Connecticut Family Law Statutes and Rules

2004 Edition

Mat #40190811

© 2004 West, a Thomson business
All rights reserved.

West, a Thomson business has created this publication to provide you with accurate and authoritative information concerning the subject matter covered. However, this publication was not necessarily prepared by persons licensed to practice law in a particular jurisdiction. West is not engaged in rendering legal or other professional advice, and this publication is not a substitute for the advice of an attorney. If you require legal or other expert advice, you should seek the services of a competent attorney or other professional.

West's and Westlaw are registered in the U.S. Patent and Trademark Office.

CONNECTICUT GENERAL STATUTES ANNOTATED is a trademark of West Publishing Corporation.

ISBN 0-314-11265-0

PREFACE

This pamphlet—available both separately and as part of *Family Law and Practice with Forms*—is designed to provide the reader with a convenient easy-to-use family law reference tool. It contains the complete text of Title 46b, Family Law, and related subject matter provisions selected from Title 1, Provisions of General Application; Title 7, Municipalities; Title 10, Education and Culture; Title 17a, Social and Human Services and Resources; Title 17b, Social Services; Title 19a, Public Health and Well-Being; Title 31, Labor; Title 36a, The Banking Laws of Connecticut; Title 38a, Insurance; Title 45a, Probate Courts and Procedure; Title 47, Land and Land Titles; Title 52, Civil Actions; Title 53, Crimes; Title 53a, Penal Code; and Title 54, Criminal Procedure. Selected provisions of the Connecticut Rules of Court governing procedure in family matters and probate practice rules also appear in this pamphlet.

This pamphlet contains statutes current through 2004 legislation approved by the Governor on or before June 11, 2004, with effective dates on or prior to July 1, 2004. For the text of subsequently enacted legislation, see Connecticut Legislative Service Pamphlets and selected 2004 Public Acts contained in this book.

A combined index covering family law, the selected related statutes, and the court rules contained herein appears at the end of the pamphlet.

For other laws, annotations, historical notes and many additional informative features and aids to research, the user should examine West's Connecticut General Statutes Annotated.

WEST
SEPTEMBER, 2004

*

RELATED PRODUCTS FROM WEST

Connecticut General Statutes Annotated
Connecticut Reporter
Connecticut Rules of Court, State and Federal
Connecticut Digest
Connecticut Business Organizations Law
Connecticut Estate and Probate Law
Connecticut Family Law

CONNECTICUT PRACTICE SERIES

Practice Book Annotated—Superior Court Civil Rules
Horton and Knox

Practice Book Annotated—Forms
Kaye and Effron

Practice Book Annotated—Criminal Procedure
Orland and Borden

Criminal Jury Instructions
Borden and Orland

Rules of Appellate Procedure
Horton and Bartschi

Trial Practice
Yules

Family Law and Practice with Forms
Rutkin, Hogan and Oldham

Land Use Law and Practice
Fuller

Criminal Law
Borden and Orland

Connecticut Unfair Trade Practices Act
Langer, Belt and Morgan

CONNECTICUT ESTATES PRACTICE SERIES

Connecticut Probate Deskbook
Wilhelm

Death Taxes in Connecticut
Wilhelm

Drafting Trusts in Connecticut
Wilhelm and Folsom

Drafting Wills in Connecticut
Wilhelm and Folsom

Incapacity, Powers of Attorney and Adoption in Connecticut
Wilhelm and Folsom

Probate Jurisdiction and Procedure in Connecticut
Wilhelm and Folsom

Probate Litigation in Connecticut
Folsom

Revocable Trusts and Trust Administration in Connecticut
Wilhelm and Folsom

Settlement of Estates in Connecticut
Wilhelm

Westlaw®

WESTCheck® and WESTMATE®

West CD–ROM Libraries™

WIN®

To order any of these Connecticut practice tools, call your West Representative or 1-800-328-9352.

INTERNET ACCESS

Contact the West Editorial Department directly with your questions and suggestions by e-mail at west.editor@thomson.com.

Visit West's home page on the World Wide Web at http://west.thomson.com.

WESTLAW ELECTRONIC RESEARCH GUIDE

Westlaw, Computer Assisted Legal Research

Westlaw is part of the research system provided by West. With Westlaw, you find the same quality and integrity that you have come to expect from West books. For the most current and comprehensive legal research, combine the strengths of West books and Westlaw.

Westlaw Adds to Your Library

Whether you wish to expand or update your research, Westlaw can help. For instance, Westlaw is the most current source for case law, including slip opinions and unreported decisions. In addition to case law, the online availability of statutes, statutory indexes, legislation, court rules and orders, administrative materials, looseleaf publications, texts, periodicals, news and business information makes Westlaw an important asset to any library. Check the online Westlaw Directory or the print *Westlaw Database Directory* for a list of available databases and services. Following is a brief description of some of the capabilities that Westlaw offers.

Natural Language Searching

You can now search most Westlaw databases using WIN®, the revolutionary Natural Language search method. As an alternative to formulating a query using terms and connectors, WIN allows you to simply enter a description of your research issue in plain English:

What is the government's obligation to warn military personnel of the danger of past exposure to radiation?

Westlaw then retrieves the set of documents that have the highest statistical likelihood of matching your description.

Retrieving a Specific Document

When you know the citation to a case or statute that is not in your library, use the Find service to retrieve the document on Westlaw. Access Find and type a citation like one of the following:

find 663 A2d 349

find CT ST s 8-10

find CT CONST art 3 s 14

Updating Your Research

You can use Westlaw to update your research in many ways:

- Retrieve cases citing a particular statute.
- Update a state or federal statute by accessing the Update service from the displayed statute using the jump marker, or by accessing the KeyCite® service.
- Retrieve newly enacted legislation by searching in the appropriate legislative service database.
- Retrieve cases not yet reported by searching in case law databases.
- Read the latest U.S. Supreme Court opinions within an hour of their release.
- Update West digests by searching with topic and key numbers.

Determining Case History and Retrieving Citing Cases

KeyCite®: Cases and other legal materials listed in KeyCite Scope can be researched through West's KeyCite service on Westlaw. Use KeyCite to check citations for form, parallel references, prior and later history, and comprehensive citator information, including citations to other decisions and secondary materials.

Additional Information

For more detailed information or assistance, contact your Westlaw Account Representative or call 1-800-REF-ATTY (1-800-733-2889).

GENERAL STATUTES OF CONNECTICUT REVISION OF 1958

The 1958 Revision of the General Statutes of Connecticut was prepared under the authority of Special Act 605 of 1957 and became effective on and after January 15, 1959.

Enactment of Revision as Public Statute Law

Section 9 of Public Act No. 13 of the 1957 Special Session provided that:

"On and after January 15, 1959, the revision of the general statutes of this state prepared in accordance with the provisions of number 605 of the special acts of 1957 and incorporating therein the public acts passed at the current special session shall be and remain the public statute laws of this state and shall be published under the title of the General Statutes of Connecticut, Revision of 1958."

Public Act No. 3 of 1959, effective January 15, 1959, provided that: "The general statutes of the state, as corrected, revised, arranged, incorporated and published under the title, 'General Statutes of Connecticut, Revision of 1958,' by the legislative commissioner under the provisions of number 605 of the special acts of 1957, are adopted, ratified, confirmed and enacted."

*

EFFECTIVE DATES OF ACTS

Sections 2–32 and 2–32a of the Connecticut General Statutes provide:

§ 2–32. Effective date of public and special acts

All public acts, except when otherwise therein specified, shall take effect on the first day of October following the session of the general assembly at which they are passed, and special acts, unless otherwise herein provided, from the date of their approval.

(1949 Rev., § 8891)

§ 2–32a. Effective date of public acts imposing state mandate

No public act which imposes a state mandate on any political subdivision of this state which requires the appropriation of funds for the budget of such political subdivision in order to comply with the provisions of such act shall be effective as to such political subdivision earlier than the first fiscal year of such political subdivision beginning after five months following the date of passage of such act.

(1972, P.A. 234, § 1, eff. May 14, 1972; 1993, P.A. 93–434, § 15, eff. June 30, 1993.)

23 Op.Atty.Gen. 148 (July 14, 1943) provided that a public act specifying an effective date takes effect from that date, and should be construed retrospectively when required by express command of the legislature or when necessary to give full effect to all provisions of the Act, and that where it was the will of the legislature that the Act be operative as of and from a date set forth therein, that is the effective date of the Act, though approved by the governor on a date subsequent to the effective date.

*

TABLE OF CONTENTS

TABLE OF CONTENTS

TITLE 31. LABOR

TITLE 36a. THE BANKING LAW OF CONNECTICUT

TITLE 38a. INSURANCE

TITLE 45a. PROBATE COURTS AND PROCEDURE

TITLE 46b. FAMILY LAW

TITLE 47. LAND AND LAND TITLES

TABLE OF CONTENTS

TITLE 52. CIVIL ACTIONS (selected provisions)

TITLE 53. CRIMES (selected provisions)

TITLE 53a. PENAL CODE (selected provisions)

TITLE 54. CRIMINAL PROCEDURE

RULES FOR THE SUPERIOR COURT

General Provisions

Procedure in Family Matters

Procedure in Juvenile Matters

TABLE OF CONTENTS

Procedure in Criminal Matters

RULES OF APPELLATE PROCEDURE

PROBATE RULES FOR PRACTICE AND PROCEDURE

FAIRFIELD JUDICIAL DISTRICT STANDING ORDERS

Family—Hon. Brian T. Fisher

TABLE OF CONTENTS

HARTFORD JUDICIAL DISTRICT STANDING ORDERS

Family—Hon. F.Herbert Gruendel

NEW HAVEN JUDICIAL DISTRICT STANDING ORDERS

Family Standing Orders

2004 PUBLIC ACTS

*

TITLE 1

PROVISIONS OF GENERAL APPLICATION

CHAPTER 1

CONSTRUCTION OF STATUTES

§ 1–1d. "Minor", "infant", "infancy", "age of majority", defined

Except as otherwise provided by statute, on and after October 1, 1972, the terms "minor", "infant" and "infancy" shall be deemed to refer to a person under the age of eighteen years and any person eighteen years of age or over shall be an adult for all purposes whatsoever and have the same legal capacity, rights, powers, privileges, duties, liabilities and responsibilities as persons heretofore had at twenty-one years of age, and "age of majority" shall be deemed to be eighteen years.

(1972, P.A. 127, § 1.)

*

TITLE 7

MUNICIPALITIES

CHAPTER 93

REGISTRARS OF VITAL STATISTICS

§ 7–48a. Birth certificate to contain name of birth mother

On and after January 1, 2002, each birth certificate shall contain the name of the birth mother, except by the order of a court of competent jurisdiction.

(2001, P.A. 01–163, § 28.)

§ 7–50. Restrictions on content of birth certificates. Exceptions. Filing of acknowledgments or adjudications of paternity. Removal or changing of paternity information

No certificate of birth shall contain any specific statement that the child was born in or out of wedlock or reference to illegitimacy of the child or to the marital status of the mother, except that information on whether the child was born in or out of wedlock and the marital status of the mother shall be recorded on a confidential portion of the certificate pursuant to section 7–48. Upon the completion of an acknowledgment of paternity at a hospital, concurrent with the hospital's electronic transmission of birth data to the department, or at a town in the case of a home birth, concurrent with the registration of the birth data by the town, the acknowledgment shall be filed in the paternity registry maintained by the department, as required by section 19a–42a, and the name of the father of a child born out of wedlock shall be entered in or upon the birth certificate or birth record of such child. All post birth acknowledgments or adjudications of paternity received by the department shall be filed in the paternity registry maintained by the department, and the name of the father of the child born out of wedlock shall be entered in or upon the birth record or certificate of such child by the department, if there is no paternity already recorded on the birth certificate. If another father's information is recorded on the certificate, the original father's information shall not be removed except upon receipt by the department of an order by a court of competent jurisdiction in which there is a finding that the individual recorded on the birth certificate, specifically referenced by name, is not the child's father, or a finding that a different individual than the one recorded, specifically referenced by name, is the child's father. The name of the father on a birth certificate or birth record shall otherwise be removed or changed only upon the filing of a rescission in such registry, as provided in section 19a–42a. The Social Security number of the father of a child born out of wedlock may be entered in or upon the birth certificate or birth record of such child if such disclosure is done in accordance with 5 USC 552a note.

(1949 Rev., § 571; 1979, P.A. 79–434, § 3; 1980, P.A. 80–483, § 17, eff. June 6, 1980; 1985, P.A. 85–323; 1994, P.A. 94–51, § 2, eff. Oct. 1, 1994; 1994, May 25 Sp.Sess., P.A. 94–1, § 44, eff. July 1, 1994; 1996, P.A. 96–180, § 3, eff. June 3, 1996; 1997, June 18 Sp.Sess., P.A. 97–7, § 4, eff. July 1, 1997; 2001, P.A. 01–163, § 11.)

§ 7–53. Birth certificates of adopted persons born in this state

Upon receipt of the record of adoption referred to in subsection (e) of section 45a–745 or of other evidence satisfactory to the department that a person born in this state has been adopted, the department shall prepare a new birth certificate of such adopted person, except that no new certificate of birth shall be prepared if the court decreeing the adoption, the adoptive parents or the adopted person, if over fourteen years of age, so requests. Such new birth certificate shall include all the information required to be set forth in a certificate of birth of this state as of the date of birth, except that the adopting parents shall be named as the parents instead of the genetic parents and, when a certified copy of the birth of such person is requested by an authorized person, a copy of the new certificate of birth as prepared by the department shall be provided. Any person seeking to examine or obtain a copy of the original record or certificate of birth shall first obtain a written order signed by the judge of the probate court for the district in which the adopted person was adopted or born in accordance with section 45a–753, or a written order of the Probate Court in accordance with the provisions of section 45a–752, stating that the court is of the opinion that the examination of the birth record of the adopted person by the adopting parents or the adopted person, if over eighteen years of age, or by the person wishing to examine the same or that the issuance of a copy of such birth certificate to the adopting parents or the adopted person, if over eighteen years of age, or to the person applying therefor will not be detrimental to the public interest or to the welfare of the adopted person or to the welfare of the genetic or adoptive parent or parents. Upon receipt of such court order, the registrar of vital statistics of any town in which the birth of such person was recorded, or the department, may issue the certified copy of the original certificate of birth on file, marked with a notation by the issuer that such original certificate of birth has been superseded by a replacement certificate of birth as on file, or may permit the examination of such record. Immediately after a new certificate of birth has been prepared, an exact copy of such certificate, together with a written notice of the evidence of adoption, shall be transmitted by the department to the registrar of vital statistics of each town in this state in which the birth of the adopted person is recorded. The new birth certificate, the original certificate of birth on file and the evidence of adoption shall be filed and indexed, under such regulations as the commissioner adopts, in accordance with chapter 54, [1] to carry out the provisions of this section and to prevent access to the records of birth and adoption and the information therein contained without due cause, except as provided in this section. Any person, except such parents or adopted person, who discloses any information contained in such records, except as provided in this section, shall be fined not more than five hundred dollars or imprisoned not more than six months, or both. Whenever a certified copy of an adoption decree from a court of a foreign country, having jurisdiction of the adopted person, is filed with the department under the provisions of this section, such decree, when written in a language other than English, shall be accompanied by an English translation, which shall be subscribed and sworn to as a true translation by an American consulate officer stationed in such foreign country.

(1949 Rev., § 580; 1957, P.A. 298, § 2; 1961, P.A. 319; 1972, P.A. 127, § 5; 1975, P.A. 75–170, § 1; 1977, P.A. 77–246, § 17; 1977, P.A. 77–604, § 63, eff. July 6, 1977; 1977, P.A. 77–614, § 323, eff. Jan. 1, 1979; 1988, P.A. 88–364, § 73, eff. June 8, 1988; 1993, P.A. 93–381, § 9, eff. July 1, 1993; 1994, P.A. 94–26; 1995, P.A. 95–257, §§ 12, 21, eff. July 1, 1995; 1996, P.A. 96–202, § 3; 2001, P.A. 01–163, § 15; 2003, P.A. 03–19, § 17, eff. May 12, 2003.)

[1] C.G.S.A. § 4–166 et seq.

§ 7–54. Certification of birth registration of persons born outside the state or country and adopted by state residents

The department shall prepare a certification of birth registration or a certificate of foreign birth for any person born outside of the country and adopted by residents of this state, provided an authenticated and exemplified copy of the order of adoption of the court of the district in which the adoption proceedings were had or such other evidence as is considered satisfactory by the probate court of the district in which such person resides shall be filed with such probate court, and such probate court notifies the department that such copy or satisfactory evidence has been so filed. Such certification of birth registration shall contain only the adopted name, sex, date of birth, place of birth and date of preparation of such certification of birth registration by the department. Such certificate of foreign birth shall contain the adopted name, sex, date of birth, place of birth, legal name of adoptive parent or parents and date of preparation of such certificate of foreign birth. No certification of birth registration or certificate of foreign birth shall be prepared by the department unless upon specific written request of the person to whom the certification of birth registration relates, if over sixteen years of age, or of the adopting parents or the court of probate of the district in which the adoption proceedings were had. When the department has prepared such certificate of birth registration or certificate of foreign birth, copies thereof shall be issued by the department in accordance with the provisions of subsection (a) of section 7–52.

(1949 Rev., § 574; 1972, P.A. 127, § 6; 1975, P.A. 75–170, § 2; 1977, P.A. 77–614, § 323, eff. Jan. 1, 1979; 1981, P.A. 81–190; 1985, P.A. 85–326; 1987, P.A. 87–148, § 1, eff. July 1, 1987; 1989, P.A. 89–98; 1993, P.A. 93–381, § 9, eff. July 1, 1993; 1995, P.A. 95–257, §§ 12, 21, eff. July 1, 1995; 2001, P.A. 01–163, § 16; 2003, P.A. 03–247, § 2.)

TITLE 10

EDUCATION AND CULTURE

CHAPTER 168

SCHOOL ATTENDANCE AND EMPLOYMENT OF CHILDREN

§ 10–198a. Policies and procedures concerning truants

(a) For purposes of this section, "truant" means a child age five to eighteen, inclusive, who is enrolled in a public or private school and has four unexcused absences from school in any one month or ten unexcused absences from school in any school year.

(b) Each local and regional board of education shall adopt and implement policies and procedures concerning truants who are enrolled in schools under the jurisdiction of such board of education. Such policies and procedures shall include, but need not be limited to, the following: (1) The holding of a meeting with the parent of each child who is a truant, or other person having control of such child, and appropriate school personnel to review and evaluate the reasons for the child being a truant, provided such meeting shall be held not later than ten school days after the child's fourth unexcused absence in a month or tenth unexcused absence in a school year, (2) coordinating services with and referrals of children to community agencies providing child and family services, (3) annually at the beginning of the school year and upon any enrollment during the school year, notifying the parent or other person having control of each child enrolled in a grade from kindergarten to eight, inclusive, in the public schools in writing of the obligations of the parent or such other person pursuant to section 10–184, (4) annually at the beginning of the school year and upon any enrollment during the school year, obtaining from the parent or other person having control of each child in a grade from kindergarten to eight, inclusive, a telephone number or other means of contacting such parent or such other person during the school day and (5) a system of monitoring individual unexcused absences of children in grades kindergarten to eight, inclusive, which shall provide that whenever a child enrolled in school in any such grade fails to report to school on a regularly scheduled school day and no indication has been received by school personnel that the child's parent or other person having control of the child is aware of the pupil's absence, a reasonable effort to notify, by telephone, the parent or such other person shall be made by school personnel or volunteers under the direction of school personnel. Any person who, in good faith, gives or fails to give notice pursuant to subdivision (5) of this subsection shall be immune from any liability, civil or criminal, which might otherwise be incurred or imposed and shall have the same immunity with respect to any judicial proceeding which results from such notice or failure to give such notice.

(c) If the parent or other person having control of a child who is a truant fails to attend the meeting held pursuant to subdivision (1) of subsection (b) of this section or if such parent or other person otherwise fails to cooperate with the school in attempting to solve the truancy problem, such policies and procedures shall require the superintendent of schools to file for each such truant enrolled in the schools under his jurisdiction a written complaint with the Superior Court pursuant to section 46b–149 alleging the belief that the acts or omissions of the child are such that his family is a family with service needs.

(d) Nothing in subsections (a) to (c), inclusive, of this section shall preclude a local or regional board of education from adopting policies and procedures pursuant to this section which exceed the requirements of said subsections.

(e) The provisions of this section shall not apply to any child receiving equivalent instruction pursuant to section 10–184.

(1990, P.A. 90–240, § 1; 1991, P.A. 91–303, § 4, eff. July 1, 1991; 1995, P.A. 95–182, § 5, eff. June 28, 1995; 1995, P.A. 95–304, § 2, eff. July 1, 1995; 1998, P.A. 98–243, § 17, eff. July 1, 1998; 2000, P.A. 00–157, § 5, eff. July 1, 2001.)

§ 10–199. Attendance officers. Duties

Any local or regional board of education may appoint one or more persons, who shall be authorized to prosecute for violations of the laws relating to attendance of children and their employment. All warrants issued upon such prosecutions shall be returnable before any court having jurisdiction. Each attendance officer shall be sworn to the faithful performance of his or her duties and shall be under the direction of the principal or superintendent of schools of the board of education by which he or she is employed. He shall investigate the absence of pupils from or the irregular attendance of pupils at school, cause such pupils as are absent or irregular in attendance to attend school regularly and present cases requiring prosecution for violation of the school laws to prosecuting officers. *(1949 Rev., § 1460; 1978, P.A. 78–218, § 126.)*

§ 10–200. Habitual truants

Each city and town may adopt ordinances concerning habitual truants from school and children between the ages of five and eighteen years wandering about its streets or public places, having no lawful occupation and not attending school, and may make such ordinances respecting such children as shall conduce to their welfare and to public order, imposing penalties, not exceeding twenty dollars, for any one breach thereof. The police in any town, city or borough, bailiffs and constables in their respective precincts shall arrest all such children found anywhere beyond the proper control of their parents or guardians, during the usual school hours of the school terms, and may stop any child under eighteen years of age during such hours and ascertain whether such child is a truant from school, and, if such child is, shall send such child to school. For purposes of this section, "habitual truant" means a child age five to eighteen, inclusive, who is enrolled in a public or private school and has twenty unexcused absences within a school year.

(1949 Rev., § 1461; 1957, P.A. 13, § 61; 1978, P.A. 78–218, § 127; 1995, P.A. 95–304, § 3, eff. July 1, 1995; 1998, P.A. 98–243, § 18, eff. July 1, 1998; 2000, P.A. 00–99, § 38, eff. Dec. 1, 2000; 2000, P.A. 00–157, § 6, eff. July 1, 2001; 2001, P.A. 01–195, § 77, eff. July 11, 2001.)

§ 10–201. Fees for arresting truants

Officers other than policemen of cities shall receive for making the arrests required by section 10–200 such fees, not exceeding the fees allowed by law for making other arrests, as may be allowed by the selectmen of the town in which such arrests are made; but unless a warrant was issued by a judge of the superior court the officer shall, before receiving a fee, present to the selectmen of the town a written statement showing the name of each child arrested, the day on which the arrest was made and, if the child was returned to school, the name or number of the school to which such child was so returned.

(1949 Rev., § 1462; 1976, P.A. 76–436, § 652, eff. July 1, 1978; 1978, P.A. 78–218, § 128.)

§ 10–202. Warrant and hearing

In all cases arising under the provisions of sections 10–200 and 10–201 a proper warrant shall be issued by a judge of the superior court in the jurisdiction where such arrest is made; and the parent or guardian of such child, shall be notified, if such parent or guardian can be found, of the day and time of hearing.

(1949 Rev., § 1463; 1974, P.A. 74–76; 1976, P.A. 76–436, § 653, eff. July 1, 1978.)

CHAPTER 169

SCHOOL HEALTH AND SANITATION

§ 10–208. Exemption from examination or treatment

No provision of section 10–206 or 10–214 shall be construed to require any pupil to undergo a physical or medical examination or treatment, or to be compelled to receive medical instruction, if the parent or legal guardian of such pupil or the pupil, if such pupil is an emancipated minor or is eighteen years of age or older, in writing, notifies the teacher or principal or other person in charge of such pupil that such parent or guardian or pupil objects, on religious grounds, to such physical or medical examination or treatment or medical instruction.

(1949 Rev., § 1469; 1978, P.A. 78–218, § 134; 1980, P.A. 80–175, § 4, eff. July 1, 1980; 1980, P.A. 80–440, § 5, eff. July 1, 1980.)

CHAPTER 170

BOARDS OF EDUCATION

§ 10–222d. Policy on bullying behavior

Each local and regional board of education shall develop a policy, for use on and after February 1, 2003, to address the existence of bullying in its schools. Such policy shall: (1) Enable students to anonymously report acts of bullying to teachers and school administrators, (2) enable the parents or guardians of students to file written reports of suspected bullying, (3) require teachers and other school staff who witness acts of bullying or receive student reports of bullying to notify school administrators, (4) require school administrators to investigate any written reports filed pursuant to subdivision (2) of this section and to review any anonymous reports, (5) include an intervention strategy for school staff to deal with bullying, (6) provide for the inclusion of language in student codes of conduct concerning bullying, (7) require the parents or guardians of students who commit any verified acts of bullying and the parents or guardians of students against whom such acts were directed to be notified, and (8) require each school to maintain a list of the number of verified acts of bullying in such school and make such list available for public inspection. The notification required pursuant to subdivision (7) of this section shall include a description of the response of school staff to such acts and any consequences that may result from the commission of further acts of bullying. For purposes of this section, "bullying" means any overt acts by a student or a group of students directed against another student with the intent to ridicule, humiliate or intimidate the other student while on school grounds or at a school-sponsored activity which acts are repeated against the same student over time.

(2002, P.A. 02–119, § 1, eff. July 1, 2002.)

§ 10–233h. Arrested students. Reports by police, disclosure, confidentiality. Police testimony at expulsion hearings

If any person who is at least seven years of age but less than twenty-one years of age and an enrolled student is arrested for a violation of section 53–206c, a class A misdemeanor or a felony, the municipal police department or Division of State Police within the Department of Public Safety that made such arrest shall, not later than the end of the weekday following such arrest, orally notify the superintendent of schools of the school district in which such person resides of the identity of such person and the offense or offenses for which he was arrested and shall, within seventy-two hours of such arrest, provide written notification of such arrest, containing a brief description of the incident, to such superintendent. The superintendent shall maintain such written report in a secure location and the information in such report shall be maintained as confidential in accordance with section 46b–124. The superintendent may disclose such information only to the principal of the school in which such person is a student or to the principal or supervisory agent of any other school in which the superintendent knows such person is a student. The principal or supervisory agent may disclose such information only to special services staff or a consultant, such as a psychiatrist, psychologist or social worker, for the purposes of assessing the risk of danger posed by such person to himself, other students, school employees or school property and effectuating an appropriate modification of such person's educational plan or placement, and for disciplinary purposes. If the arrest occurred during the school year, such assessment shall be completed not later than the end of the next school day. If an expulsion hearing is held pursuant to section 10–233d, a representative of the municipal police department or the Division of State Police, as appropriate, may testify and provide reports and information on the arrest at such hearing, provided such police participation is requested by any of the following: The local or regional board of education, the impartial hearing board, the principal of the school or the student or his parent or guardian. Such information with respect to a child under sixteen years of age shall be confidential in accordance with section 46b–124, and shall only be disclosed as provided in this section and shall not be further disclosed.

(1994, P.A. 94–221, § 10; 1995, P.A. 95–304, § 7, eff. July 1, 1995; 1997, P.A. 97–149, § 1, eff. July 1, 1997.)

*

TITLE 17a

SOCIAL AND HUMAN SERVICES AND RESOURCES

CHAPTER 319

DEPARTMENT OF CHILDREN AND FAMILIES

PART I. GENERAL PROVISIONS

§ 17a–22a. Connecticut Community KidCare: An integrated behavioral health service delivery system for children and youth with behavioral health needs. Requirements. Memorandum of understanding for joint administration. Consultation during development. Federal waivers or amendments

(a) The Commissioner of Social Services and the Commissioner of Children and Families shall, within available appropriations, develop and administer an integrated behavioral health service delivery system to be known as Connecticut Community KidCare. Said system shall provide services to children and youth with behavioral health needs who are in the custody of the Department of Children and Families, who are eligible to receive services from the HUSKY Plan, Part A [1] or the federally subsidized portion of Part B, [2] or receive services under the voluntary services program operated by the Department of Children and Families. All necessary changes to the IV-E, Title XIX and Title XXI state plans shall be made to maximize federal financial participation. The Commissioner of Social Services may amend the state Medicaid plan to facilitate the claiming of federal reimbursement for private nonmedical institutions as defined in the Social Security Act. [3] The Commissioner of Social Services may implement policies and procedures necessary to provide reimbursement for the services provided by private nonmedical institutions, as defined in 42 CFR Part 434, while in the process of adopting such policies and procedures in regulation form, provided the commissioner prints notice of intention to adopt the regulations in the Connecticut Law Journal within twenty days of implementing such policies and procedures. Policies and procedures implemented pursuant to this subsection shall be valid until the time such regulations are effective.

(b) Connecticut Community KidCare shall, within available appropriations, provide a comprehensive benefit package of behavioral health specialty services. The HUSKY Plan shall continue to provide primary behavioral health services and may provide additional behavioral health services to be determined by the Department of Social Services and shall assure an integration of such services with the behavioral health services provided by Connecticut Community KidCare.

(c) Connecticut Community KidCare shall include: (1) A system of care model in which service planning is based on the needs and preferences of the child or youth and his or her family and that places an emphasis on early identification, prevention and treatment; (2) a comprehensive behavioral health program with a flexible benefit package that shall include clinically necessary and appropriate home and community-based treatment services and comprehensive support services in the least restrictive setting; (3) community-based care planning and service delivery, including services and supports for children from birth through early childhood that link Connecticut Community KidCare to the early childhood community and promote emotional wellness; (4) comprehensive children and youth behavioral health training for agency and system staff and interested parents and guardians; (5) an efficient balance of local participation and state-wide administration; (6) integration of agency funding to support the benefit package; (7) a performance measurement system for monitoring quality and access; (8) accountability for quality, access and cost; (9) elimination of the major gaps in services and barriers to access services; (10) a system of care that is family-focused with respect for the legal rights of the child or youth and his or her parents and provides training, support and family advocacy services; (11) assurances of timely payment of service claims; (12) assurances that no child or youth shall be disenrolled or inappropriately discharged due to behavioral health care needs; and (13) identification of youths in need of transition services to adult systems.

(d) The Commissioner of Social Services and the Commissioner of Children and Families shall enter into a memorandum of understanding for the purpose of the joint administration of Connecticut Community KidCare. Such memorandum of understanding shall establish mechanisms to administer funding for, establish standards for and monitor implementation of Connecticut Community KidCare and specify that (1) the Department of Social Services, which is the agency designated as the single state agency for the administration of the Medicaid program pursuant to Title XIX of the Social Security Act [4] and is the agency responsible for the administration of the HUSKY Plan, Part B under Title XXI of the Social Security Act, [5] manage all Medicaid and HUSKY Plan modifications, waiver amendments, federal reporting and claims processing and provide financial management, and (2) the Department of Children and Families, which is the state agency responsible for administering and evaluating a comprehensive and integrated state-wide program of services for children and youth with behavioral health needs, define the services to be included in the continuum of care and develop state-wide training programs for providers, families and other persons.

(e) Said commissioners shall consult with the Commissioner of Mental Health and Addiction Services, the Commissioner of Mental Retardation, the Commissioner of Public Health and the Commissioner of Education during the development of Connecticut Community KidCare in order to (1) ensure coordination of a delivery system of behavioral health services across the life span of children, youth and adults with behavioral health needs, (2) maximize federal reimbursement and revenue, and (3) ensure the coordination of care and funding among agencies.

(f) The Commissioner of Social Services and the Commissioner of Children and Families may apply for any federal waivers or waiver amendments necessary to implement the provisions of this section.

(2000, June Sp.Sess., P.A. 00–2, § 3, eff. July 1, 2000; 2001, June Sp.Sess., P.A. 01–2, § 43, eff. July 1, 2001; 2003, P.A. 03–19, §§ 32, 33, eff. May 12, 2003.)

1 C.G.S.A. § 17b–261.

2 C.G.S.A. §§ 17b–289 to 17b–303, inclusive, and 1997, Oct. 29 Sp.Sess. P.A. 97–1, § 16.

3 42 U.S.C.A. § 301 et seq.

4 42 U.S.C.A. § 1396 et seq.

5 42 U.S.C.A. § 1397aa et seq.

§ 17a–22b. Local needs assessment by community collaborative. Lead service agencies to coordinate care of children and youth enrolled in Connecticut Community KidCare. Community collaborative composition and responsibilities

(a) Each community collaborative shall, within available appropriations, (1) complete a local needs assessment which shall include objectives and performance measures, (2) specify the number of children and youth requiring behavioral health services, (3) specify the number of children and youth actually receiving community-based and residential services and the type and frequency of such services, and (4) complete an annual self-evaluation process and a review of discharge summaries. Each community collaborative shall submit its local needs assessment to the Commissioner of Children and Families and the Commissioner of Social Services.

(b) The regional offices of the Department of Children and Families shall contract with lead service agencies, within available appropriations, to coordinate the care of all children and youth enrolled in Connecticut Community KidCare residing within their designated catchment areas, including children and youth with complex behavioral health service needs. The lead service agencies shall employ or subcontract for the employment of care coordinators to assist families in establishing and implementing individual service plans for children and youth with complex behavioral health service needs and to improve clinical outcomes and cost effectiveness. Parents shall be afforded a choice of contracted providers for authorized services.

(c) Each community collaborative may establish the number of members and the type of representatives to ensure that the membership of such collaborative is appropriately balanced. The chief elected officers of municipalities served by a community collaborative may designate a member to serve as a representative of the chief elected officials. A community collaborative, at a minimum, shall consist of representatives from the local or regional board of education, special education program, youth services bureau, local departments of social services and public health, representatives from private organizations serving children and youth and a substantial number of parents of children and youth with behavioral health needs. A community collaborative shall participate in the regional advisory councils established under section 17a–30, provide outreach to community resources, coordinate behavioral health services by forming, with the consent of the family, child specific teams for children and youth with complex behavioral health service needs, conduct community need assessments to identify service gaps and service barriers, identify priority investment areas for the state and lead service agencies and provide public education and support. A community collaborative shall establish a governance structure, determine membership and identify or establish a fiscal agent.

(d) The Commissioner of Children and Families and the Commissioner of Social Services shall, within available appropriations, provide or arrange for the administrative services necessary to operate Connecticut Community KidCare.

(2000, June Sp.Sess., P.A. 00–2, § 4, eff. July 1, 2000; 2001, June Sp.Sess, P.A. 01–2, § 44, eff. July 1, 2001.)

§ 17a–22c. Performance measures for Connecticut Community KidCare. Curricula and training. Evaluation

(a) The Commissioner of Children and Families and the Commissioner of Social Services shall establish performance measures in the areas of finance, administration, utilization, client satisfaction, quality and access for Connecticut Community KidCare.

(b) The Commissioner of Children and Families shall develop and implement, within available appropriations, culturally appropriate and competency-based curricula including best practices for the care of children and youth with, or at risk of, behavioral health needs and offer training to all willing persons involved in Connecticut Community KidCare, including, but not limited to, employees in education and child care and appropriate employees within the judicial system.

(c) The Commissioners of Children and Families and Social Services shall, within available appropriations, design and conduct a five-year independent longitudinal evaluation with evaluation goals and methods utilizing an independent evaluator. The evaluation shall assess changes in outcomes for individual children, youth and families, evaluate the effectiveness of the overall initiative in the early phases to guide future expansion of Connecticut Community KidCare and examine benefits, costs and cost avoidance achieved by it. Such evaluation may include, but is not limited to, the following: (1) Utilization of out-of-home placements; (2) adherence to system of care principles; (3) school attendance; (4) delinquency recidivism rates; (5) satisfaction of families and children and youth with Connecticut Community KidCare as assessed through client satisfaction surveys; (6) coordination of Connecticut Community KidCare with the juvenile justice, child protection, adult behavioral health and education systems; and (7) the quality of transition services.

(2001, June Sp.Sess., P.A. 01–2, § 46, eff. July 1, 2001.)

§ 17a–22d. Establishment of organization with regional local chapters to provide family-to-family support, family advocates and assistance with individual service plan process and to encourage participation in Connecticut Community KidCare planning

The Commissioner of Children and Families may, within available appropriations, provide financial assistance for the establishment of an organization, with local chapters in each region served by the Department of Children and Families, that shall provide family-to-family support and family advocates for children, youth and their families, and when requested by the family, assist the family with the individual service plan process and otherwise encourage active family participation in treatment and Connecticut Community KidCare planning. Such organization shall assure that families have input into the development and implementation of their individual service plans, including those established pursuant to section 17a–127, and into policy and planning for, and the implementation and evaluation of, Connecticut Community KidCare.

(2001, June Sp.Sess., P.A. 01–2, § 47, eff. July 1, 2001; 2003, P.A. 03–19, § 34, eff. May 12, 2003.)

§ 17a–28. Definitions. Confidentiality of and access to records; exceptions. Procedure for aggrieved persons. Regulations

(a) As used in this section:

(1) "Person" means (A) any individual named in a record, maintained by the department, who (i) is presently or at any prior time was a ward of or committed to the commissioner for any reason; (ii) otherwise received services, voluntarily or involuntarily, from the department; or (iii) is presently or was at any prior time the subject of an investigation by the department; (B) the parent of a person, as defined in subparagraph (A) of this subdivision, if such person is a minor; or (C) the authorized representative of a person, as defined in subparagraph (A) of this subdivision, if such person is deceased;

(2) "Attorney" means the licensed attorney authorized to assert the confidentiality of or right of access to records of a person;

(3) "Authorized representative" means a parent, guardian, conservator or other individual authorized to assert the confidentiality of or right of access to records of a person;

(4) "Consent" means permission given in writing by a person, his attorney or his authorized representative to disclose specified information, within a limited time period, regarding the person to specifically identified individuals;

(5) "Records" means information created or obtained in connection with the department's child protection activities or activities related to a child while in the care or custody of the department, including information in the registry of reports to be maintained by the commissioner pursuant to section 17a–101k, provided records which are not created by the department are not subject to disclosure, except as provided pursuant to subsection (f), (*l*) or (n) of this section;

(6) "Disclose" means (A) to provide an oral summary of records maintained by the department to an individual, agency, corporation or organization or (B) to allow an individual, agency, corporation or organization to review or obtain copies of such records in whole, part or summary form;

(7) "Near fatality" means an act, as certified by a physician, that places a child in serious or critical condition.

(b) Notwithstanding the provisions of section 1–210, 1–211 or 1–213, records maintained by the department shall be confidential and shall not be disclosed. Such records of any person may only be disclosed, in whole or in part, to any individual, agency, corporation or organization with the consent of the person or as provided in this section. Any unauthorized disclosure shall be punishable by a fine of not more than one thousand dollars or imprisonment for not more than one year, or both.

(c) When information concerning an incident of abuse or neglect has been made public or when the commissioner reasonably believes publication of such information is likely, the commissioner or his designee may disclose, with respect to an investigation of such abuse or neglect: (1) Whether the department has received a report in accordance with sections 17a–101a to 17a–101c, inclusive, or section 17a–103, and (2) in general terms, any action taken by the department, provided names or other individually identifiable information of the minor victim or other family member shall not be disclosed, notwithstanding such individually identifiable information is otherwise available.

(d) The Commissioner shall make available to the public, without the consent of the person, information on general terms or findings concerning an incident of abuse or neglect which resulted in a child fatality or near fatality of a child, provided disclosure of such information or findings does not jeopardize a pending investigation.

(e) The commissioner shall, upon written request, disclose the following information concerning agencies licensed by the Department of Children and Families, except foster care parents, relatives of the child who are certified to provide foster care or prospective adoptive families: (1) The name of the licensee; (2) the date the original license was issued; (3) the current status of the license; (4) whether an agency investigation or review is pending or has been completed; and (5) any licensing action taken by the department at any time during the period such license was issued and the reason for such action, provided disclosure of such information will not jeopardize a pending investigation.

(f) The commissioner or the commissioner's designee shall, upon request, promptly provide copies of records, without the consent of a person, to (1) a law enforcement agency, (2) the Chief State's Attorney or the Chief State's Attorney's designee or a state's attorney for the judicial district in which the child resides or in which the alleged abuse or neglect occurred or the state's attorney's designee, for purposes of investigating or prosecuting an allegation of child abuse or neglect, (3) the attorney appointed to represent a child in any court in litigation affecting the best interests of the child, (4) a guardian ad litem appointed to represent a child in any court in litigation affecting the best interests of the child, (5) the Department of Public Health, which licenses any person to care for children for the purposes of determining suitability of such person for licensure, (6) any state agency which licenses such person to educate or care for children pursuant to section 10–145b or 17a–101j, (7) the Governor, when requested in writing, in the course of the Governor's official functions or the Legislative Program Review and Investigations Committee, the committee of the General Assembly on judiciary and the committee of the General Assembly having cognizance of matters involving children when requested in the course of such committees' official functions in writing, and upon a majority vote of said committee, provided no names or other identifying information shall be disclosed unless it is essential to the legislative or gubernatorial purpose, (8) a local or regional board of education, provided the records are limited to educational records created or obtained by the state or Connecticut-Unified School District #2, established pursuant to section 17a–37, and (9) a party in a custody proceeding under section 17a–112, or section 46b–129, in the Superior Court where such records concern a child who is the subject of the proceeding or the parent of such child. A disclosure under this section shall be made of any part of a record, whether or not created by the department, provided no confidential record of the Superior Court shall be disclosed other than the petition and any affidavits filed therewith in the superior court for juvenile matters, except upon an order of a judge of the Superior Court for good cause shown. The commissioner shall also disclose the name of any individual who cooperates with an investigation of a report of child abuse or neglect to such law enforcement agency or state's attorney for purposes of investigating or prosecuting an allegation of child abuse or neglect. The commissioner or the commissioner's designee shall, upon request, promptly provide copies of records, without the consent of the person, to (A) the Department of Public Health for the purpose of determining the suitability of a person to care for children in a facility licensed under sections 19a–77 to 19a–80, inclusive, 19a–82 to 19a–87, inclusive, and 19a–87b, and (B) the Department of Social Services for determining the suitability of a person for any payment from the department for providing child care.

(g) When the commissioner or his designee determines it to be in a person's best interest, the commissioner or his designee may disclose records, whether or not created by the department and not otherwise privileged or confidential communications under state or federal law, without the consent of a person to:

(1) Multidisciplinary teams which are formed to assist the department in investigation, evaluation or treatment of child abuse and neglect cases or a multidisciplinary provider of professional treatment services under contract with the department for a child referred to the provider;

(2) Any agency in another state which is responsible for investigating or protecting against child abuse or neglect for the purpose of investigating a child abuse case;

(3) An individual, including a physician, authorized pursuant to section 17a–101f to place a child in protective custody if such individual has before him a child whom he reasonably suspects may be a victim of abuse or neglect and such individual requires the information in a record in order to determine whether to place the child in protective custody;

(4) An individual or public or private agency responsible for a person's care or custody and authorized by the department to diagnose, care for, treat or supervise a child who is the subject of a record of child abuse or neglect or a public or private agency responsible for a person's education for a purpose related to the individual's or agency's responsibilities;

(5) The Attorney General or any assistant attorney general providing legal counsel for the department;

(6) Individuals or public or private agencies engaged in medical, psychological or psychiatric diagnosis or treatment of a person perpetrating the abuse or who is

unwilling or unable to protect the child from abuse or neglect when the commissioner or his designee determines that the disclosure is needed to accomplish the objectives of diagnosis or treatment;

(7) A person who reports child abuse pursuant to sections 17a–101a to 17a–101c, inclusive, and section 17a–103, who made a report of abuse involving the subject child, provided the information disclosed is limited to (A) the status of the investigation and (B) in general terms, any action taken by the department;

(8) An individual conducting bona fide research, provided no information identifying the subjects of records shall be disclosed unless (A) such information is essential to the purpose of the research; (B) each person identified in a record or his authorized representative has authorized such disclosure in writing; and (C) the department has given written approval;

(9) The Auditors of Public Accounts or their representative, provided no information identifying the subjects of the records shall be disclosed unless such information is essential to an audit conducted pursuant to section 2–90;

(10) The Department of Social Services, provided the information disclosed is necessary to promote the health, safety and welfare of the child;

(11) A judge of the Superior Court for purposes of determining the appropriate disposition of a child convicted as delinquent or a child who is a member of a family with service needs; and

(12) The superintendents, or their designees, of state-operated facilities within the department.

(h) The commissioner or his designee may disclose the name, address and fees for services to a person, to individuals or agencies involved in the collection of fees for such services, except as provided in section 17b–225. In cases where a dispute arises over such fees or claims or where additional information is needed to substantiate the fee or claim, such disclosure of further information shall be limited to the following: (1) That the person was in fact committed to or otherwise served by the department; (2) dates and duration of service; and (3) a general description of the service, which shall include evidence that a service or treatment plan exists and has been carried out and evidence to substantiate the necessity for admission and length of stay in any institution or facility.

(i) Notwithstanding the provisions of subsections (f) and (*l*) of this section, the name of an individual reporting child abuse or neglect shall not be disclosed without his written consent except to (1) an employee of the department responsible for child protective services or the abuse registry; (2) a law enforcement officer; (3) an appropriate state's attorney; (4) an appropriate assistant attorney general; (5) a judge of the Superior Court and all necessary parties in a court proceeding pursuant to section 46b–129 or a criminal prosecution involving child abuse or neglect; or (6) a state child care licensing agency, executive director of any institution, school or facility or superintendent of schools pursuant to section 17a–101i.

(j) Notwithstanding the provisions of subsection (g) of this section, the name of any individual who cooperates with an investigation of a report of child abuse or neglect shall be kept confidential upon request or upon determination by the department that disclosure of such information may be detrimental to the safety or interests of the individual, except the name of any such individual shall be disclosed to the persons listed in subsection (i) of this section.

(k) Notwithstanding the confidentiality provisions of this section, the commissioner, upon request of an employee, shall disclose such records to such employee or his authorized representative which would be applicable and necessary for the purposes of an employee disciplinary hearing or appeal from a decision after such hearing.

(*l*) Information disclosed from a person's record shall not be disclosed further without the written consent of the person, except if disclosed to a party or his counsel pursuant to an order of a court in which a criminal prosecution or an abuse, neglect, commitment or termination proceeding against the party is pending. A state's attorney shall disclose to the defendant or his counsel in a criminal prosecution, without the necessity of a court order, exculpatory information and material contained in such record and may disclose, without a court order, information and material contained in such record which could be the subject of a disclosure order. All written records disclosed to another individual or agency shall bear a stamp requiring confidentiality in accordance with the provisions of this section. Such material shall not be disclosed to anyone without written consent of the person or as provided by this section. A copy of the consent form specifying to whom and for what specific use the record is disclosed or a statement setting forth any other statutory authorization for disclosure and the limitations imposed thereon shall accompany such record. In cases where the disclosure is made orally, the individual disclosing the information shall inform the recipient that such information is governed by the provisions of this section.

(m) In addition to the right of access provided in section 1–210, any person, regardless of age, his authorized representative or attorney shall have the right of access to any records made, maintained or kept on file by the department, whether or not such records are required by any law or by any rule or regulation, when those records pertain to or contain information or materials concerning the person seeking access thereto, including but not limited to records concerning investigations, reports, or medical, psychological or psychiatric examinations of the person seeking access thereto, provided that (1) information identifying an individual who reported abuse or neglect of a person, including any tape recording of an oral report pursuant to section 17a–103, shall not be released unless, upon application to the Superior Court by such person and served on the Commissioner of Children and Families, a judge determines, after in camera inspection of relevant records and a hearing, that there is reasonable cause to believe the reporter knowingly made a false report or that other interests of justice require such release; and (2) if the commissioner determines that it would be contrary to the best interests of the person or his authorized representative or attorney to review the records, he may refuse access by issuing to such person or representative or attorney a written statement setting forth the reasons for such refusal, and advise the person, his authorized representative or attorney of the right to seek judicial relief. When any person, attorney or authorized representative, having obtained access to any record, believes there are factually inaccurate entries or materials contained therein, he shall have the unqualified right to add a statement to the record setting forth what he believes to be an accurate statement of those facts, and said statement shall become a permanent part of said record.

(n) (1) Any person, attorney or authorized representative aggrieved by a violation of subsection (b), (f), (g), (h), (i), (j) or (*l*) of this section or of subsection (m) of this section, except subdivision (2) of said subsection (m), may seek judicial relief in the same manner as provided in section 52–146j; (2) any person, attorney or authorized representative denied access to records by the commissioner under subdivision (2) of subsection (m) of this section may petition the superior court for the venue district provided in section 46b–142 in which the person resides for an order requiring the commissioner to permit access to those records, and the court after hearing, and an in camera review of the records in question, shall issue such an order unless it determines that to permit such access would be contrary to the best interests of the person or authorized representative.

(*o*) The commissioner shall promulgate regulations pursuant to chapter 54,[1] within one year of October 1, 1996, to establish procedures for access to and disclosure of records consistent with the provisions of this section.

(1958 Rev., § 17–431; 1975, P.A. 75–524, § 20, eff. Jan. 1, 1976; 1977, P.A. 77–246, § 12; 1978, P.A. 78–280, § 30, eff. July 1, 1978; 1991, P.A. 91–299, § 1; 1996, P.A. 96–246, § 17; 1997, P.A. 97–104; 1997, P.A. 97–259, § 25, eff. July 1, 1997; 1997, P.A. 97–319, § 8, eff. July 1, 1997; 1998, P.A. 98–70, § 2; 1998, P.A. 98–239, § 17; 2001, P.A. 01–142, § 1.)

1 C.G.S.A. § 4–166 et seq.

§ 17a–43. Registration with photo-listing service

(a) Each child legally free for adoption, for whom the photo-listing service may recruit an adoptive family under subsection (a) of section 17a–42, shall, and any other such legally free child may, be registered with the photo-listing service within ten working days of becoming a child for whom such service may recruit an adoptive family. Each such registration shall include a recent photograph and written description of the child. Each such registration shall be reported to the court that ordered termination of parental rights.

(b) All changes in the status of a registered child shall be reported by the child care or child-placing agency to the photo-listing service within five working days after such change has occurred.

(c) Children remaining registered for a period in excess of twelve months shall have their photograph and written description updated within fifteen working days of the expiration of the twelfth month of their registration and every twelve months thereafter.

(d) A child's registration shall be withdrawn when the photo-listing service has been notified in writing that the child has been adopted, has reached his or her fourteenth birthday and will not consent to an adoption plan or has died.

(1958 Rev., § 17–444a; 1977, P.A. 77–379, § 2; 2000, P.A. 00–137, § 7.)

§ 17a–44. Status of photo-listed children. Referral to national adoption exchanges

(a) The photo-listing service shall quarterly check the status of photo-listed children for whom inquiries have been received. Periodic checks shall be made by such service to determine the progress toward adoption of such children and the status of those children registered but never photo-listed because of placement in a preadoptive or adoptive home prior to or at the time of registration.

(b) The commissioner shall refer appropriate children to national adoption exchanges when an adoptive family has not been identified within one hundred eighty days of the termination of the parental rights. The commissioner shall establish criteria by which a determination may be made that a referral to national exchanges is not necessary, and the commissioner shall monitor the status of those children not referred.

(1958 Rev., § 17–444b; 1977, P.A. 77–379, § 3; 2000, P.A. 00–137, § 8; 2001, P.A. 01–159, § 1.)

PART II. COMMITMENT OF MENTALLY ILL CHILDREN

§ 17a–75. Definitions

For the purposes of sections 17a–75 to 17a–83, inclusive, the following terms shall have the following meanings: "Business day" means Monday through Friday except when a legal holiday falls thereon; "child" means any person less than sixteen years of age; "court" means the Superior Court-Juvenile Matters or the Court of Probate, unless either court is specifically stated; "hospital for mental illness of children" means any hospital, which provides, in whole or in part, diagnostic or treatment services for mental disorders of children, but shall not include any correctional institution of this state; "mental disorder" means a mental or emotional condition which has substantial adverse effects on a child's ability to function so as to jeopardize his or her health, safety or welfare or that of others, and specifically excludes mental retardation; "parent" means parent or legal guardian, including any guardian appointed under the provisions of subsection (i) of section 46b–129 or sections 45a–132, 45a–593 to 45a–597, inclusive, 45a–603 to 45a–622, inclusive, 45a–629 to 45a–638, inclusive, 45a–707 to 45a–709, inclusive, 45a–715 to 45a–718, inclusive, 45a–724 to 45a–737, inclusive, or 45a–743 to 45a–756, inclusive.

(1958 Rev., § 17–205b; 1979, P.A. 79–511, § 1; 1981, P.A. 81–247, § 5, eff. June 2, 1981; 1981, P.A. 81–472, § 32, eff. July 8, 1981; 1998, P.A. 98–241, § 10.)

§ 17a–76. Application for commitment of mentally ill child. Jurisdiction. Transfer to Superior Court, when. Appointment of counsel. Three-judge court, members, powers

(a) Application for commitment of a mentally ill child to a hospital for mental illness shall be made to the court of probate in the district in which such child resides, or when his or her place of residence is out of state or unknown, the district in which he or she may be at the time of filing the application, except in cases where it is otherwise expressly provided by law. In any case in which the child is hospitalized under sections 17a–75 to 17a–83, inclusive, and an application for the commitment of such child is filed in accordance with the provisions of sections 17a–75 to 17a–83, inclusive, the jurisdiction shall be vested in the court of probate for the district in which the hospital where such child is a patient is located. In the event that an application has previously been filed in another court of probate with respect to the same confinement, no further action shall be taken on such previous application. Notwithstanding the provisions of section 45a–7, if the child is confined to a hospital outside the district of the court of probate in which the application for the child's commitment was made, the judge of probate from the district where the application was filed shall have jurisdiction to hold the hearing on such commitment at the hospital where such child is hospitalized. The court shall exercise jurisdiction only upon written application alleging that such child suffers from a mental disorder and is in need of treatment. Such application may be made by any person, and shall include the name and address of the hospital for mental illness to which the child's commitment is being sought and shall include the name, address and telephone number of any attorney appointed for the child by the Superior Court pursuant to section 46b–129.

(b) Any application for commitment of any child under sections 17a–75 to 17a–83, inclusive, shall be transferred from the court of probate where it has been filed to the superior court of appropriate venue upon motion of any legal party except the petitioner.

(c) The motion for such transfer shall be filed with the court of probate prior to the beginning of any hearing on the merits. The moving party shall send copies of such motion to all parties of record. The court shall grant such motion the next business day after its receipt by the court. Immediately upon granting the motion, the clerk of the court shall transmit by certified mail the original file and papers to the superior court having jurisdiction. All parties to the proceeding shall be notified of the date on which the file and papers were transferred.

(d) The court of probate shall appoint an attorney for such child from the panel of attorneys established by subsection (b) of section 17a–498 on the next business day after receipt of the application, and as soon as reasonably possible shall appoint physicians as required under section 17a–77, which appointments shall remain in full force and effect notwithstanding the fact that the matter has been transferred to the Superior Court.

(e) On any matter not transferred to the Superior Court in accordance with this section, upon the motion of the child for whom application has been made, or his or her counsel, or the judge of probate having jurisdiction over such application, filed not later than three days prior to any hearing scheduled on such application, the Probate Court Administrator shall appoint a three-judge court from among the several judges of probate to hear such application. Such three-judge court shall consist of at least one judge who is an attorney at law admitted to practice in this state. The judge of the court of probate having jurisdiction over such application under the provisions of this section shall be a member, provided such judge may disqualify himself or herself in which case all three members of such court shall be appointed by the Probate Court Administrator. Such three-judge court when convened shall have all the powers and duties set forth under sections 17a–75 to 17a–83, inclusive, and shall be subject to all of the provisions of law as if it were a single-judge court. No such child shall be involuntarily hospitalized without the vote of at least two of the three judges convened under the provisions of this section. The judges of such court shall designate a chief judge from among their members. All records for any case before the three-judge court shall be maintained in the court of probate having jurisdiction over the matter.

(1958 Rev., § 17–205c; 1979, P.A. 79–511, § 2; 1981, P.A. 81–472, §§ 33, 34, eff. July 8, 1981; 2001, P.A. 01–142, § 4.)

§ 17a–77. Hearing. Notice to child, parents, guardian. Availability of records. Physicians, appointment; certificate; report. Right of child to be at hearing. Order for commitment. Transfer to other institutions. Recommitment

(a) Upon receipt of such application, the court shall assign a time for the hearing, not later than ten business days after such receipt, unless such application has been transferred in accordance with section 17a–76, in which event such hearing shall be held by the Superior Court within ten business days of receipt of such application. The court hearing the matter shall further assign a place for hearing such application and shall cause reasonable notice thereof to be given to the child, his or her parents and the hospital for mental illness named in such application and to such relatives and others as it deems advisable. The notice shall inform the child (1) that he or she has a right to be present at the hearing; (2) that he or she has a right to present evidence and to cross-examine witnesses testifying at any hearing upon such application; (3) that the court has appointed an attorney to represent him or her, and the name, address and telephone number of such attorney. Counsel appointed to represent such child shall also be appointed guardian ad litem for such child unless the court deems it appropriate to appoint a separate guardian ad litem. The fees for counsel appointed to represent the child shall be paid by the parents or guardian or the estate of such child. The notice to the child's parents or legal guardian shall inform them that (A) they have the right to be present at the hearing; (B) they have the right to present evidence and to cross-examine witnesses testifying at the hearing upon such application and (C) they may be represented by an attorney and if they cannot afford an attorney, that the court shall appoint an attorney to represent them. The notice to the hospital for mental illness of children shall inform such hospital of the time and place of the hearing, and request that if such hospital is unable to admit such child, it shall so inform the court immediately. Prior to such hearing, counsel for the child and counsel for the parents, respectively, in accordance with the provisions of section 52–146e, shall be afforded access to all records including, without limitation, hospital records if such child is hospitalized, and shall be entitled to take notes therefrom. If such child is hospitalized at the time of any hearing held under this section, the hospital shall make available at such hearing for use by the court or his or her counsel and by counsel for the parents all records in its possession relating to the child's need for hospitalization. The reasonable compensation of counsel appointed under the provisions of this section for persons who are indigent or otherwise unable to pay shall be established by, and paid from funds appropriated to, the Judicial Department, however, if funds have not been included in the budget of the Judicial Department for such purposes, such compensation shall be established by the Probate Court Administrator and paid from the Probate Court Administration Fund.

(b) The court hearing the matter shall require a sworn certificate from at least two impartial physicians selected by the court, one of whom shall be a physician specializing in psychiatry. Both physicians shall be licensed to practice medicine in this state and shall have practiced medicine for at least one year. All appointments shall be made in accordance with procedures adopted by the Judicial Department. If such appointments have not already been made for a case transferred from the probate court under subsections (b) and (c) of section 17a–76, then such physicians shall be appointed as soon as reasonably possible by the superior court to which such matter has been transferred. Each physician shall make a report on a separate form adopted for such purpose by the Probate Court Administrator or the superior court. The certificates shall include a statement from each physician that he has personally examined such child within ten days of the hearing. The charges for such physicians shall be established by the Judicial Department and shall be paid in accordance with section 17a–82.

(c) If the child refuses to be examined by the court appointed physicians as herein provided, the court may issue a warrant for the apprehension of the child and a police officer for the town in which such court is located or if there is no such police officer then the state police shall deliver the child to a general hospital where he shall be examined by two physicians one of whom shall be a psychiatrist, in accordance with subsection (b) of this section. If, as a result of such examination, the child is committed under subsection (e) of this section, transportation of the child to any such hospital shall be in accordance with said subsection (e). If the child is not committed under subsection (e) of this section, he shall be released and the reports of such physicians shall be sent to the Court of Probate to satisfy the requirement of examination of two physicians under subsection (b) of this section.

(d) The child shall be present at any hearing for his or her commitment under the provisions of this section, provided the court may exclude him or her from such portions of the hearing at which testimony is given which the court determines would be seriously detrimental to his or her emotional or mental condition. If the child is medicated at that time, a representative from the hospital shall inform the court of such fact and of the common effects of such medication. At the request of counsel for such child or if in the opinion of at least one physician the child could be a danger to himself or herself or others or it would be detrimental to the child's health and welfare to travel to the court facility hearing the application, then such hearing shall be held at the hospital in which the child is hospitalized. In that event, such hospital shall provide adequate facilities for such hearing. All interested parties shall have the right to present evidence and cross-examine witnesses who testify at any hearing on the application.

(e) If, after such hearing, the court finds by clear and convincing evidence that the child suffers from a mental disorder, is in need of hospitalization for treatment, and such treatment is available, and such hospitalization is the least restrictive available alternative, it shall make an order for his or her commitment for a definite period not to exceed six months to a hospital for mental illness of children to be named in such order. Unless already hospitalized, such order shall direct some suitable person to convey the child to such hospital together with a copy of such order. In appointing a person to execute such order, the court shall give preference to a near relative or friend of the child, so far as it deems practicable and judicious. All costs for transportation shall be paid in accordance with section 17a–82. Such hospital shall release the child when it concludes that he or she is no longer in need of hospitalization.

(f) Any child who has been committed by any court to a hospital for mental illness of children may be transferred to any other hospital for mental illness of children upon agreement of the superintendents of the respective institutions from and to which it is desired to make such transfer. Such agreement shall be in writing, executed in triplicate and in accordance with a form prescribed by the Attorney General, which form shall be uniform throughout the state. One copy of such agreement shall be filed for record in the court by which such person was committed and one copy retained in the files of each of the institutions participating in such transfer. Any such agreement shall have the same effect as an order of the court committing the person named in such order. No such transfer shall be made until the parent or representative of the child has received written notification. The parent of any child so transferred, or his or her next friend, may make application to the court which made the order of commitment, for a revocation or modification of such agreement, and such court shall order such notice of the time and place of hearing on such application as it finds reasonable and upon such hearing may revoke, modify or affirm such transfer. Such application shall act as a stay of any such order of transfer. Such hospital shall release the child when it concludes that he or she is no longer in need of hospitalization.

(g) No later than ten days prior to the expiration of the period of commitment, or prior to the expiration of any period of recommitment under the provisions of sections 17a–75 to 17a–83, inclusive, an application for recommitment may be brought by any person to the court which heard the original application. Such application shall be brought in conformity with the provisions of this section and section 17a–76 and may result in a further commitment for a definite period not to exceed six months. In the event such an application is filed, the original commitment or recommitment order shall be extended for a sufficient time to hold a hearing under this section and section 17a–76, but in no event for more than twenty days beyond the expiration of the original commitment or recommitment. All fees and expenses incurred upon proceedings required by this section shall be payable as provided in section 17a–82.

(1958 Rev., § 17–205d; 1979, P.A. 79–511, § 3; 1980, P.A. 80–204; 1980, P.A. 80–269; 1981, P.A. 81–472, § 35, eff. July 8, 1981; 1983, P.A. 83–295, § 22, eff. Oct. 1, 1983; 1989, P.A. 89–326, § 5, eff. July 1, 1989; 1996, P.A. 96–170, § 2, eff July 1, 1998.)

§ 17a–78. Hospitalization of child for diagnosis or treatment of mental disorder. Examination. Discharge. Rights to be explained. Hearing. Duties of hospital. Order for continued hospitalization. Immediate discharge, when

(a) If a physician determines that a child is in need of immediate hospitalization for evaluation or treatment of a mental disorder, the child may be hospitalized under an emergency or diagnostic certificate as provided in this section for not more than fifteen days without order of any court, unless a written application for commitment of such child has been filed in the Court of Probate prior to the expiration of the fifteen days, in which event such hospitalization shall be continued under the emergency certificate for an additional fifteen days or twenty-five days if the matter has been transferred to the Superior Court, or until the completion of court proceedings, whichever occurs first. At the time of delivery of such child to such hospital, there shall be left, with the persons in charge of such hospital, a certificate, signed by a physician licensed to practice medicine or surgery in Connecticut and dated not more than three days prior to its delivery to the person in charge of the hospital. Such certificate shall state the findings of the physician and the date of personal examination of the child to be hospitalized, which shall be not more than three days prior to the date of the signature of the certificate.

(b) Any child hospitalized under this section shall be examined by a physician specializing in psychiatry within twenty-four hours of admission. If such physician is of the opinion that the child does not require hospitalization for emergency evaluation or treatment of a mental disorder, such child shall be immediately discharged. The physician shall record his or her findings in a permanent record.

(c) If any child is hospitalized under this section, the child and the guardian of such child shall be promptly informed by the hospital that such child has the right to consult an attorney and the right to a hearing under subsection (d) of this section, and that if such a hearing is requested or an application for commitment is filed, such child has the right to be represented by counsel, and that counsel will be provided at the state's expense if the child is unable to pay for such counsel. The reasonable compensation for counsel provided to persons unable to pay shall be established by, and paid from funds appropriated to, the Judicial Department, however, if funds have not been included in the budget of the Judicial Department for such purposes, such compensation shall be established by the Probate Court Administrator and paid from the Probate Court Administration Fund.

(d) At any time prior to the initiation of proceedings under section 17a–76, any child hospitalized under this section or his or her representative, may, in writing, request a hearing. Such hearing shall be held within seventy-two hours of receipt of such request, excluding

Saturdays, Sundays and holidays. At such hearing, the child shall have the right to be present, to cross-examine all witnesses testifying, and to be represented by counsel as provided in section 17a–76. The hearing shall be held by the court of probate having jurisdiction for commitment as provided in section 17a–76, and the hospital shall immediately notify such court of any request for a hearing by a child hospitalized under this section. At the conclusion of the hearing, if the court finds that there is probable cause to conclude that the child is subject to involuntary hospitalization under this section, considering the condition of the child at the time of the admission and at the time of the hearing, the effects of medication, if any, and the advisability of continued treatment based on testimony from the hospital staff, the court shall order that such child's hospitalization continue for the remaining time provided for in the emergency certificate or until the completion of probate proceedings under section 17a–76. If the court does not find there is probable cause to conclude that the child is subject to involuntary hospitalization under this section, the child shall be immediately discharged.

(e) The superintendent or director of any hospital for mental illness of children shall immediately discharge any child admitted under this section who is later found not to meet the standards for emergency treatment.

(1958 Rev., § 17–205e; 1979, P.A. 79–511, § 4; 1993, P.A. 93–197; 1996, P.A. 96–170, § 3, eff. July 1, 1998.)

§ 17a–79. Hospitalization of child for diagnosis or treatment of mental disorder

(a) Except as provided in subsection (b) of this section, any hospital may admit any child for diagnosis or treatment of a mental disorder upon the written request of the child's parent. A child fourteen years of age or over may be admitted under this section without consent of his or her parents if such child consents in writing, provided that the parents of such child, if any, shall be notified within five days of such admission that such child has been hospitalized under the provisions of this subsection. If the whereabouts of such parents are unknown, then such child's nearest relative shall be so notified. In the event that a child's parent or guardian requests in writing release of such child, or in the event a child age fourteen or older who has been admitted with his or her written consent requests in writing his or her release, the hospital shall release such child or commence commitment proceedings in accordance with sections 17a–76 and 17a–77 and the hospital may detain the child for five business days, in order to allow an application to be filed. In the event such an application is filed, such hospitalization shall be continued for an additional period of time to allow such application to be heard, but in no event shall such hospitalization continue for more than fifteen days, or twenty-five days, if the matter has been transferred to the Superior Court, beyond the receipt of such application by the court.

(b) No child in the custody of the Commissioner of Children and Families shall be admitted for diagnosis or treatment except in accordance with sections 17a–76 to 17a–78, inclusive, unless (1) the commissioner requests such admission, (2) legal counsel appointed by the court in accordance with section 17a–76 agrees, in writing, to such admission, and (3) the child, if fourteen years of age or over consents to such admission. The parents or guardian of the person of such child, if any, shall be notified within five days of such admission that such child has been hospitalized under the provisions of this section. If the whereabouts of such parents or guardian of the person is unknown, then the nearest relative of such child shall be notified. In the event either parent or the guardian of the person of the child requests in writing the release of such child, the hospital shall release such child, unless the Commissioner of Children and Families commences commitment proceedings in accordance with sections 17a–76 and 17a–77. The hospital may detain the child for five business days after receipt of the written request in order to allow an application to be filed. If an application is filed, hospitalization shall be continued for an additional period of time to allow the application to be heard, but in no event shall hospitalization continue for more than fifteen days, or twenty-five days, if the matter has been transferred to the Superior Court, beyond the receipt of such application by the court.

(1958 Rev., § 17–205f; 1979, P.A. 79–511, § 5; 1981, P.A. 81–247, § 6, eff. June 2, 1981; 1986, P.A. 86–311, § 1; 1993, P.A. 93–91, § 1, eff. July 1, 1993.)

§ 17a–80. Right of review of status as voluntary patient. Hearing. Child's right to be at hearing. Duties of hospital

If any child fourteen years of age or over hospitalized upon the written request of his or her parent under section 17a–79, or his or her representative, requests a hearing in writing, to review his or her status as a voluntary patient, such hearing shall be held within three business days. Any child fourteen years of age or over shall be informed in writing of his or her right to have a hearing under this section upon admission to the hospital and any child reaching the age of fourteen who is already hospitalized as a voluntary patient shall be informed within five days of his or her reaching such age. At such hearing, the child shall have the right to be present, to cross-examine all witnesses testifying, and to be represented by counsel as provided in section 17a–77. The hearing may be requested at any time prior to the initiation of proceedings under section 17a–76. The hearing shall be held by the court of probate in the district in which the hospital is located. The hospital shall immediately notify such court of any request for a hearing by a child hospitalized under section 17a–79. At the conclusion of the hearing, unless the court finds that there is clear and convincing evidence to conclude that the child suffers from a mental disorder and is in need of hospitalization for treatment, that such treatment is available and that there is no less restrictive available alternative, the court shall order such child's release from the hospital, otherwise such hospitalization may continue in accordance with section 17a–79. In no event shall a request for a hearing under this section be granted more than once in each ninety-day period. All fees and expenses incurred upon proceedings required by this section shall be paid as provided in section 17a–82. The hospital shall furnish the court of probate in the district in which such hospital is located, on a monthly basis, a list of all children admitted under the provisions of section 17a–79 who have been hospitalized for a period of one year. Within ten days thereafter, such court shall appoint an impartial physician specializing in psychiatry from the panel of physicians established under subsection (b) of section 17a–77 who shall see and examine each such child within fifteen days after the appointment. If, in the opinion of such physician, such child does not need continued hospitalization, then such child shall be released unless an application is filed for his or her hospitalization under the provisions of sections 17a–76 to 17a–78, inclusive.

(1958 Rev., § 17–205g; 1979, P.A. 79–511, § 6.)

§ 17a–81. Parental consent necessary for treatment. Exceptions

(a) Parental consent shall be necessary for treatment. In the event such consent is withheld or immediately unavailable and the physician concludes that treatment is necessary to prevent serious harm to the child, such emergency treatment may be administered pending receipt of parental consent.

(b) Involuntary patients may receive medication and treatment without their consent, or the consent of their parents, but no medical or surgical procedures may be performed without the written informed consent of: (1) The child's parent, if he or she has one; or (2) such child's next of kin; or (3) a qualified physician appointed by a judge of the Probate Court who signed the order of hospitalization, except in accordance with subsection (c) of this section.

(c) If the head of a hospital, in consultation with a physician, determines that the condition of a child, whether a voluntary or involuntary patient, is of an extremely critical nature, then emergency measures may be taken without the consent otherwise provided for in this section.

(1958 Rev., § 17–205h; 1979, P.A. 79–511, § 7.)

§ 17a–82. Payment of commitment and transportation expenses

(a) When any child is in need of hospitalization and is hospitalized in a state hospital for children under sections 17a–75 to 17a–83, inclusive, or when an applicant is indigent, all fees and expenses incurred upon the court commitment proceedings, except attorneys fees paid pursuant to the provisions of section 17a–77, shall be paid by the state, from funds appropriated to the Department of Children and Families, and if any child is hospitalized in a private hospital or if any child is found not to be mentally disordered and in need of hospitalization, such fees and expenses shall be paid by the applicant, except attorneys fees paid under the provisions of section 17a–77. Compensation shall be determined by the court hearing the matter in accordance with rules adopted by the Superior Court.

(b) The expenses, if any, of necessary transportation to a state hospital for mental illness for hospitalization of any child shall be paid for by the Department of Children and Families, if such child or legally liable relative is unable to pay for the same.

(c) The expenses of medically necessary transportation from any state facility or hospital to any other state facility or hospital shall be assumed by the state facility or hospital which initiated the transfer of such child.

(1958 Rev., § 17–205i; 1979, P.A. 79–511, § 8; 1981, P.A. 81–472, § 36, eff. July 8, 1981; 1993, P.A. 93–91, § 1, eff. July 1, 1993.)

§ 17a–83. Penalty for conspiring to commit any child to a hospital for mental illness

Any person who wilfully files or attempts to file or conspires with any person to file a fraudulent or malicious application, order or request for the commitment, hospitalization or treatment of any child pursuant to section 17a–76, 17a–78 or 17a–79, and any person who wilfully certifies falsely to the mental disorder of any child in any certificate provided for in this part, and any person who, under the provisions of sections 17a–75 to 17a–83, inclusive, relating to mentally ill minors, wilfully reports falsely to any court or judge that any child is mentally disordered, shall be fined not more than one thousand dollars or imprisoned not more than five years or both.

(1958 Rev., § 17–205j; 1979, P.A. 79–511, § 9; 1981, P.A. 81–472, § 37, eff. July 8, 1981.)

CHAPTER 319a

CHILD WELFARE

PART I. DEPENDENT AND NEGLECTED CHILDREN

§ 17a–90. Supervision over welfare of children. Portion of cost payable by parent, collection

(a) The Commissioner of Children and Families shall have general supervision over the welfare of children who require the care and protection of the state.

(b) He shall furnish protective services or provide and pay, wholly or in part, for the care and protection of children other than those committed by the Superior

Court whom he finds in need of such care and protection from the state, and such payments shall be made in accordance with the provisions of subsection (k) of section 46b–129 provided the Commissioner of Administrative Services shall be responsible for billing and collecting such sums as are determined to be owing and due from the parent of the noncommitted child in accordance with section 4a–12 and subsection (b) of section 17b–223.

(c) He shall issue such regulations as he may find necessary and proper to assure the adequate care, health and safety of children under his care and general supervision.

(d) He may provide temporary emergency care for any child whom he deems to be in need thereof.

(e) He may provide care for children in his guardianship through the resources of appropriate voluntary agencies.

(f) Whenever requested to do so by the Superior Court, he shall provide protective supervision to children.

(g) He may make reciprocal agreements with other states and with agencies outside the state in matters relating to the supervision of the welfare of children.

(1949 Rev., § 2630; 1953, Supp. § 1125c; 1955, Supp. § 1462d; 1958 Rev., § 17–32; 1965, Feb.Sp.Sess., P.A. 488, § 2; 1967, P.A. 707; 1971, P.A. 281; 1975, P.A. 75–420, § 4, eff. June 25, 1975; 1976, P.A. 76–436, § 483, eff. July 1, 1978; 1977, P.A. 77–614, § 71, eff. Oct. 1, 1977; 1977, P.A. 77–614, § 521, eff. Jan. 1, 1979; 1979, P.A. 79–631, § 51, eff. July 6, 1979; 1982, P.A. 82–43, § 3; 1987, P.A. 87–421, § 2, eff. July 1, 1987; 1993, P.A. 93–91, § 1, eff. July 1, 1993; 1998, P.A. 98–241, § 11.)

§ 17a–91. Commissioner of Children and Families' report on children committed to him and establishment of central registry and monitoring system

The Commissioner of Children and Families shall report, on February fifteenth annually, to the Governor and to the joint standing committees of the General Assembly having cognizance of matters relating to human services, the judiciary and human rights and opportunities, with respect to the status, (1) as of the January first preceding, of all children committed to the commissioner's custody, including in such report the date of commitment with respect to each child, and (2) of the central registry and monitoring system established in accordance with subsection (d) of section 17a–110.

(1958 Rev., § 17–32b; 1973, P.A. 73–156, § 23; 1975, P.A. 75–420, § 4, eff. June 25, 1975; 1976, P.A. 76–435, § 30, eff. June 9, 1976; 1977, P.A. 77–614, § 521, eff. Jan. 1, 1979; 1979, P.A. 79–631, § 52, eff. July 6, 1979; 1982, P.A. 82–314, § 60, eff. Jan. 5, 1983; 1993, P.A. 93–91, § 1, eff. July 1, 1993; 1999, P.A. 99–166, § 3.)

§ 17a–91a. Monthly report on number of children in custody of department and in subacute care who cannot be discharged

Beginning July 1, 1999, and monthly thereafter, the Department of Children and Families shall submit a report to the joint standing committees of the General Assembly having cognizance of matters relating to public health and human services on the number of children and adolescents in the custody of said department who are in subacute care in freestanding psychiatric or general hospitals and who cannot be discharged due to the lack of appropriate placements in the community.

(1999, P.A. 99–279, § 2, eff. July 1, 1999.)

§ 17a–92. Transfer of court wards to guardianship of Commissioner of Children and Families: Delegation of powers, duties and functions

Effective at 12:01 a.m., April 1, 1975, the Commissioner of Children and Families shall assume, and the Commissioner of Social Services shall cease to have guardianship, as defined in subsection (a) of section 17a–90, over all children who on that date, by virtue of any order of the Juvenile Court or Superior Court, are wards of or committed to the state of Connecticut or the Commissioner of Social Services. The Commissioner of Children and Families shall thereupon assume all liability and responsibility for such children, and exercise such powers, duties and functions regarding such children, as the Commissioner of Social Services in his capacity as guardian may now or hereafter have, except to the extent that the federal government may require that any responsibility for children be retained by the Commissioner of Social Services as a prerequisite to federal reimbursement of state expenditures for such children under Title IV—A and B of the Social Security Act.[1] The Commissioner of Children and Families may delegate any power, duty or function regarding such children, except for consent for adoption, marriage and joining of the armed services and except to the extent that the federal government may require that any responsibility for children be retained by said commissioner as a prerequisite to federal reimbursement of state expenditures for such children.

(1958 Rev., § 17–32c; 1974, P.A. 74–251, § 2; 1975, P.A. 75–544; 1977, P.A. 77–614, § 521, eff. Jan. 1, 1979; 1977, P.A. 77–614, § 587, eff. June 2, 1977; 1978, P.A. 78–303, § 85, eff. June 6, 1978; 1980, P.A. 80–483, § 155, eff. June 6, 1980; 1993, P.A. 93–91, § 1, eff. July 1, 1993.)

1 42 U.S.C.A. §§ 601 et seq., 620 et seq.

§ 17a–93. Definitions

As used in sections 17a–90 to 17a–124, inclusive, and 17a–152:

(a) "Child" means any person under eighteen years of age, except as otherwise specified, or any person under twenty-one years of age who is in full-time attendance in a secondary school, a technical school, a college or a state-accredited job training program;

(b) "Parent" means natural or adoptive parent;

(c) "Adoption" means the establishment by court order of the legal relationship of parent and child;

(d) "Guardianship" means guardianship, unless otherwise specified, of the person of a minor and refers to the obligation of care and control, the right to custody and the duty and authority to make major decisions affecting such minor's welfare, including, but not limited to, consent determinations regarding marriage, enlistment in the armed forces and major medical, psychiatric or surgical treatment;

(e) "Termination of parental rights" means the complete severance by court order of the legal relationship, with all its rights and responsibilities, between the child and his parent or parents so that the child is free for adoption except it shall not affect the right of inheritance of such child or the religious affiliation of such child;

(f) "Statutory parent" means the Commissioner of Children and Families or that child-placing agency appointed by the court for the purpose of giving a minor child or minor children in adoption;

(g) "Child-placing agency" means any agency within or without the state of Connecticut licensed or approved by the Commissioner of Children and Families in accordance with sections 17a–149 and 17a–151, and in accordance with such standards which shall be established by regulations of the Department of Children and Families;

(h) "Child care facility" means a congregate residential setting for the out-of-home placement of children or youth under eighteen years of age, licensed by the Department of Children and Families;

(i) "Protective supervision" means a status created by court order following adjudication of neglect whereby a child's place of abode is not changed but assistance directed at correcting the neglect is provided at the request of the court through the Department of Children and Families or such other social agency as the court may specify;

(j) "Receiving home" means a facility operated by the Department of Children and Families to receive and temporarily care for children in the guardianship or care of the commissioner;

(k) "Protective services" means public welfare services provided after complaints of abuse, neglect or abandonment, but in the absence of an adjudication or assumption of jurisdiction by a court;

(*l*) "Person responsible for the health, welfare or care of a child or youth" means a child's or a youth's parent, guardian or foster parent; an employee of a public or private residential home, agency or institution or other person legally responsible in a residential setting; or any staff person providing out-of-home care, including center-based child day care, family day care or group day care, as defined in section 19a–77;

(m) "Foster family" means a person or persons, licensed or certified by the Department of Children and Families or approved by a licensed child-placing agency, for the care of a child or children in a private home;

(n) "Prospective adoptive family" means a person or persons, licensed by the Department of Children and Families or approved by a licensed child-placing agency, who is awaiting the placement of, or who has a child or children placed in their home for the purposes of adoption;

(*o*) "Person entrusted with the care of a child or youth" means a person given access to a child or youth by a person responsible for the health, welfare or care of a child or youth for the purpose of providing education, child care, counseling, spiritual guidance, coaching, training, instruction, tutoring or mentoring of such child or youth.

(1958 Rev., § 17–32d; 1975, P.A. 75–420, § 4, eff. June 25, 1975; 1975, P.A. 75–567, § 39, eff. June 30, 1975; 1977, P.A. 77–614, § 521, eff. Jan. 1, 1979; 1979, P.A. 79–631, § 53, eff. July 6, 1979; 1990, P.A. 90–53; 1992, P.A. 92–14, § 2; 1993, P.A. 93–91, § 1, eff. July 1, 1993, 1995, P.A. 95–349, § 2, 2002, P.A. 02–138, § 11.)

§ 17a–94. Establishment of receiving homes

The Commissioner of Children and Families may establish, maintain and operate, throughout the state, at such locations as he finds suitable, receiving homes for children in his guardianship or care. For such purposes he may purchase, lease, hold, sell or convey real and personal property, subject to the provisions of section 4b–21, and contract for the operation and maintenance of such receiving homes with any nonprofit group or organization. Said contract may include administrative, managerial and custodial services. The expense of obtaining and maintaining the same shall be paid out of the appropriation for the Department of Children and Families. The commissioner may, subject to the provisions of chapter 67,[1] appoint such supervisory and other personnel as he finds necessary for the management of such homes. The maximum charge to be made for care of children in such homes shall be the same as the charge for care of patients in state humane institutions.

(1955, Supp. § 1463d; 1958 Rev., § 17–34; 1959, P.A. 31; 1965, Feb.Sp.Sess., P.A. 488, § 5; 1971, P.A. 260; 1975, P.A. 75–420, § 4, eff. June 25, 1975; 1977, P.A. 77–614, § 521, eff. Jan. 1, 1979; 1979, P.A. 79–631, § 54, eff. July 6, 1979; 1993, P.A. 93–91, § 1, eff. July 1, 1993; 1996, P.A. 96–180, § 45, eff. June 3, 1996.)

[1] C.G.S.A. § 5–193 et seq.

§ 17a–95. Religious and moral instruction

Equal privileges shall be granted to clergymen of all religious denominations to impart religious instruction to the children residing in receiving homes maintained and operated by the Commissioner of Children and Families, and every reasonable opportunity shall be allowed such clergymen to give religious and moral instruction to such children as belong to their respective faiths. The Commissioner of Children and Families shall prescribe reasonable times and places when and where such instruction may be given.

(1949 Rev., § 2838; 1955, Supp. § 1471d; 1958 Rev., § 17–35; 1965, Feb.Sp.Sess., P.A. 488, § 4; 1975, P.A. 75–420, § 4, eff. June 25, 1975; 1977, P.A. 77–614, § 521, eff. Jan. 1, 1979; 1979, P.A. 79–631, § 55, eff. July 6, 1979; 1993, P.A. 93–91, § 1, eff. July 1, 1993.)

§ 17a–96. Custodians of children to file reports. Placing of children in foster homes

Text of section effective until July 1, 2004, or upon enactment of the Interstate Compact for Juveniles by thirty-five jurisdictions, whichever is later. For text of section effective July 1, 2004, or upon enactment of the Interstate Compact for Juveniles by thirty-five jurisdictions, whichever is later, see § 17a–96, post.

The institutions having custody of such children and the agencies and persons licensed by authority of sections 17a–90 to 17a–124, inclusive, 17a–145 to 17a–155, inclusive, 17a–175 to 17a–182, inclusive, 17a–185 and 46b–151 to 46b–151g, inclusive, shall make such reports to the Commissioner of Children and Families at such reasonable times and in such form and covering such data as the commissioner directs. The commissioner and his deputy and agents shall supervise the placing of such children in foster homes. The commissioner may place children who have not been properly placed in homes suitable for their care and protection. In placing any child in a foster home, the commissioner shall, if practicable, select a home of like religious faith to that of the parent or parents of such child, if such faith is known or ascertainable by the exercise of reasonable care.

(1949 Rev., § 2631; 1955, Supp. § 1466d; 1958 Rev., § 17–36; 1996, P.A. 96–180, § 46, eff. June 3, 1996.)

§ 17a–96. Custodians of children to file reports. Placing of children in foster homes

Text of section effective July 1, 2004, or upon enactment of the Interstate Compact for Juveniles by thirty-five jurisdictions, whichever is later. For text of section effective until July 1, 2004, or upon enactment of the Interstate Compact for Juveniles by thirty-five jurisdictions, whichever is later, see § 17a–96, main volume.

The institutions having custody of such children and the agencies and persons licensed by authority of sections 17a–90 to 17a–124, inclusive, 17a–145 to 17a–155, inclusive, and 17a–175 to 17a–182, inclusive, 17a–185 shall make such reports to the Commissioner of Children and Families at such reasonable times and in such form and covering such data as the commissioner directs. The commissioner and his deputy and agents shall supervise the placing of such children in foster homes. The commissioner may place children who have not been properly placed in homes suitable for their care and protection. In placing any child in a foster home, the commissioner shall, if practicable, select a home of like religious faith to that of the parent or parents of such child, if such faith is known or ascertainable by the exercise of reasonable care.

(1949 Rev., § 2631; 1955, Supp. § 1466d; 1958 Rev., § 17–36; 1996, P.A. 96–180, § 46, eff. June 3, 1996; 2003, P.A. 03–255, § 3, eff. July 1, 2004.)

§ 17a–97. Repealed. (1996, P.A. 96–194, § 13.)

§ 17a–98. Supervision of children under guardianship or care of commissioner

The Commissioner of Children and Families, or any agent appointed by him, shall exercise careful supervision of each child under his guardianship or care and shall maintain such contact with the child and his foster family as is necessary to promote the child's safety and his physical, educational, moral and emotional development. The commissioner shall maintain such records and accounts as may be necessary for the proper supervision of all children under his guardianship or care.

(1949 Rev., § 2632; 1955, Supp. § 1467d; 1958 Rev., § 17–37; 1961, P.A. 341; 1965, Feb.Sp.Sess., P.A. 488, § 8; 1975, P.A. 75–420, § 4, eff. June 25, 1975; 1977, P.A. 77–614, § 521, eff. Jan. 1, 1979; 1979, P.A. 79–631, § 57, eff. July 6, 1979; 1993, P.A. 93–91, § 1, eff. July 1, 1993; 1996, P.A. 96–194, § 2.)

§ 17a–99. Delegation of guardianship authority

The Commissioner of Children and Families may delegate to his deputy commissioner his authority as guardian of children committed to him by the Superior Court, or whose guardianship is transferred to him by a court of probate, and the signature of either official on any document pertaining to any such guardianship shall be valid.

(1958 Rev., § 17–37a; 1973, P.A. 73–489; 1974, P.A. 74–251, § 19; 1975, P.A. 75–420, § 4, eff. June 25, 1975; 1976, P.A. 76–436, § 585, eff. July 1, 1978; 1977, P.A. 77–614, § 521, eff. Jan. 1, 1979; 1979, P.A. 79–631, § 58, eff. July 6, 1979; 1993, P.A. 93–91, § 1, eff. July 1, 1993.)

§ 17a–100. Ill treatment of children

Whenever it is found that any child is not properly treated in any foster family or that any such foster family is not a suitable one and is of such character as to jeopardize the welfare of any child so placed therein, the Commissioner of Children and Families, upon being satisfied of the ill treatment of the child or the unsuitableness of the foster family, shall remove the child from such foster family and take such further action as is necessary to secure the welfare of the child.

(1949 Rev., § 2633; 1955, Supp. § 1468d; 1958 Rev., § 17–38; 1975, P.A. 75–420, § 4, eff. June 25, 1975; 1977, P.A. 77–614, § 521, eff. Jan. 1, 1979; 1979, P.A. 79–631, § 59, eff. July 6, 1979; 1993, P.A. 93–91, § 1, eff. July 1, 1993; 1996, P.A. 96–194, § 3.)

§ 17a–101. Protection of children from abuse. Mandated reporters. Educational and training programs

(a) The public policy of this state is: To protect children whose health and welfare may be adversely affected through injury and neglect; to strengthen the family and to make the home safe for children by enhancing the parental capacity for good child care; to provide a temporary or permanent nurturing and safe environment for children when necessary; and for these purposes to require the reporting of suspected child abuse, investigation of such reports by a social agency, and provision of services, where needed, to such child and family.

(b) The following persons shall be mandated reporters: Any physician or surgeon licensed under the provisions of chapter 370 [1], any resident physician or intern in any hospital in this state, whether or not so licensed, any registered nurse, licensed practical nurse, medical examiner, dentist, dental hygienist, psychologist, coach of intramural or interscholastic athletics, school teacher, school principal, school guidance counselor, school paraprofessional, school coach, social worker, police officer, juvenile or adult probation officer, juvenile or adult parole officer, member of the clergy, pharmacist, physical therapist, optometrist, chiropractor, podiatrist, mental health professional or physician assistant, any person who is a licensed or certified emergency medical services provider, any person who is a licensed or certified alcohol and drug counselor, any person who is a licensed marital and family therapist, any person who is a sexual assault counselor or a battered women's counselor as defined in section 52–146k, any person who is a licensed professional counselor, any person paid to care for a child in any public or private facility, child day care center, group day care home or family day care home licensed by the state, any employee of the Department of Children and Families, any employee of the Department of Public Health who is responsible for the licensing of child day care centers, group day care homes, family day care homes or youth camps, the Child Advocate and any employee of the Office of Child Advocate.

(c) The Commissioner of Children and Families shall develop an educational training program for the accurate and prompt identification and reporting of child abuse and neglect. Such training program shall be made available to all persons mandated to report child abuse and neglect at various times and locations throughout the state as determined by the Commissioner of Children and Families.

(d) Any mandated reporter, as defined in subsection (b) of this section, who fails to report to the Commissioner of Children and Families pursuant to section 17a–101a shall be required to participate in an educational and training program established by the commissioner. The program may be provided by one or more private organizations approved by the commissioner, provided the entire costs of the program shall be paid from fees charged to the participants, the amount of which shall be subject to the approval of the commissioner.

(1958 Rev., § 17–38a; 1965, Feb.Sp.Sess., P.A. 580, §§ 1 to 3; 1967, P.A. 317; 1969, P.A. 25; 1971, P.A. 216; 1973, P.A. 73–205, § 1; 1974, P.A. 74–293, §§ 1 to 3; 1975, P.A. 75–270; 1975, P.A. 75–384, §§ 1 to 6, eff. May 30, 1975; 1975, P.A. 75–420, § 4, eff. June 25, 1975; 1976, P.A. 76–27, § 1, eff. April 7, 1976; 1976, P.A. 76–436, § 586, eff. July 1, 1978; 1977, P.A. 77–308, § 1, eff. June 2, 1977; 1977, P.A. 77–614, §§ 486, 521, eff. Jan. 1, 1979; 1977, P.A. 77–614, § 587, eff. June 2, 1977; 1978, P.A. 78–303, § 85, eff. June 6, 1978; 1979, P.A. 79–631, § 60, eff. July 6, 1979, 1980, P.A. 80–190, § 4; 1981, P.A. 81–91, § 2; 1981, P.A. 81–472, § 29, eff. July 8, 1981; 1982, P.A. 82–203; 1986, P.A. 86–337, § 6; 1988, P.A. 88–218; 1988, P.A. 88–333; 1989, P.A. 89–160, § 1, eff. July 1, 1989; 1989, P.A. 89–168, § 1; 1992, P.A. 92–76, § 1; 1993, P.A. 93–91, § 1, eff. July 1, 1993; 1993, P.A. 93–340, § 4, eff. July 1, 1993; 1994, P.A. 94–221, § 21; 1995, P.A. 95–103; 1995, P.A. 95–289, § 7; 1996, P.A. 96–246, § 1; 1999, P.A. 99–102, § 13; 2000, P.A. 00–49, § 6, eff. July 1, 2000; 2002, P.A. 02–106, § 3; 2002, P.A. 02–138, § 12.)

[1] C.G.S.A. § 20–8 et seq.

§ 17a–101a. Report of abuse, neglect or injury of child or imminent risk of serious harm to child. Penalty for failure to report

Any mandated reporter, as defined in section 17a–101, who in the ordinary course of such person's employment or profession has reasonable cause to suspect or believe that any child under the age of eighteen years (1) has been abused or neglected, as defined in section 46b–120, (2) has had nonaccidental physical injury, or injury which is at variance with the history given of such injury, inflicted upon such child, or (3) is placed at imminent risk of serious harm, shall report or cause a report to be made in accordance with the provisions of sections 17a–101b to 17a–101d, inclusive. Any person required to report under the provisions of this section who fails to make such report shall be fined not less than five hundred dollars nor more than two thousand five hundred dollars and shall be required to participate in an educational and training program pursuant to subsection (d) of section 17a–101.

(1996, P.A. 96–246, § 2; 1997, P.A. 97–319, § 9, eff. July 1, 1997; 1998, P.A. 98–241, § 3, eff. July 1, 1998; 2002, P.A. 02–106, § 4; 2002, P.A. 02–138, § 13.)

§ 17a–101b. Oral report by mandated reporter. Notification of law enforcement agency when allegation of sexual abuse or serious physical abuse. Notification of person in charge of institution, facility or school when staff member suspected of abuse or neglect

(a) An oral report shall be made by a mandated reporter as soon as practicable but not later than twelve hours after the mandated reporter has reasonable cause to suspect or believe that a child has been abused or neglected or placed in imminent risk of serious harm, by telephone or in person to the Commissioner of Children and Families or a law enforcement agency. If a law enforcement agency receives an oral report, it shall immediately notify the Commissioner of Children and Families.

(b) If the commissioner or the commissioner's designee suspects or knows that such person has knowingly made a false report, the identity of such person shall be disclosed to the appropriate law enforcement agency and to the perpetrator of the alleged abuse.

(c) If the Commissioner of Children and Families, or the commissioner's designee, receives a report alleging sexual abuse or serious physical abuse, including, but not limited to, a report that: (1) A child has died; (2) a child has been sexually assaulted; (3) a child has suffered brain damage or loss or serious impairment of a bodily function or organ; (4) a child has been sexually exploited; or (5) a child has suffered serious nonaccidental physical injury, the commissioner shall, within twelve hours of receipt of such report, notify the appropriate law enforcement agency.

(d) Whenever a mandated reporter, as defined in section 17a–101, has reasonable cause to suspect or believe that any child has been abused or neglected by a member of the staff of a public or private institution or facility that provides care for such child or a public or private school, the mandated reporter shall report as required in subsection (a) of this section. The Commissioner of Children and Families or the commissioner's designee shall notify the person in charge of such institution, facility or school or the person's designee, unless such person is the alleged perpetrator of the abuse or neglect of such child. Such person in charge, or such person's designee, shall then immediately notify the child's parent or other person responsible for the child's care that a report has been made.

(1996, P.A. 96–246, § 3; 1997, P.A. 97–319, § 10, eff. July 1, 1997; 2002, P.A. 02–138, § 14.)

§ 17a–101c. Written report by mandated reporter

Within forty-eight hours of making an oral report, a mandated reporter shall submit a written report to the Commissioner of Children and Families or his representative. When a mandated reporter is a member of the staff of a public or private institution or facility that provides care for such child or public or private school he shall also submit a copy of the written report to the person in charge of such institution, school or facility or the person's designee. In the case of a report concerning a school employee holding a certificate, authorization or permit issued by the State Board of Education under the provisions of sections 10–144o to 10–146b, inclusive, and 10–149, a copy of the written report shall also be sent by the person in charge of such institution, school or facility to the Commissioner of Education or his representative. In the case of an employee of a facility or institution that provides care for a child which is licensed by the state, a copy of the written report shall also be sent by the mandated reporter to the executive head of the state licensing agency.

(1996, P.A. 96–246, § 4; 1997, P.A. 97–319, § 11, eff. July 1, 1997; 1998, P.A. 98–239, § 18; 2003, P.A. 03–168, § 6, eff. July 1, 2003.)

§ 17a–101d. Contents of oral and written reports

All oral and written reports required in sections 17a–101a to 17a–101c, inclusive, and section 17a–103, shall contain, if known: (1) The names and addresses of the child and his parents or other person responsible for his care; (2) the age of the child; (3) the gender of the child; (4) the nature and extent of the child's injury or injuries, maltreatment or neglect; (5) the approximate date and time the injury or injuries, maltreatment or neglect occurred; (6) information concerning any previous injury or injuries to, or maltreatment or neglect of, the child or his siblings; (7) the circumstances in which the injury or injuries, maltreatment or neglect came to be known to the reporter; (8) the name of the person or persons suspected to be responsible for causing such injury or injuries, maltreatment or neglect; and (9) whatever action, if any, was taken to treat, provide shelter or otherwise assist the child.

(1996, P.A. 96–246, § 5.)

§ 17a–101e. Employers prohibited from discrimination against witness in child abuse proceeding. Penalty. Immunity for making report of child abuse in good faith. False report of child abuse. Penalty

(a) No employer shall discharge, or in any manner discriminate or retaliate against, any employee who in good faith makes a report pursuant to sections 17a–101a to 17a–101d, inclusive, and section 17a–103, testifies or is about to testify in any proceeding involving child abuse or neglect. The Attorney General may bring an action in Superior Court against an employer who violates this subsection. The court may assess a civil penalty of not more than two thousand five hundred dollars and may order such other equitable relief as the court deems appropriate.

(b) Any person, institution or agency which, in good faith, makes, or in good faith does not make, the report pursuant to sections 17a–101a to 17a–101d, inclusive, and section 17a–103 shall be immune from any liability, civil or criminal, which might otherwise be incurred or imposed and shall have the same immunity with respect to any judicial proceeding which results from such report provided such person did not perpetrate or cause such abuse or neglect.

(c) Any person who knowingly makes a false report of child abuse or neglect pursuant to sections 17a–101a to 17a–101d, inclusive, and section 17a–103, shall be fined not more than two thousand dollars or imprisoned not more than one year or both.

(1996, P.A. 96–246, § 6; 1997, P.A. 97–319, § 12, eff. July 1, 1997.)

§ 17a–101f. Examination by physician. Diagnostic tests and procedures to detect child abuse. Expenses

Any physician examining a child with respect to whom abuse or neglect is suspected shall have the right to keep such child in the custody of a hospital for no longer than ninety-six hours in order to perform diagnostic tests and procedures necessary to the detection of child abuse or neglect and to provide necessary medical care with or without the consent of such child's parents or guardian or other person responsible for the child's care, provided the physician has made reasonable attempts to (1) advise such child's parents or guardian or other person responsible for the child's care that he suspects the child has been abused or neglected and (2) obtain consent of such child's parents or guardian or other person responsible for the child's care. In addition, such physician may take or cause to be taken photographs of the area of trauma visible on a child who is the subject of such report without the consent of such child's parents or guardian or other person responsible for the child's care. All such photographs or copies thereof shall be sent to the local police department and the Department of Children and Families. The expenses for such care and such diagnostic tests and procedures, if not covered by insurance, shall be paid by the Commissioner of Children and Families, provided the state may recover such costs from the parent if the parent has been found by a court to have abused or neglected such child.

(1996, P.A. 96–246, § 8.)

§ 17a–101g. Classification and evaluation of reports. Investigation. Referral to local law enforcement authority. Home visit. Removal of child in imminent risk of harm

(a) Upon receiving a report of child abuse or neglect, as provided in sections 17a–101a to 17a–101c, inclusive, or section 17a–103, in which the alleged perpetrator is (1) a person responsible for such child's health, welfare or care, (2) a person given access to such child by such responsible person, or (3) a person entrusted with the care of a child, the Commissioner of Children and Families, or the commissioner's designee, shall cause the report to be classified and evaluated immediately. If the report contains sufficient information to warrant an investigation, the commissioner shall make the commissioner's best efforts to commence an investigation of a report concerning an imminent risk of physical harm to a child or other emergency within two hours of receipt of the report and shall commence an investigation of all other reports within seventy-two hours of receipt of the report. The department shall complete any such investigation within thirty calendar days of receipt of the report. If the report is a report of child abuse or neglect in which the alleged perpetrator is not a person specified in subdivision (1), (2) or (3) of this subsection, the Commissioner of Children and Families shall refer the report to the appropriate local law enforcement authority for the town in which the child resides or in which the alleged abuse or neglect occurred.

(b) The investigation shall include a home visit at which the child and any siblings are observed, if appropriate, a determination of the nature, extent and cause or causes of the reported abuse or neglect, a determination of the person or persons suspected to be responsible for such abuse or neglect, the name, age and condition of other children residing in the same household and an evaluation of the parents and the home. The report of such investigation shall be in writing. The investigation shall also include, but not be limited to, a review of criminal conviction information concerning the person or persons alleged to be responsible for such abuse or neglect and previous allegations of abuse or neglect relating to the child or other children residing in the household or relating to family violence.

(c) If the Commissioner of Children and Families, or his designee, has probable cause to believe that the child or any other child in the household is in imminent risk of physical harm from his surroundings and that immediate removal from such surroundings is necessary to ensure the child's safety, the commissioner, or his designee, shall authorize any employee of the department or any law enforcement officer to remove the child and any other child similarly situated from such surroundings without the consent of the child's parent or guardian. The commissioner shall record in writing the reasons for such removal and include such record with the report of the investigation conducted under subsection (b) of this section.

(d) The removal of a child pursuant to subsection (c) of this section shall not exceed ninety-six hours. During the period of such removal, the commissioner, or his designee, shall provide the child with all necessary care, including medical care, which may include an examination by a physician or mental health professional with or without the consent of the child's parents, guardian or other person responsible for the child's care, provided reasonable attempts have been made to obtain consent of the child's parents or guardian or other person responsible for the care of such child. During the course of a medical examination, a physician may perform diagnostic tests and procedures necessary for the detection of child abuse or neglect. If the child is not returned home within such ninety-six-hour period, with or without protective services, the department shall proceed in accordance with section 46b–129.

(1996, P.A. 96–246, § 9; 1997, P.A. 97–319, § 13, eff. July 1, 1997; 2002, P.A. 02–138, § 15.)

§ 17a–101h. Coordination of investigatory activities. Interview with child. Consent

Notwithstanding any provision of the general statutes to the contrary, any person authorized to conduct an investigation of abuse or neglect shall coordinate investigatory activities in order to minimize the number of interviews of any child and share information with other persons authorized to conduct an investigation of child abuse or neglect, as appropriate. The commissioner shall obtain the consent of parents or guardians or other persons responsible for the care of the child to any interview with a child, except that such consent shall not be required when the department has reason to believe such parent or guardian or other person responsible for the care of the child or member of the child's household is the perpetrator of the alleged abuse. If consent is not required to conduct the interview, such interview shall be conducted in the presence of a disinterested adult unless immediate access to the child is necessary to protect the child from imminent risk of physical harm and a disinterested adult is not available after reasonable search.

(1996, P.A. 96–246, § 10.)

§ 17a–101i. Abuse of child by school employee or staff member of public or private institution or facility providing care for children. Suspension. Notification by state's attorney re conviction. Boards of education to adopt written policy re reporting of child abuse by school employee

(a) Notwithstanding any provision of the general statutes to the contrary, after an investigation has been completed and the Commissioner of Children and Families, based upon the results of the investigation, has reasonable cause to believe that a child has been abused by a school employee who holds a certificate, permit or authorization issued by the State Board of Education, the commissioner shall notify the employing superintendent of such finding and shall provide records, whether or not created by the department, concerning such investigation to the superintendent who shall suspend such school employee. Such suspension shall be with pay and shall not result in the diminution or termination of benefits to such employee. Within seventy-two hours after such suspension the superintendent shall notify the local or regional board of education and the Commissioner of Education, or the commissioner's representative, of the reasons for and conditions of the suspension. The superintendent shall disclose such records to the Commissioner of Education and the local or regional board of education or its attorney for purposes of review of employment status or the status of such employee's certificate, permit or authorization. The suspension of a school employee employed in a position requiring a certificate shall remain in effect until the board of education acts pursuant to the provisions of section 10–151. If the contract of employment of such certified school employee is terminated, the superintendent shall notify the Commissioner of Education, or the commissioner's representative, within seventy-two hours after such termination. Upon receipt of such notice from the superintendent, the Commissioner of Education may commence certification revocation proceedings pursuant to the provisions of subsection (m) of section 10–145b. Notwithstanding the provisions of sections 1–210 and 1–211, information received by the Commissioner of Education, or the commissioner's representative, pursuant to this section shall be confidential subject to regulations adopted by the State Board of Education under section 10–145g.

(b) After an investigation has been completed and the Commissioner of Children and Families, based upon the results of the investigation, has reasonable cause to believe that a child has been abused by a staff member of a public or private institution or facility providing care for children or private school, the commissioner shall notify the executive director of such institution, school or facility and shall provide records, whether or not created by the department concerning such investigation to such executive director. Such institution, school or facility may suspend such staff person. Such suspension shall be with pay and shall not result in diminution or termination of benefits to such employee. Such suspension shall remain in effect until the incident of abuse has been satisfactorily resolved by the employer of the staff person. If such staff member has a professional license or certificate issued by the state or a permit or authorization issued by the State Board of Education, the commissioner shall forthwith notify the state agency responsible for issuing such license, certificate, permit or authorization to the staff member and provide records, whether or not created by the department, concerning such investigation.

(c) If a school employee or any person holding a certificate, permit or authorization issued by the State Board of Education under the provisions of sections 10–144o to 10–149, inclusive, is convicted of a crime involving an act of child abuse or neglect as described in section 46b–120 or a violation of section 53–21, 53a–71 or 53a–73a, the state's attorney for the judicial district in which the conviction occurred shall in writing notify the superintendent of the school district or the supervisory agent of the nonpublic school in which the person is employed and the Commissioner of Education of such conviction.

(d) For the purposes of receiving and making reports, notifying and receiving notification, or investigating, pursuant to the provisions of sections 17a–101a to 17a–101h, inclusive, and 17a–103, a superintendent of a school district or a supervisory agent of a nonpublic school may assign a designee to act on such superintendent's or agent's behalf.

(e) On or before February 1, 1997, each local and regional board of education shall adopt a written policy regarding the reporting by school employees of suspected child abuse in accordance with sections 17a–101a to 17a–101d, inclusive, and 17a–103.

(1996, P.A. 96–246, § 11; 1997, P.A. 97–319, § 14, eff. July 1, 1997; 2000, P.A. 00–220, § 30, eff. July 1, 2000; 2001, P.A. 01–142, § 5; 2001, P.A. 01–173, §§ 43, 44, eff. July 1, 2001; 2003, P.A. 03–168, § 7, eff. July 1, 2003.)

§ 17a–101j. Notification of law enforcement and prosecutorial authorities when reasonable belief of sexual abuse or serious physical abuse. Notification of agency responsible for licensure of institution or facility where abuse or neglect has occurred. Referral of parent or guardian for substance abuse treatment

(a) After the investigation has been completed and the Commissioner of Children and Families has reasonable cause to believe that sexual abuse or serious physical abuse of a child has occurred, the commissioner shall notify the appropriate local law enforcement authority and the Chief State's Attorney or the Chief State's Attorney's designee or the state's attorney for the judicial district in which the child resides or in which the abuse or neglect occurred of such belief and shall provide a copy of the report required in sections 17a–101a to 17a–101c, inclusive, and 17a–103.

(b) Whenever a report has been made pursuant to sections 17a–101a to 17a–101c, inclusive, and 17a–103, alleging that abuse or neglect has occurred at an institution or facility that provides care for children and is subject to licensure by the state for the caring of children, and the Commissioner of Children and Families, after investigation, has reasonable cause to believe abuse or neglect has occurred, the commissioner shall forthwith notify the state agency responsible for such licensure of such institution or facility and provide records, whether or not created by the department, concerning such investigation.

(c) If, after the investigation is completed, the commissioner determines that a parent or guardian inflicting abuse or neglecting a child is in need of treatment for substance abuse, the commissioner shall refer such person to appropriate treatment services.

(1996, P.A. 96–246, § 12; 1997, P.A. 97–319, § 15, eff. July 1, 1997; 2002, P.A. 02–138, § 16.)

§ 17a–101k. Registry of reports maintained by Commissioner of Children and Families. Appeal of Commissioner's determination of abuse. Confidentiality. Penalty. Disclosure of information to Department of Social Services

(a) The Commissioner of Children and Families shall maintain a registry of the reports received pursuant to sections 17a–101a to 17a–101d, inclusive, and 17a–103, and shall adopt regulations to implement the provisions of this section, including the use of the registry on a twenty-four-hour daily basis to prevent or discover abuse of children and the establishment of a hearing process for any appeal by a person of the commissioner's determination that such person is responsible for the abuse or neglect of a child pursuant to subsection (b) of section 17a–101g. The information contained in the reports and any other information relative to child abuse, wherever located, shall be confidential subject to such statutes and regulations governing their use and access as shall conform to the requirements of federal law or regulations. Any violation of this section or the regulations adopted by the commissioner under this section shall be punishable by a fine of not more than one thousand dollars or imprisonment for not more than one year.

(b) Notwithstanding the provisions of subsection (a) of this section, the Commissioner of Children and Families shall disclose to the Commissioner of Social Services, or his designee, registry information necessary for the evaluation of the temporary family assistance program operated by the Department of Social Services

(1996, P.A. 96–246, § 14; 1997, P.A. 97–319, § 16, eff. July 1, 1997, 1997, June 18 Sp.Sess., P.A. 97–2, § 142, eff. July 1, 1997; 2001, P.A. 01–142, § 2.)

§ 17a–101*l*. Visitation centers

The Commissioner of Children and Families shall, within available resources, establish visitation centers for the purpose of facilitating visits between children in the custody of the commissioner and those family members who are subject to supervised visitation. Such center shall provide a secure facility for supervised visitation or the transfer of custody of such children for visitation.

(1996, P.A. 96–246, § 26.)

§ 17a–102 Repealed. (1996, P.A. 96–246, § 38.)

§ 17a–102a. Education and training for nurses and birthing hospital staff caring for high-risk newborns re responsibilities as mandated reporters of child abuse and neglect. Regulations. Definitions.

(a) Each birthing hospital shall provide education and training for nurses and other staff who care for high-risk newborns on the roles and responsibilities of such nurses and other staff as mandated reporters of potential child abuse and neglect under section 17a–101.

(b) Not later than October 1, 2002, the Department of Children and Families shall adopt regulations, in accordance with the provisions of chapter 54, [1] on the procedures for the principal providers of daily direct care of high-risk newborns in birthing hospitals to participate in the discharge planning process and ongoing department functions concerning such newborns.

(c) For purposes of this section, "birthing hospital" means a health care facility, as defined in section 19a–630, operated and maintained in whole or in part for the purpose of caring for women during delivery of a child and for women and their newborns following birth, and "high-risk newborn" means any newborn identified as such under any regulation or policy of the Department of Children and Families.

(2001, P.A. 01–190.)

1 C.G.S.A. § 4–166 et seq.

§ 17a–103. Reports by others. False reports. Notification to law enforcement agency

(a) Any mandated reporter acting outside his professional capacity and any other person having reasonable cause to suspect or believe that any child under the age of eighteen is in danger of being abused, or has been abused or neglected, as defined in section 46b–120, may cause a written or oral report to be made to the Commissioner of Children and Families or his representative or a law enforcement agency. The Commissioner of Children and Families or his representative shall use his best efforts to obtain the name and address of a person who causes a report to be made pursuant to this section. In the case of an oral report, such report shall be recorded on tape and the commissioner or his representative shall announce to the person making such report that such report is being recorded and shall state the penalty for knowingly making a false report of child abuse or neglect under subsection (c) of section 17a–101e.

(b) Notwithstanding the provisions of section 17a–101k, if the identity of any such person who made a report pursuant to subsection (a) of this section is known, and the commissioner or his representative suspects or knows that such person has knowingly made a false report, such identity shall be disclosed to the appropriate law enforcement agency and to the perpetrator of the alleged abuse.

(c) If the Commissioner of Children and Families, or his designee, receives a report alleging sexual abuse or serious physical abuse, including, but not limited to, a report that: (1) A child has died; (2) a child has been sexually assaulted; (3) a child has suffered brain damage, loss or serious impairment of a bodily function or organ; (4) a child has been sexually exploited; or (5) a child has suffered serious nonaccidental physical injury, he shall, within twenty-four hours of receipt of such report, notify the appropriate law enforcement agency.

(1958 Rev., § 17–38c; 1973, P.A. 73–205, § 3; 1975, P.A. 75–420, § 4, eff. June 25, 1975; 1977, P.A. 77–308, § 3, eff. June 2, 1977; 1977, P.A. 77–614, § 521, eff. Jan. 1, 1979; 1979, P.A. 79–631, § 62, eff. July 6, 1979; 1993, P.A. 93–91, § 1, eff. July 1, 1993; 1996, P.A. 96–246, § 7; 1997, P.A. 97–319, § 17, eff. July 1, 1997.)

§ 17a–103a. Telephone hotline to receive reports of child abuse or neglect

The Commissioner of Children and Families shall provide a telephone hotline for child abuse that shall be dedicated to receive reports of child abuse. Such hotline shall accept all reports of abuse or neglect regardless of the relationship of the alleged perpetrator to the child who is the alleged victim and regardless of the alleged perpetrator's affiliation with any organization or other entity in any capacity. The commissioner shall classify and evaluate all reports pursuant to the provisions of section 17a–101g.

(1997, P.A. 97–319, § 20, eff. July 1, 1997; 2002, P.A. 02–138, § 17.)

§ 17a–103b. Notice to parent or guardian of substantiated complaint of child abuse

(a) Upon a substantiated complaint of abuse of a child having a single custodial parent or a guardian, the Department of Children and Families shall give, when deemed to be in the best interests of the child, to the noncustodial parent, custodial parent, guardian of the child, and parents if the Department of Children and Families has custody of a child, notice of (1) the circumstances of the complaint, including the name of the person who caused the abuse, (2) the availability of services from the department, including, but not limited to, child care subsidies and emergency shelter, and (3) the programs of the Office of Victim Services and information on obtaining a restraining order. The notice shall also inform the recipient that such child may be removed from the custody of the custodial parent by the department if such removal is authorized under the general statutes. The department shall employ all reasonable efforts to provide the notice within ten days of substantiation of a complaint.

(b) The notice required under subsection (a) of this section shall be in English or the principal language of the recipient, if known, and be delivered (1) by certified mail, return receipt requested, directed to the last-known address of each recipient, or (2) by an agent of the department. In the case of personal delivery by an agent, written acknowledgement of such delivery shall be made by the recipient.

(1998, P.A. 98–173; 1999, P.A. 99–85.)

§ 17a–103c. Report of abuse re child committed as delinquent. Notification requirements.

Upon the receipt of a report of suspected abuse of any child committed to the Commissioner of Children and Families as delinquent, the Department of Children and Families shall, no later than ten days after receipt of the complaint, provide written notification of such report to the child's legal guardian and the child's attorney in the delinquency proceeding that resulted in the commitment. If, after investigation, the department substantiates the reported abuse, the department shall, no later than ten days after receipt of the complaint, provide written notification to the child's legal guardian and the child's attorney in the delinquency proceeding that resulted in the commitment of the substantiation of the reported abuse.

(2002, P.A. 02–127, § 6.)

§ 17a–104. Treatment by Christian Science practitioner

For the purposes of sections 17a–101 to 17a–103, inclusive, and section 46b–129a, the treatment of any child by a Christian Science practitioner in lieu of treatment by a licensed practitioner of the healing arts shall not of itself constitute maltreatment.

(1958 Rev., § 17–38d; 1973, P.A. 73–205, § 8; 1996, P.A. 96–246, § 27.)

§ 17a–105. Temporary custody of abused child upon arrest of parent or guardian

Whenever any person is arrested and charged with an offense under section 53–20 or 53–21 or under part V,[1] VI[2] or VII[3] of chapter 952, the victim of which offense was a minor residing with the defendant, any judge of the Superior Court may, if it appears that the child's condition or circumstances surrounding the child's case so require and that continuation in the home is contrary to the child's welfare, issue an order to the Commissioner of Children and Families to assume immediate custody of such child and, if the circumstances so require, any other children residing with the defendant and to proceed thereon as in cases reported under section 17a–101g. Upon the issuance of such order, or not later than sixty days after the issuance of such order, the court shall make a determination whether the Department of Children and Families made reasonable efforts to keep the child with his or her parents or guardian prior to the issuance of such order and, if such efforts were not made, whether such reasonable efforts were not possible, taking into consideration the child's best interests, including the child's health and safety.

(1958 Rev., § 17–38e; 1973, P.A. 73–205, § 4; 1974, P.A. 74–183, § 170, eff. Dec. 31, 1974; 1974, P.A. 74–251, § 5; 1974, P.A. 74–293, § 4; 1975, P.A. 75–420, § 4, eff. June 25, 1975; 1976, P.A. 76–436, § 150; 1977, P.A. 77–614, § 521, eff. Jan. 1, 1979; 1977, P.A. 77–614, § 587, eff. June 2, 1977; 1978, P.A. 78–303, § 85, eff. June 6, 1978; 1982, P.A. 82–43, § 5; 1993, P.A. 93–91, § 1, eff. July 1, 1993; 1996, P.A. 96–246, § 28; 2002, May 9 Sp.Sess., P.A. 02–7, § 33, eff. Aug. 15, 2002.)

[1] C.G.S.A. § 53a–59 et seq.
[2] C.G.S.A. § 53a–65 et seq.
[3] C.G.S.A. § 53a–91 et seq.

§ 17a–105a. Child abuse and neglect unit within Division of State Police to assist investigation of child abuse and neglect

There shall be within the Division of State Police within the Department of Public Safety a child abuse and neglect unit which, within available resources, shall (1) at the request of the Commissioner of Children and Families or the head of the local law enforcement agency, or such person's designee, assist a multidisciplinary team established pursuant to section 17a–106a in the investigation of a report of child abuse or neglect, (2) investigate reports of crime involving child abuse or neglect in municipalities in which there is no organized police force, and (3) participate in a mutual support network that shares information and collaborates with local law enforcement agencies.

(1998, P.A. 98–241, § 17; 2002, P.A. 02–138, § 18.)

§ 17a–106. Cooperation in relation to prevention, identification and investigation of child abuse and neglect

All law enforcement officials, courts of competent jurisdiction, school personnel and all appropriate state agencies providing human services in relation to preventing, identifying, and investigating child abuse and neglect shall cooperate toward the prevention, identification and investigation of child abuse and neglect.

(1958 Rev., § 17–38f; 1975, P.A. 75–384, § 8, eff. May 30, 1975; 1983, P.A. 83–43; 1996, P.A. 96–194, § 4.)

§ 17a–106a. Multidisciplinary teams. Purpose. Composition. Confidentiality. Records of meetings

(a) The Commissioner of Children and Families, may as department head of the lead agency, and the appropriate state's attorney establish multidisciplinary teams for the purpose of reviewing particular cases or particular types of cases or to coordinate the prevention, intervention and treatment in each judicial district to review selected cases of child abuse or neglect. The purpose of such multidisciplinary teams is to advance and coordinate the prompt investigation of suspected cases of child abuse or neglect, to reduce the trauma of any child victim and to ensure the protection and treatment of the child. The head of the local law enforcement agency or his designee may request the assistance of the Division of State Police within the Department of Public Safety for such purposes.

(b) Each multidisciplinary team shall consist of at least one representative of each of the following: (1) The State's Attorney of the Judicial District of the team, or his designee; (2) the Commissioner of Children and Families, or his designee; (3) the head of the local or state law enforcement agencies, or his designee; (4) a health care professional with substantial experience in the diagnosis and treatment of abused or neglected children, who shall be designated by team members; (5) a member, where appropriate, of a youth service bureau; (6) a mental health professional with substantial experience in the treatment of abused or neglected children, who shall be designated by the team members; and (7) any other appropriate individual with expertise in the welfare of children that the members of the team deem necessary. Each team shall select a chairperson. A team may invite experts to participate in the review of any case and may invite any other individual with particular information germane to the case to participate in such review, provided the expert or individual shall have the same protection and obligations under subsections (f) and (g) of this section as members of the team.

(c) The Governor's Task Force for Justice for Abused Children, through the subcommittee comprised of individuals with expertise in the investigation of child abuse and neglect, shall: (1) Establish and modify standards to be observed by multidisciplinary teams; (2) review protocols of the multidisciplinary teams; and (3) monitor and evaluate multidisciplinary teams and make recommendations for modifications to the system of multidisciplinary teams.

(d) All criminal investigative work of the multidisciplinary teams shall be undertaken by members of the team who are law enforcement officers and all child protection investigative work of the teams shall be undertaken by members of the team who represent the Department of Children and Families, provided representatives of the department may coordinate all investigative work and rely upon information generated by the team. The protocols, procedures and standards of the multidisciplinary teams shall not supersede the protocols, procedures and standards of the agencies who are on the multidisciplinary team.

(e) Each multidisciplinary team shall have access to and may copy any record, transcript, document, photograph or other data pertaining to an alleged child victim within the possession of the Department of Children and Families, any public or private medical facility or any public or private health professional provided, in the case of confidential information, the coordinator of the team, or his designee, identifies the record in writing and certifies, under oath, that the record sought is necessary to investigate child abuse or neglect and that the team will maintain the record as confidential. No person who provides access to or copies of such record upon delivery of certification under this section shall be liable to any third party for such action. The multidisciplinary team shall not be deemed to be a public agency under the Freedom of Information Act [1].

(f) No person shall disclose information obtained from a meeting of the multidisciplinary team without the consent of the participant of the meeting who provided such information unless disclosure is ordered by a court of competent jurisdiction or is necessary to comply with the provisions of the constitution of the state of Connecticut.

(g) Each multidisciplinary team shall maintain records of meetings that include, but are not limited to, the name of the alleged victim and perpetrator, the names of the members of the multidisciplinary team and their positions, the decision or recommendation of the team and support services provided. In any proceeding to gain access to such records or testimony concerning matters discussed at a meeting, the privileges from disclosure applicable to the information provided by each of the participants at the meeting shall apply to all participants.

(1996, P.A. 96–246, § 22; 1998, P.A. 98–241, § 16; 1999, P.A. 99–86, § 1, eff. July 1, 1999.)

1 C.G.S.A. § 1–200 et seq.

§ 17a–106b. Impact of family violence in child abuse cases

(a) The state of Connecticut finds that family violence can result in abuse and neglect of the children living in the household where such violence occurs and that the prevention of child abuse and neglect depends on coordination of domestic violence and child protective services.

(b) The Commissioner of Children and Families may consider the existence and the impact of family violence in any child abuse investigation and may assist family members in obtaining protection from family violence.

(1996, P.A. 96–246, § 24.)

§ 17a–106c. Family Violence Coordinating Council. Members. Responsibilities

(a) There shall be a Family Violence Coordinating Council to increase awareness and understanding of family violence and its consequences and to reduce the incidence of family violence within the state. The council shall consist of the Attorney General, the Commissioner of Children and Families, the Chief State's Attorney, the Chief Court Administrator, the Commissioner of Public Health, the Commissioner of Public Safety, the executive director of the Connecticut Police Chief's Association, the executive director of the Connecticut Council on Domestic Violence, or their designees, the chairmen and ranking members of the committee on judiciary, or their designees, and six public members, one each of whom shall be appointed by the following: The president pro tempore of the Senate, the speaker of the House of Representatives and the majority and minority leaders of the House of Representatives and the Senate.

(b) The responsibility of the council shall include, but not be limited to: (1) Identifying and evaluating existing services available to address family violence; (2) identifying and promoting legislation, services and resources to prevent and address family violence; (3) studying court services and procedures relating to family violence; (4) studying law enforcement procedures and protocol related to family violence; (5) reviewing criminal justice data collection and analysis of family violence; (6) ensuring coordination of all agencies, organizations and the courts involved in family violence prevention and treatment; (7) developing and promoting multidisciplinary training programs; (8) promoting effective prevention, intervention and treatment techniques; (9) recommending treatment programs and standards to the relevant state agencies and other service providers; (10) promoting the organization of local councils on family violence; and (11) providing assistance and support to established local councils and increasing public awareness and support for family violence services and resources.

(c) Nothing contained in this section shall be construed as providing the council with authority or responsibility vested in another state or local agency or as a limitation upon the power or authority of the state or its agencies to seek administrative, legal or equitable relief as provided by law.

(1996, P.A. 96–246, § 25.)

§ 17a–107. Regulations on reports of child abuse

On or before February 1, 1987, the Commissioner of Youth Services shall adopt such regulations, in accordance with the provisions of chapter 54,[1] as are necessary to carry out the provisions of subsection (e) of section 17a–101.

(1958 Rev., § 17–38g; 1986, P.A. 86–337, § 11.)

1 C.G.S.A. § 4–166 et seq.

§ 17a–108. Financial assistance for programs which monitor child abuse and neglect cases

The Judicial Department may provide financial assistance, within available appropriations, to programs which monitor cases of child abuse and neglect.

(1958 Rev., § 17–38h; 1987, P.A. 87–328, § 1, eff. July 1, 1987; 1987, P.A. 87–589, § 77, eff. July 1, 1987.)

§ 17a–109. Commitment of children to child-caring facilities

When, because of the mental or physical condition of any child committed to the Commissioner of Children and Families under the provisions of section 46b–129, or because of a behavior problem, such child cannot be satisfactorily cared for in a foster home, said commissioner may bring a petition to the court which committed such child for the commitment of such child to a suitable child-caring facility, and, upon being satisfied that such commitment is in the best interest of such child, such court shall commit such child to such an institution.

(1949 Rev., § 2636; 1958 Rev., § 17–39; 1974, P.A. 74–251, § 7; 1975, P.A. 75–420, § 4, eff. June 25, 1975; 1977, P.A. 77–614, § 521, eff. Jan. 1, 1979; 1979, P.A. 79–631, § 63, eff. July 6, 1979; 1993, P.A. 93–91, § 1, eff. July 1, 1993; 1996, P.A. 96–194, § 5.)

§ 17a–110. Permanency planning for children. Definitions. Procedure after commitment hearing. Regulations. Central registry. Duties of commissioner

(a) As used in this section, "child" means a person under the age of eighteen years; "foster child" means a child placed temporarily in a home, pending permanent placement; "permanent home" means a home for a child with the child's genetic or adoptive parents considered to be such child's permanent residence; and "permanency placement services" means services that are designed and rendered for the purpose of relocating a foster child with such child's legal family or finding a permanent home for such child, including, but not limited to, the following: (1) Treatment services for the child and the genetic family; (2) preplacement planning; (3) appropriate court proceedings to effect permanent placement, including, but not limited to, the following: (A) Termination of parental rights; (B) revocation of commitment; (C) removal or reinstatement of guardianship; (D) temporary custody; (4) recruitment and screening of permanent placement homes; (5) home study and evaluation of permanent placement homes; (6) placement of children in permanent homes; (7) postplacement supervision and services to such homes following finalization of such placements in the courts; and (8) other services routinely performed by caseworkers doing similar work in the Department of Children and Families.

(b) At a hearing held in accordance with subsection (k) of section 46b–129 and section 17a–111b, the court shall determine the appropriateness of continuing efforts to reunify a child with the child's family. If the court finds that such efforts are not appropriate, the Department of Children and Families shall within sixty days of such finding either (1) file a petition for the termination of parental rights, (2) file a motion to revoke the commitment and vest the custody and guardianship of the child on a permanent or long-term basis in an appropriate individual or couple, or (3) file a written permanency plan with the court for permanent or long-term foster care, which plan shall include an explanation of the reason that neither termination of parental rights nor custody and guardianship is appropriate for the child. The court shall promptly convene a hearing for the purpose of reviewing such written plan. When the court finds that the efforts to reunify a child with the child's family are not appropriate, the department shall use its best efforts to maintain such child in the initial out-of-home placement, provided the department determines that such placement is in the best interests of the child, until such time as a permanent home for the child is found or the child is placed for adoption. If the permanency plan calls for placing the child for adoption or in some other permanent home, good faith efforts shall be made to place the child for adoption or in some other alternative home.

(c) Not later than January 1, 2000, the Department of Children and Families shall adopt regulations in accordance with chapter 54 [1] to establish standards for permanency plans which shall include, but not be limited to: (1) Assessment of kin, foster parents or other potential adoptive parents for adopting a child; (2) preparing children for adoption; (3) collaboration between family foster care services and adoption services; (4) transracial and cross-racial adoption; (5) open adoption; and (6) foster care and adoption subsidies.

(d) Not later than January 1, 2000, the Department of Children and Families shall, within available appropriations, establish and maintain (1) a central registry of all children for whom a permanency plan has been formulated and in which adoption is recommended, and (2) a system to monitor the progress in implementing the permanency plan for such children.

(e) Whenever the Commissioner of Children and Families deems it necessary or advisable in order to carry out the purposes of this section, the commissioner may contract with any private child-placing agency, as defined in section 45a–707, for a term of not less than three years and not more than five years, to provide any one or more permanency placement services on behalf of the Department of Children and Families. Whenever any contract is entered into under this section which requires private agencies to perform casework services, such as the preparation of applications and petitions for termination of parental rights, guardianship or other custodial matters, or which requires court appearances, the Attorney General shall provide legal services for the Commissioner of Children and Families notwithstanding that some of the services have been performed by caseworkers of private agencies, except that no such legal services shall be provided unless the Commissioner of Children and Families is a legal party to any court action hereunder.

(f) The Commissioner of Children and Families may accept funds from any source to implement the provisions of this section.

(1958 Rev., § 17–39a; 1980, P.A. 80–319, §§ 1, 2, eff. July 1, 1980; 1993, P.A. 93–91, § 1, eff. July 1, 1993; 1995, P.A. 95–238, § 2; 1996, P.A. 96–130, § 38; 1998, P.A. 98–241, § 12; 1998, June Sp.Sess., P.A. 98–1, § 113, eff. July 1, 1998; 1999, P.A. 99–166, § 1; 2003, P.A. 03–243, § 13.)

[1] C.G.S.A. § 4–166 et seq.

§ 17a–110a. Concurrent permanency planning program. Duties of commissioner. Guidelines and protocols

(a) In order to achieve early permanency for children, decrease children's length of stay in foster care, reduce the number of moves children experience in foster care and reduce the amount of time between termination of parental rights and adoption, the Commissioner of Children and Families shall establish a program for concurrent permanency planning.

(b) Concurrent permanency planning involves a planning process to identify permanent placements and prospective adoptive parents so that when termination of parental rights is granted by the court pursuant to section 17a–112 or section 45a–717, permanent placement or adoption proceedings may commence immediately.

(c) The commissioner shall establish guidelines and protocols for child-placing agencies involved in concurrent permanency planning, including criteria for conducting concurrent permanency planning based on relevant factors such as: (1) The age of the child and duration of out-of-home placement; (2) the prognosis for successful reunification with parents; (3) the availability of relatives and other concerned individuals to provide support or a permanent placement for the child; (4) special needs of the child; and (5) other factors affecting the child's best interests, goals of concurrent permanency planning, support services that are available for families, permanency options, and the consequences of not complying with case plans.

(d) Within six months of out-of-home placement, the Department of Children and Families shall complete an assessment of the likelihood of the child's being reunited with either or both birth parents, based on progress made to date. The Department of Children and Families shall develop a concurrent permanency plan for families with poor prognosis for reunification within such time period. Such assessment and concurrent permanency plan shall be filed with the court.

(e) Concurrent permanency planning programs must include involvement of parents and full disclosure of their rights and responsibilities.

(f) The commissioner shall provide ongoing technical assistance, support, and training for local child-placing agencies and other individuals and agencies involved in concurrent permanency planning.

(1999, P.A. 99–166, § 2; 2000, P.A. 00–137, § 5; 2001, P.A. 01–195, § 20, eff. July 11, 2001; 2001, P.A. 01–159, § 2.)

§ 17a–110b. Adoption resource exchange

The Commissioner of Children and Families shall, within available appropriations, establish an adoption resource exchange in this state within the Department of Children and Families. The primary purpose of the exchange shall be to link children who are awaiting placement with permanent families by providing information and referral services and by the recruitment of potential adoptive families. The department and each child-placing agency shall register any child who is free for adoption with such adoption resource exchange.

(1999, P.A. 99–252, § 1.)

§ 17a–111. Parents not entitled to earnings of child supported by Commissioner of Children and Families

Any parents whose child has been supported by the Commissioner of Children and Families for at least three years immediately preceding such child's eighteenth birthday shall not be entitled to such child's earnings or services during such child's minority.

(1949 Rev., § 2825; 1955, Supp. § 1473d; 1958 Rev., § 17–43; 1965, Feb.Sp.Sess., P.A. 488, § 10; 1974, P.A. 74–251, § 8; 1975, P.A. 75–420, § 4, eff. June 25, 1975; 1977, P.A. 77–614, § 521, eff. Jan. 1, 1979; 1979, P.A. 79–631, § 64, eff. July 6, 1979; 1993, P.A. 93–91, § 1, eff. July 1, 1993.)

§ 17a–111a. Commissioner of Children and Families to file petition to terminate parental rights, when

(a) The Commissioner of Children and Families shall file a petition to terminate parental rights pursuant to section 17a–112 if (1) the child has been in the custody of the commissioner for at least fifteen consecutive months, or at least fifteen months during the twenty-two months, immediately preceding the filing of such petition; (2) the child has been abandoned as defined in subsection (j) of section 17a–112; or (3) a court of competent jurisdiction has found that (A) the parent has killed, through deliberate, nonaccidental act, a sibling of the child or has requested, commanded, importuned, attempted, conspired or solicited to commit the killing of the child or a sibling of the child; or (B) the parent has assaulted the child or a sibling of a child, through deliberate, nonaccidental act, and such assault resulted in serious bodily injury to such child.

(b) Notwithstanding the provisions of subsection (a) of this section, the commissioner is not required to file a petition to terminate parental rights in such cases if the commissioner determines that: (1) The child has been placed under the care of a relative of such child; (2) there is a compelling reason to believe that filing such petition is not in the best interests of the child; or (3) the parent has not been offered the services contained in the permanency plan to reunify the parent with the child or such services were not available, unless a court has determined that efforts to reunify the parent with the child are not required.

(1998, P.A. 98–241, § 6, eff. July 1, 1998; 2000, P.A. 00–137, § 13.)

§ 17a–111b. Commissioner of Children and Families may petition court re reasonable efforts to reunify parent with child. Determination by court

(a) The Commissioner of Children and Families or any other party may, at any time, petition the court for a determination on whether reasonable efforts to reunify the parent with the child are appropriate. The court shall hold an evidentiary hearing on the petition within thirty days of the filing of the petition. The court may determine that such efforts are not appropriate if the court finds upon clear and convincing evidence that: (1) The parent has subjected the child to the following aggravated circumstances: (A) The child has been abandoned as defined in subsection (j) of section 17a–112; or (B) the parent has inflicted sexual molestation or exploitation or severe physical abuse on the child or engaged in a pattern of abuse of the child; (2) the parent has killed, through deliberate, nonaccidental act, another child of the parent or a sibling of the child, or has required, commanded, importuned, attempted, conspired or solicited to commit the killing of the child, another child of the parent or sibling of the child, or has committed an assault, through deliberate, nonaccidental act, that resulted in serious bodily injury of the child, another child of the parent or a sibling of the child; (3) the parental rights of the parent to a sibling have been involuntarily terminated within three years of the filing of a petition pursuant to this section, provided the commissioner has made reasonable efforts to reunify the parent with the child during a period of at least ninety days; (4) the parent was convicted by a court of competent jurisdiction of sexual assault, except a conviction of a violation of section 53a–71 or 53a–73a resulting in the conception of the child; or (5) the child was placed in the care and control of the commissioner pursuant to the provisions of sections 17a–57 to 17a–61, inclusive.

(b) If the court determined that such efforts are not appropriate, the court shall, at such hearing or at a hearing held not later than thirty days from such determination, approve a permanency plan for such child which may include a requirement that the commissioner file a petition to terminate parental rights, long-term foster care, independent living, transfer of guardianship, or adoption. The child's health and safety shall be of paramount concern in formulating such plan.

(1998, P.A. 98–241, § 7, eff. July 1, 1998; 2000, P.A. 00–137, § 14; 2001, P.A. 01–142, § 3.)

§ 17a–112. Termination of parental rights of child committed to commissioner. Cooperative postadoption agreements

(a) In respect to any child in the custody of the Commissioner of Children and Families in accordance with section 46b–129, either the commissioner, or the attorney who represented such child in a pending or prior proceeding, or an attorney appointed by the Superior Court on its own motion, or an attorney retained by such child after attaining the age of fourteen, may petition the court for the termination of parental rights with reference to such child. The petition shall be in the form and contain the information set forth in subsection (b) of section 45a–715, and be subject to the provisions of subsection (c) of said section. If a petition indicates that either or both parents consent to the termination of their parental rights, or if at any time following the filing of a petition and before the entry of a decree, a parent consents to the termination of the parent's parental rights, each consenting parent shall acknowledge such consent on a form promulgated by the Office of the Chief Court Administrator evidencing that the parent has voluntarily and knowingly consented to the termination of such parental rights. No consent to termination by a mother shall be executed within forty-eight hours immediately after the birth of such mother's child. A parent who is a minor shall have the right to consent to termination of parental rights and such consent shall not be voidable by reason of such minority. A guardian ad litem shall be appointed by the court to assure that such minor parent is giving an informed and voluntary consent.

(b) Either or both birth parents and an intended adoptive parent may enter into a cooperative postadoption agreement regarding communication or contact between either or both birth parents and the adopted child. Such an agreement may be entered into if: (1) The child is in the custody of the Department of Children and Families; (2) an order terminating parental rights has not yet been entered; and (3) either or both birth parents agree to a voluntary termination of parental rights, including an agreement in a case which began as an involuntary termination of parental rights. The postadoption agreement shall be applicable only to a birth parent who is a party to the agreement. Such agreement shall be in addition to those under common law. Counsel for the child and any guardian ad litem for the child may be heard on the proposed cooperative postadoption agreement. There shall be no presumption of communication or contact between the birth parents and an intended adoptive parent in the absence of a cooperative postadoption agreement.

(c) If the Superior Court determines that the child's best interests will be served by postadoption communication or contact with either or both birth parents, the court shall so order, stating the nature and frequency of the communication or contact. A court may grant postadoption communication or contact privileges if: (1) Each intended adoptive parent consents to the granting of communication or contact privileges; (2) the intended adoptive parent and either or both birth parents execute a cooperative agreement and file the agreement with the court; (3) consent to postadoption communication or contact is obtained from the child, if the child is at least twelve years of age; and (4) the cooperative postadoption agreement is approved by the court.

(d) A cooperative postadoption agreement shall contain the following: (1) An acknowledgment by either or both birth parents that the termination of parental rights and the adoption is irrevocable, even if the adoptive parents do not abide by the cooperative postadoption agreement; and (2) an acknowledgment by the adoptive parents that the agreement grants either or both birth parents the right to seek to enforce the cooperative postadoption agreement.

(e) The terms of a cooperative postadoption agreement may include the following: (1) Provision for communication between the child and either or both birth parents; (2) provision for future contact between either or both birth parents and the child or an adoptive parent; and (3) maintenance of medical history of either or both birth parents who are parties to the agreement.

(f) The order approving a cooperative postadoption agreement shall be made part of the final order terminating parental rights. The finality of the termination of parental rights and of the adoption shall not be affected by implementation of the provisions of the postadoption agreement. Such an agreement shall not affect the ability of the adoptive parents and the child to change their residence within or outside this state.

(g) A disagreement between the parties or litigation brought to enforce or modify the agreement shall not affect the validity of the termination of parental rights or the adoption and shall not serve as a basis for orders affecting the custody of the child. The court shall not act on a petition to change or enforce the agreement unless the petitioner had participated, or attempted to participate, in good faith in mediation or other appropriate dispute resolution proceedings to resolve the dispute and allocate any cost for such mediation or dispute resolution proceedings.

(h) An adoptive parent, guardian ad litem for the child or the court, on its own motion, may, at any time, petition for review of any order entered pursuant to subsection (c) of this section, if the petitioner alleges that such action would be in the best interests of the child. The court may modify or terminate such orders as the court deems to be in the best interest of the adopted child.

(i) The Superior Court upon hearing and notice, as provided in sections 45a–716 and 45a–717, may grant a petition for termination of parental rights based on consent filed pursuant to this section if it finds that (1) upon clear and convincing evidence, the termination is in the best interest of the child, and (2) such parent has voluntarily and knowingly consented to termination of the parent's parental rights with respect to such child. If the court denies a petition for termination of parental rights based on consent, it may refer the matter to an agency to assess the needs of the child, the care the child is receiving and the plan of the parent for the child. Consent for the termination of the parental rights of one parent does not diminish the parental rights of the other parent of the child, nor does it relieve the other parent of the duty to support the child.

(j) The Superior Court, upon hearing and notice as provided in sections 45a–716 and 45a–717, may grant a petition filed pursuant to this section if it finds by clear and convincing evidence (1) that the Department of Children and Families has made reasonable efforts to locate the parent and to reunify the child with the parent, unless the court finds in this proceeding that the parent is unable or unwilling to benefit from reunification efforts provided such finding is not required if the court has determined at a hearing pursuant to subsection (b) of section 17a–110 or section 17a–111b that such efforts are not appropriate, (2) that termination is in the best interest of the child, and (3) that: (A) The child has been abandoned by the parent in the sense that the parent has failed to maintain a reasonable degree of interest, concern or responsibility as to the welfare of the child; (B) the child (i) has been found by the Superior Court or the Probate Court to have been neglected or uncared for in a prior proceeding, or (ii) is found to be neglected or uncared for and has been in the custody of the commissioner for at least fifteen months and the parent of such child has been provided specific steps to take to facilitate the return of the child to the parent pursuant to section 46b–129 and has failed to achieve such degree of personal rehabilitation as would encourage the belief that within a reasonable time, considering the age and needs of the child, such parent could assume a responsible position in the life of the child; (C) the child has been denied, by reason of an act or acts of parental commission or omission including, but not limited to, sexual molestation or exploitation, severe physical abuse or a pattern of abuse, the care, guidance or control necessary for the child's physical, educational, moral or emotional well-being. Nonaccidental or inadequately explained serious physical injury to a child shall constitute prima facie evidence of acts of parental commission or omission sufficient for the termination of parental rights; (D) there is no ongoing parent-child relationship, which means the relationship that ordinarily develops as a result of a parent having met on a day to day basis the physical, emotional, moral and educational needs of the child and to allow further time for the establishment or reestablishment of such parent-child relationship would be detrimental to the best interest of the child; (E) the parent of a child under the age of seven years who is neglected or uncared for, has failed, is unable or is unwilling to achieve such degree of personal rehabilitation as would encourage the belief that within a reasonable period of time, considering the age and needs of the child, such parent could assume a responsible position in the life of the child and such parent's parental rights of another child were previously terminated pursuant to a petition filed by the Commissioner of Children and Families; (F) the parent has killed through deliberate, nonaccidental act another child of the parent or has requested, commanded, importuned, attempted, conspired or solicited such killing or has committed an assault, through deliberate, nonaccidental act that resulted in serious bodily injury of another child of the parent; or (G) the parent was convicted as an adult or a delinquent by a court of competent jurisdiction of a sexual assault resulting in the conception of the child, except a conviction for a violation of section 53a–71 or 53a–73a, provided the court may terminate such parent's parental rights to such child at any time after such conviction.

(k) Except in the case where termination is based on consent, in determining whether to terminate parental rights under this section, the court shall consider and shall make written findings regarding: (1) The timeliness, nature and extent of services offered, provided and made available to the parent and the child by an agency to facilitate the reunion of the child with the parent; (2) whether the Department of Children and Families has made reasonable efforts to reunite the family pursuant to the federal Adoption Assistance and Child Welfare Act of 1980,[1] as amended; (3) the terms of any applicable court order entered into and agreed upon by any individual or agency and the parent, and the extent to which all parties have fulfilled their obligations under such order; (4) the feelings and emotional ties of the child with respect to the child's parents, any guardian of such child's person and any person who has exercised physical care, custody or control of the child for at least one year and with whom the child has developed significant emotional ties; (5) the age of the child; (6) the efforts the parent has made to adjust such parent's circumstances, conduct, or conditions to make it in the best interest of the child to return such child home in the foreseeable future, including, but not limited to, (A) the extent to which the parent has maintained contact with the child as part of an effort to reunite the child with the parent, provided the court may give weight to incidental visitations, communications or contributions, and (B) the maintenance of regular contact or communication with the guardian or other custodian of the child; and (7) the extent to which a parent has been prevented from maintaining a meaningful relationship with the child by the unreasonable act or conduct of the other parent of the child, or the unreasonable act of any other person or by the economic circumstances of the parent.

(*l*) Any petition brought by the Commissioner of Children and Families to the Superior Court, pursuant to subsection (a) of section 46b–129, may be accompanied by or, upon motion by the petitioner, consolidated with a petition for termination of parental rights filed in accordance with this section with respect to such child. Notice of the hearing on such petitions shall be given in accordance with sections 45a–716 and 45a–717. The Superior Court, after hearing, in accordance with the provisions of subsection (i) or (j) of this section, may, in lieu of granting the petition filed pursuant to section 46b–129, grant the petition for termination of parental rights as provided in section 45a–717.

(m) Nothing contained in this section and sections 17a–113, 45a–187, 45a–606, 45a–607, 45a–707 to 45a–709, inclusive, 45a–715 to 45a–718, inclusive, 45a–724, 45a–725, 45a–727, 45a–733, 45a–754 and 52–231a shall negate the right of the Commissioner of Children and Families to subsequently petition the Superior Court for revocation of a commitment of a child as to whom parental rights have been terminated in accordance with the provisions of this section. The Superior Court may appoint a statutory parent at any time after it has terminated parental rights if the petitioner so requests.

(n) If the parental rights of only one parent are terminated, the remaining parent shall be the sole parent and, unless otherwise provided by law, guardian of the person.

(*o*) In the case where termination of parental rights is granted, the guardian of the person or statutory parent shall report to the court within thirty days of the date judgment is entered on a case plan, as defined by the federal Adoption Assistance and Child Welfare Act of 1980, for the child which shall include measurable objectives and time schedules. At least every three months thereafter, such guardian or statutory parent shall make a report to the court on the progress made on implementation of the plan. The court may convene a hearing upon the filing of a report and shall convene a hearing for the purpose of reviewing the plan for the child no more than twelve months from the date judgment is entered or from the date of the last permanency hearing held pursuant to subsection (k) of section 46b–129, whichever is earlier, and at least once a year thereafter until the court determines that the adoption plan has become finalized. For children where the commissioner has determined that adoption is appropriate, the report on the implementation of the plan shall include a description of the reasonable efforts the department is taking to promote and expedite the adoptive placement and to finalize the adoption of the child, including documentation of child specific recruitment efforts. At such hearing, the court shall determine whether the department has made reasonable efforts to achieve the permanency plan. If the court determines that the department has not made reasonable efforts to place a child in an adoptive placement or that reasonable efforts have not resulted in the placement of the child, the court may order the Department of Children and Families, within available appropriations, to contract with a child-placing agency to arrange for the adoption of the child. The department, as statutory parent, shall continue to provide care and services for the child while a child-placing agency is arranging for the adoption of the child.

(p) The provisions of section 17a–152, regarding placement of a child from another state, and the provisions of section 17a–175, regarding the Interstate Compact on the Placement of Children, shall apply to placements pursuant to this section.

(q) The provisions of this section shall be liberally construed in the best interests of any child for whom a petition under this section has been filed.

(1958 Rev., § 17–43a; 1959, P.A. 184, § 1; 1965, Feb.Sp.Sess., P.A. 488, § 9; 1973, P.A. 73–156, § 4; 1974, P.A. 74–164, § 3, eff. May 10, 1974; 1975, P.A. 75–420, § 4, eff. June 25, 1975; 1976, P.A. 76–226; 1976, P.A. 76–436, § 589, eff. July 1, 1978; 1977, P.A. 77–452, § 7, eff. July 1, 1978; 1982, P.A. 82–202, § 1; 1983, P.A. 83–355, § 2; 1983, P.A. 83–387, § 1; 1983, P.A. 83–478, § 1; 1984, P.A. 84–449, § 1, eff. June 12, 1984; 1987, P.A. 87–555, § 1; 1993, P.A. 93–91, § 1, eff. July 1, 1993; 1993, P.A. 93–193, § 1; 1994, P.A. 94–81, § 1; 1995, P.A. 95–238, § 3; 1996, P.A. 96–130, § 39; 1996, P.A. 96–246, § 18; 1998, P.A. 98–241, § 8, eff. July 1, 1998; 1999, P.A. 99–166, § 4; 2000, P.A. 00–75, § 1; 2000, P.A. 00–137, § 1; 2000, P.A. 00–196, § 15; 2001, P.A. 01–159, § 3; 2001, P.A. 01–195, §§ 21, 22, eff. July 11, 2001; 2003, P.A. 03–243, § 1.)

1 42 U.S.C.A. § 670 et seq.

§ 17a–113. Custody of child pending application for removal of guardian or termination of parental rights; enforcement by warrant

When application has been made for the removal of one or both parents as guardians or of any other guardian of the person of such child, or when an application has been made for the termination of the parental rights of any parties who may have parental rights with regard to any minor child, the superior court in which such proceeding is pending may, if it deems it necessary based on the best interests of the child, order the custody of such child to be given to the Commissioner of Children and Families or some proper person or to the board of managers of any child-caring institution or organization, or any children's home or similar institution licensed or approved by the Commissioner of Children and Families, pending the determination of the matter, and may enforce such order by a warrant directed to a proper officer commanding the officer to take possession of the child and to deliver such child into the custody of the person, board, home or institution designated by such order; and said court may, if either or both parents are removed as guardians or if any other guardian of the person is removed, or if said parental rights are terminated, enforce its decree, awarding the custody of the child to the person or persons entitled thereto, by a warrant directed to the proper officer commanding the officer to take possession of the child and to deliver such child into the care and custody of the person entitled thereto. Such officer shall make returns to such court of such officer's doings under either warrant. Upon the issuance of such order giving custody of the child to the Commissioner of Children and Families, or not later than sixty days after the issuance of such order, the court shall make a determination whether the Department of Children and Families made reasonable efforts to keep the child with his or her parents or guardian prior to the issuance of such order and, if such efforts were not made, whether such reasonable efforts were not possible, taking into consideration the child's best interests, including the child's health and safety.

(1958 Rev., § 17–43b; 1974, P.A. 74–164, § 17, eff. May 10, 1974; 1975, P.A. 75–420, § 4, eff. June 25, 1975;

1976, P.A. 76–436, § 590, eff. July 1, 1978; 1977, P.A. 77–614, § 521, eff. Jan. 1, 1979; 1982, P.A. 82–43, § 1; 1993, P.A. 93–91, § 1, eff. July 1, 1993; 2002, May 9 Sp.Sess., P.A. 02–7, § 34, eff. Aug. 15, 2002.)

§ 17a–114. Licensing of persons for child placement; exemption. Criminal records check. Regulations

(a) (1) No child in the custody of the Commissioner of Children and Families shall be placed with any person, unless such person is licensed by the department for that purpose. Any person licensed by the department to accept placement of a child is deemed to be licensed to accept placement as a foster family or prospective adoptive family. The commissioner shall adopt regulations, in accordance with the provisions of chapter 54,[1] to establish the licensing procedures and standards.

(2) The commissioner shall require each applicant for licensure pursuant to this section and any person sixteen years of age or older living in the household of such applicant to submit to state and national criminal history records checks prior to issuing a license to such applicant to accept placement of a child. Such criminal history records checks shall be conducted in accordance with section 29–17a. The commissioner shall also check the state child abuse registry established pursuant to section 17a–101k for the name of such applicant and for the name of any person sixteen years of age or older living in the household of such applicant for perpetrator information.

(b) Notwithstanding the requirements of subsection (a) of this section, the commissioner may place a child with a relative who is not licensed for a period of up to ninety days when such placement is in the best interests of the child, provided a satisfactory home visit is conducted, a basic assessment of the family is completed and such relative attests that such relative and any adult living within the household have not been convicted of a crime or arrested for a felony against a person, for injury or risk of injury to or impairing the morals of a child, or for the possession, use or sale of a controlled substance. Any such relative who accepts placement of a child in excess of such ninety-day period shall be subject to licensure by the commissioner, except that any such relative who, prior to July 1, 2001, had been certified by the commissioner to provide care for a related child may continue to maintain such certification if such relative continues to meet the regulatory requirements and the child remains in such relative's care. The commissioner may grant a waiver, for a child placed with a relative, on a case-by-case basis, from such procedure or standard, except any safety standard, based on the home of the relative and the needs and best interests of such child. The reason for any waiver granted shall be documented. The commissioner shall adopt regulations, in accordance with the provisions of chapter 54, to establish certification procedures and standards for a caretaker who is a relative of such child.

(1958 Rev., § 17–43c; 1988, P.A. 88–332, § 1, eff. June 3, 1988; 1993, P.A. 93–91, § 1, eff. July 1, 1993; 1994, P.A. 94–216, § 2, eff. June 7, 1994; 1999, P.A. 99–166, § 5; 2001, P.A. 01–70, § 1, eff. July 1, 2001; 2001, P.A. 01–142, § 11; 2001, P.A. 01–159, § 4; 2003, P.A. 03–243, § 7.)

[1] C.G.S.A. § 4–166 et seq.

§ 17a–114a. Liability of persons for personal injury to children placed in their care

A person licensed or certified pursuant to section 17a–114 shall be liable for any act or omission resulting in personal injury to a child placed in his care by the Commissioner of Children and Families to the same extent as a biological parent is liable for any act or omission resulting in personal injury to a biological child in his care.

(1994, P.A. 94–216, § 1, eff. June 7, 1994; 1996, P.A. 96–194, § 6.)

§ 17a–115. Arrest records

Notwithstanding any provision of the general statutes to the contrary, prior to the issuance of a license or certification to any person for the care or board of a child under the provisions of section 17a–145 or for the care of a child under the provisions of section 17a–114, the commissioner may obtain all arrest records of any such person or persons pertaining to any arrest for a felony against a person, for injury or risk of injury to or impairing the morals of a child, or for possession, use or sale of any controlled substance.

(1958 Rev., § 17–43d; 1988, P.A. 88–332, § 2, eff. June 3, 1988; 1996, P.A. 96–194, § 7.)

§ 17a–116. "Special needs" child defined

For purposes of sections 17a–116 to 17a–119, inclusive, and subsection (b) of section 45a–111, a "special needs" child is a child who is a ward of the Commissioner of Children and Families or is to be placed by a licensed child-placing agency and is difficult to place in adoption because of one or more conditions including, but not limited to, physical or mental disability, serious emotional maladjustment, a recognized high risk of physical or mental disability, age or racial or ethnic factors which present a barrier to adoption or is a member of a sibling group which should be placed together, or because the child has established significant emotional ties with prospective adoptive parents while in their care as a foster child and has been certified as a special needs child by the Commissioner of Children and Families.

(1958 Rev., § 17–44a; 1972, P.A. 86, § 1, eff. July 1, 1972; 1975, P.A. 75–420, § 4, eff. June 25, 1975; 1977, P.A. 77–614, § 521, eff. Jan. 1, 1979; 1979, P.A. 79–631, § 65, eff. July 6, 1979; 1986, P.A. 86–330, § 2, eff. April 1, 1987; 1993, P.A. 93–91, § 1, eff. July 1, 1993.)

§ 17a–116a. Information handbook re adoption of children with special needs

The Department of Children and Families shall, within available appropriations, prepare an information handbook for any individual interested in adopting a child with special needs. The department and child-placing agencies shall give the handbook to such interested individual no later than the beginning of the home study process. The handbook shall contain information concerning matters relating to adoption and adoption assistance including, but not limited to, nondiscrimination practices set forth in section 45a–726, postplacement and postadoption services, adoption subsidies, deferred subsidy agreements, modification of rates and agreements, health care support, reimbursements, assistance if the family moves out of state and the right to records and information related to the history of the child, including information available under subsection (a) of section 45a–746. The handbook shall be developed and updated by the Commissioner of Children and Families with the advice and assistance of the Connecticut Association of Foster and Adoptive Families and at least two other licensed child-placing agencies in Connecticut designated by the commissioner.

(1999, P.A. 99–252, § 2; 2000, P.A. 00–137, § 10.)

§ 17a–116b. Advisory committee promoting adoption and provision of services to minority and difficult to place children. Members, appointment, duties, reports

(a) An advisory committee on promoting the adoption of and provision of services to minority children and children who are difficult to place in adoption is established within the Department of Children and Families.

(b) The committee is composed of twelve members appointed by the commissioner. The commissioner shall appoint to the committee individuals who in the aggregate have knowledge of and experience in community education, cultural relations, family support, counseling, and parenting skills and education.

(c) A committee member serves for a two-year term and may be appointed for additional terms.

(d) A member of the committee receives no compensation.

(e) The committee shall elect one member to serve as presiding officer. The presiding officer serves for a two-year term and may be elected for additional terms.

(f) The commissioner shall set the time and place of the first committee meeting. The committee shall meet at least quarterly.

(g) To promote the adoption of and provision of services to minority children, the committee shall:

(1) Study, develop and evaluate programs and projects relating to community awareness and education, family support, counseling, parenting skills and education and reform of the child welfare system;

(2) Consult with churches and other cultural and civic organizations; and

(3) Report to the department at least annually the committee's recommendations for department programs and projects that will promote the adoption of and provision of services to minority children.

(h) On receiving the committee's recommendations, the department may adopt rules to implement a program or project recommended under this section. The department may solicit, accept and use gifts and donations to implement a program or project recommended by the committee.

(i) The department shall report to the General Assembly not later than January first of each odd-numbered year following the first year in which it receives recommendations under this section regarding committee recommendations and action taken by the department under this section.

(1999, P.A. 99–166, § 15.)

§ 17a–116c. Minority recruitment specialist for foster and adoptive families. Duties. Cultural sensitivity training

(a) The Commissioner of Children and Families shall, within available appropriations, require any employee of the Department of Children and Families whose duties concern minority adoption and foster family recruitment to complete cultural sensitivity training.

(b) The commissioner shall designate a minority recruitment specialist for foster and adoptive families within the department as a permanent position. The minority recruitment specialist, in consultation with the Connecticut Association of Foster and Adoptive Parents, Inc., shall, within available appropriations: (1) Compile education or training materials for use by the child-placing agencies in training their staffs; (2) conduct in-service training for employees of the department; (3) provide consultation, technical assistance and other appropriate services to agencies in order to strengthen and improve delivery of services to diverse minority populations; (4) conduct workshops and training programs for foster care and adoption recruiters to enable such recruiters to evaluate the effectiveness of techniques for recruiting minority foster and adoptive families; and (5) perform other duties as may be required by the commissioner to implement the federal Multiethnic Placement Act of 1994, as amended. [1]

(1999, P.A. 99–166, § 16; 2000, P.A. 00–196, § 45.)

[1] Public Law 103–382, Title 5, Part E, Subpart 1, Oct. 20, 1994.

§ 17a–116d. Interstate Compact on Adoption and Medical Assistance

The Interstate Compact on Adoption and Medical Assistance is hereby enacted into law and entered into with all other jurisdictions legally joining therein in a form substantially as follows:

INTERSTATE COMPACT ON ADOPTION AND MEDICAL ASSISTANCE

Article I. Finding.

The states which are parties to this compact find that:

(1) In order to obtain adoptive families for children with special needs, states must assure prospective adoptive parents of substantial assistance, usually on a continuing basis, in meeting the high costs of supporting and providing for the special needs and the services required by such children.

(2) The states have a fundamental interest in promoting adoption for children with special needs because the care, emotional stability, and general support and encouragement required by such children can be best, and often only, obtained in family homes with a normal parent-child relationship.

(3) The states obtain fiscal advantages from providing adoption assistance because the alternative is for the states to bear the higher cost of meeting all the needs of all children while in foster care.

(4) The necessary assurances of adoption assistance for children with special needs, in those instances where children and adoptive parents live in states other than the one undertaking to provide the assistance, include the establishment and maintenance of suitable substantive guarantees and workable procedures for interstate cooperation and payments to assist with the necessary costs of child maintenance, the procurement of services and the provision of medical assistance.

Article II. Purposes.

The purposes of this compact are to:

(1) Strengthen protections for the interests of children with special needs on behalf of whom adoption assistance is committed to be paid, when such children are in or move to states other than the one committed to provide adoption assistance.

(2) Provide substantive assurances and operating procedures which will promote the delivery of medical and other services to children on an interstate basis through programs of adoption assistance established by the laws of the states which are parties to this compact.

Article III. Definitions.

As used in this compact, unless the context clearly requires a different construction:

(1) "Child with special needs" means a minor who has not yet attained the age at which the state normally discontinues children's services, or a child who has not yet reached the age of twenty-one, where the state determines that the child's mental or physical disability warrants the continuation of assistance beyond the age of majority, for whom the state has determined the following:

(A) That the child cannot or should not be returned to the home of his or her parents;

(B) That there exists, with respect to the child, a specific factor or condition, such as his or her ethnic background, age or membership in a minority or sibling group, or the presence of factors such as a medical condition or physical, mental or emotional disability, because of which it is reasonable to conclude that such child cannot be placed with adoptive parents without providing adoption assistance; and

(C) That, except where it would be against the best interests of the child because of such factors as the existence of significant emotional ties with prospective adoptive parents while in their care as a foster child, a reasonable but unsuccessful effort has been made to place the child with appropriate adoptive parents without providing adoption assistance.

(2) "Adoption assistance" means the payment or payments for the maintenance of a child which are made or committed to be made pursuant to the adoption assistance program established by the laws of a party state.

(3) "State" means a state of the United States, the District of Columbia, the Commonwealth of Puerto Rico, the Virgin Islands, Guam, the Commonwealth of the Northern Mariana Islands or any territory or possession of the United States.

(4) "Adoption assistance state" means the state that is signatory to the adoption assistance agreement in a particular case.

(5) "Residence state" means the state in which the child is a resident by virtue of the residence of the adoptive parents.

(6) "Parents" means either the singular or plural of the word "parent".

Article IV. Adoption Assistance.

(a) Each state shall determine the amount of adoption assistance and other aid which it will give to children with special needs and their adoptive parents in accordance with its own laws and programs. The adoption assistance and other aid may be made subject to periodic reevaluation of eligibility by the adoption assistance state in accordance with its laws.

(b) The adoption assistance, medical assistance and other services and benefits to which this compact applies are those provided to children with special needs and their adoptive parents from the effective date of the adoption assistance agreement.

(c) Every case of adoption assistance shall include a written adoption assistance agreement between the adoptive parents and the appropriate agency of the state undertaking to provide the adoption assistance. Every such agreement shall contain provisions for the fixing of actual or potential interstate aspects of the assistance so provided as follows:

(1) An express commitment that the assistance so provided shall be payable without regard for the state of residence of the adoptive parents, both at the outset of the agreement period and at all times during its continuance;

(2) A provision setting forth with particularity the types of care and services toward which the adoption assistance state will make payments;

(3) A commitment to make medical assistance available to the child in accordance with Article V of this compact;

(4) An express declaration that the agreement is for the benefit of the child, the adoptive parents and the state and that it is enforceable by any or all of them; and

(5) The date or dates upon which each payment or other benefit provided thereunder is to commence, but in no event prior to the effective date of the adoption assistance agreement.

(d) Any services or benefits provided for a child by the residence state and the adoption assistance state may be facilitated by the party states on each other's behalf. To this end, the personnel of the child welfare agencies of the party states shall assist each other, as well as the beneficiaries of adoption assistance agreements, in assuring prompt and full access to all benefits expressly included in such agreements. It is further recognized and agreed that, in general, all children to whom adoption assistance agreements apply shall be eligible for benefits under the child welfare, education, rehabilitation, mental health and other programs of their state of residence on the same basis as other resident children.

(e) Adoption assistance payments on behalf of a child in another state shall be made on the same basis and in the same amounts as they would be made if the child was living in the state making the payments.

Article V. Medical Assistance.

(a) Children for whom a party state is committed, in accordance with the terms of an adoption assistance agreement to provide federally aided medical assistance under Title XIX of the Social Security Act, 42 USC Section 1396 et seq., are eligible for such medical assistance during the entire period for which the agreement is in effect. Upon application therefore, the adoptive parents of a child who is the subject of such an adoption assistance agreement shall receive a medical assistance identification document made out in the child's name. The identification shall be issued by the medical assistance program of the residence state and shall entitle the child to the same benefits pursuant to the same procedures, as any other child who is covered by the medical assistance program in the state, whether or not the adoptive parents are themselves eligible for medical assistance.

(b) The identification document shall bear no indication that an adoption assistance agreement with another state is the basis for its issuance. However, if the identification is issued pursuant to such an adoption assistance agreement, the records of the issuing state and the adoption assistance state shall show the fact, and shall contain a copy of the adoption assistance agreement and any amendment or replacement thereof, as well as all other pertinent information. The adoption assistance and medical assistance programs of the adoption assistance state shall be notified of the issuance of such identification.

(c) A state which has issued a medical assistance identification document pursuant to this compact, which identification is valid and currently in force, shall accept, process and pay medical assistance claims thereon as it would with any other medical assistance claims by eligible residents.

(d) The federally-aided medical assistance provided by a party state pursuant to this compact shall be in accordance with subsections (a) to (c), inclusive, of this article. In addition, when a child who is covered by an adoption assistance agreement is living in another party state, payment or reimbursement for any medical services and benefits specified under the terms of the adoption assistance agreement, which are not available to the child under Title XIX medical assistance program of the residence state, shall be made by the adoption assistance state as required by its law. Any payments so provided shall be of the same kind and at the same rates as provided for children who are living in the adoption assistance state. However, where the payment rate authorized for a covered service under the medical assistance program of the adoption assistance state exceeds the rate authorized by the residence state for that service, the adoption assistance state shall not be required to pay the additional amounts for the services or benefits covered by the residence state.

(e) A child referred to in subsection (a) of this article, whose residence is changed from one party state to another party state, shall be eligible for federally-aided medical assistance under the medical assistance program of the new state of residence.

Article VI. Compact Administration.

(a) In accordance with its own laws and procedures, each state which is a party to this compact shall designate a compact administrator and such deputy compact administrators as it deems necessary. The compact administrator shall coordinate all activities under this compact within his or her state. The compact administrator shall also be the principal contact for officials and agencies within and without the state for the facilitation of interstate relations involving this compact and the protection of benefits and services provided pursuant thereto. In this capacity, the compact administrator shall be responsible for assisting child welfare agency personnel from other party states and adoptive families receiving adoption and medical assistance on an interstate basis.

(b) Acting jointly, the compact administrators shall develop uniform forms and administrative procedures for the interstate monitoring and delivery of adoption and medical assistance benefits and services pursuant to this compact. The forms and procedures so developed may deal with such matters as:

(1) Documentation of continuing adoption assistance eligibility;

(2) Interstate payments and reimbursements; and

(3) Any and all other matters arising pursuant to this compact.

(c) (1) Some or all of the parties to this compact may enter into supplementary agreements for the provision of or payment for additional medical benefits and services, as provided in subsection (d) of Article V of this compact; for interstate service delivery, pursuant to subsection (d) of Article IV of this compact, or for matters related thereto. Such agreements shall not be inconsistent with this compact, nor shall they relieve the party states of any obligation to provide adoption and medical assistance in accordance with applicable state and federal law and the terms of this compact.

(2) Administrative procedures or forms implementing the supplementary agreements referred to in subdivision (1) of this subsection may be developed by joint action of the compact administrators of those states which are party to such supplementary agreements.

(d) It shall be the responsibility of the compact administrator to ascertain whether and to what extent additional legislation may be necessary in his or her own state to carry out the provisions of this article or Article IV of this compact or any supplementary agreements pursuant to this compact.

Article VII. Joinder and Withdrawal.

(a) This compact shall be open to joinder by any state. It shall enter into force as to a state when its duly constituted and empowered authority has executed it.

(b) In order that the provisions of this compact may be accessible to and known by the general public, and so that they may be implemented as law in each of the party states, the authority which has executed this compact in each party state shall cause the full text of the compact and notice of its execution to be published in his or her state. The executing authority in any party state shall also provide copies of this compact upon request.

(c) Withdrawal from this compact shall be by written notice, sent by the authority which executed it, to the appropriate officials of all other party states, but no such notice shall take effect until one year after it is given, in accordance with the requirements of this subsection.

(d) All adoption assistance agreements outstanding and to which a party state is a signatory at the time when its withdrawal from this compact takes effect shall continue to have the effects given to them pursuant to this compact until they expire or are terminated in accordance with their provisions. Until such expiration or termination, all beneficiaries of the agreements involved shall continue to have all the rights and obligations conferred or imposed by this compact, and the withdrawing state shall continue to administer this compact to the extent necessary to accord and implement fully the rights and protections preserved hereby.

Article VIII. Construction and Severability.

The provisions of this compact shall be liberally construed to effectuate the purposes thereof. The provisions of this compact shall be severable, and if any phrase, clause, sentence or provision of this compact is declared to be contrary to the Constitution of the United States or of any party state, or where the applicability thereof to any government, agency, person or circumstance is held invalid, the validity of the remainder of this compact and the applicability thereof to any government, agency, person or circumstance shall not be affected thereby. If this compact shall be held contrary to the constitution of any state party thereto, this compact shall remain in full force and effect as to the remaining states and in full force and effect as to the state affected as to all severable matters.

(1999, P.A. 99–252, § 3.)

§ 17a–116e. Compact administrator

(a) The Commissioner of Children and Families may designate an officer who shall be the compact administrator and who shall be authorized to carry out all of the powers and duties set forth in the Interstate Compact on Adoption and Medical Assistance.

(b) The compact administrator may enter into supplementary agreements with appropriate officials of other states pursuant to the Interstate Compact on Adoption and Medical Assistance. In the event that the supplementary agreement shall require or contemplate the provision of any service by this state, the supplementary agreement shall have no force or effect until approved by the head of the department or agency which shall be charged with the rendering of the service.

(c) The compact administrator, subject to the approval of the Secretary of the Office of Policy and Management, may make or arrange for any payments necessary to discharge any financial obligations imposed upon this state by the Interstate Compact on Adoption and Medical Assistance or by any supplementary agreement entered into under said compact.

(1999, P.A. 99–252, § 4.)

§ 17a–117. Subsidies for adopting parents. Adoption Subsidy Review Board

(a) The Department of Children and Families may, and is encouraged to contract with child-placing agencies to arrange for the adoption of children who are free for adoption. If (1) a child for whom adoption is indicated, cannot, after all reasonable efforts consistent with the best interests of the child, be placed in adoption through existing sources because the child is a special needs child and (2) the adopting family meets the standards for adoption which any other adopting family meets, the Commissioner of Children and Families shall, before adoption of such child by such family, certify such child as a special needs child and, after adoption, provide one or more of the following subsidies for the adopting parents: (A) A special-need subsidy, which is a lump sum payment paid directly to the person providing the required service, to pay for an anticipated expense resulting from the adoption when no other resource is available for such payment; or (B) a periodic subsidy which is a payment to the adopting family; and (C) in addition to the subsidies granted under this subsection, any medical benefits which are being provided prior to final approval of the adoption by the Court of Probate in accordance with the fee schedule and payment procedures under the state Medicaid program administered by the Department of Social Services shall continue as long as the child qualifies as a dependent of the adoptive parent under the provisions of the Internal Revenue Code.[1] Such medical subsidy may continue only until the child reaches age twenty-one. A special-need subsidy may only be granted until the child reaches age eighteen. A periodic subsidy may continue only until the child reaches age eighteen and is subject to biennial review as provided for in section 17a–118. The amount of a periodic subsidy shall not exceed the current costs of foster maintenance care.

(b) Requests for subsidies after a final approval of the adoption by the Court of Probate may be considered at the discretion of the commissioner for conditions resulting from or directly related to the totality of circumstances surrounding the child prior to placement in adoption. A written certification of the need for a subsidy shall be made by the Commissioner of Children and Families in each case and the type, amount and duration of the subsidy shall be mutually agreed to by the commissioner and the adopting parents prior to the entry of such decree. Any subsidy decision by the Commissioner of Children and Families may be appealed by a licensed child-placing agency or the adopting parent or parents to the Adoption Subsidy Review Board established under subsection (c) of this section. The commissioner shall adopt regulations establishing the procedures for determining the amount and the need for a subsidy.

(c) There is established an Adoption Subsidy Review Board to hear appeals under this section, section 17a–118 and section 17a–120. The board shall consist of the Commissioner of Children and Families, or the commissioner's designee, and a licensed representative of a child-placing agency and an adoptive parent appointed by the Governor. The Governor shall appoint an alternate licensed representative of a child-placing agency and an alternate adoptive parent. Such alternative members shall, when seated, have all the powers and duties set forth in this section and sections 17a–118 and 17a–120. Whenever an alternate member serves in place of a member of the board, such alternate member shall represent the same interest as the member in whose place such alternative member serves. All decisions of the board shall be based on the best interest of the child. Appeals under this section shall be in accordance with the provisions of chapter 54.[2]

(1958 Rev., § 17–44b; 1972, P.A. 86, § 2, eff. July 1, 1972; 1975, P.A. 75–420, § 4, eff. June 25, 1975; 1977, P.A. 77–614, § 521, eff. Jan. 1, 1979; 1979, P.A. 79–631, § 66, eff. July 6, 1979; 1986, P.A. 86–330, § 3, eff. April 1, 1987; 1993, P.A. 93–91, § 1, eff. July 1, 1993; 1993, P.A. 93–262, § 1, eff. July 1, 1993; 1994, P.A. 94–46; 1994, P.A. 94–118, § 1; 1999, P.A. 99–166, § 6; 2000, P.A. 00–4, § 1.)

1 26 U.S.C.A. § 1 et seq.

2 C.G.S.A. § 4–166 et seq.

§ 17a–118. Review and change in subsidy. Adoption Subsidy Review Board

(a) There shall be a biennial review of the subsidy by the Commissioner of Children and Families in accordance with a schedule established by the commissioner or the commissioner's designee. The adoptive parents shall, at the time of such review, submit a sworn statement that the condition which caused the child to be certified as a special needs child or a related condition continues to exist or has reoccurred and that the adoptive parent or parents are still legally responsible for the support of the child and that the child is receiving support from the adoptive family. If the subsidy is to be terminated or reduced by the Commissioner of Children and Families, notice of such proposed reduction or termination shall be given, in writing, to the adoptive parents and such adoptive parents shall, at least thirty days prior to the imposition of said reduction or termination, be given a hearing before the Adoption Subsidy Review Board. If such an appeal is taken, the subsidy shall continue without modification until the final decision of the Adoption Subsidy Review Board.

(b) A child who is a resident of the state of Connecticut when eligibility for subsidy is certified, shall remain eligible and continue to receive the subsidy regardless of the domicile or residence of the adoptive parents at the time of application for adoption, placement, legal decree of adoption or thereafter. If the Department of Children and Families is responsible for such child's placement and care, the department shall be responsible for entering into an adoption assistance agreement and paying any subsidy granted under the provisions of sections 17a–116 to 17a–120, inclusive. If a licensed child placing agency, other than the Department of Children and Families, or any public agency in another state is responsible for such child's placement and care, the adoption assistance application shall be made in the adoptive parents' state of residence and such state shall be responsible for determining that such child meets Title IV-E adoption assistance criteria and for providing adoption assistance permitted under federal law.

(1958 Rev., § 17–44c; 1972, P.A. 86, § 3, eff. July 1, 1972; 1975, P.A. 75–420, § 4, eff. June 25, 1975; 1977, P.A. 77–614, § 521, eff. Jan. 1, 1979; 1979, P.A. 79–631, § 67, eff. July 6, 1979; 1980, P.A. 80–483, § 72, eff. June 6, 1980; 1986, P.A. 86–330, § 4, eff. April 1, 1987; 1988, P.A. 88–94, § 2, eff. May 2, 1988; 1993, P.A. 93–91, § 1, eff. July 1, 1993; 2000, P.A. 00–4, § 2; 2003, P.A. 03–243, § 3.)

§ 17a–119. Moneys for subsidies. Regulations

The Department of Children and Families shall establish and maintain an ongoing program of subsidized adoption and shall encourage the use of the program and assist in finding families for children. The commissioner shall adopt regulations, in accordance with the provisions of chapter 54,[1] to administer the program by December 31, 1987. Payment of subsidies under sections 17a–116 to 17a–119, inclusive, and subsection (b) of section 45a–111, shall be made from moneys available from any source to the Department of Children and Families for child welfare purposes.

(1958 Rev., § 17–44d; 1972 P.A. 86, § 5, eff. July 1, 1972; 1975, P.A. 75–420, § 4, eff. June 25, 1975; 1977, P.A. 77–614, § 521, eff. Jan. 1, 1979; 1979, P.A. 79–631, § 68, eff. July 6, 1979; 1986, P.A. 86–330, § 5, eff. April 1, 1987; 1993, P.A. 93–91, § 1, eff. July 1, 1993.)

[1] C.G.S.A. § 4–166 et seq.

§ 17a–120. Medical expense subsidy for blind, physically or mentally disabled, emotionally maladjusted or high risk children

(a) Any child who is blind or physically disabled as defined by section 1–1f, mentally disabled, seriously emotionally maladjusted or has a recognized high risk of physical or mental disability as defined in the regulations adopted by the Commissioner of Children and Families pursuant to section 17a–118, who is to be given or has been given in adoption by a statutory parent, as defined in section 45a–707, shall be eligible for a one hundred per cent medical expense subsidy in accordance with the fee schedule and payment procedures under the state Medicaid program administered by the Department of Social Services where such condition existed prior to such adoption, provided such expenses are not reimbursed by health insurance, or federal or state payments for health care. Application for such subsidy shall be made to the Commissioner of Children and Families by such child's adopting or adoptive parent or parents. Said commissioner shall adopt regulations governing the procedures for application and criteria for determination of the existence of such condition. A written determination of eligibility shall be made by said commissioner and may be made prior to or after identification of the adopting parent or parents. Upon a finding of eligibility, an application for such medical expense subsidy by the adopting or adoptive parent or parents on behalf of the child shall be granted, and such adopting or adoptive parent or parents shall be issued a medical identification card for such child by the Department of Children and Families for the purpose of providing for payment for the medical expense subsidy. The subsidy set forth in this section shall not preclude the granting of either subsidy set forth in section 17a–117 except, if the child is eligible for subsidy under this section, his adopting parent or parents shall not be granted a subsidy or subsidies set forth in section 17a–117 that would be granted for the same purposes as the child's subsidy.

(b) There shall be an annual review of the medical expense subsidy set forth in subsection (a) of this section by the Commissioner of Children and Families. If, upon such annual review, the commissioner determines that the child continues to have a condition for which the subsidy was granted or has medical conditions related to such condition, and that the adoptive parent or parents are still legally responsible for the support of the child and that the child is receiving support from the adoptive family, the commissioner shall not terminate or reduce such subsidy. If the condition is corrected and conditions related to it no longer exist, or if the adoptive parent or parents are no longer legally responsible for the support of the child or if the child is no longer receiving any support from the adoptive family, the commissioner may reduce or terminate eligibility for such subsidy. If, following such reduction or termination, such condition or related conditions reoccur, the adopting or adoptive parent or parents may reapply for such subsidy. Upon receipt of such application and determination that such condition or related conditions have reoccurred, the commissioner shall grant such subsidy provided the adoptive parent or parents are still legally responsible for the support of the child or the child is receiving support from the adoptive family. If the subsidy is to be reduced or terminated by said commissioner, notice of such proposed reduction or termination shall be given, in writing, to the adoptive parent or parents and such adoptive parent or parents shall, at least thirty days prior to the imposition of said reduction or termination, be given a hearing before the Adoption Subsidy Review Board. If such an appeal is taken, the subsidy shall continue without modification or termination until the final decision of the Adoption Subsidy Review Board. Eligibility for such subsidy may continue until the child's twenty-first birthday if the condition that caused the child to be certified as a special needs child or related conditions continue to exist or have reoccurred and the child continues to qualify as a dependent of the legal adoptive parent under the Internal Revenue Code. In no case shall the eligibility for such subsidy continue beyond the child's twenty-first birthday.

(1958 Rev., § 17–44e; 1978, P.A. 78–266; 1981, P.A. 81–403, § 1; 1986, P.A. 86–330, § 6, eff. April 1, 1987; 1993, P.A. 93–91, § 1, eff. July 1, 1993; 1993, P.A. 93–262, § 1, eff. July 1, 1993.)

§ 17a–121. Prior subsidies not affected. Increases

Nothing in sections 17a–116 to 17a–120, inclusive, as amended by public act 86–330, shall affect any subsidy granted under the provisions of sections 17a–116, 17a–117, 17a–118, 17a–119 and 17a–120 prior to April 1, 1987, except that any adopting parent may apply for an increase in such subsidy in accordance with the provisions of this section. All subsidies granted on and after April 1, 1987, under said sections, shall be subject to the review provisions of sections 17a–118 and 17a–120. Any adopting parent who received a subsidy under said sections, prior to April 1, 1987, may apply to have said subsidy increased or modified in accordance with the provisions of said sections as amended by public act 86–330. The Commissioner of Children and Families shall notify such adopting parent of the provisions of sections 17a–116 to 17a–120, inclusive, as amended by said public act and of his right to seek an increase in such subsidy in accordance with said sections.

(1958 Rev., § 17–44f; 1986, P.A. 86–330, § 7, eff. April 1, 1987; 1993, P.A. 93–91, § 1, eff. July 1, 1993.)

§ 17a–121a. Counseling and referral services after adoption to certain adoptees and adoptive families. Postadoption services

The Department of Children and Families may provide counseling and referral services after adoption to adoptees and adoptive families for whom the department provided such services before the adoption. Postadoption services include assigning a mentor to a family, training after licensing, support groups, behavioral management counseling, therapeutic respite care, referrals to community providers, a telephone help line and training of public and private mental health professionals in postadoption issues.

(1999, P.A. 99–166, § 12; 2001, P.A. 01–159, § 5.)

§§ 17a–122, 17a–123. Repealed. (1993, P.A. 93–216, § 8.)

§ 17a–124. Repealed. (1991, P.A. 91–299, § 2.)

§ 17a–125. Out-of-Home Placements. Advisory Council

(a) There is established an Out-of-Home Placements Advisory Council. The council shall advise and make recommendations to the Governor, the General Assembly and the Commissioner of Children and Families concerning: (1) The Department of Children and Families' placement processes and policies, including, but not limited to, policies regarding foster care and therapeutic foster care, residential treatment, group home and transitional living services, emergency shelter and inpatient mental health placements; (2) the placement resources needed for the populations and age groups the department serves, including a discussion of resources needed for populations that (A) have been abused, neglected or are at-risk, (B) have mental health or substance abuse treatment needs, (C) are delinquent, (D) are members of a family with service needs, (E) are committed to the department, or (F) are receiving voluntary services or services through the noncommitted treatment program; (3) the geographic availability of placement services; (4) the availability of culturally competent services and appropriate services for children with complex medical needs or physical or developmental disabilities; (5) eligibility and utilization standards for out-of-home care options and eligibility and utilization standards for the populations and age groups the department serves; (6) the impact of the policies and processes of the department on the availability of timely and appropriate access to services; (7) an examination of quality assurance measures; (8) the amount of family or guardian input with respect to placement options and service providers; (9) the timeliness and effectiveness of client and family or guardian grievance procedures; (10) the degree of coordination with other state and local agencies and private organizations having responsibility for populations or age groups the department serves; and (11) other issues relating to out-of-home placements, as the council may deem appropriate.

(b) The advisory council shall consist of (1) the chairpersons and ranking members of the joint standing committees of the General Assembly having cognizance of matters relating to human services and the judiciary and the select committee of the General Assembly having cognizance of matters relating to children, or their designees; (2) the Child Advocate, or the Child Advocate's designee; (3) a private sector children's advocate, appointed by the Governor; (4) a nonprofit provider of group home or transitional living services for adolescents, appointed by the speaker of the House of Representatives; (5) a nonprofit children's residential treatment provider, appointed by the president pro tempore of the Senate; (6) a representative of a licensed child placing agency providing therapeutic or professional foster care services, appointed by the majority leader of the Senate; (7) a nonprofit emergency shelter provider, appointed by the minority leader of the Senate; (8) a provider of inpatient psychiatric services, appointed by the majority leader of the House of Representatives; (9) a foster parent, appointed by the minority leader of the House of Representatives; (10) one representative of a local youth services agency or police youth division, appointed by the speaker of the

House of Representatives; (11) one provider of behavioral health services for children and youth, appointed by the president pro tempore of the Senate; (12) two parents, parent advocates, or recipients or former recipients of department residential services, one appointed by the majority leader of the Senate and one appointed by the majority leader of the House of Representatives; (13) the director of the Office of Protection and Advocacy for Persons with Disabilities, or the director's designee; (14) four employees of the Department of Children and Families, one from the Residential Placement Team, one from the Office of Child Welfare Services, one from the Office of Juvenile Justice Services, and one from the Office of Mental Health, Substance Abuse and Health Services, each of whom shall be appointed by the commissioner; (15) one employee of the judicial branch having experience in matters relating to juveniles, appointed by the Chief Court Administrator; (16) the Commissioner of Mental Health and Addiction Services, or the commissioner's designee; (17) the Commissioner of Education, or the commissioner's designee; and (18) the Commissioner of Mental Retardation, or the commissioner's designee.

(c) The council shall elect a chairperson from among its members, except that the speaker of the House of Representatives and the president pro tempore of the Senate shall jointly select the chairperson for the first meeting of the council. Such chairpersons shall schedule the first meeting of the council, which shall be no later than sixty days after June 24, 1997.

(d) The membership of the council shall serve without compensation. The Department of Children and Families shall provide, within available resources, clerical support to the council.

(e) On or before January 1, 1998, and annually thereafter, the council shall report its activities for the preceding year to the joint standing committees of the General Assembly having cognizance of matters relating to human services and judiciary and the select committee on children.

(1997, P.A. 97–237, § 2, eff. June 24, 1997; 2003, P.A. 03–278, §§ 57, 121, eff. July 9, 2003.)

§ 17a–126. Subsidy for relative caregivers

(a) As used in this section, "relative caregiver" means a person who is caring for a child related to such person because the parent of the child has died or become otherwise unable to care for the child for reasons that make reunification with the parent not a viable option within the foreseeable future and "commissioner" means the Commissioner of Children and Families.

(b) The Commissioner of Children and Families shall establish a program of subsidized guardianship for the benefit of children in the care or custody of the commissioner who are living with relative caregivers and who have been in foster care or certified relative care for not less than eighteen months. The commissioner, within available appropriations, may establish a program of subsidized guardianship for the benefit of children in the care or custody of the commissioner who are living with relative caregivers and who have been in foster care or certified relative care for not less than twelve but not more than eighteen months. A relative caregiver may request a guardianship subsidy from the commissioner. If adoption of the child by the relative caregiver is an option, the commissioner shall counsel the caregiver about the advantages and disadvantages of adoption and subsidized guardianship so that the decision by the relative caregiver to request a subsidized guardianship may be a fully informed one.

(c) The subsidized guardianship program shall provide the following subsidies for the benefit of any child in the care of a relative caregiver who has been appointed the guardian or coguardian of the child by any court of competent jurisdiction: (1) A special-need subsidy, which shall be a lump sum payment for one-time expenses resulting from the assumption of care of the child when no other resource is available to pay for such expense; and (2) a medical subsidy comparable to the medical subsidy to children in the subsidized adoption program if the child lacks private health insurance. The subsidized guardianship program shall also provide a monthly subsidy on behalf of the child payable to the relative caregiver that shall be equal to the prevailing foster care rate. The commissioner may establish an asset test for eligibility under the program.

(d) The commissioner shall adopt regulations in accordance with chapter 54 [1] implementing the subsidized guardianship program established under this section. Such regulations shall require, as a prerequisite to payment of a guardianship subsidy for the benefit of a minor child, that a home study report be filed with the court having jurisdiction of the case of the minor within fifteen days of the request for a subsidy, provided that no such report shall be required to be filed if a report has previously been provided to the court or if the caregiver has been determined to be a certified relative caregiver by the commissioner. The regulations shall also establish a procedure comparable to that for the subsidized adoption program to determine the types and amounts of subsidy to be granted by the commissioner as provided in subsection (c) of this section, for annual review of the subsidy as provided in subsection (e) of this section and for appeal from decisions by the commissioner denying, modifying or terminating such subsidies.

(e) The guardianship subsidy provided under this section shall continue until the child reaches the age of eighteen or the age of twenty-one if such child is in full time attendance at a secondary school, technical school or college or is in a state accredited job training program. Annually, the subsidized guardian shall submit to the commissioner a sworn statement that the child is still living with and receiving support from the guardian. The parent of any child receiving assistance through the subsidized guardianship program shall remain liable for the support of the child as required by the general statutes.

(f) A guardianship subsidy shall not be included in the calculation of household income in determining eligibility for benefits of the relative caregiver of the subsidized child or other persons living within the household of the relative caregiver.

(g) Payments for guardianship subsidies shall be made from moneys available from any source to the commissioner for child welfare purposes. The commissioner shall develop and implement a plan that: (1) Maximizes use of the subsidized guardianship program to decrease the number of children in the legal custody of the Commissioner of Children and Families and to reduce the number of children who would otherwise be placed into foster care when there is a family member willing to provide care; (2) maximizes federal reimbursement for the costs of the subsidized guardianship program, provided whatever federal maximization method is employed shall not result in the relative caregiver of a child being subject to work requirements as a condition of receipt of benefits for the child or the benefits restricted in time or scope other than as specified in subsection (c) of this section; and (3) ensures necessary transfers of funds between agencies and interagency coordination in program implementation. The Commissioner of Children and Families shall seek all federal waivers as are necessary and appropriate to implement this plan.

(1997, P.A. 97-272, § 7, eff. July 1, 1997; 1998, June Sp.Sess., P.A. 98-1, § 90, eff. June 24, 1998; 1999, P.A. 99-251, § 1, eff. July 1, 1999.)

[1] C.G.S.A. § 4-166 et seq.

§ 17a-127. Development and implementation of individual service plan. Child specific team. Regulations

(a) The following shall be established for the purposes of developing and implementing an individual service plan: Within available appropriations, a child specific team may be developed by the family of a child or youth with complex behavioral health service needs which shall provide for family participation in all aspects of assessment, planning and implementation of services and may include, but need not be limited to, family members, the child or adolescent if appropriate, clergy, school personnel, representatives of local or regional agencies providing programs and services for children and youth, a family advocate, and other community or family representatives. The team shall designate one member to be the team coordinator. The team coordinator shall, with the consent of the parent, guardian, youth or emancipated minor, compile the results of all assessments and evaluations completed prior to the preparation of an individual service plan that document the service needs of the child or youth, make decisions affecting the implementation of an individual service plan, and make referrals to community agencies and resources in accordance with an individual service plan. The care coordinator shall not make decisions affecting the implementation of the individual service plan without the consent of the parent, guardian, youth or emancipated minor, except as otherwise provided by law.

(b) The provisions of this section shall not be construed to grant an entitlement to any child or youth with behavioral health needs to receive particular services under this section in an individual service plan if such child or youth is not otherwise eligible to receive such services from any state agency or to receive such services pursuant to any other provision of law.

(c) The Commissioner of Children and Families, in consultation with the Commissioner of Social Services, may adopt regulations in accordance with chapter 54 [1] for the purpose of implementing the provisions of this section.

(1997, P.A. 97-272, § 2; 2000, June Sp.Sess., P.A. 00-2, § 7, eff. July 1, 2000; 2001, June Sp.Sess, P.A. 01-2, § 45, eff. July 1, 2001.)

[1] C.G.S.A. § 4-166 et seq.

§ 17a-128. Liaison to Department of Social Services

The Department of Children and Families shall establish a liaison to the Department of Social Services to ensure that Medicaid eligible children and youth receive mental health services in accordance with federal law.

(1997, P.A. 97-272, § 3.)

§ 17a-129. Department not required to seek custody of certain children and youth

There shall be no requirement for the Department of Children and Families to seek custody of any child or youth with mental illness, emotional disturbance, a behavioral disorder or developmental or physical disability if such child is voluntarily placed with the department by a parent or guardian of the child for the purpose of accessing an out-of-home placement or intensive outpatient service, including, but not limited to, residential treatment programs, therapeutic foster care programs and extended day treatment programs, except as permitted pursuant to sections 17a-101g and 46b-129. Commitment to or protective supervision or protection by the department shall not be a condition for receipt of services or benefits delivered or funded by the department.

(1997, P.A. 97-272, § 4.)

§ 17a-130. Application to insurance contracts

The provisions of sections 17a-1, 17a-3, 17a-11 and sections 17a-126 to 17a-130, inclusive, shall not be construed to apply to any nongovernmental insurance policy or health care center contract or alter any contractual or statutory obligation of the insurer or health care center.

(1997, P.A. 97–272, § 8, eff. July 1, 1997.)

§ 17a–131. Cardiopulmonary resuscitation training required for persons who directly supervise children

Any person who has direct supervision of children placed by the state in a state facility or private institution shall be trained in cardiopulmonary resuscitation.

(1998, P.A. 98–256, § 13.)

§ 17a–131a. Refusal to administer or consent to the administration of psychotropic drugs to children

The refusal of a parent or other person having control of a child to administer or consent to the administration of any psychotropic drug to such child shall not, in and of itself, constitute grounds for the Department of Children and Families to take such child into custody or for any court of competent jurisdiction to order that such child be taken into custody by the department, unless such refusal causes such child to be neglected or abused, as defined in section 46b–120.

(2001, P.A. 01–124, § 2.)

§§ 17a–132 to 17a–144. Reserved for future use

§ 17a–151aa. Child placed in residential facility; written agreement re care and treatment of

(a) Any state agency that places a child, as defined in section 17a–93, in a residential facility shall enter into a written agreement with the facility at the time of the placement. Such written agreement shall establish clear standards for the child's care and treatment, including, but not limited to, requirements for monthly written reports concerning the child's care and treatment, addressed to the case worker overseeing the child's placement. The monthly written reports shall set forth child-specific goals and expectations for treatment and progress. The written agreement shall require the facility to report promptly to the placing agency any allegation that the child is abused or neglected, as defined in section 46b–120, or any incident of abuse or neglect of an individual placed in the facility. The placing agency shall ensure that a discharge plan is initiated no later than two weeks after the child's placement in the facility.

(b) In the case of a child placed by the Department of Children and Families in a residential facility in another state, the Commissioner of Children and Families shall ensure that a representative of the department makes in-person visits with the child no less frequently than every two months in order to assess the well being of the child.

(2001, June Sp.Sess., P.A. 01–2, § 25; 2004, P.A. 04–258, § 19, eff. July 1, 2004.)

CHAPTER 319j

ADDICTION SERVICES

§ 17a–688. Records, keeping and confidentiality of. Disclosure permitted, when. Minors, consent to treatment and liability for costs

(a) All records maintained by the court of cases coming before it under the provisions of sections 17a–465a, 17a–673 and 17a–680 to 17a–690, inclusive, shall be sealed and available only to the respondent or the respondent's counsel unless the court, after hearing held with notice to the respondent, determines such record should be disclosed for cause shown.

(b) Medical treatment facilities shall keep and submit such records of all persons examined, admitted or treated pursuant to sections 17a–465a, 17a–673 and 17a–680 to 17a–690, inclusive, as may be required by the department.

(c) No person, hospital or treatment facility may disclose or permit the disclosure of, nor may the department disclose or permit the disclosure of, the identity, diagnosis, prognosis or treatment of any such patient that would constitute a violation of federal statutes concerning confidentiality of alcohol or drug patient records and any regulations pursuant thereto, as such federal statutes and regulations may be amended from time to time. The department shall adopt regulations, in accordance with chapter 54,[1] to protect the confidentiality of any such information that is obtained by the department.

(d) If the person seeking treatment or rehabilitation for alcohol dependence or drug dependence is a minor, the fact that the minor sought such treatment or rehabilitation or that the minor is receiving such treatment or rehabilitation, shall not be reported or disclosed to the parents or legal guardian of the minor without the minor's consent. The minor may give legal consent to receipt of such treatment and rehabilitation. A minor shall be personally liable for all costs and expenses for alcohol and drug dependency treatment afforded to the minor at the minor's request under section 17a–682.

(e) The commissioner may use or make available to authorized persons information from patients' records for purposes of conducting scientific research, management audits, financial audits or program evaluation, provided such information shall not be utilized in a manner that discloses a patient's name or other identifying information.

(1958 Rev., § 17–155bb, § 17a–630, § 19a–126h; 1974, P.A. 74–280, § 18, eff. July 1, 1974; 1975, P.A. 75–569, § 11; 1977, P.A. 77–544, § 10, eff. July 1, 1977; 1986, P.A. 86–371, § 10, eff. July 1, 1986; 1990, P.A. 90–209, § 10; 1993, P.A. 93–381, §§ 9, 18, eff. July 1, 1993; 1993, P.A. 93–435, § 59, eff. June 28, 1993; 1995, P.A.

95–257, §§ 12, 21, eff. July 1, 1995; 1999, P.A. 99–234, § 5; 2000, P.A. 00–27, § 7, eff. May 1, 2000.)

1 C.G.S.A. § 4–166 et seq.

TITLE 17b

SOCIAL SERVICES

CHAPTER 319rr

CHILD CARE

§ 17b–743. Support order may direct payment to Commissioner of Administrative Services or local welfare department

Any court or any family support magistrate having jurisdiction to make an order for support of any person by a legally liable relative or putative father shall have authority to direct payment in accordance with such order to the Commissioner of Administrative Services or to the welfare department of any political subdivision of the state for such period as such person shall receive welfare assistance from the state or such subdivision; and such court or family support magistrate, upon its findings of any arrearage due under any support order, shall have authority to determine that portion of such arrearage the failure to pay which resulted in grants of welfare assistance, and to order payment of such portion to the Commissioner of Administrative Services or the local welfare department which granted such assistance in reimbursement therefor, as the case may be. The provisions of this section shall apply to orders made under the provisions of sections 46b–60 and 46b–81 to 46b–87, inclusive, and 53–304.

(1958 Rev., § 17–323a; 1959, P.A. 115, §§ 1, 2; 1967, P.A. 314, § 10; 1967, P.A. 656, § 15, eff. June 27, 1967; 1973, P.A. 73–373, § 33; 1977, P.A. 77–614, § 70, eff. Oct. 1, 1977; 1986, P.A. 86–359, § 28, eff. Jan. 1, 1986.)

§ 17b–744. Discontinuance of payments of support to commissioner pursuant to certain court orders

Any order payable to the Commissioner of Administrative Services for support of any beneficiary of public assistance shall, on filing by the Commissioner of Social Services with the court making such order, or with the assistant clerk of the Family Support Magistrate Division where such order was entered, of a notice of discontinuance of such assistance and on notice to the payor by registered or certified mail, a copy of which notice shall be sent to the Commissioner of Administrative Services, be payable directly to such beneficiary, beginning with the effective date of discontinuance, except that the Commissioner of Social Services may elect to continue to collect such support payments on behalf of the beneficiaries of the temporary family assistance program for three months after the date of discontinuance as provided in federal law and regulations.

(1958 Rev., § 17–323b; 1963, P.A. 25; 1967, P.A. 314, § 11; 1967, P.A. 656, § 16, eff. June 27, 1967; 1972, P.A. 294, § 21, eff. May 30, 1972; 1973, P.A. 73–373, § 34; 1974, P.A. 74–338, § 24, eff. May 31, 1974; 1975, P.A. 75–420, § 4, eff. June 25, 1975; 1976, P.A. 76–334, § 6, eff. June 2, 1976; 1977, P.A. 77–614, § 70, eff. Oct. 1, 1977; 1977, P.A. 77–614, § 608, eff. Jan. 1, 1979; 1986, P.A. 86–359, § 29, eff. Jan. 1, 1987; 1993, P.A. 93–262, § 39, eff. July 1, 1993; 1997, June 18 Sp.Sess., P.A. 97–2, § 81, eff. July 1, 1997; 2003, P.A. 03–278, § 69, eff. July 9, 2003.)

§ 17b–745. Court order for support of persons supported by the state. National Medical Support Notice. Income withholding orders. Enforcement and modification of support orders

(a) (1) The Superior Court or a family support magistrate shall have authority to make and enforce orders for payment of support to the Commissioner of Administrative Services or, in IV-D cases, to the state acting by and through the IV-D agency, directed to the husband or wife and, if the patient or person is under twenty-one or, on and after October 1, 1972, under eighteen, any parent of any patient or person being supported by the state, wholly or in part, in a state humane institution, or under any welfare program administered by the Department of Social Services, as the court or family support magistrate finds, in accordance with the provisions of subsection (b) of section 17b–179, or section 17a–90, 17b–81, 17b–223, 46b–129 or 46b–130, to be reasonably commensurate with the financial ability of any such relative. Any court or family support magistrate called upon to make or enforce such an order, including one based upon a determination consented to by the relative, shall insure that such order is reasonable in light of the relative's ability to pay.

(2) (A) The court or family support magistrate shall include in each support order in a IV–D support case a provision for the health care coverage of the child which provision may include an order for either parent to name any child under eighteen as a beneficiary of any medical or dental insurance or benefit plan carried by such parent or available to such parent on a group basis through an employer or a union. Any such employment based order shall be enforced using a National Medical Support Notice as provided in section 46b–88. If such insurance coverage is unavailable at reasonable cost, the provision for health care coverage may include an order for either parent to apply for and maintain coverage on behalf of the child under the HUSKY Plan,

Part B.[1] The noncustodial parent shall be ordered to apply for the HUSKY Plan, Part B only if such parent is found to have sufficient ability to pay the appropriate premium. In any IV–D support case in which the noncustodial parent is found to have insufficient ability to provide medical insurance coverage and the custodial party is the HUSKY Plan, Part A [2] or Part B applicant, the provision for health care coverage may include an order for the noncustodial parent to pay such amount as is specified by the court or family support magistrate to the state or the custodial party, as their interests may appear, to offset the cost of any insurance payable under the HUSKY Plan, Part A or Part B. In no event may such order include payment to offset the cost of any such premium if such payment would reduce the amount of current support required under the child support guidelines.

(B) Whenever an order of the Superior Court or family support magistrate is issued against a parent to cover the cost of such medical or dental insurance or benefit plan for a child who is eligible for Medicaid benefits, and such parent has received payment from a third party for the costs of such services but such parent has not used such payment to reimburse, as appropriate, either the other parent or guardian or the provider of such services, the Department of Social Services shall have the authority to request the court or family support magistrate to order the employer of such parent to withhold from the wages, salary or other employment income, of such parent to the extent necessary to reimburse the Department of Social Services for expenditures for such costs under the Medicaid program. However, any claims for current or past due child support shall take priority over any such claims for the costs of such services.

(3) Said court or family support magistrate shall also have authority to make and enforce orders directed to the conservator or guardian of any such patient or person, or the payee of Social Security or other benefits to which such patient or person is entitled, to the extent of the income or estate held or received by such fiduciary or payee in any such capacity.

(4) For purposes of this section, the term "father" shall include a person who has acknowledged in writing paternity of a child born out of wedlock, and the court or family support magistrate shall have authority to determine, order and enforce payment of any accumulated sums due under a written agreement to support such child in accordance with the provisions of this section.

(5) (A) Said court or family support magistrate shall also have authority to make and enforce orders for the payment by any person named herein of unpaid support contributions for which any such person is liable in accordance with the provisions of subsection (b) of section 17b–179, or section 17a–90, 17b–81, 17b–223, 46b–129 or 46b–130 or, in IV-D cases, to order such person, provided such person is not incapacitated, to participate in work activities which may include, but shall not be limited to, job search, training, work experience and participation in the job training and retraining program established by the Labor Commissioner pursuant to section 31–3t.

(B) In the determination of child support due based on neglect or refusal to furnish support prior to the action, the support due for periods of time prior to the action shall be based upon the obligor's ability to pay during such prior periods, as determined in accordance with the child support and arrearage guidelines established pursuant to section 46b–215a. The state shall disclose to the court any information in its possession concerning current and past ability to pay. If no information is available to the court concerning past ability to pay, the court may determine the support due for periods of time prior to the action as if past ability to pay is equal to current ability to pay, if current ability is known. If current ability to pay is not known, the court shall determine the past ability to pay based on the obligor's work history if known, or if not known, on the state minimum wage that was in effect during such periods, provided only actual earnings shall be used to determine ability to pay for past periods during which the obligor was a full-time high school student or was incarcerated, institutionalized or incapacitated.

(C) Any finding of support due for periods of time prior to an action in which the obligor failed to appear shall be entered subject to adjustment. Such adjustment may be made upon motion of any party, and the state in IV-D cases shall make such motion if it obtains information that would have substantially affected the court's determination of past ability to pay if such information had been available to the court. Motion for adjustment under this subparagraph may be made not later than twelve months from the date upon which the obligor receives notification of (i) the amount of such finding of support due for periods of time prior to the action, and (ii) the right not later than twelve months from the date of receipt of such notification to present evidence as to such obligor's past ability to pay support for such periods of time prior to the action. A copy of any support order entered, subject to adjustment, that is provided to each party under subsection (c) of this section, shall state in plain language the basis for the court's determination of past support, the right to request an adjustment and to present information concerning the obligor's past ability to pay, and the consequences of a failure to request such adjustment.

(6) All payments ordered by the court or family support magistrate under this section shall be made to the Commissioner of Administrative Services or, in IV–D cases, to the state acting by and through the IV–D agency, as the court or family support magistrate may determine, for the period during which the supported person is receiving assistance or care from the state, provided, in the case of beneficiaries of any program of public assistance, upon the discontinuance of such

assistance, payments shall be distributed to the beneficiary, beginning with the effective date of discontinuance. Any order of payment made under this section may, at any time after being made, be set aside or altered by the court or a family support magistrate.

(7) (A) Proceedings to obtain orders of support under this section shall be commenced by the service on the liable person or persons of a verified petition of the Commissioner of Administrative Services, the Commissioner of Social Services or their designees. The verified petition shall be filed by any of said commissioners or their designees in the judicial district of the court or Family Support Magistrate Division in which the patient, applicant, beneficiary, recipient or the defendant resides. The judge or family support magistrate shall cause a summons, signed by such judge or magistrate, by the clerk of said court, or by a commissioner of the Superior Court to be issued, requiring such liable person or persons to appear before the court or a family support magistrate at a time and place as determined by the clerk but not more than ninety days after the issuance of the summons to show cause, if any, why the request for relief in such petition should not be granted. The verified petition, summons and order shall be on forms prescribed by the Office of the Chief Court Administrator.

(B) Service of process issued under this section may be made by a state marshal, any proper officer or any investigator employed by the Department of Social Services or by the Commissioner of Administrative Services. The state marshal, proper officer or investigator shall make due return of process to the court not less than twenty-one days before the date assigned for hearing. Upon proof of the service of the summons to appear before the court or a family support magistrate, at the time and place named for hearing upon such petition, the failure of the defendant to appear shall not prohibit the court or family support magistrate from going forward with the hearing.

(8) Failure of any defendant to obey an order of the court or Family Support Magistrate Division made under this section may be punished as contempt of court. If the summons and order is signed by a commissioner of the Superior Court, upon proof of service of the summons to appear in court or before a family support magistrate and upon the failure of the defendant to appear at the time and place named for hearing upon the petition, request may be made by the petitioner to the court or family support magistrate for an order that a capias mittimus be issued. Except as otherwise provided, upon proof of the service of the summons to appear in court or before a family support magistrate at the time and place named for a hearing upon the failure of the defendant to obey the court order as contempt of court, the court or the family support magistrate may order a capias mittimus to be issued and directed to some proper officer to arrest such defendant and bring such defendant before the Superior Court for the contempt hearing. The costs of commitment of any person imprisoned therefor shall be paid by the state as in criminal cases. When any such defendant is so found in contempt, the court or family support magistrate may award to the petitioner a reasonable attorney's fee and the fees of the officer serving the contempt citation, such sums to be paid by the person found in contempt.

(9) In addition to or in lieu of contempt proceedings, the court or family support magistrate, upon a finding that any person has failed to obey any order made under this section, may issue an order directing that an income withholding order issue against such amount of any debt accruing by reason of personal services due and owing to such person in accordance with section 52–362, or against such lesser amount of such excess as said court or family support magistrate deems equitable, for payment of accrued and unpaid amounts due under such order and all amounts which thereafter become due under such order. On presentation of such income withholding order by the officer to whom delivered for service to the person or persons or corporation from whom such debt accruing by reason of personal services is due and owing, or thereafter becomes due and owing, to the person against whom such support order was issued, such income withholding order shall be a lien and a continuing levy upon such debt to the amount specified therein, which shall be accumulated by the debtor and paid directly to the Commissioner of Administrative Services or, in IV–D cases, to the state acting by and through the IV–D agency, in accordance with section 52–362, until such income withholding order and expenses are fully satisfied and paid, or until such income withholding order is modified.

(10) No entry fee, judgment fee or any other court fee shall be charged by the court to either party in actions under this section.

(11) Written statements from employers as to property, insurance, wages, indebtedness and other information obtained by the Commissioner of Social Services, or the Commissioner of Administrative Services under authority of section 17b–137, shall be admissible in evidence in actions under this section.

(b) Except as provided in sections 46b–212 to 46b–213v, inclusive, any court or family support magistrate, called upon to enforce a support order, shall insure that such order is reasonable in light of the obligor's ability to pay. Except as provided in sections 46b–212 to 46b–213v, inclusive, any support order entered pursuant to this section, or any support order from another jurisdiction subject to enforcement by the state of Connecticut, may be modified by motion of the party seeking such modification, including Support Enforcement Services in TANF support cases as defined in subdivision (14) of subsection (b) of section 46b–231, upon a showing of a substantial change in the circumstances of either party or upon a showing that the final order for child support substantially deviates from the child support guidelines established pursuant to section 46b–215a, unless there was a specific finding on the record that the application of the guidelines would be inequitable or inappropriate, provided the court or family support magistrate finds that the obligor or the obligee and any other interested party have received actual notice of the pendency of such motion and of the time and place of the hearing on such motion. There shall be a rebuttable presumption that any deviation of less than fifteen per cent from the child support guidelines is not substantial and any deviation of fifteen per cent or more from the guidelines is substantial. Modification may be made of such support order without regard to whether the order was issued before, on or after May 9, 1991. In any hearing to modify any support order from another jurisdiction the court or the family support magistrate shall conduct the proceedings in accordance with the procedure set forth in sections 46b–213o to 46b–213q, inclusive. No such support orders may be subject to retroactive modification except that the court or family support magistrate may order modification with respect to any period during which there is a pending motion for a modification of an existing support order from the date of service of notice of such pending motion upon the opposing party pursuant to section 52–50.

(c) In IV–D support cases, as defined in subdivision (13) of subsection (b) of section 46b–231, a copy of any support order established or modified pursuant to this section or, in the case of a motion for modification of an existing support order, a notice of determination that there should be no change in the amount of the support order, shall be provided to each party and the state case registry within fourteen days after issuance of such order or determination.

(1951, Supp. 554b; 1953, Supp. §§ 1112c, 1124c; 1955, Supp. §§ 1445d, 1461d; 1957, P.A. 28; 1958 Rev., § 17–324; 1959, P.A. 42, § 1; 1963, P.A. 73, § 2, eff. July 1, 1963; 1967, P.A. 314, § 12; 1967, P.A. 746, § 5; 1972, P.A. 127, § 30; 1972, P.A. 294, § 22; 1972, June Sp.Sess., P.A. 1, § 11, eff. June 19, 1972; 1974, P.A. 74–183, § 217, eff. Dec. 31, 1974; 1975, P.A. 75–420, § 4, eff. June 25, 1975; 1976, P.A. 76–334, § 7, eff. June 2, 1976; 1976, P.A. 76–435, § 20, eff. June 9, 1976; 1976, P.A. 76–436, § 186, eff. July 1, 1978; 1977, P.A. 77–594, § 4, eff. July 6; 1977, P.A. 77–614, § 70, eff. Oct. 1, 1977; 1977, P.A. 77–614, § 608, eff. Jan. 1, 1979; 1979, P.A. 79–206; 1980, P.A. 80–70, § 2; 1980, P.A. 80–149, § 1, eff. May 5, 1980; 1984, P.A. 84–159, § 3; 1984, P.A. 84–205, § 2; 1986, P.A. 86–359, § 30, eff. Jan. 1, 1987; 1987, P.A. 87–316, § 9; 1987, P.A. 87–421, § 10, eff. July 1, 1987; 1987, P.A. 87–589, § 32, eff. July 9, 1987; 1990, P.A. 90–188, § 2; 1990, P.A. 90–213, § 19, July 1, 1990; 1991, P.A. 91–76, § 2, eff. May 9, 1991; 1991, P.A. 91–391, § 1; 1992, P.A. 92–253, § 3; 1993, P.A. 93–187, § 1; 1993, P.A. 93–262, § 40, eff. July 1, 1993; 1993, P.A. 93–396, § 1; 1994, May Sp.Sess., P.A. 94–5, § 7, eff. July 1, 1994; 1995, P.A. 95–305, § 2, eff. July 1, 1995; 1997, June 18 Sp.Sess., P.A. 97–1, § 51, eff. Jan. 1, 1998; 1997, June 18 Sp.Sess., P.A. 97–2, § 82, eff. July 1, 1997; 1997, June 18 Sp.Sess., P.A. 97–7, § 11, eff. July 1, 1997; 1999, P.A. 99–279, § 28, eff. July 1, 1999; 2000, P.A. 00–99, § 56, eff. Dec. 1, 2000; 2001, P.A. 01–91, § 3; 2002, May 9 Sp.Sess., P.A. 02–7, § 40; 2003, P.A. 03–278, § 70, eff. July 9, 2003; 2003, P.A. 03–258, § 2.)

[1] C.G.S.A. §§ 17b–289 to 17b–303, inclusive, and 1997, Oct. 29 Sp.Sess., P.A. 97–1, § 16.

[2] C.G.S.A. § 17b–261.

§ 17b–746. Appeals from support orders

Any party to an action brought under the provisions of section 17b–745 shall have the right of appeal as in civil actions, except that appeals from a decision of a family support magistrate shall be taken pursuant to subsection (n) of section 46b–231. Any order for support made by the court shall not be affected by an appeal but shall continue in effect until the appeal is decided and thereafter, if the appeal is denied, until changed by further order of the court.

(1957, P.A. 536; 1958 Rev., § 17–325; 1959, P.A. 42, § 2; 1986, P.A. 86–359, § 31, eff. Jan. 1, 1987.)

§ 17b–747. Apportionment of support cost

Any court which commits a child to an institution or custodial agency shall determine the pecuniary ability of either or both parents to contribute to the support of such child and shall order such parent or parents to pay such sum for such support as is consistent with such pecuniary ability. If such commitment is to an institution or custodial agency not supported in whole or in part by the state, such order shall direct such parent or parents to pay to such institution the amount specified in such order, provided such amount shall not exceed the actual cost of the support of such child. Such institution or custodial agency may enforce such order by civil suit or by instituting contempt proceedings in the court issuing such order. If such commitment is to an institution or custodial agency supported in whole or in part by the state, such order shall direct such parent or parents to pay to the state an amount not exceeding the cost to the state of the support of such child in such institution and the Attorney General shall enforce such order by civil suit or by contempt proceedings. If such commitment is to an institution or custodial agency supported in whole or in part by the state, such court shall certify such commitment to the Commissioner of Social Services or his designee. The provisions of this section shall not apply to any commitment to the Newington Children's Hospital.

(1949 Rev., § 2844; 1955, Supp. § 1587d; 1958 Rev., § 17–319; 1961, P.A. 324; 1961, P.A. 425, § 4; 1974, P.A. 74–251, § 18; 1975, P.A. 75–420, § 4, eff. June 25, 1975; 1977, P.A. 77–614, § 608, eff. Jan. 1, 1979; 1993, P.A. 93–262, § 1, eff. July 1, 1993.)

TITLE 19a

PUBLIC HEALTH AND WELL–BEING

CHAPTER 368a

DEPARTMENT OF PUBLIC HEALTH

§ 19a–14c. Provision of outpatient mental health treatment to minors without parental consent

(a) For the purposes of this section, "outpatient mental health treatment" means the treatment of mental disorders, emotional problems or maladjustments with the object of (1) removing, modifying or retarding existing symptoms; (2) improving disturbed patterns of behavior; and (3) promoting positive personality growth and development. Treatment shall not include prescribing or otherwise dispensing any medication which is a legend drug as defined in section 20–571.

(b) A psychiatrist licensed pursuant to chapter 370,[1] a psychologist licensed pursuant to chapter 383,[2] an independent social worker certified pursuant to chapter 383b[3] or a marital and family therapist licensed pursuant to chapter 383a[4] may provide outpatient mental health treatment to a minor without the consent or notification of a parent or guardian at the request of the minor if (1) requiring the consent or notification of a parent or guardian would cause the minor to reject such treatment; (2) the provision of such treatment is clinically indicated; (3) the failure to provide such treatment would be seriously detrimental to the minor's well-being; (4) the minor has knowingly and voluntarily sought such treatment; and (5) in the opinion of the provider of treatment, the minor is mature enough to participate in treatment productively. The provider of such treatment shall document the reasons for any determination made to treat a minor without the consent or notification of a parent or guardian and shall include such documentation in the minor's clinical record, along with a written statement signed by the minor stating that (A) he is voluntarily seeking such treatment; (B) he has discussed with the provider the possibility of involving his parent or guardian in the decision to pursue such treatment; (C) he has determined it is not in his best interest to involve his parent or guardian in such decision; and (D) he has been given adequate opportunity to ask the provider questions about the course of his treatment.

(c) After the sixth session of outpatient mental health treatment provided to a minor pursuant to this section, the provider of such treatment shall notify the minor that the consent, notification or involvement of a parent or guardian is required to continue treatment, unless such a requirement would be seriously detrimental to the minor's well-being. If the provider determines such a requirement would be seriously detrimental to the minor's well-being, he shall document such determination in the minor's clinical record, review such determination every sixth session thereafter and document each such review. If the provider determines such a requirement would no longer be seriously detrimental to the minor's well-being, he shall require the consent, notification or involvement of a parent or guardian as a condition of continuing treatment. No provider shall notify a parent or guardian of treatment provided pursuant to this section or disclose any information concerning such treatment to a parent or guardian without the consent of the minor.

(d) A parent or guardian who is not informed of the provision of outpatient mental health treatment for his minor child pursuant to this section shall not be liable for the costs of the treatment provided.

(1992, P.A. 92–129, § 1; 1995, P.A. 95–289, § 8.)

1 C.G.S.A. § 20–8 et seq.
2 C.G.S.A. § 20–186 et seq.
3 C.G.S.A. § 20–195m et seq.
4 C.G.S.A. § 20–195a et seq.

CHAPTER 368e

MUNICIPAL HEALTH AUTHORITIES

§ 19a–216. Examination and treatment of minor for venereal disease. Confidentiality. Liability for costs

(a) Any municipal health department, state institution or facility, licensed physician or public or private hospital or clinic, may examine and provide treatment for venereal disease for a minor, if the physician or facility is qualified to provide such examination and treatment. The consent of the parents or guardian of the minor shall not be a prerequisite to the examination and treatment. The physician in charge or other appropriate authority of the facility or the licensed physician concerned shall prescribe an appropriate course of treatment for the minor. The fact of consultation, examination and treatment of a minor under the provisions of this section shall be confidential and shall not be divulged by the facility or physician, including the sending of a bill for the services to any person other than the minor, except for purposes of reports under section 19a–215, and except that, if the minor is not more than twelve years of age, the facility or physician shall report the name, age and address of that minor to the Commissioner of Children and Families or his designee who shall proceed thereon as in reports under section 17a–101g.

(b) A minor shall be personally liable for all costs and expenses for services afforded him at his request under this section.

(1958 Rev., § 19–89a; 1967, P.A. 206; 1969, P.A. 24; 1971, P.A. 858, § 5; 1972, P.A. 257, § 1, eff. May 18, 1972; 1973, P.A. 73–205, § 7; 1974, P.A. 74–251, § 6; 1975, P.A. 75–420, § 4, eff. June 25, 1975; 1977, P.A. 77–614, § 521, eff. Jan. 1, 1979; 1982, P.A. 82–43, § 2; 1990, P.A. 90–209, § 23; 1993, P.A. 93–91, § 1, eff. July 1, 1993; 1996, P.A. 96–246, § 29.)

CHAPTER 368i

ANATOMICAL DONATIONS

§ 19a–285. Consent by minor to medical, dental, health or hospital services for child

(a) Any minor who has been married or who has borne a child may give effective consent to medical, dental, health and hospital services for his or her child.

(b) Any such minor who has given effective consent as provided in subsection (a) of this section shall be legally liable for any fees, costs or expenses incurred as a result of the rendering of any such service.

(1958 Rev., § 19–142a; 1971, P.A. 304, §§ 1 to 3; 1973, P.A. 73–616, § 16.)

§ 19a–504a. Continuation or removal of life support system. Determination of death

(a) For the purpose of this section, "life support system" means any mechanical or electronic device utilized by any medical facility in order to replace, assist or supplement the function of any human vital organ or combination of organs.

(b) For purposes of making a determination concerning the continuation or removal of any life support system in a general hospital licensed under section 19a–491, an individual who has sustained either (1) irreversible cessation of circulatory and respiratory functions, or (2) irreversible cessation of all functions of the entire brain, including the brain stem, is dead. Determination of death shall be made in accordance with accepted medical standards.

(1984, P.A. 84–261, §§ 1, 2.)

§ 19a–505a. Hospital to provide forms for birth certificate and affidavit of parentage to parents of child born out of wedlock

Upon the birth of a child born out of wedlock, the hospital or such other institution where such birth occurs shall provide an opportunity for the mother and putative father to complete a birth certificate and an affidavit of parentage.

(1993, P.A. 93–329, § 3, eff. Oct. 1, 1993.)

CHAPTER 368w

REMOVAL OF LIFE SUPPORT SYSTEMS

Section

§ 19a–570. Definitions

For purposes of this section and sections 19a–571 to 19a–580c, inclusive:

(1) "Life support system" means any medical procedure or intervention which, when applied to an individual, would serve only to postpone the moment of death or maintain the individual in a state of permanent unconsciousness. In these circumstances, such procedures shall include, but are not limited to, mechanical or electronic devices including artificial means of providing nutrition or hydration;

(2) "Beneficial medical treatment" includes the use of medically appropriate treatment including surgery,

treatment, medication and the utilization of artificial technology to sustain life;

(3) "Terminal condition" means the final stage of an incurable or irreversible medical condition which, without the administration of a life support system, will result in death within a relatively short time, in the opinion of the attending physician;

(4) "Permanently unconscious" includes permanent coma and persistent vegetative state and means an irreversible condition in which the individual is at no time aware of himself or the environment and shows no behavioral response to the environment;

(5) "Health care agent" means an adult person to whom authority to convey health care decisions is delegated in a written document by another adult person, known as the principal;

(6) "Incapacitated" means being unable to understand and appreciate the nature and consequences of health care decisions, including the benefits and disadvantages of such treatment, and to reach and communicate an informed decision regarding the treatment;

(7) "Living will" means a written statement in compliance with section 19a–575a containing a declarant's wishes concerning any aspect of his health care, including the withholding or withdrawal of life support systems;

(8) "Next of kin" means any member of the following classes of persons, in the order of priority listed: (A) The spouse of the patient; (B) an adult son or daughter of the patient; (C) either parent of the patient; (D) an adult brother or sister of the patient; and (E) a grandparent of the patient;

(9) "Attending physician" means the physician selected by, or assigned to, the patient and who has primary responsibility for the treatment and care of the patient.

(1985, P.A. 85–606, § 1; 1991, P.A. 91–283, § 1; 1993, P.A. 93–407, § 3.)

§ 19a–571. Liability re removal of life support system of incapacitated patient. Consideration of wishes of patient

(a) Subject to the provisions of subsection (c) of this section, any physician licensed under chapter 370 [1] or any licensed medical facility who or which withholds, removes or causes the removal of a life support system of an incapacitated patient shall not be liable for damages in any civil action or subject to prosecution in any criminal proceeding for such withholding or removal, provided (1) the decision to withhold or remove such life support system is based on the best medical judgment of the attending physician in accordance with the usual and customary standards of medical practice; (2) the attending physician deems the patient to be in a terminal condition or, in consultation with a physician qualified to make a neurological diagnosis who has examined the patient, deems the patient to be permanently unconscious; and (3) the attending physician has considered the patient's wishes concerning the withholding or withdrawal of life support systems. In the determination of the wishes of the patient, the attending physician shall consider the wishes as expressed by a document executed in accordance with sections 19a–575 and 19a–575a, if any such document is presented to, or in the possession of, the attending physician at the time the decision to withhold or terminate a life support system is made. If the wishes of the patient have not been expressed in a living will the attending physician shall determine the wishes of the patient by consulting any statement made by the patient directly to the attending physician and, if available, the patient's health care agent, the patient's next of kin, the patient's legal guardian or conservator, if any, any person designated by the patient in accordance with section 1–56r and any other person to whom the patient has communicated his wishes, if the attending physician has knowledge of such person. All persons acting on behalf of the patient shall act in good faith. If the attending physician does not deem the incapacitated patient to be in a terminal condition or permanently unconscious, beneficial medical treatment including nutrition and hydration must be provided.

(b) A physician qualified to make a neurological diagnosis who is consulted by the attending physician pursuant to subdivision (2) of subsection (a) of this section shall not be liable for damages or subject to criminal prosecution for any determination made in accordance with the usual and customary standards of medical practice.

(c) In the case of an infant, as defined in 45 CFR 1340.15 (b), the physician or licensed medical facility shall comply with the provisions of 45 CFR 1340.15 (b)(2) in addition to the provisions of subsection (a) of this section.

(1985, P.A. 85–606, § 2; 1991, P.A. 91–283, § 2; 1991, June Sp.Sess., P.A. 91–11, § 19, eff. Oct. 1, 1991; 1993, P.A. 93–407, § 5; 2001, P.A. 01–195, § 162, eff. July 11, 2001; 2002, P.A. 02–105, § 7.)

[1] C.G.S.A. § 20–8 et seq.

§ 19a–572. Failure to execute document creates no presumption re wishes of patient

Sections 19a–571 and 19a–573 to 19a–575a, inclusive, create no presumption concerning the wishes of a patient who has not executed a document as described in sections 19a–575 and 19a–575a.

(1985, P.A. 85–606, § 3; 1993, P.A. 93–407, § 6.)

§ 19a–573. Comfort care and pain alleviation to be provided. Documents executed prior to October 1, 1991

(a) Notwithstanding the provisions of sections 19a–571, 19a–572, 19a–574, 19a–575, 19a–575a,

19a–577, 19a–580a and 19a–580b, comfort care and pain alleviation shall be provided in all cases.

(b) Any document executed prior to October 1, 1991, in accordance with section 19a–575, revision of 1958, revised to January 1, 1991, and section 19a–575a shall not be invalidated by any provision of public act 91–283.[1] Any document executed prior to October 1, 1991, shall not be presumed to prohibit withholding or withdrawal of life support systems as defined in section 19a–570, revision of 1958, revised to January 1, 1991, unless such prior document specifically addresses such withholding or withdrawal.

(1985, P.A. 85–606, § 4; 1991, P.A. 91–283, § 4; 1993, P.A. 93–407, § 7.)

[1] 1991, P.A. 91–283, §§ 1, 2, 4, 5, amended C.G.S.A. §§ 19a–570, 19a–571, 19a–573, and 19a–575, respectively. Gen.St., Rev. to 1993, classified 1991, P.A. 91–283, §§ 3, 6, 7, 10, 9, 14, 8, 11, 13, and 12, as C.G.S.A. §§ 19a–576, 19a–577, 19a–578, 19a–579 to 19a–579b, and 19a–580 to 19a–580c, respectively.

§ 19a–574. Nonapplicability to pregnant patient

The provisions of sections 19a–571 to 19a–573, inclusive, 19a–575 and 19a–575a shall not apply to a pregnant patient.

(1985, P.A. 85–606, § 5; 1993, P.A. 93–407, § 8.)

§ 19a–575. Form of document

Any person eighteen years of age or older may execute a document which shall contain directions as to specific life support systems which such person chooses to have administered. Such document shall be signed and dated by the maker with at least two witnesses and may be in substantially the following form:

DOCUMENT CONCERNING WITHHOLDING OR WITHDRAWAL OF LIFE SUPPORT SYSTEMS.

If the time comes when I am incapacitated to the point when I can no longer actively take part in decisions for my own life, and am unable to direct my physician as to my own medical care, I wish this statement to stand as a testament of my wishes.

"I, ... (Name), request that, if my condition is deemed terminal or if it is determined that I will be permanently unconscious, I be allowed to die and not be kept alive through life support systems. By terminal condition, I mean that I have an incurable or irreversible medical condition which, without the administration of life support systems, will, in the opinion of my attending physician, result in death within a relatively short time. By permanently unconscious I mean that I am in a permanent coma or persistent vegetative state which is an irreversible condition in which I am at no time aware of myself or the environment and show no behavioral response to the environment. The life support systems which I do not want include, but are not limited to:

Artificial respiration

Cardiopulmonary resuscitation

Artificial means of providing nutrition and hydration

(Cross out and initial life support systems you want administered)

I do not intend any direct taking of my life, but only that my dying not be unreasonably prolonged."

Other specific requests:

"This request is made, after careful reflection, while I am of sound mind."

.... (Signature)
.... (Date)

This document was signed in our presence, by the above-named .... (Name) who appeared to be eighteen years of age or older, of sound mind and able to understand the nature and consequences of health care decisions at the time the document was signed.

.... (Witness)
.... (Address)
.... (Witness)
.... (Address)

(1985, P.A. 85–606, § 6; 1991, P.A. 91–283, § 5; 1992, May Sp.Sess., P.A. 92–11, § 2, eff. June 1, 1992.)

§ 19a–575a. Form of document re health care instructions, appointment of health care agent, attorney-in-fact for health care decisions, designation of conservator of the person for future incapacity and anatomical gift

Any person eighteen years of age or older may execute a document which contains health care instructions, the appointment of a health care agent, the appointment of an attorney-in-fact for health care decisions, the designation of a conservator of the person for future incapacity and a document of anatomical gift. Any such document shall be signed and dated by the maker with at least two witnesses and may be in the substantially following form:

THESE ARE MY HEALTH CARE INSTRUCTIONS.
MY APPOINTMENT OF A HEALTH CARE AGENT,
MY APPOINTMENT OF AN ATTORNEY–IN–FACT
FOR HEALTH CARE DECISIONS,
THE DESIGNATION OF MY CONSERVATOR OF THE PERSON
FOR MY FUTURE INCAPACITY
AND
MY DOCUMENT OF ANATOMICAL GIFT

To any physician who is treating me: These are my health care instructions including those concerning the withholding or withdrawal of life support systems, together with the appointment of my health care agent and my attorney-in-fact for health care decisions, the designation of my conservator of the person for future incapacity and my document of anatomical gift. As my physician, you may rely on any decision made by my health care agent, attorney-in-fact for health care decisions or conservator of my person, if I am unable to make a decision for myself.

I, ..., the author of this document, request that, if my condition is deemed terminal or if I am determined to be permanently unconscious, I be allowed to die and not be kept alive through life support systems. By terminal condition, I mean that I have an incurable or irreversible medical condition which, without the administration of life support systems, will, in the opinion of my attending physician, result in death within a relatively short time. By permanently unconscious I mean that I am in a permanent coma or persistent vegetative state which is an irreversible condition in which I am at no time aware of myself or the environment and show no behavioral response to the environment. The life support systems which I do not want include, but are not limited to: Artificial respiration, cardiopulmonary resuscitation and artificial means of providing nutrition and hydration. I do want sufficient pain medication to maintain my physical comfort. I do not intend any direct taking of my life, but only that my dying not be unreasonably prolonged.

I appoint . . . . to be my health care agent and my attorney-in-fact for health care decisions. If my attending physician determines that I am unable to understand and appreciate the nature and consequences of health care decisions and unable to reach and communicate an informed decision regarding treatment, my health care agent and attorney-in-fact for health care decisions is authorized to:

(1) Convey to my physician my wishes concerning the withholding or removal of life support systems;

(2) Take whatever actions are necessary to ensure that any wishes are given effect;

(3) Consent, refuse or withdraw consent to any medical treatment as long as such action is consistent with my wishes concerning the withholding or removal of life support systems; and

(4) Consent to any medical treatment designed solely for the purpose of maintaining physical comfort.

If . . . . is unwilling or unable to serve as my health care agent and my attorney-in-fact for health care decisions, I appoint . . . . to be my alternative health care agent and my attorney-in-fact for health care decisions.

If a conservator of my person should need to be appointed, I designate . . . . be appointed my conservator. If . . . . is unwilling or unable to serve as my conservator, I designate . . . . No bond shall be required of either of them in any jurisdiction.

I hereby make this anatomical gift, if medically acceptable, to take effect upon my death.

I give: (check one)

. . . . (1) any needed organs or parts
. . . . (2) only the following organs or parts

to be donated for: (check one)

(1) . . . . any of the purposes stated in subsection (a) of section 19a–279f of the general statutes
(2) . . . . these limited purposes . . . .

These requests, appointments, and designations are made after careful reflection, while I am of sound mind. Any party receiving a duly executed copy or facsimile of this document may rely upon it unless such party has received actual notice of my revocation of it.

Date . . . ., 20. . .   . . L.S.

This document was signed in our presence by . . . . the author of this document, who appeared to be eighteen years of age or older, of sound mind and able to understand the nature and consequences of health care decisions at the time this document was signed. The author appeared to be under no improper influence. We have subscribed this document in the author's presence and at the author's request and in the presence of each other.

. . . .	. . . .
(Witness)	(Witness)
. . . .	. . . .
(Number and Street)	(Number and Street)
. . . .	. . . .
(City, State and Zip Code)	(City, State and Zip Code)

STATE OF CONNECTICUT)
) ss. . . . .
COUNTY OF . . . .)

We, the subscribing witnesses, being duly sworn, say that we witnessed the execution of these health care instructions, the appointments of a health care agent and an attorney-in-fact, the designation of a conservator for future incapacity and a document of anatomical gift by the author of this document; that the author subscribed, published and declared the same to be the author's instructions, appointments and designation in our presence; that we thereafter subscribed the document as witnesses in the author's presence, at the author's request, and in the presence of each other; that at the time of the execution of said document the author appeared to us to be eighteen years of age or older, of sound mind, able to understand the nature and consequences of said document, and under no improper influence, and we make this affidavit at the author's request this . . . . day of . . . ., 20. .

. . . .

(Witness) (Witness)

Subscribed and sworn to before me this .... day of .... 20..

Commissioner of the Superior Court
Notary Public
My commission expires: ....

(Print or type name of all persons signing under all signatures).

(1993, P.A. 93–407, § 1.)

§ 19a–576. Appointment of health care agent

(a) Any person eighteen years of age or older may appoint a health care agent by executing a document in accordance with section 19a–575a or section 19a–577, signed and dated by such person in the presence of two adult witnesses who shall also sign the document. The person appointed as agent shall not act as witness to the execution of such document or sign such document.

(b) For persons who reside in facilities operated or licensed by the Department of Mental Health and Addiction Services, at least one witness shall be an individual who is not affiliated with the facility and at least one witness shall be a physician or clinical psychologist with specialized training in treating mental illness.

(c) For persons who reside in facilities operated or licensed by the department of mental retardation, at least one witness shall be an individual who is not affiliated with the facility and at least one witness shall be a physician or clinical psychologist with specialized training in developmental disabilities.

(d) An operator, administrator, or employee of a hospital, residential care home, rest home with nursing supervision, or chronic and convalescent nursing home may not be appointed as a health care agent by any person who, at the time of the appointment, is a patient or a resident of, or has applied for admission to, one of the foregoing facilities. An administrator or employee of a government agency which is financially responsible for a person's medical care may not be appointed as a health care agent for such person. This restriction shall not apply if such operator, administrator or employee is related to the principal by blood, marriage or adoption.

(e) A physician shall not act as both agent for a principal and attending physician for the principal.

(1991, P.A. 91–283, § 3; 1993, P.A. 93–407, § 2; 1994, May 25 Sp.Sess., P.A. 94–1, § 22, eff. July 1, 1994; 1995, P.A. 95–257, § 11, eff. July 1, 1995; 1997, P.A. 97–112, § 2.)

§ 19a–577. Form of document re appointment of health care agent

(a) Any person eighteen years of age or older may execute a document that may, but need not be in substantially the following form:

DOCUMENT CONCERNING THE APPOINTMENT OF HEALTH CARE AGENT

"I appoint .... (Name) to be my health care agent. If my attending physician determines that I am unable to understand and appreciate the nature and consequences of health care decisions and to reach and communicate an informed decision regarding treatment, my health care agent is authorized to:

(1) Convey to my physician my wishes concerning the withholding or removal of life support systems.

(2) Take whatever actions are necessary to ensure that my wishes are given effect.

If this person is unwilling or unable to serve as my health care agent, I appoint .... (Name) to be my alternative health care agent."

"This request is made, after careful reflection, while I am of sound mind."

.... (Signature)

.... (Date)

This document was signed in our presence, by the above-named .... (Name) who appeared to be eighteen years of age or older, of sound mind and able to understand the nature and consequences of health care decisions at the time the document was signed.

.... (Witness)

.... (Address)

.... (Witness)

.... (Address)

(1991, P.A. 91–283, § 6.)

§ 19a–578. Proof of living will document or document appointing health care agent out of court. Physician to make documents and oral communications re health care and withdrawal of life support systems part of medical record

(a) Any or all of the attesting witnesses to any living will document or any document appointing a health care agent may, at the request of the declarant, make and sign an affidavit before any officer authorized to administer oaths in or out of this state, stating such facts as they would be required to testify to in court to prove such living will. The affidavit shall be written on the living will document, or if that is impracticable, on some paper attached thereto. The sworn statement of any such witness so taken shall be accepted by the court of probate as if it had been taken before such court.

(b) A physician or other health care provider who is furnished with a copy of a written living will or appointment of health care agent shall make it a part of the declarant's medical record. A physician or other health care provider shall also record in the patient's medical record any oral communication concerning any aspect of his health care, including the withholding or withdrawal of life support systems, made by the patient directly to the physician or other health care provider or to the patient's health care agent, legal guardian, conservator, next-of-kin or person designated in accordance with section 1–56r.

(1991, P.A. 91–283, § 7; 2002, P.A. 02–105, § 8.)

§ 19a–579. Living will or appointment of health care agent becomes operative, when

A living will or appointment of health care agent becomes operative when (1) the document is furnished to the attending physician and (2) the declarant is determined by the attending physician to be incapacitated.

(1991, P.A. 91–283, § 10.)

§ 19a–579a. Revocation of living will or appointment of health care agent. Absence of knowledge of revocation

(a) A living will or appointment of health care agent may be revoked at any time and in any manner by the declarant, without regard to the declarant's mental or physical condition.

(b) The attending physician or other health care provider shall make the revocation a part of the declarant's medical record.

(c) In the absence of knowledge of the revocation either of a living will or an appointment of health care agent, a person is not subject to civil or criminal liability or discipline for unprofessional conduct for carrying out the living will pursuant to the requirements of sections 19a–570, 19a–571, 19a–573 and 19a–575 to 19a–580c, inclusive.

(1991, P.A. 91–283, § 9; 1993, P.A. 93–407, § 9.)

§ 19a–579b. Revocation of appointment of spouse as health care agent upon divorce or legal separation

The appointment of the principal's spouse as health care agent shall be revoked upon the divorce or legal separation of the principal and spouse or upon the annulment or dissolution of their marriage, unless the principal specifies otherwise.

(1991, P.A. 91–283, § 14.)

§ 19a–580. Physician to notify certain persons prior to removal of life support system

Within a reasonable time prior to withholding or causing the removal of any life support system pursuant to sections 19a–570, 19a–571, 19a–573 and 19a–575 to 19a–580c, inclusive, the attending physician shall make reasonable efforts to notify the individual's health care agent, next-of-kin, legal guardian, conservator or person designated in accordance with section 1–56r, if available.

(1991, P.A. 91–283, § 8; 1993, P.A. 93–407, § 10; 2002, P.A. 02–105, § 9.)

§ 19a–580a. Transfer of patient when attending physician or health care provider unwilling to comply with wishes of patient

An attending physician or health care provider who is unwilling to comply with the wishes of the patient or sections 19a–570, 19a–571, 19a–573 and 19a–575 to 19a–580c, inclusive, shall, as promptly as practicable, take all reasonable steps to transfer care of the patient to a physician or health care provider who is willing to comply with the wishes of the patient and said sections.

(1991, P.A. 91–283, § 11; 1993, P.A. 93–407, § 11.)

§ 19a–580b. Prohibition re requiring living will or appointment of health care agent as condition of treatment or health benefits

No physician, health care provider or health care insurer shall require a person to execute a living will or appoint a health care agent as a condition of treatment or receiving health care benefits.

(1991, P.A. 91–283, § 13.)

§ 19a–580c. Probate Court to resolve disputes re provisions concerning withholding or removal of life support system

The probate court for the district in which the person is domiciled or is located at the time of the dispute shall have jurisdiction over any dispute concerning the meaning or application of any provision of sections 19a–570, 19a–571, 19a–573 and 19a–575 to 19a–580c, inclusive. With respect to any communication of a patient's wishes other than by means of a document executed in accordance with section 19a–575a the court shall consider whether there is clear and convincing evidence of such communication.

(1991, P.A. 91–283, § 12; 1993, P.A. 93–407, § 12.)

§ 19a–580d. "Do not resuscitate" orders. Regulations

The Department of Public Health shall adopt regulations, in accordance with chapter 54,[1] to provide for a system governing the recognition and transfer of "do not resuscitate" orders between health care institutions licensed pursuant to chapter 368v [2] and upon intervention by emergency medical services providers certified or licensed pursuant to chapter 368d.[3] The regulations shall include, but not be limited to, procedures concerning the use of "do not resuscitate" bracelets. The regulations shall specify that, upon request of the patient or his authorized representative, the physician who issued the "do not resuscitate" order shall assist the patient or his authorized representative in utilizing the system. The regulations shall not limit the authority of the Commissioner of Mental Retardation under subsection (g) of section 17a–238 concerning orders applied to persons receiving services under the direction of the Commissioner of Mental Retardation.

(1995, P.A. 95–113; 1995, P.A. 95–257, §§ 12, 21, eff. July 1, 1995.)

1 C.G.S.A. § 4–166 et seq.
2 C.G.S.A. § 19a–490 et seq.
3 C.G.S.A. § 19a–175 et seq.

CHAPTER 368x

AIDS TESTING AND MEDICAL INFORMATION

§ 19a–592. Testing and treatment of minor for HIV or AIDS. Confidentiality. Liability for costs

(a) Any licensed physician may examine and provide treatment for human immunodeficiency virus infection, or acquired immune deficiency syndrome for a minor, only with the consent of the parents or guardian of the minor unless the physician determines that notification of the parents or guardian of the minor will result in treatment being denied or the physician determines the minor will not seek, pursue or continue treatment if the parents or guardian are notified and the minor requests that his parents or guardian not be notified. The physician shall fully document the reasons for the determination to provide treatment without the consent or notification of the parents or guardian of the minor and shall include such documentation, signed by the minor, in the minor's clinical record. The fact of consultation, examination and treatment of a minor under the provisions of this section shall be confidential and shall not be divulged without the minor's consent, including the sending of a bill for the services to any person other than the minor until the physician consults with the minor regarding the sending of a bill.

(b) A minor shall be personally liable for all costs and expenses for services afforded him at his request under this section.

(1992, P.A. 92–119, § 1.)

CHAPTER 368y

ABORTION

§ 19a–600. Definitions

For the purposes of sections 19a–601 and 19a–602:

(1) "Counselor" means: (A) A psychiatrist, (B) a psychologist licensed under chapter 383,[1] (C) clinical social worker licensed under chapter 383b,[2] (D) a marital and family therapist licensed under chapter 383a,[3] (E) an ordained member of the clergy, (F) a physician's assistant licensed under section 20–12b, (G) a nurse-midwife licensed under chapter 377,[4] (H) a certified guidance counselor, (I) a registered professional nurse licensed under chapter 378,[5] or (J) a practical nurse licensed under chapter 378.

(2) "Minor" means a person who is less than sixteen years of age.

(1990, P.A. 90–113, § 1; 1995, P.A. 95–116, § 7; 1995, P.A. 95–289, § 9; 1996, P.A. 96–180, § 63, eff. June 3, 1996.)

1 C.G.S.A. § 20–186 et seq.
2 C.G.S.A. § 20–195m et seq.
3 C.G.S.A. § 20–195a et seq.
4 C.G.S.A. § 20–86a et seq.
5 C.G.S.A. § 20–87a et seq.

§ 19a–601. Information and counseling for minors required. Medical emergency exception

(a) Prior to the performance of an abortion upon a minor, a physician or counselor shall provide pregnancy information and counseling in accordance with this section in a manner and language that will be understood by the minor. The physician or counselor shall:

(1) Explain that the information being given to the minor is being given objectively and is not intended to coerce, persuade or induce the minor to choose to have an abortion or to carry the pregnancy to term;

(2) Explain that the minor may withdraw a decision to have an abortion at any time before the abortion is performed or may reconsider a decision not to have an abortion at any time within the time period during which an abortion may legally be performed;

(3) Explain to the minor the alternative choices available for managing the pregnancy, including: (A) Carrying the pregnancy to term and keeping the child, (B) carrying the pregnancy to term and placing the child for adoption, placing the child with a relative or obtaining voluntary foster care for the child, and (C) having an abortion, and explain that public and private agencies are available to assist the minor with whichever alternative she chooses and that a list of these agencies and the services available from each will be provided if the minor requests;

(4) Explain that public and private agencies are available to provide birth control information and that a list of these agencies and the services available from each will be provided if the minor requests;

(5) Discuss the possibility of involving the minor's parents, guardian or other adult family members in the

minor's decision-making concerning the pregnancy and whether the minor believes that involvement would be in the minor's best interests; and

(6) Provide adequate opportunity for the minor to ask any questions concerning the pregnancy, abortion, child care and adoption, and provide information the minor seeks or, if the person cannot provide the information, indicate where the minor can receive the information.

(b) After the person provides the information and counseling to a minor as required by this section, such person shall have the minor sign and date a form stating that:

(1) The minor has received information on alternatives to abortion and that there are agencies that will provide assistance and that a list of these agencies and the services available from each will be provided if the minor requests;

(2) The minor has received an explanation that the minor may withdraw an abortion decision or reconsider a decision to carry a pregnancy to term;

(3) The alternatives available for managing the pregnancy have been explained to the minor;

(4) The minor has received an explanation about agencies available to provide birth control information and that a list of these agencies and the services available from each will be provided if the minor requests;

(5) The minor has discussed with the person providing the information and counseling the possibility of involving the minor's parents, guardian or other adult family members in the minor's decision-making about the pregnancy;

(6) If applicable, the minor has determined that not involving the minor's parents, guardian or other adult family members is in the minor's best interests; and

(7) The minor has been given an adequate opportunity to ask questions.

(c) The person providing the information and counseling shall also sign and date the form and shall include such person's business address and business telephone number. The person shall keep a copy for such minor's medical record and shall give the form to the minor or, if the minor requests and if such person is not the attending physician, transmit the form to the minor's attending physician. Such medical record shall be maintained as otherwise provided by law.

(d) The provision of pregnancy information and counseling by a physician or counselor which is evidenced in writing containing the information and statements provided in this section and which is signed by the minor shall be presumed to be evidence of compliance with the requirements of this section.

(e) The requirements of this section shall not apply when, in the best medical judgment of the physician based on the facts of the case before him, a medical emergency exists that so complicates the pregnancy or the health, safety or well-being of the minor as to require an immediate abortion. A physician who does not comply with the requirements of this section by reason of this exception shall state in the medical record of the abortion the medical indications on which his judgment was based.

(1990, P.A. 90–113, § 2.)

§ 19a–602. Termination of pregnancy prior to viability. Abortion after viability prohibited; exception

(a) The decision to terminate a pregnancy prior to the viability of the fetus shall be solely that of the pregnant woman in consultation with her physician.

(b) No abortion may be performed upon a pregnant woman after viability of the fetus except when necessary to preserve the life or health of the pregnant woman.

(1990, P.A. 90–113, § 3.)

§§ 19a–603 to 19a–609. Reserved for future use

*

TITLE 31

LABOR

CHAPTER 557

EMPLOYMENT REGULATION

PART II. PROTECTION OF EMPLOYEES

§ 31–51kk. Family and medical leave: Definitions

As used in sections 31–51kk to 31–51qq, inclusive:

(1) "Eligible employee" means an employee who has been employed (A) for at least twelve months by the employer with respect to whom leave is requested; and (B) for at least one thousand hours of service with such employer during the twelve-month period preceding the first day of the leave;

(2) "Employ" includes to allow or permit to work;

(3) "Employee" means any person engaged in service to an employer in the business of the employer;

(4) "Employer" means a person engaged in any activity, enterprise or business who employs seventy-five or more employees, and includes any person who acts, directly or indirectly, in the interest of an employer to any of the employees of such employer and any successor in interest of an employer, but shall not include the state, a municipality, a local or regional board of education, or a private or parochial elementary or secondary school. The number of employees of an employer shall be determined on October first annually;

(5) "Employment benefits" means all benefits provided or made available to employees by an employer, including group life insurance, health insurance, disability insurance, sick leave, annual leave, educational benefits and pensions, regardless of whether such benefits are provided by practice or written policy of an employer or through an "employee benefit plan", as defined in Section 1002(3) of Title 29 of the United States Code;[1]

(6) "Health care provider" means (A) a doctor of medicine or osteopathy who is authorized to practice medicine or surgery by the state in which the doctor practices; (B) a podiatrist, dentist, psychologist, optometrist or chiropractor authorized to practice by the state in which such person practices and performs within the scope of the authorized practice; (C) an advanced practice registered nurse, nurse practitioner, nurse midwife or clinical social worker authorized to practice by the state in which such person practices and performs within the scope of the authorized practice; (D) Christian Science practitioners listed with the First Church of Christ, Scientist in Boston, Massachusetts; (E) any health care provider from whom an employer or a group health plan's benefits manager will accept certification of the existence of a serious health condition to substantiate a claim for benefits; (F) a health care provider as defined in subparagraphs (A) to (E), inclusive, of this subdivision who practices in a country other than the United States, who is licensed to practice in accordance with the laws and regulations of that country; or (G) such other health care provider as the Labor Commissioner determines, performing within the scope of the authorized practice. The commissioner may utilize any determinations made pursuant to chapter 568.[2]

(7) "Parent" means a biological parent, foster parent, adoptive parent, stepparent or legal guardian of an eligible employee or an eligible employee's spouse, or an individual who stood in loco parentis to an employee when the employee was a son or daughter;

(8) "Person" means one or more individuals, partnerships, associations, corporations, business trusts, legal representatives or organized groups of persons;

(9) "Reduced leave schedule" means a leave schedule that reduces the usual number of hours per workweek, or hours per workday, of an employee;

(10) "Serious health condition" means an illness, injury, impairment, or physical or mental condition that involves (A) inpatient care in a hospital, hospice, nursing home or residential medical care facility; or (B) continuing treatment, including outpatient treatment, by a health care provider;

(11) "Son or daughter" means a biological, adopted or foster child, stepchild, legal ward, or child of a person standing in loco parentis, who is (A) under eighteen years of age; or (B) eighteen years of age or older and incapable of self-care because of a mental or physical disability; and

(12) "Spouse" means a husband or wife, as the case may be.

(1996, P.A. 96–140, § 1, eff. Jan. 1, 1997.)

1 29 U.S.C.A. § 1002.

2 C.G.S.A. § 31–275 et seq.

§ 31–51*ll*. Family and medical leave: Length of leave. Eligibility

(a) Subject to section 31–51mm, an eligible employee shall be entitled to a total of sixteen workweeks of leave during any twenty-four-month period, such twenty-four-month period to be determined utilizing any one of the following methods: (1) Consecutive calendar years; (2) any fixed twenty-four-month period, such as two consecutive fiscal years or a twenty-four-month period measured forward from an employee's first date of employment; (3) a twenty-four-month period measured forward from an employee's first day of leave taken under sections 31–51kk to 31–51qq, inclusive; or (4) a rolling twenty-four-month period measured backward from an employee's first day of leave taken under sections 31–51kk to 31–51qq, inclusive, for one or more of the following:

(1) Upon the birth of a son or daughter of the employee;

(2) Upon the placement of a son or daughter with the employee for adoption or foster care;

(3) In order to care for the spouse, or a son, daughter or parent of the employee, if such spouse, son, daughter or parent has a serious health condition; or

(4) Because of a serious health condition of the employee.

(b) Entitlement to leave under subdivision (1) or (2) of subsection (a) of this section may accrue prior to the birth or placement of a son or daughter when such leave is required because of such impending birth or placement.

(c) (1) Leave under subdivision (1) or (2) of subsection (a) of this section for the birth or placement of a son or daughter may not be taken by an employee intermittently or on a reduced leave schedule unless the employee and the employer agree otherwise. Subject to subdivision (2) of this subsection concerning an alternative position, subdivision (2) of subsection (f) of this section concerning the duties of the employee and subdivision (5) of subsection (b) of section 31–51mm concerning sufficient certification, leave under subdivision (3) or (4) of subsection (a) of this section for a serious health condition may be taken intermittently or on a reduced leave schedule when medically necessary. The taking of leave intermittently or on a reduced leave schedule pursuant to this subsection shall not result in a reduction of the total amount of leave to which the employee is entitled under subsection (a) of this section beyond the amount of leave actually taken.

(2) If an employee requests intermittent leave or leave on a reduced leave schedule under subdivision (3) or (4) of subsection (a) of this section that is foreseeable based on planned medical treatment, the employer may require the employee to transfer temporarily to an available alternative position offered by the employer for which the employee is qualified and that (A) has equivalent pay and benefits and (B) better accommodates recurring periods of leave than the regular employment position of the employee, provided the exercise of this authority shall not conflict with any provision of a collective bargaining agreement between such employer and a labor organization which is the collective bargaining representative of the unit of which the employee is a part.

(d) Except as provided in subsection (e) of this section, leave granted under subsection (a) of this section may consist of unpaid leave.

(e) (1) If an employer provides paid leave for fewer than sixteen workweeks, the additional weeks of leave necessary to attain the sixteen workweeks of leave required under sections 5–248a and 31–51kk to 31–51qq, inclusive, may be provided without compensation.

(2) (A) An eligible employee may elect, or an employer may require the employee, to substitute any of the accrued paid vacation leave, personal leave or family leave of the employee for leave provided under subdivision (1), (2) or (3) of subsection (a) of this section for any part of this sixteen-week period of such leave under said subsection.

(B) An eligible employee may elect, or an employer may require the employee, to substitute any of the accrued paid vacation leave, personal leave, or medical or sick leave of the employee for leave provided under subdivision (3) or (4) of subsection (a) of this section for any part of the sixteen-week period of such leave under said subsection, except that nothing in section 5–248a or 31–51kk to 31–51qq, inclusive,[1] shall require an employer to provide paid sick leave or paid medical leave in any situation in which such employer would not normally provide any such paid leave.

(f) (1) In any case in which the necessity for leave under subdivision (1) or (2) of subsection (a) of this section is foreseeable based on an expected birth or placement of a son or daughter, the employee shall provide the employer with not less than thirty days' notice, before the date of the leave is to begin, of the employee's intention to take leave under said subdivision (1) or (2), except that if the date of the birth or placement of a son or daughter requires leave to begin in less than thirty days, the employee shall provide such notice as is practicable.

(2) In any case in which the necessity for leave under subdivision (3) or (4) of subsection (a) of this section is foreseeable based on planned medical treatment, the employee (A) shall make a reasonable effort to schedule the treatment so as not to disrupt unduly the operations of the employer, subject to the approval of the health care provider of the employee or the health care provider of the son, daughter, spouse or parent of the employee, as appropriate; and (B) shall provide the employer with not less than thirty days' notice, before the date the leave is to begin, of the employee's intention to take leave under said subdivision (3) or (4), except that if the date of the treatment requires leave to begin in less than thirty days, the employee shall provide such notice as is practicable.

(g) In any case in which a husband and wife entitled to leave under subsection (a) of this section are employed by the same employer, the aggregate number of workweeks of leave to which both may be entitled may be limited to sixteen workweeks during any twenty-four-month period, if such leave is taken: (1) Under subdivision (1) or (2) of subsection (a) of this section; or (2) to care for a sick parent under subdivision (3) of said subsection.

(h) Unpaid leave taken pursuant to sections 5–248a and 31–51kk to 31–51qq, inclusive, shall not be construed to affect an employee's qualification for exemption under chapter 558.[2]

(i) Notwithstanding the provisions of sections 5–248a and 31–51kk to 31–51qq, inclusive, all further rights granted by federal law shall remain in effect.

(1996, P.A. 96–140, § 2, eff. Jan. 1, 1997; 2003, P.A. 03–213, § 2.)

1 So in Gen.St., Rev. to 1997. Originally read "this act", which was translated elsewhere throughout the section as "sections 5–248a and 31–51kk to 31–51qq, inclusive".

2 C.G.S.A. § 31–58 et seq.

§ 31–51mm. Family and medical leave: Certification

(a) An employer may require that request for leave based on a serious health condition in subdivision (3) or (4) of subsection (a) of section 31–51*ll* be supported by a certification issued by the health care provider of the eligible employee or of the son, daughter, spouse or parent of the employee, as appropriate. The employee shall provide, in a timely manner, a copy of such certification to the employer.

(b) Certification provided under subsection (a) of this section shall be sufficient if it states:

(1) The date on which the serious health condition commenced;

(2) The probable duration of the condition;

(3) The appropriate medical facts within the knowledge of the health care provider regarding the condition;

(4) (A) For purposes of leave under subdivision (3) of subsection (a) of section 31–51*ll*, a statement that the eligible employee is needed to care for the son, daughter, spouse or parent and an estimate of the amount of time that such employee needs to care for the son, daughter, spouse or parent; and (B) for purposes of leave under subdivision (4) of subsection (a) of section 31–51*ll*, a statement that the employee is unable to perform the functions of the position of the employee;

(5) In the case of certification for intermittent leave or leave on a reduced leave schedule for planned medical treatment, the dates on which such treatment is expected to be given and the duration of such treatment;

(6) In the case of certification for intermittent leave or leave on a reduced leave schedule under subdivision (4) of subsection (a) of section 31–51*ll*, a statement of the medical necessity of the intermittent leave or leave on a reduced leave schedule, and the expected duration of the intermittent leave or reduced leave schedule; and

(7) In the case of certification for intermittent leave or leave on a reduced leave schedule under subdivision (3) of subsection (a) of section 31–51*ll*, a statement that the employee's intermittent leave or leave on a reduced leave schedule is necessary for the care of the son, daughter, parent or spouse who has a serious health condition, or will assist in their recovery, and the expected duration and schedule of the intermittent leave or reduced leave schedule.

(c) (1) In any case in which the employer has reason to doubt the validity of the certification provided under subsection (a) of this section for leave under subdivision (3) or (4) of subsection (a) of section 31–51*ll*, the employer may require, at the expense of the employer, that the eligible employee obtain the opinion of a second health care provider designated or approved by the employer concerning any information certified under subsection (b) of this section for such leave.

(2) A health care provider designated or approved under subdivision (1) of this subsection shall not be employed on a regular basis by the employer.

(d) (1) In any case in which the second opinion described in subsection (c) of this section differs from the opinion in the original certification provided under subsection (a) of this section, the employer may require, at the expense of the employer, that the employee obtain the opinion of a third health care provider designated or approved jointly by the employer and the employee concerning the information certified under subsection (b) of this section.

(2) The opinion of the third health care provider concerning the information certified under subsection (b) of this section shall be considered to be final and shall be binding on the employer and the employee.

(e) The employer may require that the eligible employee obtain subsequent recertifications on a reasonable basis, provided the standards for determining what constitutes a reasonable basis for recertification may be governed by a collective bargaining agreement between such employer and a labor organization which is the collective bargaining representative of the unit of which the worker is a part if such a collective bargaining agreement is in effect. Unless otherwise required by the employee's health care provider, the employer may not require recertification more than once during a thirty-day period and, in any case, may not unreasonably require recertification. The employer shall pay for any recertification that is not covered by the employee's health insurance.

(1996, P.A. 96–140, § 3, eff. Jan. 1, 1997.)

§ 31–51nn. Family and medical leave: Employment and benefits protection

(a) Any eligible employee who takes leave under section 31–51*ll* for the intended purpose of the leave shall be entitled on return from such leave (1) to be restored by the employer to the position of employment held by the employee when the leave commenced; (2) if the original position of employment is not available, to be restored to an equivalent position with equivalent employment benefits, pay and other terms and conditions of employment; or (3) in the case of a medical leave, if the employee is medically unable to perform the employee's original job upon the expiration of such leave, to be transferred to work suitable to such employee's physical condition if such work is available.

(b) The taking of leave under section 31–51*ll* shall not result in the loss of any employment benefit accrued prior to the date on which the leave commenced.

(c) Nothing in this section shall be construed to entitle any restored employee to (1) the accrual of any seniority or employment benefits during any period of leave; or (2) any right, benefit or position of employment other than any right, benefit or position to which the employee would have been entitled had the employee not taken the leave.

(d) As a condition of restoration under subsection (a) of this section for an employee who has taken leave under subdivision (4) of subsection (a) of section 31–51*ll*, the employer may have a uniformly applied practice or policy that requires each such employee to receive certification from the health care provider of the employee that the employee is able to resume work, except that nothing in this subsection shall supersede a valid law of this state or a collective bargaining agreement that governs the return to work of such employees.

(e) Nothing in this section shall be construed to prohibit an employer from requiring an employee on leave under section 31–51*ll* to report periodically to the employer on the status and intention of the employee to return to work.

(f) Employees may have additional rights under other state and federal law, including rights under the federal Americans with Disabilities Act of 1990.[1] Nothing in sections 5–248a and 31–51kk to 31–51qq, inclusive, shall limit any such additional rights.

(1996, P.A. 96–140, § 4, eff. Jan. 1, 1997.)

[1] 42 U.S.C.A. § 12101 et seq.

§ 31–51*oo*. Family and medical leave: Confidentiality of medical records and documents

Records and documents relating to medical certifications, recertifications or medical histories of employees or employees' family members, created for purposes of sections 5–248a and 31–51kk to 31–51qq, inclusive, shall be maintained as medical records pursuant to chapter 563a,[1] except that: (1) Supervisors and managers may be informed regarding necessary restrictions on the work or duties of an employee and necessary accommodations; (2) first aid and safety personnel may be informed, when appropriate, if the employee's physical or medical condition might require emergency treatment; and (3) government officials investigating compliance with sections 5–248a and 31–51kk to 31–51qq, inclusive, or other pertinent law shall be provided relevant information upon request.

(1996, P.A. 96–140, § 5, eff. Jan. 1, 1997.)

[1] C.G.S.A. § 31–128a et seq.

§ 31–51pp. Family and medical leave: Prohibited acts

(a) (1) It shall be a violation of sections 5–248a and 31–51kk to 31–51qq, inclusive, for any employer to interfere with, restrain or deny the exercise of, or the attempt to exercise, any right provided under said sections.

(2) It shall be a violation of sections 5–248a and 31–51kk to 31–51qq, inclusive, for any employer to discharge or cause to be discharged, or in any other manner discriminate, against any individual for opposing any practice made unlawful by said sections or because such employee has exercised the rights afforded to such employee under said sections.

(b) It shall be a violation of sections 5–248a and 31–51kk to 31–51qq, inclusive, for any person to discharge or cause to be discharged, or in any other manner discriminate, against any individual because such individual:

(1) Has filed any charge, or has instituted or caused to be instituted any proceeding, under or related to sections 5–248a and 31–51kk to 31–51qq, inclusive;

(2) Has given, or is about to give, any information in connection with any inquiry or proceeding relating to any right provided under said sections; or

(3) Has testified, or is about to testify, in any inquiry or proceeding relating to any right provided under said sections.

(c) (1) It shall be a violation of sections 31–51kk to 31–51qq, inclusive, for any employer to deny an employee the right to use up to two weeks of accumulated sick leave or to discharge, threaten to discharge, demote, suspend or in any manner discriminate against an employee for using, or attempting to exercise the right to use, up to two weeks of accumulated sick leave to attend to a serious health condition of a son or daughter, spouse or parent of the employee, or for the birth or adoption of a son or daughter of the employee. For purposes of this subsection, "sick leave" means an absence from work for which compensation is provided through an employer's bona fide written policy providing compensation for loss of wages occasioned by illness, but does not include absences from work for which compensation is provided through an employer's plan, including, but not limited to, a short or long-term disability plan, whether or not such plan is self-insured.

(2) Any employee aggrieved by a violation of this subsection may file a complaint with the Labor Commissioner alleging violation of the provisions of this subsection. Upon receipt of any such complaint, the commissioner shall hold a hearing. After the hearing, the commissioner shall send each party a written copy of the commissioner's decision. The commissioner may award the employee all appropriate relief, including rehiring or reinstatement to the employee's previous job, payment of back wages and reestablishment of employee benefits to which the employee otherwise would have been eligible if a violation of this subsection had not occurred. Any party aggrieved by the decision of the commissioner may appeal the decision to the Superior Court in accordance with the provisions of chapter 54. [1]

(3) The rights and remedies specified in this subsection are cumulative and nonexclusive and are in addition to any other rights or remedies afforded by contract or under other provisions of law.

(1996, P.A. 96–140, § 6, eff. Jan. 1, 1997; 2003, P.A. 03–213, § 1.)

1 C.G.S.A. § 4–166 et seq.

§ 31–51qq. Family and medical leave: Regulations, report

On or before January 1, 1997, the Labor Commissioner shall adopt regulations, in accordance with the provisions of chapter 54,[1] to establish procedures and guidelines necessary to implement the provisions of sections 5–248a and 31–51kk to 31–51qq, inclusive, including, but not limited to, procedures for hearings and redress, including restoration and restitution, for an employee who believes that there is a violation by the employer of such employee of any provision of said sections, and procedures for the periodic reporting by employers to the commissioner of their current experience with leaves of absence taken pursuant to said sections. In adopting such regulations, the commissioner shall make reasonable efforts to ensure compatibility of state regulatory provisions with similar provisions of the federal Family and Medical Leave Act of 1993 [2] and the regulations promulgated pursuant to said act.

(1996, P.A. 96–140, § 7, eff. Jan. 1, 1997.)

1 C.G.S.A. § 4–166 et seq.
2 29 U.S.C.A. § 2601 et seq.

CHAPTER 567

UNEMPLOYMENT COMPENSATION

§ 31–227. Payment of benefits. Deductions for child support obligations. Liability for and optimal deduction of state, federal and local income taxes

(a) Benefits shall be payable only to individuals who are unemployed and are eligible for benefits. Benefits shall be payable only out of the Unemployment Compensation Fund.

(b) All benefits shall be payable through the state public employment bureaus or such other public agencies as the administrator, by regulations, may designate and at such times and in such manner as he may prescribe.

(c) Whenever any benefit claimant dies leaving unpaid benefits due him in accordance with the provisions of this chapter, the administrator may, in his discretion, pay the amount of such unpaid benefits in the manner set forth in section 45a–273, and such payment shall discharge the administrator from liability to any person on account of such benefits.

(d) Benefits based on service in employment defined in subdivisions (1)(C) and (D) of subsection (a) of section 31–222 shall be payable in the same amount, on the same terms and subject to the same conditions as compensation payable on the basis of other service subject to this chapter; except that (1) with respect to weeks of unemployment beginning after December 31, 1977, benefits shall not be paid based on service performed in an instructional, research or principal administrative capacity for an educational institution for any week of unemployment commencing during the period between two successive academic years, or during a similar period between two regular terms, whether or not successive, or during a period of paid sabbatical leave provided for in the individual's contract, to any individual if such individual performs such services in the first of such academic years (or terms) and if there is a contract or a reasonable assurance that such individual will perform services in any such capacity for any educational institution in the second of such academic years or terms; (2) with respect to weeks of unemployment beginning after October 29, 1983, for service performed in any other capacity for an educational institution, benefits shall not be paid on the basis of such services to any individual for any week which commences during a period between two successive academic years or terms if such individual performs such services in the first of such academic years or terms and there is a reasonable assurance that such individual will perform such services in the second of such academic years or terms, except that if benefits are denied to any individual under this subdivision and such individual is not offered an opportunity to perform such services for the educational institution for the second of such academic years or terms, such individual shall be entitled to a retroactive payment of benefits for each week for which the individual filed a timely claim for benefits and for which benefits were denied solely by reason of this subdivision; (3) with respect to weeks of unemployment beginning after March 31, 1984, for services described in subdivisions (1) and (2), benefits shall not be payable on the basis of such services to any individual for any week which commences during an established and customary vacation period or holiday recess if such individual performs such services in the period immediately before such vacation period or holiday recess and there is a reasonable assurance that such individual will perform such services in the period immediately following such vacation period or holiday recess; (4) with respect to weeks of unemployment beginning after March 31, 1984, for services described in subdivisions (1) and (2), benefits shall not be payable on the basis of such services under the circumstances prescribed in subdivisions (1), (2) and (3) to any individual who performed such services in an educational institution while in the employ of an educational service agency. For purposes of this subdivision the term "educational service agency" means a governmental agency or governmental entity which is established and operated exclusively for the purpose of providing such services to one or more educational institutions.

(e) Benefits shall not be paid to any individual on the basis of any services, substantially all of which consist of participating in sports or athletic events or training or preparing to so participate, for any week which commences during the period between two successive sport seasons (or similar periods) if such individual performed such services in the first of such seasons (or similar periods) and there is a reasonable assurance that such individual will perform such services in the later of such seasons (or similar periods).

(f) (A) Benefits shall not be payable on the basis of services performed by an alien unless such alien is an individual who was lawfully admitted for permanent residence at the time such services were performed, was lawfully present for purposes of performing such services or was permanently residing in the United States under color of law at the time such services were performed (including an alien who is lawfully present in the United States as a result of the application of the provisions of Section 203(a)(7) or Section 212(d)(5) of the Immigration and Nationality Act).[1] (B) Any data or information required of individuals applying for benefits to determine whether benefits are not payable to them because of their alien status shall be uniformly required from all applicants for benefits. (C) In the case of an individual whose application for benefits would otherwise be approved, no determination that benefits to such individual are not payable because of his alien status shall be made except upon a preponderance of the evidence.

(g) With respect to benefit years beginning on or after October 1, 1981, for any week with respect to which an individual is receiving a pension, which shall include a governmental or other pension, retirement or retired pay, annuity, or any other similar periodic payment, under a plan maintained or contributed to by a base period employer, the weekly benefit rate payable to such individual for such week shall be reduced by the prorated weekly amount of the pension. Where contributions were made to the pension plan by the individual, the prorated weekly pension amount shall be reduced by the proportion which such individual's contributions bear to the total of all payments for such individual into the plan. If, as a result of the reduction made under the provisions of this subsection, the individual's weekly benefit rate is not a whole dollar amount, the weekly benefit rate payable to such individual shall be the next lower whole dollar amount. No reduction shall be made under this subsection by reason of the receipt of a pension, except in the case of pensions paid under the Social Security Act[2] or the Railroad Retirement Act of 1974,[3] if the services performed by the individual during the base period for such employer, or remuneration received for such services, did not affect the individual's eligibility for, or increase the amount of, such pension, retirement or retired pay, annuity, or similar payment.

(h) (1) An individual filing an initial claim for unemployment compensation shall, at the time of filing such claim, disclose whether or not the individual owes child support obligations as defined under subdivision (6) of this subsection. If any such individual discloses that he or she owes child support obligations and has been determined to be eligible for unemployment compensation, the administrator shall notify the state or local child support enforcement agency enforcing such obligation that the individual is eligible for unemployment compensation.

(2) The administrator shall deduct and withhold from any unemployment compensation payable to an individual who owes child support obligations (A) the amount specified by the individual to the administrator to be deducted and withheld under this subsection, if neither subparagraph (B) nor (C) is applicable, or (B) the amount determined pursuant to an agreement submitted to the administrator under Section 654(20)(B)(i) of the Social Security Act by the state or local child support enforcement agency, unless subparagraph (C) is applicable, or (C) any amount otherwise required to be so deducted and withheld from such unemployment compensation pursuant to legal process, as defined in Section 662(e) of the Social Security Act, properly served upon the administrator.

(3) Any amount deducted and withheld under subdivision (2) shall be paid by the administrator to the appropriate state or local child support enforcement agency.

(4) Any amount deducted and withheld under subdivision (2) shall for all purposes be treated as if it were paid to the individual as unemployment compensation and paid by such individual to the state or local child support enforcement agency in satisfaction of the individual's child support obligations.

(5) This subsection shall be applicable only if appropriate arrangements have been made for reimbursement by the state or local child support enforcement agency for the administrative costs incurred by the administrator under this subsection which are attribut-

able to child support obligations being enforced by such state or local child support enforcement agency.

(6) For purposes of this subsection, the term "unemployment compensation" means any compensation payable under this chapter, including amounts payable by the administrator pursuant to an agreement under any federal law providing for compensation, assistance, or allowances with respect to unemployment; "child support obligations" includes only obligations which are being enforced pursuant to a plan described in Section 654 of the Social Security Act which has been approved by the Secretary of Health and Human Services under Part D of Title IV of the Social Security Act;[4] and "state or local child support enforcement agency" means any agency of this state or a political subdivision thereof operating pursuant to a plan described in Section 654 of the Social Security Act which has been approved by the Secretary of Health and Human Services under Part D of Title IV of the Social Security Act.

(i) (1) An individual filing a new claim for unemployment compensation shall at the time of filing such claim be advised that: (A) Unemployment compensation is subject to federal, state and local income tax; (B) requirements exist pertaining to estimated tax payments; (C) the individual may elect to have federal income tax deducted and withheld from the individual's payment of unemployment compensation at the amount specified in the federal Internal Revenue Code;[5] (D) the individual may elect to have state income tax deducted and withheld from the individual's payment of unemployment compensation at the rate of three per cent; (E) the individual shall be permitted to change a previously elected withholding status one time in a benefit year; and (F) an individual who elects deductions pursuant to subparagraph (C) or (D) of this subdivision shall be subject to deductions pursuant to subparagraphs (C) and (D) of this subdivision. (2) Amounts deducted and withheld from unemployment compensation shall remain in the Unemployment Compensation Fund until transferred to the federal or state taxing authority as a payment of income tax. (3) The commissioner shall follow all procedures specified by the United States Department of Labor and the federal Internal Revenue Service pertaining to the deducting and withholding of federal and state income taxes. (4) Amounts shall be deducted and withheld in accordance with any regulations adopted by the commissioner to implement the provisions of this subsection. (5) For purposes of this subsection, "unemployment compensation" means any compensation payable under this chapter, including amounts payable by the administrator pursuant to an agreement under any federal law providing for compensation, assistance or allowances with respect to unemployment.

(j) On and after January 1, 1997, the administrator shall deduct and withhold federal income tax from benefits payable to any individual who elected to have such deductions and withholdings under subsection (i) of this section.

(1949 Rev., § 7500; 1971, P.A. 835, § 11, eff. July 1, 1971; 1977, P.A. 77–426, § 3, eff. Oct. 1, 1977; 1978, P.A. 78–368, § 7, eff. Oct. 1, 1978; 1981, P.A. 81–318, § 5, eff. June 16, 1981; 1982, P.A. 82–361, § 8, eff. Oct. 1, 1982; 1983, P.A. 83–547, § 4, eff. July 1, 1983; 1983, P.A. 83–587, § 50, eff. July 14, 1983; 1983, Dec.Sp.Sess., P.A. 83–1, § 1, eff. Dec. 9, 1983; 1990, P.A. 90–314, § 2, eff. June 12, 1990; 1996, P.A. 96–206, § 1.)

1 8 U.S.C.A. § 1153 or 8 U.S.C.A. § 1182.

2 42 U.S.C.A. § 301 et seq.

3 45 U.S.C.A. § 231 et seq.

4 42 U.S.C.A. § 651 et seq.

5 26 U.S.C.A. § 1 et seq.

*

TITLE 36a

THE BANKING LAW OF CONNECTICUT

CHAPTER 665a

DEPOSITS

PART I. DEPOSITS AND CHECKS

§ 36a–297. Deposit or share accounts of minors

A minor may contract to establish a deposit account with any bank or share account with any Connecticut credit union or federal credit union, and may be the owner, or a joint owner, co-owner or beneficiary of any deposit account or share account. A minor who is an owner, co-owner or beneficiary of any deposit account or share account shall be bound by the terms of the deposit contract or share account contract governing such account, as amended by the bank or credit union from time to time, and any payment made or withdrawal permitted by such bank or credit union in accordance with the terms of the deposit contract or share account contract governing such account shall constitute a sufficient and valid release to such bank or credit union for such payment or withdrawal and shall be binding upon such minor and any other owner, co-owner or beneficiary of such deposit account or share account to the same extent as if such minor were over the age of majority. Unless made by such minor or by a person appointed as guardian of the estate of such minor, a bank, Connecticut credit union or federal credit union may treat any claim to a deposit account or share account made solely on behalf of a minor owner, co-owner or beneficiary of such deposit account or share account as an adverse claim under section 36a–293. This section shall not affect any rights of or obligations imposed on a parent, guardian or spouse of a minor under section 45a–631.

(1949 Rev., § 5830; 1958 Rev., § 36–111; 1967, P.A. 461, § 33, eff. Jan. 1, 1968; 1994, P.A. 94–122, § 138, eff. Jan. 1, 1995; 2002, P.A. 02–73, § 33.)

*

TITLE 38a

INSURANCE

CHAPTER 699

INSURANCE CONTRACTS IN GENERAL

§ 38a–284. Insurance contracts by minors

Any minor of the age of fifteen years or more may, notwithstanding such minority, contract for life, health and accident insurance on his person for his benefit or for the benefit of his father, mother, husband, wife, child, brother or sister and may exercise all such contractual rights with respect to any such contract of insurance as might be exercised by a person of full legal age and may at any time surrender his interest in any such insurance or give a valid discharge for any benefit accruing or money payable thereunder.

(1949 Rev., § 6147; 1958 Rev., § 38–157.)

*

TITLE 45a

PROBATE COURTS AND PROCEDURE

CHAPTER 801b

PROBATE COURT PROCEDURES

PART II. PROBATE COURT PROCEEDINGS IN GENERAL

§ 45a–132. Appointment of guardian ad litem for minors and incompetent, undetermined and unborn persons

(a) In any proceeding before a court of probate or the superior court including the family support magistrate division, whether acting upon an appeal from probate or otherwise, the judge or magistrate may appoint a guardian ad litem for any minor or incompetent, undetermined or unborn person, or may appoint one guardian ad litem for two or more of such minors or incompetent, undetermined or unborn persons, if it appears to the judge or magistrate that one or more persons as individuals, or as members of a designated class or otherwise, have or may have an interest in the proceedings, and that one or more of them are minors, incompetent persons or persons undetermined or unborn at the time of the proceeding.

(b) The appointment shall not be mandatory, but shall be within the discretion of the judge or magistrate.

(c) Any order or decree passed or action taken in any such proceeding shall affect all the minors, incompetent persons or persons thereafter born or determined for whom the guardian ad litem has been appointed, in the same manner as if they had been of the age of majority and competent and present in court after legal notice at the time of the action or the issuance of the order or decree.

(d) Any appointment of a guardian ad litem may be made with or without notice and, if it appears to the judge or magistrate that it is for the best interests of a minor having a parent or guardian to have as guardian ad litem some person other than the parent or guardian, the judge or magistrate may appoint a disinterested person to be the guardian ad litem.

(e) When the appointment is made in connection with the settlement of a decedent's estate or the settlement of the account of a trustee or other fiduciary, the person so appointed shall be authorized to represent the minor or incompetent, undetermined or unborn person in all proceedings for the settlement of the estate or account and subsequent accounts of the trustee or other fiduciary, or until his appointment is terminated by death, resignation or removal.

(f) The guardian ad litem may be removed by the judge or magistrate which appointed him, without notice, whenever it appears to the judge or magistrate to be in the best interests of the ward or wards of the guardian.

(g) Any guardian ad litem appointed under the provisions of this section may be allowed reasonable compensation by the judge or magistrate appointing him and shall be paid as a part of the expenses of administration.

(1949 Rev., § 6861; 1951, Supp. § 1244b; 1955, Supp. § 2902d; 1957, P.A. 210; 1958 Rev., § 45–54; 1975, P.A. 75–384, § 7, eff. May 30, 1975; 1976, P.A. 76–436, § 640, eff. July 1, 1978; 1980, P.A. 80–476, § 65, eff. Oct. 1, 1980; 1987, P.A. 87–316, § 6.)

CHAPTER 802d

CONNECTICUT UNIFORM TRANSFERS TO MINORS ACT

Section

§§ 45a–546 to 45a–556. Repealed. (1995, P.A. 95–117, § 28.)

§ 45a–557. Short title: Connecticut Uniform Transfers to Minors Act

Sections 45a–557 to 45a–560b, inclusive, may be cited as the "Connecticut Uniform Transfers to Minors Act".

(1995, P.A. 95–117, § 1.)

§ 45a–557a. Definitions

For purposes of sections 45a–557 to 45a–560b, inclusive:

(1) "Adult" means an individual who has attained the age of twenty-one years.

(2) "Broker" means a person lawfully engaged in the business of effecting transactions in securities or commodities for the person's own account or for the account of others.

(3) "Court" means Probate Court.

(4) "Custodial property" means (A) any interest in property transferred to a custodian under sections 45a–557 to 45a–560b, inclusive, and (B) the income from and proceeds of that interest in property.

(5) "Custodian" means a person so designated under section 45a–558f or a successor or substitute custodian designated under section 45a–559c.

(6) "Financial institution" means a bank, trust company, a savings institution or credit union, chartered and supervised under state or federal law.

(7) "Guardian" means a person appointed or qualified by a court to act as guardian of a minor's estate or a person legally authorized to perform substantially the same functions.

(8) "Legal representative" means any court appointed fiduciary, including, but not limited to, a guardian, conservator, executor or administrator. A legal representative does not include a guardian ad litem.

(9) "Member of the minor's family" means the minor's parent, stepparent, spouse, grandparent, brother, sister, uncle or aunt, whether of whole or half blood or by adoption.

(10) "Minor" means an individual who has not attained the age of twenty-one years.

(11) "Person" means an individual, corporation, organization or other legal entity.

(12) "Personal representative" means an executor, administrator, successor personal representative or temporary administrator of a decedent's estate or person legally authorized to perform substantially the same functions.

(13) "State" includes any state of the United States, the District of Columbia, the Commonwealth of Puerto Rico and any territory or possession subject to the legislative authority of the United States.

(14) "Transfer" means a transaction that creates custodial property under section 45a–558f.

(15) "Transferor" means a person who makes a transfer under sections 45a–557 to 45a–560b, inclusive.

(16) "Trust company" means a financial institution, corporation or other legal entity authorized to exercise general trust powers.

(1995, P.A. 95–117, § 2.)

§ 45a–557b. Scope and jurisdiction

(a) Sections 45a–557 to 45a–560b, inclusive, apply to a transfer that refers to said sections in the designation under subsection (a) of section 45a–558f by which the transfer is made if at the time of the transfer, the transferor, the minor or the custodian is a resident of this state or the custodial property is located in this state. Courts of probate in any district in which the transferor, the minor or the custodian is resident, or in which the custodial property is located shall have jurisdiction of any disputes or matters involving custodianship under sections 45a–557 to 45a–560b, inclusive. The custodianship so created remains subject to said sections and to such probate court jurisdiction despite a subsequent change in residence of a transferor, the minor or the custodian, or the removal of custodial property from this state.

(b) A person designated as custodian under sections 45a–557 to 45a–560b, inclusive, is subject to personal jurisdiction in this state with respect to any matter relating to the custodianship.

(c) A transfer that purports to be made and which is valid under the Uniform Transfers to Minors Act, the Uniform Gifts to Minors Act,[1] or a substantially similar act, of another state is governed by the law of the state designated in the instrument of transfer and may be executed and is enforceable in this state if at the time of the transfer, the transferor, the minor or the custodian is a resident of the designated state or the custodial property is located in the designated state.

(1995, P.A. 95–117, § 3.)

[1] C.G.S.A. § 45a–546 et seq. (Repealed).

§ 45a–558. Nomination of custodian

(a) A person having the right to designate the recipient of property transferable upon the occurrence of a future event may revocably nominate a custodian to receive the property for a minor beneficiary upon the occurrence of the event by naming the custodian followed in substance by the words: "as custodian for . . . . (name of minor) under the Connecticut Uniform Transfers to Minors Act". The nomination may name one or more persons as substitute custodians to whom the property shall be transferred, in the order named, if the first nominated custodian dies before the transfer or is unable, declines or is ineligible to serve. The nomination may be made in a will, a trust, a deed, an instrument exercising a power of appointment or in a writing designating a beneficiary of contractual rights which is registered with or delivered to the payor, issuer or other obligor of the contractual rights.

(b) A custodian nominated under this section shall be a person to whom a transfer of property of that kind may be made under subsection (a) of section 45a–558f.

(c) The nomination of a custodian under this section does not create custodial property until the nominating instrument becomes irrevocable or a transfer to the nominated custodian is completed under section 45a–558f. Unless the nomination of a custodian has been revoked, upon the occurrence of the future event the custodianship becomes effective and the custodian shall enforce a transfer of the custodial property pursuant to section 45a–558f.

(1995, P.A. 95–117, § 4.)

§ 45a–558a. Transfer by gift or exercise of power

A person may make a transfer by irrevocable gift to, or the irrevocable exercise of a power of appointment in favor of, a custodian for the benefit of a minor pursuant to section 45a–558f.

(1995, P.A. 95–117, § 5.)

§ 45a–558b. Transfer authorized by will or trust

(a) A personal representative or trustee may make an irrevocable transfer pursuant to section 45a–558f to a custodian for the benefit of a minor as authorized in the governing will or trust.

(b) If the testator or settlor has nominated a custodian under section 45a–558 to receive the custodial property, the transfer shall be made to that person.

(c) If the testator or settlor has not nominated a custodian under section 45a–558, or all persons so nominated as custodian die before the transfer or are unable, decline or are ineligible to serve, the personal representative or the trustee, as the case may be, shall designate the custodian from among those eligible to serve as custodian for property of that kind under subsection (a) of section 45a–558f.

(1995, P.A. 95–117, § 6.)

§ 45a–558c. Other transfer by fiduciary

(a) Subject to subsection (c) of this section, a personal representative or trustee may make an irrevocable transfer to another adult or trust company as custodian for the benefit of a minor pursuant to section 45a–558f, in the absence of a will or under a will or trust that does not contain an authorization to do so.

(b) Subject to subsection (c) of this section, a guardian may make an irrevocable transfer to another adult or trust company as custodian for the benefit of the minor pursuant to section 45a–558f.

(c) A transfer under subsection (a) or (b) of this section may be made only if (1) the personal representative, trustee or guardian considers the transfer to be in the best interest of the minor, (2) the transfer is not prohibited by or inconsistent with provisions of the applicable will, trust agreement or other governing instrument, and (3) the transfer is authorized by the court if it exceeds five thousand dollars in value.

(d) For purposes of this section, a series of transfers shall be aggregated so that the five-thousand-dollar threshold for court approval cannot be circumvented.

(1995, P.A. 95–117, § 7.)

§ 45a–558d. Transfer by obligor

(a) Subject to subsections (b) and (c) of this section, a person not subject to section 45a–558b or 45a–558c who holds property of or owes a liquidated debt to a minor not having a guardian may make an irrevocable transfer to a custodian for the benefit of the minor pursuant to section 45a–558f.

(b) If a person having the right to do so under section 45a–558 has nominated a custodian under that section to receive the custodial property, the transfer shall be made to that person.

(c) If no custodian has been nominated under section 45a–558, or all persons so nominated as custodian die before the transfer or are unable, decline or are ineligible to serve, a transfer under this section may be made to an adult member of the minor's family or to a trust company unless the property exceeds five thousand dollars in value, in which case Probate Court approval is required. For purposes of this subsection, a series of transfers shall be aggregated so that the five-thousand-dollar threshold for court approval cannot be circumvented.

(d) This section does not authorize a guardian, existing custodian or custodian to whom an obligor makes a transfer under this section to settle, release or compromise a claim of the minor or a debt owed to the minor.

(1995, P.A. 95–117, § 8.)

§ 45a–558e. Receipt for custodial property

A written acknowledgment of delivery by a custodian constitutes a sufficient release and discharge for custodial property transferred to the custodian pursuant to sections 45a–557 to 45a–560b, inclusive.

(1995, P.A. 95–117, § 9.)

§ 45a–558f. Creation and transfer of custodial property. Designation of initial custodian. Control

(a) Custodial property is created and a transfer is made whenever:

(1) An uncertificated security or a certificated security in registered form is either: (A) Registered in the name of the transferor, an adult other than the transfer-

or or a trust company, followed in substance by the words: "as custodian for .... (name of minor) under the Connecticut Uniform Transfers to Minors Act"; or (B) delivered if in certificated form, or any document necessary for the transfer of an uncertificated security is delivered, together with any necessary endorsement to an adult other than the transferor or to a trust company as custodian, accompanied by an instrument in substantially the form set forth in subsection (b) of this section;

(2) Money is paid or delivered, or a security held in the name of a broker, financial institution or its nominee is transferred, to a broker or financial institution for credit to an account in the name of the transferor, an adult other than the transferor or a trust company, followed in substance by the words: "as custodian for .... (name of minor) under the Connecticut Uniform Transfers to Minors Act";

(3) The ownership of a life or endowment insurance policy or annuity contract is either: (A) Registered with the issuer in the name of the transferor, an adult other than the transferor or a trust company, followed in substance by the words: "as custodian for .... (name of minor) under the Connecticut Uniform Transfers to Minors Act"; or (B) assigned in writing delivered to an adult other than the transferor or to a trust company whose name in the assignment is followed in substance by the words: "as custodian for .... (name of minor) under the Connecticut Uniform Transfers to Minors Act";

(4) An irrevocable exercise of a power of appointment or an irrevocable present right to future payment under a contract is the subject of a written notification delivered to the payor, issuer or other obligor that the right is transferred to the transferor, an adult other than the transferor or a trust company, whose name in the notification is followed in substance by the words: "as custodian for .... (name of minor) under the Connecticut Uniform Transfers to Minors Act";

(5) An interest in real property is recorded in the name of the transferor, an adult other than the transferor or a trust company, followed in substance by the words: "as custodian for .... (name of minor) under the Connecticut Uniform Transfers to Minors Act";

(6) A certificate of title issued by a department or agency of a state or of the United States which evidences title to tangible personal property is either: (A) Issued in the name of the transferor, an adult other than the transferor or a trust company, followed in substance by the words: "as custodian for .... (name of minor) under the Connecticut Uniform Transfers to Minors Act"; or (B) delivered to an adult other than the transferor or to a trust company, endorsed to that person followed in substance by the words: "as custodian for .... (name of minor) under the Connecticut Uniform Transfers to Minors Act"; or

(7) An interest in any property not described in subdivisions (1) to (6), inclusive, of this subsection is transferred to an adult other than the transferor or to a trust company by a written instrument in substantially the form set forth in subsection (b) of this section.

(b) An instrument in the following form satisfies the requirements of subparagraph (B) of subdivision (1) of subsection (a) of this section and subdivision (7) of subsection (a) of this section:

"TRANSFER UNDER THE CONNECTICUT UNIFORM TRANSFERS TO MINORS ACT

I, ... (name of transferor or name and representative capacity if a fiduciary) hereby transfer to .... (name of custodian), as custodian for .... (name of minor) under the Connecticut Uniform Transfers to Minors Act, the following: (Insert a description of the custodial property sufficient to identify it.)

Dated: ....

.... (Signature)

.... (name of custodian) acknowledges receipt of the property described above as custodian for the minor named above under the Connecticut Uniform Transfers to Minors Act.

Dated: ....

..... (Signature of Custodian)"

(c) A transferor shall place the custodian in control of the custodial property as soon as practicable.

(1995, P.A. 95–117, § 10.)

§ 45a–558g. Single custodianship

A transfer may be made for only one minor, and only one person may be the custodian. All custodial property held under sections 45a–557 to 45a–560b, inclusive, by the same custodian for the benefit of the same minor constitutes a single custodianship.

(1995, P.A. 95–117, § 11.)

§ 45a–558h. Validity and effect of transfer

(a) The validity of a transfer made in a manner prescribed in sections 45a–557 to 45a–560b, inclusive, is not affected by: (1) Failure of the transferor to comply with subsection (c) of section 45a–558f concerning possession and control; (2) designation of an ineligible custodian, except designation of the transferor in the case of property for which the transferor is ineligible to serve as custodian under subsection (a) of section 45a–558f; or (3) death or incapacity of a person nominated under section 45a–558 or designated under section 45a–558f as custodian or the disclaimer of the office by that person.

(b) A transfer made pursuant to section 45a–558f is irrevocable, and the custodial property is indefeasibly vested in the minor, but the custodian has all the rights, powers, duties and authority provided in sections 45a–557 to 45a–560b, inclusive, and neither the minor nor the minor's legal representative has any right, power, duty or authority with respect to the custodial property except as provided in sections 45a–557 to 45a–560b, inclusive.

(c) By making a transfer, the transferor incorporates in the disposition all the provisions of sections 45a–557 to 45a–560b, inclusive, and grants to the custodian, and to any third person dealing with a person designated as custodian, the respective powers, rights and immunities provided in sections 45a–557 to 45a–560b, inclusive.

(1995, P.A. 95–117, § 12.)

§ 45a–558i. Care and control of custodial property

(a) A custodian shall: (1) Take control of custodial property; (2) register or record title to custodial property if appropriate; and (3) collect, hold, manage, invest and reinvest custodial property.

(b) In dealing with custodial property, a custodian shall observe the standard of care that would be observed by a prudent person of discretion and intelligence who is seeking a reasonable income and the preservation of such person's capital. The custodian shall not be limited by any other statute restricting investments by fiduciaries. However, a custodian, in the custodian's discretion and without liability to the minor or the minor's estate, may retain any custodial property received from a transferor.

(c) A custodian may invest in or pay premiums on life insurance or endowment policies on (1) the life of the minor only if the minor or the minor's estate is the sole beneficiary, or (2) the life of another person in whom the minor has an insurable interest only to the extent that the minor, the minor's estate or the custodian in the capacity of custodian, is the owner of the policy.

(d) A custodian at all times shall keep custodial property separate and distinct from all other property in a manner sufficient to identify it clearly as custodial property of the minor. Custodial property consisting of an undivided interest is so identified if the minor's interest is held as a tenant in common and is fixed. Custodial property subject to recordation is so identified if it is recorded, and custodial property subject to registration is so identified if it is either registered, or held in an account designated, in the name of the custodian, followed in substance by the words: "as a custodian for .... (name of minor) under the Connecticut Uniform Transfers to Minors Act".

(e) A custodian shall keep records of all transactions with respect to custodial property, including information necessary for the preparation of the minor's tax returns, and shall make them available for inspection at reasonable intervals by any parent or legal representative of the minor or by the minor if the minor has attained the age of twelve years.

(1995, P.A. 95–117, § 13.)

§ 45a–558j. Powers of custodian

(a) A custodian, acting in a custodial capacity, has all the rights, powers and authority over custodial property that unmarried adult owners have over their own property including, to the extent applicable and consistent with sections 45a–557 to 45a–560b, inclusive, powers pursuant to section 45a–234, but a custodian may exercise those rights, powers and authority in that custodian's fiduciary capacity only.

(b) This section does not relieve a custodian from liability for breach of the provisions of section 45a–558i.

(1995, P.A. 95–117, § 14.)

§ 45a–558k. Use of custodial property

(a) A custodian may deliver or pay to the minor or expend for the minor's benefit so much of the custodial property as the custodian considers advisable for the use and benefit of the minor, without court order and without regard to (1) the duty or ability of the custodian personally or of any other person to support the minor, or (2) any other income or property of the minor which may be applicable or available for that purpose.

(b) On petition of an interested person or the minor if the minor has attained the age of twelve years, the court may order the custodian to deliver or pay to the minor or expend for the minor's benefit so much of the custodial property as the court considers advisable for the use and benefit of the minor.

(c) A delivery, payment or expenditure under this section is in addition to, not in substitution for, and does not affect any obligation of a person to support the minor.

(1995, P.A. 95–117, § 15.)

§ 45a–559. Custodian's expenses, compensation and bond

(a) A custodian is entitled to reimbursement from custodial property for reasonable expenses incurred in the performance of the custodian's duties.

(b) Except for one who is a transferor under section 45a–558a, a custodian has a noncumulative election during each calendar year to charge reasonable compensation for services performed during that year.

(c) Except as provided in subsection (f) of section 45a–559c, a custodian need not give a bond.

(1995, P.A. 95–117, § 16.)

§ 45a–559a. Exemption of third party from liability

A third person in good faith and without court order may act on the instructions of or otherwise deal with any person purporting to make a transfer or purporting to act in the capacity of a custodian and, in the absence of knowledge, is not responsible for determining: (1) The validity of the purported custodian's designation; (2) the propriety of, or the authority under sections

45a–557 to 45a–560b, inclusive, for, any act of the purported custodian; (3) the validity or propriety under sections 45a–557 to 45a–560b, inclusive, of any instrument or instructions executed or given either by the person purporting to make a transfer or by the purported custodian; or (4) the propriety of the application of any property of the minor delivered to the purported custodian.

(1995, P.A. 95–117, § 17.)

§ 45a–559b. Liability to third persons

(a) A claim based on (1) a contract entered into by a custodian acting in a custodial capacity, (2) an obligation arising from the ownership or control of custodial property, or (3) a tort committed during the custodianship, may be asserted against the custodial property by proceeding against the custodian in the custodial capacity, whether or not the custodian or the minor is personally liable therefor.

(b) A custodian is not personally liable: (1) On a contract properly entered into in the custodial capacity unless the custodian fails to reveal that capacity and to identify the custodianship in the contract; or (2) for an obligation arising from control of custodial property or for a tort committed during the custodianship unless the custodian is personally at fault.

(c) A minor is not personally liable for an obligation arising from ownership of custodial property or for a tort committed during the custodianship unless the minor is personally at fault.

(1995, P.A. 95–117, § 18.)

§ 45a–559c. Renunciation, resignation, death or removal of custodian. Designation of successor custodian

(a) A person nominated under section 45a–558 or designated under section 45a–558f as custodian may decline to serve by delivering a valid disclaimer to the person who made the nomination or to the transferor or the transferor's legal representative. If the event giving rise to a transfer has not occurred and no substitute custodian able, willing and eligible to serve was nominated under section 45a–558, the person who made the nomination may nominate a substitute custodian under section 45a–558; otherwise the transferor or the transferor's legal representative shall designate a substitute custodian at the time of the transfer, in either case from among the persons eligible to serve as custodian for that kind of property under subsection (a) of section 45a–558f. The custodian so designated has the rights of a successor custodian.

(b) A custodian at any time may designate a trust company or an adult other than a transferor under section 45a–558a as successor custodian by executing and dating an instrument of designation before a subscribing witness other than the successor. If the instrument of designation does not contain or is not accompanied by the resignation of the custodian, the designation of the successor does not take effect until the custodian resigns, dies, becomes incapacitated or is removed.

(c) A custodian may resign at any time by delivering written notice to the minor if the minor has attained the age of twelve years and to the successor custodian and by delivering the custodial property to the successor custodian.

(d) If a custodian is ineligible, dies or becomes incapacitated without having effectively designated a successor and the minor has attained the age of twelve years, the minor may designate as successor custodian, in the manner prescribed in subsection (b) of this section, an adult member of the minor's family, a guardian of the minor or a trust company. If the minor has not attained the age of twelve years or fails to act within sixty days after the ineligibility, death or incapacity, the guardian of the minor becomes successor custodian. If the minor has no guardian or the guardian declines to act, the transferor, the legal representative of the transferor or of the custodian, an adult member of the minor's family or any other interested person may petition the court to designate a successor custodian.

(e) A custodian who declines to serve under subsection (a) of this section or resigns under subsection (c) of this section, or the legal representative of a deceased or incapacitated custodian, as soon as practicable, shall put the custodial property and records in the possession and control of the successor custodian. The successor custodian by action in a probate court may enforce the obligation to deliver custodial property and records and becomes responsible for each item as received.

(f) A transferor, the legal representative of a transferor, an adult member of the minor's family, a guardian of the person of the minor, the guardian of the minor or the minor if the minor has attained the age of twelve years may petition the court to remove the custodian under section 45a–242 and to designate a successor custodian other than a transferor under section 45a–558a or to require the custodian to give appropriate bond.

(1995, P.A. 95–117, § 19.)

§ 45a–559d. Accounting by and determination of liability of custodian

(a) A minor who has attained the age of twelve years, the minor's guardian of the person or legal representative, an adult member of the minor's family, a transferor or a transferor's legal representative may petition the court (1) for an accounting by the custodian or the custodian's legal representative, or (2) for a determination of responsibility, as between the custodial property and the custodian personally, for claims against the custodial property unless the responsibility has been adjudicated in an action under section 45a–559b to which the minor or the minor's legal representative was a party.

(b) A successor custodian may petition the court for an accounting by the predecessor custodian.

(c) The court, in a proceeding under sections 45a–557 to 45a–560b, inclusive, or in any other proceeding, may require or permit the custodian or the custodian's legal representative to account.

(d) If a custodian is removed under subsection (f) of section 45a–559c, the court shall require an accounting and order delivery of the custodial property and records to the successor custodian and the execution of all instruments required for transfer of the custodial property.

(1995, P.A. 95–117, § 20.)

§ 45a–559e. Termination of custodianship

The custodian shall transfer in an appropriate manner the custodial property to the minor, the legal representative of the minor or the personal representative of the minor's estate upon the earlier of (1) the minor's attainment of twenty-one years of age, or (2) the minor's death.

(1995, P.A. 95–117, § 21.)

§ 45a–560. Applicability

The provisions of sections 45a–557 to 45a–560b, inclusive, shall apply to a transfer within the scope of section 45a–557b made after October 1, 1995, if: (1) The transfer purports to have been made under the Connecticut Uniform Gifts to Minors Act, sections 45a–546 to 45a–556, inclusive,[1] revision of 1958, revised to January 1, 1995; or (2) the instrument by which the transfer purports to have been made uses in substance the designation "as custodian under the Uniform Gifts to Minors Act" or "as custodian under the Uniform Transfers to Minors Act" of any other state, and the application of sections 45a–557 to 45a–560b, inclusive, is necessary to validate the transfer.

(1995, P.A. 95–117, § 22.)

1 Repealed.

§ 45a–560a. Effect on existing custodianships

(a) Any transfer of custodial property as defined in sections 45a–557 to 45a–560b, inclusive, made before October 1, 1995, is validated notwithstanding that there was no specific authority in the Connecticut Uniform Gifts to Minors Act, sections 45a–546 to 45a–556, inclusive,[1] revision of 1958, revised to January 1, 1995, for the coverage of custodial property of that kind or for a transfer from that source at the time the transfer was made.

(b) The provisions of sections 45a–557 to 45a–560b, inclusive, shall apply to all transfers made before October 1, 1995, in a manner and form prescribed in the Connecticut Uniform Gifts to Minors Act, sections 45a–546 to 45a–556, inclusive, revision of 1958, revised to January 1, 1995, except insofar as the application impairs constitutionally vested rights or extends the duration of custodianships in existence on October 1, 1995.

(1995, P.A. 95–117, § 23.)

1 Repealed.

§ 45a–560b. Uniformity of application and construction

Sections 45a–557 to 45a–560b, inclusive, shall be applied and construed to effectuate their general purpose to make uniform the law with respect to the subject of sections 45a–557 to 45a–560b, inclusive, among states enacting it.

(1995, P.A. 95–117, § 24.)

§ 45a–561. Reserved for future use

CHAPTER 802e

DURABLE POWER OF ATTORNEY

§ 45a–562. Power of attorney to survive disability or incompetence

(a) The subsequent disability or incompetence of a principal shall not revoke or terminate the authority of any person who acts under a power of attorney in a writing executed by the principal, if the writing contains the words "this power of attorney shall not be affected by the subsequent disability or incompetence of the principal," or words of similar import showing the intent of the principal that the authority conferred shall be exercisable notwithstanding the principal's subsequent disability or incompetence; provided the power of attorney is executed and witnessed in the same manner as provided for deeds in section 47–5.

(b) If a conservator of the estate of the principal is appointed after the occurrence of the disability or incompetence referred to in subsection (a) of this section, the power of attorney shall cease at the time of the appointment, and the person acting under the power of attorney shall account to the conservator rather than to the principal.

(1958 Rev., § 45–69o; 1976, P.A. 76–54, § 1, eff. April 13, 1976; 1978, P.A. 78–44; 1980, P.A. 80–476, § 183, eff. Oct. 1, 1980; 1981, P.A. 81–396, § 1.)

§§ 45a–563 to 45a–567. Reserved for future use

CHAPTER 802h

PROTECTED PERSONS AND THEIR PROPERTY

PART II. GUARDIANS OF THE PERSON OF A MINOR

§ 45a–603. Residence of minor defined

For the purposes of sections 45a–132, 45a–593 to 45a–597, inclusive, 45a–603 to 45a–622, inclusive, and 45a–629 to 45a–638, inclusive, the residence of a minor means his or her actual residence and not that imputed to the minor by the residence of his or her parents or guardian.

(1949 Rev., § 6849; 1958 Rev., § 45–42; 1979, P.A. 79–460, § 3.)

§ 45a–604. Definitions

As used in sections 45a–603 to 45a–622, inclusive:

(1) "Mother" means a woman who can show proof by means of a birth certificate or other sufficient evidence of having given birth to a child and an adoptive mother as shown by a decree of a court of competent jurisdiction or otherwise;

(2) "Father" means a man who is a father under the law of this state including a man who, in accordance with section 46b–172, executes a binding acknowledgment of paternity and a man determined to be a father under chapter 815y; [1]

(3) "Parent" means a mother as defined in subdivision (1) of this section or a "father" as defined in subdivision (2) of this section;

(4) "Minor" or "minor child" means a person under the age of eighteen;

(5) "Guardianship" means guardianship of the person of a minor, and includes: (A) The obligation of care and control; and (B) the authority to make major decisions affecting the minor's education and welfare, including, but not limited to, consent determinations regarding marriage, enlistment in the armed forces and major medical, psychiatric or surgical treatment.

(6) "Guardian" means one who has the authority and obligations of "guardianship" as defined in subdivision (5) of this section;

(7) "Termination of parental rights" means the complete severance by court order of the legal relationship, with all its rights and responsibilities, between the child and the child's parent or parents so that the child is free for adoption, except that it shall not affect the right of inheritance of the child or the religious affiliation of the child.

(1958 Rev., § 45–42a; 1979, P.A. 79–460, § 1; 1981, P.A. 81–472, § 100, eff. July 8, 1981; 1996, P.A. 96–130, § 1; 1999, P.A. 99–84, § 4; 2000, P.A. 00–5; 2000, P.A. 00–157, § 7, eff. July 1, 2000; 2000, P.A. 00–196, § 31.)

1 C.G.S.A. § 46b–160 et seq.

§ 45a–605. Provisions construed in best interest of minor child

(a) The provisions of sections 45a–603 to 45a–622, inclusive, shall be liberally construed in the best interests of any minor child affected by them, provided the requirements of such sections are otherwise satisfied.

(b) All proceedings held under said sections shall, in the best interests of the minor child, be held without unreasonable delay.

(1958 Rev., § 45–42b; 1979, P.A. 79–460, § 2; 1985, P.A. 85–244, § 1, eff. May 30, 1985.)

§ 45a–606. Father and mother joint guardians

The father and mother of every minor child are joint guardians of the person of the minor, and the powers, rights and duties of the father and the mother in regard to the minor shall be equal. If either father or mother dies or is removed as guardian, the other parent of the minor child shall become the sole guardian of the person of the minor.

(1949 Rev., § 6850; 1958 Rev., § 45–43; 1959, P.A. 177; 1969, P.A. 691, § 1; 1972, P.A. 127, § 66; 1973, P.A. 73–156, § 19; 1974, P.A. 74–164, § 13, eff. May 10, 1974; 1975, P.A. 75–420, § 4, eff. June 25, 1975; 1977, P.A. 77–614, § 521, eff. Jan. 1, 1979; 1979, P.A. 79–460, § 4.)

§ 45a–607. Temporary custody of minor pending application to probate court for removal of guardian or termination of parental rights

(a) When application has been made for the removal of one or both parents as guardians or of any other guardian of the person of a minor child, or when an application has been made for the termination of the parental rights of any parties who may have parental rights with regard to any minor child, or when, in any proceeding the court has reasonable grounds to believe that any minor child has no guardian of his or her person, the court of probate in which the proceeding is pending may issue an order awarding temporary custody of the minor child to a person other than the parent or guardian, with or without the parent's or guardian's consent, but such order may only be issued in accordance with the provisions of this section.

(b) In the case of a minor child in the custody of the parent or other guardian, no application for custody of such minor child may be granted ex parte, except in accordance with subdivision (2) of this subsection. In the case of a minor child in the custody of a person other than the parent or guardian, no application for custody may be granted ex parte, except in accordance with subdivisions (1) to (3), inclusive, of this subsection.

(1) An application for immediate temporary custody shall be accompanied by an affidavit made by the custodian of such minor child under penalty of false statement, stating the circumstances under which such custody was obtained, the length of time the affiant has had custody and specific facts which would justify the conclusion that determination cannot await the hearing required by subsection (c) of this section. Upon such application, the court may grant immediate temporary custody to the affiant or some other suitable person if the court finds that: (A) The minor child was not taken or kept from the parent, parents or guardian, and (B) there is a substantial likelihood that the minor child will be removed from the jurisdiction prior to a hearing under subsection (c) of this section, or (C) to return the minor child to the parent, parents or guardian would place the minor child in circumstances which would result in serious physical illness or injury, or the threat thereof, or imminent physical danger prior to a hearing under subsection (c) of this section.

(2) In the case of a minor child who is hospitalized as a result of serious physical illness or serious physical injury, an application for immediate temporary custody shall contain a certificate signed by two physicians licensed to practice medicine in this state stating that (A) the minor child is in need of immediate medical or surgical treatment, the delay of which would be life threatening, (B) the parent, parents or guardian of the minor child refuses or is unable to consent to such treatment, and (C) determination of the need for temporary custody cannot await notice of hearing. Upon such application, the court may grant immediate temporary custody to some suitable person if it finds that (i) a minor child has suffered from serious physical illness or serious physical injury and is in need of immediate medical or surgical treatment, (ii) the parent, parents or guardian refuses to consent to such treatment, and (iii) to delay such treatment would be life threatening.

(3) If an order of temporary custody is issued ex parte, notice of the hearing required by subsection (c) of this section shall be given promptly, and the hearing shall be held within five business days of the date of such ex parte order of temporary custody, provided the respondent shall be entitled to continuance upon request. Upon the issuance of an order granting temporary custody of the minor child to the Commissioner of Children and Families, or not later than sixty days after the issuance of such order, the court shall make a determination whether the Department of Children and Families made reasonable efforts to keep the minor child with his or her parent, parents or guardian prior to the issuance of such order and, if such efforts were not made, whether such reasonable efforts were not possible, taking into consideration the minor child's best interests, including the minor child's health and safety. Upon issuance of an ex parte order of temporary custody, the court shall promptly notify the Commissioner of Children and Families, who shall cause an investigation to be made forthwith, in accordance with section 17a–101g, and shall present the commissioner's report to the court at the hearing on the application for temporary custody. The hearing on an ex parte order of temporary custody shall not be postponed, except with the consent of the respondent, or, if notice cannot be given as required by this section, a postponement may be ordered by the court for the purpose of a further order of notice.

(c) Except as provided in subsection (b) of this section, upon receipt of an application for temporary custody under this section, the court shall promptly set the time and place for hearing to be held on such application. The court shall order notice of the hearing on temporary custody to be given by regular mail to the Commissioner of Children and Families and by personal service in accordance with section 52–50 to both parents and to the minor child, if over twelve years of age, at least five days prior to the date of the hearing, except that in lieu of personal service on a parent or the father of a minor child born out of wedlock who is either an applicant or who signs under penalty of false statement a written waiver of personal service on a form provided by the Probate Court Administrator, the court may order notice to be given by certified mail, return receipt requested, deliverable to addressee only, at least five days prior to the date of the hearing. If the whereabouts of the parents are unknown, or if such delivery cannot reasonably be effected, then notice shall be ordered to be given by publication. Such notice may be combined with the notice under section 45a–609 or with the notice required under section 45a–716. If the parents are not residents of the state or are absent from the state, the court shall order notice to be given by certified mail, return receipt requested, deliverable to addressee only, at least five days prior to the date of the hearing. If the whereabouts of the parents are unknown, or if delivery cannot reasonably be effected, the court may order notice to be given by publication. Any notice by publication under this subsection shall be in a newspaper which has a circulation at the last-known place of residence of the parents. In either case, such notice shall be given at least five days prior to the date of the hearing, except in the case of notice of hearing on immediate temporary custody under subsection (b) of this section. If the applicant alleges that the whereabouts of a respondent are unknown, such allegation shall be made under penalty of false statement and shall also state the last-known address of the respondent and the efforts which have been made by the applicant to obtain a current address. The applicant shall have the burden of ascertaining the names and addresses of all parties in interest and of proving to the satisfaction of the court that he or she used all proper diligence to discover such names and addresses. Except in the case of newspaper notice, such notice shall include: (1) The time and place of the hearing, (2) a copy of the application for removal or application for termination of parental rights, (3) a copy of the motion for temporary custody, (4) any affidavit or verified petition filed with the motion for temporary custody, (5) any other documents filed by the applicant, (6) any other orders or notices made by the court of probate, and (7) any request for investigation by the Department of Children and Families or any other person or agency. Such notice shall also inform the respondent of the right to have an attorney represent him or her and, if he or she is unable to obtain or pay for an attorney, the respondent may request the court of probate to appoint an attorney to represent him or her. Newspaper notice shall include such facts as the court may direct.

(d) If, after hearing, the court finds by a fair preponderance of the evidence (1) that the parent or other guardian has performed acts of omission or commission as set forth in section 45a–610, and (2) that, because of such acts, the minor child is suffering from serious physical illness or serious physical injury, or the immediate threat thereof, or is in immediate physical danger, so as to require that temporary custody be granted, the court may order the custody of the minor child to be given to one of the following, taking into consideration the standards set forth in section 45a–617: (A) The Commissioner of Children and Families; (B) the board of managers of any child-caring institution or organization; (C) any children's home or similar institution licensed or approved by the Commissioner of Children and Families; or (D) any other person. The fact that an order of temporary custody may have been issued ex parte under subsection (b) of this section shall be of no weight in a hearing held under this subsection. The burden of proof shall remain upon the applicant to establish the applicant's case. The court may issue the order without taking into consideration the standards set forth in this section and section 45a–610 if the parent or other guardian consents to the temporary removal of the minor child, or the court finds that the minor child has no guardian of his or her person. Upon the issuance of an order giving custody of the minor child to the Commissioner of Children and Families, or not later than sixty days after the issuance of such order, the court shall make a determination whether the Department of Children and Families made reasonable efforts to keep the minor child with his or her parent, parents or guardian prior to the issuance of such order and, if such efforts were not made, whether such reasonable efforts were not possible, taking into consideration the minor child's best interests, including the minor child's health and safety.

(e) Such order for temporary custody shall be effective until disposition of the application for removal of parents or guardians as guardian or for termination of parental rights or until a guardian is appointed for a minor child who has no guardian, unless modified or terminated by the court of probate. Any respondent, temporary custodian or attorney for the minor child may petition the court of probate issuing such order at any time for modification or revocation thereof, and such court shall set a hearing upon receipt of such petition in the same manner as subsection (c) of this section. If the court finds after such hearing that the conditions upon which it based its order for temporary custody no longer exist, and that the conditions set forth in subsection (b) of this section do not exist, then the order shall be revoked and the minor child shall be returned to the custody of the parent or guardian.

(f) A copy of any order issued under this section shall be mailed immediately to the last known address of the parent or other guardian from whose custody the minor child has been removed.

(1949 Rev., § 6851; 1958 Rev., § 45–44; 1963, P.A. 151; 1974, P.A. 74–164, § 16, eff. May 10, 1974; 1975, P.A. 75–420, § 4, eff. June 25, 1975; 1977, P.A. 77–21; 1977, P.A. 77–614, § 521, eff. Jan. 1, 1979; 1979, P.A. 79–460, § 7; 1983, P.A. 83–481, § 1; 1984, P.A. 84–294, § 2; 1986, P.A. 86–264, § 1; 1993, P.A. 93–91, § 1, eff. July 1, 1993; 1996, P.A. 96–246, § 31; 1999, P.A. 99–84, § 23; 2000, P.A. 00–75, § 5; 2002, May 9 Sp.Sess., P.A. 02–7, § 31, eff. Aug. 15, 2002.)

§ 45a–608. Temporary custody of minor. Rights and duties

Any person or organization awarded the temporary custody of a minor under section 45a–607, shall have the following rights and duties regarding the minor: (1) The obligation of care and control; (2) the authority to make decisions regarding routine medical treatment or school counseling and emergency medical, psychological, psychiatric or surgical treatment; and (3) other rights and duties which the court of probate having jurisdiction may approve.

(1958 Rev., § 45–44a; 1979, P.A. 79–460, § 8; 1993, P.A. 93–183.)

§ 45a–609. Application for removal of parent as guardian. Hearing. Notice. Examination

(a) Upon application for removal of a parent or parents as guardian, the court shall set a time and place for hearing to be held within thirty days of the application, unless the court requests an investigation in accordance with the provisions of section 45a–619. In that case, the court shall set a day for hearing not more than thirty days following receipt of the results of the investigation.

(b) The court shall order notice of the hearing to be given by regular mail to the Commissioner of Children and Families and by personal service in accordance with section 52–50 to both parents and to the minor, if over twelve years of age, at least ten days before the time of the hearing, except that in lieu of personal service on a parent or the father of a child born out of wedlock who is either a petitioner or who signs under oath a written waiver of personal service on a form provided by the Probate Court Administrator, the court may order notice to be given by certified mail, return receipt requested, deliverable to addressee only, at least ten days prior to the date of the hearing. If such delivery cannot reasonably be effected, then notice shall be ordered to be given by publication. If the parents reside out of or are absent from the state, the court shall order notice to be given by certified mail, return receipt requested, deliverable to addressee only, at least ten days prior to the date of the hearing. If the whereabouts of the parents are unknown, or if delivery cannot reasonably be effected, the court may order notice to be given by publication. Any notice by publication under this subsection shall be in some newspaper which has a circulation at the parents' last-known place of residence. In either case, such notice shall be given at least ten days before the time of the hearing. If the applicant alleges that the whereabouts of a respondent are unknown, such allegation shall be made under penalty of false statement and shall also state the last-known address of the respondent and the efforts which have been made by the applicant to obtain a current address. The applicant shall have the burden of ascertaining the names and addresses of all parties in interest and of proving to the satisfaction of the court that he or she used all proper diligence to discover such names and addresses. Except in the case of newspaper notice, the notice of hearing shall include the following: (1) The notice of hearing, (2) the application for removal of parent as guardian, (3) any supporting documents and affidavits filed with such application, (4) any other orders or notice made by the Court of Probate, and (5) any request for investigation by the Department of Children and Families or any other person or agency. Such notice shall also inform the respondent of the right to have an attorney represent him or her in the matter, and if he or she is unable to obtain or to pay an attorney, the respondent may request the Court of Probate to appoint an attorney to represent him or her. Newspaper notice shall include such facts as the court may direct.

(c) If a parent is over eighteen years of age he or she may sign and file a written waiver of notice with the court.

(d) Upon finding at the hearing or at any time during the pendency of the proceeding that reasonable cause exists to warrant an examination, the court, on its own motion or on motion by any party, may order the child to be examined at a suitable place by a physician, psychiatrist or licensed clinical psychologist appointed by the court. The court may also order examination of a parent or custodian whose competency or ability to care for a child before the court is at issue. The expenses of any examination, if ordered by the court on its own motion, shall be paid for by the applicant, or if ordered on motion by a party, shall be paid for by the party moving for such an examination. If such applicant or party is unable to pay the expense of any such examination, it shall be paid from the Probate Court Administration Fund, or, if the matter has been removed to the Superior Court, from funds appropriated to the Judicial Department.

(1958 Rev., § 45–44b; 1979, P.A. 79–460, § 9; 1983, P.A. 83–481, § 2; 1986, P.A. 86–264, § 2; 1993, P.A. 93–91, § 1, eff. July 1, 1993; 1996, P.A. 96–202, § 6; 1999, P.A. 99–84, § 24; 2000, P.A. 00–75, § 6.)

§ 45a–610. Removal of parent as guardian

If the Court of Probate finds that notice has been given or a waiver has been filed, as provided in section 45a–609, it may remove a parent as guardian, if the court finds by clear and convincing evidence one of the following: (1) The parent consents to his or her removal as guardian; or (2) the minor child has been abandoned by the parent in the sense that the parent has failed to maintain a reasonable degree of interest, concern or responsibility for the minor child's welfare; or (3) the minor child has been denied the care, guidance or control necessary for his or her physical, educational, moral or emotional well-being, as a result of acts of parental commission or omission, whether the acts are the result of the physical or mental incapability of the parent or conditions attributable to parental habits, misconduct or neglect, and the parental acts or deficiencies support the conclusion that the parent cannot exercise, or should not in the best interests of the minor child be permitted to exercise, parental rights and duties at the time; or (4) the minor child has had physical injury or injuries inflicted upon the minor child by a person responsible for such child's health, welfare or care, or by a person given access to such child by such responsible person, other than by accidental means, or has injuries which are at variance with the history given of them or is in a condition which is the result of maltreatment such as, but not limited to, malnutrition, sexual molestation, deprivation of necessities, emotional maltreatment or cruel punishment; or (5) the minor child has been found to be neglected or uncared for, as defined in section 46b–120. If, after removal of a parent as guardian under this section, the minor child has no guardian of his or her person, such a guardian may be appointed under the provisions of section 45a–616. Upon the issuance of an order appointing the Commissioner of Children and Families as guardian of the minor child, or not later than sixty days after the issuance of such order, the court shall make a determination whether the Department of Children and Families made reasonable efforts to keep the minor child with his or her parents prior to the issuance of such order and, if such efforts were not made, whether such reasonable efforts were not possible, taking into consideration the minor child's best interests, including the minor child's health and safety.

(1958 Rev., § 45–44c; 1979, P.A. 79–460, § 10; 1983, P.A. 83–481, § 3; 1984, P.A. 84–294, § 3; 2000, P.A.

00–75, § 3; 2001, P.A. 01–195, § 28, eff. July 11, 2001; 2002, May 9 Sp.Sess., P.A. 02–7, § 32, eff. Aug. 15, 2002.)

§ 45a–611. Reinstatement of parent as guardian of the person of minor

(a) Any parent who has been removed as the guardian of the person of a minor may apply to the court of probate which removed him or her for reinstatement as the guardian of the person of the minor, if in his or her opinion the factors which resulted in removal have been resolved satisfactorily.

(b) In the case of a parent who seeks reinstatement, the court shall hold a hearing following notice to the guardian, to the parent or parents and to the minor, if over twelve years of age, as provided in section 45a–609. If the court determines that the factors which resulted in the removal of the parent have been resolved satisfactorily, the court may remove the guardian and reinstate the parent as guardian of the person of the minor, if it determines that it is in the best interests of the minor to do so. At the request of a parent, guardian, counsel or guardian ad litem representing one of the parties, filed within thirty days of the decree, the court shall make findings of fact to support its conclusions.

(c) The provisions of this section shall also apply to the reinstatement of any guardian of the person of a minor other than a parent.

(1958 Rev., § 45–44d; 1979, P.A. 79–460, § 15; 1992, P.A. 92–118, § 5.)

§ 45a–612. Visitation rights of parent removed as guardian

The court of probate may grant the right of visitation to any person who has been removed as guardian of any minor child or children, any relative of the minor child or children or any parent who has been denied temporary custody of any minor child or children pending the hearing on a removal or termination of parental rights application pursuant to the provisions of sections 45a–132, 45a–593 to 45a–597, inclusive, 45a–603 to 45a–622, inclusive, and 45a–629 to 45a–638, inclusive. Such order shall be according to the best judgment of the court upon the facts of the case and subject to such conditions and limitations as it deems equitable. In making, modifying or terminating such an order, the court shall be guided by the best interest of the child, giving consideration to the wishes of such child if he is of sufficient age and capable of forming an intelligent opinion. The grant of such visitation rights shall not prevent any court of competent jurisdiction from thereafter acting upon the custody of such child, the parental rights with respect to such child or the adoption of such child, and any such court may include in its decree an order terminating such visitation rights.

(1958 Rev., § 45–44e; 1982, P.A. 82–237; 1993, P.A. 93–62.)

§ 45a–613. Removal of guardian or coguardian of the person of a minor

(a) Any guardian or coguardians of the person of a minor appointed under section 45a–616 or appointed by a court of comparable jurisdiction in another state, may be removed by the court of probate which made the appointment, and another guardian or coguardian appointed, in the same manner as that provided in sections 45a–603 to 45a–622, inclusive, for removal of a parent as guardian.

(b) Any removal of a guardian under subsection (a) of this section shall be preceded by notice to the guardian or coguardians, the parent or parents and the minor if over twelve years of age, as provided by section 45a–609.

(c) If a new guardian is appointed, the court shall send a copy of that order to the parent or parents of the minor.

(1958 Rev., § 45–45a; 1979, P.A. 79–460, § 11; 1986, P.A. 86–200, § 2; 1986, P.A. 86–264, § 6.)

§ 45a–614. Removal of parent as guardian of minor

The following persons may apply to the court of probate for the district in which the minor resides for the removal as guardian of one or both parents of the minor: (1) Any adult relative of the minor, including those by blood or marriage; (2) the court on its own motion; or (3) counsel for the minor.

(1958 Rev., § 45–43a; 1979, P.A. 79–460, § 5.)

§ 45a–615. False or malicious application for removal of guardian. Penalty

Any person who wilfully files a false or malicious application for removal of a parent or other guardian as guardian of the person of a minor, who wilfully conspires with another person to file or cause to be filed such an application or who wilfully testifies either in court or by report to the court falsely in any proceeding for removal of a parent or other guardian as guardian of the person of a minor, shall be fined not more than one thousand dollars or imprisoned not more than one year, or both.

(1958 Rev., § 45–43b; 1979, P.A. 79–460, § 6.)

§ 45a–616. Appointment of guardian or coguardians for minor; rights same as of sole surviving parent

(a) If any minor has no parent or guardian of his or her person, the court of probate for the district in which the minor resides may, on its own motion, appoint a guardian or coguardians of the person of the minor, taking into consideration the standards provided in section 45a–617. Such court shall take of such guardian or coguardians a written acceptance of guardianship and, if the court deems it necessary for the protection of the minor, a probate bond.

(b) If any minor has a parent or guardian, who is the sole guardian of the person of the child, the court of probate for the district in which the minor resides may, on the application of the parent or guardian of such child or of the Commissioner of Children and Families with the consent of such parent or guardian and with regard to a child within the care of the commissioner, appoint one or more persons to serve as coguardians of the child. When appointing a guardian or guardians under this subsection, the court shall take into consideration the standards provided in section 45a–617. The court may order that the appointment of a guardian or guardians under this subsection take effect immediately or, upon request of the parent or guardian, upon the occurrence of a specified contingency, including, but not limited to, the mental incapacity, physical debilitation or death of that parent or guardian. Upon the occurrence of such contingency and notice thereof by written affidavit to the probate court by the appointed guardian or guardians, such appointment shall then take effect and continue until the further order of the court, provided the court may hold a hearing to verify the occurrence of such contingency. The court shall take of such guardian or coguardians a written acceptance of guardianship, and if the court deems it necessary for the protection of the minor, a probate bond.

(c) Upon receipt by the court of an application pursuant to this section, the court shall set a time and place for a hearing to be held within thirty days of the application, unless the court requests an investigation in accordance with the provisions of section 45a–619, in which case the court shall set a day for hearing not more than thirty days following receipt of the results of the investigation. The court shall order notice of the hearing to be given to the minor, if over twelve years of age, by certified mail, return receipt requested, deliverable to the addressee only, at least ten days prior to the date of the hearing. In addition, notice by regular mail shall be given to the petitioner and all other parties in interest known by the court.

(d) The rights and obligations of the guardian or coguardians shall be those described in subdivisions (5) and (6) of section 45a–604 and shall be shared with the parent or previously appointed guardian of the person of the minor. The rights and obligations of guardianship may be exercised independently by those who have such rights and obligations. In the event of a dispute between guardians or between a coguardian and a parent, the matter may be submitted to the court of probate which appointed the guardian or coguardian.

(e) Upon the death of the parent or guardian, any appointed guardians of the person of a minor child shall become the sole guardians or coguardians of the person of that minor child.

(1949 Rev., § 6852; 1958 Rev., § 45–45; 1971, P.A. 223, § 1, eff. July 1, 1971; 1974, P.A. 74–251, § 13; 1975, P.A. 75–420, § 4, eff. June 25, 1975; 1977, P.A. 77–614, § 521, eff. Jan. 1, 1979; 1977, P.A. 77–614, § 587, eff. June 2, 1977; 1978, P.A. 78–303, § 85, eff. June 6, 1978; 1979, P.A. 79–460, § 13; 1980, P.A. 80–227, § 2, eff. July 1, 1981; 1986, P.A. 86–200, § 1; 1986, P.A. 86–264, § 5; 1996, P.A. 96–238, § 17, eff. July 1, 1996.)

§ 45a–617. Appointment of guardian or coguardians of the person of a minor

When appointing a guardian or coguardians of the person of a minor, the court shall take into consideration the following factors: (1) The ability of the prospective guardian or coguardians to meet, on a continuing day to day basis, the physical, emotional, moral and educational needs of the minor; (2) the minor's wishes, if he or she is over the age of twelve or is of sufficient maturity and capable of forming an intelligent preference; (3) the existence or nonexistence of an established relationship between the minor and the prospective guardian or coguardians; and (4) the best interests of the child.

(1958 Rev., § 45–45b; 1979, P.A. 79–460, § 12; 1996, P.A. 96–238, § 18, eff. July 1, 1996.)

§ 45a–618. Enforcement of decree and award of custody by warrant

In any proceeding under sections 45a–603 to 45a–622, inclusive, or if an application has been made for termination of parental rights or if parental rights are terminated, the court of probate having jurisdiction may enforce its decree and award the custody of the minor to the person or organization entitled to custody, by a warrant directed to a proper officer commanding him to take possession of the minor and to deliver the minor into the care and custody of the person or organization entitled to custody. The officer shall make return to the court of his actions under the warrant.

(1958 Rev., § 45–45c; 1979, P.A. 79–460, § 14.)

§ 45a–619. Investigation by Commissioner of Children and Families

In any proceeding under sections 45a–603 to 45a–624, inclusive, in which the applicant has alleged that the minor has been abused or neglected, as those terms are defined in section 46b–120, or in which the probate judge has reason to believe that the minor may have been abused or neglected, the Court of Probate shall request the Commissioner of Children and Families or any organization, agency or individual licensed or approved by the commissioner, to make an investigation and written report to it, within ninety days from the receipt of such request, unless the request concerns an application for immediate temporary custody or temporary custody, in which case the commissioner shall render the report by such date as is reasonably ordered by the court. The report shall indicate the physical, mental and emotional status of the minor and shall contain such facts as may be relevant to the court's determination of whether the proposed court action will be in the best interests of the minor, including the physical, social, mental, and financial condition of the parties, and such other factors which the commissioner or agency finds relevant to the court's determination of whether the proposed action will be in the best interests of the minor. In any other proceeding under sections 45a–603 to 45a–624, inclusive, the court shall request an investigation and report unless this requirement is waived for cause shown. The report shall be admissible in evidence, subject to the right of any interested party to require that the person making it appear as a witness, if available, and subject to examination.

(1958 Rev., § 45–45d; 1979, P.A. 79–460, § 16; 1993, P.A. 93–91, § 1, eff. July 1, 1993; 2000, P.A. 00–75, § 7.)

§ 45a–620. Appointment of counsel. Appointment of guardian ad litem to speak on behalf of best interests of minor

The Court of Probate may appoint counsel to represent or appear on behalf of any minor in proceedings brought under sections 45a–603 to 45a–622, inclusive, and sections 45a–715 to 45a–717, inclusive. In any proceeding in which abuse or neglect, as defined in section 46b–120, is alleged by the applicant, or reasonably suspected by the court, a minor shall be represented by counsel appointed by the court to represent the minor. In all cases in which the court deems appropriate, the court shall also appoint a person, other than the person appointed to represent the minor, as guardian ad litem for such minor to speak on behalf of the best interests of the minor, which guardian ad litem is not required to be an attorney-at-law but shall be knowledgeable about the needs and protection of children. The Court of Probate shall appoint counsel to represent any respondent who notifies the court that he or she is unable to obtain counsel, or is unable to pay for counsel. The cost of such counsel shall be paid by the person whom he or she represents, except that if such person is unable to pay for such counsel and files an affidavit with the court demonstrating his or her inability to pay, the reasonable compensation of appointed counsel shall be established by, and paid from funds appropriated to, the Judicial Department, however, if funds have not been included in the budget of the Judicial Department for such purposes, such compensation shall be established by the Probate Court Administrator and paid from the Probate Court Administration Fund. In the case of a minor, such affidavit may be filed by a suitable person having knowledge of the financial status of such minor.

(1958 Rev., § 45–45e; 1979, P.A. 79–460, § 17; 1983, P.A. 83–481, § 4; 1984, P.A. 84–294, § 4; 1990, P.A. 90–31, § 3, eff. May 2, 1990; 1996, P.A. 96–170, § 16, eff. July 1, 1998; 2000, P.A. 00–75, § 4.)

§ 45a–621. Appointment of guardian ad litem

The court of probate shall appoint a guardian ad litem to make any application under sections 45a–603 to 45a–622, inclusive, to represent or appear on behalf of any parent who is less than eighteen years of age or incompetent.

(1958 Rev., § 45–45f; 1979, P.A. 79–460, § 18.)

§ 45a–622. Appointment of temporary guardian. Application. Rights and obligations

(a) Any parent or guardian of the person of a minor may apply to the court of probate for the district in which the minor lives for the appointment of a temporary guardian of the person to serve for no longer than one year if the appointing parent or guardian is unable to care for the minor for any reason including, but not limited to, illness and absence from the jurisdiction. The temporary guardian will cease to serve when the appointing parent or guardian notifies the probate court and the temporary guardian to that effect.

(b) The rights and obligations of the temporary guardian shall be those described in subdivisions (5) and (6) of section 45a–604. A temporary guardian is not liable as a guardian pursuant to section 52–572.

(1958 Rev., § 45–45g; 1979, P.A. 79–460, § 19; 1980, P.A. 80–483, § 147, eff. June 6, 1980; 1996, P.A. 96–202, § 7.)

§ 45a–623. Transfer of contested proceeding to Superior Court or another judge of probate

In any proceeding under sections 45a–603 to 45a–622, inclusive, that is contested, the Court of Probate shall, upon motion of any party other than a party who made application for the removal of a parent as a guardian, under rules adopted by the judges of the Supreme Court, transfer the case to the Superior Court. In addition to the provisions of this section, the Court of Probate may, on the court's own motion or that of any interested party, transfer the case to another judge of probate, which judge shall be appointed by the Probate Court Administrator from a panel of qualified probate judges who specialize in children's matters. Such panel shall be proposed by the Probate Court Administrator and approved by the executive committee of the Connecticut Probate Assembly. The location of the hearing shall be in the original court of probate, except upon agreement of all parties and the Department of Children and Families, where applicable. If the case is transferred and venue altered, the clerk of the court of probate shall transmit to the clerk of the Superior Court or the probate court to which the case was transferred the original files and papers in the case.

(1993, P.A. 93–344; 1995, P.A. 95–316, § 7; 2000, P.A. 00–75, § 8.)

§ 45a–624. Designation of standby guardian of minor

A parent or guardian, as principal, may designate a standby guardian of a minor in accordance with the provisions of sections 45a–624 to 45a–624g, inclusive. Such designation, in a form as provided in section 45a–624b, shall take effect upon the occurrence of a specified contingency, including, but not limited to, the mental incapacity, physical debilitation or death of the principal, provided a written statement signed under penalty of false statement has been executed pursuant to section 45a–624c that such contingency has occurred. A designation of a standby guardian shall be in writing and signed and dated by the principal with at least two witnesses. The principal shall provide a copy of such designation to the standby guardian.

(1994, P.A. 94–207, § 1; 1999, P.A. 99–84, § 25.)

§ 45a–624a. Consent of parents required for designation of standby guardian

If both parents are alive, both parents of the minor shall consent to the designation of a standby guardian, unless either parent has been removed as guardian or had his parental rights terminated. In any such event, the remaining parent may designate a standby guardian pursuant to sections 45a–624 to 45a–624g, inclusive.

(1994, P.A. 94–207, § 2.)

§ 45a–624b. Form for designation of standby guardian

The designation of a standby guardian shall be in substantially the following form:

I .... (insert name of principal) do hereby appoint .... (insert name and address of the standby guardian) as the standby guardian of .... (insert names of minor children) to take effect upon the occurrence of the following contingency or contingencies .... (insert specific contingency or contingencies).

This designation is made after careful reflection, while I am of sound mind.

Date ...., 20...	.... L.S.
....	....
(Witness)	(Witness)
....	....
(Number and Street)	(Number and Street)
....	....
(City, State and Zip Code)	(City, State and Zip Code)

(1994, P.A. 94–207, § 8.)

§ 45a–624c. Written statement that designation of standby guardian in full force and effect

The written statement referred to in section 45a–624 shall be in substantially the following form:

STATEMENT THAT DESIGNATION OF A STANDBY GUARDIAN

IS IN FULL FORCE AND EFFECT

STATE OF)

) SS:

COUNTY OF)

I,.... of...., state under penalty of false statement:

THAT...., of...., as principal, did on...., 20.., appoint me as standby guardian dated...., 20.., to execute a statement that a specified contingency had occurred;

THAT specified contingency was: ....

THAT specified contingency has occurred.

IN WITNESS WHEREOF, I have hereunto set my hand and seal under penalty of false statement.

....

Witness

....

....L.S.

Witness

(1994, P.A. 94–207, § 3; 1999, P.A. 99–84, § 26.)

§ 45a–624d. Authority of standby guardian

When a designation of a standby guardian becomes effective upon the occurrence of a specified contingency, such standby guardian shall have the authority and obligations of a guardian as defined in subdivision (5) of section 45a–604. Such designation shall be effective for a period of one year. Such authority and obligations of a standby guardian shall cease when the specified contingency no longer exists or after the expiration of such one–year period, whichever is sooner.

(1994, P.A. 94–207, § 4; 1995, P.A. 95–50, § 1, eff. May 22, 1995.)

§ 45a–624e. Authority of standby guardian after death of principal

If a designation of a standby guardian is effective at the time of death of the principal, such designation shall remain in effect for a period of ninety days after such death. At the end of such ninety-day period, the authority of such standby guardian shall cease, unless such standby guardian files an application for guardianship with the probate court in the district in which the minor resides and temporary custody of the minor is granted to such standby guardian or the court appoints such standby guardian as guardian of the person of the minor.

(1994, P.A. 94–207, § 5.)

§ 45a–624f. Revocation of designation of standby guardian

The principal may revoke a designation of a standby guardian at any time by written revocation and notification of the revocation to the standby guardian.

(1994, P.A. 94–207, § 6.)

§ 45a–624g. Probate court to resolve disputes concerning designation of standby guardian

The probate court for the district in which the minor resides at the time of any dispute concerning the meaning or application of any provision of sections

45a–624 to 45a–624f, inclusive, shall have jurisdiction over such dispute.

(1994, P.A. 94–207, § 7.)

§ 45a–625. Guardian of person of minor to report to probate court re condition of minor

Any person appointed as guardian of the person of a minor pursuant to sections 45a–603 to 45a–624g, inclusive, shall report at least annually to the probate court which appointed the guardian regarding the condition of the minor.

(1999, P.A. 99–84, § 9.)

§§ 45a–626 to 45a–627. Reserved for future use

PART III. GUARDIANS OF THE ESTATE OF A MINOR

§ 45a–628. Reserved for future use

§ 45a–629. Appointment of guardian for minor's estate

(a) When a minor is entitled to property, the court of probate for the district in which the minor resides may assign a time and place for a hearing on the appointment of a guardian of the estate of the minor. The court shall cause reasonable notice of hearing to be given to (1) the parents or guardian of the person of the minor, (2) the minor, if the minor is twelve years of age or older, and (3) such other persons as it determines. Any person entitled to notice of the hearing may waive such notice.

(b) If the court finds that there is no guardian of the estate of the minor, it may appoint one or both of the parents or any guardian of the person of the minor to be guardian of his or her estate. If neither parent nor the guardian of the person of the minor will accept the appointment, or if the parents or guardian of the person of the minor are not proper persons to act as guardian of his or her estate, the court may appoint any proper person or persons chosen by the minor if the minor is twelve years of age or over. If the minor neglects to make choice or fails to choose a proper person or persons or is not of sufficient age, the court of probate shall appoint some proper person or persons, who, as guardian of the estate of the minor, shall have charge of all the minor's property, whether acquired before or after the guardian's appointment, but shall have no control over such minor's person. If any minor who has a guardian marries and owns or thereafter acquires property, the guardianship of such property shall continue during such person's minority. Any guardian so appointed shall give a probate bond.

(1949 Rev., § 6854; 1958 Rev., § 45–47; 1974, P.A. 74–82, § 1; 1980, P.A. 80–227, § 3, eff. July 1, 1981; 1980, P.A. 80–476, § 106, eff. Oct. 1, 1980; 1985, P.A. 85–193, § 3; 1986, P.A. 86–264, § 7; 1999, P.A. 99–84, § 5.)

§ 45a–630. Application for appointment of guardian of the estate of a minor

In the case of any application for the appointment of a guardian of the estate of a minor pursuant to the provisions of sections 45a–132, 45a–593 to 45a–597, inclusive, 45a–603 to 45a–622, inclusive, and 45a–629 to 45a–638, inclusive, the application shall state that such minor either is, or is not, receiving aid or care from the state, whichever is true, and a copy of each application which states the minor is receiving such aid or care shall be sent by the court to the Commissioner of Administrative Services at least ten days in advance of any hearing on such application. Said commissioner or his designee may participate at any hearing on such application.

(1958 Rev., § 45–47a; 1979, P.A. 79–358, § 1.)

§ 45a–631. Limitation on receipt or use of minor's property by parent, guardian or spouse. Release

(a) A parent of a minor, guardian of the person of a minor or spouse of a minor shall not receive or use any property belonging to the minor in an amount exceeding ten thousand dollars in value unless appointed guardian of the estate of the minor, except that such parent, guardian or spouse may hold property as a custodian under the provisions of sections 45a–557 to 45a–560b, inclusive, without being so appointed.

(b) A release given by both parents or by the parent who has legal custody of a minor or by the guardian or spouse shall, if the amount does not exceed ten thousand dollars in value, be valid and binding upon the minor.

(1949 Rev., § 6855; 1949, Supp. § 585a; 1953, Supp. § 2192c; 1955, Supp. § 2901d; 1957, P.A. 417; 1958 Rev., § 45–49; 1963, P.A. 179, § 1, eff. May 29, 1963; 1967, P.A. 216; 1974, P.A. 74–82, § 2; 1980, P.A. 80–476, § 108, eff. Oct. 1, 1980; 1995, P.A. 95–117, § 27; 2000, P.A. 00–78.)

§ 45a–632. Appointment of guardian of estate of nonresident minor

When a minor who resides outside this state and who has no guardian within this state owns property in this state, the court of probate for the district in which the property or any part of it lies may appoint a guardian of the minor who shall have charge of and manage the property. A probate bond shall be required of such guardian.

(1949 Rev., § 6857; 1958 Rev., § 45–50; 1980, P.A. 80–227, § 4, eff. July 1, 1981; 1980, P.A. 80–476, § 109, eff. Oct. 1, 1980.)

§ 45a–633. Lease of minor's real estate by guardian or coguardians of estate

The guardian or coguardians of the estate of any minor may apply to the court of probate of the district in this state which appointed him, and may, upon application and hearing, after public notice, lease his ward's real property upon terms and for a length of time, not exceeding the ward's minority, which are approved by the court.

(1949 Rev., § 6859; 1958 Rev., § 45–52; 1980, P.A. 80–476, § 110, eff. Oct. 1, 1980; 1981, P.A. 81–472, § 79, eff. July 8, 1981; 1986, P.A. 86–200, § 4.)

§ 45a–634. Inventory of ward's property by guardian of estate

(a) Each guardian of an estate appointed by a court of probate shall make and file in the court appointing or approving such guardian, under penalty of false statement within two months after the acceptance by the guardian of the trust, an inventory of all the property belonging to such guardian's ward, appraised, or caused to be appraised, by such guardian, at fair market value as of the date of his or her appointment. Such inventory shall include the value of the ward's interest in all property in which the ward has a legal or equitable present interest, including, but not limited to, the ward's interest in any joint bank accounts or other jointly held property.

(b) Any guardian who fails to return the inventory to the court within that time shall be fined not more than twenty dollars.

(1949 Rev., § 6860; 1958 Rev., § 45–53; 1980, P.A. 80–476, § 111, eff. Oct. 1, 1980; 1987, P.A. 87–565, § 1; 1999, P.A. 99–84, § 27.)

§ 45a–635. Removal by foreign guardian of ward's personal property

(a) When any personal property in this state belongs to any person residing out of this state who has a guardian, trustee or other legal custodian of his estate, appointed under the laws of the place of his residence, the custodian may apply in writing to the court of probate of the district in which the principal part of the property in this state is located, alleging: (1) That he has been legally appointed custodian in the jurisdiction in which the person to whom the property belongs resides; and (2) that he has therein given a probate bond valid according to the requirements of such jurisdiction, and security thereon, or an increase in an existing bond and security, in an amount equal to the value of all such property of the person to be removed from this state; and (3) that a removal of the property from this state will not conflict with the terms and limitations by which the person owns it.

(b) If the probate court finds the allegations true and the applicant files in the probate court for record an exemplified copy of the record of the court by which he was appointed, the probate court may, after a hearing upon the application, upon such notice as it orders to the person having the property in his custody and to the owner of the property, and after proof that all known debts chargeable against it and contracted in this state have been paid or satisfied, appoint the applicant to be guardian, conservator or trustee of such estate without further bond. The probate court may authorize the person having the property in his custody to deliver it to the applicant, who may demand, sue for and recover it and remove it from this state.

(1949 Rev., § 6862; 1958 Rev., § 45–55; 1980, P.A. 80–227, § 6, eff. July 1, 1981; 1980, P.A. 80–476, § 112, eff. Oct. 1, 1980.)

§ 45a–636. Removal by foreign guardian of proceeds of sale of ward's real estate

If any foreign guardian of the estate of a minor who is also residing outside this state has obtained an order from any court of probate in this state having jurisdiction to sell real property of the minor which is situated in this state and has given a probate bond, the court of probate may, upon application and proceedings as specified in section 45a–635, authorize the foreign guardian to receive the proceeds of the sale of the real property sold under order and to remove the proceeds from this state into the jurisdiction in which the guardian and his ward reside. The guardian and his surety shall thereupon be discharged from all liability on the bond.

(1949 Rev., § 6863; 1958 Rev., § 45–56; 1980, P.A. 80–227, § 7, eff. July 1, 1981; 1980, P.A. 80–476, § 113, eff. Oct. 1, 1980.)

§ 45a–637. Guardians of estate of minors may make partition

If any minor has an interest in any real property as a tenant in common with any other person, the guardian of the estate of the minor may, by an instrument in writing executed as deeds of land are executed, make partition of the real property with the other parties in interest. Such deed of partition described in this section shall not be valid until the approval of the court of probate having jurisdiction of the property of the minor is endorsed on it. The deed of partition and the approval of the court of probate shall be recorded in the land records of the town or towns where the land is situated.

(1949 Rev., § 6864; 1958 Rev., § 45–57; 1980, P.A. 80–476, § 114, eff. Oct. 1, 1980.)

§ 45a–638. Court may order guardian to convey real property

The court of probate in which the guardian of any minor has been appointed may, concurrently with courts of equity, order such guardian to convey the interest of his ward in any real property which ought in equity to be conveyed to another person.

(1958 Rev., § 45-57a; 1980, P.A. 80-476, § 115, eff. Oct. 1, 1980.)

§§ 45a-639 to 45a-643. Reserved for future use

PART IV. CONSERVATORS

§ 45a-644. Definitions

For the purposes of sections 45a-644 to 45a-662, inclusive, the following terms shall have the following meanings:

(a) "Conservator of the estate" means a person, a municipal or state official, or a private profit or nonprofit corporation except a hospital or nursing home as defined in section 19a-521, appointed by the court of probate under the provisions of sections 45a-644 to 45a-662, inclusive, to supervise the financial affairs of a person found to be incapable of managing his or her own affairs or of a person who voluntarily asks the court of probate for the appointment of a conservator of the estate, and includes a temporary conservator of the estate appointed under the provisions of section 45a-654.

(b) "Conservator of the person" means a person, a municipal or state official, or a private profit or nonprofit corporation, except a hospital or nursing home as defined in section 19a-521, appointed by the probate court under the provisions of sections 45a-644 to 45a-662, inclusive, to supervise the personal affairs of a person found to be incapable of caring for himself or herself or of a person who voluntarily asks the court of probate for the appointment of a conservator of the person, and includes a temporary conservator of the person appointed under the provisions of section 45a-654.

(c) "Incapable of caring for one's self" means a mental, emotional or physical condition resulting from mental illness, mental deficiency, physical illness or disability, chronic use of drugs or alcohol, or confinement, which results in the person's inability to provide medical care for physical and mental health needs, nutritious meals, clothing, safe and adequately heated and ventilated shelter, personal hygiene and protection from physical abuse or harm and which results in endangerment to such person's health.

(d) "Incapable of managing his or her affairs" means that a person has a mental, emotional or physical condition resulting from mental illness, mental deficiency, physical illness or disability, chronic use of drugs or alcohol, or confinement, which prevents that person from performing the functions inherent in managing his or her affairs, and the person has property which will be wasted or dissipated unless proper management is provided, or that funds are needed for the support, care or welfare of the person or those entitled to be supported by that person and that the person is unable to take the necessary steps to obtain or provide funds which are needed for the support, care or welfare of the person or those entitled to be supported by such person.

(e) "Involuntary representation" means the appointment of a conservator of the person or the estate, or both, after a finding by the court of probate that the respondent is incapable of managing his or her affairs or incapable of caring for himself or herself.

(f) "Respondent" means an adult person for whom an application for involuntary representation has been filed or an adult person who has requested voluntary representation.

(g) "Voluntary representation" means the appointment of a conservator of the person or estate, or both, upon request of the respondent, without a finding that the respondent is incapable of managing his or her affairs or incapable of caring for himself or herself.

(h) "Ward" means a person for whom involuntary representation is granted under sections 45a-644 to 45a-662, inclusive.

(1958 Rev., § 45-70a; 1977, P.A. 77-446, § 1; 1980, P.A. 80-476, § 123, eff. Oct. 1, 1980; 1984, P.A. 84-271, § 1; 1993, P.A. 93-184.)

§ 45a-645. Naming of own conservator for future incapacity

(a) Any person who has attained at least eighteen years of age, and who is of sound mind, may designate in writing a person or persons whom he desires to be appointed as conservator of his person or estate or both, if he is thereafter found to be incapable of managing his affairs.

(b) The designation shall be executed, witnessed and revoked in the same manner as provided for wills in sections 45a-251 and 45a-257; provided, any person who is so designated as a conservator shall not qualify as a witness.

(c) Such written instrument may excuse the person or persons so designated from giving the probate bond required under the provisions of section 45a-650, if appointed thereafter as a conservator.

(1949 Rev., § 6874; 1955, Supp. § 2907d; 1958 Rev., § 45-70; 1965, Feb.Sp.Sess., P.A. 590, § 1; 1969, P.A. 447, § 2; 1969, P.A. 730, § 14, eff. July 1, 1969; 1973, P.A. 73-34 § 1; 1975, P.A. 75-128; 1977, P.A. 77-446, § 13; 1977, P.A. 77-614, § 70, eff. Oct. 1, 1977; 1980, P.A. 80-476, § 124, eff. Oct. 1, 1980.)

§ 45a-646. Application for voluntary representation

Any person may make application to the court of probate in the district in which he resides or has his domicile for voluntary representation either for the appointment of a conservator of the person or a conservator of the estate, or both. If the application excuses bond, no bond shall be required by the court unless later requested by the respondent or unless facts are brought to the attention of the court that a bond is necessary for the protection of the respondent. Upon receipt of the application, the court shall set a time and place for hearing and shall give such notice as it may direct to the petitioner, the petitioner's spouse, if any, the Commissioner of Administrative Services, if the respondent is receiving aid or care from the state, and to other interested parties, if any. After seeing the respondent in person and hearing his or her reasons for the application and after explaining to the respondent that granting the petition will subject the respondent or respondent's property, as the case may be, to the authority of the conservator, the court may grant voluntary representation and thereupon shall appoint a conservator of the person or estate or both, and shall not make a finding that the petitioner is incapable. The conservator of the person or estate or both, shall have all the powers and duties of a conservator of the person or estate of an incapable person appointed pursuant to section 45a–650. If the respondent subsequently becomes disabled or incapable, the authority of the conservator shall not be revoked as a result of such disability or incapacity.

(1958 Rev., § 45–70e; 1977, P.A. 77–446, § 5; 1979, P.A. 79–358, § 4; 1980, P.A. 80–476, § 125, eff. Oct. 1, 1980; 1987, P.A. 87–87; 1991, P.A. 91–49, § 4.)

§ 45a–647. Release from voluntary representation

Any person who is under voluntary representation as provided by section 45a–646 shall be released from voluntary representation upon giving thirty days' written notice to the court of probate.

(1958 Rev., § 45–70f; 1977, P.A. 77–446, § 10; 1980, P.A. 80–476, § 126, eff. Oct. 1, 1980.)

§ 45a–648. Application for involuntary representation. Penalty for fraudulent or malicious application or false testimony

(a) An application for involuntary representation may be filed by any person alleging that a respondent is incapable of managing his or her affairs or incapable of caring for himself or herself and stating the reasons for the alleged incapability. The application shall be filed in the court of probate in the district in which the respondent resides or has his domicile.

(b) Any person who wilfully files a fraudulent or malicious application for involuntary representation or appointment of a temporary conservator or any person who conspires with another person to file or cause to be filed such an application or any person who wilfully testifies either in court or by report to the court falsely to the incapacity of any person in any proceeding provided for in sections 45a–644 to 45a–662, inclusive, shall be fined not more than one thousand dollars or imprisoned not more than one year or both.

(1958 Rev., § 45–70b; 1977, P.A. 77–446, § 2; 1980, P.A. 80–476, § 127, eff. Oct. 1, 1980; 1984, P.A. 84–271, § 3.)

§ 45a–649. Notice of hearing. Appointment of counsel

(a) Upon an application for involuntary representation, the court shall issue a citation to the following enumerated parties to appear before it at a time and place named in the citation, which shall be served on the parties at least seven days before the hearing date, which date shall not be more than thirty days after the receipt of the application by the Court of Probate unless continued for cause shown. Notice of the hearing shall be sent within thirty days after receipt of the application. (1) The court shall direct that personal service be made, by a state marshal, constable or an indifferent person, upon the following: (A) The respondent, except that if the court finds personal service on the respondent would be detrimental to the health or welfare of the respondent, the court may order that such service be made upon counsel for the respondent, if any, and if none, upon the attorney appointed under subsection (b) of this section; (B) the respondent's spouse, if any, if the spouse is not the applicant, except that in cases where the application is for involuntary representation pursuant to section 17b–456, and there is no spouse, the court shall order notice by certified mail to the children of the respondent and if none, the parents of the respondent and if none, the brothers and sisters of the respondent or their representatives, and if none, the next of kin of such respondent. (2) The court shall order such notice as it directs to the following: (A) The applicant; (B) the person in charge of welfare in the town where the respondent is domiciled or resident and if there is no such person, the first selectman or chief executive officer of the town if the respondent is receiving assistance from the town; (C) the Commissioner of Social Services, if the respondent is in a state-operated institution or receiving aid, care or assistance from the state; (D) the Commissioner of Veterans' Affairs if the respondent is receiving veterans' benefits or the Veterans' Home, or both, if the respondent is receiving aid or care from such home, or both; (E) the Commissioner of Administrative Services, if the respondent is receiving aid or care from the state; (F) the children of the respondent and if none, the parents of the respondent and if none, the brothers and sisters of the respondent or their representatives; (G) the person in charge of the hospital, nursing home or some other institution, if the respondent is in a hospital, nursing home or some other institution.(3) The court, in its discretion, may order such notice as it directs to other persons having an interest in the respondent and to such persons the respondent requests be notified.

(b) (1) The notice required by subdivision (1) of subsection (a) of this section shall specify (A) the nature of involuntary representation sought and the legal consequences thereof, (B) the facts alleged in the application, and (C) the time and place of the hearing. (2) The notice shall further state that the respondent has a right to be present at the hearing and has a right to be represented by an attorney at his or her own expense. If the respondent is unable to request or obtain counsel for any reason, the court shall appoint an attorney to represent the respondent in any proceeding under this title involving the respondent. If the respondent is unable to pay for the services of such attorney, the reasonable compensation for such attorney shall be established by, and paid from funds appropriated to, the Judicial Department, however, if funds have not been included in the budget of the Judicial Department for such purposes, such compensation shall be established by the Probate Court Administrator and paid from the Probate Court Administration Fund. If the respondent notifies the court in any manner that he or she wants to attend the hearing on the application but is unable to do so because of physical incapacity, the court shall schedule the hearing on the application at a place which would facilitate attendance by the respondent but if not practical, then the judge shall visit the respondent, if he or she is in the state of Connecticut, before the hearing. Notice to all other persons required by this section shall state only the nature of involuntary representation sought, the legal consequences thereof and the time and place of the hearing.

(1958 Rev., § 45–70c; 1977, P.A. 77–446, § 3; 1977, P.A. 77–614, § 521, eff. Jan. 1, 1979; 1977, P.A. 77–614, § 587, eff. June 2, 1977; 1978, P.A. 78–303, § 85, eff. June 6, 1978; 1979, P.A. 79–358, § 3; 1979, P.A. 79–501, § 1; 1980, P.A. 80–476, § 128, eff. Oct. 1, 1980; 1981, P.A. 81–223; 1983, P.A. 83–295, § 25, eff. Oct. 1, 1983; 1984, P.A. 84–271, § 4; 1986, P.A. 86–195, § 1; 1989, P.A. 89–64; 1990, P.A. 90–31, § 6, eff. May 2, 1990; 1993, P.A. 93–262, § 1, eff. July 1, 1993; 1996, P.A. 96–170, § 17, eff. July 1, 1998; 2000, P.A. 00–99, § 86, eff. Dec. 1, 2000; 2001, P.A. 01–127, § 2; 2004, P.A. 04–169, § 20, eff. June 1, 2004.)

§ 45a–650. Hearing. Appointment of conservator. Limitation re powers and duties

(a) At any hearing for involuntary representation, the court shall receive evidence regarding the condition of the respondent, including a written report or testimony by one or more physicians licensed to practice medicine in the state who have examined the respondent within thirty days preceding the hearing. The report or testimony shall contain specific information regarding the disability and the extent of its incapacitating effect. The court may also consider such other evidence as may be available and relevant, including but not limited to a summary of the physical and social functioning level or ability of the respondent, and the availability of support services from the family, neighbors, community, or any other appropriate source. Such evidence may include, if available, reports from the social work service of a general hospital, municipal social worker, director of social service, public health nurse, public health agency, psychologist, coordinating assessment and monitoring agencies, or such other persons as the court deems qualified to provide such evidence. The court may waive the requirement that medical evidence be presented if it is shown that the evidence is impossible to obtain because of the absence of the respondent or his or her refusal to be examined by a physician or that the alleged incapacity is not medical in nature. If this requirement is waived, the court shall make a specific finding in any decree issued on the petition stating why medical evidence was not required. In any matter in which the Commissioner of Social Services seeks the appointment of a conservator pursuant to chapter 319dd [1] and represents to the court that an examination by an independent physician, psychologist or psychiatrist is necessary to determine whether the elderly person is capable of managing his or her personal or financial affairs, the court shall order such examination unless the court determines that such examination is not in the best interests of the elderly person. The court shall order such examination notwithstanding any medical report submitted to the court by the elderly person or the caretaker of such elderly person.

(b) Notwithstanding the provisions of section 45a–7, the court may hold the hearing on the application at a place within the state other than its usual courtroom if it would facilitate attendance by the respondent.

(c) If the court finds by clear and convincing evidence that the respondent is incapable of managing his or her affairs, the court shall appoint a conservator of his or her estate unless it appears to the court that such affairs are being managed properly without the appointment of a conservator. If the court finds by clear and convincing evidence that the respondent is incapable of caring for himself or herself, the court shall appoint a conservator of his or her person unless it appears to the court that the respondent is being cared for properly without the appointment of a conservator.

(d) When determining whether a conservator should be appointed and in selecting a conservator to be appointed for the respondent, the court shall be guided by the best interests of the respondent. In making such determination, the court shall consider whether the respondent had previously made alternative arrangements for the care of his person or for the management of his affairs, including, but not limited to, the execution of a valid durable power of attorney, the appointment of a health-care agent or other similar document. The respondent may, by oral or written request, if at the time of the request he or she has sufficient capacity to form an intelligent preference, nominate a conservator who shall be appointed unless the court finds the appointment of the nominee is not in the best interests of the respondent. In such case, or in the absence of any such nomination, the court may appoint any qualified person, authorized public official or corporation in accordance with subsections (a) and (b) of section 45a–644.

(e) Upon the request of the respondent or his or her counsel, made within thirty days of the date of the decree, the court shall make and furnish findings of fact to support its conclusion.

(f) If the court appoints a conservator of the estate of the respondent, it shall require a probate bond. The court may, if it deems it necessary for the protection of the respondent, require a bond of any conservator of the person appointed hereunder.

(g) The court may limit the powers and duties of either the conservator of the person or the conservator of the estate, to include some, but not all, of the powers and duties set forth in subsections (a) and (b) of section 45a–644, sections 45a–655 and 45a–656, and shall make specific findings to justify such a limitation, in the best interests of the ward. In determining whether or not any limitations should be imposed, the court shall consider the abilities of the ward, the prior appointment of any attorney-in-fact, health care agent, trustee or other fiduciary acting on behalf of the ward, any support services which are otherwise available to the ward, and any other relevant evidence. The court may modify its decree upon any change in circumstances.

(1958 Rev., § 45–70d; 1977, P.A. 77–446, § 4; 1980, P.A. 80–227, § 8, eff. July 1, 1981; 1980, P.A. 80–476, § 129, eff. Oct. 1, 1980; 1984, P.A. 84–271, § 5; 1997, P.A. 97–90, § 4; 1998, P.A. 98–219, § 17; 2001, P.A. 01–209, § 6, eff. July 1, 2001.)

[1] C.G.S.A. § 17b–450 et seq.

§ 45a–651. Appointment of Commissioner of Social Services as conservator for certain persons with limited resources. Legal representation

(a) (1) If no suitable conservator can be found after due diligence and the court finds that the health or welfare of the respondent is in jeopardy, the Commissioner of Social Services shall accept appointment within available appropriations, as conservator of the estate of any respondent sixty years of age or older found incapable under sections 45a–644 to 45a–662, inclusive, of managing his or her affairs, whose liquid assets, excluding burial insurance in an amount up to one thousand five hundred dollars, do not exceed one thousand five hundred dollars at the time of such appointment. (2) If no suitable conservator can be found after due diligence and the court finds that the health or welfare of the respondent is in jeopardy, the Commissioner of Social Services shall accept appointment, within available appropriations, as conservator of the person, of any respondent sixty years of age or older found incapable under said sections of caring for himself or herself, whose liquid assets, excluding burial insurance in an amount up to one thousand five hundred dollars, do not exceed one thousand five hundred dollars at the time of such appointment.

(b) The Commissioner of Social Services may delegate any power, duty or function arising from the appointment of such commissioner as either conservator of the estate or of the person respectively, to an employee of the Department of Social Services.

(c) When so appointed, such commissioner or designees shall have all the powers and duties of a conservator as provided in sections 45a–644 to 45a–662, inclusive. The department may contract with any public or private agency or person to assist in the carrying out of the duties as conservator of the estate or the person.

(d) During the term of appointment of the Commissioner of Social Services as conservator, if a suitable person or legally qualified person, corporation or municipal or state official is found to replace such commissioner as conservator, such person, corporation or official may be appointed successor conservator subject to the approval of the court of probate.

(e) The Commissioner of Social Services shall adopt regulations in accordance with the provisions of chapter 54 [1] setting forth the terms and conditions of the acceptance and the termination of appointment as conservator of the estate or person in accordance with this section.

(f) In any proceeding to appoint the Commissioner of Social Services as conservator, the court shall appoint an attorney to represent the person for whom such commissioner has been appointed conservator if such person is without legal representation.

(1958 Rev., § 45–70g; 1984, P.A. 84–271, § 2; 1988, P.A. 88–206, § 1; 1993, P.A. 93–262, § 64, eff. July 1, 1993; 2000, P.A. 00–39, § 1, eff. May 1, 2000.)

[1] C.G.S.A. § 4–166 et seq.

§ 45a–652. Application for appointment of conservator of the estate

In the case of any application for the appointment of a conservator of the estate, as said terms are defined in section 45a–644, and, in the case of any application for involuntary representation, as defined in subsection (d) of section 45a–644, the application shall state that the respondent, as defined in subsection (e) of section 45a–644, either is or is not, receiving such aid or care from the state, whichever is true, and a copy of each application which states the respondent is receiving such aid or care shall be sent by the court to the Commissioner of Administrative Services, in accordance with the provisions of subsection (a) of section 45a–649 or section 45a–646, as the case may be.

(1958 Rev., § 45–71a; 1979, P.A. 79–358, § 2.)

§ 45a–653. Contracts and funds of alleged incapable person pending application for appointment of conservator. Notice of application

(a) If an application for the appointment of a conservator has been made, and if, while the application is pending, the applicant records a notice of the application with the town clerk of any town within which real property of the alleged incapable person is situated and with the town clerk of the town in which the alleged incapable person resides, any conveyance of such real property by such person and any contract made by such person between the time the notice of the application is recorded and the time of the adjudication of the court upon the application shall not be valid without the approval of the court.

(b) If, during the pendency of the application, the applicant lodges with any bank, trust company or other depositary a notice of the application, such bank, trust company or depositary shall not allow any funds of the alleged incapable person to be withdrawn, between the time the notice of the application is lodged and the time of the adjudication of the court upon the application, without the approval of the court.

(c) A notice recorded or lodged pursuant to this section shall state that an application for appointment of a conservator is pending and shall include the name of the alleged incapable person, the name of the applicant, the probate district in which the application is pending, and the date of application. The notice shall be signed and acknowledged by the applicant. The notice shall not include the allegation of facts on which the application is based.

(1949 Rev., § 6876; 1958 Rev., § 45–73; 1980, P.A. 80–476, § 135, eff. Oct. 1, 1980; 1991, P.A. 91–406, § 18, eff. July 2, 1991; 1994, P.A. 94–111; 1996, P.A. 96–180, § 124, eff. June 3, 1996.)

§ 45a–654. Appointment of temporary conservator

(a) Upon written application for appointment of a temporary conservator brought by any person deemed by the court to have sufficient interest in the welfare of the respondent, including but not limited to the spouse or any relative of the respondent, the first selectman, chief executive officer or head of the department of welfare of the town of residence or domicile of any respondent, the Commissioner of Social Services, the board of directors of any charitable organization, as defined in section 21a–190a, or the chief administrative officer of any nonprofit hospital or such officer's designee, the Court of Probate may appoint a temporary conservator, if it finds that: (1) The respondent is incapable of managing his affairs or incapable of caring for himself and (2) irreparable injury to the mental or physical health or financial or legal affairs of the respondent will result if a temporary conservator is not appointed pursuant to this section. The court may, in its discretion, require the temporary conservator to give a probate bond. The temporary conservator shall have charge of the property or of the person of the respondent or both for such period of time or for such specific occasion as the court finds to be necessary, provided a temporary appointment shall not be valid for more than thirty days, unless at any time while the appointment of a temporary conservator is in effect, an application is filed for appointment of a conservator of the person or estate under section 45a–650. The court may extend the appointment of the temporary conservator until the disposition of such application, or for an additional thirty days, whichever occurs first.

(b) Except as provided in subsection (e) of this section, an appointment of a temporary conservator shall not be made unless a report is presented to the judge, signed by a physician licensed to practice medicine or surgery in this state, stating: (1) That the physician has examined such person and the date of such examination, which shall not be more than three days prior to the date of presentation to the judge; (2) that it is the opinion of the physician that the respondent is incapable of managing his affairs or of caring for himself; and (3) the reasons for such opinion.

(c) The court may, ex parte and without prior notice to the respondent, appoint a temporary conservator upon making the findings required by subsection (a) of this section. After making such appointment, the court shall immediately: (1) Appoint an attorney to represent the respondent, provided if the respondent is unable to pay for the services of such attorney, the reasonable compensation for such attorney shall be established by, and paid from funds appropriated to, the Judicial Department, however, if funds have not been included in the budget of the Judicial Department for such purposes, such compensation shall be established by the Probate Court Administrator and paid from the Probate Court Administration Fund; and (2) give notice by mail, or such other notice as the court deems appropriate, to the respondent, the respondent's next of kin and such attorney, which notice shall include: (A) A copy of the application for appointment of temporary conservator and the accompanying physician's report; and (B) a copy of the decree appointing a temporary conservator. If the court determines that notice to the respondent under this subsection would be detrimental to the health or welfare of the respondent, the court may give such notice only to the respondent's next of kin and the respondent's attorney. Thereafter, the court shall, upon the written request of the respondent, the respondent's next of kin or the respondent's attorney, or may upon its own motion, hold a hearing. Such hearing shall be held within seventy-two hours of receipt of such request, excluding Saturdays, Sundays and holidays, and upon such notice as the court deems appropriate. After hearing, the court may confirm or revoke the appointment of the temporary conservator.

(d) If the court determines that an ex parte appointment of a temporary conservator pursuant to subsection (c) of this section is not appropriate but finds substantial evidence that appointment of a temporary conservator may be necessary, the court shall hold a hearing on the application. Unless continued by the court for cause, such hearing shall be held within seventy-two hours of receipt of the application, excluding Saturdays, Sundays and holidays. Prior to such hearing, the court shall appoint an attorney to represent the respondent in accordance with subsection (c) of this section and shall give such notice as it deems appropriate to the respondent, the respondent's next of kin and such attorney, which notice shall include a copy of the application for appointment of a temporary conservator and the accompanying physician's report. After hearing and upon making the findings required by subsection (a) of this section, the court may appoint a temporary conservator.

(e) The court may waive the medical evidence requirement under subsection (b) of this section if the court finds that the evidence is impossible to obtain because of the refusal of the respondent to be examined by a physician. In any such case the court may, in lieu of medical evidence, accept other competent evidence. In any case in which the court waives the requirement of medical evidence as provided in this subsection, the court shall (1) make a specific finding in any decree issued on the application stating why medical evidence was not required and (2) if a hearing has not been held, schedule a hearing under subsection (c) of this section, which hearing shall take place within seventy two hours of the issuance of the court's decree.

(f) On termination of the temporary conservatorship, the temporary conservator shall file a written report with the court of his actions as temporary conservator.

(1955, Supp. § 2908d; 1957, P.A. 449; 1958 Rev., § 45–72; 1965, Feb.Sp.Sess., P.A. 590, § 2; 1967, P.A. 385; 1975, P.A. 75–72; 1977, P.A. 77–446, § 6; 1977, P.A. 77–614, § 521, eff. Jan. 1, 1979; 1979, P.A. 79–631, eff. Oct. 1, 1980; 1980, P.A. 80–227, § 9, eff. July 1, 1981; 1980, P.A. 80–476, § 130, eff. Oct. 1, 1980; 1984, P.A. 84–202; 1984, P.A. 84–271, § 6; 1984, P.A. 84–294, § 8; 1990, P.A. 90–230, § 58, eff. June 8, 1990; 1993, P.A. 93–262, § 65, eff. July 1, 1993; 1995, P.A. 95–89; 1996, P.A. 96–170, § 9, eff. July 1, 1998.)

§ 45a–655. Duties of conservator of the estate. Application for distribution of gifts of income and principal from the estate

(a) A conservator of the estate appointed under section 45a–646, 45a–650 or 45a–654 shall, within two months after the date of his or her appointment, make and file in the Court of Probate, an inventory under penalty of false statement of the estate of his or her ward, with the properties thereof appraised or caused to be appraised, by such conservator, at fair market value as of the date of his or her appointment. Such inventory shall include the value of the ward's interest in all property in which the ward has a legal or equitable present interest, including, but not limited to, the ward's interest in any joint bank accounts or other jointly held property. The conservator shall manage all the estate and apply so much of the net income thereof, and, if necessary, any part of the principal of the property, which is required to support the ward and those members of the ward's family whom he or she has the legal duty to support and to pay the ward's debts, and may sue for and collect all debts due the ward.

(b) Any conservator of the estate of a married person may apply such portion of the property of the ward to the support, maintenance and medical treatment of the ward's spouse which the court of probate, upon hearing after notice, decides to be proper under the circumstances of the case.

(c) Notwithstanding the provisions of section 45a–177, the court may, and at the request of any interested party shall, require annual accountings from any conservator of the estate and the court shall hold a hearing on any such account with notice to all persons entitled to notice under section 45a–649.

(d) In the case of any person receiving public assistance, state-administered general assistance or Medicaid, the conservator of the estate shall apply toward the cost of care of such person any assets exceeding limits on assets set by statute or regulations adopted by the Commissioner of Social Services. Notwithstanding the provisions of subsections (a) and (b) of this section, in the case of an institutionalized person who has applied for or is receiving such medical assistance, no conservator shall apply and no court shall approve the application of (1) the net income of the ward to the support of the ward's spouse in an amount that exceeds the monthly income allowed a community spouse as determined by the Department of Social Services pursuant to 42 USC 1396r–5(d)(2)—(4), or (2) any portion of the property of the ward to the support, maintenance and medical treatment of the ward's spouse in an amount that exceeds the amount determined allowable by the department pursuant to 42 USC 1396r–5(f)(1) and (2), notwithstanding the provisions of 42 USC 1396r–5(f)(2)(A)(iv), unless such limitations on income would result in significant financial duress.

(e) Upon application of a conservator of the estate, after hearing with notice to the Commissioner of Administrative Services, the Commissioner of Social Services and to all parties who may have an interest as determined by the court, the court may authorize the conservator to make gifts or other transfers of income and principal from the estate of the ward in such amounts and in such form, outright or in trust, whether to an existing trust or a court-approved trust created by the conservator, as the court orders to or for the benefit of individuals, including the ward, and to or for the benefit of charities, trusts or other institutions described in sections 2055(a) and 2522(a) of the Internal Revenue Code of 1986, [1] or any corresponding internal revenue code of the United States, as from time to time amended. Such gifts or transfers shall be authorized only if the court finds that: (1) In the case of individuals not related to the ward by blood or marriage, the ward had made a previous gift to that individual prior to being declared incapable; (2) in the case of a charity, either (A) the ward had made a previous gift to such charity, had pledged a gift in writing to such charity, or had otherwise demonstrated support for such charity prior to being declared incapable; or (B) the court determines that the gift to the charity is in the best interests of the ward, is consistent with proper estate planning, and there is no reasonable objection by a party having an interest in the ward's estate as determined by the court; (3) the estate of the ward and any proposed trust of which the ward is a beneficiary is more than sufficient to carry out the duties of the conservator as set forth in subsections (a) and (b) of this section, both for the present and foreseeable future, including due provision for the continuing proper care, comfort and maintenance of such ward in accordance with such ward's established standard of living and for the support of persons the ward is legally obligated to support; (4) the purpose of the gifts is not to diminish the estate of the ward so as to qualify the ward for federal or state aid or benefits; and (5) in the case of a ward capable of making an informed decision, the ward has no objection to such gift. The court shall give consideration to the following: (A) The medical condition of the ward, including the prospect of restoration to capacity; (B) the size of the ward's estate; (C) the provisions which, in the judgment of the court, such ward would have made if he or she had been capable, for minimization of income and estate taxes consistent with proper estate planning; and (D) in the case of a trust, whether the trust should be revocable or irrevocable, existing or created by the conservator and court approved. The court should also consider the provisions of an existing estate plan, if any. In the case of a gift or transfer in trust, any transfer to a court-approved trust created by the conservator shall be subject to continuing probate court jurisdiction in the same manner as a testamentary trust including periodic rendering of accounts pursuant to section 45a–177. Notwithstanding any other provision of this section, the court may authorize the creation and funding of a trust that complies with section 1917(d)(4) of the Social Security Act, 42 USC 1396p(d)(4), as from time to time amended. The provisions of this subsection shall not be construed to validate or invalidate any gifts made by a conservator of the estate prior to October 1, 1998.

(1949 Rev., § 6878; 1958 Rev., § 45–75; 1973, P.A. 73–34, § 2; 1977, P.A. 77–446, § 7; 1980, P.A. 80–476, § 131, eff. Oct. 1, 1980; 1981, P.A. 81–349, § 2, eff. June 16, 1981; 1983, P.A. 83–62; 1985, P.A. 85–523, § 1, eff. July 8, 1985; 1987, P.A. 87–565, § 2; 1989, P.A. 89–211, § 45; 1992, P.A. 92–233, § 2; 1993, P.A. 93–262, § 1, eff. July 1, 1993; 1997, June 18 Sp.Sess., P.A. 97–2, § 103, eff. July 1, 1997; 1998, P.A. 98–232, § 2; 1999, P.A. 99–84, § 28; 2001, June Sp.Sess., P.A. 01–2, § 6, eff. July 1, 2001.)

1 26 U.S.C.A. § 1 et seq.

§ 45a–656. Duties of conservator of the person

(a) The conservator of the person shall have: (1) The duty and responsibility for the general custody of the respondent; (2) the power to establish his or her place of abode within the state; (3) the power to give consent for his or her medical or other professional care, counsel, treatment or service; (4) the duty to provide for the care, comfort and maintenance of the ward; (5) the duty to take reasonable care of the respondent's personal effects; and (6) the duty to report at least annually to the probate court which appointed the conservator regarding the condition of the respondent. The preceding duties, responsibilities and powers shall be carried out within the limitations of the resources available to the ward, either through his own estate or through private or public assistance.

(b) The conservator of the person shall not have the power or authority to cause the respondent to be committed to any institution for the treatment of the mentally ill except under the provisions of sections 17a–75 to 17a–83, inclusive, 17a–456 to 17a–484, inclusive, 17a–495 to 17a–528, inclusive, 17a–540 to 17a–550, inclusive, 17a–560 to 17a–576, inclusive, 17a–615 to 17a–618, inclusive, and 17a–621 to 17a–664, inclusive, and chapter 359.[1]

(1958 Rev., § 45–75a; 1977, P.A. 77–446, § 8; 1980, P.A. 80–476, § 132, eff. Oct. 1, 1980; 1994, P.A. 94–27, § 13, eff. July 1, 1994.)

1 C.G.S.A. § 19–443 et seq. Repealed or transferred. See C.G.S.A. § 21a–240 et seq.

§ 45a–656a. Duty of conservator of estate of resident of licensed residential care home re: payment of room and board

(a) Any conservator of the estate of a person who is a resident of a licensed residential care home, as defined in section 19a–490, where such conservator is payee on behalf of such person, shall, not later than ten business days after receipt of any income used for room and board, forward payment to the operator of the residential care home for the cost of room and board of such person.

(b) If any such conservator neglects to forward payment to the operator of the home within ten business days as required under subsection (a) of this section for two consecutive months, the operator of the home may petition the court of probate having jurisdiction for removal of the conservator. The court may, after notice and a hearing, remove such conservator.

(1997, P.A. 97–73; 1997, P.A. 97–112, § 2; 1998, P.A. 98–219, § 28.)

§ 45a–657. Court to resolve conflicts between conservators

If a person has both a conservator of the person and a conservator of the estate who are not the same person and a conflict arises between the two concerning the duties and responsibilities or authority of either, the matter shall be submitted to the court of probate which appointed the conservators. Upon hearing, the court shall order the course of action which in the court's discretion is in the best interests of the person under conservatorship.

(1958 Rev., § 45–75b; 1977, P.A. 77–446, § 9; 1980, P.A. 80–476, § 133, eff. Oct. 1, 1980.)

§ 45a–658. Appointment or removal of conservator to be recorded on land records

(a) The court appointing a conservator of the property or person of any person who has been adjudged incapable and who owns real property in this state or any interest in such property or mortgage or lien on such property shall forthwith order the conservator to immediately record, in the land records of each town where the real property is situated, a certificate setting forth the name and residence of the person, the name of the conservator, the date of his appointment and the court by which the appointment was made. Upon the resignation or removal of the conservator, unless another conservator is immediately appointed by the same court to succeed him, the court shall forthwith order the conservator to record in the land records of each town where the real property is situated a certificate setting forth the name and residence of the person and of the conservator, the date of resignation or removal and the court in which the proceedings took place.

(b) The conservator shall record the notice pursuant to the order and, upon failure to do so within two months after the appointment, resignation or removal, shall be fined not more than fifty dollars.

(c) The record in the court of the appointment, resignation or removal of the conservator shall not be constructive notice of the incapacity or capacity of the owner of the real property or of an interest in real property or of a mortgage or lien on such property to make valid contracts relative to such property, until the certificate is recorded as provided in subsection (a) of this section.

(1949 Rev., § 6877; 1958 Rev., 45–74; 1980, P.A. 80–476, § 134, eff. Oct. 1, 1980; 1991, P.A. 91–49, § 5.)

§ 45a–659. Conservator of nonresident's property

(a) If any person domiciled out of and owning real property or tangible personal property in this state is incapable of managing his or her affairs, the court of probate for the district in which the property or some part of it is situated may, on the written application of a husband, wife or relative or of a conservator, committee or guardian having charge of the person or estate of the incapable person in the state where the incapable person is domiciled and after notice pursuant to section 45a–649 or such reasonable notice as the court may order, and a hearing as required pursuant to section 45a–650 appoint a conservator of the estate for the real property and tangible personal property in this state of the incapable person pursuant to section 45a–650.

(b) If a conservator of the estate has been appointed for such an incapable person in the state of such person's domicile, (1) the court may, on application of the out-of-state conservator to act as conservator for real or tangible personal property of the incapable person in this state, appoint such person as conservator of the estate without a hearing, on presentation to the court of a certified copy of the conservator's appointment in the state of the incapable person's domicile, and (2) if the application is for the appointment of a person other than the out-of-state conservator to act as conservator of the estate, the court, at its hearing on the application, may accept a certified copy of the out-of-state appointment of a conservator as evidence of incapacity. As used in this subsection, a "conservator of the estate" in an out-of-state jurisdiction includes any person serving in the equivalent capacity in such state.

(c) The conservator of the estate for the property in this state shall give a probate bond, and shall, within two months after the date of his or her appointment, make and file in the court of probate, under penalty of false statement, an inventory of all the real property and tangible personal property in this state of the incapable person, appraised or caused to be appraised, by such conservator, at fair market value as of the date of the conservator's appointment.

(d) The proceeds of any sale of either real or tangible personal property, or both, may be transferred to the conservator, committee or guardian having charge of the person and estate of the incapable person in the state where the incapable person is domiciled, following the application and proceedings which are required by section 45a–635.

(1949 Rev., § 6879; 1958 Rev., § 45–76; 1980, P.A. 80–476, § 136, eff. Oct. 1, 1980; 1987, P.A. 87–565, § 3; 1994, P.A. 94–24; 1999, P.A. 99–84, § 29.)

§ 45a–660. Termination of conservatorship. Review by court

(a) (1) If the court of probate having jurisdiction finds a ward to be capable of caring for himself or herself, the court shall, upon hearing and after notice, order that the conservatorship of the person be terminated. If the court finds upon hearing and after notice which the court prescribes, that a ward is capable of managing his or her own affairs, the court shall order that the conservatorship of the estate be terminated and that the remaining portion of his or her property be restored to the ward. (2) If the court finds upon hearing and after notice which the court prescribes, that a ward has no assets of any kind remaining except for that amount allowed by subsection (c) of section 17b–80, the court may order that the conservatorship of the estate be terminated. The court shall thereupon order distribution of the remaining assets to the conservator of the person or, if there is no conservator or the conservator declines or is unable to accept or the conservator is the Commissioner of Social Services, to some suitable person, to be determined by the court, to hold for the benefit of the ward, upon such conservator or person giving such probate bond, if any, as the court orders. (3) If any ward having a conservator dies, his or her property other than property which has accrued from the sale of his or her real property shall be delivered to his or her executor or administrator. The unexpended proceeds of his or her real property sold as aforesaid shall go into the hands of the executor or administrator, to be distributed as such real property would have been.

(b) (1) In any case under subsection (a) of this section the conservator shall file in the court his or her final account, and the court shall audit the account and allow the account if it is found to be correct. If the ward is living, the ward and his or her attorney, if any, shall be entitled to notice by regular mail of any hearing held on the final account. (2) The court of probate having jurisdiction shall send written notice annually to the ward and his or her attorney that the ward has a right to a hearing under this section. Upon receipt of request for such hearing the court shall set a time and date for the hearing, which date shall not be more than thirty days from the receipt of the application unless continued for cause shown.

(c) The court shall review each conservatorship at least every three years, and shall either continue, modify or terminate the order for conservatorship. The court shall receive and review written evidence as to the condition of the ward. The conservator, the attorney for the ward and a physician licensed to practice medicine in this state, shall each submit a written report to the court within forty-five days of the court's request for such report. If the ward is unable to request or obtain an attorney, the court shall appoint an attorney. If the ward is unable to pay for the services of the attorney, the reasonable compensation of such attorney shall be established by, and paid from funds appropriated to, the Judicial Department, however, if funds have not been included in the budget of the Judicial Department for such purposes, such compensation shall be established by the Probate Court Administrator and paid from the Probate Court Administration Fund. The physician shall examine the ward within the forty-five-day period preceding the date of submission of his report.

(d) If the court determines, after receipt of the reports from the attorney for the ward, the physician and the conservator, that there has been no change in the condition of the ward since the last preceding review by the court, a hearing on the condition of the ward shall not be required, but the court, in its discretion, may hold such hearing. If the attorney for the ward, the physician or conservator requests a hearing, the court shall hold a hearing within thirty days of such request.

(1949 Rev., § 6880; 1958 Rev., § 45–77; 1967, P.A. 196, § 1, eff. July 1, 1967; 1977, P.A. 77–446, § 12; 1980, P.A. 80–476, § 137, eff. Oct. 1, 1980; 1984, P.A. 84–271, § 7; 1986, P.A. 86–195, § 2; 1987, P.A. 87–97; 1987, P.A. 87–565, § 4; 1991, P.A. 91–71, § 1; 1993, P.A. 93–262, § 1, eff. July 1, 1993; 1996, P.A. 96–170, § 18, eff. July 1, 1998.)

§ 45a–661. Transfer of records upon removal of person under representation

When any person under voluntary or involuntary representation becomes a settled inhabitant of any town in the state in a probate district other than the one in which a conservator was appointed, and is an actual resident in such district, the court of probate in which the conservator was appointed shall, upon motion of the conservator, the first selectman or the chief executive officer of the town in which the person under conservatorship resides or of the husband or wife or a relative of the person under conservatorship, transfer the file to the probate district in which the person under conservatorship resides at the time of the application. A transfer of the file shall be accomplished by the probate court in which the conservator was originally appointed by making copies of all recorded documents in the court and certifying each of them and then causing them to be delivered to the court for the district in which the person under conservatorship resides. When the transfer is made, the court of probate in which the person under conservatorship resides at the time of transfer shall thereupon assume jurisdiction over the conservatorship and all further accounts shall be filed with such court.

(1958 Rev., § 45–77a; 1977, P.A. 77–446, § 11; 1980, P.A. 80–476, § 138, eff. Oct. 1, 1980.)

§ 45a–662. Conveyance of property by order of court

The court of probate in which the conservator of any incapable person has been appointed may, concurrently with courts of equity, order such conservator to convey the interest of his ward in any real property which ought in equity to be conveyed to another person.

(1958 Rev., § 45–77b; 1980, P.A. 80–476, § 139, eff. Oct. 1, 1980.)

§ 45a–663. Compensation of conservator if ward unable to pay

If a ward is unable to pay for the services of a conservator appointed pursuant to the provisions of sections 45a–593 to 45a–700, inclusive, the reasonable compensation of such conservator shall be paid from the Probate Court Administration Fund established under section 45a–82, pursuant to rules and regulations and at rates established by the probate court administrator.

(1992, P.A. 92–46, § 1.)

§§ 45a–664 to 45a–667. Reserved for future use

CHAPTER 803

TERMINATION OF PARENTAL RIGHTS AND ADOPTION

PART I. TERMINATION AND ADOPTION IN GENERAL

Section

PART I. TERMINATION AND ADOPTION IN GENERAL

§ 45a–706. Rule of construction

The provisions of sections 45a–706 to 45a–709, inclusive, 45a–715 to 45a–718, inclusive, 45a–724 to 45a–734, inclusive, 45a–736, 45a–737 and 52–231a shall be liberally construed in the best interests of any child for whom a petition has been filed under said sections. *(1958 Rev., § 45–61a; 1973, P.A. 73–156, § 1; 1980, P.A. 80–476, § 140, eff. Oct. 1, 1980; 1996, P.A. 96–130, § 2.)*

§ 45a–707. Definitions

As used in sections 45a–187, 45a–706 to 45a–709, inclusive, 45a–715 to 45a–718, inclusive, and 45a–724 to 45a–737, inclusive:

(1) "Adoption" means the establishment by court order of the legal relationship of parent and child;

(2) "Child care facility" means a congregate residential setting for the out-of-home placement of children or youth under eighteen years of age, licensed by the Department of Children and Families;

(3) "Child-placing agency" means any agency within or without the state of Connecticut licensed or approved by the Commissioner of Children and Families in accordance with sections 17a–149 and 17a–151, and in accordance with standards established by regulations of the Commissioner of Children and Families;

(4) "Guardianship" means guardianship, unless otherwise specified, of the person of a minor and refers to the obligation of care and control, the right to custody and the duty and authority to make major decisions affecting the minor's welfare, including, but not limited to, consent determinations regarding marriage, enlistment in the armed forces and major medical, psychiatric or surgical treatment;

(5) "Parent" means a biological or adoptive parent;

(6) "Relative" means any person descended from a common ancestor, whether by blood or adoption, not more than three generations removed from the child;

(7) "Statutory parent" means the Commissioner of Children and Families or the child-placing agency appointed by the court for the purpose of the adoption of a minor child or minor children;

(8) "Termination of parental rights" means the complete severance by court order of the legal relationship, with all its rights and responsibilities, between the child and the child's parent or parents so that the child is free for adoption except it shall not affect the right of inheritance of the child or the religious affiliation of the child.

(1958 Rev., § 45–61b; 1973, P.A. 73–156, § 2; 1974, P.A. 74–164, § 1, eff. May 10, 1974; 1975, P.A. 75–420, § 4, eff. June 25, 1975; 1977, P.A. 77–614, § 521, eff. Jan. 1, 1979; 1977, P.A. 77–614, § 587, eff. June 2, 1977; 1978, P.A. 78–303, § 85, eff. June 6, 1978; 1979, P.A. 79–631, § 76, eff. July 6, 1979; 1980, P.A. 80–476, § 141, eff. Oct. 1, 1980; 1993, P.A. 93–91, § 1, eff. July 1, 1993; 1995, P.A. 95–349, § 3; 1996, P.A. 96–130, § 3; 1999, P.A. 99–166, § 8.)

§ 45a–708. Guardian ad litem for minor or incompetent parent

(a) When, with respect to any petition for termination of parental rights filed under section 17a–112, section 45a–715 or section 45a–716, it appears that either parent of the child is a minor or incompetent, the court shall appoint a guardian ad litem for such parent. The guardian ad litem shall be an attorney-at-law authorized to practice law in Connecticut or any duly authorized officer of a child-placing agency if the child-placing agency is not the petitioner.

(b) The guardian ad litem may be allowed reasonable compensation by the court appointing him which shall be assessed against the petitioner.

(c) If the court finds the petitioner is unable to pay the compensation, the reasonable compensation shall be established by, and paid from funds appropriated to, the Judicial Department, however, in the case of a Probate Court matter, if funds have not been included in the budget of the Judicial Department for such compensation, such compensation shall be established by the Probate Court Administrator and paid from the Probate Court Administration Fund.

(1958 Rev., § 45–61e; 1973, P.A. 73–156, § 6; 1974, P.A. 74–164, § 5, eff. May 10, 1974; 1976, P.A. 76–436, § 643, eff. July 1, 1978; 1980, P.A. 80–476, § 142, eff. Oct. 1, 1980; 1983, P.A. 83–295, § 24, eff. Oct. 1, 1983; 1990, P.A. 90–31, § 4, eff. May 2, 1990; 1996, P.A. 96–130, § 4; 1996, P.A. 96–170, § 21, eff. July 1, 1998.)

§ 45a–709. Validity of proceedings prior to statutory changes

(a) Notwithstanding any provision of sections 17a–91, 17a–112, 17a–113, 17a–148, 45a–187, 45a–606, 45a–607, 45a–706 to 45a–708, inclusive, 45a–715 to 45a–718, inclusive, 45a–724, 45a–727, 45a–732 to 45a–734, inclusive, and 52–231a, to the contrary, any adoption completed after October 1, 1973, in which the application and agreement of adoption were received by the court of probate before October 1, 1973, shall be valid, provided the adoption would have been valid under the general statutes in effect on September 30, 1973.

(b) Applications for termination of parental rights, appointment of statutory parents or for adoptions or any actions taken in accordance with the applications which were received by the court of probate prior to May 10, 1974, shall be valid if they conform to the provisions of sections 17a–91, 17a–112, 17a–148, 45a–606, 45a–706 to 45a–708, inclusive, 45a–715 to 45a–718, inclusive, 45a–724, 45a–727, 45a–731 to 45a–734, inclusive, and 52–231a in effect on May 9, 1974.

(1958 Rev., § 45–61k; 1974, P.A. 74–164, § 15, eff. May 10, 1974; 1980, P.A. 80–476, § 143, eff. Oct. 1, 1980.)

§§ 45a–710 to 45a–714. Reserved for future use

PART II. TERMINATION OF PARENTAL RIGHTS

§ 45a–715. Petition to terminate parental rights. Cooperative postadoption agreements

(a) Any of the following persons may petition the Court of Probate to terminate parental rights of all persons who may have parental rights regarding any minor child or for the termination of parental rights of only one parent provided the application so states: (1) Either or both parents, including a parent who is a minor; (2) the guardian of the child; (3) the selectmen of any town having charge of any foundling child; (4) a duly authorized officer of any child care facility or child-placing agency or organization or any children's home or similar institution approved by the Commissioner of Children and Families; (5) a relative of the child if the parent or parents have abandoned or deserted the child; (6) the Commissioner of Children and Families, provided the custodial parent of such minor child has consented to the termination of parental rights and the child has not been committed to the commissioner, and no application for commitment has been made; provided in any case hereunder where the child with respect to whom the petition is brought has attained the age of twelve, the child shall join in the petition.

(b) A petition for termination of parental rights shall be entitled "In the interest of .... (Name of child), a person under the age of eighteen years", and shall set forth with specificity: (1) The name, sex, date and place of birth, and present address of the child; (2) the name and address of the petitioner, and the nature of the relationship between the petitioner and the child; (3) the names, dates of birth and addresses of the parents of the child, if known, including the name of any putative father named by the mother, and the tribe and reservation of an American Indian parent; (4) if the parent of the child is a minor, the names and addresses of the parents or guardian of the person of such minor; (5) the names and addresses of: (A) The guardian of the person of the child; (B) any guardians ad litem appointed in a prior proceeding; (C) the tribe and reservation of an American Indian child; and (D) the child-placing agency which placed the child in his current placement; (6) the facts upon which termination is sought, the legal grounds authorizing termination, the effects of a termination decree and the basis for the jurisdiction of the court; (7) the name of the persons or agencies which have agreed to accept custody or guardianship of the child's person upon disposition.

(c) If the information required under subdivisions (2) and (6) of subsection (b) of this section is not stated, the petition shall be dismissed. If any other facts required under subdivision (1), (3), (4), (5) or (7) of subsection (b) of this section are not known or cannot be ascertained by the petitioner, he shall so state in the petition. If the whereabouts of either parent or the putative father named under subdivision (3) of subsection (b) of this section are unknown, the petitioner shall diligently search for any such parent or putative father. The petitioner shall file an affidavit with the petition indicating the efforts used to locate the parent or putative father.

(d) If a petition indicates that either or both parents consent to the termination of their parental rights, or if at any time following the filing of a petition and before the entry of a decree a parent consents to the termination of his parental rights, each consenting parent shall acknowledge such consent on a form promulgated by the Office of the Chief Court Administrator evidencing to the satisfaction of the court that the parent has voluntarily and knowingly consented to the termination of his parental rights. No consent to termination by a mother shall be executed within forty-eight hours immediately after the birth of her child. A parent who is a minor shall have the right to consent to termination of parental rights and such consent shall not be voidable by reason of such minority. A guardian ad litem shall be appointed by the court to assure that such minor parent is giving an informed and voluntary consent.

(e) A petition under this section shall be filed in the court of probate for the district in which the petitioner or the child resides or, in the case of a minor who is under the guardianship of any child care facility or child-placing agency, in the court of probate for the district in which the main office or any local office of the agency is located. If the petition is filed with respect to a child born out of wedlock, the petition shall state whether there is a putative father to whom notice shall be given under subdivision (2) of subsection (b) of section 45a–716.

(f) If any petitioner under subsection (a) is a minor or incompetent, the guardian ad litem, appointed by the court in accordance with section 45a–708, must approve the petition in writing, before action by the court.

(g) Before a hearing on the merits in any case in which a petition for termination of parental rights is contested in a court of probate, the court of probate shall, on the motion of any legal party except the petitioner or may on its own motion or that of the petitioner, under rules adopted by the judges of the Supreme Court, transfer the case to the Superior Court. In addition to the provisions of this section, the probate court may, on the court's own motion or that of any interested party, transfer the case to another judge of probate, which judge shall be appointed by the Probate Court Administrator from a panel of qualified probate judges who specialize in children's matters. Such panel shall be proposed by the Probate Court Administrator and approved by the executive committee of the Connecticut Probate Assembly. The location of the hearing shall be in the original probate court, except upon agreement of all parties and the Department of Children and Families, where applicable. If the case is transferred, the clerk of the Court of Probate shall transmit to the clerk of the superior court or the probate court to which the case was transferred, the original files and papers in the case. The superior court or the probate court to which the case was transferred, upon hearing after notice as provided in sections

45a–716 and 45a–717, may grant the petition as provided in section 45a–717.

(h) Either or both birth parents and an intended adoptive parent may enter into a cooperative postadoption agreement regarding communication or contact between either or both birth parents and the adopted child. Such an agreement may be entered into if: (1) The child is in the custody of the Department of Children and Families; (2) an order terminating parental rights has not yet been entered; and (3) either or both birth parents agree to a voluntary termination of parental rights, including an agreement in a case which began as an involuntary termination of parental rights. The postadoption agreement shall be applicable only to a birth parent who is a party to the agreement. Such agreement shall be in addition to those under common law. Counsel for the child and any guardian ad litem for the child may be heard on the proposed cooperative postadoption agreement. There shall be no presumption of communication or contact between the birth parents and an intended adoptive parent in the absence of a cooperative postadoption agreement.

(i) If the Court of Probate determines that the child's best interests will be served by postadoption communication or contact with either or both birth parents, the court shall so order, stating the nature and frequency of the communication or contact. A court may grant postadoption communication or contact privileges if: (1) Each intended adoptive parent consents to the granting of communication or contact privileges; (2) the intended adoptive parent and either or both birth parents execute a cooperative agreement and file the agreement with the court; (3) consent to postadoption communication or contact is obtained from the child, if the child is at least twelve years of age; and (4) the cooperative postadoption agreement is approved by the court.

(j) A cooperative postadoption agreement shall contain the following: (1) An acknowledgment by either or both birth parents that the termination of parental rights and the adoption is irrevocable, even if the adoptive parents do not abide by the cooperative postadoption agreement; and (2) an acknowledgment by the adoptive parents that the agreement grants either or both birth parents the right to seek to enforce the cooperative postadoption agreement.

(k) The terms of a cooperative postadoption agreement may include the following: (1) Provision for communication between the child and either or both birth parents; (2) provision for future contact between either or both birth parents and the child or an adoptive parent; and (3) maintenance of medical history of either or both birth parents who are a party to the agreement.

(*l*) The order approving a cooperative postadoption agreement shall be made part of the final order terminating parental rights. The finality of the termination of parental rights and of the adoption shall not be affected by implementation of the provisions of the postadoption agreement, nor is the cooperative postadoption contingent upon the finalization of an adoption. Such an agreement shall not affect the ability of the adoptive parents and the child to change their residence within or outside this state.

(m) A disagreement between the parties or litigation brought to enforce or modify the agreement shall not affect the validity of the termination of parental rights or the adoption and shall not serve as a basis for orders affecting the custody of the child. The court shall not act on a petition to change or enforce the agreement unless the petitioner had participated, or attempted to participate, in good faith in mediation or other appropriate dispute resolution proceedings to resolve the dispute and allocate any cost for such mediation or dispute resolution proceedings.

(n) An adoptive parent, guardian ad litem for the child or the court on its own motion may, at any time, petition for review of communication or contact ordered pursuant to subsection (i) of this section, if the adoptive parent believes that the best interests of the child are being compromised. The court may order the communication or contact be terminated, or order such conditions in regard to communication or contact as the court deems to be in the best interest of the adopted child.

(1958 Rev., § 45–61c; 1973, P.A. 73–156, § 3; 1974, P.A. 74–164, § 2, eff. May 10, 1974; 1975, P.A. 75–420, § 4, eff. June 25, 1975; 1976, P.A. 76–436, § 641, eff. July 1, 1978; 1977, P.A. 77–614, § 521, eff. Jan. 1, 1979; 1979, P.A. 79–223; 1979, P.A. 79–631, §§ 33, 77, 85, eff. July 6, 1979; 1980, P.A. 80–476, § 144, eff. Oct. 1, 1980; 1983, P.A. 83–355, § 1; 1984, P.A. 84–449, § 2, eff. June 12, 1984; 1986, P.A. 86–264, § 8; 1993, P.A. 93–170, § 2; 1993, P.A. 93–91, § 1, eff. July 1, 1993; 1995, P.A. 95–349, § 4; 1996, P.A. 96–130, § 5; 2000, P.A. 00–75, § 9; 2000, P.A. 00–137, § 4; 2001, P.A. 01–195, § 98, eff. July 11, 2001.)

§ 45a–716. Hearing on petition to terminate parental rights. Notice

(a) Upon receipt of a petition for termination of parental rights, the Court of Probate or the Superior Court, on a case transferred to it from the Court of Probate in accordance with the provisions of subsection (g) of section 45a–715, shall set a time and place for hearing the petition. The time for hearing shall be not more than thirty days after the filing of the petition.

(b) The court shall cause notice of the hearing to be given to the following persons as applicable: (1) The parent or parents of the minor child, including any parent who has been removed as guardian on or after October 1, 1973, under section 45a–606; (2) the father of any minor child born out of wedlock, provided at the time of the filing of the petition (A) he has been adjudicated the father of such child by a court of competent jurisdiction, or (B) he has acknowledged in writing that he is the father of such child, or (C) he has contributed regularly to the support of such child, or (D) his name appears on the birth certificate, or (E) he has filed a claim for paternity as provided under section 46b–172a, or (F) he has been named in the petition as the father of the child by the mother; (3) the guardian or any other person whom the court shall deem appropriate; (4) the Commissioner of Children and Families. If the recipient of the notice is a person described in subdivision (1) or (2) of this subsection or is any other person whose parental rights are sought to be terminated in the petition, the notice shall contain a statement that the respondent has the right to be represented by counsel and that if the respondent is unable to pay for counsel, counsel will be appointed for the respondent. The reasonable compensation for such counsel shall be established by, and paid from funds appropriated to, the Judicial Department, however, in the case of a Probate Court matter, if funds have not been included in the budget of the Judicial Department for such purposes, such compensation shall be established by the Probate Court Administrator and paid from the Probate Court Administration Fund.

(c) Except as provided in subsection (d) of this section, notice of the hearing and a copy of the petition, certified by the petitioner, the petitioner's agent or attorney, or the court clerk, shall be served at least ten days before the date for the hearing by personal service or service at the person's usual place of abode on the persons enumerated in subsection (b) of this section who are within the state, and by certified mail, return receipt requested, on the Commissioner of Children and Families. If the address of any person entitled to personal service or service at the person's usual place of abode is unknown, or if personal service or service at the person's usual place of abode cannot be reasonably effected within the state or if any person enumerated in subsection (b) of this section is out of the state, a judge or clerk of the court shall order notice to be given by registered or certified mail, return receipt requested, or by publication at least ten days before the date of the hearing. Any publication shall be in a newspaper of general circulation in the place of the last-known address of the person to be notified, whether within or without this state, or if no such address is known, in the place where the termination petition has been filed.

(d) In any proceeding pending in the Court of Probate, in lieu of personal service on a parent or the father of a child born out of wedlock who is either a petitioner or who signs under penalty of false statement a written waiver of personal service on a form provided by the Probate Court Administrator, the court may order notice to be given by certified mail, return receipt requested, deliverable to addressee only and at least ten days prior to the date of the hearing. If such delivery cannot reasonably be effected, or if the whereabouts of the parents is unknown, then notice shall be ordered to be given by publication, as provided in subsection (c) of this section.

(1958 Rev., § 45–61d; 1973, P.A. 73–156, § 5; 1974, P.A. 74–164, § 4, eff. May 10, 1974; 1975, P.A. 75–420, § 4, eff. June 25, 1975; 1976, P.A. 76–436, § 642, eff. July 1, 1978; 1977, P.A. 77–614, § 521, eff. Jan. 1, 1979; 1979, P.A. 79–592, § 1; 1979, P.A. 79–631, § 78, eff. July 6, 1979; 1980, P.A. 80–476, § 145, eff. Oct. 1, 1980; 1980, P.A. 80–483, § 119, eff. June 6, 1980; 1983, June Sp.Sess., P.A. 83–11, § 1, eff. April 1, 1984; 1984, P.A. 84–449, § 3, eff. June 12, 1984; 1985, P.A. 85–335; 1986, P.A. 86–264, § 3; 1992, P.A. 92–118, § 6; 1993, P.A. 93–170, § 3; 1993, P.A. 93–91, § 1, eff. July 1, 1993; 1996, P.A. 96–130, § 6; 1996, P.A. 96–170, § 6, eff. July 1, 1998; 1999, P.A. 99–84, § 31; 2000, P.A. 00–137, § 11; 2000, P.A. 00–196, § 32.)

§ 45a–717. Termination of parental rights. Conduct of hearing. Investigation and report. Grounds for termination

(a) At the hearing held on any petition for the termination of parental rights filed in the Court of Probate under section 45a–715, or filed in the Superior Court under section 17a–112, or transferred to the Superior Court from the Court of Probate under section 45a–715, any party to whom notice was given shall have the right to appear and be heard with respect to the petition. If a parent who is consenting to the termination of such parent's parental rights appears at the hearing on the petition for termination of parental rights, the court shall explain to the parent the meaning and consequences of termination of parental rights. Nothing in this subsection shall be construed to require the appearance of a consenting parent at the hearing regarding the termination of such parent's parental rights except as otherwise provided by court order.

(b) If a party appears without counsel, the court shall inform such party of the party's right to counsel and upon request, if he or she is unable to pay for counsel, shall appoint counsel to represent such party. No party may waive counsel unless the court has first explained the nature and meaning of a petition for the termination of parental rights. Unless the appointment of counsel is required under section 46b–136, the court may appoint counsel to represent or appear on behalf of any child in a hearing held under this section to speak on behalf of the best interests of the child. If the respondent parent is unable to pay for such respondent's own counsel or if the child or the parent or guardian of the child is unable to pay for the child's counsel, in the case of a Superior Court matter, the reasonable compensation of counsel appointed for the respondent parent or the child shall be established by, and paid from funds appropriated to, the Judicial Department and, in the case of a Probate Court matter, the reasonable compensation of counsel appointed for the respondent parent or the child shall be established by, and paid from funds appropriated to, the Judicial

Department, however, in the case of a Probate Court matter, if funds have not been included in the budget of the Judicial Department for such purposes, such compensation shall be established by the Probate Court Administrator and paid from the Probate Court Administration Fund.

(c) The court shall, if a claim for paternity has been filed in accordance with section 46b–172a, continue the hearing under the provisions of this section until the claim for paternity is adjudicated, provided the court may combine the hearing on the claim for paternity with the hearing on the termination of parental rights petition.

(d) Upon finding at the hearing or at any time during the pendency of the petition that reasonable cause exists to warrant an examination, the court, on its own motion or on motion by any party, may order the child to be examined at a suitable place by a physician, psychiatrist or licensed clinical psychologist appointed by the court. The court may also order examination of a parent or custodian whose competency or ability to care for a child before the court is at issue. The expenses of any examination if ordered by the court on its own motion shall be paid for by the petitioner or, if ordered on motion by a party, shall be paid for by the party moving for such an examination unless such party or petitioner is unable to pay such expenses in which case, they shall be paid for by funds appropriated to the Judicial Department, however, in the case of a Probate Court matter, if funds have not been included in the budget of the Judicial Department for such purposes, such expenses shall be established by the Probate Court Administrator and paid from the Probate Court Administration Fund. The court may consider the results of the examinations in ruling on the merits of the petition.

(e) (1) The court may, and in any contested case shall, request the Commissioner of Children and Families or any child-placing agency licensed by the commissioner to make an investigation and written report to it, within ninety days from the receipt of such request. The report shall indicate the physical, mental and emotional status of the child and shall contain such facts as may be relevant to the court's determination of whether the proposed termination of parental rights will be in the best interests of the child, including the physical, mental, social and financial condition of the biological parents, and any other factors which the commissioner or such child-placing agency finds relevant to the court's determination of whether the proposed termination will be in the best interests of the child. (2) If such a report has been requested, upon the expiration of such ninety-day period or upon receipt of the report, whichever is earlier, the court shall set a day for a hearing not more than thirty days thereafter. The court shall give reasonable notice of such adjourned hearing to all parties to the first hearing, including the child, if over fourteen years of age, and to such other persons as the court shall deem appropriate. (3) The report shall be admissible in evidence, subject to the right of any interested party to require that the person making it appear as a witness, if available, and subject himself to examination.

(f) At the adjourned hearing or at the initial hearing where no investigation and report has been requested, the court may approve a petition for termination of parental rights based on consent filed pursuant to this section terminating the parental rights and may appoint a guardian of the person of the child, or if the petitioner requests, the court may appoint a statutory parent, if it finds, upon clear and convincing evidence that (1) the termination is in the best interest of the child and (2) such parent has voluntarily and knowingly consented to termination of the parent's parental rights with respect to such child. If the court denies a petition for termination of parental rights based on consent, it may refer the matter to an agency to assess the needs of the child, the care the child is receiving and the plan of the parent for the child. Consent for the termination of the parental right of one parent does not diminish the parental rights of the other parent of the child nor does it relieve the other parent of the duty to support the child.

(g) At the adjourned hearing or at the initial hearing where no investigation and report has been requested, the court may approve a petition terminating the parental rights and may appoint a guardian of the person of the child, or, if the petitioner requests, the court may appoint a statutory parent, if it finds, upon clear and convincing evidence, that (1) the termination is in the best interest of the child, and (2) (A) the child has been abandoned by the parent in the sense that the parent has failed to maintain a reasonable degree of interest, concern or responsibility as to the welfare of the child; (B) the child has been denied, by reason of an act or acts of parental commission or omission, including, but not limited to sexual molestation and exploitation, severe physical abuse or a pattern of abuse, the care, guidance or control necessary for the child's physical, educational, moral or emotional well-being. Nonaccidental or inadequately explained serious physical injury to a child shall constitute prima facie evidence of acts of parental commission or omission sufficient for the termination of parental rights; (C) there is no ongoing parent-child relationship which is defined as the relationship that ordinarily develops as a result of a parent having met on a continuing, day-to-day basis the physical, emotional, moral and educational needs of the child and to allow further time for the establishment or reestablishment of the parent-child relationship would be detrimental to the best interests of the child; (D) the parent of a child who (i) has been found by the Superior Court or the Probate Court to have been neglected or uncared for in a prior proceeding, or (ii) is found to be neglected or uncared for and has been in the custody of the commissioner for at least fifteen months and such parent has been provided specific steps to take to facilitate the return of the child to the parent pursuant to section 46b–129 and has failed to achieve such degree of personal rehabilitation as would encourage the belief that within a reasonable time, considering the age and needs of the child, such parent could assume a responsible position in the life of the child; (E) the parent of a child, under the age of seven years who is neglected or uncared for, has failed, is unable or is unwilling to achieve such degree of personal rehabilitation as would encourage the belief that within a reasonable amount of time, considering the age and needs of the child, such parent could assume a responsible position in the life of the child and such parent's parental rights of another child were previously terminated pursuant to a petition filed by the Commissioner of Children and Families; (F) the parent has killed through deliberate, nonaccidental act another child of the parent or has requested, commanded, importuned, attempted, conspired or solicited such killing or has committed an assault, through deliberate, nonaccidental act that resulted in serious bodily injury of another child of the parent; or (G) the parent was convicted as an adult or a delinquent by a court of competent jurisdiction of sexual assault resulting in the conception of a child except for a violation of section 53a–71 or 53a–73a provided the court may terminate such parent' s parental rights to such child at any time after such conviction.

(h) Except in the case where termination is based on consent, in determining whether to terminate parental rights under this section, the court shall consider and shall make written findings regarding: (1) The timeliness, nature and extent of services offered, provided and made available to the parent and the child by a child-placing agency to facilitate the reunion of the child with the parent; (2) the terms of any applicable court order entered into and agreed upon by any individual or child-placing agency and the parent, and the extent to which all parties have fulfilled their obligations under such order; (3) the feelings and emotional ties of the child with respect to the child's parents, any guardian of the child's person and any person who has exercised physical care, custody or control of the child for at least one year and with whom the child has developed significant emotional ties; (4) the age of the child; (5) the efforts the parent has made to adjust such parent's circumstances, conduct or conditions to make it in the best interest of the child to return the child to the parent's home in the foreseeable future, including, but not limited to, (A) the extent to which the parent has maintained contact with the child as part of an effort to reunite the child with the parent, provided the court may give weight to incidental visitations, communications or contributions and (B) the maintenance of regular contact or communication with the guardian or other custodian of the child; and (6) the extent to which a parent has been prevented from maintaining a meaningful relationship with the child by the unreasonable act or conduct of the other parent of the child, or the unreasonable act of any other person or by the economic circumstances of the parent.

(i) If the parental rights of only one parent are terminated, the remaining parent shall be sole parent and, unless otherwise provided by law, guardian of the person.

(j) In the case where termination of parental rights is granted, the guardian of the person or statutory parent shall report to the court within thirty days of the date judgment is entered on a case plan, as defined by the federal Adoption Assistance and Child Welfare Act of 1980,[1] as amended from time to time, for the child. At least every three months thereafter, such guardian or statutory parent shall make a report to the court on the implementation of the plan. The court may convene a hearing upon the filing of a report and shall convene a hearing for the purpose of reviewing the plan no more than twelve months from the date judgment is entered or from the date of the last permanency hearing held pursuant to subsection (k) of section 46b–129 if the child or youth is in the care and custody of the Commissioner of Children and Families, whichever is earlier, and at least once a year thereafter until such time as any proposed adoption plan has become finalized. If the Commissioner of Children and Families is the statutory parent for the child, at such a hearing the court shall determine whether the department has made reasonable efforts to achieve the permanency plan.

(k) Redesignated (j). (1998, P.A. 98–241, § 9.)

(1958 Rev., § 45–61f; 1973, P.A. 73–156, § 7; 1974, P.A. 74–164, § 6, eff. May 10, 1974; 1975, P.A. 75–420, § 4, eff. June 25, 1975; 1976, P.A. 76–436, § 644, eff. July 1, 1978; 1977, P.A. 77–614, § 521, eff. Jan. 1, 1979; 1979, P.A. 79–592, § 3; 1979, P.A. 79–631, § 79, eff. July 6, 1979; 1980, P.A. 80–476, § 146, eff. Oct. 1, 1980; 1982, P.A. 82–202, § 2; 1983, P.A. 83–387, § 2; 1983, P.A. 83–478, § 2; 1983, June Sp.Sess., P.A. 83–11, § 2, eff. April 1, 1984; 1984, P.A. 84–171, § 6, eff. May 11, 1984; 1984, P.A. 84–449, § 4, eff. June 12, 1984; 1990, P.A. 90–31, § 5, eff. May 2, 1990; 1993, P.A. 93–193, § 2; 1993, P.A. 93–91, § 1, eff. July 1, 1993; 1994, P.A. 94–81, § 2; 1995, P.A. 95–238, § 5; 1995, P.A. 95–316, § 8; 1996, P.A. 96–130, § 7; 1996, P.A. 96–170, § 7, eff. July 1, 1998; 1996, P.A. 96–246, § 19; 1998, P.A. 98–241, § 9, eff. July 1, 1998; 2000, P.A. 00–75, § 2; 2000, P.A. 00–137, § 12; 2001, P.A. 01–159, § 6.)

1 42 U.S.C.A. § 670 et seq.

§ 45a–718. Appointment and duties of statutory parent. Removal or resignation

(a) If a child is free for adoption as provided in section 45a–725, and no appointment of a statutory parent has been made under section 17a–112 or section 45a–717, the Court of Probate shall appoint a statutory parent for the child upon petition for appointment of a statutory parent by the guardian of the person of the child or a duly authorized officer of any child care facility or child-placing agency. The petition shall be filed in the Court of Probate for the district in which the petitioner or child resides or in the district in which the main office or any local office of the petitioner or the proposed statutory parent is located. The statutory parent shall be the Commissioner of Children and Families or a child-placing agency. Notice of the proceeding shall be sent to the guardian of the person, the child, if over the age of twelve, the applicant, the Commissioner of Children and Families and the proposed statutory parent by registered or certified mail or otherwise, at least ten days before the date of the hearing. Notice is not required for any party who files in court a written waiver of notice.

(b) The statutory parent shall be the guardian of the person of the child, shall be responsible for the welfare of the child and the protection of his interests and shall retain custody of the child until he attains the age of eighteen unless, before that time, he is legally adopted or committed to the Commissioner of Children and Families or a licensed child-placing agency.

(c) Any statutory parent may resign or be removed for good cause shown. Upon filing of an application for the removal of a statutory parent or filing of a resignation of a statutory parent in the Court of Probate in which the statutory parent was appointed, the court shall schedule a hearing, on the removal application or resignation. Notice of such hearing shall be sent in accordance with section 45a–716, except that notice need not be sent to any parties whose rights have previously been terminated. At the hearing the court may accept the resignation, remove the statutory parent, or deny the application for removal. If a statutory parent is removed or resigns, the Court of Probate shall appoint a new statutory parent or a guardian of the person.

(1958 Rev., § 45–61h; 1973, P.A. 73–156, § 9; 1974, P.A. 74–164, § 8, eff. May 10, 1974; 1975 P.A. 75–420, § 4, eff. June 25, 1975; 1977, P.A. 77–604, § 53, eff. July 6, 1977; 1977, P.A. 77–614, § 521, eff. Jan. 1, 1979; 1979, P.A. 79–631, § 80, eff. July 6, 1979; 1980, P.A. 80–476, § 147, eff. Oct. 1, 1980; 1986, P.A. 86–194; 1987, P.A. 87–589, § 12, eff. July 9, 1987; 1993, P.A. 93–91, § 1, eff. July 1, 1993; 1995, P.A. 95–349, § 5.)

§ 45a–719. Reopening judgment terminating parental rights. Best interest of child. Final decree of adoption

The court may grant a motion to open or set aside a judgment terminating parental rights pursuant to section 52–212 or 52–212a or pursuant to common law or may grant a petition for a new trial on the issue of the termination of parental rights, provided the court shall consider the best interest of the child, except that no such motion or petition may be granted if a final decree of adoption has been issued prior to the filing of any such motion or petition. Any person who has legal custody of the child or who has physical custody of the child pursuant to an agreement, including an agreement with the department of children and families or a licensed child-placing agency, may provide evidence to the court concerning the best interest of the child at any hearing held on the motion to reopen or set aside a judgment terminating parental rights. For the purpose of this section, "best interest of the child" shall include, but not be limited to, a consideration of the age of the child, the nature of the relationship of the child with the caretaker of the child, the length of time the child has been in the custody of the caretaker, the nature of the relationship of the child with the birth parent, the length of time the child has been in the custody of the birth parent, any relationship that may exist between the child and siblings or other children in the caretaker's household, and the psychological and medical needs of the child. The determination of the best interest of the child shall not be based on a consideration of the socioeconomic status of the birth parent or the caretaker.

(1993, P.A. 93–91, § 1, eff. July 1, 1993; 1993, P.A. 93–170, § 1.)

§§ 45a–720 to 45a–723. Reserved for future use

PART III. ADOPTION

§ 45a–724. Who may give child in adoption

(a) The following persons may give a child in adoption:

(1) A statutory parent appointed under the provisions of section 17a–112, section 45a–717 or section 45a–718 may, by written agreement, subject to the approval of the Court of Probate as provided in section 45a–727, give in adoption to any adult person any minor child of whom he or she is the statutory parent; provided, if the child has attained the age of twelve, the child shall consent to the agreement.

(2) Subject to the approval of the Court of Probate as provided in section 45a–727, any parent of a minor child may agree in writing with his or her spouse that the spouse shall adopt or join in the adoption of the child; if that parent is (A) the surviving parent if the other parent has died; (B) the mother of a child born out of wedlock, provided that if there is a putative father who has been notified under the provisions of section 45a–716, the rights of the putative father have been terminated; (C) a former single person who adopted a child and thereafter married; or (D) the sole guardian of the person of the child, if the parental rights, if any, of any person other than the parties to such agreement have been terminated.

(3) Subject to the approval of the Court of Probate as provided in section 45a–727, any parent of a minor child may agree in writing with one other person who shares parental responsibility for the child with such parent that the other person shall adopt or join in the adoption of the child, if the parental rights, if any, of any other

person other than the parties to such agreement have been terminated.

(4) Subject to the approval of the Court of Probate as provided in section 45a–727, the guardian or guardians of the person of any minor child who is free for adoption in accordance with section 45a–725 may agree in writing with a relative that the relative shall adopt the child. For the purposes of this subsection "relative" shall include, but not be limited to, a person who has been adjudged by a court of competent jurisdiction to be the father of a child born out of wedlock, or who has acknowledged his paternity under the provisions of section 46b–172a, with further relationship to the child determined through the father.

(b) If all parties consent to the adoption under subdivision (2), (3) or (4) of subsection (a) of this section, then the application to be filed under section 45a–727 shall be combined with the consent termination of parental rights to be filed under section 45a–717. An application made under subdivision (2), (3) or (4) of subsection (a) of this section shall not be granted in the case of any child who has attained the age of twelve without the child's consent.

(1958 Rev., § 45–61i; 1973, P.A. 73–156, § 10; 1974, P.A. 74–164, § 9, eff. May 10, 1974; 1980, P.A. 80–476, § 148, eff. Oct. 1, 1980; 1986, P.A. 86–264, § 9; 1996, P.A. 96–130, § 8; 1998, P.A. 98–52, § 3; 2000, P.A. 00–228, § 2.)

§ 45a–724a. Placement for adoption with child-placing agency by Commissioner of Children and Families

Upon the termination of parental rights by the court pursuant to section 17a–112 or 45a–717, the court, at the request of the Commissioner of Children and Families as statutory parent, may order any child-placing agency to place the child for adoption.

(1999, P.A. 99–166, § 13.)

§ 45a–725. When child free for adoption

A minor child shall be considered free for adoption and the Court of Probate may grant an application for the appointment of a statutory parent if any of the following have occurred: (a) The child has no living parents; (b) all parental rights have been terminated under Connecticut law; (c)(1) in the case of any child from outside the United States, its territories or the Commonwealth of Puerto Rico placed for adoption by the Commissioner of Children and Families or by any child-placing agency, the petitioner has filed an affidavit that the child has no living parents or that the child is free for adoption and that the rights of all parties in connection with the child have been properly terminated under the laws of the jurisdiction in which the child was domiciled before being removed to the state of Connecticut; or (2) in the case of any child from any of the United States, its territories or the Commonwealth of Puerto Rico placed by the Commissioner of Children and Families or a child-placing agency, the petitioner has filed an affidavit that the child has no living parents or has filed in court a certified copy of the court decree in which the rights of all parties in connection with the child have been terminated under the laws of the jurisdiction in which the child was domiciled before being removed to the state of Connecticut, and the child-placing agency obtained guardianship or other court authority to place the child for adoption. If no such affidavit or certified decree has been filed, then termination of parental rights proceedings shall be required.

(1958 Rev., § 45–61j; 1974, P.A. 74–164, § 7, eff. May 10, 1974; 1975, P.A. 75–420, § 4, eff. June 25, 1975; 1977, P.A. 77–614, § 521, eff. Jan. 1, 1979; 1979, P.A. 79–631, § 81, eff. July 6, 1979; 1980, P.A. 80–476, § 149, eff. Oct. 1, 1980; 1993, P.A. 93–91, § 1, eff. July 1, 1993; 1996, P.A. 96 130, § 9; 1998, P.A. 98–52, § 4.)

§ 45a–726. Placement of adoptive children by Commissioner of Children and Families or child-placing agency

(a) If the Commissioner of Children and Families or a child-placing agency is appointed as statutory parent for any child free for adoption, the commissioner or such agency shall not refuse to place or delay placement of such child with any prospective adoptive parent solely on the basis of a difference in race, color or national origin.

(b) The Commissioner of Children and Families or the child-placing agency, in determining placement for each child, shall focus on the particular needs of the child and the capacity of the prospective adoptive parent to meet such needs. Whenever possible, siblings should be placed with the same prospective adoptive parent unless it is determined not to be in the best interests of a sibling.

(c) The Commissioner of Children and Families shall not discriminate in preparing a home study or in placing a child with a prospective adoptive parent based on whether the prospective parent is or is not willing to become a foster parent pending an adoption placement.

(1958 Rev., § 45–61l; 1986, P.A. 86–330, § 1, eff. Oct. 1, 1986; 1993, P.A. 93–91, § 1, eff. July 1, 1993; 1996, P.A. 96–130, § 10; 1999, P.A. 99–166, § 9; 2000, P.A. 00–137, § 9.)

§ 45a–726a. Consideration of sexual orientation of prospective adoptive or foster parent

Notwithstanding any provision of sections 4a–60a and 46a–81a to 46a–81p, inclusive, the Commissioner of Children and Families or a child-placing agency may consider the sexual orientation of the prospective adoptive or foster parent or parents when placing a child for adoption or in foster care. Nothing in this section shall be deemed to require the Commissioner of Children and Families or a child-placing agency to place a child for adoption or in foster care with a prospective adoptive or foster parent or parents who are homosexual or bisexual.

(1991, P.A. 91–58, § 18; 1993, P.A. 93–91, § 1, eff. July 1, 1993; 1996, P.A. 96–130, § 11.)

§ 45a–726b. Recruitment of minority families not to delay placement of adoptive child

The recruitment of minority families may not be a reason to delay placement of a child with an available family of a race or ethnicity different from that of the child.

(1999, P.A. 99–166, § 14.)

§ 45a–727. Application and agreement for adoption. Investigation, report. Adoptive parents entitled to receive copy of records and other information re history of child. Assessment of fees. Hearing and decree

(a) (1) Each adoption matter shall be instituted by filing an application in a Court of Probate, together with the written agreement of adoption, in duplicate. One of the duplicates shall be sent immediately to the Commissioner of Children and Families.

(2) The application shall incorporate a declaration that to the best of the knowledge and belief of the declarant there is no other proceeding pending or contemplated in any other court affecting the custody of the child to be adopted, or if there is such a proceeding, a statement in detail of the nature of the proceeding and affirming that the proposed adoption would not conflict with or interfere with the other proceeding. The court shall not proceed on any application which does not contain such a declaration. The application shall be signed by one or more of the parties to the agreement, who may waive notice of any hearing on it. For the purposes of this declaration, visitation rights granted by any court shall not be considered as affecting the custody of the child.

(3) An application for the adoption of a minor child not related to the adopting parents shall not be accepted by the Court of Probate unless (A) the child sought to be adopted has been placed for adoption by the Commissioner of Children and Families or a child-placing agency, and the placement for adoption has been approved by the commissioner or a child-placing agency; (B) the placement requirements of this section have been waived by the Adoption Review Board as provided in section 45a–764; (C) the application is for adoption of a minor child by a stepparent as provided in section 45a–733; or (D) the application is for adoption of a child by another person who shares parental responsibility for the child with the parent as provided in subdivision (3) of subsection (a) of section 45a–724. The commissioner or a child-placing agency may place a child in adoption who has been identified or located by a prospective parent, provided any such placement shall be made in accordance with regulations promulgated by the commissioner pursuant to section 45a–728. If any such placement is not made in accordance with such regulations, the adoption application shall not be approved by the Court of Probate.

(4) The application and the agreement of adoption shall be filed in the Court of Probate for the district where the adopting parent resides or in the district where the main office or any local office of the statutory parent is located.

(5) The provisions of section 17a–152, regarding placement of a child from another state, and section 17a–175, regarding the interstate compact on the placement of children, shall apply to adoption placements.

(b) (1) The Court of Probate shall request the commissioner or a child-placing agency to make an investigation and written report to it, in duplicate, within sixty days from the receipt of such request. A duplicate of the report shall be sent immediately to the Commissioner of Children and Families.

(2) The report shall be filed with the Court of Probate within the sixty-day period. The report shall indicate the physical and mental status of the child and shall also contain such facts as may be relevant to determine whether the proposed adoption will be in the best interests of the child, including the physical, mental, genetic and educational history of the child and the physical, mental, social and financial condition of the parties to the agreement and the biological parents of the child, if known, and whether the best interests of the child would be served in accordance with the criteria set forth in section 45a–727a. The report shall include a history of physical, sexual or emotional abuse suffered by the child, if any. The report may set forth conclusions as to whether or not the proposed adoption will be in the best interests of the child.

(3) The physical, mental and genetic history of the child shall include information about: (A) The child's health status at the time of placement; (B) the child's birth, neonatal, and other medical, psychological, psychiatric, and dental history information; (C) a record of immunizations for the child; and (D) the available results of medical, psychological, psychiatric and dental examinations of the child. The report shall include information, to the extent known, about past and existing relationships between the child and the child's siblings, biological parents, extended family, and other persons who have had physical possession of or legal access to the child. The educational history of the child shall include, to the extent known, information about the enrollment and performance of the child in educational institutions, results of educational testing and standardized tests for the child, and special educational needs, if any, of the child.

(4) The adoptive parents are entitled to receive copies of the records and other information relating to

the history of the child maintained by the commissioner or child-placing agency. The adoptive parents are entitled to receive copies of the records, provided if required by law, the copies have been edited to protect the identity of the biological parents and any other person whose identity is confidential and other identifying information relating to the history of the child. It is the duty of the person placing the child for adoption to edit, to the extent required by law, the records and information to protect the identity of the biological parents and any other person whose identity is confidential.

(5) The report shall be admissible in evidence subject to the right of any interested party to require that the person making it appear as a witness, if available, and such person shall be subject to examination.

(6) For any report under this section the Court of Probate may assess against the adopting parent or parents a reasonable fee covering the cost and expenses of making the investigation. The fee shall be paid to the state or to the child-placing agency making the investigation and report, provided the report shall be made within the sixty-day period or other time set by the court.

(c) (1) Upon the expiration of the sixty-day period or upon the receipt of such report, whichever is first, the Court of Probate shall set a day for a hearing upon the agreement and shall give reasonable notice of the hearing to the parties to the agreement, the child-placing agency if such agency is involved in the adoption, the Commissioner of Children and Families and the child, if over twelve years of age.

(2) At the hearing the court may deny the application, enter a final decree approving the adoption if it is satisfied that the adoption is in the best interests of the child or order a further investigation and written report to be filed, in duplicate, within whatever period of time it directs. A duplicate of such report shall be sent to the commissioner. The court may adjourn the hearing to a day after that fixed for filing the report. If such report has not been filed with the court within the specified time, the court may thereupon deny the application or enter a final decree in the manner provided in this section.

(3) The Court of Probate shall not disapprove any adoption under this section solely because of an adopting parent's marital status or because of a difference in race, color or religion between a prospective adopting parent and the child to be adopted or because the adoption may be subsidized in accordance with the provisions of section 17a–117.

(4) The Court of Probate shall ascertain as far as possible the date and the place of birth of the child and shall incorporate such facts in the final decree, a copy of which shall be sent to the Commissioner of Children and Families.

(1949 Rev., § 6867; 1957, P.A. 203, § 1; 1958 Rev., § 45–63; 1961, P.A. 156; 1965, Feb.Sp.Sess., P.A. 488, § 13; 1969, P.A. 529; 1973, P.A. 73–156, § 12; 1974, P.A. 74–164, § 10, eff. May 10, 1974; 1975, P.A. 75–163, § 4; 1975, P.A. 75–164, § 1, eff. May 27, 1975; 1980, P.A. 80–476, § 150, eff. Oct. 1, 1980; 1985, P.A. 85–285, § 1; 1986, P.A. 86–264, § 10; 1989, P.A. 89–363, § 1; 1993, P.A. 93–91, § 1, eff. July 1, 1993; 1996, P.A. 96–130, § 12; 1999, P.A. 99–166, § 10; 2000, P.A. 00–196, § 33; 2000, P.A. 00–228, § 3.)

§ 45a–727a. State policy re best interests of child; public policy re marriage

The General Assembly finds that:

(1) The best interests of a child are promoted by having persons in the child's life who manifest a deep concern for the child's growth and development;

(2) The best interests of a child are promoted when a child has as many persons loving and caring for the child as possible;

(3) The best interests of a child are promoted when the child is part of a loving, supportive and stable family, whether that family is a nuclear, extended, split, blended, single parent, adoptive or foster family; and

(4) It is further found that the current public policy of the state of Connecticut is now limited to a marriage between a man and a woman.

(2000, P.A. 00–228, § 1.)

§ 45a–727b. Endorsement of rights and responsibilities of unmarried persons to child subject to adoption, but not marriage or union of such persons

Nothing in this section and sections 45a–724, 45a–727, 45a–727a and 45a–731 shall be construed to establish or constitute an endorsement of any public policy with respect to marriage, civil union or any other form of relation between unmarried persons or with respect to any rights of or between such persons other than their rights and responsibilities to a child who is a subject of an adoption as provided for in sections 45a–724 and 45a–727.

(2000, P.A. 00–228, § 5.)

§ 45a–728. Regulations re adoption placement of children identified or located by prospective parents

The Commissioner of Children and Families shall adopt regulations in accordance with chapter 54 [1] concerning adoption placement of children who have been identified or located by prospective adoptive parents. Such regulations shall provide that for adoptions involving an identified expectant mother, counseling of the birth mother shall be required within seventy two hours of birth of the child, or as soon as medically possible after the birth, and that permissible payment of expenses for birth parent counseling shall include the cost of transportation. Such counseling may be provided by a person with a master's or doctoral degree in counseling, psychology or related mental health disciplines from an accredited college or university.

(1958 Rev., § 45–63b; 1985, P.A. 85–285, § 2, eff. June 4, 1985; 1991, P.A. 91–252, § 1; 1993, P.A. 93–50; 1993, P.A. 93–81, § 2; 1993, P.A. 93–91, § 1, eff. July 1, 1993; 1996, P.A. 96–130, § 13.)

1 C.G.S.A. § 4–166 et seq.

§ 45a–728a. Participation in birth and visitation of newborn identified for adoption by prospective adoptive parents

Prospective adoptive parents may participate in the labor and birth of the child identified for adoption and may visit with such newborn child, provided the birth mother, the child-placing agency and her physician agree and such participation and visitation are consistent with the medically necessary procedures of the hospital.

(1991, P.A. 91–252, § 2; 1996, P.A. 96–130, § 14.)

§ 45a–728b. Discharge of newborn identified for adoption from hospital. Prospective adoptive parents permitted to attend hospital programs re infant care

Any licensed hospital discharging a newborn infant identified for adoption to a child-placing agency shall arrange for the physical transfer of custody of such infant to take place in a safe, secure and private room on the hospital premises. The prospective adoptive parents may be present at the discharge with the approval of the child-placing agency. At the time of discharge, the hospital shall provide such prospective adoptive parents or child-placing agency with any nonidentifying information customarily provided to birth parents upon discharge concerning the care, feeding and health of the infant. The hospital shall provide the child-placing agency with the medical information concerning the birth mother and the infant within a reasonable time. Such prospective adoptive parents shall be permitted to participate in any program of instruction regarding infant care and child development that is made available by such licensed hospital to birth parents, provided such prospective adoptive parents pay the cost of such participation in such program.

(1991, P.A. 91–252, § 3; 1992, P.A. 92–179; 1996, P.A. 96–130, § 15.)

§ 45a–728c. Payment of expenses of birth mother by prospective adoptive parents

With respect to adoption placement of children who have been identified or located by prospective adoptive parents, payment for the living expenses of the birth mother by the prospective adoptive parents shall be permitted in an amount not to exceed one thousand five hundred dollars or such amount as may be approved in unusual circumstances by the probate court for the district where the child-placing agency is located or where the prospective adoptive parents reside. In addition to the payment of living expenses, payment by the prospective adoptive parents of reasonable telephone and maternity clothing expenses of the birth mother shall be permitted.

(1993, P.A. 93–81, § 1.)

§ 45a–728d. Advertising by birth parent and prospective adoptive parent for purpose of identified adoption

Any birth parent may advertise through any public media in this state for the placement of his or her child for the purposes of identified adoption. Any prospective adoptive parent may advertise through any public media in this state for placement of a child into his or her care for the purposes of identified adoption.

(1993, P.A. 93–101; 1996, P.A. 96–130, § 16.)

§ 45a–729. Penalty for violation of provisions re adoption placement

Any person who places a child for adoption in violation of section 45a–727 or 45a–764 or assists in such a placement shall be fined not more than five thousand dollars or imprisoned not less than one year nor more than five years or both.

(1958 Rev., § 45–63c; 1985, P.A. 85–285, § 3, eff. June 4, 1985.)

§ 45a–730. Validation of foreign adoption. Petition filed in Probate Court

(a) Notwithstanding the provisions of section 45a–727, when the adoption of a minor child born outside the United States or its territories has been finalized in a jurisdiction other than the United States or its territories, and such minor is unable to obtain citizenship in the United States because the adoptive parents did not personally see and observe the child prior to or during the adoption proceedings, a petition for validation of such adoption may be filed with a court of probate.

(b) The petition may be made by an adoptive parent or a duly authorized officer of any child-placing agency.

(c) The petition shall be filed in the court of probate in which the petitioner resides or in the district in which the main office or any local office of the child-placing agency is located.

(d) The petition shall be accompanied by an authenticated and exemplified copy of the adoption unless, upon a showing of good cause, the court waives such requirement.

(e) Upon receipt of the petition the court shall hold a hearing on said petition within forty-five days and shall order such notice as it may direct.

(f) The court may validate the adoption of the minor child if it finds after hearing that: (1) The adoption of the child born outside the United States or its territories occurred outside the United States or its territories and (2) United States Immigration and Naturalization Services refuses to naturalize said minor because the adoptive parents did not personally see and observe the child prior to or during the adoption proceedings, and (3) it is in the best interest of the child.

(g) Any validation pursuant to a petition filed under this section shall not be construed to validate an adoption otherwise invalid in accordance with the law of the place of adoption.

(1958 Rev., § 45–63d; 1987, P.A. 87–28; 1996, P.A. 96–130, § 17.)

§ 45a–731. Effects of final decree of adoption. Surviving rights

A final decree of adoption, whether issued by a court of this state or a court of any other jurisdiction, shall have the following effect in this state:

(1) All rights, duties and other legal consequences of the biological relation of child and parent shall thereafter exist between the adopted person and the adopting parent and the relatives of such adopting parent. Such adopted person shall be treated as if such adopted person were the biological child of the adopting parent, for all purposes including the applicability of statutes which do not expressly exclude an adopted person in their operation or effect;

(2) The adopting parent and the adopted person shall have rights of inheritance from and through each other and the biological and adopted relatives of the adopting parent. The right of inheritance of an adopted person extends to the heirs of such adopted person, and such heirs shall be the same as if such adopted person were the biological child of the adopting parent;

(3) The adopted person and the biological children and other adopted children of the adopting parent shall be treated, unless otherwise provided by statute, as siblings, having rights of inheritance from and through each other. Such rights of inheritance extend to the heirs of such adopted person and of the biological children and other adopted children, and such heirs shall be the same as if each such adopted person were the biological child of the adopting parent;

(4) The adopted person shall, except as hereinafter provided, be treated as if such adopted person were the biological child of the adopting parent for purposes of the applicability of all documents and instruments, whether executed before or after the adoption decree is issued, which do not expressly exclude an adopted person in their operation or effect. The words "child", "children", "issue", "descendant", "descendants", "heir", "heirs", "lawful heirs", "grandchild" and "grandchildren", when used in any will or trust instrument shall include legally adopted persons unless such document clearly indicates a contrary intention. Nothing in this section shall be construed to alter or modify the provisions of section 45a–257 concerning revocation of a will when a child is born as the result of artificial insemination;

(5) Except in the case of an adoption as provided in subdivision (2) or (3) of subsection (a) of section 45a–724, the legal relationship between the adopted person and the adopted person's biological parent or parents and the relatives of such biological parent or parents is terminated for all purposes, including the applicability of statutes which do not expressly include such an adopted person in their operation and effect. The biological parent or parents of the adopted person are relieved of all parental rights and responsibilities;

(6) Except in the case of an adoption as provided in subdivision (2) or (3) of subsection (a) of section 45a–724, the biological parent or parents and their relatives shall have no rights of inheritance from or through the adopted person, nor shall the adopted person have any rights of inheritance from or through the biological parent or parents of the adopted person and the relatives of such biological parent or parents, except as provided in this section;

(7) Except in the case of an adoption as provided in subdivision (2) or (3) of subsection (a) of section 45a–724, the legal relationship between the adopted person and the adopted person's biological parent or parents and the relatives of such biological parent or parents is terminated for purposes of the construction of documents and instruments, whether executed before or after the adoption decree is issued, which do not expressly include the individual by name or by some designation not based on a parent and child or blood relationship, except as provided in this section;

(8) Notwithstanding the provisions of subdivisions (1) to (7), inclusive, of this section, when one of the biological parents of a minor child has died and the surviving parent has remarried subsequent to such parent's death, adoption of such child by the person with whom such remarriage is contracted shall not affect the rights of such child to inherit from or through the deceased parent and the deceased parent's relatives;

(9) Nothing in this section shall deprive an adopted person who is the biological child of a veteran who served in time of war as defined in section 27–103 of aid under the provisions of section 27–140 or deprive a child receiving benefits under the Social Security Act, 42 USC Sec. 301 et seq., as amended from time to time, from continued receipt of benefits authorized under said act;

(10) Except as provided in subdivision (11) of this section, the provisions of law in force prior to October 1, 1959, affected by the provisions of this section shall apply to the estates or wills of persons dying prior to said date and to inter vivos instruments executed prior to said date and which on said date were not subject to the grantor's power to revoke or amend;

(11) The provisions of subdivisions (1) to (9), inclusive, of this section shall apply to the estate or wills of persons dying prior to October 1, 1959, and to inter vivos instruments executed prior to said date and which on said date were not subject to the grantor's power to revoke or amend, unless (A) a contrary intention of the testator or grantor is demonstrated by clear and convincing evidence, or (B) distribution of the estate or under the will or under the inter vivos instrument has been or will be made pursuant to court order entered prior to October 1, 1991;

(12) No fiduciary, distributee of the estate or person to whom a legacy has been paid shall be liable to any other person for any action taken or benefit received prior to October 1, 1991, provided any such action was taken or benefit was received in good faith by such fiduciary, distributee or legatee with respect to the applicability of statutes concerning the rights of inheritance or rights to take of adopted persons under any instrument executed prior to October 1, 1959;

(13) No fiduciary shall have the obligation to determine the rights of inheritance or rights to take of an adopted person under an instrument executed prior to October 1, 1959, unless the fiduciary receives a written claim for benefits by or on behalf of such adopted person.

(1958 Rev., § 45–64a; 1973, P.A. 73–156, § 14; 1980, P.A. 80–476, § 151, eff. Oct. 1, 1980; 1981, P.A. 81–43; 1991, P.A. 91–83; 1996, P.A. 96–130, § 18; 2000, P.A. 00–228, § 4; 2001, P.A. 01–195, § 32, eff. July 11, 2001.)

§ 45a–731a. Issuance of final adoption decree notwithstanding death of child

If (1) a minor child, free for adoption pursuant to section 45a–725 on or after January 1, 1995, was placed with prospective adoptive parents by the Commissioner of Children and Families or a licensed child-placing agency, (2) an application for adoption was filed with the court of probate having jurisdiction, and (3) the child died prior to April 30, 1995, the court may enter a final decree approving such adoption, notwithstanding the death of such minor child prior to the final adoption decree, provided such adoption is solely for the purpose of establishing a name for the child and rights concerning burial. No other right or responsibility shall inure as a result of an adoption approved pursuant to this section.

(1995, P.A. 95–316, § 16.)

§ 45a–732. Husband and wife to join in adoption

A married person shall not adopt a child unless both husband and wife join in the adoption agreement, except that the court of probate may approve an adoption agreement by either of them upon finding that there is sufficient reason why the other should not join in the agreement.

(1949 Rev., § 6868; 1958 Rev., § 45–62; 1973, P.A. 73–156, § 11; 1980, P.A. 80–476, § 152, eff. Oct. 1, 1980.)

§ 45a–733. Procedure on application for adoption by stepparent

(a) Notwithstanding the provisions of section 45a–727, in the case of a child sought to be adopted by a stepparent, the Court of Probate may waive all requirements of notice to the Commissioner of Children and Families and shall waive, unless good cause is shown for an investigation and report, all requirements for investigation and report by the Commissioner of Children and Families or by a child-placing agency. Upon receipt of the application and agreement, the Court of Probate may set a day for a hearing upon the agreement and shall give reasonable notice of the hearing to the parties to the agreement and to the child, if over twelve years of age.

(b) At the hearing the court may deny the application, enter a final decree approving the adoption if it is satisfied that the adoption is in the best interests of the child, or, for good cause shown, order an investigation by the Commissioner of Children and Families or a child-placing agency.

(1958 Rev., § 45–63a; 1971, P.A. 514, § 1, eff. June 23, 1971; 1973, P.A. 73–156, § 13; 1974, P.A. 74–164, § 11, eff. May 10, 1974; 1975, P.A. 75–420, § 4 eff. June 25, 1975; 1977, P.A. 77–614, § 521, eff. Jan. 1, 1979; 1979, P.A. 79–631, § 82, eff. July 6, 1979; 1980, P.A. 80–476, § 153, eff. Oct. 1, 1980; 1986, P.A. 86–264, § 11; 1993, P.A. 93–335; 1993, P.A. 93–91, § 1, eff. July 1, 1993; 1996, P.A. 96–130, § 19.)

§ 45a–734. Adoption of adults. Inheritance

(a) Any person eighteen years of age or older may, by written agreement with another person at least eighteen years of age but younger than himself or herself, unless the other person is his or her wife, husband, brother, sister, uncle or aunt of the whole or half-blood, adopt the other person as his or her child, provided the written agreement shall be approved by the court of probate for the district in which the adopting parent resides or, if the adopting parent is not an inhabitant of this state, for the district in which the adopted person resides.

(b) The Court of Probate may, upon presentation of the agreement of adoption for approval, cause public notice to be given of the time and place of hearing on the agreement. If at the hearing the court finds that it will be for the welfare of the adopted person and for the public interest that the agreement be approved, it may pass an order of approval of it and cause the agreement and the order to be recorded. Thereupon the adopted person shall become the legal child of the adopting person, and the adopting person shall become the legal parent of the adopted person, and the provisions of section 45a–731 shall apply.

(c) A married person shall not adopt a person under the provisions of this section unless both husband and wife join in the adoption agreement, except that the Court of Probate may approve an adoption agreement by either of them upon finding that there is sufficient reason why the other should not join in the agreement.

(d) When one of the biological parents of an adult has died and the surviving parent remarries, the person with whom the remarriage is celebrated may become an adopting parent without the biological parent's joining in the adoption except to consent in writing. Upon the approval of the court, the adopted person shall be in law the child of both.

(1949 Rev., § 6871; 1958 Rev., § 45–67; 1961, P.A. 77; 1963, P.A. 460; 1973, P.A. 73–156, § 16; 1980, P.A. 80–476, § 154, eff. Oct. 1, 1980; 1996, P.A. 96–130, § 20.)

§ 45a–735. Husband or wife of adopted adult to consent

An agreement of adoption between persons of the age of majority shall not be approved without the written consent of the husband or wife, if any, of the adopted person.

(1949 Rev., § 6872; 1958 Rev., § 45–68; 1980, P.A. 80–476, § 155, eff. Oct. 1, 1980.)

§ 45a–736. Change of name of adopted person

Any court of probate, as part of its approval of any agreement of adoption or declaration of an intention to adopt, may change the name of the person adopted, as requested by the adopting parent or parents.

(1949 Rev., § 6873; 1958 Rev., §§ 45–69, 45–66a.)

§ 45a–737. Obliteration of original name on institutional records, new name substituted

Upon the request of an adopting parent of a child adopted under the provisions of section 45a–727, any public or quasi-public institution, including but not limited to schools and hospitals, shall obliterate the original family name of an adopted child and substitute the new name of the child on its records; except that the person in charge of the records may apply to the court of probate having jurisdiction over the adoption and show cause why the name shall not be substituted. The court may grant or deny the order for the substitution of names as it deems to be in the best interests of the child.

(1958 Rev., §§ 45–69a, 45–66b; 1975, P.A. 75–150; 1980, P.A. 80–476, § 156, eff. Oct. 1, 1980.)

§§ 45a–738 to 45a–742. Reserved for future use

PART IV. AVAILABILITY AND CONFIDENTIALITY OF ADOPTION RECORDS

§ 45a–743. Definitions

For the purposes of sections 7–53, 45a–743 to 45a–757, inclusive, and 46b–124, the following terms have the following meanings:

(1) "Adoptable Person" means a person who has not been adopted but whose biological parents had their parental rights terminated under the laws of the state of Connecticut.

(2) "Adopted person" means (A) a person who was adopted under the laws of the state of Connecticut or (B) a person who was adopted in another jurisdiction but whose biological parents have had their parental rights terminated in the state of Connecticut.

(3) "Authorized applicant" means (A) an adult adopted or adult adoptable person, (B) any biological parent of an adult adopted or adult adoptable person, including any person claiming to be the father who was not a party to the proceedings for the termination of parental rights, (C) any adult biological sibling of any adult adopted or adult adoptable person, and (D) if the adopted or adult adoptable person is deceased, any adult descendants, including legally adopted descendants.

(4) "Department" means the Department of Children and Families.

(5) "Information" includes information in the records of the courts of probate, Superior Court, the department or child-placing agency or child care facility, the registrars of vital statistics and the Department of Public Health.

(6) "Biological parent" means the biological mother or father of a person.

(7) "Relative" means any person descended from a common ancestor, whether by blood or adoption, not more than three generations removed from the child.

(8) Deleted. (1996, P.A. 96–130, § 21.)

(1958 Rev., § 45–68c; 1977, P.A. 77–246, § 2; 1977, P.A. 77–614, § 323, eff. Jan. 1, 1979; 1977, P.A. 77–614, § 587, eff. June 2, 1977; 1978, P.A. 78–303, § 85, eff. June 6, 1978; 1980, P.A. 80–476, § 157, eff. Oct. 1, 1980; 1987, P.A. 87–555, § 3; 1993, P.A. 93–91, § 1, eff. July 1, 1993; 1993, P.A. 93–381, § 9, eff. July 1, 1993; 1995, P.A. 95–179, § 1; 1995, P.A. 95–257, §§ 12, 21, eff. July 1, 1995; 1995, P.A. 95–316, § 14; 1996, P.A. 96–130, § 21.)

§ 45a–744. Legislative policy

It is the policy of the state of Connecticut to make available to adopted and adoptable persons who are adults (1) information concerning their background and status; to give the same information to their adoptive parent or parents; and, in any case where such adult persons are deceased, to give the same information to their adult descendants, including adopted descendants except a copy of their original birth certificate as provided by section 7–51; (2) to provide for consensual release of additional information which may identify the biological parents or relatives of such adult adopted or adoptable persons when release of such information is in the best interests of such persons; (3) except as provided in subdivisions (4) and (5), to protect the right to privacy of all parties to termination of parental rights, statutory parent and adoption proceedings; (4) to make available to any biological parent of an adult adopted or adult adoptable person, including a person claiming to be the father who was not a party to the proceedings for termination of parental rights, information which would tend to identify such adult adopted or adult adoptable person; and (5) to make available to any adult biological sibling of an adult adopted or adult adoptable person information which would tend to identify such adult adopted or adult adoptable person.

(1958 Rev., § 45-68b; 1977, P.A. 77-246, § 1; 1980, P.A. 80-476, § 158, eff. Oct. 1, 1980; 1987, P.A. 87-555, § 2; 1995, P.A. 95-179, § 2; 1996, P.A. 96-130, § 22.)

§ 45a-745. Adoption record

(a) For each final decree of adoption decreed by a court of probate, the clerk of the court shall prepare a record on a form prescribed by the Department of Public Health. The record shall include all facts necessary to locate and identify the original birth certificate of the adopted person and to establish the new birth certificate of the adopted person, and shall include official notice from the court of the adoption, including identification of the court action and proceedings.

(b) Each petitioner for adoption, the attorney for the petitioner and each social or welfare agency or other person concerned with the adoption shall supply the clerk with information which is necessary to complete the adoption record. The supplying of the information shall be a prerequisite to the issuance of a final adoption decree by the court.

(c) Not later than the fifteenth day of each calendar month, the clerk of the Court of Probate shall forward to the Department of Public Health the record provided for in subsection (a) of this section for all final adoption decrees issued during the preceding month.

(d) When the Department of Public Health receives a record of adoption for a person born outside the state, the record shall be forwarded to the proper registration authority of the place of birth.

(e) The Department of Public Health, upon receipt of a record of adoption for a person born in this state, shall establish a new certificate of birth in the manner prescribed in section 7-53, except that no new certificate of birth shall be established if the court decreeing the adoption, the adoptive parents or the adopted person, if over fourteen years of age, so requests.

(1957, P.A. 298, § 1; 1958 Rev., §§ 45-64, 45-68a; 1976, P.A. 76-12; 1977, P.A. 77-614, § 323, eff. Jan. 1, 1979; 1980, P.A. 80-476, § 159, eff. Oct. 1, 1980; 1993, P.A. 93-381, § 9, eff. July 1, 1993; 1995, P.A. 95-257, §§ 12, 21, eff. July 1, 1995; 1996, P.A. 96-130, § 23.)

§ 45a-746. Information available to adoptive parents and adult adopted or adoptable person

(a) To the extent reasonably available, the following information concerning the biological parents of any adopted or adoptable person shall be recorded by the child-placing agency or department which has access to the information, in writing on a form provided by the department: (1) Age of biological parents in years, not dates of birth, at the birth of the adopted or adoptable person; (2) heritage of the biological parent or parents, which shall include (A) nationality, (B) ethnic background and (C) race; (3) education, which shall be number of years of school completed by the biological parent or parents; (4) general physical appearance of the biological parent or parents at the time of the birth of the adopted or adoptable person in terms of height, weight, color of hair, eyes, skin and other information of a similar nature; (5) talents, hobbies and special interests of the biological parent or parents; (6) existence of any other child or children born to either biological parent of the adopted or adoptable person; (7) reasons for placing the child for adoption or for biological parental rights being terminated; (8) religion of biological parent or parents; (9) field of occupation of biological parent or parents in general terms; (10) health history of biological parent or parents and blood relatives, on a standardized form provided by the department; (11) manner in which plans for the adopted or adoptable person's future were made by biological parent or parents; (12) relationship between the biological parents; (13) any psychological, psychiatric or social evaluations, including the date of the evaluation, any diagnosis, and a summary of any findings; and (14) any other relevant nonidentifying information. In addition, such information to the extent reasonably available and applicable concerning the biological and adoptive grandparents, adoptive siblings, and siblings of the whole blood and half-blood and such siblings of the biological parents shall be recorded by the child-placing agency or department which has access to the information in writing on a form provided by the department.

(b) The information in subsection (a) of this section, if available, shall be given in writing to the adopting parents not later than the date of finalization of the adoption proceedings.

(c) The information in subsection (a) of this section and any other nonidentifying information furnished to the child-placing agency from time to time shall be made available in writing upon written request to the following persons provided the child-placing agency or department is satisfied as to the identity of such persons: (1) The adopted or adoptable person who is an adult; (2) the adoptive parents of the adopted person, provided if the adopted person is an adult, such adopted person must give notarized permission to the parents; (3) the guardian or legally authorized representative of an adopted or adoptable person; (4) if the adopted or adoptable person is deceased, any adult descendants, including legally adopted descendants, of such person, provided a certificate of death of such person is presented. Any information requested pursuant to this section shall be provided to the applicant within sixty days of receipt of the request. The child-placing agency, department or court shall notify in writing any person making such request if the information cannot be made available within sixty days and shall state the reason for the delay.

(d) At any time, upon written request, any biological parent shall be given in writing, for purposes of verifying, correcting and adding information, any information in subdivisions (1) to (14), inclusive, of subsection (a) of this section, provided the child-placing agency, department or court is satisfied as to the identity of the parent making this request. Such information shall be provided within sixty days of receipt of such request unless the child-placing agency, department or court notifies the person requesting such information that it cannot be made available within sixty days and states the reason for the delay. Any such biological parent who believes such information to be inaccurate or incomplete may add a statement to the record setting forth what he or she believes to be an accurate or complete version of such information or updated information. Such statement shall become a permanent part of the record and shall be included with any information disclosed pursuant to this section.

(e) None of the information provided for in this section shall be made available if it is of such a nature that it would tend to identify a biological parent or parents of the adopted person, except as provided in sections 45a–750, 45a–751, 45a–751a, 45a–751b and 45a–753.

(f) The provisions of chapter 55 [1] shall not apply to the provisions of this section.

(1958 Rev., § 45–68e; 1977, P.A. 77–246, § 3; 1980, P.A. 80–476, § 161, eff. Oct. 1, 1980; 1981, P.A. 81–40, § 1; 1987, P.A. 87–555, § 4; 1994, May 25 Sp.Sess., P.A. 94–1, § 40, eff. July 1, 1994; 1996, P.A. 96–130, § 24; 1999, P.A. 99–166, § 11.)

[1] C.G.S.A. § 4–190 et seq.

§ 45a–747. Information regarding adoption completed before October 1, 1977

For any adoption completed before October 1, 1977, information in section 45a–746, if available, shall be given in writing to the adoptive parent or parents of an adopted person upon their written request to the child-placing agency, department, court of probate or superior court which has the information. Any such request shall be accompanied by a statement made by such adopted person under oath authorizing such disclosure.

(1958 Rev., § 45–68f; 1977, P.A. 77–246, § 4; 1977, P.A. 77–604, § 78, eff. Oct. 1, 1977; 1980, P.A. 80–476, § 162, eff. Oct. 1, 1980; 1987, P.A. 87–555, § 5; 1996, P.A. 96–130, § 25.)

§ 45a–748. Agency or department to make effort to obtain information

Each child-placing agency or the department shall be required to make a reasonable effort to obtain the information provided for in section 45a–746 for each child being placed for adoption or for whom there is a probability of adoption, but the lack of such information shall not be a bar to the granting of a decree of adoption, provided the child-placing agency or department has made a reasonable effort to obtain the information. If the judge of probate decides that a reasonable effort has not been made to obtain the information or that the information is being unreasonably withheld, the judge may order the child-placing agency or department to make a reasonable effort to obtain the information or to release the information. Any child-placing agency or department aggrieved by the order may appeal to the Superior Court.

(1958 Rev., § 45–68g; 1977, P.A. 77–246, § 5; 1980, P.A. 80–476, § 163, eff. Oct. 1, 1980; 1987, P.A. 87–555, § 6; 1996, P.A. 96–130, § 26.)

§ 45a–749. Request for information

A person entitled to nonidentifying information under subsection (c) of section 45a–746 may request the information provided in said section by applying in person or in writing to the child-placing agency in this state or the department which has the information. Such information shall not be released unless the child-placing agency or department is satisfied as to the identity of the person requesting information under the provisions of this section. For the purposes of this section, any records at the Court of Probate or the Superior Court or the Department of Public Health shall be available to an authorized representative of the child-placing agency or department to which the request has been made. Such information may be released in writing or in person.

(1958 Rev., § 45–68h; 1977, P.A. 77–246, § 6; 1977, P.A. 77–604, §§ 58, 79, eff. Oct. 1, 1977; 1978, P.A. 78–151; 1980, P.A. 80–476, § 164, eff. Oct. 1, 1980; 1987, P.A. 87–555, § 7; 1993, P.A. 93–381, § 9, eff. July 1, 1993; 1995, P.A. 95–257, §§ 12, 21, eff. July 1, 1995; 1996, P.A. 96–130, § 27.)

§ 45a–750. Identifying information

(a) A certificate of birth registration or a certified copy of the certificate of birth shall be issued in accordance with subsection (c) of section 7–51 or section 7–52 to any adoptable person by the Department of Public Health whether or not such person knows the names of his or her birth parents, provided such department is satisfied as to the identity of the person for whom the certificate is being requested. Any child-placing agency, the department or any court having information which is needed to locate such certificate shall furnish it to the Department of Public Health.

(b) Any person for whom there is only a removal of custody or removal of guardianship, and such removal took place in this state shall be given information which may identify the biological parent or parents or any relative of such person, upon request, in person or in writing, in accordance with subsection (f) of section 45a–751b, provided such information with respect to any relative shall not be released unless the consents required in subsection (e) of section 45a–751b are obtained.

(c) The provisions of chapter 55 [1] shall not apply to the provisions of this section or section 45a–751. Any information provided in this section shall not be released unless the child-placing agency, department or court is satisfied as to the identity of the person requesting the information.

(d) Deleted. (1996, P.A. 96–130, § 28.)

(e) Redesignated (c). (1996, P.A. 96–130, § 28.)

(1958 Rev., § 45–68i; 1977, P.A. 77–246, § 14; 1980, P.A. 80–476, § 165, eff. Oct. 1, 1980; 1987, P.A. 87–555, § 8; 1993, P.A. 93–381, § 9, eff. July 1, 1993; 1995, P.A. 95–179, § 3; 1995, P.A. 95–257, §§ 12, 21, eff. July 1, 1995; 1996, P.A. 96–130, § 28; 2001, P.A. 01–163, § 35.)

[1] C.G.S.A. § 4–190 et seq.

§ 45a–751. Release of identifying information by child-placing agency or department

(a) Any authorized applicant may, by applying in person or in writing to the child-placing agency or department, request the release of information that identifies or would tend to identify biological relatives who are unknown as the result of an adoption or termination of parental rights. The child-placing agency or department shall attempt to locate the person or persons sought in the request.

(b) Following such attempt, the child-placing agency or department shall furnish the information requested unless: (1) The consents required by section 45a–751b are not given; or (2) the child-placing agency or department determines at any time that the release of the requested information would be seriously disruptive to or endanger the physical or emotional health of the applicant; or (3) the child-placing agency or department determines at any time that the release of the requested information would be seriously disruptive to or endanger the physical or emotional health of the person whose identity is being requested.

(c) If the child-placing agency or department within sixty days of receipt of the request denies the request pursuant to subsection (b) of this section, the child-placing agency or department shall inform the applicant in writing of its determination. If a determination to grant or to deny the request is not reached within sixty days, the child-placing agency or department shall state the reason for the delay.

(d) Deleted. (1996, P.A. 96–130, § 29.)

(1958 Rev., § 45–68j; 1977, P.A. 77–246, § 15; 1980, P.A. 80–476, § 166, eff. Oct. 1, 1980; 1987, P.A. 87–555, § 9, eff. July 1, 1987; 1990, P.A. 90–230, § 57, eff. June 8, 1990; 1992, P.A. 92–118, § 7; 1993, P.A. 93–208, § 2; 1995, P.A. 95–179, § 4; 1995, P.A. 95–316, § 15; 1996, P.A. 96–130, § 29.)

§ 45a–751a. Conditions re release of information. Counseling

(a) If the authorized applicant is a resident of this state and it appears that counseling is advisable with release of the information, the child-placing agency or department may request that such person appear for an interview.

(b) If the authorized applicant is not a resident of Connecticut and it appears that counseling is advisable with release of the information, the child-placing agency or department may refer the person to an out-of-state child-placing agency or appropriate governmental agency or department, approved by the department or accredited by the Child Welfare League of America, the National Conference of Catholic Charities, the Family Services Association of America or the Council on Accreditation of Services of Families and Children.

(c) If an out-of-state referral is made, the information shall be released to the out-of-state child-placing agency or department for release to the authorized applicant, provided such information shall not be released if such child-placing agency or department determines that release of the requested information would be seriously disruptive to or endanger the physical or emotional health of the adult adopted or adoptable person or the person whose identity is being requested and provided such information shall not be released unless the consents required by subsection (b) of section 45a–751b are given and the out-of-state child-placing agency or department is satisfied as to the identity of the person.

(1996, P.A. 96–130, § 30.)

§ 45a–751b. Disclosure of identifying information. Consent required

(a) If parental rights were terminated on or after October 1, 1995, any information tending to identify the adult adopted or adoptable person, a biological parent, including a person claiming to be the father who was not a party to the proceedings for termination of parental rights, or adult biological sibling shall not be disclosed unless written consent is obtained from the person whose identity is being requested.

(b) If parental rights were terminated on or before September 30, 1995, (1) any information tending to identify the biological parents, including a person claiming to be the father who was not a party to the proceedings for the termination of parental rights, shall not be disclosed unless written consent is obtained from each biological parent who was party to such proceedings and (2) identifying information shall not be disclosed to a biological parent, including a person claiming to be the father who was not a party to the proceedings for termination of parental rights, without the written consent of each biological parent who was a party to such proceedings and the consent of the adult adopted or adoptable person whose identity is being requested.

(c) If the whereabouts of any person whose identity is being sought are unknown, the court shall appoint a guardian ad litem pursuant to subsection (c) of section 45a–753.

(d) When the authorized applicant requesting identifying information has contact with a biological sibling who is a minor, identifying information shall not be disclosed unless consent is obtained from the adoptive parents or guardian or guardian ad litem of the sibling.

(e) Any information tending to identify any adult relative other than a biological parent shall not be disclosed unless written consent is obtained from such adult relative. The consent of any biological parents common to the person making the request and the person to be identified shall be required unless (1) the parental rights of such parents have been terminated and not reinstated, guardianship has been removed and not reinstated or custody has been removed and not reinstated with respect to such adult relative or (2) the adoption was finalized on or after June 12, 1984. No consent shall be required if the person to be identified is deceased. If the person to be identified is deceased, the information that may be released shall be limited as provided in subsection (e) of section 45a–753.

(f) Any adult person for whom there is only removal of custody or removal of guardianship as specified in subsection (b) of section 45a–750 may apply in person or in writing to the child-placing agency, the department, the court of probate or the superior court which has the information. Such information shall be made available within sixty days of receipt of such request unless the child-placing agency, department or court notifies the person requesting the information that it cannot be made available within sixty days and states the reason for the delay. If the person making such request is a resident of this state and it appears that counseling is advisable with release of the information, the child-placing agency or department may request that the person appear for an interview. If the person making such request is not a resident of this state, and if it appears that counseling is advisable with release of the information, the child-placing agency, department or court may refer the person to an out-of-state agency or appropriate governmental agency or department, approved by the department or accredited by the Child Welfare League of America, the National Conference of Catholic Charities, the Family Services Association of America or the Council on Accreditation of Services of Families and Children. If an out-of-state referral is made, the information shall be released to the out-of-state child-placing agency or department for release to the applicant, provided such information shall not be released unless the out-of-state child-placing agency or department is satisfied as to the identity of the person.

(1996, P.A. 96–130, § 31.)

§ 45a–752. Appeal to probate court. Advisory panel. Report. Hearing. Decision

(a) Any person requesting information under section 45a–746 who is of the opinion that any item of information is being withheld by the child-placing agency or department, or any person requesting information under section 45a–751 who has been refused release of the information, may petition the Court of Probate for a hearing on the matter. No petition shall be filed if the consents required by section 45a–751b have been denied. Such petition may be filed in the court of probate in the probate district where the adoption was finalized or where the child-placing agency or department has an office or, in the case of a petition by a person who resides in this state, may be filed in the court of probate for the district in which such person resides.

(b) When a petition, filed under the provisions of subsection (a) of this section, is received by the court and if such court is satisfied as to the identity of the petitioner, the court shall first refer the matter within thirty days of receipt of the petition to an advisory panel consisting of four members appointed from a list of panel members provided by the Probate Court Administrator. This list shall include adult adopted persons, biological parents, adoptive parents and social workers experienced in adoption matters. In convening this panel, the court shall make a reasonable effort to include one member from each category of qualified persons. Such panel members shall serve without compensation. Within thirty days of referral of the matter the panel shall begin interviewing witnesses, including the petitioner if the petitioner wants to be heard, and reviewing such other evidence it may deem relevant, and within forty-five days following its initial meeting, shall render a report including recommendations to the judge of probate having jurisdiction. The court shall set a day for a hearing on the petition which hearing shall be held not more than thirty days after receiving the panel's report and shall give notice of the hearing to the petitioner and the child-placing agency. The court shall render a decision within forty-five days after the last hearing on the merits as to whether the requested information should be released under the relevant statutes. If the applicant requests the assistance of the child placing agency or department in locating a person to be identified, the provisions of section 45a–753 shall apply.

(1958 Rev., § 45–68k; 1977, P.A. 77–246, § 8; 1980, P.A. 80–476, § 167, eff. Oct. 1, 1980; 1987, P.A. 87–555, § 10; 1996, P.A. 96–130, § 32.)

§ 45a–753. Obtaining consent of person whose identity is requested. Petition to court. Report. Hearing

(a) If a request is received pursuant to section 45a–751, the child-placing agency or department which has agreed to attempt to locate the person or persons whose identity is being requested or the child-placing agency or department which furnished a report ordered by the court following a petition made under subsection (f) of this section shall not be required to expend more than ten hours time within sixty days of receipt of the request unless the child-placing agency or department notifies the authorized applicant of a delay and states the reason for the delay. The child-placing agency or department may charge the applicant reasonable compensation and be reimbursed for expenses in locating any person whose identity is being requested. The obtaining of such consent shall be accomplished in a manner which will protect the confidentiality of the communication and shall be done without disclosing the identity of the applicant. For the purposes of this section any records at the Court of Probate or the Superior Court shall be available to an authorized representative of the child-placing agency or department to which the request has been made.

(b) If the child-placing agency or department is out-of-state and unwilling to expend time for such purpose, the court of probate which finalized the adoption or terminated parental rights or the superior court which terminated parental rights shall upon petition appoint a licensed or approved child-placing agency or the department to complete the requirements of this section.

(c) If the relative whose identity is requested cannot be located or appears to be incompetent but has not been legally so declared, the Court of Probate or the Superior Court shall appoint a guardian ad litem under the provisions of section 45a–132, at the expense of the person making the request. The guardian ad litem shall decide whether to give consent on behalf of the relative whose identity is being requested.

(d) If the relative whose identity has been requested has been declared legally incapable or incompetent by a court of competent jurisdiction, then the legal representative of such person may consent to the release of such information.

(e) Such guardian ad litem or legal representative shall give such consent unless after investigation he concludes that it would not be in the best interest of the adult person to be identified for such consent to be given. If release of the information requires the consent of such guardian ad litem or legal representative, or if the person whose identity is sought is deceased, only the following information may be released: (1) All names by which the person whose identity is being sought has been known, and all known addresses; (2) the date and place of such person's birth; (3) all places where such person was employed; (4) such person's Social Security number; (5) the names of educational institutions such person attended; and (6) any other information that may assist in the search of a person who cannot be located.

(f) (1) If (A) the person whose identity is being sought cannot be located or is incompetent or (B) the child-placing agency or department has not located the person within sixty days, the authorized applicant may petition for access to the information to the court of probate or the superior court which terminated the parental rights or to the court of probate which approved the adoption.

(2) Within fifteen days of receipt of the petition, the court shall order the child-placing agency or department which has access to such information to present a report. The report by the child-placing agency or department shall be completed within sixty days after receipt of the order from the court.

(3) If the child-placing agency or department is out-of-state and unwilling to provide the report, the court shall refer the matter to a child-placing agency in this state or to the department for a report.

(4) The report shall determine through an interview with the adult adopted or adult adoptable person and through such other means as may be necessary whether (A) release of the information would be seriously disruptive to or endanger the physical or emotional health of the authorized applicant, and (B) release of the information would be seriously disruptive to or endanger the physical or emotional health of the person whose identity is being requested.

(5) Upon receipt of the report, or upon expiration of sixty days, whichever is sooner, the court shall set a time and place for hearing not later than fifteen days after receipt of the report or expiration of such sixty days, whichever is sooner. The court shall immediately give notice of the hearing to the authorized applicant and to the child-placing agency or the department.

(6) At the hearing, the authorized applicant may give such evidence to support the petition as the authorized applicant deems appropriate.

(7) Within fifteen days after the conclusion of the hearing, the court shall issue a decree as to whether the information requested shall be given to the authorized applicant.

(8) The requested information shall be provided to the authorized applicant unless the court determines that: (A) Consent has not been granted by a guardian ad litem appointed by the court to represent the person whose identity has been requested; (B) release of the information would be seriously disruptive to or endanger the physical or emotional health of the authorized applicant; or (C) release of the information would be

seriously disruptive to or endanger the physical or emotional health of the person whose identity is being requested.

(9) If the court denies the petition and determines that it would be in the best interests of the person whose identity is being requested to be notified that the authorized applicant has petitioned the court for identifying information, the court shall request the child-placing agency or department to so notify the person whose identity is being requested. The notification shall be accomplished in a manner which will protect the confidentiality of the communication and shall be done without disclosing the identity of the authorized applicant. If the person whose identity is being requested is so notified, the authorized applicant who petitioned the court shall be informed that this notification was given.

(1958 Rev., § 45–68l; 1977, P.A. 77–246, § 16; P.A. 80–476, § 168, eff. Oct. 1, 1980; 1981, P.A. 81–472, § 148, eff. July 8, 1981; 1987, P.A. 87–555, § 11; 1995, P.A. 95–179, § 5; 1996, P.A. 96–130, § 33.)

§ 45a–754. Records to be maintained in locked files. Disclosure for health or medical reasons

(a) The state shall furnish each court of probate with an index and a book in which shall be recorded only applications, agreements, orders, waivers, affidavits and returns of notice of hearing, appointments of guardians ad litem and decrees in termination of parental rights, removal of parent as guardian, appointment of statutory parent and adoption matters.

(b) The Probate Court shall also maintain locked files which shall be used for the filing of sealed envelopes, each of which shall contain all the papers filed in court regarding the removal of a parent as guardian, petitions for termination of parental rights, appointment of statutory parent and adoption.

(c) In the case of an application for the removal of a parent as guardian, a petition for termination of parental rights, an application for a statutory parent or an application for adoption, the envelopes shall be marked only with the words "Adoption Matter" and the names of the adopting parents and the name borne by the minor before the adoption. In the case of a removal of parent as guardian or in the case of a termination of parental rights matter which does not result in an adoption matter, the envelopes shall be marked only with the words "Removal Of Parent As Guardian" or "Termination Of Parental Rights Matter" and the name of the minor.

(d) Access to such records shall be in accordance with sections 45a–743 to 45a–753, inclusive. The records may also be disclosed upon order of the judge of probate to a petitioner who requires such information for the health or medical treatment of any adopted person. If such information is so required and is not within the records, the biological parent or parents or blood relatives may be contacted in accordance with the procedures in said section 45a–753.

(e) Any person who discloses any information contained in the indexes, record books and papers, except as provided in sections 45a–706 to 45a–709, inclusive, 45a–715 to 45a–718, inclusive, 45a–724 to 45a–737, inclusive, and 45a–743 to 45a–757, inclusive, shall be fined not more than five hundred dollars or imprisoned not more than six months or both.

(1949 Rev., § 6870; 1953, Supp. § 2196c; 1955, Supp. § 2906d; 1958 Rev., §§ 45–66, 45–68m; 1972, P.A. 127, § 67; 1974, P.A. 74–164, § 19, eff. May 10, 1974; 1975, P.A. 75–201; 1977, P.A. 77–246, § 9; 1977, P.A. 77–604, § 80, eff. Oct. 1, 1977; 1980, P.A. 80–476, § 169, eff. Oct. 1, 1980; 1987, P.A. 87–555, § 12; 1996, P.A. 96–130, § 34.)

§ 45a–755. Registries. Filing of registration

(a) Notwithstanding the provisions of sections 45a–746 to 45a–754, inclusive, the department and each child-placing agency which was party to, or participated in, either applications for approval of adoption agreements or termination of parental rights shall maintain registries. Such registries shall contain registrations of voluntary consents, refusals of consent and revocations of consent to the release of information which would identify the registrant. In the case where no child-placing agency was party to or involved in either proceeding, the Department of Children and Families shall establish and maintain such registry. At any time following the termination of parental rights, the registration may be filed by: (1) A biological parent who was a party to the proceeding for the termination of parental rights; (2) an adult adopted person, an adult adoptable person, an adult adopted biological sibling of an adoptable or adopted person, or an adult nonadopted biological sibling of an adoptable or adopted person; (3) lineal ascendants and descendants of a deceased biological parent; (4) an adoptive parent for the purpose of obtaining medical information which affects an adopted person; or (5) a person claiming to be the father who was not a party to the proceeding for the termination of parental rights. No registrations shall be accepted unless the child-placing agency or department is satisfied as to the identity of the registrants.

(b) Notwithstanding the provisions of sections 45a–746 to 45a–754, inclusive, the department and each child-placing agency which was a party to, or participated in, either applications for approval of adoption agreements or termination of parental rights shall maintain registries for medical information. The department and each such child-placing agency shall receive medical information concerning an adopted person provided by a biological parent or blood relative of such adopted person. Upon receipt of such information, the department or child-placing agency shall notify such adopted person or, if such person is a minor, the adoptive parent of such adopted person of the availability of such information, provided the department or child-placing agency has the address or telephone number of such adopted person or adoptive parent. No information that would tend to identify the biological parent or blood relative providing the medical information shall be disclosed without the consents required by subsection (a) of this section.

(1958 Rev., § 45–68o; 1987, P.A. 87–555, § 13; 1993, P.A. 93–208, § 1; 1993, P.A. 93–346; 1993, P.A. 93–91, § 1, eff. July 1, 1993; 1996, P.A. 96–130, § 35.)

§ 45a–756. Agreement to release identifying information. Notification. Fee

If there is a match of consents whereby the registrants agree to the releasing of identifying information to each other, in accordance with section 45a–755, the child-placing agency or department shall notify each registrant of the name, address and other identifying information as provided by the other registrant. The child-placing agency or department may charge a fee to cover the cost of maintaining the registry and the release of any identifying information.

(1958 Rev., § 45–68p; 1987, P.A. 87–555, § 14; 1996, P.A. 96–130, § 36.)

§ 45a–757. Records maintained on a permanent basis

Records kept or information received by courts of probate, Superior Court, the department, the Department of Public Health, agencies and the registrars of vital statistics, which contain or may contain information necessary to comply with the provisions of sections 45a–743 to 45a–757, inclusive, shall be maintained on a permanent basis.

(1958 Rev., § 45–68n; 1977, P.A. 77–246, § 13; 1977, P.A. 77–614, § 323, eff. Jan. 1, 1979; 1977, P.A. 77–614, § 587, eff. June 2, 1977; 1978, P.A. 78–303, § 85, eff. June 6, 1978; 1980, P.A. 80–476, § 170, eff. Oct. 1, 1980; 1993, P.A. 93–381, § 9, eff. July 1, 1993; 1995, P.A; 95–257, §§ 12, 21, eff. July 1, 1995.)

§§ 45a–758 to 45a–762. Reserved for future use

PART V. ADOPTION REVIEW BOARD

§ 45a–763. Adoption Review Board established

(a) An Adoption Review Board is established, to consist of the Commissioner of Children and Families or his designee, the probate court administrator or his designee, and an officer of a child-placing agency which is located in the state and licensed by the Commissioner of Children and Families, who shall be appointed by the governor to serve for a term of four years from the date of his appointment.

(b) Each designee or officer shall be a person who is familiar with and experienced in adoption procedures, policies and practices.

(c) The members of the board shall select a chairman from among their membership who shall serve for a term of two years from his election or until his successor is elected.

(d) The members of the board shall receive no compensation for their services as such.

(1958 Rev., § 45–69c; 1975, P.A. 75–163, § 1; 1980, P.A. 80–476, § 171, eff. Oct. 1, 1980; 1981, P.A. 81–472, § 80, eff. July 8, 1981; 1993, P.A. 93–91, § 1, eff. July 1, 1993.)

§ 45a–764. Powers of Adoption Review Board. Notice and hearing

(a) Notwithstanding the provisions of section 45a–727, the Adoption Review Board may, upon application, notice and hearing as hereinafter provided, for cause shown that it is in the best interests of the minor child, waive the requirement that the minor child be placed by the Commissioner of Children and Families or a child-placing agency.

(b) Any judge of probate who has had presented to him an application for adoption which may not proceed because the child has not been so placed may apply in writing to the Adoption Review Board for a waiver of such requirement.

(c) Upon receipt of the application, the chairman of the board shall set a time and place for a hearing and cause notice to be sent by registered or certified mail to the judge of probate and to all parties entitled to notice in the adoption proceeding.

(d) The hearing shall be held not less than ten days nor more than thirty days after the receipt of the application. The parties entitled to notice shall be given notice at least ten days prior to the hearing.

(e) Any party to the adoption proceedings shall have the right to present such evidence as is deemed necessary and relevant to the board. After hearing the evidence the board may deny the application or approve the application in which case the chairman shall notify the court of probate that the adoption may proceed and that the requirement of placement by the Commissioner of Children and Families or a child-placing agency is waived.

(f) If the court of probate thereafter grants the adoption application, there shall be included in the decree a finding that the placement requirements of section 45a–727 have been waived by the Adoption Review Board.

(g) No such waiver may be granted if the board determines that the adoption proceeding would violate the public policy of the state against the obtaining of children by illegal means for adoption purposes.

(1958 Rev., § 45–69d; 1975, P.A. 75–163, § 2; 1980, P.A. 80–476, § 172, eff. Oct. 1, 1980; 1993, P.A. 93–91, § 1, eff. July 1, 1993.)

§ 45a–765. Records to be confidential

All proceedings, documents, correspondence and findings by the board shall be returned to the probate court initiating the application and shall be confidential and placed in sealed envelopes as required by section 45a–754.

(1958 Rev., § 45–69e; 1975, P.A. 75–163, § 3; 1980, P.A. 80–476, § 173, eff. Oct. 1, 1980.)

§§ 45a–766 to 45a–770. Reserved for future use

CHAPTER 803a

CHILDREN CONCEIVED THROUGH ARTIFICIAL INSEMINATION

Section

§ 45a–771. Child born as a result of artificial insemination legitimate

(a) It is declared that the public policy of this state has been an adherence to the doctrine that every child born to a married woman during wedlock is legitimate.

(b) Sections 45a–771 to 45a–779, inclusive, shall be construed as a codification and clarification of such doctrine with respect to any child conceived as a result of heterologous artificial insemination.

(1958 Rev., § 45–69f; 1975, P.A. 75–233, § 1; 1976, P.A. 76–279, § 1; 1980, P.A. 80–476, § 174, eff. Oct. 1, 1980.)

§ 45a–772. A.I.D. Who may perform. Consent required

(a) The technique known as heterologous artificial insemination, or artificial insemination with the semen of a donor, referred to in sections 45a–771 to 45a–779, inclusive, as A.I.D., may be performed in this state only by persons certified to practice medicine in this state pursuant to chapter 370.[1]

(b) A.I.D. shall not be performed unless the physician receives in writing the request and consent of the husband and wife desiring the utilization of A.I.D. for the purpose of conceiving a child or children.

(1958 Rev., § 45–69g; 1975, P.A. 75–233, §§ 2, 3; 1980, P.A. 80–476, § 175, eff. Oct. 1, 1980.)

[1] C.G.S.A. § 20–8 et seq.

§ 45a–773. Request and consent to be filed in probate court. Confidentiality

(a) Whenever a child is born who was conceived by the use of A.I.D., a copy of the request and consent required under subsection (b) of section 45a–772, together with a statement of the physician who performed the A.I.D., that to the best of his knowledge the child was conceived by the use of A.I.D., shall be filed with the judge of probate in the district in which the child was born or in which the child resides.

(b) The information contained in such statement may be disclosed only to the persons executing the consent. No other person shall have access to the information except upon order of the probate court for cause shown.

(1958 Rev., § 45–69h; 1975, P.A. 75–233, § 4; 1976, P.A. 76–435, § 8, eff. June 9, 1976; 1980, P.A. 80–476, § 176, eff. Oct. 1, 1980.)

§ 45a–774. Status of child born as result of A.I.D.

Any child or children born as a result of A.I.D. shall be deemed to acquire, in all respects, the status of a naturally conceived legitimate child of the husband and wife who consented to and requested the use of A.I.D.

(1958 Rev., § 45–69i; 1975, P.A. 75–233, § 5; 1980, P.A. 80–476, § 177, eff. Oct. 1, 1980.)

§ 45a–775. No rights in donor of sperm

A donor of sperm used in A.I.D., or any person claiming by or through him, shall not have any right or interest in any child born as a result of A.I.D.

(1958 Rev., § 45–69j; 1975, P.A. 75–233, § 6; 1980, P.A. 80–476, § 178, eff. Oct. 1, 1980.)

§ 45a–776. Status of child determined by jurisdiction of birth

(a) Any child conceived as a result of A.I.D. performed in Connecticut and born in another jurisdiction shall have his status determined by the law of the other jurisdiction unless the mother of the child is domiciled in Connecticut at the time of the birth of the child.

(b) If a child is conceived by A.I.D. in another jurisdiction but is born in Connecticut to a husband and wife who, at the time of conception, were not domiciliaries of Connecticut, but are domiciliaries at the time of the birth of the child, the child shall have the same status as is provided in section 45a–774, even if the provisions of subsection (b) of section 45a–772 and section 45a–773 may not have been complied with.

(1958 Rev., § 45–69k; 1975, P.A. 75–233, §§ 7, 8; 1976, P.A. 76–279, §§ 3, 4; 1980, P.A. 80–476, § 179, eff. Oct. 1, 1980.)

§ 45a–777. Inheritance by child conceived as a result of A.I.D.

(a) A child born as a result of A.I.D. may inherit the estate of his mother and her consenting spouse or their relatives as though he were the natural child of the mother and consenting spouse and he shall not inherit the estate from his natural father or his relatives.

(b) The mother and her consenting husband or their relatives may inherit the estate of a child born as a result of A.I.D., if the child dies intestate, and the natural father or his relatives shall not inherit from him.

(1958 Rev., § 45–69l; 1975, P.A. 75–233, § 9; 1980, P.A. 80–476, § 180, eff. Oct. 1, 1980.)

§ 45a–778. Words of inheritance to apply to child conceived through A.I.D.

(a) The words "child", "children", "issue", "descendant", "descendants", "heir", "heirs", "unlawful heirs", "grandchild" and "grandchildren", when used in any will or trust instrument, shall, unless the document clearly indicates a contrary intention, include children born as a result of A.I.D.

(b) The provisions of this section shall apply to wills and trust instruments whether or not executed before, on or after October 1, 1975, unless the instrument indicates an intent to the contrary.

(1958 Rev., § 45–69m; 1975, P.A. 75–233, § 10; 1980, P.A. 80–476, § 181, eff. Oct. 1, 1980.)

§ 45a–779. Status of child conceived through A.I.D., born prior to October 1, 1975

Nothing in sections 45a–771 to 45a–779, inclusive, shall be construed as a change or modification of the rights or status of children born before October 1, 1975, but shall be construed as a clarification and codification of the rights and status which the children had on said date.

(1958 Rev., § 45–69n; 1975, P.A. 75–233, § 12; 1976, P.A. 76–279, § 2; 1980, P.A. 80–476, § 182, eff. Oct. 1, 1980.)

TITLE 46b

FAMILY LAW

CHAPTER 815

COURT PROCEEDINGS IN FAMILY RELATIONS MATTERS

§ 46b–1. Family relations matters defined

Matters within the jurisdiction of the Superior Court deemed to be family relations matters shall be matters affecting or involving: (1) Dissolution of marriage, contested and uncontested, except dissolution upon conviction of crime as provided in section 46b–47; (2) legal separation; (3) annulment of marriage; (4) alimony, support, custody and change of name incident to dissolution of marriage, legal separation and annulment; (5) actions brought under section 46b–15; (6) complaints for change of name; (7) civil support obligations; (8) habeas corpus and other proceedings to determine the custody and visitation of children; (9) habeas corpus brought by or on behalf of any mentally ill person except a person charged with a criminal offense; (10) appointment of a commission to inquire whether a person is wrongfully confined as provided by section 17a–523; (11) juvenile matters as provided in section 46b–121; (12) all rights and remedies provided for in chapter 815j;[1] (13) the establishing of paternity; (14) appeals from probate concerning: (A) Adoption or termination of parental rights; (B) appointment and removal of guardians; (C) custody of a minor child; (D) appointment and removal of conservators; (E) orders for custody of any child; and (F) orders of commitment of persons to public and private institutions and to other appropriate facilities as provided by statute; (15) actions related to prenuptial and separation agreements and to matrimonial decrees of a foreign jurisdiction; (16) custody proceeding brought under the provisions of chapter 815p;[2] and (17) all such other matters within the jurisdiction of the Superior Court concerning children or family relations as may be determined by the judges of said court.

(1958 Rev., §§ 51–182c, 51–330; 1959, P.A. 531, § 3; 1967, P.A. 183, § 3; 1973, P.A. 73–373, § 36; 1976, P.A. 76–436, § 89, eff. July 1, 1978; 1977, P.A. 77–336, § 2; 1977, P.A. 77–452, § 15, eff. July 1, 1978; 1977, P.A. 77–576, § 37, eff. July 1, 1978; 1978, P.A. 78–318, § 26; 1978, P.A. 78–379, § 13, eff. July 1, 1978; 1986, P.A. 86–337, § 9; 2003, P.A. 03–19, § 101, eff. May 12, 2003.)

[1] C.G.S.A. § 46b–40 et seq.
[2] C.G.S.A. § 46b–115 et seq.

§ 46b–2. Family matters, both civil and criminal, placed on family docket first

All proceedings involving a family relations matter shall be first placed on the family relations docket of the superior court; and except for juvenile matters which are provided for in section 46b–133, the judge before whom such proceeding is brought, may transfer such matter to the criminal or civil docket of said court if he deems that such docket is more suitable for the disposition of the case. Any case so entered or transferred to either docket shall be proceeded upon as are other cases of a like nature standing on such docket.

(1958 Rev., § 51–331; 1976, P.A. 76–436, § 89a, eff. July 1, 1978.)

§ 46b–3. Domestic relations officers and other employees

(a) The judges of the superior court shall appoint such domestic relations officers and other personnel as they deem necessary for the proper operation of the family relations sessions. The salaries and duties of such officers shall be determined by the judges in accordance with the compensation plan established under section 51–12. For the purposes of any investigation or pretrial conference the judge presiding at any family relations session may employ the services of any probation officer, including those under the direction of the Office of Adult Probation, physician, psychologist, psychiatrist or family counselor. Each person serving on July 1, 1978, in the court of common pleas appointed under the provisions of section 51–156c, revised to 1975, shall continue to serve in the superior court. In no event shall the compensation of such person be affected solely as a result of the transfer of jurisdiction provided in section 51–164s. The Chief Court Administrator may assign, reassign and modify the assignments of such family relations personnel as he deems necessary to be in the best interest of the disposition of family relations matters. Such family relations personnel shall also be available to assist the courts of probate in cases involving judicial consent to marriage of a minor.

(b) Family relations personnel are authorized to collect fees in accordance with the provisions of section 52–259.

(1958 Rev., §§ 51–182e, 51–332; 1959, P.A. 531, § 5; P.A. 76–436, §§ 10a, 92, eff. July 1, 1978; 1978, P.A. 78–280, § 93, eff. July 1, 1978; 1979, P.A. 79–585, § 7, eff. July 1, 1979; 1981, Nov.Sp.Sess., P.A. 81–6, § 3; 1982; 1982, P.A. 82–325, §§ 5 to 7, eff. June 1, 1982.)

§ 46b–4. Judge may retain jurisdiction until final disposition

Any judge who hears a family relations matter may retain jurisdiction thereof until its final disposition if, in his opinion, the ends of justice require.

(1958 Rev., §§ 51–182f, 51–333; 1959, P.A. 531, § 6; 1978, P.A. 78–280, §§ 1, 94, eff. July 1, 1978.)

§ 46b–5. Transfer of family relations matters to and from general docket

If the Chief Court Administrator deems it necessary for the proper dispatch of business, he may direct that, for such period as he may fix, any portion of the matters claimed for a family relations docket, except appeals be entered upon the general docket of the court, or transferred from the family relations docket to the general docket, and may likewise direct that any such cases entered on or transferred to the general docket shall be transferred to the family relations docket. Any case so entered or transferred to either docket shall be proceeded with as are other cases of a like nature standing upon that docket.

(1958 Rev., §§ 51–182i, 51–336; 1959, P.A. 531, § 9; 1967, P.A. 656, § 33, eff. June 27, 1967; 1971, P.A. 870, § 14; 1974, P.A. 74–183, § 280, eff. Dec. 31, 1974; 1976, P.A. 76–436, §§ 10a, 94, eff. July 1, 1978.)

§ 46b–6. Investigations

In any pending family relations matter the court or any judge may cause an investigation to be made with respect to any circumstance of the matter which may be helpful or material or relevant to a proper disposition of the case. Such investigation may include an examination of the parentage and surroundings of any child, his age, habits and history, inquiry into the home conditions, habits and character of his parents or guardians and evaluation of his mental or physical condition. In any action for dissolution of marriage, legal separation or annulment of marriage such investigation may include an examination into the age, habits and history of the parties, the causes of marital discord and the financial ability of the parties to furnish support to either spouse or any dependent child.

(1958 Rev., §§ 51–182j; 51–337; 1959, P.A. 531, § 10; 1973, P.A. 73–373, § 37; 1976, P.A. 76–436, § 95, eff. July 1, 1978.)

§ 46b–7. Report of investigation to be filed

Whenever, in any family relations matter, including appeals from the superior court, an investigation has been ordered, the case shall not be disposed of until the report has been filed as hereinafter provided, and counsel and the parties have had a reasonable opportunity to examine it prior to the time the case is to be heard. Any report of an investigation shall be made in quadruplicate and shall be filed with the clerk and mailed to counsel of record.

(1958 Rev., §§ 51–182k, 51–338; 1959, P.A. 531, § 11; 1976, P.A. 76–436, § 96, eff. July 1, 1978; 1978, P.A. 78–280, § 96, eff. July 1, 1978; 1979, P.A. 79–431, § 1.)

§ 46b–8. Motion for modification of support order combined with motion for contempt

Whenever a motion for modification of an order for support and alimony is made to the superior court by a moving party against whom a motion for contempt for noncompliance with such order is pending, the court shall accept such motion and hear both motions concurrently.

(1958 Rev., §§ 51–182p, 51–341; 1973, P.A. 73–308.)

§ 46b–9. Hearing by referee in action for dissolution of marriage, legal separation or annulment

In any action for dissolution of marriage, legal separation or annulment the court may refer the case or any matter in which the issues have been closed to a state referee who shall have been a judge of the referring court or who shall have been a judge of the court of common pleas; provided the referring court shall retain jurisdiction to hear and decide any pendente lite or contempt matters until such time as the referee hears and decides the case or matter. The Chief Court Administrator, or his designee, may authorize the presiding judge to refer to such state referee any action for the dissolution of marriage, legal separation or annulment which is on the family relations uncontested assignment list. Such uncontested assignment list matters shall be heard on the date on which they are assigned to be heard on the uncontested assignment list, and if they are not heard on such date the reference shall be automatically revoked. Any hearing by such referee shall be conducted as provided in section 52–434.

(1958 Rev., §§ 51–182m, 51–340; 1959, P.A. 531, § 13; 1974, P.A. 74–183, § 285, eff. Dec. 31, 1974; 1975, P.A. 75–261; 1975, P.A. 75–319, § 1, eff. June 12, 1975; 1978, P.A. 78–379, § 14, eff. July 1, 1978.)

§ 46b–10. Attempt at reconciliation in action for dissolution of marriage, legal separation or annulment

In any action for dissolution of marriage, legal separation or annulment, at any time before final judgment any judge may require that either or both parties appear before any judge, referee or other disinterested person for the purpose of attempting a reconciliation or adjustment of differences between the parties. Any person designated under the provisions of this section may be a family relations counselor or family relations caseworker and such person shall have all the powers provided in chapter 910.[1] Such person shall report to the court only the fact of whether or not reconciliation can be effected and shall not divulge information given to him by the parties except with the consent of all parties.

(1958 Rev., 51–182l, 51–339; 1959, P.A. 531, § 12; 1983, P.A. 83–295, § 13, eff. Oct. 1, 1983.)

1 C.G.S.A. § 52–425 et seq.

§ 46b–11. Closed hearings and records

Any case which is a family relations matter may be heard in chambers or, if a jury case, in a courtroom from which the public and press have been excluded, if the judge hearing the case determines that the welfare of any children involved or the nature of the case so requires. The records and other papers in any family relations matter may be ordered by the court to be kept confidential and not to be open to inspection except upon order of the court or judge thereof for cause shown.

(1958 Rev., §§ 51–182h; 51–335; 1959, P.A. 531, § 8; 1976, P.A. 76–436, § 93, eff. July 1, 1978; 1978, P.A. 78–280, § 95, eff. July 1, 1978.)

§§ 46b–12 to 46b–14. Reserved for future use

CHAPTER 815a

FAMILY MATTERS

§ 46b–15. Relief from physical abuse by family or household member or person in dating relationship. Application. Court orders. Duration. Copies. Expedited hearing for violation of order. Other remedies

(a) Any family or household member as defined in section 46b–38a who has been subjected to a continuous threat of present physical pain or physical injury by another family or household member or person in, or has recently been in, a dating relationship who has been subjected to a continuous threat of present physical pain or physical injury by the other person in such relationship may make an application to the Superior Court for relief under this section.

(b) The application form shall allow the applicant, at the applicant's option, to indicate whether the respondent holds a permit to carry a pistol or revolver or possesses one or more firearms. The application shall be accompanied by an affidavit made under oath which includes a brief statement of the conditions from which relief is sought. Upon receipt of the application the court shall order that a hearing on the application be held not later than fourteen days from the date of the order. The court, in its discretion, may make such orders as it deems appropriate for the protection of the applicant and such dependent children or other persons as the court sees fit. Such order may include temporary child custody or visitation rights and such relief may include but is not limited to an order enjoining the respondent from (1) imposing any restraint upon the person or liberty of the applicant; (2) threatening, harassing, assaulting, molesting, sexually assaulting or attacking the applicant; or (3) entering the family dwelling or the dwelling of the applicant. If an applicant alleges an immediate and present physical danger to the applicant, the court may issue an ex parte order granting such relief as it deems appropriate. If a postponement of a hearing on the application is requested by either party and granted, the order shall not be continued except upon agreement of the parties or by order of the court for good cause shown.

(c) Every order of the court made in accordance with this section shall contain the following language: "This order may be extended by the court beyond six months. In accordance with section 53a–107, entering or remaining in a building or any other premises in violation of this order constitutes criminal trespass in the first degree. This is a criminal offense punishable by a term of imprisonment of not more than one year, a fine of not more than two thousand dollars or both."

(d) No order of the court shall exceed six months, except that an order may be extended by the court upon motion of the applicant for such additional time as the court deems necessary. If the respondent has not appeared upon the initial application, service of a motion to extend an order may be made by first-class mail directed to the respondent at his or her last known address.

(e) The applicant shall cause notice of the hearing pursuant to subsection (b) of this section and a copy of the application and the applicant's affidavit and of any ex parte order issued pursuant to subsection (b) of this section to be served on the respondent not less than five days before the hearing. The cost of such service shall be paid for by the judicial branch. Upon the granting of an ex parte order, the clerk of the court shall provide two certified copies of the order to the applicant. Upon the granting of an order after notice and hearing, the clerk of the court shall provide two certified copies of the order to the applicant and a copy to the respondent. Every order of the court made in accordance with this section after notice and hearing shall contain the following language: "This court had jurisdiction over the parties and the subject matter when it issued this protection order. Respondent was afforded both notice and opportunity to be heard in the hearing that gave rise to this order. Pursuant to the Violence Against Women Act of 1994, 18 USC 2265, this order is valid and enforceable in all fifty states, any territory or possession of the United States, the District of Columbia, the Commonwealth of Puerto Rico and tribal lands." Immediately after making service on the respondent, the proper officer shall provide a true and attested copy of any ex parte order, including the applicant's affidavit and a cover sheet stating the date and time the respondent was served, to the law enforcement agency for the town in which the applicant resides. If the respondent does not reside in such town, the proper officer shall immediately transmit by facsimile a true and attested copy of the order, including the applicant's affidavit, to the law enforcement agency for the town in which the respondent resides. The clerk of the court shall send, by facsimile or other means, a copy of any ex parte order and of any order after notice and hearing, or the information contained in any such order, to the law enforcement agency for the town in which the applicant resides and, if the respondent resides in a town different than the town in which the applicant resides, to the law enforcement agency for the town in which the respondent resides, within forty-eight hours of the issuance of such order. If the applicant is employed in a town different than the town in which the applicant resides, the clerk of the court shall send, by facsimile or other means, a copy of any such order, or the information contained in any such order, to the law enforcement agency for the town in which the applicant is employed within forty-eight hours of the issuance of such order. If the applicant is employed in a town different than the town in which the applicant resides, or in which the respondent resides, the proper officer shall transmit by facsimile a true and attested copy of any such order, including the applicant's affidavit, to the law enforcement agency for the town in which the applicant is employed.

(f) A caretaker who is providing shelter in his or her residence to a person sixty years or older shall not be enjoined from the full use and enjoyment of his or her home and property. The Superior Court may make any other appropriate order under the provisions of this section.

(g) When a motion for contempt is filed for violation of a restraining order, there shall be an expedited hearing. Such hearing shall be held within five court days of service of the motion on the respondent, provided service on the respondent is made not less than twenty-four hours before the hearing. If the court finds the respondent in contempt for violation of an order, the court may impose such sanctions as the court deems appropriate.

(h) An action under this section shall not preclude the applicant from seeking any other civil or criminal relief.

(1981, P.A. 81–272, § 2; 1986, P.A. 86–337, § 7; 1987, P.A. 87–567, § 4, eff. July 1, 1987; 1991, P.A. 91–6, § 1, eff. Feb. 21, 1991; 1991, P.A. 91–381, § 3, eff. Jan. 1, 1992; 1995, P.A. 95–193, § 1; 1996, P.A. 96–180, § 158, eff. June 3, 1996; 1997, P.A. 97–126, § 1; 1999, P.A. 99–186, § 4; 2000, P.A. 00–196, § 24; 2001, P.A. 01–130, §§ 11, 12; 2002, May 9 Sp.Sess., P.A. 02–7, § 77, eff. Aug. 15, 2002; 2002, P.A. 02–127, § 7; 2002, P.A. 02–132, § 54, eff. Jan. 1, 2003; 2003, P.A. 03–202, § 4.)

§ 46b–15a. Protective order issued by another state. Registration. Notice. Hearing. Confirmation

(a) For the purposes of this section, "foreign order of protection" means any protection order, as defined in 18 USC 2266, as from time to time amended, or similar restraining or protective order issued by a court of another state, the District of Columbia, a commonwealth, territory or possession of the United States or an Indian tribe.

(b) A valid foreign order of protection that is consistent with 18 USC 2265, as from time to time amended, shall be accorded full faith and credit by a court of this state and may be enforced as if it were the order of a court in this state. A foreign order of protection shall be presumed valid if such order appears authentic on its face. The fact that a foreign order of protection has not been entered into the automated registry of protective orders maintained pursuant to section 51–5c, the Connecticut on-line law enforcement communication teleprocessing system maintained by the Department of Public Safety or the National Crime Information Center (NCIC) computerized index of criminal justice information shall not be grounds for refusing to enforce such order in this state.

(c) A law enforcement officer shall enforce a foreign order of protection in accordance with its terms and the law of this state, and shall arrest any person suspected of violating such order and charge such person with a violation of section 53a–223b. Nothing in this subsection shall affect the responsibility of a law enforcement officer to make an arrest pursuant to section 46b–38b.

(d) It shall be an affirmative defense in any action seeking enforcement of a foreign order of protection or any criminal prosecution involving the violation of a foreign order of protection that such order is not consistent with or entitled to full faith and credit pursuant to 18 USC 2265, as from time to time amended.

(e) A child custody provision in a foreign order of protection may be enforced in this state if such provision (1) complies with the Uniform Child Custody Jurisdiction Act [1] or the Uniform Child Custody Jurisdiction and Enforcement Act,[2] and (2) is consistent with the Parental Kidnapping Prevention Act of 1980, 28 USC 1738A, as from time to time amended.

(f) A foreign order of protection may be registered in this state by sending to the Superior Court in this state: (1) A letter or other document requesting registration; (2) two copies, including one certified copy, of the foreign order of protection sought to be registered and a statement under penalty of perjury that, to the best of the knowledge and belief of the petitioner, the order has not been modified; and (3) the name and address of the person seeking registration, except if the disclosure of such name and address would jeopardize the safety of such person.

(g) On receipt of the documents required in subsection (f) of this section, the registering court shall: (1) Cause the foreign order of protection to be filed as a foreign judgment, together with one copy of any accompanying documents and information, regardless of their form; and (2) cause the foreign order of protection to be entered in the automated registry of protective orders maintained pursuant to section 51–5c, together with any accompanying information required or permitted to be contained in the registry of protective orders pursuant to the procedures adopted by the Chief Court Administrator under section 51–5c.

(1999, P.A. 99–186, § 7; 2000, P.A. 00–196, § 47; 2003, P.A. 03–98, § 1.)

[1] C.G.S.A. § 46b–90 et seq. (Repealed effective July 1, 2000).
[2] C.G.S.A. § 46b–115 et seq.

§ 46b–15b. Duties of Superior Court re applicants for restraining orders in domestic violence situations

The Superior Court shall provide any person who applies for a restraining order in a domestic violence situation with information on steps necessary to continue such order beyond the initial period and shall provide an applicant with information on how to contact domestic violence counselors and counseling organizations.

(2002, P.A. 02–127, § 2.)

§ 46b–16. Petition to superior court for ex parte order re temporary care and custody of child when parent arrested for custodial interference. Duration of order

(a) When (1) a parent or relative has been arrested for violation of section 53a–97 or 53a–98 or arrested pursuant to chapter 964 [1] for an offense of intentional interference of the lawful custody of a child under the laws of another state or territory, and (2) a child has been in the care of such parent or relative, the legal custodian of the child or the department of children and families may petition the superior court or probate court which has venue over the matter for immediate temporary custody of the child.

(b) If the court finds that there is a substantial likelihood that the child will be removed from the jurisdiction of the court prior to a hearing to determine custody, an order of temporary custody may be issued ex parte by the court granting the temporary care and custody of the child to a suitable person or agency pending a hearing to determine custody pursuant to chapter 815j [2] or 815p. [3] Such hearing shall be held not more than five days from the issuance of the ex parte order or less than three days from the return of service, whichever is later.

(c) If the parent or relative arrested for violation of section 53a–97 or 53a–98 is in custody of the state, the state shall produce such parent or relative for the hearing to determine custody of the child pursuant to chapter 815j or 815p.

(d) The sole duty of the department of children and families under this section shall be to provide care for the child during the period of custody pending determination of the custodial rights of the parents or guardians.

(1986, P.A. 86–311, § 2; 1993, P.A. 93–91, § 1, eff. July 1, 1993; 2003, P.A. 03–19, § 102, eff. May 12, 2003.)

[1] C.G.S.A. § 54–157 et seq.
[2] C.G.S.A. § 46b–40 et seq.
[3] C.G.S.A. § 46b–115 et seq.

§§ 46b–17 to 46b–19. Reserved for future use

CHAPTERS 815b to 815d [RESERVED FOR FUTURE USE]

CHAPTER 815e

MARRIAGE

§ 46b–20. Definitions

As used in this chapter:

(a) "Registrar" means the registrar of vital statistics;

(b) "Applicant" means applicant for a marriage license;

(c) "License" means marriage license.

(1978, P.A. 78–230, § 1, eff. Oct. 1, 1978.)

§ 46b–21. Kindred who may not marry

No man may marry his mother, grandmother, daughter, granddaughter, sister, aunt, niece, stepmother or stepdaughter, and no woman may marry her father, grandfather, son, grandson, brother, uncle, nephew, stepfather or stepson. Any marriage within these degrees is void.

(1949 Rev., § 7301; 1958 Rev., § 46–1; 1978, P.A. 78–230, § 3, eff. Oct. 1, 1978.)

§ 46b–22. Who may join persons in marriage. Penalty for unauthorized performance

(a) All judges and retired judges, either elected or appointed and including federal judges and judges of other states who may legally join persons in marriage in their jurisdictions, family support magistrates, state referees and justices of the peace may join persons in marriage in any town in the state and all ordained or licensed clergymen, belonging to this state or any other state, so long as they continue in the work of the ministry may join persons in marriage. All marriages solemnized according to the forms and usages of any religious denomination in this state, including marriages witnessed by a duly constituted Spiritual Assembly of the Baha'is, are valid. All marriages attempted to be celebrated by any other person are void.

(b) No public official legally authorized to issue marriage licenses may join persons in marriage under authority of a license issued by himself, or his assistant or deputy; nor may any such assistant or deputy join persons in marriage under authority of a license issued by such public official.

(c) Any person violating any provision of this section shall be fined not more than fifty dollars.

(1949 Rev., § 7306; 1951, Supp. § 1281b; 1953 Supp. § 2251c; 1955, Supp. § 3001d; 1958 Rev., § 46–3; 1967, P.A. 129, § 1, eff. May 23, 1967; 1978, P.A. 78–230, § 4, eff. Oct. 1, 1978; 1979, P.A. 79–37, § 1, eff. April 17, 1979; 1987, P.A. 87–316, § 3; 2001, June Sp.Sess., P.A. 01–4, § 27, eff. July 1, 2001.)

§ 46b–22a. Validation of marriages performed by unauthorized justice of the peace

All marriages, celebrated before July 9, 2003, otherwise valid except that the justice of the peace joining such persons in marriage did not have a valid certificate of qualification, are validated, provided the justice of the peace who joined such persons in marriage represented himself or herself to be a duly qualified justice of the peace and such persons reasonably relied upon such representation.

(1982, P.A. 82–166, § 1, eff. May 17, 1982; 1984, P.A. 84–171, § 1, eff. May 11, 1984; 1985, P.A. 85–83, § 1, eff. April 29, 1985; 1987, P.A. 87–587, § 13, eff. July 7, 1987; 1989, P.A. 89–4, § 1, eff. March 13, 1989; 1991, P.A. 91–12, § 1, eff. March 28, 1991; 1993, P.A. 93–87, § 1, eff. June 2, 1993; 1995, P.A. 95–6, § 1, eff. April 13,

1995; 1996, P.A. 96–258, § 4, eff. June 10, 1996; 1997, P.A. 97–10, § 1, eff. April 18, 1997; 1999, P.A. 99–20, § 1, eff. May 12, 1999; 2001, P.A. 01–4, § 1, eff. April 27, 2001; 2002, P.A. 02–71, § 3, eff. June 3, 2002; 2003, P.A. 03–238, § 1, eff. July 9, 2003.)

§ 46b–23. Joining persons in marriage knowingly without authority

Any person who undertakes to join persons in marriage, knowing that he is not authorized to do so, shall be fined not more than five hundred dollars or imprisoned not more than one year or both.

(1949 Rev., § 8595; 1958 Rev., § 46–4.)

§ 46b–24. License required. Period of validity. Penalty

(a) No persons may be joined in marriage in this state until both have complied with the provisions of sections 46b–24, 46b–25 and 46b–29 to 46b–33, inclusive, and have been issued a license by the registrar for the town in which (1) the marriage is to be celebrated, or (2) either person to be joined in marriage resides, which license shall bear the certification of the registrar that the persons named therein have complied with the provisions of said sections.

(b) Such license, when certified by the registrar, is sufficient authority for any person authorized to perform a marriage ceremony in this state to join such persons in marriage, provided the ceremony is performed within a period of not more than sixty-five days after the date of application.

(c) Anyone who joins any persons in marriage without having received such license from them shall be fined not more than one hundred dollars.

(1958 Rev., § 46–5a; 1967, P.A. 313, § 1, eff. June 8, 1967; 1978, P.A. 78–230, § 5, eff. Oct. 1, 1978; 2003, P.A. 03–188, § 3.)

§ 46b–24a. Validation of marriages occurring in town other than town where license issued

All marriages celebrated before July 9, 2003, otherwise valid except that the license for any such marriage was issued in a town other than the town in this state in which such marriage was celebrated, are validated.

(1979, P.A. 79–298, § 1; 1982, P.A. 82–166, § 3, eff. May 17, 1982; 1989, P.A. 89–151, § 1, eff. June 1, 1989; 1991, P.A. 91–12, § 2, eff. March 28, 1991; 1993, P.A. 93–87, § 2, eff. June 2, 1993; 1995, P.A. 95–6, § 2, eff. April 13, 1995; 1997, P.A. 97–10, § 2, eff. April 18, 1997; 1999, P.A. 99–20, § 2, eff. May 12, 1999; 2001, P.A. 01–4, § 2, eff. April 27, 2001; 2002, P.A. 02–71, § 4, eff. June 3, 2002; 2003, P.A. 03–238, § 2, eff. July 9, 2003.)

§ 46b–25. Application for license

No license may be issued by the registrar until both persons have appeared before the registrar and made application for a license. The license shall be dated, signed and sworn to by each applicant and shall state each applicant's name, age, race, birthplace, residence, whether single, widowed or divorced and whether under the supervision or control of a conservator or guardian. The Social Security numbers of the bride and the groom shall be recorded in the "administrative purposes" section of the license. If the license is signed and sworn to by the applicants on different dates, the earlier date shall be deemed the date of application.

(1958 Rev., § 46–5b; 1967, P.A. 313, § 2, eff. June 8, 1967; 1978, P.A. 78–230, § 6, eff. Oct. 1, 1978; 1996, P.A. 96–3; 1997, June 18 Sp.Sess., P.A. 97–7, § 16, eff. July 1, 1997; 2001, P.A. 01–163, § 34.)

§§ 46b–26, 46b–27. Repealed. (2003, P.A. 03–188, § 6.)

§ 46b–28. When marriages in foreign country are valid

All marriages in which one or both parties are citizens of this state, celebrated in a foreign country, shall be valid, provided: (1) Each party would have legal capacity to contract such marriage in this state and the marriage is celebrated in conformity with the law of that country; or (2) the marriage is celebrated, in the presence of the ambassador or minister to that country from the United States or in the presence of a consular officer of the United States accredited to such country, at a place within his consular jurisdiction, by any ordained or licensed clergyman engaged in the work of the ministry in any state of the United States or in any foreign country.

(1949 Rev., § 7303; 1958 Rev., § 46–6; 1965, Feb.Sp. Sess., P.A. 94; 1978, P.A. 78–230, § 14, eff. Oct. 1, 1978.)

§ 46b–29. Marriage of persons under conservatorship or guardianship

(a) No marriage license may be issued to any applicant under the supervision or control of a conservator, appointed in accordance with sections 45a–644 to 45a–662, inclusive, unless the written consent of the conservator, signed and acknowledged before a person authorized to take acknowledgments of conveyances under the provisions of section 47–5a, or authorized to take acknowledgments in any other state or country, is filed with the registrar.

(b) Any person married without the consent provided for in subsection (a) of this section shall acquire no rights by such marriage in the property of any person who was under such control or supervision at the time of the marriage.

(1958 Rev., § 46–5e; 1967, P.A. 313, § 5, eff. June 8, 1967; 1977, P.A. 77–14; 1978, P.A. 78–230, § 9, eff. Oct. 1, 1978; 1986, P.A. 86–323, § 13; 2000, P.A. 00–196, § 25.)

§ 46b–30. Marriage of minors

(a) No license may be issued to any applicant under sixteen years of age, unless the judge of probate for the district in which the minor resides endorses his written consent on the license.

(b) No license may be issued to any applicant under eighteen years of age, unless the written consent of a parent or guardian of the person of such minor, signed and acknowledged before a person authorized to take acknowledgments of conveyances under the provisions of section 47–5a, or authorized to take acknowledgments in any other state or country, is filed with the registrar. If no parent or guardian of the person of such minor is a resident of the United States, the written consent of the judge of probate for the district in which the minor resides, endorsed on the license, shall be sufficient.

(1958 Rev., § 46–5f; 1967, P.A. 313, § 6, eff. June 8, 1967; 1978, P.A. 78–230, § 10, eff. Oct. 1, 1978.)

§ 46b–31. Repealed. (1979, P.A. 79–298, § 2.)

§ 46b–32. Failure to make license available; penalty

Any registrar who places on file any application for a license, or issues any license, except as provided in sections 46b–24, 46b–25 and 46b–29 to 46b–33, inclusive, or who conceals or refuses to make any application available to public examination while his office is open for business during the period until the license is issued, shall be fined not more than one hundred dollars or imprisoned not more than thirty days or both.

(1958 Rev., § 46–5i; 1967, P.A. 313, § 9, eff. June 8, 1967; 1978, P.A. 78–230, § 12, eff. Oct. 1, 1978; 2003, P.A. 03–188, § 4.)

§ 46b–33. Copy of law to applicants

Each registrar shall issue a copy of sections 46b–24, 46b–25 and 46b–29 to 46b–33, inclusive, to any person making application for a license.

(1958 Rev., § 46–5j; 1967, P.A. 313, § 10, eff. June 8, 1967; 1978, P.A. 78–230, § 13, eff. Oct. 1, 1978; 2003, P.A. 03–188, § 5.)

§ 46b–34. Marriage certificate. Affidavit in lieu of certificate

(a) Each person who joins any person in marriage shall certify upon the license certificate the fact, time and place of the marriage, and return it to the registrar of the town where it was issued, before or during the first week of the month following the marriage. Any person who fails to do so shall be fined not more than ten dollars.

(b) If any person fails to return the certificate to the registrar, as required under subsection (a) of this section, the persons joined in marriage may provide the registrar with a notarized affidavit attesting to the fact that they were joined in marriage and stating the date and place of the marriage. Upon the recording of such affidavit by the registrar, the marriage of the affiants shall be deemed to be valid as of the date of the marriage stated in the affidavit.

(1949 Rev., § 7304; 1958 Rev., § 46–7; 1978, P.A. 78–230, § 15, eff. Oct. 1, 1978; 2002, P.A. 02–71, § 5, eff. June 3, 2002.)

§ 46b–35. Certificates prima facie evidence

The certificates required by sections 46b–24 to 46b–27, inclusive, and 46b–29 to 46b–34, inclusive, or an affidavit recorded pursuant to subsection (b) of section 46b–34, shall be prima facie evidence of the facts stated in them.

(1949 Rev., § 7305; 1958 Rev., § 46–8; 1967, P.A. 313, § 12, eff. June 8, 1967; 1978, P.A. 78–230, § 16, eff. Oct. 1, 1978; 2002, P.A. 02–71, § 6, eff. June 3, 2002.)

§ 46b–36. Wife and husband property rights not affected by marriage

Neither husband nor wife shall acquire by the marriage any right to or interest in any property held by the other before or acquired after such marriage, except as to the share of the survivor in the property as provided by sections 45a–436 and 45a–437. The separate earnings of the wife shall be her sole property. She shall have power to make contracts with her husband or with third persons, to convey to her husband or to third persons her real and personal estate and to receive conveyances of real and personal estate from her husband or from third persons as if unmarried. She may bring suit in her own name upon contracts or for torts and she may be sued for a breach of contract or for a tort; and her property, except such as is exempt by law, may be taken on attachment and execution, but shall not be taken for the debts of her husband, except as provided in section 46b–37. The husband shall not be liable for her debts contracted before marriage, nor upon her contracts made after marriage, except as provided in said section.

(1949 Rev., § 7307; 1958 Rev., § 46–9.)

§ 46b–36a. Short title: Connecticut Premarital Agreement Act

Sections 46b–36a to 46b–36j, inclusive, may be cited as the Connecticut Premarital Agreement Act.

(1995, P.A. 95–170, § 9.)

Historical and Statutory Notes

Effective Dates

1995 Act. 1995, P.A. 95–170, § 11, provided:

"This act shall take effect October 1, 1995, and shall apply to any premarital agreement executed on or after that date."

§ 46b–36b. Definitions

As used in sections 46b–36a to 46b–36j, inclusive:

(1) "Premarital agreement" means an agreement between prospective spouses made in contemplation of marriage.

(2) "Property" means an interest, present or future, legal or equitable, vested or contingent, in real or personal property, tangible or intangible, including income and debt.

(1995, P.A. 95–170, § 1.)

§ 46b–36c. Form of premarital agreement

A premarital agreement shall be in writing and signed by both parties. It shall be enforceable without consideration.

(1995, P.A. 95–170, § 2.)

§ 46b–36d. Content of premarital agreement

(a) Parties to a premarital agreement may contract with respect to:

(1) The rights and obligations of each of the parties in any of the property of either or both of them whenever and wherever acquired or located;

(2) The right to buy, sell, use, transfer, exchange, abandon, lease, consume, expend, assign, create a security interest in, mortgage, encumber, dispose of, or otherwise manage and control property;

(3) The disposition of property upon separation, marital dissolution, death, or the occurrence or nonoccurrence of any other event;

(4) The modification or elimination of spousal support;

(5) The making of a will, trust or other arrangement to carry out the provisions of the agreement;

(6) The ownership rights in and disposition of the death benefit from a life insurance policy;

(7) The right of either party as a participant or participant's spouse under a retirement plan;

(8) The choice of law governing the construction of the agreement; and

(9) Any other matter, including their personal rights and obligations.

(b) No provision made under subdivisions (1) to (9), inclusive, of subsection (a) of this section may be in violation of public policy or of a statute imposing a criminal penalty.

(c) The right of a child to support may not be adversely affected by a premarital agreement. Any provision relating to the care, custody and visitation or other provisions affecting a child shall be subject to judicial review and modification.

(1995, P.A. 95–170, § 3.)

§ 46b–36e. Effect of marriage on premarital agreement

A premarital agreement becomes effective upon marriage unless otherwise provided in the agreement.

(1995, P.A. 95–170, § 4.)

§ 46b–36f. Amendment or revocation of premarital agreement after marriage

After marriage, a premarital agreement may be amended or revoked only by a written agreement signed by the parties. The amended agreement or the revocation shall be enforceable without consideration.

(1995, P.A. 95–170, § 5.)

§ 46b–36g. Enforcement of premarital agreement

(a) A premarital agreement or amendment shall not be enforceable if the party against whom enforcement is sought proves that:

(1) Such party did not execute the agreement voluntarily; or

(2) The agreement was unconscionable when it was executed or when enforcement is sought; or

(3) Before execution of the agreement, such party was not provided a fair and reasonable disclosure of the amount, character and value of property, financial obligations and income of the other party; or

(4) Such party was not afforded a reasonable opportunity to consult with independent counsel.

(b) If a provision of a premarital agreement modifies or eliminates spousal support and such modification or elimination causes one party to the agreement to be eligible for support under a program of public assistance at the time of separation or marital dissolution, a court, notwithstanding the terms of the agreement, may require the other party to provide support to the extent necessary to avoid such eligibility.

(c) An issue of unconscionability of a premarital agreement shall be decided by the court as a matter of law.

(1995, P.A. 95–170, § 6.)

§ 46b–36h. Enforcement of premarital agreement when marriage void

If the marriage is held void or voidable, an agreement that would otherwise have been a premarital agreement shall be enforceable only to the extent necessary to avoid an inequitable result.

(1995, P.A. 95–170, § 7.)

§ 46b–36i. Statute of limitations re claims under premarital agreement

Any statute of limitations applicable to an action asserting a claim for relief under a premarital agreement is tolled during the marriage of the parties to the agreement, except that equitable defenses limiting the time for enforcement, including laches and estoppel, shall be available to either party.

(1995, P.A. 95–170, § 8.)

§ 46b–36j. Premarital agreements made prior to October 1, 1995, not affected

Nothing in sections 46b–36a to 46b–36j, inclusive, shall be deemed to affect the validity of any premarital agreement made prior to October 1, 1995.

(1995, P.A. 95–170, § 10.)

§ 46b–37. Joint duty of spouses to support family. Liability for purchases and certain expenses. Abandonment

(a) Any purchase made by either a husband or wife in his or her own name shall be presumed, in the absence of notice to the contrary, to be made by him or her as an individual and he or she shall be liable for the purchase.

(b) Notwithstanding the provisions of subsection (a) of this section, it shall be the joint duty of each spouse to support his or her family, and both shall be liable for: (1) The reasonable and necessary services of a physician or dentist; (2) hospital expenses rendered the husband or wife or minor child while residing in the family of his or her parents; (3) the rental of any dwelling unit actually occupied by the husband and wife as a residence and reasonably necessary to them for that purpose; and (4) any article purchased by either which has in fact gone to the support of the family, or for the joint benefit of both.

(c) Notwithstanding the provisions of subsection (a) of this section, a spouse who abandons his or her spouse without cause shall be liable for the reasonable support of such other spouse while abandoned.

(d) No action may be maintained against either spouse under the provisions of this section, either during or after any period of separation from the other spouse, for any liability incurred by the other spouse during the separation, if, during the separation the spouse who is liable for support of the other spouse has provided the other spouse with reasonable support.

(e) Abandonment without cause by a spouse shall be a defense to any liability pursuant to the provisions of subdivisions (1) to (4), inclusive, of subsection (b) of this section for expenses incurred by and for the benefit of such spouse. Nothing in this subsection shall affect the duty of a parent to support his or her minor child.

(1949 Rev., § 7308; 1957, P.A. 191; 1958 Rev., § 46–10; 1977, P.A. 77–288, § 1; 1978, P.A. 78–230, § 17, eff. Oct. 1, 1978; 1988, P.A. 88–364, § 58, eff. June 8, 1988; 1992, P.A. 92–140; 2001, P.A. 01–195, § 35, eff. July 11, 2001.)

§ 46b–38. Repealed. (1986, P.A. 86–337, § 12.)

§ 46b–38a. Family violence prevention and response: Definitions

For the purposes of sections 46b–38a to 46b–38f, inclusive:

(1) "Family violence" means an incident resulting in physical harm, bodily injury or assault, or an act of threatened violence that constitutes fear of imminent physical harm, bodily injury or assault between family or household members. Verbal abuse or argument shall not constitute family violence unless there is present danger and the likelihood that physical violence will occur.

(2) "Family or household member" means (A) spouses, former spouses; (B) parents and their children; (C) persons eighteen years of age or older related by blood or marriage; (D) persons sixteen years of age or older other than those persons in subparagraph (C) presently residing together or who have resided together; (E) persons who have a child in common regardless of whether they are or have been married or have lived together at any time; and (F) persons in, or have recently been in, a dating relationship.

(3) "Family violence crime" means a crime as defined in section 53a–24 which, in addition to its other elements, contains as an element thereof an act of family violence to a family member and shall not include acts by parents or guardians disciplining minor children unless such acts constitute abuse.

(4) "Institutions and services" means peace officers, service providers, mandated reporters of abuse, agencies and departments that provide services to victims and families and services designed to assist victims and families.

(1986, P.A. 86–337, § 1; 1987, P.A. 87–567, § 1, eff. July 1, 1987; 1988, P.A. 88–364, § 59, eff. June 8, 1988; 1999, P.A. 99–186, § 2.)

§ 46b–38b. Investigation of family violence crime by peace officer. Arrest. Assistance to victim. Guidelines. Education and training program

(a) Whenever a peace officer determines upon speedy information that a family violence crime, as defined in subdivision (3) of section 46b–38a, except a family violence crime involving a dating relationship, has been committed within such officer's jurisdiction, such officer shall arrest the person or persons suspected of its commission and charge such person or persons with the appropriate crime. The decision to arrest and charge shall not (1) be dependent on the specific consent of the victim, (2) consider the relationship of the parties, or (3) be based solely on a request by the victim. Whenever a peace officer determines that a family violence crime has been committed, such officer may seize any firearm at the location where the crime is alleged to have been committed that is in the possession of any person arrested for the commission of such crime or suspected of its commission or that is in plain view. Not later than seven days after any such seizure, the law enforcement agency shall return such firearm in its original condition to the rightful owner thereof unless such person is ineligible to possess such firearm or unless otherwise ordered by the court.

(b) No peace officer investigating an incident of family violence shall threaten, suggest or otherwise indicate the arrest of all parties for the purpose of discouraging requests for law enforcement intervention by any party. Where complaints are received from two or more opposing parties, the officer shall evaluate each complaint separately to determine whether he should seek a warrant for an arrest.

(c) No peace officer shall be held liable in any civil action regarding personal injury or injury to property brought by any party to a family violence incident for an arrest based on probable cause.

(d) It shall be the responsibility of the peace officer at the scene of a family violence incident to provide immediate assistance to the victim. Such assistance shall include but not be limited to: (1) Assisting the victim to obtain medical treatment if such is required; (2) notifying the victim of the right to file an affidavit or warrant for arrest; and (3) informing the victim of services available and referring the victim to the Office of Victim Services. In cases where the officer has determined that no cause exists for an arrest, assistance shall include: (A) Assistance included in subdivisions (1) to (3), inclusive, of this subsection; and (B) remaining at the scene for a reasonable time until in the reasonable judgment of the officer the likelihood of further imminent violence has been eliminated.

(e) On or before October 1, 1986, each law enforcement agency shall develop, in conjunction with the Division of Criminal Justice, and implement specific operational guidelines for arrest policies in family violence incidents. Such guidelines shall include but not be limited to: (1) Procedures for the conduct of a criminal investigation; (2) procedures for arrest and for victim assistance by peace officers; (3) education as to what constitutes speedy information in a family violence incident; (4) procedures with respect to the provision of services to victims; and (5) such other criteria or guidelines as may be applicable to carry out the purposes of sections 46b–1, 46b–15, 46b–38a to 46b–38f, inclusive, and 54–1g. Such procedures shall be duly promulgated by said law enforcement agency.

(f) The Police Officer Standards and Training Council, in conjunction with the Division of Criminal Justice, shall establish an education and training program for law enforcement officers, supervisors and state's attorneys on the handling of family violence incidents. Such training shall: (1) Stress the enforcement of criminal law in family violence cases and the use of community resources and include training for peace officers at both recruit and in-service levels; (2) include: (A) The nature, extent and causes of family violence; (B) legal rights of and remedies available to victims of family violence and persons accused of family violence; (C) services and facilities available to victims and batterers; (D) legal duties imposed on police officers to make arrests and to offer protection and assistance; (E) techniques for handling incidents of family violence that minimize the likelihood of injury to the officer and promote safety of the victim.

(1986, P.A. 86–337, § 2; 1987, P.A. 87–554; 1987, P.A. 87–567, § 2, eff. July 1, 1987; 1987, P.A. 87–589, § 13, eff. July 9, 1987; 1995, P.A. 95–108, § 15; 1996, P.A. 96–246, § 32; 1999, P.A. 99–186, § 3; 2000, P.A. 00–196, § 58; 2002, P.A. 02–120, § 1.)

§ 46b–38c. Family violence response and intervention units. Local units. Duties and functions. Protective orders. Pretrial family violence education program

(a) There shall be family violence response and intervention units in the Connecticut judicial system to respond to cases involving family violence. The units shall be coordinated and governed by formal agreement between the chief state's attorney and the judicial department.

(b) The Court Support Services Division, in accordance with the agreement between the Chief State's Attorney and the Judicial Department, shall establish within each geographical area of the Superior Court a local family violence intervention unit to implement sections 46b–1, 46b–15, 46b–38a to 46b–38f, inclusive, and 54–1g. The Court Support Services Division shall oversee direct operations of the local units.

(c) Each such local family violence intervention unit shall: (1) Accept referrals of family violence cases from a judge or prosecutor, (2) prepare written or oral reports on each case for the court by the next court date to be presented at any time during the court session on that date, (3) provide or arrange for services to victims and offenders, (4) administer contracts to carry out such services, and (5) establish centralized reporting procedures. All information provided to a family relations officer in a local family violence intervention unit shall be solely for the purposes of preparation of the report and the protective order forms for each case and recommendation of services and shall otherwise be confidential and retained in the files of such unit and not be subject to subpoena or other court process for use in any other proceeding or for any other purpose, except that if the victim has indicated that the defendant holds a permit to carry a pistol or revolver or possesses one or more firearms, the family relations officer shall disclose such information to the court and the prosecuting authority for appropriate action.

(d) In all cases of family violence, a written or oral report and recommendation of the local family violence intervention unit shall be available to a judge at the first court date appearance to be presented at any time during the court session on that date. A judge of the Superior Court may consider and impose the following conditions to protect the parties, including, but not limited to: (1) Issuance of a protective order pursuant to subsection (e) of this section; (2) prohibition against subjecting the victim to further violence; (3) referral to a family violence education program for batterers; and (4) immediate referral for more extensive case assessment. Such protective order shall be an order of the court, and the clerk of the court shall cause (A) a certified copy of such order to be sent to the victim, and (B) a copy of such order, or the information contained in such order, to be sent by facsimile or other means within forty-eight hours of its issuance to the law enforcement agency for the town in which the victim resides and, if the defendant resides in a town different than the town in which the victim resides, to the law enforcement agency for the town in which the defendant resides. If the victim is employed in a town different than the town in which the victim resides, the clerk of the court shall, upon the request of the victim, send, by facsimile or other means, a copy of such order, or the information contained in such order, to the law enforcement agency for the town in which the victim is employed within forty-eight hours of the issuance of such order.

(e) A protective order issued under this section may include provisions necessary to protect the victim from threats, harassment, injury or intimidation by the defendant, including, but not limited to, an order enjoining the defendant from (1) imposing any restraint upon the person or liberty of the victim, (2) threatening, harassing, assaulting, molesting or sexually assaulting the victim, or (3) entering the family dwelling or the dwelling of the victim. Such order shall be made a condition of the bail or release of the defendant and shall contain the following language: "In accordance with section 53a–223, any violation of this order constitutes criminal violation of a protective order which is punishable by a term of imprisonment of not more than five years, a fine of not more than five thousand dollars, or both. Additionally, in accordance with section 53a–107, entering or remaining in a building or any other premises in violation of this order constitutes criminal trespass in the first degree which is punishable by a term of imprisonment of not more than one year, a fine of not more than two thousand dollars, or both. Violation of this order also violates a condition of your bail or release, and may result in raising the amount of bail or revoking release." Every order of the court made in accordance with this section after notice and hearing shall also contain the following language: "This court had jurisdiction over the parties and the subject matter when it issued this protection order. Respondent was afforded both notice and opportunity to be heard in the hearing that gave rise to this order. Pursuant to the Violence Against Women Act of 1994, 18 USC 2265, this order is valid and enforceable in all fifty states, any territory or possession of the United States, the District of Columbia, the Commonwealth of Puerto Rico and tribal lands." The information contained in and concerning the issuance of any protective order issued under this section shall be entered in the registry of protective orders pursuant to section 51–5c.

(f) In cases referred to the local family violence intervention unit, it shall be the function of the unit to (1) identify victim service needs and, by contract with victim service providers, make available appropriate services and (2) identify appropriate offender services and where possible, by contract, provide treatment programs for offenders.

(g) There shall be a pretrial family violence education program for persons who are charged with family violence crimes. The court may, in its discretion, invoke such program on motion of the defendant when it finds: (1) That the defendant has not previously been convicted of a family violence crime which occurred on or after October 1, 1986; (2) the defendant has not had a previous case assigned to the family violence education program; (3) the defendant has not previously invoked or accepted accelerated rehabilitation under section 54–56e for a family violence crime which occurred on or after October 1, 1986; and (4) that the defendant is not charged with a class A, class B or class C felony, or an unclassified felony carrying a term of imprisonment of more than ten years, or unless good cause is shown, a class D felony or an unclassified offense carrying a term of imprisonment of more than five years. Participation by any person in the accelerated pretrial rehabilitation program under section 54–56e prior to October 1, 1986, shall not prohibit eligibility of such person for the pretrial family violence education program under this section. The court may require that the defendant answer such questions under oath, in open court or before any person designated by the clerk and duly authorized to administer oaths, under the penalties of perjury as will assist the court in making these findings. The court, on such motion, may refer the defendant to the family violence intervention unit, and may continue his case pending the submission of the report of the unit to the court. The court shall also give notice to the victim or victims that the defendant has requested assignment to the family violence education program, and, where possible, give the victim or victims opportunity to be heard. Any defendant who accepts placement in the family violence education program shall agree to the tolling of any statute of limitations with respect to the crime or crimes with which he is charged, and to a waiver of his right to a speedy trial. Any such defendant shall appear in court and shall be released to the custody of the family violence intervention unit for such period, not exceeding two years, and under such conditions as the court shall order. If the defendant refuses to accept, or, having accepted, violates such conditions, his case shall be brought to trial. If the defendant satisfactorily completes the family violence education program and complies with the conditions imposed for the period set by the court, he may apply for dismissal of the charges against him and the court, on finding satisfactory compliance, shall dismiss such charges. Upon dismissal all records of such charges shall be erased pursuant to section 54–142a.

(h) A fee of two hundred dollars shall be paid to the court by any person who enters the family violence education program, except that no person shall be excluded from such program for inability to pay the fee, provided (1) the person files with the court an affidavit of indigency or inability to pay and (2) the court enters a finding thereof. All such fees shall be credited to the general fund.

(i) The Judicial Department shall establish an ongoing training program for judges, Court Support Services Division personnel and clerks to inform them about the policies and procedures of sections 46b–1, 46b–15, 46b–38a to 46b–38f, inclusive, and 54–1g, including, but not limited to, the function of the family violence intervention units and the use of restraining and protective orders.

(1986, P.A. 86–337, § 3; 1987, P.A. 87–567, § 3, eff. July 1, 1987; 1989, P.A. 89–219, § 1, eff. July 1, 1989; 1991, P.A. 91–6, § 2, eff. Feb. 21, 1991; 1991, P.A. 91–24, § 3, eff. Oct. 1, 1991; 1991, P.A. 91–381, § 4, eff. Oct. 1, 1991; 1993, P.A. 93–280, § 2; 1993, P.A. 93–343; 1996, P.A. 96–180, § 125, eff. June 3, 1996; 1996, P.A. 96–246, §§ 33, 34; 1997, P.A. 97–126, § 2; 2001, P.A. 01–130, § 13; 2002, P.A. 02–132, § 13, 14; 2002, P.A. 02–132, § 55, eff. Jan. 1, 2003; 2003, P.A. 03–202, § 5.)

§ 46b–38d. Family violence offense report by peace officer. Compilation of statistics by Commissioner of Public Safety. Report to governor and general assembly

(a) A peace officer who responds to a family violence incident shall complete a family violence offense report, whether or not an arrest occurs.

(b) Each police department, including resident troopers and constables, shall report all family violence incidents where an arrest occurs to the Commissioner of Public Safety, who shall compile statistics of family violence crimes and cause them to be published annually in the Connecticut Uniform Crime Reports. An offense shall be counted for each incident reported to the police. A zero shall be reported if no incidents have occurred during the reporting periods.

(c) For the purpose of establishing accurate data on the extent and severity of family violence in the state and on the degree of compliance with the requirements of sections 46b–38a to 46b–38f, inclusive, the Commissioner of Public Safety shall prescribe a form for making family violence offense reports. The form shall include, but is not limited to, the following: (1) Name of the parties; (2) relationship of the parties; (3) sex of the parties; (4) date of birth of the parties; (5) time and date of the incident; (6) whether children were involved or whether the alleged act of family violence was committed in the presence of children; (7) type and extent of the alleged abuse; (8) existence of substance abuse; (9) number and types of weapons involved; (10) existence of any prior court orders; (11) any other data that may be necessary for a complete analysis of all circumstances leading to the arrest.

(d) A copy of the family violence offense report shall be forwarded to the state's attorney for the appropriate judicial district in cases where an arrest has been made.

(e) The Department of Public Safety shall tabulate and compile data from the family violence offense reports and report such compilation annually for the five years following October 1, 1986, to the governor and the general assembly.

(f) Any person required to report under the provisions of this section who fails to make such report shall be fined not more than five hundred dollars.

(1986, P.A. 86–337, § 4.)

§ 46b–38e. Repealed. (1991, P.A. 91–381, § 6.)

§ 46b–38f. Statistical summary of family violence cases maintained by Court Support Services Division. Reports

(a) The Court Support Services Division shall maintain a statistical summary of all family violence cases referred to the family violence intervention units. Such summary shall include, but not be limited to, the number of family violence cases referred, the nature of the cases and the charges and dispositions.

(b) The statistical summary reports prepared by the Court Support Services Division shall be submitted to the Department of Public Safety on a monthly basis. The Department of Public Safety shall compile and report annually for a period of five years to the Governor and the General Assembly the tabulated data of family violence crime reports.

(1986, P.A. 86–337, § 8; 2002, P.A. 02–132, § 15.)

§ 46b–38g. Programs for children impacted by domestic violence

The Chief Court Administrator shall, within available appropriations, establish programs for children impacted by domestic violence.

(1993, P.A. 93–280, § 1.)

§ 46b–38h. Designation of conviction of certain crimes as involving domestic violence for purposes of criminal history record information

If any person is convicted of a violation of section 53a–59, 53a–59a, 53a–60, 53a–60a, 53a–60b, 53a–60c, 53a–70, 53a–70a, 53a–70b, 53a–71, 53a–72a, 53a–72b, 53a–181c, 53a–181d, 53a–181e, 53a–223, 53a–223a or 53a–223b, against a family or household member, as defined in section 46b–38a, or a person in a dating relationship, the court shall include a designation that such conviction involved domestic violence on the court record for the purposes of criminal history record information, as defined in subsection (a) of section 54–142g.

(1999, P.A. 99–186, § 1; 2003, P.A. 03–202, § 6.)

§ 46b–39. Reserved for future use

CHAPTERS 815f to 815i [RESERVED FOR FUTURE USE]

CHAPTER 815j

DISSOLUTION OF MARRIAGE, LEGAL SEPARATION AND ANNULMENT

PART I. GENERAL PROVISIONS

PART II. ENFORCEMENT OF FOREIGN MATRIMONIAL JUDGMENTS

PART III. SUPPORT OF CHILD AND SPOUSE. TRANSFER OF PROPERTY

PART I. GENERAL PROVISIONS

§ 46b–40. Grounds for dissolution of marriage; legal separation; annulment

(a) A marriage is dissolved only by (1) the death of one of the parties or (2) a decree of annulment or dissolution of the marriage by a court of competent jurisdiction.

(b) An annulment shall be granted if the marriage is void or voidable under the laws of this state or of the state in which the marriage was performed.

(c) A decree of dissolution of a marriage or a decree of legal separation shall be granted upon a finding that one of the following causes has occurred: (1) The marriage has broken down irretrievably; (2) the parties have lived apart by reason of incompatibility for a continuous period of at least the eighteen months immediately prior to the service of the complaint and that there is no reasonable prospect that they will be reconciled; (3) adultery; (4) fraudulent contract; (5) wilful desertion for one year with total neglect of duty; (6) seven years' absence, during all of which period the absent party has not been heard from; (7) habitual intemperance; (8) intolerable cruelty; (9) sentence to imprisonment for life or the commission of any infamous crime involving a violation of conjugal duty and punishable by imprisonment for a period in excess of one year; (10) legal confinement in a hospital or hospitals or other similar institution or institutions, because of mental illness, for at least an accumulated period totaling five years within the period of six years next preceding the date of the complaint.

(d) In an action for dissolution of a marriage or a legal separation on the ground of habitual intemperance, it shall be sufficient if the cause of action is proved to have existed until the time of the separation of the parties.

(e) In an action for dissolution of a marriage or a legal separation on the ground of wilful desertion for one year, with total neglect of duty, the furnishing of financial support shall not disprove total neglect of duty, in the absence of other evidence.

(f) For purposes of this section, "adultery" means voluntary sexual intercourse between a married person and a person other than such person's spouse.

(1958 Rev., § 46–32; 1973, P.A. 73–373, § 1; 1974, P.A. 74–169, § 1, eff. May 13, 1974; 1978, P.A. 78–230, § 18, eff. Oct. 1, 1978; 1991, P.A. 91–19, § 1; 1995, P.A. 95–257, § 48, eff. July 1, 1995.)

§ 46b–41. Complaint includes cross-complaints or cross actions

Whenever the word "complaint" is used in this chapter or section 46b–1 or 51–348a, it shall include cross-complaints or cross actions where appropriate.

(1958 Rev., § 46–36a; 1974, P.A. 74–169, § 15, eff. May 13, 1974.)

§ 46b–42. Jurisdiction

The superior court shall have exclusive jurisdiction of all complaints seeking a decree of annulment, dissolution of a marriage or legal separation.

(1958 Rev., § 46–33; 1973, P.A. 73–373, § 2.)

§ 46b–43. Capacity of minor to prosecute or defend

Any married minor may, in his own name, prosecute or defend to final judgment an action for annulment or dissolution of a marriage or for legal separation and may participate in all judicial proceedings with respect thereto.

(1958 Rev., §§ 46–15a, 46–34; 1971, P.A. 8; 1973, P.A. 73–373, § 41; 1978, P.A. 78–230, § 19, eff. Oct. 1, 1978.)

§ 46b–44. Residency requirement

(a) A complaint for dissolution of a marriage or for legal separation may be filed at any time after either party has established residence in this state.

(b) Temporary relief pursuant to the complaint may be granted in accordance with sections 46b–56 and 46b–83 at any time after either party has established residence in this state.

(c) A decree dissolving a marriage or granting a legal separation may be entered if: (1) One of the parties to the marriage has been a resident of this state for at least the twelve months next preceding the date of the filing of the complaint or next preceding the date of the decree; or (2) one of the parties was domiciled in this state at the time of the marriage and returned to this state with the intention of permanently remaining before the filing of the complaint; or (3) the cause for the dissolution of the marriage arose after either party moved into this state.

(d) For the purposes of this section, any person who has served or is serving with the armed forces, as defined by section 27–103, or the merchant marine, and who was a resident of this state at the time of his or her entry shall be deemed to have continuously resided in this state during the time he or she has served or is serving with the armed forces or merchant marine.

(1958 Rev., § 46–35; 1973, P.A. 73–373, § 3; 1974, P.A. 74–169, § 2, eff. May 13, 1974; 1978, P.A. 78–230, § 20, eff. Oct. 1, 1978; 1992, May Sp.Sess., P.A. 92–11, § 36, eff. June 1, 1992.)

§ 46b–45. Service and filing of complaint

(a) A proceeding for annulment, dissolution of marriage or legal separation shall be commenced by the service and filing of a complaint as in all other civil actions in the superior court for the judicial district in which one of the parties resides. The complaint may also be made by the Attorney General in a proceeding for annulment of a void marriage. The complaint shall be served on the other party.

(b) If any party is an inmate of a mental institution in this state, a copy of the complaint shall be served on the Commissioner of Administrative Services personally or by registered or certified mail. If any party is confined in an institution in any other state, a copy shall be so served on the superintendent of the institution in which the party is confined.

(1958 Rev., § 46–36; 1973, P.A. 73–373, § 4; 1974, P.A. 74–169, § 3, eff. May 13, 1974; 1977, P.A. 77–614, § 70, eff. Jan. 1, 1979; 1978, P.A. 78–230, § 21, eff. Oct. 1, 1978; 1978, P.A. 78–280, § 2, eff. July 1, 1978.)

§ 46b–45a. Allegation of pregnancy in pleadings. Disagreement as to paternity. Hearing

(a) If, during the pendency of a dissolution or annulment of marriage, the wife is pregnant, she may so allege in the pleadings. The parties may in their pleadings allege and answer that the child born of the pregnancy will or will not be issue of the marriage.

(b) If the parties to a dissolution or annulment of marriage disagree as to whether or not the husband is the father of the child born of the pregnancy, the court shall hold a hearing within a reasonable period after the birth of the child to determine paternity.

(1984, P.A. 84–386.)

§ 46b–46. Notice to nonresident party. Jurisdiction over nonresident for alimony and support

(a) On a complaint for dissolution, annulment, legal separation or custody, if the defendant resides out of or is absent from the state or the whereabouts of the defendant are unknown to the plaintiff, any judge or clerk of the Supreme Court or of the Superior Court may make such order of notice as such judge or clerk deems reasonable. After notice has been given and proved to the court, the court may hear the complaint if it finds that the defendant has actually received notice that the complaint is pending. If it does not appear that the defendant has had such notice, the court may hear the case, or, if it sees cause, order such further notice to be given as it deems reasonable and continue the complaint until the order is complied with. Nothing in this section shall be construed to affect the jurisdictional requirements of chapter 815p [1] in a complaint for custody.

(b) The court may exercise personal jurisdiction over the nonresident party as to all matters concerning temporary or permanent alimony or support of children, only if: (1) The nonresident party has received actual notice under subsection (a) of this section; and (2) the party requesting alimony meets the residency requirement of section 46b–44.

(1949 Rev., § 7330; 1958 Rev., §§ 46–17, 46–39; 1973, P.A. 73–373, § 9; 1975, P.A. 75–276; 1978, P.A. 78–230, § 24, eff. Oct. 1, 1978; 1991, P.A. 91–391, § 3; 1995, P.A. 95–310, § 1, eff. Jan. 1, 1996; 1997, June 18 Sp.Sess., P.A. 97–1, § 52, eff. Jan. 1, 1998; 2003, P.A. 03–19, § 104, eff. May 12, 2003.)

[1] C.G.S.A. § 46b–115 et seq.

§ 46b–47. Complaint for dissolution of marriage on ground of confinement for mental illness; procedure

(a) A copy of the writ and complaint in an action or cross action for dissolution of marriage or legal separation on the ground of confinement for mental illness shall be served on the adverse party, on the conservator, if any, and on the Commissioner of Administrative Services at Hartford. Service on the conservator, if resident outside the state, and on the commissioner, may be made by registered or certified mail. If the adverse party is confined in any other state, a copy shall be served on the superintendent of the institution in which the adverse party is confined.

(b) If the conservator does not appear in court, or if the adverse party has no conservator, the court shall appoint a guardian ad litem for the adverse party.

(c) On motion of either party, the court shall appoint two or more psychiatrists who are diplomates of the American Board of Psychiatry and Neurology and who are not on the staff of any state hospital for mental illness, who shall investigate the mental status of such person. Within a reasonable time thereafter, the psychiatrists shall report to the court the facts found by them together with their opinion as to the probability of further indefinite prolonged hospitalization for the mental illness. The testimony of no psychiatrists other than those appointed by the court shall be received upon the trial of such action.

(d) The fees and expenses of the psychiatrists and of the guardian ad litem shall be fixed by the court and shall be paid by the plaintiff.

(1949 Rev., § 7331; 1951, Supp. § 1284b; 1953, Supp., § 2254c; 1955, Supp. § 3003d; 1957, P.A. 502, § 2; 1958 Rev., §§ 46–19, 46–40; 1973, P.A. 73–373, § 11; 1974, P.A. 74–169, § 7, eff. May 13, 1974; 1975, P.A. 75–420, § 4, 6, eff. June 25, 1975; 1977, P.A. 77–614, § 521, eff. Jan. 1, 1979; 1978, P.A. 78–230, § 25, eff. Oct. 1, 1978; 1995, P.A. 95–257, § 48, eff. July 1, 1995.)

§ 46b–48. Dissolution of marriage or annulment upon conviction of crime against chastity; procedure

When any married person has been convicted in any court of an offense against chastity which would be ground for dissolution or annulment of the marriage, any person aggrieved may petition the superior court within four months of the conviction, and upon notice to the person convicted, the court may grant a dissolution or annulment of the marriage or such other relief as the court determines. No provision of this section shall be construed to affect the right of any aggrieved person to apply to the civil side of the court for similar relief.

(1949 Rev., § 7329; 1958 Rev., §§ 46–18, 46–37; 1971, P.A. 870, § 126; 1973, P.A. 73–373, § 10; 1978, P.A. 78–230, § 22, eff. Oct. 1, 1978.)

§ 46b–49. Private hearing

When it considers it necessary in the interests of justice and the persons involved, the court shall, upon the motion of either party or of counsel for any minor children, direct the hearing of any matter under this chapter and sections 17b–743, 17b–744, 45a–257, 46b–1, 46b–6, 47–14g, 51–348a and 52–362 to be private. The court may exclude all persons except the officers of the court, a court reporter, the parties, their witnesses and their counsel.

(1958 Rev., § 46–45; 1973, P.A. 73–373, § 13; 1978, P.A. 78–230, § 30, eff. Oct. 1, 1978; 1997, June 18 Sp.Sess., P.A. 97–1, § 53, eff. Jan. 1, 1998.)

§ 46b–50. Number of witnesses in uncontested action

In any action under this chapter, where the complaint for dissolution of marriage or separation is uncontested, the judge in his sole discretion shall decide the number of witnesses required, if any, in addition to the plaintiff or defendant on a cross complaint, except as provided in subsection (a) of section 46b–51.

(1958 Rev., §§ 46–30b, 46–46; 1972, P.A. 164, § 3; 1973, P.A. 73–373, §§ 40, 44; 1974, P.A. 74–338, §§ 12, 93, eff. May 31, 1974; 1978, P.A. 78–230, § 31, eff. Oct. 1, 1978.)

§ 46b–51. Stipulation of parties and finding of irretrievable breakdown

(a) In any action for dissolution of marriage or legal separation the court shall make a finding that a marriage breakdown has occurred where (1) the parties, and not their attorneys, execute a written stipulation that their marriage has broken down irretrievably, or (2) both parties are physically present in court and stipulate that their marriage has broken down irretrievably and have submitted an agreement concerning the custody, care, education, visitation, maintenance or support of their children, if any, and concerning alimony and the disposition of property. The testimony of either party in support of that conclusion shall be sufficient.

(b) In any case in which the court finds, after hearing, that a cause enumerated in subsection (c) of section 46b–40 exists, the court shall enter a decree dissolving the marriage or granting a legal separation. In entering the decree, the court may either set forth the cause of action on which the decree is based or dissolve the marriage or grant a legal separation on the basis of irretrievable breakdown. In no case shall the decree granted be in favor of either party.

(1958 Rev., § 46–48; 1973, P.A. 73–373, § 8; 1974, P.A. 74–169, § 6, eff. May 13, 1974; 1974, P.A. 74–338, § 92, eff. May 31, 1974; 1978, P.A. 78–230, § 33, eff. Oct. 1, 1978.)

§ 46b–52. Recrimination and condonation abolished

The defenses of recrimination and condonation to any action for dissolution of marriage or legal separation are abolished.

(1978, P.A. 78–230, § 2, eff. Oct. 1, 1978.)

§ 46b–53. Conciliation procedures; privileged communications

(a) On or after the return day of a complaint seeking the dissolution of a marriage or a legal separation and prior to the expiration of the ninety-day period specified in section 46b–67 either spouse or the counsel for any minor children of the marriage may submit a request for conciliation to the clerk of the court. The clerk shall forthwith enter an order that the parties meet with a conciliator mutually acceptable to them or, if the parties cannot agree as to a conciliator, with a conciliator named by the court. The conciliator shall, in any case, be a clergyman, a physician, a domestic relations officer or a person experienced in marriage counseling.

(b) Within such ninety-day period or within thirty days of the request, whichever is later, there shall be two mandatory consultations with the conciliator by each party to explore the possibility of reconciliation or of resolving the emotional problems which might lead to continuing conflicts following the dissolution of the marriage. Failure of the plaintiff or defendant to attend these consultations except for good cause shall preclude further action on the complaint until the expiration of six months from the date of the return day; provided the court may order the termination of such stay, upon the motion of either party and for good cause shown. Further consultations may be held with the consent of both parties, or, if the conciliator recommends one or more additional consultations and either one of the parties agrees, the court may order such additional consultations.

(c) All communications during these consultations shall be absolutely privileged, except that the conciliator shall report to the court whether or not the parties attended the consultations.

(d) The reasonable fees of the conciliator shall be paid by one or both of the parties as the court directs. No fee shall be charged by a domestic relations officer for such services. If the parties are unable to pay the fees which may be charged by the conciliator, only a domestic relations officer may be named as the conciliator.

(1958 Rev., § 46–41; 1973, P.A. 73–373, § 6; 1974, P.A. 74–169, § 5, eff. May 13, 1974; 1975, P.A. 75–530, § 11, eff. June 30, 1975; 1978, P.A. 78–230, § 26, eff. Oct. 1, 1978; 2002, P.A. 02–132, § 80.)

§ 46b–53a. Mediation program for persons filing for dissolution of marriage. Privileged communications

(a) A program of mediation services for persons filing for dissolution of marriage may be established in such judicial districts of the superior court as the Chief Court Administrator may designate. Mediation services shall address property, financial, child custody and visitation issues.

(b) All oral or written communications made by either party to the mediator or made between the parties in the presence of the mediator, while participating in the mediation program conducted pursuant to subsection (a) of this section, are privileged and inadmissible as evidence in any court proceedings unless the parties otherwise agree.

(1987, P.A. 87–316, § 8; 1987, P.A. 87–589, § 36, eff. July 9, 1987; 1993, P.A. 93–92.)

§ 46b–54. Counsel for minor children. Duties

(a) The court may appoint counsel for any minor child or children of either or both parties at any time after the return day of a complaint under section 46b–45, if the court deems it to be in the best interests of the child or children. The court may appoint counsel on its own motion, or at the request of either of the parties or of the legal guardian of any child or at the request of any child who is of sufficient age and capable of making an intelligent request.

(b) Counsel for the child or children may also be appointed on the motion of the court or on the request of any person enumerated in subsection (a) of this section in any case before the court when the court finds that the custody, care, education, visitation or support of a minor child is in actual controversy, provided the court may make any order regarding a matter in controversy prior to the appointment of counsel where it finds immediate action necessary in the best interests of any child.

(c) Counsel for the child or children shall be heard on all matters pertaining to the interests of any child, including the custody, care, support, education and visitation of the child, so long as the court deems such representation to be in the best interests of the child.

(1958 Rev., § 46–43; 1973, P.A. 73–373, § 16; 1974, P.A. 74–169, § 9, eff. May 13, 1974; 1975, P.A. 75–530, § 13, eff. June 30, 1975; 1978, P.A. 78–230, § 28, eff. Oct. 1, 1978.)

§ 46b–55. Attorney General as party. Paternity establishment

(a) The Attorney General shall be and remain a party to any action for dissolution of marriage, legal separation or annulment, and to any proceedings after judgment in such action, if any party to the action, or any child of any party, is receiving or has received aid or care from the state. The Attorney General may also be a party to such action for the purpose of establishing, enforcing or modifying an order for support or alimony if any party to the action is receiving support enforcement services pursuant to Title IV–D of the Social Security Act.[1]

(b) If any child born during a marriage, which is terminated by a divorce decree or decree of dissolution of marriage, is found not to be issue of such marriage, the child or his representative may bring an action in the superior court to establish the paternity of the child within one year after the date of the judgment of divorce or decree of dissolution of the marriage of his natural mother, notwithstanding the provisions of section 46b–160.

(1958 Rev., §§ 46–26b, 46–63; 1971, P.A. 712, §§ 1 to 4; 1973, P.A. 73–373, § 42; 1974, P.A. 74–183, § 271, eff. Dec. 31, 1974; 1976, P.A. 76–436, § 234, eff. July 1, 1978; 1978, P.A. 78–230, § 47, eff. Oct. 1, 1978; 1986, P.A. 86–359, § 32, eff. Jan. 1, 1987.)

1 42 U.S.C.A. § 651 et seq.

§ 46b–56. Superior Court orders re custody, care, therapy, counseling and drug and alcohol screening of minor children or parents in actions for dissolution of marriage, legal separation and annulment. Access to records of minor children by noncustodial parent. Parenting education program

(a) In any controversy before the Superior Court as to the custody or care of minor children, and at any time after the return day of any complaint under section 46b–45, the court may at any time make or modify any proper order regarding the education and support of the children and of care, custody and visitation if it has jurisdiction under the provisions of chapter 815p.[1] Subject to the provisions of section 46b–56a, the court may assign the custody of any child to the parents jointly, to either parent or to a third party, according to its best judgment upon the facts of the case and subject to such conditions and limitations as it deems equitable. The court may also make any order granting the right of visitation of any child to a third party, including, but not limited to, grandparents.

(b) In making or modifying any order with respect to custody or visitation, the court shall (1) be guided by the best interests of the child, giving consideration to the wishes of the child if the child is of sufficient age and capable of forming an intelligent preference, provided in making the initial order the court may take into consideration the causes for dissolution of the marriage or legal separation if such causes are relevant in a determination of the best interests of the child, and (2) consider whether the party satisfactorily completed participation in a parenting education program established pursuant to section 46b–69b. Upon the issuance of any order assigning custody of the child to the Commissioner of Children and Families, or not later than sixty days after the issuance of such order, the court shall make a determination whether the Department of Children and Families made reasonable efforts to keep the child with his or her parents prior to the issuance of such order and, if such efforts were not made, whether such reasonable efforts were not possible, taking into consideration the child's best interests, including the child's health and safety.

(c) In determining whether a child is in need of support and, if in need, the respective abilities of the parents to provide support, the court shall take into consideration all the factors enumerated in section 46b–84.

(d) When the court is not sitting, any judge of the court may make any order in the cause which the court might make under subsection (a) of this section, including orders of injunction, prior to any action in the cause by the court.

(e) A parent not granted custody of a minor child shall not be denied the right of access to the academic, medical, hospital or other health records of such minor child unless otherwise ordered by the court for good cause shown.

(f) Notwithstanding the provisions of subsection (b) of this section, when a motion for modification of custody or visitation is pending before the court or has been decided by the court and the investigation ordered by the court pursuant to section 46b–6 recommends psychiatric or psychological therapy for a child, and such therapy would, in the court's opinion, be in the best interests of the child and aid the child's response to a modification, the court may order such therapy and reserve judgment on the motion for modification.

(g) As part of a decision concerning custody or visitation, the court may order either parent or both of the parents and any child of such parents to participate in counseling and drug or alcohol screening, provided such participation is in the best interest of the child.

(1958 Rev., § 46–42; 1973, P.A. 73–373, § 15; 1974, P.A. 74–169; § 8, eff. May 13, 1974; 1975, P.A. 75–530, § 12, eff. June 30, 1975; 1977, P.A. 77–488, § 2; 1978, P.A. 78–230, § 27, eff. Oct. 1, 1978; 1978, P.A. 78–318, § 28; 1980, P.A. 80–29; 1981, P.A. 81–402, § 1; 1984, P.A. 84–42; 1993, P.A. 93–319, § 3; 1999, P.A. 99–137; 2001, P.A. 01–186, § 12; 2002, May 9 Sp.Sess., P.A. 02–7, § 35, eff. August 15, 2002; 2003, P.A. 03–19, § 105, eff. May 12, 2003.)

[1] C.G.S.A. § 46b–115 et seq.

§ 46b–56a. Joint custody. Definition. Presumption. Conciliation

(a) For the purposes of this section, "joint custody" means an order awarding legal custody of the minor child to both parents, providing for joint decision-making by the parents and providing that physical custody shall be shared by the parents in such a way as to assure the child of continuing contact with both parents. The court may award joint legal custody without awarding joint physical custody where the parents have agreed to merely joint legal custody.

(b) There shall be a presumption, affecting the burden of proof, that joint custody is in the best interests of a minor child where the parents have agreed to an award of joint custody or so agree in open court at a hearing for the purpose of determining the custody of the minor child or children of the marriage. If the court declines to enter an order awarding joint custody pursuant to this subsection, the court shall state in its decision the reasons for denial of an award of joint custody.

(c) If only one parent seeks an order of joint custody upon a motion duly made, the court may order both parties to submit to conciliation at their own expense with the costs of such conciliation to be borne by the parties as the court directs according to each party's ability to pay.

(1981, P.A. 81–402, § 2.)

§ 46b–56b. Presumption re best interest of child to be in custody of parent

In any dispute as to the custody of a minor child involving a parent and a nonparent, there shall be a presumption that it is in the best interest of the child to be in the custody of the parent, which presumption may be rebutted by showing that it would be detrimental to the child to permit the parent to have custody.

(1985, P.A. 85–244, § 2, eff. May 30, 1985; 1986, P.A. 86–224; 1986, P.A. 86–403, § 81, eff. June 11, 1986.)

§ 46b–56c. Educational Support Orders

(a) For purposes of this section, an educational support order is an order entered by a court requiring a parent to provide support for a child or children to attend for up to a total of four full academic years an institution of higher education or a private occupational school for the purpose of attaining a bachelor's or other undergraduate degree, or other appropriate vocational instruction. An educational support order may be entered with respect to any child who has not attained twenty-three years of age and shall terminate not later than the date on which the child attains twenty-three years of age.

(b) (1) On motion or petition of a parent, the court may enter an educational support order at the time of entry of a decree of dissolution, legal separation or annulment, and no educational support order may be entered thereafter unless the decree explicitly provides that a motion or petition for an educational support order may be filed by either parent at a subsequent date. If no educational support order is entered at the time of entry of a decree of dissolution, legal separation or annulment, and the parents have a child who has not attained twenty-three years of age, the court shall inform the parents that no educational support order may be entered thereafter. The court may accept a parent's waiver of the right to file a motion or petition for an educational support order upon a finding that the parent fully understands the consequences of such waiver.

(2) On motion or petition of a parent, the court may enter an educational support order at the time of entry of an order for support pendente lite pursuant to section 46b–83.

(3) On motion or petition of a parent, the court may enter an educational support order at the time of entering an order of support pursuant to section 46b–61 or 46b–171 or similar section of the general statutes, or at any time thereafter.

(4) On motion or petition of a parent, the court may enter an educational support order at the time of entering an order pursuant to any other provision of the general statutes authorizing the court to make an order of support for a child, subject to the provisions of sections 46b–212 to 46b–213v, inclusive.

(c) The court may not enter an educational support order pursuant to this section unless the court finds as a matter of fact that it is more likely than not that the parents would have provided support to the child for higher education or private occupational school if the family were intact. After making such finding, the court, in determining whether to enter an educational support order, shall consider all relevant circumstances, including: (1) The parents' income, assets and other obligations, including obligations to other dependents; (2) the child's need for support to attend an institution of higher education or private occupational school considering the child's assets and the child's ability to earn income; (3) the availability of financial aid from other sources, including grants and loans; (4) the reasonableness of the higher education to be funded considering the child's academic record and the financial resources available; (5) the child's preparation for, aptitude for and commitment to higher education; and (6) evidence, if any, of the institution of higher education or private occupational school the child would attend.

(d) At the appropriate time, both parents shall participate in, and agree upon, the decision as to which institution of higher education or private occupational school the child will attend. The court may make an order resolving the matter if the parents fail to reach an agreement.

(e) To qualify for payments due under an educational support order, the child must (1) enroll in an accredited institution of higher education or private occupational school, as defined in section 10a–22a, (2) actively pursue a course of study commensurate with the child's vocational goals that constitutes at least one-half the course load determined by that institution or school to constitute full-time enrollment, (3) maintain good academic standing in accordance with the rules of the institution or school, and (4) make available all academic records to both parents during the term of the order. The order shall be suspended after any academic period during which the child fails to comply with these conditions.

(f) The educational support order may include support for any necessary educational expense, including room, board, dues, tuition, fees, registration and application costs, but such expenses shall not be more than the amount charged by The University of Connecticut for a full-time in-state student at the time the child for whom educational support is being ordered matriculates, except this limit may be exceeded by agreement of the parents. An educational support order may also include the cost of books and medical insurance for such child.

(g) The court may direct that payments under an educational support order be made (1) to a parent to be forwarded to the institution of higher education or private occupational school, (2) directly to the institution or school, or (3) otherwise as the court determines to be appropriate.

(h) On motion or petition of a parent, an educational support order may be modified or enforced in the same manner as is provided by law for any support order.

(i) This section does not create a right of action by a child for parental support for higher education.

(j) An educational support order under this section does not include support for graduate or postgraduate education beyond a bachelor's degree.

(k) The provisions of this section shall apply only in cases when the initial order for parental support of the child is entered on or after October 1, 2002.

(2002, P.A. 02–128, § 1.)

§ 46b–57. Third party intervention re custody of minor children. Preference of child

In any controversy before the Superior Court as to the custody of minor children, and on any complaint under this chapter or section 46b–1 or 51–348a, if there is any minor child of either or both parties, the court, if it has jurisdiction under the provisions of chapter 815p,[1] may allow any interested third party or parties to intervene upon motion. The court may award full or partial custody, care, education and visitation rights of such child to any such third party upon such conditions and limitations as it deems equitable. Before allowing any such intervention, the court may appoint counsel for the child or children pursuant to the provisions of section 46b–54. In making any order under this section, the court shall be guided by the best interests of the child, giving consideration to the wishes of the child if the child is of sufficient age and capable of forming an intelligent preference.

(1958 Rev., § 46–47; 1973, P.A. 73–373, § 17; 1974, P.A. 74–169, § 10, eff. May 13, 1974; 1978, P.A. 78–230, § 32, eff. Oct. 1, 1978; 1978, P.A. 78–318, § 29; 2003, P.A. 03–19, § 106, eff. May 12, 2003.)

[1] C.G.S.A. § 46b–115 et seq.

§ 46b–58. Custody, maintenance and education of adopted children

The authority of the superior court to make and enforce orders and decrees as to the custody, maintenance and education of minor children in any controversy before the court between husband and wife brought under the provisions of this chapter is extended to children adopted by both parties and to any natural child of one of the parties who has been adopted by the other.

(1958 Rev., §§ 46–26a, 46–58; 1963, P.A. 414; 1973, P.A. 73–373, § 31; 1978, P.A. 78–230, § 43, eff. Oct. 1, 1978.)

§ 46b–59. Court may grant right of visitation to any person

The superior court may grant the right of visitation with respect to any minor child or children to any person, upon an application of such person. Such order shall be according to the court's best judgment upon the facts of the case and subject to such conditions and limitations as it deems equitable, provided the grant of such visitation rights shall not be contingent upon any order of financial support by the court. In making, modifying or terminating such an order, the court shall be guided by the best interest of the child, giving consideration to the wishes of such child if he is of sufficient age and capable of forming an intelligent opinion. Visitation rights granted in accordance with this section shall not be deemed to have created parental rights in the person or persons to whom such visitation rights are granted. The grant of such visitation rights shall not prevent any court of competent jurisdiction from thereafter acting upon the custody of such child, the parental rights with respect to such child or the adoption of such child and any such court may include in its decree an order terminating such visitation rights.

(1978, P.A. 78–69; 1979, P.A. 79–8; 1983, P.A. 83–95.)

§ 46b–59a. Mediation of disputes re enforcement of visitation rights

The Office of the Chief Court Administrator may establish programs of mediation for the timely resolution of disputes involving the enforcement of visitation rights.

(1986, P.A. 86–359, § 42, eff. July 1, 1987; 1986, P.A. 86–403, § 117, eff. June 11, 1986.)

§ 46b–59b. Court may not grant visitation to parent convicted of murder. Exception

Notwithstanding any provisions of this chapter, no court shall make an order granting the right of visitation to a parent who has been convicted of murder under section 53a–54a, 53a–54b, 53a–54c or 53a–54d, or in any other jurisdiction, of any crime the essential elements of which are substantially the same as any of such crimes, unless the child who is the subject of the visitation order is of sufficient age to signify such child's wishes and such child assents to such order. Until any such visitation order is granted, no person shall visit, with the child present, such parent who has been convicted of murder without the consent of the child's parent, guardian or legal custodian.

(1998, P.A. 98–81, § 19, eff. July 1, 1998; 2001, P.A. 01–211, § 16.)

§ 46b–60. Orders re children and alimony in annulment cases

In connection with any petition for annulment under this chapter, the superior court may make such order regarding any child of the marriage and concerning alimony as it might make in an action for dissolution of marriage. The issue of any void or voidable marriage shall be deemed legitimate. Any child born before, on or after October 1, 1976, whose birth occurred prior to the marriage of his parents shall be deemed a child of the marriage.

(1958 Rev., § 46–55; 1973, P.A. 73–373, § 24; 1976, P.A. 76–265; 1978, P.A. 78–230, § 40, eff. Oct. 1, 1978.)

§ 46b–61. Orders re children where parents live separately. Commencement of proceedings

In all cases in which the parents of a minor child live separately, the superior court for the judicial district where the parties or one of them resides may, on the application of either party and after notice given to the other, make any order as to the custody, care, education, visitation and support of any minor child of the parties, subject to the provisions of sections 46b–54, 46b–56, 46b–57 and 46b–66. Proceedings to obtain such orders shall be commenced by service of an application, a summons and an order to show cause.

(1958 Rev., § 46–62; 1973, P.A. 73–373, § 19; 1974, P.A. 74–169, § 12, eff. May 13, 1974; 1978, P.A. 78–230, § 46, eff. Oct. 1, 1978; 1978, P.A. 78–280, § 2, eff. July 1, 1978; 1999, P.A. 99–215, § 4, eff. Jan. 1, 2000.)

§ 46b–62. Orders for payment of attorney's fees in certain actions

In any proceeding seeking relief under the provisions of this chapter and sections 17b–743, 17b–744, 45a–257, 46b–1, 46b–6, 46b–212 to 46b–213v, inclusive, 47–14g, 51–348a and 52–362, the court may order either spouse or, if such proceeding concerns the custody, care, education, visitation or support of a minor child, either parent to pay the reasonable attorney's fees of the other in accordance with their respective financial abilities and the criteria set forth in section 46b–82. If, in any proceeding under this chapter and said sections, the court appoints an attorney for a minor child, the court may order the father, mother or an intervening party, individually or in any combination, to pay the reasonable fees of the attorney or may order the payment of the attorney's fees in whole or in part from the estate of the child. If the child is receiving or has received state aid or care, the reasonable compensation of the attorney shall be established by, and paid from funds appropriated to, the Judicial Department.

(1958 Rev., § 46–59; 1973, P.A. 73–373, § 27; 1978, P.A. 78–230, § 44, eff. Oct. 1, 1978; 1986, P.A. 86–264, § 16; 1988, P.A. 88–41; 1997, June 18 Sp.Sess., P.A. 97–1, § 54, eff. Jan. 1, 1998.)

§ 46b–63. Restoration of birth name or former name of spouse

(a) At the time of entering a decree dissolving a marriage, the court, upon request of either spouse, shall restore the birth name or former name of such spouse.

(b) At any time after entering a decree dissolving a marriage, the court, upon motion of either spouse, shall modify such judgment and restore the birth name or former name of such spouse.

(1958 Rev., § 46–60; 1973, P.A. 73–373, § 14; 1978, P.A. 78–101; 1980, P.A. 80–48; 1988, P.A. 88–364, § 90, eff. June 8, 1988.)

§ 46b–64. Orders of court prior to return day of complaint

Any provision in this chapter that the court may make any order after the return day of a complaint shall not preclude the court from making such order prior to the return day, upon the filing of a motion and the issuance of an order to show cause, if the court deems it necessary or appropriate.

(1958 Rev., § 46–64c; 1975, P.A. 75–530, § 15, eff. June 30, 1975; 1978, P.A. 78–230, § 50, eff. Oct. 1, 1978.)

§ 46b–65. Filing of declaration of resumption of marital relations; dissolution of marriage after legal separation decree when no declaration filed

(a) If the parties to a decree of legal separation at any time resume marital relations and file their written declaration of resumption, signed, acknowledged and witnessed, with the clerk of the superior court for the judicial district in which the separation was decreed, the declaration shall be entered upon the docket, under the entries relating to the complaint, and the decree shall be vacated and the complaint shall be deemed dismissed.

(b) If no declaration has been filed under subsection (a) of this section, then at any time after the entry of a decree of legal separation, either party may petition the superior court for the judicial district in which the decree was entered for a decree dissolving the marriage and the court shall enter the decree in the presence of the party seeking the dissolution.

(1958 Rev., § 46–61; 1973, P.A. 73–373, § 12; 1978, P.A. 78–230, § 45, eff. Oct. 1, 1978; 1978, 78–280, § 2, eff. July 1, 1978.)

§ 46b–66. Review of agreements; incorporation into decree

(a) In any case under this chapter where the parties have submitted to the court an agreement concerning the custody, care, education, visitation, maintenance or support of any of their children or concerning alimony or the disposition of property, the court shall inquire into the financial resources and actual needs of the spouses and their respective fitness to have physical custody of or rights of visitation with any minor child, in order to determine whether the agreement of the spouses is fair and equitable under all the circumstances. If the court finds the agreement fair and equitable, it shall become part of the court file, and if the agreement is in writing, it shall be incorporated by reference into the order or decree of the court. If the court finds the agreement is not fair and equitable, it shall make such orders as to finances and custody as the circumstances require. If the agreement is in writing and provides for the care, education, maintenance or support of a child beyond the age of eighteen, it may also be incorporated or otherwise made a part of any such order and shall be enforceable to the same extent as any other provision of such order or decree, notwithstanding the provisions of section 1–1d.

(b) Agreements providing for the care, education, maintenance or support of a child beyond the age of eighteen entered into on or after July 1, 2001, shall be modifiable to the same extent as any other provision of any order or decree in accordance with section 46b–86.

(1958 Rev., §§ 46–26c, 46–49; 1972, P.A. 164, § 1; 1973, P.A. 73–373, § 18; 1974, P.A. 74–169, § 11, eff. May 13, 1974; 1977, P.A. 77–488, § 1; 1978, P.A. 78–230, § 34, eff. Oct. 1, 1978; 2001, P.A. 01–135, § 1, eff. July 1, 2001.)

§ 46b–66a. Order of court re conveyance of title to real property. Effect of decree

(a) At the time of entering a decree annulling or dissolving a marriage or for legal separation pursuant to a complaint under section 46b–45, the superior court may order the husband or wife to convey title to real property to the other party or to a third person.

(b) When any party is found to have violated an order of the court entered under subsection (a) of this section, the court may, by decree, pass title to the real property to either party or to a third person, without any act by either party, when in the judgment of the court it is the proper action to take.

(c) When the decree is recorded on the land records in the town where the real property is situated, it shall effect the transfer of the title of such property as if it were a deed of the party or parties.

(1986, P.A. 86–126.)

§ 46b–67. Waiting period. Effect of decree

(a) Following the expiration of ninety days after the day on which a complaint for dissolution or legal separation is made returnable, or after the expiration of six months, where proceedings have been stayed under section 46b–53, the court may proceed on the complaint, or whenever dissolution is claimed under cross complaint, amended complaint or amended cross complaint, the case may be heard and a decree granted thereon after the expiration of the ninety days and twenty days after the cross complaint, amended complaint or amended cross complaint has been filed with the court, provided the requirement of the twenty-day delay shall not apply (1) whenever opposing counsel, having appeared, consents to the cross complaint, amended complaint or amended cross complaint, or (2) where the defendant has not appeared and the amendment does not set forth either a cause of action or a claim for relief not in the original complaint. Nothing in this section shall prevent any interlocutory proceedings within the ninety-day period.

(b) A decree of annulment or dissolution shall give the parties the status of unmarried persons and they may marry again. A decree of legal separation shall have the effect of a decree dissolving the marriage except that neither party shall be free to marry. Neither the ninety-day period specified in this section nor the six-month period referred to in section 46b–53 shall apply in actions for annulment and the court may proceed on any cause of action for annulment in the manner generally applicable in civil actions.

(1958 Rev., § 46–44; 1973, P.A. 73–373, § 7; 1978, P.A. 78–230, § 29, eff. Oct. 1, 1978; 1978, P.A. 78–331, § 50, eff. June 6, 1978.)

§ 46b–68. Repealed. (1997, June 18 Sp.Sess., P.A. 97–8, § 87, eff. July 1, 1997.)

§ 46b–69. Statutes applicable to matrimonial actions

The provisions of this chapter and sections 17b–743, 17b–744, 45a–257, 46b–1, 46b–6, 47–14g, 51–348a and 52–362 shall apply to all actions for dissolution of marriage, annulment and legal separation filed after May 13, 1974, to all actions for annulment, legal separation or dissolution of marriage commenced prior to said date and to appeals from, and motions for modification of, any alimony, support or custody order entered pursuant to a decree of dissolution of a marriage, divorce, legal separation or annulment rendered prior to said date. The provisions of this chapter and sections 17b–743, 17b–744, 45a–257, 46b–1, 46b–6, 47–14g, 51–348a and 52–362 in effect on October 1, 1973, shall continue to apply to any action for dissolution of marriage, annulment or legal separation in which a decree of the Superior Court has been rendered after October 1, 1973, in which an appeal is pending or in which the date of taking an appeal has not expired on May 13, 1974, except an appeal from any order of alimony or custody. Sections 46–13 to 46–30,[1] inclusive, of the general statutes of Connecticut, revision of 1958, revised to 1972, shall continue to apply to any action for divorce, dissolution of a marriage, annulment or legal separation in which a decree has been rendered and in which an appeal is pending or in which the time for taking an appeal had not expired on October 1, 1973, except an appeal from any order of alimony, support or custody.

(1958 Rev., § 46–64b; 1974, P.A. 74–169, § 16, eff. May 13, 1974; 1978, P.A. 78–230, § 49, eff. Oct. 1, 1978; 1997, June 18 Sp.Sess., P.A. 97–1, § 55, eff. Jan. 1, 1998.)

[1] C.G.S.A. §§ 46–13 to 46–30 have been repealed or transferred. See Disposition Table.

§ 46b–69a. Wage executions and earning assignments

Executions and earning assignments in accordance with section 52–362 shall be available in all actions for dissolution of marriage, annulment and legal separation.

(1983, P.A. 83–400, § 2.)

§ 46b–69b. Parenting education program

(a) The Judicial Department shall establish a parenting education program for parties involved in any action before the Superior Court under section 46b–1, except actions brought under section 46b–15 and chapter 815t.[1] For the purposes of this section, "parenting education program" means a course designed by the Judicial Department to educate persons, including unmarried parents, on the impact on children of the restructuring of families. The course shall include, but not be limited to, information on the developmental stages of children, adjustment of children to parental separation, dispute resolution and conflict management, guidelines for visitation, stress reduction in children and cooperative parenting.

(b) The court shall order any party to an action specified in subsection (a) of this section to participate in such program whenever a minor child is involved in such action unless (1) the parties agree, subject to the approval of the court, not to participate in such program, (2) the court, on motion, determines that participation is not deemed necessary, or (3) the parties select and participate in a comparable parenting education program. A family support magistrate may order parties involved in any action before the Family Support Magistrate Division to participate in such parenting education program, upon a finding that such participation is necessary and provided both parties are present when such order is issued. No party shall be required to participate in such program more than once. A party shall be deemed to have satisfactorily completed such program upon certification by the service provider of the program.

(c) The Judicial Department shall, by contract with service providers, make available the parenting education program and shall certify to the court the results of each party's participation in the program.

(d) Any person who is ordered to participate in a parenting education program shall pay directly to the service provider a participation fee, except that no person may be excluded from such program for inability to pay such fee. Any contract entered into between the Judicial Department and the service provider pursuant to subsection (c) of this section shall include a fee schedule and provisions requiring service providers to allow persons who are indigent or unable to pay to participate in such program and shall provide that all costs of such program shall be covered by the revenue generated from participants' fees. The total cost for such program shall not exceed two hundred dollars per person. Such amount shall be indexed annually to reflect the rate of inflation. The program shall not exceed a total of ten hours.

(e) Any service provider under contract with the Judicial Department pursuant to this section shall provide safety and security for participants in the program, including victims of family violence.

(1993, P.A. 93–319, § 1; 1994, May 25 Sp.Sess., P.A. 94–1, § 99, eff. July 1, 1994; 1997, June 18 Sp.Sess., P.A. 97–7, § 35, eff. July 1, 1997; 2002, P.A. 02–132, § 16.)

1 C.G.S.A. § 46b–120 et seq.

§ 46b–69c. Advisory committee. Recommendations to Judicial Department

(a) There is established an advisory committee to (1) make recommendations to the Judicial Department on the development of, and annually thereafter on modifications to, the curriculum for the parenting education program established pursuant to subsection (a) of section 46b–69b, and (2) advise on other matters involving the service providers, including the qualifications and selection of such providers.

(b) Not later than January 15, 2003, the advisory committee shall make recommendations to the Judicial Department on the expansion of the parenting education program to include a separate program for children whose parents are involved in a dissolution of marriage action. Such program shall be designed to help children cope more effectively with the problems that result from a dissolution and shall have as its goal the prevention or reduction of children's anxiety, aggression, depression and behavioral problems and an increase in social competencies critical to children's postdissolution adjustment.

(c) The advisory committee shall consist of not more than ten members to be appointed by the Chief Justice of the Supreme Court and shall include members who represent the Commission on Children, the family law section of the Connecticut Bar Association, educators specializing in children studies, agencies representing victims of family violence, service providers and the Judicial Department. The members shall serve for terms of two years and may be reappointed for succeeding terms. The members shall elect a chairperson from among their number and shall receive no compensation for their services.

(d) The Court Support Services Division of the Judicial Department shall provide staff services to the advisory committee.

(1993, P.A. 93–319, § 2, eff. July 1, 1993; 2002, P.A. 02–132, § 81, eff. July 1, 2002; 2002, P.A. 02–132, § 17.)

PART II. ENFORCEMENT OF FOREIGN MATRIMONIAL JUDGMENTS

§ 46b–70. Foreign matrimonial judgment defined

As used in sections 46b–70 to 46b–75, inclusive, "foreign matrimonial judgment" means any judgment, decree or order of a court of any state in the United States in an action for divorce, legal separation, annulment or dissolution of marriage, for the custody, care, education, visitation, maintenance or support of children or for alimony, support or the disposition of property of the parties to an existing or terminated marriage, in which both parties have entered an appearance.

(1958 Rev., § 46–65; 1977, P.A. 77–428, § 1.)

§ 46b–71. Filing of foreign matrimonial judgment; enforcement in this state

(a) Any party to an action in which a foreign matrimonial judgment has been rendered, shall file, with a certified copy of the foreign matrimonial judgment, in the court in this state in which enforcement of such judgment is sought, a certification that such judgment is final, has not been modified, altered, amended, set aside or vacated and that the enforcement of such judgment has not been stayed or suspended, and such certificate shall set forth the full name and last-known address of the other party to such judgment and the name and address of the court in the foreign state which rendered such judgment.

(b) Such foreign matrimonial judgment shall become a judgment of the court of this state where it is filed and shall be enforced and otherwise treated in the same manner as a judgment of a court in this state; provided such foreign matrimonial judgment does not contravene the public policy of the state of Connecticut. A foreign matrimonial judgment so filed shall have the same effect and may be enforced or satisfied in the same manner as any like judgment of a court of this state and is subject to the same procedures for modifying, altering, amending, vacating, setting aside, staying or suspending said judgment as a judgment of a court of this state; provided, in modifying, altering, amending, setting aside, vacating, staying or suspending any such foreign matrimonial judgment in this state the substantive law of the foreign jurisdiction shall be controlling.

(1958 Rev., § 46–65a; 1977, P.A. 77–428, § 2; 1989, P.A. 89–3.)

§ 46b–72. Notification of filing

Within five days after the filing of such judgment and certificate, the party filing such judgment shall notify the other party of the filing of such foreign matrimonial judgment by registered mail at his last-known address or by personal service. Execution shall not issue on any such foreign matrimonial judgment for a period of twenty days from the filing thereof and no steps shall be taken to enforce such judgment until proof of service has been filed with the court.

(1958 Rev., § 46–65b; 1977, P.A. 77–428, § 3.)

§ 46b–73. Stay of enforcement; modifications; hearing

(a) If either party files an affidavit with the court that an appeal from the foreign matrimonial judgment is pending in the foreign state, or will be taken, or that a stay of execution has been granted, the court shall stay enforcement of the foreign matrimonial judgment until the appeal is concluded, the time for appeal expires or the stay of execution expires or is vacated.

(b) If a party files an affidavit with the court that such foreign matrimonial judgment has been modified, altered or amended, the court shall enforce such foreign matrimonial judgment as modified, altered or amended.

(c) Upon motion made to the court of this state in which the foreign matrimonial judgment has been filed, either party shall be entitled to a hearing on any disputed issue of fact or law concerning the enforceability of said judgment in this state, including any challenge to the jurisdiction of the court which rendered such foreign matrimonial judgment.

(1958 Rev., § 46–65c; 1977, P.A. 77–428, § 4.)

§ 46b–74. Right to action on judgment unimpaired

The right of a party to a foreign matrimonial judgment to proceed by an action on the judgment instead of proceeding under sections 46b–70 to 46b–75, inclusive, remains unimpaired.

(1958 Rev., § 46–65d; 1977, P.A. 77–428, § 5.)

§ 46b–75. Uniformity of interpretation

Sections 46b–70 to 46b–75, inclusive, shall be so construed as to effectuate their general purpose to make uniform the laws of those states which enact them.

(1958 Rev., § 46–65e; 1977, P.A. 77–428, § 6.)

§§ 46b–76 to 46b–79. Reserved for future use

PART III. SUPPORT OF CHILD AND SPOUSE. TRANSFER OF PROPERTY

§ 46b–80. Prejudgment remedies available; lis pendens; notice; effect

(a) The following procedures shall be available to secure the financial interests of either spouse in connection with any complaint under section 46b–45 or 46b–56 or any application under section 46b–61, including, but not limited to, present and future financial interests in connection with an order for alimony or support pendente lite or other order for periodic payments: (1) Any remedy afforded by chapter 903a[1] concerning prejudgment remedies, whether or not a money demand is made in such complaint or application; and (2) at any time after the service of such a complaint or application, if either party claims an interest in real property in which the other party has an interest, either spouse may cause a notice of lis pendens to be recorded in the office of the town clerk of each town in which is located real property in which the other spouse has an interest. The notice shall contain the names of the spouses, the nature of the complaint or application, the court having jurisdiction, the date of the complaint or application and a description of the real property. Such notice shall, from the time of the recording only, be notice to any person thereafter acquiring any interest in such property of the pendency of the complaint or application. Each person whose conveyance or encumbrance is subsequently executed or subsequently recorded or whose interest is thereafter obtained by descent, or otherwise, shall be deemed to be a subsequent purchaser or encumbrancer, and shall be bound by all proceedings taken after the recording of such notice, to the same extent as if he were made a party to the complaint or application. A notice of lis pendens recorded in accordance with this section may be discharged by the court upon substitution of a bond with surety in an amount established by the court if the court finds that the claim of the spouse against property subject to the notice of lis pendens can be satisfied by money damages.

(b) All notices of lis pendens recorded pursuant to the provisions of subsection (a) of this section shall be subject to the provisions of subsection (c) of section 52–325 and sections 52–325a to 52–325c, inclusive.

(1958 Rev., § 46–38; 1973, P.A. 73–373, § 5; 1974, P.A. 74–169, § 4, eff. May 13, 1974; 1977, P.A. 77–392; 1978, P.A. 78–230, § 23, eff. Oct. 1, 1978; 1981, P.A. 81–8, § 5, eff. March 31, 1981; 1999, P.A. 99–215, § 5, eff. Jan. 1, 2000; 2003, P.A. 03–130, § 2.)

1 C.G.S.A. § 52–278a et seq.

§ 46b–81. Assignment of property and transfer of title

(a) At the time of entering a decree annulling or dissolving a marriage or for legal separation pursuant to a complaint under section 46b–45, the superior court may assign to either the husband or wife all or any part of the estate of the other. The court may pass title to real property to either party or to a third person or may order the sale of such real property, without any act by either the husband or the wife, when in the judgment of the court it is the proper mode to carry the decree into effect.

(b) A conveyance made pursuant to the decree shall vest title in the purchaser, and shall bind all persons entitled to life estates and remainder interests in the same manner as a sale ordered by the court pursuant to the provisions of section 52–500. When the decree is recorded on the land records in the town where the real property is situated, it shall effect the transfer of the title of such real property as if it were a deed of the party or parties.

(c) In fixing the nature and value of the property, if any, to be assigned, the court, after hearing the witnesses, if any, of each party, except as provided in subsection (a) of section 46b–51, shall consider the length of the marriage, the causes for the annulment, dissolution of the marriage or legal separation, the age, health, station, occupation, amount and sources of income, vocational skills, employability, estate, liabilities and needs of each of the parties and the opportunity of each for future acquisition of capital assets and income. The court shall also consider the contribution of each of the parties in the acquisition, preservation or appreciation in value of their respective estates.

(1958 Rev., § 46–51; 1973, P.A. 73–373, § 20; 1975, P.A. 75–331; 1978, P.A. 78–230, § 36, eff. Oct. 1, 1978.)

§ 46b–82. Alimony

(a) At the time of entering the decree, the Superior Court may order either of the parties to pay alimony to the other, in addition to or in lieu of an award pursuant to section 46b–81. The order may direct that security be given therefor on such terms as the court may deem desirable, including an order pursuant to subsection (b) of this section or an order to either party to contract with a third party for periodic payments or payments contingent on a life to the other party. The court may order that a party obtain life insurance as such security unless such party proves, by a preponderance of the evidence, that such insurance is not available to such party, such party is unable to pay the cost of such insurance or such party is uninsurable. In determining whether alimony shall be awarded, and the duration and amount of the award, the court shall hear the witnesses, if any, of each party, except as provided in subsection (a) of section 46b–51, shall consider the length of the marriage, the causes for the annulment, dissolution of the marriage or legal separation, the age, health, station, occupation, amount and sources of income, vocational skills, employability, estate and needs of each of the parties and the award, if any, which the court may make pursuant to section 46b–81, and, in the case of a parent to whom the custody of minor children has been awarded, the desirability of such parent's securing employment.

(b) Any postjudgment procedure afforded by chapter 906 [1] shall be available to secure the present and future financial interests of a party in connection with a final order for the periodic payment of alimony.

(1958 Rev., § 46–52; 1973, P.A. 73–373, § 21; 1978, P.A. 78–230, § 37, eff. Oct. 1, 1978; 1983, P.A. 83–527, § 1, eff. Oct. 1, 1983; 2003, P.A. 03–130, § 3; 2003, P.A. 03–202, § 23.)

1 C.G.S.A. § 52–350a et seq.

§ 46b–83. Alimony, support and use of family home or other residential dwelling unit awarded pendente lite

At any time after the return day of a complaint under section 46b–45 or 46b–56 or after filing an application under section 46b–61, and after hearing, alimony and support pendente lite may be awarded to either of the parties from the date of the filing of an application therefor with the Superior Court. Full credit shall be given for all sums paid to one party by the other from the date of the filing of such a motion to the date of rendition of such order. In making an order for alimony pendente lite the court shall consider all factors enumerated in section 46b–82, except the grounds for the complaint or cross complaint, to be considered with respect to a permanent award of alimony. In making an order for support pendente lite the court shall consider all factors enumerated in section 46b–84. The court may also award exclusive use of the family home or any other dwelling unit which is available for use as a residence pendente lite to either of the parties as is just and equitable without regard to the respective interests of the parties in the property.

(1958 Rev., § 46–50; 1973, P.A. 73–373, § 22; 1974, P.A. 74–169, § 13, eff. May 13, 1974; 1975, P.A. 75–530, § 14, eff. June 30, 1975; 1978, P.A. 78–230, § 35, eff. Oct. 1, 1978; 1993, P.A. 93–7; 1999, P.A. 99–215, § 6, eff. Jan. 1, 2000.)

§ 46b–84. Parents' obligation for maintenance of minor child. Order for health insurance coverage

(a) Upon or subsequent to the annulment or dissolution of any marriage or the entry of a decree of legal separation or divorce, the parents of a minor child of the marriage, shall maintain the child according to their respective abilities, if the child is in need of maintenance. Any postjudgment procedure afforded by chapter 906 [1] shall be available to secure the present and future financial interests of a party in connection with a final order for the periodic payment of child support.

(b) If there is an unmarried child of the marriage who has attained the age of eighteen, is a full-time high school student and resides with a parent, the parents shall maintain the child according to their respective abilities if the child is in need of maintenance until such time as such child completes the twelfth grade or attains the age of nineteen, whichever first occurs. The provisions of this subsection shall apply only in cases where the decree of dissolution of marriage, legal separation or annulment is entered on or after July 1, 1994.

(c) The court may make appropriate orders of support of any child with mental retardation, as defined in section 1–1g, or a mental disability or physical disability, as defined in subdivision (15) of section 46a–51, who resides with a parent and is principally dependent upon such parent for maintenance until such child attains the age of twenty-one. The child support guidelines established pursuant to section 46b–215a shall not apply to orders entered under this subsection. The provisions of this subsection shall apply only in cases where the decree of dissolution of marriage, legal separation or annulment is entered on or after October 1, 1997, or where the initial support orders in actions not claiming any such decree are entered on or after October 1, 1997.

(d) In determining whether a child is in need of maintenance and, if in need, the respective abilities of the parents to provide such maintenance and the amount thereof, the court shall consider the age, health, station, occupation, earning capacity, amount and sources of income, estate, vocational skills and employability of each of the parents, and the age, health, station, occupation, educational status and expectation, amount and sources of income, vocational skills, employability, estate and needs of the child.

(e) At any time at which orders are entered in a proceeding for dissolution of marriage, annulment, legal separation, custody, or support, whether before, at the time of, or after entry of a decree or judgment, if health insurance coverage for a child is ordered by the court to be maintained, the court shall provide in the order that (1) the signature of the custodial parent or custodian of the insured dependent shall constitute a valid authorization to the insurer for purposes of processing an insurance reimbursement payment to the provider of the medical services, to the custodial parent or to the custodian, (2) neither parent shall prevent or interfere with the timely processing of any insurance reimbursement claim and (3) if the parent receiving an insurance reimbursement payment is not the parent or custodian who is paying the bill for the services of the medical provider, the parent receiving such insurance reimbursement payment shall promptly pay to the parent or custodian paying such bill any insurance reimbursement for such services. For purposes of subdivision (1), the custodial parent or custodian is responsible for providing the insurer with a certified copy of the order of dissolution or other order requiring maintenance of insurance for a child provided if such custodial parent or custodian fails to provide the insurer with a copy of such order, the Commissioner of Social Services may provide the insurer with a copy of such order. Such insurer may thereafter rely on such order and is not responsible for inquiring as to the legal sufficiency of the order. The custodial parent or custodian shall be responsible for providing the insurer with a certified copy of any order which materially alters the provision of the original order with respect to the maintenance of insurance for a child. If presented with an insurance reimbursement claim signed by the custodial parent or custodian, such insurer shall reimburse the provider of the medical services, if payment is to be made to such provider under the policy, or shall otherwise reimburse the custodial parent or custodian.

(f) After the granting of a decree annulling or dissolving the marriage or ordering a legal separation, and upon complaint or motion with order and summons made to the Superior Court by either parent or by the Commissioner of Administrative Services in any case arising under subsection (a) or (b) of this section, the court shall inquire into the child's need of maintenance and the respective abilities of the parents to supply maintenance. The court shall make and enforce the decree for the maintenance of the child as it considers just, and may direct security to be given therefor, including an order to either party to contract with a third party for periodic payments or payments contingent on a life to the other party. The court may order that a party obtain life insurance as such security unless such party proves, by a preponderance of the evidence, that such insurance is not available to such party, such party is unable to pay the cost of such insurance or such party is uninsurable. The court shall include in each support order a provision for the health care coverage of the child which provision may include an order for either parent to name any child who is subject to the provisions of subsection (a) or (b) of this section as a beneficiary of any medical or dental insurance or benefit plan carried by such parent or available to such parent on a group basis through an employer or a union. Any such employment-based order in a IV–D support case shall be enforced using a National Medical Support Notice as provided in section 46b–88. If such insurance coverage is unavailable at reasonable cost, the provision for health care coverage may include an order for either parent to apply for and maintain coverage on behalf of the child under the HUSKY Plan, Part B.[2] The noncustodial parent shall be ordered to apply for the HUSKY Plan, Part B only if such parent is found to have sufficient ability to pay the appropriate premium. In any IV–D support case in which the noncustodial parent is found to have insufficient ability to provide medical insurance coverage and the custodial party is the HUSKY Plan, Part A [3] or Part B applicant, the provision for health care coverage may include an order for the noncustodial parent to pay such amount as is specified by the court or family support magistrate to the state or the custodial party, as their interests may appear, to offset the cost of any insurance payable under the HUSKY Plan, Part A or Part B. In no event may such order include payment to offset the cost of any such premium if such payment would reduce the amount of current support required under the child support guidelines.

(g) Whenever an obligor is before the court in proceedings to establish, modify or enforce a support order, and such order is not secured by an income withholding order, the court may require the obligor to execute a bond or post other security sufficient to perform such order for support, provided the court finds that such a bond is available for purchase within the financial means of the obligor. Upon failure of such obligor to comply with such support order, the court may order the bond or the security forfeited and the proceeds thereof paid to the state in TANF cases or to the obligee in non-TANF cases. In any IV–D case in which the obligor is found by the court to owe past-due support, the court may issue an order for the periodic payment of such support or, if such obligor is not incapacitated, order such obligor to participate in work activities which may include, but shall not be limited to, job search, training, work experience and participation in the job training and retraining program established by the Labor Commissioner pursuant to section 31–3t.

(h) In IV–D support cases, as defined in subdivision (13) of subsection (b) of section 46b–231, a copy of any support order established or modified pursuant to this section or, in the case of a motion for modification of an existing support order, a notice of determination that there should be no change in the amount of the support order, shall be provided to each party and the state case registry within fourteen days after issuance of such order or determination.

(1958 Rev., § 46–57; 1973, P.A. 73–373, § 26; 1974, P.A. 74–169, § 14, eff. May 13, 1974; 1977, P.A. 77–614, § 70, eff. Oct. 1, 1977; 1978, P.A. 78–230, § 42, eff. Oct. 1, 1978; 1983, P.A. 83–527, § 2, eff. Oct. 1, 1983; 1984, P.A. 84–205, § 1; 1984, P.A. 84–230; 1987, P.A. 87–207, § 2; 1989, P.A. 89–195, § 2; 1991, P.A. 91–4, § 1, eff. Feb. 21, 1991; 1994, P.A. 94–61, § 1, eff. July 1, 1994; 1994, May Sp.Sess., P.A. 94–5, § 9, eff. July 1, 1994; 1994, May 25 Sp.Sess., P.A. 94–1, § 63, eff. July 1, 1994; 1997, P.A. 97–321, § 1; 1997, June 18 Sp.Sess., P.A. 97–2, § 104, eff. July 1, 1997; 1997, June 18 Sp.Sess., P.A. 97–7, § 17, eff. July 1, 1997; 1999, P.A. 99–279, § 29, eff. July 1, 1999; 2002, May 9 Sp.Sess., P.A. 02–7, § 42; 2003, P.A. 03–130, § 4; 2003, P.A. 03–202, § 24.)

1 C.G.S.A. § 52–350a et seq.

2 C.G.S.A. §§ 17b–289 to 17b–303, inclusive, and 1997, Oct. 29 Sp.Sess. P.A. 97–1, § 16.

3 C.G.S.A. § 17b–261.

§ 46b–85. Order for support of mentally ill spouse

At the time of granting dissolution of a marriage to which one party is mentally ill or at any time thereafter, on application of either party or of the guardian or conservator of the mentally ill spouse, or of any person, town or other municipality charged with the support of the mentally ill spouse, or the Commissioner of Administrative Services if the state is charged, the court may make such order requiring support of the mentally ill spouse, or security for support, as may be proper. The court may set aside or alter any such order, at any time thereafter, on application of either party or of the guardian of the mentally ill spouse, or of any person, town or other municipality charged with support, or the Commissioner of Administrative Services if the state is charged. Any order providing for the support of the mentally ill party shall be enforceable in the same manner as orders relating to alimony.

(1949 Rev., § 7332; 1953, Supp. § 2255c; 1955, Supp. § 3004d; 1957, P.A. 502, § 3; 1958 Rev., §§ 46–20, 46–53; 1973, P.A. 73–373, § 30; 1977, P.A. 77–614, § 70, eff. Oct. 1, 1977; 1978, P.A. 78–230, § 38, eff. Oct. 1, 1978; 1995, P.A. 95–257, § 48, eff. July 1, 1995.)

§ 46b–86. Modification of alimony or support orders and judgments

(a) Unless and to the extent that the decree precludes modification, the court may order either party to maintain life insurance for the other party or a minor child of the parties or any final order for the periodic payment of permanent alimony or support or an order for alimony or support pendente lite may at any time thereafter be continued, set aside, altered or modified by said court upon a showing of a substantial change in the circumstances of either party or upon a showing that the final order for child support substantially deviates from the child support guidelines established pursuant to section 46b–215a, unless there was a specific finding on the record that the application of the guidelines would be inequitable or inappropriate. There shall be a rebuttable presumption that any deviation of less than fifteen per cent from the child support guidelines is not substantial and any deviation of fifteen per cent or more from the guidelines is substantial. Modification may be made of such support order without regard to whether the order was issued before, on or after May 9, 1991. In determining whether to modify a child support order based on a substantial deviation from such child support guidelines the court shall consider the division of real and personal property between the parties set forth in the final decree and the benefits accruing to the child as the result of such division. After the date of judgment, modification of any child support order issued before or after July 1, 1990, may be made upon a showing of such substantial change of circumstances, whether or not such change of circumstances was contemplated at the time of dissolution. By written agreement, stipulation or by decision of the court, those items or circumstances that were contemplated and are not to be changed may be specified in the written agreement, stipulation or decision of the court. This section shall not apply to assignments under section 46b–81 or to any assignment of the estate or a portion thereof of one party to the other party under prior law. No order for periodic payment of permanent alimony or support may be subject to retroactive modification, except that the court may order modification with respect to any period during which there is a pending motion for modification of an alimony or support order from the date of service of notice of such pending motion upon the opposing party pursuant to section 52–50.

(b) In an action for divorce, dissolution of marriage, legal separation or annulment brought by a husband or wife, in which a final judgment has been entered providing for the payment of periodic alimony by one party to the other, the superior court may, in its discretion and upon notice and hearing, modify such judgment and suspend, reduce or terminate the payment of periodic alimony upon a showing that the party receiving the periodic alimony is living with another person under circumstances which the court finds should result in the modification, suspension, reduction or termination of alimony because the living arrangements cause such a change of circumstances as to alter the financial needs of that party.

(c) When one of the parties, or a child of the parties, is receiving or has received aid or care from the state under its aid to families with dependent children program or temporary assistance for needy families program or under its foster care program as provided in Title IV–E of the Social Security Act,[1] or where one of the parties has applied for child support enforcement services under Title IV–D of the Social Security Act [2] as provided in section 17b–179, such motion to modify shall be filed with the Family Support Magistrate Division for determination in accordance with subsection (m) of section 46b–231.

(1958 Rev., § 46–54; 1973, P.A. 73–373, § 23; 1978, P.A. 78–230, § 39, eff. Oct. 1, 1978; 1986, P.A. 86–359, § 2, eff. Jan. 1, 1987; 1987, P.A. 87–104; 1989, P.A. 89–360, § 12, eff. July 1, 1989; 1990, P.A. 90–188, § 1; 1990, P.A. 90–213, § 46, eff. July 1, 1990; 1991, P.A. 91–76, § 1, eff. May 9, 1991; 1997, June 18 Sp.Sess., P.A. 97–2, § 105, eff. July 1, 1997; 2001, P.A. 01–135, § 2, eff. July 1, 2001.)

1 42 U.S.C.A. § 670 et seq.
2 42 U.S.C.A. § 651 et seq.

§ 46b–87. Contempt of orders

When any person is found in contempt of an order of the superior court entered under section 46b–60 to 46b–62, inclusive, 46b–81 to 46b–83, inclusive, or 46b–86, the court may award to the petitioner a reasonable attorney's fee and the fees of the officer serving the contempt citation, such sums to be paid by the person found in contempt, provided if any such person is found not to be in contempt of such order, the court may award a reasonable attorney's fee to such person. The costs of commitment of any person imprisoned for contempt of court by reason of failure to comply with such an order shall be paid by the state as in criminal cases.

(1958 Rev., § 46–56; 1973, P.A. 73–373, § 25; 1978, P.A. 78–230, § 41, eff. Oct. 1, 1978; 1988, P.A. 88–196.)

§ 46b–87a. Forms and instructions for application for contempt order based on violation of visitation order

The Office of the Chief Court Administrator shall prepare forms, including instructions in plain language, for applying to the court for a contempt citation based upon a violation of a visitation order or for modification of a visitation order and shall make such forms available to litigants.

(1992, P.A. 92–253, § 10.)

§ 46b–88. National Medical Support Notice. Duties of issuing agency, employer and administrator of group health plan

(a) For the purposes of this section:

(1) "Issuing agency" means an agency providing child support enforcement services, as defined in subsection (b) of section 46b–231, and includes the Bureau of Child Support Enforcement within the Department of Social Services and Support Enforcement Services within Judicial Branch Court Operations; and

(2) "NMSN" means the National Medical Support Notice required under Title IV–D of the Social Security Act [1] and the Employee Retirement Income Security Act [2] used by state child support agencies to enforce health care coverage support provisions in child support orders.

(b) (1) Whenever a court or family support magistrate enters a support order in a Title IV–D support case, as defined in subsection (b) of section 46b–231, that requires a noncustodial parent to provide employment-based health care coverage for a child, and the noncustodial parent's employer is known to the issuing agency, such agency shall enforce the health care coverage provisions of the order through the use of a NMSN.

(2) In addition to other notice and requirements contained therein, the NMSN shall serve as notice to the employer that: (A) The employee is obligated to provide employment-based health care coverage for the child; (B) the employer may be required to withhold any employee contributions required by the group health plan or plans in which the child is eligible to be enrolled; and (C) the employer is required to forward the NMSN to the administrator of each group health plan providing such coverage for enrollment determination purposes.

(3) In addition to other notice requirements contained therein, the NMSN shall serve as notice to the group health plan that: (A) Receipt of the NMSN from an employer constitutes receipt of a medical support order; and (B) an appropriately completed NMSN constitutes a qualified medical child support order for health care coverage enrollment purposes.

(4) In any case in which the noncustodial parent is a newly hired employee, the NMSN shall be transferred by the issuing agency to the employer no later than two business days after the date of the entry of the employee in the State Directory of New Hires established under section 31–254, together with any necessary income withholding notice.

(c) (1) An employer who receives a NMSN from the issuing agency shall: (A) No later than twenty business days, after the date of NMSN, either (i) return the notice to such agency indicating why the health care coverage is not available, or (ii) transfer the notice to the administrator of each appropriate group health plan for which the child may be eligible; (B) upon notification from any such group health plan that the child is eligible for enrollment, withhold from the employee's income any employee contribution required under such plan and send the withheld payments directly to the plan, except as provided in subsection (d) of this section; and (C) notify the issuing agency whenever the employee's employment terminates. (2) Any employer who discharges an employee from employment, refuses to employ, or takes disciplinary action against an employee because of a medical child support withholding, or fails to withhold income or transmit withheld income to the group health plan as required by the NMSN shall be subject to the penalties related to employer processing of child support income withholding, as provided in subsections (f) and (j) of section 52–362. (3) The issuing agency shall notify the employer promptly when there is no longer a current order for medical support.

(d) The NMSN shall inform the employer of the duration of the withholding requirement, of any limitations on withholding prescribed by federal or state law, and of any withholding priorities that apply when available income is insufficient to satisfy all cash and medical support obligations. The employer shall notify the issuing agency when any such withholding limitations or priorities prevent the employer from withholding the amount required to obtain coverage under the group health plan for which the child is otherwise eligible.

(e) (1) The administrator of a group health plan who receives a NMSN from an employer pursuant to subsection (c) of this section shall deem the NMSN to be a "qualified medical child support order" and an application by the issuing agency for enrollment of the child. Enrollment of the child may not be denied because the child: (A) Was born out of wedlock, (B) is not claimed as a dependent on the participant's federal income tax return, (C) does not reside with the participant or in the plan's service area, or (D) is receiving benefits or is eligible for benefits under a state medical assistance plan required by the Social Security Act. An enrollment shall be made without regard to open season enrollment restrictions, and if enrollment of a child is dependent on the enrollment of a participant who is not enrolled, both the child and the participant shall be enrolled. (2) No later than forty business days after the date of the NMSN the plan administrator shall notify the issuing agency whether coverage is available or, if necessary, of the steps to be taken to begin such coverage. The administrator shall also provide to the custodial parent a description of the coverage available and of any forms or documents necessary to begin coverage. The issuing agency, in consultation with the custodial parent, shall promptly select from any available plan options when necessary. Upon completion of enrollment, the group health plan administrator shall return the NMSN to the employer for a determination of whether any necessary employee contributions are available.

(f) A NMSN issued pursuant to this section shall be deemed part of the court order requiring employment-based health care coverage. The NMSN shall have the same force and effect as a court order directed to an employer or group health plan administrator and may be enforced by the court or family support magistrate in the same manner as an order of the court or family support magistrate. The requirements imposed on employers and group health plan administrators under this section and the NMSN shall be in addition to any requirements imposed on said employer or administrator under other provisions of the general statutes.

(2002, May 9 Sp.Sess., P.A. 02–7, § 38.)

1 42 U.S.C.A. § 651 et seq.

2 29 U.S.C.A. § 1001 et seq.

§ 46b–89. Reserved for future use

CHAPTERS 815k to 815n [RESERVED FOR FUTURE USE]

CHAPTER 815*o*

UNIFORM CHILD CUSTODY JURISDICTION ACT [REPEALED]

§§ 46b–90 to 46b–114. Repealed. (1999, P.A. 99–185, § 39, eff. July 1, 2000.)

CHAPTER 815p

UNIFORM CHILD CUSTODY JURISDICTION AND ENFORCEMENT ACT

PART I. GENERAL PROVISIONS

Section

PART I. GENERAL PROVISIONS

§ 46b–115. Short title: Uniform Child Custody Jurisdiction and Enforcement Act

This chapter may be cited as the Uniform Child Custody Jurisdiction and Enforcement Act.

(1999, P.A. 99–185, § 1, eff. July 1, 2000.)

§ 46b–115a. Definitions

As used in this chapter:

(1) "Abandoned" means left without provision for reasonable and necessary care or supervision;

(2) "Child" means an individual who has not attained eighteen years of age;

(3) "Child custody determination" means a judgment, decree, or other order of a court providing for the legal custody, physical custody or visitation with respect to a child. The term includes a permanent, temporary, initial and modification order. The term does not include an order relating to child support or other monetary obligation of an individual;

(4) "Child custody proceeding" means a proceeding in which legal custody, physical custody or visitation with respect to a child is an issue. The term includes a proceeding for dissolution of marriage, divorce, separation, neglect, abuse, dependency, guardianship, paternity, termination of parental rights and protection from domestic violence, in which the issue may appear. The term does not include a proceeding involving juvenile delinquency, contractual emancipation or enforcement under sections 46b–115u to 46b–115gg, inclusive;

(5) "Commencement" means the filing of the first pleading in a proceeding;

(6) "Court" means any entity, including the Superior Court or Probate Court in this state, if such entity has jurisdiction to establish, enforce or modify a child custody determination;

(7) "Home state" means the state in which a child lived with a parent or person acting as a parent for at least six consecutive months immediately before the commencement of a child custody proceeding. In the case of a child less than six months old, the term means the state in which the child lived from birth with any such parent or person acting as a parent. A period of temporary absence of any such person is counted as part of the period;

(8) "Initial determination" means the first child custody determination concerning a particular child;

(9) "Issuing court" means the court that has made a child custody determination for which enforcement is sought under this chapter;

(10) "Issuing state" means the state in which a child custody determination has been made;

(11) "Modification" means a child custody determination that changes, replaces, supersedes or is otherwise made after a previous determination concerning the same child, whether or not it is made by the court that made the prior custody determination;

(12) "Person" shall have the same meaning as contained in subsection (k) of section 1–1 and shall include a public agency;

(13) "Person acting as a parent" means a person, other than a parent, who: (A) Has physical custody of the child or has had physical custody for a period of six consecutive months, including any temporary absence, any part of which period occurred within one year immediately before the commencement of a child custody proceeding, and (B) has been awarded legal

custody by a court or claims a right to legal custody under the laws of this state;

(14) "Physical custody" means the physical care and supervision of a child;

(15) "State" means a state of the United States, the District of Columbia, Puerto Rico, the United States Virgin Islands, or any territory or possession subject to the jurisdiction of the United States.

(1999, P.A. 99–185, § 2, eff. July 1, 2000; 2000, P.A. 00–49, § 1, eff. July 1, 2000.)

§ 46b–115b. Proceedings governed by other law

The chapter does not govern an adoption proceeding or a proceeding pertaining to the authorization of emergency medical care for a child.

(1999, P.A. 99–185, § 3, eff. July 1, 2000.)

§ 46b–115c. Application to Indian tribes

A child custody proceeding that pertains to an Indian child as defined in the Indian Child Welfare Act, 25 USC Section 1901 et seq., is not subject to this chapter to the extent that it is governed by the Indian Child Welfare Act.

(1999, P.A. 99–185, § 4, eff. July 1, 2000.)

§ 46b–115d. International application of chapter

For purposes of this chapter, any child custody order of a foreign country shall be treated in the manner provided in section 46b–115hh.

(1999, P.A. 99–185, § 5, eff. July 1, 2000.)

§ 46b–115e. Effect of child custody determination

A child custody determination made by a court of this state that had jurisdiction under this chapter binds all persons who have been served in accordance with the laws of this state or notified in accordance with section 46b–115g or who have submitted to the jurisdiction of the court, and who have been given an opportunity to be heard. As to those persons, the determination is conclusive as to all decided issues of law and fact except to the extent the determination is modified.

(1999, P.A. 99–185, § 6, eff. July 1, 2000.)

§ 46b–115f. Priority

If a question of the existence or exercise of jurisdiction under this chapter is raised in a child custody proceeding, the question, upon request of a party, must be given calendar priority and handled expeditiously.

(1999, P.A. 99–185, § 7, eff. July 1, 2000.)

§ 46b–115g. Notice to persons outside state; submission to jurisdiction

(a) Notice required for the exercise of jurisdiction over a person outside this state shall be given in a manner reasonably calculated to give actual notice, and may be: (1) By personal delivery outside this state in the manner prescribed for service of process within this state; (2) in the manner prescribed by the law of the place in which the service is made for service of process in that place in an action in any of its courts of general jurisdiction; (3) any form of mail addressed to the person to be served and requesting a receipt; or (4) as directed by the court including publication, if other means of notification are ineffective.

(b) Except as otherwise provided by any provision of the general statutes, notice under this section shall be served, mailed or delivered or last published at least twelve days before any hearing in this state.

(c) Proof of service outside this state may be made by affidavit of the individual who made the service, or in the manner prescribed by the law of this state, the order pursuant to which the service is made, or the law of the place in which the service is made. If service is made by mail, proof may be a receipt signed by the addressee or other evidence of delivery to the addressee.

(d) Except as otherwise provided by any provision of the general statutes, notice is not required if a person submits to the jurisdiction of the court.

(1999, P.A. 99–185, § 8, eff. July 1, 2000.)

§ 46b–115h. Communication between courts

(a) A court of this state may communicate with a court in another state concerning a proceeding arising under this chapter.

(b) The court may allow the parties to participate in the communication. If the parties are not able to participate in the communication, they must be given the opportunity to present facts and legal arguments before a decision on jurisdiction is made.

(c) Communication between courts on schedules, calendars, court records and similar matters may occur without informing the parties. A record need not be made of the communication.

(d) Except as otherwise provided in subsection (c) of this section, a record must be made of a communication under this section. The parties must be informed promptly of the communication and granted access to the record.

(e) For the purposes of this section, "record" means information that is inscribed on a tangible medium or that is stored in an electronic or other medium and is retrievable in perceivable form.

(1999, P.A. 99–185, § 9, eff. July 1, 2000.)

§ 46b–115i. Taking testimony in another state

(a) In addition to other procedures available to a party, a party to a child custody proceeding, guardian ad litem or legal representative of the child may offer testimony of witnesses who are located in another state, including testimony of the parties and the child, by deposition or other means allowable in this state for testimony taken in another state. The court on its own motion may order that the testimony of a person be taken in another state and may prescribe the manner in which and the terms upon which the testimony is taken.

(b) A court of this state may permit an individual residing in another state to be deposed or to testify by telephone, audiovisual means, or other electronic means before a designated court or at another location in that state. A court of this state shall cooperate with courts of other states in designating an appropriate location for the deposition or testimony.

(c) Documentary evidence transmitted from another state to a court of this state by technological means that do not produce an original writing may not be excluded from evidence on an objection based on the means of transmission.

(1999, P.A. 99–185, § 10, eff. July 1, 2000.)

§ 46b–115j. Cooperation between courts; preservation of records

(a) A court of this state may request the appropriate court of another state to: (1) Hold an evidentiary hearing; (2) order a person to produce or give evidence pursuant to procedures of that state; (3) order that an evaluation be made with respect to the custody of a child involved in a pending proceeding; (4) forward to the court of this state a certified copy of the transcript of the record of the hearing, the evidence otherwise presented, and any evaluation prepared in compliance with the request; and (5) order a party to a child custody proceeding or any person having physical custody of the child to appear in the proceeding with or without the child.

(b) Upon request of a court of another state, a court of this state may hold a hearing or enter an order described in subsection (a) of this section.

(c) Travel and other necessary and reasonable expenses incurred under subsections (a) and (b) of this section may be assessed against the parties.

(d) A court of this state shall preserve the pleadings, orders, decrees, records of hearings, evaluations and other pertinent records with respect to a child custody proceeding until the child attains eighteen years of age. Upon appropriate request by a court or law enforcement official of another state, the court shall forward a certified copy of those records.

(1999, P.A. 99–185, § 11, eff. July 1, 2000.)

PART II. JURISDICTION

§ 46b–115k. Initial child custody jurisdiction

(a) Except as otherwise provided in section 46b–115n, a court of this state has jurisdiction to make an initial child custody determination if:

(1) This state is the home state of the child on the date of the commencement of the child custody proceeding;

(2) This state was the home state of the child within six months of the commencement of the child custody proceeding, the child is absent from the state, and a parent or a person acting as a parent continues to reside in this state;

(3) A court of another state does not have jurisdiction under subdivisions (1) or (2) of this subsection, the child and at least one parent or person acting as a parent have a significant connection with this state other than mere physical presence, and there is substantial evidence available in this state concerning the child's care, protection, training and personal relationships;

(4) A court of another state which is the home state of the child has declined to exercise jurisdiction on the ground that this state is the more appropriate forum under a provision substantially similar to section 46b–115q or section 46b–115r, the child and at least one parent or person acting as a parent have a significant connection with this state other than mere physical presence, and there is substantial evidence available in this state concerning the child's care, protection, training and personal relationships;

(5) All courts having jurisdiction under subdivisions (1) to (4), inclusive, of this subsection have declined jurisdiction on the ground that a court of this state is the more appropriate forum to determine custody under a provision substantially similar to section 46b–115q or section 46b–115r; or

(6) No court of any other state would have jurisdiction under subdivisions (1) to (5), inclusive, of this subsection.

(b) Subsection (a) of this section is the exclusive jurisdictional basis for making a child custody determination by a court of this state.

(c) Physical presence of, or personal jurisdiction over, a party or a child is not necessary or sufficient to make a child custody determination.

(1999, P.A. 99–185, § 12, eff. July 1, 2000.)

§ 46b–115*l*. Jurisdiction

(a) Except as otherwise provided in section 46b–115n, a court of this state which has made a child custody determination pursuant to sections 46b–115k to 46b–115m, inclusive, has exclusive, continuing jurisdiction over the determination until: (1) A court of this state or a court of another state determines that the child, the child's parents and any person acting as a parent do not presently reside in this state; or (2) a court of this state determines that (A) this state is not the home state of the child, (B) a parent or a person acting as a parent continues to reside in this state but the child no longer has a significant relationship with such parent or person, and (C) substantial evidence is no longer available in this state concerning the child's care, protection, training and personal relationships.

(b) A court of this state which has made a child custody determination but does not have exclusive, continuing jurisdiction under this section may modify that determination only if it has jurisdiction to make an initial determination under section 46b–115k.

(1999, P.A. 99–185, § 13, eff. July 1, 2000.)

§ 46b–115m. Modification of custody determination of another state

(a) Except as otherwise provided in section 46b–115n, a court of this state may not modify a child custody determination made by a court of another state unless a court of this state has jurisdiction to make an initial determination under subdivisions (1) to (4), inclusive, of subsection (a) of section 46b–115k and one of the following occurs: (1) The court of the other state determines that it no longer has exclusive, continuing jurisdiction under a provision substantially similar to section 46b–115*l*; (2) a court of another state determines that a court of this state would be a more convenient forum under a provision substantially similar to section 46b–115q; or (3) a court of this state or another state determines that the child, the child's parents and any person acting as a parent do not presently reside in the other state.

(b) Notwithstanding the provisions of this chapter, a court of this state may modify a child custody determination made by a court of another state if: (1) The child resides in this state with a parent; (2) the child has been, or is under a threat of being, abused or mistreated by a person who resides in the state which would have jurisdiction under the provisions of this chapter; and (3) the court of this state determines that it is in the child's best interest to modify the child custody determination.

(1999, P.A. 99–185, § 14, eff. July 1, 2000.)

§ 46b–115n. Temporary emergency jurisdiction

(a) A court of this state has temporary emergency jurisdiction if the child is present in this state and (1) the child has been abandoned, or (2) it is necessary in an emergency to protect the child because the child, a sibling or a parent has been, or is under a threat of being, abused or mistreated. As used in this subsection with respect to a child, "abused" shall have the same meaning as in section 46b–120.

(b) If there is no previous child custody determination that is enforceable under this chapter and a child custody proceeding has not been commenced in a court of a state having jurisdiction under a provision substantially similar to section 46b–115k, 46b–115*l* or 46b–115m, a child custody determination made under this section remains in effect until an order is obtained from a court of a state having jurisdiction under a provision substantially similar to section 46b–115k, 46b–115*l* or 46b–115m. A child custody determination made under this section shall be a final determination if: (1) A child custody proceeding has not been or is not commenced in a court of a state having jurisdiction under a provision substantially similar to section 46b–115k, 46b–115*l* or 46b–115m; (2) this state has become the home state of the child; and (3) the child custody determination provides that it is a final determination.

(c) If there is a previous child custody determination that is enforceable under this chapter or if a child custody proceeding has been commenced in a court of a state having jurisdiction under a provision substantially similar to section 46b–115k, 46b–115*l* or 46b–115m, the court of this state which issues an order pursuant to this section shall specify that such order is effective for a period of time which the court deems adequate to allow the person seeking an order to obtain such order from the other state which has jurisdiction. Such order shall be effective for that period of time specified in the order or until an order is obtained from the other state whichever occurs first.

(d) If the court, in any proceeding commenced pursuant to this section, is informed that a child custody proceeding has been commenced, or that a child custody determination has been made, by a court of another state having jurisdiction pursuant to a provision substantially similar to section 46b–115k, 46b–115*l* or 46b–115m, such court shall immediately communicate with the court of the other state and take appropriate action, including the making of temporary orders for a specified period of time, to resolve the emergency and to protect the safety of the child and the parties.

(1999, P.A. 99–185, § 15, eff. July 1, 2000.)

§ 46b–115*o*. Notice and opportunity to be heard; joinder

(a) Before a child custody determination is made under this chapter, notice and an opportunity to be heard in accordance with the standard established in section 46b–115g shall be given to the parties, any parent whose parental rights have not been previously terminated and any person who has physical custody of the child.

(b) This chapter does not govern the enforceability of a child custody determination made without notice or an opportunity to be heard.

(c) The obligation to join a party and the right to intervene as a party in a child custody proceeding under this chapter are governed by section 46b–57.

(1999, P.A. 99–185, § 16, eff. July 1, 2000.)

§ 46b–115p. Simultaneous proceedings

(a) Except as otherwise provided in section 46b–115n, if at the time of the commencement of the proceeding in this state a proceeding concerning the custody of the child has been commenced in a court of another state having jurisdiction pursuant to a provision substantially similar to section 46b–115k, 46b–115*l* or 46b–115m, a court of this state shall not exercise jurisdiction. A court of this state may exercise jurisdiction if the proceeding in the other state has been terminated or is stayed by the court of the other state because such court has determined pursuant to a provision substantially similar to section 46b–115q, that a court in this state is a more convenient forum.

(b) Except as otherwise provided in section 46b–115n, the court shall, after review of relevant information provided to it, determine whether a child custody proceeding has been commenced in another state. If such proceeding has been commenced, the court in this state shall take appropriate action to communicate with the other court and to resolve which court shall have jurisdiction. If the court of this state determines that the court of the other state has jurisdiction pursuant to a provision substantially similar to section 46b–115k, 46b–115*l* or 46b–115m, the court of this state shall stay its proceeding while the court of the other state determines whether the court of this state is the more appropriate forum. If the court of the other state determines that the court of this state is not a more appropriate forum, the court of this state shall dismiss the proceeding.

(c) Except as otherwise provided in section 46b–115n, the court, in a proceeding to modify a child custody determination, shall after review of relevant information provided to it, determine whether a proceeding to enforce the determination has been commenced in another state. If the court determines that such enforcement proceeding has commenced, the court may (1) stay the proceeding for modification pending the entry of an order of the court of the other state enforcing, staying, denying or dismissing the proceeding for enforcement; (2) enjoin the parties from continuing with the proceeding for enforcement; or (3) proceed with the modification under conditions it considers appropriate.

(d) Except as otherwise provided in section 46b–115n, the court, in a proceeding to enforce a child custody determination, shall proceed, with regard to simultaneous proceedings, in accordance with the provisions of section 46b–115z.

(1999, P.A. 99–185, § 17, eff. July 1, 2000.)

§ 46b–115q. Inconvenient forum

(a) A court of this state which has jurisdiction under this chapter to make a child custody determination may decline to exercise its jurisdiction at any time if it determines that it is an inconvenient forum under the circumstances and that a court of another state is a more appropriate forum. The issue of inconvenient forum may be raised upon a motion of a party, the guardian ad litem for the child or the attorney for the child, the court's own motion or a request of another court.

(b) In determining whether a court of this state is an inconvenient forum and that it is more appropriate for a court of another state to exercise jurisdiction, the court shall allow the parties to submit information and shall consider all relevant factors including: (1) Whether family violence has occurred and is likely to continue in the future and which state could best protect the parties and the child; (2) the length of time the child has resided outside this state; (3) the distance between the court in this state and the court in the state that would assume jurisdiction; (4) the relative financial circumstances of the parties; (5) any agreement of the parties as to which state should assume jurisdiction; (6) the nature and location of the evidence required to resolve the pending litigation, including testimony of the child; (7) the ability of the court of each state to decide the issue expeditiously and the procedures necessary to present the evidence; and (8) the familiarity of the court of each state with the facts and issues in the pending litigation.

(c) If a court of this state determines that it is an inconvenient forum and that a court of another state is a more appropriate forum, it shall stay the proceedings upon condition that a child custody proceeding be promptly commenced in another designated state and may impose any other condition the court considers just and proper.

(d) A court of this state may decline to exercise its jurisdiction under this chapter if a child custody determination is incidental to an action for dissolution of marriage, divorce or another proceeding while still retaining jurisdiction over the dissolution of marriage, divorce or other proceeding.

(1999, P.A. 99–185, § 18, eff. July 1, 2000.)

§ 46b–115r. Jurisdiction declined by reason of conduct; assessment of fees and costs

(a) Except as otherwise provided in section 46b–115n, if a court of this state has jurisdiction under this chapter because a person seeking to invoke its jurisdiction has engaged in unjustifiable conduct, the court shall decline to exercise its jurisdiction unless:

(1) The parents and all persons acting as parents have acquiesced in the exercise of jurisdiction;

(2) A court of the state otherwise having jurisdiction under a provision substantially similar to section 46b–115k, 46b–115*l* or 46b–115m determines that this state is a more appropriate forum under a statute similar to section 46b–115q; or

(3) No court of any other state would have jurisdiction under the criteria specified in sections 46b–115k to 46b–115m, inclusive.

(b) If a court of this state declines to exercise its jurisdiction pursuant to subsection (a) of this section, it may fashion an appropriate remedy to ensure the safety of the child and prevent a repetition of the unjustifiable conduct, including staying the proceeding until a child custody proceeding is commenced in a court having jurisdiction under a provision substantially similar to section 46b–115k, 46b–115*l* or 46b–115m.

(c) If a court dismisses a petition or stays a proceeding because it declines to exercise its jurisdiction pursuant to subsection (a) of this section, it shall assess against the party seeking to invoke its jurisdiction reasonable expenses including costs, communication expenses, attorneys' fees, investigative fees, expenses for witnesses, travel expenses and child care during the course of the proceedings, unless the party from whom fees are sought establishes that the assessment would be clearly inappropriate. The court may not assess fees, costs or expenses against the state unless authorized by law.

(1999, P.A. 99–185, § 19, eff. July 1, 2000.)

§ 46b–115s. Information required by the court

(a) In a child custody proceeding, each party, in its first pleading or in an attached affidavit, shall give information, if reasonably ascertainable and not confidential under state law, under oath as to the child's present address or location, the places where the child has lived during the past five years, and the names and present addresses of the persons with whom the child has lived during the past five years. The pleading or affidavit must state whether the party:

(1) Has participated, as a party or witness or in any other capacity, in any other proceeding concerning the custody of or visitation with the child and, if so, identify the court, the case number, and the date of the child custody determination;

(2) Knows of any civil or criminal proceeding that could affect the current proceeding, including proceedings for enforcement and proceedings relating to family violence, protective orders, termination of parental rights and adoptions, and if so, identify the court, the case number and the nature of the proceeding; and

(3) Knows the names and addresses of any person not a party to the proceeding who has physical custody of the child or claims rights of legal custody or physical custody of, or visitation with, the child and if so, the names and addresses of those persons.

(b) If the information required by subsection (a) of this section is not provided, the court upon motion of a party or on its own motion may stay the proceeding until such information is provided.

(c) If the party provides any of the information required in subdivisions (1) to (3) of subsection (a) of this section, such party shall also provide any additional information under oath as required by the court. The court may examine the parties under oath as to details of the information provided and other matters pertinent to the court's jurisdiction and the disposition of the case.

(d) Each party has a continuing duty to inform the court of any proceeding in this state or another state that could affect the current proceeding.

(e) If a party under oath alleges in an affidavit or a pleading or on a form prescribed by the Office of the Chief Court Administrator that the health, safety or liberty of a party or child would be jeopardized by disclosure of location information, the information must be sealed and shall not be disclosed to the other party or the public unless the court, after a hearing, determines that it is in the interest of justice that such disclosure be made. The party making such allegation shall (1) provide obvious notice to the clerk of the court that such allegation is being made; (2) not file location information that poses the risk unless ordered by the court; (3) identify, in writing, documents previously filed with the court that contain location information that poses the risk; and (4) if, at the time the allegation is made, the party is not represented by counsel in the proceeding, provide the clerk of the court with a mailing address that may be disclosed to the public. Except as otherwise provided by rule of court, as used in this subsection, "obvious notice" means notice as provided on a form prescribed by the Office of the Chief Court Administrator or a notice to the clerk of the court which is set forth in the bottom margin of the first page of such filed document.

(1999, P.A. 99–185, § 20, eff. July 1, 2000; 2000, P.A. 00–49, § 2, eff. July 1, 2000; 2000, P.A. 00–191, § 13, eff. July 1, 2000; 2001, P.A. 01–186, § 16; 2003, P.A. 03–19, § 107, eff. May 12, 2003.)

§ 46b–115t. Appearance of parties and child

(a) In a child custody proceeding in this state, the court may order a party to the proceeding who is in this state to appear before the court in person with or without the child. The court may order any person who is in this state and who has physical custody or control of the child to appear in person with the child.

(b) If the court orders the appearance of a party who is outside this state, the court may order that a notice is given in accordance with section 46b–115g and that such notice include a statement directing the party to appear in person with or without the child and informing the party that failure to appear may result in a decision adverse to such party.

(c) The court may enter any orders necessary to ensure the safety of the child or of any person ordered to appear pursuant to this section.

(d) The court may order a party to pay for reasonable and necessary travel and expenses of a party to the child custody proceeding or the child who is outside the state.

(1999, P.A. 99–185, § 21, eff. July 1, 2000.)

PART III. ENFORCEMENT

§ 46b–115u. Definitions

As used in sections 46b–115u to 46b–115gg, inclusive, "petitioner" means a person who seeks enforcement of a child custody determination, and "respondent" means a person against whom a proceeding has been commenced for enforcement of a child custody determination.

(1999, P.A. 99–185, § 22, eff. July 1, 2000.)

§ 46b–115v. Enforcement under Hague Convention

A court of this state may enforce an order by a federal court or another state court for the return of a child made pursuant to the Hague Convention on the Civil Aspects of International Child Abduction in accordance with section 46b–115jj.

(1999, P.A. 99–185, § 23, eff. July 1, 2000.)

§ 46b–115w. Registration of child custody determination

(a) A child custody determination issued by a court of another state may be registered in this state, with or without a simultaneous request for enforcement, by sending to the Superior Court in this state: (1) A letter or other document requesting registration; (2) two copies, including one certified copy, of the determination sought to be registered, and a statement under penalty of perjury that to the best of the knowledge and belief of the petitioner the order has not been modified; and (3) except as otherwise provided in section 46b–115s, the name and address of the petitioner and any parent or person acting as parent who has been awarded custody or visitation in the child custody determination sought to be registered.

(b) On receipt of the documents required by subsection (a) of this section, the registering court shall cause the determination to be filed as a foreign judgment, together with one copy of any accompanying documents and information, regardless of their form.

(c) Within five days after the registering court's receipt of the documents required by subsection (a) of this section, the petitioner shall notify the persons named pursuant to subdivision (3) of subsection (a) of this section of the registration of the documents by certified mail, return receipt requested at their respective last-known addresses or by personal service, and provide them with an opportunity to contest the registration in accordance with this section. The notice required in this subsection shall state that: (1) A registered determination is enforceable as of the date of the registration in the same manner as a determination issued by a court of this state; (2) a hearing to contest the validity of the registered determination must be requested within twenty days after service of notice; and (3) failure to contest the registration will, upon proof of notice, result in confirmation of the child custody determination and preclude further contest of that determination with respect to any matter that could have been asserted.

(d) A hearing to contest the validity of the registered determination shall be requested within twenty days after service of the notice. Such hearing shall be held within twenty days of the receipt of such request. At that hearing, the court shall confirm the registered order unless the respondent establishes that: (1) The issuing court did not have jurisdiction under a provision substantially similar to section 46b–115k, 46b–115*l* or 46b–115m; (2) the child custody determination sought to be registered has been vacated, stayed or modified by a court having jurisdiction to do so pursuant to a statute substantially similar to sections 46b–115k to 46b–115m, inclusive; or (3) the respondent was entitled to notice of the proceedings before the court that issued the order for which registration is sought, but such notice was not given in a manner reasonably calculated to give actual notice.

(e) If a timely request for a hearing to contest the validity of the registration is not made, the registration is confirmed as a matter of law with respect to those who have received proper notice and all persons served must be notified of the confirmation by the petitioner.

(f) Confirmation of a registered order, whether by operation of law or after notice and hearing, precludes further contest of the order with respect to any matter that could have been asserted at the time of registration.

(1999, P.A. 99–185, § 24, eff. July 1, 2000; 2000, P.A. 00–49, § 3, eff. July 1, 2000; 2000, P.A. 00–191, § 14, eff. July 1, 2000.)

§ 46b–115x. Enforcement of child custody determination

A court of this state shall recognize and enforce, but not modify except in accordance with section 46b–115m, a child custody determination of a court of another state if (1) the court of the other state exercised jurisdiction under a provision substantially similar to section 46b–115k, 46b–115*l* or 46b–115m, the determination was made under factual circumstances meeting the jurisdictional standards of this chapter and the determination has not been modified in accordance with this chapter, or (2) the child custody determination was registered in this state pursuant to section 46b–115w. A child custody determination which satisfies the criteria in subdivision (1) or (2) of this section shall have the same effect and shall be enforced in the same manner as a child custody determination rendered by the Superior Court.

(1999, P.A. 99–185, § 25, eff. July 1, 2000.)

§ 46b–115y. Temporary visitation order

(a) A court of this state which does not have jurisdiction to modify a child custody determination may issue a temporary order enforcing (1) the visitation schedule made by the court of another state, or (2) the visitation provisions of a child custody determination of another state which does not provide for a specific visitation schedule.

(b) If a court of this state makes an order pursuant to subdivision (2) of subsection (a) of this section, it shall specify in the order a period that it considers adequate to allow the petitioner to obtain an order from a court having jurisdiction under a provision substantially similar to section 46b–115k, 46b–115*l* or 46b–115m. The order remains in effect until an order is obtained from the other court or the period expires, whichever comes first.

(1999, P.A. 99–185, § 26, eff. July 1, 2000.)

§ 46b–115z. Simultaneous proceedings

If a proceeding for enforcement under this chapter is commenced in a court of this state and the court determines that a proceeding to modify the determination is pending in a court of another state having jurisdiction to modify the determination under a provision substantially similar to section 46b–115k, 46b–115*l* or 46b–115m, the enforcing court shall immediately communicate with the modifying court. The court of this state shall proceed with the action for enforcement of the child custody determination unless the court, after consultation with the modifying court, stays or dismisses the proceeding.

(1999, P.A. 99–185, § 27, eff. July 1, 2000.)

§ 46b–115aa. Expedited enforcement of child custody determination

(a) A petitioner seeking to enforce a child custody determination must verify the petition and attach copies of certified copies of all orders or notice sought to be enforced and of any order confirming registration if such child custody determination has been registered.

(b) A petition for enforcement of a child custody determination shall state: (1) Whether the court that issued the determination identified the jurisdictional basis it relied upon in exercising jurisdiction and, if so, what the basis was; (2) whether the determination for which enforcement is sought has been vacated, stayed or modified by a court whose decision must be enforced under this chapter and, if so, identify the court, the case number and the nature of the proceeding; (3) whether any proceeding has been commenced that could affect the current proceeding, including proceedings relating to family violence, protective orders, termination of parental rights and adoptions and, if so, identify the court, the case number, and the nature of the proceeding; (4) the present physical address of the child and the respondent, if known; (5) whether relief in addition to the immediate physical custody of the child and attorneys' fees are sought, including a request for assistance from law enforcement officials, and, if so, the relief sought; and (6) if the child custody determination has been registered and confirmed under section 46b–115w, the date and place of registration.

(c) Upon the filing of a petition, the court shall issue an order directing the respondent to appear in person with or without the child at a hearing, the time and place of which shall be specified, and may enter any order necessary to ensure the safety of the parties and the child. The order shall advise the respondent that at the hearing, the court will order that the petitioner take immediate physical custody of the child and the payment of fees, costs and expenses under section 46b–115ee, and any other relief that the court may deem appropriate, unless the respondent appears and establishes that: (1) The child custody determination has not been registered and confirmed pursuant to section 46b–115w and (A) the court issuing the order for which enforcement is sought did not have jurisdiction under section 46b–115k, 46b–115*l* or 46b–115m or a provision substantially similar to said sections; (B) the child custody determination for which enforcement is sought has been vacated, stayed or modified by a court having jurisdiction to do so under sections 46b–115k to 46b–115t, inclusive; or (C) the respondent was entitled to notice, but notice of the proceedings before the court that issued the order for which enforcement is sought was not given in accordance with section 46b–115g or in a manner reasonably calculated to provide actual notice; or (2) the child custody determination for which enforcement is sought was registered and confirmed pursuant to section 46b–115w, but has been vacated, stayed or modified by a court of a state having jurisdiction to do so under section 46b–115k, 46b–115*l* or 46b–115m or a provision substantially similar to said sections. The hearing must be held on the next business day after service of the order unless otherwise ordered for good cause shown. The court may extend the date of the hearing at the request of the petitioner.

(1999, P.A. 99–185, § 28, eff. July 1, 2000.)

§ 46b–115bb. Service of petition and order

Except as otherwise provided in section 46b–115dd, the petition and order shall be served upon the respondent and any person who has physical custody of the child by personal service.

(1999, P.A. 99–185, § 29, eff. July 1, 2000.)

§ 46b–115cc. Hearing and order

(a) Unless the court issues a temporary emergency order pursuant to section 46b–115n, the court shall enforce the child custody determination and if appropriate, order the petitioner to take immediate physical custody of the child unless the respondent establishes that: (1) The child custody determination has not been registered and confirmed pursuant to section 46b–115w and (A) the court issuing the order for which enforcement is sought did not have jurisdiction under section 46b–115k, 46b–115*l* or 46b–115m or a provision substantially similar to said sections; (B) the child custody determination for which enforcement is sought has been vacated, stayed or modified by a court having jurisdiction to do so under section 46b–115k, 46b–115*l* or 46b–115m or a provision substantially similar to said sections; or (C) the respondent was entitled to notice, but notice of the proceedings before the court that issued the order for which enforcement is sought was not given in accordance with section 46b–115g or in a manner reasonably calculated to give actual notice; or (2) the child custody determination for which enforcement is sought was registered and confirmed pursuant to section 46b–115w, but has been vacated, stayed or modified by a court of a state having jurisdiction to do so under section 46b–115k, 46b–115*l* or 46b–115m.

(b) The court shall award the fees, costs and expenses as provided in section 46b–115ee and may grant additional relief, including a request for the assistance of law enforcement officials.

(c) If a party called to testify refuses to answer on the ground that the testimony may be self-incriminating, the court may draw an adverse inference from the refusal.

(d) A privilege against disclosure of communications between spouses and a defense of immunity based on the relationship of husband and wife or parent and child may not be invoked in a proceeding under sections 46b–115u to 46b–115gg, inclusive.

(1999, P.A. 99–185, § 30, eff. July 1, 2000.)

§ 46b–115dd. Order to take physical custody of child

(a) Upon the filing of a petition seeking enforcement of a child custody determination, the petitioner may file a verified application for the issuance of an order to take physical custody of the child if the child will suffer imminent, serious physical harm or will be removed from the state. The application for the order shall include the statements required by subsection (b) of section 46b–115aa. If the court, after reviewing the petition, testimony of the petitioner or other witnesses and other facts before it, finds there is a substantial likelihood that the child will suffer imminent serious physical harm or be removed from this state, it may issue an order to an appropriate law enforcement official to take physical custody of the child and place the child in the care of an appropriate person pending a hearing pursuant to subsection (b) of this section. In making the decision on placement of the child, the court may impose conditions to ensure the appearance of the child and the person with whom the child is placed at the hearing. Such order shall include the court's findings and the facts upon which the court made its findings. The petition and the order shall be served upon the respondent at the time the child is taken into physical custody or immediately thereafter.

(b) The court shall hold a hearing on the petition on the next business day after the order and the petition is served unless there are compelling circumstances.

(1999, P.A. 99–185, § 31, eff. July 1, 2000.)

§ 46b–115ee. Costs, fees and expenses

The court shall award the prevailing party necessary and reasonable expenses incurred by or on behalf of the party, including costs, communication expenses, attorneys' fees, investigative fees, expenses for witnesses, travel expenses, and child care during the course of the proceedings, unless the party from whom fees or expenses are sought establishes that the award would be clearly inappropriate.

(1999, P.A. 99–185, § 32, eff. July 1, 2000; 2000, P.A. 00–196, § 46.)

§ 46b–115ff. Recognition and enforcement of order issued by another state

A court of this state shall accord full faith and credit to an enforcement order issued by another state in accordance with statutes substantially similar to this chapter which enforces a child custody determination by a court of another state unless the order has been vacated, stayed or modified by a court having jurisdiction to do so under sections 46b–115k to 46b–115t, inclusive.

(1999, P.A. 99–185, § 33, eff. July 1, 2000.)

§ 46b–115gg. Appeals

An order enforcing a child custody determination may not be stayed pending appeal unless the court enters a temporary emergency order under section 46b–115n.

(1999, P.A. 99–185, § 34, eff. July 1, 2000.)

PART IV. FOREIGN CHILD CUSTODY

§ 46b–115hh. Definitions

As used in sections 46b–115*ii* and 46b–115jj: "Foreign child custody determination" means any judgment, decree or other order of a court or tribunal of competent jurisdiction of a foreign state providing for legal custody, physical custody or visitation with respect to a child. The term includes a permanent, temporary, initial and modification order. The term does not include an order relating to child support or other monetary obligation of an individual.

(1999, P.A. 99–185, § 36, eff. July 1, 2000.)

§ 46b–115ii. Foreign child custody determination

A court of this state shall treat a foreign child custody determination made under factual circumstances in substantial conformity with the jurisdictional standards of this chapter, including reasonable notice and opportunity to be heard to all affected persons, as a child custody determination of another state under sections 46b–115 to 46b–115t, inclusive, unless such determination was rendered under child custody law which violates fundamental principles of human rights or unless such determination is repugnant to the public policy of this state.

(1999, P.A. 99–185, § 37, eff. July 1, 2000.)

§ 46b–115jj. Enforcement of foreign child custody order re return of child under Hague Convention

A court of this state shall enforce a foreign child custody determination or an order of a federal court or another state court for return of a child under The Hague Convention on the Civil Aspects of International Child Abduction made under factual circumstances in substantial conformity with the jurisdictional standards of this chapter, including reasonable notice and opportunity to be heard to all affected persons, as a child custody determination of another state under sections 46b–115u to 46b–115gg, inclusive, unless such determination was rendered under child custody law which violates fundamental principles of human rights or unless such determination is repugnant to the public policy of this state.

(1999, P.A. 99–185, § 38, eff. July 1, 2000.)

§§ 46b–116 to 46b–119. Reserved for future use

CHAPTER 815t

JUVENILE MATTERS

PART I. GENERAL PROVISIONS

PART I. GENERAL PROVISIONS

§ 46b–120. Definitions

The terms used in this chapter shall, in its interpretation and in the interpretation of other statutes, be defined as follows: (1) "Child" means any person under sixteen years of age and, for purposes of delinquency matters, "child" means any person (A) under sixteen years of age, or (B) sixteen years of age or older who, prior to attaining sixteen years of age, has violated any federal or state law or municipal or local ordinance, other than an ordinance regulating behavior of a child in a family with service needs, and, subsequent to attaining sixteen years of age, violates any order of the Superior Court or any condition of probation ordered by the Superior Court with respect to such delinquency proceeding; (2) "youth" means any person sixteen or seventeen years of age; (3) "youth in crisis" means any youth who, within the last two years, (A) has without just cause run away from the parental home or other properly authorized and lawful place of abode, (B) is beyond the control of parents, guardian or other custodian, or (C) has four unexcused absences from school in any one month or ten unexcused absences in any school year; (4) "abused" means that a child or youth (A) has been inflicted with physical injury or injuries other than by accidental means, or (B) has injuries that are at variance with the history given of them, or (C) is in a condition that is the result of maltreatment such as, but not limited to, malnutrition, sexual molestation or exploitation, deprivation of necessities, emotional maltreatment or cruel punishment; (5) a child may be found "mentally deficient" who, by reason of a deficiency of intelligence that has existed from birth or from early age, requires, or will require, for his protection or for the protection of others, special care, supervision and control; (6) a child may be convicted as "delinquent" who has violated (A) any federal or state law or municipal or local ordinance, other than an ordinance regulating behavior of a child in a family with service needs, (B) any order of the Superior Court, or (C) conditions of probation as ordered by the court; (7) a child or youth may be found "dependent" whose home is a suitable one for the child or youth, save for the financial inability of parents, parent, guardian or other person maintaining such home, to provide the specialized care the condition of the child or youth requires; (8) "family with service needs" means a family that includes a child who (A) has without just cause run away from the parental home or other properly authorized and lawful place of abode, (B) is beyond the control of parent, parents, guardian or other custodian, (C) has engaged in indecent or immoral conduct, (D) is a truant or habitual truant or who, while in school, has been continuously and overtly defiant of school rules and regulations, or (E) is thirteen years of age or older and has engaged in sexual intercourse with another person and such other person is thirteen years of age or older and not more than two years older or younger than such child; (9) a child or youth may be found "neglected" who (A) has been abandoned, or (B) is being denied proper care and attention, physically, educationally, emotionally or morally, or (C) is being permitted to live under conditions, circumstances or associations injurious to the well-being of the child or youth, or (D) has been abused; (10) a child or youth may be found "uncared for" who is homeless or whose home cannot provide the specialized care that the physical, emotional or mental condition of the child requires. For the purposes of this section, the treatment of any child by an accredited Christian Science practitioner in lieu of treatment by a licensed practitioner of the healing arts, shall not of itself constitute neglect or maltreatment; (11) "delinquent act" means the violation of any federal or state law or municipal or local ordinance, other than an ordinance regulating the behavior of a child in a family with service needs, or the violation of any order of the Superior Court; (12) "serious juvenile offense" means (A) the violation by a child, including attempt or conspiracy to violate sections 21a–277, 21a–278, 29–33, 29–34, 29–35, 53–21, 53–80a, 53–202b, 53–202c, 53–390 to 53–392, inclusive, 53a–54a to 53a–57, inclusive, 53a–59 to 53a–60c, inclusive, 53a–70 to 53a–71, inclusive, 53a–72b, 53a–86, 53a–92 to 53a–94a, inclusive, 53a–95, 53a–101, 53a–102a, 53a–103a, 53a–111 to 53a–113, inclusive, subdivision (1) of subsection (a) of section 53a–122, subdivision (3) of subsection (a) of section 53a–123, 53a–134, 53a–135, 53a–136a, 53a–166, 53a–167c, subsection (a) of section 53a–174, 53a–196a, 53a–211, 53a–212, 53a–216 or 53a–217b, or (B) running away, without just cause, from any secure placement other than home while referred as a delinquent child to the Court Support Services Division or committed as a delinquent child to the Commissioner of Children and Families for a serious juvenile offense; (13) "serious juvenile offender" means any child convicted as delinquent for commission of a serious juvenile offense; (14) "serious juvenile repeat offender" means any child charged with the commission of any felony if such child has previously been convicted delinquent at any age for two violations of any provision of title 21a, 29, 53 or 53a that is designated as a felony; (15) "alcohol-dependent child" means any child who has a psychoactive substance dependence on alcohol as that condition is defined in the most recent edition of the American Psychiatric Association's "Diagnostic and Statistical Manual of Mental Disorders"; and (16) "drug-dependent child" means any child who has a psychoactive substance dependence on drugs as that condition is defined in the most recent edition of the American Psychiatric Association's "Diagnostic and Statistical Manual of Mental Disorders". No child shall be classified as drug dependent who is dependent (A) upon a morphine-type substance as an incident to current medical treatment of a demonstrable physical disorder other than drug dependence, or (B) upon amphetamine-type, ataractic, barbiturate-type, hallucinogenic or other stimulant and depressant substances as an incident to current medical treatment of a demonstrable physical or psychological disorder, or both, other than drug dependence.

(1949 Rev., § 2802; 1958 Rev., §§ 17–53, 51–301; 1959, P.A. 28, § 52; 1967, P.A. 630, § 1, eff. June 22, 1967; 1969, P.A. 794, § 1; 1971, P.A. 72, § 14; 1975, P.A. 75–602, § 1, eff. Jan. 1, 1976; 1976, P.A. 76–436, § 668, eff. July 1, 1978; 1977, P.A. 77–577, § 4; 1979, P.A. 79–567, § 1; 1979, P.A. 79–581, § 1; 1985, P.A. 85–226, § 1; 1987, P.A. 87–373, § 13; 1990, P.A. 90–161, § 1, eff. July 1, 1990; 1990, P.A. 90–240, § 2; 1990, P.A. 90–325, § 19; 1991, P.A. 91–303, § 11, eff. July 1, 1991; 1992, June Sp.Sess., P.A. 92–1, § 2; 1992, June Sp.Sess., P.A. 92–3; 1993, P.A. 93–91, § 1, eff. July 1, 1993; 1993, P.A. 93–340, § 16, eff. Oct. 1, 1993; 1995, P.A. 95–225, § 9, eff. Oct. 1, 1995; 1997, P.A. 97–319, § 18, eff. July 1, 1997; 1998, P.A. 98–256, § 1; 2000, P.A. 00–177, § 1, eff. July 1, 2001; 2002, P.A. 02–109, § 1, eff. June 7, 2002; 2002, P.A. 02–132, § 18.)

§ 46b–121. "Juvenile matters" defined. Authority of court

(a) Juvenile matters in the civil session include all proceedings concerning uncared-for, neglected or dependent children and youth within this state, termination of parental rights of children committed to a state agency, matters concerning families with service needs, contested matters involving termination of parental rights or removal of guardian transferred from the Probate Court, the emancipation of minors and youth in crisis, but does not include matters of guardianship and adoption or matters affecting property rights of any child, youth or youth in crisis over which the Probate Court has jurisdiction, provided appeals from probate concerning adoption, termination of parental rights and removal of a parent as guardian shall be included. Juvenile matters in the criminal session include all proceedings concerning delinquent children in the state and persons sixteen years of age and older who are under the supervision of a juvenile probation officer while on probation or a suspended commitment to the Department of Children and Families, for purposes of enforcing any court orders entered as part of such probation or suspended commitment.

(b) In juvenile matters, the Superior Court shall have authority to make and enforce such orders directed to parents, including any person who acknowledges before said court paternity of a child born out of wedlock, guardians, custodians or other adult persons owing some legal duty to a child, youth or youth in crisis therein, as it deems necessary or appropriate to secure the welfare, protection, proper care and suitable support of a child, youth or youth in crisis subject to its jurisdiction or otherwise committed to or in the custody of the Commissioner of Children and Families. In addition, with respect to proceedings concerning delinquent children, the Superior Court shall have authority to make and enforce such orders as it deems necessary or appropriate to punish the child, deter the child from the commission of further delinquent acts, assure that the safety of any other person will not be endangered and provide restitution to any victim. Said court shall also have authority to grant and enforce injunctive relief, temporary or permanent in all proceedings concerning juvenile matters. If any order for the payment of money is issued by said court, including any order assessing costs issued under section 46b–134 or 46b–136, the collection of such money shall be made by said court, except orders for support of children committed to any state agency or department, which orders shall be made payable to and collected by the Department of Administrative Services. Where the court after due diligence is unable to collect such moneys within six months, it shall refer such case to the Department of

Administrative Services for collection as a delinquent account. In juvenile matters, the court shall have authority to make and enforce orders directed to persons liable hereunder on petition of said Department of Administrative Services made to said court in the same manner as is provided in section 17b–745, in accordance with the provisions of section 17b–81, 17b–223, subsection (b) of section 17b–179, section 17a–90, 46b–129 or 46b–130, and all of the provisions of section 17b–745 shall be applicable to such proceedings. Any judge hearing a juvenile matter may make any other order in connection therewith that a judge of the Superior Court is authorized to grant and such order shall have the same force and effect as any other order of the Superior Court. In the enforcement of its orders, in connection with any juvenile matter, the court may issue process for the arrest of any person, compel attendance of witnesses and punish for contempt by a fine not exceeding one hundred dollars or imprisonment not exceeding six months.

(1949 Rev., § 2805; 1953, Supp. § 1188c; 1955, Supp. § 1576d; 1958 Rev., §§ 17–59, 51–302; 1969, P.A. 483; 1975, P.A. 75–171, § 1, eff. May 27, 1975; 1975, P.A. 75–602, § 3, eff. Jan. 1, 1976; 1976, P.A. 76–436, § 14, eff. July 1, 1978; 1977, P.A. 77–576, § 41, eff. July 1, 1978; 1977, P.A. 77–614, § 71, eff. Oct. 1, 1977; 1979, P.A. 79–567, § 2; 1980, P.A. 80–70, § 3; 1982, P.A. 82–472, § 128, eff. June 14, 1982; 1987, P.A. 87–421, § 9, eff. July 1, 1987; 1989, P.A. 89–219, § 2, eff. July 1, 1989; 1989, P.A. 89–273, § 1; 1993, P.A. 93–91, § 1, eff. July 1, 1993; 1995, P.A. 95–225, § 10, eff. Oct. 1, 1995; 1995, P.A. 95–254, § 2, eff. Oct. 1, 1995; 1998, P.A. 98–256, § 10; 2000, P.A. 00–170, § 33, eff. July 1, 2000; 2000, P.A. 00–177, § 2, eff. July 1, 2001.)

§ 46b–121a. Referral of juvenile matters to state referees

The Superior Court may refer any juvenile matter to a state referee who shall have been a judge of the Superior Court. Any hearing by such referee shall be conducted as provided in section 52–434. Such referee shall have and exercise the powers of the Superior Court in respect to trial, judgment and appeal in cases and matters referred pursuant to this section.

(1995, P.A. 95–225, § 29, eff. Oct. 1, 1995.)

§ 46b–121b. Handling of juvenile matters

(a) The Division of Criminal Justice shall have charge of all proceedings concerning juvenile matters in the criminal session of the Superior Court and all proceedings concerning families with service needs in the civil session of the Superior Court.

(b) The Attorney General shall have charge of all proceedings concerning juvenile matters in the civil session of the Superior Court.

(1995, P.A. 95–225, § 45, eff. July 1, 1996.)

§§ 46b–121c to 46b–121g. Reserved for future use

§ 46b–121h. Goals of juvenile justice system

It is the intent of the General Assembly that the juvenile justice system provide individualized supervision, care, accountability and treatment in a manner consistent with public safety to those juveniles who violate the law. The juvenile justice system shall also promote prevention efforts through the support of programs and services designed to meet the needs of juveniles charged with the commission of a delinquent act. The goals of the juvenile justice system shall be to:

(1) Hold juveniles accountable for their unlawful behavior;

(2) Provide secure and therapeutic confinement to those juveniles who present a danger to the community;

(3) Adequately protect the community and juveniles;

(4) Provide programs and services that are community-based and are provided in close proximity to the juvenile's community;

(5) Retain and support juveniles within their homes whenever possible and appropriate;

(6) Base probation treatment planning upon individual case management plans;

(7) Include the juvenile's family in the case management plan;

(8) Provide supervision and service coordination where appropriate and implement and monitor the case management plan in order to discourage reoffending;

(9) Provide follow-up and nonresidential postrelease services to juveniles who are returned to their families or communities;

(10) Promote the development and implementation of community-based programs including, but not limited to, mental health services, designed to prevent unlawful behavior and to effectively minimize the depth and duration of the juvenile's involvement in the juvenile justice system; and

(11) Create and maintain programs for juvenile offenders that are gender specific in that they comprehensively address the unique needs of a targeted gender group.

(1995, P.A. 95–225, § 1, eff. July 1, 1996; 2001, P.A. 01–181, § 2.)

§ 46b–121i. Duties and responsibilities of the Judicial Department in providing programs and services to the juvenile justice system

(a) The Judicial Department shall:

(1) Coordinate programs and services of the juvenile justice system with other state and municipal agencies, boards and commissions;

(2) Develop and use intake and assessment procedures for the evaluation of juveniles;

(3) Provide case management for juveniles;

(4) Provide pretrial diversion and postconviction programs;

(5) Coordinate community-based services for juveniles and their families which promote appropriate reintegration of the juvenile with his family, school and community; and

(6) Provide other programs and services necessary to the juvenile justice system.

(b) In developing its programs, the Judicial Department shall:

(1) Develop risk and assessment instruments for use in determining the need for detention or other placement at the time a juvenile enters the system;

(2) Develop a case classification process to include the establishment of classification program levels and case management standards for each program level. A program level is based on the needs of the juvenile, his potential to be dangerous and his risk of offending further;

(3) Develop a purchase-of-care system, which will facilitate the development of a state-wide community-based continuum of care, with the involvement of the private sector and the local public sector. Care services may be purchased from private providers to provide a wider diversity of services. This system shall include accessing Title IV–E funds of the federal Social Security Act, as amended,[1] new Medicaid funds and other funding sources to support eligible community-based services. Such services developed and purchased shall include, but not be limited to, evaluation services which shall be available on a geographically accessible basis across the state.

(1995, P.A. 95–225, §§ 2, 4, eff. July 1, 1996.)

1 42 U.S.C.A. § 670 et seq.

§ 46b–121j. Programs and probation treatment services for juvenile offenders

(a) The Court Support Services Division shall design and make available to the Judicial Department programs and probation treatment services for juvenile offenders. The programs and treatment services shall be based upon the individual or family assessment and evaluation process and case management plan.

(b) Probation treatment services shall address:

(1) Behavioral impairments and other emotional disturbances and other mental health or psychiatric disorders;

(2) Histories of physical or sexual abuse;

(3) Drug and alcohol addiction;

(4) Health and medical needs;

(5) Education, special education and related services.

(c) Available programs shall include:

(1) Individual, group and family counseling services and all other programs and services as appropriate with any case management plan related to subsection (b) of this section.

(2) The design and delivery of probation treatment programs following the requirements stated within Title XIX and Title IV–E of the federal Social Security Act, as amended,[1] the Special Education Act[2] and other funding guidelines, as appropriate. It is the intent of the General Assembly that these funding sources shall be utilized to support service needs of eligible juveniles.

(1995, P.A. 95–225, § 3, eff. July 1, 1996; 2002, P.A. 02–132, § 19.)

1 42 U.S.C.A. §§ 1396 et seq. and 670 et seq.

2 So in original. See 20 U.S.C.A. § 1400 et seq.

§ 46b–121k. Programs, services and facilities for juvenile offenders

(a) The Court Support Services Division shall be charged with the duty of developing constructive programs for the prevention and reduction of delinquency and crime among juvenile offenders. To that end, the executive director of the Court Support Services Division shall cooperate with other agencies to encourage the establishment of new programs and to provide a continuum of services for juvenile offenders who do not require secure placement. The programs shall be tailored to the type of juvenile including the juvenile's offense history, age, gender, mental health and chemical dependency problem, and other characteristics. The Court Support Services Division shall develop programs that provide: (1) Intensive general educational programs, with an individual educational plan for each juvenile; (2) specific educational components in the management of anger and nonviolent conflict resolution; (3) treatment for chemical dependency; (4) mental health screening, assessment and treatment; and (5) sexual offender treatment.

(b) The Judicial Department may contract to establish regional secure residential facilities and regional highly supervised residential and nonresidential facilities for juveniles referred by the court. Such facilities shall operate within contracted-for capacity limits. Such facilities shall be exempt from the licensing requirements of section 17a–145.

(c) The Court Support Services Division shall collaborate with private residential facilities providing residential programs and with community-based nonresidential postrelease programs.

(d) Any program developed by the Court Support Services Division that is designed to prevent or reduce delinquency and crime among juvenile offenders shall be gender specific, as necessary, and shall comprehensively address the unique needs of a targeted gender group.

(1995, P.A. 95–225, § 6, eff. July 1, 1996; 1998, P.A. 98–256, § 2; 2001, P.A. 01–181, § 3; 2002, P.A. 02–132, § 20.)

§ 46b–121*l*. Early intervention projects for juvenile offenders

(a) The Court Support Services Division shall fund projects for a program of early intervention initiatives designed for juvenile offenders. The projects may include, but not be limited to, the following initiatives:

(1) A peer tutoring project designed for juvenile offenders required to perform community services;

(2) Specialized residential services for juvenile offenders on probation who have been expelled from school;

(3) Social services and counseling for female juvenile offenders;

(4) Training in cognitive skill building;

(5) A self-supporting entrepreneurship program; and

(6) A mentoring program designed to match juveniles with positive adult role models.

(b) The primary purpose of these projects shall be to provide a network of community services for juvenile offenders. The Court Support Services Division shall develop evaluation protocols designed to assess the impact of components of these projects on deterring juvenile crime in the communities where the projects operate.

(1995, P.A. 95–225, § 7, eff. July 1, 1996; 2002, P.A. 02–132, § 21.)

§ 46b–121m. Evaluation of the costs and benefits of programs serving juvenile offenders

(a) The Chief Court Administrator shall enter into an agreement with the Connecticut Policy and Economic Council to evaluate the costs and benefits of programs serving juvenile offenders, whether offered by private providers or state or municipal agencies, to determine the cost-effectiveness of such programs in reducing recidivism.

(b) For the purposes of subsection (a) of this section, there is established an advisory board to be composed of the Commissioner of Children and Families, the Commissioner of Correction and the Chief Court Administrator, or their designees, and the chairpersons and ranking members of the joint standing committees of the General Assembly on judiciary and human services.

(c) The evaluation shall identify the types of programs that are effective and not effective in reducing criminal offending in a cost-beneficial way. The evaluation shall use uniform data collection and a common methodological approach to compare programs serving juvenile offenders. The evaluation shall include, but not be limited to, a determination of the extent to which each program:

(1) Targets diverted and adjudicated juvenile offenders;

(2) Includes assessment methods to determine services, programs, and intervention strategies most likely to change behaviors and norms of juvenile offenders;

(3) Provides maximum structured supervision in the community using natural surveillance and community guardians such as employers, relatives, teachers, clergy and community mentors to the greatest extent possible;

(4) Promotes good work ethic values and educational skills and competencies necessary for the juvenile offender to function effectively and positively in the community;

(5) Maximizes the efficient delivery of treatment services aimed at reducing risk factors associated with the commission of juvenile offenses;

(6) Maximizes the reintegration of the juvenile offender into the community upon release from confinement;

(7) Maximizes the juvenile offender's opportunities to make full restitution to the victims and amends to the community;

(8) Supports and encourages increased court discretion in imposing community-based intervention strategies;

(9) Is compatible with research that shows which prevention and early intervention strategies work with juvenile offenders;

(10) Is outcome-based in that it describes what outcomes will be achieved or what outcomes have already been achieved;

(11) Includes an evaluation component; and

(12) Recognizes the diversity of local needs.

(d) Not later than January 1, 2001, the council shall submit a preliminary report on its activities to the joint standing committees of the General Assembly on judiciary and human services.

(2000, P.A. 00–172.)

§ 46b–122. Juvenile matters separated from other court business if practicable. Exclusion of persons from hearing

All matters which are juvenile matters, as provided in section 46b–121, shall be kept separate and apart from all other business of the Superior Court as far as is practicable, except matters transferred under the provisions of section 46b–127, which matters shall be transferred to the regular criminal docket of the Superior Court. Any judge hearing a juvenile matter may, during such hearing, exclude from the room in which such hearing is held any person whose presence is, in the court's opinion, not necessary, except that in delinquency proceedings any victim of the delinquent act, the parents or guardian of such victim and any victim advocate appointed pursuant to section 54–221 shall not be excluded unless the judge specifically orders otherwise.

(1958 Rev., § 51–303; 1976, P.A. 76–436, § 8, eff. July 1, 1978; 1977, P.A. 77–576, § 42, eff. July 1, 1978; 1978, P.A. 78–379, § 10, eff. July 1, 1978; 1995, P.A. 95–225, § 11, eff. Oct. 1, 1995; 2003, P.A. 03–202, § 7.)

§ 46b–123. Appointment of staff for juvenile matters

The judges of the superior court, or in the discretion of the chief court administrator, a committee of said judges designated by the chief court administrator, shall appoint such probation officers, probation aides, clerks, detention personnel, clerical assistants and other personnel, including supervisory staff, as they deem necessary for the treatment and handling of juvenile matters within the venue districts established under section 46b–142. The Chief Court Administrator may assign, reassign and modify the assignments of such personnel and assign such duties within the superior court as he deems necessary for the efficient operation of the courts. Any person serving in any such capacity in the juvenile court on July 1, 1978, shall continue to serve in the superior court at the compensation he was receiving in the juvenile court under the compensation plan established pursuant to section 51–12, for the remainder of any term to which he was appointed. In no event shall the compensation of any such person be affected solely as a result of the transfer of jurisdiction in section 51–164s. Any of such appointees may be discharged by the appointing authority for cause and after hearing. The salaries of each of such officials shall be fixed by the judges, subject to the provisions of section 51–12.

(1949 Rev., § 2821; 1957, P.A. 651, § 17; 1958 Rev., §§ 17–57, 51–304; 1967, P.A. 630, § 4, eff. June 22, 1967; 1969, P.A. 794, § 2; 1975, P.A. 75–327; 1976, P.A. 76–436, §§ 10a, 12, eff. July 1, 1978; 1984, P.A. 84–198, § 4, eff. May 23, 1984.)

§ 46b–123a. Transfer of personnel to Division of Criminal Justice

All persons employed as court advocates, inspectors or investigators, and associated staff, by the Judicial Department on July 1, 1996, shall be transferred to the Division of Criminal Justice on said date.

(1995, P.A. 95–225, § 49, eff. July 1, 1996.)

§ 46b–123b. Transfer of juvenile justice centers to Judicial Department

Juvenile justice centers within the Office of Policy and Management for administrative purposes shall, on and after July 1, 1996, or upon the cessation of receipt of federal funds, whichever is later, be within the Judicial Department.

(1995, P.A. 95–225, § 44, eff. July 1, 1996.)

§ 46b–124. Confidentiality of records of juvenile matters. Exceptions

(a) For the purposes of this section, "records of cases of juvenile matters" includes, but is not limited to, court records, records regarding juveniles maintained by the Court Support Services Division, records regarding juveniles maintained by an organization or agency that has contracted with the judicial branch to provide services to juveniles, records of law enforcement agencies including fingerprints, photographs and physical descriptions, and medical, psychological, psychiatric and social welfare studies and reports by probation officers, public or private institutions, social agencies and clinics.

(b) All records of cases of juvenile matters, as provided in section 46b–121, except delinquency proceedings, or any part thereof, and all records of appeals from probate brought to the superior court for juvenile matters pursuant to subsection (b) of section 45a–186, shall be confidential and for the use of the court in juvenile matters, and open to inspection or disclosure to any third party, including bona fide researchers commissioned by a state agency, only upon order of the Superior Court, except that (1) the records concerning any matter transferred from a court of probate pursuant to section 45a–623 or subsection (g) of section 45a–715 or any appeal from probate to the superior court for juvenile matters pursuant to subsection (b) of section 45a–186 shall be available to the court of probate from which such matter was transferred or from which such appeal was taken, (2) such records shall be available to (A) the attorney representing the child or youth, including the Division of Public Defender Services, in any proceeding in which such records are relevant, (B) the parents or guardian of the child or youth until such time as the child or youth reaches the age of majority or becomes emancipated, (C) an adult adopted person in accordance with the provisions of sections 45a–736, 45a–737 and 45a–743 to 45a–757, inclusive, (D) employees of the Division of Criminal Justice who in the performance of their duties require access to such records, (E) employees of the judicial branch who in the performance of their duties require access to such records, (F) another court under the provisions of subsection (d) of section 46b–115j, (G) the subject of the record, upon submission of satisfactory proof of the subject's identity, pursuant to guidelines prescribed by the Office of the Chief Court Administrator, provided the subject has reached the age of majority or has been emancipated, and (H) the Department of Children and Families. Any records of cases of juvenile matters, or any part thereof, provided to any persons, governmental and private agencies, and institutions pursuant to this section shall not be disclosed, directly or indirectly, to any third party not specified in subsection (d) of this section, except as provided by court order or in the report required under section 54–76d or 54–91a.

(c) All records of cases of juvenile matters involving delinquency proceedings, or any part thereof, shall be confidential and for the use of the court in juvenile matters and shall not be disclosed except as provided in this section.

(d) Records of cases of juvenile matters involving delinquency proceedings shall be available to (1) judicial branch employees who, in the performance of their duties, require access to such records, and (2) employees and authorized agents of state or federal agencies involved in (A) the delinquency proceedings, (B) the provision of services directly to the child, or (C) the design and delivery of treatment programs pursuant to section 46b–121j. Such employees and authorized agents include, but are not limited to, law enforcement officials, state and federal prosecutorial officials, school officials in accordance with section 10–233h, court officials including officials of both the regular criminal docket and the docket for juvenile matters, officials of the Division of Criminal Justice, the Division of Public Defender Services, the Department of Children and Families, the Court Support Services Division, the Board of Parole and agencies under contract with the judicial branch, and an advocate appointed pursuant to section 54–221 for a victim of a crime committed by the child. Such records shall also be available to (i) the attorney representing the child, including the Division of Public Defender Services, in any proceeding in which such records are relevant, (ii) the parents or guardian of the child, until such time as the subject of the record reaches the age of majority, (iii) the subject of the record, upon submission of satisfactory proof of the subject's identity, pursuant to guidelines prescribed by the Office of the Chief Court Administrator, provided the subject has reached the age of majority, (iv) law enforcement officials and prosecutorial officials conducting legitimate criminal investigations, and (v) a state or federal agency providing services related to the collection of moneys due or funding to support the service needs of eligible juveniles, provided such disclosure shall be limited to that information necessary for the collection of and application for such moneys. Records disclosed pursuant to this subsection shall not be further disclosed, except that information contained in such records may be disclosed in connection with bail or sentencing reports in open court during criminal proceedings involving the subject of such information.

(e) Records of cases of juvenile matters involving delinquency proceedings, or any part thereof, may be disclosed upon order of the court to any person who has a legitimate interest in the information and is identified in such order. Records disclosed pursuant to this subsection shall not be further disclosed.

(f) Records of cases of juvenile matters involving delinquency proceedings, or any part thereof, shall be available to the victim of the crime committed by such child to the same extent as the record of the case of a defendant in a criminal proceeding in the regular criminal docket of the Superior Court is available to a victim of the crime committed by such defendant. The court shall designate an official from whom such victim may request such information. Records disclosed pursuant to this subsection shall not be further disclosed.

(g) Information concerning a child who has escaped from a detention center or from a facility to which he has been committed by the court or for whom an arrest warrant has been issued with respect to the commission of a felony may be disclosed by law enforcement officials.

(h) Nothing in this section shall be construed to prohibit any person employed by the judicial branch from disclosing any records, information or files in his possession to any person employed by the Division of Criminal Justice as a prosecutorial official, inspector or investigator who, in the performance of his duties, requests such records, information or files, or to prohibit any such employee of said division from disclosing any records, information or files in his possession to any such employee of the judicial branch who, in the performance of his duties, requests such records, information or files.

(i) A state's attorney shall disclose to the defendant or his counsel in a criminal prosecution, without the necessity of a court order, exculpatory information and material contained in any record disclosed to such state's attorney pursuant to this section and may disclose, without a court order, information and material contained in any such record which could be the subject of a disclosure order.

(1958 Rev., §§ 17–57a, 51–305; 1969, P.A. 794, § 3; 1975, P.A. 75–602, § 2, eff. Jan. 1, 1976; 1976, P.A. 76–436, § 13, eff. July 1, 1978; 1977, P.A. 77–246, § 11; 1977, P.A. 77–486, § 1, eff. Oct. 1, 1977; 1977, P.A. 77–486, § 2, eff. July 1, 1978; 1978, P.A. 78–280, § 92, eff. July 1, 1978; 1978, P.A. 78–318, § 27; 1979, P.A. 79–456; 1980, P.A. 80–165, § 1; 1981, P.A. 81–472, § 82, eff. July 8, 1981; 1982, P.A. 82–140, § 1; 1993, P.A. 93–48, 1994, P.A. 94–221, § 15; 1994, July Sp.Sess., P.A. 94–2, § 10; 1995, P.A. 95–225, § 12, eff. Oct. 1, 1995; 1995, P.A. 95–254, § 3, eff. Oct. 1, 1995; 1995, P.A. 95–261, § 1; 1996, P.A. 96–246, § 35; 1998, P.A. 98–70, § 1; 1999, P.A. 99–185, § 35, eff. July 1, 2000; 2002, P.A. 02–132, § 22; 2003, P.A. 03–202, § 8.)

§ 46b–125. Juvenile probation officers and juvenile matters investigators. Rights in retirement system. Duties and authority

(a) All persons employed as full-time juvenile probation officers in service in this state on January 1, 1941, and appointed without examination in the first instance juvenile probation officers of this court, shall retain full rights in any pension system or retirement fund in which they participated or to which they contributed.

(b) Probation officers shall make such investigations and reports as the court directs or the law requires. They shall execute the orders of the court; and, for that purpose, such probation officers, and any other employees specifically designated by the court to assist the probation officers in the enforcement of such orders, shall have the authority of a state marshal. They shall preserve a record of all cases investigated or coming under their care, and shall keep informed concerning the conduct and condition of each person under supervision and report thereon to the court as it may direct. Any juvenile probation officer authorized by the Office of the Chief Court Administrator, and any juvenile matters investigator authorized by the Office of the Chief State's Attorney, may arrest any juvenile on probation without a warrant or may deputize any other officer with power to arrest to do so by giving such officer a written statement setting forth that the juvenile has, in the judgment of the juvenile probation officer or juvenile matters investigator, violated the conditions of the juvenile's probation. When executing such orders of the court, except when using deadly physical force, juvenile probation officers and juvenile matters investigators shall be deemed to be acting in the capacity of a peace officer, as defined in subdivision (9) of section 53a–3.

(1949 Rev., § 2822; 1958 Rev., §§ 17–58, 51–306; 1969, P.A. 794, § 5; 1977, P.A. 77–614, § 66, eff. Oct. 1, 1977; 1984, P.A. 84–198, § 5, eff. May 23, 1984; 1993, P.A. 93–391; 2000, P.A. 00–99, § 90; 2001, P.A. 01–84, § 3, eff. July 1, 2001; 2001, P.A. 01–195, § 36, eff. July 11, 2001.)

§ 46b–126. Secure facilities for care and treatment of children

There shall be established or designated by the Department of Children and Families a secure facility or facilities within the state devoted to the care and treatment of children, which children are under the jurisdiction of the Superior Court. A consideration for admission to such a facility shall be adjudication for a serious juvenile offense.

(1958 Rev., §§ 17–60, 51–307; 1971, P.A. 170; 1976, P.A. 76–194, § 4; 1976, P.A. 76–436, § 17, eff. July 1, 1978; 1977, P.A. 77–326; 1977, P.A. 77–452, § 23, eff. July 1, 1978; 1979, P.A. 79–581, § 2; 1983, P.A. 83–402, § 1; 1984, P.A. 84–252; 1986, P.A. 86–185, § 1; 1989, P.A. 89–273, § 2; 1990, P.A. 90–136, § 1; 1990, P.A. 90–187, § 1, eff. July 1, 1991; 1993, P.A. 93–91, § 1, eff. July 1, 1993; 1995, P.A. 95–225, § 39, eff. Oct. 1, 1995.)

§ 46b–127. Transfer of child charged with a felony to the regular criminal docket

(a) The court shall automatically transfer from the docket for juvenile matters to the regular criminal docket of the Superior Court the case of any child charged with the commission of a capital felony, a class A or B felony or a violation of section 53a–54d, provided such offense was committed after such child attained the age of fourteen years and counsel has been appointed for such child if such child is indigent. Such counsel may appear with the child but shall not be permitted to make any argument or file any motion in opposition to the transfer. The child shall be arraigned in the regular criminal docket of the Superior Court at the next court date following such transfer. The file of any case so transferred shall remain sealed until the end of the tenth working day following such arraignment unless the state's attorney has filed a motion pursuant to this subsection in which case such file shall remain sealed until the court makes a decision on the motion. A state's attorney may, not later than ten working days after such arraignment, file a motion to transfer the case of any child charged with the commission of a class B felony to the docket for juvenile matters for proceedings in accordance with the provisions of this chapter. The court sitting for the regular criminal docket shall, after hearing and not later than ten working days after the filing of such motion, decide such motion.

(b) Upon motion of a juvenile prosecutor and order of the court, the case of any child charged with the commission of a class C or D felony or an unclassified felony shall be transferred from the docket for juvenile matters to the regular criminal docket of the Superior Court, provided such offense was committed after such child attained the age of fourteen years and the court finds ex parte that there is probable cause to believe the child has committed the act for which he is charged. The file of any case so transferred shall remain sealed until such time as the court sitting for the regular criminal docket accepts such transfer. The court sitting for the regular criminal docket may return any such case to the docket for juvenile matters not later than ten working days after the date of the transfer for proceedings in accordance with the provisions of this chapter. The child shall be arraigned in the regular criminal docket of the Superior Court by the next court date following such transfer.

(c) Upon the effectuation of the transfer, such child shall stand trial and be sentenced, if convicted, as if he were sixteen years of age. Such child shall receive credit against any sentence imposed for time served in a juvenile facility prior to the effectuation of the transfer. A child who has been transferred may enter a guilty plea to a lesser offense if the court finds that such plea is made knowingly and voluntarily. Any child transferred to the regular criminal docket who pleads guilty to a lesser offense shall not resume his status as a juvenile regarding said offense. If the action is dismissed or nolled or if such child is found not guilty of the charge for which he was transferred or of any lesser included offenses, the child shall resume his status as a juvenile until he attains the age of sixteen years.

(d) Any child transferred to the regular criminal docket of the Superior Court who is detained shall be in the custody of the Commissioner of Correction upon the finalization of such transfer. A transfer shall be final (1) upon the expiration of ten working days after the arraignment if no motion has been filed by the state's attorney pursuant to subsection (a) of this section or, if such motion has been filed, upon the decision of the court to deny such motion, or (2) upon the court accepting the transfer pursuant to subsection (b) of this section. Any child returned to the docket for juvenile matters who is detained shall be in the custody of the Judicial Department.

(e) The transfer of a child to a Department of Correction facility shall be limited to the provisions of subsection (d) of this section and said subsection shall not be construed to permit the transfer of or otherwise reduce or eliminate any other population of juveniles in detention or confinement within the Judicial Department or the Department of Children and Families.

(1958 Rev., §§ 17–60b, 51–308; 1975, P.A. 75–620, §§ 1 to 4, eff. Jan. 1, 1976; 1976, P.A. 76–194, § 3; 1976, P.A. 76–436, §§ 18 to 20, eff. July 1, 1978; 1979, P.A. 79–581, § 3; 1983, P.A. 83–402, § 2; 1986, P.A. 86–185, § 2; 1990, P.A. 90–136, § 2; 1990, P.A. 90–187, § 2, eff. July 1, 1991; 1994, July Sp.Sess., P.A. 94–2, § 6; 1995, P.A. 95–225, § 13, eff. Oct. 1, 1995; 1997, P.A. 97–4, § 1, eff. March 20, 1997; 1997, P.A. 97–319, § 21, eff. July 1, 1997; 1998, P.A. 98–256, § 3.)

§ 46b–128. Investigation of delinquency complaint. Nonjudicial disposition. Petition of delinquency. Summoning of child and parent or guardian

(a) Whenever the Superior Court is in receipt of any written complaint filed by any person, any public or private agency or any federal, state, city or town department maintaining that a child's conduct constitutes delinquency within the meaning of section 46b–120, it shall make a preliminary investigation to determine whether the facts, if true, would be sufficient to be a juvenile matter and whether the interests of the public or the child require that further action be taken. If so, the court may authorize the filing of a verified petition of alleged delinquency or it may make without such petition whatever nonjudicial disposition is practicable, including the ordering of such child to do work of which he is capable in public buildings or on public property, particularly in cases in which the complaint alleges that the conduct of such child resulted in the wilful destruction of property, provided the facts establishing jurisdiction are admitted and that a competent acceptance of such a disposition has been given by the child and his parent or guardian. If a nonjudicial disposition is made, the term of any nonjudicial supervision shall be established by the juvenile probation supervisor provided such period of supervision shall not exceed one hundred eighty days. Each verified petition of delinquency filed by the court shall set forth plainly (1) the facts which bring the child within the jurisdiction of the court, (2) the name, date of birth, sex and residence of the child, (3) the names and residence of his parent or parents, guardian or other person having control of the child, and (4) a prayer for appropriate action by the court in conformity with the provisions of this chapter.

(b) Upon the filing of a delinquency petition, the court may, either forthwith or after investigation, cause a summons, which summons shall have a copy of said verified petition attached thereto, signed by the judge or by the clerk or assistant clerk of such court, to be issued, requiring the child and the parent or parents, guardian or other person having control of the child to appear in court at the time and place therein specified. Whenever it appears to the judge that orders addressed to an adult, as set forth in section 46b–121, are necessary for the welfare of such child, a similar summons shall be issued and served upon such adult if such adult is not already in court. Service of summons, together with a copy of the verified petition, may be made by any one of the following methods: (1) By the delivery of a true and attested copy thereof to the person summoned, or at such person's usual place of abode; (2) by restricted delivery addressed to the person summoned, return receipt requested; or (3) by first class mail addressed to the person summoned. Any notice sent by first class mail shall include a provision informing the party that appearance in court as a result of the notice may subject the appearing party to the jurisdiction of the court. If service is made by first class mail and the party does not appear, no order may be entered by the court in the case. If, after reasonable effort, personal service has not been made, such substitute service, by publication or otherwise, as the judge may order, shall be sufficient. Service may be made by any officer authorized by law to serve process, or by a probation officer, probation aide or indifferent person, and the court may allow suitable expenses and a reasonable fee therefor. The court may punish for contempt, as provided in section 46b–121, any parent, guardian or other person so summoned who fails to appear in court at the time and place so specified.

(1949 Rev., § 2807; 1958 Rev., § 17–61, 51–309; 1967, P.A. 630, § 6, eff. June 22, 1967; 1969, P.A. 794, § 6; 1975, P.A. 75–157; 1975, P.A. 75–226, § 1; 1976, P.A. 76–436, § 15, eff. July 1, 1978; 1995, P.A. 95–225, § 14, eff. Oct. 1, 1995; 2000, P.A. 00–196, § 27.)

§ 46b–129. Commitment of child or youth. Petition for neglected, uncared-for, dependent child or youth. Hearing re temporary custody, order to appear or petition. Review of permanency plan. Revocation of commitment

(a) Any selectman, town manager, or town, city, or borough welfare department, any probation officer, or the Commissioner of Social Services, the Commissioner of Children and Families or any child-caring institution or agency approved by the Commissioner of Children and Families, a child or such child's representative or attorney or a foster parent of a child, having information that a child or youth is neglected, uncared-for or dependent, may file with the Superior Court which has venue over such matter a verified petition plainly stating such facts as bring the child or youth within the jurisdiction of the court as neglected, uncared-for, or dependent, within the meaning of section 46b–120, the name, date of birth, sex, and residence of the child or youth, the name and residence of such child's parents or guardian, and praying for appropriate action by the court in conformity with the provisions of this chapter. Upon the filing of such a petition, except as otherwise provided in subsection (k) of section 17a–112, the court shall cause a summons to be issued requiring the parent or parents or the guardian of the child or youth to appear in court at the time and place named, which summons shall be served not less than fourteen days before the date of the hearing in the manner prescribed by section 46b–128, and said court shall further give notice to the petitioner and to the Commissioner of Children and Families of the time and place when the petition is to be heard not less than fourteen days prior to the hearing in question.

(b) If it appears from the specific allegations of the petition and other verified affirmations of fact accompanying the petition and application, or subsequent thereto, that there is reasonable cause to believe that (1) the child or youth is suffering from serious physical illness or serious physical injury or is in immediate physical danger from the child's or youth's surroundings, and (2) that as a result of said conditions, the child's or youth's safety is endangered and immediate removal from such surroundings is necessary to ensure the child's or youth's safety, the court shall either (A) issue an order to the parents or other person having responsibility for the care of the child or youth to appear at such time as the court may designate to determine whether the court should vest in some suitable agency or person the child's or youth's temporary care and custody pending disposition of the petition, or (B) issue an order ex parte vesting in some suitable agency or person the child's or youth's temporary care and custody. A preliminary hearing on any ex parte custody order or order to appear issued by the court shall be held within ten days from the issuance of such order. The service of such orders may be made by any officer authorized by law to serve process, or by any probation officer appointed in accordance with section 46b–123, investigator from the Department of Administrative Services, state or local police officer or indifferent person. Such orders shall include a conspicuous notice to the respondent written in clear and simple language containing at least the following information: (i) That the order contains allegations that conditions in the home have endangered the safety and welfare of the child or youth; (ii) that a hearing will be held on the date on the form; (iii) that the hearing is the opportunity to present the parents' position concerning the alleged facts; (iv) that an attorney will be appointed for parents who cannot afford an attorney; (v) that such parents may apply for a court-appointed attorney by going in person to the court address on the form and are advised to go as soon as possible in order for the attorney to prepare for the hearing; and (vi) if such parents have any questions concerning the case or appointment of counsel, any such parent is advised to go to the court or call the clerk's office at the court as soon as possible. Upon application for appointed counsel, the court shall promptly determine eligibility and, if the respondent is eligible, promptly appoint counsel. The expense for any temporary care and custody shall be paid by the town in which such child or youth is at the time residing, and such town shall be reimbursed therefor by the town found liable for the child's or youth's support, except that where a state agency has filed a petition pursuant to the provisions of subsection (a) of this section, the agency shall pay such expense. The agency shall give primary consideration to placing the child or youth in the town where such child or youth resides. The agency shall file in writing with the clerk of the court the reasons for placing the child or youth in a particular placement outside the town where the child or youth resides. Upon issuance of an ex parte order, the court shall provide to the commissioner and the parent or guardian specific steps necessary for each to take to address the ex parte order for the parent or guardian to retain or regain custody of the child or youth. Upon the issuance of such order, or not later than sixty days after the issuance of such order, the court shall make a determination whether the Department of Children and Families made reasonable efforts to keep the child or youth with his or her parents or guardian prior to the issuance of such order and, if such efforts were not made, whether such reasonable efforts were not possible, taking into consideration the child's or youth's best interests, including the child's or youth's health and safety.

(c) In any proceeding under this section, any grandparent of the child may make a motion to intervene and the court shall grant such motion except for good cause shown. Upon the granting of such motion, such grandparent may appear by counsel or in person.

(d) The preliminary hearing on the order of temporary custody or order to appear or the first hearing on a petition filed pursuant to subsection (a) of this section shall be held in order for the court to: (1) Advise the parent or guardian of the allegations contained in all petitions and applications that are the subject of the hearing; (2) assure that an attorney, and where appropriate, a separate guardian ad litem has been appointed to represent the child or youth in accordance with section 46b–129a and section 46b–136; (3) upon request, appoint an attorney to represent the respondent when the respondent is unable to afford representation, as determined by the court; (4) advise the parent or guardian of the right to a hearing on the petitions and applications, to be held within ten days from the date of the preliminary hearing if the hearing is pursuant to an order of temporary custody or an order to show cause; (5) accept a plea regarding the truth of such allegations; (6) make any interim orders, including visitation, that the court determines are in the best interests of the child or youth. The court, after a hearing pursuant to this subsection, shall order specific steps the commissioner and the parent or guardian shall take for the parent or guardian to regain or to retain custody of the child or youth; (7) take steps to determine the identity of the father of the child or youth, including ordering genetic testing, if necessary, and order service of the petition and notice of the hearing date, if any, to be made upon him; (8) if the person named as the father appears, and admits that he is the father, provide him and the mother with the notices which comply with section 17b–27 and provide them with the opportunity to sign a paternity acknowledgment and affirmation on forms which comply with section 17b–27. These documents shall be executed and filed in accordance with chapter 815y [1] and a copy delivered to the clerk of the superior court for juvenile matters; and (9) in the event that the person named as a father appears and denies that he is the father of the child or youth, advise him that he may have no further standing in any proceeding concerning the child, and either order genetic testing to determine paternity or direct him to execute a written denial of paternity on a form promulgated by the Office of the Chief Court Administrator. Upon execution of such a form by the putative father, the court may remove him from the case and afford him no further standing in the case or in any subsequent proceeding regarding the child or youth until such time as paternity is established by formal acknowledgment or adjudication in a court of competent jurisdiction.

(e) If any parent or guardian fails, after service of such order, to appear at the preliminary hearing the court may enter or sustain an order of temporary custody.

(f) Upon request, or upon its own motion, the court shall schedule a hearing on the order for temporary custody or the order to show cause to be held within ten days from the date of the preliminary hearing. Such hearing shall be held on consecutive days except for compelling circumstances or at the request of the parent or guardian.

(g) At a contested hearing on the order for temporary custody or order to appear, credible hearsay evidence regarding statements of the child or youth made to a mandated reporter or to a parent may be offered by the parties and admitted by the court upon a finding that the statement is reliable and trustworthy and that admission of such statement is reasonably necessary. A signed statement executed by a mandated reporter under oath may be admitted by the court without the need for the mandated reporter to appear and testify unless called by a respondent or the child, provided the statement: (1) Was provided at the preliminary hearing and promptly upon request to any counsel appearing after the preliminary hearing; (2) reasonably describes the qualifications of the reporter and the nature of his contact with the child; and (3) contains only the direct observations of the reporter, and statements made to the reporter that would be admissible if the reporter were to testify to them in court and any opinions reasonably based thereupon. If a respondent or the child gives notice at the preliminary hearing that he intends to cross-examine the reporter, the person filing the petition shall make the reporter available for such examination at the contested hearing.

(h) If any parent or guardian fails, after due notice of the hearing scheduled pursuant to subsection (g) of this section and without good cause, to appear at the scheduled date for a contested hearing on the order of temporary custody or order to appear, the court may enter or sustain an order of temporary custody.

(i) When a petition is filed in said court for the commitment of a child or youth, the Commissioner of Children and Families shall make a thorough investigation of the case and shall cause to be made a thorough physical and mental examination of the child or youth if requested by the court. The court after hearing may also order a thorough physical or mental examination, or both, of a parent or guardian whose competency or ability to care for a child or youth before the court is at issue. The expenses incurred in making such physical and mental examinations shall be paid as costs of commitment are paid.

(j) Upon finding and adjudging that any child or youth is uncared-for, neglected or dependent, the court may commit such child or youth to the Commissioner of Children and Families. Such commitment shall remain in effect until further order of the court pursuant to the provisions of subsection (k) of this section, provided such commitment may be revoked or parental rights terminated at any time by the court, or the court may vest such child's or youth's care and personal custody in any private or public agency which is permitted by law to care for neglected, uncared-for or dependent children or youth or with any person or persons found to be suitable and worthy of such responsibility by the court. The court shall order specific steps which the parent must take to facilitate the return of the child or youth to the custody of such parent. The commissioner shall be the guardian of such child or youth for the duration of the commitment, provided the child or youth has not reached the age of eighteen years or, in the case of a child or youth in full-time attendance in a secondary school, a technical school, a college or a state-accredited job training program, provided such child or youth has not reached the age of twenty-one years, by consent of such youth, or until another guardian has been legally appointed, and in like manner, upon such vesting of the care of such child or youth, such other public or private agency or individual shall be the guardian of such child or youth until such child or youth has reached the age of eighteen years or, in the case of a child or youth in full-time attendance in a secondary school, a technical school, a college or a state-accredited job training program, until such child or youth has reached the age of twenty-one years or until another guardian has been legally appointed. Said commissioner may place any child or youth so committed to the commissioner in a suitable foster home or in the home of a person related by blood to such child or youth or in a licensed child-caring institution or in the care and custody of any accredited, licensed or approved child-caring agency, within or without the state, provided a child shall not be placed outside the state except for good cause and unless the parents or guardian of such child are notified in advance of such placement and given an opportunity to be heard, or in a receiving home maintained and operated by the Commissioner of Children and Families. In placing such child or youth, said commissioner shall, if possible, select a home, agency, institution or person of like religious faith to that of a parent of such child or youth, if such faith is known or may be ascertained by reasonable inquiry, provided such home conforms to the standards of said commissioner and the commissioner shall, when placing siblings, if possible, place such children together. As an alternative to commitment, the court may place the child or youth in the custody of the parent or guardian with protective supervision by the Commissioner of Children and Families subject to conditions established by the court. Upon the issuance of an order committing the child or youth to the Commissioner of Children and Families, or not later than sixty days after the issuance of such order, the court shall make a determination whether the Department of Children and Families made reasonable efforts to keep the child or youth with his or her parents or guardian prior to the issuance of such order and, if such efforts were not made, whether such reasonable efforts were not possible, taking into consideration the child's or youth's best interests, including the child's or youth's health and safety.

(k) (1) Nine months after placement of the child or youth in the care and custody of the commissioner pursuant to a voluntary placement agreement, or removal of a child or youth pursuant to section 17a–101g or an order issued by a court of competent jurisdiction, whichever is earlier, the commissioner shall file a motion for review of a permanency plan and to maintain or revoke the commitment. Nine months after a permanency plan has been approved by the court pursuant to this subsection, the commissioner shall file a motion for review of the permanency plan and to maintain or revoke the commitment. Any party seeking to oppose the commissioner's permanency plan or the maintaining or revocation of commitment shall file a motion in opposition within thirty days after the filing of the commissioner's motion for review of the permanency plan and to maintain or revoke commitment. A permanency hearing on any motion for review of the permanency plan and to maintain or revoke commitment shall be held within ninety days of the filing of such motion. The court shall hold evidentiary hearings in connection with any contested motion for review of the permanency plan and to maintain or revoke commitment. The burden of proof shall be upon the commissioner to establish that the commitment should be maintained. After the initial permanency hearing, subsequent permanency hearings shall be held not less frequently than every twelve months while the child or youth remains in the custody of the Commissioner of Children and Families. The court shall provide notice to the child or youth, and the parent or guardian of such child or youth of the time and place of the court hearing on any such motion not less than fourteen days prior to such hearing.

(2) At a permanency hearing held in accordance with the provisions of subdivision (1) of this subsection, the court shall determine whether it is appropriate to continue to make reasonable efforts to reunify the child or youth with the parent, unless the court has previously determined that such efforts are not appropriate pursuant to this subdivision or section 17a–111b. In making this determination, the court shall consider the best interests of the child, including the child's need for permanency. If the court finds upon clear and convincing evidence that further efforts are not appropriate, the commissioner has no duty to make further efforts to reunify the child or youth with the parent. If the court finds that further efforts are appropriate, such efforts shall ensure that the child or youth's health and safety are protected and such efforts shall be specified by the court, including the services to be provided to the parent, what steps the parent may take to address the problem that prevents the child or youth from safely reuniting with the parent and a time period, not longer than six months, for such steps to be accomplished.

(3) At a permanency hearing held in accordance with the provisions of subdivision (1) of this subsection, the court shall approve a permanency plan that is in the best interests of the child or youth and takes into consideration the child's or youth's need for permanency. The child's or youth's health and safety shall be of paramount concern in formulating such plan. Such permanency plan may include the goal of (A) revocation of commitment and placement of the child or youth with the parent or guardian, with or without protective supervision; (B) transfer of guardianship; (C) long-term foster care with a relative licensed as a foster parent or certified as a relative caregiver; (D) adoption and filing of termination of parental rights; or (E) such other planned permanent living arrangement ordered by the court, provided the Commissioner of Children and Families has documented a compelling reason why it would not be in the best interest of the child or youth for the permanency plan to include the goals in subparagraphs (A) to (D), inclusive, of this subdivision. Such other planned permanent living arrangement may include, but not be limited to, placement of a child or youth in an independent living program or long term foster care with an identified foster parent.

(4) At a permanency hearing held in accordance with the provisions of subdivision (1) of this subsection, the court shall review the status of the child, the progress being made to implement the permanency plan, deter-

mine a timetable for attaining the permanency plan and determine whether the commissioner has made reasonable efforts to achieve the permanency plan. The court shall maintain commitment if it is in the best interests of the child or youth. The court shall revoke commitment if a cause for commitment no longer exists and it is in the best interests of the child or youth.

(5) If the court approves the permanency plan of adoption: (A) The Commissioner of Children and Families may conduct a thorough adoption assessment and child-specific recruitment; and (B) the court may order that the child be photo-listed within thirty days if the court determines that such photo-listing is in the best interest of the child. As used in this subdivision, "thorough adoption assessment" means conducting and documenting face-to-face interviews with the child, foster care providers, and other significant parties and "child specific recruitment" means recruiting an adoptive placement targeted to meet the individual needs of the specific child, including, but not limited to, use of the media, use of photo-listing services and any other in-state or out-of-state resources that may be used to meet the specific needs of the child, unless there are extenuating circumstances that indicate that these efforts are not in the best interest of the child.

(*l*) The Commissioner of Children and Families shall pay directly to the person or persons furnishing goods or services determined by said commissioner to be necessary for the care and maintenance of such child or youth the reasonable expense thereof, payment to be made at intervals determined by said commissioner; and the Comptroller shall draw his order on the Treasurer, from time to time, for such part of the appropriation for care of committed children or youth as may be needed in order to enable the commissioner to make such payments. Said commissioner shall include in his annual budget a sum estimated to be sufficient to carry out the provisions of this section. Notwithstanding that any such child or youth has income or estate, the commissioner may pay the cost of care and maintenance of such child or youth. The commissioner may bill to and collect from the person in charge of the estate of any child or youth aided under this chapter, including his decedent estate, or the payee of such child's or youth's income, the total amount expended for care of such child or youth or such portion thereof as any such estate or payee is able to reimburse.

(m) The commissioner, a parent or the child's attorney may file a motion to revoke a commitment, and, upon finding that cause for commitment no longer exists, and that such revocation is in the best interest and welfare of such child or youth, the court may revoke the commitment of any child or youth. No such motion shall be filed more often than once every six months.

(n) Upon service on the parent, guardian or other person having control of the child or youth of any order issued by the court pursuant to the provisions of subsections (b) and (j) of this section, the child or youth concerned shall be surrendered to the person serving the order who shall forthwith deliver the child or youth to the person, agency, department or institution awarded custody in such order. Upon refusal of the parent, guardian or other person having control of the child or youth to surrender the child or youth as provided in the order, the court may cause a warrant to be issued charging the parent, guardian or other person having control of the child or youth with contempt of court. If the person arrested is found in contempt of court, the court may order such person confined until he purges himself of contempt, but for not more than six months, or may fine such person not more than five hundred dollars, or both.

(*o*) A foster parent shall have the right to be heard for the purposes of this section in Superior Court in matters concerning the placement or revocation of commitment of a foster child living with such parent. A foster parent shall receive notice of any motion to revoke commitment or any hearing on such motion. A foster parent who has cared for a child or youth for not less than six months shall have the right to be heard and comment on the best interests of such child or youth in any matter under this section which is brought not more than one year after the last day the foster parent provided such care.

(p) Upon motion of any sibling of any child committed to the Department of Children and Families pursuant to this section, such sibling shall have the right to be heard concerning visitation with, and placement of, any such child. In awarding any visitation or modifying any placement, the court shall be guided by the best interests of all siblings affected by such determination.

(q) The provisions of section 17a–152, regarding placement of a child from another state, and section 17a–175, regarding the Interstate Compact on the Placement of Children, shall apply to placements pursuant to this section.

(1949 Rev., § 2634, subs. (a) to (e); 1949, Supp. § 264(a) to (e); 1953, Supp. § 1129c(a) to (e); 1955, Supp. § 1469d, subs. (a) to (e); 1957, P.A. 50; 1958 Rev., §§ 17–60a, 51–310; 1959, P.A. 293; 1967, P.A. 698; 1969, P.A. 794, § 7; 1971, P.A. 150; 1971, P.A. 184; 1971, P.A. 231; 1971, P.A. 253; 1972, P.A. 127, § 24; 1972, P.A. 294, § 18; 1973, P.A. 73–205, § 5; 1973, P.A. 73–546, § 2; 1973, P.A. 73–625, § 3, eff. June 17, 1973; 1974, P.A. 74–251, §§ 10, 11; 1975, P.A. 75–420, § 4, eff. June 25, 1975; 1975, P.A. 75–492, § 1, eff. July 3, 1975; 1975, P.A. 75–602, § 4, eff. Jan. 1, 1976; 1976, P.A. 76–436, §§ 16, 668, eff. July 1, 1978; 1977, P.A. 77–272; 1977, P.A. 77–273; 1977, P.A. 77–614, § 71, eff. Oct. 1, 1977; 1977, P.A. 77–614, § 521, eff. Jan. 1, 1979; 1977, P.A. 77–614, § 587, eff. June 2, 1977; 1978, P.A. 78–223, § 1, eff. July 1, 1978; 1978, P.A. 78–303, § 85, eff. June 6, 1978; 1979, P.A. 79–423; 1979, P.A. 79–579; 1979, P.A. 79–631, § 84; 1980, P.A. 80–483, § 121, eff. June 6, 1980; 1982, P.A. 82–181, §§ 1, 2; 1984, P.A. 84–449, § 5, eff. June 12, 1984; 1993,

P.A. 93–91, § 1, eff. July 1, 1993; 1993, P.A. 93–262, § 1, eff. July 1, 1993; 1995, P.A. 95–238, § 4; 1996, P.A. 96–246, §§ 20, 21; 1997, P.A. 97–319, § 19, eff. July 1, 1997; 1998, P.A. 98–185; 1998, P.A. 98–241, § 5; 1998, June Sp.Sess., P.A. 98–1, § 102, eff. July 1, 1998; 2000, P.A. 00–137, §§ 2, 3, 15; 2001, P.A. 01–142, §§ 6 to 8; 2001, P.A. 01–149, § 1; 2001, P.A. 01–195, §§ 37, 38, eff. July 11, 2001; 2001, June Sp.Sess., P.A. 01–2, § 33; 2002, May 9 Sp.Sess., P.A. 02–7, §§ 29, 30, eff. Aug. 15, 2002; 2003, P.A. 03–243, § 2.)

1 C.G.S.A. § 46b–160 et seq.

§ 46b–129a. Examination by physician. Appointment of counsel and guardian ad litem

In proceedings in the Superior Court under section 46b–129: (1) The court may order the child, the parents, the guardian, or other persons accused by a competent witness with abusing the child, to be examined by one or more competent physicians, psychiatrists or psychologists appointed by the court; (2) a child shall be represented by counsel knowledgeable about representing such children who shall be appointed by the court to represent the child and to act as guardian ad litem for the child. The primary role of any counsel for the child including the counsel who also serves as guardian ad litem, shall be to advocate for the child in accordance with the Rules of Professional Conduct. When a conflict arises between the child's wishes or position and that which counsel for the child believes is in the best interest of the child, the court shall appoint another person as guardian ad litem for the child. The guardian ad litem shall speak on behalf of the best interest of the child and is not required to be an attorney-at-law but shall be knowledgeable about the needs and protection of children. In the event that a separate guardian ad litem is appointed, the person previously serving as both counsel and guardian ad litem for the child shall continue to serve as counsel for the child and a different person shall be appointed as guardian ad litem, unless the court for good cause also appoints a different person as counsel for the child. No person who has served as both counsel and guardian ad litem for a child shall thereafter serve solely as the child's guardian ad litem. The counsel and guardian ad litem's fees, if any, shall be paid by the parents or guardian, or the estate of the child, or, if such persons are unable to pay, by the court; (3) the privilege against the disclosure of communications between husband and wife shall be inapplicable and either may testify as to any relevant matter; and (4) evidence that the child has been abused or has sustained a nonaccidental injury shall constitute prima facie evidence that shall be sufficient to support an adjudication that such child is uncared for or neglected.

(1996, P.A. 96–246, § 13; 2001, P.A. 01–148, § 1.)

§ 46b–130. Reimbursement for expense of care and maintenance. Assignment of right of support to Commissioner of Children and Families

The parents of a minor child for whom care or support of any kind has been provided under the provisions of this chapter, shall be liable to reimburse the state for such care or support to the same extent, and under the same terms and conditions as are the parents of recipients of public assistance. Upon receipt of foster care maintenance payments under Title IV–E of the Social Security Act [1] by a minor child, the right of support, present, past, and future from a parent of such child shall, by this section, be assigned to the Commissioner of Children and Families. Referral by the commissioner shall promptly be made to the Child Support Enforcement Unit of the Department of Social Services for pursuit of support for said minor child in accordance with the provisions of section 17b–179. Any child who reimburses the state under the provisions of subsection (k) of section 46b–129 for any care or support he received shall have a right of action to recover such payments from his parents.

(1958 Rev., §§ 17–62a, 51–311; 1973, P.A. 73–546, § 1; 1985, P.A. 85–548, § 6; 1990, P.A. 90–230, § 64, eff. June 8, 1990; 1993, P.A. 93–91, § 1, eff. July 1, 1993; 1993, P.A. 93–262, § 1, eff. July 1, 1993; 1997, June 18 Sp.Sess., P.A. 97–2, § 106, eff. July 1, 1997; 1998, P.A. 98–241, § 13, eff. July 1, 1998.)

1 42 U.S.C.A. § 670 et seq.

§ 46b–131. Repealed. (1984, P.A. 84–369, § 3.)

§ 46b–132. Temporary detention places

Where accommodations for the temporary detention of children in state-operated detention homes are unavailable, the Chief Court Administrator or his designee shall arrange with some agency or person for the use of suitable accommodations to serve as a temporary detention place as may be required. The court may allow such agency or person reasonable compensation for the expenses and services incident to such detention. The Chief Court Administrator or his designee may employ any other suitable method or arrangement for detention. Each child while detained as herein provided shall be under the orders, direction and supervision of the court.

(1949 Rev., § 2809; 1955, Supp. § 1577d; 1958 Rev., §§ 17–64, 51–313; 1976, P.A. 76–436, §§ 10a, 21, eff. July 1, 1978.)

§ 46b–132a. Medical care of children in detention centers

When deemed in the best interests of a child placed in a juvenile detention center, the administrator of such detention center may authorize, under policies promulgated by the Chief Court Administrator, such medical assessment and treatment and dentistry as is necessary to ensure the continued good health or life of the child.

The administrator of the detention center shall make reasonable efforts to inform the child's parents or guardian prior to taking such action, and in all cases shall send notice to the parents or guardian by letter to their last-known address informing them of the actions taken and of the outcome, provided failure to notify shall not affect the validity of the authorization.

(1998, P.A. 98–256, § 9.)

§ 46b–133. Arrest of child. Release or detention of arrested child. Alcohol or drug testing or treatment as condition of release. Admission of child to overpopulated juvenile detention center

(a) Nothing in this part shall be construed as preventing the arrest of a child, with or without a warrant, as may be provided by law, or as preventing the issuance of warrants by judges in the manner provided by section 54–2a, except that no child shall be taken into custody on such process except on apprehension in the act, or on speedy information, or in other cases when the use of such process appears imperative. Whenever a child is arrested and charged with a crime, such child may be required to submit to the taking of his photograph, physical description and fingerprints. Notwithstanding the provisions of section 46b–124, the name, photograph and custody status of any child arrested for the commission of a capital felony or class A felony may be disclosed to the public.

(b) Whenever a child is brought before a judge of the Superior Court, such judge shall immediately have the case proceeded upon as a juvenile matter. Such judge may admit such child to bail or release him in the custody of his parent or parents, his guardian or some other suitable person to appear before the Superior Court when ordered. If detention becomes necessary or desirable, the same shall be in the manner prescribed by this chapter.

(c) Upon the arrest of any child by an officer, such officer may release him to the custody of his parent or parents, guardian or some other suitable person or agency or may immediately turn him over to a juvenile detention center. When a child is arrested for the commission of a delinquent act and the child is not placed in detention or referred to a diversionary program, an officer shall serve a written complaint and summons on the child and his parent, guardian or other person having control of the child. Such parent, guardian or other person shall execute a written promise to appear in court at the time and place specified in such summons. If any person so summoned wilfully fails to appear in court at the time and place so specified, the court may issue a warrant for the child's arrest or a capias to assure the appearance in court of such parent, guardian or other person. The court may punish for contempt, as provided in section 46b–121, any parent, guardian or other person so summoned who wilfully fails to appear in court at the time and place so specified.

(d) The court or detention supervisor may turn such child over to a youth service program created for such purpose, if such course is practicable, or such child may be detained pending a hearing which shall be held on the business day next following his arrest. No child shall be detained after such hearing or held in detention pursuant to a court order unless it appears from the available facts that there is probable cause to believe that the child has committed the acts alleged and that there is (1) a strong probability that the child will run away prior to court hearing or disposition, (2) a strong probability that the child will commit or attempt to commit other offenses injurious to him or to the community before court disposition, (3) probable cause to believe that the child's continued residence in his home pending disposition will not safeguard the best interests of the child or the community because of the serious and dangerous nature of the act or acts he is alleged to have committed, (4) a need to hold the child for another jurisdiction or (5) a need to hold the child to assure his appearance before the court, in view of his previous failure to respond to the court process. Such probable cause may be shown by sworn affidavit in lieu of testimony. No child shall be released from detention who is alleged to have committed a serious juvenile offense except by order of a judge of the Superior Court. In no case shall a child be confined in a community correctional center or lockup, or in any place where adults are or may be confined, except in the case of a nursing infant; nor shall any child at any time be held in solitary confinement. When a female child is held in custody, she shall, as far as possible, be in the charge of a woman attendant.

(e) The police officer who brings a child into detention shall have first notified, or made a reasonable effort to notify, the parents or guardian of the child in question of the intended action and shall file at the detention center a signed statement setting forth the alleged delinquent conduct of the child. Unless the arrest was for a serious juvenile offense, the child may be released by a detention supervisor to the custody of his parent or parents, guardian or some other suitable person.

(f) In conjunction with any order of release from detention the court may, when it has reason to believe a child is alcohol-dependent or drug-dependent as defined in section 46b–120, and where necessary, reasonable and appropriate, order the child to participate in a program of periodic alcohol or drug testing and treatment as a condition of such release. The results of any such alcohol or drug test shall be admissible only for the purposes of enforcing the conditions of release from detention.

(g) Whenever the population of a juvenile detention center equals or exceeds the maximum capacity for such center, as determined by the Judicial Department, the detention supervisor in charge of intake shall only admit a child who: (1) Is charged with the commission of a serious juvenile offense, (2) is the subject of an order to detain or an outstanding court order to take such child into custody, (3) is ordered by a court to be held in detention, or (4) is being transferred to such center to await a court appearance.

(1949 Rev., § 2810; 1958 Rev., §§ 17–65, 51–314; 1959, P.A. 28, § 54; 1974, P.A. 74–183, § 211, eff. Dec. 31, 1974; 1976, P.A. 76–426; 1976, P.A. 76–436, §§ 22, 668, eff. July 1, 1978; 1977, P.A. 77–452, § 24, eff. July 1, 1978; 1980, P.A. 80–236; 1982, P.A. 82–220; 1983, P.A. 83–504; 1984, P.A. 84–369, § 1; 1989, P.A. 89–273, § 3; 1990, P.A. 90–161, § 2, eff. July 1, 1990; 1995, P.A. 95–225, § 15, eff. Oct. 1, 1995; 1998, P.A. 98–256, § 4.)

§ 46b–133a. Right to trial or dismissal upon nolle prosequi of delinquency charge. Erasure of records

(a) A nolle prosequi may not be entered as to any count of delinquency if the juvenile objects to the nolle prosequi and demands either a trial or dismissal, except with respect to prosecutions in which a nolle prosequi is entered upon a representation to the court by the juvenile prosecutor that a material witness has died, disappeared or become disabled or that material evidence has disappeared or has been destroyed and that a further investigation is therefore necessary.

(b) Whenever a nolle prosequi has been entered as to any count of delinquency, or whenever any count of delinquency has been dismissed without prejudice, if at least thirteen months have elapsed since such nolle or dismissal without prejudice, all police and court records pertaining to such count shall be erased. Whenever any such count has been continued at the request of the juvenile prosecutor and a period of thirteen months has elapsed since the granting of such continuance during which period there has been no prosecution or other disposition of the matter, the count shall be construed to have been nolled as of the date of termination of such thirteen-month period and such erasure may thereafter be effected as provided in this subsection for nolled cases.

(1984, P.A. 84–369, § 2; 1995, P.A. 95–225, § 16, eff. Oct. 1, 1995; 1998, P.A. 98–256, § 5.)

§ 46b–133b. Suspension of delinquency proceedings for treatment for alcohol or drug dependency

(a) The court, on motion of a child charged with a delinquency offense, but not yet convicted, may order that such child be examined to determine whether the child is alcohol-dependent or drug-dependent as defined in section 46b–120. Such motion shall be filed with the court within ten days after a plea is entered, except if waived by the court or pursuant to an agreement by the parties. The results of any examination ordered pursuant to this subsection shall be utilized only for the purposes of determining whether the delinquency proceeding should be suspended under this section.

(b) The court, upon motion of the child charged with a delinquency offense but not yet convicted, may order the suspension of the delinquency proceedings for a period of up to one year, order periodic alcohol and drug testing of such child during the period of suspension and order treatment for alcohol or drug dependency if the court, after consideration of information before it concerning the alcohol or drug dependency of the child, finds that (1) the child is alcohol-dependent or drug-dependent as defined in section 46b–120, (2) the child presently needs and is likely to benefit from treatment for the dependency and (3) the suspension of the delinquency proceedings will advance the interests of justice. During the period of suspension, a child shall be placed under the supervision of a juvenile probation officer for treatment for alcohol or drug dependency and such officer shall monitor the compliance of the child with the orders of the court.

(c) If the court denies the motion for suspension of the delinquency proceedings, the juvenile prosecutor may proceed with the delinquency proceedings. Any order of the court granting or denying a motion for suspension of the delinquency proceedings shall not be deemed a final order for purposes of appeal.

(d) At any time before the end of the period of the suspension of the delinquency proceedings, but not later than one month before the end of the period of suspension, a juvenile probation officer shall notify the court of the impending conclusion of the suspension and submit a report on whether the child has completed the treatment program and has complied with all other conditions of the suspension order imposed by the court.

(e) If the court, on motion of the child or on its own motion, finds that the child has completed the treatment program and has complied with all other conditions of suspension, it may dismiss the charge for which the delinquency proceedings had been suspended. If the court denies the motion and terminates the suspension of the delinquency proceedings, the juvenile prosecutor may proceed with such proceedings.

(f) The provisions of this section shall not apply to any child charged with a serious juvenile offense as defined in section 46b–120 or any child who was previously ordered treated under this section.

(1990, P.A. 90–161, § 4, eff. July 1, 1990; 1995, P.A. 95–225, § 17, eff. Oct. 1, 1995.)

§ 46b–133c. Serious juvenile repeat offender prosecution. Sentencing

(a) Whenever a child is referred for the commission of a felony committed after such child attained the age of fourteen years and such child is a serious juvenile repeat offender, as defined in section 46b–120, the juvenile prosecutor may request the court to designate the proceeding as a serious juvenile repeat offender prosecution.

(b) If a juvenile prosecutor requests that a proceeding be designated a serious juvenile repeat offender prosecution, the court shall hold a hearing not later than thirty days after the filing of such request unless good cause is shown by the juvenile prosecutor or by the child as to why the hearing should not be held within such period. If good cause is shown, the hearing shall be held not later than ninety days after the filing of such request. The court shall decide whether to designate the proceeding as a serious juvenile repeat offender prosecution not later than thirty days after the completion of such hearing. The court shall grant the request to designate the proceeding as a serious juvenile repeat offender prosecution if the juvenile prosecutor shows by clear and convincing evidence that such designation will serve the public safety. The decision to designate the proceeding as a serious juvenile repeat offender prosecution shall not be a final judgment for purposes of appeal.

(c) A proceeding designated as a serious juvenile repeat offender prosecution pursuant to subsection (b) of this section shall be held before the court without a jury provided the child has waived his right to a trial by jury. If a child is convicted of or pleads guilty to a felony in such proceeding, the court shall: (1) Sentence the child in accordance with section 46b–140 or 46b–141a and (2) sentence the child in accordance with section 53a–28 with the execution of such sentence stayed on the condition that the child not violate the conditions of the sentence imposed pursuant to subdivision (1) of this subsection or commit a subsequent crime.

(d) If a child is convicted of or pleads guilty to a misdemeanor in a proceeding designated as a serious juvenile repeat offender prosecution pursuant to subsection (b) of this section, the court shall sentence the child in accordance with section 46b–140 or 46b–141a.

(e) Whenever it appears that a child who has been sentenced pursuant to subsection (c) of this section has violated the conditions of the sentence imposed pursuant to subdivision (1) of said subsection (c) or has committed a subsequent crime, the court may, without notice, order that the child be immediately taken into custody in accordance with the provisions of section 46b–125. The court shall notify the child and such child's parent or guardian and the attorney of record, if any, in writing of the reasons alleged to exist for the lifting of the stay of execution of the sentence imposed pursuant to subdivision (2) of said subsection (c). If the child challenges such reasons, the court shall hold a hearing at which the child shall be entitled to be heard and be represented by counsel. After such hearing, if the court finds that the child has violated the conditions of the sentence imposed pursuant to subdivision (1) of said subsection (c) or committed a subsequent crime, it shall order the child to serve a sentence not to exceed that imposed pursuant to subdivision (2) of said subsection (c) unless it determines there are mitigating circumstances that justify continuing the stay of execution and specifically states such mitigating circumstances in writing for the record. The child shall receive credit against any sentence imposed pursuant to subdivision (2) of said subsection (c) for time served in a juvenile facility pursuant to the sentence imposed pursuant to subdivision (1) of said subsection (c).

(f) Whenever a proceeding has been designated a serious juvenile repeat offender prosecution pursuant to subsection (b) of this section and the child does not waive his right to a trial by jury, the court shall transfer the case from the docket for juvenile matters to the regular criminal docket of the Superior Court. Upon transfer, such child shall stand trial and be sentenced, if convicted, as if he were sixteen years of age, except that no such child shall be placed in a correctional facility but shall be maintained in a facility for children and youth until he attains sixteen years of age or until he is sentenced, whichever occurs first. Such child shall receive credit against any sentence imposed for time served in a juvenile facility prior to the effectuation of the transfer. A child who has been transferred may enter a guilty plea to a lesser offense if the court finds that such plea is made knowingly and voluntarily. Any child transferred to the regular criminal docket who pleads guilty to a lesser offense shall not resume his status as a juvenile regarding said offense. If the action is dismissed or nolled or if such child is found not guilty of the charge for which he was transferred, the child shall resume his status as a juvenile until he attains sixteen years of age.

(1995, P.A. 95–225, § 25, eff. Oct. 1, 1995.)

§ 46b–133d. Serious sexual offender prosecution. Sentencing

(a) For the purposes of this section, "special juvenile probation" means a period of probation imposed by the superior court for juvenile matters upon a child in a proceeding designated as a serious sexual offender prosecution during which the child is supervised by a juvenile probation officer prior to such child attaining eighteen years of age and by an adult probation officer after such child attains eighteen years of age.

(b) Whenever a child is referred for the commission of any crime of a sexual nature, and such case is not transferred to the regular criminal docket pursuant to section 46b–127, the juvenile prosecutor may request the court to designate the proceeding as a serious sexual offender prosecution.

(c) If a juvenile prosecutor requests that a proceeding be designated a serious sexual offender prosecution, the court shall hold a hearing not later than thirty days after the filing of such request unless good cause is shown by the juvenile prosecutor or by the child as to why the hearing should not be held within such period. If good cause is shown, the hearing shall be held not later than ninety days after the filing of such request. The court shall decide whether to designate the proceeding as a serious sexual offender prosecution not later than thirty days after the completion of such hearing. The court shall grant the request to designate the proceeding as a serious sexual offender prosecution if the juvenile prosecutor shows by a preponderance of the evidence that such designation will serve the public safety. The decision to designate the proceeding as a serious sexual offender prosecution shall not be a final judgment for purposes of appeal.

(d) A proceeding designated as a serious sexual offender prosecution pursuant to subsection (c) of this section shall be held before the court without a jury provided the child has waived the right to a trial by jury. If a child is convicted of or pleads guilty or nolo contendere to a charge in a proceeding that has been designated as a serious sexual offender prosecution, the court shall: (1) Sentence the child in accordance with section 46b–140 or 46b–141a, (2) sentence the child to a period of special juvenile probation of at least five years, to commence upon the release of the child from the institution, agency or program in whose care the child had been placed, and (3) sentence the child in accordance with section 53a–28 with the execution of such sentence stayed on the condition that the child not violate the conditions of the sentence imposed pursuant to subdivisions (1) and (2) of this subsection or commit a subsequent crime.

(e) Whenever it appears that a child who has been sentenced pursuant to subsection (d) of this section has violated the conditions of the sentence imposed pursuant to subdivision (2) of said subsection or has committed a subsequent crime, the court may, without notice, order that the child be immediately taken into custody in accordance with the provisions of sections 46b–125 and 53a–32. If such violation of probation or subsequent crime occurs prior to the person attaining eighteen years of age, the matter shall be handled by the superior court for juvenile matters. If such violation of probation or subsequent crime occurs after the person has attained eighteen years of age, the matter shall be handled by the regular criminal docket of the Superior Court. Whenever such matter is handled by the superior court for juvenile matters, the court shall notify the child and such child's parent or guardian and the attorney of record, if any, in writing of the reasons alleged to exist for the lifting of the stay of execution of the sentence imposed pursuant to subdivision (3) of subsection (d) of this section. If the child challenges such reasons, the court shall hold a hearing at which the child shall be entitled to be heard and be represented by counsel. After such hearing, if the court finds that the child has violated the conditions of the sentence imposed pursuant to subdivision (2) of subsection (d) of this section or committed a subsequent crime, it shall order the child to serve a sentence not to exceed that imposed pursuant to subdivision (3) of subsection (d) of this section unless it determines there are mitigating circumstances that justify continuing the stay of execution and specifically states such mitigating circumstances in writing for the record. The child shall receive credit against any sentence imposed pursuant to subdivision (3) of subsection (d) of this section for time served in a juvenile facility pursuant to the sentence imposed pursuant to subdivision (1) of said subsection.

(f) When a proceeding has been designated a serious sexual offender prosecution pursuant to subsection (c) of this section and the child does not waive the right to a trial by jury, the court shall transfer the case from the docket for juvenile matters to the regular criminal docket of the Superior Court. Upon transfer, such child shall stand trial and be sentenced, if convicted, as if such child were sixteen years of age, except that no such child shall be placed in a correctional facility but shall be maintained in a facility for children and youth until such child attains sixteen years of age or until such child is sentenced, whichever occurs first. Such child shall receive credit against any sentence imposed for time served in a juvenile facility prior to the effectuation of the transfer. A child who has been transferred may enter a guilty plea to a lesser offense if the court finds that such plea is made knowingly and voluntarily. Any child transferred to the regular criminal docket who pleads guilty to a lesser offense shall not resume such child's status as a juvenile regarding such offense. If the action is dismissed or nolled or if such child is found not guilty of the charge for which such child was transferred, the child shall resume such child's status as a juvenile until such child attains sixteen years of age.

(1999, June Sp.Sess., P.A. 99–2, § 47.)

§ 46b–133e. Suspension of delinquency proceedings for participation in school violence prevention program

(a) The court, upon motion of a child charged with an offense involving the use or threatened use of physical violence in or on the real property comprising a public or private elementary or secondary school or at a school-sponsored activity as defined in subsection (h) of section 10–233a, may order the suspension of the delinquency proceedings for a period of one year and order the child to participate in a school violence prevention program during the period of suspension if the court, after consideration of information before it, finds that (1) the child presently needs and is likely to benefit from participation in a school violence prevention program, and (2) the suspension of the delinquency proceedings will advance the interests of justice.

(b) As a condition of eligibility for suspension of prosecution and placement in a school violence prevention program pursuant to this section, (1) the child shall agree to participate in a program of anger management and nonviolent conflict resolution consisting of at least eight group counseling sessions, and to satisfactorily complete such program, (2) the child shall agree to comply with any orders of the court, and (3) the parents or guardian of such child shall certify under penalty of false statement that, to the best of such parents' or guardian's knowledge and belief, neither such parent or guardian nor such child possesses any firearms, dangerous weapons, controlled substances or other property or materials the possession of which is prohibited by law or in violation of the law.

(c) The cost of participation in such program shall be paid by the parent or guardian of such child, except that no child shall be excluded from such program for inability to pay such cost provided (1) the parent or guardian of such child files with the court an affidavit of indigency or inability to pay, and (2) the court enters a finding thereof.

(d) During the period of suspension, a child shall be placed under the supervision of a juvenile probation officer for placement in a school violence prevention program and such officer shall monitor the compliance of the child with the orders of the court including, but not limited to, maintaining contact with the child and officials of the child's school.

(e) If the court denies the motion for suspension of the delinquency proceedings, the juvenile prosecutor may proceed with the delinquency proceedings. Any order of the court granting or denying a motion for suspension of the delinquency proceedings shall not be deemed a final order for purposes of appeal.

(f) At any time before the end of the period of the suspension of the delinquency proceedings, but not later than one month before the end of the period of suspension, a juvenile probation officer shall notify the court of the impending conclusion of the suspension and submit a report on whether the child has satisfactorily completed the school violence prevention program and has complied with all other conditions of the suspension order imposed by the court.

(g) If the court, on motion of the child or on its own motion, finds that the child has satisfactorily completed the school violence prevention program and has complied with all other conditions of suspension, and one year has elapsed since the child was placed in such program, it may dismiss the charge for which the delinquency proceedings had been suspended. If the court denies the motion and terminates the suspension of the delinquency proceedings, the juvenile prosecutor may proceed with such proceedings.

(1999, P.A. 99–259, § 1, eff. Jan. 1, 2000.)

§ 46b–134. Investigation by probation officer prior to disposition of delinquency case. Physical, mental and diagnostic examination

Prior to the disposition of the case of any child convicted of a delinquent act, investigation shall be made of the facts as specified in this section by the probation officer, and until such investigation has been completed and the results thereof placed before the judge, no disposition of the child's case shall be made. Such investigation shall consist of an examination of the parentage and surroundings of the child and the child's age, habits and history, and shall include also an inquiry into the home conditions, habits and character of the child's parents or guardians. Such investigation shall include an inquiry into the circumstances of the offense, the attitude of the complainant or victim, the criminal record, the present condition of the child and any damages suffered by the victim including medical expenses, loss of earnings and property loss. If the child is or legally should be in attendance at school, such investigation shall further contain a report of the child's school attendance, adjustment and behavior, the child's individualized education program if the child has been identified pursuant to sections 10–76a to 10–76gg, inclusive, as requiring special education and related services and any recommendations from school officials on conditions of probation if the child is placed on probation pursuant to section 46b–140, which shall be furnished by the school officials to the court upon its request. The court shall, when it is found necessary to the disposition, cause a complete physical or mental examination, or both, to be made of the child by persons professionally qualified to do so. Such examination may include testing to determine whether the child is alcohol-dependent or drug-dependent as defined in section 46b–120. If the court causes a complete physical or mental examination, or both, to be made of a child whose parents, guardian or custodian is found able to pay in whole or in part the cost thereof, it shall assess as costs against such parents, guardian or custodian, including any agency vested with the legal custody of the child, the expense so incurred and paid for by the court in having such examination performed, to the extent of their financial ability to do so. Prior to the disposition of the case of any child convicted of a delinquent act, the court may cause a complete diagnostic examination to be made, unless such information is otherwise available. Such information shall include physical and psychological diagnoses and may include medical, psychiatric, neurological, learning disability diagnoses and such other diagnoses as the court deems necessary. If such child is committed to the Department of Children and Families, such information shall be shared with the Department of Children and Families.

(1949 Rev., § 2811; 1958 Rev., §§ 17–66, 51–315; 1969, P.A. 794, § 9; 1978, P.A. 78–188, § 7, eff. July 1, 1978; 1979, P.A. 79–581, § 5; 1982, P.A. 82–298, § 7; 1989, P.A. 89–273, § 4; 1990, P.A. 90–161, § 3, eff. July 1, 1990; 1993, P.A. 93–91, § 1, eff. July 1, 1993; 1994, P.A. 94–221, § 13; 1995, P.A. 95–225, § 18, eff. Oct. 1, 1995; 2003, P.A. 03–86, § 1.)

§ 46b–135. Right to counsel and cross-examination

(a) At the commencement of any proceeding concerning the alleged delinquency of a child, the parent or parents or guardian and the child shall have the right to counsel and be so informed by the judge, and that if they are unable to afford counsel that counsel will be provided for them. Such counsel and such parent or parents or guardian or child shall have the rights of confrontation and cross-examination.

(b) At the commencement of any proceeding on behalf of a neglected, uncared-for or dependent child or youth, the parent or parents or guardian of the child or youth shall have the right to counsel, and shall be so informed by the judge, and that if they are unable to afford counsel, counsel will be provided for them, and such counsel and such parent or guardian of the child or youth shall have the rights of confrontation and cross-examination.

(1958 Rev., §§ 17–66b, 51–316; 1967, P.A. 630, § 8, eff. June 22, 1967; 1969, P.A. 794, §§ 11, 12; 1975, P.A. 75–602, § 5, eff. Jan. 1, 1976; 1976, P.A. 76–436, § 23, eff. July 1, 1978; 1995, P.A. 95–225, § 19, eff. Oct. 1, 1995.)

§ 46b–136. Appointment of attorney to represent child or youth and parent or guardian

In any proceeding on a juvenile matter the judge before whom such proceeding is pending shall, even in the absence of a request to do so, provide an attorney to represent the child or youth, his parent or parents, guardian or other person having control of the child or youth, if such judge determines that the interests of justice so require, and in any proceeding in which the custody of a child is at issue, such judge shall provide an attorney to represent the child and may authorize such attorney or appoint another attorney to represent such child or youth, parent, guardian or other person on an appeal from a decision in such proceeding. Where, under the provisions of this section, the court so appoints counsel for any such party who is found able to pay, in whole or in part the cost thereof, it shall assess as costs against such parents, guardian, or custodian, including any agency vested with the legal custody of the child or youth, the expense so incurred and paid for by the court in providing such counsel, to the extent of their financial ability to do so.

(1958 Rev., §§ 17–66c, 51–3; 1967, P.A. 630, § 9, eff. June 22, 1967; 1969, P.A. 794, § 10; 1973, P.A. 73–188; 1975, P.A. 75–277; 1975, P.A. 75–602, § 6, eff. Jan. 1, 1976; 1976, P.A. 76–235, § 1, eff. May 25, 1976; 1976, P.A. 76–436, § 24, eff. July 1, 1978.)

§ 46b–137. Admissibility of confession or other statement in juvenile proceedings

(a) Any admission, confession or statement, written or oral, made by a child to a police officer or Juvenile Court official shall be inadmissible in any proceeding concerning the alleged delinquency of the child making such admission, confession or statement unless made by such child in the presence of his parent or parents or guardian and after the parent or parents or guardian and child have been advised (1) of the child's right to retain counsel, or if unable to afford counsel, to have counsel appointed on the child's behalf, (2) of the child's right to refuse to make any statements and (3) that any statements he makes may be introduced into evidence against him.

(b) Any confession, admission or statement, written or oral, made by the parent or parents or guardian of the child or youth after the filing of a petition alleging such child or youth to be neglected, uncared-for or dependent, shall be inadmissible in any proceeding held upon such petition against the person making such admission or statement unless such person shall have been advised of his right to retain counsel, and that if he is unable to afford counsel, counsel will be appointed to represent him, that he has a right to refuse to make any statement and that any statements he makes may be introduced in evidence against him.

(1958 Rev., §§ 17–66d, 51–318; 1967, P.A. 630, § 10, eff. June 22, 1967; 1969, P.A. 794, §§ 13, 14; 1975, P.A. 75–183; 1975, P.A. 75–602, § 7, eff. Jan. 1, 1976; 1976, P.A. 76–436, § 591, eff. July 1, 1978; 1995, P.A. 95–225, § 20, eff. Oct. 1, 1995; 1998, P.A. 98–256, § 11.)

§ 46b–138. Summoning of witnesses. Conversation privileged

For the purpose of hearing any juvenile matter, the court may summon witnesses and compel their attendance. The conversations of the judge with a child or youth whose case is before the court shall be privileged.

(1949 Rev., § 2812; 1958 Rev., §§ 17–67, 51–319; 1975, P.A. 75–602, § 8, eff. Jan. 1, 1976; 1976, P.A. 76–436, § 25, eff. July 1, 1978; 1978, P.A. 78–379, § 11, eff. July 1, 1978.)

§ 46b–138a. Testimony of accused juvenile, parent or guardian in juvenile proceeding

In any juvenile proceeding in the superior court, the accused child shall be a competent witness, and at his or her option may testify or refuse to testify in such proceedings. The parent or guardian of such child shall be a competent witness but may elect or refuse to testify for or against the accused child except that a parent or guardian who has received personal violence from the child may, upon the child's trial for offenses arising from such personal violence, be compelled to testify in the same manner as any other witness. No unfavorable inferences shall be drawn by the court from the accused child's silence.

(1979, P.A. 79–263.)

§ 46b–138b. Statement of victim or victim's representative at delinquency proceeding

In any proceeding concerning the alleged delinquency of a child, any victim of the alleged delinquent conduct, the parents or guardian of such victim, an advocate for such victim, appointed under section 54–221, or such victim's counsel shall have the right to appear before the court for the purpose of making a statement to the court concerning the disposition of the case.

(1989, P.A. 89–273, § 11; 1995, P.A. 95–225, § 21, eff. Oct. 1, 1995.)

§ 46b–139. Expert medical witnesses; interpreter

(a) When any licensed physician or certified or licensed psychologist is summoned to give expert testimony in any juvenile matter, the court shall determine a reasonable fee to be paid to such physician or psychologist in lieu of all other witness fees payable to such physician or psychologist.

(b) Any judge of the superior court hearing a juvenile matter may call in a competent interpreter to interpret the evidence in any such hearing and each interpreter so necessarily employed shall be paid from funds appropriated to the judicial department.

(1958 Rev., §§ 17–67a, 51–320; 1969, P.A. 794, § 15; 1976, P.A. 76–436, § 26, eff. July 1, 1978; 1977, P.A. 77–576, § 25, eff. July 1, 1978.)

§ 46b–140. Disposition upon conviction of child as delinquent

(a) In determining the appropriate disposition of a child convicted as delinquent, the court shall consider: (1) The seriousness of the offense, including the existence of any aggravating factors such as the use of a firearm in the commission of the offense and the impact of the offense on any victim; (2) the child's record of delinquency; (3) the child's willingness to participate in available programs; (4) the existence of other mitigating factors; and (5) the culpability of the child in committing the offense including the level of the child's participation in the planning and carrying out of the offense.

(b) Upon conviction of a child as delinquent, the court may: (1) Place the child in the care of any institution or agency which is permitted by law to care for children; (2) order the child to participate in an alternative incarceration program; (3) order the child to participate in a wilderness school program operated by the Department of Children and Families; (4) order the child to participate in a youth service bureau program; (5) place the child on probation; (6) order the child or the parents or guardian of the child or both to make restitution to the victim of the offense in accordance with subsection (d) of this section; (7) order the child to participate in a program of community service in accordance with subsection (e) of this section; or (8) withhold or suspend execution of any judgment.

(c) The court may order, as a condition of probation, that the child (1) reside with a parent, relative or guardian or in a suitable foster home or other residence approved by the court, (2) attend school and class on a regular basis and comply with school policies on student conduct and discipline, (3) refrain from violating any federal or state law or municipal or local ordinance, (4) undergo any medical or psychiatric evaluation or treatment deemed necessary by the court, (5) submit to random drug or alcohol testing, or both, (6) participate in a program of alcohol or drug treatment, or both, (7) make restitution to the victim of the offense in accordance with subsection (d) of this section, (8) participate in an alternative incarceration program or other program established through the Court Support Services Division, (9) participate in a program of community service, and (10) satisfy any other conditions deemed appropriate by the court. The court shall cause a copy of any such order to be delivered to the child, the child's parents or guardian and the child's probation officer. If the child is convicted as delinquent for a violation of section 53–247, the court may order, as a condition of probation, that the child undergo psychiatric or psychological counseling or participate in an animal cruelty prevention and education program provided such a program exists and is available to the child.

(d) If the child has engaged in conduct which results in property damage or personal injury, the court may order the child or the parent or parents or guardian of the child, if such parent or parents or guardian had knowledge of and condoned the conduct of the child, or both the child and the parent or parents or guardian, to make restitution to the victim of such offense, provided the liability of such parent or parents or guardian shall be limited to an amount not exceeding the amount such parent or parents or guardian would be liable for in an action under section 52–572. Restitution may consist of monetary reimbursement for the damage or injury, based on the child's or the parent's, parents' or guardian's ability to pay, as the case may be, in the form of a lump sum or installment payments, paid to the court clerk or such other official designated by the court for distribution to the victim.

(e) The court may order the child to participate in a program of community service under the supervision of the court or any organization designated by the court. Such child shall not be deemed to be an employee and the services of such child shall not be deemed employment.

(f) If the court further finds that its probation services or other services available to the court are not adequate for such child, the court shall commit such child to the Department of Children and Families in accordance with the provisions of section 46b–141. Prior to making such commitment, the court shall consult with the department to determine the placement which will be in the best interest of such child.

(g) Any child or youth coming within the jurisdiction of the court, who is found to be mentally ill, may be committed by said court to the Commissioner of Children and Families and, if the court convicts a child as delinquent and finds such child to be mentally deficient, it may commit such child to an institution for mentally deficient children or youth or delinquents. Whenever it is found that a child convicted by the court as delinquent or adjudged by the court to be a member of a family with service needs who is fourteen years of age or older would not benefit from continued school attendance, the court may order such child to be placed on vocational probation if such court finds that such child may properly be employed for part or full-time at some useful occupation and that such employment would be favorable to such child's welfare, and the probation officer shall supervise such employment. For the purposes of this section, the limitations of subsection (a) of section 31–23 on the employment of minors under the age of sixteen years shall not apply for the duration of such vocational probation.

(h) Whenever the court commits a child to the Department of Children and Families, there shall be delivered with the mittimus a copy of the results of the investigations made as required by section 46b–134. The court may, at any time, require from the department in whose care a child has been placed such report as to such child and such child's treatment.

(i) If the delinquent act for which the child is committed to the Department of Children and Families is a serious juvenile offense, the court may set a minimum period of twelve months during which the child shall be placed in a residential facility operated by or under contract with said department, as determined by the Commissioner of Children and Families. The setting of such minimum period shall be in the form of an order of the court included in the mittimus. For good cause shown in the form of an affidavit annexed thereto, the Department of Children and Families, the parent or guardian of the child or the child may petition the court for modification of any such order.

(j) Except as otherwise provided in this section, the court may order a child be (1) committed to the Department of Children and Families and be placed directly in a residential facility within this state and under contract with said department, or (2) committed to the Commissioner of Children and Families for placement by the commissioner, in said commissioner's discretion, (A) with respect to the juvenile offenders determined by the Department of Children and Families to be the highest risk, in the Connecticut Juvenile Training School, if the juvenile offender is a male, or in another state facility, presumptively for a minimum period of twelve months, or (B) in a private residential or day treatment facility within or outside this state, or (C) on parole. The commissioner shall use a risk and needs assessment classification system to ensure that male children who are in the highest risk level will be placed in the Connecticut Juvenile Training School.

(k) On or after May 21, 2004, no female child committed to the Department of Children and Families shall be placed in the Connecticut Juvenile Training School. Any female child placed in the Connecticut Juvenile Training School before May 21, 2004 shall be transferred to another appropriate facility not later than ninety days after May 21, 2004.

(*l*) Notwithstanding any provisions of the general statutes concerning the confidentiality of records and information, whenever a child convicted as delinquent is committed to the Department of Children and Families, the Commissioner of Children and Families shall have access to the following information: (1) Educational records of such child; (2) records regarding such child's past treatment for physical or mental illness, including substance abuse; (3) records regarding such child's prior placement in a public or private residential facility; (4) records created or obtained by the Judicial Department regarding such child; and (5) records, as defined in subsection (a) of section 17a–28. The Commissioner of Children and Families shall review such information to determine the appropriate services and placement which will be in the best interest of the child.

(1949 Rev., § 2813; 1955, Supp. § 1578d; 1957, P.A. 41; 1958 Rev. §§ 17–68, 51–321; 1969, P.A. 498, § 1, eff. June 18, 1969; 1969, P.A. 664, § 9; 1975, P.A. 75–226, § 2; 1975, P.A. 75–567, § 77, eff. Jan. 1, 1976; 1975, P.A. 75–602, § 9, eff. Jan. 1, 1976; 1976, P.A. 76–436, § 27, eff. July 1, 1978; 1978, P.A. 78–188, § 6, eff. July 1, 1978; 1979, P.A. 79–581, § 6; 1984, P.A. 84–10; 1984, P.A. 84–389, § 1; 1989, P.A. 89–273, § 5; 1989, P.A. 89–390, § 20, eff. Jan. 1, 1990; 1990, P.A. 90–161, § 5, eff. July 1, 1990; 1990, P.A. 90–240, § 5; 1990, P.A. 90–325, § 19; 1993, P.A. 93–91, § 1, eff. July 1, 1993; 1994, P.A. 94–136, § 2; 1994, P.A. 94–221, § 14; 1995, P.A. 95–225, § 22, eff. Oct. 1, 1995; 1998, P.A. 98–70, § 3; 1998, P.A. 98–256, § 6; 1999, P.A. 99–26, § 12; 2001, P.A. 01–211, § 14; 2002, P.A. 02–132, § 23; 2003, P.A. 03–208, § 3; 2004, P.A. 04–152, § 1, eff. May 21, 2004.)

§ 46b–140a. Modification of conditions of probation or suspended commitment. Violation of conditions

(a) At any time during the period of probation or suspended commitment, after hearing and for good cause shown, the court may modify or enlarge the conditions, whether originally imposed by the court under this section or otherwise, and may extend the period as deemed appropriate by the court. The court shall cause a copy of any such order to be delivered to the child or youth and to such child or youth's parent or guardian and probation officer.

(b) The period of participation in an alternative incarceration program, as a condition of probation or suspended commitment, unless terminated sooner, shall not exceed the original period of probation or suspended commitment.

(c) At any time during the period of probation or suspended commitment, the court may issue a warrant for the arrest of a child or youth for violation of any of the conditions of probation or suspended commitment, or may issue a notice to appear to answer to a charge of such violation, which notice shall be personally served upon the child or youth. Any such warrant shall authorize all officers named therein to return the child or youth to the custody of the court or to any suitable juvenile detention facility designated by the court.

(d) If such violation is established, the court may continue or revoke the order of probation or suspended commitment or modify or enlarge the conditions and, if such order of probation or suspended commitment is revoked, require the child or youth to serve the commitment imposed or impose any lesser commitment. No such revocation shall be ordered, except upon consideration of the whole record and unless such violation is established by reliable and probative evidence.

(e) Upon a determination by the court that a child or youth has violated probation by failing to comply with the requirements of electronic monitoring, the Court Support Services Division shall notify the local law enforcement agency of such violation.

(1998, P.A. 98–256, § 8; 2000, P.A. 00–141, § 5; 2003, P.A. 03–278, § 98, eff. July 9, 2003.)

§ 46b–141. Length of commitments. Motion for extension of commitment. Permanency hearing. Permanency plan. Reopening and termination

(a) Except as otherwise limited by subsection (i) of section 46b–140, commitment of children convicted as delinquent by the Superior Court to the Department of Children and Families shall be for (1) an indeterminate time up to a maximum of eighteen months, or (2) when so convicted for a serious juvenile offense, up to a maximum of four years at the discretion of the court, unless extended as hereinafter provided.

(b) The Commissioner of Children and Families may file a motion for an extension of the commitment as provided in subdivision (1) of subsection (a) beyond the eighteen-month period on the grounds that such extension is for the best interest of the child or the community. The court shall give notice to the parent or guardian and to the child at least fourteen days prior to the hearing upon such motion. The court may, after hearing and upon finding that such extension is in the best interest of the child or the community, continue the commitment for an additional period of not more than eighteen months. Not later than twelve months after a child is committed to the Department of Children and Families in accordance with subdivision (1) of subsection (a) of this section the court shall hold a permanency hearing in accordance with subsection (d) of this section. After the initial permanency hearing, subsequent permanency hearings shall be held not less frequently than every twelve months while the child remains committed to the Department of Children and Families.

(c) The court shall hold a permanency hearing in accordance with subsection (d) of this section for each child convicted as delinquent for a serious juvenile offense as provided in subdivision (2) of subsection (a) of this section within twelve months of commitment to the Department of Children and Families and every twelve months thereafter if the child remains committed to the Department of Children and Families. Such hearing may include the submission of a motion to the court by the commissioner to either (1) modify such commitment, or (2) extend the commitment beyond such four-year period on the grounds that such extension is for the best interest of the child or the community. The court shall give notice to the parent or guardian and to the child at least fourteen days prior to the hearing upon such motion. The court, after hearing, may modify such commitment or, upon finding that such extension is in the best interest of the child or the community, continue the commitment for an additional period of not more than eighteen months.

(d) At least sixty days prior to each permanency hearing required pursuant to subsection (b) or (c) of this section, the Commissioner of Children and Families shall file a permanency plan with the court. At each permanency hearing, the court shall review and approve a permanency plan that is in the best interest of the child and takes into consideration the child's need for permanency. Such permanency plan may include the goal of: (1) Revocation of commitment and placement of the child with the parent or guardian, (2) transfer of guardianship, (3) permanent placement with a relative, (4) adoption, or (5) such other planned permanent living arrangement ordered by the court, provided the Commissioner of Children and Families has documented a compelling reason why it would not be in the best interest of the child for the permanency plan to include the goals in subdivisions (1) to (4), inclusive, of this subsection. Such other planned permanent living arrangement may include, but not be limited to, placement of the child in an independent living program. At any such permanency hearing, the court shall also determine whether the Commissioner of Children and Families has made reasonable efforts to achieve the permanency plan.

(e) All other commitments of delinquent, mentally deficient or mentally ill children by the court pursuant to the provisions of section 46b–140, may be for an indeterminate time. Commitments may be reopened and terminated at any time by said court, provided the Commissioner of Children and Families shall be given notice of such proposed reopening and a reasonable opportunity to present the commissioner's views thereon. The parents or guardian of such child may apply not more than twice in any calendar year for such reopening and termination of commitment. Any order of the court made under the provisions of this section shall be deemed a final order for purposes of appeal, except that no bond shall be required and no costs shall be taxed on such appeal.

(1949 Rev., § 2814; 1955, Supp. § 1579d; 1958 Rev., §§ 17–69, 51–322; 1969, P.A. 664, § 10; 1971, P.A. 151; 1976, P.A. 76–436, § 31, eff. July 1, 1978; 1979, P.A. 79–581, § 7; 1981, P.A. 81–472, § 84, eff. July 8, 1981;

1984, P.A. 84–389, § 2; 1992, P.A. 92–167, § 1, eff. June 1, 1992; 1993, P.A. 93–91, § 1, eff. July 1, 1993; 1995, P.A. 95–225, § 23, eff. Oct. 1, 1995; 2001, June Sp.Sess, P.A. 01–2, § 34; 2003, P.A. 03–19, § 108, eff. May 12, 2003.)

§ 46b–141a. Placement of delinquent child in alternative incarceration program

(a) Whenever a child is convicted as delinquent, the court, in lieu of committing such child to the Department of Children and Families or to a juvenile detention center, may, in its discretion, order an assessment for placement in an alternative incarceration program to be conducted by the Court Support Services Division. If the Court Support Services Division recommends placement in an alternative incarceration program, it shall also submit to the court a proposed alternative incarceration plan. Upon completion of the assessment, the court shall determine whether such child shall be ordered to participate in such program as an alternative to commitment. If the court determines that the child shall participate in such program, the court shall suspend any commitment to the Department of Children and Families or to a juvenile detention center and shall make participation in the alternative incarceration program a condition of probation.

(b) An alternative incarceration program shall include, but not be limited to, fines, restitution, community service, halfway houses, alternative incarceration centers, day incarceration centers, drug, alcohol and mental health programs, electronic monitoring, intensive probation, vocational probation, boot camps, structured wilderness programs, pretrial diversion options aimed at creating alternatives to unnecessary detention, and school and job training programs.

(1994, P.A. 94–136, § 3; 1995, P.A. 95–225, § 24, eff. Oct. 1, 1995; 2002, P.A. 02–132, § 24.)

§ 46b–141b. Probation treatment plan

(a) When a juvenile is referred to the Court Support Services Division, the division shall conduct an intake risk assessment and make a case classification evaluation. If the Court Support Services Division deems it appropriate, the proposed probation plan may be submitted to a professional evaluation team. Such team shall be composed of a juvenile probation officer, a representative of the Court Support Services Division who is familiar with the alternative incarceration programs operated by the division or a representative from a contracted agency, and, where applicable, a school employee and any other interested parties in the discretion of the court. The evaluation team shall develop a probation treatment plan for each juvenile within fifteen days of the date of the referral of the case to the professional evaluation team, unless the court orders otherwise. The probation treatment plan shall include the following components: (1) Type of residential or nonresidential placement; (2) projected length of placement for the juvenile and the projected cost; and (3) type of services needed by the juvenile and the projected cost.

(b) The probation treatment plan shall be submitted to the court for consideration and approval prior to the court's final entry of a probation treatment order. In addition to any probation order, the court may order a medical and psychiatric or psychological examination of the juvenile. The court may assess the cost of the examination to the family based on its ability to pay.

(c) In ordering implementation of a probation treatment plan, the court may reasonably designate from the programs and services under contract with the Judicial Department the scope and extent of the services to be provided by the Court Support Services Division and the juvenile probation unit.

(d) The Court Support Services Division shall proceed to implement the probation treatment plan immediately upon its approval by the court.

(1995, P.A. 95–225, § 5, eff. July 1, 1996; 2002, P.A. 02–132, § 25.)

§ 46b–141c. Reimbursement of costs of probation supervision

The Judicial Department may require the parent or parents or guardian of any child who receives probation supervision to fully or partially reimburse the department for the costs of such child's supervision and may assess such person a monthly supervision fee for such purpose. If the department finds that the parents or guardian are indigent and unable to pay a probation supervision fee, it shall waive such fee.

(1995, P.A. 95–225, § 46, eff. Oct. 1, 1995.)

§ 46b–142. Venue of petitions. Appeal to Appellate Court. Expedited hearing in termination of parental rights appeals

(a) The Chief Court Administrator, in consultation with the judges of the Superior Court, shall establish districts for the purpose of establishing venue in juvenile matters. All petitions concerning delinquent children shall be heard within the district where the delinquency is alleged to have occurred or where the child resides, in the discretion of the court. All other petitions shall be heard within the district where the child or youth resided at the time of the filing of the petition, but for the purposes of this section any child or youth born in any hospital or institution where the mother is confined at the time of birth shall be deemed to have residence in the district wherein such child's or youth's mother was living at the time of her admission to such hospital or institution.

(b) The Department of Children and Families, or any party at interest aggrieved by any final judgment or order of the court, may appeal to the Appellate Court in accordance with the provisions of section 52–263. The clerk in charge of such juvenile matters shall forthwith, after notice of any appeal, prepare and file with the clerk of the Appellate Court the certified copy of the record of the case from which such appeal has been taken. The name of the child or youth involved in any such appeal shall not appear on the record of the appeal, and the records and papers of any juvenile case filed in the Appellate Court shall be open for inspection only to persons having a proper interest therein and upon order of the court.

(c) Pending such appeal, the Superior Court may cause the child or youth to be detained in some suitable place as the court may direct, or may release the child or youth in the care of a parent, probation officer or other suitable person, and may require the appellant to enter into a bond or recognizance to the state, with surety or security conditioned that the child or youth shall appear before the Appellate Court and abide by the order and judgment.

(d) Notwithstanding subsections (a), (b) and (c) of this section, the Department of Children and Families, or any party to the action aggrieved by a final judgment in a termination of parental rights proceeding, shall be entitled to an expedited hearing before the Appellate Court. A final decision of the Appellate Court shall be issued as soon as practicable after the date on which the certified copy of the record of the case is filed with the clerk of the Appellate Court.

(1949 Rev., § 2815; 1957, P.A. 651, § 15; 1958 Rev., §§ 17–70, 51–323; 1959, P.A. 531, § 14; 1967 P.A. 252; 1967, P.A. 630, § 11, eff. June 22, 1967; 1969, P.A. 794, § 16; 1974, P.A. 74–251, § 15; 1975, P.A. 75–420, § 4, eff. June 25, 1975; 1975, P.A. 75–567, § 78, eff. Jan. 1, 1976; 1975, P.A. 75–602, § 10, eff. Jan. 1, 1976; 1976, P.A. 76–436, §§ 10a, 32, eff. July 1, 1978; 1977, P.A. 77–614, § 521, eff. Jan. 1, 1979; 1978, P.A. 78–379, § 12, eff. July 1, 1978; 1983, June Sp.Sess., P.A. 83–29, § 36, eff. July 1, 1983; 1986, P.A. 86–108; 1993, P.A. 93–91, § 1, eff. July 1, 1993; 2001, P.A. 01–148, § 2.)

§ 46b–143. Notice of appeal

The clerk in charge of juvenile matters shall note the time of filing an appeal from a juvenile matter and forthwith forward to the clerk of the appellate court a certified copy of the appeal and order made thereon. He shall also send a copy by registered or certified mail to the Commissioner of Social Services or to the Commissioner of Children and Families, to the petitioner upon whose application the proceedings in the superior court were instituted, unless he is the appellant, to any person or agency having custody of any child or youth who is a subject of the proceeding, and to all other interested persons as designated in the appeal; and if the addresses of any such persons do not appear in the appeal, he shall call the matter to the attention of a judge of the superior court who shall make such an order of notice as he deems advisable.

(1958 Rev., §§ 17–70a, 51–324, 1959, P.A. 531, § 15; 1974, P.A. 74–251, § 16; 1975, P.A. 75–420, § 4, eff. June 25, 1975; 1975, P.A. 75–602, § 11, eff. Jan. 1, 1976; 1976, P.A. 76–436, § 28, eff. July 1, 1978; 1977, P.A. 77–614, § 521, eff. Jan. 1, 1979; 1978, P.A. 78–280, § 1, eff. July 1, 1978; 1983, June Sp.Sess., P.A. 83–29, § 37, eff. July 1, 1983; 1993, P.A. 93–91, § 1, eff. July 1, 1993; 1993, P.A. 93–262, § 1, eff. July 1, 1993.)

§ 46b–144. Religious faith. Service of commitment process

In committing a child or youth to a custodial agency, other than such child's or youth's natural guardians, the court shall, as far as practicable, select as such agency some person of like faith to that of the parent or parents of the child or youth or some agency or institution governed by persons of such faith, unless such agency or institution is a state or municipal agency or institution. In the order of committal, the court shall designate some indifferent person to serve the commitment process, and such indifferent person may be accompanied by any suitable relative or friend of such child or youth. If the person designated to serve such commitment process is an officer, such officer shall not serve such commitment process while dressed in the uniform of any police officer, and no such officer shall, while serving any such commitment process, wear plainly displayed any police officer's badge.

(1949 Rev., § 2816; 1958 Rev., §§ 17–71, 51–325; 1975, P.A. 75–602, § 12, eff. Jan. 1, 1976; 2000, P.A. 00–99, § 91; 2001, P.A. 01–195, § 39, eff. July 11, 2001.)

§ 46b–145. Prohibition on prosecution of child before regular criminal docket. Exceptions

No child shall be prosecuted for an offense before the regular criminal docket of the Superior Court except as provided in section 46b–127 and subsection (f) of section 46b–133c.

(1949 Rev., § 2817; 1958 Rev., §§ 17–72, 51–326; 1976, P.A. 76–436, § 29, eff. July 1, 1978; 1995, P.A. 95–225, § 26, eff. Oct. 1, 1995.)

§ 46b–146. Erasure of police and court records

Whenever any child has been found delinquent or a member of a family with service needs, and has subsequently been discharged from the supervision of the Superior Court or from the custody of the Department of Children and Families or from the care of any other institution or agency to whom he has been committed by the court, such child, his parent or guardian, may file a petition with the Superior Court and, if such court finds that at least two years or, in the case of a child convicted as delinquent for the commission of a serious juvenile offense, four years have elapsed from the date of such discharge, that no subsequent juvenile proceeding has been instituted against such child, that such child has not been found guilty of a crime and that such child has reached sixteen years of age within such period, it shall order all police and court records pertaining to such child to be erased. Upon the entry of such an erasure order, all references including arrest, complaint, referrals, petitions, reports and orders, shall be removed from all agency, official and institutional files, and a finding of delinquency or that the child was a member of a family with service needs shall be deemed never to have occurred. The persons in charge of such records shall not disclose to any person information pertaining to the record so erased, except that the fact of such erasure may be substantiated where, in the opinion of the court, it is in the best interests of such child to do so. No child who has been the subject of such an erasure order shall be deemed to have been arrested ab initio, within the meaning of the general statutes, with respect to proceedings so erased. Copies of the erasure order shall be sent to all persons, agencies, officials or institutions known to have information pertaining to the delinquency or family with service needs proceedings affecting such child. Whenever a child is dismissed as not delinquent or as not being a member of a family with service needs, all police and court records pertaining to such charge shall be ordered erased immediately, without the filing of a petition.

(1958 Rev., §§ 17–72a, 51–327; 1969, P.A. 794, § 4; 1971, P.A. 204; 1976, P.A. 76–436, § 30, eff. July 1, 1978; 1977, P.A. 77–452, § 25, eff. July 1, 1978; 1989, P.A. 89–273, § 6; 1993, P.A. 93–91, § 1, eff. July 1, 1993; 1995, P.A. 95–225, § 27, eff. Oct. 1, 1995; 1998, P.A. 98–256, § 7.)

§ 46b–147. Proceedings inadmissible as evidence in criminal proceedings

The disposition of any child under the provisions of this chapter, evidence given in such cases, except evidence of crime which, if committed by a person of sufficient age, would be punishable by imprisonment in the Connecticut Correctional Institution, Somers, and all orders therein, shall be inadmissible as evidence in any criminal proceedings against such child.

(1949 Rev., § 2818; 1958 Rev., §§ 17–78, 51–328.)

§ 46b–147a. Reports on cases of children charged with serious juvenile offenses

The judicial department shall prepare a quarterly report which tracks the cases of children charged with the commission of serious juvenile offenses and includes information pertaining to the offenses charged, patterns and frequency of court involvement, and the disposition of the cases. The judicial department shall submit such reports to the general assembly and all judges assigned to the juvenile session of the superior court.

(1989, P.A. 89–273, § 10.)

§ 46b–148. Violation of valid court order by child of family with service needs

When a child whose family has been adjudicated as a family with service needs in accordance with section 46b–149 violates any valid order which regulates future conduct of the child made by the court following such an adjudication, a probation officer, on receipt of a complaint setting forth facts alleging such a violation, or on his own motion on the basis of his knowledge of such a violation, may file a petition with the court alleging that the child has committed a delinquent act by reason of having violated a valid court order and setting forth the facts claimed to constitute such a violation. Such child may be processed as any other delinquent child under this chapter, except that (1) such child shall not be held in detention prior to a hearing on such petition for more than seventy-two hours excluding Saturdays, Sundays and holidays; and (2) in entering any order that directs or authorizes placement in a facility under the auspices of the Court Support Services Division or commitment to the Department of Children and Families, the judge shall make a determination that there is no less restrictive alternative appropriate to the needs of the child and the community.

(1949 Rev., § 2819; 1958 Rev., §§ 17–74, 51–329; 1976, P.A. 76–436, § 33, eff. July 1, 1978; 1982, P.A. 82–335; 1985, P.A. 85–226, § 2; 1989, P.A. 89–273, § 7; 1998, P.A. 98–183, § 4; 2002, P.A. 02–132, § 26.)

§ 46b–149. Family with service needs. Complaint. Review by probation officer. Filing of petition. Hearing. Order

(a) Any selectman, town manager, police officer or welfare department of any town, city or borough, probation officer, superintendent of schools, the Commissioner of Children and Families, any child-caring institution or agency approved or licensed by the Commissioner of Children and Families, any youth service bureau, a parent or foster parent of a child, or a child or his representative or attorney, who believes that the acts or omissions of a child are such that his family is a family with service needs, may file a written complaint setting forth those facts with the superior court which has venue over that matter.

(b) The court shall refer a complaint filed under subsection (a) of this section to a probation officer, who shall promptly determine whether it appears that the alleged facts, if true, would be sufficient to meet the definition of a family with service needs, provided a complaint alleging that a child is a truant or habitual truant shall not be determined to be insufficient to meet the definition of a family with service needs solely because it was filed during the months of April, May or June. If such probation officer so determines, he shall promptly either (1) refer the matter, with the consent of the child and his parents or guardian, to a suitable community-based or other service provider, or (2) file a petition with the court in the manner prescribed in subsection (c) of this section. In either case, the probation officer shall inform the complainant in writing of his action. If it appears that the allegations are not true, or that the child's family does not meet the definition of a family with service needs, the probation officer shall inform the complainant in writing of such finding. In any case in which the probation officer does not file a petition, he shall also inform the complainant of the right of such person to file a petition pursuant to subsection (c) of this section. Any person who has filed a complaint pursuant to subsection (a) of this section, and who has been notified by a probation officer that such officer does not intend to file a petition for a family with service needs may, within thirty days after mailing of such notice, file a petition under subsection (c) of this section.

(c) A petition alleging that a family constitutes a family with service needs shall be verified and filed with the Superior Court which has venue over the matter. The petition shall set forth plainly: (1) The facts which bring the child within the jurisdiction of the court, (2) the name, date of birth, sex and residence of the child, (3) the name and residence of his parent or parents, guardian or other person having control of him, and (4) a prayer for appropriate action by the court in conformity with the provisions of this section.

(d) When a petition is filed under subsection (c) of this section, the court may issue a summons to the child and his parents, guardian or other person having control of him to appear in court at a specified time and place. The summons shall be signed by a judge or by the clerk or assistant clerk of the court, and a copy of the petition shall be attached to it. Whenever it appears to the judge that orders addressed to an adult, as set forth in section 46b–121, are necessary for the welfare of such child, a similar summons shall be issued and served upon such adult if he is not already in court. Service of summons shall be made in accordance with section 46b–128. The court may punish for contempt, as provided in section 46b–121, any parent, guardian or other person so summoned who fails to appear in court at the time and place so specified. If a petition is filed under subsection (c) of this section alleging that a family is a family with service needs because a child is a truant or habitual truant, the court may not dismiss such petition solely because it was filed during the months of April, May or June.

(e) When a petition is filed under subsection (c) of this section alleging that a family constitutes a family with service needs because it includes a child who has been habitually truant, the court shall order that the local or regional board of education for the town in which the child resides, or the private school in the case of a child enrolled in a private school, shall cause an educational evaluation of such child to be performed if no such evaluation has been performed within the preceding year. Any costs incurred for the performance of such evaluation shall be borne by such local or regional board of education or such private school.

Text of subsection (f) effective until July 1, 2004, or upon enactment of the Interstate Compact for Juveniles by thirty-five jurisdictions, whichever is later.

(f) If it appears from the allegations of a petition or other sworn affirmations that there is: (1) A strong probability that the child may do something that is injurious to himself prior to court disposition; (2) a strong probability that the child will run away prior to the hearing; or (3) a need to hold the child for another jurisdiction, a judge may vest temporary custody of such child in some suitable person or agency. No nondelinquent juvenile runaway from another state may be held in a state-operated detention home in accordance with the provisions of sections 46b–151 to 46b–151g, inclusive, Interstate Compact on Juveniles. A hearing on temporary custody shall be held not later than ten days after the date on which a judge signs an order of temporary custody. Following such hearing, the judge may order that the child's temporary custody continue to be vested in some suitable person or agency. Any expenses of temporary custody shall be paid in the same manner as provided in subsection (b) of section 46b–129.

Text of subsection (f) effective July 1, 2004, or upon enactment of the Interstate Compact for Juveniles by thirty-five jurisdictions, whichever is later.

(f) If it appears from the allegations of a petition or other sworn affirmations that there is: (1) A strong probability that the child may do something that is injurious to himself prior to court disposition; (2) a strong probability that the child will run away prior to the hearing; or (3) a need to hold the child for another jurisdiction, a judge may vest temporary custody of such child in some suitable person or agency. No nondelinquent juvenile runaway from another state may be held in a state-operated detention home in accordance with the provisions of section 1 of public act 03–255, the Interstate Compact for Juveniles. A hearing on temporary custody shall be held not later than ten days after the date on which a judge signs an order of temporary custody. Following such hearing, the judge may order that the child's temporary custody continue to be vested in some suitable person or agency. Any expenses of temporary custody shall be paid in the same manner as provided in subsection (b) of section 46b–129.

(g) If it appears that the interests of the child or the family may be best served, prior to adjudication, by a referral to community-based or other services, the judge may permit the matter to be continued for a period not to exceed three months. If it appears at the conclusion of the continuance that the matter has been satisfactorily resolved, the judge may dismiss the petition.

(h) If the court finds, based on clear and convincing evidence, that the family of a child is a family with service needs, the court may, in addition to issuing any orders under section 46b–121, (1) refer the child to the Department of Children and Families for any voluntary services provided by said department or, if the family is a family with service needs solely as a result of a finding that a child is a truant or habitual truant, to the authorities of the local or regional school district or private school for services provided by such school district or such school, which services may include summer school, or to community agencies providing child and family services; (2) commit that child to the care and custody of the Commissioner of Children and Families for an indefinite period not to exceed eighteen months; (3) order the child to remain in his own home or in the custody of a relative or any other suitable person (A) subject to the supervision of a probation officer or (B) in the case of a family which is a family with service needs solely as a result of a finding that a child is a truant or habitual truant, subject to the supervision of a probation officer and the authorities of the local or regional school district or private school; or (4) if the family is a family with service needs as a result of the child engaging in sexual intercourse with another person and such other person is thirteen years of age or older and not more than two years older or younger than such child, (A) refer the child to a youth service bureau or other appropriate service agency for participation in a program such as a teen pregnancy program or a sexually transmitted disease program and (B) require such child to perform community service such as service in a hospital, an AIDS prevention program or an obstetrical and gynecological program. If the court issues any order which regulates future conduct of the child, parent or guardian, the child, parent or guardian, shall receive adequate and fair warning of the consequences of violation of the order at the time it is issued, and such warning shall be provided to the child, parent or guardian, to his attorney and to his legal guardian in writing and shall be reflected in the court record and proceedings.

(i) (1) The Commissioner of Children and Families may petition the court for an extension of a commitment under this section on the grounds that an extension would be in the best interest of the child. The court shall give notice to the child and his parent or guardian at least fourteen days prior to the hearing upon that petition. The court may, after hearing and upon finding that such extension is in the best interest of the child, continue the commitment for an additional indefinite period of not more than eighteen months. (2) The Commissioner of Children and Families may at any time petition the court to discharge a child, committed under this section, and any child committed to the commissioner under this section, or the parent or guardian of such child, may at any time but not more often than once every six months petition the court which committed the child to revoke such commitment. The court shall notify the child, his parent or guardian and the commissioner of any petition filed under this subsection, and of the time when a hearing on such petition will be held. Any order of the court made under this subsection shall be deemed a final order for purposes of appeal, except that no bond shall be required nor costs taxed on such appeal.

(1979, P.A. 79–567, § 3; 1980, P.A. 80–401, § 1; 1985, P.A. 85–226, § 3; 1988, P.A. 88–214, § 1, eff. May 26, 1988; 1989, P.A. 89–273, § 8; 1990, P.A. 90–240, § 3; 1991, P.A. 91–303, § 12, eff. July 1, 1991; 1992, P.A. 92–167, § 2, eff. June 1, 1992; 1993, P.A. 93–91, § 1, eff. July 1, 1993; 1993, P.A. 93–340, § 17, eff. Oct. 1, 1993; 1993, P.A. 93–435, § 26, eff. June 28, 1993; 1994, May 25 Sp.Sess., P.A. 94–1, § 94, eff. July 1, 1994; 1995, P.A. 95–339, § 6, eff. July 1, 1995; 1996, P.A. 96–178, § 11, eff. July 1, 1996; 1998, P.A. 98–183, § 5; 2003, P.A. 03–255, § 4, eff. July 1, 2004.)

§ 46b–149a. Duties of police officer re child of family with service needs

(a) Any police officer who receives a report from the parent or guardian of a child that such child is a member of a family with service needs, as defined in section 46b–120, shall promptly attempt to locate the child. If the officer locates such child, or any child he believes has run away from his parent or guardian's home without permission, or any nondelinquent juvenile runaway from another state, he shall report the location of the child to the parent or guardian, and may respond in one of the following ways: (1) He may transport the child to the home of the child's parent or guardian or any other person; (2) he may refer the child to the superior court for juvenile matters in the district where the child is located; (3) he may hold the child in protective custody for a maximum period of twelve hours until the officer can determine a more suitable disposition of the matter, provided (A) the child is not held in any locked room or cell and (B) the officer may release the child at any time without taking further action; or (4) he may transport or refer a child to any public or private agency serving children, with or without the agreement of the child. If a child is transported or referred to an agency pursuant to this section, such agency may provide services to the child unless or until the child's parent or guardian at any time refuses to agree to those services. Such agency shall be immune from any liability, civil or criminal, which might otherwise be incurred or imposed; provided such services are provided in good faith and in a nonnegligent manner.

(b) Any police officer acting in accordance with the provisions of this section shall be deemed to be acting in the course of his official duties.

(1979, P.A. 79–567, § 6; 1980, P.A. 80–401, § 2; 1988, P.A. 88–214, § 2, eff. May 26, 1988; 1989, P.A. 89–273, § 9; 1998, P.A. 98–183, § 6.)

§ 46b–149b. Immunity of police officer or municipal official from personal liability

(a) Any police officer or any official of a municipal or community agency, who in the course of such police officer's or official's employment under subsection (d) of section 17a–15 or section 46b–120, 46b–121, 46b–149, 46b–149a, 46b–150f or 46b–150g provides assistance to a child or a family in need thereof, shall not be liable to such child or such family for civil damages for any personal injuries which result from the voluntary termination of service by the child or the family.

(b) Each municipal police department and the Division of State Police within the Department of Public Safety shall implement a uniform protocol for providing intervention and assistance in matters involving youths in crisis. Such uniform protocol shall be developed by the Police Officer Standards and Training Council established under section 7–294b.

(1980, P.A. 80–401, § 3; 2002, P.A. 02–109, § 4; 2003, P.A. 03–257, § 4.)

§ 46b–149c. Truancy and other family with service needs cases. Duties of judicial branch

With respect to truancy and other family with service needs cases, the judicial branch shall:

(1) Coordinate programs and services with other state agencies;

(2) Establish protocols in cooperation with the Office of Policy and Management, the Department of Children and Families and the Department of Education for referral to community-based intervention programs prior to referral of a case to the superior court for juvenile matters;

(3) Develop and use procedures to evaluate the risk and service needs of children whose cases have been referred to the superior court for juvenile matters; and

(4) Collaborate with community-based programs.

(1998, P.A. 98–183, § 1.)

§ 46b–149d. Demonstration project to establish school and community-based truancy prevention initiative. Sites. Grant eligibility. Establishment of truancy or family with service needs docket. Duties of Court Support Services Division

(a) A demonstration project to establish a school and community-based truancy prevention initiative is authorized, which shall address the needs of public school children who exhibit patterns of unexcused absences from school. The Office of Policy and Management, in consultation with the Department of Education and the judicial branch, shall issue a request for proposals and award competitive grants. The Office of Policy and Management, in consultation with the Department of Education and the judicial branch, shall select at least two demonstration project sites.

(b) To be eligible for such a competitive grant the program shall include:

(1) A description of the policies that the community's board of education has adopted pursuant to section 10–198a, as well as the board's plans to work with the leadership of community truancy prevention initiatives to: (A) Monitor school attendance; (B) enhance any existing in-school truancy prevention programs; (C) establish after-school and summer school programs for truants; (D) provide mentoring programs for children at risk of being truant; (E) implement school and community-based intervention programs that target families with elementary school children who exhibit persistent patterns of absenteeism or truancy; (F) provide in-school alternative education initiatives for chronic truants; and (G) provide monthly truancy reports to the Office of Policy and Management.

(2) Participation of youth service bureaus, juvenile review boards or other community-based service networks, to provide such services as truancy coordinators, mentorship programs and peer mediation for children as well as truancy case management for boards of education prior to the referral of a truant to a juvenile court. Such proposal may also provide for diversion of truants from the juvenile court in appropriate cases. Case management will include development of student intervention action plans, family counseling and parental education programs and, when appropriate, referrals for mental health and substance abuse assessments for the child and parents.

(c) The Chief Court Administrator may establish a truancy or family with service needs docket for communities that have been awarded a grant and established a community-based truancy prevention initiative pursuant to this section. The Court Support Services Division shall, within available appropriations, make available to such communities a risk and needs assessment tool and funding for nonjudicial diversion of appropriate truancy cases to youth service bureaus and juvenile review boards. For court sanctioned intervention programs, the Court Support Services Division shall: (1) Provide parenting education programs; (2) expand existing programs to serve truancy cases; (3) provide intensive outreach and monitoring, including intensive probation services for chronic truancy cases; (4) provide for mental health assessment and outpatient mental health and substance abuse services; and (5) provide for short-term emergency residential placement for children with multiple referrals to the juvenile court for truancy, being beyond control and for being runaways.

(1998, P.A. 98–183, § 2; 2002, P.A. 02–132, § 27; 2003, P.A. 03–278, § 99, eff. July 9, 2003.)

§ 46b–150. Emancipation of minor. Procedure

Any minor who has reached such minor's sixteenth birthday and is residing in this state, or any parent or guardian of such minor, may petition the superior court for juvenile matters or the probate court for the district in which either the minor or the parents or guardian of such minor resides for a determination that the minor named in the petition be emancipated. The petition shall be verified and shall state plainly: (1) The facts which bring the minor within the jurisdiction of the court, (2) the name, date of birth, sex and residence of the minor, (3) the name and residence of the minor's parent, parents or guardian, and (4) the name of the petitioner and the petitioner's relationship to the minor. Upon the filing of the petition in the Superior Court, the court shall cause a summons to be issued to the minor and the minor's parent, parents or guardian, in the manner provided in section 46b–128. Service on an emancipation petition filed in the superior court for juvenile matters pursuant to this section shall not be required on the petitioning party. Upon the filing of the petition in the Probate Court, the court shall assign a time, not later than thirty days thereafter, and a place for hearing such petition. The court shall cause a citation and notice to be served on the minor and the minor's parent, if the parent is not the petitioner, at least seven days prior to the hearing date, by a state marshal, constable or indifferent person. The court shall direct notice by certified mail to the parent, if the parent is the petitioner. The court shall order such notice as it directs to the Commissioner of Children and Families, and other persons having an interest in the minor.

(1979, P.A. 79–397, § 1; 1998, P.A. 98–219, § 8; 2000, P.A. 00–99, § 92; 2001, P.A. 01–148, § 3; 2001, P.A. 01–195, § 40, eff. July 11, 2001.)

§ 46b–150a. Investigation of petition for emancipation. Report. Appointment of counsel. Probate Court may order examination

(a) With respect to a petition filed in Superior Court pursuant to section 46b–150, the Superior Court may, if it deems it appropriate, (1) require a probation officer, the Commissioner of Children and Families or any other person to investigate the allegations in the petition and file a report of that investigation with the court, (2) appoint counsel for the minor who may serve as guardian ad litem for the minor, (3) appoint counsel for the minor's parents or guardian, or (4) make any other orders regarding the matter which the court deems appropriate.

(b) With respect to a petition filed in Probate Court pursuant to section 46b–150, the Probate Court shall request an investigation by the Commissioner of Children and Families, unless this requirement is waived by the court for cause shown. The court shall appoint counsel to represent the minor. The costs of such counsel shall be paid by the minor, except that if such minor is unable to pay for such counsel and files an affidavit with the court demonstrating inability of the minor to pay, the reasonable compensation shall be established by, and paid from funds appropriated to, the Judicial Department. If funds have not been included in the budget of the Judicial Department for such purposes, such compensation shall be established by the Probate Court Administrator and paid from the Probate Court Administration Fund.

(c) Upon finding at the hearing or any time during the pendency of the proceeding in the Probate Court, that reasonable cause exists to warrant an examination, the court on its own motion or on motion of any party, may order the minor to be examined at a suitable place by a physician, psychiatrist or licensed psychologist appointed by the court. The court may also order examination of a parent whose competency or ability to care for a minor before the court is at issue. The expenses of any examination if ordered by the court on its own motion shall be paid for by the petitioner or if ordered on motion by a party, shall be paid for by the party moving for such an examination, unless such party or petitioner is unable to pay such expenses in which case they shall be paid for by funds appropriated to the Judicial Department. However, in the case of a probate matter, if funds have not been included in the budget of the Judicial Department for such purposes, such expenses shall be established by the Probate Court Administrator and paid from the Probate Court Administration Fund. The court may consider the results of the examinations in ruling on the merits of the petition.

(1979, P.A. 79–397, § 2; 1993, P.A. 93–91, § 1, eff. July 1, 1993; 1998, P.A. 98–219, § 9; 1998, June Sp.Sess., P.A. 98–1, § 108, eff. June 24, 1998; 2000, P.A. 00–75, § 10.)

§ 46b–150b. Order of emancipation

If the Superior Court or the Probate Court, after hearing, finds that: (1) The minor has entered into a valid marriage, whether or not that marriage has been terminated by dissolution; or (2) the minor is on active duty with any of the armed forces of the United States of America; or (3) the minor willingly lives separate and apart from his parents or guardian, with or without the consent of the parents or guardian, and that the minor is managing his own financial affairs, regardless of the source of any lawful income; or (4) for good cause shown, it is in the best interest of the minor, any child of the minor or the parents or guardian of the minor, the court may enter an order declaring that the minor is emancipated.

(1979, P.A. 79–397, § 3; 1980, P.A. 80–283, § 1; 1995, P.A. 95–225, § 28, eff. Oct. 1, 1995; 1998, P.A. 98–219, § 10.)

§ 46b–150c. Appeal

Any person named in a petition filed pursuant to section 46b–150a who is aggrieved by the order of the Probate Court may appeal to the Superior Court as provided in section 45a–186. Any person named in a petition filed pursuant to section 46b–150a who is aggrieved by order of the Superior Court may appeal to the Appellate Court in the manner provided in subsection (b) of section 46b–142.

(1979, P.A. 79–397, § 4; 1983, June Sp.Sess., P.A. 83–29, § 38, eff. July 1, 1983; 1998, P.A. 98–219, § 11.)

§ 46b–150d. Effect of emancipation

An order that a minor is emancipated shall have the following effects: (a) The minor may consent to medical, dental or psychiatric care, without parental consent, knowledge or liability; (b) the minor may enter into a binding contract; (c) the minor may sue and be sued in his own name; (d) the minor shall be entitled to his own earnings and shall be free of control by his parents or guardian; (e) the minor may establish his own residence; (f) the minor may buy and sell real and personal property; (g) the minor may not thereafter be the subject of a petition under section 46b–129 as an abused, dependent, neglected or uncared for child or youth; (h) the minor may enroll in any school or college, without parental consent; (i) the minor shall be deemed to be over eighteen years of age for purposes of securing an operator's license under section 14–36 and a marriage license under subsection (b) of section 46b–30 without parental consent; (j) the minor shall be deemed to be over eighteen years of age for purposes of registering a motor vehicle under section 14–12; (k) the parents of the minor shall no longer be the guardians of the minor under section 45a–606; (*l*) the parents of a minor shall be relieved of any obligations respecting his school attendance under section 10–184; (m) the parents shall be relieved of all obligation to support the minor; (n) the minor shall be emancipated for the purposes of parental liability for his acts under section 52–572; (*o*) the minor may execute releases in his own name under section 14–118; and (p) the minor may enlist in the armed forces of the United States without parental consent.

(1979, P.A. 79–397, § 5; 1979, P.A. 79–631, § 98, eff. July 6, 1979; 1980, P.A. 80–283, § 2; 1980, P.A. 80–483, § 120, eff. June 6, 1980; 1984, P.A. 84–429, § 76; 1990, P.A. 90–61; 2002, P.A. 02–109, § 2, eff. June 7, 2002.)

§ 46b–150e. Emancipation under common law

Nothing in sections 46b–150 to 46b–150e, inclusive, shall affect the status of minors who are or may become emancipated under the common law of this state. *(1979, P.A. 79–397, § 6.)*

§ 46b–150f. Youth in crisis. Petition. Court orders. Violations

(a) Any selectman, town manager, police officer or welfare department of any town, city or borough, any probation officer, any superintendent of schools, any child-caring institution or agency approved or licensed by the Commissioner of Children and Families, any youth service bureau, a parent or foster parent of a youth, or a representative of youth, who believes that the acts or omissions of a youth are such that such youth is a youth in crisis may file a written complaint setting forth those facts with the Superior Court which has venue over the matter.

(b) A petition alleging that a youth is a youth in crisis shall be verified and filed with the Superior Court which has venue over the matter. The petition shall set forth plainly: (1) The facts which bring the youth within the jurisdiction of the court; (2) the name, date of birth, sex and residence of the youth; (3) the name and residence of the parent or parents, guardian or other person having control of the youth; and (4) a prayer for appropriate action by the court in conformity with the provisions of this section.

(c) Upon determination that a youth is a youth in crisis in accordance with policies established by the Chief Court Administrator, the court may make and enforce orders, including, but not limited to, orders: (1) Directing the Commissioner of Motor Vehicles to suspend the motor vehicle operator's license of the youth in crisis for a period of time, as directed by the court, but not to exceed one year; (2) requiring work or specified community service; (3) mandating that the youth in crisis attend an educational program in the local community approved by the court; (4) requiring mental health services; (5) referring the youth in crisis to a youth service bureau, provided one exists in the local community; and (6) reviewing the option of emancipation, pursuant to section 46b–150, of the youth in crisis or the parent or guardian of such youth in crisis. A youth in crisis found to be in violation of any order under this section shall not be considered to be delinquent and shall not be punished by the court by incarceration in any state-operated detention facility or correctional facility.

(d) The Judicial Department may use any funds appropriated for purposes of this chapter for costs incurred by the department or the court pursuant to this section.

(2000, P.A. 00–177, § 3, eff. July 1, 2001; 2001, P.A. 01–195, § 100, eff. July 11, 2001; 2002, P.A. 02–109, § 5, eff. July 1, 2002; 2003, P.A. 03–257, § 5.)

§ 46b–150g. Duties of police officer re youth in crisis

(a) Any police officer who receives a report from the parent or guardian of a youth in crisis, as defined in subparagraph (A) of subdivision (3) of section 46b–120, shall attempt to locate the youth in crisis. If the officer locates such youth in crisis, such officer shall report the location of the youth to the parent or guardian in accordance with the provisions of federal and state law after such officer determines that such report does not place the youth in any physical or emotional harm. In addition, the police officer shall respond in one of the following ways: (1) Transport the youth in crisis to the home of the child's parent or guardian or a suitable and worthy adult; (2) refer the youth in crisis to the probate court in the district where the youth in crisis is located, provided the probate judge for such probate court is willing to accept the referral; (3) hold the youth in crisis in protective custody for a maximum period of twelve hours until the officer can determine a more suitable disposition of the matter, provided (A) the youth in crisis is not held in any cell designed or used for adults, and (B) the officer may release the youth in crisis to the parent or guardian of the youth if the officer determines that returning the youth does not place the youth in any physical or emotional harm; (4) transport or refer a youth in crisis to any public or private agency serving children, with or without the agreement of the youth in crisis; (5) refer the youth in crisis to a youth service bureau, provided one exists in the local community; or (6) if the police officer is unable to transport, refer or hold the youth in crisis pursuant to subdivisions (1) to (5), inclusive, of this subsection, refer the youth in crisis to the superior court for juvenile matters in the district where the youth in crisis is located. If a youth in crisis is transported or referred to an agency pursuant to this section, such agency shall provide temporary services to the youth in crisis unless or until the parent or guardian of the youth in crisis at any time refuses to agree to those services.

(b) Any police officer acting in accordance with the provisions of this section shall be deemed to be acting in the course of the police officer's official duties.

(2000, P.A. 00–177, § 4, eff. July 1, 2001; 2003, P.A. 03–257, § 3.)

PART II. INTERSTATE COMPACT ON JUVENILES

§ 46b–151. Declaration of policy

This section repealed by 2003, P.A. 03–255, § 5, effective July 1, 2004, or upon enactment of the Interstate Compact for Juveniles by thirty-five jurisdictions, whichever is later.

It is hereby found and declared:

(1) That juveniles who are not under proper supervision and control, or who have absconded, escaped or run away, are likely to endanger their own health, morals and welfare, and the health, morals and welfare of others; and

(2) that the cooperation of this state with other states is necessary to provide for the welfare and protection of juveniles and of the people of this state.

It shall therefore be the policy of this state, in adopting the interstate compact on juveniles, to cooperate fully with other states:

(1) In returning juveniles to such other states whenever their return is sought; and

(2) in accepting the return of juveniles whenever a juvenile residing in this state is found or apprehended in another state and in taking all measures to initiate proceedings for the return of such juveniles.

(1957, P.A. 363, § 1; 1958, Rev., § 17–75.)

§ 46b–151a. Compact

This section repealed by 2003, P.A. 03–255, § 5, effective July 1, 2004, or upon enactment of the Interstate Compact for Juveniles by thirty-five jurisdictions, whichever is later.

The governor is hereby authorized and directed to execute a compact on behalf of this state with any other state or states legally joining therein in the form substantially as follows:

INTERSTATE COMPACT ON JUVENILES

ARTICLE I

That juveniles who are not under proper supervision and control, or who have absconded, escaped or run away, are likely to endanger their own health, morals and welfare, and the health, morals and welfare of others. The cooperation of the states party to this compact is therefore necessary to provide for the welfare and protection of juveniles and of the public with respect to (1) cooperative supervision of delinquent juveniles on probation or parole; (2) the return, from one state to another, of delinquent juveniles who have escaped or absconded; (3) the return, from one state to another, of nondelinquent juveniles who have run away from home; and (4) additional measures for the protection of juveniles and of the public, which any two or more of the party states may find desirable to undertake cooperatively. In carrying out the provisions of this compact the party states shall be guided by the noncriminal, reformative and protective policies which guide their laws concerning delinquent, neglected or dependent juveniles generally. It shall be the policy of the states party to this compact to cooperate and observe their respective responsibilities for the prompt return and acceptance of juveniles and delinquent juveniles who become subject to the provisions of this compact. The provisions of this compact shall be reasonably and liberally construed to accomplish the foregoing purposes.

ARTICLE II

That all remedies and procedures provided by this compact shall be in addition to and not in substitution for other rights, remedies and procedures, and shall not be in derogation of parental rights and responsibilities.

ARTICLE III

That, for the purposes of this compact, "delinquent juvenile" means any juvenile who has been adjudged delinquent and who, at the time the provisions of this compact are invoked, is still subject to the jurisdiction of the court that has made such adjudication or to the jurisdiction or supervision of an agency or institution pursuant to an order of such court; "probation or parole" means any kind of conditional release of juveniles authorized under the laws of the states party hereto; "court" means any court having jurisdiction over delinquent, neglected or dependent children; "state" means any state, territory or possession of the United States, the District of Columbia, and the Commonwealth of Puerto Rico; and "residence" or any variant thereof means a place at which a home or regular place of abode is maintained.

ARTICLE IV

(a) That the parent, guardian, person or agency entitled to legal custody of a juvenile who has not been adjudged delinquent but who has run away without the consent of such parent, guardian, person or agency may petition the appropriate court in the demanding state for the issuance of a requisition for his return. The petition shall state the name and age of the juvenile, the name of the petitioner and the basis of entitlement to the juvenile's custody, the circumstances of his running away, his location if known at the time application is made, and such other facts as may tend to show that the juvenile who has run away is endangering his own welfare or the welfare of others and is not an emancipated minor. The petition shall be verified by affidavit, shall be executed in duplicate, and shall be accompanied by two certified copies of the document or documents on which the petitioner's entitlement to the juvenile's custody is based, such as birth certificates, letters of guardianship, or custody decrees. Such further affidavits and other documents as may be deemed proper may be submitted with such petition. The judge of the court to which this application is made may hold a hearing thereon to determine whether for the purposes of this compact the petitioner is entitled to the legal custody of the juvenile, whether or not it appears that the juvenile has in fact run away without consent, whether or not he is an emancipated minor, and whether or not it is in the best interest of the juvenile to compel his return to the state. If the judge determines, either with or without a hearing, that the juvenile should be returned, he shall present to the appropriate court or to the executive authority of the state where the juvenile is alleged to be located a written requisition for the return of such juvenile. Such requisition shall set forth the name and age of the juvenile, the determination of the court that the juvenile has run away without the consent of a parent, guardian, person or agency entitled to his legal custody, and that it is in the best interest and for the protection of such juvenile that he be returned. In the event that a proceeding for the adjudication of the juvenile as a delinquent, neglected or dependent juvenile is pending in the court at the time when such juvenile runs away, the court may issue a requisition for the return of such juvenile upon its own motion, regardless of the consent of the parent, guardian, person or agency entitled to legal custody, reciting therein the nature and circumstances of the pending proceeding. The requisition shall in every case be executed in duplicate and shall be signed by the judge. One copy of the requisition shall be filed with the compact administrator of the demanding state, there to remain on file subject to the provisions of law governing records of such court. Upon the receipt of a requisition demanding the return of a juvenile who has run away, the court or the executive authority to whom the requisition is addressed shall issue an order to any peace officer or other appropriate person directing him to take into custody and detain such juvenile. Such detention order must substantially recite the facts necessary to the validity of its issuance hereunder. No juvenile detained upon such order shall be delivered over to the officer whom the court demanding him shall have appointed to receive him, unless he shall first be taken forthwith before a judge of a court in the state, who shall inform him of the demand made for his return, and who may appoint counsel or guardian ad litem for him. If the judge of such court shall find that the requisition is in order, he shall deliver such juvenile over to the officer whom the court demanding him shall have appointed to receive him. The judge, however, may fix a reasonable time to be allowed for the purpose of testing the legality of the proceeding. Upon reasonable information that a person is a juvenile who has run away from another state party to this compact without the consent of a parent, guardian, person or agency entitled to his legal custody, such juvenile may be taken into custody without a requisition and brought forthwith before a judge of the appropriate court, who may appoint counsel or guardian ad litem for such juvenile and who shall determine after a hearing whether sufficient cause exists to hold the person, subject to the order of the court, for his own protection and welfare, for such a time not exceeding ninety days as will enable his return to another state party to this compact pursuant to a requisition for his return from a court of that state, provided no nondelinquent juvenile runaway may be detained in a state-operated detention home. If, at the time when a state seeks the return of a juvenile who has run away, there is pending in the state wherein he is found any criminal charge, or any proceeding to have him adjudicated a delinquent juvenile for an act committed in such state, or if he is suspected of having committed within such state a criminal offense or an act of juvenile delinquency, he shall not be returned without the consent of such state until discharged from prosecution or other form of proceeding, imprisonment, detention or supervision for such offense or juvenile delinquency. The duly accredited officers of any state party to this compact, upon the establishment of their authority and identity of the juvenile being returned, shall be permitted to transport such juvenile through any and all states party to this compact, without interference. Upon his return to the state from which he ran away, the juvenile shall be subject to such further proceedings as may be appropriate under the laws of that state.

(b) That the state to which a juvenile is returned under this article shall be responsible for payment of the transportation costs of such return.

(c) That "juvenile" as used in this article means any person who is a minor under the law of the state of residence of the parent, guardian, person or agency entitled to the legal custody of such minor.

ARTICLE V

(a) That the appropriate person or authority from whose probation or parole supervision a delinquent juvenile has absconded or from whose institutional custody he has escaped shall present to the appropriate court or to the executive authority of the state where the delinquent juvenile is alleged to be located a written requisition for the return of such delinquent juvenile. Such requisition shall state the name and age of the delinquent juvenile, the particulars of his adjudication as a delinquent juvenile, the circumstances of the breach of the terms of his probation or parole or of his escape from an institution or agency vested with his legal custody or supervision, and the location of such delinquent juvenile, if known, at the time the requisition is made. The requisition shall be verified by affidavit, shall be executed in duplicate, and shall be accompanied by two certified copies of the judgment, formal adjudication, or order of commitment which subjects such delinquent juvenile to probation or parole or to the legal custody of the institution or agency concerned. Such further affidavits and other documents as may be deemed proper may be submitted with such requisition. One copy of the requisition shall be filed with the compact administrator of the demanding state, there to remain on file subject to the provisions of law governing records of the appropriate court. Upon the receipt of a requisition demanding the return of a delinquent juvenile who has absconded or escaped, the court or the executive authority to whom the requisition is addressed shall issue an order to any peace officer or other appropriate person directing him to take into custody and detain such delinquent juvenile. Such detention order must substantially recite the facts necessary to the validity of its issuance hereunder. No delinquent juvenile detained upon such order shall be delivered over to the officer whom the appropriate person or authority demanding him shall have appointed to receive him, unless he shall first be taken forthwith before a judge of an appropriate court in the state, who shall inform him of the demand made for his return and who may appoint counsel or guardian ad litem for him. If the judge of such court shall find that the requisition is in order, he shall deliver such delinquent juvenile over to the officer whom the appropriate person or authority demanding him shall have appointed to receive him. The judge, however, may fix a reasonable time to be allowed for the purpose of testing the legality of the proceeding. Upon reasonable information that a person is a delinquent juvenile who has absconded while on probation or parole, or escaped from an institution or agency vested with his legal custody or supervision in any state party to this compact, such person may be taken into custody in any other state party to this compact without a requisition. But in such event, he must be taken forthwith before a judge of the appropriate court, who may appoint counsel or guardian ad litem for such person and who shall determine, after a hearing, whether sufficient cause exists to hold the person subject to the order of the court for such a time, not exceeding ninety days, as will enable his detention under a detention order issued on a requisition pursuant to this article. If, at the time when a state seeks the return of a delinquent juvenile who has either absconded while on probation or parole or escaped from an institution or agency vested with his legal custody or supervision, there is pending in the state wherein he is detained any criminal charge or any proceeding to have him adjudicated a delinquent juvenile for an act committed in such state, or if he is suspected of having committed within such state a criminal offense or an act of juvenile delinquency, he shall not be returned without the consent of such state until discharged from prosecution or other form of proceeding, imprisonment, detention or supervision for such offense or juvenile delinquency. The duly accredited officers of any state party to this compact, upon the establishment of their authority and the identity of the delinquent juvenile being returned, shall be permitted to transport such delinquent juvenile through any and all states party to this compact, without interference. Upon his return to the state from which he escaped or absconded, the delinquent juvenile shall be subject to such further proceedings as may be appropriate under the laws of that state.

(b) That the state to which a delinquent juvenile is returned under this article shall be responsible for the payment of the transportation costs of such return.

ARTICLE VI

That any delinquent juvenile who has absconded while on probation or parole, or escaped from an institution or agency vested with his legal custody or supervision in any state party to this compact, and any juvenile who has run away from any state party to this compact, who is taken into custody without a requisition in another state party to this compact under the provisions of article IV (a) or of article V (a), may consent to his immediate return to the state from which he absconded, escaped or ran away. Such consent shall be given by the juvenile or delinquent juvenile and his counsel or guardian ad litem if any, by executing or subscribing a writing, in the presence of a judge of the appropriate court, which states that the juvenile or delinquent juvenile and his counsel or guardian ad litem, if any, consent to his return to the demanding state. Before such consent shall be executed or subscribed, however, the judge, in the presence of counsel or guardian ad litem, if any, shall inform the juvenile or delinquent juvenile of his rights under this compact. When the consent has been duly executed, it shall be forwarded to and filed with the compact administrator of the state in which the court is located and the judge shall direct the officer having the juvenile or delinquent juvenile in custody to deliver him to the duly accredited officer or officers of the state demanding his return, and shall cause to be delivered to such officer or officers a copy of the consent. The court may, however, upon the request of the state to which the juvenile or delinquent juvenile is being returned, order him to return unaccompanied to such state and shall provide him with a copy of such court order; in such event a copy of the consent shall be forwarded to the compact administrator of the state to which said juvenile or delinquent juvenile is ordered to return.

ARTICLE VII

(a) That the duly constituted judicial and administrative authorities of a state party to this compact (herein called "sending state") may permit any delinquent juvenile within such state, placed on probation or parole, to reside in any other state party to this compact (herein called "receiving state") while on probation or parole, and the receiving state shall accept such delinquent juvenile, if the parent, guardian or person entitled to the legal custody of such delinquent juvenile is residing or undertakes to reside within the receiving state. Before granting such permission, opportunity shall be given to the receiving state to make such investigations as it deems necessary. The authorities of the sending state shall send to the authorities of the receiving state copies of pertinent court orders, social case studies and all other available information which may be of value to and assist the receiving state in supervising a probationer or parolee under this compact. A receiving state, in its discretion, may agree to accept supervision of a probationer or parolee in cases where the parent, guardian or person entitled to the legal custody of the delinquent juvenile is not a resident of the receiving state, and if so accepted the sending state may transfer supervision accordingly.

(b) That each receiving state will assume the duties of visitation and of supervision over any such delinquent juvenile and in the exercise of those duties will be governed by the same standards of visitation and supervision that prevail for its own delinquent juveniles released on probation or parole.

(c) That, after consultation between the appropriate authorities of the sending state and of the receiving state as to the desirability and necessity of returning such a delinquent juvenile, the duly accredited officers of a sending state may enter a receiving state and there apprehend and retake any such delinquent juvenile on probation or parole. For that purpose, no formalities will be required other than establishing the authority of the officer and the identity of the delinquent juvenile to be retaken and returned. The decision of the sending state to retake a delinquent juvenile on probation or parole shall be conclusive upon and not reviewable within the receiving state, but if, at the time the sending state seeks to retake a delinquent juvenile on probation or parole, there is pending against him within the receiving state any criminal charge or any proceeding to have him adjudicated a delinquent juvenile for any act committed in such state, or if he is suspected of having committed within such state a criminal offense or an act of juvenile delinquency, he shall not be returned without the consent of the receiving state until discharged from prosecution or other form of proceeding, imprisonment, detention or supervision for such offense or juvenile delinquency. The duly accredited officers of the sending state shall be permitted to transport delinquent juveniles being so returned through any and all states party to this compact, without interference.

(d) That the sending state shall be responsible under this article for paying the costs of transporting any delinquent juvenile to the receiving state or of returning any delinquent juvenile to the sending state.

ARTICLE VIII

(a) That the provisions of articles IV (b), V (b) and VII (d) of this compact shall not be construed to alter or affect any internal relationship among the departments, agencies and officers of and in the government of a party state, or between a party state and its subdivisions, as to the payment of costs, or responsibilities therefor.

(b) That nothing in this compact shall be construed to prevent any party state or subdivision thereof from asserting any right against any person, agency or other entity in regard to costs for which such party state or subdivision thereof may be responsible pursuant to articles IV (b), V (b) or VII (d) of this compact.

ARTICLE IX

That, to every extent possible, it shall be the policy of states party to this compact that no juvenile or delinquent juvenile shall be placed or detained in any prison, jail or lockup nor be detained or transported in association with criminal, vicious or dissolute persons.

ARTICLE X

That the duly constituted administrative authorities of a state party to this compact may enter into supplementary agreements with any other state or states party hereto for the cooperative care, treatment and rehabilitation of delinquent juveniles whenever they shall find that such agreements will improve the facilities or programs available for such care, treatment and rehabilitation. Such care, treatment and rehabilitation may be provided in an institution located within any state entering into such supplementary agreement. Such supplementary agreements shall (1) provide the rates to be paid for the care, treatment and custody of such delinquent juveniles, taking into consideration the character of facilities, services and subsistence furnished; (2) provide that the delinquent juvenile shall be given a court hearing prior to his being sent to another state for care, treatment and custody; (3) provide that the state receiving such a delinquent juvenile in one of its institutions shall act solely as agent for the state sending such delinquent juvenile; (4) provide that the sending state shall at all times retain jurisdiction over delinquent juveniles sent to an institution in another state; (5) provide for reasonable inspection of such institutions by the sending state; (6) provide that the consent of the parent, guardian, person or agency entitled to the legal custody of said delinquent juvenile shall be secured prior to his being sent to another state; and (7) make provision for such other matters and details as shall be necessary to protect the rights and equities of such delinquent juveniles and of the cooperating states.

ARTICLE XI

That any state party to this compact may accept any and all donations, gifts and grants of money, equipment and services from the federal or any local government, or any agency thereof and from any person, firm or corporation, for any of the purposes and functions of this compact, and may receive and utilize the same subject to the terms, conditions and regulations governing such donations, gifts and grants.

ARTICLE XII

That the governor of each state party to this compact shall designate an officer who, acting jointly with like officers of other party states, shall promulgate rules and regulations to carry out more effectively the terms and provisions of this compact.

ARTICLE XIII

That this compact shall become operative immediately upon its execution by any state as between it and any other state or states so executing. When executed it shall have the full force and effect of law within such state, the form of execution to be in accordance with the laws of the executing state.

ARTICLE XIV

That this compact shall continue in force and remain binding upon each executing state until renounced by it. Renunciation of this compact shall be by the same authority which executed it, by sending six months' notice in writing of its intention to withdraw from the compact to the other states party hereto. The duties and obligations of a renouncing state under article VII hereof shall continue as to parolees and probationers residing therein at the time of withdrawal until retaken or finally discharged. Supplementary agreements entered into under article X hereof shall be subject to renunciation as provided by such supplementary agreements, and shall not be subject to the six months' renunciation notice of the present article.

ARTICLE XV

That the provisions of this compact shall be severable and if any phrase, clause, sentence or provision of this compact is declared to be contrary to the constitution of any participating state or of the United States or the applicability thereof to any government, agency, person or circumstance is held invalid, the validity of the remainder of this compact and the applicability thereof to any government, agency, person or circumstance shall not be affected thereby. If this compact shall be held contrary to the constitution of any state participating therein, the compact shall remain in full force and effect as to the remaining states and in full force and effect as to the state affected as to all severable matters.

(1957, P.A. 363, § 2; 1958, Rev., § 17–76; 1988, P.A. 88–214, § 3, eff. May 26, 1988; 1990, P.A. 90–230, § 24; 1998, June Sp.Sess., P.A. 98–1, § 72, eff. June 24, 1998.)

§ 46b–151b. Amendment to compact concerning interstate rendition of juveniles alleged to be delinquent

This section repealed by 2003, P.A. 03–255, § 5, effective July 1, 2004, or upon enactment of the Interstate Compact for Juveniles by thirty-five jurisdictions, whichever is later.

The governor is authorized and directed to execute, with any other state or states legally joining in the same, an amendment to the Interstate Compact on Juveniles in the form substantially as follows:

AMENDMENT TO THE INTERSTATE COMPACT ON JUVENILES CONCERNING INTERSTATE RENDITION OF JUVENILES ALLEGED TO BE DELINQUENT

(a) This amendment shall provide additional remedies and shall be binding only as among and between those party states which specifically execute the same.

(b) All provisions and procedures of articles V and VI of section 46b–151a shall be construed to apply to any juvenile charged with being a delinquent by reason of a violation of any criminal law. Any juvenile charged with being a delinquent by reason of violating any criminal law shall be returned to the requesting state upon a requisition to the state where the juvenile may be found. A petition in such case shall be filed in a court of competent jurisdiction in the requesting state where the violation of criminal law is alleged to have been committed. The petition may be filed regardless of whether the juvenile has left the state before or after the filing of the petition. The requisition described in article V of section 46b–151a shall be forwarded by the judge of the court in which the petition has been filed.

(1958 Rev., § 17–76a; 1983, P.A. 83–281, § 1, eff. June 7, 1983; 1991, P.A. 91–406, § 19.)

§ 46b–151c. Compact administrator

This section repealed by 2003, P.A. 03–255, § 5, effective July 1, 2004, or upon enactment of the Interstate Compact for Juveniles by thirty-five jurisdictions, whichever is later.

Pursuant to said compact, the governor is hereby authorized and empowered to designate an officer who shall be the compact administrator and who, acting jointly with like officers of other party states, shall promulgate rules and regulations to carry out more effectively the terms of the compact. Said compact administrator shall serve subject to the pleasure of the governor. The compact administrator is hereby authorized, empowered and directed to cooperate with all departments, agencies and officers of and in the government of this state and its subdivisions in facilitating the proper administration of the compact or of any supplementary agreement or agreements entered into by this state thereunder.

(1957, P.A. 363, § 3; 1958, Rev., § 17–77.)

§ 46b–151d. Supplementary agreements

This section repealed by 2003, P.A. 03–255, § 5, effective July 1, 2004, or upon enactment of the Interstate Compact for Juveniles by thirty-five jurisdictions, whichever is later.

The compact administrator is hereby authorized and empowered to enter into supplementary agreements with appropriate officials of other states pursuant to the compact. In the event that such supplementary agreement shall require or contemplate the use of any institution or facility of this state or require or contemplate the provisions of any service by this state, said supplementary agreement shall have no force or effect until approved by the head of the department or agency under whose jurisdiction said institution or facility is operated or whose department or agency will be charged with the rendering of such service.

(1957, P.A. 363, § 4; 1958, Rev., § 17–78.)

§ 46b–151e. Payments by state

This section repealed by 2003, P.A. 03–255, § 5, effective July 1, 2004, or upon enactment of the Interstate Compact for Juveniles by thirty-five jurisdictions, whichever is later.

The compact administrator, subject to the approval of the comptroller, may make or arrange for any payments necessary to discharge any financial obligations imposed upon this state by the compact or by any supplementary agreement entered into thereunder.

(1957, P.A. 363, § 5; 1958, Rev., § 17–79.)

§ 46b–151f. Enforcement of compact

This section repealed by 2003, P.A. 03–255, § 5, effective July 1, 2004, or upon enactment of the Interstate Compact for Juveniles by thirty-five jurisdictions, whichever is later.

The courts, departments, agencies and officers of this state and its subdivisions shall enforce this compact and shall do all things appropriate to the effectuation of its purposes and intent which may be within their respective jurisdictions.

(1957, P.A. 363, § 6; 1958, Rev., § 17–80.)

§ 46b–151g. Additional procedure for return of juveniles

This section repealed by 2003, P.A. 03–255, § 5, effective July 1, 2004, or upon enactment of the Interstate Compact for Juveniles by thirty-five jurisdictions, whichever is later.

In addition to any procedure provided in Articles IV and VI of the compact for the return of any runaway juvenile, the particular states, the juvenile or his parents, the courts, or other legal custodian involved may agree upon and adopt any other plan or procedure legally authorized under the laws of this state and the other respective party states for the return of any such runaway juvenile.

(1957, P.A. 363, § 7; 1958, Rev., § 17–81.)

§§ 46b–152 to 46b–159. Reserved for future use

CHAPTER 815y

PATERNITY MATTERS

Section

§ 46b–160. Petition by mother or expectant mother. Venue. Continuance of case. Evidence. Jurisdiction over nonresident putative father. Personal service. Petition to include answer form, notice and application for appointment of counsel. Genetic tests. Default judgment, when

(a) Proceedings to establish paternity of a child born or conceived out of lawful wedlock, including one born to, or conceived by, a married woman but begotten by a man other than her husband, shall be commenced by the service on the putative father of a verified petition of the mother or expectant mother. The verified petition, summons and order shall be filed in the superior court for the judicial district in which either she or the putative father resides, except that in IV–D support cases, as defined in subdivision (13) of subsection (b) of section 46b–231 and in petitions brought under sections 46b–212 to 46b–213v, inclusive, such petition shall be filed with the clerk for the Family Support Magistrate Division serving the judicial district where either she or the putative father resides. In cases involving public assistance recipients the petition shall also be served upon the Attorney General who shall be and remain a party to any paternity proceeding and to any proceedings after judgment in such action. The court or any judge, or family support magistrate, assigned to said court shall cause a summons, signed by such judge or magistrate, by the clerk of said court, or by a commissioner of the Superior Court to be issued, requiring the putative father to appear in court at a time and place as determined by the clerk but not more than ninety days after the issuance of the summons to show cause why the request for relief in such petition should not be granted. A state marshal, proper officer or investigator shall make due returns of process to the court not less than twenty-one days before the date assigned for hearing. Such petition, summons and order shall be on forms prescribed by the Office of the Chief Court Administrator. In the case of a child or expectant mother being supported wholly or in part by the state, service of such petition may be made by any investigator employed by the Department of Social Services and any proper officer authorized by law. Such petition may be brought at any time prior to the child's eighteenth birthday, provided liability for past support shall be limited to the three years next preceding the date of the filing of any such petition. If the putative father fails to appear in court at such time and place, the court or family support magistrate shall hear the petitioner and, upon a finding that process was served on the putative father, shall enter a default judgment of paternity against such father and such other orders as the facts may warrant. Such court or family support magistrate may order continuance of such hearing; and if such mother or expectant mother continues constant in her accusation, it shall be evidence that the respondent is the father of such child. The court or family support magistrate shall, upon motion by a party, issue an order for temporary support of the child by the respondent pending a final judgment of the issue of paternity if such court or magistrate finds that there is clear and convincing evidence of paternity which evidence shall include, but not be limited to, genetic test results indicating a ninety-nine per cent or greater probability that such respondent is the father of the child.

(b) If the putative father resides out of or is absent from the state, notice required for the exercise of jurisdiction over such putative father shall be actual notice, and shall be in the manner prescribed for personal service of process by the law of the place in which service is made.

(c) In any proceeding to establish paternity, the court or family support magistrate may exercise personal jurisdiction over a nonresident putative father if the court or magistrate finds that the putative father was personally served in this state or that the putative father resided in this state and while residing in this state (1) paid prenatal expenses for the mother and support for the child, (2) resided with the child and held himself out as the father of the child, or (3) paid support for the child and held himself out as the father of the child, provided the nonresident putative father has received actual notice of the pending petition for paternity pursuant to subsection (c) of this section.

(d) The petition, when served pursuant to subsection (c) of this section, shall be accompanied by an answer form, a notice to the putative father and an application for appointment of counsel, written in clear and simple language designed for use by pro se defendants.

(e) (1) The answer form shall require the putative father to indicate whether he admits that he is the father, denies that he is the father or does not know whether he is the father of the child. Any response to the answer form shall not be deemed to waive any jurisdictional defense.

(2) The notice to the putative father shall inform him that (A) he has a right to be represented by an attorney, and if he is indigent, the court will appoint an attorney for him, (B) if he is found to be the father, he will be required to financially support the child until the child attains the age of eighteen years, (C) if he does not admit he is the father, the court or family support magistrate may order a genetic test to determine paternity and that the cost of such test shall be paid by the state in IV–D support cases, and in non-IV–D cases

shall be paid by the petitioner, except that if he is subsequently adjudicated to be the father of the child, he shall be liable to the state or the petitioner, as the case may be, for the amount of such cost and (D) if he fails to return the answer form or fails to appear for a scheduled genetic test without good cause, a default judgment shall be entered.

(3) The application for appointment of counsel shall include a financial affidavit.

(f) If the court or family support magistrate may exercise personal jurisdiction over the nonresident putative father pursuant to subsection (d) of this section and the answer form is returned and the putative father does not admit paternity, the court shall order the mother, the child and the putative father to submit to genetic tests. Such order shall be served upon the putative father in the same manner as provided in subsection (c) of this section. The genetic test of the putative father, unless he requests otherwise, shall be made in the state where the putative father resides at a location convenient to him. The costs of such test shall be paid by the state in IV–D support cases, and in non-IV–D cases shall be paid by the petitioner, except that if the putative father is subsequently adjudicated the father of the child, he shall be liable to the state or the petitioner, as the case may be, for the amount of the costs.

(g) The court or family support magistrate shall enter a default judgment against a nonresident putative father if such putative father (1) fails to answer or otherwise respond to the petition, or (2) fails to appear for a scheduled genetic test without good cause, provided a default judgment shall not be entered against a nonresident putative father unless (A) there is evidence that the nonresident putative father has received actual notice of the petition pursuant to subsection (c) of this section and (B) there is verification that the process served upon the putative father included the answer form, notice to the defendant and an application for appointment of counsel required by subsection (e) of this section. Upon entry of a default judgment, a copy of the judgment and a form for a motion to reopen shall be served upon the father in the same manner as provided in subsection (c) of this section.

(1958 Rev., § 52–435a; 1965, Feb.Sp.Sess., P.A. 406, § 1, eff. July 1, 1965; 1967, P.A. 520, § 1; 1974, P.A. 74–183, § 108, eff. Dec. 31, 1974; 1975, P.A. 75–406, § 3, eff. June 25, 1975; 1975, P.A. 75–420, § 4, eff. June 25, 1975; 1976, P.A. 76–334, § 9, eff. June 2, 1976; 1976, P.A. 76–436, § 498, eff. July 1, 1978; 1977, P.A. 77–614, § 521, eff. Jan. 1, 1979; 1978, P.A. 78–379, § 21, eff. July 1, 1978; 1979, P.A. 79–560, § 16, eff. July 1, 1979; 1985, P.A. 85–548, § 3; 1988, P.A. 88–364, § 60, eff. June 8, 1988; 1989, P.A. 89–360, §§ 13, 44, eff. July 1, 1989; 1993, P.A. 93–187, § 2; 1993, P.A. 93–262, § 68, eff. July 1, 1993, 1993, P.A. 93–329, § 2, eff. Oct. 1, 1993; 1993, P.A. 93–396, § 15; 1997, June 18 Sp.Sess., P.A. 97–1, § 56, eff. Jan. 1, 1998; 1997, June 18 Sp.Sess., P.A. 97–7, § 19, eff. July 1, 1997; 2000, P.A. 00–99, § 93; 2001, P.A. 01–195, § 41, eff. July 11, 2001.)

§ 46b–161. Procedure in action brought by expectant mother

In the case of any such petition brought prior to the birth of the child, no final trial on the issue of paternity shall be had, except as to hearing on probable cause, until after the birth of the child. In such hearing on probable cause the court, on the day on which the defendant has been summoned to appear, shall determine whether probable cause exists, and if so, the court shall order the defendant to become bound to the complainant, with surety to appear on a date certain for final determination, or further continuance as circumstances may then require.

(1958 Rev., § 52–438a; 1967, P.A. 520, § 2.)

§ 46b–162. Action by state or town

The state or any town interested in the support of a child born out of wedlock may, if the mother neglects to bring such petition, institute such proceedings against the person accused of begetting the child, and may take up and pursue any petition commenced by the mother for the maintenance of the child, if she fails to prosecute to final judgment. Such petition may be made by the Commissioner of Social Services or the town welfare administrator on information or belief. The mother of the child may be subpoenaed for testimony on the hearing of the petition.

(1958 Rev., § 52–440a; 1965, Feb.Sp.Sess., P.A. 406, § 3, eff. July 1, 1965; 1975, P.A. 75–420, § 4, eff. June 25, 1975; 1977, P.A. 77–614, § 521, eff. Jan. 1, 1979; 1979, P.A. 79–560, § 17, eff. July 1, 1979; 1993, P.A. 93–262, § 69, eff. July 1, 1993.)

§ 46b–163. Action not defeated by stillbirth or other premature termination of pregnancy

No provision of section 46b–160 or 46b–161 shall be construed to defeat any action commenced thereunder because of stillbirths or other premature termination of the pregnancy. In either such event, the court shall enter such order as it shall, after hearing, determine proper.

(1958 Rev., § 52–438b; 1967, P.A. 520, § 3.)

§ 46b–164. Repealed. (1997, June 18 Sp.Sess., P.A. 97–7, § 37, eff. July 1, 1997.)

§ 46b–165. Testimony of mother

The mother of any child for whom adjudication of paternity is sought in paternity proceedings shall not be excused from testifying because her evidence may tend to disgrace or incriminate her; nor shall she thereafter be prosecuted for any criminal act about which (1) she testifies in connection with such proceedings, or (2) she makes any statement prior to such proceedings with respect to the issue of paternity.

(1958 Rev., § 52–435b; 1965, Feb.Sp.Sess., P.A. 406, § 4, eff. July 1, 1965; 1971, P.A. 439, § 2.)

§ 46b–166. Testimony of putative father

The putative father of any child for whom adjudication of paternity is sought in paternity proceedings shall not be excused from testifying because his evidence may tend to disgrace or incriminate him; nor shall he thereafter be prosecuted for any criminal act about which (1) he testifies in connection with such proceedings or (2) he makes any statement prior to such proceedings with respect to the issue of paternity.

(1958 Rev., § 52–435c; 1971, P.A. 439, § 1.)

§ 46b–167. Evidence of putative father's good character admissible

Evidence of the good character of the accused for morality and decency, prior to the alleged commission of the offense, shall be admissible in his favor in paternity proceedings, and may be rebutted by evidence showing a contrary character at such time.

(1949 Rev., § 8186; 1958 Rev., § 52–437.)

§ 46b–168. Genetic tests when paternity is in dispute. Assessment of costs

(a) In any proceeding in which the question of paternity is at issue the court or a family support magistrate, on motion of any party, may order genetic tests which shall mean deoxyribonucleic acid tests, to be performed by a hospital, accredited laboratory, qualified physician or other qualified person designated by the court, to determine whether or not the putative father or husband is the father of the child. The results of such tests, whether ordered under this section or required by the IV-D agency under section 46b–168a, shall be admissible in evidence to either establish definite exclusion of the putative father or husband or as evidence that he is the father of the child without the need for foundation testimony or other proof of authenticity or accuracy, unless objection is made in writing not later than twenty days prior to the hearing at which such results may be introduced in evidence.

(b) In any proceeding in which the question of paternity is at issue, the results of such genetic tests, whether ordered under this section or required by the IV-D agency under section 46b–168a, shall constitute a rebuttable presumption that the putative father is the father of the child if the results of such tests indicate a ninety-nine per cent or greater probability that he is the father of the child, provided the petitioner has presented evidence that sexual intercourse occurred between the mother and the putative father during the period of time in which the child was conceived.

(c) The costs of making tests provided by this section shall be chargeable against the party making the motion, provided if the court finds that such party is indigent and unable to pay such costs, such costs shall be paid by the state. If the costs of making such tests are paid by the state and the respondent making the motion is subsequently adjudicated to be the father of the child, such respondent shall be liable to the state for the amount of such costs.

(1957, P.A. 367; 1958 Rev., § 52–184; 1981, P.A. 81–433, § 1, eff. July 1, 1981; 1989, P.A. 89–360, § 41, eff. July 1, 1989; 1993, P.A. 93–329, § 10, eff. Oct. 1, 1993; 1994, P.A. 94–93; 1997, June 18 Sp.Sess., P.A. 97–7, § 20, eff. July 1, 1997.)

§ 46b–168a. Genetic tests in IV–D support cases when paternity at issue. Assessment of costs. Regulations

(a) In any IV–D support case, as defined in subdivision (13) of subsection (b) of section 46b–231, in which the paternity of a child is at issue, or in any case in which a support enforcement agency is providing services to a petitioner in a proceeding under sections 46b–212 to 46b–213v, inclusive, in which the paternity of a child is at issue, the IV–D agency or the support enforcement agency shall require the child and all other parties other than individuals who have good cause for refusing to cooperate or who are subject to other exceptions to submit to genetic tests which shall mean deoxyribonucleic acid tests, to be performed by a hospital, accredited laboratory, qualified physician or other qualified person designated by such agency, to determine whether or not the putative father or husband is the father of the child, upon the request of any such party, provided such request is supported by a sworn statement by the party which either (1) alleges paternity and sets forth facts establishing a reasonable possibility of the requisite sexual contact between the parties, or (2) denies paternity and sets forth facts establishing a reasonable possibility of the nonexistence of sexual contact between the parties.

(b) The costs of making the tests provided by this section shall be paid by the state, provided if the putative father is the requesting party and he is subsequently adjudicated to be the father of the child, he shall be liable to the state for the amount of such costs to the extent of his ability to pay, in accordance with regulations adopted by the Commissioner of Social Services pursuant to subdivision (3) of subsection (c) of this section. Any court or family support magistrate may order such father to pay the state in accordance with this subsection. The contesting party shall make advance payment for any additional testing required in the event of a contest of the original test results.

(c) The Commissioner of Social Services shall adopt regulations, in accordance with the provisions of chapter 54, [1] to establish criteria for determining (1) good cause or other exceptions for refusing to cooperate under subsection (a) of this section, which shall include, but not be limited to, domestic violence, sexual abuse and lack of information and shall take into account the best interests of the child, (2) the sufficiency of the facts establishing a reasonable possibility of the existence or nonexistence of the requisite sexual contact between the parties, as required under subsection (a) of this section, and (3) the ability of the requesting party to pay the costs of the genetic tests in accordance with subsection (b) of this section.

(1997, June 18 Sp.Sess., P.A. 97–7, § 21, eff. July 1, 1997; 2003, P.A. 03–89, § 4.)

1 C.G.S.A. § 4–166 et seq.

§ 46b–169. Compelling disclosure of name of putative father. Institution of action

(a) If the mother of any child born out of wedlock, or the mother of any child born to any married woman during marriage which child shall be found not to be issue of the marriage terminated by a decree of divorce or dissolution or by decree of any court of competent jurisdiction, fails or refuses to disclose the name of the putative father of such child under oath to the Commissioner of Social Services, if such child is a recipient of public assistance, or to a selectman of a town in which such child resides, if such child is a recipient of general assistance, or otherwise to a guardian or a guardian ad litem of such child, such mother may be cited to appear before any judge of the superior court and compelled to disclose the name of the putative father under oath and to institute an action to establish the paternity of said child.

(b) Any woman who, having been cited to appear before a judge of the superior court pursuant to subsection (a), fails to appear or fails to disclose or fails to prosecute a paternity action may be found to be in contempt of said court and may be fined not more than two hundred dollars or imprisoned not more than one year or both.

(1958 Rev., § 52–440b; 1971, P.A. 439, § 4; 1974, P.A. 74–183, § 110, eff. Dec. 31, 1974; 1975, P.A. 75–406, § 6, eff. June 25, 1975; 1975, P.A. 75–420, § 4, eff. June 25, 1975; 1976, P.A. 76–436, § 500, eff. July 1, 1978; 1977, P.A. 77–614, § 521, eff. Jan. 1, 1979; 1979, P.A. 79–560, § 18, eff. July 1, 1979; 1988, P.A. 88–364, § 61, eff. June 8, 1988; 1993, P.A. 93–262, § 70, eff. July 1, 1993.)

§ 46b–170. Withdrawal or settlement

No such petition shall be withdrawn except upon approval of a judge or in IV–D support cases as defined in subsection (b) of section 46b–231 and petitions brought under sections 46b–212 to 46b–213v, inclusive, the family support magistrate assigned to the judicial district in which the petition was brought. Any agreement of settlement, before or after a petition has been brought, other than an agreement made under the provisions of section 46b–172, between the mother and putative father shall take effect only upon approval of the terms thereof by a judge of the Superior Court, or family support magistrate assigned to the judicial district in which the mother or the putative father resides and, in the case of children supported by the state or the town, on the approval of the Commissioner of Social Services or the Attorney General. When so approved, such agreements shall be binding upon all persons executing them, whether such person is a minor or an adult.

(1958 Rev., § 52–439a; 1965, Feb.Sp.Sess., P.A. 406, § 2, eff. July 1, 1965; 1974, P.A. 74–183, § 109, eff. Dec. 31, 1974; 1975, P.A. 75–406, § 5, eff. June 25, 1975; 1975, P.A. 75–420, § 4, eff. June 25, 1975; 1976, P.A. 76–436, § 499, eff. July 1, 1978; 1977, P.A. 77–614, § 521, eff. Jan. 1, 1979; 1979, P.A. 79–560, § 19, eff. July 1, 1979; 1988, P.A. 88–364, § 62, eff. June 8, 1988; 1989, P.A. 89–360, § 14, eff. July 1, 1989; 1993, P.A. 93–262, § 71, eff. July 1, 1993; 1993, P.A. 93–396, § 16; 1997, June 18 Sp.Sess., P.A. 97–1, § 57, eff. Jan. 1, 1998.)

§ 46b–171. Judgment and order of court or family support magistrate

(a) (1) If the defendant is found to be the father of the child, the court or family support magistrate shall order the defendant to stand charged with the support and maintenance of such child, with the assistance of the mother if such mother is financially able, as said court finds, in accordance with the provisions of section 17b–81, 17b–223, 17b–745, subsection (b) of section 17b–179, section 17a–90, 46b–129, 46b–130 or 46b–215 to be reasonably commensurate with the financial ability of the defendant, and to pay a certain sum periodically until the child attains the age of eighteen years. The court or family support magistrate shall order the defendant to pay such sum to the complainant, or, if a town or the state has paid such expense, to the town or the state, as the case may be, and shall grant execution for the same and costs of suit taxed as in other civil actions, together with a reasonable attorney's fee; and may require the defendant to become bound with sufficient surety to perform such orders for support and maintenance.

(2) In addition, the court or family support magistrate shall include in each support order in a IV–D support case a provision for the health care coverage of the child which provision may include an order for either parent to name any child under the age of eighteen years as a beneficiary of any medical or dental insurance or benefit plan carried by such parent or available to such parent on a group basis through an employer or union. Any such employment-based order shall be enforced using a National Medical Support Notice as provided in section 46b–88. If such insurance coverage is unavailable at reasonable cost, the provision for health care coverage may include an order for either parent to apply for and maintain coverage on behalf of the child under the HUSKY Plan, Part B.[1] The noncustodial parent shall be ordered to apply for the HUSKY Plan, Part B only if such parent is found to have sufficient ability to pay the appropriate premium. In any IV–D support case in which the noncustodial

parent is found to have insufficient ability to provide medical insurance coverage and the custodial party is the HUSKY Plan, Part A [2] or Part B applicant, the provision for health care coverage may include an order for the noncustodial parent to pay such amount as is specified by the court or family support magistrate to the state or the custodial party, as their interests may appear, to offset the cost of any insurance payable under the HUSKY Plan, Part A or Part B. In no event may such order include payment to offset the cost of any such premium if such payment would reduce the amount of current support required under the child support guidelines.

(3) The court or family support magistrate shall also have authority to make and enforce orders for the payment by any person named herein of unpaid support contributions for which the defendant is liable in accordance with the provisions of section 17b–81, 17b–223, subsection (b) of section 17b–179, section 17a–90, 46b–129 or 46b–130 and, in IV–D cases, to order such person, provided such person is not incapacitated, to participate in work activities which may include, but shall not be limited to, job search, training, work experience and participation in the job training and retraining program established by the Labor Commissioner pursuant to section 31–3t.

(4) If the defendant fails to comply with any order made under this section, the court or family support magistrate may commit the defendant to a community correctional center, there to remain until the defendant complies therewith; but, if it appears that the mother does not apply the periodic allowance paid by the defendant toward the support of such child, and that such child is chargeable, or likely to become chargeable, to the town where it belongs, the court, on application, may discontinue such allowance to the mother, and may direct it to be paid to the selectmen of such town, for such support, and may issue execution in their favor for the same. The provisions of section 17b–743 shall apply to this section. The clerk of the court which has rendered judgment for the payment of money for the maintenance of any child under the provisions of this section shall, within twenty-four hours after such judgment has been rendered, notify the selectmen of the town where the child belongs.

(5) Any support order made under this section may at any time thereafter be set aside, altered or modified by any court issuing such order upon a showing of a substantial change in the circumstances of the defendant or the mother of such child or upon a showing that such order substantially deviates from the child support guidelines established pursuant to section 46b–215a, unless there was a specific finding on the record that the application of the guidelines would be inequitable or inappropriate. There shall be a rebuttable presumption that any deviation of less than fifteen per cent from the child support guidelines is not substantial and any deviation of fifteen per cent or more from the guidelines is substantial. Modification may be made of such support order without regard to whether the order was issued before, on or after May 9, 1991. No such support orders may be subject to retroactive modification, except that the court may order modification with respect to any period during which there is a pending motion for a modification of an existing support order from the date of service of the notice of such pending motion upon the opposing party pursuant to section 52–50.

(6) Failure of the defendant to obey any order for support made under this section may be punished as for contempt of court and the costs of commitment of any person imprisoned therefor shall be paid by the state as in criminal cases.

(b) Whenever the Superior Court or family support magistrate reopens a judgment of paternity entered pursuant to this section in which a person was found to be the father of a child who is or has been supported by the state and the court or family support magistrate finds that the person adjudicated the father is not the father of the child, the Department of Social Services shall refund to such person any money paid to the state by such person during the period such child was supported by the state.

(c) In IV–D support cases, as defined in subdivision (13) of subsection (b) of section 46b–231, a copy of any support order established or modified pursuant to this section or, in the case of a motion for modification of an existing support order, a notice of determination that there should be no change in the amount of the support order, shall be provided to each party and the state case registry within fourteen days after issuance of such order or determination.

(1949 Rev., § 8180; 1957, P.A. 462, § 1; 1958 Rev., § 52–442; 1959, P.A. 115, § 3; 1959, P.A. 639, § 1, eff. June 29, 1959; 1969, P.A. 297; 1989, P.A. 89–360, §§ 15, 42, eff. July 1, 1989; 1990, P.A. 90–188, § 3; 1991, P.A. 91–76, § 3, eff. May 9, 1991; 1993, P.A. 93–329, § 11, eff. Oct. 1, 1993; 1997, June 18 Sp.Sess., P.A. 97–7, § 22, eff. July 1, 1997; 1999, P.A. 99–279, § 30, eff. July 1, 1999; 2002, May 9 Sp.Sess., P.A. 02–7, § 43.)

[1] C.G.S.A. §§ 17b–289 to 17b–303, inclusive, and 1997, Oct. 29 Sp.Sess. P.A. 97–1, § 16.

[2] C.G.S.A. § 17b–261.

§ 46b–172. Acknowledgment of paternity and agreement to support; judgment

(a) (1) In lieu of or in conclusion of proceedings under section 46b–160, a written acknowledgment of paternity executed and sworn to by the putative father of the child when accompanied by (A) an attested waiver of the right to a blood test, the right to a trial and the right to an attorney, and (B) a written affirmation of paternity executed and sworn to by the mother of the child shall have the same force and effect as a judgment of the Superior Court. It shall be considered a legal finding of paternity without requiring or permitting judicial ratification, and shall be binding on the person executing the same whether such person is an adult or a minor, subject to subdivision (2) of this subsection. Such acknowledgment shall not be binding unless, prior to the signing of any affirmation or acknowledgement of paternity, the mother and the putative father are given oral and written notice of the alternatives to, the legal consequences of, and the rights and responsibilities that arise from signing such affirmation or acknowledgement. The notice to the mother shall include, but shall not be limited to, notice that the affirmation of paternity may result in rights of custody and visitation, as well as a duty of support, in the person named as father. The notice to the putative father shall include, but not be limited to, notice that such father has the right to contest paternity, including the right to appointment of counsel, a genetic test to determine paternity and a trial by the Superior Court or a family support magistrate and that acknowledgment of paternity will make such father liable for the financial support of the child until the child's eighteenth birthday. In addition, the notice shall inform the mother and the father that DNA testing may be able to establish paternity with a high degree of accuracy and may, under certain circumstances, be available at state expense. The notices shall also explain the right to rescind the acknowledgment, as set forth in subdivision (2) of this subsection, including the address where such notice of rescission should be sent, and shall explain that the acknowledgment cannot be challenged after sixty days, except in court upon a showing of fraud, duress or material mistake of fact.

(2) The mother and the acknowledged father shall have the right to rescind such affirmation or acknowledgment in writing within the earlier of (A) sixty days, or (B) the date of an agreement to support such child approved in accordance with subsection (b) of this section or an order of support for such child entered in a proceeding under subsection (c) of this section. An acknowledgment executed in accordance with subdivision (1) of this subsection may be challenged in court or before a family support magistrate after the rescission period only on the basis of fraud, duress or material mistake of fact which may include evidence that he is not the father, with the burden of proof upon the challenger. During the pendency of any such challenge, any responsibilities arising from such acknowledgment shall continue except for good cause shown.

(3) All written notices, waivers, affirmations and acknowledgments required under subdivision (1) of this subsection, and rescissions authorized under subdivision (2) of this subsection, shall be on forms prescribed by the Department of Public Health, provided such acknowledgment form includes the minimum requirements specified by the Secretary of the United States Department of Health and Human Services. All acknowledgments and rescissions executed in accordance with this subsection shall be filed in the paternity registry established and maintained by the Department of Public Health under section 19a–42a.

(4) An acknowledgment of paternity signed in any other state according to its procedures shall be given full faith and credit by this state.

(b) An agreement to support the child by payment of a periodic sum until the child attains the age of eighteen years, together with provisions for reimbursement for past due support based upon ability to pay in accordance with the provisions of section 17b–81, 17b–223, subsection (b) of section 17b–179, section 17a–90, 46b–129 or 46b–130, and reasonable expense of prosecution of the petition, when filed with, and approved by a judge of said court, or in IV–D support cases and matters brought under sections 46b–212 to 46b–213v, inclusive, a family support magistrate at any time, shall have the same force and effect, retroactively or prospectively in accordance with the terms of said agreement, as an order of support entered by that court, and shall be enforceable and subject to modification in the same manner as is provided by law for orders of the court in such cases. Past due support in such cases shall be limited to the three years next preceding the date of the filing of such agreements to support. Payments under such agreement shall be made to the petitioner, except that in IV–D support cases, as defined in subsection (b) of section 46b–231, payments shall be made to the Bureau of Child Support Enforcement or its designated agency. Such written agreements to support shall be on forms prescribed by the Office of the Chief Court Administrator and shall be sworn to, and shall be binding on the person executing the same whether he is an adult or a minor.

(c) At any time after the signing of any acknowledgment of paternity, upon the application of any interested party, the court or any judge thereof or any family support magistrate in IV–D support cases and in matters brought under sections 46b–212 to 46b–213v, inclusive, shall cause a summons, signed by such judge or magistrate, by the clerk of said court or by a commissioner of the Superior Court, to be issued, requiring the acknowledged father to appear in court at a time and place as determined by the clerk but not more than ninety days after the issuance of the summons, to show cause why the court or the family support magistrate assigned to the judicial district in IV–D support cases should not enter judgment for support of the child by payment of a periodic sum until the child attains the age of eighteen years, together with provision for reimbursement for past due support based upon ability to pay in accordance with the provisions of section 17b–81, 17b–223, subsection (b) of section 17b–179, section 17a–90, 46b–129 or 46b–130, a provision for health coverage of the child as required by section 46b–215, and reasonable expense of the action under this subsection. Such court or family support magistrate, in IV–D cases, shall also have the authority to order the acknowledged father who is subject to a plan for reimbursement of past-due support and is not incapacitated, to participate in work activities which may include, but shall not be limited to, job search, training, work experience and participation in the job training and retraining program established by the Labor Commissioner pursuant to section 31–3t. The application, summons and order shall be on forms prescribed by the Office of the Chief Court Administrator. Proceedings to obtain such orders of support shall be commenced by the service of such summons on the acknowledged father. A state marshal or proper officer shall make due return of process to the court not less than twenty-one days before the date assigned for hearing. The prior judgment as to paternity shall be res judicata as to that issue for all paternity acknowledgments filed with the court on or after March 1, 1981, but before July 1, 1997, and shall not be reconsidered by the court unless the person seeking review of the acknowledgment petitions the superior court for the judicial district having venue for a hearing on the issue of paternity within three years of such judgment. In addition to such review, if the acknowledgment of paternity was filed prior to March 1, 1981, the acknowledgment of paternity may be reviewed by denying the allegation of paternity in response to the initial petition for support, whenever it is filed. All such payments shall be made to the petitioner, except that in IV–D support cases, as defined in subsection (b) of section 46b–231, payments shall be made to the state, acting by and through the IV–D agency.

(d) Whenever a petition is filed for review of an acknowledgment of paternity of a child who is or has been supported by the state, and review of such acknowledgment of paternity is granted by the court pursuant to subsection (c) of this section, and upon review, the court or family support magistrate finds that the petitioner is not the father of the child, the Department of Social Services shall refund to the petitioner any money paid by the petitioner to the state during any period such child was supported by the state.

(e) In IV–D support cases, as defined in subdivision (13) of subsection (b) of section 46b–231, a copy of any support order established pursuant to this section shall be provided to each party and the state case registry within fourteen days after issuance of such order or determination.

(1958 Rev., § 52–442a; 1965, Feb.Sp.Sess., P.A. 406, § 5, eff. July 1, 1965; 1971, P.A. 439, § 3; 1974, P.A. 74–183, § 111, eff. Dec. 31, 1974; 1975, P.A. 75–406, § 7, eff. June 25, 1975; 1976, P.A. 76–436, § 501, eff. July 1, 1978; 1981, P.A. 81–274; 1982, P.A. 82–6; 1986, P.A. 86–359, § 40, eff. Jan. 1, 1987; 1989, P.A. 89–360, § 43, eff. July 1, 1989; 1990, P.A. 90–213, § 20, eff. July 1, 1990; 1991, P.A. 91–391, § 4; 1993, P.A. 93–187, § 3; 1993, P.A. 93–262, § 1, eff. July 1, 1993; 1993, P.A. 93–329, § 12, eff. Oct. 1, 1993; 1993, P.A. 93–396, § 17; 1993, P.A. 93–435, § 59, eff. June 28, 1993; 1997, June 18 Sp.Sess., P.A. 97–1, § 58, eff. Jan. 1, 1998; 1997, June 18 Sp.Sess., P.A. 97–7, § 23, eff. July 1, 1997; 1999, P.A. 99–193, § 7, eff. July 1, 1999; 2000, P.A. 00–99, § 94, eff. December 1, 2000; 2001, P.A. 01–195, § 42, eff. July 11, 2001.)

§ 46b–172a. Claim for paternity by putative father. Hearing. Three-judge court. Rights and responsibilities upon adjudication or acknowledgment of paternity. Claim for paternity after death of putative father

(a) Any person claiming to be the father of a child born out of wedlock may at any time but no later than sixty days after the date of notice under section 45a–716, file a claim for paternity with the court of probate for the district in which either the mother or the child resides, on forms provided by such court. The claim shall contain the claimant's name and address, the name and last-known address of the mother and the month and year of the birth or expected birth of the child. Within five days after the filing of a claim for paternity, the judge of the court of probate shall cause a certified copy of such claim to be mailed by certified mail to the mother or prospective mother of such child at the last-known address shown on the claim for paternity. The claim for paternity shall be admissible in any action for paternity under section 46b–160, and shall estop the claimant from denying his paternity of such child and shall contain language that he acknowledges liability for contribution to the support and education of the child after its birth and for contribution to the pregnancy-related medical expenses of the mother.

(b) If a claim for paternity is filed by the father of any minor child born out of wedlock, the court of probate shall schedule a hearing on such claim, send notice of the hearing to all parties involved and proceed accordingly.

(c) The child shall be made a party to the action. Said child shall be represented by a guardian ad litem appointed by the court in accordance with section 45a–708. Payment shall be made in accordance with such section from funds appropriated to the Judicial Department, however, if funds have not been included in the budget of the Judicial Department for such purposes, such payment shall be made from the Probate Court Administration Fund.

(d) In the event that the mother or the claimant father is a minor, the court shall appoint a guardian ad litem to represent him or her in accordance with the provisions of section 45a–708. Payment shall be made in accordance with said section from funds appropriated to the Judicial Department, however, if funds have not been included in the budget of the Judicial Department for such purposes, such payment shall be made from the Probate Court Administration Fund.

(e) Upon the motion of the putative father, the mother, or his or her counsel, or the judge of probate having jurisdiction over such application, filed not later than three days prior to any hearing scheduled on such claim, the Probate Court Administrator shall appoint a three-judge court from among the several judges of probate to hear such claim. Such three-judge court shall consist of at least one judge who is an attorney-at-law admitted to practice in this state. The judge of the court of probate having jurisdiction over such application under the provisions of this section shall be a member, provided such judge may disqualify himself in which case all three members of such court shall be appointed by the Probate Court Administrator. Such three-judge court when convened shall have all the powers and duties set forth under sections 17a–75 to 17a–83, inclusive, 17a–450 to 17a–484, inclusive, 17a–495 to 17a–528, inclusive, 17a–540 to 17a–550, inclusive, 17a–560 to 17a–576, inclusive, and 17a–615 to 17a–618, inclusive, and shall be subject to all of the provisions of law as if it were a single-judge court. The judges of such court shall designate a chief judge from among their members. All records for any case before the three-judge court shall be maintained in the court of probate having jurisdiction over the matter as if the three-judge court had not been appointed.

(f) By filing a claim under this section, the putative father submits to the jurisdiction of the court of probate.

(g) Once alleged parental rights of the father have been adjudicated in his favor under subsection (b) of this section, or acknowledged as provided for under section 46b–172, his rights and responsibilities shall be equivalent to those of the mother, including those rights defined under section 45a–606. Thereafter, disputes involving custody, visitation or support shall be transferred to the Superior Court under chapter 815j,[1] except that the probate court may enter a temporary order for custody, visitation or support until an order is entered by the Superior Court.

(h) Failing perfection of parental rights as prescribed by this section, any person claiming to be the father of a child born out of wedlock (1) who has not been adjudicated the father of such child by a court of competent jurisdiction, or (2) who has not acknowledged in writing that he is the father of such child, or (3) who has not contributed regularly to the support of such child or (4) whose name does not appear on the birth certificate shall cease to be a legal party in interest in any proceeding concerning the custody or welfare of the child, including but not limited to guardianship and adoption, unless he has shown a reasonable degree of interest, concern or responsibility for the child's welfare.

(i) Notwithstanding the provisions of this section, after the death of the father of a child born out of wedlock, a party deemed by the court to have a sufficient interest may file a claim for paternity on behalf of such father with the probate court for the district in which either the putative father resided or the party filing the claim resides. If a claim for paternity is filed pursuant to this subsection, the court of probate shall schedule a hearing on such claim, send notice of the hearing to all parties involved and proceed accordingly.

(1979, P.A. 79–592, § 2; 1980, P.A. 80–483, §§ 123, 124, eff. June 6, 1980; 1990, P.A. 90–31, § 8, eff. May 2, 1990; 1991, P.A. 91–109, § 3; 1993, P.A. 93–381, § 9, eff. July 1, 1993; 1994, P.A. 94–27, § 15, eff. July 1, 1994; 1995, P.A. 95–257, §§ 12, 21, eff. July 1, 1995; 1996, P.A. 96–170, § 8, eff. July 1, 1998; 1997, June 18 Sp.Sess., P.A. 97–7, § 24, eff. July 1, 1997; 1998, P.A. 98–52, § 2; 1999, P.A. 99–84, § 8.)

[1] C.G.S.A. § 46b–40 et seq.

§ 46b–173. Repealed. (1995, P.A. 95–133, § 3.)

§ 46b–174. Enforcement and modification of prior orders and agreements

The superior court shall have jurisdiction to enforce and modify all paternity orders and paternity support agreements issued by or filed with the court of common pleas or circuit court prior to or after October 1, 1963, and existing on July 1, 1978.

(1958 Rev., § 52–442c; 1965, Feb.Sp.Sess., P.A. 406, § 7, eff. July 1, 1965; 1974, P.A. 74–183, § 113, eff. Dec. 31, 1974; 1976, P.A. 76–436, § 100, eff. July 1, 1978.)

§ 46b–175. Repealed. (1988, P.A. 88–364, § 122, eff. June 8, 1988.)

§ 46b–176. Continued liability of person committed for failure to comply with order

No person committed to a community correctional center for failure to comply with an order of the court as provided in sections 46b–160, 46b–162 and 46b–171, or any of them, shall be entitled to any of the privileges allowed other prisoners on civil process, or to take the oath provided for poor debtors, within six months from the date of such commitment, but shall be kept at hard labor during such six months; and the mother of such child, the state or the town chargeable with its support may, at any time after the liberation of such prisoner, or after his taking said oath, recover the sum or sums due from him in pursuance of such order of court.

(1949 Rev., § 8184; 1957, P.A. 462, § 5; 1958 Rev., § 52–443; 1969, P.A. 297.)

§ 46b–177. Support of defendant while imprisoned

The complainant shall not be required to pay or give security for the support of the defendant during his confinement in a community correctional center, nor shall such defendant be discharged from imprisonment by reason of payment or security not being made or given for his support, but the jailer shall furnish such support and may recover the cost of the same from such defendant, or, in case of his inability to pay such cost, from the town where he belongs; and, if he belongs to no town in this state, such cost shall be paid by the state.

(1949 Rev., § 8185; 1958 Rev., § 52–444; 1969, P.A. 297.)

§ 46b–178. Wage execution

Executions and earning assignments in accordance with section 52–362 shall be available in paternity proceedings.

(1957, P.A. 208; 1958 Rev., § 52–445; 1983, P.A. 83–400, § 3.)

§ 46b–179. Foreign paternity judgments

As used in sections 46b–179a to 46b–179d, inclusive, foreign paternity judgment means any judgment, decree or order of a court of any state in the United States, other than a court of this state, in an action which results in a final determination on the issue of paternity except any such judgment, decree or order obtained by default in appearance.

(1984, P.A. 84–500, § 1.)

§ 46b–179a. Registry of foreign paternity judgments. Filing of certified copy and certification of final judgment

(a) Support Enforcement Services of the Superior Court shall maintain a registry in the Family Support Magistrate Division of paternity judgments from other states. Any party to an action in which a paternity judgment from another state was rendered may register the foreign paternity judgment in the registry maintained by Support Enforcement Services without payment of a filing fee or other cost to the party.

(b) The party shall file a certified copy of the foreign paternity judgment and a certification that such judgment is final and has not been modified, altered, amended, set aside or vacated and that the enforcement of such judgment has not been stayed or suspended. Such certificate shall set forth the full name and last-known address of the other party to the judgment.

(1984, P.A. 84–500, § 2; 1997, June 18 Sp.Sess., P.A. 97–1, § 59, eff. Jan. 1, 1998; 2001, P.A. 01–91, § 4.)

§ 46b–179b. Enforcement of foreign paternity judgment

Such foreign paternity judgment, on the filing with the registry maintained by Support Enforcement Services, shall become a judgment of the Family Support Magistrate Division of the Superior Court and shall be enforced and otherwise treated in the same manner as a judgment of the Family Support Magistrate Division. A foreign paternity judgment so filed shall have the same effect and may be enforced in the same manner as any like judgment of a family support magistrate of this state, provided no such judgment shall be enforced for a period of twenty days after the filing thereof.

(1984, P.A. 84–500, § 3; 1997, June 18 Sp.Sess., P.A. 97–1, § 60, eff. Jan. 1, 1998; 2001, P.A. 01–91, § 5.)

§ 46b–179c. Notification of filing judgment. Proof of service to be filed with court

Within five days of the filing of the judgment and certification in accordance with section 46b–179a, the party filing such judgment shall notify the other party to the paternity action of the filing of such judgment by registered mail at his last-known address or by personal service. The Family Support Magistrate Division shall not enforce any such foreign paternity judgment until proof of service has been filed with the court.

(1984, P.A. 84–500, § 4; 1997, June 18 Sp.Sess., P.A. 97–1, § 61, eff. Jan. 1, 1998.)

§ 46b–179d. Enforcement of foreign paternity judgment stayed by other pending actions

If either party files an affidavit with the Family Support Magistrate Division that an appeal from the foreign paternity judgment is pending in the foreign state, or will be taken, or that a stay of execution has been granted, the Family Support Magistrate Division will stay enforcement of the foreign paternity judgment until the appeal is concluded, the time for appeal expires or the stay of execution expires or is vacated.

(1984, P.A. 84–500, § 5; 1997, June 18 Sp.Sess., P.A. 97–1, § 62, eff. Jan. 1, 1998.)

CHAPTER 816

SUPPORT

PART I. UNIFORM RECIPROCAL ENFORCEMENT OF SUPPORT

Section

PART Ia. UNIFORM INTERSTATE FAMILY SUPPORT ACT

PART I. UNIFORM RECIPROCAL ENFORCEMENT OF SUPPORT

§§ 46b–180 to 46b–186. Repealed. (1997, June 18 Sp.Sess., P.A. 97–1, § 74, eff. Jan. 1, 1998.)

§ 46b–187. Repealed. (1986, P.A. 86–359, § 43, eff. Jan. 1, 1987.)

§§ 46b–188 to 46b–198. Repealed. (1997, June 18 Sp.Sess., P.A. 97–1, § 74, eff. Jan. 1, 1998.)

§§ 46b–198a to 46b–198c. Repealed. (1997, June 18 Sp.Sess., P.A. 97–1, § 74, eff. Jan. 1, 1998.)

§§ 46b–199 to 46b–206. Repealed. (1997, June 18 Sp.Sess., P.A. 97–1, § 74, eff. Jan. 1, 1998.)

§ 46b–207. Support services

The court is authorized to establish and maintain Support Enforcement Services and such offices thereof as it determines are necessary for the proper handling of the administrative details incident to proceedings under sections 46b–212 to 46b–213v, inclusive, and may appoint such personnel as necessary for the proper administration of the nonjudicial functions of proceedings under sections 46b–212 to 46b–213v, inclusive.

(1953, Supp. § 2462c; 1955, Supp. § 3264d; 1958 Rev., § 17–354; 1980, P.A. 80–180, § 5; 1990, P.A. 90–213, § 30, eff. July 1, 1990; 1997, June 18 Sp.Sess., P.A. 97–1, § 63, eff. Jan. 1, 1998; 2001, P.A. 01–91, § 6.)

§ 46b–208. Powers of support service investigators

The support service investigators of Support Enforcement Services of the Superior Court shall, while acting within the scope of their duties as such, pursuant to matters under sections 46b–212 to 46b–213v, inclusive, have the powers of service and of execution of summons and orders for withholding, and the conduct of investigations.

(1958 Rev., § 17–354a; 1972, P.A. 188, § 4; 1976, P.A. 76–17, § 2; 1976, P.A. 76–436, § 587, eff. July 1, 1978; 1980, P.A. 80–180, § 6; 1986, P.A. 86–359, § 24, eff. Jan. 1, 1987; 1989, P.A. 89–302, § 4, eff. March 1, 1990; 1990, P.A. 90–213, § 31, eff. July 1, 1990; 1997, June 18 Sp.Sess., P.A. 97–1, § 64, eff. Jan. 1, 1998; 2001, P.A. 01–91, § 7.)

§§ 46b–209, 46b–210. Repealed. (1997, June 18 Sp. Sess., P.A. 97–1, § 74, eff. Jan. 1, 1998.)

§ 46b–211. Participation in proceedings not to confer jurisdiction for other proceedings

Participation in any proceedings under this part shall not confer upon any court jurisdiction of any of the parties thereto in any other proceeding.

(1958 Rev., § 17–355b; 1961, P.A. 475, § 6.)

PART Ia. UNIFORM INTERSTATE FAMILY SUPPORT ACT

§ 46b–212. Short title: Uniform Interstate Family Support Act

Sections 46b–212 to 46b–213v, inclusive, may be cited as the Uniform Interstate Family Support Act.

(1997, June 18 Sp.Sess., P.A. 97–1, § 1, eff. Jan. 1, 1998.)

§ 46b–212a. Definitions

As used in sections 46b–212 to 46b–213v, inclusive:

(1) "Child" means an individual, whether over or under the age of majority, who is or is alleged to be owed a duty of support by the individual's parent or who is or is alleged to be the beneficiary of a support order directed to the parent.

(2) "Child support order" means a support order for a child, including a child who has attained the age of majority under the law of the issuing state.

(3) "Duty of support" means an obligation imposed or imposable by law to provide support for a child, spouse or former spouse, including an unsatisfied obligation to provide support.

(4) "Governor" means an individual performing the functions of Governor or the executive authority of a state covered by sections 46b–212 to 46b–213v, inclusive.

(5) "Home state" means the state in which a child lived with a parent or a person acting as parent for at least six consecutive months immediately preceding the time of filing of a petition or comparable pleading for support and, if such child is less than six months old, the state in which such child lived from birth with such parent or person acting as parent. A period of temporary absence of such parent or person acting as parent is counted as part of the six-month or other period.

(6) "Income" includes earnings or other periodic entitlements to money from any source and any other property subject to withholding for support under the laws of this state.

(7) "Income withholding order" means an order or other legal process directed to an obligor's employer, as defined in section 52–362, to withhold support from the income of the obligor.

(8) "Initiating state" means a state from which a proceeding is forwarded under sections 46b–212 to 46b–213v, inclusive, or a law or procedure substantially similar to said sections, the Uniform Reciprocal Enforcement of Support Act [1] or the Revised Uniform Reciprocal Enforcement of Support Act.

(9) "Initiating tribunal" means the authorized tribunal in an initiating state.

(10) "Issuing state" means the state in which a tribunal issues a support order or renders a judgment determining paternity.

(11) "Issuing tribunal" means the tribunal which issues a support order or renders a judgment determining paternity.

(12) "Law" includes decisional and statutory law and rules and regulations having the force of law.

(13) "Obligee" means: (A) An individual to whom a duty of support is or is alleged to be owed or in whose favor a support order has been issued or a judgment determining paternity has been rendered; (B) a state or political subdivision to which the rights under a duty of support or support order have been assigned or which

has independent claims based on financial assistance provided to an individual obligee; or (C) an individual seeking a judgment determining paternity of the individual's child.

(14) "Obligor" means an individual, or the estate of a decedent: (A) Who owes or is alleged to owe a duty of support; (B) who is alleged but has not been adjudicated to be a parent of a child; or (C) who is liable under a support order.

(15) "Register" means to file a support order or judgment determining paternity in the registry of support orders of the Family Support Magistrate Division of the Superior Court. Such a support order or judgment shall be filed by delivery of the order or judgment for filing to Support Enforcement Services of the Superior Court which shall maintain the registry on behalf of the Family Support Magistrate Division.

(16) "Registering tribunal" means a tribunal in which a support order is registered.

(17) "Responding state" means a state in which a proceeding is filed or to which a proceeding is forwarded for filing under sections 46b–212 to 46b–213v, inclusive, or a law or procedure substantially similar to said sections, the Uniform Reciprocal Enforcement of Support Act or the Revised Uniform Reciprocal Enforcement of Support Act.

(18) "Responding tribunal" means the authorized tribunal in a responding state.

(19) "Spousal-support order" means a support order for a spouse or former spouse of the obligor.

(20) "State" means a state of the United States, the District of Columbia, Puerto Rico, the U.S. Virgin Islands or any territory or insular possession subject to the jurisdiction of the United States. The term "state" includes an Indian tribe and a foreign jurisdiction that has enacted a law or established procedures for issuance and enforcement of support orders which are substantially similar to the procedure under sections 46b–212 to 46b–213v, inclusive, the Uniform Reciprocal Enforcement of Support Act or the Revised Uniform Enforcement of Support Act.

(21) "Support enforcement agency" means a public official or agency authorized to seek: (A) Enforcement of support orders or laws relating to the duty of support; (B) establishment or modification of child support; (C) determination of paternity; or (D) the location of obligors or their assets.

(22) "Support order" means a judgment, decree or order, whether temporary, final or subject to modification, for the benefit of a child, a spouse or a former spouse, which provides for monetary support, health care, arrearages or reimbursement, and may include related costs and fees, interest, income withholding, attorney's fees and other relief.

(23) "Tribunal" means a court, administrative agency or quasi-judicial entity authorized to establish, enforce or modify support orders or to determine paternity.

(1997, June 18 Sp.Sess., P.A. 97–1, § 2, eff. Jan. 1, 1998; 2001, P.A. 01–91, § 8; 2003, P.A. 03–19, § 109, eff. May 12, 2003.)

1 C.G.S.A. § 46b–180 et seq. (Repealed).

§ 46b–212b. Tribunals of state

The Superior Court and the Family Support Magistrate Division of the Superior Court are the tribunals of this state. The Family Support Magistrate Division is the tribunal for the filing of petitions under sections 46b–212 to 46b–213v, inclusive, provided clerical, administrative and other nonjudicial functions in proceedings before the Family Support Magistrate Division may be performed by Support Enforcement Services of the Superior Court.

(1997, June 18 Sp.Sess., P.A. 97–1, § 3, eff. Jan. 1, 1998; 2001, P.A. 01–91, § 9.)

§ 46b–212c. Remedies cumulative

Remedies provided by sections 46b–212 to 46b–213v, inclusive, are cumulative and do not affect the availability of remedies under any other law.

(1997, June 18 Sp.Sess., P.A. 97–1, § 4, eff. Jan. 1, 1998.)

§ 46b–212d. Jurisdiction over nonresident

Subject to the provisions of subsection (b) of section 46b–46, in a proceeding to establish, enforce or modify a support order or to determine paternity, a tribunal of this state may exercise personal jurisdiction over a nonresident individual if: (1) The individual is personally served with process within this state; (2) the individual submits to the jurisdiction of this state by consent, by entering a general appearance and failing to object to jurisdiction in a timely manner, or by filing a responsive document having the effect of waiving any contest to personal jurisdiction; (3) the individual resided with the child in this state; (4) the individual resided in this state and provided prenatal expenses or support for the child; (5) the child resides in this state as a result of the acts or directives of the individual; (6) the individual engaged in sexual intercourse in this state and the child may have been conceived by that act of intercourse; or (7) there is any other basis consistent with the constitutions of this state and the United States for the exercise of personal jurisdiction.

(1997, June 18 Sp.Sess., P.A. 97–1, § 5, eff. Jan. 1, 1998.)

§ 46b–212e. Procedure when exercising jurisdiction over nonresident

The Family Support Magistrate Division exercising personal jurisdiction over a nonresident under section 46b–212d, may apply section 46b–213a to receive evidence from another state, and section 46b–213c to obtain discovery through a tribunal of another state. In all other respects, sections 46b–212m to 46b–213s, inclusive, do not apply and the Family Support Magistrate Division shall apply the procedural and substantive law of this state, including the rules on choice of law other than those established by sections 46b–212 to 46b–213v, inclusive.

(1997, June 18 Sp.Sess., P.A. 97–1, § 6, eff. Jan. 1, 1998.)

§ 46b–212f. Family Support Magistrate Division as initiating and responding tribunal

Under sections 46b–212 to 46b–213v, inclusive, the Family Support Magistrate Division may serve as an initiating tribunal to forward proceedings to another state and as a responding tribunal for proceedings initiated in another state.

(1997, June 18 Sp.Sess., P.A. 97–1, § 7, eff. Jan. 1, 1998.)

§ 46b–212g. Simultaneous proceedings in another state

(a) If a petition or comparable pleading is filed in this state after a petition or comparable pleading is filed in another state, the Family Support Magistrate Division may exercise jurisdiction to establish a support order only if: (1) The petition or comparable pleading in this state is filed before the expiration of the time allowed in the other state for filing a responsive pleading challenging the exercise of jurisdiction by the other state; (2) the contesting party timely challenges the exercise of jurisdiction in the other state; and (3) if relevant, this state is the home state of the child.

(b) The Family Support Magistrate Division may not exercise jurisdiction to establish a support order if the petition or comparable pleading is filed before a petition or comparable pleading is filed in another state if: (1) The petition or comparable pleading in the other state is filed before the expiration of the time allowed in this state for filing a responsive pleading challenging the exercise of jurisdiction by this state; (2) the contesting party timely challenges the exercise of jurisdiction in this state; and (3) provided it is relevant, the other state is the home state of the child.

(1997, June 18 Sp.Sess., P.A. 97–1, § 8, eff. Jan. 1, 1998.)

§ 46b–212h. Continuing, exclusive jurisdiction of Family Support Magistrate Division or Superior Court, when

(a) The Family Support Magistrate Division or the Superior Court issuing a support order consistent with the law of this state has continuing exclusive jurisdiction over a child support order: (1) As long as this state remains the residence of the obligor, the individual obligee or the child for whose benefit the support order is issued; or (2) until all of the parties who are individuals have filed written consents with the Family Support Magistrate Division for a tribunal of another state to modify the order and assume continuing exclusive jurisdiction.

(b) The Family Support Magistrate Division or the Superior Court issuing a child support order consistent with the law of this state may not exercise its continuing jurisdiction to modify the order if the order has been modified by a tribunal of another state pursuant to a law substantially similar to sections 46b–212 to 46b–213v, inclusive.

(c) If a child support order of this state is modified by a tribunal of another state pursuant to a law substantially similar to sections 46b–212 to 46b–213v, inclusive, the Family Support Magistrate Division and the Superior Court lose continuing exclusive jurisdiction with regard to prospective enforcement of the order issued in this state, and may only: (1) Enforce the order that was modified as to amounts accruing before the modification; (2) enforce nonmodifiable aspects of that order; and (3) provide other appropriate relief for violations of that order which occurred before the effective date of the modification.

(d) The Family Support Magistrate Division and the Superior Court shall recognize the continuing exclusive jurisdiction of a tribunal of another state which has issued a child support order pursuant to a law substantially similar to sections 46b–212 to 46b–213v, inclusive.

(e) A temporary support order issued ex parte or pending resolution of a jurisdictional conflict does not create continuing exclusive jurisdiction in the issuing tribunal.

(f) The Family Support Magistrate Division or Superior Court issuing a support order consistent with the law of this state has continuing exclusive jurisdiction over a spousal support order throughout the existence of the support obligation. The Family Support Magistrate Division and the Superior Court may not modify a spousal support order issued by a tribunal of another state having continuing exclusive jurisdiction over that order under the law of that state.

(1997, June 18 Sp.Sess., P.A. 97–1, § 9, eff. Jan. 1, 1998.)

§ 46b–212i. Enforcement and modification of support order by Family Support Magistrate Division

(a) The Family Support Magistrate Division may serve as an initiating tribunal to request a tribunal of another state to enforce or modify a support order issued in that state.

(b) The Family Support Magistrate Division having continuing exclusive jurisdiction over a support order may act as a responding tribunal to enforce or modify the order. If a party subject to the continuing exclusive jurisdiction of the Family Support Magistrate Division no longer resides in the issuing state, in subsequent proceedings the Family Support Magistrate Division may apply the provisions of section 46b–213a to receive evidence from another state and the provisions of section 46b–213c to obtain discovery through a tribunal of another state.

(c) If the Family Support Magistrate Division or Superior Court lacks continuing exclusive jurisdiction over a spousal support order, it may not serve as a responding tribunal to modify a spousal support order of another state.

(1997, June 18 Sp.Sess., P.A. 97–1, § 10, eff. Jan. 1, 1998.)

§ 46b–212j. Recognition of controlling child support orders

(a) If a proceeding is brought under sections 46b–212 to 46b–213v, inclusive, and only one tribunal has issued a child support order, the order of that tribunal controls and shall be recognized.

(b) If a proceeding is brought under sections 46b–212 to 46b–213v, inclusive, and two or more child support orders have been issued by tribunals of this state or another state with regard to the same obligor and child, the family support magistrate shall apply the following rules in determining which order to recognize for purposes of continuing, exclusive jurisdiction:

(1) If only one of the tribunals would have continuing, exclusive jurisdiction under sections 46b–212 to 46b–213v, inclusive, the order of that tribunal controls and shall be recognized.

(2) If more than one of the tribunals would have continuing, exclusive jurisdiction under 46b–212 to 46b–213v, inclusive, an order issued by a tribunal in the current home state of the child controls and shall be recognized, but if an order has not been issued in the current home state of the child, the order most recently issued controls and shall be recognized.

(3) If none of the tribunals would have continuing, exclusive jurisdiction under sections 46b–212 to 46b–213v, inclusive, the family support magistrate having jurisdiction over the parties shall issue a child support order which controls and shall be recognized.

(c) If two or more child support orders have been issued for the same obligor and child or the individual obligee resides in this state, a party may request a family support magistrate to determine which order controls and is required to be recognized under subsection (b) of this section. The request shall be accompanied by a certified copy of every support order in effect. The requesting party shall give notice of the request to each party whose rights may be affected by the determination.

(d) The tribunal that issued an order recognized under this section is the tribunal having continuing, exclusive jurisdiction.

(e) The family support magistrate which determines by order the identity of the controlling order under subsection (b) of this section or which issues a new controlling order under subdivision (3) of subsection (b) of this section shall state in the order the basis upon which the tribunal made its determination.

(f) The family support magistrate shall order the party obtaining the order determining the identity of the controlling order to file, within thirty days after issuance of an order determining the identity of the controlling order, a certified copy of such order with each tribunal that issued or registered an earlier order of child support. The failure to file such order pursuant to this subsection shall not affect the validity or enforceability of the controlling order.

(1997, June 18 Sp.Sess., P.A. 97–1, § 11, eff. Jan. 1, 1998.)

§ 46b–212k. Multiple child support orders for two or more obligees

In responding to multiple registrations or petitions for enforcement of two or more child support orders in effect at the same time with regard to the same obligor and different individual obligees, at least one of which was issued by a tribunal of another state, the Family Support Magistrate Division shall enforce those orders in the same manner as if the multiple orders had been issued by the Family Support Magistrate Division.

(1997, June 18 Sp.Sess., P.A. 97–1, § 12, eff. Jan. 1, 1998.)

§ 46b–212*l*. Credit for support payments

Amounts collected and credited for a particular period pursuant to a support order issued by a tribunal of another state must be credited against the amounts accruing or accrued for the same period under a support order issued by the Family Support Magistrate Division or the Superior Court.

(1997, June 18 Sp.Sess., P.A. 97–1, § 13, eff. Jan. 1, 1998.)

§ 46b–212m. Proceedings. Procedure

(a) Except as otherwise provided in sections 46b–212 to 46b–213v, inclusive, sections 46b–212m to 46b–213d, inclusive, apply to all proceedings under sections 46b–212 to 46b–213v, inclusive.

(b) Sections 46b–212 to 46b–213v, inclusive, provide for the following proceedings: (1) Establishment of an order for spousal support or child support pursuant to section 46b–213e; (2) enforcement of a support order and income withholding order of another state without registration pursuant to section 46b–213f; (3) registration of an order for spousal support or child support of another state for enforcement pursuant to sections 46b–213g to 46b–213r, inclusive; (4) modification of an order for child support or spousal support issued by a tribunal of this state pursuant to sections 46b–212f to 46b–212i, inclusive; (5) registration of an order for child support of another state for modification pursuant to sections 46b–213g to 46b–213r, inclusive; (6) determination of paternity pursuant to section 46b–213s; and (7) assertion of jurisdiction over nonresidents pursuant to sections 46b–212d and 46b–212e.

(c) An individual petitioner or a support enforcement agency may commence a proceeding authorized under sections 46b–212 to 46b–213v, inclusive, by filing a petition in an initiating tribunal for forwarding to a responding tribunal or by filing a petition or a comparable pleading directly in a tribunal of another state which has or can obtain personal jurisdiction over the respondent.

(1997, June 18 Sp.Sess., P.A. 97–1, § 14, eff. Jan. 1, 1998.)

§ 46b–212n. Action by minor parent

A minor parent, or a guardian or other legal representative of a minor parent, may maintain a proceeding on behalf of or for the benefit of the minor's child.

(1997, June 18 Sp.Sess., P.A. 97–1, § 15, eff. Jan. 1, 1998.)

§ 46b–212*o*. Applicability of state law

Except as otherwise provided by sections 46b–212 to 46b–213v, inclusive, a responding tribunal of this state: (1) Shall apply the procedural and substantive law, including the rules on choice of law, generally applicable to similar proceedings originating in this state and may exercise all powers and provide all remedies available in those proceedings; and (2) shall determine the duty of support and the amount payable in accordance with the law and support guidelines of this state.

(1997, June 18 Sp.Sess., P.A. 97–1, § 16, eff. Jan. 1, 1998.)

§ 46b–212p. Duties of initiating tribunal

(a) Except with respect to the initial petition in a IV–D support case, upon filing of a petition authorized by sections 46b–212 to 46b–213v, inclusive, an initiating tribunal of this state shall forward three copies of the petition and its accompanying documents: (1) To the responding tribunal or appropriate support enforcement agency in the responding state; or (2) if the identity of the responding tribunal is unknown, to the state information agency of the responding state with a request that they be forwarded to the appropriate tribunal and that receipt be acknowledged. If a petition is the initial petition in a IV–D support case, the initiating tribunal shall forward the three copies of the petition and its accompanying documents to the interstate central registry in the responding state.

(b) If a responding state has not enacted a law or procedure substantially similar to sections 46b–212 to 46b–213v, inclusive, the family support magistrate may issue a certificate or other document and make findings required by the law of the other responding state. If the responding state is a foreign jurisdiction, the family support magistrate may specify the amount of support sought and provide other documents necessary to satisfy the requirements of the responding state.

(1997, June 18 Sp.Sess., P.A. 97–1, § 17, eff. Jan. 1, 1998.)

§ 46b–212q. Duties and powers of responding tribunal

(a) When the Family Support Magistrate Division receives a petition or comparable pleading from an initiating tribunal or directly pursuant to subsection (c) of section 46b–212m, the Family Support Magistrate Division, or Support Enforcement Services acting on its behalf shall promptly cause the petition or pleading to be filed and notify the petitioner by first class mail where and when it was filed.

(b) In matters arising under this section, family support magistrates shall have the same powers and authority as provided by law for IV-D support cases.

(c) The family support magistrate may not condition the payment of a support order issued under sections 46b–212 to 46b–213v, inclusive, upon compliance by a party with provisions for visitation.

(d) If the Family Support Magistrate Division issues an order under sections 46b–212 to 46b–213v, inclusive, the Family Support Magistrate Division, or Support Enforcement Services acting on its behalf, shall send a copy of the order by first class mail to the petitioner and the respondent and to the initiating tribunal, if any.

(1997, June 18 Sp.Sess., P.A. 97–1, § 18, eff. Jan. 1, 1998; 2001, P.A. 01–91, § 10.)

§ 46b–212r. Inappropriate tribunal

If a petition or comparable pleading is received by an inappropriate tribunal of this state, the tribunal shall promptly forward the pleading and accompanying documents to an appropriate tribunal in this state or another state and notify the petitioner by first class mail where and when the pleading was sent.

(1997, June 18 Sp.Sess., P.A. 97–1, § 19, eff. Jan. 1, 1998.)

§ 46b–212s. Duties of support enforcement agency

(a) A support enforcement agency of this state, upon request, shall provide services to a petitioner in a proceeding under sections 46b–212 to 46b–213v, inclusive.

(b) A support enforcement agency that is providing services to the petitioner as appropriate shall: (1) Take all steps necessary to enable an appropriate tribunal in this state or another state to obtain jurisdiction over the respondent; (2) request an appropriate tribunal to set a date, time and place for a hearing; (3) make a reasonable effort to obtain all relevant information, including information as to income and property of the parties; (4) within five days, exclusive of Saturdays, Sundays and legal holidays, after receipt of a written notice from an initiating, responding or registering tribunal, send a copy of the notice by first class mail to the petitioner; (5) within five days, exclusive of Saturdays, Sundays and legal holidays, after receipt of a written communication from the respondent or the respondent's attorney, send a copy of the communication by first class mail to the petitioner; and (6) notify the petitioner if jurisdiction over the respondent cannot be obtained.

(c) The provisions of sections 46b–212 to 46b–213v, inclusive, do not create a relationship of attorney and client or other fiduciary relationship between a support enforcement agency or the attorney for the agency and the individual being assisted by the agency.

(1997, June 18 Sp.Sess., P.A. 97–1, § 20, eff. Jan. 1, 1998.)

§ 46b–212t. Legal services by Attorney General. Private counsel

(a) The Attorney General shall provide necessary legal services on behalf of the support enforcement agency in providing services to a petitioner under sections 46b–212 to 46b–213v, inclusive.

(b) An individual may employ private counsel to represent the individual in proceedings authorized by sections 46b–212 to 46b–213v, inclusive.

(1997, June 18 Sp.Sess., P.A. 97–1, § 21, eff. Jan. 1, 1998.)

§ 46b–212u. Duty of Commissioner of Social Services

If the Commissioner of Social Services determines the support enforcement agency is neglecting or refusing to provide services to an individual, the commissioner may provide those services directly to the individual.

(1997, June 18 Sp.Sess., P.A. 97–1, § 22, eff. Jan. 1, 1998.)

§ 46b–212v. Duties of state information agency

(a) Support Enforcement Services of the Superior Court is the state information agency under sections 46b–212 to 46b–213v, inclusive.

(b) The state information agency shall: (1) Compile and maintain a current list, including addresses, of the tribunals in this state which have jurisdiction under sections 46b–212 to 46b–213v, inclusive, and any support enforcement agencies in this state and transmit a copy to the state information agency of every other state; (2) maintain a registry of tribunals and support enforcement agencies received from other states; (3) forward to the appropriate tribunal in the place in this state in which the individual obligee or the obligor resides, or in which the obligor's property is believed to be located, all documents concerning a proceeding under sections 46b–212 to 46b–213v, inclusive, received from an initiating tribunal or the state information agency of the initiating state; and (4) obtain information concerning the location of the obligor and the obligor's property within this state not exempt from execution.

(c) In addition to its duties as the state information agency Support Enforcement Services of the Superior Court shall maintain a registry of support orders and judgments in the Family Support Magistrate Division of the Superior Court and shall perform such clerical, administrative and other nonjudicial functions on behalf of the Family Support Magistrate Division as may be required, or as are otherwise agreed upon, pursuant to sections 46b–62, 46b–69, 46b–179a, 46b–179b, 46b–207, 46b–208, 46b–212 to 46b–213v, inclusive, 46b–231, 52–362 and 52–362f.

(1997, June 18 Sp.Sess., P.A. 97–1, § 23, eff. Jan. 1, 1998; 2001, P.A. 01–91, § 11.)

§ 46b–212w. Pleadings and accompanying documents

(a) A petitioner seeking to establish or modify a support order or to determine paternity in a proceeding under sections 46b–212 to 46b–213v, inclusive, must verify the petition. Unless otherwise ordered under section 46b–212x, the petition or accompanying documents must provide, so far as known, the name, residential address and Social Security numbers of the obligor and the obligee, and the name, sex, residential address, Social Security number and date of birth of each child for whom support is sought. The petition must be accompanied by a certified copy of any support order in effect. The petition may include any other information that may assist in locating or identifying the respondent.

(b) The petition must specify the relief sought. The petition and accompanying documents must conform substantially with the requirements imposed by the forms mandated by federal law for use in cases filed by a support enforcement agency.

(1997, June 18 Sp.Sess., P.A. 97–1, § 24, eff. Jan. 1, 1998.)

§ 46b–212x. Nondisclosure of information in exceptional circumstances

Upon a finding, which may be made ex parte, that the health, safety or liberty of a party or child would be unreasonably put at risk by the disclosure of identifying information, or if an existing order so provides, a tribunal shall order that the address of the child or party or other identifying information not be disclosed in a pleading or other document filed in a proceeding under sections 46b–212 to 46b–213v, inclusive.

(1997, June 18 Sp.Sess., P.A. 97–1, § 25, eff. Jan. 1, 1998.)

§ 46b–212y. Costs and fees

(a) The petitioner may not be required to pay a filing fee or other costs.

(b) If an obligee prevails, a responding tribunal may assess against an obligor filing fees, reasonable attorney's fees, other costs and necessary travel and other reasonable expenses incurred by the obligee and the

obligee's witnesses. The tribunal may not assess fees, costs or expenses against the obligee or the support enforcement agency of either the initiating or the responding state, except as provided by other law.
(1997, June 18 Sp.Sess., P.A. 97–1, § 26, eff. Jan. 1, 1998.)

§ 46b–212z. Limited immunity of petitioner

(a) Participation by a petitioner in a proceeding before a responding tribunal, whether in person, by private attorney or through services provided by the support enforcement agency, does not confer personal jurisdiction over the petitioner in another proceeding.

(b) A petitioner is not amenable to service of civil process while physically present in this state to participate in a proceeding under sections 46b–212 to 46b–213v, inclusive.

(c) The immunity granted by this section does not extend to civil litigation based on acts unrelated to a proceeding under sections 46b–212 to 46b–213v, inclusive, committed by a party while present in this state to participate in the proceeding.
(1997, June 18 Sp.Sess., P.A. 97–1, § 27, eff. Jan. 1, 1998.)

§ 46b–213. Nonpaternity as defense

A party whose paternity of a child has been previously determined by or pursuant to law may not plead nonpaternity as a defense to a proceeding under sections 46b–212 to 46b–213v, inclusive.
(1997, June 18 Sp.Sess., P.A. 97–1, § 28, eff. Jan. 1, 1998.)

§ 46b–213a. Special rules of evidence and procedure

(a) The physical presence of the petitioner in a responding tribunal of this state is not required for the establishment, enforcement or modification of a support order or the rendition of a judgment determining paternity.

(b) A verified petition, affidavit, document substantially complying with federally-mandated forms and a document incorporated by reference in any of them, not excluded under the hearsay rule if given in person, is admissible in evidence if given under oath by a party or witness residing in another state.

(c) A copy of the record of child support payments certified as a true copy of the original by the custodian of the record may be forwarded to a responding tribunal. The copy is evidence of facts asserted in it and is admissible to show whether payments were made.

(d) Copies of bills for testing for paternity and for prenatal and postnatal health care of the mother and child, furnished to the adverse party at least ten days before trial, are admissible in evidence to prove the amount of the charges billed and that the charges were reasonable, necessary and customary.

(e) Documentary evidence transmitted from another state to a tribunal of this state by telephone, telecopier or other means that do not provide an original writing may not be excluded from evidence on an objection based on the means of transmission.

(f) In a proceeding under sections 46b–212 to 46b–213v, inclusive, the family support magistrate may permit a party or witness residing in another state to testify by telephone or other electronic means, if available, and such costs for such testimony shall be assessed to the party requesting such method of providing testimony.

(g) If a party called to testify at a civil hearing refuses to answer on the ground that the testimony may be self-incriminating, the trier of fact may draw an adverse inference from the refusal.

(h) A privilege against disclosure of communications between spouses does not apply in a proceeding under sections 46b–212 to 46b–213v, inclusive.

(i) The defense of immunity based on the relationship of husband and wife or parent and child does not apply in a proceeding under sections 46b–212 to 46b–213v, inclusive.
(1997, June 18 Sp.Sess., P.A. 97–1, § 29, eff. Jan. 1, 1998.)

§ 46b–213b. Communication between tribunals

A family support magistrate may communicate with a tribunal of another state in writing, or by telephone or other means, to obtain information concerning the laws of that state, the legal effect of a judgment, decree or order of that tribunal and the status of a proceeding in the other state. A family support magistrate may furnish similar information by similar means to a tribunal of another state.
(1997, June 18 Sp.Sess., P.A. 97–1, § 30, eff. Jan. 1, 1998.)

§ 46b–213c. Assistance with discovery

A family support magistrate may: (1) Request a tribunal of another state to assist in obtaining discovery; and (2) upon request, compel a person over whom it has jurisdiction to respond to a discovery order issued by a tribunal of another state.
(1997, June 18 Sp.Sess., P.A. 97–1, § 31, eff. Jan. 1, 1998.)

§ 46b–213d. Receipt and disbursement of support payments

The Child Support Enforcement Bureau of the Department of Social Services or its designated collection agent, and any tribunal shall disburse promptly any amounts received pursuant to a support order, as directed by the order. The bureau, agent or tribunal shall furnish to a requesting party or tribunal of another state a certified statement by the custodian of the record of the amounts and dates of all payments received.

(1997, June 18 Sp.Sess., P.A. 97–1, § 32, eff. Jan. 1, 1998.)

§ 46b–213e. Issuance of support order

(a) If a support order entitled to recognition under sections 46b–212 to 46b–213v, inclusive, has not been issued, a family support magistrate may issue a support order if: (1) The individual seeking the order resides in another state; or (2) the support enforcement agency seeking the order is located in another state.

(b) The family support magistrate may issue a temporary child support order if: (1) The respondent has signed a verified statement acknowledging paternity; (2) the respondent has been determined by or pursuant to law to be the parent; or (3) there is clear and convincing evidence of paternity which evidence shall include, but not be limited to, genetic test results indicating a ninety-nine per cent or greater probability that such respondent is the father of the child.

(c) Upon finding, after notice and opportunity to be heard, that an obligor owes a duty of support, the tribunal shall issue a support order directed to the obligor and may issue other orders pursuant to section 46b–212q.

(1997, June 18 Sp.Sess., P.A. 97–1, § 33, eff. Jan. 1, 1998.)

§ 46b–213f. Administrative enforcement of orders

(a) A party seeking to enforce a support order or an income withholding order, or both, issued by a tribunal of another state may send the documents required for registering the order to Support Enforcement Services.

(b) Upon receipt of the documents, Support Enforcement Services, with the assistance of the Bureau of Child Support Enforcement within the Department of Social Services, as appropriate, without initially seeking to register the order, shall consider and, if appropriate, use any administrative procedure authorized by the law of this state to enforce a support order or an income withholding order, or both. If the obligor does not contest administrative enforcement, the order need not be registered. If the obligor contests the validity or administrative enforcement of the order, the support enforcement agency shall file the order with Support Enforcement Services of the Superior Court to be recorded in the registry of support orders of the Family Support Magistrate Division.

(1997, June 18 Sp.Sess., P.A. 97–1, § 34, eff. Jan. 1, 1998; 1999, P.A. 99–193, § 8, eff. June 23, 1999; 2000, P.A. 00–196, § 28; 2001, P.A. 01–91, § 12.)

§ 46b–213g. Registration of order for enforcement

A support order or an income withholding order issued by a tribunal of another state may be registered in this state for enforcement with the registry of support orders of the Family Support Magistrate Division maintained by Support Enforcement Services of the Superior Court.

(1997, June 18 Sp.Sess., P.A. 97–1, § 35, eff. Jan. 1, 1998; 2000, P.A. 00–196, § 29; 2001, P.A. 01–91, § 13.)

§ 46b–213h. Procedure to register order for enforcement

(a) A support order or income withholding order of another state may be registered in this state by sending the following documents and information to Support Enforcement Services for filing in the registry of support orders of the Family Support Magistrate Division: (1) A letter of transmittal to Support Enforcement Services requesting registration and enforcement; (2) two copies, including one certified copy, of all orders to be registered, including any modification of an order; (3) a sworn statement by the party seeking registration or a certified statement by the custodian of the records showing the amount of any arrearage; (4) the name of the obligor and, if known: (A) The obligor's address and Social Security number; (B) the name and address of the obligor's employer and any other source of income of the obligor; and (C) a description and the location of property of the obligor in this state not exempt from execution; (5) the name and address of the obligee and, if applicable, the agency or person to whom support payments are to be remitted; and (6) a statement disclosing whether or not any other action or proceeding is currently pending concerning the support of the child who is the subject of such support order.

(b) On receipt of a request for registration, Support Enforcement Services shall cause the order to be filed as a foreign judgment in the registry of support orders of the Family Support Magistrate Division, together with one copy of the documents and information, regardless of their form.

(c) A petition or comparable pleading seeking a remedy that is required to be affirmatively sought under other law of this state may be filed at the same time as the request for registration or later. The pleading shall specify the grounds for the remedy sought.

(1997, June 18 Sp.Sess., P.A. 97–1, § 36, eff. Jan. 1, 1998; 2001, P.A. 01–91, § 14.)

§ 46b–213i. Effect of registration for enforcement

(a) A support order or income withholding order issued in another state is registered when the order is filed with Support Enforcement Services for registration in the registry of support orders.

(b) A registered order issued in another state is enforceable in the same manner and is subject to the same procedures as an order issued by a tribunal of this state.

(c) Except as otherwise provided in sections 46b–213g to 46b–213r, inclusive, a tribunal of this state shall recognize and enforce, but may not modify, a registered order if the issuing tribunal had jurisdiction.

(1997, June 18 Sp.Sess., P.A. 97–1, § 37, eff. Jan. 1, 1998; 2001, P.A. 01–91, § 15.)

§ 46b–213j. Choice of law

(a) The law of the issuing state governs the nature, extent, amount and duration of current payments and other obligations of support and the payment of arrearages under the order.

(b) In a proceeding for arrearages, the statute of limitations under the laws of this state or of the issuing state, whichever is longer, applies.

(1997, June 18 Sp.Sess., P.A. 97–1, § 38, eff. Jan. 1, 1998.)

§ 46b–213k. Notice of registration of order

(a) When a support order or income withholding order issued in another state is registered, the Family Support Magistrate Division or Support Enforcement Services acting on its behalf, shall notify the nonregistering party. Notice must be given by first class, certified or registered mail or by any means of personal service authorized by the law of this state. The notice must be accompanied by a copy of the registered order and the documents and relevant information accompanying the order.

(b) The notice must inform the nonregistering party: (1) That a registered order is enforceable as of the date of registration in the same manner as an order issued by a tribunal of this state; (2) that a hearing before the Family Support Magistrate Division to contest the validity or enforcement of the registered order must be requested within twenty days after the date of mailing or personal service of the notice; (3) that failure to contest the validity or enforcement of the registered order in a timely manner will result in confirmation of the order and enforcement of the order and the alleged arrearages and precludes further contest of that order with respect to any matter that could have been asserted; and (4) of the amount of any alleged arrearages.

(c) Upon registration of an income withholding order for enforcement, the Family Support Magistrate Division, or Support Enforcement Services acting on its behalf, shall notify the obligor's employer pursuant to section 52–362.

(1997, June 18 Sp.Sess., P.A. 97–1, § 39, eff. Jan. 1, 1998; 2001, P.A. 01–91, § 16.)

§ 46b–213*l*. Procedure to contest validity or enforcement of registered order

(a) A nonregistering party seeking to contest the validity or enforcement of a registered order in this state shall request a hearing before the Family Support Magistrate Division within twenty days after the date of mailing or personal service of notice of the registration. The nonregistering party may seek to vacate the registration, to assert any defense to an allegation of noncompliance with the registered order, or to contest the remedies being sought or the amount of any alleged arrearages pursuant to section 46b–213m.

(b) If the nonregistering party fails to contest the validity or enforcement of the registered order in a timely manner, the order is confirmed by operation of law.

(c) If a nonregistering party requests a hearing to contest the validity or enforcement of the registered order, the Family Support Magistrate Division shall schedule the matter for hearing and give notice to the parties by first class mail of the date, time and place of the hearing.

(1997, June 18 Sp.Sess., P.A. 97–1, § 40, eff. Jan. 1, 1998.)

§ 46b–213m. Contest of registration or enforcement

(a) A party contesting the validity or enforcement of a registered order or seeking to vacate the registration has the burden of proving one or more of the following defenses: (1) The issuing tribunal lacked personal jurisdiction over the contesting party; (2) the order was obtained by fraud; (3) the order has been vacated, suspended or modified by a later order; (4) the issuing tribunal has stayed the order pending appeal; (5) there is a defense under the law of this state to the remedy sought; (6) full or partial payment has been made; or (7) the statute of limitations under section 46b–213j precludes enforcement of some or all of the arrearages.

(b) If a party presents evidence establishing a full or partial defense under subsection (a) of this section, a tribunal may stay enforcement of the registered order, continue the proceeding to permit production of additional relevant evidence and issue other appropriate orders. An uncontested portion of the registered order may be enforced by all remedies available under the law of this state.

(c) If the contesting party does not establish a defense under subsection (a) of this section to the validity or enforcement of the order, the registering tribunal shall issue an order confirming the order.

(1997, June 18 Sp.Sess., P.A. 97–1, § 41, eff. Jan. 1, 1998.)

§ 46b–213n. Confirmation of registered order

Confirmation of a registered order, whether by operation of law or after notice and hearing, precludes further contest of the order with respect to any matter that could have been asserted at the time of registration.

(1997, June 18 Sp.Sess., P.A. 97–1, § 42, eff. Jan. 1, 1998.)

§ 46b–213*o*. Procedure re registration of child support order of another state for modification

A party or support enforcement agency seeking to modify, or to modify and enforce, a child support order issued in another state shall register that order in this state in the same manner provided in sections 46b–213g to 46b–213j, inclusive, if the order has not been registered. A petition for modification may be filed at the same time as a request for registration, or later. The pleading must specify the grounds for modification.

(1997, June 18 Sp.Sess., P.A. 97–1, § 43, eff. Jan. 1, 1998.)

§ 46b–213p. Effect of registration for modification

A family support magistrate may enforce a child support order of another state registered for purposes of modification, in the same manner as if the order had been issued by a family support magistrate, but the registered order may be modified only if the requirements of section 46b–213q have been met.

(1997, June 18 Sp. Sess., P.A. 97–1, § 44, eff. Jan. 1, 1998.)

§ 46b–213q. Modification of child support order of another state

(a) After a child support order issued in another state has been registered in this state, a family support magistrate may modify that order only if subsection (e) of this section does not apply and, after notice and hearing, such magistrate finds that: (1) The following requirements are met: (A) The child, the individual obligee and the obligor do not reside in the issuing state; (B) a petitioner who is a nonresident of this state seeks modification; and (C) the respondent is subject to the personal jurisdiction of the Family Support Magistrate Division; or (2) the child or party who is an individual is subject to the personal jurisdiction of the Family Support Magistrate Division and all of the parties who are individuals have filed written consents in the issuing tribunal for a family support magistrate to modify the support order and assume continuing exclusive jurisdiction over the order provided if the issuing state is a foreign jurisdiction that has not enacted a law or established procedures substantially similar to sections 46b–212 to 46b–213v, inclusive, the consent otherwise required of an individual residing in this state is not required for the family support magistrate to assume jurisdiction to modify a child support order.

(b) Modification of a registered child support order is subject to the same requirements, procedures and defenses that apply to the modification of an order issued by the Family Support Magistrate Division and the order may be enforced and satisfied in the same manner.

(c) A family support magistrate may not modify any aspect of a child support order that may not be modified under the law of the issuing state. If two or more tribunals have issued child support orders for the same obligor and child, the order that controls and shall be so recognized under section 46b–212j establishes the aspects of the support order which are nonmodifiable.

(d) On issuance of an order modifying a child support order issued in another state, the Family Support Magistrate Division becomes the tribunal of continuing exclusive jurisdiction.

(e) (1) If all of the parties who are individuals reside in this state and the child does not reside in the issuing state, the Family Support Magistrate Division has jurisdiction to enforce and to modify the issuing state's child support order in a proceeding to register that order.

(2) The Family Support Magistrate Division exercising jurisdiction under this subsection shall apply the provisions of sections 46b–212a to 46b–212l, inclusive, and sections 46b–213g to 46b–213r, inclusive, and the procedural and substantive law of this state to the proceeding for enforcement or modification. Sections 46b–212m to 46b–213f, inclusive, sections 46b–213s to 46b–213u, inclusive, and section 46b–213w shall not apply to such proceeding.

(f) The family support magistrate shall order the party obtaining the modification of a child support order to file, within thirty days after issuance of such modification order, a certified copy of such order with each tribunal that issued or registered an earlier order of child support. The failure to file such orders pursuant to this subsection shall not affect the validity or enforceability of the controlling order.

(1997, June 18 Sp.Sess., P.A. 97–1, § 45, eff. Jan. 1, 1998; 1999, P.A. 99–193, § 9, eff. June 23, 1999.)

§ 46b–213r. Recognition of order modified in another state

The Family Support Magistrate Division or Superior Court shall recognize a modification of its earlier child support order by a tribunal of another state which assumed jurisdiction pursuant to a law substantially similar to sections 46b–212 to 46b–213v, inclusive, and, upon request, except as otherwise provided in said sections, shall: (1) Enforce the order that was modified only as to amounts accruing before the modification; (2) enforce only nonmodifiable aspects of that order; (3) provide other appropriate relief only for violations of that order which occurred before the effective date of modification; and (4) recognize the modifying order of the other state, upon registration, for the purpose of enforcement.

(1997, June 18 Sp.Sess., P.A. 97–1, § 46, eff. Jan. 1, 1998.)

§ 46b–213s. Proceeding to determine paternity

(a) The Family Support Magistrate Division may serve as an initiating or responding tribunal in a proceeding brought under sections 46b–212 to

46b–213v, inclusive, or a law substantially similar to said sections, the Uniform Reciprocal Enforcement of Support Act [1] or the Revised Uniform Reciprocal Enforcement of Support Act to determine that the petitioner is a parent of a particular child or to determine that a respondent is a parent of such child.

(b) In a proceeding to determine paternity, the Family Support Magistrate Division shall apply the procedural and substantive law of this state and the rules of this state on choice of law.

(1997, June 18 Sp.Sess., P.A. 97–1, § 47, eff. Jan. 1, 1998.)

1 C.G.S.A. § 46b–180 et seq. (Repealed).

§ 46b–213t. Surrender and extradition of individual criminally charged with failure to provide support

(a) The Governor of this state may: (1) Demand that the governor of another state surrender an individual found in the other state who is charged criminally in this state with having failed to provide for the support of an obligee; or (2) on the demand by the governor of another state, surrender an individual found in this state who is charged criminally in the other state with having failed to provide for the support of an obligee.

(b) A provision for extradition of individuals not inconsistent with sections 46b–212 to 46b–213v, inclusive, applies to the demand even if the individual whose surrender is demanded was not in the demanding state when the crime was allegedly committed and has not fled therefrom.

(1997, June 18 Sp.Sess., P.A. 97–1, § 48, eff. Jan. 1, 1998.)

§ 46b–213u. Conditions of rendition

(a) Before making a demand that the governor of another state surrender an individual charged criminally in this state with having failed to provide for the support of an obligee, the Governor of this state may require a state's attorney or assistant state's attorney to demonstrate that at least sixty days previously the obligee had initiated proceedings for support pursuant to sections 46b–212 to 46b–213v, inclusive, or that the proceeding would be of no avail.

(b) If, under sections 46b–212 to 46b–213v, inclusive, or a law substantially similar to said sections, the Uniform Reciprocal Enforcement of Support Act [1] or the Revised Uniform Reciprocal Enforcement of Support Act, the governor of another state makes a demand that the Governor of this state surrender an individual charged criminally in that state with having failed to provide for the support of a child or other individual to whom a duty of support is owed, the Governor may require a state's attorney or assistant state's attorney to investigate the demand and report whether a proceeding for support has been initiated or would be effective. If it appears that a proceeding would be effective, but has not been initiated, the Governor may delay honoring the demand for a reasonable time to permit the initiation of a proceeding.

(c) If a proceeding for support has been initiated and the individual whose rendition is demanded prevails, the Governor may decline to honor the demand. If the petitioner prevails and the individual whose rendition is demanded is subject to a support order, the Governor may decline to honor the demand if the individual is complying with the support order.

(1997, June 18 Sp.Sess., P.A. 97–1, § 49, eff. Jan. 1, 1998.)

1 C.G.S.A. § 46b–180 et seq. (Repealed).

§ 46b–213v. Uniformity of application and construction

Sections 46b–212 to 46b–213v, inclusive, shall be applied and construed to effectuate their general purpose to make uniform the law with respect to the subject of said sections, among states enacting this uniform act.

(1997, June 18 Sp.Sess., P.A. 97–1, § 50, eff. Jan. 1, 1998.)

§ 46b–213w. Duties of employer re income withholding order issued in another state. Notice and claim form distributed by Department of Social Services. Contents of form. Multiple income withholding orders. Penalty for noncompliance. Contest by obligor

(a) An income withholding order issued in another state may be sent to the person or entity defined as the obligor's employer under section 52–362 without first filing a petition or comparable pleading or registering the order in the registry of support orders of the Family Support Magistrate Division.

(b) Upon receipt of an income withholding order issued in another state, the obligor's employer shall immediately provide to the obligor (1) a copy of the order and (2) a copy of the notice and claim form provided by the Department of Social Services pursuant to subsection (c) of this section.

(c) The Department of Social Services shall distribute to all employers in this state a standard notice and claim form, written in clear and simple language, which shall include:

(1) Notice that money will be withheld from the employee's wages for child support and health insurance;

(2) Notice of the amount of disposable earnings that are exempt from the income withholding order;

(3) Notice that the amount of the income withholding order may not exceed the maximum permitted by federal law under Section 1673 of Title 15 of the United States Code, together with a statement of the obligor's right to claim any other applicable state or federal exemptions;

(4) Notice of the right to object to the validity or enforcement of such income withholding order in a court in this state and of the right to seek modification of the underlying support order in the court of continuing exclusive jurisdiction;

(5) Notice of the right to seek the assistance of the Child Support Enforcement Bureau of the Department of Social Services and the toll-free telephone number at which the bureau can be contacted;

(6) A claim form which shall include (A) a list of the most common defenses and exemptions to such income withholding order in a manner which allows the obligor to check any of the defenses and exemptions which apply; (B) a space where the obligor may briefly explain the obligor's claim or defense; (C) a space where the obligor may initiate a request for services to modify the support order; (D) a space for the obligor to provide the obligor's address and the name of the town in which the obligor principally conducts the obligor's work for the employer; (E) a space for the obligor to sign the obligor's name; (F) the address of the Bureau of Child Support Enforcement of the Department of Social Services to which the claim form is to be sent in order to contest the validity or enforcement of the income withholding order or to initiate a request for modification; and (G) space for the employer to state the date upon which the form was actually delivered to the obligor.

(d) The employer shall treat an income withholding order issued in another state which appears valid if it had been issued by a tribunal of this state.

(e) Except as otherwise provided in subsections (f) and (g), the employer shall withhold and distribute the funds as directed in the withholding order by complying with terms of the order which specify: (1) The duration and amount of periodic payments of current child support, stated as a sum certain; (2) the person or agency designated to receive payments and the address to which the payments are to be forwarded; (3) medical support, whether in the form of periodic cash payment, stated as a sum certain, or ordering the obligor to provide health insurance coverage for the child under a policy available through the obligor's employment, subject to the provisions of subsection (e) of section 38a–497a; (4) the amount of periodic payments of fees and costs for a support enforcement agency, the issuing tribunal and the obligee's attorney, stated as sums certain; and (5) the amount of periodic payments of arrearages and interest on arrearages, stated as sums certain.

(f) The employer shall comply with the law of this state for withholding from income with respect to: (1) The prohibition against an employer's fee for processing an income withholding order; (2) the maximum amount permitted to be withheld from the obligor's income; and (3) the time period within which the employer must implement the withholding order and forward the child support payment.

(g) If an employer receives multiple income withholding orders with respect to the earnings of the same obligor, the employer satisfies the terms of the multiple orders if the employer complies with the law of this state to establish the priorities for withholding and allocating income withheld for multiple child support obligees.

(h) An employer who complies with an income withholding order issued in another state in accordance with this section shall be immune from civil liability with regard to the employer's withholding of child support from the obligor's income.

(i) An employer who wilfully fails to comply with an income withholding order issued by another state and received for enforcement is subject to the same penalties that may be imposed for noncompliance with an order issued by a tribunal of this state.

(j) An obligor may contest the validity or enforcement of an income withholding order issued in another state and received directly by an employer in this state in the same manner as if the order had been issued by a tribunal of this state or by mailing to the Bureau of Child Support Enforcement of the Department of Social Services the claim form delivered to the obligor pursuant to subsection (b) of this section, signed by the obligor and containing his address and a copy of the income withholding order. The obligor shall also deliver a copy of such claim form to the employer. If a claim form contesting the validity or enforcement of an income withholding order is received by the employer within fourteen days of the receipt by the obligor of the notice and claim form, imposition of the withholding order shall be stayed and the employer shall not implement the withholding order for a period of thirty days. If the employer receives from the Bureau of Child Support Enforcement a notice that it has received the claim form, the employer shall not implement the withholding order until the claim is decided by a family support magistrate.

(k) Upon receipt of a claim form contesting the validity or enforcement of an income withholding order, the Bureau of Child Support Enforcement shall within seven days notify the employer of the receipt of the claim form. The bureau shall also give notice of the contest and of the fact that the order is stayed until the claim is decided by a family support magistrate to (1) the support enforcement agency providing services to the obligee; (2) the obligor's employer; (3) the person or agency designated to receive payments in the income withholding order; and (4) if the obligee's address is known, the obligee. In addition, the bureau shall immediately cause the income withholding order to be registered in this state with the appropriate clerk of the Family Support Magistrate Division and shall comply with the registration requirements of section 46b–213h.

The bureau shall also immediately file the claim form on behalf of the obligor with the Family Support Magistrate Division of the Superior Court. The clerk shall promptly enter the appearance of the obligor, schedule a hearing, and give notice of the hearing to the obligor, the Bureau of Child Support Enforcement, the party initiating the income withholding order, and, if the obligee's address is known, the obligee. The clerk shall proceed in accordance with subsection (d) of section 52–361. The family support magistrate shall promptly hear and determine the claim and enter its determination within forty-five days from the date of the filing of the claim form. In addition to any notice given by the clerk, upon entry of the decision of the family support magistrate on the claim, the bureau shall give notice of the decision to the employer, the party initiating the income withholding order, the obligor and, if the obligee's address is known, the obligee.

(*l*) If the claim form requests services to modify the support order, the Bureau of Child Support Enforcement shall assist the obligor to file a motion for modification with the appropriate tribunal of the state of continuing exclusive jurisdiction in accordance with the law of that jurisdiction. The receipt of the request for modification shall constitute a request for Title IV–D services, but the bureau may require the making of a formal application. Such assistance shall include, but is not limited to, providing the obligor with information about how such a motion is filed, contacting the state of continuing exclusive jurisdiction on behalf of the obligor to obtain appropriate forms, and transmitting such forms and applicable information to the appropriate tribunal in such state.

(m) Venue for contested claims under this section shall be the family support magistrate division of the superior court in the judicial district in which the obligor resides, provided (1) if the obligor does not reside in this state, venue shall be in the judicial district in which the obligor principally conducts his work for the employer who is subject to the income withholding order, and (2) if there is an existing action concerning support of the child or children who are the subject of the income withholding order, the claim shall be filed in that action.

(1997, June 18 Sp.Sess., P.A. 97–1, § 73, eff. Jan. 1, 1998; 2001 P.A. 01–207, § 8, eff. July 1, 2001.)

§ 46b–214. Reserved for future use

PART II. OBLIGATION OF RELATIVES

§ 46b–215. Relatives obliged to furnish support, when. Orders

(a) (1) The Superior Court or a family support magistrate shall have authority to make and enforce orders for payment of support against any person who neglects or refuses to furnish necessary support to such person's spouse or a child under the age of eighteen, according to such person's ability to furnish such support, notwithstanding the provisions of section 46b–37.

(2) Any such support order in a IV–D support case shall include a provision for the health care coverage of the child which provision may include an order for either parent to name any child under eighteen as a beneficiary of any medical or dental insurance or benefit plan carried by such parent or available to such parent on a group basis through an employer or a union. Any such employment-based order shall be enforced using a National Medical Support Notice as provided in section 46b–88. If such insurance coverage is unavailable at reasonable cost, the provision for health care coverage may include an order for either parent to apply for and maintain coverage on behalf of the child under the HUSKY Plan, Part B.[1] The noncustodial parent shall be ordered to apply for the HUSKY Plan, Part B only if such parent is found to have sufficient ability to pay the appropriate premium. In any IV–D support case in which the noncustodial parent is found to have insufficient ability to provide medical insurance coverage and the custodial party is the HUSKY Plan, Part A [2] or Part B applicant, the provision for health care coverage may include an order for the noncustodial parent to pay such amount as is specified by the court or family support magistrate to the state or the custodial party, as their interests may appear, to offset the cost of any insurance payable under the HUSKY Plan, Part A or Part B. In no event may such order include payment to offset the cost of any such premium if such payment would reduce the amount of current support required under the child support guidelines.

(3) Proceedings to obtain orders of support under this section shall be commenced by the service on the liable person or persons of a verified petition with summons and order, in a form prescribed by the Office of the Chief Court Administrator, of the husband or wife, child or any relative or the conservator, guardian or support enforcement officer, town or state, or any selectmen or the public official charged with the administration of public assistance of the town, or in TANF support cases, as defined in subdivision (14) of subsection (b) of section 46b–231, the Commissioner of Social Services. The verified petition, summons and order shall be filed in the judicial district in which the petitioner or respondent resides or does business, or if filed in the Family Support Magistrate Division, in the judicial district in which the petitioner or respondent resides or does business.

(4) For purposes of this section, the term "child" shall include one born out of wedlock whose father has acknowledged in writing paternity of such child or has been adjudged the father by a court of competent jurisdiction, or a child who was born before marriage whose parents afterwards intermarry.

(5) Said court or family support magistrate shall also have authority to make and enforce orders directed to

the conservator or guardian of any person, or payee of Social Security or other benefits to which such person is entitled, to the extent of the income or estate held by such fiduciary or payee in any such capacity.

(6) Said court or family support magistrate shall also have authority to determine, order and enforce payment of any sums due under a written agreement to support against the person liable for such support under such agreement.

(7) (A) Said court or family support magistrate shall also have authority to determine, order and enforce payment of any support due because of neglect or refusal to furnish support prior to the action.

(B) In the determination of support due based on neglect or refusal to furnish support prior to the action, the support due for periods of time prior to the action shall be based upon the obligor's ability to pay during such prior periods, as determined in accordance with the child support and arrearage guidelines established under section 46b–215a. The state shall disclose to the court any information in its possession concerning current and past ability to pay. If no information is available to the court concerning past ability to pay, the court may determine the support due for periods of time prior to the action as if past ability to pay is equal to current ability to pay, if current ability is known. If current ability to pay is not known, the court shall determine the past ability to pay based on the obligor's work history, if known, or if not known, on the state minimum wage that was in effect during such periods, provided only actual earnings shall be used to determine ability to pay for past periods during which the obligor was a full-time high school student or was incarcerated, institutionalized or incapacitated.

(C) Any finding of support due for periods of time prior to an action in which the obligor failed to appear shall be entered subject to adjustment. Such adjustment may be made upon motion of any party, and the state in IV-D cases shall make such motion if it obtains information that would have substantially affected the court's determination of past ability to pay if such information had been available to the court. Motion for adjustment under this subparagraph may be made not later than twelve months date from the date upon which the obligor receives notification of (i) the amount of such finding of support due for periods of time prior to the action, and (ii) the right not later than twelve months from the date of receipt of such notification to present evidence as to such obligor's past ability to pay support for such periods of time prior to the action. A copy of any support order entered, subject to adjustment, shall state in plain language the basis for the court's determination of past support, the right to request an adjustment and to present information concerning the obligor's past ability to pay, and the consequences of a failure to request such adjustment.

(8) (A) The judge or family support magistrate shall cause a summons, signed by such judge or magistrate, by the clerk of said court or Family Support Magistrate Division, or by a commissioner of the Superior Court to be issued requiring such liable person or persons to appear in court or before a family support magistrate, at a time and place as determined by the clerk but not more than ninety days after the issuance of the summons. Service may be made by a state marshal, any proper officer or any investigator employed by the Department of Social Services or by the Commissioner of Administrative Services. The state marshal, proper officer or investigator shall make due return of process to the court not less than twenty-one days before the date assigned for hearing. Upon proof of the service of the summons to appear in court or before a family support magistrate at the time and place named for hearing upon such petition, the failure of the defendant or defendants to appear shall not prohibit the court or family support magistrate from going forward with the hearing. If the summons and order is signed by a commissioner of the Superior Court, upon proof of service of the summons to appear in court or before a family support magistrate and upon the failure of the defendant to appear at the time and place named for hearing upon the petition, request may be made by the petitioner to the court or family support magistrate for an order that a capias mittimus be issued.

(B) In the case of a person supported wholly or in part by a town, the welfare authority of the town shall notify the responsible relatives of such person of the amount of assistance given, the beginning date thereof and the amount of support expected from each of them, if any, and if any such relative does not contribute in such expected amount, the superior court for the judicial district in which such town is located or a family support magistrate sitting in the judicial district in which such town is located may order such relative or relatives to contribute to such support, from the time of the beginning date of expense shown on the notice, such sum as said court or family support magistrate deems reasonably within each such relative's ability to support such person.

(C) The court, or any judge thereof, or family support magistrate when said court or family support magistrate is not sitting, may require the defendant or defendants to become bound, with sufficient surety, to the state, town or person bringing the complaint, to abide such judgment as may be rendered on such complaint. Failure of the defendant or defendants to obey any order made under this section, may be punished as contempt of court and the costs of commitment of any person imprisoned therefor shall be paid by the state as in criminal cases. Except as otherwise provided, upon proof of the service of the summons to appear in court or before a family support magistrate at the time and place named for a hearing upon the failure of the defendant or defendants to obey such court order or order of the family support magistrate, the court or family support magistrate may order a capias mittimus be issued, and directed to some proper officer to arrest such defendant or defendants and bring such defendant or defendants before the Superior Court for the contempt hearing. When any person is found in contempt under this section, the court or family support magistrate may award to the petitioner a reasonable attorney's fee and the fees of the officer serving the contempt citation, such sums to be paid by the person found in contempt.

(9) In addition to or in lieu of such contempt proceedings, the court or family support magistrate, upon a finding that any person has failed to obey any order made under this section, may: (A) Order a plan for payment of any past-due support owing under such order, or, in IV–D cases, if such obligor is not incapacitated, order such obligor to participate in work activities which may include, but shall not be limited to, job search, training, work experience and participation in the job training and retraining program established by the Labor Commissioner pursuant to section 31–3t; (B) suspend any professional, occupational, recreational, commercial driver's or motor vehicle operator's license as provided in subsections (b) to (e), inclusive, of section 46b–220, provided such failure was without good cause; (C) issue an income withholding order against such amount of any debt accruing by reason of personal services as provided by sections 52–362, 52–362b and 52–362c; and (D) order executions against any real, personal, or other property of such person which cannot be categorized solely as either, for payment of accrued and unpaid amounts due under such order.

(10) No entry fee, judgment fee or any other court fee shall be charged by the court or the family support magistrate to either party in proceedings under this section.

(11) Any written agreement to support which is filed with the court or the Family Support Magistrate Division shall have the effect of an order of the court or a family support magistrate.

(b) The Attorney General of the state of Connecticut and the attorney representing a town, shall become a party for the interest of the state of Connecticut and such town, in any proceedings for support which concerns any person who is receiving or has received public assistance or care from the state or any town. The Attorney General shall represent the IV–D agency in non-TANF IV–D support cases if the IV–D agency determines that such representation is required pursuant to guidelines issued by the Commissioner of Social Services.

(c) The court or a family support magistrate shall direct all payments on orders of support in IV–D cases to be made to the state acting by and through the IV–D agency.

(d) No order for support made by the court or a family support magistrate shall be stayed by an appeal but such order shall continue in effect until a determination is made thereon upon such appeal; if however as a result of such appeal or further hearing, the amount of such order is reduced or vacated, such defendant shall be credited or reimbursed accordingly.

(e) Any court or family support magistrate, called upon to enforce a support order, shall insure that such order is reasonable in light of the obligor's ability to pay. Any support order entered pursuant to this section, or any support order from another jurisdiction subject to enforcement by the state of Connecticut, may be modified by motion of the party seeking such modification upon a showing of a substantial change in the circumstances of either party or upon a showing that such support order substantially deviates from the child support guidelines established pursuant to section 46b–215a, unless there was a specific finding on the record that the application of the guidelines would be inequitable or inappropriate, provided the court or family support magistrate finds that the obligor or the obligee and any other interested party have received actual notice of the pendency of such motion and of the time and place of the hearing on such motion. There shall be a rebuttable presumption that any deviation of less than fifteen per cent from the child support guidelines is not substantial and any deviation of fifteen per cent or more from the guidelines is substantial. Modification may be made of such support order without regard to whether the order was issued before, on or after May 9, 1991. No such support orders may be subject to retroactive modification, except that the court or family support magistrate may order modification with respect to any period during which there is a pending motion for a modification of an existing support order from the date of service of the notice of such pending motion upon the opposing party pursuant to section 52–50. In any hearing to modify any support order from another jurisdiction the court or the family support magistrate shall conduct the proceedings in accordance with the procedure set forth in sections 46b–213*o* to 46b–213q, inclusive.

(f) In IV–D support cases, as defined in subdivision (13) of subsection (b) of section 46b–231, a copy of any support order established or modified pursuant to this section or, in the case of a motion for modification of an existing support order, a notice of determination that there should be no change in the amount of the support order, shall be provided to each party and the state case registry within fourteen days after issuance of such order or determination.

(1949 Rev., § 2610; 1951, Supp. § 550b; 1955, Supp. § 1444d; 1957, Sept. Sp.Sess., P.A. 11, § 20; 1958 Rev., § 17–320; 1959, P.A. 34; 1961, P.A. 307; 1967, P.A. 746, § 4; 1972, P.A. 127, § 29; 1974, P.A. 74–183, § 216, eff. Dec. 31, 1974; 1975, P.A. 75–103; 1976, P.A. 76–334, § 10, eff. June 2, 1976; 1976, P.A. 76–436,

§ 185, eff. July 1, 1978; 1977, P.A. 77–452, § 9, eff. July 1, 1978; 1977, P.A. 77–594, § 3, eff. July 6, 1977; 1977, P.A. 77–614, § 70, eff. Oct. 1, 1977; 1977, P.A. 77–614, § 608, eff. Jan. 1, 1979; 1983, P.A. 83–295, § 14, eff. Oct. 1, 1983; 1984, P.A. 84–159, § 4; 1986, P.A. 86–359, § 33, eff. Jan. 1, 1987; 1987, P.A. 87–316, § 10; 1987, P.A. 87–589, § 31, eff. July 9, 1987; 1989, P.A. 89–195, § 3; 1990, P.A. 90–188, § 5; 1990, P.A. 90–213, § 32, eff. July 1, 1990; 1991, P.A. 91–76, § 5, eff. May 9, 1991; 1991, P.A. 91–391, § 6; 1993, P.A. 93–187, § 4; 1993, P.A. 93–262, § 72, eff. July 1, 1993; 1993, P.A. 93–396, § 18; 1995, P.A. 95–310, § 2, eff. Jan. 1, 1996; 1997, June 18 Sp.Sess., P.A. 97–1, § 65, eff. Jan. 1, 1998; 1997, June 18 Sp.Sess., P.A. 97–2, § 107, eff. July 1, 1997; 1997, June 18 Sp.Sess., P.A. 97–7, § 25, eff. July 1, 1997; 1999, P.A. 99–279, § 31, eff. July 1, 1999; 2000, P.A. 00–99, § 95, eff. December 1, 2000; 2002, May 9 Sp.Sess., P.A. 02–7, § 44; 2003, P.A. 03–258, § 3.)

[1] C.G.S.A. §§ 17b–289 to 17b–303, inclusive, and 1997, Oct. 29 Sp.Sess., P.A. 97–1, § 16.

[2] C.G.S.A. § 17b–261.

§ 46b–215a. Commission for Child Support Guidelines. Duties. Members

The Commission for Child Support Guidelines is established to review the child support guidelines promulgated pursuant to section 8 of public act 85–548,[1] to establish criteria for the establishment of guidelines to ensure the appropriateness of child support awards and to issue updated guidelines not later than October 1, 1993, and every four years thereafter. Not later than January 1, 1992, the commission shall also establish criteria and promulgate guidelines to ensure that such orders of payment on any arrearage and past due support shall be based on the obligor's ability to pay. Such guidelines shall also ensure the appropriateness of periodic payments of arrearages when the obligor (1) is the child's legal guardian and resides with the child or (2) is not the child's legal guardian but has resided with the child either for at least six months immediately preceding the order of payment of arrearage or for at least six months of the twelve months immediately preceding such order. In such cases, the commission shall consider exemptions similar to those in the uniform contribution scale adopted pursuant to section 4a–12. Updated arrearage guidelines shall be issued at the same time as the child support guidelines. The commission shall consist of eleven members as follows: The Chief Court Administrator or his designee, the Commissioner of Social Services or his designee, the Attorney General or his designee, the chairpersons and ranking members of the joint standing committee on judiciary or their designees and a representative of the Connecticut Bar Association, a representative of legal services, a person who represents the financial concerns of child support obligors and a representative of the Permanent Commission on the Status of Women, all of whom shall be appointed by the governor. The chairperson of the commission shall be elected by the members of the commission.

(1989, P.A. 89–203, § 1, eff. July 1, 1989; 1991, P.A. 91–391, § 7; 1992, P.A. 92–253, § 1; 1993, P.A. 93–262, § 1, eff. July 1, 1993; 1993, P.A. 93–329, § 5, eff. Oct. 1, 1993.)

[1] 1985, P.A. 85–548, § 8, is special in nature and has not been codified but remains in full force and effect.

§ 46b–215b. Guidelines to be used in determination of amount of support and payment on arrearages and past due support

(a) The child support and arrearage guidelines promulgated pursuant to section 8 of public act 85–548 [1] and any updated guidelines issued pursuant to section 46b–215a shall be considered in all determinations of child support amounts and payment on arrearages and past due support within the state. In all such determinations, there shall be a rebuttable presumption that the amount of such awards which resulted from the application of such guidelines is the amount of support or payment on any arrearage or past due support to be ordered. A specific finding on the record that the application of the guidelines would be inequitable or inappropriate in a particular case, as determined under criteria established by the Commission for Child Support Guidelines under section 46b–215a, shall be required in order to rebut the presumption in such case.

(b) In any determination pursuant to subsection (a) of this section, when a party has been determined by the Social Security Administration, or a state agency authorized to award disability benefits, to qualify for disability benefits under the federal Supplemental Security Income Program, the Social Security disability program, the state supplement to the federal Supplemental Security Income Program, the state-administered general assistance program or the general assistance program, parental earning capacity shall not be a basis for deviating from the presumptive support amount that results from the application of the child support guidelines to such party's income.

(c) In any proceeding for the establishment or modification of a child support award, the child support guidelines shall be considered in addition to and not in lieu of the criteria for such awards established in sections 46b–84, 46b–86, 46b–130, 46b–171, 46b–172, 46b–215, 17b–179 and 17b–745.

(1989, P.A. 89–203, § 2, eff. Oct. 1, 1989; 1991, P.A. 91–391, § 8; 1997, June 18 Sp.Sess., P.A. 97–1, § 66, eff. Jan. 1, 1998; 2003, P.A. 03–130, § 1.)

[1] 1985, P.A. 85–548, § 8, is special in nature and has not been codified but remains in full force and effect.

§ 46b–215c. Guidelines to be approved by legislative regulation review committee

(a) Notwithstanding the provisions of sections 46b–215 and 46b–215b, updated child support guidelines issued by the Commission for Child Support Guidelines pursuant to section 46b–215a shall be submitted by the commission to the standing legislative regulation review committee and adopted as regulations in accordance with the provisions of chapter 54.[1]

(b) Nothing in this section shall affect the validity of a child support order issued pursuant to any guidelines promulgated pursuant to section 46b–215a prior to the approval of any such guidelines pursuant to the provisions of this section.

(1991, P.A. 91–209, § 1, eff. June 10, 1991; 1992, P.A. 92–253, § 2.)

1 C.G.S.A. § 4–166 et seq.

§ 46b–215d. Certain earnings not considered income for purposes of guidelines

Notwithstanding the child support guidelines established pursuant to section 46b–215a, in cases in which an obligor is an hourly wage earner and has worked less than forty-five hours per week at the time of the establishment of the support order, any additional income earned from working more than forty-five hours per week shall not be considered income for purposes of such guidelines.

(1999, P.A. 99–193, § 3, eff. June 23, 1999; 1999, P.A. 99–279, § 32, eff. June 29, 1999.)

§ 46b–216. Support of surviving husband or wife by heirs

The estate of any person dying without issue, leaving a husband or wife surviving, shall be liable for the support of such surviving spouse until remarriage if such survivor becomes poor and there is no person or persons of sufficient ability, under the provisions of section 46b–215, to provide such support. Each person to whom any such estate is given or descends shall, to an amount equal to the estate so received by him, be liable to contribute to such support, and, if he neglects to provide such support, and sufficient support cannot be obtained from any of the persons liable under the provisions of said section 46b–215, such survivor, the Commissioner of Social Services, the selectmen of the town in which such survivor resides, or any person liable under the provisions of said section 46b–215, to contribute to such support but unable to wholly furnish the same, or any person other than the defendant or defendants, liable under this section to contribute to such support, may bring a complaint to the superior court for the judicial district in which such survivor resides, against all or any of the persons, except the plaintiff, to whom any of such estate has been given or has descended. Said court may order the defendant or defendants to contribute to such support from the time of serving such complaint such sum, not exceeding the value of the property received by such defendant or defendants from the estate of such deceased, as may be reasonable and necessary, and may issue execution monthly or quarterly for the same, which, when collected, shall be paid to such survivor, said commissioner or such selectmen, for such support, as the court orders. When such complaint is brought by the survivor, commissioner or selectmen, the court, or any judge thereof when said court is not sitting, may require the defendant or defendants to become bound with sufficient surety to such survivor, the state or town to abide the judgment rendered on such complaint.

(1949 Rev., § 2611; 1958 Rev., § 17–321; 1975, P.A. 75–420, § 4, eff. June 25, 1975; 1977, P.A. 77–614, § 608, eff. Jan. 1, 1979; 1978, P.A. 78–280, § 2, eff. July 1, 1978; 1993, P.A. 93–262, § 1, eff. July 1, 1993.)

§ 46b–217. Relief from support

Any defendant in an action brought under either section 46b–215 or 46b–216 may, at any time thereafter, prefer his complaint to said court against such survivor, the Commissioner of Social Services, selectmen or other persons, plaintiffs in such action, to be relieved from such contribution. In any action brought under said section 46b–215, the defendant in a IV–D support case as defined in subsection (b) of section 46b–231 may prefer his complaint to the family support magistrate serving the judicial district where the order was entered against the plaintiff in such action to be relieved from such contribution. If said court or family support magistrate finds that he, being liable under said section 46b–215, is required to contribute an amount beyond his ability or beyond what is requisite for such support, or that he, being liable under said section 46b–216, is required to contribute beyond the amount received by him from the estate of such deceased or beyond what is requisite for such support, it may again direct how much, if anything, he shall contribute therefor. If the contribution of the person or persons liable to support such poor person, as fixed by the court, is insufficient for such support, the remainder of such support shall be furnished by the state or such town.

(1949 Rev., § 2612; 1958, Rev., § 17–322; 1975, P.A. 75–420, § 4, eff. June 25, 1975; 1977, P.A. 77–614, § 608, eff. Jan. 1, 1979; 1986, P.A. 86–359, § 35, eff. Jan. 1, 1987; 1993, P.A. 93–262, § 73, eff. July 1, 1993.)

§ 46b–218. Filing of identification and location information with the state case registry

(a) For purposes of this section:

(1) "Identification and location information" means current information on the location and identity of a party to any paternity or child support proceeding, including, but not limited to, the party's Social Security number, residential and mailing addresses, telephone number, driver's license number, employer's name, address and telephone number, and such other information as may be required for the state case registry to comply with federal law and regulations;

(2) "Paternity or child support proceeding" means any court action or administrative process authorized by

state statute in which the paternity or support of a child is established; and

(3) "State case registry" means the database included in the automated system established and maintained by the Bureau of Child Support Enforcement under subsection (*l*) of section 17b–179 which database shall contain information on each support order established or modified in the state.

(b) Each party to any paternity or child support proceeding shall file identification and location information with the state case registry upon entry of an order and whenever such information changes.

(c) All identification and location information provided to the state case registry under subsection (b) of this section shall be subject to the provisions of section 17b–90.

(1958 Rev., § 17–324a; 1969, P.A. 654; 1971, P.A. 225; 1974, P.A. 74–183, § 218, eff. Dec. 31, 1974; 1976, P.A. 76–436, § 187, eff. July 1, 1978; 1977, P.A. 77–452, § 55, eff. July 1, 1978; 1990, P.A. 90–213, § 33, eff. July 1, 1990; 1999, P.A. 99–193, § 10, eff. June 23, 1999.)

§ 46b–219. No liability for support of deserting parent

No person shall be liable under any provision of the general statutes for the support of a parent who wilfully deserted such person continuously during the ten-year period prior to such person reaching his majority. For the purposes of this section, wilful desertion means total neglect of parental responsibility in failing to provide reasonable support and care within the financial capability of the parent. Any person claiming the provisions of this section as a defense shall have the burden of proof of such wilful desertion.

(1957, P.A. 475; 1958 Rev., § 17–326.)

§ 46b–220. Suspension of license of delinquent child support obligor. Conditions. Reinstatement

(a) For the purposes of this section:

(1) "Delinquent child support obligor" means (A) an obligor who owes overdue support, accruing after the entry of a court order, in an amount which exceeds ninety days of periodic payments on a current support or arrearage payment order; (B) an obligor who has failed to make court ordered medical or dental insurance coverage available within ninety days of the issuance of a court order or who fails to maintain such coverage pursuant to court order for a period of ninety days; or (C) an obligor who has failed, after receiving appropriate notice, to comply with subpoenas or warrants relating to paternity or child support proceedings;

(2) "License" means each license, certification or permit to engage in a profession or occupation regulated pursuant to the provisions of title 19a, 20 or 21, a motor vehicle operator's license or a commercial driver's license issued by the Commissioner of Motor Vehicles in accordance with chapter 246,[1] and licensees and permits issued by the Department of Environmental Protection pursuant to part III of chapter 490 of title 26;[2]

(3) "Licensing authority" means any board, commission, department or official with authority to issue a license;

(4) "Obligor" means any person owing a duty of child support;

(5) "Obligee" means the person or entity to whom child support payments are owed;

(6) "Past-due support" means any one or a combination of the following: (A) Court ordered current support or arrearage payments which have become due and payable and remain unpaid; (B) unpaid support which has been reduced to a judgment or otherwise found to be due by a court of competent jurisdiction, whether or not presently payable; (C) support due for periods prior to an action to establish a child support order, provided such amounts are based upon the obligor's ability to pay during the prior periods if known or, if not known, on the obligor's current ability to pay if known, or, if not known, upon assistance rendered to the obligor's child;

(7) "Overdue support" means a delinquency accruing after the entry of an initial court order establishing a child support obligation.

(b) The Superior Court and any family support magistrate may issue a suspension order, which suspends the license of a delinquent child support obligor, to enforce a child support order. Such suspension order shall specify the conditions which must be met to avoid license suspension and shall be effective only on the filing of an affidavit, sufficient under subsection (c) of this section as to the obligor's delinquency. Such order shall also specify the conditions of reinstatement of any such suspended license in the event of suspension by the court or family support magistrate. In IV-D cases the order shall specify that the Department of Social Services shall notify the licensing authority of the suspension order and of compliance with or rescission of such order. In non-IV-D cases, the order shall specify the procedure for notification of the licensing authority of the suspension order and of compliance with or rescission of such order and the person required to provide such notification. No judge or family support magistrate may issue a suspension order unless he finds (1) the obligor has received actual notice of the proceeding and that a motor vehicle operator's license or professional, occupational or recreational license which he holds may be suspended, (2) the noncompliance with his child support obligations was wilful and without good cause, (3) the suspension order is fair and equitable, (4) the obligor has sufficient financial resources to comply with the conditions specified in the suspension order. A copy of any suspension order issued against a nonappearing obligor shall be sent to the obligor by first class mail, postage prepaid by the Department of Social Services, or, in any non-IV-D case, any person specified in the suspension order.

(c) If the obligor fails to comply with the conditions of a suspension order within thirty days of the issuance of such order, the Department of Social Services, a support enforcement officer, the attorney for the obligee or the obligee, as provided in the suspension order, shall file with the court or assistant clerk of the Family Support Magistrate Division, an affidavit stating that the conditions of the suspension order have not been met, and provide the obligor with a copy of such affidavit. Such affidavit shall be filed within forty-five days of the expiration of such thirty-day period. Such suspension order shall be effective upon the filing of such affidavit.

(d) If (1) the obligor satisfies the conditions of the suspension order within thirty days of the issuance of such suspension order or (2) the affidavit is not filed within forty-five days of the expiration of such thirty-day period, such order shall be null and void and shall have no further effect.

(e) Upon receipt of an effective court order directing suspension of a license, the Department of Social Services or, in any non-IV-D case, any person specified in such order shall provide the licensing authority with a copy of the suspension order and affidavit. The licensing authority shall, upon receipt of such order and affidavit, suspend such license. Upon the obligor's compliance with the conditions of the license suspension order concerning reinstatement, or upon any subsequent order of the court or family support magistrate to rescind such license suspension, the licensing authority shall immediately reinstate such license. No licensing authority may charge a fee for the reinstatement of any such license which exceeds the actual administrative cost of such reinstatement.

(1995, P.A. 95–310, § 4, eff. Jan. 1, 1996; 1997, June 18 Sp.Sess., P.A. 97–7, § 32, eff. July 1, 1997.)

[1] C.G.S.A. § 14–1 et seq.
[2] C.G.S.A. § 26–27 et seq.

§ 46b–221. Notice to delinquent child support obligors by Commissioner of Social Services re availability of remedy of license suspension

The Commissioner of Social Services may provide notice to all IV-D delinquent child support obligors of the availability of the remedy of suspension of motor vehicle operator's licenses and professional, occupational and recreational licenses pursuant to section 46b–220. Such notice shall comply with the provisions of section 52–362g.

(1995, P.A. 95–310, § 6, eff. Jan. 1, 1996; 1997, June 18 Sp.Sess., P.A. 97–7, § 33, eff. July 1, 1997.)

§ 46b–222. Regulations

The Department of Social Services may adopt regulations in accordance with the provisions of chapter 54 [1] to implement the provisions of section 46b–220.

(1995, P.A. 95–310, § 7, eff. Jan. 1, 1996.)

[1] C.G.S.A. § 4–166 et seq.

§ 46b–223. Rules of Court

The judges of the Superior Court may adopt any rules they deem necessary to implement the provisions of section 46b–220, including the application of said section to the practice of law, and the Office of the Chief Court Administrator shall prescribe any forms required to implement said section.

(1995, P.A. 95–310, § 8, eff. Jan. 1, 1996.)

§§ 46b–224 to 46b–230. Reserved for future use

PART III. FAMILY SUPPORT MAGISTRATE'S ACT

§ 46b–231. Definitions. Family Support Advisory Committee. Family Support Magistrate Division. Family support magistrates; appointment, salaries, powers and duties. Orders. Appeal. Attorney General; duties re actions for support

(a) **Short title: Family Support Magistrate's Act.** This section shall be known and may be cited as the "Family Support Magistrate's Act".

(b) **Definitions.** For the purposes of this section:

(1) "Chief Family Support Magistrate" means the family support magistrate designated by the Chief Court Administrator as provided in subsection (g) of this section;

(2) "Child support enforcement services" means the services provided by the IV–D agency or an agency under cooperative or purchase of service agreement therewith pursuant to Title IV–D of the Social Security Act,[1] including, but not limited to, location; establishment of paternity; establishment, modification and enforcement of child and medical support orders and the collection and distribution of support payments;

(3) "Commissioner" means the Commissioner of Social Services or a designee or authorized representative;

(4) "Bureau of Child Support Enforcement" means a division within the Department of Social Services established pursuant to section 17b–179;

(5) "Department" means the Department of Social Services or any bureau, division or agency of the Department of Social Services;

(6) "Family Support Magistrate Division" means a division of the Superior Court created by this section for the purpose of establishing and enforcing child and spousal support in IV–D cases and in cases brought

pursuant to sections 46b–212 to 46b–213v, inclusive, utilizing quasi-judicial proceedings;

(7) "Family support magistrate" means a person, appointed as provided in subsection (f) of this section to establish and enforce child and spousal support orders;

(8) "Foster care cases" are cases in which children are receiving foster care under part I of chapter 319a or part I of chapter 815t,[2] but does not include cases in which children reside in detention facilities, forestry camps, training schools or other facilities operated primarily for the detention of children adjudicated as delinquent;

(9) "Law" includes both common and statute law;

(10) "Obligee" means any person to whom a duty of support is owed;

(11) "Obligor" means any person owing a duty of support;

(12) "IV–D agency" means the Bureau of Child Support Enforcement within the Department of Social Services, created by section 17b–179 and authorized to administer the child support program mandated by Title IV–D of the Social Security Act;

(13) "IV–D support cases" are those in which the IV–D agency is providing child support enforcement services under Title IV–D of the Social Security Act, including all foster care cases referred to the Bureau of Child Support Enforcement under section 46b–130; and

(14) "Support order" means a judgment, decree or order, whether temporary, final or subject to modification, issued by a court of competent jurisdiction, for the support and maintenance of a child, including a child who has attained the age of majority under the law of the issuing state, or a child and parent with whom the child is living, which provides for monetary support, health care, arrearages or reimbursement, and which may include related costs and fees, interest and penalties, income withholding, attorneys' fees and other relief.

(c) **Remedies.** The remedies herein provided are in addition to and not in substitution for any other remedy.

(d) **Family Support Magistrate Division established.** There is created the Family Support Magistrate Division of the Superior Court for the purpose of the impartial administration of child and spousal support.

(e) **Family Support Advisory Committee established.** Repealed by P.A. 91–190, § 8, 9.

(f) **Magistrates.** The Family Support Magistrate Division shall include nine family support magistrates who shall be appointed by the Governor to serve in that capacity for a term of three years. A family support magistrate may be reappointed upon completion of his term of office by the Governor. To be eligible for appointment, a family support magistrate must have engaged in the practice of law for five years prior to his appointment and shall be experienced in the field of family law. He shall devote full time to his duties as a family support magistrate and shall not engage in the private practice of law. A family support magistrate may be removed from office by the Governor for cause.

(g) **Chief magistrate.** A Chief Family Support Magistrate shall be designated by the Chief Court Administrator of the Superior Court from among the nine family support magistrates appointed by the Governor pursuant to subsection (f) of this section. Under the direction of the Chief Court Administrator, the Chief Family Support Magistrate shall supervise the Family Support Magistrate Division and submit an annual report to the Chief Court Administrator and perform such other duties as provided in this section.

(h) **Salaries of chief magistrate and magistrates.** (1) On and after April 1, 2000, the Chief Family Support Magistrate shall receive a salary of ninety-nine thousand five hundred eighty-seven dollars, and other family support magistrates shall receive an annual salary of ninety-four thousand five hundred eighty-seven dollars.

(2) On and after April 1, 2001, the Chief Family Support Magistrate shall receive a salary of one hundred three thousand six hundred dollars, and other family support magistrates shall receive an annual salary of ninety-eight thousand six hundred dollars.

(3) On and after April 1, 2002, the Chief Family Support Magistrate shall receive a salary of one hundred eight thousand eight hundred twenty-one dollars, and other family support magistrates shall receive an annual salary of one hundred three thousand five hundred sixty-nine dollars.

(i) **Retirement and disability coverage.** (1) Family support magistrates shall be included under the provisions of chapters 65 and 66[3] regarding retirement and disability of state employees. Each such individual shall receive full retirement credit for each year or portion thereof for which retirement benefits are paid while serving as a family support magistrate.

(2) Any family support magistrate may elect to be included within the provisions of sections 51–49, 51–49a, 51–49b, 51–49c, 51–49d, 51–49h, 51–50a and 51–50b, or to continue to be subject to the provisions of subdivision (1) of this subsection. Any family support magistrate who has so elected may revoke such election and elect to be included in the provisions of chapters 65 and 66 regarding retirement and disability of state employees. Thereupon any payments transferred from the State Employees Retirement Fund to the Judges, Family Support Magistrates and Compensation Commissioners Retirement Fund shall be transferred from the Judges, Family Support Magistrates and Compensation Commissioners Retirement Fund to the State Employees Retirement Fund.

(j) **Assistant clerks and other employees.** The Chief Court Administrator shall designate assistant clerks for the Family Support Magistrate Division to serve in judicial districts created pursuant to section 51–344 and such other assistant clerks and other employees as may be necessary for the operation of the Family Support Magistrate Division. The administrative judge for each judicial district may also assign clerks or administrative clerks for the judicial district to serve as assistant clerks or administrative clerks in his judicial district for the Family Support Magistrate Division.

(k) **Hearings to be recorded.** The Chief Court Administrator shall arrange for the recording of all hearings before the family support magistrate by contract or otherwise.

(*l*) **Rules of procedure to be adopted.** The judges of the Superior Court shall adopt rules of procedure in accordance with the provisions of section 51–14 for the handling by magistrates of IV–D support cases and in cases brought pursuant to sections 46b–212 to 46b–213v, inclusive. Such rules of procedure shall conform when applicable to rules adopted for the Superior Court.

(m) **Magistrates' powers and duties.** The Chief Family Support Magistrate and the family support magistrates shall have the powers and duties enumerated in this subsection.

(1) A family support magistrate in IV–D support cases may compel the attendance of witnesses or the obligor under a summons issued pursuant to sections 17b–745, 46b–172, and 46b–215 or under a subpoena issued pursuant to section 52–143, or a citation for failure to obey an order of a family support magistrate or a judge of the Superior Court. If a person is served with a summons, subpoena or citation issued by the family support magistrate or the assistant clerk of the Family Support Magistrate Division and fails to appear, a family support magistrate may issue a capias mittimus directed to some proper officer to arrest the obligor or the witness and bring him before a family support magistrate. Whenever such a capias mittimus is ordered, the family support magistrate shall establish a recognizance to the state of Connecticut in the form of a bond of such character and amount as to assure the appearance of the obligor at the next regular session of the Family Support Magistrate Division in the judicial district in which the matter is pending. If the obligor posts such a bond, and thereafter fails to appear before the family support magistrate at the time and place he is ordered to appear, the family support magistrate may order the bond forfeited, and the proceeds thereof paid to the state in TANF cases or the obligee in non-TANF cases.

(2) Family support magistrates shall hear and determine matters involving child and spousal support in IV–D support cases including petitions for support brought pursuant to sections 17b–81, 17b–179, 17b–745 and 46b–215; applications for show cause orders in IV–D support cases brought pursuant to subsection (b) of section 46b–172, and actions for interstate enforcement of child and spousal support and paternity under sections 46b–212 to 46b–213v, inclusive, and shall hear and determine all motions for modifications of child and spousal support in such cases. In all IV–D cases, family support magistrates shall have the authority to order any obligor who is subject to a plan for reimbursement of past-due support and is not incapacitated, to participate in work activities which may include, but shall not be limited to, job search, training, work experience and participation in the job training and retraining program established by the Labor Commissioner pursuant to section 31–3t. A family support magistrate shall not modify an order for periodic payment on an arrearage due the state for state assistance which has been discontinued to increase such payments, unless the family support magistrate first determines that the state has made a reasonable effort to notify the current recipient of child support, at the most current address available to the IV–D agency, of the pendency of the motion to increase such periodic arrearage payments and of the time and place of the hearing on such motion. If such recipient appears, either personally or through a representative, at such hearing, the family support magistrate shall determine whether the order in effect for child support is reasonable in relation to the current financial circumstances of the parties, prior to modifying an order increasing such periodic arrearage payments.

(3) Family support magistrates shall review and approve or modify all agreements for support in IV–D support cases filed with the Family Support Magistrate Division in accordance with sections 17b–179, 17b–745, 46b–172, 46b–215 and subsection (c) of section 53–304.

(4) Motions for modification of existing child and spousal support orders entered by the Superior Court in IV–D support cases, including motions to modify existing child and spousal support orders entered in actions brought pursuant to chapter 815j,[4] shall be brought in the Family Support Magistrate Division and decided by a family support magistrate. Family support magistrates, in deciding if a spousal or child support order should be modified, shall make such determination based upon the criteria set forth in section 46b–84 and section 46b–215b. A person who is aggrieved by a decision of a family support magistrate modifying a Superior Court order is entitled to appeal such decision in accordance with the provisions of subsection (n) of this section.

(5) Proceedings to establish paternity in IV–D support cases shall be filed in the family support magistrate division for the judicial district where the mother or putative father resides. The matter shall be heard and determined by the family support magistrate in accordance with the provisions of chapter 815y.[5]

(6) Agreements for support obtained in IV–D support cases shall be filed with the assistant clerk of the

family support magistrate division for the judicial district where the mother or the father of the child resides, pursuant to subsection (b) of section 46b–172, and shall become effective as an order upon filing with the clerk. Such support agreements shall be reviewed by the family support magistrate who shall approve or disapprove the agreement. If the support agreement filed with the clerk is disapproved by a family support magistrate, such disapproval shall have a retroactive effect.

(7) Family support magistrates shall enforce orders for child and spousal support entered by such family support magistrate and by the Superior Court in IV–D support cases by citing an obligor for contempt. Family support magistrates, in IV–D cases, shall have the authority to order any obligor who is subject to a plan for reimbursement of past-due support and is not incapacitated, to participate in work activities which may include, but shall not be limited to, job search, training, work experience and participation in the job training and retraining program established by the Labor Commissioner pursuant to section 31–3t. Family support magistrates shall also enforce income withholding orders entered pursuant to section 52–362, including any additional amounts to be applied toward liquidation of any arrearage, as required under subsection (e) of said section. Family support magistrates may require the obligor to furnish recognizance to the state of Connecticut in the form of a cash deposit or bond of such character and in such amount as the Family Support Magistrate Division deems proper to assure appearance at the next regular session of the Family Support Magistrate Division in the judicial district in which the matter is pending. Upon failure of the obligor to post such bond, the family support magistrate may refer the obligor to a community correctional center until he has complied with such order, provided that the obligor shall be heard at the next regular session of the Family Support Magistrate Division in the court to which he was summoned. If no regular session is held within seven days of such referral, the family support magistrate shall either cause a special session of the Family Support Magistrate Division to be convened, or the obligor shall be heard by a Superior Court judge in the judicial district. If the obligor fails to appear before the family support magistrate at the time and place he is ordered to appear, the family support magistrate may order the bond, if any, forfeited, and the proceeds thereof paid to the state in TANF cases or the obligee in non-TANF cases, as the family support magistrate may determine, and the family support magistrate may issue a capias mittimus for the arrest of the obligor, ordering him to appear before the family support magistrate. A family support magistrate may determine whether or not an obligor is in contempt of the order of the Superior Court or of a family support magistrate and may make such orders as are provided by law to enforce a support obligation, except that if the family support magistrate determines that incarceration of an obligor for failure to obey a support order may be indicated, the family support magistrate shall inform the obligor of his right to be represented by an attorney and his right to a court-appointed attorney to represent him if he is indigent. If the obligor claims he is indigent and desires an attorney to represent him, the family support magistrate shall conduct a hearing to determine if the obligor is indigent; and if he so finds, he will appoint an attorney to represent him.

(8) Agreements between parties as to custody and visitation of minor children in IV–D support cases may be filed with the assistant clerk of the Family Support Magistrate Division. Such agreements shall be reviewed by a family support magistrate, who shall approve the agreement unless he finds such agreement is not in the best interests of the child. Agreements between parties as to custody and visitation in IV–D support cases shall be enforced in the same manner as agreements for support are enforced, pursuant to subdivision (7) of this subsection.

(9) Whenever an obligor is before a family support magistrate in proceedings to establish, modify or enforce a support order in a IV–D support case and such order is not secured by an income withholding order, the magistrate may require the obligor to execute a bond or post other security sufficient to perform such order for support, provided the magistrate finds that such a bond is available for purchase within the financial means of the obligor. Upon failure of such obligor to comply with such support order, the family support magistrate may order the bond or the security forfeited and the proceeds thereof paid to the state in TANF cases or to the obligee in non-TANF cases.

(10) In any proceeding in the Family Support Magistrate Division, if the family support magistrate finds that a party is indigent and unable to pay a fee or fees payable to the court or to pay the cost of service of process, the family support magistrate shall waive such fee or fees and the cost of service of process shall be paid by the state.

(11) A family support magistrate may dismiss any action or proceeding which the family support magistrate may hear and determine.

(12) A family support magistrate may order parties to participate in the parenting education program in accordance with the provisions of section 46b–69b.

(n) **Appeal procedure.** (1) A person who is aggrieved by a final decision of a family support magistrate is entitled to judicial review by way of appeal under this section.

(2) Proceedings for such appeal shall be instituted by filing a petition in superior court for the judicial district in which the decision of the family support magistrate was rendered not later than fourteen days after filing of the final decision with an assistant clerk assigned to the Family Support Magistrate Division or, if a rehearing is

requested, not later than fourteen days after filing of the notice of the decision thereon. In a IV–D support case, such petitions shall be accompanied by a certification that copies of the petition have been served upon the IV–D agency as defined in subsection (b) of this section and all parties of record. Service upon the IV–D agency may be made by the appellant mailing a copy of the petition by certified mail to the office of the Attorney General in Hartford.

(3) Within fourteen days after the filing of the petition, or within such further time as may be allowed by the court, the Family Support Magistrate Division shall transmit to the reviewing court the original or a certified copy of the entire record of the proceeding appealed from, which shall include the decision of the family support magistrate. The court may require or permit subsequent corrections or additions to the record.

(4) The aggrieved party shall file with his appeal a statement that no transcript is required for the purpose of determining the issues raised on appeal or a statement that he has ordered a transcript. A transcript may be filed by any party to an appeal and shall be filed within thirty days from the filing of said appeal unless the time for filing such transcript is extended by order of the Superior Court or the family support magistrate. Costs of preparing the transcript shall be paid by the party ordering the preparation of the transcript.

(5) If, before the date set for hearing, application is made to the Superior Court for leave to present additional evidence, and it is shown to the satisfaction of the court that the additional evidence is material and that there were good reasons for failure to present it in the proceeding before the family support magistrate, the Superior Court may permit additional evidence be taken before it upon conditions determined by the court.

(6) The appeal shall be conducted by the Superior Court without a jury and shall be confined to the record and such additional evidence as the Superior Court has permitted to be introduced. The Superior Court, upon request, shall hear oral argument and receive written briefs.

(7) The Superior Court may affirm the decision of the family support magistrate or remand the case for further proceedings. The Superior Court may reverse or modify the decision if substantial rights of the appellant have been prejudiced because the decision of the family support magistrate is: (A) In violation of constitutional or statutory provisions; (B) in excess of the statutory authority of the family support magistrate; (C) made upon unlawful procedure; (D) affected by other error of law; (E) clearly erroneous in view of the reliable, probative, and substantial evidence on the whole record; or (F) arbitrary or capricious or characterized by abuse of discretion or clearly unwarranted exercise of discretion.

(8) Any order entered by the court pursuant to an appeal under this subsection may be retroactive to the date of the original order entered by the family support magistrate.

(9) Upon all such appeals which are denied, costs may be taxed in favor of the prevailing party at the discretion of the Superior Court, but no costs shall be taxed against the state.

(10) In any case in which any party claims that he cannot pay the costs of an appeal or defending an appeal under this section, he shall, within the time permitted for filing the appeal, or the time permitted for filing of a transcript of testimony if preparation of such transcript is required, file with the clerk of the superior court to which the appeal is to be taken an application for waiver of payment of such fees, costs and necessary expenses. The application shall conform to rules adopted pursuant to section 51–14. After such hearing as the Superior Court determines is necessary, the Superior Court shall enter its judgment on the application, which judgment shall contain a statement of the facts the Superior Court has found, with its conclusions thereon. The filing of the application for the waiver shall toll the time limits for the filing of an appeal until such time as a judgment on such application is entered.

(*o*) **Appeals to Appellate and Supreme Courts.** Upon final determination of any appeal from a decision of a family support magistrate by the Superior Court, there shall be no right to further review except to the Appellate Court. The procedure on such appeal to the Appellate Court shall, except as otherwise provided herein, be in accordance with the procedures provided by rule or law for the appeal of judgments rendered by the Superior Court unless modified by rule of the judges of the Appellate Court. There shall be no right to further review except to the Supreme Court pursuant to the provisions of section 51–197f.

(p) **Order of support continued during appeal or until changed by further order.** The filing of an appeal from a decision of a family support magistrate does not affect the order of support of a family support magistrate, but it shall continue in effect until the appeal is decided, and thereafter, unless denied, until changed by further order of a family support magistrate or the Superior Court.

(q) **Order issued by Superior Court supersedes previous orders.** When an order for child or spousal support has been entered against an obligor by the Superior Court in an action originating in the Superior Court, such order shall supersede any previous order for child or spousal support against such obligor entered by a family support magistrate and shall also supersede any previous agreement for support executed by such obligor and filed with the Family Support Magistrate Division.

(r) **Force and effect of order for support. Garnishment provision.** Orders for support entered by a family support magistrate shall have the same force and effect as orders of the Superior Court, except where otherwise provided in sections 17b–81, 17b–93, 17b–179, 17b–743, 17b–744, 17b–745 and 17b–746, subsection (a) of section 46b–55, sections 46b–59a, 46b–86 and 46b–172, this chapter, subsection (b) of section 51–348, section 52–362, subsection (a) of section 52–362d, subsection (a) of section 52–362e and subsection (c) of section 53–304, and shall be considered orders of the Superior Court for the purpose of establishing and enforcing support orders of the family support magistrate, as provided in sections 17b–81, 17b–93, 17b–179, 17b–745, 52–362, 52–362d, 52–362e and 53–304, except as otherwise provided in this section. All orders for support issued by family support magistrates in any matter before a magistrate shall contain an order for withholding to enforce such orders as set forth in section 52–362.

(s) **Duties of support enforcement officers.** Support enforcement officers of Support Enforcement Services of the Superior Court shall:

(1) Supervise the payment of any child or spousal support order made by a family support magistrate. Supervision of such orders is defined as the utilization of all procedures available by law to collect child or spousal support, including issuance and implementation of income withholdings ordered by the Superior Court or a family support magistrate pursuant to section 52–362, issuance of an order requiring any party to appear before a family support magistrate on an action to modify a support order pursuant to subdivision (4) of this subsection, and if necessary, bringing an application for contempt to a family support magistrate and, in connection with such application, issuing an order requiring the obligor to appear before a family support magistrate to show cause why such obligor should not be held in contempt for failure to pay an order for child or spousal support entered by the Superior Court or a family support magistrate;

(2) In non-TANF cases, have the authority to bring petitions for support orders pursuant to section 46b–215, file agreements for support with the assistant clerk of the Family Support Magistrate Division, and bring applications for show cause orders pursuant to section 46b–172, and in IV–D cases and cases under sections 46b–212 to 46b–213v, inclusive, enforce foreign support orders registered with the Family Support Magistrate Division pursuant to sections 46b–213f to 46b–213i, inclusive, and file agreements for support with the assistant clerk of the Family Support Magistrate Division;

(3) In connection with any order or agreement entered by, or filed with, the Family Support Magistrate Division, or any order entered by the Superior Court in a IV–D support case upon order, investigate the financial situation of the parties and report findings to the family support magistrate regarding: (A) Any pending motion to modify such order or agreement, or (B) any request or application for modification of such order or agreement made by an obligee;

(4) In non-TANF IV–D cases, review child support orders at the request of either parent or custodial party subject to a support order or, in TANF cases, review child support orders at the request of the Bureau of Child Support Enforcement, and initiate an action before a family support magistrate to modify such support order if it is determined upon such review that the order substantially deviates from the child support guidelines established pursuant to section 46b–215a or 46b–215b. The requesting party shall have a right to such review every three years without proving a substantial change in circumstances; more frequent reviews shall be made only if the requesting party demonstrates a substantial change in circumstances. There shall be a rebuttable presumption that any deviation of less than fifteen per cent from the child support guidelines is not substantial and any deviation of fifteen per cent or more from the guidelines is substantial. Modification may be made of such support order without regard to whether the order was issued before, on or after May 9, 1991. In determining whether to modify a child support order based on a substantial deviation from such child support guidelines, consideration shall be given to the division of real and personal property between the parties set forth in any final decree entered pursuant to chapter 815j and the benefits accruing to the child as the result of such division. No order for periodic payment of support may be subject to retroactive modification, except that the family support magistrate may order modification with respect to any period during which there is a pending motion for modification of a support order from the date of service of notice of such pending motion to the opposing party pursuant to section 52–50.

(t) **Duties of Attorney General.** The Attorney General shall:

(1) Represent the interest of the state in all actions for child or spousal support in all cases in which the state is furnishing or has furnished aid or care to one of the parties to the action or a child of one of the parties;

(2) In interstate support enforcement under sections 46b–212 to 46b–213v, inclusive, provide necessary legal services on behalf of the support enforcement agency in providing services to a petitioner;

(3) Represent the IV–D agency in providing support enforcement services in non-TANF IV–D support cases pursuant to sections 17b–179, 17b–745 and 46b–215.

(u) (1) The Department of Social Services may in IV–D cases (A) bring petitions for support orders pursuant to section 46b–215, (B) obtain acknowledgments of paternity, (C) bring applications for show cause orders pursuant to section 46b–172, (D) file agreements for support with the assistant clerk of the Family Support Magistrate Division, and (E) issue withholding orders entered by the Superior Court or a family support magistrate in accordance with subsection (b) of section 52–362.

(2) The Department of Social Services shall provide notice not less than once every three years to the parents subject to a support order in a IV–D case informing the parents of their right to request a review under subdivision (4) of subsection (s) of this section.

(1986, P.A. 86–359, § 1; 1986, P.A. 86–403, §§ 113, 114, eff. June 11, 1986; 1987, P.A. 87–316, § 7; 1989, P.A. 89–195, § 1; 1989, P.A. 89–302, § 5, eff. March 1, 1990; P.A. 89–360, §§ 9 to 11, eff. July 1, 1989; 1990, P.A. 90–132; 1990, P.A. 90–189; 1990, P.A. 90–213, § 34, eff. July 1, 1990; 1991, P.A. 91–76, § 6, eff. May 9, 1991; 1991, P.A. 91–190, § 8, eff. July 1, 1991; 1992, P.A. 92–226, § 3, eff. June 22, 1992; 1992, May Sp.Sess., P.A. 92–16, § 86, eff. June 19, 1992; 1993, P.A. 93–187, § 5; 1993, P.A. 93–262, § 1, eff. July 1, 1993; 1993, P.A. 93–329, § 8, eff. Oct. 1, 1993; 1993, P.A. 93–396, § 5; 1993, P.A. 93–435, § 59, eff. June 28, 1993; 1995, P.A. 95–191, § 1, eff. July 1, 1995; 1995, P.A. 95–310, § 3, eff. Jan. 1, 1996; 1997, P.A. 97–252; 1997, June 18 Sp.Sess., P.A. 97–1, § 67, eff. Jan. 1, 1998; 1997, June 18 Sp.Sess., P.A. 97–2, § 108, eff. July 1, 1997; 1997, June 18 Sp.Sess., P.A. 97–7, §§ 26, 36, eff. July 1, 1997; 1997, July 21 Sp.Sess., P.A. 97–1, § 6, eff. July 23, 1997; 1998, P.A. 98–197, § 3, eff. July 1, 1998; 1999, P.A. 99–193, § 11, eff. July 1, 1999; 1999, P.A. 99–193, § 12; 1999, June Sp.Sess., P.A. 99–1, § 38, eff. July 1, 1999; 2000, P.A. 00–231, § 9, eff. Jan. 3, 2001; 2001, P.A. 01–91, § 17; 2003, P.A. 03–89, § 5; 2003.)

1 42 U.S.C.A. § 651 et seq.
2 C.G.S.A. § 17a–90 et seq. or C.G.S.A. § 46b–120 et seq.
3 C.G.S.A. § 5–142 et seq. and C.G.S.A. § 5–152 et seq.
4 C.G.S.A. § 46b–40 et seq.
5 C.G.S.A. § 46b–160 et seq.

§ 46b–232. Alteration or setting aside of support order by family support magistrate, when

A family support magistrate may alter or set aside (1) any order for payment of support issued by a family support magistrate at any time or (2) any order for payment of support issued by the superior court at any time upon referral of such order by the superior court.

(1986, P.A. 86–359, § 34, eff. Jan. 1, 1987.)

§ 46b–233. Longevity payments

Each family support magistrate, who has completed not less than ten years of service as such magistrate, or other state service or service as an elected officer of the state, or any combination of such service, shall receive semiannual longevity payments based on such service completed as of the first day of July and the first day of January of each year as follows:

(1) A family support magistrate who has completed ten or more years but less than fifteen years of service shall receive one-quarter of three per cent of the annual salary payable under subsection (h) of section 46b–231;

(2) A family support magistrate who has completed fifteen or more years but less than twenty years of service shall receive one-half of three per cent of the annual salary payable under said subsection (h) of section 46b–231;

(3) A family support magistrate who has completed twenty or more years but less than twenty-five years of service shall receive three-quarters of three per cent of the annual salary payable under said subsection (h) of section 46b–231; and

(4) A family support magistrate who has completed twenty-five or more years of service shall receive three per cent of the annual salary payable under said subsection (h) of section 46b–231.

(1989, P.A. 89–360, § 17, eff. July 1, 1989; 1993, P.A. 93–379, § 6, eff. June 30, 1993.)

§ 46b–233a. Retirement of family support magistrates. Credit for prior service. Amounts used in determining salary

(a) Each family support magistrate who had elected under the provisions of subdivision (2) of subsection (i) of section 46b–231 shall, for retirement purposes, be entitled to credit for any or all the prior years of service accrued by him on June 22, 1992, while serving in the office of family support magistrate, provided such magistrate shall pay to the comptroller five per cent of the salary for his office for each prior year of service he claims for retirement credit. Each such magistrate shall be entitled to have his retirement contributions to the state employees retirement system under chapter 66 [1] credited toward the payment due for the prior year or years of service he claims for retirement credit under this section.

(b) For purposes of determining both the retirement salary of family support magistrates and the allowance payable to their surviving spouses under subsection (b) of section 51–51, "salary" shall be composed of the total of the following amounts: The annual salary payable at the time of retirement or death, fixed in accordance with subsection (h) of section 46b–231; and for family support magistrates to whom a longevity payment has been made or is due and payable, in each case under section 51–51 (1) one and one-half per cent of the annual salary the family support magistrate was receiving at the time of retirement or death, for those who have completed ten or more but less than fifteen years of service as a family support magistrate, (2) three per cent of the annual salary the family support magistrate was receiving at the time of retirement or death, for those who have completed fifteen or more but less than twenty years of service as a family support magistrate, (3) four and one-half per cent of the annual salary the family support magistrate was receiving at the time of retirement or death, for those who have completed twenty or more but less than twenty-five years of service as a family support magistrate, and (4) six per cent of the annual salary the family support magistrate was receiving at the time of retirement or death, for those who have completed twenty-five or more years of service as a family support magistrate.

(1992, P.A. 92–226, §§ 9, 16, eff. June 22, 1992.)

[1] C.G.S.A. § 5–152 et seq.

§ 46b–234. Repealed. (1999, P.A. 99–193, § 15, eff. June 23, 1999.)

§ 46b–235. Applicability of sections in relation to any bargaining unit designation, award, settlement, benefit, existing employment practice or classification of any employee

The provisions of subsection (a) of section 4a–2, subsection (a) of section 4a–12, sections 17b–137, 17b–179, 17b–745, 46b–172, 46b–207, 46b–208, 46b–215, 46b–218, 46b–231 and 46b–235, subsection (a) of section 51–348a, subsection (d) of section 52–50, sections 52–259a, 52–362, 52–362c to 52–362f, inclusive, and 53–304 shall not be construed to alter, modify, impair or change existing collective bargaining agreements, any bargaining unit designation, award, settlement, benefit, existing employment practice or classification of any employee in the event of transfer from one division, bureau or agency or department to another division, agency or department.

(1990, P.A. 90–213, § 45, eff. July 1, 1990; 1997, June 18 Sp.Sess., P.A. 97–1, § 68, eff. Jan. 1, 1998; 1999, P.A. 99–193, § 14, eff. June 23, 1999.)

§ 46b–236. Family support referees

(a) Each family support magistrate who ceases or has ceased to hold office because of retirement other than under the provisions of section 5–169 or 51–49 and who is an elector and a resident of this state shall be a family support referee for the remainder of his term of office as a family support magistrate and shall be eligible for appointment as a family support referee during the remainder of his life in the manner prescribed by law for the appointment of a family support magistrate. Each such family support referee shall exercise the powers of a family support magistrate.

(b) Each family support referee shall receive, for acting as a family support referee, in addition to the retirement salary, the sum of one hundred eighty dollars and expenses, including mileage, for each day a family support referee is so engaged.

(1994, May Sp.Sess., P.A. 94–6, § 13, eff. June 21, 1994; 1995, P.A. 95–350; 1999, June Sp.Sess., P.A. 99–1, § 39, eff. July 1, 1999.)

*

TITLE 47

LAND AND LAND TITLES

CHAPTER 821

LAND TITLES

§ 47–14g. Divorce or marriage dissolution of husband and wife joint tenants

Whenever a husband and wife are joint tenants in the same real estate, either together or in conjunction with others, a divorce or dissolution of the marriage, unless the divorce decree or decree of dissolution otherwise provides, severs their interests and converts them into tenants in common as to each other but not as to any remaining joint tenant or joint tenants. Such severance does not become effective as to any other persons until a certified copy of the decree or abstract of it, indicating the effective date of the divorce or dissolution, has been recorded in the land records of the town where the real cstatc is located.

(1959, P.A. 677, § 7, eff. June 29, 1959; 1967, P.A. 276; 1973, P.A. 73–373, § 32; 1979, P.A. 79–602, § 30.)

TITLE 52

CIVIL ACTIONS

CHAPTER 895

CIVIL JURISDICTION

§ 52–11. Complaints for change of name

(a) The superior court in each judicial district shall have jurisdiction of complaints praying for a change of name, brought by any person residing in the judicial district, and may change the name of the complainant, who shall thereafter be known by the name prescribed by said court in its decree.

(b) Whenever the court, pursuant to this section, orders a change of name of a person, the clerk of the court shall notify the Commissioner of Public Safety of the issuance of such order if the clerk finds that such person is listed in the registry established and maintained pursuant to section 54–257.

(1949 Rev., § 7756; 1976, P.A. 76–436, § 176, eff. July 1, 1978; 1978, P.A. 78–33, § 2; 1978, P.A. 78–280, § 1, eff. July 1, 1978; 2003, P.A. 03–202, § 17.)

CHAPTER 899

EVIDENCE

§ 52–146. Wife as a witness against her husband

A wife may be compelled to testify in any action brought against her husband for necessaries furnished her while living apart from him.

(1949 Rev., § 7869.)

§ 52–146k. Privileged communications between battered women's or sexual assault counselor and victim

(a) As used in this section:

(1) "Battered women's center" means any office, shelter, host home or center offering assistance to battered women through crisis intervention, emergency shelter referral and medical and legal advocacy, and which meets the department of social services criteria of service provision for such centers.

(2) "Battered women's counselor" means any person engaged in a battered women's center (A) who has undergone a minimum of twenty hours of training which shall include, but not be limited to, the dynamics of battering, crisis intervention, communication skills, working with diverse populations, an overview of the state criminal justice system and information about state and community resources for battered women, (B) who is certified as a counselor by the battered women's center which provided such training, (C) who is under the control of a direct service supervisor of a battered women's center, and (D) whose primary purpose is the rendering of advice, counsel and assistance to, and the advocacy of the cause of, battered women.

(3) "Confidential communication" means information transmitted between a victim of a battering or a sexual assault and a battered women's counselor or sexual assault counselor in the course of that relationship and in confidence by a means which, so far as the victim is aware, does not disclose the information to a third person other than any person who is present to further the interests of the victim in the consultation or any person to whom disclosure is reasonably necessary for the transmission of the information or for the accomplishment of the purposes for which such counselor is consulted, and includes all information received by, and any advice, report or working paper given or made by, such counselor in the course of the relationship with the victim.

(4) "Rape crisis center" means any office, institution or center offering assistance to victims of sexual assault and their families through crisis intervention, medical and legal advocacy and follow-up counseling and which meets the Department of Public Health criteria of service provision for such centers.

(5) "Sexual assault counselor" means any person engaged in a rape crisis center who (A) has undergone a minimum of twenty hours of training which shall include, but not be limited to, the dynamics of sexual assault and incest, crisis intervention, communication skills, working with diverse populations, an overview of the state criminal justice system, information about hospital and medical systems and information about state and community resources for sexual assault victims, (B) is certified as a counselor by the sexual assault center which has provided such training, (C) is under the control of a direct services supervisor of a rape crisis center, and (D) whose primary purpose is the rendering of advice, counseling and assistance to, and the advocacy of the cause of, victims of sexual assault.

(6) "Victim" means any person who consults a battered women's counselor or a sexual assault counselor for the purpose of securing advice, counseling or assistance concerning a mental, physical or emotional condition caused by a battering or a sexual assault.

(b) On or after October 1, 1983, a battered women's counselor or a sexual assault counselor shall not disclose any confidential communications made to such counselor at any time by a victim in any civil or criminal case or proceeding or in any legislative or administrative proceeding unless the victim making the confidential communications waives the privilege, provided under no circumstances shall the location of the battered women's center or rape crisis center or the identity of the battered women's counselor or sexual assault counselor be disclosed in any civil or criminal proceeding. Any request made on or after October 1, 1983, by the defendant or the state for such confidential communications shall be subject to the provisions of this subsection.

(c) When a victim is deceased or has been adjudged incompetent by a court of competent jurisdiction, the guardian of the victim or the executor or administrator of the estate of the victim may waive the privilege established by this section.

(d) A minor may knowingly waive the privilege established by this section. In any instance where the minor is, in the opinion of the court, incapable of knowingly waiving the privilege, the parent or guardian of the minor may waive the privilege on behalf of the minor, provided such parent or guardian is not the defendant and does not have a relationship with the defendant such that he has an interest in the outcome of the proceeding.

(e) The privilege established by this section shall not apply: (1) In matters of proof concerning chain of custody of evidence; (2) in matters of proof concerning the physical appearance of the victim at the time of the injury; or (3) where the battered women's counselor or sexual assault counselor has knowledge that the victim has given perjured testimony and the defendant or the state has made an offer of proof that perjury may have been committed.

(f) The failure of any party to testify as a witness pursuant to the provisions of this section shall not result in an inference unfavorable to the state's cause or to the cause of the defendant.

(1983, P.A. 83–429; 1985, P.A. 85–112; 1993, P.A. 93–262, § 1, eff. July 1, 1993; 1993, P.A. 93–381, § 9, eff. July 1, 1993; 1995, P.A. 95–257, §§ 12, 21, eff. July 1, 1995.)

§ 52–146p. Disclosure of privileged communications between marital and family therapist and person consulting such therapist prohibited. Exceptions

(a) As used in this section:

(1) "Person" means an individual who consults a marital and family therapist for purposes of diagnosis or treatment;

(2) "Marital and family therapist" means an individual certified as a marital and family therapist pursuant to chapter 383a;[1]

(3) "Communications" means all oral and written communications and records thereof relating to the diagnosis and treatment of a person between such person and a marital and family therapist or between a member of such person's family and a marital and family therapist;

(4) "Consent" means consent given in writing by the person or his authorized representative;

(5) "Authorized representative" means (A) an individual empowered by a person to assert the confidentiality of communications which are privileged under this section, or (B) if a person is deceased, his personal representative or next of kin, or (C) if a person is incompetent to assert or waive his privileges under this section, (i) a guardian or conservator who has been or is appointed to act for the person, or (ii) for the purpose of maintaining confidentiality until a guardian or conservator is appointed, the person's nearest relative.

(b) Except as provided in subsection (c) of this section, all communications shall be privileged and a marital and family therapist shall not disclose any such communications unless the person or his authorized representative consents to waive the privilege and allow such disclosure. In circumstances where more than one person in a family is receiving therapy, each such family member shall consent to the waiver. In the absence of such a waiver from each such family member, a marital and family therapist shall not disclose communications with any family member. The person or his authorized representative may withdraw any consent given under the provisions of this section at any time in a writing addressed to the individual with whom or the office in which the original consent was filed. The withdrawal of consent shall not affect communications disclosed prior to notice of the withdrawal.

(c) Consent of the person shall not be required for the disclosure of such person's communications:

(1) Where mandated by any other provision of the general statutes;

(2) Where a marital and family therapist believes in good faith that the failure to disclose such communications presents a clear and present danger to the health or safety of any individual;

(3) Where a marital and family therapist makes a claim for collection of fees for services rendered, the name and address of the person and the amount of the fees may be disclosed to individuals or agencies involved in such collection, provided notification that such disclosure will be made is sent, in writing, to the person not less than thirty days prior to such disclosure. In cases where a dispute arises over the fees or claims or where additional information is needed to substantiate the claim, the disclosure shall be limited to the following: (A) That the person was receiving services from a marital and family therapist, (B) the dates of such services, and (C) a general description of the types of services.

(1992, P.A. 92–225, § 1, eff. July 1, 1992.)

[1] C.G.S.A. § 20–195a et seq.

CHAPTER 906

POSTJUDGMENT PROCEDURES

§ 52–362. Income withholding and unemployment compensation for support

(a) For purposes of this section:

(1) "Dependent" means a spouse, former spouse or child entitled to payments under a support order, provided Support Enforcement Services of the Superior Court or the state acting under an assignment of a dependent's support rights or under an application for child support enforcement services shall, through an officer of Support Enforcement Services or the Bureau of Child Support Enforcement within the Department of Social Services or an investigator of the Department of Administrative Services or the Attorney General, take any action which the dependent could take to enforce a support order;

(2) "Disposable earnings" means that part of the earnings of an individual remaining after deduction from those earnings of amounts required to be withheld for the payment of federal, state and local income taxes, employment taxes, normal retirement contributions, union dues and initiation fees, and group life and health insurance premiums;

(3) "Earnings" means any debt accruing to an obligor by reason of such obligor's personal services, including any compensation payable by an employer to an employee for such personal services whether denominated as wages, salary, commission, bonus or otherwise, including unemployment compensation if a purchase of service agreement between the Commissioner of Social Services and the Labor Commissioner is in effect pursuant to subsection (e) of section 17b–179;

(4) "Employer" means any person, including the Labor Commissioner, who owes earnings to an obligor;

(5) "Income" means any periodic form of payment due to an individual, regardless of source, including, but not limited to, disposable earnings, workers' compensation and disability benefits, payments pursuant to a pension or retirement program and interest;

(6) "Obligor" means a person required to make payments under a support order;

(7) "Support order" means a court order, or order of a family support magistrate including an agreement approved by a court or a family support magistrate, that requires the payment to a dependent of either current support payments, payments on an arrearage, or both;

(8) "Unemployment compensation" means any compensation payable under chapter 567,[1] including amounts payable by the administrator of the unemployment compensation law pursuant to an agreement under any federal law providing for compensation, assistance or allowances with respect to unemployment.

(b) The Superior Court and any family support magistrate shall issue an order for withholding pursuant to this section against the income of an obligor to enforce a support order when the support order is entered or modified or when the obligor is before the court in an enforcement proceeding. The court shall order the withholding to be effective immediately or may, for cause or pursuant to an agreement by the parties, order a contingent withholding to be effective only on accrual of a delinquency in an amount greater than or equal to thirty days' obligation. Any finding that there is cause not to order withholding to be effective immediately shall be based on at least (1) a written determination that, and explanation by the court or family support magistrate of why, implementing immediate income withholding would not be in the best interests of the child, and (2) proof of timely payment of previously ordered support in cases involving the modification of such support. Before the court or family support magistrate issues an order for withholding which is effective immediately against an obligor who is before the court or a family support magistrate, it shall inform the obligor of the minimum amount of income which is exempt from withholding under state and federal law, of such obligor's right to claim any applicable state or federal exemptions with respect thereto and of such obligor's right to offer any evidence as to why a withholding order effective immediately should not issue. If the court or family support magistrate issues an order for withholding to be effective immediately against a nonappearing obligor, notice shall be served subsequently upon the obligor in accordance with section 52–57 or sent by certified mail, return receipt requested, to the obligor's last known address, informing such obligor: (A) That a support order has been issued to be enforced by an income withholding order, (B) that an income withholding order has been issued effective immediately as part of the support order, (C) of the minimum amount of income exempt from withholding under state and federal law and of such obligor's right at the hearing on the support order to claim any other applicable state or federal exemptions with respect thereto, (D) of such obligor's right to a hearing, upon motion to the court, to offer any evidence as to why the withholding order effective immediately should not continue in effect, (E) of the amount of income received by such obligor which formed the basis for the support order against such obligor, and (F) of such obligor's right to move to modify the support order if such obligor's income has changed substantially or if the support order substantially deviates from the child support guidelines established pursuant to section 46b–215a.

(c) (1) If an obligor is delinquent on support payments on any prior order of support in an amount greater than or equal to thirty days' obligation, whether or not such order is subject to a contingent income withholding, such obligor shall become subject to with holding and the dependent shall cause a delinquency notice to be served on such obligor. The delinquency notice shall include a claim form and be in clear and simple language informing the obligor that (A) such obligor is delinquent under the support order in a specified amount and any additional amounts accruing until the effective date of the withholding order, (B) a withholding order has become effective against such obligor's income, (C) such obligor has fifteen days to request a hearing before the court or family support magistrate, and at such hearing such obligor may contest the claimed delinquency and the imposition of the income withholding, seek modification of the withholding order, and claim any lawful exemption with respect to such obligor's income, (D) such obligor has a right to seek modification of the support order by a proper motion filed with the court or family support magistrate, (E) eighty-five per cent of the first one hundred forty-five dollars of disposable income per week are exempt, and (F) the amount of the withholding order may not exceed the maximum percentage of disposable income which may be withheld pursuant to Section 1673 of Title 15 of the United States Code, together with a statement of such obligor's right to claim any other applicable state or federal exemptions with respect thereto. The claim form shall contain a checklist identifying the most common defenses and exemptions such that the obligor may check any which apply to the obligor and a space where the obligor may briefly explain the claim or request a modification of or raise a defense to the support order.

(2) An obligor shall become subject to withholding to enforce a prior order of support upon the request of the dependent regardless of any delinquency, and whether or not such order is subject to a contingent income withholding. In such cases, the dependent shall cause a notice to be served on such obligor which notice shall comply in all respects with the delinquency notice required under subdivision (1) of this subsection except that such notice shall not be required to allege a delinquency.

(d) An obligor may claim a defense based upon mistake of fact, may claim an exemption in accordance with subsection (e) of this section with respect to the withholding order, or may file by motion a modification or defense to the support order being enforced by the withholding, by delivering a signed claim form, or other written notice or motion, with the address of the obligor thereon, indicating the nature of the claim or grounds of the motion, to the clerk of the Superior Court or the assistant clerk of the Family Support Magistrate Division within fifteen days of receipt of notice. On receipt of the claim or motion, the clerk shall promptly enter the appearance of the obligor, set the matter for a short calendar hearing, send a file-stamped copy of the claim or motion to the person or agency of the state to whom the support order is payable and notify all parties of the hearing date set. The court or family support magistrate shall promptly hear and determine the claim or motion and notify the obligor within forty-five days from the date of the notice required under subsection (c) of this section of its determination. Unless the obligor successfully shows cause why the withholding order should not continue in effect, the court or family support magistrate shall order that the outstanding withholding order continue in effect against the nonexempt income of the obligor to the extent provided under subsection (e) of this section. The order shall be a final judgment for purposes of appeal. The effect of the withholding order shall not be stayed on appeal except by order of the court or a family support magistrate.

(e) A withholding order shall issue in the amount necessary to enforce a support order against only such nonexempt income of the obligor as exceeds the greater of (1) eighty-five per cent of the first one hundred forty-five dollars per week of disposable income, or (2) the amount exempt under Section 1673 of Title 15 of the United States Code, or against any lesser amount which the court or family support magistrate deems equitable. The withholding order shall secure payment of past and future amounts due under the support order and an additional amount computed in accordance with the child support guidelines established in accordance with section 46b–215a, to be applied toward liquidation of any arrearage accrued under such order, unless contested by the obligor after a notice has been served pursuant to subsection (c) of this section, in which case the court or family support magistrate may determine the amount to be applied toward the liquidation of the arrearage found to have accrued under prior order of the court or family support magistrate. In no event shall such additional amount be applied if there is an existing arrearage order from the court or family support magistrate in a IV–D support case, as defined in subdivision (13) of subsection (b) of section 46b–231. Any investigator or other authorized employee of the Bureau of Child Support Enforcement within the Department of Social Services, or any officer of Support Enforcement Services of the Superior Court, may issue a withholding order entered by the Superior Court or a family support magistrate pursuant to subsection (b) of this section, and shall issue a withholding order pursuant to this subsection when the obligor becomes subject to withholding under subsection (c) of this section. On service of the order of withholding on an existing or any future employer or other payer of income, and until the support order is fully satisfied or modified, the order of withholding is a continuing lien and levy on the obligor's income as it becomes due.

(f) Commencing no later than the first pay period in the case of an employer, or the date of periodic payment in the case of a payer of income other than an employer, that occurs after fourteen days following the date of service of an order for withholding and within seven business days of the date the obligor is paid thereafter, an employer or other payer of income shall pay sums withheld pursuant to the withholding order to the state disbursement unit, as required by subsection (p) of this section. The employer or other payer of income (1) shall specify the dates on which each withholding occurred and the amount withheld for each obligor on each such date, and (2) may combine all withheld amounts into a single payment to the state disbursement unit with the portion thereof which is attributable to each individual obligor being separately designated. If an employer or other payer of income fails to withhold from income due an obligor pursuant to an order for withholding or fails to make those payments, such employer or other payer of income is liable to such person for the full amount of income not withheld since receipt of proper notice in an action therefor, and the amount secured in the action shall be applied by such person toward the arrearage owed by the obligor. Such employer or other payer of income shall be subject to a finding of contempt by the court or family support magistrate for failure to honor such order for withholding, provided service of the order is made in accordance with section 52–57 or by certified mail, return receipt requested.

(g) All orders for withholding issued pursuant to this section shall take precedence over any execution issued pursuant to section 52–361 of the general statutes revised to 1983, or section 52–361a. Two or more orders for withholding may be levied concurrently under this section, but if the total levy in any week exceeds the maximum permitted under this section, all sums due shall be allocated by the state disbursement unit in proportion to the amount of such orders, giving priority in such allocation to current support.

(h) Service of any process under this section, including any notice, may be made in accordance with section 52–57, or by certified mail, return receipt requested. If service is made on behalf of the state, it may be made by an authorized employee of Support Enforcement Services, or by an investigator or other officer of the Bureau of Child Support Enforcement within the Department of Social Services or by an investigator of the Department of Administrative Services or by the Attorney General. Service of income withholding orders by Support Enforcement Services or by an investigator or other officer of said bureau upon an employer under this section may be made in accordance with section 52–57, by certified mail, return receipt requested, or by first class mail.

(i) An applicant for employment or an employee subject to an order for withholding issued pursuant to this section shall have the same protection from discipline, suspension or discharge by an employer as provided in section 52–361a.

(j) There shall be a fine of not more than one thousand dollars imposed on any employer who discharges from employment, refuses to employ, takes disciplinary action against or discriminates against an employee subject to an order for withholding issued pursuant to this section because of the existence of such order for withholding and the obligations or additional obligations which it imposes upon the employer.

(k) The employer shall notify promptly the dependent or Support Enforcement Services as directed when the obligor terminates employment, makes a claim for workers' compensation benefits or makes a claim for unemployment compensation benefits and shall provide the obligor's last-known address and the name and address of the obligor's new employer, if known.

(*l*) When an obligor who is subject to withholding under this section is identified as a newly hired employee pursuant to subsection (d) of section 31–2c, the state agency enforcing the obligor's child support order shall, within two business days after the date information regarding such employee is entered into the state directory of new hires, issue a withholding order to the employer of the employee in accordance with subsection (e) of this section.

(m) The provisions of this section shall be in addition to and not in lieu of any other remedy available at law to enforce or punish for failure to obey a support order.

(n) When a support order is issued in another state and the obligor has income subject to withholding derived in this state, such income shall be subject to withholding in accordance with the provisions of this section, upon the registration of the support order in accordance with sections 46b–213g to 46b–213j, inclusive. Notice of rights to the obligor and the obligor's right to contest such order are governed by sections 46b–213k to 46b–213m, inclusive.

(*o*) An employer who withholds the income of an obligor pursuant to a withholding order issued under subsection (e) or (*l*) of this section that is regular on its face shall not be subject to civil liability to any individual or agency for conduct in compliance with such order.

(p) All withholding orders issued under this section shall be payable to the state disbursement unit established and maintained by the Commissioner of Social Services in accordance with subsection (j) of section 17b–179. The state disbursement unit shall insure distribution of all money collected under this section to the dependent, the state and the support enforcement agencies of other states, as their interests may appear, within two business days. Each dependent who is not receiving child support enforcement services, as defined in subsection (b) of section 46b–231, shall be notified upon the issuance of a withholding order pursuant to this section, that such services are offered free of charge by the State of Connecticut upon application to the Bureau of Child Support Enforcement within the Department of Social Services.

(q) The judges of the Superior Court may adopt any rules they deem necessary to implement the provisions of this section and sections 46b–69a, 46b–178 and 52–361a and such judges, or their designee, shall prescribe any forms required to implement such provisions.

(1955, Supp. § 3204d; 1959, P.A. 655; 1963, P.A. 33; 1969, P.A. 447, § 3; 1973, P.A. 73–373, § 38; 1976, P.A. 76–66; 1976, P.A. 76–436, § 142, eff. July 1, 1978; 1977, P.A. 77–389; 1977, P.A. 77–594, § 6, eff. July 6, 1977; 1977, P.A. 77–614, § 70, eff. Oct. 1, 1977; 1978, P.A. 78–217, § 1; 1980, P.A. 80–149, § 2, eff. May 5, 1980; 1981, P.A. 81–266, § 1, eff. June 1, 1981; 1982, P.A. 82–433, § 2; 1983, P.A. 83–295, § 17, eff. Oct. 1, 1983; 1983, P.A. 83–400, § 1; 1983, P.A. 83–581, § 34, eff. July 14, 1983; 1984, P.A. 84–455, §§ 4, 5; 1984, P.A. 84–527, §§ 17, 18; 1984, P.A. 84–546, §§ 115, 116, eff. June 14, 1984; 1985, P.A. 85–548, § 1; 1986 P.A. 86–359, § 36, eff. Jan. 1, 1987; 1987, P.A. 87–483, § 1, eff. July 1, 1987; 1989, P.A. 89–302, § 1, eff. March 1, 1990; 1990, P.A. 90–213, § 38, eff. July 1, 1990; 1991, P.A. 91–391, § 10; 1992, P.A. 92–253, § 4; 1993, P.A. 93–262, § 1, eff. July 1, 1993; 1996, P.A. 96–268, § 9, eff. July 1, 1996; 1997, June 18 Sp.Sess., P.A. 97–1, § 71, eff. Jan. 1, 1998; 1997, June 18 Sp.Sess., P.A. 97–7, § 28, eff. July 1, 1997; 1999, P.A. 99–193, § 6; 2000, P.A. 00–68, §§ 4, 5; 2000, P.A. 00–196, § 35; 2001, June Sp.Sess, P.A. 01–2, §§ 27, 28, eff. July 1, 2001; 2001, P.A 01–91, §§ 19, 20, 21, 22; 2003, P.A. 03–89, §§ 6, 7.)

1 C.G.S.A. § 31–222 et seq.

§ 52–362b. Priority of voluntary wage deduction authorization for support over wage executions

A voluntary wage deduction authorization for payment of amounts due for support in public welfare cases shall have the same priority over executions issued under section 52–361a as is provided for executions issued under section 52–362.

(1969, P.A. 220; 1983, P.A. 83–581, § 35, eff. July 14, 1983.)

§ 52–362c. Voluntary wage deduction authorization for support

A voluntary wage deduction authorization for payment of amounts due for support shall have the same force and effect as a wage withholding order issued under section 52–362 and all payments under such authorization shall be made to the state disbursement unit established and maintained by the Commissioner of Social Services in accordance with subsection (j) of section 17b–179. A voluntary wage deduction authorization under this section shall have the same priority over execution issued under section 52–361a as is provided for wage withholding issued under section 52–362.

(1972, P.A. 214; 1974, P.A. 74–183, § 101, eff. Dec. 31, 1974; 1976, P.A. 76–436, § 490, eff. July 1, 1978; 1982, P.A. 82–472, § 141, eff. June 14, 1982; 1983, P.A. 83–581, § 36, eff. July 14, 1983; 1989, P.A. 89–195, § 4; 1989, P.A. 89–360, § 16, eff. July 1, 1989; 1990, P.A. 90–213, § 39, eff. July 1, 1990; 1993, P.A. 93–396, § 9; 1999, P.A. 99–193, § 13.)

§ 52–362d. Lien against property of obligor for unpaid child support. Notice of intent. Foreclosure. Information re unpaid support reported to participating consumer reporting agency. Offset for child support arrearage against money payable by state to obligor. Notification by Connecticut Lottery Corporation. Hearing. Regulations

(a) Whenever an order of the Superior Court or a family support magistrate for support of a minor child or children is issued and such payments have been ordered to be made to the state acting by and through the IV–D agency and the person against whom such support order was issued owes past-due support in the amount of five hundred dollars or more, the state shall have a lien on any property, real or personal, in which such person has an interest to enforce payment of such past-due support after first providing such person with notice of intent to place such lien, and an opportunity for a hearing before a hearing officer to contest the amount of such past-due support. The lien for past-due child support shall be secured by the IV–D agency pursuant to procedures contained in the general statutes applicable to the type of property to be secured. Any such lien on real property may, at any time during which the obligor owes the amount of past-due child support secured by such lien, be foreclosed in an action brought in a court of competent jurisdiction by the Commissioner of Social Services in a title IV–D case or by the person to whom the child support is due. A lien for past-due support arising in any other state shall be given full faith and credit by this state provided such other state has complied with its procedural rules relating to recording or serving of liens.

(b) On October 1, 1991, and monthly thereafter, the Department of Social Services shall compile a list of all obligors who owe overdue support in the amount of one thousand dollars or more accruing after the entry of an initial court order establishing a child support obligation. Any overdue support in an amount of one thousand dollars or more shall be subject to the reporting provisions of this section. The state shall report to any participating consumer reporting agency, as defined in 15 USC 1681a(f), information regarding the amount of such overdue support owed by an obligor if the amount of such overdue support is one thousand dollars or more, on a computer tape in a format acceptable to the consumer reporting agency. Such information shall be reported by the department only after notice has been sent by the department to such obligor of the proposed action, and such obligor is given an opportunity for a hearing before a hearing officer of the department to contest the amount of the alleged arrearage. Any such notice sent to such obligor shall contain a telephone number and address of the Department of Social Services and shall contain the following language in bold type: "If you are no longer in arrears or have received this notice in error, please contact the department at the following address or telephone number." On a monthly basis, the Department of Social Services shall provide to each consumer reporting agency informed of the original arrearage of an obligor updated information concerning any such obligor and the status of payments, including a list of obligors who no longer owe overdue support, in such acceptable computer format. The department shall designate one or more persons in the department to receive telephone or other requests from an obligor or a consumer reporting agency regarding verification of information supplied to a consumer reporting agency. The department shall respond to any such request within five working days of its receipt. Upon satisfactory verification that an obligor is no longer in arrears, the department shall send a statement to such obligor, and such statement shall constitute proof to a creditor that such obligor is no longer in arrears as of the date of the statement. A participating consumer reporting agency which receives such updated information from the department that an obligor no longer owes any overdue support shall record such information within thirty days of receipt of such notification unless the information was in a format which was unusable by the agency or contained an error which prevented the agency from matching the updated information to previously supplied data. Any consumer reporting agency which negligently or wilfully fails to use reasonable efforts to comply with any requirement imposed under this subsection with respect to an obligor shall be liable to such obligor in an amount equal to the sum of (1) any actual damages sustained by the obligor as a result of such failure, and (2) a reasonable attorney's fee as determined by the court.

(c) When any person redeems a winning lottery ticket worth five thousand dollars or more, at the central office of the Connecticut Lottery Corporation, the Connecticut Lottery Corporation shall check the name and other identifying information of such person against a list of obligors supplied by the Commissioner of Social Services. If such person is included on the list of obligors, the Connecticut Lottery Corporation shall request confirmation from the Commissioner of Social Services that such person is in fact an obligor, and upon notification by the Commissioner of Social Services that money is due from any such person as a result of a claim for support which has been assigned to the state pursuant to section 17b–77, or is to be paid to the state acting by and through the IV–D agency, the Connecticut Lottery Corporation shall withhold from any lottery winnings payable to such person under the provisions of chapter 226 or chapter 229a [1] the amount of such claim for support owed to an individual for any portion of support which has not been assigned to the state and then the amount of such claim for support owed to the state, provided the Connecticut Lottery Corporation shall notify such person that (1) lottery winnings have been withheld as a result of the amount due for such support, and (2) such person has the right to a hearing before a hearing officer designated by the Commissioner of Social Services if such person contests the amount of the alleged claim for support. The Connecticut Lottery Corporation shall pay such persons in accordance with any decisions of the hearing officer or the court upon appeal of the hearing officer's decision.

(d) Whenever an order of the Superior Court or a family support magistrate of this state, or an order of another state that has been registered in this state, for support of a minor child or children is issued and such payments have been ordered through the IV–D agency, and the obligor against whom such support order was issued owes overdue support under such order in the amount of five hundred dollars or more, the IV–D agency, as defined in subdivision (12) of subsection (b) of section 46b–231, or Support Enforcement Services of the Superior Court may notify (1) any state or local agency with authority to distribute benefits to such obligor including, but not limited to, unemployment compensation and workers' compensation, (2) any person having or expecting to have custody or control of or authority to distribute any amounts due such obligor under any judgment or settlement, (3) any financial institution holding assets of such obligor, and (4) any public or private entity administering a public or private retirement fund in which such obligor has an interest that such obligor owes overdue support in a IV–D support case. Upon receipt of such notice, such agency, person, institution or entity shall withhold delivery or distribution of any such benefits, amounts, assets or funds until receipt of further notice from the IV–D agency.

(e) In IV–D cases in which a notice is sent pursuant to subsection (d) of this section, the IV–D agency shall notify the obligor that such benefits, amounts, assets or funds have been withheld as a result of overdue support in a IV–D support case in accordance with an order of the Superior Court or family support magistrate of this state, or an order of another state that has been registered in this state. The IV–D agency shall further notify the agency, person, institution or entity to whom notice was sent pursuant to subsection (d) of this section as follows: (1) Upon expiration of the time for requesting a hearing specified in section 17b–60, to make payment to the state from any such benefits, amounts, assets or funds withheld in accordance with subsection (d) of this section provided, in the case of retirement funds, such payment shall only be made in accordance with a withholding order issued under section 52–362 when the obligor is entitled to receive retirement benefits from such fund; (2) upon payment of such overdue support by such obligor, to release or distribute, as appropriate, such benefits, amounts, assets or funds to such obligor; or (3) upon issuance of a decision by the hearing officer or the court upon appeal of such officer's decision, to take such other action as may be ordered by such officer or such court, and such agency, person, institution or entity shall forthwith comply with such notice received from the IV–D agency.

(f) Support collected pursuant to this section shall be distributed as required by Title IV–D of the Social Security Act. [2]

(g) The Commissioner of Social Services shall adopt regulations, in accordance with chapter 54, [3] setting forth procedures providing for adequate notice of (1) the right to a hearing before a hearing officer, and (2) procedures for a fair hearing for any person alleged by the commissioner to owe past-due or overdue child support to the state, or to an individual when the payments have been ordered payable to the state acting by and through the IV–D agency, if the commissioner has filed a lien on the property of such person or claimed an offset against money payable by the state to enforce a claim for payment of such past-due or overdue support, or intends to seize any benefits, amounts, assets or funds withheld in accordance with subsection (d) of this section or report such overdue support to a consumer credit agency.

(1985, P.A. 85–548, § 7; 1986, P.A. 86–359, § 38, eff. Jan. 1, 1987; 1988, P.A. 88–257, § 1, eff. Jan. 1, 1989; 1990, P.A. 90–206; 1990, P.A. 90–213, § 40, eff. July 1, 1990; 1991, P.A. 91–139; 1993, P.A. 93–262, § 1, eff. July 1, 1993; 1993, P.A. 93–329, § 1, eff. Oct. 1, 1993; 1997, June 18 Sp.Sess., P.A. 97–7, § 29, eff. July 1, 1997; 2001, P.A. 01–207, §§ 9, 10, eff. July 1, 2001; 2001, P.A. 01–91, § 23; 2003, P.A. 03–109, § 1.)

1 C.G.S.A. §§ 12–557b et seq., 12–800 et seq.

2 42 U.S.C.A. § 651 et seq.

3 C.G.S.A. § 4–166 et seq.

§ 52–362e. Withholding federal income tax refunds in amount equal to support arrearage. Procedures. Eligibility. Regulations

(a) Subject to the provisions of section 52–362h, whenever an order of the Superior Court or a family support magistrate for support of a minor child or children is issued, and, in TFA cases as defined in subdivision (13) of subsection (b) of section 46b–231, the person against whom such order was issued owes past-due support of one hundred fifty dollars or more, or in non-TANF IV-D support cases, as defined in subdivision (13) of subsection (b) of said section 46b–231, the person against whom such order was issued owes past-due support of five hundred dollars or more, the state shall submit to the Internal Revenue Service through the federal Office of Child Support Enforcement the name of such person and request the withholding from refunds of federal income taxes owed to such person of an amount equal to the past-due support, and payment of such withheld amount to the state for distribution to the state for reimbursement of public assistance in TANF cases and in non-TANF IV-D support cases for distribution to the guardian or custodial parent of such minor child or children, after first deducting from the amount payable to such guardian or custodial parent a collection fee determined by the Secretary of the Treasury to be sufficient to reimburse the Internal Revenue Service for the cost of the offset procedure.

(b) Subject to the provisions of subsection (c) of this section, whenever an order of the Superior Court or a family support magistrate for support of a minor child or children is issued, and, in TANF cases, the person against whom such support order is issued owes past-due support of one hundred fifty dollars or more, or in non-TANF IV-D support cases the person against whom such order is issued owes past-due support of five hundred dollars or more, the Department of Social Services shall submit to the Commissioner of Administrative Services the name of such person and request the withholding from refunds of state income taxes owed to such person of an amount equal to the past-due support, and payment of such withheld amount by the Commissioner of Revenue Services to the state for distribution to the state for reimbursement of public assistance in TANF cases and in non-TANF IV-D support cases for distribution to the guardian or custodial parent of such minor child or children. Whenever an order of the Superior Court or family support magistrate is issued against a parent to cover the cost of health insurance for a child who is eligible for Medicaid and such parent has received payment from a third party for the costs of services provided under such health coverage for such child but such parent has not used such payments to reimburse, as appropriate, either the other parent or guardian or the provider of such services, the Commissioner of Social Services shall submit to the Commissioner of Administrative Services the name of such person and request the withholding from refunds of state income taxes owed to such person of an amount necessary to reimburse the Department of Social Services for such costs under the Medicaid program, and payment of such amount shall be withheld by the Commissioner of Revenue Services and distributed to the Department of Social Services for reimbursement. However, any claims for current or past due child support shall take priority over any such claims for the costs of such services.

(c) Support collected pursuant to this section shall be distributed as required by Title IV–D of the Social Security Act. [1]

(d) The Commissioner of Social Services shall adopt regulations, in accordance with chapter 54, [2] setting forth procedures in compliance with federal law and regulations under Title IV-D of the Social Security Act providing for adequate notice of (1) the right to a review by Support Enforcement Services of the Superior Court, (2) the right to a fair hearing before a hearing officer, (3) a list of available defenses including the defense described in section 52–362h, and (4) procedures for a fair hearing for any person who is alleged to owe past-due support and is subject to the provisions of this section.

(1985, P.A. 85–548, § 10; 1986, P.A. 86–359, § 39, eff. Jan. 1, 1987; 1990, P.A. 90–213, § 41, eff. July, 1, 1990;

1991, P.A. 91–391, § 11; 1992, P.A. 92–253, § 5; 1993, P.A. 93–262, § 1, eff. July 1, 1993; 1993, P.A. 93–396, § 19; 1994, May Sp.Sess., P.A. 94–5, § 10, eff. July 1, 1994; 1995, P.A. 95–305, § 4, eff. July 1, 1995; 1997, June 18 Sp.Sess., P.A. 97–2, § 110, eff. July 1, 1997; 1997, June 18 Sp.Sess., P.A. 97–7, § 30, eff. July 1, 1997; 2001, P.A. 01–91, § 24; 2003, P.A. 03–109, § 2.)

[1] 42 U.S.C.A. § 651 et seq.

[2] C.G.S.A. § 4–166 et seq.

§ 52–362f. Enforcement of child support orders by income withholding

(a) As used in this section, unless the context requires otherwise:

(1) "Agency" means the Bureau of Child Support Enforcement within the Department of Social Services of this state and, when the context requires, means either the court or agency of any other jurisdiction with functions similar to those defined in this section, including the issuance and enforcement of support orders.

(2) "Child" means any child, whether above or below the age of majority, with respect to whom a support order exists.

(3) "Court" means the Superior Court of this state, including the Family Support Magistrate Division, or the court or agency of any other jurisdiction with functions similar to those defined in this section, including the issuance and enforcement of support orders.

(4) "Income" means earnings as defined in subdivision (3) of subsection (a) of section 52–362.

(5) "Income derived in this jurisdiction" means any earnings, the payer of which is subject to the jurisdiction of this state for the purpose of imposing and enforcing an order for withholding under section 52–362.

(6) "Jurisdiction" means any state or political subdivision, territory or possession of the United States, the District of Columbia, and the Commonwealth of Puerto Rico.

(7) "Obligee" means any person or entity which is entitled to receive support under an order of support and shall include an agency of another jurisdiction to which a person has assigned his or her right to support.

(8) "Obligor" means any person required to make payments under the terms of a support order for a child, spouse, or former spouse.

(9) "Payer" means any payer of income.

(10) "Support order" means any order, decree, or judgment for the support, or for the payment of arrearages on such support, of a child, spouse, or former spouse issued by a court or agency of another jurisdiction, whether interlocutory or final, whether or not prospectively or retroactively modifiable, whether incidental to a proceeding for divorce, judicial or legal separation, separate maintenance, paternity, guardianship, civil protection, or otherwise.

(b) The remedies herein provided are in addition to and not in substitution for any other remedies.

(c) When a support order has been issued in this state and the obligor has earnings subject to income withholding in another jurisdiction, (1) the agency shall on application of a resident of this state, (2) Support Enforcement Services shall on behalf of any client for whom Support Enforcement Services is providing services, (3) an obligee or obligor of a support order issued by this state may, or (4) an agency to whom the obligee has assigned support rights may, promptly request the agency of another jurisdiction in which the obligor of a support order derives income to enter the order for the purpose of obtaining income withholding against such income. The agency or Support Enforcement Services, as the case may be, shall compile and transmit promptly to the agency of the other jurisdiction all documentation required to enter a support order for this purpose. The agency or Support Enforcement Services also shall transmit immediately to the agency of the other jurisdiction a certified copy of any subsequent modifications of the support order. If the agency or Support Enforcement Services receives notice that the obligor is contesting income withholding in another jurisdiction, it shall immediately notify the individual obligee of the date, time and place of the hearings and of the obligee's right to attend.

(d) When a support order is issued in another jurisdiction and the obligor has income subject to withholding in accordance with the provisions of section 52–362, Support Enforcement Services shall, upon receiving a support order of another jurisdiction with the documentation specified in this subsection from an agency of another jurisdiction, or from an obligee, an obligor or an attorney for either the obligee or obligor, file such support order and documents in the registry maintained by Support Enforcement Services. Documentation required for the entry of a support order for another jurisdiction for the purpose of withholding of income shall comply with the requirements of section 46b–213i. If the documentation received by Support Enforcement Services does not conform to those requirements, Support Enforcement Services shall remedy any defect which it can without the assistance of the obligee or requesting agency or person. If Support Enforcement Services is unable to make such corrections, the requesting agency or person shall immediately be notified of the necessary additions or corrections. Support Enforcement Services shall accept the documentation required by this subsection as long as the substantive requirements of this subsection are met.

(e) A support order registered under subsection (d) of this section shall be enforceable by withholding in the manner and with the effect as set forth for registered support orders of another jurisdiction pursuant to section 52–362. A support order from another jurisdiction filed under this section shall not be subject to modification by a court or other agency of this state except as provided in sections 46b–213o to 46b–213q, inclusive. Entry of the order shall not confer jurisdiction on any court of this state for any purpose other than withholding of income.

(f) Upon registration of a support order from another jurisdiction pursuant to subsection (d) of this section, Family Support Magistrate Division or Support Enforcement Services of the Superior Court acting on its behalf shall proceed as provided in section 46b–213k.

(g) An income withholding order under this section shall direct payment to the Bureau of Child Support Enforcement or its designated collection agent. The bureau or its designated agent shall promptly distribute payments received pursuant to an income withholding order or garnishment based on a support order of another jurisdiction entered under this section to the agency or person designated pursuant to subdivision (5) of subsection (a) of section 46b–213h. A support order entered pursuant to subsection (d) of this section does not nullify and is not nullified by a support order made by a court of this state pursuant to any other section of the general statutes or a support order made by a court of any other state. Amounts collected by any withholding of income shall be credited against the amounts accruing or accrued for any period under any support orders issued either by this state or by another jurisdiction.

(h) The agency or Support Enforcement Services, upon receiving a certified copy of any amendment or modification to a support order entered pursuant to subsection (d) of this section, shall file such certified copy with the clerk of Support Enforcement Services, and Support Enforcement Services shall amend or modify the order for withholding to conform to the modified support order.

(i) If the agency or Support Enforcement Services determines that the obligor has obtained employment in another state or has a new or additional source of income in another state, it shall notify the agency which requested the income withholding of the changes within ten days of receiving that information and shall forward to such agency all information it has or can obtain with respect to the obligor's new address and the name and address of the obligor's new employer or other source of income. The agency or Support Enforcement Services shall include with the notice a certified copy of the order for withholding in effect in this state.

(j) Any person who is the obligor on a support order of another jurisdiction may obtain a voluntary income withholding by filing with the agency a request for such withholding and a certified copy of the support order issued by such jurisdiction. The agency shall file such request for a voluntary withholding with the certified copy of the support order from the jurisdiction that entered such order with the clerk of Support Enforcement Services of the Superior Court and Support Enforcement Services, acting on behalf of the Family Support Magistrate Division, shall issue an order for withholding. Any order for withholding thus issued shall be subject to all applicable provisions of this section.

(1987, P.A. 87–483, § 2, eff. July 1, 1987; 1989, P.A. 89–302, § 3, eff. March 1, 1990; 1990, 90–213, § 42; 1993, P.A. 93–262, § 1, eff. July 1, 1993; 1993, P.A. 93–396, § 10; 1997, June 18 Sp.Sess., P.A. 97–1, § 72, eff. Jan. 1, 1998; 2001, P.A. 01–91, § 25; 2003; 2003, P.A. 03–19, §§ 120, 121, eff. May 12, 2003.)

§ 52–362g. Notice by IV–D agency for collection of current or past due child support payments

Any written notice sent by or on behalf of the IV–D agency for the purpose of collection of current or past due child support payments shall, if such notice contains possible sanctions for failure to make payments, describe the obligor's right to (1) move for modification of the court order, (2) a hearing prior to imposition of any sanctions and (3) appointment of counsel prior to incarceration for contempt if the obligor is indigent.

(1991, P.A. 91–391, § 12.)

§ 52–362h. Defense re withholding support arrearage from federal and state income tax refunds

For the purpose only of submission to the Internal Revenue Service for the withholding from federal income tax refunds or submission to the Commissioner of Administrative Services for the withholding from state income tax refunds, beginning with the tax year 1992, past due support for a minor child shall not be considered owing to the state if the person against whom such withholding is sought at the time of the withholding (1) is the legal guardian of the minor child and resides with the child or (2) is not the legal guardian of the minor child but has resided with the child either for six months immediately preceding the withholding or for at least six months of the tax year in question. Any notice given to an obligor shall inform him of the circumstances in which a submission for such withholding from a federal or state tax refund shall not be made and shall permit the obligor to obtain a hearing at which he may attempt to demonstrate the existence of such circumstances.

(1991, P.A. 91–391, § 13; 1992, P.A. 92–253, § 6.)

§ 52–362i. Court may require cash deposit of support to be held in escrow by Connecticut Child Enforcement Enforcement Bureau [1] or Support Enforcement Services, when

If the court or family support magistrate finds that (1) an obligor is delinquent on payment of child support, and (2) future support payments are in jeopardy, or (3) the obligor has exhibited or expressed an intention not to pay any such support, the court or family support magistrate may order the obligor to provide a cash deposit not to exceed the amount of four times the current monthly support and arrearage obligation, to be held in escrow by the Connecticut Child Support Enforcement Bureau or Support Enforcement Services. Any funds from such cash deposit may be disbursed by the Connecticut Child Support Enforcement Bureau or Support Enforcement Services to the custodial parent upon a determination by said support enforcement bureau or Support Enforcement Services that the obligor has failed to pay the full amount of the monthly support obligation. Payment shall be in an amount that, when combined with the obligor's payment, would not exceed the monthly support obligation. Payment from such cash deposit shall not preclude a finding of delinquency during the period of time in which the obligor failed to pay current support.

(1993, P.A. 93–329, § 6; 2001, P.A. 01–91, § 26.)

1 So in original, to conform to Gen.St., Rev. to 2003. Probably should read "Connecticut Child Support Enforcement Bureau"

§ 52–362j. "Past-due support", "overdue support", defined

For the purposes of sections 52–362d, 52–362e, 52–362g, and 52–362h:

(1) "Past-due support" means any one or a combination of the following: (A) Court ordered current support or arrearage payments which have become due and payable and remain unpaid; (B) unpaid support which has been reduced to a judgment or otherwise found to be due by a court of competent jurisdiction, whether or not presently payable; (C) support due for periods prior to an action to establish a child support order.

(2) "Overdue support" means a delinquency accruing after the entry of an initial court order establishing a child support obligation.

(1997, June 18 Sp.Sess., P.A. 97–7, § 31, eff. July 1, 1997; 2003, P.A. 03–258, § 5.)

CHAPTER 925

STATUTORY RIGHTS OF ACTION AND DEFENSES

§ 52–572. Parental liability for torts of minors

(a) The parent or parents or guardian, other than a temporary guardian appointed pursuant to section 45a–622, of any unemancipated minor or minors, which minor or minors wilfully or maliciously cause damage to any property or injury to any person, or, having taken a motor vehicle without the permission of the owner thereof, cause damage to the motor vehicle, shall be jointly and severally liable with the minor or minors for the damage or injury to an amount not exceeding five thousand dollars, if the minor or minors would have been liable for the damage or injury if they had been adults.

(b) This section shall not be construed to relieve the minor or minors from personal liability for the damage or injury.

(c) The liability provided for in this section shall be in addition to and not in lieu of any other liability which may exist at law.

(d) As used in this section, "damage" shall include depriving the owner of his property or motor vehicle or of the use, possession or enjoyment thereof.

(1955, Supp. § 3231d; 1959, P.A. 244; 1959, P.A. 549; 1969, P.A. 326; 1971, P.A. 314; 1972, P.A. 127, § 75; 1979, P.A. 79–58; 1982, P.A. 82–160, § 236; 1993, P.A. 93–26; 1996, P.A. 96–202, § 8.)

§ 52–572c. Parent-child immunity abrogated in certain negligence actions

In all actions for negligence in the operation of a motor vehicle, and in all actions accruing on or after October 1, 1979, for negligence in the operation of an aircraft or vessel, as defined in section 15–127, resulting in personal injury, wrongful death or injury to property, the immunity between parent and child in such negligence action brought by a parent against his child or by or on behalf of a child against his parent is abrogated.

(1967, P.A. 596, § 1, July 1, 1967; 1979, P.A. 79–5.)

§ 52–572d. Interspousal immunity abrogated in motor vehicle negligence actions accruing out of state

In all actions brought by one resident spouse against the other resident spouse for negligence in the operation of a motor vehicle resulting in personal injury, wrongful death or injury to property, it shall not be a defense or a bar to the cause of action that such an action by one spouse against another would not lie in the state where the injury or death occurred. The rights of such spouses, including the standard of care to be applied in such action, shall be determined as if the injury or death had occurred in this state.

(1969, P.A. 623, § 1; 1974, P.A. 74–338, § 48, eff. May 31, 1974.)

*

TITLE 53

CRIMES

CHAPTER 939

OFFENSES AGAINST THE PERSON

§ 53–23. Abandonment of child under the age of six years

(a) Any person having the charge of any child under the age of six years who exposes such child in any place, with intent wholly to abandon such child, shall be fined not more than five hundred dollars and imprisoned not more than five years.

(b) The act of a parent or agent leaving an infant thirty days or younger with a designated employee pursuant to section 17a–58 shall not constitute a violation of this section.

(1949 Rev., § 8366; 2000, P.A. 00–207, § 7.)

CHAPTER 944

(OFFENSES AGAINST CHASTITY) CONCEALMENT OF DELIVERY OF CHILD

§ 53–237a. Concealment of delivery: Class A misdemeanor

(a) A person is guilty of concealment of delivery who intentionally conceals the delivery of any child, whether such child was delivered alive or dead.

(b) Concealment of delivery is a class A misdemeanor.

(1971, P.A. 871, § 56.)

CHAPTER 946

OFFENSES AGAINST PUBLIC POLICY

§ 53–304. Nonsupport. Support orders and agreements. Administration of oaths by family relations counselors and support enforcement officers

(a) Any person who neglects or refuses to furnish reasonably necessary support to the person's spouse, child under the age of eighteen or parent under the age of sixty-five shall be deemed guilty of nonsupport and shall be imprisoned not more than one year, unless the person shows to the court before which the trial is had that, owing to physical incapacity or other good cause, the person is unable to furnish such support. Such court may suspend the execution of any community correctional center sentence imposed, upon any terms or conditions that it deems just, may suspend the execution of the balance of any such sentence in a like manner, and, in addition to any other sentence or in lieu thereof, may order that the person convicted shall pay to the Commissioner of Administrative Services directly or through Support Enforcement Services of the Superior Court, such support, in such amount as the court may find commensurate with the necessities of the case and the ability of such person, for such period as the court shall determine. Any such order of support may, at any time thereafter, be set aside or altered by such court for cause shown. Failure of any defendant to make any payment may be punished as contempt of court and, in addition thereto or in lieu thereof, the court may order the issuance of a wage withholding in the same manner as is provided in section 17b–748, which withholding order shall have the same precedence as is provided in section 52–362. The amounts withheld under such withholding order shall be remitted to the Department of Administrative Services by the person or corporation to whom the withholding order is presented at such intervals as such withholding order directs. For purposes of this section, the term "child" shall include one born out of wedlock whose father has acknowledged in writing his paternity of such child or has been adjudged the father by a court of competent jurisdiction.

(b) Any person who violates any provision of this section may be prosecuted before any court of this state in the same manner as if such offense had been committed within the territorial jurisdiction of such court.

(c) A written agreement to support or any modification of an agreement to support filed with said court or the assistant clerk of the Family Support Magistrate Division shall have the same force and effect as an order of support by the Superior Court and shall be enforceable in the same manner as is provided herein for orders of support issued by the court.

(d) Family relations counselors and support enforcement officers employed by the Judicial Department may administer oaths in all affidavits, statements, complaints and reports made to or by such family relations counselors and support enforcement officers in the performance of their duties.

(1949 Rev., § 8586; 1955, Supp. § 3295d; 1957, P.A. 158; 1959, P.A. 115, § 4; 1959, P.A. 308; 1963, P.A. 497, § 1, eff. June 19, 1963; 1967, P.A. 746, § 6; 1969, P.A. 297; 1971, P.A. 290; 1972, P.A. 127, § 76; 1974,

P.A. 74-183, § 122, eff. Dec. 31, 1974; 1976, P.A. 76-436, § 512, eff. July 1, 1978; 1978, P.A. 78-331, § 33, eff. July 1, 1978; 1980, P.A. 80-56, § 1, eff. April 17, 1980; 1983, P.A. 83-295, § 18, eff. Oct. 1, 1983; 1986, P.A. 86-359, § 37, eff. Jan. 1, 1987; 1990, P.A. 90-213, § 43, eff. July 1, 1990; 1993, P.A. 93-396, § 11; 2000, P.A. 00-68, § 6; 2001, P.A. 01-91, § 27; 2002, P.A. 02-132, § 28.)

§ 53-305. Bond on appeal

If the accused appeals, such court, in addition to requiring a recognizance or appearance bond, may order such accused to give a bond conditioned for his furnishing support pending the determination of such appeal.

(1949 Rev., § 8587; 1967, P.A. 656, § 55, eff. June 27, 1967.)

§ 53-306. Failure to comply with terms or make payment

If any person convicted under section 53-304 fails to comply fully with the terms and conditions imposed under the provisions of said section or to make any payment required by any bond given pursuant to an appeal under section 53-305, the suspension of the execution of any community correctional center sentence imposed may be revoked and such person may be committed, and any such action shall not affect the validity of any such bond.

(1949 Rev., § 8588; 1967, P.A. 656, § 56, eff. June 27, 1967; 1969, P.A. 297.)

§ 53-308. Forfeited bonds in nonsupport cases

When any bond or recognizance conditioned for the appearance of any person accused in any information or complaint charging a violation of any of the provisions of section 53-304 becomes forfeited or whenever any person convicted under the provisions of said section gives a bond and fails to comply with the provisions of the same, the court before which such information or complaint is pending or in which such conviction was had, upon collection or settlement of such forfeited bond or recognizance, may order the avails or any portion thereof to be paid to the spouse or for the support of the children or both, in such manner and installments as such court may find reasonable, or may order the avails or any portion thereof to be paid to the selectmen of the town, Support Enforcement Services of the Superior Court, or the Commissioner of Administrative Services, who shall administer the same for the benefit of the spouse or children or both, as they or he may find reasonable.

(1949 Rev., § 8590; 1959, P.A. 28, § 136, eff. Jan. 1, 1961; 1967, P.A. 138; 1969, P.A. 447, § 4; 1969, P.A. 730, § 14, eff. July 1, 1969; 1971, P.A. 171; 1974, P.A. 74-183, § 123, eff. Dec. 31, 1974; 1976, P.A. 76-436, § 513, eff. July 1, 1978; 1977, P.A. 77-614, § 70, eff. Oct. 1, 1977; 1978, P.A. 78-331, § 34, eff. July 1, 1978; 1993, P.A. 93-396, § 12; 2001, P.A. 01-91, § 28.)

TITLE 53a

PENAL CODE

CHAPTER 951

PENAL CODE: STATUTORY CONSTRUCTION; PRINCIPLES OF CRIMINAL LIABILITY

§ 53a–18. Use of reasonable physical force or deadly physical force generally

The use of physical force upon another person which would otherwise constitute an offense is justifiable and not criminal under any of the following circumstances:

(1) A parent, guardian or other person entrusted with the care and supervision of a minor or an incompetent person, except a person entrusted with the care and supervision of a minor for school purposes as described in subdivision (6) of this section, may use reasonable physical force upon such minor or incompetent person when and to the extent that he reasonably believes such to be necessary to maintain discipline or to promote the welfare of such minor or incompetent person.

(2) An authorized official of a correctional institution or facility may, in order to maintain order and discipline, use such physical force as is reasonable and authorized by the rules and regulations of the department of correction.

(3) A person responsible for the maintenance of order in a common carrier of passengers, or a person acting under his direction, may use reasonable physical force when and to the extent that he reasonably believes such to be necessary to maintain order, but he may use deadly physical force only when he reasonably believes such to be necessary to prevent death or serious physical injury.

(4) A person acting under a reasonable belief that another person is about to commit suicide or to inflict serious physical injury upon himself may use reasonable physical force upon such person to the extent that he reasonably believes such to be necessary to thwart such result.

(5) A duly licensed physician or psychologist, or a person acting under his direction, may use reasonable physical force for the purpose of administering a recognized form of treatment which he reasonably believes to be adapted to promoting the physical or mental health of the patient, provided the treatment (A) is administered with the consent of the patient or, if the patient is a minor or an incompetent person, with the consent of his parent, guardian or other person entrusted with his care and supervision, or (B) is administered in an emergency when the physician or psychologist reasonably believes that no one competent to consent can be consulted and that a reasonable person, wishing to safeguard the welfare of the patient, would consent.

(6) A teacher or other person entrusted with the care and supervision of a minor for school purposes may use reasonable physical force upon such minor when and to the extent he reasonably believes such to be necessary to (A) protect himself or others from immediate physical injury, (B) obtain possession of a dangerous instrument or controlled substance, as defined in subdivision (9) of section 21a–240, upon or within the control of such minor, (C) protect property from physical damage or (D) restrain such minor or remove such minor to another area, to maintain order.

(1969, P.A. 828, § 18, eff. Oct. 1, 1971; 1971, P.A. 871, § 4; 1973, P.A. 73–205, § 6; 1989, P.A. 89–186, § 1, eff. July 1, 1989; 1990, P.A. 90–43; 1992, P.A. 92–260, § 3.)

CHAPTER 952

PENAL CODE: OFFENSES

PART II. SENTENCES AND SENTENCING PROCEDURE

§ 53a–40d. Persistent offenders of crimes involving assault, stalking, trespass, threatening, harassment, criminal violation of a protective order or criminal violation of a restraining order. Authorized sentences

(a) A persistent offender of crimes involving assault, stalking, trespass, threatening, harassment, criminal violation of a protective order or criminal violation of a restraining order is a person who (1) stands convicted of assault under section 53a–61, stalking under section 53a–181d, threatening under section 53a–62, harassment under section 53a–183, criminal violation of a protective order under section 53a–223 criminal violation of a restraining order under section 53a–223b or criminal trespass under section 53a–107 or 53a–108, and (2) has, within the five years preceding the commission of the present crime, been convicted of a capital felony, a class A felony, a class B felony, except a conviction under section 53a–86 or 53a–122, a class C felony, except a conviction under section 53a–87, 53a–152 or 53a–153, or a class D felony under sections 53a–60 to 53a–60c, inclusive, 53a–72a, 53a–72b, 53a–95, 53a–103,

53a–103a, 53a–114, 53a–136 or 53a–216, assault under section 53a–61, stalking under section 53a–181d, threatening under section 53a–62, harassment under section 53a–183, criminal violation of a protective order under section 53a–223, criminal violation of a restraining order under section 53a–223b, or criminal trespass under section 53a–107 or 53a–108 or has been released from incarceration with respect to such conviction, whichever is later.

(b) When any person has been found to be a persistent offender of crimes involving assault, stalking, trespass, threatening, harassment, criminal violation of a protective order or criminal violation of a restraining order, and the court is of the opinion that such person's history and character and the nature and circumstances of such person's criminal conduct indicate that an increased penalty will best serve the public interest, the court shall, in lieu of imposing the sentence authorized for the crime under section 53a–36 or section 53a–35a, as applicable, impose the sentence of imprisonment authorized by said section 53a–36 or section 53a–35a for the next more serious degree of misdemeanor or felony, except that if the crime is a class A misdemeanor the court shall impose the sentence of imprisonment for a class D felony, as authorized by section 53a–35a. *(1995, P.A. 95–193, § 2; 2002, P.A. 02–127, § 4.)*

§ 53a–40e. Standing criminal restraining order

(a) If any person is convicted of a violation of section 53a–59, 53a–59a, 53a–60, 53a–60a, 53a–60b, 53a–60c, 53a–70, 53a–70a, 53a–70b, 53a–71, 53a–72a, 53a–72b, 53a–181c, 53a–181d or 53a–181e, or of attempt or conspiracy to violate any of said sections or section 53a–54a, against a family or household member as defined in subdivision (2) of section 46b–38a, the court may, in addition to imposing the sentence authorized for the crime under section 53a–35a, if the court is of the opinion that the history and character and the nature and circumstances of the criminal conduct of such offender indicate that a standing criminal restraining order will best serve the interest of the victim and the public, issue a standing criminal restraining order which shall remain in effect until modified or revoked by the court for good cause shown.

(b) Such standing criminal restraining order may include but is not limited to enjoining the offender from (1) imposing any restraint upon the person or liberty of the victim; (2) threatening, harassing, assaulting, molesting, sexually assaulting or attacking the victim or (3) entering the family dwelling or the dwelling of the victim.

(c) Every standing criminal restraining order of the court made in accordance with this section shall contain the following language: "This order shall remain in effect until modified or revoked by the court for good cause shown. In accordance with section 53a–223a, violation of a standing criminal restraining order issued by the court pursuant to subsection (a) of this section shall be punishable by a term of imprisonment of not less than one year nor more than five years, a fine of not more than five thousand dollars or both."

(1996, P.A. 96–228, § 1; 1998, P.A. 98–15; 1998, June Sp.Sess., P.A. 98–1, § 41, eff. June 24, 1998; 1999, P.A. 99–186, § 13.)

PART VII. KIDNAPPING AND RELATED OFFENSES

§ 53a–91. Definitions

The following definitions are applicable to this part:

(1) "Restrain" means to restrict a person's movements intentionally and unlawfully in such a manner as to interfere substantially with his liberty by moving him from one place to another, or by confining him either in the place where the restriction commences or in a place to which he has been moved, without consent. As used herein "without consent" means, but is not limited to, (A) deception and (B) any means whatever, including acquiescence of the victim, if he is a child less than sixteen years old or an incompetent person and the parent, guardian or other person or institution having lawful control or custody of him has not acquiesced in the movement or confinement.

(2) "Abduct" means to restrain a person with intent to prevent his liberation by either (A) secreting or holding him in a place where he is not likely to be found, or (B) using or threatening to use physical force or intimidation.

(3) "Relative" means a parent, ancestor, brother, sister, uncle or aunt.

(1969, P.A. 828, § 92, eff. Oct. 1, 1971; 1992, P.A. 92–260, § 35.)

§ 53a–97. Custodial interference in the first degree: Class D felony

(a) A person is guilty of custodial interference in the first degree when he commits custodial interference in the second degree as provided in section 53a–98: (1) Under circumstances which expose the child or person taken or enticed from lawful custody or the child held after a request by the lawful custodian for his return to a risk that his safety will be endangered or his health materially impaired; or (2) by taking, enticing or detaining the child or person out of this state.

(b) Custodial interference in the first degree is a class D felony.

(1969, P.A. 828, § 99, eff. Oct. 1, 1971; 1981, P.A. 81–280, § 2; 1992, P.A. 92–260, § 39; 1995, P.A. 95–206, § 1.)

§ 53a–98. Custodial interference in the second degree: Class A misdemeanor

(a) A person is guilty of custodial interference in the second degree when: (1) Being a relative of a child who is less than sixteen years old and intending to hold such child permanently or for a protracted period and knowing that he has no legal right to do so, he takes or entices such child from his lawful custodian; (2) knowing that he has no legal right to do so, he takes or entices from lawful custody any incompetent person or any person entrusted by authority of law to the custody of another person or institution; or (3) knowing that he has no legal right to do so, he holds, keeps or otherwise refuses to return a child who is less than sixteen years old to such child's lawful custodian after a request by such custodian for the return of such child.

(b) Custodial interference in the second degree is a class A misdemeanor.

(1969, P.A. 828, § 100, eff. Oct. 1, 1971; 1981, P.A. 81–280, § 1.)

§ 53a–99. Substitution of children: Class D felony

(a) A person is guilty of substitution of children when, having been temporarily entrusted with a child less than one year old and, intending to deceive a parent, guardian or other lawful custodian of such child, he substitutes, produces or returns to such parent, guardian or custodian a child other than the one entrusted.

(b) Substitution of children is a class D felony.

(1969, P.A. 828, § 101, eff. Oct. 1, 1971.)

PART VIII. BURGLARY, CRIMINAL TRESPASS, ARSON, CRIMINAL MISCHIEF AND RELATED OFFENSES

§ 53a–110b. Transferred to C.G.S.A. § 53a–223 in Gen.St., Rev. to 2001

§ 53a–110c. Transferred to C.G.S.A. § 53a–223a in Gen.St., Rev. to 2001

PART XVIII. BIGAMY AND INCEST

§ 53a–190. Bigamy: Class D felony

(a) A person is guilty of bigamy when he marries or purports to marry another person in this state if either is lawfully married; or so marries or purports to marry another person in any other state or country in violation of the laws thereof, and knowingly cohabits and lives with such other person in this state as husband and wife.

(b) It shall be an affirmative defense to the charge of bigamy that at the time of the subsequent marriage or purported marriage: (1) The actor reasonably believed, based on persuasive and reliable information, that the prior spouse was dead; or (2) a court had entered a judgment purporting to terminate or annul any prior disqualifying marriage and the actor did not know that such judgment was invalid; or (3) the single person did not know that the other person was legally married.

(c) Bigamy is a class D felony.

(1969, P.A. 828, § 192, eff. Oct. 1, 1971; 1971, P.A. 871, § 47; 1992, P.A. 92–260, § 73.)

§ 53a–191. Incest: Class D felony

(a) A person is guilty of incest when he marries a person whom he knows to be related to him within any of the degrees of kindred specified in section 46b–21.

(b) Incest is a class D felony.

(1969, P.A. 828, § 193, eff. Oct. 1, 1971; 1980, P.A. 80–346, § 2; 1992, P.A. 92–260, § 74.)

§ 53a–223. Criminal violation of a protective order: Class D felony

(a) A person is guilty of criminal violation of a protective order when an order issued pursuant to subsection (e) of section 46b–38c, or section 54–1k or 54–82r has been issued against such person, and such person violates such order.

(b) Criminal violation of a protective order is a class D felony.

(1958 Rev., § 53a–110b; 1991, P.A. 91–381, § 1, eff. Oct. 1, 1991; 1995, P.A. 95–214, § 5; 1999, P.A. 99–240, § 4; 2002, P.A. 02–127, § 3.)

§ 53a–223a. Criminal violation of a standing criminal restraining order: Class D felony

(a) A person is guilty of criminal violation of a standing criminal restraining order when an order issued pursuant to subsection (a) of section 53a–40e has been issued against such person, and such person violates such order.

(b) Criminal violation of a standing criminal restraining order is a class D felony.

(1958 Rev., § 53a–110c; 1996, P.A. 96–228, § 2; 1998, June Sp.Sess., P.A. 98–1, § 37, eff. June 24, 1998.)

§ 53a–223b. Criminal violation of a restraining order: Class A misdemeanor

(a) A person is guilty of criminal violation of a restraining order when (1) (A) a restraining order has been issued against such person pursuant to section 46b–15, or (B) a foreign order of protection, as defined in section 46b–15a, has been issued against such person, after notice and an opportunity to be heard has been provided to such person, in a case involving the use, attempted use or threatened use of physical force against another, and (2) such person, having knowledge of the terms of the order, (A) does not stay away from a person or place in violation of the order, (B) contacts a person in violation of the order, (C) imposes any restraint upon the person or liberty of a person in violation of the order, or (D) threatens, harasses, assaults, molests, sexually assaults or attacks a person in violation of the order.

(b) Criminal violation of a restraining order is a class A misdemeanor.

(2002, P.A. 02–127, § 1; 2003, P.A. 03–98, § 6.)

§§ 53a–223c to 53a–249. Reserved for future use

TITLE 54

CRIMINAL PROCEDURE

CHAPTER 961

TRIAL AND PROCEEDINGS AFTER CONVICTION

PART I. DISCOVERY, TRIAL AND WITNESSES

§ 54–84a. Privilege of spouse

If any person on trial for crime has a husband or wife, he or she shall be a competent witness but may elect or refuse to testify for or against the accused, except that either spouse who has received personal violence from the other or is the spouse of one who is charged with violation of any of sections 53–20, 53–21, 53–23, 53–304, 53a–70, 53a–70a, 53a–71 and 53a–83 to 53a–88, inclusive, may, upon his or her trial for offenses arising out of such personal violence or from violation of the provisions of any of said sections, be compelled to testify in the same manner as any other witness.

(1980, P.A. 80–313, § 45.)

*

RULES FOR THE SUPERIOR COURT

Including Amendments Received Through August 1, 2004

GENERAL PROVISIONS

CHAPTER 3. APPEARANCES

§ 3–1. Appearance for Plaintiff on Writ or Complaint in Civil and Family Cases

When a writ has been signed by an attorney at law admitted to practice in the courts of this state, such writ shall contain the attorney's name, juris number, mailing address, and telephone number, all of which shall be typed or printed on the writ, and the attorney's appearance shall be entered for the plaintiff, unless such attorney by endorsement on the writ shall otherwise direct, or unless such attorney shall type or print on the writ the name, address, juris number and telephone number of the professional corporation or firm, of which such attorney shall be a member, entering its appearance for the plaintiff. The signature on the complaint of any person proceeding without the assistance of counsel pursuant to Section 8–1 shall be deemed to constitute the appearance pro se of such party.

§ 3–2. Time to File Appearance

(a) After the writ has been filed the attorney for any party to any action, or any party himself or herself, may enter his or her appearance in writing with the clerk of the court location to which such action is returnable. Except where otherwise prescribed herein or by statute, an appearance for a party in a civil or family case should be filed on or before the second day following the return day. Appearances filed thereafter in such cases shall be accepted but an appearance for a party after the entry against such party of a nonsuit or judgment after default for failure to appear shall not affect the entry of the nonsuit or any judgment after default.

(b) An appearance in a criminal case or in a juvenile matter should be filed promptly but may be filed at any stage of the proceeding.

§ 3–3. Form and Signing of Appearance

Each appearance shall (1) be typed or printed on size 8-½″ × 11″ paper, (2) be headed with the name and number of the case, the name of the court location to which it is returnable and the date, (3) be legibly signed by the individual preparing the appearance with the individual's own name and (4) state the party or parties for whom the appearance is being entered and the official (with position or department, if desired), firm, professional corporation or individual whose appearance is being entered, together with the juris number assigned thereto if any, the mailing address and the telephone number. This section shall not apply to appearances entered pursuant to Section 3–1.

§ 3–4. Filing Appearance With the Clerk—Copies

Appearances shall be filed with the clerk of the court location where the matter is pending. Whenever an appearance is filed in any civil or family action returnable to a judicial district of the superior court, only an original need be filed and the clerk with whom it is filed shall cause notice thereof to be given to all other counsel and pro se parties of record in the action. Whenever an appearance is filed in any criminal case or juvenile matter, only the original need be filed. Whenever an appearance is filed in any civil action returnable to a geographical area of the superior court, an original and sufficient copies for each party to the action must be filed. This section shall not apply to appearances entered pursuant to Section 3–1.

§ 3–5. Service of Appearances on Other Parties—when Required

(a) In summary process actions the attorney for the defendant or, if there is no such attorney, the defendant himself or herself, in addition to complying with Section 3-4, shall mail or deliver a copy of the appearance to the attorney for the plaintiff or, if there is no such attorney, to the plaintiff himself or herself.

(b) In delinquency and family with service needs proceedings, such attorney shall mail or deliver a copy of the appearance to the juvenile prosecutor; in other juvenile proceedings, such attorney shall mail or deliver a copy of the appearance to the attorney for the petitioner and to all other attorneys and pro se parties.

(c) In criminal cases the attorney for the defendant shall mail or deliver a copy of the appearance to the prosecuting authority.

(d) Service of such appearances shall be made in accordance with Sections 10-12 through 10-17. Proof of service shall be endorsed on the appearance filed with the clerk.

§ 3-6. Appearances for Bail or Detention Hearing Only

(a) An attorney, prior to the entering of an appearance by any other attorney, may enter an appearance for the defendant in a criminal case for the sole purpose of representing the defendant at a hearing for the fixing of bail. Such appearance shall be in writing and shall be styled, "for the purpose of the bail hearing only." Upon entering such an appearance, that attorney shall be entitled to confer with the prosecuting authority in connection with the bail hearing.

(b) An attorney may enter an appearance in a delinquency proceeding for the sole purpose of representing the respondent at any detention hearing; such appearance shall be in writing and styled "for the purpose of detention hearing only."

§ 3-7. Consequence of Filing Appearance

(a) Except by leave of the judicial authority, no attorney shall be permitted to appear in court or to be heard in behalf of a party until the attorney's appearance has been entered. No attorney shall be entitled to confer with the prosecuting authority as counsel for the defendant in a criminal case until the attorney's appearance has been so entered.

(b) After the filing of an appearance the attorney or pro se party shall receive copies of all notices required to be given to parties by statute or by these rules.

(c) The filing of an appearance by itself shall not waive the right to attack defects in jurisdiction or any claimed violation of constitutional rights.

§ 3-8. Appearance for Represented Party

Whenever an attorney files an appearance for a party, or the party files an appearance for himself or herself, and there is already an appearance of an attorney or party on file for that party, the attorney or party filing the new appearance shall state thereon whether such appearance is in place of or in addition to the appearance or appearances already on file. If the new appearance is stated to be in place of any appearance or appearances on file, the party or attorney filing that new appearance shall serve, in accordance with Sections 10-12 through 10-17, a copy of that new appearance on any attorney or party whose appearance is to be replaced by the new appearance. Unless a written objection is filed within ten days after the filing of an in-lieu-of appearance, the appearance or appearances to be replaced by the new appearance shall be deemed to have been withdrawn and the clerk shall make appropriate entries for such purpose on the file and docket. The provisions of this section regarding parties filing appearances for themselves does not apply to criminal cases.

§ 3-9. Withdrawal of Appearance; Duration of Appearance

(a) An attorney or party whose appearance has been filed shall be deemed to have withdrawn such appearance upon failure to file a written objection within ten days after written notice has been given or mailed to such attorney or party that a new appearance has been filed in place of the appearance of such attorney or party in accordance with Section 3-8.

(b) An attorney may withdraw his or her appearance for a party or parties in any action after the appearance of other counsel representing the same party or parties has been entered. An application for withdrawal in accordance with this subsection shall state that such an appearance has been entered and that such party or parties are being represented by such other counsel at the time of the application. Such an application may be granted by the clerk as of course, if such an appearance by other counsel has been entered.

(c) All appearances of counsel shall be deemed to have been withdrawn 180 days after the entry of judgment in any action seeking a dissolution of marriage, annulment, or legal separation, provided no appeal shall have been taken. In the event of an appeal or the filing of a motion to open a judgment within such 180 days, all appearances of counsel shall be deemed to have been withdrawn after final judgment on such appeal or motion or within 180 days after the entry of the original judgment, whichever is later. Nothing herein shall preclude or prevent any attorney from filing a motion to withdraw with leave of the court during that period subsequent to the entry of judgment. In the absence of a specific withdrawal, counsel will continue of record for all postjudgment purposes until 180 days have elapsed from the entry of judgment or, in the event an appeal or a motion to open a judgment is filed within such 180 day period, until final judgment on that appeal or determination of that motion, whichever is later.

(d) Except as provided in subsections (a), (b) and (c), no attorney shall withdraw his or her appearance after it has been entered upon the record of the court without the leave of the court.

(e) All appearances in juvenile matters shall be deemed to continue during the period of delinquency or family with service needs probation or supervision, or during the period of any commitment or protective supervision or during the period until final adoption following termination of parental rights; however, in the absence of a specific request, no attorney appointed in a prior proceeding shall automatically continue to represent the parent for any subsequent petition to terminate parental rights. The attorney shall represent the client in connection with appeals, subject to Section 35–4(b), and with petitions for extensions, revocations or postjudgment motions and shall have access to any documents filed in court. The attorney for the child shall continue to represent the child in all proceedings relating to the child, including termination of parental rights.

§ 3–10. Motion to Withdraw Appearance

(a) No motion for withdrawal of appearance shall be granted unless good cause is shown and until the judicial authority is satisfied that reasonable notice has been given to the party or parties represented by the attorney and to other attorneys of record.

(b) In civil and family cases a motion to withdraw shall include the last known address of any party as to whom the attorney seeks to withdraw his or her appearance and shall have attached to it a notice to such party advising of the following: (1) the attorney is filing a motion which seeks the court's permission to no longer represent the party in the case; (2) if the party wishes to be heard, he or she should contact the clerk's office to find out the date and time of the hearing; (3) the party may appear in court on that date and address the court concerning the motion; (4) if the motion to withdraw is granted, the party should either obtain another attorney or file an appearance on his or her own behalf with the court and (5) if the party does neither, the party will not receive notice of court proceedings in the case and a nonsuit or default judgment may be rendered against such party.

(c) In criminal and juvenile matters, the motion to withdraw shall comply with subsections (b)(1), (2) and (3) of this section and the client shall also be advised by the attorney that if the motion to withdraw is granted the client should request court appointed counsel, obtain another attorney or file an appearance on his or her own behalf with the court and be further advised that if none is done, there may be no further notice of proceeding and the court may act.

(d) In addition to the above, each motion to withdraw appearance and each notice to the party or parties who are the subject of the motion shall state whether the case has been assigned for pre-trial or trial and, if so, the date so assigned.

(e) The attorney's appearance for the party shall be deemed to have been withdrawn upon the granting of the motion without the necessity of filing a withdrawal of appearance.

[Amended June 26, 2000, effective January 1, 2001; amended June 25, 2001, effective January 1, 2002.]

PROCEDURE IN FAMILY MATTERS

CHAPTER 25. GENERAL PROVISIONS

Table of Sections

---

§ 25-1. Definitions Applicable to Proceedings on Family Matters

The following shall be "family matters" within the scope of these rules: Any actions brought pursuant to General Statutes § 46b-1, including but not limited to dissolution of marriage, legal separation, dissolution of marriage after legal separation, annulment of marriage, alimony, support, custody, and change of name incident to dissolution of marriage, habeas corpus and other proceedings to determine the custody and visitation of children except those which are properly filed in the superior court as juvenile matters, the establishing of paternity, enforcement of foreign matrimonial judgments, actions related to prenuptial and separation agreements and to matrimonial decrees of a foreign jurisdiction, actions brought pursuant to General Statutes § 46b-15, custody proceedings brought under the provisions of the Uniform Child Custody Jurisdiction Act and proceedings for enforcement of support brought under the provisions of the Uniform Interstate Family Support Act.

[Amended June 28, 1999, effective January 1, 2000.]

§ 25-2. Complaints for Dissolution of Marriage, Legal Separation, or Annulment

(a) Every complaint in a dissolution of marriage, legal separation or annulment action shall state the date and place, including the city or town, of the marriage and the facts necessary to give the court jurisdiction.

(b) Every such complaint shall also state whether there are minor children issue of the marriage and whether there are any other minor children born to the wife since the date of marriage of the parties, the name and date of birth of each, and the name of any individual or agency presently responsible by virtue of judicial award for the custody or support of any child. These requirements shall be met whether a child is issue of the marriage or not and whether custody of children is sought in the action. In every case in which the state of Connecticut or any town thereof is contributing or has contributed to the support or maintenance of a party or child of said party, such fact shall be stated in the complaint and a copy thereof served on the attorney general or town clerk in accordance with the provisions of Sections 10–12 through 10–17. Although the attorney general or town clerk shall be a party to such cases, he or she need not be named in the writ of summons or summoned to appear.

(c) The complaint shall also set forth the plaintiff's demand for relief and the automatic orders as required by Section 25–5.

[Amended June 25, 2001, effective January 1, 2002.]

§ 25–3. Action for Custody of Minor Child

Every application in an action for custody of a minor child, other than actions for dissolution of marriage, legal separation or annulment, shall state the name and date of birth of such minor child or children, the names of the parents and legal guardian of such minor child or children, and the facts necessary to give the court jurisdiction. The application shall comply with Section 25–5. Such application shall be commenced by an order to show cause. Upon presentation of the application and an affidavit concerning children, the judicial authority shall cause an order to be issued requiring the adverse party or parties to appear on a day certain and show cause, if any there be, why the relief requested in the application should not be granted. The application, order and affidavit shall be served on the adverse party not less than twelve days before the date of the hearing, which shall not be held more than thirty days from the filing of the application.

[Amended June 28, 1999, effective January 1, 2000; amended June 26, 2000, effective January 1, 2001.]

§ 25–4. Action for Visitation of Minor Child

Every application in an action for visitation of a minor child, other than actions for dissolution of marriage, legal separation or annulment, shall state the name and date of birth of such minor child or children, the names of the parents and legal guardian of such minor child or children, and the facts necessary to give the court jurisdiction. The application shall comply with Section 25–5. Such application shall be commenced by an order to show cause. Upon presentation of the application and an affidavit concerning children, the judicial authority shall cause an order to be issued requiring the adverse party or parties to appear on a day certain and show cause, if any there be, why the relief requested in the application should not be granted. The application, order and affidavit shall be served on the adverse party not less than twelve days before the date of the hearing, which shall not be held more than thirty days from the filing of the application.

[Amended June 28, 1999, effective January 1, 2000; amended June 26, 2000, effective January 1, 2001.]

§ 25–5. Automatic Orders upon Service of Complaint or Application

(a) The following automatic orders shall apply to both parties, with service of the automatic orders to be made with service of process of a complaint for dissolution of marriage, legal separation, or annulment, or of an application for custody or visitation. An automatic order shall not apply if there is a prior, contradictory order of a judicial authority. The automatic orders shall be effective with regard to the plaintiff or the applicant upon the signing of the complaint or the application and with regard to the defendant or the respondent upon service and shall remain in place during the pendency of the action, unless terminated, modified, or amended by further order of a judicial authority upon motion of either of the parties:

(1) Neither party shall sell, transfer, encumber (except for the filing of a lis pendens), conceal, assign, remove, or in any way dispose of, without the consent of the other party in writing, or an order of a judicial authority, any property, individually or jointly held by the parties, except in the usual course of business or for customary and usual household expenses or for reasonable attorneys' fees in connection with this action.

(2) Neither party shall incur unreasonable debts hereafter, including, but not limited to, further borrowing against any credit line secured by the family residence, further encumbrancing any assets, or unreasonably using credit cards or cash advances against credit cards.

(3) The parties shall each complete and exchange sworn financial statements substantially in accordance with a form prescribed by the chief court administrator within thirty days of the return day. The parties may thereafter enter and submit to the court a stipulated interim order allocating income and expenses, in accordance with the uniform child support guidelines.

(4) The case management date for this case is ________. The parties shall comply with Section 25–50 to determine if their actual presence at the court is required on that date.

(5) Neither party shall permanently remove the minor child or children from the state of Connecticut, without written consent of the other or order of a judicial authority.

(6) The parties, if they share a minor child or children, shall participate in the parenting education program within sixty days of the return day or within sixty days from the filing of the application.

(7) Neither party shall cause the other party or the children of the marriage to be removed from any medical, hospital and dental insurance coverage, and each party shall maintain the existing medical, hospi-

tal and dental insurance coverage in full force and effect.

(8) Neither party shall change the beneficiaries of any existing life insurance policies, and each party shall maintain the existing life insurance, automobile insurance, homeowners or renters insurance policies in full force and effect.

(9) If the parties are living together on the date of service of these orders, neither party may deny the other party use of the current primary residence of the parties, whether it be owned or rented property, without order of a judicial authority. This provision shall not apply if there is a prior, contradictory order of a judicial authority.

(10) If the parties share a child or children, a party vacating the family residence shall notify the other party or the other party's attorney, in writing, within forty-eight hours of such move, of an address where the relocated party can receive communication. This provision shall not apply if there is a prior, contradictory order of a judicial authority.

(11) If the parents of minor children live apart during this dissolution proceeding, they shall assist their children in having contact with both parties, which is consistent with the habits of the family, personally, by telephone, and in writing unless there is a prior order of a judicial authority.

(b) The automatic orders of a judicial authority as enumerated in subsection (a) shall be set forth immediately following the party's requested relief in any complaint for dissolution of marriage, legal separation, or annulment, or in any application for custody or visitation, and shall set forth the following language in uppercase letters: FAILURE TO OBEY THESE ORDERS MAY BE PUNISHABLE BY CONTEMPT OF COURT. IF YOU OBJECT TO OR SEEK MODIFICATION OF THESE ORDERS DURING THE PENDENCY OF THE ACTION, YOU HAVE THE RIGHT TO A HEARING BEFORE A JUDGE WITHIN A REASONABLE TIME. The clerk shall not accept for filing any complaint for dissolution of marriage, legal separation, or annulment, or any application for custody or visitation, that does not comply with this subsection.

(c) The automatic orders of a judicial authority as enumerated in subdivisions (a)(1), (2), and (3) shall not apply in custody and visitation cases.

[Amended June 29, 1998, effective January 1, 1999; subd. (a)(1) amended on an interim basis pursuant to § 1-9(c), effective January 1, 1999; amended June 28, 1999, effective January 1, 2000; amended August 22, 2001, effective January 1, 2002.]

§ 25-6. Parties and Appearances

The provisions of Sections 8-1, 8-2, 9-1, 9-3 through 9-6, inclusive, 9-18, 9-19, 9-22, 9-24 and 10-12 through 10-17 of the rules of practice shall apply to family matters as defined in Section 25-1.

§ 25-7. Pleadings in General—Amendments to Complaint or Application

If Sections 25-2, 25-3 or 25-4 are not complied with, the judicial authority, whenever its attention is called to the matter, shall order that the complaint or the application, as the case may be, be amended upon such terms and conditions as it may direct. Where an amendment is filed concerning support or maintenance contributed by the state of Connecticut, no further action shall be taken by the judicial authority until such amendment shall be served upon the attorney general and opportunity given him or her to be heard upon the matter. Nothing in this section shall be construed to affect the automatic orders in Section 25-5 above.

[Amended June 28, 1999, effective January 1, 2000.]

§ 25-8. Pleadings in General—Amendment; New Ground for Dissolution of Marriage

(a) In any action for a dissolution of marriage an amendment to the complaint which states a ground for dissolution of marriage alleged to have arisen since the commencement of the action may be filed with permission of the judicial authority.

(b) The provisions of Sections 10-59, 10-60 and 10-61 of the rules of practice shall apply to family matters as defined in Section 25-1.

§ 25-9. Pleadings in General—Answer, Cross Complaint, Claims for Relief by Defendant

The defendant in a dissolution of marriage, legal separation, or annulment matter may file, in addition to the above mentioned pleadings, one of the following pleadings which shall comply with Sections 10-1, 10-3, 10-5, 10-7, 10-8 and 10-12 through 10-17, 10-18 and 10-19 inclusive:

(1) An answer may be filed which denies or admits the allegations of the complaint, or which states that the defendant has insufficient information to form a belief and leaves the pleader to his or her proof, and which may set forth the defendant's claims for relief.

(2) An answer and cross complaint may be filed which denies or admits the allegations of the complaint, or which states that the defendant has insufficient information to form a belief and leaves the pleader to his or her proof, and which alleges the grounds upon which a dissolution, legal separation or annulment is sought by the defendant and specifies therein the claims for relief.

[Amended June 28, 1999, effective January 1, 2000.]

§ 25-10. Pleadings in General—Answer to Cross Complaint

A plaintiff in a dissolution of marriage, legal separation, or annulment matter seeking to contest the grounds of a cross complaint shall file an answer admitting or denying the allegations of such cross complaint or leaving the pleader to his or her proof. If a decree is rendered on the cross complaint, the judicial authority may award to the plaintiff such relief as is claimed in the complaint.

[Amended June 28, 1999, effective January 1, 2000.]

§ 25-11. Pleadings in General—Order of Pleadings

The order of pleadings shall be:

(1) the plaintiff's complaint;

(2) the defendant's motion to dismiss the complaint;

(3) the defendant's motion to strike the complaint or claims for relief;

(4) the defendant's answer, cross complaint and claims for relief;

(5) the plaintiff's motion to strike the defendant's answer, cross complaint, or claims for relief;

(6) the plaintiff's answer.

§ 25-12. Motion to Dismiss

(a) Any defendant, wishing to assert grounds to dismiss the action under Section 25-13(2), (3), (4) or (5) must do so by filing a motion to dismiss within thirty days of the filing of an appearance.

(b) Any claim based on Section 25-13(2), (3), (4) or (5) is waived if not raised by a motion to dismiss filed in the sequence provided in Section 25-11, within the time provided in this section.

§ 25-13. Motion to Dismiss—Grounds on Motion to Dismiss

(a) The motion to dismiss shall be used to assert (1) lack of jurisdiction over the subject matter, (2) lack of jurisdiction over the person, (3) improper venue, (4) insufficiency of process and (5) insufficiency of service of process. This motion shall always be filed with a supporting memorandum of law and, where appropriate, with supporting affidavits as to facts not apparent on the record.

(b) If an adverse party objects to this motion he or she shall, at least five days before the motion is to be considered on the short calendar, file and serve in accordance with Sections 10-12 through 10-17 a memorandum of law and, where appropriate, supporting affidavits as to facts not apparent on the record.

§ 25-14. Motion to Dismiss—Waiver and Subject Matter Jurisdiction

Any claim of lack of jurisdiction over the subject matter cannot be waived; and whenever it is found after suggestion of the parties or otherwise that the court lacks jurisdiction of the subject matter, the judicial authority shall dismiss the action.

§ 25-15. Motion to Dismiss—Further Pleading by Defendant

If any motion to dismiss is denied with respect to any jurisdictional issue, the defendant may plead further without waiving his or her right to contest jurisdiction further.

§ 25-16. Motion to Strike—In General

(a) Whenever any party wishes to contest (1) the legal sufficiency of the allegations of any complaint or cross complaint, or of any one or more counts thereof, to state a claim upon which relief can be granted, or (2) the legal sufficiency of any claim for relief in any such complaint or cross complaint, or (3) the legal sufficiency of any such complaint or cross complaint, or any count thereof, because of the absence of any necessary party, or (4) the joining of two or more causes of action which cannot properly be united in one complaint or cross complaint, whether the same be stated in one or more counts, or (5) the legal sufficiency of any answer to any complaint or cross complaint, or any part of that answer contained therein, that party may do so by filing a motion to strike the contested pleading or part thereof.

(b) A motion to strike on the ground of the nonjoinder of a necessary party must give the name and residence of the missing party or such information as the moving party has as to his or her identity and residence and must state his or her interest in the cause of action.

§ 25-17. Motion to Strike—Date for Hearing

The motion shall be placed on the short calendar to be held not less than fifteen days following the filing of the motion, unless the judicial authority otherwise directs.

§ 25-18. Motion to Strike—Reasons

Each motion to strike raising any of the claims of legal insufficiency enumerated in the Sections 25-12, 25-13, and 25-16 shall separately set forth each such claim of insufficiency and shall distinctly specify the reason or reasons for each such claimed insufficiency.

§ 25–19. Motion to Strike—Memorandum of Law

(a) Each motion to strike must be accompanied by an appropriate memorandum of law citing the legal authorities upon which the motion relies.

(b) If an adverse party objects to this motion such party shall, at least five days before the date the motion is to be considered on the short calendar, file and serve in accordance with Sections 10–12 through 10–17 a memorandum of law.

§ 25–20. Motion to Strike—When Memorandum of Decision Required

Whenever a motion to strike is filed and more than one ground of decision is set up therein, the judicial authority, in rendering the decision thereon, shall specify in writing the grounds upon which that decision is based.

§ 25–21. Motion to Strike—Substitute Pleading; Judgment

Within fifteen days after the granting of any motion to strike, the party whose pleading has been stricken may file a new pleading; provided that in those instances where an entire complaint or cross complaint has been stricken, and the party whose pleading has been so stricken fails to file a new pleading within that fifteen-day period, the judicial authority may upon motion enter judgment against said party on said stricken complaint or cross complaint.

§ 25–22. Motion to Strike—Stricken Pleading Part of Another Cause or Defense

Whenever the judicial authority grants a motion to strike the whole or any portion of any pleading or count which purports to state an entire cause of action, and such pleading or portion thereof states or constitutes a part of another cause of action, the granting of that motion shall remove from the case only the cause of action which was the subject of the granting of that motion, and it shall not remove such pleading or count or any portion thereof so far as the same is applicable to any other cause of action.

§ 25–23. Motions, Requests, Orders of Notice, and Short Calendar

The provisions of Sections 11–1, 11–2, 11–4, 11–5, 11–6, 11–8, 11–10, 11–11, 11–12, 11–19, 12–1, 12–2, and 12–3 of the rules of practice shall apply to family matters as defined in Section 25–1.

[Amended May 14, 2003, effective July 1, 2003.]

Commentary

The above cite to Section 11–20 is no longer necessary in light of Sections 25–59 and 25–59A below.

§ 25–24. Motions

(a) Any appropriate party may move for alimony, child support, custody, visitation, appointment of counsel for the minor child, counsel fees, or for an order with respect to the maintenance of the family or for any other equitable relief.

(b) Each such motion shall state clearly, in the caption of the motion, whether it is a pendente lite or a postjudgment motion.

§ 25–25. Motion for Exclusive Possession

Each motion for exclusive possession shall state the nature of the property, whether it is rental property or owned by the parties or one of them, the length of tenancy or ownership of each party, the current family members residing therein and the grounds upon which the moving party seeks exclusive possession.

§ 25–26. Modification of Custody, Alimony or Support

(a) Upon an application for a modification of an award of alimony pendente lite, alimony or support of minor children, filed by a person who is then in arrears under the terms of such award, the judicial authority shall, upon hearing, ascertain whether such arrearage has accrued without sufficient excuse so as to constitute a contempt of court, and, in its discretion, may determine whether any modification of current alimony and support shall be ordered prior to the payment, in whole or in part as the judicial authority may order, of any arrearage found to exist.

(b) Either parent or both parents of minor children may be cited or summoned by any party to the action to appear and show cause, if any they have, why orders of custody, visitation, support or alimony should not be entered or modified.

(c) If any applicant is proceeding without the assistance of counsel and citation of any other party is necessary, the applicant shall sign the application and present the application, proposed order and summons to the clerk; the clerk shall review the proposed order and summons and, unless it is defective as to form, shall sign the proposed order and summons and shall assign a date for a hearing on the application.

(d) Each motion for modification of custody, visitation, alimony or child support shall state clearly in the caption of the motion whether it is a pendente lite or a postjudgment motion.

(e) Each motion for modification shall state the specific factual and legal basis for the claimed modification and shall include the outstanding order and date thereof to which the motion for modification is addressed.

(f) On motions addressed to financial issues the provisions of Section 25–30 shall be followed.

§ 25–27. Motion for Contempt

(a) All motions for contempt must state (1) the date and specific language of the order of the judicial authority on which the motion is based; (2) the specific acts alleged to constitute the contempt of that order, including the amount of any arrears claimed due as of the date of the motion or a date specifically identified in the motion; (3) the movant's claims for relief for the contempt.

(b) All motions for contempt must state clearly in the caption of the motion whether it is a pendente lite or a postjudgment motion, and the subject matter and the type of order alleged to have been violated.

[Amended June 28, 1999, effective January 1, 2000.]

§ 25–28. Order of Notice

(a) On a complaint for dissolution of marriage, legal separation, or annulment, or on an application for custody or visitation, when the adverse party resides out of or is absent from the state or the whereabouts of the adverse party is unknown to the plaintiff or the applicant, any judge or clerk of the court may make such order of notice as he or she deems reasonable. If such notice is by publication, it shall not include the automatic orders set forth in Section 25–5, but shall instead include a statement that automatic orders have issued in the case pursuant to Section 25–5 and that such orders are set forth in the complaint or the application on file with the court. Such notice having been given and proved, the judicial authority may hear the complaint or the application if it finds that the adverse party has actually received notice that the complaint or the application is pending. If actual notice is not proved, the judicial authority in its discretion may hear the case or continue it for compliance with such further order of notice as it may direct.

(b) With regard to any postjudgment motion for modification or for contempt or any other motion requiring an order of notice, where the adverse party resides out of or is absent from the state any judge or clerk of the judicial authority may make such order of notice as he or she deems reasonable. Such notice having been given and proved, the court may hear the motion if it finds that the adverse party has actually received notice that the motion is pending.

[Amended June 28, 1999, effective January 1, 2000.]

§ 25–29. Notice of Orders for Support or Alimony

In all dissolution of marriage, legal separation, annulment, custody or visitation actions, such notice as the judicial authority shall direct shall be given to nonappearing parties of any orders for support or alimony. No such order shall be effective until the order of notice shall have been complied with or the nonappearing party has actually received notice of such orders.

§ 25–30. Statements to Be Filed

(a) At least five days before the hearing date of a motion or order to show cause concerning alimony, support, or counsel fees, or at the time a dissolution of marriage, legal separation or annulment action or action for custody or visitation is scheduled for a hearing, each party shall file, where applicable, a sworn statement substantially in accordance with a form prescribed by the chief court administrator, of current income, expenses, assets and liabilities. When the attorney general has appeared as a party in interest, a copy of the sworn statements shall be served upon him or her in accordance with Sections 10–12 through 10–17. Unless otherwise ordered by the judicial authority, all appearing parties shall file sworn statements within thirty days prior to the date of the decree. Notwithstanding the above, the court may render pendente lite and permanent orders, including judgment, in the absence of the opposing party's sworn statement.

(b) At least ten days before the scheduled family special masters session, alternative dispute resolution session, or judicial pretrial, the parties shall serve on each appearing party, but not file with the court, written proposed orders, and, at least ten days prior to the date of the final limited contested or contested hearing, the parties shall file with the court and serve on each appearing party written proposed orders.

(c) The written proposed orders shall be comprehensive and shall set forth the party's requested relief including, where applicable, the following:

(1) a parenting plan;

(2) alimony;

(3) child support;

(4) property division;

(5) counsel fees;

(6) life insurance;

(7) medical insurance; and

(8) division of liabilities.

(d) The proposed orders shall be neither factual nor argumentative but shall, instead, only set forth the party's claims.

(e) Where there is a minor child who requires support, the parties shall file a completed child support and arrearage guidelines worksheet at the time of any court hearing concerning child support; or at the time of a final hearing in an action for dissolution of marriage, legal separation, annulment, custody or visitation.

(f) At the time of any hearing, including pendente lite and postjudgment proceedings, in which a moving party seeks a determination, modification, or enforcement of any alimony or child support order, a party shall submit an Advisement of Rights Re: Wage Withholding Form (JD–FM–71).

[Amended June 24, 2002, effective January 1, 2003.]

§ 25–31. Discovery and Depositions

The provisions of Sections 13–1 through 13–11 inclusive, 13–13 through 13–16 inclusive, and 13–17 through 13–32 of the rules of practice inclusive, shall apply to family matters as defined in Section 25–1.

§ 25–32. Mandatory Disclosure and Production

(a) Unless otherwise ordered by the judicial authority for good cause shown, upon request by a party involved in an action for dissolution of marriage, legal separation, annulment or support, or a postjudgment motion for modification of alimony or support, opposing parties shall exchange the following documents within thirty days of such request:

(1) all federal and state income tax returns filed within the last three years, including personal returns and returns filed on behalf of any partnership or closely-held corporation of which a party is a partner or shareholder;

(2) IRS forms W–2, 1099 and K–1 within the last three years including those for the past year if the income tax returns for that year have not been prepared;

(3) copies of all pay stubs or other evidence of income for the current year and the last pay stub from the past year;

(4) statements for all accounts maintained with any financial institution, including banks, brokers and financial managers, for the past 24 months;

(5) the most recent statement showing any interest in any Keogh, IRA, profit sharing plan, deferred compensation plan, pension plan, or retirement account;

(6) the most recent statement regarding any insurance on the life of any party;

(7) a summary furnished by the employer of the party's medical insurance policy, coverage, cost of coverage, spousal benefits, and COBRA costs following dissolution;

(8) any written appraisal concerning any asset owned by either party.

(b) Such duty to disclose shall continue during the pendency of the action should a party appear. This section shall not preclude discovery under any other provisions of these rules.

[Amended June 29, 1998, effective January 1, 1999.]

§ 25–33. Judicial Appointment of Expert Witnesses

Whenever the judicial authority deems it necessary, on its own motion it may appoint any expert witnesses of its own selection. The judicial authority shall give notice of its intention to appoint such expert, and give the parties an opportunity to be heard concerning such appointment. An expert witness shall not be appointed by the judicial authority unless the expert consents to act. An expert witness so appointed shall be informed of his or her duties by the judicial authority in writing, a copy of which shall be filed with the clerk, or the witness shall be informed of his or her duties at a conference in which the parties shall have an opportunity to participate. Such expert witness shall advise the parties of his or her findings, if any, and may thereafter be called to testify by the judicial authority or by any party and shall be subject to cross-examination by each party. The judicial authority may determine the reasonable compensation for such witness and direct payment out of such funds as may be provided by law or by the parties or any of them as the judicial authority may direct. Nothing in this section shall prohibit the parties from retaining their own expert witnesses.

§ 25–34. Procedure for Short Calendar

(a) Oral argument on any motion or the presentation of testimony thereon shall be allowed if the appearing parties have followed administrative policies for marking the motion ready and for screening with Family Services.

(b) If the matter will require more than one hour of court time, it may be specifically assigned for a date certain.

(c) Failure to appear and present argument on the date set by the judicial authority shall constitute a waiver of the right to argue unless the judicial authority orders otherwise. Unless for good cause shown, no motion may be reclaimed after a period of three months from the date of filing. This subsection shall not apply to those motions where counsel appeared on the date set by the judicial authority and entered into a scheduling order for discovery, depositions and a date certain for hearing.

§ 25–35. Disclosure of Conference Recommendation

In the event the parties or their counsel confer with a family relations counselor on finances concerning alimony and child support in connection with either a pendente lite, postjudgment or dissolution hearing, the recommendations of the family relations counselor concerning alimony and child support shall not be reported to the judicial authority by the parties or their counsel or the family relations counselor unless, before such conference, the parties or their counsel have stipulated that the recommendation of the family relations counselor may be made known to the judicial authority.

§ 25-36. Motion for Decree Finally Dissolving Marriage after Decree of Legal Separation

Every motion for a decree finally dissolving and terminating the marriage, after a decree of legal separation, shall state the number of the case in which the separation was granted, the date of the decree of legal separation and whether the parties have resumed marital relations since the entry of the decree, and it shall be accompanied by an application for an order of notice to the adverse party.

§ 25-37. Motion for Decree Finally Dissolving Marriage after Decree of Legal Separation—Notice and Hearing

Upon presentation of such motion to the judicial authority it shall fix a time for hearing the same and make an order of notice, by personal service if the adverse party is within the state and that party's place of residence is known, otherwise in such manner as it shall deem reasonable.

§ 25-38. Judgment Files

The provisions of Sections 17-4, 17-9 and 17-43 shall apply to family matters as defined in Section 25-1. The provisions of Section 3-9 concerning withdrawal of appearance of an attorney 180 days after the entry of judgment shall not apply to family matters actions until the provisions of this section concerning the filing of judgment files have been satisfied.

§ 25-39. Miscellaneous Rules

Except as otherwise provided in Section 25-51, the provisions of Sections 17-20, 7-19, 18-5, 18-9, 20-1, 20-3, and 23-67 of the rules of practice shall apply to family matters as defined in Section 25-1.

§ 25-40. Habeas Corpus in Family; The Petition

(a) A petition for a writ of habeas corpus shall be under oath and shall state:

(1) the specific facts upon which each claim of custody or visitation is based such that the judicial authority would immediately order the child or children to be brought before the court;

(2) any previous petitions for the writ of habeas corpus, and any existing custody or visitation orders, involving the same child or children and the dispositions taken thereon; and

(3) the specific facts upon which the court has jurisdiction.

§ 25-41. Habeas Corpus in Family—Preliminary Consideration

(a) The judicial authority shall promptly review any petition for a writ of habeas corpus to determine whether the writ should issue. The judicial authority shall issue the writ if it appears that:

(1) the court has jurisdiction;

(2) the petition is meritorious; and

(3) another proceeding is not more appropriate.

(b) The judicial authority shall notify the petitioner if it declines to issue the writ pursuant to this section.

§ 25-42. Habeas Corpus in Family—Dismissal

The judicial authority may, at any time, upon its own motion or upon motion of the respondent, dismiss the petition, or any count thereof, if it determines that:

(1) the court lacks jurisdiction;

(2) the petition, or a count thereof, fails to state a claim upon which habeas corpus relief can be granted;

(3) the petition presents the same ground as a prior petition previously denied and fails to state new facts or proffer new evidence not reasonably available at the time of the prior petition;

(4) the claims asserted in the petition are moot or premature;

(5) any other legally sufficient ground for dismissal of the petition exists.

§ 25-43. Habeas Corpus in Family—The Return

The return shall respond to the allegations of the petition and shall allege any facts in support of any claim of procedural default, abuse of the writ, or any other claim that the petitioner is not entitled to relief.

§ 25-44. Habeas Corpus in Family—Reply to the Return

(a) If the return alleges any defense or claim that the petitioner is not entitled to relief, and such allegations are put in dispute by the petition, the petitioner shall file a reply.

(b) The reply shall admit or deny any allegations that the petitioner is not entitled to relief.

§ 25-45. Habeas Corpus in Family—Schedule for Filing Pleadings

The return or responsive pleading and any reply to the return shall be filed as the judicial authority may order.

§ 25-46. Habeas Corpus in Family—Summary Judgment as to Writ of Habeas Corpus

At any time after the pleadings are closed, any party may move for summary judgment, which shall be rendered if the pleadings, affidavits and any other evidence submitted, show that there is no genuine issue of material fact between the parties requiring a trial and the moving party is entitled to judgment as a matter of law.

§ 25-47. Habeas Corpus in Family—Discovery

Discovery shall be as in all other family matters.

§ 25-48. Dockets, Pretrials and Assignment for Disposition

The provisions of Sections 14-2, 14-3, 14-23, and 14-25 of the rules of practice shall apply to family matters as defined in Section 25-1.

§ 25-49. Definitions

For purposes of these rules the following definitions shall apply:

(1) "Uncontested matter" means a case in which no aspect of the matter is in dispute.

(2) "Limited contested matter" means a case in which the matters in dispute are limited to monetary awards, real property or personal property.

(3) "Contested matter" means a case in which child custody, visitation rights, paternity or the grounds for the action are in dispute, and matters of monetary awards or the disposition of real or personal property may be in dispute.

[Amended June 28, 1999, effective January 1, 2000.]

§ 25-50. Case Management

(a) The presiding judge or a designee shall determine by the case management date which track each case shall take and assign each case for disposition. That date shall be set on a schedule approved by the presiding judge.

(b) If the matter is uncontested, and a form prescribed by the Office of the Chief Court Administrator has been filed, the clerk shall assign the matter to a date certain for disposition.

(c) With the approval of the presiding judge, a case management conference may be conducted by the filing of a stipulated scheduling order when only financial issues are outstanding. If there is a dispute with respect to financial issues, the matter may be directed to any alternative dispute resolution mechanism, private or court-annexed, or thereafter have assigned a date certain for family special masters and further judicial pretrial. Thereafter, the matter may be assigned for trial for a date certain if not resolved.

(d) In cases where custody or visitation issues are outstanding, the parties and counsel must appear for a case management conference on the case management date. If custody or visitation issues require judicial intervention, the appointment of counsel or a guardian ad litem for the minor child, or case study or evaluation by family services or by a private provider of services, a target date shall be assigned for completion of such study and the final conjoint thereon and thereafter a date certain shall be assigned for disposition.

(e) With respect to subsections (c) and (d), if a trial is required, such order may include a date certain for a trial management conference between counsel or pro se parties for the purpose of premarking exhibits and complying with other orders of the judicial authority to expedite the trial process.

[Amended June 28, 1999, effective January 1, 2000.]

§ 25-51. When Motion for Default for Failure to Appear Does Not Apply

(a) Any case claiming a dissolution of marriage, legal separation, or annulment in which the defendant has failed to file an appearance may be assigned a date certain for disposition as an uncontested matter pursuant to Section 25-50. If the defendant has not filed an appearance by the date assigned for disposition, the case may proceed to judgment without further notice to such defendant. Section 17-20 concerning motions for default shall not apply to such cases.

(b) If the defendant files an appearance by the date assigned for disposition, the presiding judge or a designee shall determine which track the case shall take pursuant to Section 25-50.

§ 25-52. Failure to Appear for Scheduled Disposition

If a party fails to appear in person or by counsel for a scheduled disposition, the opposing party may introduce evidence and the case may proceed to judgment without further notice to such party who failed to appear.

§ 25-53. Reference of Family Matters

In any family matter the court may, upon its own motion or upon motion of a party, refer any contested, limited contested, or uncontested matter for hearing and decision to a judge trial referee who shall have been a judge of the referring court. Such matters shall be deemed to have been referred for all further proceedings and judgment, including matters pertaining to any appeal therefrom, except that the referring court may retain jurisdiction to hear and decide any pendente lite or contempt matters.

§ 25-54. Order of Trial; Argument by Counsel

The provisions of Sections 15-5, 15-6 and 15-7, shall apply to family matters as defined in Section 25-1.

§ 25-55. Medical Evidence

A party who plans to offer a hospital record in evidence shall have the record in the clerk's office twenty-four hours prior to trial. The judge shall order that all such records be available for inspection in the clerk's office to any counsel of record under the supervision of the clerk. Counsel must recognize their responsibility to have medical testimony available when needed and shall, when necessary, subpoena medical witnesses to that end. Such records shall be submitted in accordance with the provisions of Section 7-18.

[Amended June 28, 1999, effective January 1, 2000.]

§ 25-56. Production of Documents at Hearing or Trial

(a) At the trial management conference prior to the commencement of an evidentiary hearing or trial, but in no event later than five days before the scheduled hearing date, either party may serve on the other a request for production of documents and tangible things, in a manner consistent with Sections 13-9 through 13-11. Service may be made in the same manner as a subpoena or consistent with Sections 10-12 through 10-14.

(b) If a party fails to produce the requested documents and items, the party filing the request shall be permitted to introduce into evidence such copies as that party might have, without having to authenticate the copies offered.

(c) If a party fails to produce the requested documents and items and the requesting party does not have copies to offer into evidence, the judicial authority may impose such sanctions on the nonproducing party as the judicial authority deems appropriate pursuant to Section 13-14 and as are available to the judicial authority for the enforcement of subpoenas.

§ 25-57. Affidavit Concerning Children

Before the judicial authority renders any order in any matter pending before it involving the custody, visitation or support of a minor child or children, an affidavit shall be filed with the judicial authority averring (1) whether the wife is believed to be pregnant, (2) the name and date of birth of any minor child born since the date of the filing of the complaint or the application; (3) information which meets the requirements of the Uniform Child Custody Jurisdiction and Enforcement Act, General Statutes § 46b-115, et seq.; (4) that there is no other proceeding in which either party has participated as a party, witness, or otherwise concerning custody of the child in any state; and (5) that no person not a party has physical custody or claims custody or visitation rights with respect to the child. This section shall not apply to modifications of existing support orders or in situations involving allegations of contempt of support orders.

[Amended July 23, 1998, effective January 1, 1999; June 28, 1999, effective January 1, 2000; amended August 24, 2001, effective January 1, 2002.]

§ 25-58. Reports of Dissolution of Marriage and Annulment

Before a hearing is commenced for a dissolution or annulment of marriage, the parties concerned, or their attorneys, shall provide, on forms prescribed by the chief court administrator and furnished by the clerk, such information as is required by the judges of the superior court.

[Amended June 28, 1999, effective January 1, 2000.]

§ 25-59. Closure of Courtroom in Family Matters

<Text of section effective until January 1, 2005>

(a) Except as otherwise provided by law, there shall be a presumption that courtroom proceedings shall be open to the public.

(b) Except as provided in this section and except as otherwise provided by law, the judicial authority shall not order that the public be excluded from any portion of a courtroom proceeding.

(c) Upon motion of any party, or upon its own motion, the judicial authority may order that the public be excluded from any portion of a courtroom proceeding only if the judicial authority concludes that such order is necessary to preserve an interest which is determined to override the public's interest in attending such proceeding. The judicial authority shall first consider reasonable alternatives to any such order and any such order shall be no broader than necessary to protect such overriding interest. An agreement of the parties to close the courtroom shall not constitute a sufficient basis for the issuance of such an order.

(d) In connection with any order issued pursuant to subsection (c) of this section, the judicial authority shall articulate the overriding interest being protected and shall specify its findings underlying such order. If any findings would reveal information entitled to remain confidential, those findings may be set forth in a sealed portion of the record. The time, date and scope of any such order shall be in writing and shall be signed by the judicial authority and be entered by the court clerk in the court file. The judicial authority shall order that a transcript of its decision be included in the file or prepare a memorandum setting forth the reasons for its order.

(e) A motion to close a courtroom proceeding shall be filed not less than fourteen days before the proceeding is scheduled to be heard. Such motion shall be placed on the short calendar so that notice to the public is given of the time and place of the hearing on the motion and to afford the public an opportunity to be heard on the motion under consideration. The motion itself may be filed under seal, where appropriate, by leave of the judicial authority. When placed on a short calendar, motions filed under this rule shall be listed in a separate section titled "Motions to Seal or Close" and shall also be listed with the time, date and place of the hearing on the Judicial Branch web site. A copy of the short calendar page containing the aforesaid section shall, upon issuance of the short calendar, be posted on a bulletin board adjacent to the clerk's office and accessible to the public.

[Amended May 14, 2003, effective July 1, 2003.]

<For text of section effective January 1, 2005, see § 25–59, post>

Commentary

The public and press enjoy a right of access to attend trials in civil as well as criminal cases. *Globe Newspaper Co. v. Superior Court*, 457 U.S. 596, 606 (1982); *Press–Enterprises Co. v. Superior Court*, 478 U.S. 1 (1986) (*Press Enterprises II*); *Westmoreland v. CBS, Inc.*, 752 F.2d 16 (2d Cir. 1984).

For a further discussion of court closure, see the Commentary to Sections 11–20 and 42–49.

It is intended that the above rule also apply to family support magistrates.

§ 25–59. Closure of Courtroom in Family Matters (Later effective version)

<Text of section effective January 1, 2005>

(a) Except as otherwise provided by law, there shall be a presumption that courtroom proceedings shall be open to the public.

(b) Except as provided in this section and except as otherwise provided by law, the judicial authority shall not order that the public be excluded from any portion of a courtroom proceeding.

(c) Upon motion of any party, or upon its own motion, the judicial authority may order that the public be excluded from any portion of a courtroom proceeding only if the judicial authority concludes that such order is necessary to preserve an interest which is determined to override the public's interest in attending such proceeding. The judicial authority shall first consider reasonable alternatives to any such order and any such order shall be no broader than necessary to protect such overriding interest. An agreement of the parties to close the courtroom shall not constitute a sufficient basis for the issuance of such an order.

(d) In connection with any order issued pursuant to subsection (c) of this section, the judicial authority shall articulate the overriding interest being protected and shall specify its findings underlying such order. If any findings would reveal information entitled to remain confidential, those findings may be set forth in a sealed portion of the record. The time, date and scope of any such order shall be set forth in a writing signed by the judicial authority which upon issuance the court clerk shall immediately enter in the court file. The judicial authority shall order that a transcript of its decision be included in the file or prepare a memorandum setting forth the reasons for its order.

(e) A motion to close a courtroom proceeding shall be filed not less than fourteen days before the proceeding is scheduled to be heard. Such motion shall be placed on the short calendar so that notice to the public is given of the time and place of the hearing on the motion and to afford the public an opportunity to be heard on the motion under consideration. The motion itself may be filed under seal, where appropriate, by leave of the judicial authority. When placed on a short calendar, motions filed under this rule shall be listed in a separate section titled "Motions to Seal or Close" and shall also be listed with the time, date and place of the hearing on the judicial branch web site. A copy of the short calendar page containing the aforesaid section shall, upon issuance of the short calendar, be posted on a bulletin board adjacent to the clerk's office and accessible to the public.

[Amended May 14, 2003, effective July 1, 2003; amended June 21, 2004, effective January 1, 2005.]

<For text of section effective until January 1, 2005, see § 25–59, ante>

Commentary

As used in paragraph (a) above, the words "except as otherwise provided by law" are intended to exempt from the operation of this rule all established procedures for the closure of courtroom proceedings as required or permitted by statute; *e.g.* Gen. Stat. §§ 19a–583(a)(10)(D) (pertaining to court proceedings as to disclosure of confidential HIV-related information), 36a–21(b) (pertaining to court proceedings at which certain records of the Department of Banking are disclosed), 46b–11 (pertaining to hearings in family relations matters), 54–86c(b) (pertaining to the disclosure of exculpatory information or material), 54–86f (pertaining to the admissibility of evidence of sexual conduct) and 54–86g (pertaining to the testimony of a victim of child abuse); other rules of practice; *e.g.* Practice Book Sec. 40–43; and/or controlling state or federal case law.

The above amendment to subsection (d) establishes a mechanism by which the public and the press, who are empowered by this rule to object to pending motions to close the courtroom in family matters, will receive timely notice of the court's disposition of such motions.

§ 25–59A. Sealing Files or Limiting Disclosure of Documents in Family Matters

<Text of section effective until January 1, 2005>

(a) Except as otherwise provided by law, there shall be a presumption that documents filed with the court shall be available to the public.

(b) Except as provided in this section and except as otherwise provided by law, including Section 13–5, the judicial authority shall not order that any files, affidavits, documents, or other materials on file with the court or filed in connection with a court proceeding be sealed or their disclosure limited.

(c) Upon written motion of any party, or upon its own motion, the judicial authority may order that files, affidavits, documents, or other materials on file or lodged with the court or in connection with a court proceeding be sealed or their disclosure limited only if the judicial authority concludes that such order is necessary to preserve an interest which is determined to override the public's interest in viewing such materials. The judicial authority shall first consider reasonable alternatives to any such order and any such order shall be no broader than necessary to protect such overriding interest. An agreement of the parties to seal or limit the disclosure of documents on file with the court or filed in connection with a court proceeding shall not constitute a sufficient basis for the issuance of such an order.

(d) In connection with any order issued pursuant to subsection (c) of this section, the judicial authority shall articulate the overriding interest being protected and shall specify its findings underlying such order and the duration of such order. If any findings would reveal information entitled to remain confidential, those findings may be set forth in a sealed portion of the record. The time, date, scope and duration of any such order shall forthwith be reduced to writing and be signed by the judicial authority and entered by the court clerk in the court file. The judicial authority shall order that a transcript of its decision be included in the file or prepare a memorandum setting forth the reasons for its order.

(e) Except as otherwise ordered by the judicial authority, a motion to seal or limit the disclosure of affidavits, documents, or other materials on file or lodged with the court or filed in connection with a court proceeding shall be calendared so that notice to the public is given of the time and place of the hearing on the motion and to afford the public an opportunity to be heard on the motion under consideration. The procedures set forth in Sections 7–4B and 7–4C shall be followed in connection with a motion to file affidavits, documents or other materials under seal or to limit their disclosure.

(f)(1) A motion to seal the contents of an entire court file shall be placed on the short calendar to be held not less than fifteen days following the filing of the motion, unless the judicial authority otherwise directs, so that notice to the public is given of the time and place of the hearing on the motion and to afford the public an opportunity to be heard on the motion under consideration. The procedures set forth in Sections 7–4B and 7–4C shall be followed in connection with such motion.

(2) The judicial authority may issue an order sealing the contents of an entire court file only upon a finding that there is not available a more narrowly tailored method of protecting the overriding interest, such as redaction or sealing a portion of the file. The judicial authority shall state in its decision or order each of the more narrowly tailored methods that was considered and the reason each such method was unavailable or inadequate.

(g) The provisions of this section shall not apply to settlement conferences or negotiations or to documents submitted to the court in connection with such conferences or negotiations. The provisions of this section shall apply to settlement agreements which have been filed with the court or have been incorporated into a judgment of the court.

(h) Sworn statements of current income, expenses, assets and liabilities filed with the court pursuant to Section 25–30 shall be under seal and be disclosable only to the judicial authority, to court personnel and to the parties to the action and their attorneys, except as otherwise ordered by the judicial authority. When such sworn statements are filed the clerk shall place them in a sealed envelope clearly identified with the words "Financial Affidavit." All such sworn statements that are filed in a case may be placed in the same sealed envelope. Any person may file a motion to unseal these documents. When such motion is filed, the provisions of paragraphs (a) through (e) of this section shall apply and the party who filed the documents shall have the burden of proving that they should remain sealed. The judicial authority shall order that the automatic sealing pursuant to this paragraph shall terminate with respect to all such sworn statements then on file with the court when any hearing is held at which financial issues are in dispute. This shall not preclude a party from filing a motion to seal or limit disclosure of such sworn statements pursuant to this section.

(i) When placed on a short calendar, motions filed under this rule shall be listed in a separate section titled "Motions to Seal or Close" and shall also be listed with the time, date and place of the hearing on the Judicial Branch web site. A copy of the short calendar page containing the aforesaid section shall, upon issuance of the short calendar, be posted on a bulletin board adjacent to the clerk's office and accessible to the public.

[Adopted May 14, 2003, effective July 1, 2003.]

<For text of section effective January 1, 2005, see § 25–59A, post>

Commentary

The public and press enjoy a right of access to attend trials in civil as well as criminal cases. See *Nixon v. Warner Communications, Inc.*, 435 U.S. 589, 597–608, 98 S. Ct. 1306, 55 L. Ed. 2d 570 (1978). The guarantee of open public proceedings in civil trials applies as well to the sealing of court documents. See *Publicker Industries, Inc. v. Cohen*, 733 F.2d 1059, 1070–1071 (3d Cir. 1984).

See also the Commentary to Section 42–49A.

Paragraph (h) is proposed to minimize the potential for abuse that can result when personal financial information is made available to persons who engage in identity theft or other illegal activities.

It is intended that paragraph (h) not apply retroactively to sworn statements that have been filed before the effective date of this rule.

It is intended that the above rule also apply to family support magistrates.

It is intended that the use of pseudonyms in place of the name of a party or parties not be permitted in family cases.

§ 25–59A. Sealing Files or Limiting Disclosure of Documents in Family Matters (Later effective version)

<Text of section effective January 1, 2005>

(a) Except as otherwise provided by law, there shall be a presumption that documents filed with the court shall be available to the public.

(b) Except as provided in this section and except as otherwise provided by law, including Section 13–5, the judicial authority shall not order that any files, affidavits, documents, or other materials on file with the court or filed in connection with a court proceeding be sealed or their disclosure limited.

(c) Upon written motion of any party, or upon its own motion, the judicial authority may order that files, affidavits, documents, or other materials on file or lodged with the court or in connection with a court proceeding be sealed or their disclosure limited only if the judicial authority concludes that such order is necessary to preserve an interest which is determined to override the public's interest in viewing such materials. The judicial authority shall first consider reasonable alternatives to any such order and any such order shall be no broader than necessary to protect such overriding interest. An agreement of the parties to seal or limit the disclosure of documents on file with the court or filed in connection with a court proceeding shall not constitute a sufficient basis for the issuance of such an order.

(d) In connection with any order issued pursuant to subsection (c) of this section, the judicial authority shall articulate the overriding interest being protected and shall specify its findings underlying such order and the duration of such order. If any findings would reveal information entitled to remain confidential, those findings may be set forth in a sealed portion of the record. The time, date, scope and duration of any such order shall be set forth in a writing signed by the judicial authority which upon issuance the court clerk shall immediately enter in the court file. The judicial authority shall order that a transcript of its decision be included in the file or prepare a memorandum setting forth the reasons for its order.

(e) Except as otherwise ordered by the judicial authority, a motion to seal or limit the disclosure of affidavits, documents, or other materials on file or lodged with the court or filed in connection with a court proceeding shall be calendared so that notice to the public is given of the time and place of the hearing on the motion and to afford the public an opportunity to be heard on the motion under consideration. The procedures set forth in Sections 7–4B and 7–4C shall be followed in connection with a motion to file affidavits, documents or other materials under seal or to limit their disclosure.

(f) (1) A motion to seal the contents of an entire court file shall be placed on the short calendar to be held not less than fifteen days following the filing of the motion, unless the judicial authority otherwise directs, so that notice to the public is given of the time and place of the hearing on the motion and to afford the public an opportunity to be heard on the motion under consideration. The procedures set forth in Sections 7–4B and 7–4C shall be followed in connection with such motion.

(2) The judicial authority may issue an order sealing the contents of an entire court file only upon a finding that there is not available a more narrowly tailored method of protecting the overriding interest, such as redaction or sealing a portion of the file. The judicial authority shall state in its decision or order each of the more narrowly tailored methods that was

considered and the reason each such method was unavailable or inadequate.

(g) The provisions of this section shall not apply to settlement conferences or negotiations or to documents submitted to the court in connection with such conferences or negotiations. The provisions of this section shall apply to settlement agreements which have been filed with the court or have been incorporated into a judgment of the court.

(h) Sworn statements of current income, expenses, assets and liabilities filed with the court pursuant to Section 25–30 shall be under seal and be disclosable only to the judicial authority, to court personnel, to the parties to the action and their attorneys, and to any guardians ad litem and attorneys appointed for any minor children involved in the matter, except as otherwise ordered by the judicial authority. When such sworn statements are filed the clerk shall place them in a sealed envelope clearly identified with the words "Financial Affidavit." All such sworn statements that are filed in a case may be placed in the same sealed envelope. Any person may file a motion to unseal these documents. When such motion is filed, the provisions of paragraphs (a) through (e) of this section shall apply and the party who filed the documents shall have the burden of proving that they should remain sealed. The judicial authority shall order that the automatic sealing pursuant to this paragraph shall terminate with respect to all such sworn statements then on file with the court when any hearing is held at which financial issues are in dispute. This shall not preclude a party from filing a motion to seal or limit disclosure of such sworn statements pursuant to this section.

(i) When placed on a short calendar, motions filed under this rule shall be listed in a separate section titled "Motions to Seal or Close" and shall also be listed with the time, date and place of the hearing on the judicial branch web site. A copy of the short calendar page containing the aforesaid section shall, upon issuance of the short calendar, be posted on a bulletin board adjacent to the clerk's office and accessible to the public.

[Adopted May 14, 2003, effective July 1, 2003; amended June 21, 2004, effective January 1, 2005.]

<*For text of section effective until January 1, 2005, see § 25–59A, ante*>

Commentary

As used in paragraph (a) above, the words "except as otherwise provided by law" are intended to exempt from the operation of this rule all established procedures for the sealing or *ex parte* filing, *in camera* inspection and/or nondisclosure to the public of documents, records and other materials, as required or permitted by statute; *e.g.* Gen. Stat. §§ 12–242vv (pertaining to taxpayer information), 52–146c *et seq.* (pertaining to the disclosure of psychiatric records) and 54–56g (pertaining to the pretrial alcohol education program); other rules of practice; *e.g.* Practice Book Secs. 7–18, 13–5(6)–(8) and 40–13(c); and/or controlling state or federal case law; *e.g. Matza v. Matza*, 226 Conn. 166 (1993) (establishing a procedure whereby an attorney seeking to withdraw from a case due to his client's anticipated perjury at trial may support his motion to withdraw by filing a sealed affidavit for the court's review).

The above amendment to subsection (d) establishes a mechanism by which the public and the press, who are empowered by this rule to object to pending motions to seal files or limit the disclosure of documents in family matters, will receive timely notice of the court's disposition of such motions.

The above change to subsection (h) adds to those categories of individuals to whom financial affidavits filed with the court pursuant to Section 25–30 are disclosable the following: guardians ad litem and attorneys appointed for the minor children.

§ 25–60. Family Division Evaluations and Studies

(a) Whenever, in any family matter, an evaluation or study has been ordered, the case shall not be disposed of until the report has been filed as hereinafter provided, and counsel and the parties have had a reasonable opportunity to examine it prior to the time the case is to be heard, unless the judicial authority shall order that the case be heard before the report is filed, subject to modification on the filing of the report.

(b) Any report of an evaluation or study shall be made in quadruplicate, shall be filed with the clerk, who will impound such reports, and shall be mailed to counsel of record. Said report shall be available for inspection only to counsel of record and to the parties to the action, unless otherwise ordered by the judicial authority.

(c) Said report shall be admissible in evidence provided the author of the report is available for cross-examination.

§ 25–61. Family Division

The Family Services Unit shall, at the request of the judicial authority, provide assistance with regard to issues concerning custody, visitation, finances, mediation, case management and such other matters as the judicial authority may direct.

§ 25–62. Appointment of Guardian Ad Litem

The judicial authority may appoint a guardian ad litem for a minor involved in any family matter. Unless the judicial authority orders that another person be appointed guardian ad litem, a family relations counselor shall be designated as guardian ad litem. The guardian ad litem is not required to be an attorney. If the guardian ad litem is not a family relations counselor, the judicial authority may order compensation for services rendered in accordance with the established judicial branch fee schedule.

§ 25-63. Right to Counsel in Family Civil Contempt Proceedings

(a) A person who is before the court in a civil contempt proceeding involving the failure to comply with the order of a judicial authority in a family matter and who faces potential incarceration shall be advised of his or her right to be represented by counsel and his or her right to court appointed counsel if he or she is indigent. If the person is unable to obtain counsel by reason of his or her indigency he or she shall have counsel appointed to represent him or her unless:

(1) He or she waives such appointment pursuant to Section 25-64; or

(2) At the time of the application for the appointment of counsel, the judicial authority eliminates incarceration as a possible result of the proceeding and makes a statement to that effect on the record.

(b) The person shall be further advised that no person shall continue to be detained in a correctional facility pursuant to an order of civil contempt for longer than thirty days, unless at the expiration of such thirty days he or she is presented to the judicial authority. On each such presentment, the contemnor shall be given an opportunity to purge himself or herself of the contempt by compliance with the order of the judicial authority. If the contemnor does not so act, the judicial authority may direct that the contemnor remain in custody under the terms of the order of the judicial authority then in effect, or may modify the order if the interests of justice so dictate.

(c) Any attorney appointed to represent the contemnor shall represent such contemnor only on the contempt, and shall not be appointed for any other purpose.

§ 25-64. Right to Counsel in Family Civil Contempt Proceedings—Waiver

A person shall be permitted to waive his or her right to counsel and shall be permitted to represent himself or herself at any stage of the proceedings, either prior to or following the appointment of counsel. A waiver will be accepted only after the judicial authority makes a thorough inquiry and is satisfied that the person:

(1) Has been clearly advised of his or her right to the assistance of counsel, including his or her right to the assignment of counsel when he or she is so entitled;

(2) Possesses the intelligence and capacity to appreciate the consequences of the decision to represent himself or herself;

(3) Comprehends the nature of the proceedings, the range of permissible sanctions and any additional facts essential to a broad understanding of the case; and

(4) Has been made aware of the risks and disadvantages of self-representation.

§ 25-65. Family Support Magistrates; Procedure

(a) The procedure in any matter which is to be heard and determined by a family support magistrate shall conform, where applicable, to the procedure in and for the superior court except as otherwise provided herein.

(b) Any pleading or motion filed in a family support magistrate matter shall indicate, in the lower right hand corner of the first page of the document, that it is a family support magistrate matter.

(c) Matters to be heard and determined by a family support magistrate shall be placed on the family support magistrate list.

(d) Matters on the family support magistrate list shall be assigned automatically by the family support magistrate clerk without the necessity of a written claim. No such matters shall be so assigned unless filed at least five days before the opening of court on the day the list is to be called.

(e) Matters upon the family support magistrate list shall not be continued except by order of a family support magistrate.

§ 25-66. Appeal from Decision of Family Support Magistrate

Any person who is aggrieved by a final decision of a family support magistrate may appeal such decision in accordance with the provisions of Public Act 86-359 of the General Statutes. The appeal shall be instituted by the filing of a petition which shall include the reasons for the appeal.

§ 25-67. Support Enforcement Services

In cases where the payment of alimony and support has been ordered, a support enforcement officer, where provided by statute, shall:

(1) Whenever there is a default in any payment of alimony or support of children under judgments of dissolution of marriage or separation, or of support under judgments of support, where necessary, (A) bring an application to a family support magistrate for a rule requiring said party to appear before a family support magistrate to show cause why such party should not be held in contempt, or (B) take such other action as is provided by rule or statute.

(2) In connection with subdivision (1) above, or at any other time upon direction of a family support magistrate, investigate the financial situation of the parties and report his or her findings thereon to a family support magistrate which may authorize the officer to bring an application for a rule requiring any party to appear before a family support magistrate to show cause why there should not be a modification of the judgment.

(3) In non-AFDC IV–D cases, review child support orders at the request of either parent subject to a support order or, in AFDC cases, review child support orders at the request of the bureau of child support enforcement and initiate and facilitate, but not advocate on behalf of either party, an action before a family support magistrate to modify such support order if it is determined upon such review that the order substantially deviates from the child support guidelines established pursuant to General Statutes §§ 46b–215a or 46b–215b. The requesting party shall have the right to such review every three years without proving a substantial change in circumstances; more frequent reviews shall be made only if the requesting party demonstrates a substantial change in circumstances.

[Amended June 29, 1998, effective January 1, 1999.]

§ 25–68. Right to Counsel in State Initiated Paternity Actions

(a) A putative father named in a state initiated paternity action shall be advised by the judicial authority of his right to be represented by counsel and his right to court appointed counsel if indigent. If he is unable to obtain counsel by reason of his indigency he shall have counsel appointed to represent him unless he waives such appointment pursuant to Section 25–64.

(b) In cases under this section a copy of the paternity petition shall be served on the attorney general in accordance with the provisions of Sections 10–12 through 10–17. The attorney general shall be a party to such cases, but he or she need not be named in the petition or summoned to appear.

§ 25–69. Social Services; Additional Duties

(a) Under the supervision and direction of the judicial authority, a family relations counselor shall, where there is a motion for change of custody of a child, or where his or her knowledge of the family situation causes him or her to believe that the welfare of the child requires a hearing on a change of custody, upon direction of the judicial authority, be permitted to investigate the domestic and financial situation of the parties and report his or her findings. The judicial authority may thereafter, on its own motion if necessary, hold a hearing thereon after such notice to the parties as it deems proper.

(b) Under the supervision and direction of the judicial authority, the family relations counselor shall conduct such investigations or mediation conferences in domestic relations matters as may be directed by the judicial authority.

(c) Under the supervision and direction of the judicial authority, the family relations counselor may, where necessary, bring an application to the court for a rule requiring a party to appear before the court to show cause why such party should not be held in contempt for failure to comply with an order of the judicial authority for visitation.

(d) Family relations caseworkers, family relations counselors and support enforcement officers shall investigate all criminal matters involving family relations cases referred to them by the prosecuting attorney or by the judicial authority.

PROCEDURE IN JUVENILE MATTERS

2003 JUVENILE MATTERS DISPOSITION TABLE

The table below shows where the subject matter of the Superior Court Rules, Procedure in Juvenile Matters, was redesignated in new sections of Chapters 26 through 35a, effective January 1, 2003.

Former Sections	New Sections
26–1	26–1
27–1	27–1A
27–2	Repealed
27–3	Repealed
27–4	27–4

Former Sections	New Sections
27–5	27–5
27–6	27–6
	27–7(b)
27–7	27–7
27–8	27–4A
28–1	27–8A
29–1	29–1
29–2	29–2
30–1	30–1A
30–2	Repealed
30–3	30–3
30–4	30–4
30–5	30–5
30–6	30–6
30–7	30–7
30–8	30–8
30–9	30–9
30–10	30–10
30–11	30–11
31–1	30a–1
31–2	30a–2
	See 30a–4
31–3	30a–2
31–4	Repealed
31–5	See 30a–5
31–6	30a–5
31–7	Repealed
31–8	See 30a–5
31–9	30a–6
31–10	31a–18
31–11	31a–13
31–12	31a–14
31–13	31a–15
32–1	33a–1
32–2	33a–2
32–3	33a–3
32–4	33a–4
32–5	33a–5
32–6	33a–6
32–7	See 33a–6
32–8	Repealed
32–9	33a–8
33–1	35a–1
33–2	33a–7
	35a–2
33–3	32a–8
	35a–7
33–4	35a–8
33–5	35a–9
33–6	35a–10
33–7	35a–11
33–8	35a–12
33–9	Repealed
33–10	Repealed
33–11	35a–16
33–12	35a–3
33–13	35a–19
34–1	32a–1
	33a–4(b)
34–2	32a–2
34–3	32a–3
34–4	32a–4
35–1	31a–1
	34a–1
35–2	Repealed
35–3	31a–16
	34a–20
35–4	35a–21
35–5	30a–7
	32a–7

CHAPTER 26. DEFINITIONS

Table of Sections

§ 26–1. Definitions Applicable to Proceedings on Juvenile Matters

In these definitions and in the rules of practice and procedure on juvenile matters, the singular shall include the plural and the plural, the singular where appropriate.

(a)(1) "Child" means any person under sixteen years of age and, for purposes of delinquency matters and family with service needs matters, "child" means any person (A) under sixteen years of age whose delinquent act or family with service needs conduct occurred prior to the person's sixteenth birthday or, (B) sixteen years of age or older who, prior to attaining sixteen years of age, has violated any federal or state law or municipal or local ordinance, other than an ordinance regulating behavior of a child in a family with service needs, and, subsequent to attaining sixteen years of age, violates any order of a judicial authority or any condition of probation ordered by a judicial authority with respect to such delinquency proceeding; (2) "Youth" means any person sixteen or seventeen years of age; (3) "Youth in crisis" means any youth who, within the last two years, (A) has without just cause run away from the parental home or other properly authorized and lawful place of abode; (B) is beyond the control of parents, guardian or other custodian; or (C) has four unexcused absences from school in any one month or ten unexcused absences in any school year; (4) The definitions of the terms "abused," "mentally deficient," "delinquent," "delinquent act," "dependent," "neglected," "uncared for," "alcohol-dependent," "family with service needs" "drug-dependent" "serious juvenile offense," "serious juvenile offender," and "serious juvenile repeat offender" shall be as set forth in General Statutes § 46b–120. (5) "Indian child" means an unmarried person under age eighteen who is either a member of a federally recognized Indian tribe or is eligible for membership in a federally recognized Indian tribe and is the biological child of a member of a federally recognized Indian tribe, and is involved in custody proceedings, excluding delinquency proceedings.

(b) "Commitment" means an order of the judicial authority whereby custody and/or guardianship of a child or youth are transferred to the Commissioner of the Department of Children and Families.

(c) "Complaint" means a written allegation or statement presented to the judicial authority that a child's or youth's conduct as a delinquent or situation as a child from a family with service needs or youth in crisis brings the child or youth within the jurisdiction of the judicial authority as prescribed by General Statutes § 46b–121.

(d) "Detention" means a secure building or staff secure facility for the temporary care of a child who is the subject of a delinquent complaint.

(e) "Guardian" means a person who has a judicially created relationship with a child which is intended to be permanent and self sustaining as evidenced by the transfer to the caretaker of the following parental rights with respect to the child: protection, education, care and control of the person, custody of the person and decision making.

(f) "Hearing" means an activity of the court on the record in the presence of a judicial authority and shall include (1) "Adjudicatory hearing": A court hearing to determine the validity of the facts alleged in a petition or information to establish thereby the judicial authority's jurisdiction to decide the matter which is the subject of the petition or information; (2) "Contested hearing on an order of temporary custody" means a hearing on an *ex parte* order of temporary custody or an order to show cause which is held within ten days from the day of a preliminary hearing on such orders. Contested hearings shall be held on consecutive days except for compelling circumstances or at the request of the parent or guardian; (3) "Dispositive hearing": The judicial authority's jurisdiction to adjudicate the matter which is the subject of the petition or information having been established, a court hearing in which the judicial authority, after considering the social study or predispositional study and the total circumstances of the child, orders whatever action is in the best interests of the child and, where applicable, the community. In the discretion of the judicial authority, evidence concerning adjudication and disposition may be presented in a single hearing, (4) "Preliminary hearing" means a hearing on an *ex parte* order of temporary custody or an order to appear or the first hearing on a petition alleging that a child or youth is uncared for, neglected, or dependent. A preliminary hearing on any *ex parte* custody order or order to appear shall be held within ten days from the issuance of the order. (5) "Plea hearing" is a hearing at which (i) A parent or guardian who is a named respondent in a neglect, uncared for or dependency petition, upon being advised of his or her rights admits, denies, or pleads nolo contendere to allegations contained in the petition; or (ii) a child or youth who is a named respondent in a delinquency petition or information enters a plea of not guilty, guilty, or nolo contendere upon being advised of the charges against him or her contained in the information or petition, or a hearing at which a child or youth who is a named respondent in a family with service needs or youth in crisis petition admits or denies the allegations contained in the petition upon being advised of the allegations.

(g) "Parent" means a biological mother or father or adoptive, mother or father except a biological or adoptive mother or father whose parental rights have been terminated; or the father of any child born out of wedlock, provided at the time of the filing of the petition (A) he has been adjudicated the father of such child by a court which possessed the authority to make such adjudication, or (B) he has acknowledged in writing to be the father of such child, or (C) he has contributed regularly to the support of such child, or (D) his name appears on the birth certificate, or (E) he has filed a claim for paternity as provided under General Statutes § 46b–172a, or (F) he has been named in the petition as the father of the minor child by the mother.

(h) "Parties" includes: (1) The child or youth who is the subject of a proceeding and those additional persons as defined herein; (2) "Legal party": Any person, including a parent, whose legal relationship to the matter pending before the judicial authority is of such a nature and kind as to mandate the receipt of proper legal notice as a condition precedent to the establishment of the judicial authority's jurisdiction to adjudicate the matter pending before it; and (3) "Intervening party": Any person whose interest in the matter before the judicial authority is not of such a nature and kind as to entitle legal service as a prerequisite to the judicial authority's jurisdiction to adjudicate the matter pending before it but whose participation therein, at the discretion of the judicial authority, may promote the interests of justice. An "intervening party" may in any proceeding before the judicial authority be given notice thereof in any manner reasonably appropriate to that end, but no such "intervening party" shall be entitled, as a matter of right, to provision of counsel by the court.

(i) "Permanency plan" means a plan developed by the Commissioner of Children and Families for the permanent placement of a child in the commissioner's care. Permanency plans shall be reviewed by the judicial authority as prescribed in General Statutes §§ 17a–110(b), 17a–111b(b), 46b–129(k) and 46b–141 as amended by P.A. 01–142.

(j) "Petition" means a formal pleading, executed under oath alleging that the respondent is within the judicial authority's jurisdiction to adjudicate the matter which is the subject of the petition by reason of cited statutory provisions and seeking a disposition. Except for a petition for erasure of record, such petitions invoke a judicial hearing and shall be executed by any one of the parties authorized to do so by statute, provided a delinquency petition may be executed by either a probation officer or juvenile prosecutor.

(k) "Information" means a formal pleading executed by a prosecutor alleging that a child or youth in a delinquency matter is within the judicial authority's jurisdiction;

(*l*) "Probation" means a legal status created in delinquency cases following conviction whereby a respondent child is permitted to remain in the home or in the physical custody of a relative or other fit person subject to supervision by the court through the court's probation officers and upon such terms as the judicial authority determines, subject to the continuing jurisdiction of the judicial authority.

(m) "Respondent" means a child who is alleged to be a delinquent or a child from a family with service needs, or a youth in crisis, or a parent or a guardian of a child who is the subject of a petition alleging that the child is uncared for, neglected, or dependent or requesting termination of parental rights.

(n) "Specific steps" means those judicially determined steps the parent or guardian and the commissioner of children and families should take in order for the parent or guardian to retain or regain custody of a child or youth.

(*o*) "Supervision" includes: (1) "Nonjudicial supervision": A legal status without the filing of a petition or a court conviction or adjudication but following the child or youth's admission to a complaint wherein a probation officer exercises supervision over the child or youth with the consent of the child or youth and the parent; (2) "Protective supervision": A disposition following adjudication in neglected, uncared for or dependent cases created by an order of the judicial authority requesting a supervising agency other than the court to assume the responsibility of furthering the welfare of the family and best interests of the child when the child's place of abode remains with the parent or any suitable or worthy person, subject to the continuing jurisdiction of the court; and (3) "Judicial supervision": A legal status equivalent to probation for a child adjudicated to be from a family with service needs or subject to supervision pursuant to an order of suspended proceedings under General Statutes § 46b–133b.

(p) "Take into Custody Order" means an order by a judicial authority that a child be taken into custody and immediately turned over to a detention supervisor.

[Amended June 24, 2002, effective January 1, 2003.]

Commentary

This section has been transferred, with revisions, from Section 26–1. The amendments conform the definition of "child" with that which is set forth in Public Act 98–241 as codified by General Statutes § 46b–120. Separate definitions for "youth" and "youth in crisis" are now included pursuant to P.A. 02–109. Several phrases in (a)(4) are added pursuant to Public Act 95–225 as codified by General Statutes § 46b–120. It should be noted, however, that General Statutes § 17a–110(a) defines "child" as a person under the age of eighteen.

The amendment to subsection (d) includes the alternative detention centers within the definition of "detention." See General Statutes § 46b–132.

The amendments to subsection (e) conform it to Public Act 98–241 as codified by General Statutes § 17a–1(13) and the federal Adoption and Safe Families Act of 1997 (ASFA) which redefine the term "guardian."

With regard to subsection (f), the terms "plea hearing", "adjudicatory hearing," "trial," and "dispositive hearing" have different meanings in child protection, delinquency, Family with Service Needs and Youth in Crisis Cases. The definitions have been modified to encompass all of the references. As to new subparagraph (2), see General Statutes § 46b–129(f)(g)(h). As to new subparagraph (4), see General Statutes § 46b–129(d) which sets forth the purposes of the preliminary hearing. General Statutes § 46b–129(b) pertains to procedural requirements concerning requests for or issuance of orders of temporary custody.

The former subsection (g) was repealed because the process is now usually initiated by a summons. See General Statutes § 46b–133.

The amendment to what is now subsection (g) conforms it to Public Act 98–241, as codified by General Statutes § 17a–1(12) which deleted the word "natural" and replaced it with "biological." General Statutes §§ 46b–129 and 46b–172a set forth the procedures by which paternity may be established.

The amendment to subsection (h) conforms it to Public Act 98–241 as codified by General Statutes § 46b–129(c) which provides for intervention by grandparents.

With regard to subsection (i), General Statutes §§ 17a–111b(b), 46b–129(k)(2),(3), and 46b–141 require that permanency plans be reviewed by the judicial authority subsequent to a judicial determination that continued efforts to reunify the parent with the child are no longer necessary and that the judicial authority shall approve permanency plans in the best interests of the child and take into consideration the child's need for permanency. General Statutes § 46b–129(k)(1) specifies that motions for review of permanency plans shall be filed nine months after the date the child is voluntarily placed in the care and custody of the Commissioner of the Department of Children and Families or removed from the home by order of a court of competent jurisdiction. The judicial authority shall conduct hearings on motions for review of permanency plans within ninety days of the filing. Section 46b–141 as amended by P.A. 01–2 of the June Special Session requires that the Commissioner of the Department of Children and Families file a permanency plan for any delinquent committed to DCF at least sixty days prior to the expiration of the commitment, and further requires that the judicial authority hold a permanency hearing within 12 months of the commitment and every twelve months thereafter so long as the child remains committed.

The amendments to subsection (*l*), among other things, conform it to Public Act 95–225 which changed the term "adjudication" to "conviction."

With regard to subsection (n), General Statutes § 46b–129(b) requires that the judicial authority provide specific steps at the time an ex parte order for temporary custody is issued. General Statutes § 46b–129(j) requires that the judicial authority order specific steps at the time that a child is committed to the commissioner's care.

Subsection (q) was repealed because the term "vocational probation" is infrequently used.

CHAPTER 27. RECEPTION AND PROCESSING OF NONJUDICIAL DELINQUENCY, FAMILY WITH SERVICE NEEDS, OR YOUTH IN CRISIS COMPLAINTS, OR PETITIONS

Table of Sections

§ 27–1. Complaints; In General [Repealed]

[Repealed June 24, 2002, effective January 1, 2003.]

§ 27–1A. Referrals for Nonjudicial Handling

(a) Any police summons accompanied by a police report alleging an act of delinquency shall be in writing and signed by the police officer and filed with the clerk of the superior court for juvenile matters. After juvenile identification and docket numbers are entered, the summons and report shall be referred to the probation department for possible nonjudicial handling. Any family with service needs or youth in crisis complaint or petition may be designated by the probation department for nonjudicial handling.

(b) If the probation officer initiates a delinquency, family with service needs or youth in crisis petition that may be eligible for nonjudicial handling, the probation officer shall cause a summons to be issued or mailed to the child and parent or guardian containing a notice to appear setting forth with reasonable particularity the allegations of the petition and fixing a time and location of the court and date not less than seven days, excluding Saturdays, Sundays, and holidays, subsequent to service or mailing.

(c) Matters eligible for nonjudicial handling shall be designated as such on the docket. If the prosecuting authority objects to the designation, the judicial authority shall determine if such designation is appropriate. The judicial authority may refer to the Office of Juvenile Probation a matter so designated and may, sua sponte, refer a matter for nonjudicial handling prior to adjudication.

[Adopted June 24, 2002, effective January 1, 2003.]

Commentary

This section has been transferred, with revisions, from Section 27–1. It clarifies that cases initiated by police summons can also be handled nonjudicially. This section also was revised to include Youth In Crisis cases.

§ 27-2. Complaints—Insufficient Allegations in Complaints [Repealed]

[Repealed June 24, 2002, effective January 1, 2003.]

§ 27-3. Complaints—Sufficient Allegations in Complaints [Repealed]

[Repealed June 24, 2002, effective January 1, 2003.]

§ 27-4. Additional Offenses and Misconduct

Any additional police summons, complaint or petition regarding a child which is received by the court prior to action by the judicial authority on any pending request for nonjudicial handling shall be consolidated with the initial offenses or misconduct for purposes of eligibility for nonjudicial handling.

[Amended June 24, 2002, effective January 1, 2003.]

§ 27-4A. Ineligibility for Nonjudicial Handling

A child shall not be eligible for nonjudicial handling if one or more of the following apply, unless waived by the judicial authority:

(1) The alleged misconduct:

(a) is a serious juvenile offense under General Statutes § 46b-120, or any other felony or violation of General Statutes § 53a-54d;

(b) concerns the theft or unlawful use or operation of a motor vehicle; or

(c) concerns the sale of, or possession of with intent to sell, any illegal drugs or the use or possession of a firearm.

(2) The child was previously adjudged delinquent or a child from a family with service needs.

(3) The child admitted nonjudicially at least twice previously to have been delinquent or a child from a family with service needs.

(4) The alleged misconduct was committed by a child while on probation or under judicial supervision.

(5) If the nature of the alleged misconduct warrants judicial intervention.

[Adopted June 24, 2002, effective January 1, 2003.]

Commentary

This section has been transferred, with revisions, from Section 27-8, but eliminates those provisions which seemed to require that a child admit responsibility for the alleged misconduct before the case could be determined ineligible for nonjudicial handling.

§ 27-5. Initial Interview For Nonjudicial Handling Eligibility

(a) At the initial interview to determine eligibility for nonjudicial handling, held at the time of arraignment or notice date, the probation officer shall inquire of the child and parent or guardian whether they have read the court documents and understand the nature of the complaint set forth therein. Any allegations of misconduct being considered for nonjudicial handling, including any additional allegations not contained in the summons or notice to appear because they were filed with the court after the issuance of that notice shall likewise be explained in simple and nontechnical language.

(b) The probation officer shall inform the child and parent or guardian of their rights under Section 30a-1. If either the child or the parent or guardian state that they wish to be represented by counsel, or if the probation officer determines that a judicial hearing is necessary, the interview shall end. Any further interview to consider nonjudicial handling shall take place with counsel present unless waived.

[Amended June 24, 2002, effective January 1, 2003.]

Commentary

This section refers only to interviews for nonjudicial handling. Children whose misconduct cannot be considered for nonjudicial handling should not be interviewed by a probation officer until they have been presented before the judicial authority for an initial plea and have been advised of their rights.

§ 27-6. Denial of Responsibility

Where the child denies responsibility for the alleged misconduct, the interview shall end and the child and the parent or guardian shall be informed that, if the evidence warrants, the case will be set down for a judicial hearing to determine the child's responsibility for the alleged misconduct, for which hearing the child must have counsel unless waived and for which hearing the judicial authority will provide counsel if the parties cannot afford counsel.

[Amended June 24, 2002, effective January 1, 2003.]

§ 27-7. Denial of Responsibility—Written Statement of Responsibility

(a) Where the child and the parent or guardian affirm that they are ready to go forward with the investigation, with or without counsel, and to make a statement concerning the child's responsibility for the alleged misconduct, such affirmation must be embodied in a written statement of responsibility executed by both child and parent, or guardian, and, in the case of the child, in the presence of the parent or guardian.

(b) If a child orally acknowledges responsibility for the alleged misconduct but refuses to execute a written statement of responsibility, such an oral admission shall not be accepted as the equivalent of an admission, and the case shall be dealt with in the manner prescribed in Section 27-6. If the written statement of responsibility is executed, the probation officer shall accept it as authorization to proceed with those aspects of investigation which are essential to the compiling of the predispositional study.

(c) The age, intelligence and maturity of the child and the mutuality of interests between parent or guardian and child shall be weighed in determining their competency to execute such written statement of responsibility.

[Amended June 24, 2002, effective January 1, 2003.]

Commentary

Subsection (b) of this section has been transferred, with revisions, from Section 27–6(b).

§ 27–8. Initial Interview—Scheduling of Judicial Plea/Dispositional Hearing [Repealed]

[Repealed June 24, 2002, effective January 1, 2003.]

Commentary

This section has been transferred to Section 27–4A.

§ 27–8A. Nonjudicial Supervision

(a) If a child has acknowledged responsibility, for the alleged misconduct which is not one for which a judicial hearing is mandated pursuant to Section 27–4A, and the probation officer has then found from investigation of the child's total circumstances that some form of court accountability less exacting than that arising out of a court appearance appears to be in the child's best interests, the officer may, subject to the conditions imposed by subsection (b) hereof, place the child on nonjudicial supervision for a term established by the juvenile probation supervisor for a period not to exceed 180 days.

(b) Whenever the probation officer seeks to effect nonjudicial supervision, the parent and the child shall have a right to a conference with the probation officer's administrative superior, or a court hearing. Whenever a parent or child elects to pursue either or both rights, supervision shall be held in abeyance until the outcome thereof.

(c) Such nonjudicial supervision when completed shall constitute a resolution of the case, and thereafter a child may not again be presented for formal court action on the same summons, complaint or petition or the facts therein set forth, provided however, that a judicial hearing may be initiated on the original summons, complaint or petition during said supervision if there has been a failure to comply with terms of the supervision and any oral or written statement of responsibility shall not be used against the child. When the judicial authority refers the file for nonjudicial handling, the referral order should provide that upon successful completion of any nonjudicial handling, the matter will be dismissed and erased for all purposes except for subsequent consideration for nonjudicial handling under Section 27–4A.

[Adopted June 24, 2002, effective January 1, 2003.]

Commentary

This section has been transferred, with revisions, from Section 28–1, which was in a chapter by itself. The final sentence in subsection (c) replaced the prior reference to erasure because General Statutes § 46b–146 does not mention the applicability of erasure of cases that are handled nonjudicially. However, it is felt that fairness dictates that some provision for erasure should definitely address nonjudicially handled cases, which are less serious matters than those that are handled judicially.

CHAPTER 28. DELINQUENCY AND FAMILY WITH SERVICE NEEDS NONJUDICIAL SUPERVISION [REPEALED]

Table of Sections

---

§ 28–1. Nonjudicial Supervision [Repealed]

[Repealed June 24, 2002, effective January 1, 2003.]

Commentary

This section has been transferred to Section 27–8A.

CHAPTER 29. RECEPTION AND PROCESSING OF DELINQUENCY, CHILD FROM FAMILY WITH SERVICE NEEDS AND YOUTH IN CRISIS PETITIONS AND DELINQUENCY INFORMATIONS

Table of Sections

---

§ 29-1. Contents of Delinquency, Family with Service Needs, and Youth In Crisis Petitions or Delinquency Informations

(a) A delinquency petition or information shall set forth in plain, concise and definite language the offense which the petitioner contends the child has committed. The petition or information shall further state the citation of any provision of law which is the basis of the petition or information, together with a statement that the offense occurred on or about a particular date or period of time at a particular location.

(b) A family with service needs or youth in crisis petition shall set forth in plain, concise and definite language the specific misconduct which the petitioner contends the child or youth has committed. The petition shall further state the citation of any provision of law which is the basis of the petition, together with a statement that the misconduct occurred on or about a particular date or period of time at a particular location.

[Amended June 24, 2002, effective January 1, 2003.]

Commentary

Changes wrought by the passage of the 1995 Juvenile Justice Reform Act contemplate not only the use of petitions to commence delinquency cases, but also the filing of informations by the prosecuting authority subsequent to the issuance of warrants or summonses pursuant to General Statutes § 46b-133(a), (b) and (c). In practicality, most delinquency cases now commence in response to the issuance of a summons by a police officer and not by a simple referral of alleged delinquent conduct to the judicial authority. Public Act 00-177 created a status offense known as "youth in crisis" and procedural rules have been amended to include these types of actions.

§ 29-1A. Processing of Delinquency Petitions and Informations

The procedures promulgated in General Statutes §§ 46b-128 or 46b-133(a), (b) and (c) shall apply. Any police summons and report which requires judicial processing should be returned to the clerk for preparation of a formal information based on the police summons or report. The information, summons and report shall be submitted to the juvenile prosecutor for review and verified signature. The juvenile prosecutor may thereafter file an amendment or a substituted information.

[Adopted June 24, 2002, effective January 1, 2003.]

§ 29-1B. Processing of Family With Service Needs and Youth In Crisis Petitions

The procedures promulgated in General Statutes §§ 46b-149 and 46b-150f shall apply. Court process shall be initiated by a petition filed by a probation officer and signed and verified by the juvenile prosecutor.

[Adopted June 24, 2002, effective January 1, 2003.]

Commentary

Sections 29-1A and 29-1B clarify the various procedures to initiate court process and to include Youth In Crisis petitions. Petitions or informations alleging violation of probation or violation of orders of a judicial authority are delinquency cases and are included in Section 29-1A.

§ 29-2. Service of Petitions

(a) Notice of summons, together with a copy of the verified delinquency, family with service needs or youth in crisis petition, may be made to the child or youth and parent, guardian or other person having control of the child or youth by service in accordance with any one of the methods set out in General Statutes § 46b-128. Any notice sent by first class mail shall include a provision informing the party that appearance in court as a result of the notice may subject the appearing party to the jurisdiction of the court. If the child or youth does not appear on the plea date, service shall be made in accordance with General Statutes § 46b–128 or § 46b–149(d), as appropriate.

(b) Petitions alleging delinquency, family with service needs or youth in crisis misconduct shall be served or delivered not less than seven days before the date of the hearing which shall be held not more than thirty days from the date of filing of the petition.

[Amended June 24, 2002, effective January 1, 2003.]

Commentary

This section was revised to include Youth In Crisis petitions.

CHAPTER 30. DETENTION

Table of Sections

---

§ 30–1. Notice and Statement by Person Bringing Child to Detention [Repealed]

[Repealed June 24, 2002, effective January 1, 2003.]

§ 30–1A. Admission To Detention

Whenever an officer or other person intends to admit a child into detention, the provisions of General Statutes § 46b–133 shall apply.

[Adopted June 24, 2002, effective January 1, 2003.]

Commentary

Former sections 30–1 and 30–2 were inconsistent and incomplete statements of the statutory requirements for admitting a child into detention.

§ 30–2. Release [Repealed]

[Repealed June 24, 2002, effective January 1, 2003.]

§ 30–3. Advisement of Rights

Upon admission to detention, the child shall be advised of the right to remain silent and the right to counsel and be further advised of the right to a detention hearing in accordance with Sections 30–5 through 30–8, which hearing may be waived only with the written consent of the child and the child's attorney.

[Amended June 24, 2002, effective January 1, 2003.]

§ 30–4. Notice to Parents by Detention Personnel

If, upon admission, the officer or other person who brings the child to detention has not complied with the duty of notifying the parent or guardian as set forth in Section 30–1A, the detention supervisor or a designated representative shall make efforts to immediately notify the parent or guardian in the manner calculated most speedily to effect such notice and, upon the parent's or guardian's appearance at the detention facility, shall advise the parent or guardian of his or her rights and note the child's rights, including the child's right to a detention hearing.

[Amended June 24, 2002, effective January 1, 2003.]

§ 30–5. Detention Time Limitations

(a) No child shall be held in detention for more than twenty-four hours, excluding Saturdays, Sundays, and holidays, unless a delinquent petition or information alleging delinquent conduct has been filed and an order for such continued detention has been signed by the judicial authority.

(b) A hearing to determine probable cause and the need for further detention shall be held no later than the next business day following the arrest. However, a judicial finding of probable cause must be made within 48 hours of arrest, including Saturdays, Sundays and holidays. If there is no such finding of said probable cause within 48 hours of the arrest, the child shall be released from detention subject to an information and subsequent arrest by warrant or take into custody order.

[Amended June 24, 2002, effective January 1, 2003.]

Commentary

This section has been amended to insure that a child is presented at a detention release hearing no later than the next business day following an arrest. The former language seemed to require only that the judicial authority sign an order for continued detention.

§ 30-6. Basis for Detention

No child shall be held in detention unless it appears from the available facts that there is probable cause to believe that the child is responsible for the acts alleged and that there is (1) a strong probability that the child will run away prior to court hearing or disposition, or (2) a strong probability that the child will commit or attempt to commit other offenses injurious to the child or to the community before court disposition, or (3) probable cause to believe that the child's continued residence in the home pending disposition will not safeguard the best interests of the child or the community because of the serious and dangerous nature of the act or acts set forth in the attached delinquency petition, or (4) a need to hold the child for another jurisdiction, or (5) a need to hold the child to assure the child's appearance before the court, in view of a previous failure to respond to the court process. The court in exercising its discretion to detain under § 46b-133(d) may consider a suspended detention order with graduated sanctions as an alternative to detention in accordance with graduated sanctions procedures established by the judicial branch.

[Amended June 24, 2002, effective January 1, 2003.]

Commentary

The last sentence has been added to authorize the use of less restrictive alternatives to detention.

§ 30-7. Place of Detention Hearings

The initial detention hearing may be conducted in the superior court for juvenile matters at the detention facility where the child is held and, thereafter, detention hearings shall be held at the case venue.

[Amended June 24, 2002, effective January 1, 2003.]

§ 30-8. Initial Order for Detention; Waiver of Hearing

Such initial order of detention may be signed without a hearing only if there is a written waiver of the detention hearing by the child and the child's attorney and there is a finding by the judicial authority that the circumstances outlined in Section 30-5 pertain to the child in question. An order of detention entered without a hearing shall authorize the detention of the child for a period not to exceed ten days, including the date of admission, and may further authorize the detention supervisor or a designated representative to release the child to the custody of a parent, guardian or some other suitable person, with or without conditions of release, if detention is no longer necessary, except that no child shall be released from detention who is alleged to have committed a serious juvenile offense except by order of a judicial authority of the superior court. Such an ex parte order of detention shall not be renewable without a detention hearing before the judicial authority.

[Amended June 24, 2002, effective January 1, 2003.]

§ 30-9. Information Allowed at Detention Hearing

At the detention hearing the judicial authority may consider any information which is material and relevant to the issue of detention. Probable cause may be proven by sworn affidavit in lieu of testimony. The probation department may ascertain such factors as might pertain to any need for detention. Any written reports or social records made available to the judicial authority shall be made available to counsel of record and, in the absence of counsel, to the parties unless the judicial authority finds that the availability of such materials would be psychologically destructive to the relationship between members of the family. Either through direct access or by quotation or summation by the judicial authority, the parties should be made aware of such findings in the reports or social records as directly enter into the judicial authority's decision.

[Amended June 24, 2002, effective January 1, 2003.]

§ 30-10. Orders of a Judicial Authority after Initial Detention Hearing

(a) At the conclusion of the initial detention hearing, the judicial authority shall issue an order for detention on finding that at least one of the factors outlined in Section 30-5 applies to the child.

(b) If the child is placed in detention, such order for detention shall be for a period not to exceed fifteen days, including the date of admission, or until the dispositional hearing is held, whichever is the shorter period, unless, following a further detention review hearing, the order is renewed. Such detention review hearing may not be waived.

(c) If the child is not placed in detention but released on a suspended order of detention on conditions, such suspended order of detention shall continue to the dispositional hearing or until further order of the judicial authority. Said suspended order of detention may be reviewed by the judicial authority every fifteen days. Upon a finding of probable cause that the child has violated any condition, a judicial authority may issue a take into custody order or order such child to appear in court for a hearing on revocation of the suspended order of detention. Such an order to appear shall be served upon the child in accordance with General Statutes § 46b-128(b), or, if the child is represented, by serving the order to appear upon the child's counsel, who shall notify the child of the order and the hearing date. After a hearing and upon a finding that the child has violated reasonable conditions imposed on release, the judicial authority may impose different or additional conditions of release or may remand the child to detention.

(d) In conjunction with any order of release from detention the judicial authority may, in accordance with General Statutes § 46b–133(f), order the child to participate in a program of periodic drug testing and treatment as a condition of such release. The results of any such drug test shall be admissible only for the purposes of enforcing the conditions of release from detention.

[Amended June 24, 2002, effective January 1, 2003.]

Commentary

The language in subsection (b) has been amended to clarify the distinction between an initial detention hearing and a subsequent detention review hearing. Subsection (c) was amended to set forth the means of enforcing conditions of suspended detention orders so that a take into custody order is not the only alternative.

§ 30–11. Detention after Dispositional Hearing

While awaiting implementation of the judicial authority's order, a child may be held in detention subsequent to the dispositional hearing, provided a hearing to review the circumstances and conditions of such detention order shall be conducted every fifteen days and such hearing may not be waived.

CHAPTER 30a. DELINQUENCY, FAMILY WITH SERVICE NEEDS AND YOUTH IN CRISIS HEARINGS

Table of Sections

---

§ 30a–1. Initial Plea Hearing

(a) The judicial authority shall begin the hearing by determining whether all necessary parties are present and that the rules governing service for nonappearing parties have been complied with, and shall note these facts for the record. The judicial authority shall then inform the parties of the substance of the petition or information.

(b) In age appropriate language, the judicial authority prior to any plea shall advise the child or youth and parent or guardian of the following rights:

(1) That the child or youth is not obligated to say anything and that anything that is said may be used against the child or youth.

(2) That the child or youth and the parent or guardian is entitled to the services of an attorney and that if the child or youth or parent or guardian is unable to pay, an application for a public defender or court-appointed attorney should be completed and filed with the office of the public defender or the clerk of the court to request an attorney without cost.

(3) That the child or youth will not be questioned unless he or she consents, that the child or youth can consult with an attorney before being questioned and may have an attorney present during questioning, and that the child or youth can stop answering questions at any time.

(4) That the child or youth has the right to a trial and the rights of confrontation and cross-examination of witnesses.

(c) Notwithstanding any prior statement acknowledging responsibility for the acts alleged, the judicial authority shall inquire of the child whether the child presently admits or denies the allegations of the petition or information.

[Adopted June 24, 2002, effective January 1, 2003.]

Commentary

Subsections (a) and (c) of this section have been transferred, with revisions, from Section 31–1(a) and (b). The word "information" has been added since most delinquency matters are now initiated by such, rather than a petition. Subsection (b) has been added to clarify the constitutional and statutory rights accorded the child or youth and the parent or guardian. See General Statutes § 46b–135.

§ 30a–2. Pretrial Conference

(a) When counsel is requested, or responsibility is denied, the case may be continued for a pretrial conference. At the pretrial, the parties may agree that a substitute information will be filed, or that certain charges will be nolled or dismissed. If the child or youth and parent or guardian subsequently execute a written statement of responsibility at the pretrial conference, or the attorney for the child or youth conveys to the prosecutor an agreement on the adjudicatory grounds, a predispositional study shall be compiled by the probation department and the case shall be assigned for a plea and dispositional hearing.

(b) If a plea agreement has been reached by the parties which contemplates the entry of an admission in a family with service needs or youth in crisis case, or a plea of guilty or nolo contendere in a delinquency case, and the recommendation of a particular disposition, the agreement shall be disclosed in open court at the time the plea is offered. Thereupon the judicial authority may accept or reject any agreement, or may defer the decision on acceptance or rejection of the agreement until it has had an opportunity to review the predispositional study.

[Adopted June 24, 2002, effective January 1, 2003.]

Commentary

This section has been transferred, with revisions, from Section 31–2. To clarify standard pretrial practice and to eliminate, for the sake of expediting the movement of cases, the onerous practice that a written statement of responsibility must be executed pursuant to an agreement to admit, plead guilty or nolo contendere. Subsection (b) provides for the use of oral plea agreements and allows the judicial authority to postpone acceptance of the plea until it has had an opportunity to consider the predispositional study. As a result of the 1995 Juvenile Justice Reform Act, the use of the word "admission" for delinquency matters is obsolete, as statutory amendments now refer to a plea of guilty.

§ 30a–3. Pretrial Conference—Standards of Proof; Burden of Going Forward

(a) The standard of proof for a delinquency conviction is evidence beyond a reasonable doubt and for a family with service needs adjudication is clear and convincing evidence.

(b) The burden of going forward with evidence shall rest with the juvenile prosecutor, or with the petitioner's counsel, as the case may be.

[Adopted June 24, 2002, effective January 1, 2003; amended June 30, 2003, effective January 1, 2004.]

Commentary

The above change sets forth the standards of proof in delinquency and family with service needs cases.

§ 30a–4. Plea Canvass

To assure that any plea or admission is voluntary and knowingly made, the judicial authority shall address the child or youth in age appropriate language to determine that the child or youth substantially understands:

(1) The nature of the charges;

(2) The factual basis of the charges;

(3) The possible penalty, including any extensions or modifications;

(4) That the plea or admission must be voluntary and not the result of force, threats, or promises, apart from the plea agreement;

(5) That the child or youth has (i) the right to deny responsibility or plead not guilty or to persist if that denial or plea has already been made, (ii) the right to be tried by a judicial authority, (iii) that at trial the child or youth has the right to the assistance of counsel, the right to confront and cross examine witnesses against him or her, and the right not to be compelled to incriminate himself or herself.

[Adopted June 24, 2002, effective January 1, 2003.]

Commentary

This section insures that a child or youth entering an admission or plea of guilty or nolo contendere is fully advised of the effect and possible consequences of the admission or plea. See *In Re Jason C.*, 255 Conn. 565 (2001). (Juvenile is entitled to be advised of the possibility of commitment extensions when making plea.)

§ 30a–5. Dispositional Hearing

(a) The dispositional hearing may follow immediately upon a conviction or an adjudication.

(b) The judicial authority may admit into evidence any testimony which is considered relevant to the issue of the disposition, in any form the judicial authority finds of probative value, but no disposition shall be made by the judicial authority until the predispositional study, unless waived, has been submitted. A written predispositional study may be waived by the judicial authority for good cause shown upon the request of the parties, provided that the basis for the waiver and the probation officer's oral summary of any investigation are both placed on the record.

(c) The prosecutor and the child or youth and parent or guardian shall have the right to produce witnesses on behalf of any dispositional plan they may wish to offer.

(d) Prior to any disposition, the child or youth shall be allowed a reasonable opportunity to make a personal statement to the judicial authority in mitigation of any disposition.

[Adopted June 24, 2002, effective January 1, 2003.]

Commentary

Subsections (a) and (b) of this section have been transferred, with revisions, from Section 31–6. See General Statutes § 46b–134. New subsection (c) clarifies that not only the child, youth, parent or guardian has the right to produce witnesses at the dispositional hearing, but the prosecutor does as well. As to subsection (d), see *State v. Hedman*, 62 Conn.App. 403 (2001).

§ 30a-6. Dispositional Hearing—Statement on Behalf of Victim

Whenever a victim of an alleged delinquent act, the parent or guardian of such victim, a General Statutes § 54-221 advocate or such victim's counsel exercises the right to appear before the judicial authority for the purpose of making a statement to the judicial authority concerning the disposition of the case, all parties, including the probation officer, shall be so notified. No statement shall be received unless the alleged delinquent has signed a statement of responsibility, confirmed a plea agreement or been convicted as a delinquent.

[Adopted June 24, 2002, effective January 1, 2003.]

Commentary

This section has been transferred from Section 31-9.

§ 30a-7. Recording of Hearings

A verbatim stenographic or electronic recording shall be kept of any hearing, the transcript of which shall form part of the record of the case.

[Adopted June 24, 2002, effective January 1, 2003.]

Commentary

This section has been transferred, with revisions, from subsection (a) of section 35-5. Some grammatical corrections have been made, and the title has been changed to clarify that the entire hearing, not just testimony, must be recorded.

§ 30a-8. Records

(a) Except as otherwise provided by statute, all records maintained in juvenile matters brought before the judicial authority, either current or closed, including transcripts of hearings, shall be kept confidential.

(b) Except as otherwise provided by statute, no material contained in the court records, including the predispositional study, medical or clinical reports, school reports, police reports, or the reports of social agencies, may be copied or otherwise reproduced in written form in whole or in part by the parties or their counsel without the express consent of the judicial authority.

[Adopted June 24, 2002, effective January 1, 2003.]

Commentary

This section is similar to Section 32a-7 in the rules for child protection proceedings. Changes were made to achieve consistency with General Statutes § 46b-124, which has been amended to allow for broader rules of disclosure than Section 35-5(b) and (c) permitted.

CHAPTER 31. DELINQUENCY AND FAMILY WITH SERVICE NEEDS HEARING [REPEALED]

Table of Sections

---

§ 31-1. Adjudicatory Hearing; Actions by Judicial Authority [Repealed]

[Repealed June 24, 2002, effective January 1, 2003.]

Commentary

Subsections (a) and (b) of this section have been transferred to Section 30a-1. The subject matter of subsection (c) is dealt with in Section 30a-4.

§ 31-2. Adjudicatory Hearing—Continuance for Pretrial Conference [Repealed]

[Repealed June 24, 2002, effective January 1, 2003.]

Commentary

This section has been transferred to Section 30a-2.

§ 31-3. Adjudicatory Hearing—Burden of Going Forward [Repealed]

[Repealed June 24, 2002, effective January 1, 2003.]

Commentary

This section has been transferred to Section 30a-3.

§ 31-4. Adjudicatory Hearing—Physical Presence of Child [Repealed]

[Repealed June 24, 2002, effective January 1, 2003.]

§ 31-5. Dispositional Hearing; Factors to Be Considered by Judicial Authority [Repealed]

[Repealed June 24, 2002, effective January 1, 2003.]

Commentary

The subject matter of this section is dealt with in Section 30a-5.

§ 31-6. Dispositional Hearing—When Held; Evidence and Predispositional Study [Repealed]

[Repealed June 24, 2002, effective January 1, 2003.]

Commentary

This section has been transferred to Section 30a-5.

§ 31-7. Dispositional Hearing—Availability of Predispositional Study to Counsel and Parties [Repealed]

[Repealed June 24, 2002, effective January 1, 2003.]

§ 31-8. Dispositional Hearing—Dispositional Plan Offered by Child or Parent [Repealed]

[Repealed June 24, 2002, effective January 1, 2003.]

Commentary

The subject matter of this section is dealt with in 30a-5.

§ 31-9. Dispositional Hearing—Statement on Behalf of Victim [Repealed]

[Repealed June 24, 2002, effective January 1, 2003.]

Commentary

This section has been transferred to Section 30a-6.

§ 31-10. Modification of Probation and Supervision [Repealed]

[Repealed June 24, 2002, effective January 1, 2003.]

Commentary

This section has been transferred to Section 31a-18.

§ 31-11. Take into Custody [Repealed]

[Repealed June 24, 2002, effective January 1, 2003.]

Commentary

This section has been transferred to Section 31a-13.

§ 31-12. Physical and Mental Examinations [Repealed]

[Repealed June 24, 2002, effective January 1, 2003.]

Commentary

This section has been transferred to Section 31a-14.

§ 31-13. Mentally Ill Children [Repealed]

[Repealed June 24, 2002, effective January 1, 2003.]

Commentary

This section has been transferred to Section 31a-15.

CHAPTER 31a. DELINQUENCY, FAMILY WITH SERVICE NEEDS AND YOUTH IN CRISIS MOTIONS AND APPLICATIONS

Table of Sections

---

§ 31a–1. Motions and Amendments

(a) A motion other than one made during a hearing shall be in writing and have annexed to it a proper order and, where appropriate, shall be in the form called for by Section 4–1. A motion shall state in paragraphs successively numbered the specific grounds upon which it is made. A copy of the written motion shall be served on the opposing party or counsel pursuant to Sections 10–12 through 10–17.

(b) Motions shall be filed no later than ten days after the date the matter is scheduled for trial except with the permission of the judicial authority. All motions shall be calendared to be heard by the judicial authority within fifteen days after filing provided reasonable notice is given to parties in interest, or notices are waived. Any motion filed in a case on trial or assigned for trial may be disposed of by the judicial authority at its discretion or ordered upon the docket.

(c) If the moving party determines and reports that all counsel and pro se parties agree to the granting of a motion or the consideration of a motion without the need for oral argument or testimony, or the motion states on its face that there is such an agreement, the motion may be granted without a hearing.

(d) A petition or information may be amended at any time by the judicial authority on its own motion or in response to the motions of any party prior to any final adjudication. When an amendment has been so ordered, a continuance shall be granted whenever the judicial authority finds that the new allegations in the petition justify the need for additional time to permit the parties to respond adequately to the additional or changed facts and circumstances.

[Adopted June 24, 2002, effective January 1, 2003.]

Commentary

Subsections (a), (b) and (d) have been transferred, with revisions, from subsections 35–1(b) and (c). These amendments to juvenile procedure are intended to create entirely separate chapters for delinquency, family with service needs, and youth in crisis matters, distinct from procedure applicable to neglect, uncared for, dependent and termination matters. Subsection (c) is new and is intended to provide for the judicial authority's ruling on motions without oral argument or testimony in the interest of expediency.

§ 31a–2. Motion for Bill of Particulars

The child or youth may file a motion, or the judicial authority may order at any time, that the prosecuting authority file a bill of particulars. The judicial authority shall order that a bill of particulars disclose information sufficient to enable the child or youth to prepare the defense, including but not being limited to reasonable notice of the offense charged and the date, time and place of its commission. When any bill of particulars is ordered, an amended or substitute information, if necessary, shall be filed incorporating its provisions.

[Adopted June 24, 2002, effective January 1, 2003.]

§ 31a–3. Motion to Dismiss

The child or youth may file a motion to dismiss if the motion is capable of determination without a trial of the general issue on grounds (1) to (9) of Section 41–8 of the rules of procedure in criminal matters, subject to the conditions of Section 41–10 and 41–11.

[Adopted June 24, 2002, effective January 1, 2003.]

§ 31a–4. Motion to Suppress

The child or youth may file a motion to suppress potential testimony or other evidence if required under the constitution or laws of the United States or the State of Connecticut in accordance with the provisions of Sections 41–13 through 41–17 of the rules of procedure in criminal matters.

[Adopted June 24, 2002, effective January 1, 2003.]

§ 31a–5. Motion for Judgment of Acquittal

(a) After the close of the juvenile prosecutor's case in chief, upon motion of the child or youth or upon its own motion, the judicial authority shall order the entry of a judgment of acquittal as to any principal offense charged and as to any lesser included offense for which the evidence would not reasonably permit an adjudication or finding of guilty. Such judgment of acquittal shall not apply to any lesser included offense for which the evidence would reasonably permit a finding of guilty.

(b) The judicial authority shall either grant or deny the motion before calling upon the child or youth to present defendant's case in chief. If the motion is not granted, the defendant may offer evidence without having reserved the right to do so.

[Adopted June 24, 2002, effective January 1, 2003.]

Commentary

This section is a modified version of the rule in criminal proceedings, since motions after the close of all the evidence in non-jury proceedings would not be necessary.

§ 31a–6. Motion for Transfer of Venue

The child or youth or juvenile prosecutor may file a motion, or the judicial authority may order at any time, that a juvenile matter be transferred to a different venue in accordance with Sections 41–23 and 41–25 of the rules of procedure in criminal matters.

[Adopted June 24, 2002, effective January 1, 2003.]

§ 31a–7. Motion in Limine

The judicial authority to whom a matter has been referred for trial may in its discretion entertain a motion in limine made by the child or youth or juvenile prosecutor regarding the admission or exclusion of anticipated evidence. Such motion shall be in writing and shall describe the anticipated evidence and the prejudice which may result therefrom. The judicial authority may grant the relief sought in the motion or such other relief as it may deem appropriate, may deny the motion with or without prejudice to its later renewal, or may reserve decision thereon until a later time in the proceeding.

[Adopted June 24, 2002, effective January 1, 2003.]

§ 31a–8. Motion for Sequestration

A child or youth or juvenile prosecutor may file a motion for sequestration. The judicial authority upon such motion shall cause any witness to be sequestered during the hearing on any issue or motion or during any part of the trial in which such witness is not testifying.

[Adopted June 24, 2002, effective January 1, 2003.]

§ 31a–9. Severance of Offenses

If it appears that a child or youth is prejudiced by a joinder of offenses, the judicial authority may, upon its own motion or the motion of the child or youth, order separate trials of the counts or provide whatever other relief justice may require.

[Adopted June 24, 2002, effective January 1, 2003.]

§ 31a–10. Trial Together on Petitions or Informations

The judicial authority may, upon its own motion or the motion of the child or youth or juvenile prosecutor, order that two or more petitions or informations against the same child or youth, be tried together. Petitions or informations against different children or youths may not be tried together unless all parties agree to waive the confidentiality rules.

[Adopted June 24, 2002, effective January 1, 2003.]

Commentary

This new rule allows the judicial authority to try together two or more cases involving the same child or youth. Although permitted in adult criminal proceedings, juvenile confidentiality rules would prohibit trying together cases involving two or more children or youths absent a waiver by the child, youth and parent or guardian.

§ 31a–11. Motion for New Trial

(a) Upon motion of the child or youth, the judicial authority may grant a new trial if it is required in the interest of justice in accordance with Section 42–53 of the rules of criminal procedure.

(b) Unless otherwise permitted by the judicial authority in the interests of justice, a motion for a new trial shall be made within five days after an adjudication or finding of guilty or within any further time the judicial authority allows during the five-day period.

(c) A request for a new trial on the ground of newly discovered evidence shall require a petition for a new trial and shall be brought in accordance with General Statutes § 52–270. The judicial authority may grant the petition even though an appeal is pending.

[Adopted June 24, 2002, effective January 1, 2003.]

Commentary

Sections 31a–2 through 31a–11 are new and are intended to incorporate rules similar to those in criminal procedure that are useful and often employed, as a matter of practice, in delinquency, family with service needs or youth in crisis cases. Motions filed prior to trial must be filed in accordance with Section 31a–1.

§ 31a–12. Motion to Transfer to Adult Criminal Docket

The juvenile prosecutor may file a motion to transfer prosecution to the adult criminal docket in accordance with General Statutes § 46b–127.

[Adopted June 24, 2002, effective January 1, 2003.]

§ 31a–13. Take into Custody Order

(a) Upon application in a delinquency proceeding, a Take into Custody Order may be issued by the judicial authority:

(1) Upon a finding of probable cause to believe that the child is responsible for: (i) a delinquent act, including violation of probation or supervision conditions or the failure of the child, duly notified, to attend a pretrial, probation or evaluation appointment, or (ii) for failure to comply with any duly warned condition of a suspended order of detention. The judicial authority also must find at the time it issues a take into custody order that a ground for detention pursuant to Section 30–6 exists before issuing the order.

(2) For failure to appear in court in response to a delinquency petition or summons served in hand or to a direct notice previously provided in court.

(b) Any application for a Take into Custody Order must be supported by a sworn statement alleging facts to substantiate probable cause, and where applicable, a petition or information charging a delinquent act.

(c) Any child detained under a Take into Custody Order is subject to Sections 30–1 through 30–11.

[Adopted June 24, 2002, effective January 1, 2003.]

Commentary

This section has been transferred, with revisions, from Section 31–11.

§ 31a–14. Physical and Mental Examinations

(a) No physical and/or mental examination or examinations by any physician, psychologist, psychiatrist or social worker shall be ordered by the judicial authority of any child denying delinquent behavior or status as a child from family with service needs or youth in crisis prior to the adjudication, except (1) with the agreement of the child's parent or guardian and attorney, (2) when the child has executed a written statement of responsibility, (3) when the judicial authority finds that there is a question of the child's competence to understand the nature of the proceedings or to participate in the defense, or a question of the child having been mentally capable of unlawful intent at the time of the commission of the alleged act, or (4) where the child has been detained and as an incident of detention is administered a physical examination to establish the existence of any contagious or infectious condition.

(b) Upon a showing that the mental health of a child is at issue, either prior to adjudication for the reasons set forth in subsection (a) herein or subsequent thereto as a determinate of disposition, the judicial authority may order a child's detention for a period not to exceed thirty days in a hospital or other institution empowered by law to treat mentally ill children for study and a report on the child's mental condition.

[Adopted June 24, 2002, effective January 1, 2003.]

Commentary

This section has been transferred, with revisions, from Section 31–12. This section has been amended to provide for an agreement to an examination without the need for written permission, since these are often ordered upon oral motion during court hearings. There is no procedure for establishing competency in juvenile court.

§ 31a–15. Mentally Ill Children

No child shall be committed by a judicial authority as mentally ill pursuant to General Statutes § 46b–140 until such a study has been made and a sworn report filed with the judicial authority or in lieu thereof without the sworn certificate of at least two impartial physicians, one of whom shall be a physician specializing in psychiatry, selected by the judicial authority who have personally examined the child within ten days of the hearing that in their opinion the child's mental condition necessitates placement in a designated hospital for mental illness. If, after such hearing, the judicial authority finds by clear and convincing evidence that the child suffers from a mental disorder, as defined in General Statutes § 17a–75, is in need of hospitalization for treatment and such treatment is available as the least restrictive alternative, the judicial authority shall make an order for commitment for a definite period not to exceed six months to a designated hospital for mental illness of children. No child or youth shall be committed as mentally deficient pursuant to General Statutes § 46b–140 except in accordance with procedures of General Statutes § 17a–274(b), (g), and (h).

[Adopted June 24, 2002, effective January 1, 2003.]

Commentary

This section has been transferred, with revisions, from Section 31–13.

§ 31a–16. Discovery

(a) The child or youth or the juvenile prosecutor shall be permitted pretrial discovery in accordance with subsections (b), (c) and (d) of this section by interrogatory, production, inspection or deposition of a person in delinquency, family with service needs or youth in crisis matters if the information or material sought is not otherwise obtainable and upon a finding that proceedings will not be unduly delayed.

(b) Motions or requests for discovery shall be filed with the court in accordance with Section 31a–1. The clerk shall calendar any such motion or request for a hearing. Objections to such motions or requests may be filed with the court and served in accordance with Sections 10–12 through 10–17 within ten days of the filing of the motion or request unless the judicial authority, for good cause shown, allows a later filing. Upon its own motion or upon the request or motion of a party, the judicial authority may, after a hearing, order discovery. The judicial authority shall fix the times for filing and for responding to discovery motions and requests and, when appropriate, shall fix the hour, place, manner, terms and conditions of responses to the motions and requests, provided that the party seeking discovery shall be allowed a reasonable opportunity to obtain information needed for the preparation of the case.

(c) Motions or requests for discovery should not be filed unless the moving party has attempted unsuccessfully to obtain an agreement to disclose from the party or person from whom information is being sought.

(d) The provisions of Sections 40–2 through 40–6, inclusive, 40–7(b), 40–8, through 40–16, inclusive, and

40-26 through 40-58, inclusive, of the rules of procedure in criminal matters shall be applied by the judicial authority in determining whether to grant, limit or set conditions on the requested discovery, issue any protective orders, or order appropriate sanctions for any clear misuse of discovery or arbitrary delay or refusal to comply with a discovery request.

[Adopted June 24, 2002, effective January 1, 2003.]

Commentary

This section has been transferred, with revisions, from Section 35-3. The changes to this section create separate rules for discovery in delinquency, family with service needs and youth in crisis cases. The rule patterns common practice and adopts many of the rules of criminal discovery, except filing and compliance time lines, which are either contained in this section or to be determined by the judicial authority after hearing. All motions or written requests for discovery in juvenile proceedings will be scheduled for a hearing by the judicial authority to avoid burdensome, irrelevant or repetitive discovery requests since juvenile proceedings should be expeditious in the best interests of the child or youth. Note that General Statutes § 46b-124(h) requires the juvenile prosecutor to disclose exculpatory material without the need for the defense to file any motion or request.

§ 31a-17. Disclosure of Defenses In Delinquency Proceedings

The child in a delinquency case shall disclose defenses to the charged offenses in accordance with Section 40-17 through 40-25 of the rules of criminal procedures. Such disclosures shall be made within 10 days after the matter is scheduled for trial except with the permission of the judicial authority.

[Adopted June 24, 2002, effective January 1, 2003.]

Commentary

This section provides for disclosure of defenses of mental disease, defect or extreme emotional disturbance or alibi to the prosecuting authority on a timely basis. Disclosure of defenses is a practice in delinquency proceedings, and should be codified into the rules of juvenile procedure.

§ 31a-18. Modification of Probation and Supervision

Any modification of the terms of probation or supervision, including discharge, shall be given in writing to the child, attorney, juvenile prosecutor and parent who may, in the event of disagreement, in writing request the judicial authority within five days of the receipt thereof for a hearing on the propriety of the modification. In the absence of any request, the modification of the terms of probation may be effected by the probation officer with the approval of the supervisor and the judicial authority.

[Adopted June 24, 2002, effective January 1, 2003.]

Commentary

This section has been transferred from Section 31-10.

§ 31a-19. Motion for Extension of Delinquency Commitment; Motion For Review of Permanency Plan

(a) The Commissioner of Children and Families may file a motion for an extension of a delinquency commitment beyond the eighteen-month or four-year period on the grounds that such extension is for the best interest of the child or the community. The clerk of the court shall give notice to the parent or guardian and to the child at least fourteen days prior to the hearing upon such motion. The judicial authority may, after hearing and upon finding such extension is in the best interest of the child or the community, continue the commitment for an additional period of not more than eighteen months.

(b) No later than twelve months after a child is committed as a delinquent to the Department of Children and Families, the judicial authority shall hold a permanency hearing. Such a hearing will be held every twelve months thereafter if the child remains committed. Such hearing may include the submission of a motion to the judicial authority by the commissioner to either modify or extend the commitment.

(c) At least sixty days prior to each permanency hearing required under subsection (b) of this section, the Commissioner of Children and Families shall file a permanency plan with the judicial authority. At each permanency hearing, the judicial authority shall review and approve a permanency plan that is in the best interest of the child and takes into consideration the child's need for permanency. The judicial authority shall also determine whether the Commissioner of Children and Families has made reasonable efforts to achieve the permanency plan.

[Adopted June 24, 2002, effective January 1, 2003.]

Commentary

This section conforms to General Statutes § 46b-141 as amended by P.A. 01-2, Section 34, of the June 2001 Special Session. That statute changes petitions for extensions of delinquency commitments to motions, and includes the requirement for twelve month permanency plan reviews for all committed delinquents.

CHAPTER 32. NEGLECTED, UNCARED FOR AND DEPENDENT CHILDREN AND TERMINATION OF PARENTAL RIGHTS [REPEALED]

Table of Sections

---

§ 32–1. Initiation of Judicial Proceeding; Contents of Petitions and Summary of Facts [Repealed]

[Repealed June 24, 2002, effective January 1, 2003.]

Commentary

This section has been transferred to Section 33a–1.

§ 32–2. Initiation of Judicial Proceeding—Summons Accompanying Petitions [Repealed]

[Repealed June 24, 2002, effective January 1, 2003.]

Commentary

This section has been transferred to Section 33a–2.

§ 32–3. Initiation of Judicial Proceeding—Venue [Repealed]

[Repealed June 24, 2002, effective January 1, 2003.]

Commentary

This section has been transferred to Section 33a–3.

§ 32–4. Initiation of Judicial Proceeding—Identity or Location of Parent Unknown [Repealed]

[Repealed June 24, 2002, effective January 1, 2003.]

Commentary

This section has been transferred to Section 33a–4.

§ 32–5. Initiation of Judicial Proceeding—Address of Person Entitled to Personal Service Unknown [Repealed]

[Repealed June 24, 2002, effective January 1, 2003.]

Commentary

This section has been transferred to Section 33a–5.

§ 32–6. Order of Temporary Custody; Application and Sworn Statement [Repealed]

[Repealed June 24, 2002, effective January 1, 2003.]

Commentary

This section has been transferred to Section 33a–6.

§ 32–7. Order of Temporary Custody—Statement in Temporary Custody Order of Respondent's Rights and of Subsequent Hearing [Repealed]

[Repealed June 24, 2002, effective January 1, 2003.]

Commentary

See Section 33a–6.

§ 32–8. Order of Temporary Custody—Authority of Temporary Custodian [Repealed]

[Repealed June 24, 2002, effective January 1, 2003.]

§ 32–9. Order of Temporary Custody—Emergency, Life–Threatening Medical Situations—Procedures [Repealed]

[Repealed June 24, 2002, effective January 1, 2003.]

Commentary

This section has been transferred to Section 33a–8.

CHAPTER 32a. RIGHTS OF PARTIES NEGLECTED, UNCARED FOR AND DEPENDENT CHILDREN AND TERMINATION OF PARENTAL RIGHTS

Table of Sections

§ 32a–1. Right to Counsel and to Remain Silent

(a) The judicial authority shall advise and explain to the parents or guardian of a child or youth their right to silence and to counsel prior to commencement of any proceeding.

(b) The parents or guardian of a child or youth and the child or youth have the rights of confrontation and cross-examination and may be represented by counsel in each and every phase of any and all proceedings in juvenile matters, including appeals, and if they are unable to afford counsel, counsel will be appointed to represent them if such is their request. The judicial authority shall appoint counsel for these parties or any of them (1) upon request and upon a finding that the party, is, in fact, financially unable to employ counsel, or (2) in the case of counsel for the child, whether a request is made or not, in any proceeding on a juvenile matter in which the custody of a child is at issue, or if in the opinion of the judicial authority the interests of the child and the parents conflict, or (3) in the case of counsel for the child and the parent, whether a request is made or not, if in the opinion of the judicial authority a fair hearing necessitates such an appointment.

(c) Where the judicial authority so appoints counsel for any such party who is found able to pay, in whole or in part, the cost thereof, it shall assess as costs against such parent or custodian, including any agency vested with the legal custody of the child, the expense so incurred and paid for by the court in providing such counsel, to the extent of their financial ability to do so. Reimbursement to the appointed attorney of unrecovered costs shall be made to that attorney by the judicial branch upon the attorney's certification of his unrecovered expenses to the judicial branch.

(d) Notices of initial hearings on petitions, shall contain a statement of the respondent's right to counsel.

(e) Any confession, admission or statement, written or oral, made by the parent or parents or guardian of the child or youth after the filing of a petition alleging such child or youth to be neglected, uncared-for or dependent, shall be inadmissible in any proceeding held upon such petition against the person making such admission or statement unless such person shall have been advised of his right to retain counsel, and that if he is unable to afford counsel, counsel will be appointed to represent him, that he has a right to refuse to make any statement and that any statements he makes may be introduced in evidence against him.

[Adopted June 24, 2002, effective January 1, 2003.]

Commentary

This section has been transferred, with revisions, from Section 34–1. Subsections (a) and (b) are transferred from Section 34–1(a) and (b). The prior rule seemed to indicate that a child or youth has a right to remain silent in neglect/uncared for or dependency proceedings. A child may, however, be called to testify as to the factual basis of allegations in these proceedings. See *State v. Jarzbek*, 204 Conn. 683(1987) and its progeny. See also, General Statutes § 46b–135(b).

Subsection (c) addresses reimbursements to appointed attorneys if the party ordered to reimburse the state fails to do so. In such cases, the matter should be referred to the Department of Administrative Services for collection.

Subsection (d), in part, no longer applies, since motions, not petitions, are used to maintain or revoke commitments or modify dispositions.

New subsection (e) is the exact language of General Statutes § 46b–137(b), which describes the right to remain silent in neglect matters. Without these amendments, the rule inappropriately narrows the right as set forth in statute. Although no statute explicitly provides parents in termination of parental rights cases with the right to remain silent, it is logical to extend the right to those cases in light of the fundamental right that is being affected and since the nature of some acts that lead to the filing of a termination petition make the right to remain silent more significant. There was a need to clarify this provision so it only applies to neglect/uncared for or dependency proceedings. Delinquent children's rights are addressed in a separate section on delinquency.

§ 32a–2. Hearing Procedure; Subpoenas

(a) All hearings are essentially civil proceedings except where otherwise provided by statute. Testimony may be given in narrative form and the proceedings shall at all times be as informal as the requirements of due process and fairness permit.

(b) Issuance, service, and compliance with subpoenas are governed by General Statutes § 52–143 et seq.

(c) Any pro se indigent party may request the clerk of the court to issue subpoenas for persons to testify before the judicial authority. Pro se indigent parties and court-appointed counsel shall obtain prior approval from the judicial authority to issue subpoenas and seek reimbursement for the costs thereof.

[Adopted June 24, 2002, effective January 1, 2003.]

Commentary

This section has been transferred, with revisions, from Section 34–2. Subsections (b) and revisions to (c) clarify the process for issuing and serving subpoenas.

§ 32a–3. Standards of Proof

(a) The standard of proof applied in a neglect, uncared for or dependency proceeding is a fair preponderance of the evidence.

(b) The standard of proof applied in a decision to terminate parental rights or a finding that efforts to reunify a parent with a child are no longer appropriate, is clear and convincing evidence.

(c) Any child custody proceedings, except delinquency, involving removal of an Indian child from a parent or Indian custodian for placement shall, in addition, comply with the Indian Child Welfare Act (ICWA), 25 USC § 1901 et seq.

[Adopted June 24, 2002, effective January 1, 2003.]

Commentary

This section has been transferred, with revisions, from Section 34–3. Changes to subsections (a) and (b) conform this section with case law and Public Act 01–142. Subsection (c) clarifies the necessity for the judicial authority to comply with the Indian Child Welfare Act.

§ 32a–4. Child Witness

(a) All oral testimony shall be given under oath. For child witnesses, the oath may be "you promise that you will tell the truth." The judicial authority may, however, admit the testimony of a child without the imposition of a formal oath if the judicial authority finds that the oath would be meaningless to the particular child, or would otherwise inhibit the child from testifying freely and fully.

(b) Any party who intends to call a child as a witness shall first file a motion seeking permission of the judicial authority.

(c) In any proceeding when testimony of a child is taken, an adult who is known to the child and with whom the child feels comfortable shall be permitted to sit in close proximity to the child during the child's testimony without obscuring the child from view and the attorneys shall ask questions and pose objections while seated and in a manner which is not intimidating to the child. The judicial authority shall minimize any distress to a child in court.

(d) The judicial authority with the consent of all parties may privately interview the child. Counsel may submit questions and areas of concern for examination. The knowledge gained in such a conference shall be shared on the record with counsel and, if there is no legal representative, with the parent.

(e) When the witness is the child of the respondent, the respondent may be excluded from the hearing room upon a showing by clear and convincing evidence that the child witness would be so intimidated or inhibited that trustworthiness of the child witness is seriously called into question. In such an instance, if the respondent is without counsel, the judicial authority shall summarize for the respondent the nature of the child's testimony.

[Adopted June 24, 2002, effective January 1, 2003.]

Commentary

This section has been transferred, with revisions, from Section 34–4. These changes ensure that the parent is aware of the testimony against him or her if the child testifies outside of the presence of the parent. The discretion not to require the child to testify is supported by case law: *In re Noel M.*, 23 Conn.App. 410, 421 (1990); *In re Lauren R.*, 49 Conn.App. 763 (1998); *In re Brandon W.*, 56 Conn.App. 418 (2000). In these cases, it was held that the right to confrontation and cross-examination in a child protection case is statutory, not constitutional.

§ 32a–5. Child in the Court

For good cause shown, the child who is the subject of the hearing may be excluded from the courtroom.

[Adopted June 24, 2002, effective January 1, 2003.]

Commentary

This section allows for the child's presence when appropriate. Children, who are parties to the action, have the right to be present if they so request.

§ 32a–6. Interpreter

The judicial authority shall provide an official interpreter to the parties as necessary to ensure their understanding of, and participation in, the proceedings.

[Adopted June 24, 2002, effective January 1, 2003.]

Commentary

This section ensures that all parties understand and are able to participate in the proceedings.

§ 32a–7. Records

(a) Except as otherwise provided by statute. All records maintained in juvenile matters brought before the judicial authority, either current or closed, including the transcripts of hearings, shall be kept confidential.

(b) Except as otherwise provided by statute. no material contained in the court record, including the social study, medical or clinical reports, school reports, police reports and the reports of social agencies, may be copied or otherwise reproduced in written form in whole or in part by the parties or their counsel without the express consent of the judicial authority.

[Adopted June 24, 2002, effective January 1, 2003.]

Commentary

This section has been transferred, with revisions, from Section 35–5. These changes achieve consistency with General Statutes § 46b–124. Subsection (a) of Section 35–5 has been transferred to Section 35a–1(d).

§ 32a–8. Use of Confidential Alcohol or Drug Abuse Treatment Records As Evidence

(a) Upon a determination by the judicial authority that good cause exists pursuant to federal law and regulations, the judicial authority may admit evidence of any party's alcohol or drug treatment by a facility subject to said regulations.

(b) A party seeking to introduce substance abuse treatment records shall submit a motion to the judicial authority requesting permission to subpoena such records and explaining the need for them, and shall also file a motion to disclose such confidential records and permit testimony regarding them. The motion for permission to subpoena such records may be signed ex parte by the judicial authority. If the judicial authority approves the motion, such records may be subpoenaed and submitted to the court under seal, and the judicial authority shall set a date for the parties and service providers to be heard on the motion to disclose confidential alcohol or drug abuse treatment records.

[Adopted June 24, 2002, effective January 1, 2003.]

Commentary

Subsection (a) has been transferred, with revisions, from Section 33–3(c) to provide more detailed references to applicable federal law and regulations. (See 42 U.S.C. 290dd–2; 42 C.F.R. §§ 2.63 and 2.64.) Subsection (b) has been added to note the proper procedure to subpoena such records into court prior to the hearing on the motion to disclose confidential alcohol or drug abuse treatment records. It should be noted that this section does not pertain to the use of all other confidential records, such as medical, psychiatric or psychological treatment records, as evidence. For a general discussion of the disclosure of confidential treatment records and communications in juvenile proceedings, see *In re Marvin M.*, 48 Conn.App. 563, cert. denied 245 Conn. 916 (1998) and *In re Romance M.*, 30 Conn.App. 839, cert. granted on other grounds, 226 Conn. 916 (1993).

CHAPTER 33. HEARINGS CONCERNING NEGLECTED, UNCARED FOR AND DEPENDENT CHILDREN AND TERMINATION OF PARENTAL RIGHTS [REPEALED]

Table of Sections

§ 33–1. Adjudicatory Hearing; Actions by Judicial Authority [Repealed]

[Repealed June 24, 2002, effective January 1, 2003.]

Commentary

This section has been transferred to Section 35a–1.

§ 33–2. Adjudicatory Hearing—Continuance for Case Status Conference [Repealed]

[Repealed June 24, 2002, effective January 1, 2003.]

Commentary

This section has been transferred to Section 33a–7 and 35a–2.

§ 33–3. Adjudicatory Hearing—Evidence [Repealed]

[Repealed June 24, 2002, effective January 1, 2003.]

Commentary

Subsections (a) and (b) of this section have been transferred to Section 35a–7. Subsection (c) has been transferred to Section 32a–8.

§ 33–4. Adjudicatory Hearing—Burden of Proceeding [Repealed]

[Repealed June 24, 2002, effective January 1, 2003.]

Commentary

This section has been transferred to Section 35a–8.

§ 33–5. Dispositional Hearing; Evidence and Social Study [Repealed]

[Repealed June 24, 2002, effective January 1, 2003.]

Commentary

This section has been transferred to Section 35a–9.

§ 33–6. Dispositional Hearing—Availability of Social Study to Counsel and Parties [Repealed]

[Repealed June 24, 2002, effective January 1, 2003.]

Commentary

This section has been transferred to Section 35a 10.

§ 33–7. Dispositional Hearing—Dispositional Plan Offered by Respondents [Repealed]

[Repealed June 24, 2002, effective January 1, 2003.]

Commentary

This section has been transferred to Section 35a–11.

§ 33–8. Protective Supervision—Conditions and Modification [Repealed]

[Repealed June 24, 2002, effective January 1, 2003.]

Commentary

This section has been transferred to Section 35a–12.

§ 33–9. Extension Petitions [Repealed]

[Repealed June 24, 2002, effective January 1, 2003.]

§ 33–10. Revocation of Commitments [Repealed]

[Repealed June 24, 2002, effective January 1, 2003.]

§ 33–11. Modifications [Repealed]

[Repealed June 24, 2002, effective January 1, 2003.]

Commentary

This section has been transferred to Section 35a–16.

§ 33–12. Coterminous Petitions [Repealed]

[Repealed June 24, 2002, effective January 1, 2003.]

Commentary

This section has been transferred to Section 35a–3.

§ 33–13. Transfer from Probate Court of Petitions for Removal of Parent as Guardian [Repealed]

[Repealed June 24, 2002, effective January 1, 2003.]

Commentary

This section has been transferred to Section 35a–19.

CHAPTER 33a. PETITIONS FOR NEGLECT, UNCARED FOR, DEPENDENCY AND TERMINATION OF PARENTAL RIGHTS: INITIATION OF PROCEEDINGS, ORDERS OF TEMPORARY CUSTODY AND PRELIMINARY HEARINGS

Table of Sections

---

§ 33a-1. Initiation of Judicial Proceeding; Contents of Petitions and Summary of Facts

(a) The petitioner shall set forth with reasonable particularity, including statutory references, the specific conditions which have resulted in the situation which is the subject of the petition.

(b) A summary of the facts substantiating the allegations of the petition shall be attached thereto and shall be incorporated by reference.

[Adopted June 24, 2002, effective January 1, 2003.]

Commentary

This section has been transferred from Section 32-1.

§ 33a-2. Service of Summons, Petitions and Ex Parte Orders

(a) A summons accompanying a petition alleging that a child is neglected, uncared for or dependent, along with the summary of facts, shall be served by the petitioner on the respondents and provided to the Office of the Attorney General at least fourteen days before the date of the initial plea hearing on the petition, which shall be held not more than forty-five days from the date of filing the petition.

(b) A summons accompanying a petition for termination of parental rights, along with the summary of facts, shall be served by the petitioner on the respondents and provided to the Office of the Attorney General at least ten days prior to the date of the initial plea hearing on the petition, which shall be held not more than thirty days from the filing of the petition.

(c) A summons accompanying simultaneously filed coterminous petitions, along with the summary of facts, shall be served by the petitioner on the respondents and provided to the Office of the Attorney General at least ten days prior to the date of the initial plea hearing on the petition, which shall be held not more than thirty days from the filing of the petitions.

(d) A summons accompanying any petition filed with an application for order of temporary custody shall be served by the petitioner on the respondents and provided to the Office of the Attorney General as soon as practicable after the issuance of any ex parte order or order to appear, along with such order, any sworn statements supporting the order, the summary of facts, the specific steps provided by the judicial authority, and the notice required by Practice Book Section 33a-6.

[Adopted June 24, 2002, effective January 1, 2003.]

Commentary

This section has been transferred, with revisions, from Section 32-2. These changes clarify that the summary of facts must be served along with the petition; that the petition and summary of facts must be provided to the Attorney General's office; that service requirements for coterminous petitions are the same as those for termination of parental rights petitions; and establish service rules for petitions accompanied by temporary custody applications.

§ 33a-3. Venue

All child protection petitions shall be filed within the juvenile matters district where the child or youth resided at the time of the filing of the petition, but any child or youth born in any hospital or institution where the mother is confined at the time of birth shall be deemed to have residence in the district wherein such child's mother was living at the time of her admission to such hospital or institution. When placement of a child has been effected prior to filing of a petition, venue shall be in the district wherein the custodial parent is living at the time of the filing of the petition.

[Adopted June 24, 2002, effective January 1, 2003.]

Commentary

This section has been transferred, with revisions, from Section 32–3. The first sentence of this section is taken from General Statutes § 46b–142(a), which governs venue. The second sentence, which is not statutory, clarifies venue when a child is in foster placement prior to the filing of a petition: for example, when the child is already in placement pursuant to a voluntary placement or a 96 hour hold. Since a parent can move between the time of placement and the date of the filing of a petition, it is appropriate to use the parent's most current residence for venue purposes, as that is the location where services will most likely be provided.

§ 33a–4. Identity or Location of Respondent Unknown

(a) If the identity or present location of a respondent is unknown when a petition is filed, an affidavit shall be attached reciting the efforts to identify and locate that respondent. The judicial authority shall require reasonable efforts to identify and locate the absent respondent. Notice by publication to unidentified persons shall be required in any petition for termination of parental rights.

(b) The judicial authority may appoint counsel for an unidentified parent or an absent parent who has received only constructive notice of termination proceedings, for the limited purposes of conducting a reasonable search for the unidentified or absent parents and reporting to the judicial authority before any adjudication.

[Adopted June 24, 2002, effective January 1, 2003.]

Commentary

Subsection (a) has been transferred, with revisions, from Section 32–4. Subsection (b) has been transferred from Section 34–1(c). These changes, and corresponding changes in subsequent sections, replace the word "parent" with "respondent." The change to subsection (a) clarifies that notice by publication to an unidentified parent is required in a termination of parental rights action.

§ 33a–5. Address of Person Entitled to Personal Service Unknown

If the address of any person entitled to personal service is unknown, service may be by publication as ordered by the judicial authority.

[Adopted June 24, 2002, effective January 1, 2003.]

Commentary

This section has been transferred, with revisions, from Section 32–5.

§ 33a–6. Order of Temporary Custody; Ex Parte Orders and Orders to Appear

(a) If the judicial authority finds, based upon the specific allegations of the petition and other verified affirmations of fact provided by the applicant, that there is reasonable cause to believe that: (1) the child is suffering from serious physical illness or serious physical injury or is in immediate physical danger from his surroundings and (2) that as a result of said conditions, the child's safety is endangered and immediate removal from such surroundings is necessary to ensure the child's safety, the judicial authority shall, upon proper application at the time of filing of the petition or at any time subsequent thereto, either (A) issue an order to the respondents or other persons having responsibility for the care of the child or youth to appear at such time as the judicial authority may designate to determine whether the judicial authority should vest in some suitable agency or person the child's or youth's temporary care and custody pending disposition of the petition, or (B) issue an order ex parte vesting in some suitable agency or person the child's or youth's temporary care and custody.

(b) A preliminary hearing on any ex parte custody order or order to appear issued by the judicial authority shall be held as soon as practicable but no more than ten days from the issuance of such order.

(c) If the application is filed subsequent to the filing of the petition, a motion to amend the petition or to modify protective supervision shall be filed no later than the next business date before such preliminary hearing.

(d) Upon issuance of an ex parte order or order to appear, the judicial authority shall provide to the commissioner and the respondents specific steps necessary for each to take for the respondents to retain or regain custody of the child or youth.

(e) An ex parte order or order to appear shall be accompanied by a conspicuous notice to the respondents written in clear and simple language containing at least the following information: (i) That the order contains allegations that conditions in the home have endangered the safety and welfare of the child; (ii) that a hearing will be held on the date on the form; (iii) that the hearing is the opportunity to present the parents' position concerning the alleged facts; (iv) that the respondent has the right to remain silent; (v) that an attorney will be appointed for parents who cannot afford an attorney; (vi) that such parents may apply for a court-appointed attorney by going in person to the court address on the form and are advised to go as soon as possible in order for the attorney to prepare for the hearing; and (vii) if such parents have any questions concerning the case or appointment of counsel, any such parent is advised to go to the court or call the clerk's office at the court as soon as possible.

(f) Upon application for appointed counsel, the judicial authority shall promptly determine eligibility and, if the respondent is eligible, promptly appoint counsel. In the absence of such a request prior to the preliminary hearing, the judicial authority shall ensure that standby counsel is available at such hearing to assist and/or represent the respondents.

[Adopted June 24, 2002, effective January 1, 2003.]

Commentary

This section has been transferred, with revisions, from Section 32–6. Much of the suggested language is derived from General Statutes § 46b–129(b), as amended by Public Act 98–241. The following changes are not based on the statute: the language in subsection (b) clarifying that a preliminary hearing must be held "as soon as practicable" but no more than ten days after issuance of ex parte Order of Temporary Custody ("OTC"); the new service rule for OTCs in subsection (e); the requirement in subsection (e)(iv) that the mandatory notice to respondents include a statement of their right to remain silent, and the second sentence in subsection (f), codifying the current practice of providing standby counsel at preliminary hearings.

§ 33a–7. Preliminary Hearing

(a) At the preliminary hearing on the order of temporary custody or order to appear, or at the first hearing on a petition for neglect, uncared for, dependency, or termination of parental rights, the judicial authority shall:

(1) first determine whether all necessary parties are present and that the rules governing service for nonappearing parties have been complied with, and shall note these facts for the record.

(2) inform the respondents of the allegations contained in all petitions and applications that are the subject of the hearing;

(3) inform the respondents of their right to remain silent;

(4) ensure that an attorney, and where appropriate, a separate guardian ad litem, has been appointed to represent the child or youth in accordance with General Statutes §§ 46b–129a(2) and 46b–136;

(5) advise the respondents of their right to counsel and their right to have counsel appointed if unable to afford representation and, upon request, appoint an attorney to represent any respondent who is unable to afford representation, as determined by the judicial authority;

(6) advise the respondents of the right to a hearing on the petitions and applications, to be held within ten days from the date of the preliminary hearing if the hearing is pursuant to an ex parte order of temporary custody or an order to appear;

(7) notwithstanding any prior statements acknowledging responsibility, inquire of the custodial respondent in neglect, uncared for and dependency matters, and of all respondents in termination matters, whether the allegations of the petition are presently admitted or denied;

(8) make any interim orders, including visitation, that the judicial authority determines are in the best interests of the child or youth, and order specific steps the commissioner and the respondents shall take for the respondents to regain or to retain custody of the child or youth;

(9) take steps to determine the identity of the father of the child or youth, including ordering genetic testing, if necessary, and order service of the petition and notice of the hearing date, if any, to be made upon him;

(10) If the person named as the father appears, and admits that he is the father, provide him and the mother with the notices which comply with General Statutes § 17b–27 and provide them with the opportunity to sign a paternity acknowledgment and affirmation on forms which comply with General Statutes § 17b–27, which documents shall be executed and filed in accordance with Chapter 815y of the General Statutes and a copy delivered to the clerk of the superior court for juvenile matters; and

(11) In the event that the person named as a father appears and denies that he is the father of the child or youth, advise him that he may have no further standing in any proceeding concerning the child, and either order genetic testing to determine paternity or direct him to execute a written denial of paternity on a form promulgated by the Office of the Chief Court Administrator. Upon execution of such a form by the putative father, the judicial authority may remove him from the case and afford him no further standing in the case or in any subsequent proceeding regarding the child or youth until such time as paternity is established by formal acknowledgment or adjudication in a court of competent jurisdiction.

(b) At the preliminary hearing on the order of temporary custody or order to appear, the judicial authority may provide parties an opportunity to present argument with regard to the sufficiency of the sworn statements.

(c) If any respondent fails, after proper service, to appear at the preliminary hearing, the judicial authority may enter or sustain an order of temporary custody.

(d) Upon request, or upon its own motion, the judicial authority shall schedule a hearing on the order for temporary custody or the order to show cause to be held as soon as practicable but no more than ten days from the date of the preliminary hearing. Such hearing shall be held on consecutive days except for compelling circumstances or at the request of the respondents.

(e) When the allegations are denied, necessitating testimony in support of the petitioner's allegations, the case shall be continued for a case status conference and a subsequent hearing before a judicial authority who has not read the case status conference memo. Said case status conference may be waived by the judicial authority, on its own motion or upon request of the parties.

[Adopted June 24, 2002, effective January 1, 2003.]

Commentary

Subsection (e) has been transferred, in part, from Section 33-2. Much of the language is derived from General Statutes § 46b-129(d), (e) and (f), as amended by Public Act 98-241. The following changes are not based on those sources: subsection (a)(3), which codifies courts' current practice of advising respondents at the preliminary hearing of their right to remain silent; subsection (b), which establishes a limited right to be heard at a preliminary hearing on the sufficiency of the affidavits supporting an order of temporary custody; and the language in subsection (c) clarifying that a contested hearing must be held "as soon as practicable" after a preliminary hearing.

§ 33a-8. Emergency, Life-Threatening Medical Situations—Procedures.

When an emergency medical situation exists which requires the immediate assumption of temporary custody of a child in order to save the child's life, the application for a temporary custody order shall be filed together with a neglect or uncared for petition. Two physicians under oath must attest to the need for such medical treatment. Oral permission by the judicial authority may be given after receiving sworn oral testimony of two physicians that the specific surgical or medical intervention is absolutely necessary to preserve the child's life. The judicial authority may grant the temporary custody order ex parte or may schedule an immediate hearing prior to issuing said order. At any hearing the two physicians shall be available for testifying, and the judicial authority shall appoint counsel for the child.

[Adopted June 24, 2002, effective January 1, 2003.]

Commentary

This section has been transferred, with revisions, from Section 32-9. See General Statutes § 45a-607(b)(2).

CHAPTER 34. RIGHTS OF PARTIES [REPEALED]

Table of Sections

---

§ 34-1. Right to Counsel and to Remain Silent [Repealed]

[Repealed June 24, 2002, effective January 1, 2003.]

Commentary

Subsections (a) and (b) and (e) have been transferred to Section 32a-1. Subsection (c) has been transferred to Section 33a-4(b). Subsection (d), in part, is no longer necessary since motions, not petitions, are used to maintain or revoke commitments or modify dispositions. Subsection (f) is no longer necessary as it inappropriately narrows the right to remain silent in neglect matters and is replaced by Section 32a-1(e).

§ 34-2. Hearing Procedure; Subpoenas [Repealed]

[Repealed June 24, 2002, effective January 1, 2003.]

Commentary

This section has been transferred to Section 32a-2.

§ 34-3. Standards of Proof [Repealed]

[Repealed June 24, 2002, effective January 1, 2003.]

Commentary

This section has been transferred in part to Section 32a-3.

§ 34-4. Child Witness [Repealed]

[Repealed June 24, 2002, effective January 1, 2003.]

Commentary

This section has been transferred to Section 32a-4.

CHAPTER 34a. PLEADINGS, MOTIONS AND DISCOVERY NEGLECTED, UNCARED FOR AND DEPENDENT CHILDREN AND TERMINATION OF PARENTAL RIGHTS

Table of Sections

§ 34a-1. Motions, Requests and Amendments

(a) Except as otherwise provided, the sections in chapters 1 through 7 shall apply to juvenile matters in the superior court as defined by General Statutes § 46b-121.

(b) The provisions of Sections 8-2, 9-5, 9-22, 10-12(a), 10-13, 10-14, 10-17, 10-18, 10-29, 10-62, 11-4, 11-5, 11-6, 11-7, 11-8, 11-10, 11-11, 11-12, 11-13, 12-1, 12-2 and 12-3 of the rules of practice shall apply to juvenile matters as defined by General Statutes § 46b-121.

(c) A motion or request, other than a motion made orally during a hearing, shall be in writing. An objection to a request shall also be in writing. A motion, request or objection to a request shall have annexed to it a proper order and where appropriate shall be in the form called for by Section 4-1. The form and manner of notice shall adequately inform the interested parties of the time, place and nature of the hearing. A motion request, or objection to a request whose form is not therein prescribed shall state in paragraphs successively numbered the specific grounds upon which it is made. A copy of all written motions requests, or objections to requests shall be served on the opposing party or counsel pursuant to Sections 10-12(a) and (c), 10-13, 10-14 and 10-17. All motions or objections to requests shall be given an initial hearing by the judicial authority within fifteen days after filing provided reasonable notice is given to parties in interest, or notices are waived; any motion in a case on trial or assigned for trial may be disposed of by the judicial authority at its discretion or ordered upon the docket.

(d) A petition may be amended at any time by the judicial authority on its own motion or in response to a motion prior to any final adjudication. When an amendment has been so ordered, a continuance shall be granted whenever the judicial authority finds that the new allegations in the petition justify the need for additional time to permit the parties to respond adequately to the additional or changed facts and circumstances.

(e) If the moving party determines and reports that all counsel and pro se parties agree to the granting of a motion or agree that the motion may be considered without the need for oral argument or testimony and the motion states on its face that there is such an agreement, the judicial authority may consider and rule on the motion without a hearing.

[Adopted June 24, 2002, effective January 1, 2003.]

Commentary

This section has been transferred, with revisions, from Section 35-1. The changes in this section conform to and clarify current practice. The reference to "liberally construing" pleadings has been deleted; General Statutes § 17a-112(p) only refers to liberally construing pleadings in termination petitions. There is no corresponding statutory reference to "liberally construing" pleadings in neglect/uncared for cases. Written objections to motions are necessary only when the rule on a specific motion requires that a written objection be filed.

§ 34a-2. Short Calendar—Frequency

Short calendar sessions shall be held in each juvenile matters court location at least once every two weeks, the date, hour and place to be fixed by the presiding judge upon due notice to the clerk.

[Adopted June 24, 2002, effective January 1, 2003.]

Commentary

This section establishes more frequent short calendar sessions.

§ 34a–3. Short Calendar—Assignments Automatic

Matters to be placed on the short calendar shall be assigned automatically by the clerk. No such matters shall be so assigned unless filed at least five days before the opening of court on the short calendar day, unless for good cause shown.

[Adopted June 24, 2002, effective January 1, 2003.]

Commentary

This section limits last minute filings.

§ 34a–4. Short Calendar—Continuances When Counsel's Presence or Oral Argument Required

Matters on the short calendar docket requiring oral argument or counsel's presence shall not be continued except for good cause shown; and no such matter in which adverse parties are interested shall be continued unless the parties shall agree thereto before the day of the short calendar session and notify the clerk, subject to the approval of the judicial authority. In the absence of such an agreement, unless the judicial authority shall otherwise order, any counsel appearing may argue the matter and submit it for decision, or request that it be denied.

[Adopted June 24, 2002, effective January 1, 2003.]

Commentary

This section establishes an equitable and orderly process for continuing matters.

§ 34a–5. Continuances and Advancements

(a) Motions for continuances or changes in scheduled court dates must be submitted in writing in compliance with Section 34a–1(c) and filed no later than seven days prior to the scheduled date. Such motions must state the precise reason for the request, the name of the judge scheduled to hear the case, and whether or not all other parties consent to the request. After consulting with the presiding judge, a court services officer or clerk will handle bona fide emergency requests submitted less than seven days prior to scheduled court dates.

(b) Trials that are not completed within the allotted prescheduled time will be subject to continuation at the next available court date.

[Adopted June 24, 2002, effective January 1, 2003.]

Commentary

This section establishes an equitable and orderly process by which to request and grant continuances.

§ 34a–6. Pleadings Allowed and Their Order

The order of pleadings shall be as follows:

(1) The petition.

(2) The respondent's or child's motion to dismiss.

(3) The respondent's or child's motion to strike.

[Adopted June 24, 2002, effective January 1, 2003.]

Commentary

Sections 34a–6 through 34a–19 set forth the pleadings that are pertinent and permissible in a juvenile proceeding as opposed to a strictly civil proceeding. These sections also establish timeframes for such pleadings to comply with the statutory requirement that child protection matters proceed to disposition as expeditiously as possible.

§ 34a–7. Waiving Right to Plead

In all cases, when the judicial authority does not otherwise order, the filing of any pleading provided for by the preceding section will waive the right to file any pleading which might have been filed in due order and which precedes it in the order of pleading provided in that section.

[Adopted June 24, 2002, effective January 1, 2003.]

§ 34a–8. Time to Plead

Commencing on the plea date stated on the petition, pleadings shall first advance within 15 days from the plea date stated on the petition, and any subsequent pleadings, motions and requests shall advance at least one step within each successive period of fifteen days from the preceding pleading or the filing of the decision of the judicial authority thereon if one is required.

[Adopted June 24, 2002, effective January 1, 2003.]

If the respondent enters a pro forma denial before the plea date stated on the petition, the respondent is not precluded from filing any pleadings within the time frame specified.

§ 34a–9. Motion to Dismiss

Any respondent or child, wishing to contest the court's jurisdiction, may do so even after having entered a general appearance, but must do so by filing a motion to dismiss within 15 days of the plea date stated on the petition.

[Adopted June 24, 2002, effective January 1, 2003.]

§ 34a–10. Grounds of Motion to Dismiss

(a) The motion to dismiss shall be used to assert: (1) lack of jurisdiction over the subject matter; (2)

lack of jurisdiction over the person; (3) improper venue; (4) insufficiency of process; and (5) insufficiency of service of process. A motion to dismiss shall always be filed with a supporting memorandum of law, and where appropriate, with supporting affidavits as to facts not apparent on the record.

(b) Any adverse party who objects to a motion to dismiss shall, at least five days before the motion is to be considered on the short calendar, file and serve in accordance with Sections 10–12(a) and (c), 10–13, 10–14 and 10–17 a memorandum of law and, where appropriate, supporting affidavits as to facts not apparent on the record.

[Adopted June 24, 2002, effective January 1, 2003.]

§ 34a–11. Waiver Based on Certain Grounds

Any claim of lack of jurisdiction over the person, improper venue, insufficiency of process, or insufficiency of service of process is waived if not raised by a motion to dismiss filed in the sequence provided in Sections 34a–3 and 34a–4 and within the time provided by Section 34a–6.

[Adopted June 24, 2002, effective January 1, 2003.]

§ 34a–12. Waiver and Subject Matter Jurisdiction

Any claim of lack of jurisdiction over the subject matter cannot be waived; and whenever it is found after suggestion of the parties or otherwise that the judicial authority lacks jurisdiction of the subject matter, the judicial authority shall dismiss the action.

[Adopted June 24, 2002, effective January 1, 2003.]

§ 34a–13. Further Pleading by Respondent or Child

If a motion to dismiss is denied with respect to any jurisdictional issue, the respondent or child may plead further without waiving the right to contest jurisdiction further.

[Adopted June 24, 2002, effective January 1, 2003.]

§ 34a–14. Response to Summary of Facts

In addition to the entry of a pro forma plea of denial, a parent, legal guardian or child may, within thirty days of the plea date, file a written response to the Summary of Facts attached to the petition specifying that certain allegations in said summary of facts are irrelevant, immaterial, false or otherwise improper.

[Adopted June 24, 2002, effective January 1, 2003.]

§ 34a–15. Motion to Strike

(a) Whenever any party wishes to contest: (1) the legal sufficiency of the allegations of any petition, or of any one or more counts thereof, to state a claim upon which relief can be granted; or (2) the legal sufficiency of any prayer for relief in any such petition; or (3) the legal sufficiency of any such petition, or any count thereof, because of the absence of any necessary party; or (4) the joining of two or more causes of action which cannot properly be united in one petition whether the same be stated in one or more counts, that party may do so by filing a motion to strike the contested petition or part thereof.

(b) A motion to strike on the ground of the nonjoinder of a necessary party must give the name and residence of the missing party or such information as the moving party has as to the identity and residence of the missing party and must state the missing party's interest in the cause of action.

[Adopted June 24, 2002, effective January 1, 2003.]

§ 34a–16. Reasons in Motion to Strike

Each motion to strike raising any of the claims of legal insufficiency enumerated in the preceding sections shall separately set forth each such claim of insufficiency and shall distinctly specify the reason or reasons for each such claimed insufficiency.

[Adopted June 24, 2002, effective January 1, 2003.]

§ 34a–17. Memorandum of Law—Motion and Objection

(a) Each motion to strike must be accompanied by an appropriate memorandum of law citing the legal authorities upon which the motion relies.

(b) Any adverse party who objects to this motion shall, at least five days before the date the motion is to be considered on the short calendar, file and serve in accordance with Sections 10–12(a) and (c), 10–13, 10–14 and 10–17 a memorandum of law.

[Adopted June 24, 2002, effective January 1, 2003.]

§ 34a–18. When Memorandum of Decision Required on Motion to Strike

Whenever a motion to strike is filed and more than one ground of decision is set forth therein, the judicial authority, in rendering the decision thereon, shall specify in writing the grounds upon which that decision is based.

[Adopted June 24, 2002, effective January 1, 2003.]

§ 34a–19. Substitute Pleading; Judgment

Within fifteen days after the granting of any motion to strike, the petitioner may file a new petition; provided that in those instances where an entire petition has been stricken, and the petitioner fails to file a new petition within that fifteen-day period, the judicial authority may, upon motion, enter judgment against said party on said stricken petition.

[Adopted June 24, 2002, effective January 1, 2003.]

§ 34a–20. Discovery

(a) Access to the records of the Department of Children and Families shall be permitted in accordance with General Statutes § 17a–28 and other applicable provisions of the law.

(b) Pretrial discovery by interrogatory, production, inspection or deposition of a person may be allowed with the permission of the judicial authority only if the information or material sought is not otherwise obtainable and upon a finding that proceedings will not be unduly delayed.

(c) Upon its own motion or upon the request of a party, the judicial authority may limit discovery methods, and specify overall timing and sequence, provided that the parties shall be allowed a reasonable opportunity to obtain information needed for the preparation of their case. The judicial authority may grant the requested discovery, order reciprocal discovery, order appropriate sanctions permitted under Section 13–14 for any clear misuse of discovery or arbitrary delay or refusal to comply with a discovery request, and deny, limit, or set conditions on the requested discovery, including any protective orders under Section 13–5.

(d) If the judicial authority permits discovery, the provisions of Sections 13–1 through 13–11 inclusive, 13–14, 13–16, 13–21 through 13–32 inclusive may be incorporated in the discovery order in the discretion of the judicial authority. Motions for discovery or disclosure of confidential records should not be filed unless the moving party has attempted unsuccessfully to obtain an appropriate release or agreement to disclose from the party or person whose records are being sought.

(e) If, subsequent to compliance with any filed request or order for discovery and prior to or during trial, a party discovers additional or new material or information previously requested and ordered subject to discovery or inspection, or discovers that the prior compliance was totally or partially incorrect or, though correct when made, is no longer true and the circumstances are such that a failure to amend the compliance is in substance a knowing concealment, that party shall promptly notify the other party, or the other party's attorney and file and serve in accordance with Section 10–12 through 10–17 a supplemental or corrected compliance.

[Adopted June 24, 2002, effective January 1, 2003.]

Commentary

This section has been transferred, with revisions, from Section 35–3. Changes to this section eliminate the need for burdensome and/or repetitive discovery requests with the goal of expediting child protection proceedings to disposition.

§ 34a–21. Court Ordered Evaluations

(a) The judicial authority, after hearing on a motion for a court ordered evaluation or after an agreement has been reached to conduct such an evaluation, may order a mental or physical examination of a child or youth. The judicial authority after hearing or after an agreement has been reached may also order a thorough physical or mental examination of a parent or guardian whose competency or ability to care for a child or youth is at issue.

(b) At the time of appointment of any court appointed evaluator, counsel and the court services officer shall complete the evaluation form and agree upon appropriate questions to be addressed by the evaluator and materials to be reviewed by the evaluator. If the parties cannot agree, the judicial authority shall decide the issue of appropriate questions to be addressed and materials to be reviewed by the evaluator. A representative of the court shall contact the evaluator and arrange for scheduling and for delivery of the referral package.

(c) Any party who wishes to alter, update, amend or modify the initial terms of referral shall seek prior permission of the judicial authority. There shall be no ex parte communication with the evaluator by counsel prior to completion of the evaluation.

(d) After the evaluation has been completed and filed with the court, counsel may communicate with the evaluator subject to the following terms and conditions:

(1) Counsel shall identify themselves as an attorney and the party she or he represents;

(2) Counsel shall advise the evaluator that with respect to any substantive inquiry into the evaluation or opinions contained therein, the evaluator has the right to have the interview take place in the present of counsel of his/her choice, or in the presence of all counsel of record;

(3) Counsel shall have a duty to disclose to other counsel the nature of any ex parte communication with the evaluator and whether it was substantive or procedural. The disclosure shall occur within a reasonable time after the communication and prior to the time of the evaluator's testimony;

(4) All counsel shall have the right to contact the evaluator and discuss procedural matters relating to the time and place of court hearings or evaluation sessions, the evaluator's willingness to voluntarily attend without subpoena, what records are requested, and the parameters of the proposed examination of the evaluator as a witness.

[Adopted June 24, 2002, effective January 1, 2003.]

Commentary

See General Statutes § 46b–129(i) authorizing evaluations; see also *In re David W.*, 254 Conn. 676 (2000).

§ 34a–22. Motion for Contempt

All motions for contempt must state: (1) the date and specific language of the order of the judicial authority on which the motion is based; (2) the specific acts alleged to constitute the contempt of that order, including the amount of any arrears claimed due as of the date of the motion or a date specifically identified in the motion; (3) the movant's claims for relief for the contempt.

[Adopted June 24, 2002, effective January 1, 2003.]

Commentary

This section is patterned on Section 25–27 of the rules for procedures in family matters.

§ 34a–23. Motion for Emergency Relief

(a) Notwithstanding the above provisions, any party may file a motion for emergency relief, seeking an order directed to the parents, including any person who acknowledged before a judicial authority paternity of a child born out of wedlock, guardians, custodians or other adult persons owing some legal duty to the child, as deemed necessary or appropriate to secure the welfare, protection, proper care and suitable support of a child or youth before this court for the protection of the child. Such orders include, but are not limited to, an order for access to the family home, an order seeking medical exam or mental health exam or treatment of the child, an order to remedy a dangerous condition in the family or foster home, an order to provide or to accept and cooperate with certain services, or an order prohibiting the removal of the child from the state or the home. Such motions may be heard at the next short calendar; however, if the exigencies of the situation demand, the judicial authority may order immediate ex parte relief, pending an expeditious hearing.

(b) No motion for emergency relief shall be granted without notice to each party unless the applicant certifies one of the following to the court in writing:

(1) facts showing that within a reasonable time prior to presenting the motion the moving party gave notice to all other parties of the time when and the place where the motion would be presented and provided a copy of the motion; or

(2) the moving party in good faith attempted but was unable to give notice to the other parties, specifying the efforts made to contact such parties; or

(3) facts establishing good cause why the moving party should not be required to give notice to other parties.

[Adopted June 24, 2002, effective January 1, 2003.]

Commentary

Subsection (b) is patterned on the notice provisions for ex parte temporary injunctions contained in Section 4–5(a).

CHAPTER 35. GENERAL PROVISIONS [REPEALED]

Table of Sections

---

§ 35–1. Petitions, Motions and Amendments [Repealed]

[Repealed June 24, 2002, effective January 1, 2003.]

Commentary

This section has been transferred to Sections 31a–1 and 34a–1.

§ 35–2. Continuances and Advancements [Repealed]

[Repealed June 24, 2002, effective January 1, 2003.]

§ 35–3. Discovery [Repealed]

[Repealed June 24, 2002, effective January 1, 2003.]

Commentary

This section has been transferred to Sections 31a–16 and 34a–20.

§ 35–4. Appeal [Repealed]

[Repealed June 24, 2002, effective January 1, 2003.]

Commentary

This section has been transferred to Section 35a–21.

§ 35–5. Recording of Testimony; Records [Repealed]

[Repealed June 24, 2002, effective January 1, 2003.]

Commentary

Subsection (a) of this section has been transferred to Section 30a–7 and 35a–1(d). Subsections (b) and (c) have been transferred to Section 32a–7.

CHAPTER 35a. HEARINGS CONCERNING NEGLECTED, UNCARED FOR AND DEPENDENT CHILDREN AND TERMINATION OF PARENTAL RIGHTS

Table of Sections

§ 35a–1. Adjudicatory Hearing; Actions by Judicial Authority

(a) The judicial authority shall first determine whether all necessary parties are present and that the rules governing service for nonappearing parties have been complied with, and shall note these facts for the record. The judicial authority shall then inform the unrepresented parties of the substance of the petition.

(b) Notwithstanding any prior statements acknowledging responsibility, the judicial authority shall inquire whether the allegations of the petition are presently admitted or denied. This inquiry shall be made of the custodial parent in neglect, uncared for or dependent matters; and of all appearing parents in termination matters.

(c) A written plea of nolo contendere signed by the respondent may be accepted by the judicial authority. Before accepting an admission or plea of nolo contendere, the judicial authority shall determine whether the right to counsel has been waived, and that the parties understand the content and consequences of their admission or plea. If the allegations are admitted or the plea accepted, the judicial authority shall make its finding as to the validity of the facts alleged in the petition and may proceed to a dispositional hearing.

(d) A verbatim stenographic or electronic recording of all hearings shall be kept, any transcript of which shall be part of the record of the case.

[Adopted June 24, 2002, effective January 1, 2003.]

Commentary

This section has been transferred from Section 33–1. Subsection (d) was transferred from Section 35–5(a).

§ 35a–2. Case Status Conference or Judicial Pretrial

(a) When the allegations of the petition are denied, necessitating testimony in support of the petitioner's allegations, the case shall be continued for a case status conference and/or a judicial pretrial Said case status conference or judicial pretrial may be waived by the judicial authority upon request of all the parties.

(b) Parties with decision-making authority to settle must be present or immediately accessible during a case status conference or judicial pretrial. Continuances will be granted only in accordance with Section 34a–5.

(c) At the case status conference and/or judicial pretrial, all attorneys and pro se parties will be prepared to discuss the following matters:

1. Settlement;
2. Simplification and narrowing of the issues;

3. Amendments to the pleadings;

4. Such other actions as may aid in the disposition of the case;

5. The setting of firm trial dates;

6. Preliminary witness lists;

7. Identification of necessary arrangements for trial including, but not limited to, habeas for incarcerated parties, transportation, interpreters, and special equipment.

(d) When necessary, the judicial authority may issue a trial management order including, but not limited to, an order fixing a date prior to trial by which all parties are to exchange proposed witness and exhibit lists and copies of proposed exhibits not previously exchanged. Failure to comply with this order may result in the imposition of sanctions as the ends of justice may require.

[Adopted June 24, 2002, effective January 1, 2003.]

Commentary

Subsection (a) has been transferred, with revisions, from 33–2. This section is patterned, in part, on Section 14–13. This section clarifies procedures for case status conferences and judicial pretrials and allows for the imposition of trial management orders.

§ 35a–3. Coterminous Petitions

When coterminous petitions are filed, the judicial authority first determines by a fair of preponderance of the evidence whether the child is neglected, uncared for or dependent; if so, then the judicial authority determines whether statutory grounds exist to terminate parental rights by clear and convincing evidence; if so, then the judicial authority determines whether termination is in the best interest of the child by clear and convincing evidence. If the judicial authority determines that termination grounds do not exist or termination is not in the best interest of the child, then the judicial authority may consider by a fair preponderance of the evidence any of the dispositional alternatives available under the neglect, uncared for or dependent petition.

[Adopted June 24, 2002, effective January 1, 2003.]

Commentary

This section has been transferred, with revisions, from Section 33-12. Changes to this section are made for clarification.

§ 35a–4. Intervening Parties

(a) In making a determination upon a motion to intervene by any grandparent of the child, the judicial authority shall consider:

(1) the timeliness of the motion as judged by all the circumstances of the case;

(2) whether the applicant has a direct and immediate interest in the case.

(b) Other persons including, but not limited to, siblings may move to intervene in the dispositional phase of the trial and the judicial authority may grant said motion if it determines that such intervention is in the best interest of the child or in the interests of justice.

(c) In making a determination upon a motion to intervene by any other applicant, the judicial authority shall consider:

(1) the timeliness of the motion as judged by all the circumstances of the case;

(2) whether the applicant has a direct and immediate interest in the case;

(3) whether the applicant's interest is not adequately represented by existing parties;

(4) whether the intervention may cause delay in the proceedings or other prejudice to the existing parties;

(5) the necessity for or value of the intervention in terms of resolving the controversy before the judicial authority.

(d) Upon the granting of such motion, such grandparent or other applicant may appear by counsel or in person. Intervenors are responsible for obtaining their own counsel and are not entitled to appointment of counsel at state expense by the court.

[Adopted June 24, 2002, effective January 1, 2003.]

Commentary

This section clarifies that parties other than parents, guardians or children may intervene and standardizes the manner in which intervention may occur. Although these individuals have a statutory right to be heard, the judicial authority has discretion as to whether they may intervene as a party. The judicial authority may also decide not to permit a grandparent to intervene for good cause shown. See General Statutes § 46b–129(c), Public Act 01–149 and *Horton v. Meskill*, 187 Conn. 187, 193–94 (1982). Subsection (e) makes clear that intervening parties do not have a statutory right to court appointed counsel.

§ 35a–5. Foster Parents' and Siblings' Right to Be Heard

(a) Any foster parent has the right to be heard concerning the placement or revocation of commitment of a foster child living with such foster parent.

(b) Upon motion of any sibling of any child committed to the Department of Children and Families pursuant to General Statutes § 46b–129 the sibling shall have the right to be heard concerning visitation with and placement of any such child.

[Adopted June 24, 2002, effective January 1, 2003.]

Commentary

This section conforms with Public Acts 01–142, Section 8, and 01–149.

§ 35a–6. Post–Disposition Role of Former Guardian

When a court of competent jurisdiction has ordered legal guardianship of a child to a person other than the biological parents of the child prior to the juvenile court proceeding, the juvenile court shall determine at the time of the commitment of the child to the Department of Children and Families whether good cause exists to allow said legal guardian to participate in future proceedings as a party and what, if any further actions the Department of Children and Families and the guardian are required to take.

[Adopted June 24, 2002, effective January 1, 2003.]

Commentary

This section clarifies the future actions and role of a guardian. A judicial authority may issue specific steps for a parent and a guardian.

§ 35a–7. Evidence

(a) In the adjudicatory phase, the judicial authority is limited to evidence of events preceding the filing of the petition or the latest amendment, except where the judicial authority must consider subsequent events as part of its determination as to the existence of a ground for termination of parental rights.

(b) In the discretion of the judicial authority, evidence on adjudication and disposition may be heard in a non-bifurcated hearing, provided disposition may not be considered until the adjudicatory phase has concluded.

[Adopted June 24, 2002, effective January 1, 2003.]

Commentary

This section has been transferred, with revisions, from Section 33–3. The addition to subsection (b) is made for clarification. Post-adjudicatory date evidence may be considered in the adjudicatory phase in a termination of parental rights case alleging the grounds of no ongoing parent-child relationship or failure to rehabilitate. *In re Amber B.*, 56 Conn.App. 776 (2000); *In re Stanley D.*, 61 Conn.App. 224 (2000); *In re Latifa K.*, 67 Conn.App. 742 (2002). Subsection (c) of former Section 33–3 is addressed in greater detail in Section 32a–8, Use of Confidential Records as Evidence.

§ 35a–8. Burden of Proceeding

(a) The petitioner shall be prepared to substantiate the allegations of the petition. If a custodial parent fails to appear, the judicial authority may default that parent, evidence may be introduced and judgment rendered. In the event of a coterminous hearing, the judicial authority shall ensure that the parents are given adequate time to appear.

(b) The clerk shall give notice by mail to the defaulted party and the party's attorney of the default and of any action taken by the judicial authority. The clerk shall note on the docket the date that such notice is given or mailed.

[Adopted June 24, 2002, effective January 1, 2003.]

Commentary

This section has been transferred, with revisions, from Section 33–4. The changes in subsection (a) make it clear that, if a party does not appear, the disposition may go forward. See Section 17–33. Subsection (b) requires the clerk to give notice of a default. See Section 17–36.

§ 35a–9. Dispositional Hearing; Evidence and Social Study

The judicial authority may admit into evidence any testimony relevant and material to the issue of the disposition, including events occurring through the close of the evidentiary hearing, but no disposition may be made by the judicial authority until any mandated social study has been submitted to the judicial authority. Said study shall be marked as an exhibit subject to the right of any party to require that the author, if available, appear for cross-examination.

[Adopted June 24, 2002, effective January 1, 2003.]

Commentary

This section has been transferred with revisions, from Section 33–5.

§ 35a–10. Availability of Social Study to Counsel and Parties

The mandated social study, update or any other written report or evaluation made available to the judicial authority shall be made available for inspection to all counsel of record and, in the absence of counsel, to the parties themselves before the scheduled case status conference, pretrial or hearing date. The mandated social study, updates, reports and records and any copies thereof made available in the discretion of the judicial authority, together with any notes, copies or abstractions thereof, shall be returned to the clerk immediately following the disposition unless they may be required for subsequent proceedings. All persons who have access to such materials shall be responsible for preserving the confidentiality thereof.

[Adopted June 24, 2002, effective January 1, 2003.]

Commentary

This section has been transferred, with revisions, from Section 33–6. The changes to this section ensure that such documents are available to prepare for trial and appeal.

§ 35a–11. Dispositional Plan Offered by Respondents

The respondents shall have the right to produce witnesses on behalf of any dispositional plan they may wish to offer.

[Adopted June 24, 2002, effective January 1, 2003.]

Commentary

This section has been transferred from Section 33–7.

§ 35a–12. Protective Supervision—Conditions and Modification

When protective supervision is ordered, the judicial authority will set forth any conditions of said supervision including duration, specific steps and review dates. Parental noncompliance with the order of protective supervision shall be a ground for a motion to modify the disposition. Upon finding that the circumstances so warrant, the judicial authority on its own motion or acting on a motion of any party and after notice is given and hearing has been held, may modify a previously entered disposition of protective supervision in accordance with the applicable general statutes. A protective supervision order shall be reviewed by the judicial authority at least thirty days prior to its expiration. At said review, an updated social study shall be provided to the judicial authority. If an extension of protective supervision is being sought by the commissioner of the Department of Children and Families or any other party in interest, including counsel for the minor child, then a written motion for the same shall be filed not less than thirty days prior to such expiration. Such motion shall be heard either at the in court review of protective supervision if within thirty days of such expiration or at a hearing to be held within ten days after the filing of such motion. For good cause shown and under extenuating circumstances, such written motion may be filed in a period of less than thirty days prior to the expiration of the protective supervision and the same shall be docketed accordingly. The motion shall set forth the reason(s) for the extension of the protective supervision and the period of the extension being sought.

[Adopted June 24, 2002, effective January 1, 2003.]

Commentary

This section has been transferred, with revisions, from Section 33–8. The changes to this section codify existing practices and procedures relevant to protective supervision dispositions and discourage last minute oral motions for extensions.

§ 35a–13. Findings as to Continuation in the Home, Efforts to Prevent Removal

Whenever the judicial authority orders a child to be removed from the home, the judicial authority shall make written findings: (1) at the time of the order that continuation in the home is contrary to the welfare of the child; and (2) at the time of the order or within sixty days thereafter whether the Commissioner of the Department of Children and Families has made reasonable efforts to prevent removal or whether such efforts were not possible.

[Adopted June 24, 2002, effective January 1, 2003.]

Commentary

This section sets out the findings that are required by statute.

§ 35a–14. Motions for Review of Permanency Plan and to Maintain or Revoke the Commitment

(a) Motions for review of the permanency plan and to maintain or revoke the commitment shall be filed nine months after the placement of the child or youth in the custody of the Commissioner of the Department of Children and Families pursuant to a voluntary placement agreement, or removal of a child pursuant to Conn. General Statutes § 17a–101g or an order of a court of competent jurisdiction whichever is earlier. At the date custody is vested by order of a court of competent jurisdiction, or if no order of temporary custody is issued, at the date when commitment is ordered, the judicial authority shall set a date by which the subsequent motion for review of plan and to maintain or revoke the commitment shall be filed. Nothing in this section shall preclude any party from filing a motion for revocation of commitment separate from a motion for review of permanency plan and to maintain or revoke the commitment subject to subsection (c) of this rule.

(b) Once a motion for review of the permanency plan and to maintain or revoke the commitment has been filed, the clerk of the court shall set a hearing within ninety days thereafter. Any party who is in opposition to a motion shall file a written objection and state the reasons therefor within thirty days after the filing of the Commissioner's motion or a motion for revocation of commitment which shall be considered at the hearing. If there is no objection or motion for revocation filed, then the motion or motions shall be granted by the judicial authority at the date of said hearing.

(c) Whether to maintain or revoke the commitment is a dispositional question, based on the prior adjudication, and the judicial authority shall determine whether it is in the best interest of the child to maintain or revoke upon a fair preponderance of the evidence. The party seeking to maintain the commitment has the burden of proof that it is in the best interest of the child to maintain the commitment. The party seeking revocation of commitment has the burden of proof that no cause for commitment exists. If the burden is met, the party opposing the revocation has the burden of proof that revocation would not be in the best interest of the child. If a motion for revocation is denied, a new motion shall not be filed by the movant until at least six months has elapsed from the date of the filing of the prior motion unless waived by the judicial authority.

(d) The Commissioner of the Department of Children and Families shall propose a permanency plan that conforms to the statutory requirements and shall provide a social study to support said plan, including information indicating what steps the Commissioner has taken to implement it. At the hearing on the motion for review of permanency plan, the judicial authority shall determine whether efforts to reunify the child with the parent have been made, whether such efforts are still appropriate, and whether the Commissioner has made reasonable efforts to achieve the permanency plan for the child. The judicial authority shall also determine whether the proposed goal of the permanency plan is in the best interest of the child by a fair preponderance of the evidence, taking into consideration the child's need for permanency. The child's health and safety shall be of paramount concern in formulating such plan. If a permanency plan is not approved by the judicial authority, it shall order the filing of a revised plan and set a hearing to review said revised plan within sixty days.

(e) If the judicial authority determines at the hearing on the motion for review of permanency plan and to maintain or revoke the commitment that further efforts to reunify the child with the parent are appropriate, the judicial authority shall provide the parent with specific steps the parent shall take to address problems preventing reunification. Six months after such hearing, the judicial authority shall hold another hearing to assess the parent's progress. If the judicial authority finds that the parent has failed to make sustained and significant progress, the judicial authority shall redetermine whether further reunification efforts are appropriate. If the judicial authority determines efforts are not appropriate, it shall order the filing of a revised permanency plan and set a hearing to review said revised plan.

(f) As long as a child remains in the custody of the Commissioner of the Department of Children and Families, the Commissioner shall file a motion for review of permanency plan and to maintain or revoke commitment nine months after the prior permanency plan hearing. No later than twelve months after the approval of a permanency plan, the judicial authority shall hold a subsequent permanency review hearing in accordance with subsection (d), unless such child has been adopted, returned home or guardianship of the child has been transferred pursuant to an order of the judicial authority.

(g) A determination that further efforts to reunify the child with the parent are not appropriate need not be made at subsequent permanency review hearings if the judicial authority has previously determined that such efforts are not appropriate. A determination as to whether the Commissioner of the Department of Children and Families has made reasonable efforts to achieve the permanency plan must be made at each hearing on the motion for review of permanency plan.

(h) Whenever an approved permanency plan needs revision, the Commissioner of the Department of Children and Families shall file a motion for review of the revised permanency plan. The Commissioner is not precluded from initiating a proceeding in the best interests of the child considering the needs for safety and permanency.

[Adopted June 24, 2002, effective January 1, 2003.]

Commentary

This section provides for rules in accordance with provisions set forth in General Statutes § 46b–129(k) as amended by P.A. 01–142. It replaces Sections 33–9 and 33–10.

§ 35a–15. Reunification Efforts—Aggravating Factors

Whenever the Commissioner seeks a finding of the existence of an aggravating factor negating the requirement that reasonable efforts be made to reunify a child with a parent, the Commissioner shall file a petition, or motion if a case is already pending, requesting such finding and the judicial authority shall proceed in accordance with General Statutes § 17a–111b.

[Adopted June 24, 2002, effective January 1, 2003.]

§ 35a–16. Modifications

Motions to modify dispositions are dispositional in nature based on the prior adjudication and the judicial authority shall determine whether a modification is in the best interest of the child upon a fair preponderance of the evidence. Unless filed by the commissioner of children and families, any modification motion to return the child to the custody of the parent without protective supervision shall be treated as a motion for revocation of commitment.

[Adopted June 24, 2002, effective January 1, 2003.]

Commentary

This section has been transferred, with revisions, from Section 33–11. The changes in this section were made for clarification.

§ 35a–17. Motions to Review Plan for Child Whose Parents' Rights Have Been Terminated

Where a petition for termination of parental rights is granted, the guardian of the child or statutory parent shall report to the judicial authority within 30 days of the date judgment is entered on a permanency plan and on the status of the child. At least every three months thereafter, such guardian or statutory parent shall make a report to the judicial authority on the implementation of the plan, or earlier if the plan changes before the elapse of three months. A hearing shall be held before the judicial authority for the purpose of reviewing the plan for the child no more than twelve months from the date judgment is entered or from the date of the last permanency hearing held in accordance with General Statutes § 46b–129(k), whichever is earlier, and at least once a year thereafter until such time as a proposed adoption or transfer of guardianship is finalized. At each court hearing, the judicial authority will make factual findings whether or not reasonable efforts to achieve permanency or promote adoption have been made.

[Adopted June 24, 2002, effective January 1, 2003.]

Commentary

This section incorporates requirements of Public Act 01–159 and federal requirements.

§ 35a–18. Opening Default

Any order or decree entered through a default may be set aside within four months succeeding the date of such entry of the order or decree upon the written motion of any party or person prejudiced thereby, showing reasonable cause, or that a defense in whole or in part existed at the time of the rendition of such order or of such decree, and that the party so defaulted was prevented by mistake, accident or other reasonable cause from prosecuting or appearing to make the same. Such written motion shall be verified by the oath of the complainant, and shall state in general terms the nature of the claim or defense and shall particularly set forth the reason why the party failed to appear. The judicial authority shall order reasonable notice of the pendency of such motion to be given to all parties to the action, and may enjoin enforcement of such order or decree until the decision upon such written motion, unless said action shall prejudice or place the child's health, safety or welfare in jeopardy. A hearing on said motion shall be held as a priority matter but no later than 15 days after the same has been filed with the clerk of the juvenile court, unless otherwise agreed to by the parties and sanctioned by the judicial authority. In the event that said motion is granted the matter shall be scheduled for an immediate pretrial or case status conference within fourteen days thereof, and failing a resolution at that time, then the matter shall be scheduled for a trial as expeditiously as possible.

[Adopted June 24, 2002, effective January 1, 2003.]

Commentary

This allowance to reopen a default decree or judgment modifies Section 17–43 to accommodate the need to proceed expeditiously toward permanency in the best interest of the child.

§ 35a–19. Transfer from Probate Court of Petitions for Removal of Parent as Guardian or Termination of Parental Rights

(a) When a contested application for removal of parent as guardian or petition for termination of parental rights or application to commit a child to a hospital for the mentally ill has been transferred from the court of probate to the superior court, the clerk shall transmit to the probate court from which the transfer was made a copy of any orders or decrees thereafter rendered, including orders regarding reinstatement pursuant to General Statutes § 45a–611 and visitation pursuant to General Statutes § 45a–612, and a copy of any appeal of a superior court decision in the matter.

(b) The date of receipt by the superior court of a transferred petition shall be the filing date for determining initial hearing dates in the superior court. The date of receipt by the superior court of any court of probate issued ex parte order of temporary custody not heard by that court shall be the issuance date in the superior court.

(c)(1) Any appearance filed for any party in the court of probate shall continue in the superior court until withdrawn or replaced. The superior court clerk shall notify appearing parties in applications for removal of guardian by mail of the date of the initial hearing. Not less than ten days before the initial hearing, the superior court clerk shall cause a copy of the transfer order and probate petition for removal of guardian, and an advisement of rights notice to be served on any non-appearing party or any party not served within the last twelve months with an accompanying order of notice and summons to appear at an initial hearing.

(2) Not less than 10 days before the initial hearing, the superior court clerk shall cause a copy of the transfer order and probate petition for termination of parental rights, and an advisement of rights notice to be served on all parties, regardless of prior service, with an accompanying order of notice and summons to appear at an initial hearing not less than ten days before the date of the hearing.

(3) The superior court clerk shall mail notice of the initial hearing date for all transferred petitions to all counsel of record and to the commissioner of the Department of Children and Families or to any other agency which has been ordered by the probate court to conduct an investigation pursuant to General Statutes § 45a–619. The commissioner or any other in-

vestigating agency will be notified of the need to have a representative present at the initial hearing.

[Adopted June 24, 2002, effective January 1, 2003.]

Commentary

This section has been transferred, with revisions, from Section 33–13. Service must be in accordance with General Statutes § 45a–716(c) for termination petitions, therefore, service must be made in ten, rather than the fourteen days. See also General Statutes §§ 45a–715(g) and 45a–623, which mandate that the judges of the Supreme Court adopt rules for the transfer of petitions for removal of guardian and termination of parental rights.

§ 35a–20. Petitions for Reinstatement of Parent as Guardian

Whenever a parent or legal guardian whose guardianship rights to a child were removed and transferred to another person by the superior court for juvenile matters seeks reinstatement as that child's guardian, the parent or legal guardian may file a petition with the court that ordered the transfer of guardianship.

The clerk of the court shall assign such petition a hearing date and issue a summons. The petitioner shall cause a copy of such petition and summons to be served on the child's current legal guardian(s). Before acting on such petition, the judicial authority shall determine if the court still has custody jurisdiction and shall request, if necessary, that the Commissioner of the Department of Children and Families conduct an investigation and submit written findings and recommendations before rendering a decision.

[Adopted June 24, 2002, effective January 1, 2003.]

Commentary

This section establishes a process for a parent whose guardianship is revoked to be reinstated.

§ 35a–21. Appeals

(a) Appeals from final judgments or decisions of the superior court in juvenile matters shall be taken within twenty days from the issuance of notice of the rendition of the judgment or decision from which the appeal is taken in the manner provided by the rules of appellate procedure.

(b) If an indigent party wishes to appeal a final decision and if the trial counsel declines to represent the party because in counsel's professional opinion the appeal lacks merit, counsel shall file a timely motion to withdraw and to extend time in which to take an appeal. The judicial authority shall then forthwith appoint another attorney to review this record who, if willing to represent the party on appeal, will be appointed for this purpose. If the second attorney determined that there is no merit to an appeal, that attorney shall make this known to the judicial authority at the earliest possible moment, and the party will be informed by the clerk forthwith that the party has the balance of the extended time to appeal in which to secure counsel who, if qualified, may be appointed to represent the party on the appeal.

(c) The time to take an appeal shall not be extended past forty days from the date of the issuance of notice of the rendition of the judgment or decision.

[Adopted June 24, 2002, effective January 1, 2003.]

Commentary

This section has been transferred, with revisions, from Section 35–4. Subsection (c) has been added to make it clear that no party may be granted more than 40 days from the issuance of notice of the judgment or decision to commence an appeal.

PROCEDURE IN CRIMINAL MATTERS

CHAPTER 40. DISCOVERY AND DEPOSITIONS

---

§ 40–40. Protective Orders—Relief

Upon the filing of a motion for a protective order by either party and after a hearing thereon, the judicial authority may at any time order that disclosure or inspection be denied, restricted or deferred, or that reasonable conditions be imposed as to the manner of inspection, photographing, copying or testing, to the extent necessary to protect the evidentiary values of any information or material.

§ 40–41. Protective Orders—Grounds

In deciding the motion for a protective order the judicial authority may consider the following:

(1) The timeliness of the motion;

(2) The protection of witnesses and others from physical harm, threats of harm, bribes, economic reprisals and other intimidation;

(3) The maintenance of secrecy regarding informants as required for effective investigation of criminal activity;

(4) The protection of confidential relationships, privileges and communications recognized by law; and

(5) Any other relevant considerations.

§ 40-42. Protective Orders—In Camera Proceedings

Upon the hearing of any motion under Sections 40-40 through 40-43, the judicial authority may permit all or part of any showing of cause for denial or deferral of access to be made in camera and out of the presence of the opposing party. Any in camera proceedings shall be recorded verbatim. If the judicial authority allows any access to be denied or deferred, the entire record of the in camera proceedings shall be sealed and preserved in the court's records, to be made available to the appellate court in the event of an appeal.

§ 40-43. Protective Orders—Excision

If the moving party claims in a motion for a protective order that a portion of any information or materials requested or required to be disclosed is not subject to disclosure or inspection or contains irrelevant material, that party shall deliver such information or materials to the judicial authority for inspection in camera out of the presence of the other party. If the judicial authority excises any portion of such information or materials, a record of the in camera proceedings shall be made and sealed and preserved in the court's records, to be made available to the appellate court in the event of an appeal. That portion of the information or materials made available to the other party shall show that an excision has been made.

RULES OF APPELLATE PROCEDURE

Including Amendments Received Through August 1, 2004

CHAPTER 70. ARGUMENTS AND MEDIA COVERAGE OF COURT PROCEEDINGS

§ 70–10. Cameras and Electronic Media; Coverage of Supreme and Appellate Court Proceedings by News Media

(a) The broadcasting, televising, recording or photographing of court proceedings by news media in the courtroom will be allowed subject to the limitations set forth herein.

(b) Any member of the news media seeking permission to broadcast, televise, record or photograph a court proceeding appearing on a printed docket of the court, excluding any hearing on a motion, shall, not later than two weeks before the term for which such printed docket is prepared, file a written request with the appellate clerk and at the same time shall send by certified mail a copy of such written request to each counsel or pro se party of record. Endorsed on the request filed with the appellate clerk shall be a certification of such mailing. If any counsel or pro se party of record wishes to be excluded from any broadcasting, televising, recording or photographing in a court proceeding appearing on a printed docket of the court, he or she shall file a written request with the appellate clerk not later than six days before the term for which such printed docket is prepared. The request shall set forth in detail the reasons why the request should be granted. The printed docket shall indicate the dates by which requests for coverage and requests for exclusion must be filed. The appellate clerk shall refer any such requests to the appellate jurists for review and their decision on the requests shall be final. Before the appellate jurists approve of any request for coverage, they shall be satisfied that the permitted coverage will not interfere with the rights of the parties to a fair hearing. The right, however, to permit or to exclude coverage, whether partially or totally, at any time in the interests of the administration of justice shall remain with the appellate jurists.

(c) Generally, no broadcasting, televising, recording or photographing of any proceedings in appeals taken from trial court judgments in the following cases shall be permitted:

(1) Family relations matters as defined in General Statutes § 46b–1;

(2) Cases involving trade secrets;

(3) Cases involving sexual offense charges;

(4) Cases which were closed to the public to comply with the provisions of state law.

(d) No broadcasting, televising, recording or photographic equipment permitted under these rules shall be operated during a recess.

(e) No audio broadcasting or audio recording of conferences in the courtroom among members of the court, between cocounsel or between counsel and client shall be permitted.

(f)(1) Only one television camera operator, utilizing one portable mounted television camera, shall be permitted in the courtroom. The television camera and operator shall be positioned only in such location in the courtroom as shall be designated by the appellate jurists. To the extent possible, that location shall provide access to optimum coverage. While court proceedings are in progress, the television camera operator shall operate the television camera only in that designated location. Videotape recording equipment and other equipment which are not component parts of a television camera shall be located outside the courtroom.

(2) Only one still camera photographer, carrying not more than two still cameras with not more than one lens for each camera, shall be permitted in the courtroom. The still camera photographer shall be positioned only in such location in the courtroom as shall be designated by the court. To the extent possible, that location shall provide access to optimum coverage. While court proceedings are in progress, the still camera photographer shall photograph court proceedings only from that location.

(3) Only one audio system for television, broadcasting and recording purposes shall be permitted in the courtroom. Audio pickup for such purposes shall be accomplished from the existing audio system in the court facility. If there is no technically suitable audio system in the court facility, microphones and related wiring essential for media purposes shall be unobtrusive and shall be located in places designated in advance by the appellate jurists.

(g) No broadcasting, televising, recording OR photographic equipment shall be placed in or removed from the courtroom while the court is in session. Television film magazines or still camera film or lenses may be changed within the courtroom, provided that it is done in a quiet and unobtrusive manner.

(h) Only still camera, television and audio equipment which does not produce distracting sound or light shall be employed to cover the proceeding. The operator of such equipment shall not employ any artificial lighting device to supplement the existing light in the courtroom.

(i) Participating members of the broadcasting, televising, recording and photographic media shall make their respective pooling arrangements, including the establishment of necessary procedures and selection of pool representatives, without calling upon the appellate jurists to mediate any dispute as to the appropriate media representative or equipment for a particular proceeding. If any such medium shall not agree on equipment, procedures and personnel, the appellate jurists shall not permit that medium to have coverage.

(j) Except as provided by these rules, established restrictions upon broadcasting, televising, recording and photographing in areas adjacent to courtrooms shall remain in full force.

(k) The conduct of all attorneys with respect to publicity shall be governed by Disciplinary Rule 3.6 of the Rules of Professional Conduct.

[Amended February 19, 2003, effective January 1, 2004.]

CHAPTER 79. APPEALS IN JUVENILE MATTERS

Table of Sections

§ 79–1. Time to Take; Form; Filing; Costs

Appeals from judgments of the superior court in juvenile matters shall be taken within twenty days from the issuance of notice of the rendition of the judgment from which the appeal is taken.

The appeal shall be filed with the clerk in charge of juvenile matters with sufficient copies so that the clerk may distribute copies as required by Section 79–2.

An appellant who is indigent may make written application to the court before which the juvenile matter was heard for waiver of fees as provided in Section 63–6 or 63–7.

§ 79–2. Clerk's Duties

In addition to the clerk's duties as specified in Section 63–3, the clerk of the superior court in charge of juvenile matters shall also send a copy of the endorsed appeal form and the docket sheet to the commissioner of children and families, to the petitioner upon whose application the proceedings in the superior court were instituted, unless such party is the appellant, to any person or agency having custody of any child who is a subject of the proceeding, and to all other interested persons; and if the addresses of any such persons do not appear of record, such juvenile clerk shall call the matter to the attention of a judge of the superior court who shall make such an order of notice as such judge deems advisable.

§ 79–3. Inspection of Records

The records and papers of any juvenile matter shall be open for inspection only to counsel of record and to others having a proper interest therein only upon order of the court. The name of the child or youth involved in any appeal from a juvenile matter shall not appear on the record of the appeal.

§ 79–4. Hearings; Confidentiality

(a) For the purpose of maintaining confidentiality, upon the hearing of an appeal from a juvenile matter, the court may exclude any person from the court whose presence is unnecessary.

(b) All proceedings shall be conducted in a manner that will preserve the anonymity of the child or youth.

[Amended October 15, 2003, effective January 1, 2004.]

PROBATE RULES FOR PRACTICE AND PROCEDURE

Including Amendments Received Through August 1, 2004

Table of Rules

RULE 3. CONSERVATORS

3.1 Definitions for Purposes of This Rule

.01. BANK: The term BANK shall mean any corporate banking institution authorized to act in this state as conservator of an estate.

.02. INTERESTED PARTIES: The term INTERESTED PARTIES shall mean persons, agencies or institutions who shall appear to the court of probate to be legitimately interested in the welfare of the RESPONDENT.

.03. MAIL NOTICE: The term MAIL NOTICE shall have the same definition as is given to that term in Rule 1.1.04.

.04. NEWSPAPER NOTICE: The term NEWSPAPER NOTICE shall have the same definition as is given to that term in Rule 1.1.05.

.05. PROBATE BOND: The term PROBATE BOND shall have the same definition as is given to that term in Rule 2.1.05.

3.2 Public Notice of Application to Appoint a Conservator

Upon application for the appointment of a conservator for a RESPONDENT, the court shall determine whether notice to the public is warranted. If the court so determines, the clerk of the court of probate shall give NEWSPAPER NOTICE to the public of the pending proceedings. Such NEWSPAPER NOTICE shall be printed at least once and shall appear not later than two days before the date of hearing on the application for appointment of a conservator.

3.3 Conservator of Person or Estate

In the application for the appointment of a conservator, the petitioner shall state whether the conservator is sought for the person of the RESPONDENT or his or her estate or both.

3.4 Medical Evidence

Ordinarily, the judge of probate shall require the medical evidence as to the incapacity of the RESPONDENT. If medical evidence is required, the judge of probate or guardian ad litem appointed to represent the RESPONDENT shall inform the RESPONDENT of his or her right to cross-examine any physicians who give medical evidence at the hearing and of the RESPONDENT'S right to introduce medical evidence by a physician of the RESPONDENT'S choice.

3.5 Appointment of GUARDIAN AD LITEM in Conservatorship Proceedings

Upon the application for the appointment of a conservator, the judge of probate may appoint a GUARDIAN AD LITEM to represent a RESPONDENT who is not represented by counsel.

The judge shall appoint an attorney to represent an elderly person for whom a conservator is sought under Gen.Stat. § 17a–436, if that person has no other legal representation.

3.6 Qualifications for Conservator

Any person, legally authorized state official or private, non-profit corporation other than a hospital or nursing home whom the court finds to be able to act responsibly and capably in a fiduciary manner may be appointed conservator of the estate, conservator of the person, or both, except as limited by statute. In addition, a private, for profit corporation may be appointed conservator of the estate. In the event that the RESPONDENT is over 60 years of age, the Commissioner of Human Resources is authorized by Gen.Stat. § 45a–651 to be conservator of the person.

Under Gen.Stat. §§ 4a–14 and 4a–15, the estate administrator from the Department of Administrative Services may act as conservator of the estate of any incapable who is receiving financial aid from the state if the estate consists of personal property which does not exceed $10,000.

3.7 Bond for Conservator

The amount of and security for a PROBATE BOND required of a conservator is to be determined by the judge of probate in accordance with Rule 2.

3.8 Inventory and Accounting by Conservator of the Estate

Each such conservator shall promptly comply with an order of the court of probate concerning the filing of an account. Unless excused from filing a periodic account by statutory provisions, he or she shall file an account at least once during each three-year period. In addition, the court may require, and at the request of any interested party, shall require an annual accounting. One example of when the court may require an annual accounting would be where there are complaints from relatives, creditors, or other interested parties. When the conservator's appointment has terminated for any reason, he or she shall file a final account within two months after such termination. The accounts filed by a conservator of the estate shall conform to Rule 6.

[Amended effective November 1, 1979; October 1, 1981; revised 1990; 1992.]

RULE 4. GUARDIANS AD LITEM

4.1 Definitions for Purposes of This Rule

.01. CAUSE FOR APPOINTMENT OF A GUARDIAN AD LITEM: The term CAUSE FOR APPOINTMENT OF A GUARDIAN AD LITEM shall mean any facts showing that the rights of a minor, incompetent person, undetermined or unborn person, or class of such persons may be substantially affected in a proceeding before a court of probate. At any point in a proceeding, a court may appoint a GUARDIAN AD LITEM to represent the interest of a minor, an incompetent, unborn, or unascertained person, or a person whose identity or whereabouts or address is unknown, if the court determines that representation of the interest otherwise would be inadequate. If not precluded by conflict of interests, a GUARDIAN AD LITEM may be appointed to represent several persons or interests.

.02. GUARDIAN AD LITEM: The term GUARDIAN AD LITEM shall have the same definition as is given to that term in Rule 1.1.09.

4.2 Appointment of a GUARDIAN AD LITEM

.01. The judge of probate shall appoint a GUARDIAN AD LITEM whenever CAUSE FOR APPOINTMENT OF A GUARDIAN AD LITEM exists, unless cause is shown for not making such an appointment in which case the judge shall make a finding in the final decree on the matter as to why such appointment was not made.

.02. In any proceeding involving a minor child in which child abuse is alleged as a reason for terminating parental rights or removing guardians of the person, the court shall appoint a GUARDIAN AD LITEM.

4.3 Duties and Functions of the GUARDIAN AD LITEM

The GUARDIAN AD LITEM shall take all action necessary for the protection of the rights of the person he or she represents, including review of all pertinent documents, investigation of facts of the estate in respect to which the GUARDIAN AD LITEM has been appointed, insuring that he or she will receive notice of all events affecting the estate and appear at hearings as necessary. The judge of probate may, if he or she deems such action advisable, instruct the GUARDIAN AD LITEM concerning his or her responsibilities and require the GUARDIAN AD LITEM to take specific steps on behalf of the person he or she represents.

The GUARDIAN AD LITEM has a duty to make proper objections to any actions by a fiduciary or the court of probate when the GUARDIAN AD LITEM believes it essential to do so for the protection of rights of the person he or she represents. All such objections shall be in writing setting forth the reasons therefor.

The GUARDIAN AD LITEM shall make a report to the court in writing setting forth the results of his or her investigation and advice on behalf of the person represented.

4.4 Who Shall Be Appointed GUARDIAN AD LITEM

The court of probate shall appoint as GUARDIAN AD LITEM any proper adult person who does not have interests conflicting with those of the person or class of persons for whom a GUARDIAN AD LITEM is to be appointed.

4.5 Limitations on Authority of GUARDIAN AD LITEM

The GUARDIAN AD LITEM may recommend to the court of probate a waiver, modification or compromise of the rights of the person for whom he or she has been appointed a GUARDIAN AD LITEM, and the court of probate may adopt such recommendation. The GUARDIAN AD LITEM may not deal with or administer property of that person.

4.6 Appeals and Employment of Counsel

The GUARDIAN AD LITEM may appeal from any ruling of the court of probate by which the person he or she represents is aggrieved and may incur necessary expenses therefor, subject to the approval of the court of probate.

4.7 Compensation of GUARDIAN AD LITEM

The GUARDIAN AD LITEM shall be allowed reasonable compensation, which shall be an expense of the estate being administered.

[Amended effective November 1, 1979; revised 1992.]

RULE 5. GUARDIANS

5.1 Definitions for Purposes of This Rule

.01. BANK: The term BANK shall mean any corporate banking institution authorized to act as a guardian of an estate.

.02. INTERESTED PARTY: The term INTERESTED PARTY shall mean any person, agency, or institution who shall appear to the court of probate to be interested in the welfare of a minor.

.03. MAIL NOTICE: The term MAIL NOTICE shall have the same definition as is given to that term in Rule 1.1.04.

.04. PROBATE BOND: The term PROBATE BOND shall have the same definition as is given to that term in Rule 2.1.05.

.05. MINOR RESPONDENT: The term MINOR RESPONDENT shall mean a person under the age of majority for whom an application for appointment of a guardian has been made or for whom a guardian has been appointed.

5.2 Appointment of Guardian of the Person

The court of probate, upon application of an INTERESTED PARTY, or on its own motion, may appoint a proper adult person as guardian of the person of a MINOR RESPONDENT who has no parent or guardian of the person.

5.3 Bond for Guardian of the Person

A guardian of the person may be required to give a PROBATE BOND if the court of probate deems it necessary for the protection of the minor.

5.4 Appointment and Qualifications of Guardian of the Estate

Upon application of an INTERESTED PARTY or upon its own motion for appointment of guardian of the estate for a MINOR RESPONDENT having an interest in real or personal property, the court of probate shall appoint a guardian of the MINOR RESPONDENT'S estate, if such appointment is required by statute or is in the best interest of the MINOR RESPONDENT. Any adult person whom the court of probate finds to be able to act responsibly and capably in a fiduciary capacity may be appointed a guardian of the estate subject to applicable statutory provisions. The court of probate may, in its discretion, appoint a BANK as guardian of the estate.

5.5 Bond for Guardian of the Estate

The appointment of a person as guardian of the estate is not effective until he or she has filed a PROBATE BOND with the court of probate.

5.6 Notice of Hearing on Appointment of Guardian of the Estate

Where the MINOR RESPONDENT has parents or a guardian of his or her person or is a beneficiary of the Veterans' Administration, the court of probate shall order that MAIL NOTICE be sent to any such parents, guardian of the person, or Veterans' Administration and MINOR RESPONDENT, if twelve years of age or over, of the hearing on application for appointment of guardian of the estate.

5.7 Inventory and Accounting by Guardian of the Estate

Each guardian of the estate shall file an inventory of the estate within two months after his or her appointment.

Each guardian of the estate shall promptly comply with an order of the court of probate concerning the filing of an account. Unless excused from filing a periodic account by statutory provisions, he or she shall file an account at least once during each three-year period. Any guardian of the estate whose appointment has terminated for any reason shall file a final account with the court of probate within two months after such termination without any order of the court. The accounts filed by a guardian of the estate shall conform to Rule 6.

5.8 Limitations on Application of This Rule

Rule 5 does not apply to guardians for the mentally retarded.

[Amended effective November 1, 1979; October 1, 1981; revised 1990; 1992.]

FAIRFIELD JUDICIAL DISTRICT STANDING ORDERS *

Including Amendments Received Through August 1, 2004

FAMILY—HON. BRIAN T. FISHER

Table of Standing Orders

Trial Management Order

Counsel and pro se parties in the above captioned matter are ordered to submit to the trial judge, **one week prior to the assigned trial date**, documents in compliance with this Trial Management Order. Only one packet is to be submitted by each party. The compliance shall contain the following documents:

1. **A copy of the claims for relief, current financial affidavits, and statement of arrearages claimed for any pendente lite orders.**

2. Current sworn financial affidavits, which include detailed income statements, a complete list of liabilities, fair market value of all assets and current value of all retirement and employment benefits.

3. A list of pending motions, outstanding discovery requests and proposed motions in limine.

4. A list setting forth the names and addresses of each witness to be called at trial, including the relationship of each witness to the case (e.g. party, fact witness, expert); and whether a scheduling problem exists as to the testimony of any such witness. Witnesses not listed will **not** be allowed to testify except for good cause shown.

5. A list of exhibits reasonably expected to be introduced, indexed by number for plaintiff (i.e. Plaintiff's 1), letter for defendant (i.e. Defendant's A), and M+numeral for minor child(ren) (i.e. M # 1). The list shall briefly describe each exhibit and indicate whether any party objects to the admission of such exhibit. If there is an objection, the exhibit should be marked for identification. The actual exhibits shall not be included with the list to be sent to the court but shall be exchanged by the parties within the time specified. Exhibits not listed will **not** be admissible except for good cause shown. Counsel are to report to the courtroom clerk at 9:00 a.m. in order to complete the marking of exhibits for the trial.

6. Identification of all anticipated evidentiary disputes. Citations of authorities for any unusual issues with a short statement as to the holding of cases, and copies of all unpublished cases.

7. Per your request, your case was assigned trial dates to which you will be held accountable. If for some reason more or fewer days are needed, specify the number and the reasons for the change.

8. If custody and visitation are agreed upon, a written and signed stipulation should be included detailing the agreement signed by the parties.

9. Written proposed orders (Conn. Prac. Bk Sec. 25–30) which shall be comprehensive and shall set forth the party's requested relief including where applicable the following:

   1. a parenting plan;
   2. child support;
   3. alimony;
   4. medical insurance;
   5. life insurance;
   6. property division;
   7. retirement benefits;
   8. division of liabilities;
   9. tax issues;
   10. counsel fees.

10. In addition to documents mentioned earlier herein, the following documents where applicable are to be submitted on the day of trial:

* © 2004 Connecticut Judicial Branch, reprinted with permission

a. dissolution of marriage report;
b. affidavit concerning children;
c. child support guidelines worksheet;
d. advisement of rights form;
e. certificate of attendance at parenting education.

11. Ex parte communication with the court is strictly prohibited.

12. When both parties are represented by counsel, a trial management conference with counsel and the Court will take place immediately before commencement of the trial in chambers. When one or both parties are pro se, the trial management conference will take place immediately before commencement of trial in open court.

Variations from this order may be made only with the approval of the court.

____

BRIAN T. FISHER
PRESIDING JUDGE—FAMILY

Notice of Trial

SUPERIOR COURT
STATE OF CONNECTICUT
1061 Main Street, Bridgeport, Connecticut 06604
Telephone: (203) 579–6540

DATE: ________

DOCKET NO. ___

NAME OF CASE: ________

The undersigned attorneys or pro se parties of record acknowledge that notice of trial to be held on ________ has been received on the above date. **MOTIONS FOR CONTINUANCE MUST BE FILED AT LEAST ONE WEEK BEFORE THE SCHEDULED TRIAL DATE. SUCH REQUESTS WILL NOT BE GRANTED UNLESS FOR GOOD CAUSE SHOWN.**

The undersigned also acknowledge that failure of counsel or a pro se party to appear for trial on the trial date will result in either the dismissal of the case, with prejudice, or the matter may proceed as an uncontested dissolution.

The undersigned also acknowledge receipt of both the Standing Trial Management Order and Trial Management Conference Procedure.

____

Counsel for Plaintiff/Pro Se

____

Counsel for Defendant/Pro Se

____

Counsel for Minor Child(ren)

HARTFORD JUDICIAL DISTRICT STANDING ORDERS *

Including Amendments Received Through August 1, 2004

FAMILY—HON. F. HERBERT GRUENDEL

Table of Standing Orders

Family Standing Orders

EX PARTE MATTERS

1. All ex parte matters are to be filed in the Family Clerk's Office. The clerk will pull the file and bring it to the judge with the motion. No ex parte motion will be brought directly to a judge by a party or counsel.

2. **The clerk shall inquire whether there is an attorney on the other side, whether that attorney has notice of the filing of the ex parte matter** and if the other attorney objects. Counsel should be directed to notify the attorney on the other side of the case by the applying **counsel unless counsel represents that notifying opposing counsel would endanger** the applying party. After an attorney on the other side has notice of the ex parte matter **and an opportunity to object**, the clerk shall take the papers to the judge with the court file, if one already exists. This procedure applies to TROs as well as to the ex parte motions.

3. The following judge will review all ex parte matters, applications for temporary restraining orders and fee waivers:

September 2003	**Judge Gruendel**
October 2003	**Judge Caruso**
November 2003	**Judge Gruendel**
December 2003	**Judge Caruso**
January 2004	**Judge Gruendel**
February 2004	**Judge Caruso**
March 2004	**Judge Gruendel**
April 2004	**Judge Caruso**
May 2004	**Judge Gruendel**
June 2004	**Judge Caruso**
July 2004	**Judge Gruendel**
August 2004	**Judge Caruso**

TEMPORARY RESTRAINING ORDERS

1. The Clerk's Office shall inquire as to the existence of any criminal and/or family matters. If the applicant states that there is a criminal matter, the clerk will complete a computer criminal check when possible. The clerk will make notes as to the status of any criminal case. If a family file exists, that file should be pulled and brought to the judge with the TRO application. Notes on criminal searches must be kept confidential and must be disposed of after the judge reviews them because some of the information obtained in a criminal search is not public information.

2. When custody is requested on a TRO application, the applicant must fully complete a custody affidavit.

FEE WAIVERS

1. Fee waivers may be granted by the Clerk's Office on the judge's behalf on post-judgment motions

* © 2004 Connecticut Judicial Branch, reprinted with permission.

for filing fees and for marshal's fees "up to $60" when the applicant:

Is receiving AFDC or City Assistance *and*

Has minimal assets.

OR

If the party falls within 125% of the Federal Poverty Guidelines, as posted in the Family Clerk's Office *and*

Has minimal assets.

2. Fee waivers may not be granted by the Clerk's Office on the judge's behalf for publication, new actions or parenting education.

3. When the applicant for a Restraining Order does not apply for a fee waiver with the TRO and then requests a fee waiver after the judge has granted the TRO, the clerk may grant the fee waiver on the judge's behalf if the applicant is on state/city assistance or falls within 125% of the Federal Poverty Guidelines..

4. Fee waiver applications must be completed fully. If income is zero, the party must explain on the fee waiver application how he or she is living.

5. If a fee waiver request is for a Parenting Education Program, the clerk must send the file to the judge with the request. The clerk should ask the party to indicate the other parent's weekly gross income and make a note of that amount on the file cover or complete an affidavit to be made available in the Clerk's Office stating the place of employment and the approximate income of the other parent.

CHILDREN'S LAW CENTER

1. **Children's Law Center: Fees are to be waived automatically for all copies requested by the Children's Law Center. All clients represented by the Children's Law Center are indigent.**

2. **When a judge appoints the Children's Law Center in a case, the courtroom clerk, in addition to recording the appointment on the docket and in the order when written up, will indicate "CLC" on the order and circle it. The clerk will then give to a designated Family Office supervisor the case name, docket number, name of attorney appointed, name of judge, date and any other pertinent information.**

3. **Whenever any pleadings or other papers are filed, they must be served not only on the opposing party/opposing attorney, but *also* on *all* attorneys of record, *including the guardian ad litem and/or attorney for the minor child.***

MOTIONS TO MODIFY

Motions to modify must state the substance of the initial order and must state the substantial change in circumstances alleged.

APPLICATIONS FOR NAME CHANGE

1. Applications for name change after a disposition shall not appear on short calendar, but shall be brought to the judge as ex parte requests. No fee shall be charged for such a name change.

2. **Applications for inmate change of name shall require the inmate to be habeased in for a hearing date. Inmates seeking a name change must appear in court and must be canvassed.**

3. **Any party seeking a name change shall complete an affidavit stating that he or she has not been convicted of any crime requiring registration with any sex offender registry.**

MISCELLANEOUS CALENDAR (#3) AND CONTEMPT CALENDAR (#4)

1. Cases must be marked "ready" even if a date certain has been assigned to the motion and served upon the opposing party.

2. When a case on the Wednesday calendar is not marked ready according to proper practice, the case shall not be allowed to go forward unless both sides appear and they have an agreement. The moving party shall be instructed to reclaim the motion when appropriate.

3. Continuance Policy: The clerk may grant a continuance only if (1) the parties agree, (2) a citation has not been issued, and (3) the matter is not a "Family Division Report" or a "case held on docket."

JUDGMENT FILES

Judgment files: incorporate by reference or not as the parties desire.

SECOND ORDER OF NOTICE

The clerk may grant second order of notice upon presentation. The clerk will pull the file, take out the original order of notice, change the return date on all papers, make a copy of all papers and give the originals to the party for service.

PROPER VENUE

The Family Clerk's Office shall not accept for filing any family case for which Hartford is not the proper venue without approval of the Presiding Family Judge.

EX PARTE COMMUNICATIONS

Lawyers will not have ex parte communications with judges except as allowed by the Practice Book and the Code of Judicial Ethics.

EVIDENTIARY MATERIAL FILED WITH MOTION

Except for ex parte motions or as required by the Practice Book, evidentiary material should not be attached to motions.

ATTORNEY FOR MINOR CHILD/GUARDIAN AD LITEM

1. Whenever an attorney for the minor child or guardian ad litem is appointed, the judge making or approving the appointment will continue the case for three weeks to have the parties report back whether arrangements satisfactory to the AMC/GAL have been made for payment of fees. If such arrangements have been made, the parties need not report back on the continuance date.

2. When a judge appoints an attorney for a minor child or a guardian ad litem, he or she should do so substantially in accordance with the form attached hereto. Forms should be available on all family courtroom benches.

READY MARKINGS

1. When marking a matter "ready" for pretrial, trial, or short calendar, parties must represent that the attorney for the minor child and/or the guardian ad litem has been notified of the marking.

2. When family division reports other than successful mediations appear on the short calendar, the judges will not read them except with the permission of all parties. The purpose of the reports is so that the judge can determine what additional steps need to be taken.

FEE WAIVERS

All fee waivers ordered on new writs shall automatically include a waiver of the $5.00 fee required by § 10 of Bill No. 7507 of the 2001 Legislative Session, effective July 2, 2001.

UNSEALING FINANCIAL AFFIDAVITS

The court hearing any contested matter involving financial orders shall, at the commencement of the hearing, order that all financial affidavits previously submitted shall be unsealed. The courtroom clerk is expected to bring this issue to the judge's attention if the order is not made.

WITHDRAWAL OF APPEARANCE

An attorney's appearance will not be deemed withdrawn without a motion for permission to withdraw unless another attorney (but not the client alone) files an in lieu of appearance..

____

The Honorable F. Herbert Gruendel
Presiding Judge

____

Date Signed

*

NEW HAVEN JUDICIAL DISTRICT STANDING ORDERS *

Including Amendments Received Through August 1, 2004

FAMILY STANDING ORDERS

Table of Standing Orders

Family Case Management Procedures

All initial case management conferences will be conducted by family caseflow. At the case management date uncontested dissolutions may be heard. Any case which does not have a case management stipulation filed or for which no conference has been held by family caseflow on the case management date, shall be dismissed at the end of the case management date. All cases in which there is a custody contest will be set for a status conference at the first available date with the judge. All cases will have a case management order which must be followed. Motions to modify case management orders will be heard at short calendar.

In addition to scheduling uncontested matters, the family caseflow coordinator may also schedule family relations pretrials, special masters and judicial pretrials and trials. Family relations pretrials and special master pretrials may be scheduled on the case management date or on a report back date as approved in a case management order.

Family relations pretrials will not be held on Thursdays. Special master pretrials will be held on Tuesdays and Fridays. Judicial pretrials will be scheduled any day except Thursdays. Six judicial pretrials may be scheduled each Friday morning, at half hour intervals commencing at 9:15 a.m. It is expected that for special masters pretrials and judicial pretrials that the parties will comply with the requirements of the pretrial orders. (See annexed.)

All parties and lawyers must be present for special masters and judicial pretrials. Counsel and pro se parties will report to the caseflow office and indicate that everyone is present and that the conditions of the pretrial order have been complied with and the case may proceed to pretrial. Those not complying with the terms of the pretrial order will be referred to uncontested dissolutions resulting from settlements achieved at special masters and special pretrials.

Uncontested hearings will be scheduled for any day except Thursdays.

Trials will be assigned to a particular judge on the assigned day and counsel should report to the assigned judge's courtroom by 10:00 a.m. All trials will be conducted in accordance with the standing trial management order.

Requests for continuances will not be entertained on the date of a scheduled special masters or judicial pretrial or trial and will be granted by the presiding judge prior to the scheduled date in the event of emergency only. Family Relations pretrials may be rescheduled prior to the date scheduled by counsel supplying caseflow with an agreed new date *and* report back date.

IF ANY CASE GETS SETTLED PRIOR TO A SCHEDULED TRIAL OR PRETRIAL, PLEASE NOTIFY CASEFLOW IMMEDIATELY SO THE TIME MAY BE USED TO SCHEDULE ANOTHER MATTER.

The caseflow coordinator may schedule status conferences with a judge in cases where it is necessary at 9:30 on any day except Thursdays.

Family Standing Orders will be posted on the Judicial website at www.jud.state.ct.us and in the Courthouse.

____

Presiding Judge, Family

* © 2004 Connecticut Judicial Branch, reprinted with permission.

Pretrials by Special Masters

As of 6/1/2004, the New Haven Superior Court has implemented a new procedure for its Special Masters Program. This is done to insure that the Special Masters time is not wasted and the cases are ripe for a special masters pretrial. Under the new procedure a status conference will be scheduled at 2:00 PM one week prior to the Special Masters date. At that time compliance with the standing orders must be completed. If not, counsel must appear to explain why the matter will not be proceeding the following week for a Special Master's pretrial. If compliance has been met and counsel will be proceeding forward with the Special Masters, they may call the Family Caseflow Coordinator and mark the status conference off.

All counsel and parties assigned a special masters pretrial are ordered to attend. Counsel and pro se parties are ordered to exchange between themselves and submit to the special masters document in compliance with these Standing Orders. The following documents shall be exchanged between counsel and pro se parties at least **ONE WEEK** prior to the scheduled pretrial and submitted to the special masters at the time of the pretrial:

1. Current sworn financial affidavits, which include detailed income statements, a complete list of liabilities, fair market value of all assets and current value of all retirement and employment benefits.

2. Written proposed orders in accordance with Practice Book Sec. 25–30(c) which shall be comprehensive and shall set forth the party's requested relief.

3. If there are minor children, a proposed parenting plan governing custody and visitation and a child support guidelines worksheet indicating the presumptive amount of child support and the appropriate percentages for child care and reimbursed medical expenses.

4. Copies of tax returns and W–2 statements for the past three years.

5. Appraisals, if any, of real or personal property where values are in dispute.

6. Pension valuations, if any, and recent pension statements.

Failure to fully comply with this order may subject the offending party to sanctions, including fines and the preclusion at trial of evidence and witnesses.

Presiding Judge, Family

[Amended effective June 1, 2004.]

Procedures for Short Calendar

COURT BEGINS AT 9:30 A.M. PARTIES ARE EXPECTED TO BE READY FOR FAMILY RELATIONS OR HEARING AT THAT TIME. THERE WILL NOT BE A FORMAL CALL OF THE CALENDAR.

ALL CONTESTED MATTERS, EXCEPT MOTIONS CONCERNING QUESTIONS OF LAW, SHALL REPORT TO FAMILY RELATIONS FOR DISCUSSION. FAMILY RELATIONS COUNSELORS ARE AVAILABLE AT 9:00 A.M.

MOTIONS REGARDING QUESTIONS OF LAW NEED NOT REPORT TO FAMILY RELATIONS. HOWEVER, THE MOVING PARTY MUST COMPLETE A **"REPORT TO CLERK"** (Word Doc.) FORM WHICH MUST BE SUBMITTED TO THE COURTROOM CLERK.

AGREEMENTS WILL BE CALLED FIRST IN THE ORDER RECEIVED BY THE COURTROOM CLERK. FOLLOWING AGREEMENTS, CONTESTED MATTERS WILL BE HEARD ACCORDING TO THE LENGTH OF TIME INDICATED ON THE "REPORT TO CLERK."

WHEN PARTIES RETURN FROM FAMILY RELATIONS THE MOVING PARTY MUST SUBMIT THE FULLY COMPLETED "REPORT TO CLERK" FORM TO THE COURTROOM CLERK. THESE FORMS ARE AVAILABLE IN THE COURTROOM OR AT FAMILY RELATIONS. IF THE FORM IS INCOMPLETE, THE CLERK WILL RETURN IT TO THE PARTIES FOR COMPLETION.

THE COURT WILL LIMIT THE ARGUMENT TO THE TIME INDICATED ON THE "REPORT TO CLERK." IF MORE TIME IS NEEDED, THE MATTER WILL BE PLACED AT THE END OF THE DOCKET. IF MORE THAN ONE HOUR IS NECESSARY, THE COURT MAY SPECIALLY ASSIGN THE MATTER FOR ANOTHER DAY.

AT 10:30 A.M. THE COURT WILL CALL THOSE CASES IN WHICH THE OPPOSING PARTY HAS FAILED TO APPEAR. IF THE MOVING PARTY IS PRESENT, AND THE NON–APPEARING PARTY WAS PROPERLY SERVED, AND ALL REQUIRED DOCUMENTS ARE PRESENTED TO THE COURT, THE COURT WILL PROCEED WITH A HEARING ON THE MATTER ACCORDING TO THE TIME INDICATED ON THE "REPORT TO CLERK." IF THE NON–MOVING PARTY IS PRESENT BUT THE MOVING PARTY IS NOT, THE PARTY WHO IS PRESENT MAY BE HEARD IF THE MATTER WAS MARKED READY.

PRESIDING JUDGE, FAMILY

Standing Trial Management Orders

One week prior to the assigned trial date, counsel and pro se parties in the above captioned matter are ordered to submit to the trial judge through the family caseflow office and provide copies to all parties, documents in compliance with this Trial Management Order. The following documents shall be submitted:

1. Current sworn financial affidavits, which include detailed income statements, a complete list of liabilities, fair market value of all assets and current value of all retirement and employment benefits.

2. A list of pending motions, outstanding discovery requests and proposed motions in limine.

3. A list setting forth the names and addresses of each witness to be called at trial, including the relationship of each witness to the case (e.g. party, fact witness, expert); and whether a scheduling problem exists as to the testimony of any such witness.

4. If a Family Relations counselor is going to testify, the counselor must have one week prior notice.

5. A list of exhibits reasonably expected to the introduced, indexed by number for plaintiff (i.e. Plaintiff's 1), letter for defendant (i.e. Defendant's A), and M + numeral for minor child(ren) (i.e. M#1). The list shall briefly describe each exhibit and indicate whether any party objects to the admission of such exhibit. If there is an objection, the exhibit should be marked for identification.

6. If custody and visitation are agreed upon, a written stipulation detailing the agreement signed by the parties must be filed.

7. Written proposed orders (in accordance with Practice Book § 25–30(c)) which shall be comprehensive and shall set forth the party's requested relief.

Failure to fully comply with this order may subject the offending party to sanctions, including the preclusions of evidence and witnesses.

____

Presiding Judge, Family

Preparation of Family Judgment Files in Uncontested Cases

The Chief Clerk's Office at New Haven JD has a program for preparation of uncontested dissolution of marriage judgment files. Under this program, the judgment files are prepared by the clerks in courtrooms 3D, 3E and 6D at the time of entry of judgment. A certified copy of a judgment file will then be available in the clerk's office in ten days.

It will still be necessary for counsel and/or pro se parties to prepare judgment files for judgments of legal separation, annulment or for lengthy oral agreements.

____

Chief Clerk

Report to Clerk

REPORT TO CLERK

JUDICIAL DISTRICT OF NEW HAVEN

☐ Check here if Pro Bono

☐ The following case is ready for argument regarding a question of law:

☐ The following case has returned from Family Relations:

____________________ (Case Name) FA-__________ (Docket No.) __________ (Calendar Pos.)

Check One:

________ Requesting a continuance

________ Ready with a written agreement

________ Ready to proceed and requires ________ min./hr. time for argument

________ Ready unopposed (the other side is not here)

________ Ready for final judgment (divorce or custody/visitation action)

The following are present:

____ Plaintiff ____ Plaintiff's Attorney ________________ (Name)

____ Defendant ____ Defendant's Attorney ________________ (Name)

____ Other Counsel ________________________ (Name(s)Of Counsel for Minor Children, etc.)

Once you hand this Report to the clerk, both parties must remain in the courtroom unless you tell the clerk and opposing parties where you will be. You must report back to the clerk when all parties have returned to the courtroom ready to proceed. Continuance requests and agreements will be taken first, then contested matters, depending upon their length of time. Matters requiring more than one hour of court time may be specifically assigned for a date certain pursuant to Connecticut Practice Book Section 25–34(b).

You are not ready unless you have given all papers required including Financial Affidavits, both pages of the Child Support Guidelines Worksheets, and a written agreement where necessary to the clerk.

NEW 2/02

*

CHILD ABUSE—REPORTS—NOTICE

P.A. No. 04–48

S.B. No. 308

AN ACT CONCERNING NOTIFICATION OF CHILD NEGLECT REPORTS.

Be it enacted by the Senate and House of Representatives in General Assembly convened:

Section 1. Section 17a–103c of the general statutes is repealed and the following is substituted in lieu thereof (Effective October 1, 2004):

Upon the receipt of a report of suspected abuse or neglect of any child committed to the Commissioner of Children and Families as delinquent, the Department of Children and Families shall, no later than ten days after receipt of ~~the complaint~~ such report, provide written notification of such report to the child's legal guardian and the child's attorney in the delinquency proceeding that resulted in the commitment. If, after investigation, the department substantiates the reported abuse or neglect, the department shall, no later than ten days after ~~receipt of the complaint~~ substantiation of such abuse or neglect, provide written notification of the substantiated report of abuse or neglect to the child's legal guardian and the child's attorney in the delinquency proceeding that resulted in the commitment. ~~of the substantiation of the reported abuse.~~

Approved May 4, 2004.

DOMESTIC VIOLENCE—ARREST—SELF DEFENSE

P.A. No. 04–66

S.H.B. No. 5293

AN ACT CONCERNING DUAL ARRESTS IN FAMILY VIOLENCE CASES.

Be it enacted by the Senate and House of Representatives in General Assembly convened:

Section 1. Section 46b–38b of the general statutes is repealed and the following is substituted in lieu thereof (Effective October 1, 2004):

(a) Whenever a peace officer determines upon speedy information that a family violence crime, ~~as defined in subdivision (3) of section 46b–38a,~~ except a family violence crime involving a dating relationship, has been committed within such officer's jurisdiction, such officer shall arrest the person or persons suspected of its commission and charge such person or persons with the appropriate crime. The decision to arrest and charge shall not (1) be dependent on the specific consent of the victim, (2) consider the relationship of the parties, or (3) be based solely on a request by the victim. Whenever a peace officer determines that a family violence crime has been committed, such officer may seize any firearm at the location where the crime is alleged to have been committed that is in the possession of any person arrested for the commission of such crime or suspected of its commission or that is in plain view. Not later than seven days after any such seizure, the law enforcement agency shall return such firearm in its original condition to the rightful owner thereof unless such person is ineligible to possess such firearm or unless otherwise ordered by the court.

(b) No peace officer investigating an incident of family violence shall threaten, suggest or otherwise indicate the arrest of all parties for the purpose of discouraging requests for law enforcement intervention by any party. Where complaints are ~~received from~~ made by two or more opposing parties, the officer shall evaluate each complaint separately to determine whether ~~he~~ such officer should make an arrest or seek a warrant for an arrest. Notwithstanding the provisions of subsection (a) of this section, when a peace officer reasonably believes that a party in an incident of family violence has used force as a means of self defense, such officer is not required to arrest such party under this section.

(c) No peace officer shall be held liable in any civil action regarding personal injury or injury to property brought by any party to a family violence incident for an arrest based on probable cause.

(d) It shall be the responsibility of the peace officer at the scene of a family violence incident to provide immediate assistance to the victim. Such assistance shall include, but not be limited to: (1) Assisting the victim to obtain medical treatment if such treatment is required; (2) notifying the victim of the right to file an affidavit or warrant for arrest; and (3) informing the victim of services available and referring the victim to the Office of Victim Services. In cases where the officer has determined that no cause exists for an arrest, assistance shall include: (A) Assistance ~~included~~ as provided in subdivisions (1) to (3), inclusive, of this subsection; and (B) remaining at the scene for a reasonable time until, in the reasonable judgment of the officer, the likelihood of further imminent violence has been eliminated.

(e) ~~On or before October 1, 1986, each~~ Each law enforcement agency shall develop, in conjunction with the Division of Criminal Justice, and implement specific operational guidelines for arrest policies in family violence incidents. Such guidelines shall include, but not be limited to: (1) Procedures for the conduct of a criminal investigation; (2) procedures for arrest and for victim assistance by peace officers; (3) education as to what constitutes speedy information in a family violence incident; (4) procedures with respect to the provision of services to victims; and (5) such other criteria or guidelines as may be applicable to carry out the purposes of sections 46b–1, as amended, 46b–15, as amended, 46b–38a to 46b–38f, inclusive, and 54–1g. Such procedures shall be duly promulgated by ~~said~~ such law enforcement agency.

(f) The Police Officer Standards and Training Council, in conjunction with the Division of Criminal Justice, shall establish an education and training program for law enforcement officers, supervisors and state's attorneys on the handling of family violence incidents. ~~Such training~~ Training under such program shall: (1) Stress the enforcement of criminal law in family violence cases and the use of community resources, and include training for peace officers at both recruit and in-service levels; and (2) include, but not be limited to: (A) The nature, extent and causes of family violence; (B) legal rights of and remedies available to victims of family violence and persons accused of family violence; (C) services and facilities available to victims and batterers; (D) legal duties imposed on police officers to make arrests and to offer protection and assistance; and (E) techniques for handling incidents of family violence that minimize the likelihood of injury to the officer and promote the safety of the victim.

Approved May 10, 2004.

SOCIAL SERVICES—GENERAL ASSISTANCE PROGRAM—ADMINISTRATION

P.A. No. 04–76

S.H.B. No. 5508

AN ACT CONCERNING REVISIONS TO THE GENERAL STATUTES NECESSITATED BY THE ELIMINATION OF THE GENERAL ASSISTANCE PROGRAM.

Be it enacted by the Senate and House of Representatives in General Assembly convened:

Section 1. Section 4–71c of the general statutes is repealed and the following is substituted in lieu thereof (Effective October 1, 2004):

The Secretary of the Office of Policy and Management shall annually compute the cost of an increase in assistance payments under the state-administered general assistance program, state supplement program, medical assistance program, temporary family assistance program and food stamp program based on the percentage increase, if any, in the most recent calendar year average in the consumer price index for urban consumers provided if the increase in such index exceeds five per cent, the computation shall be based on a five per cent increase.

Sec. 2. Section 8–72 of the general statutes is repealed and the following is substituted in lieu thereof (Effective October 1, 2004):

Each developer or housing authority shall manage and operate its housing projects in an efficient manner so as to enable it to fix the rentals for dwelling accommodations at the lowest possible rates consistent with providing decent, safe and sanitary dwelling accommodations, and no housing authority or nonprofit corporation shall construct or operate any such project for profit. To this end an authority or a nonprofit corporation shall fix the rentals for dwelling in its projects at no higher rates than it finds to be necessary in order to produce revenues which, together with all other available money, revenues, income and receipts of the authority or nonprofit corporation from whatever sources derived, will be sufficient (a) to pay, as the same become due, the principal and interest on the bonds of the authority or nonprofit corporation; (b) to meet the cost of, and to provide for, maintaining and operating the projects, including the cost of any insurance, and the administrative expenses of the authority or nonprofit corporation; provided nothing in this section shall be construed as prohibiting any authority or nonprofit corporation from providing for variable rentals based on family income. In the operation or management of housing projects an authority or nonprofit corporation shall, at all times, rent or lease the dwelling accommodations therein at rentals within the financial reach of families of low income. The Commissioner of Economic and Community Development may establish maximum income limits for admission and continued occupancy of tenants, provided such maximum income limits and all revisions thereof for housing projects operated pursuant to any contract with any agency of the federal government shall be subject to the prior approval of such federal agency. The Commissioner of Economic and Community Development shall define the income of a family to provide the basis for determining eligibility for the admission, rentals and for the continued occupancy of families under the maximum income limits fixed and approved. The definition of family income, by the Commissioner of Economic and Community Development, may provide for the exclusion of all or part of the income of family members which, in the judgment of said commissioner, is not generally available to meet the cost of basic living needs of the family. No housing authority or developer shall refuse to rent any dwelling accommodation to an otherwise qualified applicant on the ground that one or more of the proposed occupants are children born out of wedlock. Each housing authority and developer shall provide a receipt to each applicant for admission to its housing projects stating the time and date of application and shall maintain a list of such applications, which shall be a public record as defined in section 1–200. The Commissioner of Economic and Community Development shall, by regulation, provide for the manner in which such list shall be created, maintained and revised. No provision of this part shall be construed as limiting the right of the authority to vest in an obligee the right, in the event of a default by such authority, to take possession of a housing project or cause the appointment of a receiver thereof or acquire title thereto through foreclosure proceedings, free from all the restrictions imposed by this chapter with respect to rental rates and tenant selection. The Commissioner of Economic and Community Development shall approve an operation or management plan of each housing project, which shall provide an income adequate for debt service, if any, administration, including a state service charge, other operating costs and establishment of reasonable reserves for repairs, maintenance and replacements, vacancy and collection losses. Said commissioner shall have the right of inspection of any housing during the period between the date on which construction thereof begins and the date the state loan is fully paid or, in the case of a grant, during the period for which any housing project built pursuant to such grant is used for housing for families of low and moderate income. An authority or developer shall semiannually submit to said commissioner a sworn statement setting forth such information with respect to the tenants and rentals for each housing project hereunder and the costs of operating each housing project under its jurisdiction as said commissioner requires. Any person who makes a false statement concerning the income of the family for which application for admission to or continued occupancy of housing projects is made may be fined not more than five hundred dollars or imprisoned not more than six months or both. With regard to a family who, since the last annual recertification, received any public assistance or state-administered general assistance and received earnings from employment, the authority or developer shall not require any interim recertification due to an earnings increase. At the annual recertification, the authority or developer shall base rent levels on such family's average income throughout the preceding twelve months. During the subsequent twelve-month period, the authority or developer shall not require any interim recertifications due to increased earnings from employment. However, if a family's income has decreased, nothing in this section shall preclude an interim recertification or recertification based on the reduced income level.

Sec. 3. Subsection (s) of section 12–574 of the general statutes is repealed and the following is substituted in lieu thereof (Effective October 1, 2004):

(s) Any person or business organization issued a license to conduct dog racing pursuant to subsection (c) of section 12–574c shall employ persons who, at the time of employment, are recipients of assistance under the state-administered general assistance program, state supplement program, medical assistance program, temporary family assistance program or food stamps program to fill not less than twenty per cent of the positions created by the conversion of a jai alai fronton to a dog race track if such persons have been trained for such employment by public or publicly-funded agencies in coordination with such licensee.

Sec. 4. Subsections (a) and (b) of section 16a–41h of the general statutes are repealed and the following is substituted in lieu thereof (Effective October 1, 2004):

(a) Each electric and gas company, as defined in section 16–1, as amended, having at least seventy-five thousand customers, shall include in its monthly bills a request to each customer to add a one-dollar donation to the bill payment. Each company shall transmit all such donations received each month to Operation Fuel, Inc., a state-wide nonprofit organization designed to respond to people within the state who are in financial crisis and need emergency energy assistance. Donations shall be distributed to nonprofit social services agencies and private fuel banks in accordance with guidelines established by the board of directors of Operation Fuel, Inc., provided such funds shall be distributed on a priority basis to low-income elderly and working poor households which are not eligible for public assistance or state-administered general assistance but who are faced with a financial crisis and are unable to make timely payments on winter fuel, electricity or gas bills.

(b) If Operation Fuel, Inc. ceases to exist, such electric and gas companies shall jointly establish a nonprofit, tax-exempt corporation for the purpose of holding in trust and distributing such customer donations. The board of directors of such corporation shall consist of eleven members appointed as follows: Four by the companies, each of which shall appoint one member; one by the president pro tempore of the Senate; one by the minority leader of the Senate; one by the speaker of the House of Representatives; one by the minority leader of the House of Representatives; and three by the Governor. The board shall distribute such funds to nonprofit organizations and social service agencies which provide emergency energy or fuel assistance. The board shall target available funding on a priority basis to low-income elderly and working poor households which are not eligible for public assistance or state-administered general assistance but who are faced with a financial crisis and are unable to make timely payments on winter fuel, electricity or gas bills.

Sec. 5. Subsection (b) of section 16a–44b of the general statutes is repealed and the following is substituted in lieu thereof (Effective October 1, 2004):

(b) Funds allocated for the purposes of sections 16a–44b to 16a–44d, inclusive, shall be distributed among the towns in the following manner: (1) Ten per cent of the amount shall be distributed pro rata on the basis of the ratio of the total population of each town to the total population of the state. (2) Fifty per cent of the amount shall be divided among those towns whose adjusted equalized net grand list per capita falls below that of the town at the seventy-fifth percentile among all towns in the state, as determined by ranking in ascending order of all towns in the state according to their adjusted equalized net grand list per capita. The distribution shall be made to each town pro rata on the basis of the following ratio: The difference between the adjusted equalized net grand list per capita for the town at the seventy-fifth percentile and that of such town multiplied by the population of such town shall be the numerator of the fraction. For each town whose adjusted equalized net grand list per capita falls below that of the town at the seventy-fifth percentile, the resulting products of all such towns shall be added together and the sum shall be the denominator of the fraction. (3) Twenty per cent of the amount shall be distributed pro rata on the basis of the ratio of the average number of monthly paid maintenance cases for such town to the average number of monthly paid maintenance cases in the state. (4) Twenty per cent of the amount shall be distributed pro rata on the basis of the ratio of the number of elderly persons in such town receiving assistance under section 12–129b and chapter 204a [1] to the number of elderly persons in the state receiving such assistance. For the purposes of this section, "adjusted equalized net grand list per capita" and "total population" shall be defined as in section 10–261, as amended, and "average number of monthly paid maintenance cases" means the monthly number of recipients of temporary family assistance, state-administered general assistance, and assistance to the aged, the blind and the totally disabled, ~~Connecticut assistance and medical aid program for the disabled and general assistance,~~ averaged over the most recent fiscal year for which information is available.

[1] C.G.S.A. § 12–170d et seq.

Sec. 6. Subsection (b) of section 17a–460c of the general statutes, as amended by section 36 of public act 03–19, is repealed and the following is substituted in lieu thereof (Effective October 1, 2004):

(b) The agreements and other contractual arrangements identified in subsection (a) of this section may include plans and arrangements certified by the Department of Social Services, the Department of Mental Health and

Addiction Services, or the federal Centers for Medicare and Medicaid Services, to provide services to Medicaid, Medicare, state-administered general assistance, Department of Mental Health and Addiction Services or Centers for Medicare and Medicaid Services beneficiaries, as well as private plans and arrangements satisfactory to the commissioner.

Sec. 7. Section 17b–10 of the general statutes is repealed and the following is substituted in lieu thereof (Effective October 1, 2004):

(a) The Department of Social Services shall prepare and routinely update state medical services and public assistance manuals. ~~and general assistance policy manuals.~~ The pages of such manuals shall be consecutively numbered and indexed, containing all departmental policy regulations and substantive procedure. Said manuals shall be published by the department and distributed so that they are available to (1) all district, subdistrict and field offices of the Department of Social Services; (2) each town hall in the state; (3) all legal assistance programs in the state; and (4) any interested member of the public who requests a copy. All policy manuals of the department, as they exist on May 23, 1984, including the supporting bulletins but not including statements concerning only the internal management of the department and not affecting private rights or procedures available to the public, shall be construed to have been adopted as regulations in accordance with the provisions of chapter 54.[1] After May 23, 1984, any policy issued by the department, except a policy necessary to conform to a requirement of a federal or joint federal and state program administered by the department, including, but not limited to, the state supplement program to the Supplemental Security Income Program, shall be adopted in regulation form in accordance with the provisions of chapter 54. After May 23, 1984, the department shall adopt in regulation form in accordance with the provisions of chapter 54, any new policy necessary to conform to a requirement of a federal or joint state and federal program administered by the department, including, but not limited to, the state supplement program to the Supplemental Security Income Program, but the department may operate under such policy while it is in the process of adopting the policy in regulation form, provided the Department of Social Services prints notice of intent to adopt the regulations in the Connecticut Law Journal within twenty days after adopting the policy. Such policy shall be valid until the time final regulations are effective.

~~(b) By July 1, 1986, the Department of Social Services shall rewrite the general assistance policy manual using plain language as described in section 42–152 and sections 38a–295 to 38a–300, inclusive. The manual shall include an index for frequent referencing and a separate section or manual which specifies procedures to follow to clarify policy. The department shall keep records of policy and procedural questions raised by town welfare officials and staff during telephone conversations and office visits.~~

~~(c)~~ (b) By January 1, 1987, the Department of Social Services shall replace its state public assistance policy manual with a new manual which is adopted in accordance with the provisions of chapter 54 and which sets forth in clear and concise language the policies and procedures to be used by the department in implementing and enforcing federal and state laws. The department may operate under a policy in the new recipient eligibility and benefit policy manual while it is in the process of adopting the manual in regulation form, provided the department shall print a notice of intent to adopt regulations relating to recipient eligibility and benefits in the Connecticut Law Journal within twenty days of issuing the policy.

[1] C.G.S.A. § 4–166 et seq.

Sec. 8. Subsection (c) of section 17b–30 of the general statutes is repealed and the following is substituted in lieu thereof (Effective October 1, 2004):

(c) Said system shall be utilized for office use only in the following programs: ~~(1) General assistance; (2) temporary~~ (1) Temporary family assistance; and ~~(3)~~ (2) any other program to be determined at the discretion of the Commissioner of Social Services.

Sec. 9. Subsection (b) of section 17b–90 of the general statutes, as amended by section 1 of public act 03–89, is repealed and the following is substituted in lieu thereof (Effective October 1, 2004):

(b) No person shall, except for purposes directly connected with the administration of programs of the Department of Social Services and in accordance with the regulations of the commissioner, solicit, disclose, receive or make use of, or authorize, knowingly permit, participate in or acquiesce in the use of, any list of the names of, or any information concerning, persons applying for or receiving assistance from the Department of Social Services or persons participating in a program administered by said department, directly or indirectly derived from the records, papers, files or communications of the state or its subdivisions or agencies, or acquired in the course of the performance of official duties. The Commissioner of Social Services shall disclose (1) to any authorized representative of the Labor Commissioner such information directly related to unemployment compensation, administered pursuant to chapter 567 [1] or information necessary for implementation of sections 17b–688b, 17b–688c and 17b–688h, as amended, and section 122 of public act 97–2 of the June 18 special session*, [2] (2) to any authorized representative of the Commissioner of Mental Health and Addiction Services any information necessary for the implementation and operation of the basic needs supplement program or for the management of and payment for behavioral health services for applicants for and recipients of ~~general assistance and~~ state-administered general assistance, (3) to any authorized representative of the Commissioner of Administrative Services, or the Commissioner of Public Safety such information as the state Commissioner of Social Services determines is directly related to and necessary for the Department of Administrative Services or the Department of Public Safety for purposes of performing their functions of collecting social services recoveries and overpayments or amounts due as support in social services cases, investigating social services fraud or locating absent parents of public assistance recipients, (4) to any authorized representative of the Commissioner of Children and Families necessary information concerning a child or the immediate family of a child receiving services from the Department of Social Services, including safety net services, if the Commissioner of Children and Families or the Commissioner of Social Services has determined that imminent danger to such child's health, safety or welfare exists to target the services of the family services programs administered by the Department of Children and Families, (5) to a town official or other contractor or authorized representative of the Labor Commissioner such information concerning an applicant for or a recipient of financial or medical assistance under ~~general assistance or~~ state-administered general assistance deemed necessary by said commissioners to carry out their respective responsibilities to serve such persons under the programs administered by the Labor Department that are designed to serve applicants for or recipients of ~~general assistance or~~ state-administered general assistance, (6) to any authorized representative of the Commissioner of Mental Health and Addiction Services for the purposes of the behavioral health managed care program established by section 17a–453, or (7) to a health insurance provider, in IV-D support cases, as defined in section 46b–231, as amended, information concerning a child and the custodial parent of such child that is necessary to enroll such child in a health insurance plan available through such provider when the noncustodial parent of such child is under court order to provide health insurance coverage but is unable to provide such information, provided the Commissioner of Social Services determines, after providing prior notice of the disclosure to such custodial parent and an opportunity for such parent to object, that such disclosure is in the best interests of the child. No such representative shall disclose any information obtained pursuant to this section, except as specified in this section. Any applicant for assistance provided through said department shall be notified that, if and when such applicant receives benefits, the department will be providing law enforcement officials with the address of such applicant upon the request of any such official pursuant to section 17b–16a.

[1] C.G.S.A. § 31–222 et seq.

[2] 1997, June 18 Sp. Sess., P.A. 97–2, § 122, was not classified to the General Statutes, but remains in full force and effect according to its terms.

Sec. 10. Section 17b–92 of the general statutes is repealed and the following is substituted in lieu thereof (Effective October 1, 2004):

(a) A relocation adjustment payment under Section 114 of the federal Housing Act of 1949,[1] as amended, shall not be considered income, earnings, assets or rent in the determination of eligibility under any public assistance program ~~or any general assistance program~~ provided, if a recipient of such assistance receives a relocation adjustment payment in excess of two hundred fifty dollars, the Commissioner of Social Services shall not be required to provide such recipient with similar assistance for moving expenses or other expenses directly related to relocation. In those instances where a recipient has received a relocation adjustment payment in excess of two hundred fifty dollars and has also been provided with similar assistance for moving expenses or other expenses directly related to relocation, under any public assistance program ~~or any general assistance program~~ such recipient shall be required to transfer or assign to the Commissioner of Social Services an amount equal to the relocation assistance that had been received from the Commissioner of Social Services.

(b) Any payment made pursuant to section 47–88d to a recipient of public assistance ~~or general assistance~~ shall not be considered income, earnings, assets or rent in the determination of eligibility for any public assistance program ~~or any general assistance program~~ and shall not be deducted from the amount of assistance to which the recipient would otherwise be entitled.

[1] 42 U.S.C.A. § 4601 et seq.

Sec. 11. Section 17b–104 of the general statutes, as amended by section 38 of public act 03–19 and section 60 of public act 03–3 of the June 30 special session, is repealed and the following is substituted in lieu thereof (Effective October 1, 2004):

(a) The Commissioner of Social Services shall administer the program of state supplementation to the Supplemental Security Income Program provided for by the Social Security Act [1] and state law. The commissioner may delegate any powers and authority to any deputy, assistant, investigator or supervisor, who shall have, within the scope of the power and authority so delegated, all of the power and authority of the Commissioner of Social Services. On and after January 1, 1994, the commissioner shall establish a standard of need based on the cost of living in this state for the temporary family assistance program ~~,~~ and the state-administered general assistance program. ~~and the general assistance program.~~ The commissioner shall make a reinvestigation, at least every twelve months, of all cases receiving aid from the state, except that such reinvestigation may be conducted every twenty-four months for recipients of assistance to the elderly or disabled with stable circumstances, and shall maintain all case records of the several programs administered by the Department of Social Services so that such records show, at all times, full information with respect to eligibility of the applicant or recipient. In the determination of need under any public assistance program, such income or earnings shall be disregarded as federal law requires, and such income or earnings may be disregarded as federal law permits. The commissioner shall encourage and promulgate such incentive earning programs as are permitted by federal law and regulations.

(b) On July 1, 1988, and annually thereafter, the commissioner shall increase the payment standards over those of the previous fiscal year under the aid to families with dependent children program, temporary family assistance program ~~,~~ and the state-administered general assistance program ~~and for the general assistance program~~ by the percentage increase, if any, in the most recent calendar year average in the consumer price index for urban consumers over the average for the previous calendar year, provided the annual increase, if any, shall not exceed five per cent, except that the payment standards for the fiscal years ending June 30, 1992, June 30, 1993, June 30, 1994, June 30, 1995, June 30, 1996, June 30, 1997, June 30, 1998, June 30, 1999, June 30, 2000, June 30, 2001, June 30, 2002, June 30, 2003, June 30, 2004, and June 30, 2005, shall not be increased. On January 1, 1994, the payment standards shall be equal to the standards of need in effect July 1, 1993.

(c) On and after July 1, 1995, the payment standards for families receiving assistance under the temporary family assistance program ~~,~~ and the state-administered general assistance program ~~and general assistance program~~ shall be equal to seventy-three per cent of the AFDC standards of need in effect June 30, 1995.

(d) For a family living in subsidized housing, income shall be attributed to such family which shall be eight per cent of the payment standard for such family.

[1] 42 U.S.C.A. § 301 et seq.

Sec. 12. Section 17b–111 of the general statutes is repealed and the following is substituted in lieu thereof (Effective October 1, 2004):

On and after July 1, 1998, the commissioner shall implement a state-administered general assistance program and on or before April 1, 1997, the commissioner shall implement said program in the fourteen towns in which the regional or district offices of the Department of Social Services are located, subject to the restrictions of section 17b–118, as amended. The commissioner may contract for the implementation of such program. ~~A town, with a regional or district office of the department and a general assistance office, may petition the commissioner to allow such town to continue the operation of its general assistance program. The commissioner, in examining such petition, shall consider the cost effectiveness of such town's general assistance program.~~

Sec. 13. Section 17b–118 of the general statutes, as amended by section 97 of public act 03–3 of the June 30 special session, is repealed and the following is substituted in lieu thereof (Effective October 1, 2004):

~~(a) No assistance or care shall be given under sections 17b–111, 17b–118, 17b–118a, 17b–118b, 17b–119, 17b–122 and 17b–124 to 17b–132, inclusive, to an employable person by the state or the town liable to support such person in accordance with section 17b–111. On and after July 1, 1995, financial assistance granted under the general assistance program and state-administered general assistance, to a person who has been determined to be a transitional individual, as defined in section 17b–689, shall be limited to a twenty-four-month period of eligibility with no more than ten months of assistance in the first twelve months of eligibility and no more than six months of assistance in the second twelve months of eligibility. Persons with dependent children under eighteen years of age and transitional individuals who are not classified as such solely due to mental illness or substance abuse who are eligible for assistance under sections 17b–111, 17b–118, 17b–118a, 17b–118b, 17b–119, 17b–122,~~

~~17b–124 to 17b–132, inclusive, 17b–136 to 17b–138, inclusive, 17b–221 to 17b–250, inclusive, 17b–256, 17b–263, 17b–340 to 17b–350, inclusive, and 17b–743 to 17b–747, inclusive, shall not be subject to the durational limits on assistance established pursuant to this section. The Commissioner of Social Services shall adopt regulations, in accordance with the provisions of chapter 54, to implement the provisions of this subsection.~~

~~(b) Prior to or upon discontinuance of assistance, a person previously determined to be a transitional individual may petition the commissioner to review the determination of his status. In such review, the commissioner shall consider factors, including but not limited to: (1) Age; (2) education; (3) vocational training; (4) mental and physical health; and (5) employment history and shall make a determination of such person's ability to obtain gainful employment. The commissioner shall notify the town providing assistance to such person of his determination. The commissioner shall adopt regulations, in accordance with the provisions of chapter 54, to establish a standardized procedure of determining employability. Upon determination by the commissioner that a transitional individual is not unemployable, the person shall be ineligible to receive financial assistance from the town or from the state for one year, unless he produces medical verification of a substantial deterioration in his physical or mental condition or a new condition of such severity and duration that it precludes employment for a period of at least six months.~~

~~(c)~~ Notwithstanding any provision of the general statutes, when a person who is ineligible for financial assistance due to his employability status ~~or the time limits imposed under subsection (a) of this section,~~ is currently in or enters a residential substance abuse treatment facility, the town shall pay his room and board while at such facility as an expense reimbursable under the general assistance program by the Department of Social Services or the Department of Mental Health and Addiction Services, provided the person is eligible to receive medical assistance. The town shall be responsible for these costs until the date upon which the administration of the general assistance program is assumed by the state or is officially delegated to a town by the Commissioner of Social Services, at which time the Department of Social Services or the Department of Mental Health and Addiction Services shall assume these costs. Such assistance shall be paid directly to the treatment facility at a rate established by the Department of Social Services or negotiated by the Department of Mental Health and Addiction Services.

~~(d) The provisions of this section shall take effect no later than August 31, 1997.~~

Sec. 14. Section 17b–118a of the general statutes is repealed and the following is substituted in lieu thereof (Effective October 1, 2004):

A person (1) at least eighteen years of age and under twenty-one years of age, (2) living with his family which is receiving benefits under the temporary family assistance program, and (3) who would be an eligible dependent in such program if under the age of eighteen shall be eligible for state-administered general assistance in the amount of assistance such person would be eligible for under the temporary family assistance program.

Sec. 15. Section 17b–180a of the general statutes is repealed and the following is substituted in lieu thereof (Effective October 1, 2004):

The Department of Social Services shall implement an expedited application and eligibility determination process for the temporary family assistance program to reduce state-administered general assistance program expenditures for those applicants potentially eligible for temporary family assistance.

Sec. 16. Section 17b–274 of the general statutes, as amended by section 19 of public act 03–2 and section 84 of public act 03–3 of the June 30 special session, is repealed and the following is substituted in lieu thereof (Effective October 1, 2004):

(a) The Division of Criminal Justice shall periodically investigate pharmacies to ensure that the state is not billed for a brand name drug product when a less expensive generic substitute drug product is dispensed to a Medicaid recipient. The Commissioner of Social Services shall cooperate and provide information as requested by such division.

(b) A licensed medical practitioner may specify in writing or by a telephonic or electronic communication that there shall be no substitution for the specified brand name drug product in any prescription for a Medicaid, state-administered general assistance, ~~general assistance~~ or ConnPACE recipient, provided (1) the practitioner specifies the basis on which the brand name drug product and dosage form is medically necessary in comparison to a chemically equivalent generic drug product substitution, and (2) the phrase "brand medically necessary" shall be in the practitioner's handwriting on the prescription form or, if the prohibition was communicated by telephonic communication, in the pharmacist's handwriting on such form, and shall not be preprinted or stamped or initialed on such form. If the practitioner specifies by telephonic communication that there shall be no substitution for the specified brand name drug product in any prescription for a Medicaid, state-administered general assistance, ~~general assistance~~ or ConnPACE recipient, written certification in the practitioner's handwriting bearing the phrase "brand medically necessary" shall be sent to the dispensing pharmacy within ten days. A pharmacist shall dispense a generically equivalent drug product for any drug listed in accordance with the Code of Federal Regulations Title 42 Part 447. 332 for a drug prescribed for a Medicaid, state-administered general assistance, ~~general assistance~~ or ConnPACE recipient unless the phrase "brand medically necessary" is ordered in accordance with this subsection and such pharmacist has received approval to dispense the brand name drug product in accordance with subsection (c) of this section.

(c) The Commissioner of Social Services shall implement a procedure by which a pharmacist shall obtain approval from an independent pharmacy consultant acting on behalf of the Department of Social Services, under an administrative services only contract, whenever the pharmacist dispenses a brand name drug product to a Medicaid, state-administered general assistance, ~~general assistance~~ or ConnPACE recipient and a chemically equivalent generic drug product substitution is available, provided such procedure shall not require approval for other than initial prescriptions for such drug product. In cases where the brand name drug is less costly than the chemically equivalent generic drug when factoring in manufacturers' rebates, the pharmacist shall dispense the brand name drug. If such approval is not granted or denied within two hours of receipt by the commissioner of the request for approval, it shall be deemed granted. Notwithstanding any provision of this section, a pharmacist shall not dispense any initial maintenance drug prescription for which there is a chemically equivalent generic substitution that is for less than fifteen days without the department's granting of prior authorization, provided prior authorization shall not otherwise be required for atypical antipsychotic drugs if the individual is currently taking such drug at the time the pharmacist receives the prescription. The pharmacist may appeal a denial of reimbursement to the department based on the failure of such pharmacist to substitute a generic drug product in accordance with this section.

(d) A licensed medical practitioner shall disclose to the Department of Social Services or such consultant, upon request, the basis on which the brand name drug product and dosage form is medically necessary in comparison to a chemically equivalent generic drug product substitution. The Commissioner of Social Services shall establish a procedure by which such a practitioner may appeal a determination that a chemically equivalent generic drug product substitution is required for a Medicaid, state-administered general assistance, ~~general assistance~~ or ConnPACE recipient.

Sec. 17. Section 17b–274a of the general statutes is repealed and the following is substituted in lieu thereof (Effective October 1, 2004):

The Commissioner of Social Services may establish maximum allowable costs to be paid under the Medicaid, state-administered general assistance, ~~general assistance,~~ ConnPACE and Connecticut AIDS drug assistance programs for generic prescription drugs based on, but not limited to, actual acquisition costs. The department shall implement and maintain a procedure to review and update the maximum allowable cost list at least annually, and shall report annually to the joint standing committee of the General Assembly having cognizance of matters relating to appropriations and the budgets of state agencies on its activities pursuant to this section.

Sec. 18. Section 17b–274b of the general statutes is repealed and the following is substituted in lieu thereof (Effective October 1, 2004):

The Commissioner of Social Services may implement a pharmaceutical purchasing initiative by contracting with an established entity for the purchase of drugs through the lowest pricing available notwithstanding the provisions of section 17b–280, as amended, for Medicaid, state-administered general assistance, ~~general assistance,~~ ConnPACE and Connecticut AIDS drug assistance recipients. Any entity with whom the commissioner contracts for the purposes of this section shall have an established pharmaceutical network and a demonstrated capability of processing the prescription volume anticipated for Medicaid, state-administered general assistance, ~~general assistance,~~ ConnPACE and Connecticut AIDS drug assistance recipients. The department shall report annually on the status of the pharmaceutical purchasing initiative to the joint standing committee of the General Assembly having cognizance of matters relating to appropriations and the budgets of state agencies.

Sec. 19. Section 17b–274c of the general statutes is repealed and the following is substituted in lieu thereof (Effective October 1, 2004):

The Commissioner of Social Services may establish a voluntary mail order option for any maintenance prescription drug covered under the Medicaid, state-administered general assistance, ~~general assistance,~~ ConnPACE or Connecticut AIDS drug assistance programs.

Sec. 20. Section 17b–280 of the general statutes, as amended by section 2 of public act 03–2 and section 52 of public act 03–3 of the June 30 special session, is repealed and the following is substituted in lieu thereof (Effective October 1, 2004):

(a) The state shall reimburse for all legend drugs provided under the Medicaid, state-administered general assistance, ~~general assistance,~~ ConnPACE and Connecticut AIDS drug assistance programs at the rate established by the Health Care Finance Administration as the federal acquisition cost, or, if no such rate is established, the commissioner shall establish and periodically revise the estimated acquisition cost in accordance with federal regulations. Effective October 1, 2003, the commissioner shall also establish a professional fee of three dollars and thirty cents for each prescription to be paid to licensed pharmacies for dispensing drugs to Medicaid, state-administered general assistance, ~~general assistance,~~ ConnPACE and Connecticut AIDS drug assistance recipients in accordance with federal regulations; and on and after September 4, 1991, payment for legend and nonlegend drugs provided to Medicaid recipients shall be based upon the actual package size dispensed. Effective October 1, 1991, reimbursement for over-the-counter drugs for such recipients shall be limited to those over-the-counter drugs and products published in the Connecticut Formulary, or the cross reference list, issued by the commissioner. The cost of all over-the-counter drugs and products provided to residents of nursing facilities, chronic disease hospitals, and intermediate care facilities for the mentally retarded shall be included in the facilities' per diem rate.

(b) The Department of Social Services may provide an enhanced dispensing fee to a pharmacy enrolled in the federal Office of Pharmacy Affairs Section 340B drug discount program established pursuant to 42 USC 256b or a pharmacy under contract to provide services under said program.

Sec. 21. Section 17b–491a of the general statutes is repealed and the following is substituted in lieu thereof (Effective October 1, 2004):

(a) The Commissioner of Social Services may establish a plan for the prior authorization of (1) any initial prescription for a drug covered under the Medicaid, state-administered general assistance, ~~general assistance~~ or ConnPACE program that costs five hundred dollars or more for a thirty-day supply, or (2) any early refill of a prescription drug covered under any of said programs. The Commissioner of Social Services shall establish a procedure by which prior authorization under this subsection shall be obtained from an independent pharmacy consultant acting on behalf of the Department of Social Services, under an administrative services only contract. If prior authorization is not granted or denied within two hours of receipt by the commissioner of the request for prior authorization, it shall be deemed granted.

(b) The Commissioner of Social Services shall, to increase cost-efficiency or enhance access to a particular prescription drug, establish a plan under which the commissioner may designate specific suppliers of a prescription drug from which a dispensing pharmacy shall order the prescription to be delivered to the pharmacy and billed by the supplier to the department. For each prescription dispensed through designated suppliers, the department shall pay the dispensing pharmacy a handling fee not to exceed four hundred per cent of the dispensing fee established pursuant to section 17b–280, as amended. In no event shall the provisions of this subsection be construed to allow the commissioner to purchase all prescription drugs covered under the Medicaid, state-administered general assistance, ~~general assistance~~ and ConnPACE programs under one contract.

(c) Notwithstanding the provisions of section 17b–262 and any regulation adopted thereunder, on or after July 1, 2000, the Commissioner of Social Services may establish a schedule of maximum quantities of oral dosage units permitted to be dispensed at one time for prescriptions covered under the Medicaid ~~,~~ and state-administered general assistance ~~and general assistance~~ programs based on a review of utilization patterns.

(d) A plan or schedule established pursuant to subsection (a), (b) or (c) of this section and any revisions thereto shall be submitted to the joint standing committees of the General Assembly having cognizance of matters relating to public health, human services and appropriations and the budgets of state agencies. Within sixty days of receipt of such a plan or schedule or revisions thereto, said joint standing committees of the General Assembly shall approve or deny the plan or schedule or any revisions thereto and advise the commissioner of their approval or denial of the plan or schedule or any revisions thereto. The plan or schedule or any revisions thereto shall be deemed approved unless all committees vote to reject such plan or schedule or revisions thereto within sixty days of receipt of such plan or schedule or revisions thereto.

Sec. 22. Section 17b–491b of the general statutes is repealed and the following is substituted in lieu thereof (Effective October 1, 2004):

The maximum allowable cost paid for Factor VIII pharmaceuticals under the Medicaid, state-administered general assistance, ~~general assistance~~ and ConnPACE programs shall be the actual acquisition cost plus eight per cent. The Commissioner of Social Services may designate specific suppliers of Factor VIII pharmaceuticals from which a dispensing pharmacy shall order the prescription to be delivered to the pharmacy and billed by the supplier to the Department of Social Services. If the commissioner so designates specific suppliers of Factor VIII pharmaceuticals, the department shall pay the dispensing pharmacy a handling fee equal to eight per cent of the actual acquisition cost for such prescription.

Sec. 23. Section 17b–694 of the general statutes is repealed and the following is substituted in lieu thereof (Effective October 1, 2004):

(a) The Labor Commissioner, in consultation with the Commissioners of Social Services and Mental Health, shall administer a grant program, within available appropriations, to fund employment placement projects for recipients of ~~general assistance or~~ state-administered general assistance, cash assistance or medical assistance or recipients of Medicaid who are eighteen to twenty years of age. A grant may be awarded to (1) a municipality or group of towns which form a region based on a project plan providing education, training or other assistance in securing employment, (2) a private substance abuse or mental health services provider based on a project plan incorporating job placement in the treatment process, or (3) a nonprofit organization providing employment services when no municipality or group of towns elect to apply for such a grant for a given geographic area. A plan may include cash incentives as a supplement to wages for recipients who work.

(b) In order to receive funding, a project plan shall be submitted to the commissioner no later than August first, annually. Funds shall be disbursed by the commissioner no later than September first, annually. Projects shall be funded based on the number of recipients to be served and the level of services to be provided.

Sec. 24. Section 17b–730 of the general statutes is repealed and the following is substituted in lieu thereof (Effective October 1, 2004):

(a) The Commissioner of Social Services is authorized to take advantage of any federal statutes and regulations relating to child day care and shall have the power to administer any federally-assisted child day care program in the event that said federal statutes or regulations require that said federally-assisted program be administered by a single state agency.

(b) The Commissioner of Social Services is authorized to take advantage of Title V of Public Law 88–452, entitled "Economic Opportunity Act of 1964", [1] with respect to providing work training, aid and assistance to persons eligible for state-administered general assistance or public assistance, and to administer the same in such manner as is required for the receipt of federal funds therefor.

[1] 42 U.S.C.A. § 2701 et seq.

Sec. 25. Section 17b–802 of the general statutes is repealed and the following is substituted in lieu thereof (Effective October 1, 2004):

(a) The Commissioner of Social Services shall establish, within available appropriations, and administer a security deposit guarantee program for persons who (1) (A) are recipients of temporary family assistance, aid under the state supplement program, or state-administered general assistance, ~~or general assistance,~~ or (B) have a documented showing of financial need, and (2) (A) are residing in emergency shelters or other emergency housing, cannot remain in permanent housing due to any reason specified in subsection (a) of section 17b–808, or are served a notice to quit in a summary process action instituted pursuant to chapter 832,[1] or (B) have a rental assistance program or federal Section 8 certificate or voucher. Under such program, the Commissioner of Social Services may provide security deposit guarantees for use by such persons in lieu of a security deposit on a rental dwelling unit. Eligible persons may receive a security deposit guarantee in an amount not to exceed the equivalent of two months' rent on such rental unit. No person may apply for and receive a security deposit guarantee more than once in any eighteen-month period without the express authorization of the Commissioner of Social Services, except as provided in subsection (b) of this section. The Commissioner of Social Services may establish priorities for allocating security deposit guarantees between eligible persons described in subparagraphs (A) and (B) of subdivision (2) of this subsection.

(b) In the case of any person who qualifies for a guarantee, the Commissioner of Social Services, or any emergency shelter under contract with the Department of Social Services to assist in the administration of the security deposit guarantee program established pursuant to subsection (a) of this section, may execute a written agreement to pay the landlord for any damages suffered by the landlord due to the tenant's failure to comply with such tenant's obligations as defined in section 47a–21, as amended, provided the amount of any such payment shall not exceed the amount of the requested security deposit. Notwithstanding the provisions of subsection (a) of this section, if a person who has previously received a grant for a security deposit or a security deposit guarantee becomes eligible for a subsequent security deposit guarantee within eighteen months after a claim has been paid on a prior security deposit guarantee, such person may receive a security deposit guarantee. The amount of the subsequent security deposit guarantee for which such person would otherwise have been eligible shall be reduced by (1) any amount of a previous grant which has not been returned to the department pursuant to section 47a–21, as amended, or (2) the amount of any payment made to the landlord for damages pursuant to this subsection.

(c) Any payment made pursuant to this section to any person receiving temporary family assistance, aid under the state supplement program ~~, general assistance~~ or state-administered general assistance shall not be deducted from the amount of assistance to which the recipient would otherwise be entitled.

(d) On and after July 1, 2000, no special need or special benefit payments shall be made by the commissioner for security deposits from the temporary family assistance, state supplement, or state-administered general assistance ~~or general assistance~~ programs.

(e) The Commissioner of Social Services may, within available appropriations, on a case-by-case basis, provide a security deposit grant to a person eligible for the security deposit guarantee program established under subsection (a) of this section, in an amount not to exceed the equivalent of one month's rent on such rental unit provided the commissioner determines that emergency circumstances exist which threaten the health, safety or welfare of a child who resides with such person. Such person shall not be eligible for more than one such grant without the authorization of said commissioner. Nothing in this section shall preclude the approval of such one-month security deposit grant in conjunction with a one-month security deposit guarantee.

(f) The Commissioner of Social Services may provide a security deposit grant to a person receiving such grant through any emergency shelter under an existing contract with the Department of Social Services to assist in the administration of the security deposit program, but in no event shall a payment be authorized after October 1, 2000. Nothing in this section shall preclude the commissioner from entering into a contract with one or more emergency shelters for the purpose of issuing security deposit guarantees.

(g) The Commissioner of Social Services shall adopt regulations, in accordance with the provisions of chapter 54,[2] to administer the program established pursuant to this section and to set eligibility criteria for the program, but may implement the program until June 30, 2003, while in the process of adopting such regulations provided notice of intent to adopt the regulations is published in the Connecticut Law Journal within twenty days after implementation.

[1] C.G.S.A. § 47a–23 et seq.
[2] C.G.S.A. § 4–166 et seq.

Sec. 26. Subsection (c) of section 17b–853 of the general statutes is repealed and the following is substituted in lieu thereof (Effective October 1, 2004):

(c) So much of the cost of a human resource development program as is not met by either a federal grant-in-aid or by a state grant-in-aid pursuant to this section may be paid by a municipality, any agency, board, commission or department thereof, or any public authority, or any private organization, in cash or in kind, including, but not limited to, in the discretion of the Commissioner of Social Services, additional plant and equipment, added services and increases in financial assistance furnished thereby, provided only such increments in plant and equipment, services and financial assistance as (1) are used for or in connection with human resource development programs, and (2) are funded otherwise than by federal or state financial assistance ~~and (3) are not general assistance payments~~ may be considered as payment by a municipality under this section.

Sec. 27. Section 19a–492b of the general statutes is repealed and the following is substituted in lieu thereof (Effective October 1, 2004):

(a) A home health care agency that receives payment for rendering care to persons receiving medical assistance from the state, ~~general assistance medical benefits from a town,~~ assistance from the Connecticut home-care program for the elderly pursuant to section 17b–342, or funds obtained through Title XVIII of the Social Security Amendments of 1965[1] shall be prohibited from discriminating against such persons who apply for enrollment to such home health care agency on the basis of source of payment.

(b) Any home health care agency which violates the provisions of this section shall be subject to suspension or revocation of license.

[1] See Short Title note under 42 U.S.C.A. § 1305.

Sec. 28. Subsection (a) of section 19a–533 of the general statutes is repealed and the following is substituted in lieu thereof (Effective October 1, 2004):

(a) As used in this section, "nursing home" means any chronic and convalescent facility or any rest home with nursing supervision, as defined in section 19a–521, which has a provider agreement with the state to provide services to recipients of funds obtained through Title XIX of the Social Security Amendments of 1965;[1] and "indigent person" means any person who is eligible for or who is receiving medical assistance benefits from the state. ~~or general assistance benefits from a town.~~

[1] 42 U.S.C.A. § 1396 et seq.

Sec. 29. Subdivision (7) of section 19a–659 of the general statutes is repealed and the following is substituted in lieu thereof (Effective October 1, 2004):

(7) "Medical assistance" means medical assistance provided under the ~~general assistance program, the~~ state-administered general assistance program or the Medicaid program.

Sec. 30. Subdivision (4) of section 19a–673 of the general statutes, as amended by section 5 of public act 03–266, is repealed and the following is substituted in lieu thereof (Effective October 1, 2004):

(4) "Uninsured patient" means any person who is liable for one or more hospital charges whose income is at or below two hundred fifty per cent of the poverty income guidelines who (A) has applied and been denied eligibility for any medical or health care coverage provided under the state-administered general assistance program or the Medicaid program due to failure to satisfy income or other eligibility requirements, and (B) is not eligible for coverage for hospital services under the Medicare or CHAMPUS programs, or under any Medicaid or health insurance program of any other nation, state, territory or commonwealth, or under any other governmental or privately sponsored health or accident insurance or benefit program including, but not limited to, workers' compensation and awards, settlements or judgments arising from claims, suits or proceedings involving motor vehicle accidents or alleged negligence.

Sec. 31. Subsection (c) of section 20–619 of the general statutes is repealed and the following is substituted in lieu thereof (Effective October 1, 2004):

(c) A prescribing practitioner may specify in writing or by a telephonic or other electronic communication that there shall be no substitution for the specified brand name drug product in any prescription, provided (1) in any prescription for a Medicaid, state-administered general assistance, ~~general assistance~~ or ConnPACE recipient, such practitioner specifies the basis on which the brand name drug product and dosage form is medically necessary in comparison to a chemically equivalent generic drug product substitution, and (2) the phrase "BRAND MEDICALLY NECESSARY", shall be in the practitioner's handwriting on the prescription form or on an electronically-produced copy of the prescription form or, if the prohibition was communicated by telephonic or other electronic communication that did not reproduce the practitioner's handwriting, a statement to that effect appears on the form. The phrase "BRAND MEDICALLY NECESSARY" shall not be preprinted or stamped or initialed on the form. If the practitioner specifies by telephonic or other electronic communication that did not reproduce the practitioner's handwriting that there shall be no substitution for the specified brand name drug product in any prescription for a Medicaid, state-administered general assistance, ~~general assistance~~ or ConnPACE recipient, written certification in the practitioner's handwriting bearing the phrase "BRAND MEDICALLY NECESSARY" shall be sent to the dispensing pharmacy within ten days.

Sec. 32. Subsections (a) and (b) of section 31–3d of the general statutes, as amended by section 97 of public act 03–3 of the June 30 special session, are repealed and the following is substituted in lieu thereof (Effective October 1, 2004):

(a) The Labor Commissioner shall develop and implement work training opportunities programs in cooperation with municipalities, public and private agencies and business and industry in order to expand education, training, supportive services and job development for the placement of the chronically unemployed with specific emphasis on the needs of persons receiving or eligible to receive ~~general assistance under the provisions of sections 17b–118, 17b–118a, 17b–118b, 17b–119, 17b–122, 17b–124 to 17b–132, inclusive, 17b–136 to 17b–138, inclusive, 17b–221 to 17b–250, inclusive, 17b–256, 17b–263, 17b–340 to 17b–350, inclusive, 17b–689, 17b–689b and 17b–743 to 17b–747, inclusive~~ state-administered general assistance program benefits. For the purposes of funding such programs, the commissioner may, in addition to expending available appropriations, apply for, receive and expend funds from federal governmental and private sources.

(b) Participants in such programs shall receive compensation for time spent in training at rates established or approved by the Labor Commissioner. Participants who are state-administered general assistance recipients may earn a net amount up to thirty dollars per week in education and training programs established under this section, section 31–3b or subsection (a) of section 17b–689, as amended, without affecting the amount of their grants. Amounts in excess of thirty dollars earned by state-administered general assistance recipients for each week of such education or training shall be deducted from such recipients' grants. Medical benefits of such recipients shall not be affected by participation in such education or training. Job placement of participants who have completed training shall be limited to positions for which compensation is payable at rates consistent with industry practice or in conformity with collective bargaining agreements.

Sec. 33. Subsection (b) of section 31–3k of the general statutes is repealed and the following is substituted in lieu thereof (Effective October 1, 2004):

(b) Each board, within its region, shall:

(1) Carry out the duties and responsibilities of a private industry council under the Job Training Partnership Act,[1] provided the private industry council within the region elects by a vote of its members to become a board and the Labor Commissioner approves the council as a regional work force development board.

(2) Within existing resources and consistent with the state employment and training information system and any guidelines issued by the commissioner under subsection (b) of section 31–2, and with the annual plan developed by the commission under section 31–3h, as amended, and approved by the Governor, (A) assess regional needs and identify regional priorities for employment and training programs, including, but not limited to, an assessment of the special employment needs of unskilled and low-skilled unemployed persons, including persons receiving state-administered general assistance or short-term unemployment assistance, (B) conduct planning for regional employment and training programs, (C) coordinate such programs to ensure that the programs respond to the needs of labor, business and industry, municipalities within the region, the region as a whole, and all of its citizens, (D) serve as a clearinghouse for information on all employment and training programs in the region, (E) prepare and submit an annual plan containing the board's priorities and goals for regional employment and training programs to the commissioner and the commission for their review and approval, (F) review grant proposals and plans submitted to state agencies for employment and training programs that directly affect the region to determine whether such proposals and plans are consistent with the annual regional plan prepared under subparagraph (E) of this subdivision and inform the commission and each state agency concerned of the results of the review, (G) evaluate the effectiveness of employment and training programs within the region in meeting the goals contained in the annual regional plan prepared under subparagraph (E) of this subdivision and report its findings to the commissioner and the commission on an annual basis, (H) ensure the effective use of available employment and training resources in the region, and (I) allocate funds where applicable for program operations in the region.

(3) Provide information to the commissioner concerning (A) all employment and training programs, grants or funds to be effective or available in the region in the following program year, (B) the source and purpose of such programs, grants or funds, (C) the projected amount of such programs, grants or funds, (D) persons, organizations and institutions eligible to participate in such programs or receive such grants or funds, (E) characteristics of clients eligible to receive services pursuant to such programs, grants or funds, (F) the range of services available pursuant to such programs, grants or funds, (G) goals of such programs, grants or funds, (H) where applicable, schedules for submitting requests for proposals, planning instructions, proposals and plans, in connection with such programs, grants or funds, (I) the program period for such programs, grants or funds, and (J) any other data relating to such programs, grants or funds that the commissioner or the commission deems essential for effective state planning.

(4) Carry out the duties and responsibilities of the local board for purposes of the federal Workforce Investment Act of 1998, P. L. 105–220, as from time to time amended.[2]

(5) Establish a worker training education committee comprised of persons from the education and business communities within the region, including, but not limited to, regional community-technical colleges and regional vocational-technical schools.

[1] 29 U.S.C.A. § 1501 et seq.
[2] 29 U.S.C.A. § 2801 et seq.

Sec. 34. Subsection (c) of section 31–11x of the general statutes is repealed and the following is substituted in lieu thereof (Effective October 1, 2004):

(c) The Labor Commissioner shall adopt regulations, in accordance with the provisions of chapter 54,[1] establishing criteria for the distribution of funds under this section and shall adopt regulations, in accordance with chapter 54, to further implement the purposes of this section. The criteria shall include requirements that: (1) The program receiving state assistance: (A) Involves the Commissioner of Social Services in the planning of the program; (B) involves residents in the region to be served by the program in the planning and operation of the program; (C) involves the business community in the region to be served by the program in its development and operation; and (D) gives priority to persons who receive ~~general assistance or~~ state-administered general assistance benefits; and (2) a program receiving financial assistance has adequate internal administrative controls, accounting procedures, personnel standards, evaluation procedures, availability of in-service training and technical assistance programs and other policies as are necessary to promote the effective use of funds received under said programs.

[1] C.G.S.A. § 4–166 et seq.

Sec. 35. Subsection (e) of section 31–254 of the general statutes is repealed and the following is substituted in lieu thereof (Effective October 1, 2004):

(e) On a biweekly basis, the Department of Social Services shall compile a list of individuals who are receiving public assistance under the temporary assistance for needy families, Medicaid, food stamp, state supplement and state-administered general assistance programs and shall transmit such list to the Labor Department. The Labor Department shall promptly identify any new employee who is such an individual and said department shall transmit to the Department of Social Services the name, address and Social Security number of each such new employee and the name, address and state and federal tax registration or identification numbers of the employer.

Sec. 36. Subsection (b) of section 38a–472 of the general statutes is repealed and the following is substituted in lieu thereof (Effective October 1, 2004):

(b) Whenever there is in existence a contract by an insurer for payment to, or on behalf of, an applicant or recipient of medical assistance under the ~~general assistance program, the~~ state-administered general assistance program or the Medicaid program under said contract on account of bills incurred by the applicant or recipient for medical services, including, but not limited to, physician services, nursing services, pharmaceutical services, surgical care and hospital care, the assignment of the benefits of the contract by such applicant or recipient or his legally liable relative pursuant to section 17b–265 shall, upon receipt of notice from the assignee, be authority for payment by the insurer directly to the assignee. If notice is provided by the assignee to the insurer in accordance with the provisions of section 17b–265, the insurer shall be liable to the assignee for any amount payable to the assignee under the contract.

Sec. 37. Subdivision (3) of section 46a–63 of the general statutes is repealed and the following is substituted in lieu thereof (Effective October 1, 2004):

(3) "Lawful source of income" means income derived from social security, supplemental security income, housing assistance, child support, alimony or public or state-administered general assistance.

Sec. 38. Subsection (a) of section 46b–169 of the general statutes is repealed and the following is substituted in lieu thereof (Effective October 1, 2004):

(a) If the mother of any child born out of wedlock, or the mother of any child born to any married woman during marriage which child shall be found not to be issue of the marriage terminated by a decree of divorce or dissolution or by decree of any court of competent jurisdiction, fails or refuses to disclose the name of the putative father of such child under oath to the Commissioner of Social Services, if such child is a recipient of public assistance, ~~or to a selectman of a town in which such child resides, if such child is a recipient of general assistance,~~ or otherwise to a guardian or a guardian ad litem of such child, such mother may be cited to appear before any judge of the Superior Court and compelled to disclose the name of the putative father under oath and to institute an action to establish the paternity of said child.

Sec. 39. Subsection (b) of section 46b–215b of the general statutes, as amended by section 1 of public act 03–130, is repealed and the following is substituted in lieu thereof (Effective October 1, 2004):

(b) In any determination pursuant to subsection (a) of this section, when a party has been determined by the Social Security Administration, or a state agency authorized to award disability benefits, to qualify for disability benefits under the federal Supplemental Security Income Program, the Social Security disability program, the state supplement to the federal Supplemental Security Income Program, or the state-administered general assistance program, ~~or the general assistance program,~~ parental earning capacity shall not be a basis for deviating from the presumptive support amount that results from the application of the child support guidelines to such party's income.

Sec. 40. Subsection (b) of section 52–259b of the general statutes is repealed and the following is substituted in lieu thereof (Effective October 1, 2004):

(b) There shall be a rebuttable presumption that a person is indigent and unable to pay a fee or fees or the cost of service of process if (1) such person receives public assistance or (2) such person's income after taxes, mandatory wage deductions and child care expenses is one hundred twenty-five per cent or less of the federal poverty level. For purposes of this subsection, "public assistance" includes, but is not limited to, ~~general assistance,~~ state-administered general assistance, temporary family assistance, aid to the aged, blind and disabled, food stamps and Supplemental Security Income.

Sec. 41. Subsection (b) of section 54–210 of the general statutes is repealed and the following is substituted in lieu thereof (Effective October 1, 2004):

(b) Payment of compensation under this chapter may be made to a person who is a recipient of public assistance ~~,~~ or state-administered general assistance ~~or general assistance~~ for necessary and reasonable expenses related to injuries resulting from a crime and not provided for by the income assistance program in which such person is a participant. Unless required by federal law, no such payment shall be considered an asset for purposes of eligibility for such assistance.

Sec. 42. Section 7–406 of the general statutes, as amended by section 97 of public act 03–3 of the June 30 special session, is repealed and the following is substituted in lieu thereof (Effective October 1, 2004):

The board of finance or other corresponding board in each town, or, if there is no such board, the selectmen, shall annually prepare and have published a town report. Such report shall be available for distribution and shall contain, in addition to reports of town officers or boards required by law to be included, a statement of the amount received by such town under the provisions of part IIa of chapter 240 [1] together with an itemized account of the disposition of such amount, and such other matter as the board of finance or other corresponding board deems advisable. Towns with a population of five thousand or less, as computed by the Secretary of the Office of Policy and Management, shall publish their receipts and expenditures and the names of all persons, firms or corporations, other than recipients of support under sections 17b–118, as amended, 17b–118a, ~~17b–118b,~~ 17b–119, as amended, 17b–122, 17b–124 to 17b–132, inclusive, as amended, 17b–136 to 17b–138, inclusive, ~~17b–221~~ 17b–222 to 17b–250, inclusive, as amended, 17b–256, 17b–263, 17b–340 to 17b–350, inclusive, as amended, 17b–689, as amended, 17b–689b and 17b–743 to 17b–747, inclusive, receiving money from such towns, together with the total amount of payments in excess of fifty dollars to each, unless such town has a bookkeeping system approved by the secretary setting forth all the receipts and expenditures in detail, in which case it shall not be necessary for the town to publish in its report the names of all persons, firms or corporations receiving money from such towns, together with the total amount of payments in excess of fifty dollars to each.

[1] C.G.S.A. § 13a–175a et seq.

Sec. 43. Section 10a–194a of the general statutes, as amended by section 97 of public act 03–3 of the June 30 special session, is repealed and the following is substituted in lieu thereof (Effective October 1, 2004):

The authority shall report the terms and conditions of all financings and refinancings of nursing homes to the Commissioner of Social Services who shall make rate adjustments in accordance with the provisions of sections 17b–118, as amended, 17b–118a, ~~17b–118b,~~ 17b–119, as amended, 17b–122, 17b–124 to 17b–132, inclusive, as amended, 17b–136 to 17b–138, inclusive, ~~17b–221~~ 17b–222 to 17b–250, inclusive, as amended, 17b–256, 17b–263, 17b–340 to 17b–350, inclusive, as amended, 17b–689, as amended, 17b–689b and 17b–743 to 17b–747, inclusive.

Sec. 44. Subsection (b) of section 17a–600 of the general statutes, as amended by section 97 of public act 03–3 of the June 30 special session, is repealed and the following is substituted in lieu thereof (Effective October 1, 2004):

(b) The expense of confinement, support and treatment of any acquittee committed to the jurisdiction of the board shall be computed and paid for in accordance with the provisions of sections 17a–528, 17b–118, as amended, 17b–118a, ~~17b–118b,~~ 17b–119, as amended, 17b–122, 17b–124 to 17b–132, inclusive, as amended, 17b–136 to 17b–138, inclusive, ~~17b–221~~ 17b–222 to 17b–250, inclusive, as amended, 17b–256, 17b–263, 17b–340 to 17b–350, inclusive, as amended, 17b–689, as amended, 17b–689b and 17b–743 to 17b–747, inclusive.

Sec. 45. Section 17b–13 of the general statutes, as amended by section 97 of public act 03–3 of the June 30 special session, is repealed and the following is substituted in lieu thereof (Effective October 1, 2004):

The Commissioner of Social Services is designated as the agency of the state to administer or supervise the administration of financial aid for emergency relief purposes which the United States government has authorized or may authorize to be given to the several states. The State Treasurer is directed to receive all money granted by the United States or by any agency thereof and to hold the same separate from all other funds of the state. Funds granted to the state for emergency relief purposes shall be disbursed by the Treasurer, upon voucher of the Comptroller, under direction of and subject to the regulations of said commissioner. Unless otherwise provided by the terms of the federal authorization, such money shall be distributed by said commissioner to the several towns of this state for emergency relief in the state and shall be used by such towns in accordance with, and shall be subject to, the provisions of sections 17b–118, as amended, 17b–118a, ~~17b–118b,~~ 17b–119, as amended, 17b–122, 17b–124 to 17b–132, inclusive, as amended, 17b–136 to 17b–138, inclusive, ~~17b–221~~ 17b–222 to 17b–250, inclusive, as amended, 17b–256, 17b–263, 17b–340 to 17b–350, inclusive, as amended, 17b–689, as amended, 17b–689b and 17b–743 to 17b–747, inclusive. The remaining cost of providing such relief, after deduction of the federal contribution thereto, shall be borne by the state and the towns in accordance with the provisions of section 17b–134, as amended; but such cost shall not include administrative expense unless included in the federal authorization.

Sec. 46. Subsection (b) of section 17b–124 of the general statutes, as amended by section 97 of public act 03–3 of the June 30 special session, is repealed and the following is substituted in lieu thereof (Effective October 1, 2004):

(b) Each person having in his possession or control any property of any person for whom an application has been filed for medical assistance under sections 17b–118, as amended, 17b–118a, ~~17b–118b,~~ 17b–119, as amended, 17b–122, 17b–124 to 17b–132, inclusive, as amended, 17b–136 to 17b–138, inclusive, ~~17b–221~~ 17b–222 to 17b–250, inclusive, as amended, 17b–256, 17b–263, 17b–340 to 17b–350, inclusive, as amended, 17b–689, as amended, 17b–689b and 17b–743 to 17b–747, inclusive, or being indebted to him, or having knowledge of any property or income, including wages, belonging to him, or having knowledge of any other information relevant to such person's eligibility for such assistance, and any officer having control of the books and accounts of any corporation which has possession or control of any property or income, including wages, belonging to any such person, or is indebted to him, or having knowledge of such information, shall, upon presentation by a medical provider or its attorney of a signed certificate stating that an application signed by such person has been made for medical assistance, make full disclosure to such provider as to any such property or income, including wages or indebtedness or such other information relevant to such person's eligibility. Any person who violates any provision of this section shall be fined not more than one hundred dollars and shall pay just damages to the provider injured thereby.

Sec. 47. Subsection (a) of section 42 of public act 03–3 of the June 30 special session is repealed and the following is substituted in lieu thereof (Effective October 1, 2004):

(a) Notwithstanding the provisions of sections ~~17b–7,~~ 17b–111, 17b–111b, 17b–118, as amended, and 17b–118a, ~~17b–118b and 17b–221,~~ the Commissioner of Social Services shall operate a state-administered general assistance program in accordance with this section and section 44 of ~~this act~~ public act 03–3 of the June 30 special session and sections 17b–78, as amended, 17b–119, as amended, 17b–131, as amended, 17b–257, as amended, and 17b–689, as amended. Notwithstanding any provision of the general statutes, on and after October 1, 2003, no town shall be reimbursed by the state for any general assistance medical benefits incurred after September 30, 2003, and on and after March 1, 2004, no town shall be reimbursed by the state for any general assistance cash benefits or general assistance program administrative costs incurred after February 29, 2004.

Sec. 48. Section 17b–126 of the general statutes, as amended by section 97 of public act 03–3 of the June 30 special session, is repealed and the following is substituted in lieu thereof (Effective October 1, 2004):

If any person receiving such aid neglects or refuses to sign such agreement, the selectmen are authorized to file a lien against such property, or against the real property of any legally liable relative of any person receiving aid or support under sections ~~17b–221~~ 17b–222 to 17b–250, inclusive, as amended, 17b–256, 17b–263, 17b–340 to 17b–350, inclusive, as amended, 17b–689, as amended, 17b–689b and 17b–743 to 17b–747, inclusive, to secure the disbursements of such town made prior to filing such lien and any disbursements thereafter made, and such lien from the time of filing shall have the same force and effect and may be foreclosed in the same manner as any agreement provided for in section 17b–125.

Sec. 49. Subsection (c) of section 17b–127 of the general statutes, as amended by section 97 of public act 03–3 of the June 30 special session, is repealed and the following is substituted in lieu thereof (Effective October 1, 2004):

(c) Any person who defrauds the town to obtain any monetary award to which such person is not entitled, assists another person in so defrauding the town or with intent to defraud, or violates any other provision of sections 17b–118, as amended, 17b–118a, ~~17b–118b,~~ 17b–119, as amended, 17b–122, 17b–124 to 17b–132, inclusive, as amended, 17b–136 to 17b–138, inclusive, ~~17b–221~~ 17b–222 to 17b–250, inclusive, as amended, 17b–256, 17b–263, 17b–340 to 17b–350, inclusive, as amended, 17b–689, as amended, 17b–689b and 17b–743 to 17b–747, inclusive, shall be subject to the penalties for larceny under sections 53a–122 and 53a–123, depending on the amount involved. Any person convicted of violating this section shall be terminated from participation in the program for a period of at least one year.

Sec. 50. Subsection (b) of section 17b–128 of the general statutes, as amended by section 97 of public act 03–3 of the June 30 special session, is repealed and the following is substituted in lieu thereof (Effective October 1, 2004):

(b) Any town that overpays a person receiving financial assistance under sections 17b–118, as amended, 17b–118a, ~~17b–118b,~~ 17b–119, as amended, 17b–122, 17b–124 to 17b–132, inclusive, as amended, 17b–136 to 17b–138, inclusive, ~~17b–221~~ 17b–222 to 17b–250, inclusive, as amended, 17b–256, 17b–263, 17b–340 to 17b–350, inclusive, as amended, 17b–689, as amended, 17b–689b and 17b–743 to 17b–747, inclusive, shall recover such overpayment from such person's ongoing assistance. The amount of such recovery shall not exceed ten per cent of such person's ongoing benefit in any month.

Sec. 51. Section 17b–129 of the general statutes, as amended by section 97 of public act 03–3 of the June 30 special session, is repealed and the following is substituted in lieu thereof (Effective October 1, 2004):

(a) If any beneficiary of aid under sections 17b–118, as amended, 17b–118a, ~~17b–118b,~~ 17b–119, as amended, 17b–122, 17b–124 to 17b–132, inclusive, as amended, 17b–136 to 17b–138, inclusive, ~~17b–221~~ 17b–222 to 17b–250, inclusive, as amended, 17b–256, 17b–263, 17b–340 to 17b–350, inclusive, as amended, 17b–689, as amended, 17b–689b and 17b–743 to 17b–747, inclusive, has a cause of action, a town that provided aid to such beneficiary shall have a claim against the proceeds of such cause of action for the amount of such aid or fifty per cent of the proceeds received by such beneficiary after payment of all expenses connected with the cause of action, whichever is less, which shall have priority over all other unsecured claims and unrecorded encumbrances. Such claim shall be a lien, subordinate to any interest the state may possess under section 17b–94, against the proceeds from such cause of action, for the amount established in accordance with this section, and such lien shall have priority over all other claims except attorney's fees for such causes of action, expenses of suit, costs of hospitalization connected with the cause of action by whomever paid, over and above hospital insurance or other such benefits, and, for such period of hospitalization as was not paid for by the town, physician's fees for services during any such period as are connected with the cause of action over and above medical insurance or other such benefits. Where the state also has a claim against the proceeds of such cause of action under section 17b–94, the total amount of the claims by the state under said section and the town under this subsection shall not exceed fifty per cent of the proceeds received by the recipient after the allowable expenses and the town's claim shall be reduced accordingly. The proceeds of such causes of action shall be assignable to the town for payment of such lien irrespective of any other provision of law except section 17b–94. Upon presentation to the attorney for the beneficiary of an assignment of such proceeds executed by the beneficiary or his conservator or guardian, such assignment shall constitute an irrevocable direction to the attorney to pay the town in accordance with its terms.

(b) In the case of an inheritance of an estate by a beneficiary of aid under sections 17b–118, as amended, 17b–118a, ~~17b–118b,~~ 17b–119, as amended, 17b–122, 17b–124 to 17b–132, inclusive, as amended, 17b–136 to 17b–138, inclusive, ~~17b–221~~ 17b–222 to 17b–250, inclusive, as amended, 17b–256, 17b–263, 17b–340 to 17b–350, inclusive, as amended, 17b–689, as amended, 17b–689b and 17b–743 to 17b–747, inclusive, fifty per cent of the assets of the estate payable to the beneficiary or the amount of such assets equal to the amount of assistance paid, whichever is less, shall be assignable to the town. Where the state also has an assignment of such assets under section 17b–94, the total amount of the claims of the state under said section and the town under this subsection shall not exceed fifty per cent of the assets of the estate payable to the beneficiary and the town's assigned share shall be reduced accordingly. The Court of Probate shall accept any such assignment executed by the beneficiary and filed by the town with the court prior to the distribution of such inheritance, and to the extent of such inheritance not already distributed, the court shall order distribution in accordance therewith. If the town receives any assets of an estate pursuant to any such assignment, the town shall be subject to the same duties and liabilities concerning such assigned assets as the beneficiary.

(c) No claim shall be made, or lien applied, against any payment made pursuant to chapter 135,[1] any payment made pursuant to section 47–88d or 47–287, any court-ordered retroactive rent abatement, including any made pursuant to subsection (e) of section 47a–14h, as amended, or section 47a–4a, 47a–5 or 47a–57, or any security deposit refund pursuant to subsection (d) of section 47a–21, as amended, paid to a beneficiary of assistance under sections 17b–118, as amended, 17b–118a, ~~17b–118b,~~ 17b–119, as amended, 17b–122, 17b–124 to 17b–132, inclusive, as amended, 17b–136 to 17b–138, inclusive, ~~17b–221~~ 17b–222 to 17b–250, inclusive, as amended, 17b–256, 17b–263, 17b–340 to 17b–350, inclusive, as amended, 17b–689, as amended, 17b–689b and 17b–743 to 17b–747, inclusive.

[1] C.G.S.A. § 8–266 et seq.

Sec. 52. Section 17b–250 of the general statutes, as amended by section 97 of public act 03–3 of the June 30 special session, is repealed and the following is substituted in lieu thereof (Effective October 1, 2004):

When any person has been transferred from the Connecticut Correctional Institution, Somers, the Connecticut Correctional Institution, Niantic, or its maximum security division, the John R. Manson Youth Institution, Cheshire, or a community correctional center to a state hospital, such person's hospital expense prior to the termination of his sentence shall be charged to the state. If any person, transferred from a correctional institution or community correction center is committed to or otherwise remains in a state hospital after the expiration of his sentence, such person's hospital expense shall be paid to the state in the manner provided for payment in sections 17b–118, as amended, 17b–118a, ~~17b–118b,~~ 17b–119, as amended, 17b–122, 17b–124 to 17b–132, inclusive, as amended, 17b–136 to 17b–138, inclusive, ~~17b–221~~ 17b–222 to 17b–250, inclusive, as amended, 17b–256, 17b–263, 17b–340 to 17b–350, inclusive, as amended, 17b–689, as amended, 17b–689b and 17b–743 to 17b–747, inclusive.

Sec. 53. Subsection (a) of section 17b–351 of the general statutes is repealed and the following is substituted in lieu thereof (Effective October 1, 2004):

(a) Notwithstanding the provisions of sections ~~17b–7,~~ 17b–8 or 17b–9, as amended, any nursing home participating in the Title XVIII and Title XIX programs[1] may, on a one-time basis, increase its licensed bed capacity and implement a capital construction project to accomplish such an increase without being required to request or obtain approval of the increase in services, licensed bed capacity or the capital expenditures program from the Department of Social Services provided that the project (1) shall not require licensure by the Department of Public Health of more than ten additional nursing home beds, and (2) the total capital cost of said program shall not exceed thirty thousand dollars per bed, adjusted for inflation annually by said department.

[1] 42 U.S.C.A. § 1395 et seq. and § 1396 et seq.

Sec. 54. Section 18–87 of the general statutes, as amended by section 97 of public act 03–3 of the June 30 special session, is repealed and the following is substituted in lieu thereof (Effective October 1, 2004):

The Commissioner of Correction may transfer any inmate of any of the institutions of the Department of Correction to any other appropriate state institution with the concurrence of the superintendent of such institution or to the Department of Children and Families when the Commissioner of Correction finds that the welfare or health of the inmate requires it. When an inmate, after the expiration of his sentence, is committed to or otherwise remains in the institution to which he was transferred, the expense of his treatment and support shall be paid as provided by sections 17b–118, as amended, 17b–118a, ~~17b–118b,~~ 17b–119, as amended, 17b–122, 17b–124 to 17b–132, inclusive, as amended, 17b–136 to 17b–138, inclusive, ~~17b–221~~ 17b–222 to 17b–250, inclusive, as amended, 17b–256, 17b–263, 17b–340 to 17b–350, inclusive, as amended, 17b–689, as amended, 17b–689b, and 17b–743 to 17b–747, inclusive. No transfer of any person who has attained the age of eighteen years shall be made to the Department of Children and Families, and no transfer of any person who has not attained the age of eighteen to the Department of Children and Families shall be made unless the Commissioner of Children and Families finds that such person would benefit from a transfer to the Department of Children and Families and agrees to accept such person and such person has given his written consent to such transfer. Such person transferred to the Department of Children and Families shall be deemed to be committed to the custody of the Commissioner of Children and Families. The Commissioner of Children and Families shall have the power to terminate the commitment and release such person at any time he determines such termination and release would be in such person's best interest, and shall have the power to return such person to the jurisdiction of the Commissioner of Correction. The transfer of any person under this section to the Department of Children and Families shall not result in the person so transferred being in the custody of the Commissioner of Correction and the Commissioner of Children and Families for a total of less than the minimum nor more than the maximum term he would have been in the custody of the Commissioner of Correction had he not been so transferred.

Sec. 55. Section 19a–255 of the general statutes, as amended by section 97 of public act 03–3 of the June 30 special session, is repealed and the following is substituted in lieu thereof (Effective October 1, 2004):

Any resident of the state afflicted with tuberculosis in any form, who requires medical care for tuberculosis and who applies for care, shall be received: (1) In a state chronic disease hospital; (2) in a private hospital or clinic; or (3) by a physician or other health care provider without regard to the financial condition of the patient. The cost of care and treatment of such patients shall be computed in accordance with the provisions of sections 17b–118, as amended, 17b–118a, ~~17b–118b,~~ 17b–119, as amended, 17b–122, 17b–124 to 17b–132, inclusive, as amended, 17b–136 to 17b–138, inclusive, ~~17b–221~~ 17b–222 to 17b–250, inclusive, as amended, 17b–256, 17b–263, 17b–340 to 17b–350, inclusive, as amended, 17b–689, as amended, 17b–689b and 17b–743 to 17b–747, inclusive, and section 4–67c and shall be paid by the state if such cost is deemed appropriate by the Commissioner of Public Health to the treatment of tuberculosis.

Sec. 56. Subsection (f) of section 52–57 of the general statutes, as amended by section 97 of public act 03–3 of the June 30 special session, is repealed and the following is substituted in lieu thereof (Effective October 1, 2004):

(f) When the other methods of service of process provided under this section or otherwise provided by law cannot be effected, in actions concerning the establishment, enforcement or modification of child support orders other than actions for dissolution of marriage, including, but not limited to, such actions under sections 17b–118, as amended, 17b–118a, ~~17b–118b,~~ 17b–119, as amended, 17b–122, 17b–124 to 17b–132, inclusive, as amended, 17b–136 to 17b–138, inclusive, ~~17b–221~~ 17b–222 to 17b–250, inclusive, as amended, 17b–256, 17b–263, 17b–340 to 17b–350, inclusive, as amended, 17b–689, as amended, 17b–689b, 17b–743 to 17b–747, inclusive, and 46b–212 to 46b–213v, inclusive, and chapters 815, 815p, 815t, 815y and 816,[1] and actions to implement garnishments for support under section 52–362, as amended, service of process may be made upon a party to the action by one of the following methods, provided proof of receipt of such process by such party is presented to the court in accordance with rules promulgated by the judges of the Superior Court:

[1] C.G.S.A. §§ 46b–1 et seq., 46b–115 et seq., 46b–120 et seq., 46b–160 et seq., and 46b–180 et seq.

(1) By certified mail to a party to the action addressed to the employer of such party. Any service of process so sent shall include on the outside envelope the words "To be delivered to the employee in accordance with subsection (f) of section 52–57". The employer shall accept any such service of process sent by certified mail and promptly deliver such certified mail to the employee; or

(2) When a party to an action under this subsection is employed by an employer with fifteen or more employees, by personal service upon an official of the employer designated as an agent to accept service of process in actions brought under this subsection. Every employer with fifteen or more employees doing business in this state shall designate an official to accept service of process for employees who are parties to such actions. The person so served shall promptly deliver such process to the employee.

Sec. 57. Subsection (n) of section 54–56d of the general statutes, as amended by sections 17 and 97 of public act 03–3 of the June 30 special session, is repealed and the following is substituted in lieu thereof (Effective October 1, 2004):

(n) The cost of the examination effected by the Commissioner of Mental Health and Addiction Services and of testimony of persons conducting the examination effected by the commissioner shall be paid by the Department of Mental Health and Addiction Services. The cost of the examination and testimony by physicians appointed by the court shall be paid by the Judicial Department. If the defendant is indigent, the fee of the person selected by the defendant to observe the examination and to testify on his behalf shall be paid by the Public Defender Services Commission. The expense of treating a defendant placed in the custody of the Commissioner of Mental Health and Addiction Services, the Commissioner of Children and Families or the Commissioner of Mental Retardation pursuant to subdivision (2) of subsection (h) of this section or subsection (i) of this section shall be computed and paid for in the same manner as is provided for persons committed by a probate court under the provisions of sections 17b–118, as amended, 17b–118a, ~~17b–118b,~~ 17b–119, as amended, 17b–122, 17b–124 to 17b–132, inclusive, as amended, 17b–136 to 17b–138, inclusive, ~~17b–221~~ 17b–222 to 17b–250, inclusive, as amended, 17b–256, 17b–263, 17b–340 to 17b–350, inclusive, as amended, 17b–689, as amended, 17b–689b and 17b–743 to 17b–747, inclusive.

Sec. 58. Subsection (a) of section 8–358 of the general statutes, as amended by section 97 of public act 03–3 of the June 30 special session, is repealed and the following is substituted in lieu thereof (Effective October 1, 2004):

~~(a) If a person residing in a dwelling unit in any project receiving financial assistance pursuant to sections 8–355 to 8–359, inclusive, is a recipient of general assistance as a one person household under sections 17b–118, 17b–118a, 17b–118b, 17b–119, 17b–122, 17b–124 to 17b–132, inclusive, 17b–136 to 17b–138, inclusive, 17b–221 to 17b–250, inclusive, 17b–256, 17b–263, 17b–340 to 17b–350, inclusive, 17b–689, 17b–689b and 17b–743 to 17b–747, inclusive, the rental payment for such person's dwelling unit shall be an amount equal to the shelter component of the general assistance grant as determined by the town in accordance with regulations adopted by the Commissioner of Social Services pursuant to section 17b–78. Otherwise, the~~

(a) The maximum amount which a person or family residing in a dwelling unit in a project receiving financial assistance under sections 8–355 to 8–359, inclusive, shall pay as its contribution to the total rent for the dwelling unit shall be thirty per cent of the adjusted monthly income, as defined by the commissioner pursuant to subsection (b) of this section, of the household in which the person resides or of the family, less the amount of such household's or family's utility allowance.

Sec. 59. (Effective October 1, 2004) Sections 8–206b, 17b–7, 17b–111b, 17b–118b, 17b–221 and 17b–810 of the general statutes are repealed.

Approved May 10, 2004.

FOSTER CARE—LICENSES AND PERMITS—SPECIAL STUDY FOSTER CARE

P.A. No. 04–88

S.B. No. 300

AN ACT CONCERNING SPECIAL STUDY FOSTER CARE.

Be it enacted by the Senate and House of Representatives in General Assembly convened:

Section 1. Section 17a–114 of the general statutes, as amended by section 7 of public act 03–243, is repealed and the following is substituted in lieu thereof (Effective October 1, 2004):

(a) As used in this section, "licensed" means a person holds a license issued by the Department of Children and Families to provide foster care, including foster care of a specific child, and "special study foster parent" means a person who is twenty-one years of age or older and who does not hold a license issued by the Department of Children and Families to provide foster care.

~~(a)~~ (b)(1) No child in the custody of the Commissioner of Children and Families shall be placed with any person, unless such person is licensed by the department. ~~for that purpose.~~ Any person licensed by the department ~~to accept placement of a child is deemed to be licensed to accept placement as a foster family or prospective adoptive family~~ may be a prospective adoptive parent. The commissioner shall adopt regulations, in accordance with the provisions of chapter 54,[1] to establish the licensing procedures and standards.

(2) The commissioner shall require each applicant for licensure pursuant to this section and any person sixteen years of age or older living in the household of such applicant to submit to state and national criminal history records checks prior to issuing a license to such applicant to accept placement of a child. Such criminal history records checks shall be conducted in accordance with section 29–17a. The commissioner shall also check the state child abuse registry established pursuant to section 17a–101k for the name of such applicant and for the name of any person sixteen years of age or older living in the household of such applicant for perpetrator information.

~~(b)~~ (c) Notwithstanding the requirements of subsection ~~(a)~~ (b) of this section, the commissioner may place a child with a relative who is not licensed or, if the child is fourteen years of age or older, with a special study foster parent for a period of up to ninety days when such placement is in the best interests of the child, provided a satisfactory home visit is conducted, a basic assessment of the family is completed and such relative or special study foster parent attests that such relative or special study foster parent and any adult living within the household ~~have~~ has not been convicted of a crime or arrested for a felony against a person, for injury or risk of injury to or impairing the morals of a child, or for the possession, use or sale of a controlled substance. Any such relative or special study foster parent who accepts placement of a child in excess of such ninety-day period shall be subject to licensure by the commissioner, except that any such relative who, prior to July 1, 2001, had been certified by the commissioner to provide care for a related child may continue to maintain such certification if such relative continues to meet the regulatory requirements and the child remains in such relative's care. The commissioner may grant a waiver from such procedure or standard, except any safety standard, for a child placed with a relative, on a case-by-case basis, from such procedure or standard, except any safety standard, based on the home of the relative and the needs and best interests of such child. The reason for any waiver granted shall be documented in writing. The commissioner shall adopt regulations, in accordance with the provisions of chapter 54, to establish certification procedures and standards for a caretaker who is a relative of such child.

[1] C.G.S.A. § 4–166 et seq.

Approved May 10, 2004.

ORGAN DONATION—FAMILY MEDICAL LEAVE

P.A. No. 04–95

S.S.B. No. 327

AN ACT CONCERNING FAMILY AND MEDICAL LEAVE FOR ORGAN DONATION.

Be it enacted by the Senate and House of Representatives in General Assembly convened:

Section 1. Section 5–248a of the general statutes is repealed and the following is substituted in lieu thereof (Effective October 1, 2004):

(a) Each permanent employee, as defined in subdivision (21) of section 5–196, shall be entitled to the following: (1) A maximum of twenty-four weeks of family leave of absence within any two-year period upon the birth or adoption of a child of such employee, or upon the serious illness of a child, spouse or parent of such employee; and (2) a maximum of twenty-four weeks of medical leave of absence within any two-year period upon the serious illness of such employee or in order for such employee to serve as an organ or bone marrow donor.Any such leave of absence shall be without pay. Upon the expiration of any such leave of absence, the employee shall be entitled (A) to return to the employee's original job from which the leave of absence was provided or, if not available, to an equivalent position with equivalent pay, except that in the case of a medical leave, if the employee is medically unable to perform the employee's original job upon the expiration of such leave, the Personnel Division of the Department of Administrative Services shall endeavor to find other suitable work for such employee in state service, and (B) to all accumulated seniority, retirement, fringe benefit and other service credits the employee had at the commencement of such leave. Such service credits shall not accrue during the period of the leave of absence.

(b) The leave of absence benefits granted by this section shall be in addition to any other paid leave benefits and benefits provided under subdivision (7) of subsection (a) of section 46a–60 which are otherwise available to the employee.

(c) Any permanent employee who requests a medical leave of absence due to the employee's serious illness or a family leave of absence due to the serious illness of a child, spouse or parent pursuant to subsection (a) of this section shall be required by the employee's appointing authority, prior to the inception of such leave, to provide sufficient written certification from the physician of such employee, child, spouse or parent of the nature of such illness and its probable duration. For the purposes of this section, "serious illness" means an illness, injury, impairment or physical or mental condition that involves (1) inpatient care in a hospital, hospice or residential care facility, or (2) continuing treatment or continuing supervision by a health care provider.

(d) Any permanent employee who requests a medical leave of absence in order to serve as an organ or bone marrow donor pursuant to subsection (a) of this section shall be required by the employee's appointing authority, prior to the inception of such leave, to provide sufficient written certification from the physician of such employee of the proposed organ or bone marrow donation and the probable duration of the employee's recovery period from such donation.

~~(d)~~ (e) Any permanent employee who requests a family leave of absence pursuant to subsection (a) of this section shall submit to the employee's appointing authority, prior to the inception of such leave, a signed statement of the employee's intent to return to the employee's position in state service upon the termination of such leave.

~~(e)~~ (f) Notwithstanding the provisions of subsection (b) of section 38a–554, as amended, the state shall pay for the continuation of health insurance benefits for the employee during any leave of absence taken pursuant to this section. In order to continue any other health insurance coverages during such leave, the employee shall contribute that portion of the premium the employee would have been required to contribute had the employee remained an active employee during the leave period.

Sec. 2. Section 31–51*ll* of the general statutes, as amended by section 2 of public act 03–213, is repealed and the following is substituted in lieu thereof (Effective October 1, 2004):

(a)(1) Subject to section 31–51mm, an eligible employee shall be entitled to a total of sixteen workweeks of leave during any twenty-four-month period, such twenty-four-month period to be determined utilizing any one of the following methods: ~~(1)~~ (A) Consecutive calendar years; ~~(2)~~ (B) any fixed twenty-four-month period, such as two consecutive fiscal years or a twenty-four-month period measured forward from an employee's first date of employment; ~~(3)~~ (C) a twenty-four-month period measured forward from an employee's first day of leave taken under sections 31–51kk to 31–51qq, inclusive; or ~~(4)~~ (D) a rolling twenty-four-month period measured backward from an employee's first day of leave taken under sections 31–51kk to 31–51qq, inclusive.~~,~~

(2) Such leave may be taken for one or more of the following:

~~(1)~~ (A) Upon the birth of a son or daughter of the employee;

~~(2)~~ (B) Upon the placement of a son or daughter with the employee for adoption or foster care;

~~(3)~~ (C) In order to care for the spouse, or a son, daughter or parent of the employee, if such spouse, son, daughter or parent has a serious health condition; ~~or~~

~~(4)~~ (D) Because of a serious health condition of the employee; or

(E) In order to serve as an organ or bone marrow donor.

(b) Entitlement to leave under ~~subdivision (1) or (2)~~ subparagraph (A) or (B) of subdivision (2) of subsection (a) of this section may accrue prior to the birth or placement of a son or daughter when such leave is required because of such impending birth or placement.

(c)(1) Leave under ~~subdivision (1) or (2)~~ subparagraph (A) or (B) of subdivision (2) of subsection (a) of this section for the birth or placement of a son or daughter may not be taken by an employee intermittently or on a reduced leave schedule unless the employee and the employer agree otherwise. Subject to subdivision (2) of this subsection concerning an alternative position, subdivision (2) of subsection (f) of this section concerning the duties of the employee and subdivision (5) of subsection (b) of section 31–51mm concerning sufficient certification, leave under ~~subdivision (3) or (4)~~ subparagraph (C) or (D) of subdivision (2) of subsection (a) of this section for a serious health condition may be taken intermittently or on a reduced leave schedule when medically necessary. The taking of leave intermittently or on a reduced leave schedule pursuant to this subsection shall not result in a reduction of the total amount of leave to which the employee is entitled under subsection (a) of this section beyond the amount of leave actually taken.

(2) If an employee requests intermittent leave or leave on a reduced leave schedule under ~~subdivision (3) or (4)~~ subparagraph (C), (D) or (E) of subdivision (2) of subsection (a) of this section that is foreseeable based on planned medical treatment, the employer may require the employee to transfer temporarily to an available alternative position offered by the employer for which the employee is qualified and that (A) has equivalent pay and benefits and (B) better accommodates recurring periods of leave than the regular employment position of the employee, provided the exercise of this authority shall not conflict with any provision of a collective bargaining agreement between such employer and a labor organization which is the collective bargaining representative of the unit of which the employee is a part.

(d) Except as provided in subsection (e) of this section, leave granted under subsection (a) of this section may consist of unpaid leave.

(e)(1) If an employer provides paid leave for fewer than sixteen workweeks, the additional weeks of leave necessary to attain the sixteen workweeks of leave required under sections 5–248a, as amended by this act, and 31–51kk to 31–51qq, inclusive, may be provided without compensation.

(2)(A) An eligible employee may elect, or an employer may require the employee, to substitute any of the accrued paid vacation leave, personal leave or family leave of the employee for leave provided under ~~subdivision (1), (2) or (3)~~ subparagraph (A), (B) or (C) of subdivision (2) of subsection (a) of this section for any part of this sixteen-week period of such leave under said subsection.

(B) An eligible employee may elect, or an employer may require the employee, to substitute any of the accrued paid vacation leave, personal leave, or medical or sick leave of the employee for leave provided under ~~subdivision (3) or (4)~~ subparagraph (C), (D) or (E) of subdivision (2) of subsection (a) of this section for any part of the sixteen-week period of such leave under said subsection, except that nothing in section 5–248a, as amended by this act, or 31–51kk to 31–51qq, inclusive, shall require an employer to provide paid sick leave or paid medical leave in any situation in which such employer would not normally provide any such paid leave.

(f)(1) In any case in which the necessity for leave under ~~subdivision (1) or (2)~~ subparagraph (A) or (B) of subdivision (2) of subsection (a) of this section is foreseeable based on an expected birth or placement of a son or daughter, the employee shall provide the employer with not less than thirty days' notice, before the date of the leave is to begin, of the employee's intention to take leave under said ~~subdivision (1) or (2)~~ subparagraph (A) or (B), except that if the date of the birth or placement of a son or daughter requires leave to begin in less than thirty days, the employee shall provide such notice as is practicable.

(2) In any case in which the necessity for leave under ~~subdivision (3) or (4)~~ subparagraph (C), (D) or (E) of subdivision (2) of subsection (a) of this section is foreseeable based on planned medical treatment, the employee (A) shall make a reasonable effort to schedule the treatment so as not to disrupt unduly the operations of the employer, subject to the approval of the health care provider of the employee or the health care provider of the son, daughter, spouse or parent of the employee, as appropriate; and (B) shall provide the employer with not less than thirty days' notice, before the date the leave is to begin, of the employee's intention to take leave under said ~~subdivision (3) or (4)~~ subparagraph (C), (D) or (E), except that if the date of the treatment requires leave to begin in less than thirty days, the employee shall provide such notice as is practicable.

(g) In any case in which a husband and wife entitled to leave under subsection (a) of this section are employed by the same employer, the aggregate number of workweeks of leave to which both may be entitled may be limited to sixteen workweeks during any twenty-four-month period, if such leave is taken: (1) Under ~~subdivision (1) or (2)~~ subparagraph (A) or (B) of subdivision (2) of subsection (a) of this section; or (2) to care for a sick parent under ~~subdivision (3)~~ subparagraph (C) of said subsection (a).

(h) Unpaid leave taken pursuant to sections 5–248a, as amended by this act, and 31–51kk to 31–51qq, inclusive, shall not be construed to affect an employee's qualification for exemption under chapter 558.[1]

(i) Notwithstanding the provisions of sections 5–248a, as amended by this act, and 31–51kk to 31–51qq, inclusive, all further rights granted by federal law shall remain in effect.

[1] C.G.S.A. § 31–58 et seq.

Sec. 3. Section 31–51mm of the general statutes is repealed and the following is substituted in lieu thereof (Effective October 1, 2004):

(a) An employer may require that request for leave based on a serious health condition in ~~subdivision (3) or (4)~~ subparagraph (C) or (D) of subdivision (2) of subsection (a) of section 31–51*ll*, as amended by this act, be supported by a certification issued by the health care provider of the eligible employee or of the son, daughter, spouse or parent of the employee, as appropriate. The employee shall provide, in a timely manner, a copy of such certification to the employer.

(b) Certification provided under subsection (a) of this section shall be sufficient if it states:

(1) The date on which the serious health condition commenced;

(2) The probable duration of the condition;

(3) The appropriate medical facts within the knowledge of the health care provider regarding the condition;

(4)(A) For purposes of leave under ~~subdivision (3)~~ subparagraph (C) of subdivision (2) of subsection (a) of section 31–51*ll*, as amended by this act, a statement that the eligible employee is needed to care for the son, daughter, spouse or parent and an estimate of the amount of time that such employee needs to care for the son, daughter, spouse or parent; and (B) for purposes of leave under ~~subdivision (4)~~ subparagraph (D) of subdivision (2) of subsection (a) of section 31–51*ll*, as amended by this act, a statement that the employee is unable to perform the functions of the position of the employee;

(5) In the case of certification for intermittent leave or leave on a reduced leave schedule for planned medical treatment, the dates on which such treatment is expected to be given and the duration of such treatment;

(6) In the case of certification for intermittent leave or leave on a reduced leave schedule under ~~subdivision (4)~~ subparagraph (D) of subdivision (2) of subsection (a) of section 31–51*ll*, as amended by this act, a statement of the medical necessity of the intermittent leave or leave on a reduced leave schedule, and the expected duration of the intermittent leave or reduced leave schedule; and

(7) In the case of certification for intermittent leave or leave on a reduced leave schedule under ~~subdivision (3)~~ subparagraph (C) of subdivision (2) of subsection (a) of section 31–51*ll*, as amended by this act, a statement that the employee's intermittent leave or leave on a reduced leave schedule is necessary for the care of the son, daughter, parent or spouse who has a serious health condition, or will assist in their recovery, and the expected duration and schedule of the intermittent leave or reduced leave schedule.

(c)(1) In any case in which the employer has reason to doubt the validity of the certification provided under subsection (a) of this section for leave under ~~subdivision (3) or (4)~~ subparagraph (C) or (D) of subdivision (2) of subsection (a) of section 31–51*ll*, as amended by this act, the employer may require, at the expense of the employer, that the eligible employee obtain the opinion of a second health care provider designated or approved by the employer concerning any information certified under subsection (b) of this section for such leave.

(2) A health care provider designated or approved under subdivision (1) of this subsection shall not be employed on a regular basis by the employer.

(d)(1) In any case in which the second opinion described in subsection (c) of this section differs from the opinion in the original certification provided under subsection (a) of this section, the employer may require, at the expense of the employer, that the employee obtain the opinion of a third health care provider designated or approved jointly by the employer and the employee concerning the information certified under subsection (b) of this section.

(2) The opinion of the third health care provider concerning the information certified under subsection (b) of this section shall be considered to be final and shall be binding on the employer and the employee.

(e) The employer may require that the eligible employee obtain subsequent recertifications on a reasonable basis, provided the standards for determining what constitutes a reasonable basis for recertification may be governed by a collective bargaining agreement between such employer and a labor organization which is the collective bargaining representative of the unit of which the worker is a part if such a collective bargaining agreement is in effect. Unless otherwise required by the employee's health care provider, the employer may not require recertification more than once during a thirty-day period and, in any case, may not unreasonably require recertification. The employer shall pay for any recertification that is not covered by the employee's health insurance.

Sec. 4. Subsection (d) of section 31–51nn of the general statutes is repealed and the following is substituted in lieu thereof (Effective October 1, 2004):

(d) As a condition of restoration under subsection (a) of this section for an employee who has taken leave under ~~subdivision (4)~~ subparagraph (D) of subdivision (2) of subsection (a) of section 31–51*ll*, as amended by this act, the employer may have a uniformly applied practice or policy that requires each such employee to receive certification from the health care provider of the employee that the employee is able to resume work, except that nothing in this subsection shall supersede a valid law of this state or a collective bargaining agreement that governs the return to work of such employees.

Approved May 10, 2004.

CHILD SUPPORT—ENFORCEMENT—ORDERS OF COURT

P.A. No. 04–100

S.S.B. No. 596

AN ACT CONCERNING IMPROVED PROCESSING OF CHILD SUPPORT CASES.

Be it enacted by the Senate and House of Representatives in General Assembly convened:

Section 1. Subdivisions (1) and (2) of subsection (a) of section 17b–745 of the general statutes, as amended by section 70 of public act 03–278, are repealed and the following is substituted in lieu thereof (Effective October 1, 2004):

(a)(1) The Superior Court or a family support magistrate shall have authority to make and enforce orders for payment of support to the Commissioner of Administrative Services or, in IV-D support cases, to the state acting by and through the IV-D agency, directed to the husband or wife and, if the patient or person is ~~under twenty-one or, on and after October 1, 1972,~~ under the age of eighteen years or as otherwise provided in this subsection, to any parent of any patient or person being supported by the state, wholly or in part, in a state humane institution, or under any welfare program administered by the Department of Social Services, as the court or family support magistrate finds, in accordance with the provisions of subsection (b) of section 17b–179, or section 17a–90, 17b–81, 17b–223, 46b–129, as amended, or 46b–130, to be reasonably commensurate with the financial ability of any such relative. If such person is unmarried, a full-time high school student and residing with the custodial parent, such support shall continue according to the parents' respective abilities, if such person is in need of support, until such person completes the twelfth grade or attains the age of nineteen, whichever first occurs. Any court or family support magistrate called upon to make or enforce such an order, including one based upon a determination consented to by the relative, shall insure that such order is reasonable in light of the relative's ability to pay.

(2)(A) The court or family support magistrate shall include in each support order in a IV-D support case a provision for the health care coverage of the child which provision may include an order for either parent to name any child ~~under eighteen~~ as a beneficiary of any medical or dental insurance or benefit plan carried by such parent or available to such parent on a group basis through an employer or a union. Any such ~~employment based~~ employment-based order shall be enforced using a National Medical Support Notice as provided in section 46b–88. If such insurance coverage is unavailable at reasonable cost, the provision for health care coverage may include an order for either parent to apply for and maintain coverage on behalf of the child under the HUSKY Plan, Part B.[1] The noncustodial parent shall be ordered to apply for the HUSKY Plan, Part B only if such parent is found to have sufficient ability to pay the appropriate premium. In any IV-D support case in which the noncustodial parent is found to have insufficient ability to provide medical insurance coverage and the custodial party is the HUSKY Plan, Part A [2] or Part B applicant, the provision for health care coverage may include an order for the noncustodial parent to pay such amount as is specified by the court or family support magistrate to the state or the custodial party, as their interests may appear, to offset the cost of any insurance payable under the HUSKY Plan, Part A or Part B. In no event may such order include payment to offset the cost of any such premium if such payment would reduce the amount of current support required under the child support guidelines.

(B) Whenever an order of the Superior Court or family support magistrate is issued against a parent to cover the cost of such medical or dental insurance or benefit plan for a child who is eligible for Medicaid benefits, and such parent has received payment from a third party for the costs of such services but such parent has not used such payment to reimburse, as appropriate, either the other parent or guardian or the provider of such services, the Department of Social Services shall have the authority to request the court or family support magistrate to order the employer of such parent to withhold from the wages, salary or other employment income ~~,~~ of such parent to the extent necessary to reimburse the Department of Social Services for expenditures for such costs under the Medicaid program. However, any claims for current or past due child support shall take priority over any such claims for the costs of such services.

[1] C.G.S.A. §§ 17b–289 to 17b–303, inclusive, and 1997, Oct. 29 Sp. Sess., P.A. 97–1, § 16.
[2] C.G.S.A. § 17b–261 et seq.

Sec. 2. Subdivisions (1) and (2) of subsection (a) of section 46b–171 of the general statutes are repealed and the following is substituted in lieu thereof (Effective October 1, 2004):

(a)(1) If the defendant is found to be the father of the child, the court or family support magistrate shall order the defendant to stand charged with the support and maintenance of such child, with the assistance of the mother if such mother is financially able, as ~~said~~ the court or family support magistrate finds, in accordance with the provisions of subsection (b) of section 17b–179, or section 17a–90, 17b–81, 17b–223, 17b–745, as amended by this act, ~~subsection (b) of section 17b–179, section 17a–90,~~ 46b–129, as amended, 46b–130 or 46b–215, as amended by this act, to be reasonably commensurate with the financial ability of the defendant, and to pay a certain sum periodically until the child attains the age of eighteen years or as otherwise provided in this subsection. If such child is unmarried, a full-time high school student and residing with the custodial parent, such support shall continue according to the parents' respective abilities, if such child is in need of support, until such child completes the twelfth grade or attains the age of nineteen, whichever first occurs. The court or family support magistrate shall order the defendant to pay such sum to the complainant, or, if a town or the state has paid such expense, to the town or the state, as the case may be, and shall grant execution for the same and costs of suit taxed as in other civil actions, together with a reasonable attorney's fee; and may require the defendant to become bound with sufficient surety to perform such orders for support and maintenance.

(2) In addition, the court or family support magistrate shall include in each support order in a IV-D support case a provision for the health care coverage of the child which provision may include an order for either parent to name any child ~~under the age of eighteen years~~ as a beneficiary of any medical or dental insurance or benefit plan carried by such parent or available to such parent on a group basis through an employer or union. Any such employment-based order shall be enforced using a National Medical Support Notice as provided in section 46b–88. If such insurance coverage is unavailable at reasonable cost, the provision for health care coverage may include an order for either parent to apply for and maintain coverage on behalf of the child under the HUSKY Plan, Part B.[1] The noncustodial parent shall be ordered to apply for the HUSKY Plan, Part B only if such parent is found to have sufficient ability to pay the appropriate premium. In any IV-D support case in which the

noncustodial parent is found to have insufficient ability to provide medical insurance coverage and the custodial party is the HUSKY Plan, Part A [2] or Part B applicant, the provision for health care coverage may include an order for the noncustodial parent to pay such amount as is specified by the court or family support magistrate to the state or the custodial party, as their interests may appear, to offset the cost of any insurance payable under the HUSKY Plan, Part A or Part B. In no event may such order include payment to offset the cost of any such premium if such payment would reduce the amount of current support required under the child support guidelines.

[1] C.G.S.A. §§ 17b–289 to 17b–303, inclusive, and 1997, Oct. 29 Sp. Sess., P.A. 97–1, § 16.

[2] C.G.S.A. § 17b–261 et seq.

Sec. 3. Subsections (b) and (c) of section 46b–172 of the general statutes are repealed and the following is substituted in lieu thereof (Effective October 1, 2004):

(b) An agreement to support the child by payment of a periodic sum until the child attains the age of eighteen years or as otherwise provided in this subsection, together with provisions for reimbursement for past due support based upon ability to pay in accordance with the provisions of subsection (b) of section 17b–179, or section 17a–90, 17b–81, 17b–223, ~~subsection (b) of section 17b–179, section 17a–90,~~ 46b–129, as amended, or 46b–130, and reasonable expense of prosecution of the petition, when filed with , and approved by a judge of ~~said court~~ the Superior Court, or in IV-D support cases and matters brought under sections 46b–212 to 46b–213v, inclusive, a family support magistrate at any time, shall have the same force and effect, retroactively or prospectively in accordance with the terms of said agreement, as an order of support entered by ~~that~~ the court, and shall be enforceable and subject to modification in the same manner as is provided by law for orders of the court in such cases. If such child is unmarried, a full-time high school student and residing with the custodial parent, such support shall continue according to the parents' respective abilities, if such child is in need of support, until such child completes the twelfth grade or attains the age of nineteen, whichever first occurs. Past due support in such cases shall be limited to the three years next preceding the date of the filing of such agreements to support. Payments under such agreement shall be made to the petitioner, except that in IV-D support cases, as defined in subsection (b) of section 46b–231, payments shall be made to the Bureau of Child Support Enforcement or its designated agency. Such written agreements to support shall be on forms prescribed by the Office of the Chief Court Administrator and shall be sworn to, and shall be binding on the person executing the same whether he is an adult or a minor.

(c) At any time after the signing of any acknowledgment of paternity, upon the application of any interested party, the court or any judge thereof or any family support magistrate in IV-D support cases and in matters brought under sections 46b–212 to 46b–213v, inclusive, shall cause a summons, signed by such judge or family support magistrate, by the clerk of ~~said~~ the court or by a commissioner of the Superior Court, to be issued, requiring the acknowledged father to appear in court at a time and place as determined by the clerk but not more than ninety days after the issuance of the summons, to show cause why the court or the family support magistrate assigned to the judicial district in IV-D support cases should not enter judgment for support of the child by payment of a periodic sum until the child attains the age of eighteen years or as otherwise provided in this subsection, together with provision for reimbursement for past due support based upon ability to pay in accordance with the provisions of subsection (b) of section 17b–179, or section 17a–90, 17b–81, 17b–223, ~~subsection (b) of section 17b–179, section 17a–90,~~ 46b–129, as amended, or 46b–130, a provision for health coverage of the child as required by section 46b–215, as amended by this act, and reasonable expense of the action under this subsection. If such child is unmarried, a full-time high school student and residing with the custodial parent, such support shall continue according to the parents' respective abilities, if such child is in need of support, until such child completes the twelfth grade or attains the age of nineteen, whichever first occurs. Such court or family support magistrate, in IV-D support cases, shall also have the authority to order the acknowledged father who is subject to a plan for reimbursement of past-due support and is not incapacitated, to participate in work activities which may include, but shall not be limited to, job search, training, work experience and participation in the job training and retraining program established by the Labor Commissioner pursuant to section 31–3t. The application, summons and order shall be on forms prescribed by the Office of the Chief Court Administrator. Proceedings to obtain such orders of support shall be commenced by the service of such summons on the acknowledged father. A state marshal or proper officer shall make due return of process to the court not less than twenty-one days before the date assigned for hearing. The prior judgment as to paternity shall be res judicata as to that issue for all paternity acknowledgments filed with the court on or after March 1, 1981, but before July 1, 1997, and shall not be reconsidered by the court unless the person seeking review of the acknowledgment petitions the superior court for the judicial district having venue for a hearing on the issue of paternity within three years of such judgment. In addition to such review, if the acknowledgment of paternity was filed prior to March 1, 1981, the acknowledgment of paternity may be reviewed by denying the allegation of paternity in response to the initial petition for support, whenever it is filed. All such payments shall be made to the petitioner, except that in IV-D support cases, as defined in subsection (b) of section 46b–231, payments shall be made to the state, acting by and through the IV-D agency.

Sec. 4. Subdivisions (1) and (2) of subsection (a) of section 46b–215 of the general statutes are repealed and the following is substituted in lieu thereof (Effective October 1, 2004):

(a)(1) The Superior Court or a family support magistrate shall have authority to make and enforce orders for payment of support against any person who neglects or refuses to furnish necessary support to such person's spouse or a child under the age of eighteen or as otherwise provided in this subsection, according to such person's ability to furnish such support, notwithstanding the provisions of section 46b–37. If such child is unmarried, a full-time high school student and residing with the custodial parent, such support shall continue according to the parents' respective abilities, if such child is in need of support, until such child completes the twelfth grade or attains the age of nineteen, whichever first occurs.

(2) Any such support order in a IV-D support case shall include a provision for the health care coverage of the child which provision may include an order for either parent to name any child ~~under eighteen~~ as a beneficiary of any medical or dental insurance or benefit plan carried by such parent or available to such parent on a group basis through an employer or a union. Any such employment-based order shall be enforced using a National Medical Support Notice as provided in section 46b–88. If such insurance coverage is unavailable at reasonable cost, the provision for health care coverage may include an order for either parent to apply for and maintain coverage on behalf of the child under the HUSKY Plan, Part B.[1] The noncustodial parent shall be ordered to apply for the HUSKY Plan, Part B only if such parent is found to have sufficient ability to pay the appropriate premium. In any IV-D support case in which the noncustodial parent is found to have insufficient ability to provide medical insurance coverage and the custodial party is the HUSKY Plan, Part A [2] or Part B applicant, the provision for health care coverage may include an order for the noncustodial parent to pay such amount as is specified by the court or family support magistrate to the state or the custodial party, as their interests may appear, to offset the cost of any insurance payable under the HUSKY Plan, Part A or Part B. In no event may such order include payment to offset the cost of any such premium if such payment would reduce the amount of current support required under the child support guidelines.

[1] C.G.S.A. §§ 17b–289 to 17b–303, inclusive, and 1997, Oct. 29 Sp. Sess., P.A. 97–1, § 16.

[2] C.G.S.A. § 17b–261 et seq.

Sec. 5. Subsection (a) of section 46b–220 of the general statutes is repealed and the following is substituted in lieu thereof (Effective October 1, 2004):

(a) For the purposes of this section:

(1) "Delinquent child support obligor" means an obligor who (A) ~~an obligor who~~ owes overdue support, accruing after the entry of a court order, in an amount which exceeds ninety days of periodic payments on a current support or arrearage payment order, ~~; (B) an obligor who~~ (B) has failed to make court ordered medical or dental insurance coverage available within ninety days of the issuance of a court order or ~~who~~ fails to maintain such coverage pursuant to court order for a period of ninety days, ~~; or (C) an obligor who~~ or (C) has failed, after receiving appropriate notice, to comply with subpoenas or warrants relating to paternity or child support proceedings;

(2) "License" means each license, certification or permit to engage in a profession or occupation regulated pursuant to the provisions of title 19a, 20 or 21, a motor vehicle operator's license or a commercial driver's license issued by the Commissioner of Motor Vehicles in accordance with chapter 246,[1] and ~~licensees~~ licenses and permits issued by the Department of Environmental Protection pursuant to part III of chapter 490 [2]; ~~of title 26;~~

(3) "Licensing authority" means any board, commission, department or official with authority to issue a license;

(4) "Obligor" means any person owing a duty of child support;

(5) "Obligee" means the person or entity to whom child support payments are owed;

(6) "Past-due support" ~~means any one or a combination of the following: (A) Court ordered current support or arrearage payments which have become due and payable and remain unpaid; (B) unpaid support which has been reduced to a judgment or otherwise found to be due by a court of competent jurisdiction, whether or not~~

~~presently payable; (C) support due for periods prior to an action to establish~~ a child ~~support order, provided such amounts are based upon the obligor's ability to pay during the prior periods if known or, if not known, on the obligor's current ability to pay if known, or, if not known, upon assistance rendered to the obligor's child;~~ shall have the same meaning as provided in section 52–362j, as amended; and

(7) "Overdue support" ~~means a delinquency accruing after the entry of an initial court order establishing a child support obligation~~ shall have the same meaning as provided in section 52–362j, as amended.

[1] C.G.S.A. § 14–1 et seq.
[2] C.G.S.A. § 26–27 et seq.

Sec. 6. Subsection (m) of section 46b–231 of the general statutes is repealed and the following is substituted in lieu thereof (Effective October 1, 2004):

(m) The Chief Family Support Magistrate and the family support magistrates shall have the powers and duties enumerated in this subsection.

(1) A family support magistrate in IV-D support cases may compel the attendance of witnesses or the obligor under a summons issued pursuant to sections 17b–745, as amended by this act, 46b–172, as amended by this act, and 46b–215, as amended by this act, or under a subpoena issued pursuant to section 52–143, as amended, or a citation for failure to obey an order of a family support magistrate or a judge of the Superior Court. If a person is served with ~~a~~ any such summons, subpoena or citation issued by ~~the~~ a family support magistrate or the assistant clerk of the Family Support Magistrate Division and fails to appear, a family support magistrate may issue a capias mittimus directed to ~~some~~ a proper officer to arrest the obligor or the witness and bring him before a family support magistrate. Whenever such a capias mittimus is ordered, the family support magistrate shall establish a recognizance to the state of Connecticut in the form of a bond of such character and amount as to assure the appearance of the obligor at the next regular session of the Family Support Magistrate Division in the judicial district in which the matter is pending. If the obligor posts such a bond, and thereafter fails to appear before the family support magistrate at the time and place he is ordered to appear, the family support magistrate may order the bond forfeited, and the proceeds thereof paid to the state in TANF cases or the obligee in non-TANF cases.

(2) Family support magistrates shall hear and determine matters involving child and spousal support in IV-D support cases including petitions for support brought pursuant to sections 17b–81, 17b–179, as amended, 17b–745, as amended by this act, and 46b–215, as amended by this act; applications for show cause orders in IV-D support cases brought pursuant to subsection (b) of section 46b–172, as amended by this act, and actions for interstate enforcement of child and spousal support and paternity under sections 46b–212 to 46b–213v, inclusive, and shall hear and determine all motions for modifications of child and spousal support in such cases. In all IV-D support cases, family support magistrates shall have the authority to order any obligor who is subject to a plan for reimbursement of past-due support and is not incapacitated, to participate in work activities which may include, but shall not be limited to, job search, training, work experience and participation in the job training and retraining program established by the Labor Commissioner pursuant to section 31–3t. A family support magistrate shall not modify an order for periodic payment on an arrearage due the state for state assistance which has been discontinued to increase such payments, unless the family support magistrate first determines that the state has made a reasonable effort to notify the current recipient of child support, at the most current address available to the IV-D agency, of the pendency of the motion to increase such periodic arrearage payments and of the time and place of the hearing on such motion. If such recipient appears, either personally or through a representative, at such hearing, the family support magistrate shall determine whether the order in effect for child support is reasonable in relation to the current financial circumstances of the parties, prior to modifying an order increasing such periodic arrearage payments.

(3) Family support magistrates shall review and approve or modify all agreements for support in IV-D support cases filed with the Family Support Magistrate Division in accordance with sections 17b–179, as amended, 17b–745, as amended by this act, 46b–172, as amended by this act, 46b–215, as amended by this act, and subsection (c) of section 53–304.

(4) Motions for modification of existing child and spousal support orders entered by the Superior Court in IV-D support cases, including motions to modify existing child and spousal support orders entered in actions brought pursuant to chapter 815j,[1] shall be brought in the Family Support Magistrate Division and decided by a family support magistrate. Family support magistrates, in deciding if a spousal or child support order should be modified, shall make such determination based upon the criteria set forth in section 46b–84, as amended, and section 46b–215b, as amended. A person who is aggrieved by a decision of a family support magistrate modifying

a Superior Court order is entitled to appeal such decision in accordance with the provisions of subsection (n) of this section.

(5) Proceedings to establish paternity in IV-D support cases shall be filed in the family support magistrate division for the judicial district where the mother or putative father resides. The matter shall be heard and determined by ~~the~~ a family support magistrate in accordance with the provisions of chapter 815y.[2]

(6) Agreements for support obtained in IV-D support cases shall be filed with the assistant clerk of the family support magistrate division for the judicial district where the mother or the father of the child resides, pursuant to subsection (b) of section 46b–172, as amended by this act, and shall become effective as an order upon filing with the clerk. Such support agreements shall be reviewed by ~~the~~ a family support magistrate who shall approve or disapprove the agreement. If the support agreement filed with the clerk is disapproved by a family support magistrate, such disapproval shall have a retroactive effect.

(7) Family support magistrates shall enforce orders for child and spousal support entered by such family support magistrate and by the Superior Court in IV-D support cases by citing an obligor for contempt. Family support magistrates, in IV-D support cases, shall have the authority to order any obligor who is subject to a plan for reimbursement of past-due support and is not incapacitated, to participate in work activities which may include, but shall not be limited to, job search, training, work experience and participation in the job training and retraining program established by the Labor Commissioner pursuant to section 31–3t. Family support magistrates shall also enforce income withholding orders entered pursuant to section 52–362, as amended, including any additional amounts to be applied toward liquidation of any arrearage, as required under subsection (e) of said section. Family support magistrates may require the obligor to furnish recognizance to the state of Connecticut in the form of a cash deposit or bond of such character and in such amount as the Family Support Magistrate Division deems proper to assure appearance at the next regular session of the Family Support Magistrate Division in the judicial district in which the matter is pending. Upon failure of the obligor to post such bond, the family support magistrate may refer the obligor to a community correctional center until he has complied with such order, provided ~~that~~ the obligor shall be heard at the next regular session of the Family Support Magistrate Division in the court to which he was summoned. If no regular session is held within seven days of such referral, the family support magistrate shall either cause a special session of the Family Support Magistrate Division to be convened, or the obligor shall be heard by a Superior Court judge in the judicial district in which the matter is pending. If the obligor fails to appear before the family support magistrate at the time and place he is ordered to appear, the family support magistrate may order the bond, if any, forfeited, and the proceeds thereof paid to the state in TANF cases or the obligee in non-TANF cases, as the family support magistrate may determine, and the family support magistrate may issue a capias mittimus for the arrest of the obligor, ordering him to appear before the family support magistrate. A family support magistrate may determine whether or not an obligor is in contempt of the order of the Superior Court or of a family support magistrate and may make such orders as are provided by law to enforce a support obligation, except that if the family support magistrate determines that incarceration of an obligor for failure to obey a support order may be indicated, the family support magistrate shall inform the obligor of his right to be represented by an attorney and his right to a court-appointed attorney to represent him if he is indigent. If the obligor claims he is indigent and desires an attorney to represent him, the family support magistrate shall conduct a hearing to determine if the obligor is indigent. ~~; and if he so finds, he will appoint an attorney to represent him.~~ If, after such hearing, the family support magistrate finds that the obligor is indigent, the family support magistrate shall appoint an attorney to represent the obligor.

(8) Agreements between parties as to custody and visitation of minor children in IV-D support cases may be filed with the assistant clerk of the Family Support Magistrate Division. Such agreements shall be reviewed by a family support magistrate, who shall approve the agreement unless he finds such agreement is not in the best interests of the child. Agreements between parties as to custody and visitation in IV-D support cases shall be enforced in the same manner as agreements for support are enforced, pursuant to subdivision (7) of this subsection.

(9) Whenever an obligor is before a family support magistrate in proceedings to establish, modify or enforce a support order in a IV-D support case and such order is not secured by an income withholding order, the family support magistrate may require the obligor to execute a bond or post other security sufficient to perform such order for support, provided the family support magistrate finds that such a bond is available for purchase within the financial means of the obligor. Upon failure of such obligor to comply with such support order, the family support magistrate may order the bond or the security forfeited and the proceeds thereof paid to the state in TANF cases or to the obligee in non-TANF cases.

(10) In any proceeding in the Family Support Magistrate Division, if the family support magistrate finds that a party is indigent and unable to pay a fee or fees payable to the court or to pay the cost of service of process, the family support magistrate shall waive such fee or fees and the cost of service of process shall be paid by the state.

(11) A family support magistrate may dismiss any action or proceeding which the family support magistrate may hear and determine.

(12) A family support magistrate may order parties to participate in the parenting education program in accordance with the provisions of section 46b–69b.

(13) Family support magistrates may issue writs of habeas corpus ad testificandum in IV-D support cases for persons in the custody of the Commissioner of Correction.

[1] C.G.S.A. § 46b–40 et seq.
[2] C.G.S.A. § 46b–160 et seq.

Sec. 7. Subsection (s) of section 46b–231 of the general statutes is repealed and the following is substituted in lieu thereof (Effective October 1, 2004):

(s) Support enforcement officers of Support Enforcement Services of the Superior Court shall:

(1) Supervise the payment of any child or spousal support order made by a family support magistrate. Supervision of such orders is defined as the utilization of all procedures available by law to collect child or spousal support, including (A) issuance and implementation of income withholdings ordered by the Superior Court or a family support magistrate pursuant to section 52–362, as amended, (B) issuance of an order requiring any party to appear before a family support magistrate on an action to modify a support order pursuant to subdivision (4) of this subsection, (C) issuance of a capias mittimus directed to a proper officer to arrest an obligor or witness and bring such obligor or witness before a family support magistrate if such obligor or witness is served with a summons, subpoena, citation or order to appear issued by a family support magistrate, the assistant clerk of the Family Support Magistrate Division or a support enforcement officer and fails to appear, and (D) if necessary, bringing an application for contempt to a family support magistrate and, in connection with such application, issuing an order requiring the obligor to appear before a family support magistrate to show cause why such obligor should not be held in contempt for failure to pay an order for child or spousal support entered by the Superior Court or a family support magistrate;

(2) In non-TANF cases, have the authority to bring petitions for support orders pursuant to section 46b–215, as amended by this act, file agreements for support with the assistant clerk of the Family Support Magistrate Division, and bring applications for show cause orders pursuant to section 46b–172, as amended by this act, and in IV-D support cases and cases under sections 46b–212 to 46b–213v, inclusive, enforce foreign support orders registered with the Family Support Magistrate Division pursuant to sections 46b–213f to 46b–213i, inclusive, and file agreements for support with the assistant clerk of the Family Support Magistrate Division;

(3) In connection with any order or agreement entered by, or filed with, the Family Support Magistrate Division, or any order entered by the Superior Court in a IV-D support case, upon order, investigate the financial situation of the parties and report findings to the family support magistrate regarding: (A) Any pending motion to modify such order or agreement; , or (B) any request or application for modification of such order or agreement made by an obligee;

(4) ~~In non-TANF IV-D cases, review~~ Review child support orders (A) in non-TANF IV-D support cases (i) at the request of either parent or custodial party subject to a support order, or (ii) upon receipt of information indicating a substantial change in circumstances of any party to the support order, (B) in TANF cases, ~~review child support orders~~ at the request of the Bureau of Child Support Enforcement, or (C) as necessary to comply with federal requirements for the child support enforcement program mandated by Title IV-D of the Social Security Act,[1] and initiate an action before a family support magistrate to modify such support order if it is determined upon such review that the order substantially deviates from the child support guidelines established pursuant to section 46b–215a or 46b–215b, as amended. ~~The~~ A requesting party under subparagraph (A)(i) or (B) of this subdivision shall have a right to such review every three years without proving a substantial change in circumstances, ~~;~~ but more frequent reviews shall be made only if ~~the~~ such requesting party demonstrates a substantial change in circumstances. There shall be a rebuttable presumption that any deviation of less than fifteen per cent from the child support guidelines is not substantial and any deviation of fifteen per cent or more from the guidelines is substantial. Modification may be made of such support order without regard to whether the order was issued before, on or after May 9, 1991. In determining whether to modify a child support order based on a substantial deviation from such child support guidelines, consideration shall be given to the division of

real and personal property between the parties set forth in any final decree entered pursuant to chapter 815j[2] and the benefits accruing to the child as the result of such division. No order for periodic payment of support may be subject to retroactive modification, except that the family support magistrate may order modification with respect to any period during which there is a pending motion for modification of a support order from the date of service of notice of such pending motion to the opposing party pursuant to section 52–50.

[1] 42 U.S.C.A. § 651.
[2] C.G.S.A. § 46b–40 et seq.

Sec. 8. (NEW) (Effective from passage) Whenever the Probate Court, in a guardianship matter under chapter 802h[1] of the general statutes, or the Superior Court, in a juvenile matter under chapter 815t[2] of the general statutes, orders a change or transfer of the guardianship or custody of a child who is the subject of a preexisting support order, and the court makes no finding with respect to such support order, such guardianship or custody order shall operate to: (1) Suspend the support order if guardianship or custody is transferred to the obligor under the support order; or (2) modify the payee of the support order to be the person or entity awarded guardianship or custody of the child by the court, if such person or entity is other than the obligor under the support order.

[1] C.G.S.A. § 45a–591 et seq.
[2] C.G.S.A. § 46b–120 et seq.

Approved May 10, 2004.

COURTS—OPERATIONS

P.A. No. 04–127

S.H.B. No. 5594

AN ACT CONCERNING COURT OPERATIONS.

Be it enacted by the Senate and House of Representatives in General Assembly convened:

Section 1. Subsection (b) of section 13a–73 of the general statutes is repealed and the following is substituted in lieu thereof (Effective October 1, 2004):

(b) The commissioner may take any land he finds necessary for the layout, alteration, extension, widening, change of grade or other improvement of any state highway or for a highway maintenance storage area or garage and the owner of such land shall be paid by the state for all damages, and the state shall receive from such owner the amount or value of all benefits, resulting from such taking, layout, alteration, extension, widening, change of grade or other improvement. The use of any site acquired for highway maintenance storage area or garage purposes by condemnation shall conform to any zoning ordinance or development plan in effect for the area in which such site is located, provided the commissioner may be granted any variance or special exception as may be made pursuant to the zoning ordinances and regulations of the town ~~wherein~~ in which any such site is to be acquired. The assessment of such damages and of such benefits shall be made by the commissioner and filed by him with the clerk of the superior court ~~in~~ for the judicial district in which the land affected is located. ~~, and such clerk~~ The commissioner shall give notice of such assessment to each person having an interest of record therein by mailing to each a copy of the same, postage prepaid, and, at any time after such assessment has been made by ~~said~~ the commissioner, the physical construction of such layout, alteration, extension, widening, maintenance storage area or garage, change of grade or other improvement may be made. If notice cannot be given to any person entitled thereto because his whereabouts or existence is unknown, notice may be given by publishing a notice at least twice in a newspaper published in the judicial district and having a daily or weekly circulation in the town in which the property affected is ~~situated~~ located. Any such published notice shall state that it is a notice to the last owner of record or his surviving spouse, heirs, administrators, assigns, representatives or creditors if he is deceased, and shall contain a brief description of the property taken. Notice shall also be given by mailing to each such person at his last-known address, by registered or certified mail, a copy of such notice. If, after a search of the land and probate records, the address of any interested party cannot be found, an affidavit stating such facts and reciting the steps taken to establish the address of any such person shall be filed with the clerk of the ~~superior~~ court and accepted in lieu of service of such notice by mailing the same to the last known address of such person. Upon filing an assessment with the clerk of the ~~superior~~ court, the commissioner shall forthwith sign and file for record with the town clerk of the town ~~wherein~~ in which such real property is located a certificate setting forth the fact of such taking, a description of the real property so taken and the names and residences of the owners from whom it was taken. Upon the filing of such certificate, title to such real property in fee simple shall vest in the state of Connecticut, except that, if it is so specified in such certificate, a lesser estate, interest or right shall vest in the state. The commissioner shall permit the last owner of record of such real property upon which a residence is situated to remain in such residence, rent free, for a period of one hundred twenty days after the filing of such certificate.

Sec. 2. Subsections (a) and (b) of section 46b–127 of the general statutes are repealed and the following is substituted in lieu thereof (Effective October 1, 2004):

(a) The court shall automatically transfer from the docket for juvenile matters to the regular criminal docket of the Superior Court the case of any child charged with the commission of a capital felony, a class A or B felony or a violation of section 53a–54d, provided such offense was committed after such child attained the age of fourteen years and counsel has been appointed for such child if such child is indigent. Such counsel may appear with the child but shall not be permitted to make any argument or file any motion in opposition to the transfer. The child shall be arraigned in the regular criminal docket of the Superior Court at the next court date following such transfer, provided any proceedings held prior to the finalization of such transfer shall be private and shall be conducted in such parts of the courthouse or the building wherein court is located as shall be separate and apart from the other parts of the court which are then being held for proceedings pertaining to adults charged with crimes. The file of any case so transferred shall remain sealed until the end of the tenth working day following such arraignment unless the state's attorney has filed a motion pursuant to this subsection, in which case such file shall remain sealed until the court makes a decision on the motion. A state's attorney may, not later than ten working days after such arraignment, file a motion to transfer the case of any child charged with the commission of a class B felony to the docket for juvenile matters for proceedings in accordance with the provisions of this. The court sitting for the regular criminal docket shall, after hearing and not later than ten working days after the filing of such motion, decide such motion.

(b) Upon motion of a juvenile prosecutor and order of the court, the case of any child charged with the commission of a class C or D felony or an unclassified felony shall be transferred from the docket for juvenile matters to the regular criminal docket of the Superior Court, provided such offense was committed after such child attained the age of fourteen years and the court finds ex parte that there is probable cause to believe the child has committed the act for which he is charged. The file of any case so transferred shall remain sealed until such time as the court sitting for the regular criminal docket accepts such transfer. The court sitting for the regular criminal docket may return any such case to the docket for juvenile matters not later than ten working days after the date of the transfer for proceedings in accordance with the provisions of this chapter. The child shall be arraigned in the regular criminal docket of the Superior Court by the next court date following such transfer, provided any proceedings held prior to the finalization of such transfer shall be private and shall be conducted in such parts of the courthouse or the building wherein court is located as shall be separate and apart from the other parts of the court which are then being held for proceedings pertaining to adults charged with crimes.

Sec. 3. Subsection (d) of section 47a–23 of the general statutes is repealed and the following is substituted in lieu thereof (Effective October 1, 2004):

(d) With respect to a month-to-month or a week-to-week tenancy of a dwelling unit, a notice to quit possession based on nonpayment of rent shall, upon delivery, terminate the rental agreement for the month or week in which the notice is delivered, convert the month-to-month or week-to-week tenancy to a tenancy at sufferance and provide proper basis for a summary process action notwithstanding that such notice was delivered in the month or week after the month or week in which the rent is alleged to be unpaid.

Sec. 4. Section 47a–26c of the general statutes is repealed and the following is substituted in lieu thereof (Effective October 1, 2004):

All pleadings, including motions, shall advance at least one step within each successive period of three days from the preceding pleading or motion. If the defendant fails to plead within any such period, the complainant may file a motion for judgment for failure to plead, served upon the defendant in the manner provided in the rules adopted by the judges of the Superior Court for the service of pleadings. If the defendant fails to plead within three days after receipt of such motion by the clerk, the court shall forthwith enter judgment that the complainant recover possession or occupancy with costs.

Sec. 5. Subsection (a) of section 47a–30 of the general statutes is repealed and the following is substituted in lieu thereof (Effective October 1, 2004):

(a) When any farm employee or any domestic servant, caretaker, manager or other employee as described in subsection (b) of section 47a–36 occupies a dwelling, dwelling unit or tenement furnished by his employer and when his employment is terminated by himself or his employer, or such employee fails to report for employment, and fails to vacate the premises in which he is residing, he shall be given not less than ~~five~~ three days' notice to quit possession of such premises on the form prescribed by section 47a–23, as amended by this act.

Sec. 6. Subsection (b) of section 49–15 of the general statutes, as amended by section 9 of public act 03–202, is repealed and the following is substituted in lieu thereof (Effective October 1, 2004):

(b) Upon the filing of a bankruptcy petition by a mortgagor under ~~Chapter 13 of~~ Title 11 of the United States Code, [1] any judgment against the mortgagor foreclosing the title to real estate by strict foreclosure shall be opened automatically without action by any party or the court, provided, the provisions of such judgment, other than the establishment of law days, shall not be set aside under this subsection; but no such judgment shall be opened after the title has become absolute in any encumbrancer or the mortgagee, or any person claiming under such encumbrancer or mortgagee. The mortgagor shall file a copy of the bankruptcy petition, or an affidavit setting forth the date the bankruptcy petition was filed, with the clerk of the court in which the foreclosure matter is pending. Upon the ~~determination~~ termination of the automatic stay authorized pursuant to 11 USC 362, the mortgagor shall file with such clerk an affidavit setting forth the date the stay was terminated.

[1] 11 U.S.C.A. § 101 et seq.

Sec. 7. Subsection (b) of section 51–164n of the general statutes, as amended by section 9 of public act 03–136, section 12 of public act 03–202 and section 5 of public act 03–267, is repealed and the following is substituted in lieu thereof (Effective October 1, 2004):

(b) Notwithstanding any provision of the general statutes, any person who is alleged to have committed (1) a violation under the provisions of section 1–9, 1–10, 1–11, 4b–13, as amended, 7–13, 7–14, 7–35, 7–41, 7–83, 7–283, 7–325, 7–393, 8–25, as amended, 8–27, 9–63, 9–296, 9–305, 9–322, 9–350, 10–193, 10–197, 10–198, 10–230, 10–251, 10–254, 12–52, 12–170aa, as amended, 12–292, as amended, or 12–326g, subdivision (4) of section 12–408, as amended, subdivision (3), (5) or (6) of section 12–411, as amended, section 12–435c, 12–476a, 12–476b, 12–487, 13a–71, 13a–107, 13a–113, 13a–114, 13a–115, 13a–117b, 13a–123, as amended, 13a–124, 13a–139, 13a–140, 13a–143b, 13a–247, as amended, or 13a–253, subsection (f) of section 13b–42, as amended, section 13b–90, 13b–221, 13b–292, as amended, 13b–336, 13b–337, as amended, 13b–338, 13b–410a, 13b–410b or 13b–410c, subsection (a), (b) or (c) of section 13b–412, section 13b–414, subsection (d) of section 14–12, section 14–20a or 14–27a, subsection (e) of section 14–34a, subsection (d) of section 14–35, as amended, section 14–43, 14–49, as amended, 14–50a, as amended, or 14–58, as amended, subsection (b) of section 14–66, as amended, section 14–66a, 14–66b or 14–67a, subsection (g) of section 14–80, as amended, subsection (f) of section 14–80h, section 14–97a, 14–100b, 14–103a, 14–106a, 14–106c, 14–146, 14–152, 14–153 or 14–163b, a first violation as specified in subsection (f) of section 14–164i, section 14–219 as specified in subsection (e) of said section, section 14–240, 14–249 or 14–250, subsection (a), (b) or (c) of section 14–261a, section 14–262, as amended, 14–264, 14–267a, as amended, 14–269, 14–270, 14–275a, 14–278 or 14–279, subsection (e) of section 14–283, section 14–291, 14–293b, 14–319, 14–320, 14–321, as amended, 14–325a, 14–326, 14–330 or 14–332a, subdivision (1), (2) or (3) of section 14–386a, section 15–33, subsection (a) of section 15–115, section 16–256, 16–256e, 16a–15, as amended, or 16a–22, subsection (a) or (b) of section 16a–22h, section 17a–24, 17a–145, 17a–149, 17a–152, 17a–465, 17a–642, 17b–124, as amended, 17b–131, as amended, 17b–137 or 17b–734, subsection (b) of section 17b–736, section 19a–30, 19a–33, 19a–39 or 19a–87, subsection (b) of section 19a–87a, section 19a–91, 19a–105, 19a–107, 19a–215, 19a–219, 19a–222, 19a–224, 19a–286, 19a–287, 19a–297, 19a–301, 19a–309, 19a–335, 19a–336, 19a–338, 19a–339, 19a–340, 19a–425, 19a–502, 20–7a, 20–14, 20–158, 20–231, 20–257, 20–265 or 20–324e, subsection (a) of section 20–341, section 20–341*l*, 20–597, 20–608, 20–610, 21–30, 21–38, 21–39, 21–43, 21–47, 21–48, 21–63, 21–76a, 21a–21, 21a–25, 21a–26 or 21a–30, subsection (a) of section 21a–37, section 21a–46, 21a–61, as amended, 21a–63, as amended, or 21a–77, subsection (b) of section 21a–79, as amended, section 21a–85, 21a–154, 21a–159, as amended, 21a–201, 21a–211, 22–13, 22–14, as amended, 22–15, 22–16, 22–29, 22–34, as amended, 22–35, as amended, 22–36, as amended, 22–37, as amended, 22–38, as amended, 22–39, as amended, 22–39a, 22–39b, as amended, 22–39c, 22–39d, as amended, 22–39e, as amended, 22–49, 22–54, 22–61, 22–89, 22–90, 22–98, 22–99, 22–100, 22–111*o*, 22–279, as amended, 22–280a, 22–318a, as amended, 22–320h, 22–324a, as amended, 22–326 or 22–342, subsection (b) or (e) of section 22–344, section 22–359,

22–366, 22–391, 22–413, 22–414, as amended, 22–415, as amended, 22a–66a or 22a–246, subsection (a) of section 22a–250, subsection (e) of section 22a–256h, section 22a–449, as amended, 22a–461, 23–37, 23–38, 23–46 or 23–61b, subsection (a) or (b) of section 23–65, section 25–37, 25–40, as amended, 26–19, 26–21, 26–31, 26–40, 26–40a, as amended, 26–49, 26–54, 26–59, 26–61, 26–64, 26–79, 26–89, 26–97, 26–107, 26–117, 26–128, 26–131, 26–132, 26–138, 26–141, 26–207, 26–215, as amended, 26–224a, as amended, 26–227, as amended, 26–230, as amended, 26–294, 28–13, 29–6a, 29–109, 29–161a, 29–161b, 29–198, 29–210, 29–243, 29–277, 29–316, 29–318, 29–341, 29–381, as amended, 30–48a, 30–86a, as amended, 31–3, 31–10, 31–11, 31–12, 31–13, 31–14, 31–15, 31–16, 31–18, 31–23, 31–24, 31–25, 31–28, 31–32, 31–36, 31–38, 31–38a, 31–40, 31–44, 31–47, 31–48, 31–51, 31–51k, 31–52, 31–52a or 31–54, subsection (a) or (c) of section 31–69, section 31–70, 31–74, 31–75, 31–76, 31–76a, 31–89b or 31–134, subsection (i) of section 31–273, section 31–288, 36a–787, 42–230, 45a–450, 45a–634 or 45a–658, subdivision (13) or (14) of section 46a–54, as amended, section 46a–59, 46b–22, 46b–24, as amended, 46b–34, 47–34a, as amended, 47–47, 49–8a, as amended, 49–16 or 53–133, subsection (a) or (b) of section 53–211, or section 53–212a, 53–249a, 53–252, 53–264, 53–302a, 53–303e, 53–311a, 53–321, 53–322, 53–323, 53–331, 53–344, as amended, 53–450 or subsection (a) of section 8 of ~~this act~~ public act 03–136, or (2) a violation under the provisions of chapter 268, [1] or (3) a violation of any regulation adopted in accordance with the provisions of section 12–484, 12–487 or 13b–410, shall follow the procedures set forth in this section.

[1] C.G.S.A. § 15–121 et seq.

Sec. 8. Subsection (e) of section 54–2a of the general statutes is repealed and the following is substituted in lieu thereof (Effective October 1, 2004):

(e) Whenever a ~~rearrest~~ warrant is issued under this section or section 53a–32, the court, judge or judge trial referee may cause such warrant to be entered into a central computer system. Existence of the warrant in the computer system shall constitute prima facie evidence of the issuance of the warrant. Any person named in the warrant may be arrested based on the existence of the warrant in the computer system and shall, upon any such arrest, be given a copy of the warrant.

Sec. 9. Subsections (a) and (b) of section 51–345 of the general statutes are repealed and the following is substituted in lieu thereof (Effective October 1, 2004):

(a) Except as provided in section 51–348 and subsections (b) to (g), inclusive, of this section, all civil process shall be made returnable to a judicial district, as follows:

(1) If all the parties reside outside this state, to the judicial district where (A) the injury occurred, (B) the transaction occurred, or (C) the property is located or lawfully attached.

(2) If the defendant is not a resident, to the judicial district where the attached property is located.

(3) If either or both the plaintiff or defendant are residents of this state, to the judicial district where either the plaintiff or defendant resides, except:

(A) If either the plaintiff or the defendant resides in the town of Manchester, East Windsor, South Windsor or Enfield, the action may be made returnable at the option of the plaintiff to either the judicial district of Hartford or the judicial district of Tolland.

(B) If either the plaintiff or the defendant resides in the town of Plymouth, the action may be made returnable at the option of the plaintiff to either the judicial district of New Britain or the judicial district of Waterbury.

(C) If either the plaintiff or the defendant resides in the town of Bethany, Milford, West Haven or Woodbridge, the action may be made returnable at the option of the plaintiff to either the judicial district of New Haven or the judicial district of Ansonia-Milford.

(D) If either the plaintiff or the defendant resides in the town of Southbury, the action may be made returnable at the option of the plaintiff to either the judicial district of Ansonia-Milford or the judicial district of Waterbury.

(E) If either the plaintiff or defendant resides in the town of Darien, Greenwich, New Canaan, Norwalk, Stamford, Weston, Westport or Wilton, the action may be made returnable at the option of the plaintiff to either the judicial district of Stamford-Norwalk or the judicial district of Fairfield.

(F) If either the plaintiff or defendant resides in the town of Watertown or Woodbury, the action may be made returnable at the option of the plaintiff to either the judicial district of Waterbury or the judicial district of Litchfield.

(G) If either the plaintiff or defendant resides in the town of Avon, Canton, Farmington or Simsbury, the action may be made returnable at the option of the plaintiff to either the judicial district of Hartford or the judicial district of New Britain.

(H) If either the plaintiff or defendant resides in the town of Newington, Rocky Hill or Wethersfield, the action may be made returnable at the option of the plaintiff to either the judicial district of Hartford or the judicial district of New Britain, except for actions where venue is in the geographical area as provided in section 51–348 or in rules of court.

(I) If either the plaintiff or defendant resides in the town of Cromwell, the action may be made returnable at the option of the plaintiff to either the judicial district of Hartford or the judicial district of Middlesex.

(J) If either the plaintiff or defendant resides in the town of New Milford, the action may be made returnable at the option of the plaintiff to either the judicial district of Danbury or the judicial district of Litchfield.

(b) In all actions involving the title to land, for trespass to land and to foreclose or redeem mortgages or liens upon real property, civil process shall be made returnable to the judicial district where the real property is located, either entirely or in part, except:

(1) If the land is located in the town of Manchester, East Windsor, South Windsor or Enfield and either the plaintiff or the defendant resides in the town of Manchester, East Windsor, South Windsor or Enfield, the action may be made returnable at the option of the plaintiff to either the judicial district of Hartford or the judicial district of Tolland.

(2) If the land is located in the town of Plymouth and either the plaintiff or the defendant resides in the town of Plymouth, the action may be made returnable at the option of the plaintiff to either the judicial district of New Britain or the judicial district of Waterbury.

(3) If the land is located in the town of Bethany, Milford, West Haven or Woodbridge and either the plaintiff or the defendant resides in the town of Bethany, Milford, West Haven or Woodbridge, the action may be made returnable at the option of the plaintiff to either the judicial district of New Haven or the judicial district of Ansonia-Milford.

(4) If the land is located in the town of Southbury and either the plaintiff or the defendant resides in the town of Southbury, the action may be made returnable at the option of the plaintiff to either the judicial district of Ansonia-Milford or the judicial district of Waterbury.

(5) If the land is located in the town of Weston, Westport or Wilton and either the plaintiff or the defendant resides in any one of these towns, the action may be made returnable at the option of the plaintiff to either the judicial district of Stamford-Norwalk or the judicial district of Fairfield.

(6) If the land is located in the town of Watertown or Woodbury and either the plaintiff or the defendant resides in the town of Watertown or Woodbury, the action may be made returnable at the option of the plaintiff to either the judicial district of Waterbury or the judicial district of Litchfield.

(7) If the land is located in the town of Avon, Canton, Farmington or Simsbury and either the plaintiff or the defendant resides in the town of Avon, Canton, Farmington or Simsbury, the action may be made returnable at the option of the plaintiff to either the judicial district of Hartford or the judicial district of New Britain.

(8) If the land is located in the town of Newington, Rocky Hill or Wethersfield and either the plaintiff or the defendant resides in the town of Newington, Rocky Hill or Wethersfield, the action may be made returnable at the option of the plaintiff to either the judicial district of Hartford or the judicial district of New Britain, except for actions where venue is in the geographical area as provided in section 51–348 or in rules of court.

(9) If the land is located in the town of New Milford and either the plaintiff or the defendant resides in the town of New Milford, the action may be made returnable at the option of the plaintiff to either the judicial district of Danbury or the judicial district of Litchfield.

Approved May 21, 2004.

TERMINATION OF PARENTAL RIGHTS—CONSENT

P.A. No. 04–128

H.B. No. 5597

AN ACT CONCERNING TERMINATION OF PARENTAL RIGHTS BASED ON CONSENT.

Be it enacted by the Senate and House of Representatives in General Assembly convened:

Section 1. Subsection (a) of section 45a–187 of the general statutes is repealed and the following is substituted in lieu thereof (Effective October 1, 2004):

(a) An appeal under section 45a–186 by ~~those~~ persons of the age of majority and who are present or who have legal notice to be present, or who have been given notice of their right to request a hearing or have filed a written waiver of their right to a hearing, shall be taken within thirty days, except as otherwise provided in this section. If such persons have no notice to be present and are not present, or have not been given notice of their right to request a hearing, ~~then~~ such appeal shall be taken within twelve months, except for appeals by such persons from ~~a decree~~ an order of termination of parental rights, other than an order of termination of parental rights based on consent, or a decree of adoption, in which case appeal shall be taken within ninety days. An appeal from an order of termination of parental rights based on consent, which order is issued on or after the effective date of this section, shall be taken within twenty days.

Sec. 2. Subsection (a) of section 45a–716 of the general statutes is repealed and the following is substituted in lieu thereof (Effective October 1, 2004):

(a) Upon receipt of a petition for termination of parental rights, the Court of Probate or the Superior Court, on a case transferred to it from the Court of Probate in accordance with the provisions of subsection (g) of section 45a–715, shall set a time and place for hearing the petition. The time for hearing shall be not more than thirty days after the filing of the petition, except, in the case of a petition for termination of parental rights based on consent that is filed on or after the effective date of this section, the time for hearing shall be not more than twenty days after the filing of such petition.

Approved May 21, 2004.

JUVENILE COURTS—JURISDICTION—JUVENILES TRIED AS ADULTS

P.A. No. 04–148

S.H.B. No. 5444

AN ACT CONCERNING THE TRANSFER TO JUVENILE COURT OF THE CASES OF CHILDREN CHARGED WITH CERTAIN SEXUAL OFFENSES.

Be it enacted by the Senate and House of Representatives in General Assembly convened:

Section 1. Subsection (a) of section 46b–127 of the general statutes is repealed and the following is substituted in lieu thereof (Effective October 1, 2004):

(a) The court shall automatically transfer from the docket for juvenile matters to the regular criminal docket of the Superior Court the case of any child charged with the commission of a capital felony, a class A or B felony or a violation of section 53a–54d, provided such offense was committed after such child attained the age of fourteen years and counsel has been appointed for such child if such child is indigent. Such counsel may appear with the child but shall not be permitted to make any argument or file any motion in opposition to the transfer. The child shall be arraigned in the regular criminal docket of the Superior Court at the next court date following such transfer. The file of any case so transferred shall remain sealed until the end of the tenth working day following such arraignment unless the state's attorney has filed a motion pursuant to this subsection in which case such file shall remain sealed until the court makes a decision on the motion. A state's attorney may, not later than ten working days after such arraignment, file a motion to transfer the case of any child charged with the commission of a class B felony or a violation of subdivision (2) of subsection (a) of section 53a–70 to the docket for juvenile matters for proceedings in accordance with the provisions of this chapter. The court sitting for the regular criminal docket shall, after hearing and not later than ten working days after the filing of such motion, decide such motion.

Approved May 21, 2004.

WORKERS COMPENSATION—LUMP SUM PAYMENTS

P.A. No. 04–214

S.H.B. No. 5340

AN ACT CONCERNING LUMP SUM PAYMENTS UNDER THE WORKERS' COMPENSATION ACT AND DISQUALIFICATIONS AND OFFSETS UNDER THE UNEMPLOYMENT COMPENSATION ACT.

Be it enacted by the Senate and House of Representatives in General Assembly convened:

Section 1. Section 31–302 of the general statutes is repealed and the following is substituted in lieu thereof (Effective from passage):

Compensation payable under this chapter shall be paid at the particular times in the week and in the manner the commissioner may order, and shall be paid directly to the persons entitled to receive them unless the commissioner, for good reason, orders payment to those entitled to act for such persons, ~~; but, when he~~ except that when the commissioner finds it just or necessary, the commissioner may approve or direct the commutation, in whole or in part, of weekly compensation under the provisions of this chapter into monthly or quarterly payments, or into a single lump sum, which may be paid to the one then entitled to the compensation, and the commutation shall be binding upon all persons entitled to compensation for the injury in question. In any case of commutation, a true equivalence of value shall be maintained, with due discount of sums payable in the future; and, when commutation is made into a single lump sum, (1) the commissioner may direct that it be paid to any savings bank, trust company or life insurance company authorized to do business within this state, to be held in trust for the beneficiary or beneficiaries under the provisions of this chapter and paid in conformity with the provisions of this chapter, and (2) the parties, by agreement and with approval of the commissioner, may prorate the single lump sum over the life expectancy of the injured employee.

Sec. 2. Subdivision (16) of subsection (a) of section 31–236 of the general statutes is repealed and the following is substituted in lieu thereof (Effective October 1, 2004):

(16) For purposes of subparagraph (B) of subdivision (2) of this subsection, "wilful misconduct" means deliberate misconduct in wilful disregard of the employer's interest, or a single knowing violation of a reasonable and uniformly enforced rule or policy of the employer, when reasonably applied, provided such violation is not a result of the employee's incompetence and provided further, in the case of absence from work, "wilful misconduct" means an employee must be absent without either good cause for the absence or notice to the employer which the employee could reasonably have provided under the circumstances for three separate instances within ~~an eighteen-month~~ a twelve-month period. Except with respect to tardiness, for purposes of subparagraph (B) of subdivision (2) of this subsection, each instance in which an employee is absent for one day or two consecutive days without either good cause for the absence or notice to the employer which the employee could reasonably have provided under the circumstances constitutes a "separate instance". For purposes of subdivision (15) of this subsection, "temporary help service" means any person conducting a business that consists of employing individuals directly for the purpose of furnishing part-time or temporary help to others; and "temporary employee" means an employee assigned to work for a client of a temporary help service.

Sec. 3. Subsection (g) of section 31–227 of the general statutes is repealed and the following is substituted in lieu thereof (Effective October 1, 2004):

(g) With respect to benefit years beginning on or after October 1, 1981, for any week with respect to which an individual is receiving a pension, which shall include a governmental or other pension, retirement or retired pay, annuity, or any other similar periodic payment, under a plan maintained or contributed to by a base period employer, the weekly benefit rate payable to such individual for such week shall be reduced by the prorated weekly amount of the pension. ~~Where~~ If contributions were made to the pension plan by the individual, the prorated weekly pension amount shall be reduced by the proportion ~~which~~ that such individual's contributions bear to the total of all payments for such individual into the plan, except that if the pension is paid under the Social Security Act, [1] the individual's contributions to the plan shall reduce the prorated weekly pension amount by one hundred per cent. If, as a result of the reduction made under the provisions of this subsection, the individual's weekly benefit rate is not a whole dollar amount, the weekly benefit rate payable to such individual shall be the next lower whole dollar amount. No reduction shall be made under this subsection by reason of the receipt of a pension, except in the case of pensions paid under the Social Security Act or the Railroad Retirement Act of 1974, [2] if the services performed by the individual during the base period for such employer, or remuneration received for such services, did not affect the individual's eligibility for, or increase the amount of, such pension, retirement or retired pay, annuity, or similar payment.

[1] 42 U.S.C.A. § 301 et seq.
[2] 45 U.S.C.A. § 231 et seq.

Approved June 3, 2004.

VITAL STATISTICS—DEATH CERTIFICATES

P.A. No. 04–255

S.H.B. No. 5628

AN ACT CONCERNING FUNERAL DIRECTORS AND VITAL RECORDS.

Be it enacted by the Senate and House of Representatives in General Assembly convened:

Section 1. Section 7–42 of the general statutes is repealed and the following is substituted in lieu thereof (Effective October 1, 2004):

Each registrar of vital statistics shall ascertain as accurately as the registrar can all marriages, deaths and fetal deaths, and all births, upon the affidavit of the father or mother, occurring in the registrar's town, and record the same in such form and with such particulars as are prescribed by the department. The registrar shall give licenses to marry, according to provisions of law, shall make and perfect all records of the birth and death of the persons born or deceased in the registrar's town, and, when any birth or death happens of which no certificate is returned to the registrar, shall obtain the information required by law respecting such birth or death. The registrar shall ensure that all certificates of birth, marriage, death and fetal death are fully completed before accepting the certificate for filing. The registrar shall include the Social Security numbers of both persons on all marriage licenses. The registrar shall make available to all persons in the registrar's town who, in the registrar's judgment, are likely to need them, blank forms for the certificates and returns required by law to be made to the registrar, and shall amend or correct certificates of births, marriages, deaths and fetal deaths that occurred in the registrar's town, and the records thereof, whenever the registrar discovers transcribing, typographical or clerical errors upon the face thereof. When the registrar makes a correction on a certificate of birth, marriage, death or fetal death, the registrar shall, within ten days, forward an authenticated copy of the corrected certificate to the department and any other registrar having a copy of the certificate. The registrar shall maintain sufficient documentation, as prescribed by the commissioner, to support such correction, and shall ensure the confidentiality of such documentation as required by law. The date of the correction and a summary description of the evidence submitted in support of the correction shall be made part of the record. The certificate shall not be marked "Amended" unless an amendment is made as provided in subdivision (10) of section 7–36, as amended. The registrar shall record on each certificate of birth, marriage, death or fetal death received for record the date of its receipt, by writing on the certificate or through electronic means. The registrar of vital statistics from the town where a child was born may electronically access birth data for such child to make corrections and amendments as requested by the parent or parents, the reporting hospital, or the department, excluding amendments regarding parentage and gender change. Amendments to vital records made by the registrar of vital statistics in the town of occurrence shall be made in accordance with section 19a–42, as amended. The registrar shall keep the records of the registrar's office, when a fireproof safe is not provided for the registrar's use, in the vaults provided for the land records of the town. The registrar may, with the approval of the department, store any records not in current use in a location other than the registrar's office or such vaults, provided such location shall be approved by the Public Records Administrator, and provided such location is within the limits of such town. The registrar shall, on or before the fifteenth day of each month, send to the commissioner an authenticated copy of each certificate of birth, marriage, death and fetal death received by the registrar for the calendar month next preceding or a notification that no such certificate has been received. Such notification shall be in a format prescribed by the department. Copies of certificates of births, marriages, deaths and fetal deaths, transmitted to the commissioner as required under this section, shall be plain, complete and legible transcripts of the certificates. If a transcript is illegible or incomplete, the commissioner shall require of the registrar a complete or legible copy. Each registrar of vital statistics shall also transmit to the registrars of voters for the registrar's town a notice of the death of any person seventeen years of age or older, at the same time the registrar transmits the authenticated copy of the certificate of death for such person to the commissioner under this section.

Sec. 2. Subsection (a) of section 7–44 of the general statutes is repealed and the following is substituted in lieu thereof (Effective October 1, 2004):

(a) When it appears from the certificate of a birth, marriage, death or fetal death filed with any registrar of vital statistics that the residence of the mother of the child or that of either of the parties to the marriage or that of the deceased was in some other town in this state ~~or a town in any other state where town officials retain custody of such certificates,~~ at the time of such birth, marriage, death or fetal death, such registrar shall at once transmit an authenticated copy of such certificate of birth, marriage, death or fetal death, including all information contained on such certificate, to the registrar of the town in which the mother of such child or either of the contracting parties to such marriage or such deceased resided at the time of such birth, marriage, death or fetal death. Such copy shall be in the format prescribed by the department. Any registrar of vital statistics of any town or city in this state, receiving such authenticated copy of a birth, marriage, death or fetal death certificate from a registrar of a town or city in this ~~or any other~~ state, shall record the same, but shall not transmit a copy thereof to the commissioner.

Sec. 3. Subsection (a) of section 7–48 of the general statutes is repealed and the following is substituted in lieu thereof (Effective October 1, 2004):

(a) Not later than ten days after each live birth which occurs in this state, a birth certificate shall be filed with the registrar of vital statistics in the town in which the birth occurred and the certificate shall be registered if properly filed, by manual or electronic systems as prescribed by the commissioner. On and after January 1, 1994, each hospital with two hundred or more live births in calendar year 1990, or any subsequent calendar year, shall electronically transmit birth information data to the department in a computer format approved by the department. Each birth certificate shall contain such information as the department may require and shall be completed in its entirety. Medical and health information which is required by the department, including information regarding voluntary acknowledgments of paternity and whether the child was born out of wedlock, shall be recorded on a confidential portion of the certificate to be sent directly to the department. Such confidential records may be used for statistical and health purposes by the department or by a local director of health, as authorized by the department, for records related to the town served by the local director of health and where the mother was a resident at the time of the birth of the child. Such birth certificate and confidential records may be used internally by the hospital for records transmitted by the hospital for statistical, health and quality assurance purposes. The department shall give due consideration to national uniformity in vital statistics in prescribing the format and content of such certificate.

Sec. 4. Section 7–50 of the general statutes is repealed and the following is substituted in lieu thereof (Effective October 1, 2004):

(a) No certificate of birth shall contain any specific statement that the child was born in or out of wedlock or reference to illegitimacy of the child or to the marital status of the mother, except that information on whether the child was born in or out of wedlock and the marital status of the mother shall be recorded on a confidential portion of the certificate pursuant to section 7–48, as amended by this act. Upon the completion of an acknowledgment of paternity at a hospital, concurrent with the hospital's electronic transmission of birth data to the department, or at a town in the case of a home birth, concurrent with the registration of the birth data by the town, the acknowledgment shall be filed in the paternity registry maintained by the department, as required by section 19a–42a, as amended by this act, and the name of the father of a child born out of wedlock shall be entered in or upon the birth certificate or birth record of such child. All properly completed post birth acknowledgments or certified adjudications of paternity received by the department shall be filed in the paternity registry maintained by the department, and the name of the father of the child born out of wedlock shall be entered in or upon the birth record or certificate of such child by the department, if there is no paternity already recorded on the birth certificate. If another father's information is recorded on the certificate, the original father's information shall not be removed except upon receipt by the department of ~~an~~ a certified order by a court of competent jurisdiction in which there is a finding that the individual recorded on the birth certificate, specifically referenced by name, is not the child's father, or a finding that a different individual than the one recorded, specifically referenced by name, is the child's father. The name of the father on a birth certificate or birth record shall otherwise be removed or changed only upon the filing of a rescission in such registry, as provided in section 19a–42a, as amended by this act. The Social Security number of the father of a child born out of wedlock may be entered in or upon the birth certificate or birth record of such child if such disclosure is done in accordance with 5 USC 552a note.

(b) The department shall restrict access to and issuance of certified copies of acknowledgements of paternity as provided in section 19a–42a, as amended by this act.

Sec. 5. Section 7–62b of the general statutes is repealed and the following is substituted in lieu thereof (Effective October 1, 2004):

(a) A death certificate for each death which occurs in this state shall be completed in its entirety and filed with the registrar of vital statistics in the town in which the death occurred no later than five days after death if filing a paper certificate and no later than three days after death if filing through an electronic death registry system, in order to obtain a burial permit prior to final disposition. The death certificate shall be registered if properly filed. If the place of death is unknown but the body is found in this state, the death certificate shall be completed and filed in accordance with this section, provided the place where the body is found shall be shown as the place of death.

(b) The funeral director or embalmer licensed by the department, or the funeral director or embalmer licensed in another state and complying with the terms of a reciprocal agreement on file with the department, in charge of the burial of the deceased person shall complete the death certificate on a form provided by the department. ~~and shall file it~~ Said certificate shall be filed by a licensed embalmer or such embalmer's designee or a funeral director or such director's designee, in accordance with the provisions of this section, except when inquiry is required by the Chief Medical Examiner's Office, in which case the death certificate shall be filed in accordance with section 19a–409. The Social Security number of the deceased person shall be recorded on such certificate. Such licensed funeral director or licensed embalmer shall obtain the personal data from the next of kin or the best qualified person or source available and shall obtain a medical certification from the person responsible therefor, in accordance with the provisions of this section. Only a licensed embalmer may assume charge of the burial of a deceased person who ~~died from~~ had a communicable disease, as designated in the Public Health Code, at the time of death and such licensed embalmer shall file ~~the death certificate and a certificate~~ an affidavit, on a form provided by the department, signed and sworn to by such licensed embalmer ~~or another licensed embalmer~~ stating that the body has been disinfected in accordance with the Public Health Code.

(c) The medical certification portion of the death certificate shall be completed, signed and returned to the licensed funeral director or licensed embalmer ~~within~~ no later than twenty-four hours after death by the physician or advanced practice registered nurse in charge of the patient's care for the illness or condition which resulted in death. In the absence of such physician or advanced practice registered nurse, or with ~~his~~ the physician's or advanced practice registered nurse's approval, the medical certification may be completed and signed by ~~a designated~~ an associate physician, an advanced practice registered nurse, a physician assistant as provided in subsection (d) of section 20–12d, as amended by this act, a registered nurse as provided in section 20–101a, as amended by this act, the chief medical officer of the institution in which death occurred, or by the pathologist who performed an autopsy upon the decedent. No physician, advanced practice registered nurse, physician assistant, registered nurse, chief medical officer or pathologist shall sign and return the medical certification unless ~~he~~ such physician, advanced practice registered nurse, physician assistant, registered nurse, chief medical officer or pathologist has personally viewed and examined the body of the person to whom the medical certification relates and ~~has satisfied himself~~ is satisfied that at the time of the examination such person was in fact dead, except ~~that in the event a~~ in the event a medical certification is completed by a physician, advanced practice registered nurse, physician assistant, registered nurse, chief medical officer or pathologist other than the one who made the determination and pronouncement of death, ~~has been made by a registered nurse pursuant to section 20–101a, such~~ an additional viewing and examination of the body shall not be required. If a physician, advanced practice registered nurse, physician assistant, registered nurse, chief medical officer or pathologist refuses or otherwise fails to complete, sign and return the medical portion of the death certificate to the licensed funeral director or licensed embalmer within twenty-four hours after death, such licensed funeral director or embalmer may notify the Commissioner of Public Health of such refusal. The commissioner may, upon receipt of notification and investigation, assess a civil penalty against such physician, advanced practice registered nurse, physician assistant, registered nurse, chief medical officer or pathologist not to exceed two hundred fifty dollars. The medical certification shall state the cause of death, defined so that such death may be classified under the international list of causes of death, the duration of disease if known and such additional information as the Department of Public Health requires. The department shall give due consideration to national uniformity in vital statistics in prescribing the form and content of such information.

(d) If the cause of death cannot be determined within twenty-four hours after death and inquiry is not required by the Chief Medical Examiner, the medical certification may be completed in such manner as may be provided by regulation, adopted by the Commissioner of Public Health in accordance with chapter 54. [1] The attending physician or advanced practice registered nurse shall give the licensed funeral director or licensed embalmer notice of the reason for the delay and final disposition of the body shall not be made until a signed medical certification is obtained from the attending physician or advanced practice registered nurse.

(e) When a death is presumed to have occurred within this state but the body cannot be located, a death certificate may be prepared by the Chief Medical Examiner upon receipt of an order of a court of competent jurisdiction, which shall include the finding of facts required to complete the death certificate. Such death certificate shall be filed with the Department of Public Health and marked "presumptive" and shall show on its face the date of filing and shall identify the court and the date of decree.

(f) The Commissioner of Public Health may by regulation, adopted in accordance with chapter 54, provide for the extension of time periods prescribed for the filing of death certificates in cases where compliance therewith would result in undue hardship.

[1] C.G.S.A. § 4–166 et seq.

Sec. 6. Section 7–64 of the general statutes is repealed and the following is substituted in lieu thereof (Effective October 1, 2004):

The body of each person who dies in this state shall be buried, removed or cremated within a reasonable time after death. The person to whom the custody and control of the remains of any deceased person are granted by law shall see that the certificate of death required by law has been completed and filed in accordance with section 7–62b, as amended by this act, prior to final disposition of the body. An authorization for final disposition issued under the law of another state which accompanies a dead body or fetus brought into this state shall be authority for final disposition of the body or fetus in this state. The final disposition of a cremated body shall be recorded as the crematory. The provisions of this section shall not in any way impair the authority of directors of health in cases of death resulting from communicable diseases, nor conflict with any statutes regulating the delivery of bodies to any medical school, nor prevent the placing of any body temporarily in the receiving vault of any cemetery. The placing of any body in a family vault or tomb within any cemetery shall be deemed a burial under the provisions of this section. Any person who violates any provision of this section shall be fined not more than five hundred dollars or imprisoned not more than five years.

Sec. 7. Section 7–65 of the general statutes is repealed and the following is substituted in lieu thereof (Effective October 1, 2004):

~~No deceased person shall be buried in the town in which he dies until a burial permit, specifying~~ The embalmer or funeral director licensed by the department, or licensed in a state having a reciprocal agreement on file with the department and complying with the terms of such agreement, who assumes custody of a dead body shall obtain a burial transit removal permit from the registrar of the town in which the death occurred not later than five calendar days after death, and prior to final disposition or removal of the body from the state. The burial permit shall specify the place of burial ~~by section, lot or grave~~ or other place of interment and ~~stating~~ state that the death certificate and any other certificate required by law have been returned and recorded. ~~, has been issued by the registrar of vital statistics, and the registrar shall record the place of any burial other than a public cemetery.~~ Such registrar shall appoint suitable persons as subregistrars, who shall be authorized to issue ~~burial permits based upon certificates as hereinbefore provided, and also to issue removal permits based upon certificates as provided in sections 7–68 and 7–69, in the same manner as is required of the registrar~~ a burial transit removal permit based upon receipt of a completed death certificate as provided in section 7–62b, as amended by this act, during the hours in which the registrar of vital records is closed. All such certificates upon which a permit is issued shall be forwarded to the registrar within seven days after receiving such certificates. The appointment of subregistrars shall be made in writing, with the approval of the selectmen of such town, and shall be made with reference to locality, to best accommodate the inhabitants of the town. Such subregistrars shall be sworn, and their term of office shall not extend beyond the term of office of the appointing registrar.

The names of such subregistrars shall be reported to the Department of Public Health. The Chief Medical Examiner, Deputy Chief Medical Examiner and associate medical examiners shall be considered subregistrars of any town in which death occurs for the purpose of issuing burial permits and removal permits. The fee for such burial permit and burial transit removal permit shall be paid to the town in which the death occurred.

Sec. 8. Section 7–66 of the general statutes is repealed and the following is substituted in lieu thereof (Effective October 1, 2004):

~~The burial or removal permit required under the provisions of sections 7–65 and 7–67 to 7–70, inclusive, shall be required in each case mentioned in section 7–64 except that, in cases where any body is placed temporarily in the receiving vault of any cemetery and subsequently buried in the same cemetery, no additional burial permit shall be required for such subsequent burial, and except that, in disposing of the ashes of any body that has been cremated, either by burial or by placing such ashes in any cemetery vault, no additional burial permit shall be required.~~

The sexton of a cemetery shall specify on the burial permit the place of burial, by section, lot or grave, or other place of interment. No additional burial or burial transit removal permit shall be required for a body that is placed temporarily in a receiving vault of any cemetery and subsequently buried in the same cemetery. In each case herein provided for, the sexton of such cemetery shall endorse upon the ~~original~~ burial permit the date when the body was placed in the temporary receiving vault, ~~or when the ashes were buried or were placed in such vault,~~ and the date when and the place where such body was subsequently buried. ~~, or where such ashes were buried or placed; and he~~ The sexton shall also include a statement of the same in ~~his~~ the monthly returns to the registrar of vital statistics. If such subsequent burial is to be in any cemetery other than the cemetery where the body was temporarily deposited or if the body is to be cremated, the sexton shall return the burial permit ~~or transit permit~~ to the issuing registrar, who shall thereupon issue the necessary permits. Any person who violates any provision of this section shall be fined not more than five hundred dollars or imprisoned not more than five years.

Sec. 9. Section 7–68 of the general statutes is repealed and the following is substituted in lieu thereof (Effective October 1, 2004):

On receipt by the registrar of vital statistics of any town of a certificate of death containing the facts required by section 7–65, as amended by this act, for a permit for burial, or when it appears that such certificate is already a matter of record, or that the original burial permit, by virtue of which the body of any deceased person was brought into such town, is on file or recorded in such registrar's office, the registrar, upon request, shall issue a permit for the disinterment or removal of such body to the responsible licensed funeral director or embalmer, as indicated on the death certificate or burial permit, or to an individual designated on an order from a judge of the Superior Court, as provided in section 19a–413, stating therein the locality of the interment, disinterment or removal; but no permit for the disinterment of the body of any deceased person shall be issued in any case where death was caused by a communicable disease, except by the permission and under the direction of the town director of health.

Sec. 10. Section 7–69 of the general statutes is repealed and the following is substituted in lieu thereof (Effective October 1, 2004):

~~Except as provided in section 7–70 no~~ No person except a licensed embalmer or funeral director licensed by the department, or licensed in a state having a reciprocal agreement on file with the department and complying with the terms of such agreement, shall remove the body of a deceased person, ~~from one town to another or into the limits of any town in this state unless a permit for such removal has been obtained, as provided by section 7–68, and no~~ except that once a dead body has been embalmed or prepared in accordance with the Public Health Code and applicable provisions of the general statutes, a licensed embalmer or funeral director may authorize an unlicensed employee to transport such body. No person except a licensed embalmer or funeral director licensed by the department, or licensed in a state having a reciprocal agreement on file with the department, shall remove the body of any deceased person from this state to another state ~~unless a death certificate signed by a person licensed by the department, or licensed in a state having a reciprocal agreement on file with the department and complying with the terms of such agreement, has been procured~~ until a burial transit removal permit has been issued in accordance with section 7–65, as amended by this act. No burial ~~or~~ transit removal permit shall be issued unless the death certificate has been signed by a licensed embalmer or funeral director licensed by the department, or licensed in a state having a reciprocal agreement on file with the department and complying with the terms of such agreement. ~~Any embalmer or funeral director licensed by the department, or licensed in a state having a reciprocal agreement on file with the department, may remove the body of any deceased person from or into the limits of any town in this state, provided there shall be attached to the coffin or case containing~~

~~such body a written or printed permit, signed by the registrar of vital statistics in the town in which such person died, certifying the cause of death or disease of which such person died and the town in which such person is to be buried. The permit shall also certify that, when death was due to any communicable disease specified by the Public Health Code, the body has been~~ In the case of a deceased person who, at the time of death, had a communicable disease specified by the Public Health Code, the permit shall certify that the body was prepared in accordance with the regulations of the Public Health Code. Such permit shall be sufficient to permit the burial of such deceased person in any town in this state other than the town in which such person died, without a burial permit from the registrar of the town where such person is to be buried. If the body of a deceased person is brought into the state for burial and is accompanied by a burial transit removal permit issued by the legally constituted authorities of the state from which it was brought, such permit shall be received as sufficient authority for burial; but, if it is not accompanied by such permit, then the person or persons in charge of it shall apply for a burial permit to the registrar of vital statistics of the town in which it is to be buried, and such registrar shall issue such permit when furnished with such information as to the identity of the deceased and the cause of death as is required by section 7–62b, as amended by this act, concerning a person dying in this state. Any person who violates any provision of this section, or who knowingly signs a false permit or knowingly allows a false permit to be used in lieu of a permit required by this section, shall be fined not more than five hundred dollars or imprisoned not more than six months, or both.

Sec. 11. Section 7–72 of the general statutes is repealed and the following is substituted in lieu thereof (Effective October 1, 2004):

(a) Each ~~person~~ sexton having charge of any burial place shall, during the first week of each month, return a list of all interments, disinterments and removals made by ~~him~~ such sexton during the month next preceding, with the dates thereof, to the registrar of the town and also, within said time, file with the registrar permits received by ~~him~~ such sexton by virtue of which a body has been brought into the town from another town or state for burial, with ~~his~~ such sexton's endorsement thereon showing when and in what cemeteries the interments took place. The registrar shall inscribe upon ~~the back of~~ each certificate and each permit so received the date of its reception and record such lists and permits in books to be furnished by the Department of Public Health. When a permit has been given for the disinterment and removal of a body, the registrar shall make a memorandum on ~~his~~ the registrar's records of such removal and the place to which such body was removed.

(b) Any sexton who fails to make the appropriate filing of reports as required by subsection (a) of this section by the end of the third week of a month to the registrar of the town, shall be subject to a fine of not more than one hundred dollars per day.

Sec. 12. Subsection (a) of section 7–73 of the general statutes is repealed and the following is substituted in lieu thereof (Effective October 1, 2004):

(a) To any person performing the duties required by the provisions of the general statutes relating to registration of births, marriages, deaths and fetal deaths, the following fees shall be allowed: (1) To the registrar for completing each record of birth by procuring and inserting the full name of the child, or for the recording, indexing, copying and endorsing of each birth, marriage, death or fetal death certificate, two dollars; (2) for the license to marry, ten dollars; and (3) for issuing each burial or burial transit removal permit, three dollars.

Sec. 13. Section 7–74 of the general statutes is repealed and the following is substituted in lieu thereof (Effective October 1, 2004):

The fee for a certification of birth registration shall be five dollars and the fee for a certified copy of a certificate of birth shall be five dollars, except that the fee for such certifications and copies when issued by the department shall be fifteen dollars. The fee for a certified copy of a certificate of marriage or death shall be five dollars. Such fees shall not be required of ~~any federal agency or~~ the department.

Sec. 14. Subsection (a) of section 19a–42 of the general statutes is repealed and the following is substituted in lieu thereof (Effective October 1, 2004):

(a) To protect the integrity and accuracy of vital records, a certificate registered under chapter 93 [1] may be amended only in accordance with sections 19a–41 to 19a–45, inclusive, chapter 93, regulations adopted by the Commissioner of Public Health pursuant to chapter 54 [2] and uniform procedures prescribed by the commissioner. Only the commissioner may amend birth certificates to reflect changes concerning parentage or gender change. Amendments related to parentage or gender change shall result in the creation of a replacement certificate that supersedes the original, and shall in no way reveal the original language changed by the amendment. Any amendment to a vital record made by the registrar of vital statistics of the town in which the vital event occurred or by the commissioner shall be in accordance with such regulations and uniform procedures.

[1] C.G.S.A. § 7–36 et seq.
[2] C.G.S.A. § 4–166 et seq.

Sec. 15. Subsection (d) of section 19a–42 of the general statutes is repealed and the following is substituted in lieu thereof (Effective October 1, 2004):

(d)(1) Upon receipt of (A) an acknowledgment of paternity executed in accordance with the provisions of subsection (a) of section 46b–172 by both parents of a child born out of wedlock, or (B) a certified copy of an order of a court of competent jurisdiction establishing the paternity of a child born out of wedlock, the commissioner shall include on or amend, as appropriate, such child's birth certificate to show such paternity if paternity is not already shown on such birth certificate ~~or to change the name of the child or both. If another father is listed on the birth certificate, the department shall not remove or replace the father's information unless presented with a court order that meets the requirements specified in section 7–50. Birth certificates amended under this subsection shall not be marked "Amended"~~ and to change the name of the child if so indicated on the acknowledgment of paternity form or within the certified court order as part of the paternity action.

(2) If another father is listed on the birth certificate, the commissioner shall not remove or replace the father's information unless presented with a certified court order that meets the requirements specified in section 7–50, as amended by this act, or upon the proper filing of a rescission, in accordance with the provisions of section 46b–172. The commissioner shall thereafter amend such child's birth certificate to remove or change the father's name and to change the name of the child, as requested at the time of the filing of a rescission, in accordance with the provisions of section ~~7–50~~ 46b–172. Birth certificates amended under this subsection shall not be marked "Amended".

(3) A fee of twenty-five dollars shall be charged by the department for each amendment to a birth certificate requested pursuant to this subsection which request is not received from a hospital, a state agency or a court of competent jurisdiction.

Sec. 16. Section 19a–42a of the general statutes is repealed and the following is substituted in lieu thereof (Effective October 1, 2004):

(a) All (1) voluntary acknowledgments of paternity and rescissions of such acknowledgments executed in accordance with subsection (a) of section 46b–172, and (2) adjudications of paternity issued by a court or family support magistrate under section 46b–171, section 46b–172a or any other provision of the general statutes shall be filed in the paternity registry maintained by the Department of Public Health. All information in such registry shall be made available to the IV-D agency, as defined in subdivision (12) of subsection (b) of section 46b–231, as amended, for comparison with information in the state case registry established under subsection (*l*) of section 17b–179, as amended.

(b) Except for the IV-D agency, as provided in subsection (a) of this section, the department shall restrict access to and issuance of certified copies of acknowledgements of paternity to the following parties: (1) Parents named on the acknowledgment of paternity; (2) the person whose birth is acknowledged, if such person is over eighteen years of age; (3) an authorized representative of the Department of Social Services; (4) an attorney representing such person or a parent named on the acknowledgment; or (5) agents of a state or federal agency, as approved by the department.

Sec. 17. Section 19a–44 of the general statutes is repealed and the following is substituted in lieu thereof (Effective October 1, 2004):

To protect the integrity of vital records and to prevent the fraudulent use of birth certificates of deceased persons, the Commissioner of Public Health ~~is~~ and the local registrars of vital records are hereby authorized to match birth and death certificates and to post the facts of death to the appropriate birth certificate. Copies issued from birth certificates marked deceased shall be similarly marked.

Sec. 18. Section 19a–270 of the general statutes is repealed and the following is substituted in lieu thereof (Effective October 1, 2004):

The first selectman of any town, the mayor of any city, the administrative head of any state correctional institution or the superintendent or person in charge of any almshouse, asylum, hospital, morgue or other public institution which is supported, in whole or in part, at public expense, having in his possession or control the dead body of any person which, if not claimed as hereinafter provided, would have to be buried at public expense, or at the expense of any such institution, shall, immediately upon the death of such person, notify his relatives thereof, if known, and, if such relatives are not known, shall notify the person or persons bringing or committing him to such institution. Such official shall, within twenty-four hours from the time such body came into his possession or control, give notice thereof to the Department of Public Health and shall deliver such body to The University of Connecticut, the Yale University School of Medicine or the University of Bridgeport College of Chiropractic or its successor institution, as said department may direct and in accordance with an agreement to be made among said universities in such manner as is directed by said department and at the expense of the university receiving the body, if The University of Connecticut, Yale University, or the University of Bridgeport College of Chiropractic or its successor institution, at any time within one year, has given notice to any of such officials that such bodies would be needed for the purposes specified in section 19a–270b; provided any such body shall not have been claimed by a relative, either by blood or marriage, or a legal representative of such deceased person prior to delivery to any of said universities. The university receiving such body shall not embalm such body for a period of at least forty-eight hours after death, and any relative, either by blood or marriage, or a legal representative of such deceased person may claim such body during said period. If any such body is not disposed of in either manner herein specified, it may be cremated or buried. When any person has in his possession or control the dead body of any person which would have to be buried at public expense or at the expense of any such institution, he shall, within forty-eight hours after such body has come into his possession or control, file, with the registrar of the town within which such death occurred, a certificate of death as provided in section 7–62b, as amended by this act, unless such certificate has been filed by a funeral director. Before any such body is removed to any of said universities, the official or person contemplating such removal shall secure a ~~burial or transit~~ burial transit removal permit which shall be delivered with the body to the official in charge of such university, who shall make return of such ~~burial or transit~~ burial transit removal permit in the manner provided in section 7–72, as amended by this act. ~~; except that any such body removed to such university under the provisions of section 7–70 shall not be required to be returned to the town where death occurred, provided the permit for permanent removal as required under the provisions of section 7–69 shall be secured as soon as practicable after such removal.~~

Sec. 19. Section 19a–322 of the general statutes is repealed and the following is substituted in lieu thereof (Effective October 1, 2004):

The managers of each crematory shall keep books of record, which shall be open at reasonable times for inspection, in which shall be entered the name, age, sex and residence of each person whose body is cremated, together with the authority for such cremation and the disposition of the ashes. The owner or superintendent shall ~~immediately forward to the registrar by whom the permit required by section 19a–323 was issued a certified duplicate of such record, which duplicate the~~ complete the cremation permit required by section 19a–323, as amended by this act, retain a copy for record and immediately forward the original permit to the registrar of the town in which the death occurred. The registrar shall keep the cremation permit on file and record it with other vital statistics. When any body is removed from this state for the purpose of cremation, the person having the legal custody and control of such body shall cause a certificate to be procured from the person in charge of the crematory in which such body is incinerated, stating the facts called for in this section, and cause such certificate to be filed for record with the registrar ~~by whom the permit was issued~~ of the town in which the death occurred.

Sec. 20. Section 19a–323 of the general statutes is repealed and the following is substituted in lieu thereof (Effective October 1, 2004):

The body of any deceased person may be disposed of by incineration or cremation in this state or may be removed from the state for such purpose. If death occurred in this state, the death certificate required by law shall be filed with the registrar of vital statistics for the town in which such person died, if known, or, if not known, for the town in which the body was found. ~~, and a cremation certificate from the~~ The Chief Medical Examiner, Deputy Chief Medical Examiner, associate medical examiner, or an authorized assistant medical examiner shall complete the cremation certificate, stating that ~~he~~ such medical examiner has made inquiry into the cause and manner of death and is of the opinion that no further examination or judicial inquiry is necessary. ~~,~~ The cremation certificate shall be ~~filed with~~ submitted to the registrar of vital statistics of the town in which such person died, if known, or, if not known, of the town in which the body was found, or with the registrar of vital statistics of the town in which the funeral director having charge of the body is located. Upon receipt of the cremation certificate, the registrar shall authorize the cremation certificate, keep it on permanent record, and issue a cremation permit, except that if the cremation certificate is submitted to the registrar of the town where the funeral director is located, such certificate shall be forwarded to the registrar of the town where the person died to be kept on permanent record. The estate of the deceased person, if any, shall pay the sum of forty dollars for the issuance of the cremation certificate or an amount equivalent to the compensation then being paid by the state to authorized assistant medical examiners, if greater. ~~Upon receiving such certificate, the registrar shall issue a permit for the cremation of such body; except that no such~~ No cremation certificate shall be required for a permit to cremate the remains of bodies pursuant to section 19a–270a. ~~and except that, when~~ When the cremation certificate is issued in a town other than that where the person died, the registrar of vital statistics for such other town shall ascertain from the original burial transit removal permit that the certificates required by the state statutes have been received and recorded, that the body has been prepared in accordance with the Public Health Code and that the entry regarding the place of disposal is correct. Whenever the registrar finds that the place of disposal is incorrect, ~~he~~ the registrar shall issue a corrected burial transit removal permit and, after inscribing and recording the original permit in the manner prescribed for sextons' reports under section 7–72, as amended by this act, shall then immediately give written notice to the registrar for the town where the death occurred of the change in place of disposal stating the name and place of the crematory and the date of cremation. Such written notice shall be sufficient authorization to correct these items on the original certificate of death. No body shall be cremated until at least forty-eight hours after death, unless such death was the result of communicable disease, and no body shall be received by any crematory unless accompanied by the permit provided for in this section. The fee for a cremation permit shall be three dollars and for the written notice one dollar. The Department of Public Health shall provide forms for such permits, which shall not be the same as for regular burial permits, and such blanks and books as may be required by the registrars.

Sec. 21. Subsection (d) of section 20–12d of the general statutes is repealed and the following is substituted in lieu thereof (Effective October 1, 2004):

(d) A physician assistant licensed under this chapter may make the actual determination and pronouncement of death of a patient, provided: (1) The death is an anticipated death; (2) the physician assistant attests to such pronouncement on the certificate of death; and (3) the physician assistant or a physician licensed by the state of Connecticut certifies the death and signs the certificate of death ~~within~~ no later than twenty-four hours ~~of~~ after the pronouncement. ~~by the physician assistant.~~

Sec. 22. Subsection (b) of section 20–87a of the general statutes is repealed and the following is substituted in lieu thereof (Effective October 1, 2004):

(b) Advanced nursing practice is defined as the performance of advanced level nursing practice activities that, by virtue of postbasic specialized education and experience, are appropriate to and may be performed by an advanced practice registered nurse. The advanced practice registered nurse performs acts of diagnosis and treatment of alterations in health status, as described in subsection (a) of this section, and shall collaborate with a physician licensed to practice medicine in this state. If practicing in (1) an institution licensed pursuant to subsection (a) of section 19a–491, as amended, as a hospital, residential care home, health care facility for the handicapped, nursing home, rest home, mental health facility, substance abuse treatment facility, infirmary operated by an educational institution for the care of students enrolled in, and faculty and staff of, such institution, or facility operated and maintained by any state agency and providing services for the prevention, diagnosis and treatment or care of human health conditions, or (2) an industrial health facility licensed pursuant to subsection (h) of section 31–374 which serves at least two thousand employees, or (3) a clinic operated by a state agency, municipality, or private nonprofit corporation, or (4) a clinic operated by any educational institution prescribed by regulations adopted pursuant to section 20–99a, the advanced practice registered nurse may, in collaboration with a physician licensed to practice medicine in this state, prescribe, dispense, and administer medical therapeutics and corrective measures. In all other settings, the advanced practice registered nurse may, in collaboration with a physician licensed to practice medicine in the state, prescribe and administer medical therapeutics and corrective measures and may dispense drugs in the form of professional samples in accordance with sections 20–14c to 20–14e, inclusive, except that an advanced practice registered nurse licensed pursuant to section 20–94a and maintaining current certification from the American Association of Nurse Anesthetists who is prescribing and administrating medical therapeutics during surgery may only do so if the physician who is medically directing the prescriptive activity is physically present in the institution, clinic or other setting where the surgery is being performed. For purposes of this subsection, "collaboration" means a mutually agreed upon relationship between an advanced practice registered nurse and a physician who is educated, trained or has relevant experience that is related to the work of such advanced practice registered nurse. The collaboration shall address a reasonable and appropriate level of consultation and referral, coverage for the patient in the absence of the advanced practice registered nurse, a method to review patient outcomes and a method of disclosure of the relationship to the patient. Relative to the exercise of prescriptive authority, the collaboration between an advanced practice registered nurse and a physician shall be in writing and shall address the level of schedule II and III controlled substances that the advanced practice registered nurse may prescribe and provide a method to review patient outcomes, including, but not limited to, the review of medical therapeutics, corrective measures, laboratory tests and other diagnostic procedures that the advanced practice registered nurse may prescribe, dispense and administer. An advanced practice registered nurse licensed under the provisions of this chapter may make the determination and pronouncement of death of a patient, provided the advanced practice

<u>registered nurse attests to such pronouncement on the certificate of death and signs the certificate of death no later than twenty-four hours after the pronouncement.</u>

Sec. 23. Section 20–101a of the general statutes is repealed and the following is substituted in lieu thereof (Effective October 1, 2004):

(a) A registered nurse, licensed under this chapter, in charge in a hospice or nursing home facility as defined in section 19a–521, or a registered nurse, licensed under this chapter or a registered nurse employed by a home health care agency licensed by the state of Connecticut, in a home or residence may make the actual determination and pronouncement of death of a patient provided that the following conditions are satisfied: (1) The death is an anticipated death; (2) the registered nurse attests to such pronouncement on the certificate of death; and (3) <u>the registered nurse, an advanced practice registered nurse licensed under chapter 378,</u>[1] <u>or</u> a physician licensed ~~by the state of Connecticut~~ under chapter 370[2] certifies the death and signs the certificate of death ~~within~~ <u>no later than</u> twenty-four hours ~~of~~ <u>after</u> the pronouncement<u>.</u> ~~by the registered nurse.~~

(b) The Department of Public Health shall adopt regulations, in accordance with the provisions of chapter 54,[3] to establish the procedures for the implementation of this section. ~~The department shall be required to notify all persons affected by such implementation, including, but not limited to, hospices, nursing home facilities, physicians, home health care agencies, emergency medical technicians, funeral directors and medical examiners.~~

[1] C.G.S.A. § 20–87 et seq.
[2] C.G.S.A. § 20–8 et seq.
[3] C.G.S.A. § 4–166 et seq.

Sec. 24. Section 20–212 of the general statutes is repealed and the following is substituted in lieu thereof (Effective October 1, 2004):

No person, except a licensed embalmer, shall inject any fluid or substance into any dead human body, except that a registered student embalmer may, even if not in the presence of a licensed embalmer, make such injection or perform any other act under his instruction; and no person, firm or corporation shall enter, engage in, carry on or manage for another the business of caring for, preserving or disposing of dead human bodies until each person, firm or corporation so engaged has obtained from the Department of Public Health and holds a license as provided in this chapter; nor shall any person be employed to remove a dead human body, except a licensed embalmer, a registered student embalmer, a licensed funeral director, or a person authorized in each instance by the Chief Medical Examiner, Deputy Medical Examiner or assistant medical examiner incidental to examining the body of a deceased person, except that once a dead human body has been prepared in accordance with the Public Health Code and the applicable provisions of the general statutes, an embalmer or funeral director licensed in this state may authorize ~~a nonlicensed~~ <u>an unlicensed</u> employee to ~~remove~~ <u>transport</u> such body. ~~Nothing in this section shall be construed to affect any provision of section 7–70.~~ Nothing in this section shall be construed to prohibit any person licensed as an embalmer or as a funeral director under the laws of another state from bringing into or removing from this state a dead human body, provided any and all other laws of this state relative to such body have been complied with.

Sec. 25. Section 20–215 of the general statutes is repealed and the following is substituted in lieu thereof (Effective October 1, 2004):

No licensed embalmer shall sign ~~a certificate~~ <u>an affidavit</u> attesting the preparation or embalming of any body unless such body has been prepared or embalmed by him, or by a registered student embalmer under his personal supervision.

Sec. 26. Section 46b–25 of the general statutes is repealed and the following is substituted in lieu thereof (Effective October 1, 2004):

No license may be issued by the registrar until both persons have appeared before the registrar and made application for a license. The license shall be <u>completed in its entirety,</u> dated, signed and sworn to by each applicant and shall state each applicant's name, age, race, birthplace, residence, whether single, widowed or divorced and whether under the supervision or control of a conservator or guardian. The Social Security numbers of the bride and the groom shall be recorded in the "administrative purposes" section of the license. If the license is signed and sworn to by the applicants on different dates, the earlier date shall be deemed the date of application.

Sec. 27. Subsection (a) of section 46b–34 of the general statutes is repealed and the following is substituted in lieu thereof (Effective October 1, 2004):

(a) Each person who joins any person in marriage shall certify upon the license certificate the fact, time and place of the marriage, and return it to the registrar of the town where ~~it was issued~~ the marriage took place, before or during the first week of the month following the marriage. Any person who fails to do so shall be fined not more than ten dollars.

Sec. 28. Section 7–48a of the general statutes is repealed and the following is substituted in lieu thereof (Effective from passage):

On and after January 1, 2002, each birth certificate shall contain the name of the birth mother, except by the order of a court of competent jurisdiction, and be filed with the name of the birth mother recorded. Not later than forty-five days after receipt of an order from a court of competent jurisdiction, the Department of Public Health shall create a replacement certificate in accordance with the court's order. Such replacement certificate shall include all information required to be included in a certificate of birth of this state as of the date of the birth. When a certified copy of such certificate of birth is requested by an eligible party, as provided in section 7–51, a copy of the replacement certificate shall be provided. The department shall seal the original certificate of birth in accordance with the provisions of subsection (c) of section 19a–42. Immediately after a replacement certificate has been prepared, the department shall transmit an exact copy of such certificate to the registrar of vital statistics of the town of birth and to any other registrar as the department deems appropriate. The town shall proceed in accordance with the provisions of section 19a–42.

Sec. 29. (Effective October 1, 2004) Sections 7–70 and 46b–32 of the general statutes, as amended, are repealed.

Approved June 14, 2004.

REVISOR—TECHNICAL CORRECTIONS

P.A. No. 04–257

S.S.B. No. 604

AN ACT CONCERNING THE REVISOR'S TECHNICAL CORRECTIONS TO THE GENERAL STATUTES AND CERTAIN PUBLIC ACTS.

Be it enacted by the Senate and House of Representatives in General Assembly convened:

Section 1. Section 1–1e of the general statutes is repealed and the following is substituted in lieu thereof (Effective from passage):

Nothing in sections 1–1d, 3–94b to 3–94e, inclusive, 7–6, 7–51, 7–53, as amended, 7–54, as amended, 7–172, as amended, 9–12, as amended, 10a–207, 14–14, 14–36, as amended, 14–40a, as amended, 14–41, as amended, 14–44, as amended, 14–61, 14–73, 14–214, 14–276, 17a–1, 17a–152, 17b–75, 17b–81, 17b–223, ~~17b–748,~~ 17b–745, as amended, 18–73, 18–87, as amended, 19a–512, 20–10, 20–130, 20–146, 20–188, 20–213, 20–217, 20–236, 20–250, 20–252, 20–270, 20–291, as amended, 20–316, as amended, 20–361, 20–590, as amended, 20–592, 26–38, 29–156a, 30–1, as amended, 30–45, as amended, 30–86a, as amended, 31–222, 38a–482, 38a–609, 38a–633, 38a–786, 45a–263, 45a–502, 45a–504, 45a–606, 45a–754, 46b–129, as amended, 46b–215, as amended, 52–572, 53–304, 53–330, 53a–70 or 53a–87 shall impair or affect any act done, offense committed or right accruing, accrued or acquired, or an obligation, liability, penalty, forfeiture or punishment incurred prior to October 1, 1972, and the same may be enjoyed, asserted and enforced, as fully and to the same extent and in the same manner as they might under the laws existing prior to said date, and all matters civil or criminal pending on said date or instituted thereafter for any act done, offense committed, right accruing, accrued ~~,~~ or acquired, or obligation, liability, penalty, forfeiture ~~,~~ or punishment incurred prior to said date may be continued or instituted under and in accordance with the provisions of the law in force at the time of the commission of ~~said~~ such act done, offense committed, right accruing, accrued ~~,~~ or acquired, or obligation, liability, penalty, forfeiture or punishment incurred.

Sec. 2. Section 4–141 of the general statutes is repealed and the following is substituted in lieu thereof (Effective from passage):

As used in this chapter: "Claim" means a petition for the payment or refund of money by the state or for permission to sue the state; "just claim" means a claim which in equity and justice the state should pay, provided the state has caused damage or injury or has received a benefit; "person" means any individual, firm, partnership, corporation, limited liability company, association or other group, including political subdivisions of the state; "state agency" includes every department, division, board, office, commission, arm, agency and institution of the state government, whatever its title or function; , and "state officers and employees" includes every person elected or appointed to or employed in any office, position or post in the state government, whatever such person's title, classification or function and whether such person serves with or without remuneration or compensation, including judges of probate courts and employees of such courts. In addition to the foregoing, "state officers and employees" includes attorneys appointed as victim compensation commissioners, attorneys appointed by the Public ~~Defenders~~ Defender Services Commission as public defenders, assistant public defenders or deputy assistant public defenders , and attorneys appointed by the court as special assistant public defenders, the Attorney General, the Deputy Attorney General and any associate attorney general or assistant attorney general, any other attorneys employed by any state agency, any commissioner of the Superior Court hearing small claims matters or acting as a fact-finder, arbitrator or magistrate or acting in any other quasi-judicial position, any person appointed to a committee established by law for the purpose of rendering services to the Judicial Department, including, but not limited to, the Legal Specialization Screening Committee, the State-Wide Grievance Committee, the Client Security Fund Committee , and the State Bar Examining Committee, any member of a multidisciplinary team established by the Commissioner of Children and Families pursuant to section 17a–106a, and any physicians or psychologists employed by any state agency. "State officers and employees" shall not include any medical or dental intern, resident or fellow of The University of Connecticut when (1) the intern, resident or fellow is assigned to a hospital affiliated with the university through an integrated residency program, and (2) such hospital provides protection against professional liability claims in an amount and manner equivalent to that provided by the hospital to its full-time physician employees.

Sec. 3. Section 4–165 of the general statutes is repealed and the following is substituted in lieu thereof (Effective from passage):

No state officer or employee shall be personally liable for damage or injury, not wanton, reckless or malicious, caused in the discharge of his duties or within the scope of his employment. Any person having a complaint for such damage or injury shall present it as a claim against the state under the provisions of this chapter. For the purposes of this section, "scope of employment" shall include, but not be limited to, representation by an attorney appointed by the Public Defender Services Commission as a public defender, assistant public defender or deputy assistant public defender or an attorney appointed by the court as a special assistant public defender of an indigent accused or of a child on a petition of delinquency, representation by such other attorneys, referred to in section 4–141, of state officers and employees , in actions brought against such officers and employees in their official and individual capacities, the discharge of duties as a trustee of the state employees retirement system, the discharge of duties of a commissioner of the Superior Court hearing small claims matters or acting as a fact-finder, arbitrator or magistrate or acting in any other quasi-judicial position, and the discharge of duties of a person appointed to a committee established by law for the purpose of rendering services to the Judicial Department, including, but not limited to, the Legal Specialization Screening Committee, the State-Wide Grievance Committee, the Client Security Fund Committee and the State Bar Examining Committee; provided such actions arise out of the discharge of the duties or within the scope of employment of such officers or employees. For the purposes of this section, members or employees of the soil and water district boards established pursuant to section 22a–315 shall be considered state employees.

Sec. 4. Subsection (h) of section 7–147b of the general statutes, as amended by sections 210 and 235 of public act 03–6 of the June 30 special session, is repealed and the following is substituted in lieu thereof (Effective from passage):

(h) The form of the ballot to be mailed to each owner shall be consistent with the model ballot prepared by the Historic Preservation Council of the Connecticut Commission on Arts, Tourism, Culture, History and Film established pursuant to section 10–320b, as amended. The ballot shall be a secret ballot and shall set the date by which such ballots shall be received by the clerk of the municipality. The ballots shall be mailed by first class mail to each owner eligible to vote in such balloting at least fifteen days in advance of the day on which ballots must be returned. Notice of balloting shall be published in the form of a legal advertisement appearing in a newspaper having a substantial circulation in the municipality at least twice, at intervals of not less than two days, the first not more than fifteen days ~~nor~~ or less than ten days and the last not less than two days before the day on which the ballots must be returned. Such ballot shall be returned to the municipal clerk, inserted in an inner envelope which shall have endorsed on the face thereof a form containing a statement as follows: "I, the undersigned, do hereby state under the penalties of false statement that I am an owner of record of real property to be included in the proposed historic district and that I am, or my predecessors in title were, liable to the municipality for taxes on an assessment of not less than one thousand dollars on the last grand list of the municipality of real property within the district, or who would be or would have been so liable if not entitled to an exemption under subdivision (7), (8), (10), (11), (13), (14), (15), (16), (17), (20), (21), (22), (23), (24), (25), (26), (29) or (49) of section 12–81." Such statement shall be signed and dated. Any person who intentionally falsely signs such ballot shall be guilty of false statement as ~~defined~~ provided in section 53a–157b. The inner envelope, in which the ballot has been inserted by the owner, shall be returned to the municipal clerk in an outer envelope endorsed on the outside with the words: "Official ballot". Such outer envelope shall also contain, in the upper left corner of the face thereof, blank spaces for the name and return address of the sender. In the lower left corner of such outer envelope, enclosed in a printed box, there shall be spaces upon which the municipal clerk, before issuance of the ballot and envelopes, shall inscribe the name, street and number of the elector's voting residence and the date by which the ballot must be returned, and before issuance the municipal clerk shall similarly inscribe such envelope with his name and address for the return thereof. All outer envelopes shall be serially numbered. The ballots shall be returned to the municipal clerk by the close of business on the day specified, and such clerk shall compare each ballot to the list of property owners to whom such ballots were mailed to insure that each such ballot has been properly signed and returned.

Sec. 5. Subsection (i) of section 7–169 of the general statutes, as amended by section 1 of public act 03–178, is repealed and the following is substituted in lieu thereof (Effective from passage):

(i) Prizes offered for the winning of bingo games may consist of cash, merchandise, tickets for any lottery conducted under chapter 226,[1] the value of which shall be the purchase price printed on such tickets, or other personal property. No permittee may offer a prize which exceeds fifty dollars in value, except that (1) a permittee may offer a prize or prizes on any one day of not less than fifty-one dollars ~~nor~~ or more than two hundred dollars in value, provided the total value of such prizes on any one day does not exceed six hundred dollars, (2) a permittee may offer one or two winner-take-all games or series of games played on any day on which the permittee is allowed to conduct bingo, provided ninety per cent of all receipts from the sale of bingo cards for ~~said~~ such winner-take-all game or series of games shall be awarded as prizes and provided each prize awarded does not exceed five hundred dollars in value, (3) the holder of a Class A permit may offer two additional prizes on a weekly basis not to exceed one hundred twenty-five dollars each as a special grand prize and in the event such a special grand prize is not won, the money reserved for such prize shall be added to the money reserved for the next week's special grand prize, provided no such special grand prize may accumulate for more than sixteen weeks or exceed a total of two thousand dollars, and (4) a permittee may award door prizes the aggregate value of which shall not exceed two hundred dollars in value. When more than one player wins on the call of the same number, the designated prize shall be divided equally to the next nearest dollar. If a permittee elects, no winner may receive a prize which amounts to less than ten per cent of the announced prize and in such case the total of such multiple prizes may exceed the statutory limit of such game.

[1] C.G.S.A. § 12–557b et seq.

Sec. 6. Subsection (a) of section 8–7d of the general statutes, as amended by section 5 of public act 03–177, is repealed and the following is substituted in lieu thereof (Effective from passage):

(a) In all matters wherein a formal petition, application, request or appeal must be submitted to a zoning commission, planning and zoning commission ~~,~~ or zoning board of appeals under this chapter, a planning commission under chapter 126[1] or an inland wetlands agency under chapter 440[2] and a hearing is required or otherwise held on such petition, application, request or appeal, such hearing shall commence within sixty-five days after receipt of such petition, application, request or appeal and shall be completed within thirty-five days after such hearing commences, unless a shorter period of time is required under this chapter, ~~or~~ chapter 126 or chapter 440. Notice of the hearing shall be published in a newspaper having a general circulation in such municipality where the land that is the subject of the hearing is located at least twice, at intervals of not less than two days, the first not more than fifteen days ~~, nor~~ or less than ten days ~~,~~ and the last not less than two days before the date set for the hearing. In addition to such notice, such commission, board or agency may, by regulation, provide for notice to persons who own or occupy land that is adjacent to the land that is the subject of the hearing. All applications and maps and documents relating thereto shall be open for public inspection. At such hearing, any person or persons may appear and be heard and may be represented by agent or by attorney. All decisions on such matters shall be rendered within sixty-five days after completion of such hearing, unless a shorter period of time is required ~~pursuant to~~ under this chapter, chapter 126 or chapter 440. The petitioner or applicant may consent to one or more extensions of any period specified in this subsection, provided the total extension of all such periods shall not be for longer than sixty-five days, or may withdraw such petition, application, request or appeal.

[1] C.G.S.A. § 8–18 et seq.
[2] C.G.S.A. § 22a–28 et seq.

Sec. 7. Subsection (d) of section 9–150a of the general statutes, as amended by section 97 of public act 03–6 of the June 30 special session, is repealed and the following is substituted in lieu thereof (Effective from passage):

(d)(1) If the statement on the inner envelope has not been signed as required by section 9–140a, as amended, such inner envelope shall not be opened ~~nor~~ or the ballot removed therefrom, and such inner envelope shall be replaced in the opened outer envelope which shall be marked "Rejected" and the reason therefor endorsed thereon by the counters. (2) If such statement is signed but the individual completing the ballot is an individual described in subsection (a) of section 90 of ~~this act~~ public act 03–6 of the June 30 special session and has not met the requirements of subsection (e) of section 90 of ~~this act~~ public act 03–6 of the June 30 special session, the counters shall replace the ballot in the opened inner envelope, replace the inner envelope in the opened outer envelope and mark "Rejected as an Absentee Ballot" and endorse the reason for such rejection on the outer envelope, and the ballot shall be treated as a provisional ballot for federal offices only, pursuant to sections 83 to 89, inclusive, of ~~this act~~ public act 03–6 of the June 30 special session.

Sec. 8. Section 9–391 of the general statutes, as amended by section 22 of public act 03–241, is repealed and the following is substituted in lieu thereof (Effective from passage):

(a) Each endorsement of a candidate to run in a primary for the nomination of candidates for municipal office to be voted upon at a municipal election, or for the election of town committee members shall be made under the provisions of section 9–390, as amended, not earlier than the fifty-sixth day ~~nor~~ or later than the forty-ninth day preceding the day of such primary. The endorsement shall be certified to the clerk of the municipality by the chairman or presiding officer and the secretary of the town committee, caucus or convention, as the case may be, not later than four o'clock p.m. on the forty-eighth day preceding the day of such primary. Such certification shall contain the name and street address of each person so endorsed, the title of the office or the position as committee member and the name or number of the political subdivision or district, if any, for which each such person is endorsed. If such a certificate of a party's endorsement is not received by the town clerk by such time, such party, for purposes of sections 9–417, as amended, 9–418 and 9–419, shall be deemed to have neither made nor certified such endorsement of any candidate for such office.

(b) Each selection of delegates to a state or district convention shall be made in accordance with the provisions of section 9–390, as amended, not earlier than the one-hundred-sixty-eighth day and not later than the one-hundred-sixty-first day preceding the day of the primary for such state or district office. Such selection shall be certified to the clerk of the municipality by the chairman or presiding officer and the secretary of the town committee or caucus, as the case may be, not later than four o'clock p.m. on the one-hundred-sixtieth day preceding the day of such primary. Each such certification shall contain the name and street address of each person so selected, the position as delegate, and the name or number of the political subdivision or district, if any, for which each such person is selected. If such a certificate of a party's selection is not received by the town clerk by such time, such party, for purposes of sections 9–417, as amended, and 9–420, as amended, shall be deemed to have neither made nor certified any selection of any person for the position of delegate.

(c) Each endorsement of a candidate to run in a primary for the nomination of candidates for a municipal office to be voted upon at a state election shall be made under the provisions of section 9–390, as amended, not earlier than the eighty-fourth day ~~nor~~ or later than the seventy-seventh day preceding the day of such primary. Any certification to be filed under this section shall be received by the town clerk not later than four o'clock p.m. on the fourteenth day after the close of the town committee meeting, caucus or convention, as the case may be. If such a certificate of a party's endorsement is not received by the town clerk by such time, such party, for the purposes of sections 9–417, as amended, and 9–418, shall be deemed to have neither made nor certified any endorsement of any candidate for such office. The candidate so endorsed for a municipal office to be voted upon at a state election, other than the office of justice of the peace, shall file with the town clerk a certificate, signed by that candidate, stating that such candidate was so endorsed, the candidate's name as the candidate authorizes it to appear on the ballot, the candidate's full street address and the title and district of the office for which the candidate was endorsed. Such certificate shall be attested by the chairman or presiding officer and the secretary of the town committee, caucus or convention which made such endorsement. The endorsement of candidates for the office of justice of the peace shall be certified to the clerk of the municipality by the chairman or presiding officer and the secretary of the town committee, caucus or convention, and shall contain the name and street address of each person so endorsed and the title of the office for which each such person is endorsed.

Sec. 9. Subsection (c) of section 10–27 of the general statutes, as amended by section 40 of public act 03–76, is repealed and the following is substituted in lieu thereof (Effective from passage):

(c) State agencies, including the educational institutions, may exchange a limited number of professional personnel and students with institutions of other states and other countries and may pay the salaries of such personnel and may assign scholarships and grants-in-aid to the exchangees. The authorized exchange of personnel and students need not be parallel and simultaneous ~~nor~~ or specific with regard to the assignment of persons between institutions. If a vacancy exists on the staff of any state agency, including the educational institutions, because a leave of absence without pay has been granted, such agency may engage the services of professional personnel of other countries, and may pay such personnel so engaged from the funds which otherwise would have been paid to such staff members on leave of absence without pay.

Sec. 10. Subdivision (1) of subsection (a) of section 10–71 of the general statutes, as amended by section 8 of public act 03–76 and section 4 of public act 03–100, is repealed and the following is substituted in lieu thereof (Effective from passage):

(1) The percentage of the eligible costs for adult education a local board of education shall receive, under the provisions of this section, shall be determined as follows: (A) Each town shall be ranked in descending order from one to one hundred sixty-nine according to such town's adjusted equalized net grand list per capita, as defined in section 10–261, as amended; and (B) based upon such ranking, a percentage of not less than zero ~~nor~~ or more than sixty-five shall be determined for each town on a continuous scale, except that the percentage for a priority school district pursuant to section 10–266p, as amended, shall not be less than twenty. Any such percentage shall be increased by seven and one-half percentage points but shall not exceed sixty-five per cent for any local board of education which provides basic adult education programs for adults at facilities operated by or within the general administrative control and supervision of the Department of Mental Health and Addiction Services, provided such adults reside at such facilities.

Sec. 11. Subdivision (1) of subsection (b) of section 10–217a of the general statutes, as amended by section 1 of public act 03–6 of the June 30 special session, is repealed and the following is substituted in lieu thereof (Effective from passage):

(1) The percentage of the amount paid from local tax revenues for such services reimbursed to a local board of education shall be determined by (A) ranking each town in the state in descending order from one to one hundred sixty-nine according to such town's adjusted equalized net grand list per capita, as defined in section 10–261, as amended; (B) based upon such ranking, (i) for reimbursement paid in the fiscal year ending June 30, 1990, a percentage of not less than forty-five ~~nor~~ or more than ninety shall be determined for each town on a continuous scale, except that for any town in which the number of children under the temporary family assistance program, as defined in subdivision (17) of section 10–262f, is greater than one per cent of the total population of the town, as defined in subdivision (7) of subsection (a) of section 10–261, the percentage shall be not less than eighty, (ii) for reimbursement paid in the fiscal years ending June 30, 1991, to June 30, 2001, inclusive, a percentage of not less than ten ~~nor~~ or more than ninety shall be determined for each town on a continuous scale, except that for any town in which the number of children under the temporary family assistance program, as defined in ~~said~~ subdivision (17) of section 10–262f, is greater than one per cent of the total population of the town, as defined in subdivision (7) of subsection (a) of section 10–261, and for any town which has a wealth rank greater than thirty when towns are ranked pursuant to subparagraph (A) of this subdivision and which provides such services to greater than one thousand five hundred children who are not residents of the town, the percentage shall be not less than eighty, and (iii) for reimbursement paid in the fiscal ~~years~~ year ending June 30, 2002, and each fiscal year thereafter, a percentage of not less than ten ~~nor~~ or more than ninety shall be determined for each town on a continuous scale, except that for any town in which the number of children under the temporary family assistance program, as defined in ~~said~~ subdivision (17) of section 10–262f, for the fiscal year ending June 30, 1997, was greater than one per cent of the total population of the town, as defined in subdivision (7) of subsection (a) of section 10–261, for the fiscal year ending June 30, 1997, and for any town which has a wealth rank greater than thirty when towns are ranked pursuant to subparagraph (A) of this subdivision and which provides such services to greater than one thousand five hundred children who are not residents of the town, the percentage shall be not less than eighty.

Sec. 12. Subsection (b) of section 10–264*l* of the general statutes is repealed and the following is substituted in lieu thereof (Effective from passage):

(b) Applications for interdistrict magnet school program operating grants awarded pursuant to this section shall be submitted annually to the Commissioner of Education at such time and in such manner as the commissioner prescribes. In determining whether an application shall be approved and funds awarded pursuant to this section, the commissioner shall consider, but such consideration shall not be limited to: (1) Whether the program offered by the school is likely to increase student achievement; (2) whether the program is likely to reduce racial, ethnic and economic isolation; (3) the percentage of the student enrollment in the program from each participating district; and (4) the proposed operating budget and the sources of funding for the interdistrict magnet school. If requested by the commissioner, the applicant shall meet with the commissioner or the commissioner's designee to discuss the budget and sources of funding. The commissioner shall not award a grant to a program that is in operation prior to July 1, 2005, if more than eighty per cent of its total enrollment is from one school district, except that the commissioner may award a grant for good cause, for any one year, on behalf of an otherwise eligible magnet school program, if more than eighty per cent of the total enrollment is from one district. The commissioner shall not award a grant to a program that begins operations on or after July 1, 2005, if more than seventy-five per cent of its total enrollment is from one school district or if less than twenty-five or more than seventy-five per cent of the students enrolled are pupils of racial minorities, as defined in section 10–226a, as amended, except that the commissioner may award a grant for good cause, for one year, on behalf of an otherwise eligible interdistrict magnet school program, if more than seventy-five per cent of the total enrollment is from one district or less than twenty-five or more than seventy-five ~~percent~~ per cent of the students enrolled are pupils of racial minorities. The commissioner may not award grants pursuant to such an exception for a second consecutive year.

Sec. 13. Subsection (d) of section 10a–6 of the general statutes is repealed and the following is substituted in lieu thereof (Effective from passage):

(d) The Board of Governors shall request and receive, or be provided electronic access to, data, reports and other information from the constituent units of the state system of higher education that is necessary for the board to carry out its responsibilities pursuant to this section.

Sec. 14. Section 10a–6b of the general statutes is repealed and the following is substituted in lieu thereof (Effective from passage):

(a) The accountability measures developed by the Higher Education Coordinating Council pursuant to subsection (b) of section 10a–6a shall be used by the Department of Higher Education and each constituent unit of the state system of higher education in assessing the constituent unit's progress toward meeting the following goals to: (1) Enhance student learning and promote academic excellence; (2) join with elementary and secondary schools to improve teaching and learning at all levels; (3) ensure access to and affordability of higher education; (4) promote the economic development of the state to help business and industry sustain strong economic growth; (5) respond to the needs and problems of society; and (6) ensure the efficient use of resources. The council shall develop an implementation plan for use of the accountability measures.

(b) In developing the measures pursuant to subsection (a) of this section, the council shall consider graduation rates, student retention rates, tuition and fees, student financial need and available aid, trends in enrollment and the percentage of incoming students who are state residents, strategic plans pursuant to section 10a–11, data on graduates by academic program, faculty productivity, and any other factor that it deems relevant. In considering faculty productivity measures, the council shall consult with the committee established under section 10a–3.

(c) The council shall submit the accountability measures to the Board of Governors of Higher Education for the board's review and approval. Once the measures are approved, each constituent unit shall provide the data to the department that is necessary for purposes of applying the measures.

(d) The Commissioner of Higher Education, on behalf of the council, shall report, in accordance with section 11–4a, to the joint standing committee of the General Assembly having cognizance of matters relating to education on the accountability measures and the implementation plan developed pursuant to this section by February 1, 2000. The report shall include recommendations: (1) For any statutory changes needed for purposes of assessing the constituent units and public institutions of higher education based on the accountability measures; (2) to clarify and streamline planning and accountability reporting requirements of the constituent units and public institutions of higher education; (3) concerning goals, actions to achieve such goals and analysis of performance; and (4) for options to revise budgeting policies and programs to meet accountability goals and measures as outlined in subsections (a) and (b) of this section.

(e) The Commissioner of Higher Education shall develop, in concurrence with the Higher Education Coordinating Council, an accountability report prototype. Upon review and approval by the Board of Governors of Higher Education, the commissioner shall submit the report prototype to the joint standing committee of the General Assembly having cognizance of matters relating to education by October 1, 2000. The report prototype shall include accountability measures developed and approved under this section for which data collection mechanisms exist as determined by the commissioner.

(f) Each constituent unit of the state system of higher education shall submit to the Commissioner of Higher Education its first accountability report by January 1, 2001. The commissioner shall compile and consolidate the reports. The commissioner shall submit, in accordance with section 11–4a, an accountability report that covers the state system of higher education and each constituent unit and public institution of higher education to the joint standing committee of the General Assembly having cognizance of matters relating to education by February 1, 2001. The report shall include baseline data for the accountability measures developed under this section for which data collection mechanisms exist and comparable peer data, as determined by the commissioner after consultation with the Higher Education Coordinating Council and reviewed and approved by the Board of Governors of Higher Education. The report shall also include a timeline for the collection of data and reporting of the remaining accountability measures and for the identification of performance improvement targets.

(g) Each constituent unit of the state system of higher education shall submit an accountability report to the Commissioner of Higher Education annually, by January first. The commissioner shall compile the reports and shall submit, in accordance with section 11–4a, a consolidated accountability report for the state system of higher education to the joint standing committee of the General Assembly having cognizance of matters relating to education annually, by February first. The report shall contain accountability measures for each constituent unit and public institution of higher education pursuant to subsections (a) and (b) of this section. The report shall include updated baseline and peer comparison data, performance improvement targets for each measure, and other information as determined by the commissioner.

Sec. 15. Subsection (c) of section 10a–19b of the general statutes, as amended by section 25 of public act 03–278, is repealed and the following is substituted in lieu thereof (Effective from passage):

(c) Not later than July 1, 2002, and annually thereafter, the council, in consultation with the Departments of Education and Higher Education and the boards of trustees of the constituent units of the state system of higher education, shall report to the joint standing committees of the General Assembly having cognizance of matters relating to education and higher education and employment advancement on all articulation agreements involving higher education institutions and any progress made on the establishment of additional agreements, in accordance with section 11–4a.

Sec. 16. Section 10a–151e of the general statutes is repealed and the following is substituted in lieu thereof (Effective from passage):

On and after July 1, 1999, each constituent unit of the state system of higher education and each public institution of higher education that negotiates a contract with a vendor for the provision of course books for purchase by students shall ensure that such contract: (1) Includes a provision requiring the vendor to post its policies concerning the return of used books and the exchange rate for books used the previous semester that are in good condition, and (2) does not prevent student organizations from holding used book exchange programs.

Sec. 17. Section 10a–153 of the general statutes is repealed and the following is substituted in lieu thereof (Effective from passage):

The constituent units of the state system of higher education shall comply with the provisions of section 4a–60g when undertaking remodeling, alteration, repair or enlargement projects pursuant to the provisions of sections 4b–51, as amended, 4b–52, as amended, 4b–55, as amended, and 4b–91, as amended.

Sec. 18. Subsection (e) of section 12–62k of the general statutes is repealed and the following is substituted in lieu thereof (Effective from passage):

(e) On and after July 1, 2002, the provisions of this section and section 12–62 shall ~~supercede~~ supersede the provisions of any special act, charter or home rule ordinance to the contrary concerning the year a revaluation is required to be implemented.

Sec. 19. Subsection (d) of section 12–81f of the general statutes, as amended by section 1 of public act 03–44, is repealed and the following is substituted in lieu thereof (Effective from passage):

(d) Any person who has submitted an application and been approved in any year for the additional exemption under subsection (a) or (b) of this section shall, in the year immediately following approval, be presumed to be qualified for such exemption. During the year immediately following such approval, the assessor shall notify, in writing, each person presumed to be qualified pursuant to this subsection. If any such person has qualifying income in excess of the maximum allowed under said subsection (a) or (b), such person shall notify the assessor on or before the next filing date for such exemption and shall be denied such exemption for the assessment year immediately following and for any subsequent year until such person has reapplied and again qualified for such exemption. Any person who fails to notify the assessor of such disqualification shall make payment to the municipality in the amount of property tax loss related to the exemption improperly taken.

Sec. 20. Subsection (b) of section 13a–247 of the general statutes, as amended by section 39 of public act 03–115, is repealed and the following is substituted in lieu thereof (Effective from passage):

(b) Any person, firm or corporation violating any provision of subsection (a) of this section shall be fined not more than one hundred dollars for a first offense and not less than one hundred dollars ~~nor~~ or more than five hundred dollars for each subsequent offense.

Sec. 21. Subsection (b) of section 13b–44 of the general statutes, as amended by section 51 of public act 03–115, is repealed and the following is substituted in lieu thereof (Effective from passage):

(b) The commissioner shall cause a public hearing to be held at the expense of the department in each municipality in which such lands or interests in such lands are located. At such hearing, the commissioner shall present and explain the plan of development, and any persons who are opposed to such plan may be heard and may state their reasons for such opposition. Such hearing shall be held not earlier than thirty days after such plan has been filed in the office of the town clerk of the municipality. Notice of the time and place of such hearing shall be published in a newspaper having a substantial circulation in such municipality at least twice, at intervals of not less than two days, the first not more than fifteen days ~~nor~~ or less than ten days and the second not less than two days before such hearing.

Sec. 22. Subsection (g) of section 14–36 of the general statutes, as amended by section 1 of public act 03–171, is repealed and the following is substituted in lieu thereof (Effective from passage):

(g) Any person who violates any provision of this section shall, for a first offense, be deemed to have committed an infraction and be fined not less than seventy-five dollars ~~nor~~ or more than ninety dollars and, for any subsequent offense, shall be fined not less than two hundred fifty dollars ~~nor~~ or more than three hundred fifty dollars or be imprisoned not more than thirty days, or both.

Sec. 23. Subsection (d) of section 14–40a of the general statutes, as amended by section 4 of public act 03–171, is repealed and the following is substituted in lieu thereof (Effective from passage):

(d) Any person who violates any provision of subsection (a), (b) or (c) of this section shall, for a first offense, be deemed to have committed an infraction and be fined not less than thirty-five dollars ~~nor~~ or more than fifty dollars and, for any subsequent offense, shall be fined not more than one hundred dollars or imprisoned not more than thirty days, or both.

Sec. 24. Subsection (h) of section 15–133 of the general statutes, as amended by section 1 of public act 03–244, is repealed and the following is substituted in lieu thereof (Effective from passage):

(h) Any person who violates the provisions of subsection (d) of this section shall: (1) For conviction of a first violation, (A) be fined not less than five hundred dollars ~~nor~~ or more than one thousand dollars, and (B) be (i) imprisoned not more than six months, forty-eight consecutive hours of which may not be suspended or reduced in any manner, or (ii) imprisoned not more than six months, with the execution of such sentence of imprisonment suspended entirely and a period of probation imposed requiring as a condition of such probation that such person perform one hundred hours of community service, as defined in section 14–227e, and (C) have such person's safe boating certificate or certificate of personal watercraft operation, if any, or right to operate a vessel that requires a safe boating certificate for operation suspended for one year; (2) for conviction of a second violation not later than ten years after a prior conviction for the same offense, (A) be fined not less than one thousand dollars ~~nor~~ or more than four thousand dollars, (B) be imprisoned not more than two years, one hundred twenty consecutive days of which may not be suspended or reduced in any manner, and sentenced to a period of probation requiring as a condition of such probation that such person perform one hundred hours of community service, as defined in section 14–227e, and (C) have such person's safe boating certificate or certificate of personal watercraft operation, if any, or right to operate a vessel that requires a safe boating certificate for operation suspended for three years or until the date of such person's twenty-first birthday, whichever is longer; and (3) for conviction of a third and subsequent violation not later than ten years after a prior conviction for the same offense, (A) be fined not less than two thousand dollars ~~nor~~ or more than eight thousand dollars, (B) be imprisoned not more than three years, one year of which may not be suspended or reduced in any manner, and sentenced to a period of probation requiring as a condition of such probation that such person perform one hundred hours of community service, as defined in section 14–227e, and (C) have such person's safe boating certificate or certificate of personal watercraft operation, if any, or right to operate a vessel that requires a safe boating certificate for operation permanently revoked upon such third offense.

Sec. 25. Subsection (b) of section 15–140*l* of the general statutes, as amended by section 2 of public act 03–244, is repealed and the following is substituted in lieu thereof (Effective from passage):

(b) Any person guilty of reckless operation of a vessel in the first degree while under the influence shall be fined not less than two thousand five hundred dollars ~~nor~~ or more than five thousand dollars or imprisoned not more than two years, or both.

Sec. 26. Subsection (b) of section 15–140n of the general statutes, as amended by section 3 of public act 03–244, is repealed and the following is substituted in lieu thereof (Effective from passage):

(b) Any person guilty of reckless operation of a vessel in the second degree while under the influence shall be fined not less than five hundred dollars ~~nor~~ or more than one thousand dollars or imprisoned not more than six months, or both.

Sec. 27. Subsection (h) of section 15–144 of the general statutes, as amended by section 14 of public act 03–244, is repealed and the following is substituted in lieu thereof (Effective from passage):

(h)(1) Any person who operates or any owner who permits the operation of a vessel on the waters of this state which has not been numbered or registered in accordance with the provisions of this chapter and any other applicable section of the general statutes ~~,~~ shall have committed a violation and shall be fined not less than twenty-five ~~nor~~ dollars or more than two hundred dollars for the first offense and for each subsequent offense shall be fined not less than two hundred dollars ~~nor~~ or more than five hundred dollars. (2) No person shall use any vessel registration or registration decals that have been issued to another person pursuant to sections 15–142 to 15–144, inclusive. No person shall use a vessel registration or registration decals on any vessel other than the vessel for which such registration number or registration decals have been issued. Any person who violates any provision of this subdivision shall be fined not more than one hundred dollars or imprisoned not more than thirty days, or both. (3) Any officer empowered to enforce the provisions of this chapter and any other applicable section of the general statutes who finds a vessel which is not numbered or registered in accordance with the provisions of this chapter and such discovery is subsequent to a violation of this chapter may make application to the court for a warrant to seize such vessel and take it into custody pending proof of payment of proper numbering or registration fees. No officer shall be liable for any act performed under the provisions of this subsection.

Sec. 28. Subsection (b) of section 15–154 of the general statutes, as amended by section 7 of public act 03–244, is repealed and the following is substituted in lieu thereof (Effective from passage):

(b) When engaged in the enforcement of this chapter and chapter 446k,[1] such officer shall have the authority to stop and board any vessel which is under way or which is moored on the waters of this state for the purposes of (1) examining decals, certificates and other documents, (2) inspecting safety equipment and waste disposal systems, (3) determining if the operation of such vessel exceeds the noise levels established in subsection (b) of section 15–129, (4) searching when such officer has probable cause to believe that any provision of any law of this state or any rule or regulation of the Department of Environmental Protection relating to boating or water pollution has been violated, (5) determining compliance with sections 15–140*l*, as amended, and 15–140n, as amended, and subsections (d) and (e) of section 15–133, as amended, when such authorized officer has probable cause to believe said section or subsection has been violated, and (6) making arrests. No person operating a vessel shall refuse to stop such vessel or, if sea conditions make stopping in that area unsafe, refuse to take such vessel to a designated area after being requested or signalled to do so by such officer. Any person operating a vessel who refuses to stop or refuses to take such vessel to the designated area shall have committed an infraction. Any person, when signalled to stop by such officer in a law enforcement vessel using an audible signal device or flashing blue lights, who operates such vessel in disregard of such signal so as to (A) interfere with or endanger the operation of the law enforcement vessel or any other vessel, (B) endanger or cause damage to property or person, or (C) increase speed in an attempt to escape or elude such law enforcement officer shall be fined not less than one hundred dollars ~~nor~~ or more than five hundred dollars for a first offense and for any subsequent offense shall be fined not less than five hundred dollars ~~nor~~ or more than one thousand dollars. Proof of the registration number of the vessel shall be prima facie evidence in any prosecution that the owner was the operator.

[1] C.G.S.A. 22a–416 et seq.

Sec. 29. Subsection (a) of section 16–50m of the general statutes, as amended by section 8 of public act 03–140, is repealed and the following is substituted in lieu thereof (Effective October 1, 2004):

(a) The council shall promptly fix a commencement date and location for a public hearing on an application for a certificate complying with section 16–50*l*, as amended, (1) where no proposals are received pursuant to the request-for-proposal process, not less than thirty days after the deadline for submission of such proposals ~~nor~~ or more than sixty days after such deadline; (2) where a proposal is received pursuant to the request-for-proposal process, not less than thirty days after the deadline of submission of an application pursuant to subdivision (3) of subsection (a) of section 16–50*l*, as amended, ~~nor~~ or more than sixty days after such deadline; or (3) where the application is for a facility described in subdivision (5) or (6) of subsection (a) of section 16–50i, as amended, not less than thirty days after receipt of an application ~~nor~~ or more than one hundred fifty days after such receipt. Applications that are common to a request-for-proposal shall be heard under a consolidated public hearing process. At least one session of such hearing shall be held at a location selected by the council in the county in which the facility or any part thereof is to be located after six-thirty p.m. for the convenience of the general public. After holding at least one hearing session in the county in which the facility or any part thereof is to be located, the council may, in its discretion, hold additional hearing sessions at other locations. If the proposed facility is to be located in more than one county, the council shall fix the location for at least one public hearing session in whichever county it determines is most appropriate, provided the council may hold hearing sessions in more than one county.

Sec. 30. Subsection (a) of section 16–245d of the general statutes, as amended by section 22 of public act 03–135, is repealed and the following is substituted in lieu thereof (Effective from passage):

(a) The Department of Public Utility Control shall, by regulations adopted pursuant to chapter 54, [1] develop a standard billing format that enables customers to compare pricing policies and charges among electric suppliers. On and after January 1, 2000, each electric company or electric distribution company, as the case may be, shall, in accordance with the billing format developed by the department, include at a minimum the following information in each customer's bill: (1) The total amount owed by the customer, which shall be itemized to show, (A) the electric generation services component and any additional charges imposed by the electric supplier, if applicable, (B) the electric transmission and distribution charge, including all applicable taxes and the systems benefits charge, as provided in section 16–245*l*, as amended, (C) the competitive transition assessment, as provided in section 16–245g, as amended, (D) ~~federally-mandated~~ federally mandated congestion costs, and (E) the conservation and renewable energy charge, consisting of the conservation and load management program charge, as provided in section 16–245m, as amended, and the renewable energy investment charge, as provided in section 16–245n, as amended; (2) any unpaid amounts from previous bills which shall be listed separately from current charges; (3) except for customers subject to a demand charge, the rate and usage for the current month and each of the previous twelve months in the form of a bar graph or other visual form; (4) the payment due date; (5) the interest rate applicable to any unpaid amount; (6) the toll-free telephone number of the electric distribution company to report power losses; (7) the toll-free telephone number of the Department of Public Utility Control for questions or complaints; (8) the toll-free telephone number and address of the electric supplier; and (9) a statement about the availability of information concerning electric suppliers pursuant to section 16–245p, as amended.

[1] C.G.S.A. § 4–166 et seq.

Sec. 31. Section 17b–28e of the general statutes is repealed and the following is substituted in lieu thereof (Effective from passage):

Not later than September 30, 2002, the Commissioner of Social Services shall submit an amendment to the Medicaid state plan to implement the provisions of public act 02–1 of the May 9 special session* concerning optional services under the Medicaid program. Said state plan amendment shall ~~supercede~~ supersede any regulations of Connecticut state agencies concerning such optional services.

Sec. 32. Section 17b–222 of the general statutes is repealed and the following is substituted in lieu thereof (Effective from passage):

As used in this section and sections 17b–223, 17b–228, 17b–229 and ~~17b–748,~~ 17b–745, as amended, "state humane institution" or "humane institution" means ~~and includes~~ state mental hospitals, community mental health centers, treatment facilities for children and adolescents, or any other facility or program administered by the Departments of Mental Health and Addiction Services, Mental Retardation, or Children and Families. The person in charge of each state humane institution shall furnish the Commissioner of Administrative Services with a daily report of changes in the patient roster and the date of formal commitment of each patient.

Sec. 33. Subsection (b) of section 17b–229 of the general statutes is repealed and the following is substituted in lieu thereof (Effective from passage):

(b) The provisions of sections 17a–278, 17a–502, 17b–222, 17b–223, 17b–228, 17b–232, ~~17b–748,~~ 17b–745, as amended, 46b–215, as amended, and 53–304 shall not affect or impair the responsibility of any patient or patient's estate for his care in a state humane institution prior to July 1, 1955, and the same may be enforced by any action by which such responsibility would have been enforceable prior to July 1, 1955, but only to the extent of that portion of such estate as is not needed for the support of the spouse, parents and dependent children of such patient.

Sec. 34. Section 17b–429 of the general statutes is repealed and the following is substituted in lieu thereof (Effective from passage):

The Commissioner of Social Services shall, within available appropriations, make information available to senior citizens and disabled persons concerning any pharmaceutical company's drug program for indigent persons by utilizing the ConnPACE program, the CHOICES health insurance ~~counseling and~~ assistance program, as defined in section ~~17b–427a~~ 17b–427, as amended, and Infoline of Connecticut to deliver such information.

Sec. 35. Subsection (c) of section 19a–42 of the general statutes is repealed and the following is substituted in lieu thereof (Effective from passage):

(c) An amended certificate shall ~~supercede~~ supersede the original certificate that has been changed and shall be marked "Amended", except for amendments due to parentage or gender change. The original certificate in the case of parentage or gender change shall be physically or electronically sealed and kept in a confidential file by the department and the registrar of any town in which the birth was recorded, and may be unsealed for viewing or issuance only upon a written order of a court of competent jurisdiction. The amended certificate shall become the public record.

Sec. 36. Subsection (a) of section 19a–77a of the general statutes, as amended by section 10 of public act 03–243, is repealed and the following is substituted in lieu thereof (Effective from passage):

(a) Any retail establishment in this state may establish a drop-in supplementary child-care operation on the premises of such retail establishment in accordance with the following requirements:

(1) The hours of operation may only be between six o'clock a.m. and nine o'clock p.m.

(2) No child receiving care shall be less than three years ~~nor~~ or more than ten years of age.

(3) A child may not receive more than two hours of care per day.

(4) The operation may immediately notify appropriate law enforcement or state agencies if any child receiving care at such operation is not picked up by a parent or guardian after three hours.

(5) A parent or guardian shall be on the premises at the retail establishment at all times while the child is receiving care.

(6) The retail establishment shall provide a clean and safe area for the drop-in supplementary child-care operation.

(7) At all times the operation shall provide (A) at least one child-care staff person for every ten children, and (B) at least one child-care staff person who is twenty years of age or older who has experience in child care.

(8) The operation shall submit the names of all child-care staff to the Commissioner of Public Health, who shall request a check of such names from the state child abuse registry established pursuant to section 17a–101k for perpetrator information.

Sec. 37. Section 19a–302 of the general statutes, as amended by section 24 of public act 03–252, is repealed and the following is substituted in lieu thereof (Effective from passage):

If at any time such association fails to comply with the provisions of section 19a–301, the selectmen of the town in which such cemetery is located shall take over the care of ~~said~~ such fund and file an annual report with the Probate Court in accordance with the provisions of section 19a–301. The selectmen may appoint a cemetery committee consisting of not fewer than three ~~nor~~ or more than seven members who are residents of such town. If three members are appointed, one shall serve for a term of two years, one for a term of four years and one for a term of six years; if four members are appointed, one shall serve for a term of two years, one for a term of four years and two for a term of six years; if five members are appointed, one shall serve for a term of two years, two for a term of four years and two for a term of six years; if six members are appointed, two shall serve for a term of two years, two for a term of four years and two for a term of six years; and if seven members are appointed, two shall serve for a term of two years, two for a term of four years and three for a term of six years. Biennially thereafter, they may appoint one member for a term of six years to replace each member whose term expires. ~~Said~~ Such committee shall have all of the powers and duties of a committee established as provided in section 19a–301.

Sec. 38. Subsection (i) of section 19a–343a of the general statutes, as amended by section 8 of public act 03–231, is repealed and the following is substituted in lieu thereof (*Effective from passage*):

(i) At the evidentiary hearing upon the public nuisance complaint, the state shall have the burden of proving, by clear and convincing evidence, ~~of~~ the existence of a public nuisance upon the real property as ~~defined~~ provided in section 19a–343, as amended. If the state presents clear and convincing evidence that there have been three or more arrests, or the issuance of three or more arrest warrants indicating a pattern of criminal activity and not isolated incidents, for conduct on the real property or any portion thereof documented by a law enforcement officer for any of the offenses enumerated in subdivisions (1) to (11), inclusive, of subsection (c) of section 19a–343, as amended, within the three hundred sixty-five days preceding commencement of the action, ~~this~~ such evidence shall create a rebuttable presumption of the existence of a public nuisance. Any defendant may offer evidence by way of an affirmative defense that such defendant has taken reasonable steps to abate the public nuisance, but has been unable to abate the nuisance.

Sec. 39. Subsection (c) of section 19a–673 of the general statutes, as amended by section 5 of public act 03–266, is repealed and the following is substituted in lieu thereof (*Effective from passage*):

(c) Each collection agent, as defined in section 19a–509b, as amended, engaged in collecting a debt from a patient arising from services provided at a hospital shall provide written notice to such patient as to whether the hospital deems the patient an insured patient or an uninsured patient ~~as defined in subsection (a) of this section~~ and the reasons for such determination.

Sec. 40. Section 20–205 of the general statutes, as amended by section 2 of public act 03–198, is repealed and the following is substituted in lieu thereof (*Effective from passage*):

The provisions of this chapter shall not apply to any person in governmental employ while acting in the scope of his or her employment, ~~nor~~ or to any person who furnishes medical or surgical assistance without compensation in an emergency, ~~nor~~ or to any veterinarian, licensed in another state, who is employed as a direct consultant for not more than ten days during any calendar year with any practitioner licensed in conformity with the provisions of section 20–197, as amended. The provisions of this chapter shall not apply to any hospital, educational institution or laboratory or any state or federal institution, or any employee of, student in or person associated with any such hospital, educational institution or laboratory or state or federal institution, while engaged in research or studies involving the use of medical, surgical or dental procedures, or to the owner of any animal or livestock or his or her employee while administering to such animal or livestock.

Sec. 41. Section 22–333 of the general statutes, as amended by section 2 of public act 03–123, is repealed and the following is substituted in lieu thereof (*Effective from passage*):

Any dog, cat or other animal captured or impounded under the provisions of this chapter shall be redeemed by the owner or keeper thereof, or the agent of such owner or keeper, upon proper identification, and, if the animal in question is a dog, upon presentation to the municipal animal control officer of a license and tag for such dog, and upon the payment by such owner or keeper or his agent of (1) the redemption fee established by the municipality, which shall not exceed fifteen dollars, and (2) the cost of advertising incurred under the provisions of section 22–332, as amended; provided no dog, cat or other animal seized for doing damage under the provisions of section 22–355 shall be released except upon written order of the commissioner, the Chief Animal Control Officer or an animal control officer. When the owner or keeper of any such impounded dog, cat or other animal fails to redeem such dog, cat or other animal within twenty-four hours after receiving notification to do so, or, where the owner was unknown, within twenty-four hours after notification was effected by means of publication in a newspaper, such owner or keeper shall pay, in addition to such redemption fee and the cost of advertising, the amount determined by the municipality to be the full cost of detention and care of such impounded dog, cat or other animal. The owner or keeper of any dog, cat or other animal impounded for the purposes of quarantine, as set forth in sections 22–358 and 22–359, shall pay the amount determined by the municipality to be the full cost of detention and care of such quarantined animal. In addition, any owner or keeper of any such impounded dog, cat or other animal who fails to redeem such dog, cat or other animal within one hundred ~~and~~ twenty hours after receiving notification to do so shall have committed an infraction. The legislative body of the municipality shall set any fees imposed by the municipality under this section.

Sec. 42. Section 26–55 of the general statutes, as amended by section 3 of public act 03–192 and section 242 of public act 03–6 of the June 30 special session, is repealed and the following is substituted in lieu thereof (*Effective from passage*):

No person shall import or introduce into the state, or possess or liberate therein, any live fish, wild bird, wild mammal, reptile, amphibian or invertebrate unless such person has obtained a permit therefor from the commissioner, provided nothing in this section shall be construed to require such permit for any live fish, wild bird, wild mammal, reptile, amphibian or invertebrate that was imported, introduced into the state, possessed or liberated in the state prior to October 1, 2003. Such permit may be issued at the discretion of the commissioner under such regulations as the commissioner may prescribe. The commissioner may by regulation prescribe the numbers of live fish, wild birds, wild mammals, reptiles, amphibians or invertebrates of certain species which may be imported, possessed, introduced into the state or liberated therein. The commissioner may by regulation exempt certain species or groups of live fish from the permit requirements. The commissioner may by regulation determine which species of wild birds, wild mammals, reptiles, amphibians or invertebrates must meet permit requirements. The commissioner may totally prohibit the importation, possession, introduction into the state or liberation therein of certain species which the commissioner has determined may be a potential threat to humans, agricultural crops or established species of plants, fish, birds, mammals, reptiles, amphibians or invertebrates. The commissioner may by regulation exempt from permit requirements organizations or institutions such as zoos, research laboratories, colleges or universities, public nonprofit aquaria or nature centers where live fish, wild birds, wild mammals, reptiles, amphibians or invertebrates are held in strict confinement. Any such fish, bird, mammal, reptile, amphibian or invertebrate illegally imported into the state or illegally possessed therein shall be seized by any representative of the Department of Environmental Protection and shall be disposed of as determined by the commissioner. Any person, except as provided in section 26–55a, who violates any provision of this section or any regulation issued by the commissioner as ~~herein~~ provided in this section shall be guilty of an infraction. Importation, liberation or possession of each fish, wild bird, wild mammal, reptile, amphibian or invertebrate in violation of this section or such regulation shall be a separate and distinct offense and, in the case of a continuing violation, each day of continuance thereof shall be deemed to be a separate and distinct offense.

Sec. 43. Section 26–57 of the general statutes, as amended by section 4 of public act 03–192, is repealed and the following is substituted in lieu thereof (*Effective from passage*):

No person shall transport within the state or transport out of the state any fish, bird, mammal, reptile, amphibian or invertebrate for which a closed season is provided without a permit from the commissioner, except as provided ~~herein~~ in this section. The commissioner may issue a permit to any person to transport within the state or to transport out of the state any fish, bird, mammal, reptile, amphibian or invertebrate protected under the provisions of this chapter under such regulations as the commissioner may prescribe. No fish, bird, mammal, reptile, amphibian or invertebrate shall be transported out of the state unless each unit, package or container is conspicuously tagged or labeled, and such tag or label contains in legible writing the full name and address of the person legally authorized to transport out of the state such fish, bird, mammal, reptile, amphibian or invertebrate. Any such fish, bird, mammal, reptile, amphibian or invertebrate received by any person or by any common carrier within the state, addressed for shipment to any point without the state and not having such tag or label conspicuously attached shall be prima facie evidence of a violation of the provisions of this section. A permit shall not be required to transport within the state or to transport out of the state any fish, bird, mammal, reptile, amphibian or invertebrate which has been legally taken, bred, propagated or possessed by a person to whom a license, registration or permit has been issued under the provisions of this chapter authorizing the taking, breeding, propagating or possessing of fish, birds, mammals, reptiles, amphibians or invertebrates, and no permit shall be required to transport within the state or to transport out of the state any fish, bird, mammal, reptile, amphibian or invertebrate that has been legally taken or acquired by a person exempt from license requirements under the provisions of this chapter. Any person who violates any provision of this section shall be fined not less than ten dollars ~~nor~~ or more than two hundred dollars or imprisoned not more than sixty days, or be both fined and imprisoned.

Sec. 44. Subsection (b) of section 26–82 of the general statutes, as amended by section 6 of public act 03–192, is repealed and the following is substituted in lieu thereof (*Effective from passage*):

(b) Any person who violates any provision of this section shall be fined not less than two hundred dollars ~~nor~~ or more than five hundred dollars or imprisoned not less than thirty days ~~nor~~ or more than six months, or shall be both fined and imprisoned, for the first offense, and for each subsequent offense shall be fined not less than two hundred dollars ~~nor~~ or more than one thousand dollars or imprisoned not more than one year, or shall be both fined and imprisoned.

Sec. 45. Subsection (e) of section 28–1 of the general statutes, as amended by section 166 of public act 03–6 of the June 30 special session, is repealed and the following is substituted in lieu thereof (*Effective from passage*):

(e) "Civil preparedness forces" means any organized personnel engaged in carrying out civil preparedness functions in accordance with the provisions of this chapter or any regulation or order thereunder. All the police and fire forces of the state or any political subdivision of the state, or any part of any political subdivision, including all the auxiliaries of these forces, shall be construed to be a part of the civil preparedness forces. The Connecticut Disaster Medical Assistance Team and the Medical Reserve Corps, under the auspices of the Department of Public Health, the Connecticut Urban Search and Rescue Team, under the auspices of the Department of Public Safety, and the Connecticut behavioral health regional crisis response teams, under the auspices of the Department of Mental Health and Addiction Services and the Department of Children and Families, and their members, shall be construed to be a part of the civil preparedness forces while engaging in authorized civil preparedness duty or while assisting or engaging in authorized training for the purpose of eligibility for immunity from liability as provided in section 28–13 and for death, disability and injury benefits as provided in section 28–14. Any member of the civil preparedness forces who is called upon either by civil preparedness personnel or state or municipal police personnel to assist in any emergency shall be deemed to be engaging in civil preparedness duty while assisting in such emergency or while engaging in training under the auspices of the Office of Emergency Management, ~~or the state~~ the Division of State Police within the Department of Public Safety or a municipal police department, for the purpose of eligibility for death, disability and injury benefits as provided in section 28–14.

Sec. 46. Section 29–231 of the general statutes, as amended by section 1 of public act 03–15, is repealed and the following is substituted in lieu thereof (Effective from passage):

The provisions of this chapter shall not apply to: (1) Boilers under federal control; (2) portable boilers used in pumping, heating, steaming and drilling in the open field; (3) portable boilers used solely for agricultural purposes; (4) steam heating boilers, hot water heaters and hot water heating boilers, when used in private homes or apartment houses of not more than five families; (5) hot water heaters approved by a nationally recognized testing agency that are equipped with adequate safety devices including a temperature and pressure relief valve, having a nominal water capacity of not more than one hundred twenty gallons and a heat input of not more than two hundred thousand British thermal units per hour and used solely for hot water supply carrying a pressure of not more than one hundred sixty pounds per square inch and operating at temperatures of not more than two hundred ~~and~~ ten degrees Fahrenheit, provided such heaters are not installed in schools, day care centers, public or private hospitals, nursing or boarding homes, churches or public buildings, as defined in section 1–1; (6) antique or model boilers used in public, nonprofit engineering or scientific museums and operated for educational, historical or exhibition purposes having a shell diameter of less than twelve inches and a grate surface area of less than one square foot; and (7) public service companies, as defined in section 16–1, as amended.

Sec. 47. Section 29–381 of the general statutes, as amended by section 2 of public act 03–231, is repealed and the following is substituted in lieu thereof (Effective from passage):

(a) No owner, proprietor, manager or agent of any theater, concert or music hall or assembly hall or of any building, auditorium or ~~rooms~~ room used for public gatherings shall permit any person to occupy any aisle in any such theater, concert or music hall, assembly hall or other building used for such purpose, or permit any person to occupy the back or sides of any such building or room used ~~as aforesaid~~ for such purpose, to such an extent as to prevent the free and unobstructed passage to and from the entrance to any aisle or any of the exits in such place. ~~; but the~~ The provisions of this ~~section~~ subsection shall not apply to town halls which are on the ground floor.

(b) Before any performance or event at any theater, concert or music hall or assembly hall or at any building, auditorium or room used for public gatherings of more than one hundred persons, the owner, proprietor, manager or agent of such theater, hall, building, auditorium or room shall make a public announcement that describes the location of emergency exits.

(c) Any person who violates any provision of subsection (a) or (b) of this section shall be fined not more than fifty dollars.

Sec. 48. Section 30–88a of the general statutes, as amended by section 14 of public act 03–171, is repealed and the following is substituted in lieu thereof (Effective from passage):

Each person who attains the age of twenty-one years and has a motor vehicle operator's license, containing a full-face photograph of such person, may use, and each permittee may accept, such license as legal proof of the age of the licensee for the purposes of this chapter. Any person who, for the purpose of procuring alcoholic liquor, misrepresents his or her age or uses or exhibits ~~, for the purpose of procuring alcoholic liquor,~~ an operator's license belonging to any other person ~~,~~ shall be fined not less than two hundred ~~nor~~ dollars or more than five hundred dollars or imprisoned not more than thirty days, or both.

Sec. 49. Section 31–51*ll* of the general statutes, as amended by section 2 of public act 03–213, is repealed and the following is substituted in lieu thereof (Effective from passage):

(a)(1) Subject to section 31–51mm, an eligible employee shall be entitled to a total of sixteen workweeks of leave during any twenty-four-month period, such twenty-four-month period to be determined utilizing any one of the following methods: ~~(1)~~ (A) Consecutive calendar years; ~~(2)~~ (B) any fixed twenty-four-month period, such as two consecutive fiscal years or a twenty-four-month period measured forward from an employee's first date of employment; ~~(3)~~ (C) a twenty-four-month period measured forward from an employee's first day of leave taken under sections 31–51kk to 31–51qq, inclusive; or ~~(4)~~ (D) a rolling twenty-four-month period measured backward from an employee's first day of leave taken under sections 31–51kk to 31–51qq, inclusive. ~~,~~

(2) Leave under this subsection may be taken for one or more of the following reasons:

~~(1)~~ (A) Upon the birth of a son or daughter of the employee;

~~(2)~~ (B) Upon the placement of a son or daughter with the employee for adoption or foster care;

~~(3)~~ (C) In order to care for the spouse, or a son, daughter or parent of the employee, if such spouse, son, daughter or parent has a serious health condition; or

~~(4)~~ (D) Because of a serious health condition of the employee.

(b) Entitlement to leave under subparagraph (A) or (B) of subdivision ~~(1) or~~ (2) of subsection (a) of this section may accrue prior to the birth or placement of a son or daughter when such leave is required because of such impending birth or placement.

(c)(1) Leave under subparagraph (A) or (B) of subdivision ~~(1) or~~ (2) of subsection (a) of this section for the birth or placement of a son or daughter may not be taken by an employee intermittently or on a reduced leave schedule unless the employee and the employer agree otherwise. Subject to subdivision (2) of this subsection concerning an alternative position, subdivision (2) of subsection (f) of this section concerning the duties of the employee and subdivision (5) of subsection (b) of section 31–51mm concerning sufficient certification, leave under subparagraph (C) or (D) of subdivision ~~(3) or (4)~~ (2) of subsection (a) of this section for a serious health condition may be taken intermittently or on a reduced leave schedule when medically necessary. The taking of leave intermittently or on a reduced leave schedule pursuant to this subsection shall not result in a reduction of the total amount of leave to which the employee is entitled under subsection (a) of this section beyond the amount of leave actually taken.

(2) If an employee requests intermittent leave or leave on a reduced leave schedule under subparagraph (C) or (D) of subdivision ~~(3) or (4)~~ (2) of subsection (a) of this section that is foreseeable based on planned medical treatment, the employer may require the employee to transfer temporarily to an available alternative position offered by the employer for which the employee is qualified and that (A) has equivalent pay and benefits, and (B) better accommodates recurring periods of leave than the regular employment position of the employee, provided the exercise of this authority shall not conflict with any provision of a collective bargaining agreement between such employer and a labor organization which is the collective bargaining representative of the unit of which the employee is a part.

(d) Except as provided in subsection (e) of this section, leave granted under subsection (a) of this section may consist of unpaid leave.

(e)(1) If an employer provides paid leave for fewer than sixteen workweeks, the additional weeks of leave necessary to attain the sixteen workweeks of leave required under sections 5–248a and 31–51kk to 31–51qq, inclusive, may be provided without compensation.

(2)(A) An eligible employee may elect, or an employer may require the employee, to substitute any of the accrued paid vacation leave, personal leave or family leave of the employee for leave provided under subparagraph (A), (B) or (C) of subdivision ~~(1), (2) or (3)~~ (2) of subsection (a) of this section for any part of this sixteen-week period of such leave under said subsection.

(B) An eligible employee may elect, or an employer may require the employee, to substitute any of the accrued paid vacation leave, personal leave, or medical or sick leave of the employee for leave provided under subparagraph (C) or (D) of subdivision ~~(3) or (4)~~ (2) of subsection (a) of this section for any part of the sixteen-week period of such leave under said subsection, except that nothing in section 5–248a or sections 31–51kk to 31–51qq, inclusive, shall require an employer to provide paid sick leave or paid medical leave in any situation in which such employer would not normally provide any such paid leave.

(f)(1) In any case in which the necessity for leave under subparagraph (A) or (B) of subdivision ~~(1) or~~ (2) of subsection (a) of this section is foreseeable based on an expected birth or placement of a son or daughter, the employee shall provide the employer with not less than thirty days' notice, before the date of the leave is to begin, of the employee's intention to take leave under said ~~subdivision (1) or (2)~~ subparagraph (A) or (B), except that if the date of the birth or placement of a son or daughter requires leave to begin in less than thirty days, the employee shall provide such notice as is practicable.

(2) In any case in which the necessity for leave under subparagraph (C) or (D) of subdivision ~~(3) or (4)~~ (2) of subsection (a) of this section is foreseeable based on planned medical treatment, the employee (A) shall make a reasonable effort to schedule the treatment so as not to disrupt unduly the operations of the employer, subject to the approval of the health care provider of the employee or the health care provider of the son, daughter, spouse or parent of the employee, as appropriate; and (B) shall provide the employer with not less than thirty days' notice, before the date the leave is to begin, of the employee's intention to take leave under said ~~subdivision (3) or (4)~~ subparagraph (C) or (D), except that if the date of the treatment requires leave to begin in less than thirty days, the employee shall provide such notice as is practicable.

(g) In any case in which a husband and wife entitled to leave under subsection (a) of this section are employed by the same employer, the aggregate number of workweeks of leave to which both may be entitled may be limited to sixteen workweeks during any twenty-four-month period, if such leave is taken: (1) Under subparagraph (A) or (B) of subdivision ~~(1) or~~ (2) of subsection (a) of this section; or (2) to care for a sick parent under ~~subdivision (3) of said subsection~~ subparagraph (C) of said subdivision.

(h) Unpaid leave taken pursuant to sections 5–248a and 31–51kk to 31–51qq, inclusive, shall not be construed to affect an employee's qualification for exemption under chapter 558. [1]

(i) Notwithstanding the provisions of sections 5–248a and 31–51kk to 31–51qq, inclusive, all further rights granted by federal law shall remain in effect.

[1] C.G.S.A. § 31–58 et seq.

Sec. 50. Section 31–51mm of the general statutes is repealed and the following is substituted in lieu thereof (Effective from passage):

(a) An employer may require that request for leave based on a serious health condition in subparagraph (C) or (D) of subdivision ~~(3) or (4)~~ (2) of subsection (a) of section 31–51*ll*, as amended, be supported by a certification issued by the health care provider of the eligible employee or of the son, daughter, spouse or parent of the employee, as appropriate. The employee shall provide, in a timely manner, a copy of such certification to the employer.

(b) Certification provided under subsection (a) of this section shall be sufficient if it states:

(1) The date on which the serious health condition commenced;

(2) The probable duration of the condition;

(3) The appropriate medical facts within the knowledge of the health care provider regarding the condition;

(4)(A) For purposes of leave under subparagraph (C) of subdivision ~~(3)~~ (2) of subsection (a) of section 31–51*ll*, as amended, a statement that the eligible employee is needed to care for the son, daughter, spouse or parent and an estimate of the amount of time that such employee needs to care for the son, daughter, spouse or parent; and (B) for purposes of leave under subparagraph (D) of subdivision ~~(4)~~ (2) of subsection (a) of section 31–51*ll*, as amended, a statement that the employee is unable to perform the functions of the position of the employee;

(5) In the case of certification for intermittent leave or leave on a reduced leave schedule for planned medical treatment, the dates on which such treatment is expected to be given and the duration of such treatment;

(6) In the case of certification for intermittent leave or leave on a reduced leave schedule under subparagraph (D) of subdivision ~~(4)~~ (2) of subsection (a) of section 31–51*ll*, as amended, a statement of the medical necessity of the intermittent leave or leave on a reduced leave schedule, and the expected duration of the intermittent leave or reduced leave schedule; and

(7) In the case of certification for intermittent leave or leave on a reduced leave schedule under subparagraph (C) of subdivision ~~(3)~~ (2) of subsection (a) of section 31–51*ll*, as amended, a statement that the employee's intermittent leave or leave on a reduced leave schedule is necessary for the care of the son, daughter, parent or spouse who has a serious health condition, or will assist in their recovery, and the expected duration and schedule of the intermittent leave or reduced leave schedule.

(c)(1) In any case in which the employer has reason to doubt the validity of the certification provided under subsection (a) of this section for leave under subparagraph (C) or (D) of subdivision ~~(3) or (4)~~ (2) of subsection (a) of section 31–51*ll*, as amended, the employer may require, at the expense of the employer, that the eligible employee obtain the opinion of a second health care provider designated or approved by the employer concerning any information certified under subsection (b) of this section for such leave.

(2) A health care provider designated or approved under subdivision (1) of this subsection shall not be employed on a regular basis by the employer.

(d)(1) In any case in which the second opinion described in subsection (c) of this section differs from the opinion in the original certification provided under subsection (a) of this section, the employer may require, at the expense of the employer, that the employee obtain the opinion of a third health care provider designated or approved jointly by the employer and the employee concerning the information certified under subsection (b) of this section.

(2) The opinion of the third health care provider concerning the information certified under subsection (b) of this section shall be considered to be final and shall be binding on the employer and the employee.

(e) The employer may require that the eligible employee obtain subsequent recertifications on a reasonable basis, provided the standards for determining what constitutes a reasonable basis for recertification may be governed by a collective bargaining agreement between such employer and a labor organization which is the collective bargaining representative of the unit of which the worker is a part if such a collective bargaining agreement is in effect. Unless otherwise required by the employee's health care provider, the employer may not require recertification more than once during a thirty-day period and, in any case, may not unreasonably require recertification. The employer shall pay for any recertification that is not covered by the employee's health insurance.

Sec. 51. Subsection (d) of section 31–51nn of the general statutes is repealed and the following is substituted in lieu thereof (Effective from passage):

(d) As a condition of restoration under subsection (a) of this section for an employee who has taken leave under subparagraph (D) of subdivision ~~(4)~~ (2) of subsection (a) of section 31–51*ll*, as amended, the employer may have a uniformly applied practice or policy that requires each such employee to receive certification from the health care provider of the employee that the employee is able to resume work, except that nothing in this subsection shall supersede a valid law of this state or a collective bargaining agreement that governs the return to work of such employees.

Sec. 52. Subsection (c) of section 33–883 of the general statutes, as amended by section 28 of public act 03–18, is repealed and the following is substituted in lieu thereof (Effective from passage):

(c) After the revocation of dissolution is authorized, the corporation may revoke the dissolution by delivering to the Secretary of the State for filing a certificate of revocation of dissolution that (1) sets forth: ~~(1)~~ (A) The name of the corporation; ~~(2)~~ (B) the effective date of the dissolution that was revoked; ~~(3)~~ (C) the date that the revocation of dissolution was authorized; ~~(4)~~ (D) if the corporation's board of directors, or incorporators, revoked the dissolution, a statement to that effect; ~~(5)~~ (E) if the corporation's board of directors revoked a dissolution authorized by the shareholders, a statement that revocation was permitted by action by the board of directors alone pursuant to that authorization; ~~(6)~~ and (F) if shareholder action was required to revoke the dissolution, the information required by subdivision (3) of subsection (a) of section 33–882, as amended; and ~~(7)~~ (2) if the name of the corporation whose dissolution is to be revoked is no longer available, ~~be~~ is accompanied by an amendment of the certificate of incorporation which changes the name of the corporation to an available name.

Sec. 53. Subsection (c) of section 33–1173 of the general statutes, as amended by section 50 of public act 03–18, is repealed and the following is substituted in lieu thereof (Effective from passage):

(c) After the revocation of dissolution is authorized, the corporation may revoke the dissolution by delivering to the Secretary of the State for filing a certificate of revocation of dissolution that (1) sets forth: ~~(1)~~ (A) The name of the corporation; ~~(2)~~ (B) the effective date of the dissolution that was revoked; ~~(3)~~ (C) the date that the revocation of dissolution was authorized; ~~(4)~~ (D) if the corporation's board of directors, or incorporators, revoked the dissolution, a statement to that effect; ~~(5)~~ (E) if the corporation's board of directors revoked a dissolution authorized by members, a statement that revocation was permitted by action of the board of directors alone pursuant to that authorization; ~~(6)~~ and (F) if member action was required to revoke the dissolution, the information required by subdivision (3) of subsection (a) of section 33–1172, as amended; and ~~(7)~~ (2) if the name of the corporation whose dissolution is to be revoked is no longer available, ~~be~~ is accompanied by an amendment of the certificate of incorporation which changes the name of the corporation to an available name.

Sec. 54. Subsection (c) of section 34–38p of the general statutes is repealed and the following is substituted in lieu thereof (Effective from passage):

(c) A foreign limited partnership's appointment of the ~~secretary of the state~~ Secretary of the State and his successors in office as its initial agent upon whom process may be served shall be included in the application for registration as provided in section 34–38g. A subsequent appointment of the Secretary of the State and his successors in office as a foreign limited partnership's agent upon whom process may be served shall be filed in the office of the Secretary of the State in such form as the secretary shall prescribe.

Sec. 55. Subdivision (14) of section 34–101 of the general statutes, as amended by section 61 of public act 03–18, is repealed and the following is substituted in lieu thereof (Effective from passage):

(14) "Member" or "members" means a person or persons who have been admitted to membership in a limited liability company as provided in section 34–179 and who ~~has~~ have not disassociated from the limited liability company as provided in section 34–180.

Sec. 56. Subsection (b) of section 34–406 of the general statutes is repealed and the following is substituted in lieu thereof (Effective from passage):

(b) The name of a registered limited liability partnership or foreign registered limited liability partnership shall be such as to distinguish it upon the records of the Secretary of the State from: (1) The name of any registered limited liability partnership, limited partnership, limited liability company or corporation existing under the laws of this state; (2) the name of any foreign registered limited liability partnership, foreign limited partnership, foreign limited liability company or foreign corporation authorized to transact business in this state; or (3) any name reserved under section 34–407 or reserved or registered under section 33–656, 33–657, 33–1045, 33–1046, 33–1047, 34–13 or 34–103. ~~or subsection (a) of section 34–13.~~

Sec. 57. Subdivision (3) of subsection (a) of section 36a–468a of the general statutes, as amended by section 69 of public act 03–84, is repealed and the following is substituted in lieu thereof (Effective from passage):

(3) A terminating Connecticut credit union shall give written notice of the date, time and place of the meeting at which its members shall vote on the plan of merger. Such notice shall state that the purpose of the meeting is to consider the plan of merger and contain or be accompanied by a copy or summary of the plan. The notice shall be hand-delivered or mailed to each member at such member's last-known address as shown on the records of the credit union not less than thirty ~~nor~~ or more than fifty days prior to the date of the meeting. Unless waived by the commissioner in accordance with subdivision (2) of subsection (b) of this subsection, the affirmative vote of two-thirds of the members of the terminating Connecticut credit union voting on the plan of merger shall be required for approval of the merger. The terminating Connecticut credit union shall file with the commissioner a verified statement that the merger has been duly noticed and approved by its members in accordance with this subdivision.

Sec. 58. Subsection (c) of section 36a–468b of the general statutes, as amended by section 70 of public act 03–84, is repealed and the following is substituted in lieu thereof (Effective from passage):

(c) The converting Connecticut credit union shall give written notice of the date, time and place of the meeting at which the plan of conversion is to be considered, which notice shall be hand-delivered or mailed to each member of the converting Connecticut credit union at such member's last-known address as shown on the records of such Connecticut credit union not less than thirty ~~nor~~ or more than fifty days prior to the date of the meeting.

Sec. 59. Subdivision (4) of subsection (a) of section 36a–469c of the general statutes, as amended by section 72 of public act 03–84 and section 17 of public act 03–196, is repealed and the following is substituted in lieu thereof (Effective from passage):

(4) In the case of a converting Connecticut credit union, the plan of conversion shall require the approval of a majority of the governing board. After approving the plan of conversion, the governing board of the converting Connecticut credit union shall establish the date and time of a regular or special meeting of members for vote on the proposal. Written notice of the meeting at which the proposal is to be considered together with a mail ballot and a disclosure statement shall be hand-delivered or mailed to each member, at such member's last-known address as shown on the records of the converting Connecticut credit union, not more than thirty days ~~nor~~ or less than fourteen days prior to the date of the meeting. The disclosure statement shall include, at a minimum, a description of (A) the reasons for the proposed conversion; (B) the differences between membership rights in the converting credit union and depositor rights in the proposed mutual savings bank, mutual savings and loan association or mutual community bank; and (C) the significant differences between the authorized powers of the converting credit union and those of the proposed mutual savings bank, mutual savings and loan association or mutual community bank. The notice, disclosure statement and mail ballot shall be submitted to the commissioner for approval prior to distribution to members. Each member of the converting Connecticut credit union may cast one vote on the proposal. The affirmative vote of two-thirds of all the members voting, including those votes cast

in person and those ballots properly completed and received by the converting Connecticut credit union prior to the time of the meeting, shall be required for approval of the conversion.

Sec. 60. Subsection (b) of section 36a–470a of the general statutes, as amended by section 73 of public act 03–84, is repealed and the following is substituted in lieu thereof (Effective from passage):

(b) Within three days after a majority of the governing board has adopted a plan of dissolution of the Connecticut credit union, the governing board shall file with the commissioner a copy of such plan of dissolution, attested by the chairman or vice chairman and the secretary or treasurer, and inform the commissioner of the date on which the plan will be voted on by the members of the Connecticut credit union. The plan of dissolution shall be approved at an annual or special meeting of the members. Written notice of the date, time and place of the meeting at which the plan of dissolution is to be considered shall be hand-delivered or mailed to each member at such member's last-known address as shown on the records of the Connecticut credit union, not more than thirty ~~nor~~ or less than seven days prior to the date of the vote. The written notice shall clearly describe the plan and the reasons for the plan and shall notify the member of such member's right to vote on the plan in person, by proxy or by mail ballot, and shall have an official form of proxy or mail ballot attached. The affirmative vote of two-thirds of those members voting shall be required to approve the proposal. Upon receipt of the filing, the commissioner may by order appoint the National Credit Union Administration or its successor agency to act as liquidating agent.

Sec. 61. Section 36b–41 of the general statutes, as amended by section 88 of public act 03–19 and section 27 of public act 03–84, is repealed and the following is substituted in lieu thereof (Effective from passage):

Except as otherwise provided in sections 36b–40 to 36b–52, inclusive, all terms used in said sections shall have the meanings ascribed to them under section 36–321 of the general statutes, revision of 1958, revised to January 1, 1977. As used in said sections:

(1) "Target company" means any stock corporation which is organized under the laws of this state, has its principal executive office in this state and has, on a consolidated basis, five hundred or more employees and fifty million dollars of tangible assets in this state, other than: (A) A domestic insurance company, as defined in section 38a–1, as amended; (B) a bank, as defined in subdivision (3) of subsection (a) of section 36–419 of the general statutes, revision of 1958, revised to January 1, 1993, or a bank holding company, as defined in subdivision (1) of subsection (a) of section 36–419 of the general statutes, revision of 1958, revised to January 1, 1993; (C) a public utility company or a holding company, as defined in Section 2 of the Federal Public Utility Holding Company Act of 1935, presently constituted as Section 79b of Title 15 of the United States Code, an acquisition of or by, or merger with which, is subject to approval by the appropriate federal agency as provided in said act; (D) a bank or bank holding company subject to the Federal Bank Holding Company Act of 1956, presently constituted as Section 1841 et seq. of Title 12 of the United States Code, an acquisition of or by, or merger with which, is subject to approval by the appropriate federal agency as provided in said act; or (E) a savings and loan holding company, as defined in Section 2 of the Federal Savings and Loan Holding Company Amendments of 1967, presently constituted as Section 1730a of Title 12 of the United States Code, an acquisition of or by, or merger with which, is subject to approval by the appropriate federal agency as provided in said act.

(2) "Equity security" means (A) any stock or similar security carrying, at the time of the tender offer, the right to vote on any matter by virtue of the certificate of incorporation, bylaws or governing instrument of the target company or the right to vote for directors or persons performing substantially similar functions by operation of law; (B) any security, including debt securities, convertible into such stock or similar security; (C) any warrant or right to purchase such stock or similar security; (D) any security carrying any warrant to purchase such stock or similar security; or (E) any other security which for the protection of investors is deemed an equity security pursuant to regulation of the commissioner.

(3) "Offeror" means a person who makes or in any way participates in making a tender offer, and includes all affiliates and associates of that person. The term does not include a financial institution, a broker or dealer loaning funds or extending credit to any offeror in the ordinary course of its business, or any accountant, attorney, financial institution, broker, dealer, newspaper or magazine of general circulation, consultant or other person furnishing services or advice to or performing ministerial or administrative duties for an offeror and not otherwise participating in the takeover offer.

(4) "Affiliate" of a person means any person controlling, controlled by ~~,~~ or under common control with that person.

(5) "Associate" of a person means any person acting jointly or in concert with that person for the purpose of acquiring, holding or disposing of, or exercising any voting rights attached to, the equity securities of a target company.

(6) "Control", including the terms "controlling", "controlled by" ~~,~~ and "under common control with", means the possession of the power to direct or cause the direction of the management and policies of a person unless the power is the result of an official position or office.

(7) "Offeree" means a record or beneficial owner of equity securities which an offeror acquires or offers to acquire in connection with a tender offer.

(8) "Tender offer" means the offer to acquire, or the acquisition of, any equity security of a target company, pursuant to a tender offer or request or invitation for tenders, if after acquisition the offeror would be directly or indirectly a record or beneficial owner of more than ten per cent of any class of the outstanding equity securities of the target company, but shall not include: (A) A bid made by a dealer for that dealer's own account in the ordinary course of that dealer's business of buying and selling such equity securities; (B) broker transactions effected by or through a broker or dealer in the ordinary course of its business; (C) an offer to exchange the securities of one issuer for the securities of another issuer, if the offer is registered or exempt from registration under the Federal Securities Act of 1933; [1] (D) any offer to acquire such equity securities for the sole account of the offeror if there are no more than one hundred record owners of the voting securities of the target company at the time of the offer; (E) an offer which, if accepted by all offerees, will not result in the offeror having acquired more than two per cent of the same class of equity securities of the issuer within the preceding twelve-month period; (F) an offer by the issuer to acquire its own equity securities; (G) an isolated offer to purchase equity securities from individual security holders and not made to security holders generally; (H) an offer involving a vote of shareholders of the target company on a merger, consolidation or sale of corporate assets in consideration of cash or the issuance of securities of another corporation; and (I) any offer which the commissioner, by regulation or order, and after notice to the offeror and target company, shall exempt from the definition of tender offer as not being entered into for the purpose of, and not having the effect of, changing or influencing the control of the target company or otherwise as not comprehended within the purposes of sections 36b–40 to 36b–52, inclusive.

(9) "Commissioner" means the Banking Commissioner or any person designated by the Banking Commissioner to administer sections 36b–40 to 36b–52, inclusive.

(10) "Schedule 14D–1" means the schedule 14D–1 as prescribed by the Securities and Exchange Commission or such other form pertaining to disclosures in tender offers as the commissioner by regulation, rule or order may designate.

[1] 15 U.S.C.A. § 77a et seq.

Sec. 62. Section 38a–475 of the general statutes is repealed and the following is substituted in lieu thereof (Effective from passage):

The Insurance Department shall only precertify long-term care insurance policies which (1) alert the purchaser to the availability of consumer information and public education provided by the Department of Social Services pursuant to section ~~17a–307~~ 17b–251; (2) offer the option of home and community-based services in addition to nursing home care; (3) in all home care plans, include case management services delivered by an access agency approved by the Office of Policy and Management and the Department of Social Services as meeting the requirements for such agency as defined in regulations adopted pursuant to subsection (e) of section 17b–342, which services shall include, but need not be limited to, the development of a comprehensive individualized assessment and care plan and, as needed, the coordination of appropriate services and the monitoring of the delivery of such services; (4) provide inflation protection; (5) provide for the keeping of records and an explanation of benefit reports on insurance payments which count toward Medicaid resource exclusion; and (6) provide the management information and reports necessary to document the extent of Medicaid resource protection offered and to evaluate the Connecticut Partnership for Long-Term Care. No policy shall be precertified if it requires prior hospitalization or a prior stay in a nursing home as a condition of providing benefits. The commissioner may adopt regulations, in accordance with chapter 54, [1] to carry out the precertification provisions of this section.

[1] C.G.S.A. § 4–166 et seq.

Sec. 63. Subdivision (c) of section 38a–556 of the general statutes, as amended by section 68 of public act 03–6 of the June 30 special session, is repealed and the following is substituted in lieu thereof (Effective from passage):

(c) Every member shall participate in the association in accordance with the provisions of this subdivision. (1) A participating member shall determine the particular risks it elects to have written by or through the association. A member shall designate which of the following classes of risks it shall underwrite in the state, from which classes of risk it may elect to reinsure selected risks: (A) Individual, excluding group conversion; and (B) individual, including group conversion. (2) No member shall be permitted to select out individual lives from an employer group to be insured by or through the association. Members electing to administer risks which are insured by or through the association shall comply with the benefit determination guidelines and the accounting procedures established by the association. A risk insured by or through the association cannot be withdrawn by the participating member except in accordance with the rules established by the association. (3) Rates for coverage issued by or through the association shall not be excessive, inadequate or unfairly discriminatory. Separate scales of premium rates based on age shall apply, but rates shall not be adjusted for area variations in provider costs. Premium rates shall take into consideration the substantial extra morbidity and administrative expenses for association risks, reimbursement or reasonable expenses incurred for the writing of association risks and the level of rates charged by insurers for groups of ten lives, provided incurred losses which result from provision of coverage in accordance with section 38a–537 shall not be considered. In no event shall the rate for a given classification or group be less than one hundred twenty-five per cent ~~nor~~ or more than one hundred fifty per cent of the average rate charged for that classification with similar characteristics under a policy covering ten lives. All rates shall be promulgated by the association through an actuarial committee consisting of five persons who are members of the American Academy of Actuaries, shall be filed with the commissioner and may be disapproved within sixty days from the filing thereof if excessive, inadequate , or unfairly discriminatory.

Sec. 64. Subsection (d) of section 38a–702g of the general statutes is repealed and the following is substituted in lieu thereof (Effective from passage):

(d) Notwithstanding any other provision of sections 38a–702a to 38a–702r, inclusive, a person licensed as a surplus lines broker in the person's home state shall receive a nonresident surplus lines broker license pursuant to subsection (a) of this section. Except as provided in subsection (a) of this section, nothing in this section otherwise amends or ~~supercedes~~ supersedes any provision of sections 38a–740 to 38a–745, inclusive.

Sec. 65. Subsection (b) of section 38a–981 of the general statutes, as amended by section 3 of public act 03–119, is repealed and the following is substituted in lieu thereof (Effective from passage):

(b)(1) An insurance institution or a third-party administrator providing insurance or administrative services with respect to an employer's employee benefit plan which provides its employees with health benefits shall, upon written request of an exclusive bargaining agent for such employees, provide such bargaining agent with information regarding description of health benefits available to such employees, claim experience regarding such benefits and the cost to the employer for such coverage or administrative services, as the case may be, for employees in the bargaining unit represented by such bargaining agent. If such employees constitute a subgroup of a multi-bargaining-unit group, the information provided by the ~~insurer~~ insurance institution or administrator shall, upon written request of the exclusive bargaining agent for the subgroup, include a description of available health benefits, claim experience regarding such benefits and the cost to the employer for such coverage or administrative services, as the case may be, for the entire multi-bargaining-unit group or for subgroups within the multi-bargaining-unit group. A copy of such information shall be provided at the same time to the employer by the insurance institution or administrator. Such information shall be made available to the bargaining agent and the employer only if the bargaining agent agrees in writing to pay all reasonable costs, as determined by the insurance institution or administrator, that are incurred by the insurance institution or administrator in developing and distributing the information. The information provided to such agent shall relate to the group of employees as a whole and shall not include any information relating to specific individuals. No requests made pursuant to this subdivision may seek information which relates to a period of time more than twenty-four months prior to the date such request was made.

(2) Prior to providing any information pursuant to subdivision (1) of this subsection, an insurance institution or third-party administrator may require the bargaining agent requesting such information to provide evidence in writing that such bargaining agent is currently designated or certified by the proper state or federal authority as the exclusive bargaining representative or agent of the employees who are the subject of the request.

(3) The provisions of this subsection shall not apply to employees participating in an employee welfare benefit plan subject to the provisions of Title I of the Employee Retirement Income Security Act of 1974 (ERISA), Public Law 93–406, [1] as amended from time to time, or to the exclusive bargaining agents of such employees.

[1] 29 U.S.C.A. § 1001 et seq.

Sec. 66. Subsections (c) and (d) of section 45a–8 of the general statutes are repealed and the following is substituted in lieu thereof (Effective from passage):

(c) If suitable court facilities are not provided in accordance with subsection (a) or (b) of this section: ~~, (1) the~~ (1) The Probate Court Administrator shall submit a report to the joint standing committee of ~~cognizance of~~ the General Assembly having cognizance of matters relating to the judiciary concerning the failure of the probate district to provide the required court facilities, together with a recommendation that the probate district be abolished as a separate district and be consolidated with a contiguous district where suitable court facilities can be provided; or (2) if, in the opinion of the Probate Court Administrator, abolition of the district is not in the public interest and judicial action is necessary to enforce the provision of suitable court facilities, the Probate Court Administrator shall bring an action in the Superior Court to enforce the requirements for the provision of suitable court facilities.

(d) Any town located in a probate district that desires to (1) consolidate such probate district with one or more districts, (2) be removed from such probate district to a separate district established for any such town, or (3) be located in another probate district, may, by resolution of its legislative body, petition the General Assembly for such consolidation, separation and creation of a new probate district or relocation. The Probate Court Administrator shall provide such assistance in the preparation of the petition as the officials of the town or towns may request. At the time of submission of a petition to the General Assembly, a copy of the petition shall be sent to the judges of probate in the probate districts to be affected. No probate district may be consolidated with another district until the expiration of the term of office of any probate judge in an affected probate district.

Sec. 67. Subsection (b) of section 45a–78 of the general statutes is repealed and the following is substituted in lieu thereof (Effective from passage):

(b) The Probate Court Administrator shall, from time to time, compile into a probate practice book all rules regarding practice and procedure in the courts of probate ~~,~~ and all forms prescribed for use in probate courts. ~~He~~ The Probate Court Administrator shall cause the probate practice book to be published, shall pay for the probate practice book from the ~~trust~~ fund ~~provided for by~~ established under section 45a–82, as amended, and shall sell the probate practice book, at a price determined by ~~him~~ the Probate Court Administrator. The proceeds from the sales shall be added to and shall become a part of ~~such trust~~ said fund.

Sec. 68. Section 45a–80 of the general statutes is repealed and the following is substituted in lieu thereof (Effective from passage):

(a) The Commissioner of Public Works shall provide such office space for the conduct of the duties of the office of the Probate Court Administrator as the ~~administrator~~ Probate Court Administrator approves. The expenses of the office space shall be paid from the ~~trust~~ fund established under section 45a–82, as amended.

(b) The Probate Court Administrator shall purchase furniture, stationery, office supplies, typewriters, filing cabinets and ~~whatever~~ such other equipment, apparatus and supplies, contractual services and other services as the Probate Court Administrator deems necessary or advisable for the expeditious conduct of the duties of the office and shall pay for them from the ~~trust~~ fund established under section 45a–82, as amended, subject to the provisions of section 45a–83.

Sec. 69. Subsection (i) of section 45a–82 of the general statutes is repealed and the following is substituted in lieu thereof (Effective from passage):

(i) The State Treasurer shall, on or before October first, annually, give an accounting of the Probate Court Administration Fund, showing the receipts and disbursements and the balance or condition thereof, as of the preceding June thirtieth, to the Connecticut Probate Assembly and to the joint standing committee ~~on~~ of the General Assembly having cognizance of matters relating to the judiciary.

Sec. 70. Section 45a–83 of the general statutes is repealed and the following is substituted in lieu thereof (Effective from passage):

If at any time the ~~trust~~ fund established ~~by~~ under section 45a–82, as amended, is insufficient to pay the several charges to be paid from it, the Comptroller shall draw his order on the Treasurer for payment, from the General Fund, of such sums as are necessary to pay such charges. When the amount in the ~~trust~~ fund established ~~by~~ under said section is more than sufficient to meet the requirements imposed upon it by law, other than amounts which are required to make the retirement fund established ~~by~~ under section 45a–35 actuarially sound, all as certified by the Probate Court Administrator, there shall be paid over to the General Fund from the ~~trust~~ fund established ~~by~~ under section 45a–82, as amended, any moneys paid from the General Fund under this section.

Sec. 71. Section 45a–668 of the general statutes, as amended by section 1 of public act 03–51, is repealed and the following is substituted in lieu thereof (Effective from passage):

Guardians of the property, and limited guardians of the property, of persons who are not minors and who are persons with mental retardation, appointed as such guardians or limited guardians under chapter 779a [1] prior to October 1, 1982, shall serve on or after October 1, 1982, as conservators of the estates of such persons as if appointed conservators under the provisions of sections 45a–644 to 45a–662, inclusive, and in accordance with the provisions of said sections. Any guardian of the person or property of a ~~minor person who is mentally retarded~~ person with mental retardation who is a minor, appointed under chapter 779a, prior to October 1, 1982, may continue to serve as such guardian on or after October 1, 1982, as if appointed under and in accordance with the provisions of sections 45a–132, 45a–593 to 45a–597, inclusive, 45a–603 to 45a–662, inclusive, or 45a–629 to 45a–638, inclusive, relative to guardians of minors. Such guardianship shall terminate upon the ~~minor~~ minor's reaching the age of eighteen. Continuation of the guardianship of the estate shall be by application made pursuant to the provisions of sections 45a–644 to 45a–662, inclusive. Continuation of the guardianship of the person shall be by application made pursuant to the provisions of sections 45a–668 to 45a–684, inclusive. Any guardian of the person of a person with mental retardation who is not a minor, appointed under chapter 779a prior to October 1, 1982, may continue to serve as such guardian after October 1, 1982. Upon filing of a periodic account by any guardian appointed under the provisions of chapter 779a, prior to October 1, 1982, the court shall require a probate bond in the same manner as under sections 45a–132, 45a–593 to 45a–597, inclusive, 45a–603 to 45a–622, inclusive, 45a–629 to 45a–638, inclusive, or 45a–644 to 45a–662, inclusive. Failure to furnish a probate bond or written acceptance of guardianship required under the provisions of said sections ~~,~~ shall be cause for termination of the continued service of the fiduciary provided for in this section.

[1] C.G.S.A. § 45–78a et seq.

Sec. 72. Subdivision (5) of section 46a–11 of the general statutes, as amended by section 1 of public act 03–88, is repealed and the following is substituted in lieu thereof (Effective from passage):

(5) Request and receive information, including personal data, concerning a person with a disability from any state or private agency, with the consent of such person with a disability, or the parent or guardian of such person, as appropriate. With respect to a developmentally disabled adult who has no guardian or whose guardian is an employee of the Department of Mental Retardation, the director may request and receive such information only if:

(A) A request for advocacy services has been made on ~~his~~ such person's behalf;

(B) Such person does not indicate refusal to give consent to receipt to the information by the director;

(C) Such person resides in a facility for developmentally disabled persons, including any institution, as defined in subsection (a) of section 19a–490, as amended, or has been placed in a boarding home, group home or other residential facility pursuant to section 17a–277;

(D) Such person has received an explanation of the manner in which any information obtained concerning ~~him~~ such person will be used by the advocacy office;

(E) Such person has received an explanation of ~~his~~ such person's right to refuse to allow the director to request or receive such information; ~~,~~ and

(F) The director has documented ~~his~~ the director's conscientious efforts to provide the required explanations and verified that the developmentally disabled person has not indicated refusal to give consent.

Sec. 73. Section 46b–35 of the general statutes is repealed and the following is substituted in lieu thereof (Effective from passage):

The certificates required by sections 46b–24, ~~to 46b–27, inclusive,~~ as amended, 46b–24a, as amended, 46b–25 and 46b–29 to 46b–34, inclusive, or an affidavit recorded pursuant to subsection (b) of section 46b–34, shall be prima facie evidence of the facts stated in them.

Sec. 74. Subdivision (2) of subsection (a) of section 46b–220 of the general statutes is repealed and the following is substituted in lieu thereof (Effective from passage):

(2) "License" means each license, certification or permit to engage in a profession or occupation regulated pursuant to the provisions of title 19a, 20 or 21, a motor vehicle operator's license or a commercial driver's license issued by the Commissioner of Motor Vehicles in accordance with chapter 246, [1] and ~~licensees~~ licenses and permits issued by the Department of Environmental Protection pursuant to part III of chapter 490. [2] ~~of title 26;~~

1 C.G.S.A. § 14–1 et seq.
2 C.G.S.A. § 26–27 et seq.

Sec. 75. Section 47–34a of the general statutes, as amended by section 82 of public act 03–115, is repealed and the following is substituted in lieu thereof (Effective from passage):

(a) Any person who knowingly injures, destroys, disturbs or removes any marker properly placed on any tract of land or street or highway line by a surveyor, or by any person at the direction of a surveyor, for the purpose of designating any point, course or line in the boundary of such tract of land, street or highway, shall be fined not less than five hundred dollars ~~nor~~ or more than one thousand dollars.

(b) Notwithstanding the provisions of subsection (a) of this section, a surveyor licensed under chapter 391, [1] or a person acting at the direction of any such licensed surveyor, may remove an existing marker in order to place an upgraded marker in the same location.

(c) Any person who knowingly injures, destroys, disturbs or removes any monument that has been established by the National Geodetic Survey or Connecticut Geodetic Survey for use in the determination of spatial location relative to the Connecticut coordinate systems specified in section 13a–255, as amended, or precise elevation datum shall be fined not less than two thousand dollars ~~nor~~ or more than five thousand dollars.

1 C.G.S.A. § 20–299 et seq.

Sec. 76. Subsection (b) of section 49–15 of the general statutes, as amended by section 9 of public act 03–202, is repealed and the following is substituted in lieu thereof (Effective from passage):

(b) Upon the filing of a bankruptcy petition by a mortgagor under Chapter 13 of Title 11 of the United States Code, [1] any judgment against the mortgagor foreclosing the title to real estate by strict foreclosure shall be opened automatically without action by any party or the court, provided, the provisions of such judgment, other than the establishment of law days, shall not be set aside under this subsection; but no such judgment shall be opened after the title has become absolute in any encumbrancer or the mortgagee, or any person claiming under such encumbrancer or mortgagee. The mortgagor shall file a copy of the bankruptcy petition, or an affidavit setting forth the date the bankruptcy petition was filed, with the clerk of the court in which the foreclosure matter is pending. Upon the ~~determination~~ termination of the automatic stay authorized pursuant to 11 USC 362, the mortgagor shall file with such clerk an affidavit setting forth the date the stay was terminated.

1 11 U.S.C.A. § 1301 et seq.

Sec. 77. Subsection (a) of section 49–55a of the general statutes is repealed and the following is substituted in lieu thereof (Effective from passage):

(a) Upon the possession of the vessel by a lienor, he shall cause a notice of a vessel lien, in quadruplicate, to be filed on a form provided by the Secretary of the State with the office of ~~said~~ the secretary on which he shall also indicate the date and place of the sale of the vessel, which date of sale shall be at least sixty days next succeeding the filing of the notice. The lienor shall, within seven days of the filing, send by certified mail a copy of ~~this~~ such notice to the person indicated as the owner of the vessel, and to anyone who has filed with the Secretary of the State claiming a legal or equitable interest in the vessel. The fees for ~~this~~ such notice and procedure shall be set by the Secretary of the State.

Sec. 78. Subsection (a) of section 49–92h of the general statutes is repealed and the following is substituted in lieu thereof (Effective from passage):

(a) Upon the possession of the aircraft by a lienor, he shall cause a notice of an aircraft lien, in quadruplicate, to be filed on a form provided by the Secretary of the State with the office of ~~said~~ the secretary on which he shall also indicate the date and place of the sale of the aircraft, which date of sale shall be at least sixty days next succeeding the filing of the notice. The lienor shall, within seven days of the filing, send by certified mail a copy of ~~this~~ such notice to the person indicated as the owner of the aircraft, and to anyone who has filed with the Secretary of the State claiming a legal or equitable interest in the aircraft. The fees for ~~this~~ such notice and procedure shall be set by the ~~secretary of the state~~ Secretary of the State.

Sec. 79. Subsection (d) of section 52–50 of the general statutes is repealed and the following is substituted in lieu thereof (Effective from passage):

(d) Service of motions for modification, motions for contempt and wage withholdings in any matter involving child support, including, but not limited to, petitions for support authorized under sections ~~17b–748~~ 17b–745, as amended, and 46b–215, as amended, and those matters involving a beneficiary of care or assistance from the state, may be made by a support enforcement officer or support services investigator of the Superior Court.

Sec. 80. Section 52–367a of the general statutes, as amended by section 48 of public act 03–2, section 22 of public act 03–62, section 40 of public act 03–84 and section 12 of public act 03–224, is repealed and the following is substituted in lieu thereof (Effective from passage):

(a) As used in this section and section 52–367b, as amended, "financial institution" means any bank, savings bank, savings and loan association or credit union organized, chartered or licensed under the laws of this state or the United States and having its main office in this state, or any similar out-of-state institution having a branch office in this state.

(b) Execution may be granted pursuant to this section against any debts due from any financial institution to a judgment debtor which is not a natural person. If execution is desired against any such debt, the plaintiff requesting the execution shall make application to the clerk of the court. The application shall be accompanied by a fee of thirty-five dollars payable to the clerk of the court for the administrative costs of complying with the provisions of this section which fee may be recoverable by the judgment creditor as a taxable cost of the action. The clerk shall issue such execution containing a direction that the officer serving such execution shall make demand (1) upon the main office of any financial institution having its main office within the county of the serving officer, or (2) if such main office is not within the serving officer's county and such financial institution has one or more branch offices within such county, upon an employee of such a branch office, such employee and branch office having been designated by the financial institution in accordance with regulations adopted by the Banking Commissioner, in accordance with chapter 54,[1] for the payment of any debt due to the judgment debtor, and, after having made such demand, shall serve a true and attested copy thereof, with the serving officer's actions thereon endorsed, with the financial institution officer upon whom such demand is made.

(c) If any such financial institution upon which such execution is served and upon which such demand is made is indebted to the judgment debtor, the ~~banking~~ financial institution shall remove from the judgment debtor's account the amount of such indebtedness not exceeding the amount due on such execution. Except as provided in subsection (d) of this section, the ~~banking~~ financial institution shall immediately pay to such serving officer the amount removed from the judgment debtor's account, which amount shall be received and applied on such execution by such serving officer. Such financial institution shall act upon such execution according to section 42a–4–303 before its midnight deadline, as defined in section 42a–4–104. Nothing in this subsection shall be construed to affect any other rights or obligations of the ~~banking~~ financial institution with regard to funds in the judgment debtor's account.

(d) If the deposit account is subject to a security interest of a secured party, other than the ~~banking~~ financial institution upon which such execution is served and upon which such demand is made, pursuant to a control agreement between the ~~banking~~ financial institution and such secured party under article 9 of title 42a,[2] and if any funds are removed from the judgment debtor's account pursuant to subsection (c) of this section, the ~~banking~~ financial institution shall forthwith mail a copy of the execution when received from the serving officer, postage prepaid, to the judgment debtor and to such other secured party at the last known address of such parties with respect to the affected accounts on the records of the ~~banking~~ financial institution. The ~~banking~~ financial institution shall hold the amount removed from the judgment debtor's account pursuant to subsection (c) of this section for twenty days from the date of the mailing to the judgment debtor and such other secured party, and during such period shall not pay the serving officer.

(e) To prevent the ~~banking~~ financial institution from paying the serving officer, as provided in subsection (h) of this section, such other secured party shall give notice of its prior perfected security interest in such deposit account, by delivering to the clerk of the court that issued the execution a written claim for determination of interests in property pursuant to section 52–356c and by delivering a copy of such claim to the ~~banking~~ financial institution upon which such execution is served.

(f) Upon receipt of a written claim for determination of interests in property made pursuant to subsection (e) of this section, the clerk of the court shall enter the appearance of the secured party with the address set forth in the written claim. The clerk shall forthwith send file-stamped copies of the written claim to the judgment creditor, the judgment debtor and the ~~banking~~ financial institution upon which such execution was served with a notice stating that the disputed funds are being held until a court order is entered regarding the disposition of the funds.

(g) If a written claim for determination of interests in property is made pursuant to subsection (e) of this section, the ~~banking~~ financial institution shall continue to hold the amount removed from the judgment debtor's account until a court order is received regarding disposition of the funds.

(h) If no written claim for determination of interests in property is made pursuant to subsection (e) of this section, the ~~banking~~ financial institution shall, upon demand, forthwith pay the serving officer the amount removed from the judgment debtor's account, and the serving officer shall thereupon pay such sum, less such serving officer's fees, to the judgment creditor, except to the extent otherwise ordered by a court.

(i) If a written claim for determination of interests in property is made pursuant to subsection (e) of this section, the clerk of the court, after a judgment or order is entered pursuant to section 52–356c, shall forthwith send a copy of such judgment or order to the ~~banking~~ financial institution. Such judgment or order shall be deemed to be a final judgment for the purposes of appeal. No appeal shall be taken except within seven days of the rendering of the judgment or order. The judgment or order of the court may be implemented during such seven-day period, unless stayed by the court.

(j) If records or testimony are subpoenaed from a ~~banking~~ financial institution in connection with a hearing conducted pursuant to section 52–356c on a written claim for determination of interests in property made pursuant to subsection (e) of this section, the reasonable costs and expenses of the ~~banking~~ financial institution in complying with the subpoena shall be recoverable by the ~~banking~~ financial institution from the party requiring such records or testimony, provided the ~~banking~~ financial institution shall be under no obligation to attempt to obtain records or documentation relating to the account executed against that are held by any other ~~banking~~ financial institution. The records of a ~~banking~~ financial institution as to the dates and amounts of deposits into an account in the ~~banking~~ financial institution shall, if certified as true and accurate by an officer of the ~~banking~~ financial institution, be admissible as evidence without the presence of the officer in any hearing conducted pursuant to section 52–356c to determine the legitimacy of a claim of an interest in property made under subsection (e) of this section.

(k) If such financial institution fails or refuses to pay over to such serving officer the amount of such debt, not exceeding the amount due on such execution, such financial institution shall be liable in an action therefor to the judgment creditor named in such execution, and the amount so recovered by such judgment creditor shall be applied toward the payment of the amount due on such execution.

(*l*) Except as provided in subsection (k) of this section, no ~~banking~~ financial institution or any officer, director or employee of such ~~banking~~ financial institution shall be liable to any person with respect to any act done or omitted in good faith or through the commission of a bona fide error that occurred despite reasonable procedures maintained by the ~~banking~~ financial institution to prevent such errors in complying with the provisions of this section.

(m) Nothing in this section shall in any way restrict the rights and remedies otherwise available to a judgment debtor or to any such secured party at law or in equity.

[1] C.G.S.A. § 4–166 et seq.
[2] C.G.S.A. § 42a–9–101 et seq.

Sec. 81. Subsections (d) and (e) of section 52–367b of the general statutes, as amended by section 23 of public act 03–62 and section 13 of public act 03–224, are repealed and the following is substituted in lieu thereof (Effective from passage):

(d) If any funds are removed from the judgment debtor's account pursuant to subsection (c) of this section, upon receipt of the execution and exemption claim form from the serving officer, the financial institution shall forthwith mail copies thereof, postage prepaid, to the judgment debtor and to any secured party that is party to a control agreement between the ~~banking~~ financial institution and such secured party under article 9 of title 42a[1] at the last known address of the judgment debtor and of any such secured party with respect to the affected accounts on the records of the financial institution. The financial institution shall hold the amount removed from the judgment debtor's account pursuant to subsection (c) of this section for fifteen days from the date of the mailing to the judgment debtor and any such secured party, and during such period shall not pay the serving officer.

(e) To prevent the financial institution from paying the serving officer, as provided in subsection (h) of this section, the judgment debtor shall give notice of a claim of exemption by delivering to the financial institution, by mail or other means, the exemption claim form or other written notice that an exemption is being claimed and any such secured party shall give notice of its claim of a prior perfected security interest in such deposit account by delivering to the ~~banking~~ financial institution, by mail or other means, written notice thereof. The financial institution may designate an address to which the notice of a claim of exemption, or a secured party claim notice, shall be delivered. Upon receipt of such notice, the financial institution shall, within two business days, send a copy of such notice to the clerk of the court which issued the execution.

[1] C.G.S.A. § 42a–9–101 et seq.

Sec. 82. Subsection (a) of section 53–304 of the general statutes is repealed and the following is substituted in lieu thereof (Effective from passage):

(a) Any person who neglects or refuses to furnish reasonably necessary support to the person's spouse, child under the age of eighteen or parent under the age of sixty-five shall be deemed guilty of nonsupport and shall be imprisoned not more than one year, unless the person shows to the court before which the trial is had that, owing to physical incapacity or other good cause, the person is unable to furnish such support. ~~Such~~ The court may suspend the execution of any community correctional center sentence imposed, upon any terms or conditions that it deems just, may suspend the execution of the balance of any such sentence in a like manner, and, in addition to any other sentence or in lieu thereof, may order that the person convicted shall pay to the Commissioner of Administrative Services directly or through Support Enforcement Services of the Superior Court, such support, in such amount as the court may find commensurate with the necessities of the case and the ability of such person, for such period as the court shall determine. Any such order of support may, at any time thereafter, be set aside or altered by ~~such~~ the court for cause shown. Failure of any defendant to make any payment may be punished as contempt of court and, in addition thereto or in lieu thereof, the court may order the issuance of a wage withholding in the same manner as is provided in section ~~17b–748,~~ 17b–745, as amended, which withholding order shall have the same precedence as is provided in section 52–362, as amended. The amounts withheld under such withholding order shall be remitted to the Department of Administrative Services by the person or corporation to whom the withholding order is presented at such intervals as such withholding order directs. For the purposes of this section, ~~the term~~ "child" ~~shall include~~ includes one born out of wedlock whose father has acknowledged in writing his paternity of such child or has been adjudged the father by a court of competent jurisdiction.

Sec. 83. Subsection (b) of section 54–1m of the general statutes, as amended by section 1 of public act 03–160, is repealed and the following is substituted in lieu thereof (Effective from passage):

(b) Commencing on January 1, 2000, each municipal police department and the Department of Public Safety shall, using the form developed and promulgated pursuant to subsection ~~(i)~~ (h) of this section, record and retain the following information: (1) The number of persons stopped for traffic violations; (2) characteristics of race, color, ethnicity, gender and age of such persons, provided the identification of such characteristics shall be based on the observation and perception of the police officer responsible for reporting the stop and the information shall not be required to be provided by the person stopped; (3) the nature of the alleged traffic violation that resulted in the stop; (4) whether a warning or citation was issued, an arrest made or a search conducted as a result of the stop; and (5) any additional information that such municipal police department or the Department of Public Safety, as the case may be, deems appropriate, provided such information does not include any other identifying information about any person stopped for a traffic violation such as the person's operator's license number, name or address.

Sec. 84. Subsection (c) of section 54–128 of the general statutes is repealed and the following is substituted in lieu thereof (Effective from passage):

(c) Any person who, during the service of a period of special parole imposed in accordance with subdivision (9) of subsection (b) of section 53a–28, has been returned to the custody of the Commissioner of Correction or any institution of the Department of Correction for violation of his parole, may be retained in the institution from which he was paroled for a period equal to the unexpired portion of the period of special parole. The total length of the term of incarceration and term of special parole combined shall not exceed the maximum sentence of incarceration authorized for the offense for which the person was convicted.

Sec. 85. Subsection (d) of section 2 of public act 03–114 is repealed and the following is substituted in lieu thereof (Effective from passage):

(d) Any person under the minimum age for the purchase of alcoholic liquor under the provisions of chapter 545[1] who, for the purpose of gaining access to a gaming facility, (1) misrepresents such person's age, or (2) uses or exhibits (A) a forged, counterfeit or altered government-issued identity card, passport or motor vehicle operator's license, or (B) a government-issued identity card, passport or motor vehicle operator's license belonging to any other person, shall be fined not less than one hundred dollars ~~nor~~ or more than five hundred dollars or imprisoned not more than thirty days, or both.

[1] C.G.S.A. § 30–1 et seq.

Sec. 86. Subsection (b) of section 1 of public act 03–233 is repealed and the following is substituted in lieu thereof (Effective from passage):

(b) Any person who violates the provisions of subsection (a) of this section shall, for a first offense, be fined not less than one hundred fifty dollars ~~nor~~ or more than two hundred dollars or imprisoned not more than ninety days, or both, and, for any subsequent offense, be fined not less than two hundred dollars ~~nor~~ or more than six hundred dollars or imprisoned not more than one year, or both.

Sec. 87. Section 38 of public act 03–259 is repealed and the following is substituted in lieu thereof (Effective from passage):

~~(a)~~ A violation of section 33 or sections 35 to 37, inclusive, of ~~this act~~ public act 03–259 shall be deemed an unfair or deceptive trade practice under subsection (a) of section 42–110b, provided the provisions of section 42–110g, as amended, shall not apply to such violation.

Sec. 88. Section 3 of public act 03–266 is repealed and the following is substituted in lieu thereof (Effective from passage):

(a) No hospital shall refer to a collection agent, as defined in section ~~19–509b~~ 19a–509b, as amended, or initiate an action against an individual patient or such patient's estate to collect fees arising from care provided at a hospital on or after October 1, 2003, unless the hospital has made a determination that such individual is an uninsured patient, as defined in section 19a–673, as amended, and is not eligible for the hospital bed fund.

(b) Nothing in this section shall ~~effect~~ affect a hospital's ability to initiate an action against an individual patient or such patient's estate to collect coinsurance, deductibles or fees arising from care provided at a hospital where such coinsurance, deductibles or fees may be eligible for reimbursement through awards, settlements or judgments arising from claims, suits or proceedings. In addition, nothing in this section shall affect a hospital's ability to initiate an action against an individual patient or such patient's estate where payment or reimbursement has been made, or likely is to be made, directly to the patient.

Sec. 89. Section 7 of public act 03–267 is repealed and the following is substituted in lieu thereof (Effective from passage):

(a) A person is guilty of abuse in the first degree when such person intentionally commits abuse of an elderly, blind, disabled or mentally retarded person and causes serious physical injury to such elderly, blind, disabled or mentally retarded ~~, or disabled~~ person.

(b) Abuse in the first degree is a class C felony.

Sec. 90. Subsection (c) of section 4–67u of the general statutes, as amended by section 1 of public act 03–145, is repealed and the following is substituted in lieu thereof (Effective from passage):

(c) The State Prevention Council shall determine long-term goals, strategies and outcome measures to promote the health and well-being of children and families. Such goals include, but are not limited to: Cost-effective, research-based, early intervention strategies; an increase in pregnant women and newborns who are healthy; a decrease in the rate of child neglect and abuse; an increase in children who are ready for school; an increase in children who succeed in school; a decrease in children who are unsupervised after school; an increase in ~~youth~~ youths who choose healthy behaviors and become successful working adults; a decrease in juvenile suicide; a decrease in juvenile crime; and an increase in access to health care and stable housing. The council shall design a plan for inter-agency and intra-agency implementation of such goals and strategies and shall submit such plan, in accordance with section 11–4a, to the Secretary of the Office of Policy and Management and the joint standing committee of the General Assembly having cognizance of matters relating to appropriations and the budgets of state agencies not later than January 1, 2004.

Sec. 91. Section 7–174 of the general statutes is repealed and the following is substituted in lieu thereof (Effective from passage):

Such chief of police or first selectman, as the case may be, shall, on behalf of the executive director of the Division of Special Revenue, make or cause to be made an investigation of the qualifications of the applicant and the facts stated in the application and, if ~~he~~ such chief of police or first selectman determines that the applicant is qualified to hold, operate and conduct a bazaar or raffle under the provisions of sections 7–170 to 7–186, inclusive, that the members of the applicant designated in the application to hold, operate or conduct such bazaar or raffle are electors of such municipality, bona fide active members of the applicant and persons of good moral character and have never been convicted of a felony and that such bazaar or raffle is to be held, operated and conducted in accordance with the provisions of said sections, ~~he~~ such chief of police or first selectman shall, with the approval of the executive director, issue a permit to such applicant. Upon issuing such permit, such chief of police or first selectman shall forward to the executive director the state's share of the permit fee, if any. Any investigation required pursuant to this section of the qualifications of an applicant for a "Class No. 7" permit, authorized pursuant to section ~~7–174~~ 7–175, shall be made by the executive director of the Division of Special Revenue.

Sec. 92. Section 8–129 of the general statutes is repealed and the following is substituted in lieu thereof (Effective from passage):

The redevelopment agency shall determine the compensation to be paid to the persons entitled thereto for such real property and shall file a statement of compensation, containing a description of the property to be taken and the names of all persons having a record interest therein and setting forth the amount of such compensation, and a deposit as provided in section 8–130, with the clerk of the superior court for the judicial district in which the property affected is located. Upon filing such statement of compensation and deposit, the redevelopment agency shall forthwith cause to be recorded, in the office of the town clerk of each town in which the property is located, a copy of such statement of compensation, such recording to have the same effect ~~as~~ and to be treated the same as the recording of a lis pendens, and shall forthwith give notice, as ~~hereinafter~~ provided in this section, to each person appearing of record as an owner of property affected thereby and to each person appearing of record as a holder of any mortgage, lien, assessment or other encumbrance on such property or interest therein (a) ~~,~~ in the case of any such person found to be residing within this state, by causing a copy of such notice, with a copy of such statement of compensation, to be served upon each such person by a state marshal, constable or ~~an~~ indifferent person, in the manner set forth in section 52–57, as amended, for the service of civil process, and (b) ~~,~~ in the case of any such person who is a nonresident of this state at the time of the filing of such statement of compensation and deposit or of any such person whose whereabouts or existence is unknown, by mailing to each such person a copy of such notice and of such statement of compensation, by registered or certified mail, directed to his last-known address, and by publishing such notice and such statement of compensation at least twice in a newspaper published in the judicial district and having daily or weekly circulation in the town in which such property is located. Any such published notice shall state that it is notice to the widow or widower, heirs, representatives and creditors of the person holding such record interest, if such person is dead. If, after a reasonably diligent search, no last-known address can be found for any interested party, an affidavit stating such fact, and reciting the steps taken to locate such address, shall be filed with the clerk of the superior court and accepted in lieu of mailing to the last-known address. Not less than twelve days ~~nor~~ or more than ninety days after such notice and such statement of compensation have been so served or so mailed and first published, the redevelopment agency shall file with the clerk of the superior court a return of notice setting forth the notice given and, upon receipt of such return of notice, such clerk shall, without any delay or continuance of any kind, issue a certificate of taking setting forth the fact of such taking, a description of all the property so taken and the names of the owners and of all other persons having a record interest therein. The redevelopment agency shall cause such certificate of taking to be recorded in the office of the town clerk of each town in which such property is located. Upon the recording of such certificate, title to such property in fee simple shall vest in the municipality, and the right to just compensation shall vest in the persons entitled thereto. At any time after such certificate of taking has been so recorded, the redevelopment agency may repair, operate or insure such property and enter upon such property, and take ~~whatever~~ any action that is proposed with regard to such property by the project area redevelopment plan. The notice referred to above shall state ~~(a)~~ that (1) not less than twelve days ~~nor~~ or more than ninety days after service or mailing and first publication thereof, the redevelopment agency shall file, with the clerk of the superior court ~~of~~ for the judicial district in which such property is located, a return setting forth the notice given, ~~(b) that~~ (2) upon receipt of such return, such clerk shall issue a certificate for recording in the office of the town clerk of each town in which such property is located, ~~(c) that~~ (3) upon the recording of such certificate, title to such property shall vest in the municipality, the right to just compensation shall vest in the persons entitled thereto and the redevelopment agency may repair, operate or insure such property and enter upon such property and take ~~whatever~~ any action that may be proposed with regard thereto by the project area redevelopment plan, and ~~(d) that~~ (4) such notice shall bind the widow or widower, heirs, representatives and creditors of each person named therein who then or thereafter may be dead. When any redevelopment agency acting ~~in~~ on behalf of any municipality has acquired or rented real property by purchase, lease, exchange or gift in accordance with the provisions of this section, or in exercising its right of eminent domain has filed a statement of compensation and deposit with the clerk of the superior court and has caused a certificate of taking to be recorded in the office of the town clerk of each town in which such property is located as ~~herein~~ provided in this section, any judge of such court may, upon application and proof of such acquisition or rental or such filing and deposit and such recording, order such clerk to issue an execution commanding a state marshal to put such municipality and the redevelopment agency, as its agent, into peaceable possession of the property so acquired, rented or condemned. The provisions of this section shall not be limited in any way by the provisions of chapter 832.[1]

[1] C.G.S.A. § 47a–23 et seq.

Sec. 93. Section 8–132 of the general statutes is repealed and the following is substituted in lieu thereof (Effective from passage):

(a) Any person claiming to be aggrieved by the statement of compensation filed by the redevelopment agency may, at any time within six months after the same has been filed, apply to the superior court for the judicial district in which such property is situated for a review of such statement of compensation so far as the same affects such applicant. The court, after causing notice of the pendency of such application to be given to ~~said~~ the redevelopment agency, may appoint a judge trial referee to make a review of the statement of compensation.

(b) If the court appoints a judge trial referee, ~~such~~ the judge trial referee, after giving at least ten days' notice to the parties interested of the time and place of hearing, shall hear the applicant and ~~said~~ the redevelopment agency, shall view the property and take such testimony as ~~such~~ the judge trial referee deems material and shall thereupon revise such statement of compensation in such manner as ~~such~~ the judge trial referee deems proper and forthwith report to the court. Such report shall contain a detailed statement of findings by the judge trial referee, sufficient to enable the court to determine the considerations upon which the judge trial referee's conclusions are based. The report of the judge trial referee shall take into account any evidence relevant to the fair market value of the property, including evidence of environmental condition and required environmental remediation. The judge trial referee shall make a separate finding for remediation costs and the property owner shall be entitled to a ~~setoff~~ set-off of such costs in any pending or subsequent action to recover remediation costs for the property. The court shall review the report, and may reject it for any irregular or improper conduct in the performance of the duties of ~~such~~ the judge trial referee. If the report is rejected, the court may appoint another judge trial referee to make such review and report. If the report is accepted, its statement of compensation shall be conclusive upon such owner and the redevelopment agency.

(c) If the court does not appoint a judge trial referee, the court, after giving at least ten days' notice to the parties interested of the time and place of hearing, shall hear the applicant and ~~said~~ the redevelopment agency and take such testimony as it deems material, may view the subject property, and shall make a finding regarding the statement of compensation. The findings of the court shall take into account any evidence relevant to the fair market value of the property, including evidence of environmental condition and required environmental remediation. The court shall make a separate finding for remediation costs and the property owner shall be entitled to a set-off of such costs in any pending or subsequent action to recover remediation costs for the property. The findings of the court shall be conclusive upon such owner and the redevelopment agency.

(d) If no appeal to the Appellate Court is filed within the time allowed by law, or if ~~one~~ an appeal is filed and the proceedings have terminated in a final judgment finding the amount due the property owner, the clerk shall send a certified copy of the statement of compensation and of the judgment to the redevelopment agency, which shall, upon receipt thereof, pay such property owner the amount due as compensation. The pendency of any such application for review shall not prevent or delay ~~whatever~~ any action that is proposed with regard to such property by the project area redevelopment plan.

Sec. 94. Subdivision (3) of section 20–417a of the general statutes, as amended by section 1 of public act 03–167 and section 146 of public act 03–6 of the June 30 special session, is repealed and the following is substituted in lieu thereof (Effective July 1, 2004):

(3) "Contract" means any agreement between a new home construction contractor and a consumer for the construction or sale of a new home or any portion of a new home prior to occupancy.

Sec. 95. Section 26–40a of the general statutes, as amended by section 2 of public act 03–192 and section 146 of public act 03–6 of the June 30 special session, is repealed and the following is substituted in lieu thereof (Effective July 1, 2004):

For the purposes of this section, the following wildlife, or any hybrid thereof, shall be considered as potentially dangerous animals: The felidae, including, but not limited to, the lion, leopard, cheetah, jaguar, ocelot, jaguarundi cat, puma, lynx and bobcat; the canidae, including, but not limited to, the wolf and coyote; and the ursidae, including, but not limited to, the black bear, grizzly bear and brown bear. No person shall possess a potentially dangerous animal. Any such animal illegally possessed may be ordered seized and may be disposed of as determined by the Commissioner of Environmental Protection. The Department of Environmental Protection shall issue a bill to the owner or person in illegal possession of such potentially dangerous animal for all costs of

~~confiscation~~ seizure, care, maintenance and disposal of such animal. Additionally, any person who violates any provision of this section shall be assessed a civil penalty not to exceed one thousand dollars, to be fixed by the court, for each offense. Each violation shall be a separate and distinct offense and in the case of a continuing violation, each day's continuance thereof shall be deemed to be a separate and distinct offense. The Commissioner of Environmental Protection may request the Attorney General to institute an action in Superior Court to recover such penalty and any amounts owed pursuant to a bill issued in accordance with this section. The provisions of this section shall not apply to municipal parks, zoos and nature centers, or museums, laboratories and research facilities maintained by scientific or educational institutions; to a person possessing a Bengal cat certified by an internationally recognized multiple-cat domestic feline breeding association as being without wild parentage for a minimum of four prior generations which cat was registered with the Commissioner of Agriculture and Consumer Protection on or before October 1, 1996, provided no such cat may be imported into this state after June 6, 1996; or to persons possessing animals legally on or before May 23, 1983. In any action taken by any official of the state or any municipality to control rabies, a Bengal cat shall be considered not vaccinated for rabies in accordance with accepted veterinary practice.

Sec. 96. Subsection (b) of section 27–189 of the general statutes is repealed and the following is substituted in lieu thereof (Effective from passage):

(b) The fees of all witnesses so summoned and of the ~~deputy sheriffs~~ state marshals, constables or indifferent persons serving such subpoenas shall be the same as provided for in civil actions in the state, and shall be taxed by the president of the court-martial or by the summary court officer.

Sec. 97. Section 45a–690 of the general statutes is repealed and the following is substituted in lieu thereof (Effective from passage):

For the purposes of sections 45a–690 to 45a–700, inclusive:

~~(a)~~ (1) "Sterilization" means a surgical or other medical procedure, the purpose of which is to render an individual permanently incapable of procreating;

~~(b)~~ (2) "Informed consent" means consent that is ~~(1)~~ (A) based upon an understanding of the nature and consequences of sterilization, ~~; (2)~~ (B) given by a person competent to make such a decision, and ~~(3)~~ (C) wholly voluntary and free from coercion, express or implied;

~~(c)~~ (3) "Institution" means a state school or hospital or other residential facility operated or leased by the state of Connecticut; and

~~(d)~~ (4) "Best interest" shall include all of the following factors: (1) (A) Less drastic alternative contraceptive methods have proved unworkable or inapplicable, ~~(2)~~ (B) the individual is physiologically sexually mature, ~~(3)~~ (C) there is no evidence of infertility, (4) (D) the individual has the capability and a reasonable opportunity for sexual activity, ~~(5)~~ (E) the individual is unable to understand reproduction or contraception and there exists the likely permanence of that inability, ~~(6)~~ (F) the physical or emotional inability to care for the child, ~~(7)~~ (G) the proponents of the sterilization are seeking sterilization in good faith and their primary concern is for the best interests of the respondent rather than their own convenience or the convenience of the public, and ~~(8)~~ (H) in the case of females, procreation would endanger the life or severely impair the health of the individual.

Sec. 98. Subsection (a) of section 2 of public act 03–251 is repealed and the following is substituted in lieu thereof (Effective from passage):

(a) The advisory group for the Connecticut Juvenile Training School, established pursuant to subsection (b) of section 17a–6, as amended, and the Connecticut Juvenile Training School public safety committee, established pursuant to section 17a–27f, shall provide an on-going review of the Connecticut Juvenile Training School with recommendations for improvement or enhancement. The review shall include, but not be limited to:

(1) The number, age, ethnicity and race of the residents placed at the training school, including the court locations that sentenced them, the number sentenced from each court location and the ~~offense~~ offenses for which ~~the child was~~ they were sentenced;

(2) The percentage of ~~children~~ residents in need of substance abuse treatment and the programming interventions provided to assist residents;

(3) A review of the program and policies of the facility;

(4) The ~~educational/literacy~~ educational and literacy programs available to the residents, including the educational level of residents, the number of residents requiring special education and related services, including school attendance requirements, the number of ~~children~~ residents who are educated in the alternative school and the reasons for such education;

(5) The vocational training programs available to the residents and the actual number of residents enrolled in each training program, including all vocational attendance requirements;

(6) The delinquency recidivism rates of such residents, which ~~will~~ shall include the number of children discharged to residential placement, the number of children discharged due to expiration of the period of commitment and the number of children returned to the Connecticut Juvenile Training School;

(7) The diagnosis of each ~~child~~ resident after intake assessment;

(8) The costs associated with the operation of the training school, including staffing costs and average cost per resident; and

(9) Reintegration strategies and plans to transition the ~~children~~ residents to their home communities.

Sec. 99. Subsection (b) of section 3 of public act 03–251 is repealed and the following is substituted in lieu thereof (Effective from passage):

(b) Each report required pursuant to subsection (a) of this section shall summarize the information and recommendations specified in section 2 of ~~this act~~ public act 03–251 and shall also include such other information that the Department of Children and Families has identified ~~that requires~~ as requiring immediate legislative action.

Sec. 100. Subsections (b) and (c) of section 14–215 of the general statutes are repealed and the following is substituted in lieu thereof (Effective from passage):

(b) Except as provided in subsection (c) of this section, any person who violates any provision of subsection (a) of this section shall, for a first offense, be fined not less than one hundred fifty dollars ~~nor~~ or more than two hundred dollars or imprisoned not more than ninety days, or be both fined and imprisoned, ~~for the first offense,~~ and, for any subsequent offense, shall be fined not less than two hundred dollars ~~nor~~ or more than six hundred dollars or imprisoned not more than one year, or be both fined and imprisoned.

(c) Any person who operates any motor vehicle during the period ~~his~~ such person's operator's license or right to operate a motor vehicle in this state is under suspension or revocation on account of a violation of subsection (a) of section 14–227a, as amended, or section 53a–56b or 53a–60d or pursuant to section 14–227b, as amended, shall be fined not less than five hundred dollars ~~nor~~ or more than one thousand dollars and imprisoned not more than one year, and, in the absence of any mitigating circumstances as determined by the court, thirty consecutive days of the sentence imposed may not be suspended or reduced in any manner. The court shall specifically state in writing for the record the mitigating circumstances, or the absence thereof.

Sec. 101. Subsection (g) of section 14–227a of the general statutes, as amended by section 1 of public act 03–265 and section 47 of public act 03–278, is repealed and the following is substituted in lieu thereof (Effective from passage):

(g) Any person who violates any provision of subsection (a) of this section shall: (1) For conviction of a first violation, (A) be fined not less than five hundred dollars or more than one thousand dollars, and (B) be (i) imprisoned not more than six months, forty-eight consecutive hours of which may not be suspended or reduced in any manner, or (ii) imprisoned not more than six months, with the execution of such sentence of imprisonment suspended entirely and a period of probation imposed requiring as a condition of such probation that such person perform one hundred hours of community service, as defined in section 14–227e, and (C) have such person's motor vehicle operator's license or nonresident operating privilege suspended for one year; (2) for conviction of a second violation within ten years after a prior conviction for the same offense, (A) be fined not less than one thousand dollars or more than four thousand dollars, (B) be imprisoned not more than two years, one hundred twenty consecutive days of which may not be suspended or reduced in any manner, and sentenced to a period of probation requiring as a condition of such probation that such person perform one hundred hours of community service, as defined in section 14–227e, and (C) (i) have such person's motor vehicle operator's license or nonresident operating privilege suspended for three years or until the date of such person's twenty-first birthday, whichever is longer, or (ii) if such person has been convicted of a violation of subdivision (1) of subsection (a) of this section on account of being under the influence of intoxicating liquor or of subdivision (2) of subsection (a) of this section, have such person's motor vehicle operator's license or nonresident operating privilege suspended for one year and be prohibited for the two-year period following completion of such period of suspension from operating a motor vehicle unless such motor vehicle is equipped with a functioning, approved ignition interlock device, as defined in section ~~3 of this act~~ 2 of public act 03–265; and (3) for conviction of a third and subsequent violation within ten years after a prior conviction for the same offense, (A) be fined not less than two thousand dollars or more than eight thousand dollars, (B) be imprisoned not more than three years, one year of which may not be suspended or reduced in any manner, and sentenced to a period of probation requiring as a condition of such probation that such person perform one hundred hours of community service, as defined in section 14–227e, and (C) have such person's motor vehicle operator's license or nonresident operating privilege permanently revoked upon such third offense. For purposes of the imposition of penalties for a second or third and subsequent offense pursuant to this subsection, a conviction under the provisions of subsection (a) of this section in effect on October 1, 1981, or as amended thereafter, a conviction under the provisions of either subdivision (1) or (2) of subsection (a) of this section, a conviction under the provisions of section 53a–56b or 53a–60d or a conviction in any other state of any offense the essential elements of which are determined by the court to be substantially the same as subdivision (1) or (2) of subsection (a) of this section or section 53a–56b or 53a–60d, shall constitute a prior conviction for the same offense.

Sec. 102. Subsection (a) of section 17b–451 of the general statutes, as amended by section 3 of public act 03–267, is repealed and the following is substituted in lieu thereof (Effective from passage):

(a) Any physician or surgeon licensed under the provisions of chapter 370, [1] any resident physician or intern in any hospital in this state, whether or not so licensed, any registered nurse, any nursing home administrator, nurse's aide or orderly in a nursing home facility, any person paid for caring for a patient in a nursing home facility, any staff person employed by a nursing home facility, any patients' advocate and any licensed practical nurse, medical examiner, dentist, optometrist, chiropractor, podiatrist, social worker, clergyman, police officer, pharmacist, psychologist or physical therapist, who has reasonable cause to suspect or believe that any elderly person has been abused, neglected, exploited or abandoned, or is in a condition which is the result of such abuse, neglect, exploitation or abandonment, or ~~who~~ is in need of protective services, shall, not later than seventy-two hours after such suspicion or belief arose, report such information or cause a report to be made in any reasonable manner to the Commissioner of Social Services or to the person or persons designated by the commissioner to receive such reports. Any person required to report under the provisions of this section who fails to make such report within the prescribed time period shall be fined not more than five hundred dollars, except that, if such person intentionally fails to make such report within the prescribed time period, such person shall be guilty of a class C misdemeanor for the first offense and a class A misdemeanor for any subsequent offense.

[1] C.G.S.A. § 20–8 et seq.

Sec. 103. Section 20–14i of the general statutes is repealed and the following is substituted in lieu thereof (Effective from passage):

Any provisions to the contrary notwithstanding, chapter 378 [1] shall not prohibit the administration of medication to persons attending day programs, or residing in residential facilities, under the jurisdiction of the Departments of Children and Families, Correction, Mental Retardation and Mental Health <u>and Addiction Services</u>, or being detained in juvenile detention centers, when such medication is administered by trained persons, pursuant to the written order of a physician licensed under this chapter, a dentist licensed under chapter 379, [2] an advanced practice registered nurse licensed to prescribe in accordance with section 20–94a or a physician assistant licensed to prescribe in accordance with section 20–12d, authorized to prescribe such medication. The provisions of this section shall not apply to institutions, facilities or programs licensed pursuant to chapter 368v. [3]

[1] C.G.S.A. § 20–87 et seq.
[2] C.G.S.A. § 20–103 et seq.
[3] C.G.S.A. § 19a–485 et seq.

Sec. 104. Subsection (d) of section 20–427 of the general statutes, as amended by section 2 of public act 03–186, is repealed and the following is substituted in lieu thereof (Effective from passage):

(d) The commissioner may, after notice and hearing in accordance with the provisions of chapter 54, [1] impose a civil penalty on any person who engages in or practices the work or occupation for which a certificate of registration is required by this chapter without having first obtained such a certificate of registration or who wilfully employs or supplies for employment a person who does not have such a certificate of registration or who wilfully and falsely pretends to qualify to engage in or practice such work or occupation, or who engages in or practices any of the work or occupations for which a certificate of registration is required by this chapter after the expiration of ~~his~~ <u>such person's</u> certificate of registration or who violates any of the provisions of this chapter or the regulations adopted pursuant thereto. Such penalty shall be in an amount not more than five hundred dollars for a first violation of this subsection, not more than seven hundred fifty dollars for a second violation of this subsection occurring not more than three years after a prior violation, not more than one thousand five hundred dollars for a third or subsequent violation of this subsection occurring not more than three years after a prior violation and, in the case of radon mitigation work, such penalty shall be not less than two hundred fifty dollars. Any civil penalty collected pursuant to this subsection shall be deposited in the ~~Consumer Protection Enforcement Fund~~ consumer protection enforcement account established in section 21a–8a, as amended.

[1] C.G.S.A. § 4–166 et seq.

Sec. 105. Subsection (c) of section 20–432 of the general statutes is repealed and the following is substituted in lieu thereof (Effective from passage):

(c) Payments received under subsection (b) of this section shall be credited to the guaranty fund until the balance in such fund equals seven hundred fifty thousand dollars. Annually, if such fund has an excess, the first four hundred thousand dollars of the excess shall be deposited into the ~~Consumer Protection Enforcement Fund~~ consumer protection enforcement account established in section 21a–8a, as amended. Any excess thereafter shall be deposited in the General Fund. Any money in the guaranty fund may be invested or reinvested in the same manner as funds of the state employees retirement system, and the interest arising from such investments shall be credited to the guaranty fund.

Sec. 106. Subsection (a) of section 36a–582 of the general statutes, as amended by section 2 of public act 04–14, is repealed and the following is substituted in lieu thereof (Effective October 1, 2004):

(a) Each applicant for a check cashing license shall pay to the commissioner ~~,~~ a nonrefundable initial application fee of one thousand dollars and a nonrefundable license fee of one hundred dollars for each location. Each licensee shall pay to the commissioner a nonrefundable location transfer fee of one hundred dollars for each application to transfer a location. Each license issued pursuant to section 36a–581, as amended by ~~this act~~ public act 04–14, shall expire at the close of business on June thirtieth of each year unless such license is renewed. Each licensee shall, on or before June twentieth of each year, pay to the commissioner a renewal application fee of seven hundred fifty dollars and a renewal license fee for each location of fifty dollars for the succeeding year, commencing July first.

Sec. 107. Subdivision (1) of section 36a–715 of the general statutes is repealed and the following is substituted in lieu thereof (Effective from passage):

(1) "First mortgage loan" has the same meaning as provided in ~~subsection (1)~~ subdivision (6) of section 36a–485.

Sec. 108. Subsection (f) of section 45a–676 of the general statutes, as amended by section 5 of public act 03–51, is repealed and the following is substituted in lieu thereof (Effective from passage):

(f) In selecting a plenary guardian or limited guardian of the person with mental retardation, the court shall be guided by the best interests of the respondent, including, but not limited to, the preference of the respondent as to who should be appointed as plenary guardian or limited guardian. No person shall be excluded from serving as a plenary guardian or limited guardian solely because ~~he~~ such person is employed by the Department of Mental Retardation, except that (1) no such employee may be appointed as a plenary guardian or limited guardian of a person with mental retardation residing in a state-operated residential facility for ~~the mentally retarded~~ persons with mental retardation located in the Department of Mental Retardation region in which such person is employed; and (2) no such employee shall be so appointed unless no other suitable person to serve as plenary guardian or limited guardian can be found. Any appointment of an employee of the Department of Mental Retardation as a plenary guardian or limited guardian shall be made for a limited purpose and duration. During the term of appointment of any such employee, the Commissioner of Mental Retardation shall search for a suitable person who is not an employee of the department to replace such employee as plenary guardian or limited guardian.

Sec. 109. Subsection (e) of section 45a–677 of the general statutes, as amended by section 6 of public act 03–51 and section 97 of public act 03–278, is repealed and the following is substituted in lieu thereof (Effective from passage):

(e) A plenary guardian or limited guardian of a person with mental retardation shall not have the power or authority: (1) To cause the ward to be admitted to any institution for treatment of the mentally ill, except in accordance with the provisions of sections 17a–75 to 17a–83, inclusive, 17a–456 to 17a–484, inclusive, 17a–495 to 17a–528, inclusive, 17a–540 to 17a–550, inclusive, 17a–560 to 17a–576, inclusive, 17a–615 to 17a–618, inclusive, and 17a–621 to 17a–664, inclusive, and chapter 420b; [1] (2) to cause the ward to be admitted to any training school or other facility provided for the care and training of ~~the mentally retarded~~ persons with mental retardation if there is a conflict concerning such admission between the guardian and the person with mental retardation or next of kin, except in accordance with the provisions of sections 17a–274, as amended, and 17a–275; (3) to consent on behalf of the ward to a sterilization, except in accordance with the provisions of sections 45a–690 to 45a–700, inclusive; (4) to consent on behalf of the ward to psychosurgery, except in accordance with the provisions of section 17a–543, as amended; (5) to consent on behalf of the ward to the termination of the ward's parental rights, except in accordance with the provisions of sections 45a–706 to 45a–709, inclusive, 45a–715 to 45a–718, inclusive, 45a–724 to 45a–737, inclusive, and 45a–743 to 45a–757, inclusive; (6) to consent on behalf of the ward to the performance of any experimental biomedical or behavioral medical procedure or participation in any biomedical or behavioral experiment, unless it (A) is intended to preserve the life or prevent serious impairment of the physical health of the ward, (B) is intended to assist the ward to regain the ward's abilities and has been approved for the ward by the court, or (C) has been (i) approved by a recognized institutional review board, as defined by 45 CFR 46, 21 CFR 50 and 21 CFR 56, as amended from time to time, which is not a part of the Department of Mental Retardation, (ii) endorsed or supported by the Department of Mental Retardation, and (iii) approved for the ward by such ward's primary care physician; (7) to admit the ward to any residential facility operated by an organization by whom such guardian is employed, except in accordance with the provisions of section 17a–274, as amended; (8) to prohibit the marriage or divorce of the ward; and (9) to consent on behalf of the ward to an abortion or removal of a body organ, except in accordance with applicable statutory procedures when necessary to preserve the life or prevent serious impairment of the physical or mental health of the ward.

[1] C.G.S.A. § 21a–240 et seq.

Sec. 110. Section 45a–716 of the general statutes is repealed and the following is substituted in lieu thereof (Effective from passage):

(a) Upon receipt of a petition for termination of parental rights, the Court of Probate, or the Superior Court ~~,~~ on a case transferred to it from the Court of Probate in accordance with the provisions of subsection (g) of section 45a–715, shall set a time and place for hearing the petition. The time for hearing shall be not more than thirty days after the filing of the petition.

(b) The court shall cause notice of the hearing to be given to the following persons, as applicable: (1) The parent or parents of the minor child, including any parent who has been removed as guardian on or after October 1, 1973, under section 45a–606; (2) the father of any minor child born out of wedlock, provided at the time of the filing of the petition (A) he has been adjudicated the father of such child by a court of competent jurisdiction, ~~or~~ (B) he has acknowledged in writing that he is the father of such child, ~~or~~ (C) he has contributed regularly to the support of such child, ~~or~~ (D) his name appears on the birth certificate, ~~or~~ (E) he has filed a claim for paternity as provided under section 46b–172a, or (F) he has been named in the petition as the father of the child by the mother; (3) the guardian or any other person whom the court shall deem appropriate; and (4) the Commissioner of Children and Families. If the recipient of the notice is a person described in subdivision (1) or (2) of this subsection or is any other person whose parental rights are sought to be terminated in the petition, the notice shall contain a statement that the respondent has the right to be represented by counsel and that if the respondent is unable to pay for counsel, counsel will be appointed for the respondent. The reasonable compensation for such counsel shall be established by, and paid from funds appropriated to, the Judicial Department, however, in the case of a Probate Court matter, if funds have not been included in the budget of the Judicial Department for such purposes, such compensation shall be established by the Probate Court Administrator and paid from the Probate Court Administration Fund.

(c) Except as provided in subsection (d) of this section, notice of the hearing and a copy of the petition, certified by the petitioner, the petitioner's agent or attorney, or the ~~court~~ clerk of the court, shall be served at least ten days before the date ~~for~~ of the hearing by personal service or service at the person's usual place of abode on the persons enumerated in subsection (b) of this section who are within the state, and by certified mail, return receipt requested, on the Commissioner of Children and Families. If the address of any person entitled to personal service or service at the person's usual place of abode is unknown, or if personal service or service at the person's usual place of abode cannot be reasonably effected within the state, or if any person enumerated in subsection (b) of this section is out of the state, a judge or the clerk of the court shall order notice to be given by registered or certified mail, return receipt requested, or by publication at least ten days before the date of the hearing. Any such publication shall be in a newspaper of general circulation in the place of the last-known address of the person to be notified, whether within or without this state, or, if no such address is known, in the place where the ~~termination~~ petition has been filed.

(d) In any proceeding pending in the Court of Probate, in lieu of personal service on a parent or the father of a child born out of wedlock who is either a petitioner or who signs under penalty of false statement a written waiver of personal service on a form provided by the Probate Court Administrator, the court may order notice to be given by certified mail, return receipt requested, deliverable to addressee only, ~~and~~ at least ten days ~~prior to~~ before the date of the hearing. If such delivery cannot reasonably be effected, or if the whereabouts of the parents is unknown, ~~then~~ notice shall be ordered to be given by publication ~~,~~ as provided in subsection (c) of this section.

Sec. 111. Section 6 of public act 03–267 is repealed and the following is substituted in lieu thereof (Effective from passage):

For the purposes of sections 6 to ~~10~~ 9, inclusive, of ~~this act~~ public act 03–267:

(1) "Person" means any natural person, corporation, partnership, limited liability company, unincorporated business or other business entity;

(2) "Elderly person" means any person who is sixty years of age or older;

(3) "Blind person" means any person who is blind, as defined in section 1–1f;

(4) "Disabled person" means any person who is physically disabled, as defined in section 1–1f;

(5) "Mentally retarded person" means any person with mental retardation, as defined in section 1–1g;

(6) "Abuse" means any repeated act or omission that causes physical injury or serious physical injury to an elderly, blind, disabled or mentally retarded person, except when (A) the act or omission is a part of the treatment and care, and in furtherance of the health and safety, of the elderly, blind, disabled or mentally retarded person, or (B) the act or omission is based upon the instructions, wishes, consent, refusal to consent or revocation of consent of an elderly, blind, disabled or mentally retarded person, or the legal representative of an incapable elderly, blind, disabled or mentally retarded person. For purposes of this subdivision, "repeated" means an act or omission that occurs on two or more occasions;

(7) "Intentionally" means "intentionally" as defined in subdivision (11) of section 53a–3;

(8) "Knowingly" means "knowingly" as defined in subdivision (12) of section 53a–3;

(9) "Recklessly" means "recklessly" as defined in subdivision (13) of section 53a–3;

(10) "Physical injury" means "physical injury" as defined in subdivision (3) of section 53a–3; and

(11) "Serious physical injury" means "serious physical injury" as defined in subdivision (4) of section 53a–3.

Sec. 112. Subsection (d) of section 17b–10 of the general statutes, as amended by section 1 of public act 04–166, is repealed and the following is substituted in lieu thereof (Effective October 1, 2004):

(d) In lieu of submitting proposed regulations by the date specified in subsection (c) of this section, the department may submit to the legislative regulation review committee a notice not later than thirty-five days before such date that the department will not be able to submit the proposed regulations on or before such date and shall include in such notice (1) the reasons why the department will not submit the proposed regulations by such date, and (2) the date by which the department will submit the proposed regulations. The legislative regulation review committee may require the department to appear before the committee at a time prescribed by the committee to further explain ~~the reasons for the request~~ such reasons and to respond to any questions by the committee about the policy. The legislative regulation review committee may request the joint standing committee of the General Assembly having cognizance of matters relating to human services to review the department's policy, the department's reasons for not submitting the proposed regulations by the date specified in subsection (c) of this section and the date by which the department will submit the proposed regulations. Said joint standing committee may review the policy, such reasons and such date, may schedule a hearing thereon and may make a recommendation to the legislative regulation review committee.

Sec. 113. Section 1–24 of the general statutes, as amended by section 1 of public act 03–278, is repealed and the following is substituted in lieu thereof (Effective from passage):

The following officers may administer oaths: (1) The clerks of the Senate, the clerks of the House of Representatives and the chairpersons of committees of the General Assembly or of either branch thereof, during its session; (2) state officers, as defined in subsection (t) of section 9–1, judges and clerks of any court, family support magistrates, judge trial referees, justices of the peace, commissioners of the Superior Court, notaries public, town clerks and assistant town clerks, in all cases where an oath may be administered, except in a case where the law otherwise requires; (3) commissioners on insolvent estates, auditors, arbitrators and committees, to parties and witnesses, in all cases tried before them; (4) assessors and boards of assessment appeals, in cases coming before them; (5) commissioners appointed by governors of other states to take the acknowledgment of deeds, in the discharge of their official duty; (6) the moderator of a school district meeting, in such meeting, to the clerk of such district, as required by law; (7) the first selectman, in any matter before the board of selectmen;

(8) the Chief Medical Examiner, Deputy Medical Examiner and assistant medical examiners of the Office of the Medical Examiner, in any matter before them; (9) registrars of vital statistics, in any matter before them; (10) any chief inspector or inspector appointed pursuant to section 51–286; (11) registrars of voters, deputy registrars, assistant registrars, and moderators, in any matter before them; (12) special assistant registrars, in matters provided for in subsections (b) and (c) of section 9–19b and section 9–19c; (13) the Commissioner of Public Safety and any sworn member of any local police department or the Division of State Police within the Department of Public Safety, in all affidavits, statements, depositions, complaints or reports made to or by any member of any local police department or said Division of State Police or any constable who is under the supervision of said commissioner or any of such officers of said Division of State Police and who is certified under the provisions of sections 7–294a to 7–294e, inclusive, and performs criminal law enforcement duties; (14) judge advocates of the United States Army, Navy, Air Force and Marine Corps, law specialists of the United States Coast Guard, adjutants, assistant adjutants, acting adjutants and personnel adjutants, commanding officers, executive officers and officers whose rank is lieutenant commander or major, or above, of the armed forces, as defined in section 27–103, as amended, to persons serving with or in the armed forces, as defined in said section, or their spouses; (15) investigators, deputy investigators, investigative aides, secretaries, clerical assistants, social workers, social worker trainees, paralegals and certified legal interns employed by or assigned to the Public Defender Services Commission in the performance of their assigned duties; (16) bail commissioners employed by the Judicial Department in the performance of their assigned duties; (17) juvenile matter investigators employed by the Division of Criminal Justice in the performance of their assigned duties; (18) the chairperson of the Connecticut Siting Council or the chairperson's designee; (19) the presiding officer at an agency hearing under section 4–177b; (20) family relations counselors employed by the Judicial Department and support enforcement officers and investigators employed by the Department of Social Services Bureau of Child Support Enforcement and the Judicial Department, in the performance of their assigned duties; (21) the chairperson, vice-chairperson and members of the Board of Parole, ~~parole officers and parole supervisors~~ in the performance of their assigned duties; and (22) the Commissioner of Correction or the commissioner's designee.

Sec. 114. Subsection (a) of section 1–217 of the general statutes is repealed and the following is substituted in lieu thereof (Effective from passage):

(a) No public agency may disclose, under the Freedom of Information Act, [1] the residential address of any of the following persons:

(1) A federal court judge, federal court magistrate, judge of the Superior Court, Appellate Court or Supreme Court of the state, or family support magistrate;

(2) A sworn member of a municipal police department or a sworn member of the Division of State Police within the Department of Public Safety;

(3) An employee of the Department of Correction;

(4) An attorney-at-law who represents or has represented the state in a criminal prosecution;

(5) An attorney-at-law who is or has been employed by the Public Defender Services Division or a social worker who is employed by the Public Defender Services Division;

(6) An inspector employed by the Division of Criminal Justice;

(7) A firefighter;

(8) An employee of the Department of Children and Families;

(9) A member ~~or employee~~ of the Board of Parole;

(10) An employee of the judicial branch; or

(11) A member or employee of the Commission on Human Rights and Opportunities.

[1] C.G.S.A. § 1–200 et seq.

Sec. 115. Subsection (e) of section 14–10 of the general statutes is repealed and the following is substituted in lieu thereof (Effective from passage):

(e) In the event (1) a federal court judge, federal court magistrate or judge of the Superior Court, Appellate Court or Supreme Court of the state, (2) a member of a municipal police department or a member of the Division of State Police within the Department of Public Safety, (3) an employee of the Department of Correction, (4) an attorney-at-law who represents or has represented the state in a criminal prosecution, or (5) a member ~~or employee~~ of the Board of Parole submits a written request and furnishes such individual's business address to the commissioner, such business address only shall be disclosed or available for public inspection to the extent authorized by this section.

Sec. 116. Section 18–100d of the general statutes is repealed and the following is substituted in lieu thereof (Effective from passage):

Notwithstanding any other provision of the general statutes, any person convicted of a crime committed on or after October 1, 1994, shall be subject to supervision by personnel of the Department of Correction ~~or the Board of Parole~~ until the expiration of the maximum term or terms for which ~~he~~ such person was sentenced.

Sec. 117. Subsection (g) of section 46a–152 of the general statutes is repealed and the following is substituted in lieu thereof (Effective from passage):

(g) Nothing in this section shall be construed as limiting the justified use of physical force by a local, state or federal law enforcement official or an employee of the ~~Board of Parole~~ Department of Correction responsible for the supervision of persons released on parole while in the performance of such official's or employee's duties.

Sec. 118. Subsection (b) of section 51–5c of the general statutes is repealed and the following is substituted in lieu thereof (Effective from passage):

(b)(1) The following information contained in the registry of protective orders shall not be subject to disclosure and may be accessed only in accordance with this section, unless otherwise ordered by the court: (A) Any information that would identify a person protected by an order contained in the registry; (B) any information that is confidential pursuant to state or federal law, including, but not limited to, any information that is confidential pursuant to a court order; and (C) any information entered in the registry pursuant to an ex parte order prior to a hearing by a court having jurisdiction over the parties and the subject matter.

(2) Any employee of the Judicial Department authorized by policies and procedures adopted by the Chief Court Administrator shall have access to such information. The Chief Court Administrator may grant access to such information to personnel of the Department of Public Safety, the Department of Correction, ~~the Board of Parole,~~ the Psychiatric Security Review Board, the Division of Criminal Justice, any municipal or tribal police department within this state or any other agency, organization or person determined by the Chief Court Administrator, pursuant to policies and procedures adopted by the Chief Court Administrator, to have a legitimate interest in the information contained in the registry. Any person who obtains such information pursuant to this subdivision may use and disclose the information only in the performance of such person's duties.

(3) Except as provided in subsection (c) of this section, the information contained in the registry shall be provided to and may be accessed through the Connecticut on-line law enforcement communications teleprocessing system maintained by the Department of Public Safety. Nothing in this section shall be construed to permit public access to the Connecticut on-line law enforcement communications teleprocessing system.

Sec. 119. Section 53a–22 of the general statutes is repealed and the following is substituted in lieu thereof (Effective from passage):

(a) For purposes of this section, a reasonable belief that a person has committed an offense means a reasonable belief in facts or circumstances which if true would in law constitute an offense. If the believed facts or circumstances would not in law constitute an offense, an erroneous though not unreasonable belief that the law is otherwise does not render justifiable the use of physical force to make an arrest or to prevent an escape from custody. A peace officer or an authorized official of the Department of Correction ~~or the Board of Parole~~ who is effecting an arrest pursuant to a warrant or preventing an escape from custody is justified in using the physical force prescribed in subsections (b) and (c) of this section unless such warrant is invalid and is known by such officer to be invalid.

(b) Except as provided in subsection (a) of this section, a peace officer or authorized official of the Department of Correction ~~or the Board of Parole~~ is justified in using physical force upon another person when and to the extent that he reasonably believes such to be necessary to: (1) Effect an arrest or prevent the escape from custody of a person whom he reasonably believes to have committed an offense, unless he knows that the arrest or custody is unauthorized; or (2) defend himself or a third person from the use or imminent use of physical force while effecting or attempting to effect an arrest or while preventing or attempting to prevent an escape.

(c) A peace officer or authorized official of the Department of Correction ~~or the Board of Parole~~ is justified in using deadly physical force upon another person for the purposes specified in subsection (b) of this section only when he reasonably believes such to be necessary to: (1) Defend himself or a third person from the use or imminent use of deadly physical force; or (2) effect an arrest or prevent the escape from custody of a person whom he reasonably believes has committed or attempted to commit a felony which involved the infliction or threatened infliction of serious physical injury and if, where feasible, he has given warning of his intent to use deadly physical force.

(d) Except as provided in subsection (e) of this section, a person who has been directed by a peace officer or authorized official of the Department of Correction ~~or the Board of Parole~~ to assist such peace officer or official to effect an arrest or to prevent an escape from custody is justified in using reasonable physical force when and to the extent that he reasonably believes such to be necessary to carry out such peace officer's or official's direction.

(e) A person who has been directed to assist a peace officer or authorized official of the Department of Correction ~~or the Board of Parole~~ under circumstances specified in subsection (d) of this section may use deadly physical force to effect an arrest or to prevent an escape from custody only when: (1) He reasonably believes such to be necessary to defend himself or a third person from what he reasonably believes to be the use or imminent use of deadly physical force; or (2) he is directed or authorized by such peace officer or official to use deadly physical force, unless he knows that the peace officer or official himself is not authorized to use deadly physical force under the circumstances.

(f) A private person acting on his own account is justified in using reasonable physical force upon another person when and to the extent that he reasonably believes such to be necessary to effect an arrest or to prevent the escape from custody of an arrested person whom he reasonably believes to have committed an offense and who in fact has committed such offense; but he is not justified in using deadly physical force in such circumstances, except in defense of person as prescribed in section 53a–19.

Sec. 120. Subsection (a) of section 53a–167c of the general statutes, as amended by section 1 of public act 03–6 and section 126 of public act 03–19, is repealed and the following is substituted in lieu thereof (Effective from passage):

(a) A person is guilty of assault of public safety or emergency medical personnel when, with intent to prevent a reasonably identifiable peace officer, firefighter or employee of an emergency medical service organization, as defined in section 53a–3, emergency room physician or nurse, employee of the Department of Correction, ~~employee or~~ member of the Board of Parole, probation officer, employee of the judicial branch assigned to provide pretrial secure detention and programming services to juveniles accused of the commission of a delinquent act, employee of the Department of Children and Families assigned to provide direct services to children and youth in the care or custody of the department or employee of a municipal police department assigned to provide security at the police department's lockup and holding facility from performing his or her duties, and while such peace officer, firefighter, employee, physician, nurse, member or probation officer is acting in the performance of his or her duties, (1) such person causes physical injury to such peace officer, firefighter, employee, physician, nurse, member or probation officer, or (2) such person throws or hurls, or causes to be thrown or hurled, any rock, bottle, can or other article, object or missile of any kind capable of causing physical harm, damage or injury, at such peace officer, firefighter, employee, physician, nurse, member or probation officer, or (3) such person uses or causes to be used any mace, tear gas or any like or similar deleterious agent against such peace officer, firefighter, employee, physician, nurse, member or probation officer, or (4) such person throws or hurls, or causes to be thrown or hurled, any paint, dye or other like or similar staining, discoloring or coloring agent or any type of offensive or noxious liquid, agent or substance at such peace officer, firefighter, employee, physician, nurse, member or probation officer, or (5) such person throws or hurls, or causes to be thrown or hurled, any bodily fluid including, but not limited to, urine, feces, blood or saliva at such peace officer, firefighter, employee, physician, nurse, member or probation officer.

Sec. 121. Subsection (d) of section 54–102g of the general statutes, as amended by section 1 of public act 03–242, is repealed and the following is substituted in lieu thereof (Effective from passage):

(d) Any person who has been convicted of a criminal offense against a victim who is a minor, a nonviolent sexual offense or a sexually violent offense, as those terms are defined in section 54–250, or a felony, and is serving a period of probation or parole, and who has not submitted to the taking of a blood or other biological sample pursuant to subsection (a), (b) or (c) of this section, shall, prior to discharge from the custody of the Court Support Services Division or the ~~Board of Parole~~ Department of Correction and at such time as said division or ~~board~~ department may specify, submit to the taking of a blood or other biological sample for DNA (deoxyribonucleic acid) analysis to determine identification characteristics specific to the person.

Sec. 122. Section 54–125g of the general statutes is repealed and the following is substituted in lieu thereof (Effective from passage):

Notwithstanding the provisions of sections 18–100d, as amended by this act, 54–124c and 54–125a, any person who has six months or less to the expiration of the maximum term or terms for which such person was sentenced, may be allowed to go at large on parole provided such person agrees (1) to be subject to supervision by personnel of the ~~Board of Parole~~ Department of Correction for a period of one year, and (2) to be retained in the institution from which such person was paroled for a period equal to the unexpired portion of the term of his or her sentence if such person is found to have violated the terms or conditions of his or her parole. Any person subject to the provisions of subdivision (1) or (2) of subsection (b) of section 54–125a shall only be eligible to go at large on parole under this section after having served ninety-five per cent of the definite sentence imposed.

Sec. 123. Section 54–127 of the general statutes is repealed and the following is substituted in lieu thereof (Effective from passage):

The request of the Commissioner of Correction or any officer of the Department of Correction so designated by the commissioner, or of the Board of Parole ~~,~~ or its chairman ~~or any officer of the Board of Parole designated by the chairman~~ shall be sufficient warrant to authorize any officer of the Department of Correction ~~or of the Board of Parole, as the case may be,~~ or any officer authorized by law to serve criminal process within this state, to return any convict or inmate on parole into actual custody; and any such officer, police officer, constable or state marshal shall arrest and hold any parolee or inmate when so requested, without any written warrant.

Sec. 124. Subsection (a) of section 54–128 of the general statutes is repealed and the following is substituted in lieu thereof (Effective from passage):

(a) Any paroled ~~convict or~~ inmate who has been returned to ~~the custody of the Commissioner of Correction or~~ any institution of the Department of Correction for violation of ~~his~~ such inmate's parole may be retained in ~~the institution from which he was paroled~~ a correctional institution for a period equal to the unexpired portion of the term of ~~his~~ such inmate's sentence at the date of the request or order for ~~his~~ such inmate's return less any commutation or diminution of ~~his~~ such inmate's sentence earned except that the Board of Parole may, in its discretion, determine that ~~he~~ such inmate shall forfeit any or all of such earned time, or may be again paroled by said board.

Sec. 125. Subsection (b) of section 54–131d of the general statutes is repealed and the following is substituted in lieu thereof (Effective from passage):

(b) The Board of Parole may require as a condition of release on medical parole periodic diagnoses as described in section 54–131c. If after review of such diagnoses the board finds that a parolee released pursuant to sections 54–131a to 54–131g, inclusive, is no longer so debilitated or incapacitated as to be physically incapable of presenting a danger to society, such parolee shall be returned to ~~the custody~~ any institution of the Department of Correction.

Sec. 126. Section 13 of public act 04–139 is repealed and the following is substituted in lieu thereof (Effective from passage):

The Commissioner of Correction shall prohibit any person who has been convicted of a crime that requires registration pursuant to chapter 969 [1] of the general statutes from ~~having access to~~ using a computer with Internet access while such person is in the custody of the commissioner and confined in a correctional facility.

[1] C.G.S.A. § 54–250 et seq.

Sec. 127. Subsection (a) of section 1 of public act 04–155 is repealed and the following is substituted in lieu thereof (Effective from passage):

(a) All civil actions brought to recover damages resulting from personal injury or wrongful death, whether in tort or in contract, in which it is alleged that such injury or death resulted from the negligence of a health care provider, ~~as defined in section 52–184b of the general statutes,~~ shall be referred to mandatory mediation pursuant to this section, unless the parties have agreed to refer the civil action to an alternative dispute resolution program. For the purposes of this subsection, "health care provider" means a provider, as defined in subsection (b) of section 20–7b, or an institution, as defined in section 19a–490, as amended by section 2 of public act 03–274.

Sec. 128. Subsection (c) of section 52–192a of the general statutes, as amended by section 8 of public act 04–155, is repealed and the following is substituted in lieu thereof (Effective from passage):

(c) With respect to any civil action brought to recover damages resulting from personal injury or wrongful death, whether in tort or in contract, in which it is alleged that such injury or death resulted from the negligence of a health care provider, ~~as defined in section 52–184b,~~ and where the cause of action accrued on or after the effective date of this section, if the court ascertains from the record that the plaintiff has recovered an amount equal to or greater than the sum certain stated in the plaintiff's offer of judgment, the court shall add to the amount so recovered eight per cent annual interest on said amount, except that if the plaintiff has recovered an amount that is more than twice the sum certain stated in the plaintiff's offer of judgment, the court shall add to the amount so recovered (1) eight per cent annual interest on the portion of the amount recovered that is equal to or less than twice the sum certain stated in such offer of judgment, and (2) four per cent annual interest on the portion of the amount recovered that is more than twice the sum certain stated in such offer. For the purposes of this subsection, "health care provider" means a provider, as defined in subsection (b) of section 20–7b, or an institution, as defined in section 19a–490, as amended by section 2 of public act 03–274.

Sec. 129. Subdivision (1) of subsection (c) of section 52–251c of the general statutes, as amended by section 15 of public act 04–155, is repealed and the following is substituted in lieu thereof (Effective from passage):

(1) Whenever a claimant in a medical malpractice ~~case~~ claim or civil action enters into a contingency fee arrangement with an attorney which provides for a fee that would exceed the percentage limitations set forth in subsection (b) of this section, such arrangement shall not be valid unless the claimant's attorney files an application with the court for approval of such arrangement and the court, after a hearing, grants such application. The claimant's attorney shall attach to such application a copy of such fee arrangement and the proposed unsigned writ, summons and complaint in the case. Such fee arrangement shall provide that the attorney will advance all costs in connection with the investigation and prosecution or settlement of the case and the claimant will not be liable for the reimbursement of the attorney for any such costs if there is no recovery.

Sec. 130. Subdivision (2) of subsection (e) of section 52–251c of the general statutes, as amended by section 15 of public act 04–155, is repealed and the following is substituted in lieu thereof (Effective from passage):

(2) For the purposes of this section and with respect to a medical malpractice ~~case~~ claim or civil action in which an application was granted by a court pursuant to subsection (c) of this section, "damages awarded and received" means in a ~~medical malpractice~~ civil action in which final judgment is entered, that amount of the judgment or amended judgment entered by the court that is received by the claimant after deduction for any disbursements made or costs incurred by the attorney in connection with the investigation and prosecution or settlement of the civil action, other than ordinary office overhead and expense, for which the claimant is liable; and "settlement amount received" means in a ~~medical malpractice~~ claim or civil action in which no final judgment is entered, the amount received by the claimant pursuant to a settlement agreement after deduction for any disbursements made or costs incurred by the attorney in connection with the investigation and prosecution or settlement of the claim or civil action, other than ordinary office overhead and expense, for which the claimant is liable.

Sec. 131. Section 52–251c of the general statutes, as amended by section 15 of public act 04–155, is amended by adding subsection (f) as follows (Effective from passage):

(NEW) (f) For the purposes of this section, "medical malpractice claim or civil action" means a claim or civil action brought to recover damages resulting from personal injury or wrongful death, whether in tort or in contract, in which it is alleged that such injury or death resulted from the negligence of a health care provider, and "health care provider" means a provider, as defined in subsection (b) of section 20–7b, or an institution, as defined in section 19a–490, as amended by section 2 of public act 03–274.

Sec. 132. Section 18 of public act 04–155 is repealed and the following is substituted in lieu thereof (Effective from passage):

Whenever in a civil action to recover damages resulting from personal injury or wrongful death, whether in tort or in contract, in which it is alleged that such injury or death resulted from the negligence of a health care provider, the jury renders a verdict specifying noneconomic damages, as defined in section 52–572h of the general statutes, in an amount exceeding one million dollars, the court shall review the evidence presented to the jury to determine if the amount of noneconomic damages specified in the verdict is excessive as a matter of law in that it so shocks the sense of justice as to compel the conclusion that the jury was influenced by partiality, prejudice, mistake or corruption. If the court so concludes, it shall order a remittitur and, upon failure of the party so ordered to remit the amount ordered by the court, it shall set aside the verdict and order a new trial. For the purposes of this section, "health care provider" means a provider, as defined in subsection (b) of section 20–7b, or an institution, as defined in section 19a–490, as amended by section 2 of public act 03–274.

Sec. 133. Section 38a–395 of the general statutes, as amended by section 16 of public act 04–155, is repealed and the following is substituted in lieu thereof (Effective January 1, 2005):

(a) As used in this section:

(1) "Claim" means a request for indemnification filed by a ~~medical professional or entity~~ physician, surgeon, hospital, advanced practice registered nurse or physician assistant pursuant to a professional liability policy for a loss for which a reserve amount has been established by an insurer;

(2) "Closed claim" means a claim that has been settled, or otherwise disposed of, where the insurer has made all indemnity and expense payments on the claim; and

(3) "Insurer" means an insurer, as defined in section 38a–1, as amended, that insures a ~~medical professional or entity~~ physician, surgeon, hospital, advanced practice registered nurse or physician assistant against professional liability. "Insurer" includes, but is not limited to, a captive insurer or a self-insured person.

(b) On and after January 1, 2005, each insurer shall provide to the Insurance Commissioner a closed claim report, on such form as the commissioner prescribes, in accordance with this section. The insurer shall submit the report not later than ten days after the last day of the calendar quarter in which a claim is closed. The report shall only include information about claims settled under the laws of this state.

(c) The closed claim report shall include:

(1) Details about the insured and insurer, including: (A) The name of the insurer; (B) the professional liability insurance policy limits and whether the policy was an occurrence policy or was issued on a claims-made basis; (C) the name, address, health care provider professional license number and specialty coverage of the insured; and (D) the insured's policy number and a unique claim number.

(2) Details about the injury or loss, including: (A) The date of the injury or loss that was the basis of the claim; (B) the date the injury or loss was reported to the insurer; (C) the name of the institution or location at which the injury or loss occurred; (D) the type of injury or loss, including a severity of injury rating that corresponds with the severity of injury scale that the Insurance Commissioner shall establish based on the severity of injury scale developed by the National Association of Insurance Commissioners; and (E) the name, age and gender of any injured person covered by the claim. Any individually identifiable health information, as defined in 45 CFR 160.103, as from time to time amended, submitted pursuant to this subdivision shall be confidential. The reporting of the information is required by law. If necessary to comply with federal privacy laws, including the Health Insurance Portability and Accountability Act of 1996, ~~P.L. 104–191~~ (P.L. 104–191) (HIPAA), [1] as from time to time amended, the insured shall arrange with the insurer to release the required information.

(3) Details about the claims process, including: (A) Whether a lawsuit was filed, and if so, in which court; (B) the outcome of such lawsuit; (C) the number of other defendants, if any; (D) the stage in the process when the claim was closed; (E) the dates of the trial; (F) the date of the judgment or settlement, if any; (G) whether an appeal was filed, and if so, the date filed; (H) the resolution of the appeal and the date such appeal was decided; (I) the date the claim was closed; (J) the initial indemnity and expense reserve for the claim; and (K) the final indemnity and expense reserve for the claim.

(4) Details about the amount paid on the claim, including: (A) The total amount of the initial judgment rendered by a jury or awarded by the court; (B) the total amount of the settlement if there was no judgment rendered or awarded; (C) the total amount of the settlement if the claim was settled after judgment was rendered or awarded; (D) the amount of economic damages, as defined in section 52–572h, or the insurer's estimate of the amount in the event of a settlement; (E) the amount of noneconomic damages, as defined in section 52–572h, or the insurer's estimate of the amount in the event of a settlement; (F) the amount of any interest awarded due to failure to accept an offer of judgment; (G) the amount of any remittitur or additur; (H) the amount of final judgment after remittitur or additur; (I) the amount paid by the insurer; (J) the amount paid by the defendant due to a deductible or a judgment or settlement in excess of policy limits; (K) the amount paid by other insurers; (L) the amount paid by other defendants; (M) whether a structured settlement was used; (N) the expense assigned to and recorded with the claim, including, but not limited to, defense and investigation costs, but not including the actual claim payment; and (O) any other information the commissioner determines to be necessary to regulate the professional liability insurance industry with respect to ~~medical professionals and entities~~ physicians, surgeons, hospitals, advanced practice registered nurses or physicians assistants, ensure the industry's solvency and ensure that such liability insurance is available and affordable.

(d)(1) The commissioner shall establish an electronic database composed of closed claim reports filed pursuant to this section.

(2) The commissioner shall compile the data included in individual closed claim reports into an aggregated summary format and shall prepare a written annual report of the summary data. The report shall provide an analysis of closed claim information including a minimum of five years of comparative data, when available, trends

in frequency and severity of claims, itemization of damages, timeliness of the claims process, and any other descriptive or analytical information that would assist in interpreting the trends in closed claims.

(3) The annual report shall include a summary of rate filings for professional liability insurance for ~~medical professionals and entities~~ physicians, surgeons, hospitals, advanced practice registered nurses or physicians assistants, which have been approved by the department for the prior calendar year, including an analysis of the trend of direct losses, incurred losses, earned premiums and investment income as compared to prior years. The report shall include base premiums charged by ~~medical malpractice~~ insurers for each specialty and the number of providers insured by specialty for each insurer.

(4) Not later than March 15, 2006, and annually thereafter, the commissioner shall submit the annual report to the joint standing committee of the General Assembly having cognizance of matters relating to insurance in accordance with section 11–4a. The commissioner shall also (A) make the report available to the public, (B) post the report on its Internet site, and (C) provide public access to the contents of the electronic database after the commissioner establishes that the names and other individually identifiable information about the claimant and practitioner have been removed.

(e) The Insurance Commissioner shall provide the Commissioner of Public Health with electronic access to all information received pursuant to this section. The Commissioner of Public Health shall maintain the confidentiality of such information in the same manner and to the same extent as required for the Insurance Commissioner.

[1] 29 U.S.C.A. § 1181 et seq.

Sec. 134. Section 19 of public act 04–155 is repealed and the following is substituted in lieu thereof (Effective July 1, 2004, and applicable to taxable years commencing on or after January 1, 2004):

(a) Any resident of this state, as defined in subdivision (1) of subsection (a) of section 12–701, who is a physician licensed pursuant to chapter 370 [1] and who is subject to the tax imposed under chapter 229 [2] for any taxable year shall be entitled to a credit in determining the amount of tax liability under said chapter, for a portion, as permitted by this section, of the amount of medical malpractice insurance premiums first becoming due and actually paid during such taxable year by such person in accordance with this section.

(b) The credit allowed under this section shall be equal to one hundred per cent of the amount by which the medical malpractice insurance premiums first becoming due and actually paid during such taxable year by such person exceed twenty-five per cent of the person's Connecticut taxable income, provided such credit shall not exceed an amount equal to fifteen per cent of such premiums.

(c) The credit may only be used to reduce such qualifying taxpayer's tax liability for the year for which such credit is applicable and shall not be used to reduce such tax liability to less than zero.

(d) The amount of tax due pursuant to sections 12–705 and 12–722 shall be calculated without regard to this credit.

(e) Any physician who has had, at any time, a judgment entered against him or her as a defendant in a civil action to recover damages for personal injury or wrongful death resulting from the acts or omissions of such physician in the medical diagnosis, care or treatment of a person shall not be entitled to a credit under this section.

[1] C.G.S.A. § 20–8 et seq.
[2] C.G.S.A. § 12–700 et seq.

Sec. 135. (Effective from passage) Section 54–124d of the general statutes is repealed.

Sec. 136. (Effective from passage) Section 36 of public act 04–234 is repealed.

Approved June 14, 2004.

BUDGETS—APPROPRIATIONS

May Special Session, P.A. No. 04–2

H.B. No. 5801

AN ACT CONCERNING BUDGET IMPLEMENTATION.

Be it enacted by the Senate and House of Representatives in General Assembly convened:

Section 1. (Effective July 1, 2004) Up to $ 100,000 of federal funds available to the Department of Social Services shall be transferred to the Commission on Fire Prevention and Control, during the fiscal year ending June 30, 2005, to reimburse municipalities for the costs of emergency responses.

Sec. 2. (Effective July 1, 2004) The sum of $ 1,000,000 appropriated to DEBT SERVICE - STATE TREASURER, Debt Service, for the fiscal year ending June 30, 2005, shall be transferred to the appropriation to DEBT SERVICE - STATE TREASURER, CHEFA Day Care Security, for said fiscal year.

Sec. 3. (Effective July 1, 2004) The sum of $ 3,774,657 is appropriated to the Labor Department, from the General Fund, for the fiscal year ending June 30, 2005, for Workforce Investment Act. [1]

[1] 29 U.S.C.A. § 2801 et seq.

Sec. 4. (Effective July 1, 2004) The sum of $ 100,000 appropriated to the Department of Higher Education, for the fiscal year ending June 30, 2004, for Education and Health Initiatives, shall not lapse June 30, 2004, and shall be transferred to the Office of Workforce Competitiveness, CETC Workforce, for the fiscal year ending June 30, 2005, for Workforce Development.

Sec. 5. (Effective July 1, 2004) The sum of $ 50,000 appropriated to the Department of Higher Education, for the fiscal year ending June 30, 2005, for Education and Health Initiatives, shall be transferred to the Office of Workforce Competitiveness, CETC Workforce, for Workforce Development.

Sec. 6. Section 5–200 of the general statutes is repealed and the following is substituted in lieu thereof (Effective from passage):

(a) The Commissioner of Administrative Services or his authorized agent shall administer centralized and decentralized selection programs that will identify those applicants most qualified for appointment to or promotion in the state classified service, and establish candidate and reemployment lists for the various classes of positions within occupational groups and career progression levels. Upon a request from any appointing authority or indication of the need for additional employees, as evidenced by the presence of a temporary or provisional employee or by a request for certification of a temporary employee in any class, the commissioner or his designee shall certify the names of persons eligible for employment or reemployment. The commissioner shall: (1) Install and administer service-rating systems; (2) devise plans for, and cooperate with, appointing authorities and other supervising officials in the conduct of employee training programs to the end that the quality of service rendered by persons in the classified service may be continually improved; (3) conduct research into methods of selection, service ratings and other problems of personnel administration; (4) arrange for and, in cooperation with appointing authorities, effect transfers; (5) cooperate with appointing authorities in employee recruitment programs; (6) administer annual sick and special leaves of absence and hours of work and attendance in accordance with the provisions of this chapter and any regulations relating thereto; (7) establish personnel standards, governing promotions, classifications, reclassifications and the creation of positions, that will provide guidance to all agencies in matters of personnel management and serve as a means to evaluate agency performance in conducting personnel management; and (8) see that all appointments, promotions, layoffs, demotions, suspensions, removals and retirements are made in accordance with the applicable provisions of the general statutes and regulations issued pursuant thereto. The commissioner may fully or partially delegate the responsibilities set forth in this subsection to the heads of state agencies or their authorized agents, subject to audit, in order to improve human resource management.

(b) The commissioner shall review position classifications in accordance with subsection (c) of section 5–206.

(c) The commissioner shall cause to be kept for the classified service suitable records of (1) regulations adopted under this chapter, (2) classifications of positions, occupational groups, career progression levels and schedules of compensation provided for under this chapter, (3) standards for examining qualifications and measuring service,

(4) examinations conducted and candidate and reemployment lists established, and (5) provisional and temporary appointments and other official acts.

(d) The commissioner shall prescribe procedures for reports to be submitted to him.

(e) The commissioner shall establish and maintain a complete roster of the employees and officers in the state service, whether under the classified service or not, showing for each such employee the title of the position held, his departmental, agency or institution assignment, rate of compensation, date of appointment and each change in his status, including any increase and decrease in pay, change in title, transfers or other facts which the commissioner considers desirable and pertinent.

(f) The commissioner shall prescribe reasonable conditions and procedures under which the records of the Department of Administrative Services shall be open to public inspection during usual business hours, except as provided in section 5-225. He shall take all due precautions to prevent the securing in advance by any unauthorized person of any material to be used in any examination under this chapter, unless such material is available for all applicants. Statements of the former employers of applicants shall be considered confidential and shall not be open to inspection by any person.

(g) The commissioner and his agents shall have free access to premises and records under the control of all officers, appointing authorities and other state employees during usual business hours and shall be furnished such facilities, assistance and information as he and his agents require in carrying out their functions. This subsection shall not apply to the medical records of state employees, unless the employee gives his consent or unless the information sought is necessary to assure adjudication of any responsibility on the part of the state or unless medical interpretations of preemployment and other examinations are requested by the commissioner.

(h)(1) The commissioner shall, after completion of all established preliminary procedures necessary to prepare new and revised regulations, print and provide current and complete personnel regulations to all state agencies and to recognized state employee organizations. (2) New and revised regulations prepared as the result of legislative changes or development of new policies shall be processed in accordance with established procedures within a period of time not less than six months from their effective date and distributed in the same manner.

(i) The commissioner may designate any two or more of his staff to serve as a hearing panel with respect to any matter before the commissioner. The commissioner and any hearing panel shall have the power to make investigations, inquiries and hold hearings. Any such panel shall report and may submit recommendations to the commissioner but shall have no other power except as otherwise specified in this chapter.

(j) The commissioner shall issue such regulations as he may find necessary or appropriate for the administration of personnel pursuant to the provisions of this chapter.

(k) The commissioner shall, subject to the approval of the Secretary of the Office of Policy and Management, establish compensation schedules or plans pertaining to all state employees except employees of the Judicial and Legislative Departments and employees whose compensation is prescribed by statute. The commissioner shall prescribe higher compensation for work performed under less desirable conditions or at less desirable hours.

(*l*) The commissioner shall establish classes of positions, occupational groups and career progression levels for all state employees holding positions in the classified service.

(m) The commissioner shall maintain current compensation schedules pertaining to all employees specified in subsection (k) of this section and a comprehensive plan of position classifications pertaining to all employees specified in subsection (*l*) of this section.

(n) Any interested employee, his representative or any appointing authority may submit to the commissioner written data, views, arguments or request for a hearing in regard to specified position classifications or allocation of a class of positions to the compensation schedule. Within two months after the commissioner shall have received such data, views or arguments or shall have held any requested hearing, he shall forward to such employee, representative or appointing authority his written decision thereon, together with all written materials submitted to him by the interested employee or his representative and such other information as he considers appropriate.

(*o*) The commissioner may at any time establish, abolish, divide or combine classes of positions and allocation of classes of positions to the compensation schedule. Any such action having a fiscal impact must be approved by the Secretary of the Office of Policy and Management. The commissioner may at any time, subject to the approval of the Secretary of the Office of Policy and Management, amend or repeal any portion of any compensation schedule. The commissioner need not conduct any investigation or hearing prior to any such action.

(p) When such authority is not otherwise conferred by statute, the commissioner may issue orders to provide that (1) executive or judicial branch employees exempt from the classified service or not included in any prevailing bargaining unit contract, except unclassified employees of any board of trustees of the constituent units of higher education, be granted rights and benefits not less than those granted to employees in the classified service or covered under such contracts, or (2) retirement benefits for state employees exempt from the classified service or not included in any prevailing bargaining unit contract and employees of state-aided institutions, as defined in section 5–175, be adjusted to provide retirement benefits for such employees which are the same as those most frequently provided under the terms of approved bargaining unit contracts in effect at the time of such adjustment. When such authority is not otherwise conferred by statute, the board of trustees of any constituent unit of the state system of higher education may issue orders to provide that the unclassified employees of such board be granted rights and benefits not less than those granted to employees of the board who are covered under a prevailing bargaining unit contract. Where there is a conflict between an order granting such rights and benefits and any provision of the general statutes, such order shall prevail. Such orders shall be subject to the approval of the Secretary of the Office of Policy and Management. If the secretary approves such order, and such order is in conflict with any provision of the general statutes, the secretary shall forward a copy of such order to the joint committee of the General Assembly having cognizance of labor matters.

(q) Commencing November 1, 1989, elected officials and employees in the legislative branch and elected officials in the executive branch shall be granted rights and benefits equal to those granted to employees in the classified service covered under a prevailing collective bargaining agreement negotiated in accordance with subdivision (1) of subsection (f) of section 5–278.

~~(q)~~ (r) When requested by the appropriate appointing authority, the commissioner shall establish classes of positions for employees holding positions in the unclassified service and shall establish compensation schedules pertaining to employees of the Judicial and Legislative Departments, subject to the approval of the Secretary of the Office of Policy and Management.

~~(r)~~ (s) The commissioner and any municipality or other political subdivision of the state may enter into an agreement whereby the Department of Administrative Services shall provide such personnel administration services as may be requested by such municipality or political subdivision. Such agreement shall provide for the payment by such municipality or political subdivision, to the commissioner, of expenses incurred in the provision of such personnel services. All payments received by the commissioner pursuant to this section shall be deposited in the General Fund and credited to the appropriations of the Department of Administrative Services in accordance with the provisions of section 4–86.

~~(s)~~ (t) Notwithstanding the provisions of this chapter, any matters involving collective bargaining shall be the responsibility of the Secretary of the Office of Policy and Management.

Sec. 7. Section 5–257 of the general statutes is amended by adding subsection (f) as follows (Effective from passage):

(NEW) (f) Commencing November 1, 1989, as used in this section, "employee" includes an elected official in the executive branch.

Sec. 8. Section 6–38m of the general statutes, as amended by section 15 of public act 03–19 and section 5 of public act 03–224, is repealed and the following is substituted in lieu thereof (Effective July 1, 2004):

~~(a) There is established a state marshal account which shall be a separate nonlapsing account within the General Fund. The account shall contain any moneys required by law to be deposited into the account. Any balance remaining in said account at the end of any fiscal year shall be carried forward in the account for the next fiscal year.~~

~~(b)~~ Commencing October 1, 2001, and not later than October first each year thereafter, each state marshal shall pay an annual fee of two hundred fifty dollars to the State Marshal Commission, which fee shall be deposited in the General Fund.

~~(c) The additional fee paid to the Superior Court pursuant to section 52–259d and any fee collected pursuant to subsection (b) of this section, shall be deposited in the General Fund.~~

~~(d) The first two hundred fifty thousand dollars collected each fiscal year, pursuant to subsections (b) and (c) of this section, shall be credited to the state marshal account and be available for expenditure by the State Marshal Commission for the operating expenses of the commission. From July 1, 2001, until July 1, 2006, the Secretary of the Office of Policy and Management shall review and approve or disapprove the budget of the commission. For the fiscal year ending June 30, 2004, and each fiscal year thereafter, the State Marshals Advisory Board shall~~

~~submit to the State Marshal Commission a request for administrative support for such fiscal year. Such request shall be submitted prior to the beginning of such fiscal year.~~

~~(e) For the fiscal year ending June 30, 2002, the next one hundred ten thousand dollars collected in subsections (b) and (c) of this section shall be transferred to the Judicial Department and be available for expenditure by the Judicial Department for the operating expenses of the Commission on Racial and Ethnic Disparity. The next two hundred thirty thousand dollars shall be transferred to the Office of Policy and Management for Other Expenses for the purposes of subsections (f) and (g) of section 54–1m.~~

~~(f) The moneys made available in subsection (e) of this section may be transferred by said office to agencies requiring funds for such purposes.~~

Sec. 9. Subsection (a) of section 46a–57 of the general statutes is repealed and the following is substituted in lieu thereof (Effective from passage):

(a)(1) The Governor shall appoint three human rights referees for terms commencing October 1, 1998, and four human rights referees for terms commencing January 1, 1999. The human rights referees so appointed shall serve for a term of one year.

(2)(A) On and after October 1, 1999, the Governor shall appoint seven human rights referees with the advice and consent of both houses of the General Assembly. The Governor shall appoint three human rights referees to serve for a term of two years commencing October 1, 1999. The Governor shall appoint four human rights referees to serve for a term of three years commencing January 1, 2000. Thereafter, human rights referees shall serve for a term of three years.

(B) On and after July 1, 2001, there shall be five human rights referees. Each of the human rights referees serving on July 1, 2001, shall complete the term to which such referee was appointed. Thereafter, human rights referees shall be appointed by the Governor, with the advice and consent of both houses of the General Assembly, to serve for a term of three years.

(C) On and after July 1, 2004, there shall be seven human rights referees. Each of the human rights referees serving on July 1, 2004, shall complete the term to which such referee was appointed and shall serve until his successor is appointed and qualified. Thereafter, human rights referees shall be appointed by the Governor, with the advice and consent of both houses of the General Assembly, to serve for a term of three years.

(3) When the General Assembly is not in session, any vacancy shall be filled pursuant to the provisions of section 4–19. The Governor may remove any human rights referee for cause.

Sec. 10. Subsection (h) of section 46b–231 of the general statutes is repealed and the following is substituted in lieu thereof (Effective January 1, 2005):

~~(h)(1) On and after April 1, 2000, the Chief Family Support Magistrate shall receive a salary of ninety-nine thousand five hundred eighty-seven dollars, and other family support magistrates shall receive an annual salary of ninety-four thousand five hundred eighty-seven dollars.~~

~~(2) On and after April 1, 2001, the Chief Family Support Magistrate shall receive a salary of one hundred three thousand six hundred dollars, and other family support magistrates shall receive an annual salary of ninety-eight thousand six hundred dollars.~~

~~(3)~~ (h)(1) On and after April 1, 2002, the Chief Family Support Magistrate shall receive a salary of one hundred eight thousand eight hundred twenty-one dollars, and other family support magistrates shall receive an annual salary of one hundred three thousand five hundred sixty-nine dollars.

(2) On and after January 1, 2005, the Chief Family Support Magistrate shall receive a salary of one hundred fourteen thousand eight hundred six dollars, and other family support magistrates shall receive an annual salary of one hundred nine thousand two hundred sixty-five dollars.

(3) On and after January 1, 2006, the Chief Family Support Magistrate shall receive a salary of one hundred twenty-one thousand one hundred twenty dollars, and other family support magistrates shall receive an annual salary of one hundred fifteen thousand two hundred seventy-five dollars.

(4) On and after January 1, 2007, the Chief Family Support Magistrate shall receive a salary of one hundred twenty-seven thousand seven hundred eighty-two dollars, and other family support magistrates shall receive an annual salary of one hundred twenty-one thousand six hundred fifteen dollars.

Sec. 11. Subsection (b) of section 46b–236 of the general statutes is repealed and the following is substituted in lieu thereof (Effective January 1, 2005):

(b) Each family support referee shall receive, for acting as a family support referee, in addition to the retirement salary, the sum of ~~one hundred eighty~~ one hundred ninety dollars and expenses, including mileage, for each day a family support referee is so engaged.

Sec. 12. Subsection (a) of section 51–47 of the general statutes is repealed and the following is substituted in lieu thereof (Effective January 1, 2005):

(a) The judges of the Superior Court, judges of the Appellate Court and judges of the Supreme Court shall receive annually salaries as follows:

~~(1) On and after April 1, 2000, (A) the Chief Justice of the Supreme Court, one hundred thirty-five thousand eight hundred sixty-one dollars; (B) the Chief Court Administrator if a judge of the Supreme Court, Appellate Court or Superior Court, one hundred thirty thousand seventeen dollars; (C) each associate judge of the Supreme Court, one hundred twenty-four thousand six hundred eighty-three dollars; (D) the Chief Judge of the Appellate Court, one hundred twenty-three thousand one hundred fifty-two dollars; (E) each judge of the Appellate Court, one hundred sixteen thousand two hundred sixty-seven dollars; (F) the Deputy Chief Court Administrator if a judge of the Superior Court, one hundred thirteen thousand eight hundred ninety-six dollars; (G) each judge of the Superior Court, one hundred eleven thousand two hundred seventy-nine dollars.~~

~~(2) On and after April 1, 2001, (A) the Chief Justice of the Supreme Court, one hundred forty thousand five hundred eighty-two dollars; (B) the Chief Court Administrator if a judge of the Supreme Court, Appellate Court or Superior Court, one hundred thirty-four thousand seven hundred thirty-eight dollars; (C) each associate judge of the Supreme Court, one hundred twenty-nine thousand four hundred four dollars; (D) the Chief Judge of the Appellate Court, one hundred twenty-seven thousand eight hundred seventy-three dollars; (E) each judge of the Appellate Court, one hundred twenty thousand nine hundred eighty-eight dollars; (F) the Deputy Chief Court Administrator if a judge of the Superior Court, one hundred eighteen thousand six hundred seventeen dollars; (G) each judge of the Superior Court, one hundred sixteen thousand dollars.~~

~~(3)~~ (1) On and after April 1, 2002, (A) the Chief Justice of the Supreme Court, one hundred forty-nine thousand five hundred eighty-two dollars; (B) the Chief Court Administrator if a judge of the Supreme Court, Appellate Court or Superior Court, one hundred forty-three thousand seven hundred thirty-eight dollars; (C) each associate judge of the Supreme Court, one hundred thirty-eight thousand four hundred four dollars; (D) the Chief Judge of the Appellate Court, one hundred thirty-six thousand eight hundred seventy-three dollars; (E) each judge of the Appellate Court, one hundred twenty-nine thousand nine hundred eighty-eight dollars; (F) the Deputy Chief Court Administrator if a judge of the Superior Court, one hundred twenty-seven thousand six hundred seventeen dollars; (G) each judge of the Superior Court, one hundred twenty-five thousand dollars.

(2) On and after January 1, 2005, (A) the Chief Justice of the Supreme Court, one hundred fifty-seven thousand eight hundred nine dollars; (B) the Chief Court Administrator if a judge of the Supreme Court, Appellate Court or Superior Court, one hundred fifty-one thousand six hundred forty-four dollars; (C) each associate judge of the Supreme Court, one hundred forty-six thousand sixteen dollars; (D) the Chief Judge of the Appellate Court, one hundred forty-four thousand four hundred one dollars; (E) each judge of the Appellate Court, one hundred thirty-seven thousand one hundred thirty-seven dollars; (F) the Deputy Chief Court Administrator if a judge of the Superior Court, one hundred thirty-four thousand six hundred thirty-six dollars; (G) each judge of the Superior Court, one hundred thirty-one thousand eight hundred seventy-five dollars.

(3) On and after January 1, 2006, (A) the Chief Justice of the Supreme Court, one hundred sixty-six thousand four hundred eighty-nine dollars; (B) the Chief Court Administrator if a judge of the Supreme Court, Appellate Court or Superior Court, one hundred fifty-nine thousand nine hundred eighty-four dollars; (C) each associate judge of the Supreme Court, one hundred fifty-four thousand forty-seven dollars; (D) the Chief Judge of the Appellate Court, one hundred fifty-two thousand three hundred forty-three dollars; (E) each judge of the Appellate Court, one hundred forty-four thousand six hundred eighty dollars; (F) the Deputy Chief Court Administrator if a judge of the Superior Court, one hundred forty-two thousand forty-one dollars; (G) each judge of the Superior Court, one hundred thirty-nine thousand one hundred twenty-eight dollars.

(4) On and after January 1, 2007, (A) the Chief Justice of the Supreme Court, one hundred seventy-five thousand six hundred forty-five dollars; (B) the Chief Court Administrator if a judge of the Supreme Court, Appellate Court or Superior Court, one hundred sixty-eight thousand seven hundred eighty-three dollars; (C) each associate judge of the Supreme Court, one hundred sixty-two thousand five hundred twenty dollars; (D) the Chief Judge of the Appellate Court, one hundred sixty thousand seven hundred twenty-two dollars; (E) each judge of the Appellate Court, one hundred fifty-two thousand six hundred thirty-seven dollars; (F) the Deputy Chief Court Administrator if a judge of the Superior Court, one hundred forty-nine thousand eight hundred fifty-

three dollars; (G) each judge of the Superior Court, one hundred forty-six thousand seven hundred eighty dollars.

Sec. 13. Section 52–259 of the general statutes, as amended by section 43 of public act 03–2 and section 102 of public act 03–278, is repealed and the following is substituted in lieu thereof (Effective July 1, 2004):

There shall be paid to the clerks for entering each appeal or writ of error to the Supreme Court, or entering each appeal to the Appellate Court, as the case may be, two hundred fifty dollars, and for each civil cause in the Superior Court, ~~two hundred twenty~~ two hundred twenty-five dollars, except (1) one hundred twenty dollars for entering each case in the Superior Court in which the sole claim for relief is damages and the amount, legal interest or property in demand is less than two thousand five hundred dollars and for summary process, landlord and tenant and paternity actions, and (2) there shall be no entry fee for making an application to the Superior Court for relief under section 46b–15, as amended, or for making an application to modify or extend an order issued pursuant to section 46b–15, as amended. If the amount, legal interest or property in demand by the plaintiff is alleged to be less than two thousand five hundred dollars, a new entry fee of seventy-five dollars shall be charged if the plaintiff amends his complaint to state that such demand is not less than two thousand five hundred dollars. The fee for the entry of a small claims case shall be thirty-five dollars. If a motion is filed to transfer a small claims case to the regular docket, the moving party shall pay a fee of seventy-five dollars. There shall be paid to the clerk of the Superior Court by any party who requests that a matter be designated as a complex litigation case the sum of two hundred fifty dollars, to be paid at the time the request is filed. There shall be paid to the clerk of the Superior Court by any party who requests a finding of fact by a judge of such court to be used on appeal the sum of twenty-five dollars, to be paid at the time the request is filed. There shall be paid to the clerk of the Superior Court a fee of seventy-five dollars for a petition for certification to the Supreme Court and Appellate Court. Such clerks shall also receive for receiving and filing an assessment of damages by appraisers of land taken for public use or the appointment of a commissioner of the Superior Court, two dollars; for recording the commission and oath of a notary public or certifying under seal to the official character of any magistrate, ten dollars; for certifying under seal, two dollars; for exemplifying, twenty dollars; for making all necessary records and certificates of naturalization, the fees allowed under the provisions of the United States statutes for such services; and for making copies, one dollar a page. There shall be paid to the clerk of the Superior Court for a copy of a judgment file a fee of twenty-five dollars, inclusive of the fees for certification and copying, for a certified copy and a fee of fifteen dollars, inclusive of the fee for copying, for a copy which is not certified; and for a copy of a certificate of judgment in a foreclosure action, as provided by the rules of practice and procedure, twenty-five dollars, inclusive of the fees for certification and copying. There shall be paid to the clerk of the court a fee of one hundred dollars at the time any application for a prejudgment remedy is filed. A fee of twenty dollars for any check issued to the court in payment of any fee which is returned as uncollectible by the bank on which it is drawn may be imposed. The tax imposed under chapter 219 [1] shall not be imposed upon any fee charged under the provisions of this section.

[1] C.G.S.A. § 12–406 et seq.

Sec. 14. Subsection (a) of section 52–259a of the general statutes, as amended by section 44 of public act 03–2, is repealed and the following is substituted in lieu thereof (Effective July 1, 2004):

(a) Any member of the Division of Criminal Justice or the Division of Public Defender Services, any employee of the Judicial Department, acting in the performance of such employee's duties, the Attorney General, an assistant attorney general, the Consumer Counsel, any attorney employed by the Office of Consumer Counsel within the Department of Public Utility Control, the Department of Revenue Services, the Commission on Human Rights and Opportunities, the Freedom of Information Commission, the Board of Labor Relations, the Office of Protection and Advocacy for Persons with Disabilities, the Office of the Victim Advocate or the Department of Social Services, or any attorney appointed by the court to assist any of them or to act for any of them in a special case or cases, while acting in such attorney's official capacity or in the capacity for which such attorney was appointed, shall not be required to pay the fees specified in sections 52–258, 52–259, as amended, and 52–259c, as amended, ~~and 52–259d,~~ subsection (a) of section 52–356a, as amended, subsection (a) of section 52–361a, as amended, section 52–367a, as amended, subsection (b) of section 52–367b, as amended, and subsection (n) of section 46b–231, as amended.

Sec. 15. Subsection (f) of section 52–434 of the general statutes is repealed and the following is substituted in lieu thereof (Effective January 1, 2005):

(f) Each judge trial referee shall receive, for acting as a referee or as a single auditor or committee of any court or for performing duties assigned by the Chief Court Administrator with the approval of the Chief Justice, in addition to the retirement salary, the sum of ~~two hundred~~ two hundred eleven dollars and expenses, including mileage, for each day a state referee is so engaged, said sums to be taxed by the court making the reference in the same manner as other court expenses.

Sec. 16. (NEW) (Effective July 1, 2004) Not later than thirty days after the close of the first quarter of the fiscal year ending June 30, 2005, and not later than thirty days after the close of each quarter thereafter, the Banking Commissioner shall submit a report to the joint standing committee of the General Assembly having cognizance of matters relating to appropriations and the budgets of state agencies, through the Office of Fiscal Analysis, containing the specific amount of each fee, charge, assessment, fine, civil penalty, settlement payment and other revenue collected by the Department of Banking during the quarter covered by the report.

Sec. 17. Section 43 of public act 04–216 is repealed and the following is substituted in lieu thereof (Effective July 1, 2004):

The sum of $ 1,250,000 appropriated to the Department of Correction, for the fiscal year ending June 30, 2004, for Personal Services, shall not lapse on June 30, 2004, and such funds shall be transferred to the appropriation to the department, for the fiscal year ending June 30, 2005, for Other Expenses, for mental health assessments of residents of the Northern Correctional Center and for plaintiff attorney fees.

Sec. 18. (Effective July 1, 2004) The sum of $ 10,000 is appropriated to the Department of Environmental Protection, from the General Fund, for the fiscal year ending June 30, 2005, for artesian well repairs at Salmon River State Park.

Sec. 19. Section 4–141 of the general statutes is repealed and the following is substituted in lieu thereof (Effective October 1, 2004):

As used in this chapter: "Claim" means a petition for the payment or refund of money by the state or for permission to sue the state; "just claim" means a claim which in equity and justice the state should pay, provided the state has caused damage or injury or has received a benefit; "person" means any individual, firm, partnership, corporation, limited liability company, association or other group, including political subdivisions of the state; "state agency" includes every department, division, board, office, commission, arm, agency and institution of the state government, whatever its title or function; ~~,~~ and "state officers and employees" includes every person elected or appointed to or employed in any office, position or post in the state government, whatever such person's title, classification or function and whether such person serves with or without remuneration or compensation, including judges of probate courts and employees of such courts. In addition to the foregoing, "state officers and employees" includes attorneys appointed as victim compensation commissioners, attorneys appointed by the Public ~~Defenders~~ Defender Services Commission as public defenders, assistant public defenders or deputy assistant public defenders ~~,~~ and attorneys appointed by the court as special assistant public defenders, the Attorney General, the Deputy Attorney General and any associate attorney general or assistant attorney general, any other attorneys employed by any state agency, any commissioner of the Superior Court hearing small claims matters or acting as a fact-finder, arbitrator or magistrate or acting in any other quasi-judicial position, any person appointed to a committee established by law for the purpose of rendering services to the Judicial Department, including, but not limited to, the Legal Specialization Screening Committee, the State-Wide Grievance Committee, the Client Security Fund Committee, the advisory committee appointed pursuant to section 51–81d, as amended by this act, and the State Bar Examining Committee, any member of a multidisciplinary team established by the Commissioner of Children and Families pursuant to section 17a–106a, and any physicians or psychologists employed by any state agency. "State officers and employees" shall not include any medical or dental intern, resident or fellow of The University of Connecticut when (1) the intern, resident or fellow is assigned to a hospital affiliated with the university through an integrated residency program, and (2) such hospital provides protection against professional liability claims in an amount and manner equivalent to that provided by the hospital to its full-time physician employees.

Sec. 20. Section 4–165 of the general statutes is repealed and the following is substituted in lieu thereof (Effective October 1, 2004):

No state officer or employee shall be personally liable for damage or injury, not wanton, reckless or malicious, caused in the discharge of his duties or within the scope of his employment. Any person having a complaint for such damage or injury shall present it as a claim against the state under the provisions of this chapter. For the purposes of this section, "scope of employment" shall include, but not be limited to, representation by an attorney appointed by the Public Defender Services Commission as a public defender, assistant public defender or deputy assistant public defender or an attorney appointed by the court as a special assistant public defender of an indigent accused or of a child on a petition of delinquency, representation by such other attorneys, referred to in section 4–141, as amended by this act, of state officers and employees ~~,~~ in actions brought against such officers and employees in their official and individual capacities, the discharge of duties as a trustee of the state employees retirement system, the discharge of duties of a commissioner of the Superior Court hearing small claims matters or acting as a fact-finder, arbitrator or magistrate or acting in any other quasi-judicial position, and the discharge of duties of a person appointed to a committee established by law for the purpose of rendering services to the Judicial Department, including, but not limited to, the Legal Specialization Screening Committee, the State-Wide Grievance Committee, the Client Security Fund Committee, the advisory committee appointed pursuant to section 51–81d, as amended by this act, and the State Bar Examining Committee; provided such actions arise out of the discharge of the duties or within the scope of employment of such officers or employees. For the purposes of this section, members or employees of the soil and water district boards established pursuant to section 22a–315 shall be considered state employees.

Sec. 21. Section 51–81d of the general statutes, as amended by section 176 of public act 03–6 of the June 30 special session, is repealed and the following is substituted in lieu thereof (Effective October 1, 2004):

(a) The Superior Court, in accordance with rules established by the judges of the Superior Court, may (1) establish a Client Security Fund to (A) reimburse claims for losses caused by the dishonest conduct of attorneys admitted to the practice of law in this state and incurred in the course of an attorney-client relationship, and (B) provide for crisis intervention and referral assistance to attorneys admitted to the practice of law in this state who suffer from alcohol or other substance abuse problems or gambling problems, or who have behavioral health problems, and (2) assess any person admitted as an attorney by the Superior Court, in accordance with section 51–80, an annual fee to be deposited in ~~said~~ the Client Security Fund. Such crisis intervention and referral assistance (i) shall be provided with the assistance of an advisory committee, to be appointed by the Chief Court Administrator, that includes one or more behavioral health professionals, and (ii) shall not be deemed to constitute the practice of medicine or mental health care.

(b) The Commissioner of Revenue Services, or the commissioner's designee, shall collect any fee established pursuant to subsection (a) of this section, record such payments with the State Comptroller and deposit such payments promptly with the State Treasurer, who shall credit such payments to the Client Security Fund. The State Treasurer shall maintain the Client Security Fund separate and apart from all other moneys, funds and accounts and shall credit any interest earned from the Client Security Fund to the fund. Any interest earned from the fund shall be credited to the fund.

(c) The Client Security Fund shall be used to satisfy the claims approved in accordance with procedures established pursuant to rules of the Superior Court, to provide funding for crisis intervention and referral assistance provided pursuant to ~~subparagraph (B) of subdivision (1) of subsection (a)~~ of this section and to pay the reasonable costs of administration of the fund.

(d) No such fee shall be assessed to any attorney described in subsection (g) of section 51–81b, except that any attorney who does not engage in the practice of law as an occupation and receives less than four hundred fifty dollars in legal fees or other compensation for services involving the practice of law during the calendar year shall be obligated to pay one-half of such fee.

(e) The Commissioner of Revenue Services shall notify the Chief Court Administrator or his designee of the failure of any person to pay any fee assessed in accordance with subsection (a) of this section.

(f) All information given or received in connection with crisis intervention and referral assistance provided pursuant to this section, including the identity of any attorney seeking or receiving such crisis intervention and referral assistance, shall be confidential and shall not be disclosed to any third person other than a person to whom disclosure is reasonably necessary for the accomplishment of the purposes of such crisis intervention and referral assistance, and shall not be disclosed in any civil or criminal case or proceeding or in any legal or administrative proceeding, unless the attorney seeking or obtaining such crisis intervention and referral assistance waives such privilege or unless disclosure is otherwise required by law. Except as otherwise provided in this subsection, no attorney who provides crisis intervention and referral assistance pursuant to this section shall disclose any information given or received in connection with such crisis intervention and referral assistance unless such disclosure is required by the rules governing communications between attorney and client. Unless the privilege under this subsection has been waived or unless disclosure is otherwise required by law, no person in any civil or criminal case or proceeding or in any legal or administrative proceeding may request or require any information given or received in connection with the crisis intervention and referral assistance provided pursuant to this section.

Sec. 22. (NEW) (Effective October 1, 2004) No attorney appointed by the court pursuant to rules of the Superior Court to inventory the files of an inactive, suspended, disbarred or resigned attorney and to take necessary action to protect the interests of the inactive, suspended, disbarred or resigned attorney's clients shall be liable for damage or injury, not wanton, reckless or malicious, caused in the discharge of the appointed attorney's duties in connection with such inventory and action.

Sec. 23. (NEW) (Effective from passage, and applicable to assessment years commencing on or after October 1, 2002) (a) Notwithstanding the provisions of any general statute or any municipal charter, the assessors for the towns of Killingly and North Stonington shall, not later than thirty days after the effective date of this section, correct the October 1, 2002, and October 1, 2003, grand lists of said towns, to remove any real property that was subject to property taxation on or prior to October 1, 2002, by any town, village or similar taxing entity located in the state of Rhode Island. Said assessors shall issue a single certificate of correction for each such grand list that identifies each real property account subject to such removal, and which shall include a reference to the provisions of this section with respect to the reason for removal.

(b) If the property tax applicable to any real property account identified on a certificate of correction filed pursuant to subsection (a) of this section has not been levied or has not been paid, such tax shall be abated. If the property tax with respect to any such real property account has been paid, the town that received such payment shall, notwithstanding the provisions of section 12–129 of the general statutes refund to the taxpayer the amount of said tax payment together with any interest that may have been applied under the provisions of section 12–145 of the general statutes. Such refunds shall be issued not later than thirty days following the date on which such certificate of correction is filed on the appropriate grand list.

(c) The assessors for the towns of Killingly and North Stonington shall, not later than ten days after filing each certificate of correction, as required under subsection (a) of this section, send a notice in writing to the clerk of each district to whom a grand list for October 1, 2002, and October 1, 2003, was furnished, pursuant to section 7–328 of the general statutes. Such notice shall identify the real property accounts located in such district that have been removed from such town's October 1, 2002, and October 1, 2003, grand lists. The district clerk shall immediately file such notice on the appropriate grand list for the district. The filing of such notice shall serve to correct the grand list for such district by removing said real property accounts. If the property tax applicable to any such account identified on said notice has not been levied or has not been paid, such tax shall be abated. If the property tax levied by the district with respect to any account so identified has been paid, the district shall, notwithstanding the provisions of section 12–129 of the general statutes, refund to the taxpayer the amount of said tax together with any interest that may have been applied under the provisions of section 12–145 of the general statutes. Such refunds shall be issued not later than thirty days following the date on which such notice is filed on the appropriate grand list for such district.

(d) Notwithstanding the provisions of any general statute or any municipal charter, an assessor for any town that has a border that includes a boundary of the state of Rhode Island shall not include in the October 1, 2004, and October 1, 2005, grand list of such town any real property that was subject to property taxation on or prior to October 1, 2002, by any town, village or similar taxing entity located in the state of Rhode Island.

Sec. 24. Section 32–9s of the general statutes is repealed and the following is substituted in lieu thereof (Effective from passage and applicable to assessment years commencing on or after October 1, 2002):

The state shall make an annual grant payment to each municipality, to each district, as defined in section 7–325, which is located in a distressed municipality, targeted investment community or enterprise zone and to each special services district created pursuant to chapter 105a [1] which is located in a distressed municipality, targeted investment community or enterprise zone ~~(1)~~ in the amount of fifty per cent of the amount of that tax revenue which the municipality or district would have received except for the provisions of subdivisions (59), ~~and~~ (60) and (70) of section 12–81. ~~, and (2) in the amount of fifty per cent of the amount of the tax revenue which the municipality or district would have received except for the provisions of subdivision (70) of section 12–81.~~ On or before the first day of August of each year, each municipality and district shall file a claim with the Secretary of the Office of Policy and Management for the amount of such grant payment to which such municipality or district is entitled under this section. The claim shall be made on forms prescribed by the secretary and shall be accompanied by such supporting information as the secretary may require. Any municipality or district which neglects to transmit to the secretary such claim and supporting documentation as required by this section shall forfeit two hundred fifty dollars to the state, provided the secretary may waive such forfeiture in accordance with procedures and standards adopted by regulation in accordance with chapter 54. [2] The secretary shall review each such claim as provided in section 12–120b. Any claimant aggrieved by the results of the secretary's review shall have the rights of appeal as set forth in section 12–120b. The secretary shall, on or before the December first next succeeding the deadline for the receipt of such claims, certify to the Comptroller the amount due under this section, including any modification of such claim made prior to December first, to each municipality or district which has made a claim under the provisions of this section. The Comptroller shall draw an order on the

Treasurer on or before the following December fifteenth, and the Treasurer shall pay the amount thereof to each such municipality or district on or before the following December thirty-first. If any modification is made as the result of the provisions of this section on or after the December first following the date on which the municipality or district has provided the amount of tax revenue in question, any adjustment to the amount due to any municipality or district for the period for which such modification was made shall be made in the next payment the Treasurer shall make to such municipality or district pursuant to this section. In the fiscal year commencing July 1, 2003, and in each fiscal year thereafter, the amount of the grant payable to each municipality and district in accordance with this section shall be reduced proportionately in the event that the total amount of the grants payable to all municipalities and districts exceeds the amount appropriated.

[1] C.G.S.A. § 7–339m et seq.
[2] C.G.S.A. § 4–166 et seq.

Sec. 25. (NEW) (Effective from passage) For calendar quarters commencing on or after July 1, 2004, any retailer with sales in more than one town in this state, for which sales such retailer files a return under chapter 219 [1] of the general statutes, shall disaggregate the information in the return, in such form as may be prescribed by the Commissioner of Revenue Services, to indicate the town in which sales occurred for which tax was collected by such retailer and the amount of such tax collected, by town.

[1] C.G.S.A. § 12–406 et seq.

Sec. 26. Subdivision (2) of subsection (a) of section 12–458 of the general statutes is repealed and the following is substituted in lieu thereof (Effective from passage):

(2) On said date and coincident with the filing of such return each distributor shall pay to the commissioner for the account of the purchaser or consumer a tax (A) on each gallon of such fuels sold or used in this state during the preceding calendar month of twenty-six cents on and after January 1, 1992, twenty-eight cents on and after January 1, 1993, twenty-nine cents on and after July 1, 1993, thirty cents on and after January 1, 1994, thirty-one cents on and after July 1, 1994, thirty-two cents on and after January 1, 1995, thirty-three cents on and after July 1, 1995, thirty-four cents on and after October 1, 1995, thirty-five cents on and after January 1, 1996, thirty-six cents on and after April 1, 1996, thirty-seven cents on and after July 1, 1996, thirty-eight cents on and after October 1, 1996, thirty-nine cents on and after January 1, 1997, thirty-six cents on and after July 1, 1997, thirty-two cents on and after July 1, 1998, and twenty-five cents on and after July 1, 2000; and (B) in lieu of said taxes, each distributor shall pay a tax on each gallon of gasohol, as defined in section 14–1, sold or used in this state during such preceding calendar month, of twenty-five cents on and after January 1, 1992, twenty-seven cents on and after January 1, 1993, twenty-eight cents on and after July 1, 1993, twenty-nine cents on and after January 1, 1994, thirty cents on and after July 1, 1994, thirty-one cents on and after January 1, 1995, thirty-two cents on and after July 1, 1995, thirty-three cents on and after October 1, 1995, thirty-four cents on and after January 1, 1996, thirty-five cents on and after April 1, 1996, thirty-six cents on and after July 1, 1996, thirty-seven cents on and after October 1, 1996, thirty-eight cents on and after January 1, 1997, thirty-five cents on and after July 1, 1997, thirty-one cents on and after July 1, 1998, and twenty-four cents on and after July 1, 2000, and twenty-five cents on and after July 1, 2004; and (C) in lieu of such rate, on each gallon of diesel fuel, propane or natural gas sold or used in this state during such preceding calendar month, of eighteen cents on and after September 1, 1991, and twenty-six cents on and after August 1, 2002.

Sec. 27. (NEW) (Effective from passage) The Secretary of the Office of Policy and Management shall examine the policies and regulations relative to revaluation of property under section 12–62 of the general statutes, as amended by this act, and shall, on or before January 1, 2005, submit a report to the joint standing committee of the General Assembly having cognizance of matters relating to finance, revenue and bonding regarding any findings or recommendations to clarify, or make more effective, such policies and regulations.

Sec. 28. Section 8–64a of the general statutes is repealed and the following is substituted in lieu thereof (Effective July 1, 2004):

No housing authority which receives or has received any state financial assistance may sell, lease, transfer or destroy, or contract to sell, lease, transfer or destroy, any housing project or portion thereof in any case where such project or portion thereof would no longer be available for the purpose of low or moderate income rental housing as a result of such sale, lease, transfer or destruction, except the Commissioner of Economic and Community Development may grant written approval for the sale, lease, transfer or destruction of a housing project if the commissioner finds, after a public hearing, that (1) the sale, lease, transfer or destruction is in the best interest of the state and the municipality in which the project is located, (2) an adequate supply of low or moderate income rental housing exists in the municipality in which the project is located, (3) the housing authority has developed a plan for the sale, lease, transfer or destruction of such project in consultation with the residents of such project and representatives of the municipality in which such project is situated and has made adequate provision for said residents' and representatives' participation in such plan, and (4) any person who is displaced as a result of the sale, lease, transfer or destruction will be relocated to a comparable dwelling unit of public or subsidized housing in the same municipality or will receive a tenant-based rental subsidy and will receive relocation assistance under chapter 135.[1] The commissioner shall consider the extent to which the housing units which are to be sold, leased, transferred or destroyed will be replaced in ways which may include, but need not be limited to, newly constructed housing, rehabilitation of housing which is abandoned or has been vacant for at least one year, or new federal, state or local tenant-based or project-based rental subsidies. The commissioner shall give the residents of the housing project or portion thereof which is to be sold, leased, transferred or destroyed written notice of said public hearing by first class mail not less than ninety days before the date of the hearing. Said written approval shall contain a statement of facts supporting the findings of the commissioner. This section shall not apply to the sale, lease, transfer or destruction of a housing project pursuant to the terms of any contract entered into before June 3, 1988. This section shall not apply to phase I of Father Panik Village in Bridgeport, Elm Haven in New Haven, ~~and~~ Pequonock Gardens Project in Bridgeport, Evergreen Apartments in Bridgeport, Quinnipiac Terrace/Riverview in New Haven, Dutch Point in Hartford, Southfield Village in Stamford and, upon approval by the United States Department of Housing and Urban Development of a HOPE VI revitalization application and a revitalization plan that includes at least the one-for-one replacement of low and moderate income units, Fairfield Court in Stamford.

[1] C.G.S.A. § 8–266 et seq.

Sec. 29. Section 31–284a of the general statutes is repealed and the following is substituted in lieu thereof (Effective July 1, 2004):

(a) Notwithstanding the provisions of sections 4a–19 and 4a–20 to the contrary, the Commissioner of Administrative Services shall solicit proposals from any management firm engaged in the business of administering workers' compensation claims, or from any authorized mutual insurance company or stock company or subsidiary thereof writing workers' compensation or employer's liability insurance in this state, for the purposes of administering the workers' compensation claims filed against the state, or of insuring the state's full liability under workers' compensation and administering such claims. ~~Said~~ The commissioner may, at ~~his~~ said commissioner's discretion, reject any or all of such proposals if they are deemed to be inadequate to effectively serve the needs of the state concerning workers' compensation. ~~Any funds appropriated in section 1 of special act 81–22* for workers' compensation payments by the state and administrative expenses for the state workers' compensation program shall be available and may be transferred with the approval of the Governor to meet the necessary expenses of contracting for such services.~~

(b) The Commissioner of Administrative Services shall adopt regulations, in accordance with the provisions of chapter 54,[1] which establish the fees payable by this state for its employees under the provisions of this chapter, based on the medical procedure, combination of procedures or diagnosis of the patient, provided the fee schedule shall not apply to services rendered to a claimant who is participating in the state's managed care plan. The regulations shall limit annual growth in total medical fees payable by the state to no more than the annual percentage increase in the consumer price index for all urban workers. Said commissioner may exclude from participation in the state workers' compensation managed care program any medical provider found, through a systematic program of utilization review, to exceed generally accepted standards of the scope, duration or intensity of services rendered to patients with similar diagnostic characteristics. The state shall not make any payment to a facility owned in whole or in part by the referring practitioner.

(c) The Commissioner of Administrative Services shall have sole responsibility for establishing procedures for all executive branch agencies participating in the state of Connecticut workers' compensation program, except that all mandatory subjects of collective bargaining pertaining to modified or alternative duty shall continue to be governed by the provisions of chapter 68.[2]

[1] C.G.S.A. § 4–166 et seq.
[2] C.G.S.A. § 5–270 et seq.

Sec. 30. Subsection (e) of section 210 of public act 03–6 of the June 30 special session is repealed and the following is substituted in lieu thereof (Effective from passage):

(e) Wherever the words "State Commission on the Arts", "Connecticut Historical Commission", "Office of Tourism" ~~and~~ "Connecticut Film, Video and Media Office" and "Connecticut Commission on Arts, Tourism,

Culture, History and Film" are used in the following sections of the general statutes, or in any public or special act of the 2003 or 2004 session the words "Connecticut Commission on ~~Arts, Tourism, Culture, History and Film~~ Culture and Tourism" shall be substituted in lieu thereof: 3-110f, as amended, 3-110h, as amended, 3-110i, as amended, 4-9a, as amended, 4b-53, as amended, 4b-60, as amended, 4b-64, as amended, 4b-66a, as amended, 7-147a, as amended, 7-147b, as amended, 7-147c, as amended, 7-147j, as amended, 7-147p, as amended, 7-147q, as amended, 7-147y, as amended, 8-2j, as amended, 10-382, as amended, 10-384, as amended, 10-385, as amended, 10-386, as amended, 10-387, as amended, 10-388, as amended, 10-389, as amended, 10-391, as amended, 10a-111a, as amended, 10a-112, as amended, 10a-112b, as amended, 10a-112g, as amended, 10-384, as amended, 11-6a, as amended, 12-376d, as amended, 13a-252, as amended, 19a-315b, as amended, 19a-315c, as amended, 22a-1d, as amended, 22a-19b, as amended, 25-102qq, as amended, 25-109q, as amended, 29-259, as amended, and 32-6a, as amended.

Sec. 31. (NEW) (Effective from passage) After completion of the courthouse which is to be constructed after the effective date of this section in the town of Torrington and commencing with the payment in lieu of taxes made under section 12-19a of the general statutes for such courthouse to the town of Torrington for the grand list year the courthouse was completed, such payment shall be divided between the towns of Torrington and Litchfield as follows:

(1) For the first year such payments are made until and including the seventh such year, fifty-five per cent of such payment shall be made to the town of Torrington and forty-five per cent of such payment shall be made to the town of Litchfield; and

(2) For the eighth such year until and including the fourteenth such year, sixty five per cent of such payment shall be made to the town of Torrington and thirty-five per cent of such payment shall be made to the town of Litchfield.

Sec. 32. (NEW) (Effective from passage and applicable to assessment years commencing on or after October 1, 2003) (a) Notwithstanding any provision of the general statutes, any municipal charter, any special act or any home rule ordinance, any municipality required to effect a revaluation of real property under section 12-62 of the general statutes, as amended by this act, for the 2003, 2004 or 2005 assessment year shall not be required to effect a revaluation prior to the 2006 assessment year provided any decision not to implement a revaluation pursuant to this subsection shall be approved by the legislative body of such town or, in any town where the legislative body is a town meeting, by the board of selectmen. Any required revaluation subsequent to any delayed revaluation effected pursuant to this subsection shall be effected in accordance with the provisions of said section 12-62. The rate maker, as defined in section 12-131 of the general statutes, in any municipality that elects, pursuant to this subsection, not to implement a revaluation may prepare new rate bills under the provisions of chapter 204 [1] of the general statutes in order to carry out the provisions of this section.

(b) The assessor or board of assessors of any municipality that elects, pursuant to subsection (a) of this section, not to implement a revaluation of real property for the 2003 assessment year shall prepare a revised grand list for said assessment year, which shall reflect the assessments of real estate according to the grand list in effect for the assessment year commencing October 1, 2002, subject only to transfers of ownership, additions for new construction and reductions for demolitions. Such assessor shall send notice of any increase in the valuation of real estate over the valuation of such real estate as of October 1, 2002, or notice of the valuation of any real estate which is on the grand list to be effective for the October 1, 2003, assessment year but was not on such list in the prior assessment year, to the last-known address of the person whose valuation is so affected, and such person shall have the right to appeal such increase or valuation during the next regular session of the board of assessment appeals at which real estate appeals may be heard.

[1] C.G.S.A. § 12-122 et seq.

Sec. 33. Subsections (a) and (b) of section 12-62 of the general statutes are repealed and the following is substituted in lieu thereof (Effective October 1, 2003, and applicable to assessment years commencing on or after October 1, 2003):

(a)(1) Commencing October 1, 1997, the assessor or board of assessors of each town shall revalue all of the real estate in their respective municipalities for assessment purposes in accordance with the provisions of subsection (b) of this section. The assessments derived from each such revaluation shall be used for the purpose of levying property taxes in such municipality in the assessment year in which such revaluation becomes effective and in each assessment year thereafter until the next succeeding revaluation in accordance with the provisions of subsection (b) of this section. In the performance of these duties, except in any municipality where there is a single assessor, at least two of the assessors shall act together and all valuations shall be separately approved by a majority of the assessors.

(2) The assessor or board of assessors of each town shall view by physical inspection all of the real estate in their respective municipalities for assessment purposes within the period of time provided in subdivision (3) of this subsection.

(3) An assessor shall have fulfilled the requirement to view by physical inspection if a physical inspection of a property has been made at any time from June 27, 1997, to October 1, 2009, inclusive, and thereafter, the assessor or board of assessors shall view by physical inspection each parcel of real estate no later than ~~twelve~~ ten years following the preceding inspection.

(b) ~~(1)~~ The assessor or board of assessors of each town shall revalue all of the real estate in their respective municipalities ~~in accordance with the schedule provided in this section. Nothing in this subsection shall be construed to prohibit a town from effecting more frequent revaluations between the implementation of each revaluation required in accordance with the provisions of this section.~~

~~Town/City~~	~~Year of Next Revaluation~~	~~Year of Subsequent Revaluation~~
~~Andover~~	~~2001~~	~~2005~~
~~Ansonia~~	~~2002~~	~~2006~~
~~Ashford~~	~~2002~~	~~2006~~
~~Avon~~	~~1999~~	~~2003~~
~~Barkhamsted~~	~~1999~~	~~2003~~
~~Beacon Falls~~	~~2001~~	~~2005~~
~~Berlin~~	~~1997 or 1998~~	~~2002~~
~~Bethany~~	~~1999~~	~~2003~~
~~Bethel~~	~~1999~~	~~2003~~
~~Bethlehem~~	~~1999~~	~~2003~~
~~Bloomfield~~	~~2000~~	~~2004~~
~~Bolton~~	~~1999~~	~~2003~~
~~Bozrah~~	~~2001~~	~~2005~~
~~Branford~~	~~2000~~	~~2004~~
~~Bridgeport~~	~~1999~~	~~2003~~
~~Bridgewater~~	~~1999~~	~~2003~~
~~Bristol~~	~~1997 or 1998~~	~~2002~~
~~Brookfield~~	~~2001~~	~~2005~~
~~Brooklyn~~	~~2000~~	~~2004~~
~~Burlington~~	~~1999~~	~~2003~~
~~Canaan~~	~~997 or 1998~~	~~2002~~
~~Canterbury~~	~~2000~~	~~2004~~
~~Canton~~	~~1999~~	~~2003~~
~~Chaplin~~	~~1999~~	~~2003~~
~~Cheshire~~	~~1999~~	~~2003~~
~~Chester~~	~~1999~~	~~2003~~
~~Clinton~~	~~2000~~	~~2004~~
~~Colchester~~	~~2001~~	~~2005~~
~~Colebrook~~	~~2000~~	~~2004~~
~~Columbia~~	~~2001~~	~~2005~~
~~Cornwall~~	~~2001~~	~~2005~~
~~Coventry~~	~~2000~~	~~2004~~
~~Cromwell~~	~~1999~~	~~2003~~
~~Danbury~~	~~1997 or 1998~~	~~2002~~
~~Darien~~	~~1999~~	~~2003~~
~~Deep River~~	~~2001~~	~~2005~~
~~Derby~~	~~2000~~	~~2004~~
~~Durham~~	~~2000~~	~~2004~~
~~Eastford~~	~~1997 or 1998~~	~~2002~~

~~Town/City~~	~~Year of Next Revaluation~~	~~Year of Subsequent Revaluation~~
~~East Granby~~	~~1999~~	~~2003~~
~~East Haddam~~	~~2002~~	~~2006~~
~~East Hampton~~	~~2000~~	~~2004~~
~~East Hartford~~	~~2001~~	~~2005~~
~~East Haven~~	~~2000~~	~~2004~~
~~East Lyme~~	~~2001~~	~~2005~~
~~Easton~~	~~2002~~	~~2006~~
~~East Windsor~~	~~2002~~	~~2006~~
~~Ellington~~	~~2000~~	~~2004~~
~~Enfield~~	~~2001~~	~~2005~~
~~Essex~~	~~1999~~	~~2003~~
~~Fairfield~~	~~2001~~	~~2005~~
~~Farmington~~	~~2002~~	~~2006~~
~~Franklin~~	~~1999~~	~~2003~~
~~Glastonbury~~	~~2002~~	~~2006~~
~~Goshen~~	~~1997 or 1998~~	~~2002~~
~~Granby~~	~~1997 or 1998~~	~~2002~~
~~Greenwich~~	~~2001~~	~~2005~~
~~Griswold~~	~~2001~~	~~2005~~
~~Groton~~	~~2001~~	~~2005~~
~~Guilford~~	~~2002~~	~~2006~~
~~Haddam~~	~~2001~~	~~2005~~
~~Hamden~~	~~2000~~	~~2004~~
~~Hampton~~	~~1999~~	~~2003~~
~~Hartford~~	~~1999~~	~~2003~~
~~Hartland~~	~~2001~~	~~2005~~
~~Harwinton~~	~~1999~~	~~2003~~
~~Hebron~~	~~2001~~	~~2005~~
~~Kent~~	~~1999~~	~~2003~~
~~Killingly~~	~~2002~~	~~2006~~
~~Killingworth~~	~~2001~~	~~2005~~
~~Lebanon~~	~~1999~~	~~2003~~
~~Ledyard~~	~~2001~~	~~2005~~
~~Lisbon~~	~~2001~~	~~2005~~
~~Litchfield~~	~~1999~~	~~2003~~
~~Lyme~~	~~1999~~	~~2003~~
~~Madison~~	~~2000~~	~~2004~~
~~Manchester~~	~~2000~~	~~2004~~
~~Mansfield~~	~~2000~~	~~2004~~
~~Marlborough~~	~~2001~~	~~2005~~
~~Meriden~~	~~2001~~	~~2005~~
~~Middlebury~~	~~2001~~	~~2005~~
~~Middlefield~~	~~2001~~	~~2005~~
~~Middletown~~	~~1997 or 1998~~	~~2002~~
~~Milford~~	~~2000~~	~~2004~~
~~Monroe~~	~~1999~~	~~2003~~
~~Montville~~	~~2001~~	~~2005~~
~~Morris~~	~~2000~~	~~2004~~
~~Naugatuck~~	~~1997 or 1998~~	~~2002~~
~~New Britain~~	~~2002~~	~~2006~~
~~New Canaan~~	~~1999~~	~~2003~~
~~New Fairfield~~	~~2000~~	~~2004~~
~~New Hartford~~	~~1999~~	~~2003~~
~~New Haven~~	~~2000~~	~~2004~~

~~Town/City~~	~~Year of Next Revaluation~~	~~Year of Subsequent Revaluation~~
~~Newington~~	~~2000~~	~~2004~~
~~New London~~	~~1999~~	~~2003~~
~~New Milford~~	~~2001~~	~~2005~~
~~Newtown~~	~~2002~~	~~2006~~
~~Norfolk~~	~~1999~~	~~2003~~
~~North Branford~~	~~2001~~	~~2005~~
~~North Canaan~~	~~1997 or 1998~~	~~2002~~
~~North Haven~~	~~2000~~	~~2004~~
~~North Stonington~~	~~2000~~	~~2004~~
~~Norwalk~~	~~1999~~	~~2003~~
~~Norwich~~	~~1999~~	~~2003~~
~~Old Lyme~~	~~2000~~	~~2004~~
~~Old Saybrook~~	~~1999~~	~~2003~~
~~Orange~~	~~2000~~	~~2004~~
~~Oxford~~	~~2000~~	~~2004~~
~~Plainfield~~	~~1997 or 1998~~	~~2002~~
~~Plainville~~	~~2000~~	~~2004~~
~~Plymouth~~	~~2001~~	~~2005~~
~~Pomfret~~	~~2000~~	~~2004~~
~~Portland~~	~~2001~~	~~2005~~
~~Preston~~	~~1997 or 1998~~	~~2002~~
~~Prospect~~	~~2000~~	~~2004~~
~~Putnam~~	~~1999~~	~~2003~~
~~Redding~~	~~1997 or 1998~~	~~2002~~
~~Ridgefield~~	~~1997 or 1998~~	~~2002~~
~~Rocky Hill~~	~~1999~~	~~2003~~
~~Roxbury~~	~~1997 or 1998~~	~~2002~~
~~Salem~~	~~2001~~	~~2005~~
~~Salisbury~~	~~2000~~	~~2004~~
~~Scotland~~	~~1999~~	~~2003~~
~~Seymour~~	~~2001~~	~~2005~~
~~Sharon~~	~~1999~~	~~2003~~
~~Shelton~~	~~2001~~	~~2005~~
~~Sherman~~	~~1999~~	~~2003~~
~~Simsbury~~	~~2002~~	~~2006~~
~~Somers~~	~~2002~~	~~2006~~
~~Southbury~~	~~1997 or 1998~~	~~2002~~
~~Southington~~	~~2001~~	~~2005~~
~~South Windsor~~	~~2002~~	~~2006~~
~~Sprague~~	~~2000~~	~~2004~~
~~Stafford~~	~~2000~~	~~2004~~
~~Stamford~~	~~2001~~	~~2005~~
~~Sterling~~	~~1997 or 1998~~	~~2002~~
~~Stonington~~	~~2002~~	~~2006~~
~~Stratford~~	~~2000~~	~~2004~~
~~Suffield~~	~~1999~~	~~2003~~
~~Thomaston~~	~~1999~~	~~2003~~
~~Thompson~~	~~2000~~	~~2004~~
~~Tolland~~	~~2000~~	~~2004~~
~~Torrington~~	~~1999~~	~~2003~~
~~Trumbull~~	~~2000~~	~~2004~~
~~Union~~	~~1999~~	~~2003~~
~~Vernon~~	~~2000~~	~~2004~~
~~Voluntown~~	~~2001~~	~~2005~~

~~Town/City~~	~~Year of Next Revaluation~~	~~Year of Subsequent Revaluation~~
~~Wallingford~~	~~2000~~	~~2004~~
~~Warren~~	~~1997 or 1998~~	~~2002~~
~~Washington~~	~~1999~~	~~2003~~
~~Waterbury~~	~~1997 or 1998~~	~~2002~~
~~Waterford~~	~~1997 or 1998~~	~~2002~~
~~Watertown~~	~~1999~~	~~2003~~
~~Westbrook~~	~~2001~~	~~2005~~
~~West Hartford~~	~~1999~~	~~2003~~
~~West Haven~~	~~2000~~	~~2004~~
~~Weston~~	~~1999~~	~~2003~~
~~Westport~~	~~1999~~	~~2003~~
~~Wethersfield~~	~~1999~~	~~2003~~
~~Willington~~	~~1999~~	~~2003~~
~~Wilton~~	~~2002~~	~~2006~~
~~Winchester~~	~~2002~~	~~2006~~
~~Windham~~	~~2001~~	~~2005~~
~~Windsor~~	~~1999~~	~~2003~~
~~Windsor Locks~~	~~1999~~	~~2003~~
~~Wolcott~~	~~2000~~	~~2004~~
~~Woodbridge~~	~~2000~~	~~2004~~
~~Woodbury~~	~~1999~~	~~2003~~
~~Woodstock~~	~~2000~~	~~2004~~

~~(2) For the assessment date four years following the date of the subsequent revaluation required under subdivision (1) of this subsection and every fourth year thereafter, the assessor or board of assessors shall revalue all of the real estate in their respective municipalities.~~

~~(3) Any municipality required to revalue all real property for assessment year 1997 or 1998, which revalued such real property for the assessment year 1996, shall not be required to revalue for assessment year 1997 or 1998 but shall be required to revalue all real property for assessment year 2002~~ not later than five years after the last revaluation conducted in each municipality, except as provided in section 32 of this act. In carrying out the provisions of this subsection, any municipality which last effected revaluation by statistical means shall effect its next revaluation by physical inspection provided in no case shall a physical inspection be required more than once every ten years. In carrying out the provisions of this subsection, any municipality which last effected revaluation by physical inspection may effect its next revaluation by statistical means.

Sec. 34. Subsection (g) of section 17b–239 of the general statutes, as amended by section 68 of public act 03–3 of the June 30 special session and section 3 of public act 04–258, is repealed and the following is substituted in lieu thereof (Effective July 1, 2004):

(g) Effective June 1, 2001, the commissioner shall establish inpatient hospital rates in accordance with the method specified in regulations adopted pursuant to this section and applied for the rate period beginning October 1, 2000, except that the commissioner shall update each hospital's target amount per discharge to the actual allowable cost per discharge based upon the 1999 cost report filing multiplied by sixty two and one-half per cent if such amount is higher than the target amount per discharge for the rate period beginning October 1, 2000, as adjusted for the ten per cent incentive identified in Section 4005 of Public Law 101–508. If a hospital's rate is increased pursuant to this subsection, the hospital shall not receive the ten per cent incentive identified in Section 4005 of Public Law 101–508. For rate periods beginning October 1, 2001, through ~~September 30, 2004~~ March 31, 2008, the commissioner shall not apply an annual adjustment factor to the target amount per discharge. Effective April 1, 2005, the revised target amount per discharge for each hospital with a target amount per discharge less than three thousand seven hundred fifty dollars shall be three thousand seven hundred fifty dollars. Effective April 1, 2006, the revised target amount per discharge for each hospital with a target amount per discharge less than four thousand dollars shall be four thousand dollars. Effective April 1, 2007, the revised target amount per discharge for each hospital with a target amount per discharge less than four thousand two hundred fifty dollars shall be four thousand two hundred fifty dollars.

Sec. 35. Subsection (b) of section 17b–688c of the general statutes, as amended by section 13 of public act 04–258, is repealed and the following is substituted in lieu thereof (Effective July 1, 2004):

(b) In no event shall temporary family assistance be granted to an applicant for such assistance, who is not exempt from participation in the employment services program, prior to the applicant's attendance at an initial scheduled employment services assessment interview and participation in the development of an employment services plan. The Department of Social Services shall not ~~deny~~ delay temporary family assistance to an applicant in cases where the department schedules the initial employment services assessment interview more than ten business days after the date on which application for assistance is made, or in cases where the Labor Department does not complete an employment services plan for the benefit of the applicant within ten business days of the date on which the applicant attends an employment services assessment interview. The Commissioner of Social Services shall refer any applicant denied temporary family assistance, who may be in need of emergency benefits, to other services offered by the Department of Social Services or community services that may be available to such applicant. The Department of Social Services shall reduce the benefits awarded to a family under the temporary family assistance program when a member of the family who is required to participate in employment services fails to comply with an employment services requirement without good cause. The first instance of noncompliance with an employment services requirement shall result in a twenty-five per cent reduction of such benefits for three consecutive months. The second instance of noncompliance with such requirement shall result in a thirty-five per cent reduction of such benefits for three consecutive months. A third or subsequent instance of noncompliance with such requirement shall result in the termination of such benefits for three consecutive months. If only one member of a family is eligible for temporary family assistance and such member fails to comply with an employment services requirement, the department shall terminate all benefits of such family for three consecutive months. Notwithstanding the provisions of this subsection, the department shall terminate the benefits awarded to a family under the temporary family assistance program if a member of the family who is not exempt from the twenty-one-month time limit specified in subsection (a) of section 17b–112, as amended, fails, without good cause, to: (1) Attend any scheduled assessment appointment or interview relating to the establishment of an employment services plan, except that such individual's benefits shall be reinstated if the individual attends a subsequently scheduled appointment or interview within thirty days of the date on which the department has issued notification to the individual that benefits have been terminated, or (2) comply with an employment services requirement during a six-month extension of benefits. Any individual who fails to comply with the provisions of subdivision (1) of this subsection may submit a new application for such benefits at any time after termination of benefits.

Sec. 36. (Effective July 1, 2004) (a) The sum of $ 100,000 available for expenditure by the Department of Social Services from the TANF high performance bonus payments for welfare to work, for Emergency Shelters, shall be used for a grant to the Connecticut Association for United Spanish Action, Inc. (CAUSA).

(b) The sum of $ 50,000 available for expenditure by the Department of Social Services from the TANF high performance bonus payments for welfare to work, for Good News Garage, shall be used for a grant to the Connecticut Association for United Spanish Action, Inc. (CAUSA).

(c) The grants provided for in subsection (a) of this section shall be made during the fiscal year ending June 30, 2005.

Sec. 37. Section 46a–70 of the general statutes, as amended by public act 04–171, is repealed and the following is substituted in lieu thereof (Effective from passage):

(a) State officials and supervisory personnel shall recruit, appoint, assign, train, evaluate and promote state personnel on the basis of merit and qualifications, without regard for race, color, religious creed, sex, marital status, age, national origin, ancestry, mental retardation, mental disability, learning disability or physical disability, including but not limited to, blindness, unless it is shown by such state officials or supervisory personnel that such disability prevents performance of the work involved.

(b) All state agencies shall promulgate written directives to carry out this policy and to guarantee equal employment opportunities at all levels of state government. They shall regularly review their personnel practices to assure compliance.

(c) All state agencies shall conduct continuing orientation and training programs with emphasis on human relations and nondiscriminatory employment practices.

~~(d) The name and address of, and any related identifying information concerning, a sexual harassment complainant in any internal sexual harassment investigation conducted by an affirmative action officer or other designated person on behalf of a state agency shall be confidential and shall be disclosed only upon order of the~~

~~Superior Court, except the state agency (1) shall disclose the name of the sexual harassment complainant to the accused during the state agency's sexual harassment investigation, and (2) may disclose the name of the sexual harassment complainant to other persons participating in the state agency's sexual harassment investigation. For purposes of this subsection, "state agency" has the same meaning as "public agency" in section 1-200.~~

~~(e)~~ (d) The Commissioner of Administrative Services shall insure that the entire examination process, including qualifications appraisal, is free from bias.

~~(f)~~ (e) Appointing authorities shall exercise care to insure utilization of minority group persons.

Sec. 38. (NEW) (Effective July 1, 2004) At the request of the Commissioner of Social Services, the Secretary of the Office of Policy and Management is authorized to cancel any receivable that has resulted from an audit against a town, including any receivables associated with the prior general assistance program operated by towns. The secretary may direct the Commissioner of Social Services to estimate any potential receivables from future audits in the former general assistance programs operated by towns and authorize the commissioner to suspend any future audits. If the secretary authorizes the suspension of future audits in the program, the commissioner shall notify the towns of such suspension.

Sec. 39. (Effective from passage) (a) Notwithstanding any provision of the general statutes, no state employee shall be transferred to the Department of Information Technology, prior to October 1, 2004, for the purpose of the transformation or consolidation of the state's information technology services, except that an employee who was transferred prior to the effective date of this section and who is employed by said department on the effective date of this section shall not be subject to this section.

(b) During the fiscal year ending June 30, 2005, the Secretary of the Office of Policy and Management may transfer funds appropriated to the Department of Information Technology, for Personal Services, for said fiscal year, to the appropriation to other General Fund agencies, for Personal Services, for said fiscal year, in order to implement the provisions of subsection (a) of this section.

Sec. 40. (Effective July 1, 2004) (a) Up to $ 2.5 million appropriated to the Office of Policy and Management, for Personal Services, in section 1 of public act 03–1 of the June 30 special session, shall not lapse June 30, 2004, and such funds shall be transferred to the Capital City Economic Development account, for the fiscal year ending June 30, 2005.

(b) The sum of $ 200,000 appropriated to the Office of Policy and Management, for Justice Assistance Grants, in section 1 of public act 03–1 of the June 30 special session, shall not lapse June 30, 2004, and such funds shall be transferred to the Capital City Economic Development account, for the fiscal year ending June 30, 2005.

Sec. 41. Subsection (f) of section 17b–274d of the general statutes, as amended by public act 04–258, is repealed and the following is substituted in lieu thereof (Effective July 1, 2004):

(f) Except for mental-health-related drugs and antiretroviral drugs, ~~and medications used to treat diabetes, asthma or cancer,~~ reimbursement for a drug not included in the preferred drug list is subject to prior authorization.

Sec. 42. Subdivision (1) of subsection (a) of section 32–655 of the general statutes is repealed and the following is substituted in lieu thereof (Effective from passage):

(1) Acquire, by condemnation, gift, purchase, lease, lease-purchase, exchange or otherwise, the real property comprising the Adriaen's Landing site and the stadium facility site and such other real property determined to be necessary by the secretary for off-site infrastructure improvements related to the development of the Adriaen's Landing site or the stadium facility site or for temporary use for construction staging or replacement parking during the period of construction as contemplated by the master development plan, including the exchange of real property acquired by the secretary under authority of this chapter for other real property in circumstances where the secretary determines that such exchange will better conform site boundaries to final plans or otherwise facilitate the layout, development or financing of the public and private improvements contemplated by the master development plan.

Sec. 43. Subdivision (3) of subsection (a) of section 32–655 of the general statutes is repealed and the following is substituted in lieu thereof (Effective from passage):

(3) Lease or sublease, as lessor or lessee or sublessor or sublessee, convey, and grant temporary or permanent easements and rights-of-way and enter into access, support, common area maintenance and similar agreements with respect to, any real property in connection with the overall project and the on-site related private development, including leases or subleases, as lessor or lessee or sublessor or sublessee, of off-site real property in connection with site acquisition arrangements, on terms to be determined by the secretary;

Sec. 44. Section 25–33k of the general statutes is repealed and the following is substituted in lieu thereof (Effective October 1, 2004):

(a) For purposes of this section, "safe yield" means the maximum dependable quantity of water per unit of time that may flow or be pumped continuously from a source of supply during a critical dry period without consideration of available water limitations.

(b) No source of water supply shall be abandoned by a water company or other entity without a permit from the Commissioner of Public Health. A water company or other entity shall apply for such permit in the manner prescribed by the commissioner. Not later than thirty days before filing an application for such permit, the applicant shall notify the chief elected official of any municipality in which such source of supply is located. Not later than sixty days after receipt of such notification the municipality or municipalities receiving such notice and any water company as defined in section 25–32a may submit comments on such application to the commissioner. The commissioner shall take such comments into consideration when reviewing the application.

(c)(1) In ~~his~~ the commissioner's decision, the commissioner shall consider the water supply needs of the water company, the state and any comments submitted pursuant to subsection (b) of this section, and shall consult with the Commissioner of Environmental Protection, the Secretary of the Office of Policy and Management and the Department of Public Utility Control.

(2) The Commissioner of Public Health shall grant a permit upon a finding that ~~the source shall~~ any groundwater source with a safe yield of less than 0.75 millions of gallons per day, any reservoir with a safe yield of less than 0.75 millions of gallons per day, any reservoir system with a safe yield of less than 0.75 millions of gallons per day, or any individual source within a reservoir system when such system has a safe yield of less than 0.75 millions of gallons per day will not be needed by such water company for present or future water supply and, in the case of a water company required to file a water supply plan under section 25–32d, as amended, that such abandonment is consistent with a water supply plan filed and approved pursuant to said section. No permit shall be granted if the commissioner determines that the source would be necessary for water supply by the company owning such source in an emergency or the proposed abandonment would impair the ability of ~~the~~ such company to provide a pure, adequate and reliable water supply for present and projected future customers. As used in this section, a future source of water supply shall be considered to be any source of water supply necessary to serve areas reasonably expected to require service by the water company owning such source for a period of not more than fifty years after the date of the application for a permit under this section.

(3) The Commissioner of Public Health shall grant a permit upon a finding that any groundwater source with a safe yield of more than 0.75 millions of gallons per day, any reservoir with a safe yield of more than 0.75 millions of gallons per day, any reservoir system with a safe yield of more than 0.75 millions of gallons per day, or any individual source within a reservoir system when such system has a safe yield of more than 0.75 millions of gallons per day is of a size or condition that makes it unsuitable for present or future use as a drinking water supply by the water company, other entity or the state. In making a decision, the commissioner shall consider the general utility of the source and the viability for use to meet water supply needs. The commissioner shall consider any public water supply plans filed and approved pursuant to sections 25–32d, as amended, and 25–33h, and any other water system plan approved by the commissioner, and the efficient and effective development of public water supply in the state. In assessing the general utility of the source, the commissioner shall consider factors including, but not limited to, (1) the safe yield of the source; (2) the location of the source relative to other public water supply systems, (3) the water quality of the source and the potential for treatment, (4) water quality compatibility between systems and interconnections, (5) extent of water company-owned lands for source protection of the supply, (6) types of land uses and land use controls in the aquifer protection area or watershed and their potential impact on water quality of the source, and (7) physical limitations to water service, system hydraulics and topography.

Sec. 45. Subsection (d) of section 25–32 of the general statutes is repealed and the following is substituted in lieu thereof (Effective October 1, 2004):

(d) The commissioner may grant a permit for (1) the sale of class I or II land to another water company, to a state agency or to a municipality, ~~or~~ (2) the sale of class II land or the sale or assignment of a conservation restriction or a public access easement on class I or class II land to a private, nonprofit land-holding conservation organization, or (3) the sale of class I land to a private nonprofit land-holding conservation organization if the water company is denied a permit to abandon a source not in current use or needed by the water company pursuant to subsection (c) of section 25–33k, as amended by this act, if the purchasing entity agrees to maintain the land subject to the provisions of this section, any regulations adopted pursuant to this section and the terms of any permit issued pursuant to this section. Such purchasing entity or assignee may not sell, lease or assign any such land or conservation restriction or public access easement or sell, lease, assign or change the use of such land without obtaining a permit pursuant to this section.

Sec. 46. Section 83 of public at 03–1 of the June 30 special session is repealed and the following is substituted in lieu thereof (Effective from passage):

A holder of property subject to part III of chapter 32 [1] and section 71, 73 and 74 of ~~this act~~ public act 03–1 of the June 30 special session may not impose on the property a dormancy charge or fee, abandoned property charge or fee, unclaimed property charge or fee, escheat charge or fee, inactivity charge or fee, or any similar charge, fee or penalty for inactivity with respect to the property. Neither the property nor an agreement with respect to the property may contain language suggesting that the property may be subject to such a charge, fee or penalty for inactivity. The provisions of this section shall not apply to property subject to subdivision (1), (2), (3) or (5) of subsection (a) of section 3–57a, as amended, provided a holder of any such property may not impose an escheat charge or fee with respect to such property.

[1] C.G.S.A. § 3–56 et seq.

Sec. 47. Subsection (j) of section 3–65a of the general statutes, as amended by section 76 of public act 03–1 of the June 30 special session, is repealed and the following is substituted in lieu thereof (Effective from passage):

(j) Notwithstanding the provisions of subsection (b) of this section, the holder of personal property presumed abandoned pursuant to subdivision (5) of subsection (a) of section 3–57a, as amended, shall sell such property and pay the proceeds arising from such sale, excluding any charges that may lawfully be withheld, to the Treasurer. A holder of such property may contract with a third party to store and sell such property and to pay the proceeds arising from such sale, excluding any charges that may be lawfully withheld, to the Treasurer, provided the third party holds a surety bond or other form of insurance coverage with respect to such activities. Any holder who sells such property and remits the excess proceeds to the Treasurer or who transmits such property to a bonded or insured third party for such purposes, shall not be responsible for any claims related to the sale or transmission of the property or proceeds to the Treasurer. If the Treasurer exempts any such property from being remitted or sold pursuant to this subsection, whether by regulations or guidelines, the holder of such property may dispose of such property in any manner such holder deems appropriate and such holder shall not be responsible for any claims related to the disposition of such property or any claims to the property itself. For purposes of this subsection, charges that may lawfully be withheld include costs of storage, appraisal, advertising and sales commissions as well as lawful charges owing under the contract governing the safe deposit box rental.

Sec. 48. Section 12–20a of the general statutes is repealed and the following is substituted in lieu thereof (Effective October 1, 2004, and applicable to assessment years commencing on or after October 1, 2004):

(a) On or before January first, annually, the Secretary of the Office of Policy and Management shall determine the amount due to each municipality in the state, in accordance with this section, as a state grant in lieu of taxes with respect to real property owned by any private nonprofit institution of higher ~~education~~ learning or any nonprofit general hospital facility or free standing chronic disease hospital or an urgent care facility that operates for at least twelve hours a day and that had been the location of a nonprofit general hospital for at least a portion of calendar year 1996 to receive payments in lieu of taxes for such property, exclusive of any such facility operated by the federal government, except a campus of the United States Department of Veterans Affairs Connecticut Healthcare Systems, or the state of Connecticut or any subdivision thereof. As used in this section "private nonprofit institution of higher ~~education~~ learning" means any such institution, as defined in subsection (a) of section 10a–34, or any independent college or university, as defined in section 10a–37, that is engaged primarily in education beyond the high school level, and offers courses of instruction for which college or university-level credit may be given or may be received by transfer, the property of which is exempt from property tax under any of the subdivisions of section 12–81, as amended by this act; "nonprofit general hospital facility" means any such facility which is used primarily for the purpose of general medical care and treatment, exclusive of any hospital facility used primarily for the care and treatment of special types of disease or physical or mental conditions; and "free standing chronic disease hospital" means a facility which provides for the care and treatment of chronic diseases, excluding any such facility having an ownership affiliation with and operated in the same location as a chronic and convalescent nursing home.

(b) The grant payable to any municipality under the provisions of this section in the state fiscal year commencing July 1, 1999, and in each fiscal year thereafter, shall be equal to seventy-seven per cent of the property taxes which, except for any exemption applicable to any such institution of higher education or general hospital facility under the provisions of section 12–81, as amended by this act, would have been paid with respect to such exempt real property on the assessment list in such municipality for the assessment date two years prior to the commencement of the state fiscal year in which such grant is payable. The amount of the grant payable to each municipality in any year in accordance with this section shall be reduced proportionately in the event that the total of such grants in such year exceeds the amount appropriated for the purposes of this section with respect to such year.

(c) Notwithstanding the provisions of subsection (b) of this section, the amount of the grant payable to any municipality under the provisions of this section with respect to a campus of the United States Department of Veterans Affairs Connecticut Healthcare Systems shall be as follows: (1) For the fiscal year ending June 30, 2007, twenty per cent of the amount payable in accordance with said subsection (b); (2) for the fiscal year ending June 30, 2008, forty per cent of such amount; (3) for the fiscal year ending June 30, 2009, sixty per cent of such amount; (4) for the fiscal year ending June 30, 2010, eighty per cent of such amount; (5) for the fiscal year ending June 30, 2011, and each fiscal year thereafter, one hundred per cent of such amount.

~~(c)~~ (d) As used in this section and section 12–20b, as amended by this act, the word "municipality" means any town, consolidated town and city, consolidated town and borough, borough, district, as defined in section 7–324, and any city not consolidated with a town.

Sec. 49. Subdivision (3) of section 34 of public act 03–6 of the June 30 special session is repealed and the following is substituted in lieu thereof (Effective from passage):

(3) "Housing revitalization plan" means the master plan of development for the housing developments accepted by the housing authority of the city of New Britain on March 13, 2002, and approved by the commissioner pursuant to subsection (d) of section 35 of ~~this act~~ public act 03–6 of the June 30 special session, as amended by this act, as such plan may be amended from time to time.

Sec. 50. Subsection (a) of section 22a–208a of the general statutes is repealed and the following is substituted in lieu thereof (Effective October 1, 2004):

(a) The Commissioner of Environmental Protection may issue, deny, modify, renew, suspend, revoke or transfer a permit, under such conditions as he may prescribe and upon submission of such information as he may require, for the construction, alteration and operation of solid waste facilities, in accordance with the provisions of this chapter and regulations adopted pursuant to this chapter. Notwithstanding the provisions of this section, the commissioner shall not issue (1) a permit for a solid waste land disposal facility on former railroad property until July 1, 1989, unless the commissioner makes a written determination that such facility is necessary to meet the solid waste disposal needs of the state and will not result in a substantial excess capacity of solid waste land disposal areas or disrupt the orderly transportation of or disposal of solid waste in the area affected by the facility, or (2) an operational permit for a resources recovery facility unless the applicant has submitted a plan pursuant to section 22a–208g for the disposal or recycling of ash residue expected to be generated at the facility in the first five years of operation. In making a decision to grant or deny a permit to construct a solid waste land disposal facility, including a vertical or horizontal landfill expansion, the commissioner shall consider the character of the neighborhood in which such facility is located and may impose requirements for hours and routes of truck traffic, security and fencing and for measures to prevent the blowing of dust and debris and to minimize insects, rodents and odors. In making a decision to grant or deny a permit to construct or operate a new transfer station, the commissioner shall consider whether such transfer station will result in disproportionately high adverse human health or environmental effects. The commissioner shall not authorize under a general permit or issue an individual permit under this section to establish or construct a new volume reduction plant or transfer station located, or proposed to be located, within one-quarter mile of a child day care center, as defined in subdivision (1) of subsection (a) of section 19a–77, as amended, in a municipality with a population greater than one hundred thousand persons provided such center is operating as of July 8, 1997. The commissioner may modify or renew a permit for an existing volume reduction plant or transfer station, in accordance with the provisions of this chapter, without regard to its location. In making a decision to grant or deny a permit to construct an ash residue disposal area, the commissioner shall consider any provision which the applicant shall make for a double liner, a leachate collection or detection system and the cost of transportation and disposal of ash residue at the site under consideration.

Sec. 51. (NEW) (Effective from passage) The Secretary of the Office of Policy and Management and the Capital City Economic Development Authority may enter into a memorandum of understanding with the Connecticut Center for Science and Exploration that provides that the secretary and the authority may provide financial management and construction management services assistance for the science center.

Sec. 52. Subsection (d) of section 42a–9–109 of the general statutes, as amended by section 3 of public act 03–62, is repealed and the following is substituted in lieu thereof (Effective from passage and applicable to any pledge, lien or security interest of this state or any political subdivision of this state, which pledge, lien or interest was in existence on October 1, 2003, and applicable to any such pledge, lien or interest created after October 1, 2003):

(d) This article does not apply to:

(1) A landlord's lien, other than an agricultural lien;

(2) A lien, other than an agricultural lien, given by statute or other rule of law for services or materials, but section 42a–9–333 applies with respect to priority of the lien;

(3) An assignment of a claim for wages, salary or other compensation of an employee;

(4) A sale of accounts, chattel paper, payment intangibles or promissory notes as part of a sale of the business out of which they arose;

(5) An assignment of accounts, chattel paper, payment intangibles or promissory notes which is for the purpose of collection only;

(6) An assignment of a right to payment under a contract to an assignee that is also obligated to perform under the contract;

(7) An assignment of a single account, payment intangible or promissory note to an assignee in full or partial satisfaction of a preexisting indebtedness;

(8) A transfer of an interest in or an assignment of a claim under a policy of insurance, other than an assignment by or to a health-care provider of a health-care-insurance receivable and any subsequent assignment of the right to payment, but sections 42a–9–315 and 42a–9–322 apply with respect to proceeds and priorities in proceeds;

(9) An assignment of a right represented by a judgment, other than a judgment taken on a right to payment that was collateral;

(10) A right of recoupment or set-off, but:

(A) Section 42a–9–340 applies with respect to the effectiveness of rights of recoupment or set-off against deposit accounts; and

(B) Section 42a–9–404 applies with respect to defenses or claims of an account debtor;

(11) The creation or transfer of an interest in or lien on real property, including a lease or rents thereunder, except to the extent that provision is made for:

(A) Liens on real property in sections 42a–9–203 and 42a–9–308;

(B) Fixtures in section 42a–9–334;

(C) Fixture filings in sections 42a–9–501, as amended, 42a–9–502, 42a–9–512, as amended, 42a–9–516 and 42a–9–519, as amended; and

(D) Security agreements covering personal and real property in section 42a–9–604;

(12) An assignment of a claim arising in tort, other than a commercial tort claim, but sections 42a–9–315 and 42a–9–322 apply with respect to proceeds and priorities in proceeds;

(13) An assignment of a deposit account in a consumer transaction, but sections 42a–9–315 and 42a–9–322 apply with respect to proceeds and priorities in proceeds;

(14) A pledge or other lien by this state or a government subdivision or agency of this state in existence on or after October 1, 2003, in connection with a bond or note issue of this state or of a government subdivision or agency of this state, which pledge or other lien is governed by a statute of this state that (A) provides for the creation of a pledge or other lien by this state or a government subdivision or agency of this state in connection with any bond or note issued by this state or a government subdivision or agency of this state, and (B) expressly states that such pledge or lien shall be valid and binding as against other parties;

~~(14)~~ (15) An assignment of workers' compensation benefits governed by section 31–320; or

~~(15)~~ (16) A security interest in a deposit account that is a payroll account or a trust account and which is titled or otherwise clearly identifiable as such an account, except that this article does apply to a security interest in (A) such an account if another statute of this state expressly so provides, or (B) a deposit account of a debtor that is a statutory trust formed or a foreign statutory trust registered under chapter 615, [1] provided such deposit account is not a payroll account or a trust account which is titled or otherwise clearly identifiable as such an account.

[1] C.G.S.A. § 34–500 et seq.

Sec. 53. Subsection (d) of section 10a–185 of the general statutes is repealed and the following is substituted in lieu thereof (Effective from passage and applicable to any pledge, lien or security interest of this state or any political subdivision of this state, which pledge, lien or interest was in existence on October 1, 2003, and applicable to any such pledge, lien or interest created after October 1, 2003):

(d) Any resolution or resolutions authorizing any bonds or any issue of bonds may contain provisions, which shall be a part of the contract with the holders of the bonds to be authorized, as to: (1) Pledging the full faith and credit of the authority, the full faith and credit of a participating institution for higher education, a participating health care institution, a participating corporation or of a participating nursing home, all or any part of the revenues of a project or any revenue-producing contract or contracts made by the authority with any individual, partnership, corporation or association or other body, public or private, any federally guaranteed security and moneys received therefrom purchased with bond proceeds or any other property, revenues, funds or legally available moneys to secure the payment of the bonds or of any particular issue of bonds, subject to such agreements with bondholders as may then exist; (2) the rentals, fees and other charges to be charged, and the amounts to be raised in each year thereby, and the use and disposition of the revenues; (3) the setting aside of reserves or sinking funds, and the regulation and disposition thereof; (4) limitations on the right of the authority or its agent to restrict and regulate the use of the project; (5) the purpose and limitations to which the proceeds of sale of any issue of bonds then or thereafter to be issued may be applied, including as authorized purposes, all costs and expenses necessary or incidental to the issuance of bonds, to the acquisition of or commitment to acquire any federally guaranteed security and to the issuance and obtaining of any federally insured mortgage note, and pledging such proceeds to secure the payment of the bonds or any issue of the bonds; (6) limitations on the issuance of additional bonds, the terms upon which additional bonds may be issued and secured and the refunding of outstanding bonds; (7) the procedure, if any, by which the terms of any contract with bondholders may be amended or abrogated, the amount of bonds the holders of which must consent thereto, and the manner in which such consent may be given; (8) limitations on the amount of moneys derived from the project to be expended for operating, administrative or other expenses of the authority; (9) defining the acts or omissions to act which shall constitute a default in the duties of the authority to holders of its obligations and providing the rights and remedies of such holders in the event of a default, and (10) the mortgaging of a project and the site thereof for the purpose of securing the bondholders.

Sec. 54. Section 10a–186 of the general statutes is repealed and the following is substituted in lieu thereof (Effective from passage and applicable to any pledge, lien or security interest of this state or any political subdivision of this state, which pledge, lien or interest was in existence on October 1, 2003, and applicable to any such pledge, lien or interest created after October 1, 2003):

In the discretion of the authority any bonds issued under the provisions of this chapter may be secured by a trust agreement by and between the authority and a corporate trustee or trustees, which may be any trust company or bank having the powers of a trust company within or without the state. Such trust agreement or the resolution providing for the issuance of such bonds ~~may~~ or other instrument of the authority may secure such bonds by a pledge or ~~assign the~~ assignment of any revenues to be received, any contract or proceeds of any contract, ~~or contracts pledged and may convey or mortgage the project or any portion thereof~~ or any other property, revenues, moneys or funds available to the authority for such purpose. Any pledge made by the authority pursuant to this section shall be valid and binding from the time when the pledge is made. The lien of any such pledge shall be valid and binding as against all parties having claims of any kind in tort, contract or otherwise against the authority, irrespective of whether the parties have notice of the claims. Notwithstanding any provision of the Uniform Commercial Code,[1] no instrument by which such pledge is created need be recorded or filed. Any revenues or other receipts, funds, moneys, income, contracts or property so pledged and thereafter received by the authority shall be subject immediately to the lien of the pledge without any physical delivery thereof or further act and such lien shall have priority over all other liens. Such trust agreement or other instrument may mortgage, assign or convey any real property to secure such bonds. Such trust agreement or resolution providing for the issuance of such bonds may contain such provisions for protecting and enforcing the rights and remedies of the bondholders as may be reasonable and proper and not in violation of law, including particularly such provisions as have hereinabove been specifically authorized to be included in any resolution or resolutions of the authority authorizing bonds thereof. Any bank or trust company incorporated under the laws of this state which may act as depositary of the proceeds of bonds or of revenues or other moneys may furnish such indemnifying bonds or pledge such securities as may be required by the authority. Any such trust agreement may set forth the rights and remedies of the bondholders and of the trustee or trustees, and may restrict the individual right of action by bondholders. In addition to the foregoing, any such trust agreement or resolution may contain such other provisions as the authority may deem reasonable and proper for the security of the bondholders. All expenses incurred in carrying out the provisions of such trust agreement or resolution may be treated as a part of the cost of the operation of a project.

[1] C.G.S.A. § 42a–1–101 et seq.

Sec. 55. Subsection (i) of section 32–607 of the general statutes is repealed and the following is substituted in lieu thereof (Effective from passage and applicable to any pledge, lien or security interest of this state or any political subdivision of this state, which pledge, lien or interest was in existence on October 1, 2003, and applicable to any such pledge, lien or interest created after October 1, 2003):

(i) Any pledge made by the authority of income, revenues, state contract assistance provided under section 32–608, or other property shall be valid and binding from the time the pledge is made. ~~, and shall constitute a pledge within the meaning and for all purposes of title 42a.~~ The income, revenue, state contract assistance, such state taxes as the authority shall be entitled to receive or other property so pledged and thereafter received by the authority shall immediately be subject to the lien of such pledge without any physical delivery thereof or further act, and the lien of any such pledge shall be valid and binding as against all parties having claims of any kind in tort, contract or otherwise against the authority, irrespective of whether such parties have notice thereof.

Sec. 56. Subsection (i) of section 32–206 of the general statutes is repealed and the following is substituted in lieu thereof (Effective from passage and applicable to any pledge, lien or security interest of this state or any political subdivision of this state, which pledge, lien or interest was in existence on October 1, 2003, and applicable to any such pledge, lien or interest created after October 1, 2003):

(i) Any pledge made by the authority of income, revenues, state contract assistance as herein provided and such state taxes as the authority shall be entitled to receive pursuant to the provisions hereof, or other property shall be valid and binding from the time the pledge is made. ~~, and shall constitute a pledge within the meaning and for all purposes of title 42a.~~ The income, revenue, state contract assistance as provided in sections 32–200 to 32–212, inclusive, and such state taxes as the authority shall be entitled to receive pursuant to the provisions of said sections, or other property so pledged and thereafter received by the authority shall immediately be subject to the lien of such pledge without any physical delivery thereof or further act, and the lien of any such pledge shall be valid and binding as against all parties having claims of any kind in tort, contract or otherwise against the authority, irrespective of whether such parties have notice thereof.

Sec. 57. Subsection (a) of section 10a–109h of the general statutes is repealed and the following is substituted in lieu thereof (Effective from passage and applicable to any pledge, lien or security interest of this state or any political subdivision of this state, which pledge, lien or interest was in existence on October 1, 2003, and applicable to any such pledge, lien or interest created after October 1, 2003):

(a) Any pledge made by the university pursuant to section 10a–109g is and shall be deemed a statutory lien. ~~and, except as expressly provided in this section, is governed by article 9 of title 42a.~~ Such lien shall be valid and binding from the time when the pledge is made. The lien of any pledge shall be valid and binding as against all parties having claims of any kind in tort, contract or otherwise against the university, irrespective of whether the parties have notice of the claims. Notwithstanding any provision of the Uniform Commercial Code[1] to the contrary, neither sections 10a–109a to 10a–109y, inclusive, the indenture or resolution, nor any other instrument by which a pledge is created need be recorded. Any revenues or other receipts, funds, moneys, personal property of fixtures so pledged and thereafter received by the university shall be subject immediately to the lien of the pledge without any physical delivery thereof or further act and such lien shall have priority over all other liens, including without limitation the liens of persons who, in the ordinary course of business, furnish services or materials in respect of such assets.

[1] C.G.S.A. § 42a–1–101 et seq.

Sec. 58. Subsection (e) of section 22a–483 of the general statutes is repealed and the following is substituted in lieu thereof (Effective from passage and applicable to any pledge, lien or security interest of this state or any political subdivision of this state, which pledge, lien or interest was in existence on October 1, 2003, and applicable to any such pledge, lien or interest created after October 1, 2003):

(e) Any pledge made by the state pursuant to sections 22a–475 to 22a–483, inclusive, is a statutory pledge ~~within the meaning and for all purposes of title 42a~~ and shall be valid and binding from the time when the pledge is made, and any revenues or other receipts, funds or moneys so pledged and thereafter received by the state shall be subject immediately to the lien of such pledge without any physical delivery thereof or further act. The lien of any such pledge shall be valid and binding as against all parties having claims of any kind in tort, contract or otherwise against the state, irrespective of whether such parties have notice thereof. Neither the resolution nor any other instrument by which a pledge is created need be recorded. Any pledge made by the state pursuant to sections 22a–475 to 22a–483, inclusive, to secure revenue bonds issued to finance eligible water quality projects shall secure only revenue bonds issued for such purpose and any such pledge made by the state to secure revenue bonds issued to finance eligible drinking water projects shall secure only revenue bonds issued for such purpose.

Sec. 59. Subsection (a) of section 10a–224 of the general statutes is repealed and the following is substituted in lieu thereof (Effective from passage and applicable to any pledge, lien or security interest of this state or any political subdivision of this state, which pledge, lien or interest was in existence on October 1, 2003, and applicable to any such pledge, lien or interest created after October 1, 2003):

(a) There is created a body politic and corporate to be known as the "Connecticut Higher Education Supplemental Loan Authority". The authority is constituted a public instrumentality and political subdivision of the state and the exercise by the authority of the powers conferred by this chapter shall be deemed and held to be the performance of an essential public and governmental function. The powers of the authority shall be vested in and exercised by a board of directors which shall consist of eight members, one of whom shall be the State Treasurer, one of whom shall be the Secretary of the Office of Policy and Management and one of whom shall be the Commissioner of Higher Education, each serving ex officio, and five of whom shall be residents of the state appointed by the Governor, not more than three of such appointed members to be members of the same political party. Three of the appointed members shall be active or retired trustees, directors, officers or employees of Connecticut institutions for higher education, of whom not more than one shall be from a constituent unit of the state system of higher education. At least one of the appointed members shall be a person having a favorable reputation for skill, knowledge and experience in the higher education loan finance field, and at least one of such appointed members shall be a person having a favorable reputation for skill, knowledge and experience in state and municipal finance, either as a partner, officer or employee of an investment banking firm which originates and purchases state and municipal securities, or as an officer or employee of an insurance company or bank whose duties relate to the purchase of state and municipal securities as an investment and to the management and control of a state and municipal securities portfolio. Of the three members first appointed who are trustees, directors, officers or employees of Connecticut institutions for higher education, one shall serve until July 1, 1986, one shall serve until July 1, 1987, and one shall serve until July 1, 1988. Of the three remaining members first appointed, one shall serve until July 1, 1983, one shall serve until July 1, 1984, and one shall serve until July 1, 1985. On or before the first day of July, annually, the Governor shall appoint a member or members to succeed those whose terms expire, each for a term of six years and until his successor is appointed and has qualified. The Governor shall fill any vacancy for the unexpired term. A member of the board shall be eligible for reappointment. Any member of the board may be removed by the Governor for misfeasance, malfeasance or wilful neglect of duty. Each member of the board before entering upon his or her duties shall take and subscribe the oath or affirmation required by section 1 of article eleventh of the State Constitution. A record of each such oath shall be filed in the office of the Secretary of the State. The State Treasurer, the Secretary of the Office of Policy and Management and the Commissioner of Higher Education may each designate a deputy or any staff member to represent him as a member at meetings of the board with full power to act and vote on his behalf.

Sec. 60. Subsection (b) of section 10a–230 of the general statutes is repealed and the following is substituted in lieu thereof (Effective from passage and applicable to any pledge, lien or security interest of this state or any political subdivision of this state, which pledge, lien or interest was in existence on October 1, 2003, and applicable to any such pledge, lien or interest created after October 1, 2003):

(b) The revenue bonds and notes of every issue shall be payable solely out of the revenues of the authority pertaining to the program relating to such bonds or notes including principal and interest on authority loans and education loans, and any other revenues derived from or in connection with any other authority loans and education loans, payments by participating institutions for higher education, banks, guarantors, insurance companies or others pursuant to letters of credit or purchase agreements, investment earnings from funds or accounts maintained pursuant to the bond resolution, insurance proceeds, loan funding deposits, proceeds of sales of education loans, proceeds of refunding bonds and fees, charges and other revenues, funds and other assets of the authority ~~from such program~~ but subject only to any agreements with the holders of particular revenue bonds or notes pledging any particular revenues and subject to any agreements with any participating institution for higher education.

Sec. 61. Subsection (d) of section 10a–230 of the general statutes is repealed and the following is substituted in lieu thereof (Effective from passage and applicable to any pledge, lien or security interest of this state or any political subdivision of this state, which pledge, lien or interest was in existence on October 1, 2003, and applicable to any such pledge, lien or interest created after October 1, 2003):

(d) Any resolution or resolutions authorizing any revenue bonds or any issue of revenue bonds may contain provisions, which shall be a part of the contract with the holders of the revenue bonds to be authorized, as to: (1) Pledging all or any part of the revenues, ~~derived from~~ funds or other assets of the authority, including, but not limited to, the authority loans and education loans ~~with respect to which~~ to secure such bonds or notes; ~~are to be issued;~~ (2) pledging all or any part of the revenues paid to the authority by any guarantor or insurance company; (3) pledging any revenue producing contract or contracts made by the authority with any individual, partnership, corporation or association or other body, public or private, or any federally guaranteed security and moneys received or receivable therefrom whether such security is acquired by the authority or a participating institution for higher education to secure the payment of the revenue bonds or notes or of any particular issue of revenue bonds or notes, subject to such agreements with bondholders or noteholders as may then exist; (4) the fees and other amounts to be charged, and the sums to be raised in each year thereby, and the use, investment and disposition of such sums; (5) the establishment and setting aside of reserves or sinking funds, the setting aside of loan funding deposits, capitalized interest accounts, and cost of issuance accounts, and the regulation and disposition thereof; (6) limitations on the use of the education loans; (7) limitations on the purpose to which the proceeds of the sale of any issue of revenue bonds or notes then or thereafter to be issued may be applied, including as authorized purposes, all costs and expenses necessary or incidental to the issuance of bonds, to the acquisition of or commitment to acquire any federally guaranteed security and pledging such proceeds to secure the payment of the revenue bonds, notes or any issue of the revenue bonds or notes; (8) limitations on the issuance of additional bonds or notes, the terms upon which additional bonds or notes may be issued and secured and the terms on which additional bonds or notes rank on a parity with, or be subordinate or superior to, other bonds or notes; (9) the refunding of outstanding bonds or notes; (10) the procedure, if any, by which the terms of any contract with bondholders or noteholders may be amended or abrogated, the amount of bonds or notes the holders of which must consent thereto, and the manner in which such consent may be given; (11) limitations on the amount of moneys derived from the educational program to be expended for operating, administrative or other expenses of the authority; (12) defining the acts or omissions to act which shall constitute a default in the duties of the authority to holders of its obligations and providing the rights and remedies of such holders in the event of default; (13) the duties, obligations and liabilities of any trustee or paying agent; (14) providing for guarantees, pledges of endowments, letters of credit, property or other security for the benefit of the holders of such bonds or notes; and (15) any other matters relating to the bonds or notes which the authority deems desirable.

Sec. 62. Section 10a–233 of the general statutes is repealed and the following is substituted in lieu thereof (Effective from passage and applicable to any pledge, lien or security interest of this state or any political subdivision of this state, which pledge, lien or interest was in existence on October 1, 2003, and applicable to any such pledge, lien or interest created after October 1, 2003):

The authority shall fix, revise, charge and collect fees and is empowered to contract with any person, partnership, association or corporation, or other body, public or private, in respect thereof. Each agreement entered into by the authority with a participating institution or institutions for higher education shall provide that the fees and other amounts payable by said institution or institutions with respect to any program or programs of the authority shall be sufficient at all times, (1) to pay its or their share of the administrative costs and expenses of such program, (2) to pay the principal of, the premium, if any, and the interest on outstanding bonds or notes of the authority issued with respect to such program to the extent that other revenues of the authority pledged for the payment of the bonds or notes are insufficient to pay the bonds or notes as they become due and payable, (3) to create and maintain reserves which may but need not be required or provided for in the bond resolution relating to such bonds or notes of the authority, and (4) to establish and maintain whatever education loan servicing, control, or audit procedures are deemed to be necessary to the operations of the authority. The authority ~~shall~~ may pledge all or any part of the revenues, ~~from each program,~~ funds, contracts or other assets of the authority, as described in ~~subsection (b)~~ subsections (b) and (d) of section 10a–230, as security for ~~the~~ any issue of bonds or notes. ~~relating to such program~~ Such pledge shall be valid and binding from the time when the pledge is made; the revenues, funds, contracts or other assets so pledged by the authority shall immediately be subject to the lien of such pledge without any physical delivery thereof or further act, and the lien of any such pledge shall be valid and binding against all parties having claims of any kind in tort, contract or otherwise against the authority or any participating institution for higher education, irrespective of whether such parties have notice thereof. ~~Neither~~ Such lien shall have priority over all other liens, including, without limitation, the lien of any person who in the ordinary course of business furnishes services or materials to the authority. Notwithstanding any provisions of the Uniform Commercial Code, [1] neither the bond resolution nor any financing statement, continuation statement or other instrument by which a pledge or security interest is created or by which the authority's interest in revenues, funds, contracts or other assets is assigned need be filed in any public records in order to perfect the security interest or lien thereof as against third parties. ~~except in the records of the authority. The authority may elect, notwithstanding the exclusions provided in subdivision (14) of subsection (d) of section 42a–9–109, to have the provisions of the Connecticut Uniform Commercial Code apply to any pledge made by or to the authority to secure its bonds or notes by filing a financing statement with respect to the security interest created by the pledge.~~ The use and disposition of moneys to the credit of such sinking or other similar fund shall be subject to the provisions of the resolution authorizing the issuance of such bonds or notes or of such trust agreement. Except as may otherwise be provided in such resolution, or such trust agreement, such sinking or other similar fund shall be a fund for all such revenue bonds or notes issued to finance an educational program or programs at one or more participating institutions for higher education, without distinction or priority of one over another; provided, the authority in any such resolution or trust agreement may provide that such sinking or other similar fund shall be the fund for a particular educational program or programs at a participating institution or institutions for higher education and for the revenue bonds or notes issued to finance a particular education program or programs and may, additionally, permit and provide for the issuance of revenue bonds or notes having a subordinate lien in respect of the security herein authorized to other revenue bonds or notes of the authority and, in such case, the authority may create separate or other similar funds in respect of such subordinate lien bonds or notes.

[1] C.G.S.A. § 42a–1–101 et seq.

Sec. 63. Subsection (d) of section 10a–237 of the general statutes is repealed and the following is substituted in lieu thereof (Effective from passage and applicable to any pledge, lien or security interest of this state or any political subdivision of this state, which pledge, lien or interest was in existence on October 1, 2003, and applicable to any such pledge, lien or interest created after October 1, 2003):

(d) The portion of the proceeds of any such revenue bonds or notes issued for the additional purpose of making additional authority loans may be invested and reinvested in direct obligations of, or unconditionally guaranteed by, the United States, and certificates of deposit or time deposits secured by direct obligations of, or unconditionally guaranteed by, the United States, or obligations of a state, territory or possession of the United States, or any political subdivision of any such state, territory or possession, or of the District of Columbia, within the meaning of Section 103(a) of the Internal Revenue Code of 1986, [1] or any subsequent corresponding internal revenue code of the United States, as from time to time amended, the full and timely payment of the principal of and interest on which are secured by an irrevocable deposit of direct obligations of the United States or which, if the outstanding bonds are then rated by a nationally recognized rating agency, are rated in the highest rating category by such rating agency, maturing not later than the time or times when such proceeds will be needed for the purpose of paying all or any part of such cost and any other investment described in section 10a–238, as amended by this act. The interest, income and profits, if any, earned or realized on such investment may be applied to the payment of all or any part of such cost or may be used by the authority in any lawful manner.

[1] 26 U.S.C.A. § 103.

Sec. 64. Section 10a–238 of the general statutes, as amended by section 11 of public act 03–84, is repealed and the following is substituted in lieu thereof (Effective from passage and applicable to any pledge, lien or security interest of this state or any political subdivision of this state, which pledge, lien or interest was in existence on October 1, 2003, and applicable to any such pledge, lien or interest created after October 1, 2003):

Except as otherwise provided in subsection (c) of section 10a–237, the authority may invest any funds in (1) direct obligations of the United States or the state of Connecticut, (2) obligations as to which the timely payment of principal and interest is fully guaranteed by the United States or the state of Connecticut, ~~including~~ and Connecticut's Short-Term Investment Fund, (3) obligations of the United States Export-Import Bank, Farmers Home Administration, Federal Financing Bank, Federal Housing Administration, General Services Administration, United States Maritime Administration, United States Department of Housing and Urban Development, Farm Credit System, Resolution Funding Corporation, federal intermediate credit banks, federal banks for cooperatives, federal land bank, federal home loan banks, Federal National Mortgage Association, Government National Mortgage Association and the Student Loan Marketing Association, (4) certificates of deposit or time deposits constituting direct obligations of any bank in the state, provided that investments may be made only in those certificates of deposit or time deposits in banks which are insured by the Federal Deposit Insurance Corporation if then in existence, (5) withdrawable capital accounts or deposits of federal chartered savings and loan associations which are insured by the Federal Savings and Loan Insurance Corporation, (6) other obligations which are legal investments for savings banks in the state, (7) investment agreements with financial institutions whose long-term obligations are rated within the top two rating categories of any nationally recognized rating service or of any rating service recognized by the Banking Commissioner or whose short-term obligations are rated within the top two rating categories of any nationally recognized rating service or of any rating service recognized by the Banking Commissioner, or investment agreements fully secured by obligations of, or guaranteed by, the United States or agencies or instrumentalities of the United States, and (8) securities or obligations which are legal investments for savings banks in Connecticut, subject to repurchase agreements in the manner in which such agreements are negotiated in sales of securities in the market place, provided the authority shall not enter into any such agreement with any securities dealer or bank acting as a securities dealer unless such dealer or bank is included in the list of primary dealers, as prepared by the Federal Reserve Bank of New York, effective at the time of the agreement. Any such securities may be purchased at the offering or market price thereof at the time of such purchase. All such securities so purchased shall mature or be redeemable on a date or dates prior to the time when, in the judgment of the authority, the funds so invested will be required for expenditure. The express judgment of the authority as to the time when any funds shall be required for expenditure or be redeemable is final and conclusive.

Sec. 65. Subsection (i) of section 10a–204b of the general statutes is repealed and the following is substituted in lieu thereof (Effective from passage and applicable to any pledge, lien or security interest of the corporation, which pledge, lien or interest was in existence on October 1, 2003, and applicable to any such pledge, lien or interest created after October 1, 2003):

(i) Any pledge made by the corporation of income, revenues or other property to secure bonds, notes or other obligations of the corporation shall be valid and binding from the time the pledge is made. The income, revenue or other property so pledged and thereafter received by or on behalf of the corporation shall immediately be subject to the lien of such pledge without any physical delivery thereof or further act, and the lien of any such pledge shall be valid and binding as against all parties having claims of any kind in tort, contract or otherwise against the corporation, irrespective of whether such parties have notice thereof. Any such lien shall have priority over all other liens, including, without limitation, the lien of any person who in the ordinary course of business furnishes services or materials to the corporation. Any provision of law to the contrary notwithstanding, neither possession nor the filing of any financing or continuation statement or other instrument shall be necessary with respect to any such income, revenues or other property to establish or evidence the lien of any such pledge with respect thereto. Neither this section, nor any resolution authorizing bonds, notes or other obligations, nor any trust agreement nor any other instrument by which such a pledge is created need be recorded. Any pledge or lien described by this subsection shall be conclusively deemed to be a pledge or lien described by subdivision (14) of subsection (d) of section 42a–9–109, as amended by this act, notwithstanding that the corporation is neither a political subdivision nor an agency of the state.

Sec. 66. Subsection (c) of section 22a–516 of the general statutes is repealed and the following is substituted in lieu thereof (Effective from passage and applicable to any pledge, lien or security interest of this state or any political subdivision of this state, which pledge, lien or interest was in existence on October 1, 2003, and applicable to any such pledge, lien or interest created after October 1, 2003):

(c) Any pledge made by a municipality or an authority pursuant to the provisions of sections 22a–500 to 22a–519, inclusive, shall be valid and binding from the time when the pledge is made, and any revenues or other receipts, funds or moneys so pledged and thereafter received by such municipality or authority shall be subject immediately to the lien of such pledge without any physical delivery thereof, filing or further act. The lien of any such pledge shall be valid and binding as against all parties having claims of any kind in tort, contract, or otherwise against the municipality or the authority, irrespective of whether such parties have notice thereof and shall be a statutory lien. ~~within the meaning of the Uniform Commercial Code and article 9 of title 42a.~~ Neither the resolution nor any other instrument by which a pledge is created shall be required to be recorded.

Sec. 67. Section 3 of special act 92–25, as amended by section 9 of special act 93–40 and section 3 of special act 01–10, is amended to read as follows (Effective from passage and applicable to any pledge, lien or security interest of this state or any political subdivision of this state, which pledge, lien or interest was in existence on October 1, 2003, and applicable to any such pledge, lien or interest created after October 1, 2003):

The principal of and interest on bonds issued by the committee, and any agreement as set forth in section 2 of special act 92–25, may be secured by a pledge of any revenues and receipts of the committee derived from the project and may be additionally secured by the assignment of a lease of the project or by an assignment of the revenues and receipts derived by the committee from any such lease. The payment of principal and interest on such bonds may be additionally secured by a pledge of any other property, revenues, moneys or funds available to the committee for such purpose. The resolution authorizing the issuance of bonds and any such lease may contain or authorize agreements and provisions respecting (1) the establishment of reserves to secure such bonds, (2) the maintenance and insurance of the project covered thereby, (3) the fixing and collection of rents for any portion thereof leased by the committee to others, (4) the creation and maintenance of special funds from such revenues, (5) the rights and remedies available in the event of default, (6) provision for a trust agreement by and between the committee and a corporate trustee or trustees which may be any trust company or bank having the powers of a trust company within or without the state, which agreement may provide for the pledge or assigning of any assets or income from assets to which or in which the committee has rights or interest, the vesting in such trustee or trustees of such property, rights, powers and duties in trust as the committee may determine, which may include any or all of the rights, powers and duties of any trustee appointed by the holders of any bonds and limiting or abrogating the right of the holders of any bonds to appoint a trustee or limiting rights, powers and duties of such trustee, and may further provide for such other rights and remedies exercisable by the trustee as may be proper for the protection of the holders of any bonds and not otherwise in violation of law. Such trust agreement may provide for the restriction of rights of any individual holder of bonds of the committee and may contain any provisions which are reasonable to delineate further the respective rights, due safeguards, responsibilities and liabilities of the committee, persons and collective holders of bonds of the committee and the trustee, (7) covenants to do or refrain from doing acts and things as may be necessary or convenient or desirable in order to better secure bonds of the committee, or which, in the discretion of the committee, will tend to make any bonds to be issued more marketable, notwithstanding that such covenants or things may not be enumerated in this act, and (8) any other matters of like or different character, which in any way affect the security or protection of the bonds, all as the committee shall deem advisable and not in conflict with the provisions of this act. Each pledge, agreement or assignment of lease made for the benefit or security of any bonds of the committee shall be in effect until the principal of and interest on the bonds for the benefit of which the same were made have been fully paid, or until provision has been made for the payment in the manner provided in the resolution or resolutions authorizing the issuance. Any pledge made in respect of such bonds shall be valid and binding from the time when the pledge is made; moneys or rents so pledged and thereafter received by the committee shall immediately be subject to the lien of such pledge without any physical delivery thereof or further act; and the lien of any such pledge shall be valid and binding as against parties having claims of any kind in tort, contract or otherwise against the committee, irrespective of whether such parties have notice thereof. Neither the resolution, trust indenture nor any other instrument by which a pledge is created need be recorded. The committee may, without further approval of the legislative bodies of the municipalities which are parties to the original project agreements, assign, amend, reaffirm, or terminate any or all of such original project agreements to secure the bonds and exercise the powers set forth in this act by vote taken in accordance with the inter-community agreement. The resolution authorizing the issuance of such bonds may provide for the enforcement of any such pledge or security in any lawful manner. The committee shall be considered a political subdivision of the state for purposes of subdivision (14) of subsection (d) of section 42a–9–109 of the general statutes, as amended by this act.

Sec. 68. Section 10–66c of the general statutes is amended by adding subsection (i) as follows (Effective from passage and applicable to any pledge, lien or security interest of this state or any political subdivision of this state, which pledge, lien or interest was in existence on October 1, 2003, and applicable to any such pledge, lien or interest created after October 1, 2003):

(NEW) (i) A regional educational service center shall be considered an agency of the state for purposes of subdivision (14) of subsection (d) of section 42a–9–109, as amended by this act.

Sec. 69. Section 22a–479 of the general statutes is repealed and the following is substituted in lieu thereof (Effective from passage and applicable to any pledge, lien or security interest of this state or any political subdivision of this state, which pledge, lien or interest was in existence on October 1, 2003, and applicable to any such pledge, lien or interest created after October 1, 2003):

(a) A municipality may authorize and approve (1) the execution and delivery of project funding agreements, and (2) the issuance and sale of project obligations, grant account loan obligations and interim funding obligations, in accordance with such statutory and charter requirements as govern the authorization and approval of borrowings and the making of contracts generally by the municipality or in accordance with the provisions of subsection (e) of this section. Project loan obligations, grant account loan obligations and interim funding obligations shall be duly executed and accompanied by an approving legal opinion of bond counsel of recognized standing in the field of municipal law whose opinions are generally accepted by purchasers of municipal bonds and shall be subject to the debt limitation provisions of section 7–374; except that project loan obligations, grant account loan obligations and interim funding obligations issued in order to meet the requirements of any abatement order of the commissioner shall not be subject to the debt limitation provisions of section 7–374, provided the municipality files a certificate, signed by its chief fiscal officer, with the commissioner demonstrating to the satisfaction of the commissioner that the municipality has a plan for levying a system of charges, assessments or other revenues which are sufficient, together with other available funds of the municipality, to repay such obligations as the same become due and payable.

(b) Each recipient which enters into a project funding agreement shall protect, defend and hold harmless the state, its agencies, departments, agents and employees from and against any and all claims, suits, actions, demands, costs and damages arising from or in connection with the performance or nonperformance by the recipient, or any of its officers, employees or agents, of the recipient's obligations under any project funding agreement as such project funding agreement may be amended or supplemented from time to time. Each such recipient may insure against the liability imposed by this subsection through any insurance company organized within or without this state authorized to write such insurance in this state or may elect to act as self-insurer of such liability, provided such indemnity shall not be limited by any such insurance coverage.

(c) Whenever a recipient has entered into a project funding agreement and has authorized the issuance of project loan obligations or grant account loan obligations, it may authorize the issuance of interim funding obligations. Proceeds from the issuance and sale of interim funding obligations shall be used to temporarily finance an eligible project pending receipt of the proceeds of a project loan obligation, a grant account loan obligation or project grant. Such interim funding obligations may be issued and sold to the state for the benefit of the Clean Water Fund or issued and sold to any other lender on such terms and in such manner as shall be determined by a recipient. Such interim funding obligations may be renewed from time to time by the issuance of other notes, provided the final maturity of such notes shall not exceed six months from the date of completion of the planning and design phase or the construction phase, as applicable, of an eligible project, as determined by the commissioner. Such notes and any renewals of a municipality shall not be subject to the requirements and limitations set forth in sections 7–378, ~~and~~ 7–378a and 7–264. The provisions of section 7–374 shall apply to such notes and any renewals thereof of a municipality; except that project loan obligations, grant account loan obligations and interim funding obligations issued in order to meet the requirements of an abatement order of the commissioner shall not be subject to the debt limitation provisions of section 7–374, provided the municipality files a certificate, signed by its chief fiscal officer, with the commissioner demonstrating to the satisfaction of the commissioner that the municipality has a plan for levying a system of charges, assessments or other revenues sufficient, together with other available funds of the municipality, to repay such obligations as the same become due and payable. The officer or agency authorized by law or by vote of the recipient to issue such interim funding obligations shall, within any limitation imposed by such law or vote, determine the date, maturity, interest rate, form, manner of sale and other details of such obligations. Such obligations may bear interest or be sold at a discount and the interest or discount on such obligations, including renewals thereof, and the expense of preparing, issuing and marketing them may be included as a part of the cost of an eligible project. Upon the issuance of a project loan obligation or grant account loan obligation, the proceeds thereof, to the extent required, shall be applied forthwith to the payment of the principal of and interest on all interim funding obligations issued in anticipation thereof and upon receipt of a project grant, the proceeds thereof, to the extent required, shall be applied forthwith to the payment of the principal of and interest on all grant anticipation notes issued in anticipation thereof or, in either case, shall be deposited in trust for such purpose with a bank or trust company, which may be the bank or trust company, if any, at which such obligations are payable.

(d) Project loan obligations, grant account loan obligations, interim funding obligations or any obligation of a municipality that satisfies the requirements of Title VI of the federal Water Pollution Control Act [1] or the federal Safe Drinking Water Act [2] or other related federal act may, as determined by the commissioner, be general obligations of the issuing municipality and in such case each such obligation shall recite that the full faith and credit of the issuing municipality are pledged for the payment of the principal thereof and interest thereon. To the extent a municipality is authorized pursuant to sections 22a–475 to 22a–483, inclusive, to issue project loan obligations or interim funding obligations, such obligations may be secured by a pledge of revenues and other funds derived from its sewer system or public water supply system, as applicable. Each pledge and agreement made for the benefit or security of any of such obligations shall be in effect until the principal of, and interest on, such obligations have been fully paid, or until provision has been made for payment in the manner provided in the resolution authorizing their issuance or in the agreement for the benefit of the holders of such obligations. In any such case, such pledge shall be valid and binding from the time when such pledge is made. Any revenues or other receipts, funds or moneys so pledged and thereafter received by the municipality shall immediately be subject to the lien of such pledge without any physical delivery thereof or further act. The lien of any such pledge shall be valid and binding as against all parties having claims of any kind in tort, contract or otherwise against the municipality, irrespective of whether such parties have notice thereof. Neither the project loan obligation, interim funding obligation, project funding agreement nor any other instrument by which a pledge is created need be recorded. All securities or other investments of moneys of the state permitted or provided for under sections 22a–475 to 22a–483, inclusive, may, upon the determination of the State Treasurer, be purchased and held in fully marketable form, subject to provision for any registration in the name of the state. Securities or other investments at any time purchased, held or owned by the state may, upon the determination of the State Treasurer and upon delivery to the state, be accompanied by such documentation, including approving bond opinion, certification and guaranty as to signatures and certification as to absence of litigation, and such other or further documentation as shall from time to time be required in the municipal bond market or required by the state.

(e) Notwithstanding the provisions of the general statutes, any special act or any municipal charter ~~, a municipality may, upon the approval of~~ governing the authorization of bonds, notes or obligations or the appropriation of funds, or governing the application for, and expenditure of, grants or loans, or governing the authorization of contracts or financing agreements or governing the pledging of sewer or water revenues or funds, a municipality may, by resolution approved by its legislative body and by (1) its water pollution control authority or sewer authority, if any, authorize a project loan and project grant agreement between the municipality and the state pursuant to sections 22a–475 to 22a–483, inclusive, and appropriate funds and authorize project loan obligations ~~,~~ and interim funding obligations ~~, revenue bonds, notes or other obligations~~ of the municipality paid and secured solely by a pledge of revenues, funds and moneys of the municipality and the water pollution control authority or sewer authority, if any, derived from its sewer system, to pay for and finance the total project costs of an eligible water quality project, pursuant to a project loan and project grant agreement between the municipality and the state pursuant to sections 22a–475 to 22a–483, inclusive, ~~and~~ or (2) by its water authority, if any, authorize a project loan and project grant agreement between the municipality and the state pursuant to sections 22a–475 to 22a–483, inclusive, and appropriate funds and authorize project loan obligations ~~,~~ and interim funding obligations ~~, revenue bonds, notes or other obligations~~ of the municipality paid and secured solely by a pledge of revenues, funds and moneys of the municipality and the water authority, if any, derived from its public water supply system, to pay for and finance the total project costs of an eligible water quality project, pursuant to a project loan agreement between the municipality and the state pursuant to sections 22a–475 to 22a–483, inclusive. The provisions of chapter 103 [3] shall apply to the ~~bonds, notes or other~~ obligations authorized by this section, to the extent such section is not inconsistent with this subsection. A project loan and project grant agreement authorized by such resolution may contain covenants and agreements with respect to, and may pledge the revenues, funds and moneys derived from, the sewer system or public water system to secure such project loan obligations and interim funding obligations, including, but not limited to, covenants and agreements with respect to holding or depositing such revenues, funds and moneys in separate accounts and agreements described in section 7–266. As used in this subsection "legislative body" means (A) the board of selectmen in a town that does not have a charter, special act or home rule ordinance relating to its government, (B) the council, board of aldermen, representative town meeting, board of selectmen or other elected legislative body described in a charter, special act or home rule ordinance relating to government in a city, consolidated town and city, consolidated town and borough or a town having a charter, special act, consolidation ordinance or home rule ordinance relating to its government, (C) the board of burgesses or other elected legislative body in a borough, or (D) the district committee or other elected legislative body in a district, metropolitan district or other municipal corporation.

(f) Any recipient which is not a municipality shall execute and deliver project loan obligations and interim financing obligations in accordance with applicable law and in such form and with such requirements as may be determined by the commissioner. The Commissioner of Public Health and the Department of Public Utility Control as required by section 16–19e shall review and approve all costs that are necessary and reasonable prior to the award of the project funding agreement. The Department of Public Utility Control, where appropriate, shall include these costs in the recipient's rate structure in accordance with section 16–19e.

[1] 33 U.S.C.A. § 1341 et seq.
[2] 42 U.S.C.A. § 300f et seq.
[3] C.G.S.A. § 7–245 et seq.

Sec. 70. Section 1–125 of the general statutes is repealed and the following is substituted in lieu thereof (Effective from passage):

The directors, officers and employees of the Connecticut Development Authority, Connecticut Innovations, Incorporated, Connecticut Higher Education Supplemental Loan Authority, Connecticut Housing Finance Authority, Connecticut Housing Authority, Connecticut Resources Recovery Authority, including ad hoc members of the Connecticut Resources Recovery Authority, Connecticut Health and Educational Facilities Authority, Capital City Economic Development Authority, Connecticut Lottery Corporation and Connecticut Port Authority and any person executing the bonds or notes of the agency shall not be liable personally on such bonds or notes or be subject to any personal liability or accountability by reason of the issuance thereof, nor shall any director or employee of the agency, including ad hoc members of the Connecticut Resources Recovery Authority, be personally liable for damage or injury, not wanton, reckless, wilful or malicious, caused in the performance of his or her duties and within the scope of his or her employment or appointment as such director, officer or employee, including ad hoc members of the Connecticut Resources Recovery Authority. The agency shall protect, save harmless and indemnify its directors, officers or employees, including ad hoc members of the Connecticut Resources Recovery Authority, from financial loss and expense, including legal fees and costs, if any, arising out of any claim, demand, suit or judgment by reason of alleged negligence or alleged deprivation of any person's civil rights or any other act or omission resulting in damage or injury, if the director, officer or employee, including ad hoc members of the Connecticut Resources Recovery Authority, is found to have been acting in the discharge of his or her duties or within the scope of his or her employment and such act or omission is found not to have been wanton, reckless, wilful or malicious.

Sec. 71. Section 4a–59a of the general statutes is repealed and the following is substituted in lieu thereof (Effective from passage):

(a) No state agency may extend a contract for the purchase of supplies, materials, equipment or contractual services which expires on or after October 1, 1990, and is subject to the competitive bidding requirements of subsection (a) of section 4a–57, without complying with such requirements, unless (1) the Commissioner of Administrative Services makes a written determination, supported by documentation, that (A) soliciting competitive bids for such purchase would cause a hardship for the state, (B) such solicitation would result in a major increase in the cost of such supplies, materials, equipment or contractual services, or (C) the contractor is the sole source for such supplies, materials, equipment or contractual services, (2) such commissioner solicits at least three competitive quotations in addition to the contractor's quotation, and (3) the commissioner makes a written determination that no such competitive quotation which complies with the existing specifications for the contract is lower than or equal to the contractor's quotation. Any such contract extension shall be based on the contractor's quotation. No contract may be extended more than two times under this section.

(b) Notwithstanding the provisions of subsection (a) of this section, the Commissioner of Administrative Services may, for a period of one year from the date such contract would otherwise expire, extend any contract in effect on May 1, 2004, to perform any of the following services for the state: Janitorial, building maintenance, security and food and beverage.

Sec. 72. Section 33 of public act 04–216 is amended to read as follows (Effective from passage):

(a) Up to ~~$ 10,000,000~~ $ 7,000,000 of the unexpended balance appropriated to the Department of Transportation in section 11 12 of public act 03–1 of the June 30 special session, for Personal Services, shall not lapse on June 30, 2004, and such funds shall be transferred to the Department of Motor Vehicles to the Reflective License Plates account for expenditure for the purpose of upgrading the Department of Motor Vehicles registration and driver license data processing systems for the fiscal year ending June 30, 2005.

(b) Up to ~~$ 5,500,000~~ $ 8,500,000 of the unexpended balance appropriated to the State Treasurer, for Debt Service, in section ~~11~~ 12 of public act 03–1 of the June 30 special session, shall not lapse on June 30, 2004, and such funds shall be transferred to the Department of Motor Vehicles to the Reflective License Plates account for expenditure for the purpose of upgrading the Department of Motor Vehicles registration and driver license data processing systems for the fiscal year ending June 30, 2005.

Sec. 73. Section 45 of public act 04–216 is amended to read as follows (Effective from passage):

During the fiscal ~~year~~ years ending June 30, 2004, and June 30, 2005, the Secretary of the Office of Policy and Management may transfer funds appropriated from the Special Transportation Fund to the Departments of Transportation and Motor Vehicles, for Other Current Expenses, to the appropriations from said fund to the

Employers Social Security Tax and the State Employees Health Service Cost accounts in order to implement accounting changes necessitated by the CORE-CT system.

Sec. 74. (Effective July 1, 2004) Up to $ 133,700 of funds appropriated to the Department of Banking, for Equipment, shall not lapse on June 30, 2004, and such funds shall continue to be available for expenditure for such purpose during the fiscal year ending June 30, 2005.

Sec. 75. (Effective July 1, 2004) Up to $ 15,000 appropriated to the Commission on the Deaf and Hearing Impaired, for the Other Expenses account, in section 1 of public act 03–1 of the June 30 special session, shall not lapse on June 30, 2004, and such funds shall be available for moving expenses during the fiscal year ending June 30, 2005.

Sec. 76. Subdivision (55) of section 12–81 of the general statutes, as amended by section 40 of public act 03–6 of the June 30 special session, is repealed and the following is substituted in lieu thereof (Effective from passage and applicable to assessment years commencing on or after October 1, 2003):

(55) ~~For assessment years commencing prior to October 1, 2003, and for assessment years commencing on or after October 1, 2004, property~~ Property to the amount of one thousand dollars belonging to, or held in trust for, any resident of this state who (1) is eligible, in accordance with applicable federal regulations, to receive permanent total disability benefits under Social Security, (2) has not been engaged in employment covered by Social Security and accordingly has not qualified for benefits thereunder but who has become qualified for permanent total disability benefits under any federal, state or local government retirement or disability plan, including the Railroad Retirement Act[1] and any government-related teacher's retirement plan, determined by the Secretary of the Office of Policy and Management to contain requirements in respect to qualification for such permanent total disability benefits which are comparable to such requirements under Social Security, or (3) has attained age sixty-five or over and would be eligible in accordance with applicable federal regulations to receive permanent total disability benefits under Social Security or any such federal, state or local government retirement or disability plan as described in subparagraph (2) of this subdivision, except that such resident has attained age sixty-five or over and accordingly is no longer eligible to receive benefits under the disability benefit provisions of Social Security or such other plan because of payments received under retirement provisions thereof; or, lacking said amount of property in his own name, so much of the property belonging to, or held in trust for, his spouse, who is domiciled with him, as is necessary to equal said amount. Each assessor shall issue a certificate of correction with respect to the property of a person who would have been eligible, except for the provisions of section 40 of public act 03–6 of the June 30 special session, to receive the exemption under this subdivision for the assessment year commencing October 1, 2003. Such certificate shall reduce the assessment of such eligible person's property by the amount of said exemption.

[1] 45 U.S.C.A. § 231 et seq.

Sec. 77. Section 12–94a of the general statutes, as amended by section 41 of public act 03–6 of the June 30 special session, is repealed and the following is substituted in lieu thereof (Effective from passage and applicable to assessment years commencing on or after October 1, 2003):

On or before July first, annually, the tax collector of each municipality shall certify to the Secretary of the Office of Policy and Management, on a form furnished by said secretary, the amount of tax revenue which such municipality, except for the provisions of subdivision (55) of section 12–81, as amended by this act, would have received, together with such supporting information as said secretary may require, except that for the assessment year commencing October 1, 2003, such certification shall be made to the secretary on or before August 1, 2004. Any municipality which neglects to transmit to said secretary such claim and supporting documentation as required by this section shall forfeit two hundred fifty dollars to the state, provided said secretary may waive such forfeiture in accordance with procedures and standards adopted by regulation in accordance with chapter 54.[1] Said secretary shall review each such claim as provided in section 12–120b, as amended by this act. Any claimant aggrieved by the results of the secretary's review shall have the rights of appeal as set forth in section 12–120b, as amended by this act. The secretary shall, on or before December first, annually, certify to the Comptroller the amount due each municipality under the provisions of this section, including any modification of such claim made prior to December first, and the Comptroller shall draw an order on the Treasurer on or before the fifteenth day of December following and the Treasurer shall pay the amount thereof to such municipality on or before the thirty-first day of December following. If any modification is made as the result of the provisions of this section on or after the December first following the date on which the tax collector has provided the amount of tax revenue in question, any adjustments to the amount due to any municipality for the period for which such modification was made shall be made in the next payment the Treasurer shall make to such municipality pursuant to this section. For the purposes of this section, "municipality" means a town, city, borough, consolidated town and city or consolidated town and borough. The provisions of this section shall not apply to the assessment ~~years~~ year commencing on October 1, 2002. ~~, and October 1, 2003.~~ In the fiscal year commencing July 1, 2004, and in each fiscal year thereafter, the amount of the grant payable to each municipality in accordance with this section shall be reduced proportionately in the event that the total amount of the grants payable to all municipalities exceeds the amount appropriated.

1 C.G.S.A. § 4–166 et seq.

Sec. 78. Subdivision (4) of subsection (d) of section 12–120b of the general statutes is repealed and the following is substituted in lieu thereof (Effective July 1, 2004, and applicable to certifications by the Secretary of the Office of Policy and Management on and after July 1, 2001):

(4) ~~Not later than the date by which the secretary is required to certify to the Comptroller the amount of payment with respect to any such program, the~~ The secretary shall notify each claimant of the final modification or denial of financial assistance as claimed, in accordance with the procedure set forth in this subsection. A copy of the notice of final modification or denial shall be sent concurrently to the assessor or municipal official who approved such financial assistance. With respect to property tax exemptions under section 12–81g, as amended by this act, or subdivision (55), (59), (60) or (70) of section 12–81, and tax relief pursuant to section 12–129d or 12–170aa, as amended by this act, the notice pursuant to this subdivision shall be sent not later than one year after the date claims for financial assistance for each such program are filed with the secretary. For property tax exemptions under subdivision (72) or (74) of section 12–81, as amended, such notice shall be sent not later than the date by which a final modification to the payment for such program must be reflected in the certification of the secretary to the Comptroller. For the program of rebates under section 12–170d, such notice shall be sent not later than the date by which the secretary certifies the amounts of payment to the Comptroller.

Sec. 79. Section 12–170aa of the general statutes, as amended by section 183 of public act 03–6 of the June 30 special session, is amended by adding subsection (k) as follows (Effective July 1, 2004, and applicable to claims for reimbursement filed on and after July 1, 2001):

(NEW) (k) If the Secretary of the Office of Policy and Management makes any adjustments to the grants for tax reductions or assumed amounts of property tax liability claimed under this section subsequent to the Comptroller the payment of said grants in any year, the amount of such adjustment shall be reflected in the next payment the Treasurer shall make to such municipality pursuant to this section.

Sec. 80. Section 13b–68 of the general statutes, as amended by section 58 of public act 03–115, is repealed and the following is substituted in lieu thereof (Effective July 1, 2004):

(a) There is established a fund to be known as the "Special Transportation Fund". The fund may contain any moneys required or permitted by law to be deposited in the fund and any moneys recovered by the state for overpayments, improper payments or duplicate payments made by the state relating to any transportation infrastructure improvements which have been financed by special tax obligation bonds issued pursuant to sections 13b–74 to 13b–77, inclusive, as amended, and shall be held by the State Treasurer separate and apart from all other moneys, funds and accounts. Investment earnings credited to the assets of said fund shall become part of the assets of said fund. Any balance remaining in said fund at the end of any fiscal year shall be carried forward in said fund for the fiscal year next succeeding.

(b) There is established a fund to be known as the "Transportation Grants and Restricted Accounts Fund". Upon certification by the Comptroller and the Secretary of the Office of Policy and Management that the CORE-CT project for fiscal services is operational, the fund shall contain all transportation moneys that are restricted, not available for general use and previously accounted for in the Special Transportation Fund as "Federal and Other Grants". The Comptroller is authorized to make such transfers as are necessary to provide that, notwithstanding any provision of the general statutes, all transportation moneys that are restricted and not available for general use are in the Transportation Grants and Restricted Accounts Fund.

Sec. 81. (NEW) (Effective July 1, 2004) There is established a fund to be known as the "Grants and Restricted Accounts Fund". Upon certification by the Comptroller and the Secretary of the Office of Policy and Management that the CORE-CT project for financial services is operational, the fund shall contain all moneys that are restricted, not available for general use and previously accounted for in the General Fund as "Federal and Other Grants". The Comptroller is authorized to make such transfers as are necessary to provide that, notwithstanding any provision of the general statutes, all moneys that are restricted and not available for general use are in the Grants and Restricted Accounts Fund.

Sec. 82. Section 4–66f of the general statutes is repealed and the following is substituted in lieu thereof (Effective from passage):

Notwithstanding any provision of the general statutes or the regulations adopted thereunder, disaster assistance funds received by the Office of ~~Policy and~~ Emergency Management from the Federal Emergency Management Agency for administration may be maintained in a separate fund or separate account within the General Fund and used for any administrative functions. The balance of any such funds remaining at the end of each fiscal year shall be carried forward for the fiscal year next succeeding.

Sec. 83. Section 29 of public act 03–6 of the June 30 special session, as amended by section 9 of public act 04–254, is repealed and the following is substituted in lieu thereof (Effective July 1, 2004):

For the fiscal year ending June 30, 2005, the distribution of priority school district grants pursuant to subsection (a) of section 10–266p of the general statutes, as amended by this act, shall be as follows: (1) For priority school districts in the amount of $ 28,986,250, (2) for school readiness in the amount of $ 44,576,500, (3) for early reading in the amount of ~~$ 18,647,286~~ $ 19,700,000, (4) for extended school building hours in the amount of $ 2,994,752, and (5) for summer school in the amount of $ 3,499,699. ~~, and (6) for school improvement in the amount of $ 1,100,000.~~

Sec. 84. Section 4 of public act 01–8 of the June special session, as amended by section 70 of public act 03–3 of the June 30 special session, is repealed and the following is substituted in lieu thereof (Effective from passage):

(a) The Department of Mental Health and Addiction Services, in consultation with the Department of Social Services, shall conduct a study concerning the implementation of adult rehabilitation services under Medicaid. Not later than February 1, 2002, the departments shall jointly submit a report of their findings and recommendations to the Governor and to the joint standing committees of the General Assembly having cognizance of matters relating to public health, human services and appropriations and the budgets of state agencies, in accordance with the provisions of section 11–4a. The report shall include, but not be limited to, an implementation plan, a cost benefit analysis and a description of the plan's impact on existing services.

(b) The Department of Mental Health and Addiction Services and the Department of Social Services shall conduct a study concerning the advisability of entering into an interagency agreement pursuant to which the Department of Mental Health and Addiction Services would provide clinical management of mental health services, including, but not limited to, review and authorization of services, implementation of quality assurance and improvement initiatives and provision of case management services, for aged, blind or disabled adults enrolled in the Medicaid program to the extent permitted under federal law. Not later than February 1, 2002, the departments shall jointly submit a report of their findings and recommendations to the Governor and to the joint standing committees of the General Assembly having cognizance of matters relating to public health, human services and appropriations and the budgets of state agencies, in accordance with the provisions of section 11–4a.

(c) The Commissioner of Social Services shall take such action as may be necessary to amend the Medicaid state plan to provide for coverage of optional adult rehabilitation services supplied by ~~various~~ providers of mental health services ~~, pursuant to a contract with~~ or substance abuse rehabilitation services for adults with serious and persistent mental illness or who have alcoholism or other substance abuse conditions, that are certified by the Department of Mental Health and Addiction Services. ~~, for adults with mental health needs who are clients of said department.~~ For the fiscal years ending June 30, 2004, and June 30, 2005, up to three million dollars in each such fiscal year of any moneys received by the state as federal reimbursement for optional Medicaid adult rehabilitation services shall be credited to the Community Mental Health Restoration subaccount within the account established under section 1 of public act 01–8 of the June special session and shall be available for use for the purposes of the subaccount. The Commissioner of Social Services shall adopt regulations, in accordance with the provisions of chapter 54,[1] to implement optional rehabilitation services under the Medicaid program. The commissioner shall implement policies and procedures to administer such services while in the process of adopting such policies or procedures in regulation form, provided notice of intention to adopt the regulations is printed in the Connecticut Law Journal within forty-five days of implementation, and any such policies or procedures shall be valid until the time final regulations are effective.

(d) The Commissioner of Mental Health and Addiction Services shall have the authority to certify providers of mental health or substance abuse rehabilitation services for adults with serious and persistent mental illness or who have alcoholism or other substance abuse conditions for the purpose of coverage of optional rehabilitation services. The Commissioner of Mental Health and Addiction Services shall adopt regulations, in accordance with the provisions of chapter 54, for purposes of certification of such providers. The commissioner shall implement policies and procedures for purposes of such certification while in the process of adopting such policies or procedures in regulation form, provided notice of intention to adopt the regulations is printed in the Connecticut

Law Journal no later than twenty days after implementation and any such policies and procedures shall be valid until the time the regulations are effective.

[1] C.G.S.A. § 4–166 et seq.

Sec. 85. Subsection (a) of section 17b–280 of the general statutes, as amended by section 11 of public act 03–2, section 52 of public act 03–3 of the June 30 special session and section 10 of public act 04–258, is repealed and the following is substituted in lieu thereof (Effective July 1, 2004):

(a) The state shall reimburse for all legend drugs provided under the Medicaid, state-administered general assistance, general assistance, ConnPACE and Connecticut AIDS drug assistance programs at the rate established by the Health Care Finance Administration as the federal acquisition cost, or, if no such rate is established, the commissioner shall establish and periodically revise the estimated acquisition cost in accordance with federal regulations. The commissioner shall also establish a professional fee of three dollars and fifteen cents for each prescription to be paid to licensed pharmacies for dispensing drugs to Medicaid, ~~state-administered general assistance, general assistance,~~ ConnPACE and Connecticut AIDS drug assistance recipients in accordance with federal regulations; and on and after September 4, 1991, payment for legend and nonlegend drugs provided to Medicaid recipients shall be based upon the actual package size dispensed. Effective October 1, 1991, reimbursement for over-the-counter drugs for such recipients shall be limited to those over-the-counter drugs and products published in the Connecticut Formulary, or the cross reference list, issued by the commissioner. The cost of all over-the-counter drugs and products provided to residents of nursing facilities, chronic disease hospitals, and intermediate care facilities for the mentally retarded shall be included in the facilities' per diem rate.

Sec. 86. Subsection (h) of section 17b–340 of the general statutes, as amended by section 45 of public act 03–19 and section 50 of public act 03–3 of the June 30 special session, is repealed and the following is substituted in lieu thereof (Effective July 1, 2004):

(h)(1) For the fiscal year ending June 30, 1993, any residential care home with an operating cost component of its rate in excess of one hundred thirty per cent of the median of operating cost components of rates in effect January 1, 1992, shall not receive an operating cost component increase. For the fiscal year ending June 30, 1993, any residential care home with an operating cost component of its rate that is less than one hundred thirty per cent of the median of operating cost components of rates in effect January 1, 1992, shall have an allowance for real wage growth equal to sixty-five per cent of the increase determined in accordance with subsection (q) of section 17–311–52 of the regulations of Connecticut state agencies, provided such operating cost component shall not exceed one hundred thirty per cent of the median of operating cost components in effect January 1, 1992. Beginning with the fiscal year ending June 30, 1993, for the purpose of determining allowable fair rent, a residential care home with allowable fair rent less than the twenty-fifth percentile of the state-wide allowable fair rent shall be reimbursed as having allowable fair rent equal to the twenty-fifth percentile of the state-wide allowable fair rent. Beginning with the fiscal year ending June 30, 1997, a residential care home with allowable fair rent less than three dollars and ten cents per day shall be reimbursed as having allowable fair rent equal to three dollars and ten cents per day. Property additions placed in service during the cost year ending September 30, 1996, or any succeeding cost year shall receive a fair rent allowance for such additions as an addition to three dollars and ten cents per day if the fair rent for the facility for property placed in service prior to September 30, 1995, is less than or equal to three dollars and ten cents per day. For the fiscal year ending June 30, 1996, and any succeeding fiscal year, the allowance for real wage growth, as determined in accordance with subsection (q) of section 17–311–52 of the regulations of Connecticut state agencies, shall not be applied. For the fiscal year ending June 30, 1996, and any succeeding fiscal year, the inflation adjustment made in accordance with subsection (p) of section 17–311–52 of the regulations of Connecticut state agencies shall not be applied to real property costs. Beginning with the fiscal year ending June 30, 1997, minimum allowable patient days for rate computation purposes for a residential care home with twenty-five beds or less shall be eighty-five per cent of licensed capacity. Beginning with the fiscal year ending June 30, 2002, for the purposes of determining the allowable salary of an administrator of a residential care home with sixty beds or less the department shall revise the allowable base salary to thirty-seven thousand dollars to be annually inflated thereafter in accordance with section 17–311–52 of the regulations of Connecticut state agencies. The rates for the fiscal year ending June 30, 2002, shall be based upon the increased allowable salary of an administrator, regardless of whether such amount was expended in the 2000 cost report period upon which the rates are based. Beginning with the fiscal year ending June 30, 2000, the inflation adjustment for rates made in accordance with subsection (p) of section 17–311–52 of the regulations of Connecticut state agencies shall be increased by two per cent, and beginning with the fiscal year ending June 30, 2002, the inflation adjustment for rates made in accordance with subsection (c) of said section shall be increased by one per cent. Beginning with the fiscal year ending June 30, 1999, for the purpose of determining the allowable salary of a related party, the department shall revise the maximum salary to twenty-seven thousand eight hundred fifty-six dollars to be annually inflated thereafter in accordance with section 17–311–52 of the regulations of Connecticut state agencies and beginning with the fiscal year ending June 30, 2001, such allowable salary shall be computed on an hourly basis and the maximum number of hours allowed for a related party other than the proprietor shall be increased from forty hours to forty-eight hours per work week. For the fiscal year ending June 30, 2005, each facility shall receive a rate that is two and one-quarter per cent more than the rate the facility received in the prior fiscal year, except any facility that would have been issued a lower rate effective July 1, 2004, than for the fiscal year ending June 30, 2004, due to interim rate status or agreement with the department shall be issued such lower rate effective July 1, 2004.

(2) The commissioner shall, upon determining that a loan to be issued to a residential care home by the Connecticut Housing Finance Authority is reasonable in relation to the useful life and property cost allowance pursuant to section 17–311–52 of the regulations of Connecticut state agencies, allow actual debt service, comprised of principal, interest and a repair and replacement reserve on the loan, in lieu of allowed property costs whether actual debt service is higher or lower than such allowed property costs.

Sec. 87. Subsection (d) of section 17b–257 of the general statutes, as amended by section 18 of public act 03–2, section 43 of public act 03–3 of the June 30 special session and section 9 of public act 04–258, is repealed and the following is substituted in lieu thereof (Effective from passage):

(d) The Commissioner of Social Services shall contract with federally qualified health centers or other primary care providers as necessary to provide medical services to eligible state-administered general assistance recipients pursuant to this section. The commissioner shall, within available appropriations, make payments to such centers based on their pro rata share of the cost of services provided or the number of clients served, or both. The Commissioner of Social Services shall, within available appropriations, make payments to other providers based on a methodology determined by the commissioner. The Commissioner of Social Services may reimburse for extraordinary medical services, provided such services are documented to the satisfaction of the commissioner. For purposes of this section, the commissioner may contract with a managed care organization or other entity to perform administrative functions, including a grievance process for recipients to access review of a denial of coverage for a specific medical service, and to operate the program in whole or in part. Provisions of a contract for medical services entered into by the commissioner pursuant to this section shall supersede any inconsistent provision in the regulations of Connecticut state agencies. A recipient who has exhausted the grievance process established through such contract and wishes to seek further review of the denial of coverage for a specific medical service may request a hearing in accordance with the provisions of section 17b–60.

Sec. 88. Subsection (f) of section 1 of public act 03–1 of the September 8 special session is repealed and the following is substituted in lieu thereof (Effective from passage):

(f) An amount equal to the amount certified by the Secretary of the Office of Policy and Management for retrospective reimbursements shall be credited to the State Administered General Assistance account in the Department of Social Services for the fiscal ~~year~~ years ending June 30, 2004, and June 30, 2005. Such amount shall be available to the department to pay such retrospective reimbursement claims received during the fiscal ~~year~~ years ending June 30, 2004, and June 30, 2005.

Sec. 89. Section 18–86b of the general statutes, as amended by section 156 of public act 03–6 of the June 30 special session, is repealed and the following is substituted in lieu thereof (Effective July 1, 2004):

(a) Notwithstanding the provisions of sections 18–105 to 18–107, inclusive, the Commissioner of Correction is authorized to improve the operation of the state's correctional facilities by entering into contracts with any governmental or private vendor for supervision of not more than five hundred inmates outside the state. Any such governmental or private vendor shall agree to be bound by the provisions of the Interstate Corrections Compact, [1] and any governmental or privately-operated facility to which state inmates are transferred pursuant to a contract under this subsection shall be located in a state which has enacted and entered into the Interstate Corrections Compact.

(b)(1) Notwithstanding the provisions of sections 18–105 to 18–107, inclusive, during the fiscal ~~years~~ year ending June 30, 2004, ~~and June 30, 2005,~~ the Commissioner of Correction is authorized to improve the operation of the state's correctional facilities by entering into contracts in accordance with this subsection with any governmental or private vendor for the supervision of not more than an additional two thousand inmates outside the state.

(2) If the governmental vendor with which the commissioner has a contract under subsection (a) of this section on August 20, 2003, for the supervision of inmates outside this state is willing to accept additional inmates for supervision, the Commissioner of Correction may, notwithstanding the provisions of section 4a–57, enter into a contract with such governmental vendor for the supervision of such number of additional inmates as such governmental vendor is willing to accept. If the commissioner does not enter into such a contract with such governmental vendor or if, after contracting for the supervision of additional inmates by such governmental vendor, the number of inmates authorized to be supervised outside this state under subdivision (1) of this subsection has not been attained, the commissioner may enter into contracts with any governmental or private vendor for the supervision of all or part of the remaining number of inmates authorized to be supervised outside this state under said subdivision (1).

(3) Any such governmental or private vendor shall agree to be bound by the provisions of the Interstate Corrections Compact, and any governmental or privately-operated facility to which state inmates are transferred pursuant to a contract under this subsection shall be located in a state which has enacted and entered into the Interstate Corrections Compact.

(c)(1) Notwithstanding the provisions of sections 18–105 to 18–107, inclusive, during the fiscal years ending June 30, 2005, June 30, 2006, and June 30, 2007, the Commissioner of Correction is authorized to improve the operation of the state's correctional facilities by entering into contracts in accordance with this subsection with any governmental or private vendor for the supervision of not more than an additional one thousand inmates outside the state.

(2) Any such governmental or private vendor shall agree to be bound by the provisions of the Interstate Corrections Compact, and any governmental or privately-operated facility to which state inmates are transferred pursuant to a contract under this subsection shall be located in a state which has enacted and entered into the Interstate Corrections Compact.

(3) Prior to entering into any contract under this subsection, the commissioner shall submit such proposed contract to the joint standing committees of the General Assembly having cognizance of matters relating to appropriations and the budgets of state agencies and to the judiciary for their review and comment.

~~(c)~~ (d) A state inmate confined in any governmental or privately-operated facility pursuant to the terms of any contract with the state shall at all times be subject to the authority of the Commissioner of Correction who may at any time remove the inmate for transfer to a state correctional facility or other institution, for transfer to another governmental or privately-operated facility, for release on probation or parole, for discharge or for any other purpose permitted by the laws of this state.

[1] C.G.S.A. § 18–105 et seq.

Sec. 90. Section 35 of public act 03–6 of the June 30 special session is amended by adding subsections (e) and (f) as follows (Effective from passage):

(NEW) (e) The successor entity may, from time to time, amend an approved revitalization plan, provided any such amendment shall comply with this section and sections 34 and 36 of public act 03–6 of the June 30 special session. Any such amendment shall be proposed and approved pursuant to the provisions of subsections (c) and (d) of this section, provided no such amendment may be submitted to the commissioner for approval or approved by the commissioner unless it is developed with the advice and consultation of the local planning committee. The local planning committee shall be convened by the successor entity. The executive director of the successor entity shall designate the members of the local planning committee and its chairperson, provided the membership of such planning committee shall include not less than two residents of the developments including residents selected by a resident association, and not less than two representatives of organizations that advocate for public housing residents. Each resident association representing residents of the developments may select one representative to serve on the local planning committee. The successor entity shall (1) assure that the residents of the housing developments are able to fully participate in the planning, review and implementation process, and (2) make reasonable efforts to link residents to community resources so that such residents will have access to expertise in tenant outreach, training, organizing, legal rights and housing policy in order to promote genuine tenant participation and to protect the interests of the residents during the planning and implementation process. As used in this subsection, "successor entity" means the Connecticut Housing Finance Authority.

(NEW) (f) The local planning committee may propose amendments to the housing revitalization plan. The committee shall hold at least one public hearing prior to its approval of any amendment. At least thirty days prior to the public hearing, the committee shall mail or deliver notice to each resident household in the developments and to each resident association representing residents in the developments. In addition to any formal notice, any such public hearing shall be publicized generally in the municipality through posted notices at the developments and through publicity both through newspapers of general circulation in the municipality and through weekly community newspapers. A record shall be kept of all comments received at such hearings and at the hearing held pursuant to subsection (c) of this section, and a summary of all oral comments and copies of all written comments shall be transmitted to the commissioner at the time of submission of the proposed amendment to the plan.

Sec. 91. Subdivision (44) of section 8–250 of the general statutes, as amended by section 39 of public act 03–6 of the June 30 special session, is repealed and the following is substituted in lieu thereof (Effective from passage):

(44) Provide assistance, in such form and subject to such conditions as the authority may determine, to a local housing authority or project sponsor in connection with a housing revitalization project undertaken pursuant to ~~this section~~ sections 34 to 38, inclusive, of public act 03–6 of the June 30 special session, as amended by this act.

Sec. 92. Subsection (a) of section 51 of public act 03–6 of the June 30 special session is repealed and the following is substituted in lieu thereof (Effective from passage):

(a) As used in this section:

(1) "Commissioner" means the Commissioner of Economic and Community Development;

(2) "Connecticut Housing Finance Authority" means the authority created and operating pursuant to the provisions of chapter 134; [1]

(3) "Financially distressed development" means a housing development owned by a housing authority and subject to an asset that was transferred from the Department of Economic and Community Development to the Connecticut Housing Finance Authority pursuant to ~~subsection (a) of this~~ section 8–37u or subdivision (3) of section 32–11; and

(4) "Housing authority" means a local housing authority owning a financially distressed development.

[1] C.G.S.A. § 8–241 et seq.

Sec. 93. Subsection (b) of section 8–216 of the general statutes is repealed and the following is substituted in lieu thereof (Effective from passage):

(b) The state, acting by and in the discretion of the Commissioner of Economic and Community Development, may enter into a contract with a municipality and the housing authority of the municipality or with the Connecticut Housing Finance Authority or any subsidiary created by the authority pursuant to section 8–242a or 8–244, as amended, to make payments in lieu of taxes to the municipality on land and improvements owned or leased by the housing authority or the Connecticut Housing Finance Authority under the provisions of part II of chapter 128 [1] or under the provisions of sections 8–430 to 8–438, inclusive. On and after July 1, 1997, the time period of the contract may include the remaining years of operation of the project. Such payments shall be made annually in an amount equal to the taxes that would be paid on such property were the property not exempt from taxation, and shall be calculated by multiplying the assessed value of such property, which shall be determined by the tax assessor of such municipality in the manner used by such assessor for assessing the value of other real property, by the applicable tax rate of the municipality. Such contract shall provide that, in consideration of such grant-in-aid, the municipality shall waive during the period of such contract any payments by the housing authority or the Connecticut Housing Finance Authority to the municipality under the provisions of section 8–71, and shall further provide that the amount of the payments so waived shall be used by the housing authority or the Connecticut Housing Finance Authority for a program of social and supplementary services to the occupants or shall be applied to the operating costs or reserves of the property, or shall be used to maintain or improve the physical quality of the property.

[1] C.G.S.A. § 8–69 et seq.

Sec. 94. Section 8–68f of the general statutes is repealed and the following is substituted in lieu thereof (Effective July 1, 2004):

Each housing authority which receives financial assistance under any state housing program, and the Connecticut Housing Finance Authority or its subsidiary when said authority or subsidiary is the successor owner of housing previously owned by a housing authority under part II [1] or part VI [2] of this chapter, shall, for housing which it owns and operates, (1) provide each of its tenants with a written lease, (2) adopt a procedure for hearing tenant complaints and grievances, (3) adopt procedures for soliciting tenant comment on proposed changes in housing authority policies and procedures, including changes to its lease and to its admission and occupancy policies, and (4) encourage tenant participation in the housing authority's operation of state housing programs, including, where appropriate, the facilitation of tenant participation in the management of housing projects. If such housing authority or the Connecticut Housing Finance Authority or its subsidiary operates both a federal and a state-assisted housing program, it shall use the same procedure for hearing tenant grievances in both programs. The Commissioner of Economic and Community Development shall adopt regulations in accordance with the provisions of chapter 54 [3] to establish uniform minimum standards for the requirements in this section.

[1] C.G.S.A. § 8–69 et seq.
[2] C.G.S.A. § 8–112 et seq.
[3] C.G.S.A. § 4–166 et seq.

Sec. 95. (NEW) (Effective from passage) Whenever the Connecticut Housing Finance Authority or its subsidiary is a successor owner of housing previously owned by a housing authority under part II [1] or part VI [2] of chapter 128 of the general statutes, the authority or its successor shall be subject to the requirements of and operate such housing in compliance with all provisions of the general statutes applicable to the operation or disposition of such housing by a housing authority.

[1] C.G.S.A. § 8–69 et seq.
[2] C.G.S.A. § 8–112 et seq.

Sec. 96. (NEW) (Effective from passage) If a housing authority sold a housing property containing thirty-two rental units to a private developer between October 1, 2003, and November 30, 2003, the housing authority may apply to the Commissioner of Economic and Community Development for a waiver of the requirements of the regulations adopted pursuant to section 8–45 of the general statutes to allow for the use of state-financed housing as a relocation resource for families or persons otherwise eligible for residency in such state-financed housing except for the waiting list. Any waiver granted by the commissioner shall remain in effect until all eligible displaced tenants seeking such housing have been accommodated.

Sec. 97. Section 196 of public act 03–6 of the June 30 special session is repealed and the following is substituted in lieu thereof (Effective from passage):

Notwithstanding the provisions of the general statutes, at the request of the Secretary of the Office of Policy and Management, the Comptroller shall transfer up to $ 3,600,000 from the resources of the Banking Fund, to Other Expenses, for relocation expenses and furniture costs for the Department of Banking during the fiscal years ending June 30, 2003, and June 30, 2004. The Banking Commissioner is authorized to reimburse the Department of Public Works from funds available in Other Expenses for amounts paid by the Department of Public Works on behalf of the Department of Banking for such relocation expenses, furniture costs and rent during the fiscal years ending June 30, 2003, ~~and~~ June 30, 2004, and June 30, 2005.

Sec. 98. (Effective July 1, 2004) (a) The Secretary of the Office of Policy and Management shall immediately notify the Commissioners of Correction and Administrative Services that the sum of $ 2,000,000 shall not be expended in the Workers' Compensation account in the Department of Correction for the fiscal year ending June 30, 2004. The secretary shall monitor said account, including any stipulations, through the end of said fiscal year to ensure such sum shall not be expended.

(b) Up to $ 1,000,000 appropriated to the Department of Correction in section 1 of special act 03–1 of the June 30 special session, for Workers' Compensation Claims, and not expended in accordance with subsection (a) of this section, shall not lapse June 30, 2004. The first $ 200,000 of such funds shall be transferred to the Labor Department, for Opportunity Industrial Centers, and shall be available for expenditure during the fiscal year ending June 30, 2005, as follows: The sum of $ 100,000 for the Bridgeport Opportunity Industrial Center and the sum of $ 100,000 for the Waterbury Opportunity Industrial Center. The remainder of such funds shall continue to be available for Workers' Compensation Claims during the fiscal year ending June 30, 2005.

Sec. 99. (Effective from passage) For the fiscal year ending June 30, 2004, the Secretary of the Office of Policy and Management may authorize the carry-forward of funds in any appropriated account, if requested by an agency head and such funds are available due to delays in the payment of contractors resulting from the affidavit requirement imposed by the office of the Attorney General.

Sec. 100. Section 4–65a of the general statutes is repealed and the following is substituted in lieu thereof (Effective from passage):

(a) There shall be an Office of Policy and Management which shall be responsible for all aspects of state staff planning and analysis in the areas of budgeting, management, planning, energy policy determination and evaluation, intergovernmental policy, criminal and juvenile justice planning and program evaluation. The department head shall be the Secretary of the Office of Policy and Management, who shall be appointed by the Governor in accordance with the provisions of sections 4–5, as amended, 4–6, 4–7 and 4–8, with all the powers and duties therein prescribed. The Secretary of the Office of Policy and Management shall be the employer representative (1) in collective bargaining negotiations concerning changes to the state employees retirement system and health and welfare benefits, and (2) in all other matters involving collective bargaining, including negotiation and administration of all collective bargaining agreements and supplemental understandings between the state and the state employee unions concerning all executive branch employees except (A) employees of the Division of Criminal Justice, and (B) faculty and professional employees of boards of trustees of constituent units of the state system of higher education. The secretary may designate a member of the secretary's staff to act as the employer representative in the secretary's place.

(b) There shall be such undersecretaries as may be necessary for the efficient conduct of the business of the office. Each such undersecretary shall be appointed by the secretary and shall be qualified and experienced in the functions to be performed by him. The positions of each such undersecretary shall be exempt from the classified service.

(c) The secretary may delegate to the deputy secretary all or part of the authority, powers and duties of the secretary.

Sec. 101. (NEW) (Effective from passage) The Attorney General may delegate to the Secretary of the Office of Policy and Management the authority to appoint an attorney employed by said office to represent the state of Connecticut in matters relating to certain appeals to the Superior Court from an arbitration, decision or determination or any other labor relations issue involving the Office of Labor Relations. The Attorney General may enter into a memorandum of understanding with the Secretary of the Office of Policy and Management which shall list the types of appeals which are the subject of such delegation.

Sec. 102. (Effective July 1, 2004) The Comptroller is authorized to maintain the balances of any appropriations that would otherwise lapse at the close of the fiscal year ending June 30, 2004, for a period of one month to permit the liquidation of obligations from the prior fiscal year.

Sec. 103. Subdivision (5) of section 12–412 of the general statutes is repealed and the following is substituted in lieu thereof (Effective July 1, 2004):

(5) Sales of tangible personal property or services to and by nonprofit charitable hospitals in this state, nonprofit nursing homes, nonprofit rest homes and nonprofit residential care homes licensed by the state pursuant to chapter 368v [1] for the exclusive purposes of such institutions except any such service transaction as described in subparagraph (EE) of subdivision (37) of subsection (a) of section 12–407, as amended, and sales of tangible personal property or services to an acute care, for-profit hospital, operating as an acute care, for-profit hospital as of the effective date of this section, for the purposes of such institution in connection with the constructing and equipping of any facility of such hospital for which a certificate of need was filed before, and is pending on, the effective date of this section.

[1] C.G.S.A. § 19a–485 et seq.

Sec. 104. Subdivision (5) of section 12–412 of the general statutes, as amended by section 54 of public act 03–6 of the June 30 special session, is repealed and the following is substituted in lieu thereof (Effective from passage and applicable to sales occurring on or after July 1, 2005):

(5) Sales of tangible personal property or services to and by nonprofit charitable hospitals in this state, nonprofit nursing homes, nonprofit rest homes and nonprofit residential care homes licensed by the state pursuant to chapter 368v [1] for the exclusive purposes of such institutions except any such service transaction as described in subparagraph (EE) of subdivision (37) of subsection (a) of section 12–407, as amended, and sales of ~~medical equipment and supplies for patient care to and by acute care, for-profit hospitals for the exclusive purposes of such institutions, except any such service transaction as described in subparagraph (EE) of subdivision (37) of subsection (a) of section 12–407~~ tangible personal property or services to an acute care, for-profit hospital, operating as an acute care, for-profit hospital as of the effective date of this section, for the purposes of such institution in connection with the constructing and equipping of any facility of such hospital for which a certificate of need was filed before, and is pending on, the effective date of this section.

[1] C.G.S.A. § 19a–485 et seq.

Sec. 105. (NEW) (Effective July 1, 2004) (a) On or before September 1, 2004, the Secretary of the Office of Policy and Management, in consultation with the head of each budgeted state agency responsible for services related to health and hospitals, human services, education and correction, shall prepare a report which compares, for the previous biennium, the increases paid by the state pursuant to contracts with private providers of such services to the compensation increases due to cost of living allowances or performance-based increases paid by the state to state employees providing the same or similar services. Such report shall be included in the budget document for the biennium ending June 30, 2007, transmitted by the Governor to the General Assembly pursuant to section 4–71 of the general statutes and any funding necessary to provide an increase to such private providers that equals the mean average increase paid to such state employees for the previous biennium shall be included in the recommended current service appropriations for each affected agency for the ensuing biennium.

(b) Nothing in subsection (a) this section shall limit the Governor's ability to recommend reductions to current service appropriations in such budget document.

Sec. 106. (Effective from passage) From the effective date of this section to June 30, 2005, inclusive, the Commissioner of Social Services shall not agree to any Medicaid waiver in which the federal government, as a condition of granting the waiver, requires the state to agree to limit the normal fifty per cent federal cost sharing in the program.

Sec. 107. (Effective from passage) Notwithstanding any provision of the general statutes, from the effective date of this section to June 30, 2004, inclusive, no child shall be terminated from the HUSKY B medical program for lack of payment of any premium increase implemented by the commissioner within the fiscal year ending June 30, 2004. The Commissioner of Social Services shall examine the impact of the premium increases on enrollment and shall notify the joint committees having cognizance of matters relating to appropriations and the budgets of state agencies and human services by June 1, 2004, of any final premium increase adopted for the fiscal year ending June 30, 2005.

Sec. 108. (Effective from passage) Section 34 of public act 04–221 shall take effect from passage.

Sec. 109. (Effective from passage) The Graduate Institute, located in the towns of Milford and New London, shall have power, in accordance with its bylaws and subject to such requirements as may be prescribed for institutions of higher learning by the Board of Governors for Higher Education, as provided in section 10a–34 of the general statutes, to confer such degrees and grant such diplomas as are customary in institutions of higher learning.

Sec. 110. Subsection (b) of section 4–66c of the general statutes, as amended by section 1 of public act 04–1 of the May, 2004 special session, is repealed and the following is substituted in lieu thereof (Effective from passage):

(b) The proceeds of the sale of said bonds, to the extent hereinafter stated, shall be used, subject to the provisions of subsections (c) and (d) of this section, for the purpose of redirecting, improving and expanding state activities which promote community conservation and development and improve the quality of life for urban residents of the state as hereinafter stated: (1) For the Department of Economic and Community Development: Economic and community development projects, including administrative costs incurred by the Department of Economic and Community Development, not exceeding sixty-seven million five hundred ninety-one thousand six hundred forty-two dollars, one million dollars of which shall be used for a grant to the development center program and the nonprofit business consortium deployment center approved pursuant to section 32–411; (2) for the Department of Transportation: Urban mass transit, not exceeding two million dollars; (3) for the Department of Environmental Protection: Recreation development and solid waste disposal projects, not exceeding one million nine hundred ninety-five thousand nine hundred two dollars; (4) for the Department of Social Services: Child day care projects, elderly centers, shelter facilities for victims of domestic violence, emergency shelters and related facilities for the homeless, multipurpose human resource centers and food distribution facilities, not exceeding thirty-nine million one hundred thousand dollars, provided four million dollars of said authorization shall be effective July 1, 1994; (5) for the Department of Economic and Community Development: Housing projects, not exceeding three million dollars; (6) for the Office of Policy and Management: (A) Grants-in-aid to municipalities for a pilot demonstration program to leverage private contributions for redevelopment of designated historic preservation areas, not exceeding one million dollars; (B) grants-in-aid for urban development projects including economic and community development, transportation, environmental protection, public safety, children and families and social services projects and programs, including, in the case of economic and community development projects administered on behalf of the Office of Policy and Management by the Department of Economic and Community Development, administrative costs incurred by the Department of Economic and Community Development, not exceeding eight hundred sixty-seven million eight hundred thousand dollars, provided eighty-two million five hundred thousand dollars of said authorization shall be effective July 1, 2004. Five million dollars of the grants-in-aid authorized in subparagraph (B) of subdivision (6) of this subsection may be made available to private nonprofit organizations for the purposes described in said subparagraph (B). ~~Ten~~ Twelve million dollars of the grants-in-aid authorized in subparagraph (B) of subdivision (6) of this subsection may be made available for necessary renovations and improvements of libraries. Five million dollars of the grants-in-aid authorized in subparagraph (B) of subdivision (6) of this subsection shall be made available for small business gap financing. Ten million dollars of the grants-in-aid authorized in subparagraph (B) of subdivision (6) of this subsection may be made available for regional economic development revolving loan funds.

Sec. 111. (Effective from passage) Public act 04–81 shall take effect from passage.

Sec. 112. (Effective July 1, 2004) Section 52–259d of the general statutes and section 39 of public act 04–216 are repealed.

Approved May 12, 2004.

INDEX

General Statutes section are cited by number.

P.A. .... Public Act Number
PROB Rule .... Probate Rules for Practice and Procedure
RAP .... Rules of Appellate Procedure
SUPER CT CIV .... Superior Court Rules - Civil Matters
SUPER CT CR .... Superior Court Rules - Criminal Matters
SUPER CT FAM .... Superior Court Rules - Family Matters
SUPER CT GEN .... Superior Court Rules - General Provisions
SUPER CT JUV .... Superior Court Rules - Juvenile Matters

---

Index

Index

Index

Index

Index

Index

Index

Index

Index

Index

Index

Index